Penguin Handbooks
The Penguin Cassette Guide

Edward Greenfield has been Record Critic of the *Guardian* since 1954 and from 1964
Music Critic as well. At the end of 1960 he joined the reviewing panel of the
Gramophone, specializing in operatic and orchestral issues. He is a regular
broadcaster on music and records for the B B C, and in 1958 published a monograph
on the operas of Puccini. More recently he has written studies on the recorded work
of Joan Sutherland and André Previn.

Robert Layton studied at Oxford with Edmund Rubbra for composition and with
the late Egon Wellesz for the history of music. He spent two years in Sweden at the
universities of Uppsala and Stockholm. He joined the B B C Music Division in 1959,
and as Music Talks Producer has been responsible for such programmes as
Interpretations on Record. He has contributed 'A Quarterly Retrospect' to the
Gramophone for a number of years, and he has written books on Berwald and
Sibelius and has specialized in Scandinavian music. His recent publications include a
monograph on the Dvořák symphonies and concertos for the B B C Music Guides (of
which he is series General Editor) and the first volume of his translation of
Erik Tawaststjerna's definitive study of Sibelius.

Ivan March is an ex-professional musician. He studied at Trinity College of Music,
London, and later at the Royal Manchester College. After service in the R A F
Central Band, he played the horn professionally for the B B C and has also travelled
with the Carl Rosa and D'Oyly Carte opera companies. Now director of the Long
Playing Record Library, the largest commercial lending library for classical music on
L P and cassette tapes in the British Isles, he is a well-known lecturer, journalist, and
personality in the world of recorded music. He is a regular contributor (reviewing
both cassettes and records) to *Gramophone*.

The authors also collaborated on the much-praised *Penguin Stereo Record Guide*,
which has gone into its second edition.

The Penguin Cassette Guide

Edward Greenfield
Robert Layton
Ivan March

Edited by Ivan March

PENGUIN BOOKS

Penguin Books Ltd, Harmondsworth,
Middlesex, England
Penguin Books, 625 Madison Avenue,
New York, New York 10022, U.S.A.
Penguin Books Australia Ltd, Ringwood,
Victoria, Australia
Penguin Books Canada Ltd, 2801 John Street,
Markham, Ontario, Canada L3R 1B4
Penguin Books (N.Z.) Ltd, 182–190 Wairau Road,
Auckland 10, New Zealand

First published 1979

Made and printed in Great Britain by
Richard Clay (The Chaucer Press) Ltd, Bungay, Suffolk
Set in Monophoto Times

Contents

Preface – Tape or Disc?

Recorded music has been with us for just over a century, the disc recording system for only a few years less than that. The LP has been here for three decades, stereo for two. All these ways of reproducing sound essentially derive from Edison's original 1877 mechanical system of etching sound waves on a cylinder. When Emil Berliner's disc arrived in 1887 he merely turned the engraved signal through 90° from Edison's 'hill and dale' method to make the lateral groove of the mono record, first standardized at 78 r.p.m., later to evolve into the 33⅓ r.p.m. LP. The stereo groove marries the two signals, turning the physical information around again so that each 'channel' lies at an angle of 45° to the surface plane of the record. But the physical principle remains the same, and it says much for the robust qualities of Edison's inspiration and the mass duplicating technology that originated with Berliner that an essentially nineteenth-century conception should remain at the centre of our musical culture a hundred years later. The recording process was greatly improved at the turn of the century by the introduction of the wax master; today's increasingly automated manufacturing processes are much more sophisticated than

those of 1887, while the material of which LPs are made is infinitely more refined than the original shellac compound which served the 78 era. But in an electronic age the gramophone/phonograph record is essentially bound to the past. Its universal acceptance and the huge amount of capital invested in world-wide manufacturing plant are both strong factors standing in the way of change. Yet perhaps strongest of all is the pull of nostalgia. We have all grown up with the disc recording, and most of us are reluctant to move away from something so endearingly familiar which has been well tried and on the whole not found wanting. It is no accident that the younger generation was the first to welcome the tape medium.

The musicassette was introduced by the Philips company in 1963. It was originally envisaged as a compact, low-fi and portable means of recording and reproducing speech and music. Its designers could surely never have foreseen the degree of fidelity achieved by the best of today's pre-recorded tapes. They certainly did not anticipate the alleged 'threat' to the recording industry which the modern cassette-recorder is supposed to offer by allowing the user to make his own recordings from the radio or to copy discs on blank tape. The link here with Edison's original phonograph is inescapable. This offered a similar advantage, although Edison was not afraid of any threat to the viability of his commercial recordings. It is reasonable to believe that a background of trepidation within the present-day recording industry – a fear that the ability of the general public to make their own copies might herald the death of the commercially produced record – has held back the fullest development of the cassette as an alternative to disc. But human beings are natural collectors and there is no real reason to assume that first-class pre-recorded tapes (and LPs) will not continue to find a place in music-lovers' homes alongside the home-made product. The question that currently concerns most collectors of recorded music, especially those with high-grade reproducing equipment, is the future potential of the cassette itself as a positive alternative to the LP, and its ability to offer a comparable fidelity of reproduction in spite of its slow speed of $1\frac{7}{8}''$ per second.

There has been a wall of prejudice surrounding the answer to this question, mainly created by the sound experts and engineers, whose judgements always tend to be technical rather than aesthetic and are blinkered by present knowledge. One remembers how we were told in the earliest days of stereo that 'good' mono was better than 'low-fi' stereo. This was true only on a purely

technical level of frequency and dynamic range. Sound reproduction is above all else an illusion, and that illusion was made fundamentally more convincing by stereo just as it had been by the introduction of electric recording in the twenties. The same thinking can be applied to the development of the tape cassette. It may initially have produced a less truthful sound picture than a comparable disc, but what is of paramount importance is the balance of the sound. If this is well managed and there is no suggestion to the ear that the upper range is blanketed and the bass response 'boomy', then the listener can be readily satisfied with what he hears.

At the present stage of the art, a direct A/B comparison between the average mass-produced pre-recorded cassette and the equivalent disc reveals that the latter tends to be marginally superior in frequency range, clarity of detail and distortion content. Often the reproduction is virtually identical, but the cassette shows its slightly less extended range by displaying rather less bloom and smoothness in the treble. That is not to say that the sound on LP is always more natural, or a more agreeable listening experience. Nor is it to suggest that the balance of advantage continues to lie with the disc when other factors are taken into account such as overall background noise, continuity, ease of use, and resistance to deterioration. But most important of all is the consideration that any present limitations in cassette quality are directly attributable to the tape formulations in current use, ferric oxide, chromium dioxide or a laminated combination of the two. Even within these limitations, we have heard an amazing and continuing improvement in cassette reproduction quality during the three-year period of the preparation of this book. This applies to all companies, although it must fairly be said that the technical lead in ferric oxide has been consistently retained by British Decca (London in the USA); and the possibilities and advantages inherent in chromium-dioxide coatings have been imaginatively explored by the Advent Corporation of Cambridge, Massachusetts. But the future undoubtedly lies with more revolutionary tape formulations; we are already promised a pure ferric coating which within the next two years might well bring a quality of sound reproduction at $1\frac{7}{8}''$ per second comparable with a $15''$ per second reel-to-reel master tape. Cost is at present the limiting factor, but past experience suggests that technology in the audio industry can usually provide an answer to this problem.

To the collector of recorded music considering the integration of the compact cassette into his serious collection we would say: the disc, even if it inherently belongs to a past era, will be with us for a long time yet, but the future of tape is bright. The cassette may not be the final answer, but it is a twentieth-century conception. If its transport system is physical, that at least makes a link with the past, but the recording and reproduction chain is entirely electronic. The cassette's construction is simple and robust. It could well become almost foolproof. It is here to stay.

The Cassette Medium –
Some Advantages and Disadvantages

When the long-playing record first appeared and the manufacturers' publicity trumpeted its obvious merits, music-lovers soon discovered that there were drawbacks too. (The old 78-r.p.m. format was, and still is, the ideal way of recording a single song or a Puccini-length aria.) So it is with tape. Moreover not all the inherent advantages of the cassette medium are consistently used by the major manufacturers. We now take for granted the Dolby process which, by a simple pre-emphasis technique, reduces background hiss. But it must be applied with scrupulous care to the tape master or the high frequencies on the cassette are disagreeably muffled. Another problem which can arise in applying the Dolby process may bring a curious pulsing effect to the musical textures, especially destructive of sustained *fortissimo* passages on orchestral strings. Resonance is another source of either distortion or reduction in the refinement of detail in the cassette transfer. Where the reverberation on the original recording is excessive this can cause a muddying intermodulation of treble and bass, blurring the crispness of the upper focus. The bass drum can also cause problems: a single stroke may create an embarrassing hiatus in the overall recorded

texture. Coating faults on the tape itself can produce insecurity of texture or 'drop-outs', where the music suddenly disappears for a split second; and print-through can cause pre- and post-echo effects. All these problems are still with us, although they are much less prevalent now than they were.

Some recordings obviously transfer to cassette more readily than others, and in this respect one often finds really elderly recordings responding especially well. One thinks of the famous series of opera and operetta recordings (produced by Walter Legge) centring around artists like Schwarzkopf, Gedda and Kunz which were first issued on disc in the early fifties. Here the cassette, with its ready response in the middle-frequency area, gives a kindly bloom to voices and orchestra alike. Similarly early stereo recordings where on LP the treble response seems slightly acerbic are made to sound more agreeably balanced without loss of clarity. It is thus not surprising that the Turnabout catalogue has transferred to tape with remarkable success, often giving cassette issues which are preferable to their disc equivalents. But the best modern recording can also be vividly effective, and here the advantage of a reliably silent or near-silent background is a tremendous gain.

First-class cassette quality is inextricably linked to the level at which the transfer can be made. A really high-level transfer brings the double bonus of a low signal-to-noise ratio (i.e. the relationship between the recorded music and any attendant background noise) and a wide frequency range, which means clear detail and a bright treble response. Where the recording is an old one (made before the recording companies used the Dolby system on the master tape itself) some hiss will be inevitable, but that only becomes a real annoyance if linked to the added hiss of the cassette itself. Young ears find hiss more bothersome than older listeners, for as we reach our forties our sensitivity to the frequencies which carry this background noise declines. But almost all listeners tend to accept a steady background noise more readily than the occasional clicks and rustles characteristic of an LP, which immediately impair concentration. One of the great joys of, for instance, a piano recording on tape is security from this kind of interference. Decca have realized the importance of high-level transfers from their earliest Dolby issues, and the best Decca cassettes have a vividness of detail that is sometimes astonishing. EMI tapes too have in the last three years sought high transfer levels, and during one brief period experiments were made – with disastrous results in some cases – in compressing the

dynamic range of the cassette master. Fortunately this is now in the past, and although a few of the issues made at that time are still in the catalogue, others have been remastered. Both Philips and (perhaps surprisingly) DG continue to issue cassettes transferred at unambitious levels, with the result that although the sound may be refined (and DG tapes are often remarkably successful in achieving good detail in spite of the low level) there is a noticeable lack of sparkle and bite in the upper frequencies, with attendant hiss problems at high-level playback. Another consideration with DG tapes is that the level sometimes appears to vary marginally between batches. The reviewer receives an advance copy from Hanover and later discovers that the production run (tailored and assembled in England, but with the actual copying still done in Germany) does not quite match the first copy, perhaps with loss of presence and clarity. Such disparity is exasperating. Absolute consistency is not impossible, as Decca have regularly shown.

One of the ways of making a successful transfer at a high level without distortion is to reduce the amplitude of the sound at the bass end of the audio spectrum. If this is skilfully done the ear hardly notices. Organ recordings are an obvious area where a degree of rebalancing is entirely beneficial. However, great care has to be taken when an orchestral recording is treated in this way; if not, the upper register will harshen or will too obviously lack support in the middle and bass areas. Two other factors are also crucial: the most obvious is the quality of the blank tape in use for the cassette; and the copying speed undoubtedly affects the range and quality of the recording. There is reason to believe that standards in both these areas are sometimes sacrificed in the interests of commercial economy. Often pre-recorded tapes are played on small portable players that conceal most of these faults, and this has minimized public pressure for higher and more consistent overall standards (especially in the area of popular music). Even today a disgraceful number of cassettes – for which the manufacturers still ask premium prices – remain in the catalogue in primitive non-Dolby transfers. Some important early classical issues are among them, a clear indication of the long-standing inertia which has existed since the cassette first appeared and which has retarded its serious appreciation and growth.

A further criticism often levelled at the cassette by the keen record collector is the relative inaccessibility of the inner contents, especially within a miscellaneous collection or recital. Equally obviously, while the second movement of a symphony can be located instantly on an LP, spooling forward on a cassette is (to some) an irritating necessity. It seems incredible to us that the manufacturers of 'hardwear' and 'softwear' have not joined forces to meet this problem halfway. If the digital counter on all cassette decks could be standardized, then the cassette liner-note could indicate the *precise* layout of the contents, making allowance for the length of the run-in leader tape.

Notes are another bone of contention in the presentation of music on tape. They are seldom as generous as those provided with the equivalent disc and often they are printed in unreadably small type. Some early Enigma issues are unbelievably bad examples of the practice of photo-reduction of the LP sleeve notes, but at least this is better than providing no liner notes at all, which has happened on far too many cassettes, at all prices. Operas offer a special problem. They are normally issued in some kind of box or album, and each major company has adopted its own format. Opinions are divided over which of the various methods of packaging is preferable. Certainly the newest DG and Philips joint design seems well-thought-out; each of the cassettes fits into a plastic well and is removable in its conventional hinged 'library' box, which has a simple liner leaflet to detail the contents. Opera recordings are especially attractive for in-car use, and for each tape to be given its own box to protect it when away from the container is a useful refinement. But this means that the spine of the album is comparatively thick, taking up more room on the shelf. Both Decca and EMI favour a shallower box with a moulded interior plastic tray into which the cassettes fit neatly like pieces in a jigsaw puzzle, but there is

THE CASSETTE MEDIUM – SOME ADVANTAGES AND DISADVANTAGES

no protection for them when they are removed. Decca have chosen a book shape (9″ by 7″) and normally go to considerable trouble to provide a clearly printed libretto to fit snugly inside the lid. E M I's box is usually square (standard measurement 7½″) and the libretto is compressed photographically from that provided for the equivalent disc album. Sometimes the print is minuscule, like reading a Ruby edition of the Bible. The slimline D G/Philips album (9½″ by 4½″) offers even greater problems. D G and Philips have always provided robust, clearly printed liner notes with their single cassette issues, but the four-language librettos which accompany their opera sets are printed sideways, and too often the typeface is neither large nor bold enough for comfort. Yet tape remains an ideal medium for opera, offering the unique facility that one can so easily break off listening and return later to exactly the same spot. (The story is told, however, of a critic, who shall be nameless, driving his car into the drive during the middle of the last act of *Der Rosenkavalier* and then sitting enthralled for twenty minutes until the 'performance' concluded.)

We have dwelt at some length on the pitfalls and inadequacies of cassette production. All these problems are soluble, given the pressure of the market-place. Now let us turn to the positive side. Cassettes are inherently more flexible than discs in the matter of playing time; there is no

reason, other than the cost of the tape itself, why we should not be able to listen to *any* major symphonic work with just a single carefully-chosen turnover break. The American Advent company has taken this premise to its logical conclusion by making no break at all in some of their issues, for instance Horenstein's version of Mahler's *First Symphony*. The music is complete on one side, and the purchaser is invited to use the blank side for home recording. Decca too have experimented with double-length tapes with a major symphony on each side (Dvořák's *New World* and Tchaikovsky's *Pathétique*, for example). But it is in the world of opera that the flexibility of tape can be used to the greatest effect. Not all companies take advantage of this. D G cassette issues, for instance, still normally follow the disc format, but both Decca and E M I have shown what can be done. An excellent example is the Decca recording of Mozart's *Nozze di Figaro* conducted by Erich Kleiber. Here is a performance famous for its compulsive forward momentum (especially in Act 2). On disc it has never been heard without interruptions. The tape issue, however, presents each act complete on one of four cassette sides – and moreover the transfer has improved the recorded sound immeasurably in comparison with the quality available on the original LPs. With the longest operas the advantage can be even more striking, as in the Solti recordings of

Wagner's *Ring*, where, whenever possible, a single cassette is provided for each separate act. Continuity is obviously an enormous boon to concentration but it can be overdone. The EMI way with opera is often to prefer two cassettes to three or more, whatever the length of the piece. The Giulini version of *Don Giovanni* proves an admirable example, with each of the two acts on a single tape; but the Karajan *Der Rosenkavalier* is transferred from four discs to two cassettes, whereas the Solti version is handier on three, one to each act. For operetta and Gilbert and Sullivan, EMI have sensibly been transferring whole works on to single extended-play tapes. There is apparently some market resistance to this scheme, by the very reason of the miniature size of the overall presentation, but it seems an ideal solution, particularly when a two-act work can be accommodated with one act on each side. Obviously consumer resistance could be overcome by putting such a double-length tape issue in a box, complete with notes, and it is surprising that no company has tried this out.

During the war the BBC Brains Trust once considered which items representative of twentieth-century culture should be buried to be rediscovered by a future generation. The obvious musical choice was a 78-r.p.m. recording of Beethoven's *Choral symphony*. Today a recording of that famous work can be fitted compactly (and with no mid-movement break) on one extended-play cassette that will slip neatly into a jacket pocket. Could anything represent the last quarter of the twentieth century more effectively?

Introduction

The object of *The Penguin Cassette Guide* is to provide the serious tape collector with a comprehensive guide to the cream of the cassette tape recordings of permanent music available in the United Kingdom. We foresee that this book will also be read by *record* collectors who may be considering venturing into the field of pre-recorded tapes. Thus almost all our reviews initially discuss the basic recording as found on the equivalent L Ps and then add a comment about the comparative quality of the tape transfer. As will be seen, this can vary tremendously. The worst cassette issues sound unbelievably coarse and distorted (one wonders at times whether they passed any kind of aural quality control by their manufacturers), but the best can be virtually indistinguishable from disc reproduction. The high-speed copying process has brought problems of insecurity of pitch and texture and with some companies a lack of consistency. But this can apply to L P record surfaces too and, as with discs, a reputable dealer is usually willing to exchange a 'rogue tape' and try again, especially where the purchaser has seen a favourable review.

Of course tape is not restricted to classical music alone, and as an appendix to our classical reviews we give a list of spoken-word material which is extremely attractive for a long car journey, especially with children. Modern light background music is also useful in the car, and can serve a double function as background for a party or dinner. Ideally one needs double-length cassettes for this purpose, but there are surprisingly few available. In our appendix the field is discussed briefly. But for most readers it is the rich repertoire of serious music that will be the prime concern, and that is what our book is about.

Our coverage of the tape catalogue in the UK has been as near comprehensive as possible, and so far as we know this is the first serious attempt in the world to provide a wide-ranging critical appraisal of pre-recorded tapes. Only Dolbyized cassettes have been included. While 'pop' music may be acceptable in non-Dolby form because of its consistently high decibels, classical music, with its wide dynamic contrasts, certainly is not.

The sheer number of available recordings of artistic merit offers considerable problems in any assessment of overall and individual excellence. While in the case of a single popular repertoire work it might be ideal for the discussion to be conducted by a single reviewer, it was not always possible for one person to have access to every version, and division of reviewing responsibility inevitably leads to some clashes of opinion. Also there are certain works and certain recorded performances for which one or another of our team has a special affinity. Such a personal identification can often carry with it a special perception too. We feel that it is a strength of our basic style to let such conveyed pleasure or admiration for the merits of an individual recording come over directly to the reader, even if this produces a certain ambivalence in the matter of choice between competing recordings. Where disagreement is profound (and this has very rarely happened), then readers will find an indication of this difference of opinion in the text. We have considered and rejected the use of initials against individual reviews, since this is essentially a team project.

EVALUATION

However good a recorded performance may be, the impact it makes on the listener is greatly dependent on the skill of the engineers. In the case of cassettes this dependence is amplified by the need for great additional skill in the preparation of the secondary master tape and in monitoring the transfer process itself. Because of the variable degree of expertise shown in these procedures, a 'best-buy' recommendation on disc is not

always mirrored for its tape equivalent. We have followed the starring system already established in our companion *Penguin Stereo Record Guide*:

*** An outstanding performance in every way, well recorded and successfully transferred to cassette, losing little if any of the excellence of the equivalent L P.
** A good performance and recording of today's normal high standard, satisfactorily transferred.
* A fair performance sounding acceptable in its tape format.

Brackets round one or more of the stars indicate reservations about its inclusion and readers are advised to refer to the text. Brackets round two of the stars are often used for a recording which has great merit as a performance but which is less than satisfactorily transferred to tape; and brackets round all three stars may indicate that the tape transfer leaves a great deal to be desired.

The symbols (M) and (B) indicate whether a tape is issued in the U K at medium or bargain price. Where no bracketed initial precedes the starring it can be taken that the issue is on a premium-priced label (currently ranging between £4.50 and £5.50). Medium-priced tapes at present cost between £2.75 and £3.75; the bargain labels centre around £2, but with ever-pressing inflationary trends they seem increasingly to move upwards towards the middle-price area. It could be argued that many issues in Decca's lower price schedules (KCSP, KECC etc.), which we have treated as medium-priced, are in effect an 'upper-bargain' range because of their technical reliability.

Our evaluation is normally applied to the cassette as a whole, unless there are two main works, or groups of works, on each side of the tape, and by different composers. In a few cases where short but major works are featured, this principle has been extended to give three or four separate entries in the appropriate places.

ROSETTES

To a very few recordings we have awarded a rosette: ❀.

Unlike our general evaluation, where we have tried to be consistent, a rosette is a quite arbitrary compliment by a member of the reviewing team to a recorded performance which he finds shows special illumination, a magic, or spiritual quality that places it in a very special class. The editor has in addition awarded a rosette to a very few 'hand-picked' cassettes where the combination of musical and technical achievement is memorable, or the presentation imaginatively apt. In all cases the choice is essentially a personal one. The rosette symbol is placed immediately before the normal evaluation and catalogue number. It is quite small; we do not mean to imply an 'Academy award' but to give a token of personal appreciation for something uniquely valuable. We hope that

once a reader has discovered and perhaps acquired a 'rosette' issue, its special qualities will soon become apparent.

LAYOUT OF TEXT

We have aimed to make our style as simple as possible. Immediately before the catalogue number, the manufacturer and label are given in full except for familiar shortenings, such as DG (for Deutsche Grammophon) and HMV (for His Master's Voice).

Numbers in square brackets are US catalogue numbers. Further details are given in the note for American readers below.

We have tried to avoid using too many abbreviations in indicating the contents of the cassettes, but when a work is listed several times its title is usually shortened. For opera recordings only the principal artists are named and we have, for space reasons, omitted details of the contents of operatic highlights collections. These can be found in the *Gramophone Classical Catalogue*, published quarterly by the *Gramophone* magazine.

To make further space savings we have sometimes omitted artists' Christian names where they are not absolutely necessary for identification purposes. In addition some familiar or obvious abbreviations are used, including:

| CO | Chamber Orchestra |
| ECO | English Chamber Orchestra |

Ens.	Ensemble
LPO	London Philharmonic Orchestra
LSO	London Symphony Orchestra
PO	Philharmonic Orchestra
Qt	Quartet
RPO	Royal Philharmonic Orchestra
SO	Symphony Orchestra

We have followed common practice in the use of the original language for titles where it seems sensible. In most cases English is used for orchestral and instrumental music and the original language for vocal music and opera. There are exceptions, however; for instance, the Johann Strauss tapeography uses the German language in the interests of consistency.

ORDER OF MUSIC

The order of music under each composer's name broadly follows that adopted by the *Gramophone Classical Catalogue*: orchestral music, including concertos and symphonies; chamber music; solo instrumental music (in some cases with keyboard and organ music separated); vocal and choral music; opera; vocal collections; miscellaneous collections.

The *Gramophone Classical Catalogue* now usually elects to include stage works alongside opera; we have not generally followed this practice, preferring to list, for instance, ballet music and incidental music (where no vocal items are involved)

in the general orchestral group. Within each group our listing follows an alphabetic sequence, and couplings within a single composer's output are *usually* discussed together instead of separately with cross-references. Occasionally and inevitably because of this alphabetical approach, different recordings of a given work can become separated when a cassette is listed and discussed under the first work of its alphabetical sequence. A cross-reference is then usually given (either within the listing or in the review) to any important alternative versions. The editor feels that alphabetical consistency is essential if the reader is to learn to find his way about.

CONCERTS AND RECITALS

Most collections of music intended to be regarded as concerts or recitals involve several composers and it is quite impractical to deal with them within the alphabetical composer index. They are grouped separately, at the end of the book, in four sections. In each section, cassettes are usually arranged in alphabetical order of the performers' names: concerts of orchestral and concertante music (under the name of the orchestra, ensemble or, if more important, conductor or soloist); brass and military band collections (under the name of the band); instrumental recitals (under the name of the instrumentalist); operatic and vocal recitals (under the principal singer or vocal group as seems appropriate).

In certain cases where the compilation features many different performers it is listed alphabetically under its collective title, or the key word in that title (so *Great opera choruses* is listed under 'Opera choruses'). Often for complicated collections only brief details of contents and performers are given; fuller information can usually be found in the current *Gramophone Classical Catalogue*.

CASSETTE NUMBERS

Enormous care has gone into the checking of cassette numbers and contents to ensure that all details are correct, but the editor and publishers cannot be held responsible for any mistakes that may have crept in despite all our zealous checking. When ordering cassettes, readers are urged to provide their dealer with full details of the music and performers as well as the catalogue number.

DELETIONS

Inevitably a small number of the cassettes reviewed here will prove to have been later withdrawn by their manufacturers, though this does not always mean that copies cannot still be found in the shops.

PLAYING EQUIPMENT

As many readers will have discovered for themselves, different tape decks with broadly similar technical specifications and claims to fidelity give varying sound balances, especially when used in conjunction with alternative hi-fi reproducing chains. Currently the main difference between the newest and better decks concerns the relative brightness and softness of grain of the treble response. It is obviously vital to have a clear, clean upper range, and most modern cassette players can offer this, but the cheaper decks sometimes give an added edge to the sound which is difficult to smooth without dampening detail in the middle frequency range. The differences are not unlike those between different gramophone pickups. Each of the three authors has assembled a high-grade reproducing set-up which he finds satisfying, but because of the factors mentioned above (and the acoustic of each listening room makes its own contribution) the end results are not identical. To achieve consistency in our technical comments the editor has tried to listen to some if not all of each tape reviewed within these pages and act as final arbiter on the technical judgements expressed.

ACKNOWLEDGEMENTS

The editor and authors express herewith their gratitude to Mrs Judith Wardman, a member of Penguin's editorial staff, for her help in the preparation of this volume, and also to E. T. Bryant, M.A., F.L.A., for his assistance with the task of proof-correcting.

Advent Process CR/70 Cassettes

Advent cassettes represent a modest but ambitious enterprise by an American corporation in Cambridge, Massachusetts. Advent tapes began production in 1970, and the catalogue lists between fifty and sixty classical issues. It must be said that to European ears some of Advent's own recordings sound rather too closely balanced, but many Advent cassettes use smaller but famous international labels for their recording sources, such as Nonesuch, Desmar and Unicorn. The technical excellence of the transfers, using chrome tape as standard, is fairly consistent, although there are a few disappointments. The classical issues are tailored to take the fullest advantage of the flexibility of tape in the layout of the music itself. The duplicating system (Process CR/70) has been designed to produce a pre-recorded copy which 'when played on the finest deck achieves a signal-to-noise level comparable with the master tape'. This ambitious claim is sometimes slightly undermined by the moderate level of the transfer itself. Nevertheless the finest of Advent's issues are very impressive.

The duplicator's high performance is due in part to its operating at just four times the cassette's playing speed, rather than using the ratio of sixteen or thirty-two (and sometimes sixty-four!) which is more normal in commercial copying processes. This slow copying speed, incidentally, is necessary for practical as well as technical reasons, for we understand that high-speed copying using chrome tape induces such excessive wear on the manufacturing tape heads that it becomes uneconomic. However, it is the end product that counts. Advent tapes are austerely packaged but include concise, clearly printed liner notes. Moreover the purchaser is offered access to a series of booklets giving much fuller musical information. Many of the major Advent issues are reviewed within our pages, and these cassettes can be ordered by mail. Cambridge, Massachusetts, is as near the west coast of England as the west coast of America, and British readers should have no difficulty in obtaining them.

The address to write to is:
Process CR/70 Department,
Advent Corporation,
195 Albany Street,
Cambridge,
Massachusetts 02139,
USA.

For American Readers

The tape scene is by no means identical in Great Britain and the USA. The British Decca company issues tapes in America on the London label, and Argo issues are similarly available. Both are manufactured in England. The important DG and Philips cassettes can also be obtained in America: their catalogue numbers are often internationally identical. But RCA and CBS issues in the USA have no direct connection with their British counterparts, while Angel (the American equivalent of British EMI's HMV classical label) also has an independent tape catalogue in the USA, and tapes are manufactured domestically. Angel publicity claims suggest that the dynamic range of these cassette issues may not always coincide with the equivalent discs. At such a distance a survey of these American-produced tapes is not feasible, and readers will need to make their own experiments. However, American catalogue numbers are included throughout this survey where they are known at the time of going to press. In each case the American domestic listing is given in square brackets immediately after the British catalogue number. The abbreviation [id.] indicates that the American and British numbers are identical.

The addition of (d) immediately before the American number indicates some difference in the contents of the American issue. We have taken care to check catalogue information as far as possible, but as all the editorial work has been done in England there is always the possibility of error and American readers are advised, when ordering tapes locally, to take the precaution of giving their dealer the fullest information about the music and recordings they want.

The indications (M) or (B) immediately before the starring of a recording refer only to the British issue, as pricing systems are not always identical both sides of the Atlantic.

Where no American catalogue number is given this does not necessarily mean that a tape is not available in the USA; the transatlantic issue may not have been made at the time of the publication of this *Guide*. Readers are advised to check the current *Schwann Catalogue* and consult their local store. Most important classical recordings are made today for international circulation, but certain works are better represented in Europe than in the USA. This particularly applies to the 'bargain' and medium-priced area. Where a required recording is not readily available locally it will probably be obtainable direct from England. Readers are invited to write to:

Squires Gate Music Centre,
Squires Gate Station Approach,
Blackpool, Lancashire, England.

Adam, Adolphe
(1803–56)

Giselle (ballet; ed. Henri Büsser).
  (M) *** Decca KCSP 15384. Paris
    Conservatoire Orch., Martinon.
Giselle (older European score): highlights.
  (M) **(*) Decca Jubilee KJBC 14.
    Vienna PO, Karajan.

Adam's famous score – the first of the great romantic ballets – has been heard in various forms since its first performance in 1841, but for the ordinary ballet-lover the various interpolations and alterations of orchestration will not be of prime importance. The Büsser version has the advantage of fitting compactly on to a single disc or tape and yet including all the important music. Jean Martinon's performance is an ideal one, warm and full of poetry, with lovely string playing. The opening of Act 2 is enchanting. The recording here has splendid atmosphere and throughout has a fine tonal bloom and crispness of focus. This is undoubtedly one of Decca's best cassettes, and the overall sparkle is matched by the brilliance of the string tone.

Karajan's Vienna cassette is lovingly played, with the suave blandishments of the Karajan baton guiding the famous orchestra to produce a reading of beauty and elegance. The glowing Decca recording is first-rate and as the legend of the Wilis (the ghosts of dead girls jilted by their lovers) on which *Giselle* is based is a German one, to have a distinct impression of Austrian peasantry and hunting music will seem to many very appropriate. The lighter, French style of Martinon's account remains preferable,
but those who fancy the Karajan approach will find this Decca tape of very high quality, notably rich and resonant, yet with no lack of sparkle. It is a most sophisticated issue, with (appropriately) more body of string tone than the Martinon.

Albéniz, Isaac
(1860–1909)

Suite española (arr. Frühbeck de Burgos).
  *** Decca KSXC 6355. New
    Philharmonia Orch., Frühbeck
    de Burgos.

As we go to press this cassette has been withdrawn (one hopes temporarily), but there may well still be some copies about, and it must be listed, since it was for the cassette-tape medium what the famous Ansermet *Petrushka* was for LP, showing spectacularly that a full-ranging and sparkling orchestral sound could be captured on a $1\frac{7}{8}''$ p.s. tape, when most cassettes available at the time offered a restricted range unsupported by Dolby. It offers real light music of the best kind. Tuneful, exotically scored (by the conductor here, Rafael Frühbeck de Burgos), and giving orchestra and recording engineers alike a chance to show their paces, the *Suite española* makes highly entertaining listening. We are given here seven pieces from Albéniz's original piano suite plus *Cordoba*, which is from the same composer's *Cantos de España*. As this has a very fetching tune to end the programme graciously, no one is likely to complain. But try the opening *Castilla* for its glittering castanets or the *Asturias*

1

with its eloquent and sonorous brass chords to offset the flurry of strings.

Albinoni, Tommaso
(1671–1750)

Adagio in G minor (arr. Giazotto) *for strings and organ.*
- (M) ** Turnabout KTVC 34135. Douglas Haas (organ), Württemberg CO, Faerber – CORRETTE and HANDEL: *Concertos*; MOZART: *Sonata.* (**)
- (M) * Saga CA 5443. Sinfonia di Siena – VIVALDI: *Four Seasons.**(*)

This is Albinoni's equivalent of Bach's so-called *Air on the G string*; only the lushness of the arrangement suggests the twentieth rather than the nineteenth century. The effect is vulgar but striking too, and one can understand why the piece has had considerable popular success. The Turnabout version is played discreetly and with taste. The transfer to tape is quite effective, but unfortunately the sound quality in the couplings is much less congenial. Readers are reminded that there is also an enticingly plushy Karajan/Berlin Philharmonic version, which makes no attempt to simulate baroque style but is very agreeable just the same (DG 3300 317: see our Concerts section below, where several other versions are also reviewed).

On Saga the playing of the Sinfonia di Siena is expressive, with an agreeably rich string texture. The recording is smooth; the sound, although not wide-ranging, is quite acceptable. There is some lack of refinement of texture at the climax.

Adagio in G minor (arr. Giazotto) *for strings and organ; Oboe concerto in G minor, Op. 9/8; Double oboe concerto in F major, Op. 9/3; Violin concertos:* *in B flat major, Op. 9/1; in G minor, Op. 10/8.*
- (M) ** Philips 7317 094 [7310 085]. I Musici (with soloists).

This is an exceptionally lively cassette, with clean textures of demonstration quality, especially on side one. The approach of I Musici to the infamous *Adagio* is to try and permeate it with a genuine baroque sensibility. But Giazotto's arrangement essentially needs fuller textures than are provided here and the result is less happy than in rival performances. But the rest of the programme is much more successful, and as the tape is well filled it remains an excellent medium-priced anthology. The style throughout is vibrant and the recording vivid, if sometimes a little dry in texture. The two oboes are rather forwardly balanced in the *Double concerto*, but as Heinz Holliger is the principal the playing itself is distinguished. The quality of the presentation has the proper bright colouring, and the harpsichord comes through nicely without sounding artificially balanced. A fresh and enjoyable concert.

Arensky, Anton
(1861–1906)

Variations on a theme of Tchaikovsky, Op. 35a.
- (M) (***) HMV TC-SXLP 30239. LSO, Barbirolli – TCHAIKOVSKY: *Serenade for strings.*(***)

Barbirolli's reading of Arensky's delightful and very Tchaikovskian variations is full-blooded, even passionate, and obviously seeks to remove for ever the epithet 'slight' from descriptions of the work. There is affection too, of course, and a splendid flexibility of phrasing and dynamic. Thus the slow variation which is obviously modelled on the famous *Andante cantabile* from Tchaikovsky's *D major String quartet* is wonderfully gentle. The record is basically spacious, but the quality of the transfer is not very refined. The transfer is made at a high level, and the resonance tends to cloud the texture.

Arnold, Malcolm
(born 1921)

(i) *Flute concertos Nos. 1, Op. 45; 2, Op. 11. Sinfoniettas Nos. 1, Op. 48; 2, Op. 65.*

> **(*) HMV TC-ASD 3487. Philharmonia Orch., Dilkes, (i) with John Solum (flute).

Malcolm Arnold is not always able to keep his high spirits and exuberance from overstepping the mark, but in these works there is little trace of vulgarity and a great deal of charm and invention. The *First Sinfonietta* is distinguished by some excellent ideas, and the *Flute concertos* are both charming and resourceful; there is no doubt that Arnold's mastery of the orchestra is of a high order. John Solum plays excellently and receives good support from the Philharmonia under Neville Dilkes. The recorded sound has admirable freshness and a good sense of space; the flute is (only marginally) larger than life and the orchestral detail is vivid. The transfer is smooth and atmospheric, but the treble is soft-grained rather than sharply focused. The sound suits the two *Flute concertos* rather better than the *Sinfoniettas*, which, although they are pleasing, lack something in sparkle in the treble.

Guitar concerto, Op. 67.

> **(*) CBS 40-76715. John Williams, London Sinfonietta, Howarth – BROUWER: *Guitar concerto.***(*)

It was Julian Bream who pioneered Arnold's *Guitar concerto* in the recording studio, but his version is not available on tape, and this new version makes an admirable alternative. John Williams sounds a shade larger-than-life, but not unacceptably so. Slightly more ambience might have given the orchestral timbre a greater degree of freshness, but in any event this is basically a first-class recording. Bream gives the more romantic, dreamier performance, but John Williams has concentration and eloquence. A finely characterized reading, with good support from Elgar Howarth and the London Sinfonietta. The transfer is smooth and quite natural if lacking the last degree of range and sparkle in the treble.

Concerto for Phyllis and Cyril.

> (M) *** HMV Greensleeve TC-ESD 7065. Cyril Smith, Phyllis Sellick (pianos), City of Birmingham SO, the composer – BLISS and JACOB: *Concertos.****

Malcolm Arnold wrote his three-handed concerto especially for Phyllis Sellick and Cyril Smith, and a riotous first performance was given at a Saturday-night Prom. This recorded version, with the composer conducting, was made in the De Montfort Hall, Leicester, and although inevitably in such music which calls for outright laughter you miss an audience, the humour is still infectious. The first movement starts with Stravinskian bell sounds, which lead to a gently lyrical middle section. The central *Andante con moto* is a cool chaconne with an elaborate descant for the second piano. The finale is an outrageous send-up of pop music of the twenties, banjo-

3

strumming and all. A delightful, undemanding work, superbly played by the dedicatees. The recording has a fine sense of spectacle, and the reverberant acoustic is remarkably well captured in the vivid tape transfer.

Serenade for guitar and string orchestra.
   ** CBS 40-76634. John Williams, ECO, Groves – CASTEL-NUOVO-TEDESCO: *Concerto No. 1***; DODGSON: *Concerto No. 2.***(*)

Malcolm Arnold's *Serenade* is a short, beguiling piece, beautifully laid out for guitar and strings, and it is played with great poetry and charm by John Williams and the ECO. The sound is warm and pleasing, if not strikingly extended in range. The balance favours the distinguished soloist unduly.

Symphony No. 2, Op. 40; English dances Nos. 1–8.
   *(*) HMV TC-ASD 3353. Bournemouth SO, Groves.

The *Symphony No. 2* is a fresh, colourful work, far more complex in structure than it may initially seem. Like Shostakovich Arnold opts for an easygoing *Allegretto*, but its undemanding open-air manner conceals genuine symphonic purpose. So with the rest of the symphony, including the beautiful slow movement – much the longest – where a haunting tune with a distant echo of the second subject of Tchaikovsky's *Pathétique* builds up to a formidable climax. Groves secures a dedicated performance. The *English dances*, first of a genre that Arnold has made his own, are superb in their rumbustiousness. The cassette transfer is disappointing, lacking sparkle and refined detail in the symphony (the textures tend to sound opaque) and the right kind of demonstration brilliance in the dances, although

here the sound is quite vivid. Unnecessarily, the tape turns over before the last movement of the symphony, which is placed on side two before the dances.

Bach, Carl Philipp Emanuel (1714–88)

Magnificat, W.215.
   **(*) Argo KZRC 853. Felicity Palmer, Helen Watts, Robert Tear, Stephen Roberts, King's College Choir, Academy of St Martin-in-the-Fields, Ledger.

One would have thought that the example of father Johann Sebastian in setting the *Magnificat* would have been daunting to his son; but just before old Bach died, C.P.E. produced a setting which in terms of the *galant* style conveyed startling involvement. The magnificent opening chorus (repeated later in the setting of the *Gloria*) presents King's College Choir at its most exhilarating. This irresistible movement, here taken challengingly fast, leads to a whole series of sharply characterized numbers, including a sparkling tenor aria on *Quia fecit*. The whole is rounded off in a choral fugue as energetic as Handel's best, with barely a nod in father's direction. With vividly atmospheric recording the performance under Philip Ledger comes electrically to life, with choir, soloists, and orchestra all in splendid form. The cassette transfer has been very well managed. The sound is vivid and spacious and only at the very end is there a suspicion that the level of modulation is fractionally high.

Bach, Johann Christian (1735–82)

Harp concerto in D major (from *Harpsichord concerto, Op. 1/6*).
- (B) ** Philips Fontana 7328 612. Annie Challan (harp), Antiqua Musica Orch., Couraud – HANDEL: *Royal Fireworks suite*; HAYDN: *Symphony No. 101.***

This is the most interesting work on this inexpensive cassette. The concerto uses *God save the Queen* as a basis for its finale and is attractively inventive throughout. It is well played, and the recording has transferred smoothly.

Six 'favourite' overtures: Nos. 1–3 in D major; 4 in C major; 5–6 in G major.
- *** Oiseau-Lyre KDSLC 525. Academy of Ancient Music, dir. Christopher Hogwood (harpsichord).

J. C. Bach's *Six 'favourite' overtures* were published as a set in London in 1763 for use in the concert hall, although their original derivation was theatrical. They are all short and succinct Italian-style pieces in three movements (fast–slow–fast), and they show great variety of invention and imaginative scoring (using double wind: oboes, sometimes flutes, horns and strings). The performances here are characteristically alert and vivid and there are many features to remain in the mind: the trio for wind instruments in the finale of No. 1; the attractively robust outer movements of No. 3; the Vivaldi-like figuration of the finale of No. 4; the tripping strings in the *Andante* of No. 5. This is not a tape to play all at once, but dipped into it offers delightful music played in a refreshingly spirited (and authentic) way. The recording is excellent, and the transfer very good indeed, if fractionally mellower on side one than side two.

Bach, Johann Sebastian (1685–1750)

ORCHESTRAL MUSIC

The Art of fugue (*Die Kunst der Fuge*), *BWV 1080*.
- **(*) Philips 7699 007 [id.]. Academy of St Martin-in-the-Fields, Marriner.

Neville Marriner in the edition he prepared with Andrew Davis has varied the instrumental textures of *The Art of fugue* most intelligently, giving a fair proportion of the fugues and canons to keyboard instruments, organ as well as harpsichord. In each instance the instrument has been chosen as specially suitable to that particular movement. So the opening fugue is given to plain string quartet, the second to the full orchestra of strings (two violins, viola, cello and violone) and woodwind (two oboes, cor anglais and bassoon), and so on. The fugue for two harpsichords and its inversion are exhilarating as performed by Andrew Davis and Christopher Hogwood, while the final quadruple fugue, which Bach never completed, is left achingly in mid-air at the end, a valid procedure on record at least. Marriner's style of performance is profoundly satisfying, with finely judged tempi, unmannered phrasing and resilient rhythms. The sound is excellent, beautifully refined, until the final side, when the hitherto clear focus of the recording becomes slightly muzzy. This fault may well not appear on all copies, but it is best to check.

Brandenburg concertos Nos. 1–6, BWV 1046/51.
- **(*) Philips 7699 006 [id.]. ECO, Leppard.
- **(*) Enigma K 453547/8. Northern Sinfonia, Malcolm.
- **(*) DG 3370 021. Los Angeles PO, Zukerman.

** Decca KSXC 6774/5 [Lon. 5-6634/5]. ECO, Britten.
** Philips 7300 158/9 [id.]. Academy of St Martin-in-the-Fields, Marriner.
**Telefunken CX 4.41191/2 [id.]. Vienna Concentus Musicus, Harnoncourt.
(M) *(*) Turnabout KTVC 34044/5 [CT 2126/7]. Württemberg CO, Faerber.
(B) *(*) Classics for Pleasure TC-CFP 40010/11. Virtuosi of England, Davison.

Brandenburg concertos Nos. 1–6; Suite No. 2 in B minor, BWV 1067: Rondeau; Menuet; Badinerie. Suite No. 3 in D major, BWV 1068: Air.
(M) *(*) Decca KCSP 382/3. Stuttgart CO, Münchinger.

Although Leppard's set is placed at the top of the list, there is an element of controversy about the consistently fast tempi that he adopts throughout. Certainly the sparkling contribution from the ECO soloists is splendidly alive and buoyant, and the recording is beautifully balanced as well as vivid. The secure horns in No. 1 with their easy roulades and trills; the impeccable, crisp accuracy of John Wilbraham's trumpet in No. 2, matched by some delightful oboe playing; a characteristically piquant account of the recorder solos in No. 4 from the late David Munrow: all these give consistent pleasure to the listener. Leppard's own harpsichord solo in No. 5, however, seems curiously rigid. The recording is very good indeed, fresh and with fine body, yet with the inner detail admirably clear. To some ears this is all irresistible; others find that Leppard's vivacity can sometimes seem a little too insistent. Nevertheless this stands very high indeed among the current versions. The transfers are of excellent quality, although on each tape the sound seems to be marginally cleaner on the second side: thus

there is a hint of fluffiness in the horn-dominated texture of No. 1, yet No. 5 (on the reverse side) is cleanly focused. Similarly on the second tape, where Concertos Nos. 3 and 4 (on side two) offer demonstration quality, Nos. 2 and 6 (on side one) are slightly less sharp in detail. But taken as a whole this set is thoroughly recommendable, although the musical comments and notes are not generous.

Malcolm's are highly enjoyable, amiable performances, very well recorded. Indeed on tape they offer perhaps the highest standards of sound quality in any set of the *Brandenburgs*. The quality is clean and natural, not lacking brightness. The transfer level of the first tape is marginally lower than the second, which means that the sound has fractionally less detail; yet the *Second Concerto* is especially vivid and lively. It might be felt that the balance in No. 4 makes the harpsichord too dominant. Malcolm's direction ensures rhythmic resilience throughout, and, more clearly than in many more brilliant performances, the players here convey the joy of Bach's inspiration. Much of the solo playing – for instance the oboe – is most sensitive, but by the highest international standards there is sometimes a shortfall in polish and precision.

The discipline of the Los Angeles players under Zukerman is most impressive and the playing of Zukerman himself in the violin solos adds an individuality and sense of purpose which set a seal on the performances. But to some ears the accompanying rhythms may seem to be pursued too relentlessly, and too even in stress. It is instructive to compare movements in which Zukerman chooses unusually fast speeds against the recording of Raymond Leppard: consistently the Philips version allows extra resilience and extra breathing-space, however rapid the tempo. The sound on tape is generally very successful, comparatively full-textured in No. 1 and with splendid linear detail in Nos. 2 and 4, the latter sounding especially bright and pleasingly detailed. No. 6 too offers an admirable balance between clarity and homogeneity, and only in No. 5 is there a tendency to edginess in the upper string sound. The continuo can be heard throughout but is not strongly projected.

Britten made his recording in the Maltings Concert Hall not long before the serious fire there. The engineers had not quite accustomed themselves to the reverberant acoustic, and to compensate they put the microphones rather close to the players. The result is big beefy sound that in its way goes well with Britten's interpretations, which are not quite what one would expect. The disappointing element is the lack of delicacy in the slow movements of Nos. 1, 2, 4 and 6. However, the bubbling high spirits of the outer movements are hard to resist, and Philip Ledger, the harpsichordist, follows the pattern he set in live Britten performances with extra Britten-inspired elaborations, a continual delight. The transfer offers rather sharp-edged string tone (except in No. 6, which is almost too mellow, to the point of lugubriousness); the harpsichord too sounds rather metallic. However, a treble reduction and bass increase produce satisfactory results.

Marriner, one had predicted, would before long record a set of *Brandenburgs* to outshine all others. In some ways his Philips set does bear out one's expectations, for the stylishness of the playing, the point of phrasing, the resilience of rhythm, coupled with superb recording, are very satisfying. But, sadly, Marriner uses an edition prepared by the late Thurston Dart (here contributing to some of the concertos in the very last days before he died) which aims at re-creating the first version of these works long before Bach thought of sending them to the Margrave of Brandenburg. So No. 1, for example, has only three movements, there is a horn instead of a trumpet in No. 2, and maddeningly squeaky sopranino recorders in No. 4. Often the sounds are delightful, but this is not a definitive set of *Brandenburgs* such as Marriner will one day make. The sound on tape is of good quality, but the level is not very high and the comparative lack of brilliance in the recording means that a slight treble lift may be needed, which brings up the hiss.

The Telefunken set aims at reconstructing the authentic sound of the original performances, using stringed instruments modified to eighteenth-century sound characteristics, and wind instruments that are either genuinely old or else exact copies of originals. But the final assessment will always concern the musical qualities of a performance, over and above any claims for authenticity. In fact all attempts to produce an 'original' sound are essentially conjectural, since not only instruments but musicians – the personal element – varied from year to year and from city to city. Not that the 'old' sounds here are at all unpleasant. No. 5, for example, gains because of the better balance between the soloists; No. 1, however (never easy to record, with its horns and oboes), suffers from internal fuzziness. The mixed brass, woodwind and strings in No. 2 integrate more successfully, as does the sound of recorders and violin in No. 4. But the excessive closeness of the sound picture, which is consistent throughout (set within the resonant acoustic of the Great Hall of the Schönburg Palace in Vienna), means that there is nothing like a real *pianissimo* at any time, even in slow movements. The interpretations are variable. Generally tempi are traditional, but here and there – as in the plodding speed for the first movement of No. 2, and the insensitively fast speed for the first movement of No. 6 – the direction is less convincing. Most damaging of all is the square continuo-playing of Georg Fischer. However, there is much in this version to interest the connoisseur of 'old' sounds, and with the advantage of chrome tape (not fully used because of the comparatively low-level transfer) the sound has a fairly wide range, even if detail is not very crisp in focus.

7

The Faerber performances are well made, spontaneous and musically convincing. The wind-playing is generally excellent, and the harpsichord soloist distinguishes himself in No. 5, although the continuo-playing is less imaginative elsewhere. The overall effect is of a small group of musicians playing with skill and conviction, and the recording has worn its years lightly. However, the Turnabout transfers were early ones; we have tried current copies, but the quality remains disappointing, with a generally fizzy focus to the upper strings. No. 1, with horns, is thick-textured, and neither No. 3 nor No. 5, which share the first tape, is particularly clean in the upper range. Generally KTVC 34045 is the better of the two tapes, and the *Second Concerto* with its solo trumpet sounds well. But in No. 4, although the flutes are clear, the string textures again lack the clean detail one expects from Decca transfers.

The transfer of the Classics for Pleasure set has been made at a remarkably high level with only marginal loss of refinement, although the dynamic range has been levelled. Even so, the robust lively playing is enjoyable, and the second cassette, with Nos. 4–6, sounds especially well, with clear, realistic sound quality. The brisk, unfussy approach of the conductor, Arthur Davison, is impressive, but these performances in the last analysis lack individuality.

It was Münchinger and his Stuttgart Chamber players who in the early days of LP revolutionized our ideas of Bach playing. After that in successive new versions of the *Brandenburgs* they seemed to grow more stolid, less imaginative. The present set is the earlier of Münchinger's two stereo versions. It is very well transferred to tape and is technically one of the finest cassette editions, with plenty of tonal body and clean sound, notably brighter in the *Fourth* and *Fifth Concertos*. It is a pity that the playing itself is not more imaginative. The performances are reliable enough but squarer and less buoyant than this conductor's best work, and are

not really a rival to Faerber in the same price range. However, the Turnabout transfers offer a less satisfactory sound picture.

Flute concerto in A minor (from BWV 1056; ed. Galway); Flute concerto in E minor (from BWV 1059 and BWV 35; ed. Radeke); Suite No. 2 in B minor for flute and strings, BWV 1067.

*** RCA RK 25119. James Galway (flute), Zagreb Soloists, led by Tonko Ninic.

The two arranged concertos (one a reconstruction) prove an admirable vehicle for James Galway, and he plays the famous slow-movement cantilena of BWV 1056 (the *F minor Harpsichord concerto*) as beautifully as one might expect. He is balanced forwardly, and is in consequence slightly larger than life. In the *Suite in B minor* the orchestral textures are a little less transparent, but generally the sound is excellent and the transfer to tape is first-class in every way, with body as well as range and detail. The harpsichord continuo comes through without being insistent, which many listeners will like.

(i; v) *Flute concerto in G minor (from BWV 1056)*; (ii; iii; v) *Double concerto in D minor for violin, oboe and strings (from BWV 1060)*; (ii; iv; v) *Triple violin concerto in D major (from BWV 1064)*.

*** Argo KZRC 820 [id.]. (i) William Bennett (flute); (ii) Carmel Kaine (violin); (iii) Tess Miller (oboe); (iv) Ronald Thomas, Richard Studt (violins); (v) Academy of St Martin-in-the-Fields, Marriner.

The idea behind this tape and its companion (see p. 10) is to present Bach harpsichord concertos in reconstructions for alternative instruments that either did exist or might have existed. The purist may throw up his hands in horror, but the sparkle, charm and sensitivity of all these performances under Marriner, with soloists from among regular Academy members, should silence all but the severest Bachians. For identification BWV 1056 is the *F minor Harpsichord concerto* (here for flute), BWV 1060 is the *Double harpsichord concerto in C minor* (here for violin and oboe), and BWV 1064 is the *Triple harpsichord concerto No. 3* (here for three violins). Christopher Hogwood's realizations are admirably stylish. The recording is most beautiful, and the cassette is of demonstration quality, crisp and leonine in sound, with a clear, clean bass line.

Harpsichord concerto No. 1 in D minor, BWV 1052.
  (**) Decca KSXC 6174 [Lon. 5-6440]. Vladimir Ashkenazy (piano), LSO, Zinman – CHOPIN: *Piano concerto No. 2.*(***)

Those who fancy their Bach on a piano rather than the harpsichord will find that Ashkenazy makes no concessions to the earlier instrument. This is no piano imitation of a plucked string instrument, but the piano on its own terms, with a wide variety of colour in the first movement and gentle half-tones in the *Adagio*. Without preconceptions this can be successful and is especially so in the finale, where there are some surprisingly pianistic figurations. But in the opening movement such tonal sophistry does soften the forward momentum, and at the end of the second movement one feels the line of the melody suffers. David Zinman's accompaniment is most stylish, attentive to the soloist's needs and buoyantly rhythmic in the allegros, yet with nice light textures and no hint of heaviness. In its own way this is certainly enjoyable

music-making and obviously sincerely felt. Unfortunately (and rarely for Decca) the transfer level has been misjudged. It is too high and the quality of the orchestral tuttis is coarse.

Harpsichord concertos Nos. 1 in D minor; 2 in E major, BWV 1052/3.
  ✪(M) *** Decca Jubilee KJBC 9. George Malcolm (harpsichord), Stuttgart CO, Münchinger.

This is an outstanding tape in every way. The sound is strikingly warm and vivid, with excellent projection and detail; the balance between solo harpsichord (most naturally caught) and the orchestra is very well managed – a demonstration of just how good a cassette can be, every bit the equal of the equivalent LP. Malcolm's performances have clarity and brilliance. His registrations are nicely judged, and there is a fine control of colour and balance. Müchinger's accompaniments perhaps miss the last degree of flexibility, but they have authority and plenty of rhythmic life.

Harpsichord concertos Nos. 2 in E major, BWV 1053; 4 in A major; 5 in F minor, BWV 1055/6.
  *(*) Telefunken CX 4.41099 [id.]. Gustav Leonhardt (harpsichord), Leonhardt Consort.
Double harpsichord concerto No. 2 in C major, BWV 1061; Triple concerto in A minor for flute, violin and harpsichord, BWV 1044.
  *(*) Telefunken CX 4.41115 [id.]. Gustav Leonhardt, Anneke Uittenbosch (harpsichords), Marie Leonhardt (violin), Frans Brüggen (recorder), Leonhardt Consort.

Leonhardt's set of Bach keyboard concertos has many fine qualities, but is somewhat lacking in spontaneity and imagination. The recordings are not helped by a close balance for the solo instruments and a very resonant acoustic that makes everything (the harpsichord especially) sound larger than life. The chrome tapes offer a spectacular if not especially refined sound, and the basic level of transfer is not adventurous. On each cassette, side two sounds rather better focused than side one, which means that the *A minor Triple concerto* has better detail than the *Double harpsichord concerto*, and of the solo concertos BWV 1053 is clearer than BWV 1055/6.

Quadruple harpsichord concerto in A minor, BWV 1065; Triple harpsichord concertos Nos. 1 in D minor; 2 in C major, BWV 1063/4.

(M) * Turnabout KTVC 34106. Martin Galling, Hedwig Bilgram, Franz Lehrndorfer, Kurt-Heinz Stolze (harpsichords), Mainz CO, Kehr.

This outstanding collection is technically somewhat disappointing: the full and rather complicated textures seem to have partially defeated the transfer engineers, although the level of the transfer is not excessive. In the louder moments one has a feeling of discomfort, although on a smaller machine the reproduction can be quite effective. The beginning of side two is, however, noticeably rough. The performances are first-class, with Gunter Kehr's masterly overall control of the music-making matched by fine solo playing.

Oboe concerto in F major (from BWV 1053); Oboe d'amore concerto in A major (from BWV 1055); Triple concerto in D minor for violin, oboe, flute and strings (from BWV 1063).

*** Argo KZRC 821 [id.]. Neil Black (oboe or oboe d'amore), Carmel Kaine (violin), William Bennett (flute), Academy of St Martin-in-the-Fields, Marriner.

This second instalment of Bach harpsichord concertos in conjectural realizations for different instruments is just as attractive as the first (see pp. 8–9). Whatever the arguments about whether they could actually have existed in this form in Bach's time, there is no doubt of the charm of hearing, for example, the *Triple harpsichord concerto in D minor* arranged for violin, oboe and flute. Most beautiful is the *Oboe d'amore concerto in F*, arranged from the *E major Harpsichord concerto*. The recording is beautifully refined, and the transfers throughout are of top quality, with clear, clean sound, plenty of detail and no lack of body.

Violin concertos Nos. 1 in A minor; 2 in E major, BWV 1041/2; Double violin concerto in D minor, BWV 1043.

*** DG 923087 [id.]. David and Igor Oistrakh, Vienna SO and RPO, Goossens.

(M) ** Philips 7317 105. Felix Ayo, Roberto Michelucci, I Musici.

*(*) Telefunken CX 4.41227 [id.]. Alice Harnoncourt, Walter Pfeiffer, Vienna Concentus Musicus, Harnoncourt.

Violin concertos Nos. 1 and 2.

(M) **(*) DG Privilege 3335 109. David Oistrakh (as above) – BEETHOVEN: *Romances.***

The styles of David and Igor Oistrakh are different enough to provide a suitable contrast of timbre in their performance of the *Double concerto*; at the same time the musical partnership provided by father and son is an understanding one. The performance is available coupled to sympathetic versions of the solo concertos on an early full-priced issue. However, the transfer is very successful, with full, yet clear and well-balanced sound; in some ways it is better than the LP, which tends to sound a little dated now. The solo concertos are also available in a Privilege coupling with the Beethoven *Romances*, which is good value. The recording is lively (perhaps with a shade too much edge, but it is tameable).

On the Philips cassette it is Felix Ayo who plays the *E major Concerto*, and with rather more flair than his colleague Roberto Michelucci shows in the *A minor*; but the two players join for a spirited account of the *Double concerto*. The clear, unaffected approach to all three works gives pleasure, and the only snag is the reverberant acoustic, which rarely allows the harpsichord continuo to come through with any bite. But the Philips transfer is successful, rich yet not lacking clarity of focus. There is some lack of brightness in the treble, but a fresh sound can be achieved and the level is quite high.

On Telefunken, Alice Harnoncourt's timbre using a baroque violin is wiry, and her matter-of-fact approach does not produce very expressive performances, although the music-making is alive. There is also some tonal unsteadiness, with swelling-out effects as contrasts are made in the *Double concerto*; this may partly be exaggerated by the tape transfer.

Violin concertos Nos. (i) *1 in A minor;* (ii) *2 in E major, BWV 1041/2;* (ii; iii) *Double concerto for violin, oboe and strings, BWV 1060.*

(M) (**) CBS 40-61573. Isaac Stern (violin), with (i) members of the LSO; (ii) members of the New York PO, Leonard Bernstein (harpsichord); (iii) Harold Gomberg (oboe).

Although these are distinguished performances, this is a very poor tape, with husky coarse-grained sound and a high distortion content.

(i; iii) *Violin concerto Nos. 2 in E major, BWV 1042;* (ii; iii) *Violin con-*

certo in G minor, BWV 1056 (arr. of *Harpsichord concerto in F minor);* (i– iii) *Double violin concerto in D minor, BWV 1043.*

*** HMV TC-ASD 2783 [Angel 4 XS 36841]. (i) Itzhak Perlman (violin); (ii) Pinchas Zukerman (violin); (iii) ECO, Barenboim.

Perlman and Zukerman with their friend and colleague are inspired to give a magic performance of the great *Double concerto*, one in which their artistry is beautifully matched in all its intensity. The slow movement in particular has rarely sounded so ravishing in a recording. Perlman is also most impressive in the slow movement of the *E major* solo *Violin concerto*, but neither he nor Zukerman in the *G minor Concerto* (arranged from the *F minor Harpsichord concerto* with its sublime *Arioso* slow movement) is quite so impressive without the challenge of the other. Nonetheless, with fine accompaniment from the ECO, this is a Bach recording to treasure, and the transfer to tape is admirably crisp and lively, detailed yet with no lack of richness and body of string tone.

(i) *Triple concerto in A minor for flute, violin and harpsichord, BWV 1044;* (ii) *Suite No. 2 in B minor for flute and strings, BWV 1067.*

(M) ** Turnabout KTVC 34219. (i) Hans Möhring (flute), Susanne Lautenbacher (violin), Martin Galling (harpsichord), Stuttgart Soloists; (ii) Klaus Pohlers (flute), Mainz CO, Kehr.

The *Triple concerto* – not an easy work to bring off on record – is freshly played and recorded, the finale especially vivacious, the central movement musical rather than imaginative. The flautist in the famous *B minor Suite* is a nimble player, but some of his tempi are curious: the *Badinerie* is surely too fast. But these performances make a more than acceptable coupling and the recording is good. The transfer is generally most successful, clean and smooth. The slow movement of the *Triple concerto* sounds particularly fresh, and the quality is excellent throughout the suite. However, our copy had some fluttering disturbance which lasted for the first minute of side one (the concerto) and then disappeared. A second copy we checked had the same fault, but it may be common only to the batch.

Orchestral suites Nos. 1 in C major; 2 in B minor for flute and strings; 3 in D major; 4 in D major, BWV 1066/9.
> ⊛ *** Argo KZRC 687/8 [id.]. Academy of St Martin-in-the-Fields, Marriner.
> *(*) Telefunken CX 4.41128/9 [id.]. Vienna Concentus Musicus, Harnoncourt.

Enormous care went into the preparation of the Argo performances, with Thurston Dart's imaginative, scholarly mind searching always for a compromise between the truth of the original score and what is sensible in terms of modern re-creative performance. Hence not only the ornamentation comes into the picture but even the lightening of the scoring itself to favour the baroque practice of altering the colouring on repeats. This is especially noticeable in *Suites 3* and *4* in the use of the trumpets (which Thurston Dart tells us in his excellent notes did not appear in Bach's original). The set is a splendid memorial to Dart himself, and because the music-making is so exuberant and alive, it is the most joyous memorial: no one could ask for better. Indeed the playing throughout is quite marvellous, expressive without being romantic, buoyant and vigorous and yet retaining the music's strength and weight. William Bennett is the agile and sensitive flute soloist in the *Second Suite*, even providing decoration in the famous *Badinerie*, with splendid bravura. Throughout the performances the baroque spirit is realized at its most colourful. With tip-top

Argo sound this is a fine set indeed, and in the first-class cassette transfer, the sound is highly sophisticated, with body and clarity and only marginally less refinement than the disc in matters of transparency.

The only version using 'original instruments' is that by the Concentus Musicus. Harnoncourt's approach is clean and literal. Slow introductions are taken fast in allemande-style, minuets are taken slowly, and – hardest point to accept – there is comparatively little concession to expressiveness in the famous *Air* from *Suite No. 3*. However, the resonance of the recording helps to give this warmth. But elsewhere the quality of the sound provided by the tape transfer has a more detrimental effect. The level is so low as to take no advantage of the possibilities of chrome tape. The textures are spongy, even fluffy, and the lack of robust qualities has a serious effect on the *Third* and *Fourth Suites*. The *Second* is more successful (although here the *Sarabande* may seem a little disconcerting at first hearing with its use of *notes inégales*). The overall resonance is on the whole kind to the wind instruments, but the lack of clarity of focus in the strings is not helpful, and the prevailing *mezzo forte* of the performances tends to become monotonous.

Orchestral suites Nos. 2 in B minor; 3 in D major, BWV 1067/8.
> (M) * DG Privilege 3335 138. Berlin PO, Karajan.

Karajan seems to think of Bach harmonically rather than contrapuntally, and the rich, glossy textures are matched by similarly unstylish rhythms. Although there is some superb flute-playing in the *B minor Suite* this cannot be recommended. The transfer to tape is smoothly agreeable.

Orchestral suite No. 3 in D major, BWV 1068.
> (**) HMV TC-ASD 3321. Scottish CO, Tortelier – COUPERIN: *Les Goûts-réunis* etc.(**)

Bach's *Third Suite* is agreeably played here under Tortelier, but the HMV recording has been transferred at too high a level, and there is unacceptable coarseness in the *Overture*. A pity, for the recording is basically good and the performance, though not strong on authenticity in matters of rhythmic style and ornamentation, has splendid vigour where appropriate. Its expressive feeling is not overdone, in spite of the large-scale effect provided by the resonance as well as the actual number of players. The famous *Air* is beautifully played.

CHAMBER AND
INSTRUMENTAL MUSIC

Flute sonatas Nos. 1 in B minor; 2 in E flat major; 3 in A major; 4 in C major; 5 in E minor; 6 in E major, BWV 1030/5; Partita in A minor, BWV 1013.
    ** CRD CRD 4014/5. Stephen Preston (baroque flute), Trevor Pinnock (harpsichord), Jordi Savall (viola da gamba).
Flute sonatas Nos. 1–3.
    *** Enigma K 453556. William Bennett (flute), George Malcolm (harpsichord).

Using an authentic one-key baroque flute, Stephen Preston plays Bach's flute music with a rare delicacy. By its nature the instrument can only cope with a limited dynamic range, but Preston is finely expressive, not least in the splendid *Partita* for solo flute. Of the works with continuo the two minor-key sonatas are particularly fine. A reconstruction of the first movement of the *A major Sonata* where bars are missing, is included. Fine continuo-playing. The recording is not transferred to tape at a very ambitious level considering the modest instrumentation. However, the background is low and the sound is on the whole natural, although the flute timbre emphasizes the

middle frequencies of the instrument's tone and some might like a clearer and more sparkling outline to its image. The effect is intimate, and the harpsichord is agreeably caught. But the uninsistent focus of the continuo (the viola da gamba is very backward) undoubtedly lacks presence. Sometimes too the flute sounds a little fluffy.

William Bennett uses a modern flute, and he and George Malcolm manage without the niceties of including a viola da gamba in the continuo. The effect is undoubtedly more robust than in the CRD set, particularly as the recording places the flute well forward. However, the harpsichord is most natural in timbre, and the balance between the two instruments is wholly convincing. The playing, as might be expected of these artists, has superb character. It is strong in personality, yet does not lack finesse. Moreover, it is strikingly alive and spontaneous, and since the transfer brings demonstration quality without being in the least overblown, this can be enthusiastically recommended to all but those who seek the finer points of authenticity above all else. Bennett himself has made the reconstruction of the first movement of BWV 1032. The only drawback to this issue is the printing of the notes, which are in excruciatingly small, unreadable type.

The Musical Offering, BWV 1079.
    *** Enigma K 453550. Members of the Yorkshire Sinfonia, Parikian.
    **(*) Decca KSXC 6824 [Lon. 5-7045]. Stuttgart CO, Münchinger.

A beautifully fresh performance from the Yorkshire group under Manoug Parikian, spirited and in proper scale, is matched by an excellent recording which has transferred to cassette with splendid detail. The internal balance is good, except perhaps for the cor anglais, which is occasionally too forward (although not unagreeably so). With a high transfer level, the background is virtually silent.

Münchinger's latest version of this score is also very well recorded, with excellent presence and detail. Moreover the performance itself is far from negligible; indeed there is playing of genuine breadth and eloquence here, particularly in the *Trio sonata*. The canons are grouped together and come off well. Not that this is entirely free from the heavy-handedness that sometimes disfigures Münchinger's art, but it is a satisfying account within the German tradition and commands attention.

Guitar transcriptions: (Lute) *Suite No. 1 in E minor, BWV 996; Prelude, fugue and allegro in E flat major, BWV 998; Prelude in C minor, BWV 999; Sarabande in E minor;* (Unaccompanied) *Violin sonata No. 1 in G minor, BWV 1001: Fugue in A minor; Violin partita No. 1 in B minor, BWV 1002: Sarabande and Double; Violin partita No. 2 in D minor, BWV 1004: Chaconne.*

(M) *** DG Privilege 3335 248. Narciso Yepes (guitar).

Those who enjoy Bach on the guitar will find this a distinguished and enjoyable recital. Yepes brings the music to life compellingly without any romantic exaggerations. The programme includes the famous *Chaconne*, which transcribes effectively. The sound is first-class.

Guitar transcriptions: (Lute) *Suites Nos. 1 in E minor; 2 in C minor, BWV 996/7; 3 in A minor, BWV 995; 4 in E major, BWV 1006a; Prelude, fugue and allegro in E flat major, BWV 998; Prelude in C minor, BWV 999; Fugue in A minor, BWV 1000.*

*** CBS 40-79203. John Williams (guitar).

John Williams's set is first-class in every way. His rhythmic vitality and

sense of colour tell; the control of line and the ornamentation are equally impressive, and the recording has good presence even if the tape transfer has not quite the range of the equivalent discs. However, the quality is realistic and secure.

(Unaccompanied) *Violin sonatas Nos. 1 in G minor, BWV 1001; 2 in A minor, BWV 1003; 3 in C major, BWV 1005; Violin partitas Nos. 1 in B minor, BWV 1002; 2 in D minor, BWV 1004; 3 in E major, BWV 1006.*

*** DG 3371 030. Nathan Milstein.

This is the finest set of these works to have appeared in recent years. Every phrase is beautifully shaped and keenly alive; there is a highly developed feeling for line, and no want of virtuosity. Milstein is excellently served by the DG engineers, and the sound is natural and lifelike. The transfer to tape is immaculately done, giving the violin natural presence and timbre. There is ample body, and a slight treble cut removes a hint of edge plus any remaining hiss, to enhance the sense of realism.

(Unaccompanied) *Violin partita No. 2 in D minor, BWV 1004; Violin sonata No. 3 in C major, BWV 1005.*

** Decca KSXC 6721. Kyung-Wha Chung.

Kyung-Wha Chung is so commanding an artist that one hardly expects anything other than total mastery. However, the natural warmth of her approach here brings a feeling of romanticism that will not appeal to all ears. There are extremes of dynamics, touches of *rubato* that some will not find convincing, and, for all the technical assurance, some traces of less than secure intonation, though these are rare. She is superbly recorded by the Decca engineers, and the transfers are of excellent quality, smooth and natural in tone.

Keyboard music

Chromatic fantasia and fugue in D minor, BWV 903; French suite No. 5 in G major, BWV 816; Italian concerto in F major, BWV 971; Toccata in D major, BWV 912.
> (M) **(*) Decca Eclipse KECC 788. George Malcolm (harpsichord).

In 1955 George Malcolm made an outstanding record coupling a breathtakingly virtuoso performance of the *Chromatic fantasia* with a very lively *Italian concerto*. In his stereo remake much of the flamboyance of that original *Chromatic fantasia* has disappeared, and the present reading is more considered. The result does not sound quite so spontaneous, and it reserves all its excitement for the cumulative climax of the *Fugue*. But Malcolm's rather more didactic approach to the *Italian concerto* achieves poise without loss of forward momentum, and the buoyant performance of the attractive *Toccata in D* is balanced on the second side with a genial, even lyrical, approach to the jolly *French suite*. The sound on tape is crisp and clean, with rather more edge than on the LP. This slight reduction of the mellow naturalness of the original can be minimized with the controls, and this remains an excellent cassette.

English suites Nos. 1 in A major; 2 in A minor; 3 in G minor; 4 in F major; 5 in E minor; 6 in D minor, BWV 806/11.
> * CBS 40-79208. Glenn Gould (piano).

Glenn Gould often inspires the adjective 'wilful', and certainly these performances have much that is eccentric. At the same time there is undoubtedly a strong musical personality to which the listener cannot remain indifferent. The vocalizations are tiresome, and although phras-

ing is often imaginative, there is some bizarre ornamentation and accentuation, and the sound tends to be dry and unappealing. In cassette form the quality is not distinguished and there is a trace of insecurity.

Goldberg variations, BWV 988.
> (M) **(*) Turnabout KTVC 34015. Martin Galling (harpsichord).
> **(*) Telefunken CX 4.41198 [id.]. Gustav Leonhardt (harpsichord).

There is a sense of dignity and power in Martin Galling's fine performance, due not least to the excellent recording and warm acoustic. Galling displays admirable taste and musicianship, and his technique is first-class. The recording has transferred to tape with fine presence and is most realistic. Highly recommended.

Leonhardt offers a careful academic approach. He is beautifully recorded (this chrome tape is of top demonstration quality, exceptionally natural and realistic), but the playing, though scholarly, has not quite the life of Galling's version.

The Well-tempered Clavier, Book 1, excerpts: *Nos. 1–3, BWV 846/8; 5–8, BWV 850/3; 15–17, BWV 860/2; 21–2, BWV 866/7.*
> *** DG 3300 807. Wilhelm Kempff (piano).

Cool, clear and compelling, Kempff's performances from the first book of the *48* convey pianistic poetry as well as dedication to Bach. A fine tape with excellent sound, showing a great artist relaxed and enjoying himself.

Organ music

Chorale preludes and variations, BWV 690–713; 727; 734; 736; Concertos Nos. 1 in G major; 2 in A minor, BWV 592/3; Fantasia in G

15

major, BWV 572; Fantasia and fugue in G minor, BWV 542; Preludes and fugues: in A major, BWV 536; in E minor, BWV 533; in G major, BWV 541; Trio sonatas Nos. 4 in E minor; 5 in C major, BWV 528/9.

(M) *** Argo K 120 K 32. Peter Hurford (Casavant and Sharp organs).

This is the first issue in a projected complete recording of Bach's organ music. The layout on cassette is slightly different – two cassettes against three LPs – but the idea of presenting the works intermixed, recital-style, remains basically unaltered. Thus instead of (for instance) placing all the *Preludes and fugues* together they are separated by groups of chorales, and the *Trio sonatas* and transcribed solo *Concertos* are fitted within the overall scheme to enhance the stylistic contrast. It works well. Two different modern organs are used: for most of the programme Hurford plays on the Casavant instrument at the Church of Our Sorrows, Toronto, but in two of the *Preludes and fugues*, one of the *Concertos,* the *Trio sonatas* and certain of the *Chorales* he changes to the Ronald Sharp organ at Knox Grammar School, Sydney. Both instruments produce sound that is internally clear yet has admirable baroque colouring. Indeed the piquancy of the registration, often reedily robust in the *Chorales*, is a constant source of delight. The playing itself is fresh, vigorous and imaginative throughout, but the bigger set pieces have no want of breadth. Hurford's technical control is never in doubt, and a concern to bring the music to tingling life is the overriding feature of his interpretations. The recording is clean and sparkling, the tape transfer immaculate: the sound is never weighted down by a puddingy bass (for some, the comparative lack of resonance in the pedals may be a drawback), and there is no intermodulatory distortion. A major achievement.

Chorale preludes 'for the Christmas season', BWV 599/612; 614; 659; 696/70; 703/4; 710; 722/4; 738.

(M) *(*) Turnabout KTVC 34084. Walter Kraft.

Walter Kraft on Turnabout very generously gives us twenty-nine of Bach's *Chorale preludes* which have associations with Christmas. In many cases there is more than one version of a single chorale; for instance *Gelobet seist du, Jesu Christ* is played in four versions, and both *Gottes Sohn ist kommen* and the well-known *Nun komm der Heiden Heiland* each in three. However, this adds interest, showing Bach having second and sometimes third thoughts. Kraft uses six different organs, all dating from Bach's time and well suited to the texture of the writing. The recording is mostly excellent, with only the very slightest blurring on one or two tracks and some fascinating mechanical noises from the Silbermann organ in Ebermunster. The remarkable consistency of pitch – for nearly always there is a change of instrument at each item – is a tribute to organ builders and maintainers alike. The tape transfer has been made at a high level, and at times there are hints of discoloration in the upper partials of the organ sound. The degree of disturbance appears to vary from organ to organ, and much of it can be smoothed out with a cut-back in the controls. On the review copy there was a comparatively serious patch of fluctuation on side two.

6 Schübler chorale preludes, BWV 645/50.

(M) *** Argo KZKC 13. Simon Preston (organ of Westminster Abbey) – MOZART: *Fantasias.****

This is one of the very finest of all tape issues of organ music. The quality is flawless, and the background hiss must be blamed on the master recording, as it is present on the disc too. Including as it does *Wachet auf* and *Meine Seele erhebt den Herren*, the Bach group hardly needs a recommendation in these strong, vital performances, interestingly coupled with Mozart's *Fantasias* originally written for mechanical clock.

6 Schübler chorale preludes, BWV 645/50; Fantasia in C minor, BWV 562; Fugue on the Magnificat, BWV 773; Passacaglia in C minor, BWV 582.

(M) ** Philips Festivo 7310 069. Wolfgang Rübsam.

This collection opens with an exceptionally successful account of the *Passacaglia in C minor*, and the *Fantasia in C minor* and the *Fugue on the Magnificat* are strongly played too. However, in the *Schübler chorales* Rübsam is much more circumspect, and his registration is not nearly as imaginative as Simon Preston's (see above). The recording is of high quality and the transfer first-class: the organ sound is resonantly full-blooded, with almost complete freedom from intermodulation. Technically this is a very impressive tape.

Fantasias: in C minor, BWV 562; in G major, BWV 572; Prelude and fugue in E flat major, BWV 552; Toccata and fugue in D minor, BWV 565; Toccata and fugue in D minor (Dorian), BWV 538.

(M) *** DG 3318 018. Helmut Walcha (organ of St Laurenskerk, Alkmaar).

This impeccably transferred recital is available only on cassette and is an admirable demonstration of how convincingly an organ can be recorded on tape provided the balance is carefully managed. Here the deep bass response is comparatively light, yet the ear feels no loss in this programme: indeed Bach's polyphonic lines are revealed clearly without loss

of body and timbre. The performances are characteristic of Walcha's scholarly and didactic approach: he lays out the music soberly in front of the listener and seeks to impose no dramatic overlay. However, the keen feeling for registration is readily shown in the two *Fantasias*: the sprightly work in G major is especially felicitous, and the more sober C minor piece makes a suitable contrast to end the recital in its prevailing mood of seriousness of purpose.

Fantasia and fugue in G minor, BWV 542; Passacaglia and fugue in C minor, BWV 582; Prelude and fugue in G minor, BWV 542; Toccata and fugue in D minor, BWV 565.

(M) ** Decca KCSP 459. Karl Richter (organ of Victoria Hall, Geneva).

Richter's tempi are characteristically steady (some will feel that the famous D minor work is too relaxed), and this provides more clarity than would otherwise have been the case in the reverberant Victoria Hall, Geneva. The *Fantasia and fugue in G minor* is quite lively, but the peak performance, which Richter controls admirably, is the great *Passacaglia and fugue in C minor*. In the cassette transfer, which is impressive, there are some problems at the very opening of the *Prelude and fugue in G minor*, where the texture is not clean, and again at the opening of the *Fantasia and fugue*, but later this work offers a cleaner sound on tape than on disc, and the overall quality is good.

Toccata and fugue in D minor, BWV 565; Trio sonata No. 2 in C minor, BWV 526; Preludes and fugues: in D major, BWV 532; in G minor, BWV 534.

*** DG 923055 [id.]. Karl Richter (organ in the church at Jaegersborg, near Copenhagen).

An outstanding cassette in every way. The sound has a wide dynamic range and presence, the bass has been transferred with great skill, and the sound remains clear in the spectacular cadences. The organ at Jaegersborg is a new one; the builders have attempted to simulate the principles and action of a baroque instrument, and the result is highly effective. Richter's registration is perceptive in its choice of the right timbres for each piece (notably so in the *Trio sonata*), and his control of the fugues is no less impressive. This is one of the finest available accounts of the famous *Toccata and fugue in D minor*, and both this and BWV 534 have a splendid feeling of weight and power.

VOCAL MUSIC

Cantatas Nos. 11: Lobet Gott in seinen Reichen; 44: Sie werden euch in den Bann tun.
**(*) DG Archive 3310 355. Edith Mathis, Anna Reynolds, Peter Schreier, Dietrich Fischer-Dieskau, Munich Bach Choir and Orch., Richter.

Lobet Gott in seinen Reichen is one of the works that Bach decided in the mid-1730s to call an oratorio, and it is often billed as *Himmelfahrts-oratorio* ('Ascension oratorio'). As in the *Christmas oratorio*, Bach writes the Evangelist's account in *secco* recitative, while the non-Biblical recitatives are accompanied. The opening chorus and the arias are all borrowed from earlier works, and readers will recognize the aria *Ach bleibe doch* as being from the *Agnus Dei* of the *B Minor Mass*. (Bach drew on a lost secular cantata for the *Mass*, however, and not on the version he had fashioned for this cantata.) A beautiful work, well sung and played, though directed with a certain stiffness by Karl Richter. *Sie werden euch in den Bann tun* was composed for the Sunday after Ascension and comes from

1724. Some fine singing and an eloquent oboe obbligato in the alto aria give pleasure, though Richter is generally square. The recording is well balanced and the transfer is well made. The focus of the choral tone is rather more precise in No. 44 than in No. 11, but the overall clarity and bloom on the sound bring an agreeable naturalness and clarity to the solo voices.

Cantata No. 147: Herz und Mund und Tat und Leben. Motets: *Fürchte dich nicht, BWV 228; Der Geist hilft unsrer, BWV 226; Lobet den Herrn, BWV 230.*
(M) * HMV TC-EXE 189. Elly Ameling, Janet Baker, Ian Partridge, John Shirley-Quirk, King's College Choir, Academy of St Martin-in-the-Fields, Willcocks.

This issue has the advantage of a mid-priced label and excellent soloists. The motets are rather less successful than the cantata (as a performance, not the music itself), but this is still a refreshing coupling. Unfortunately the cassette offers poor choral sound (flabby and ill-defined), though the solo voices are adequately caught.

Christmas oratorio, BWV 248.
** HMV TC-SLS 5098. Elly Ameling, Janet Baker, Robert Tear, Dietrich Fischer-Dieskau, King's College Choir, Academy of St Martin-in-the-Fields, Ledger.
** Telefunken MO 4.35022. Treble soloists from Vienna Boys' Choir, Paul Esswood, Kurt Equiluz, Siegmund Nimsgern, Vienna Boys' Choir, Chorus Viennensis, Vienna Concentus Musicus, Harnoncourt.

With generally brisk tempi (controversially so in the alto's cradle song, *Schlafe mein Liebster*, in Part II) Philip Ledger directs an intensely refreshing performance which grows more winning the more one hears it. It was Ledger who played the harpsichord continuo in many of Benjamin Britten's performances of this work, and some of Britten's imagination comes through here, helped by four outstanding and stylish soloists. The King's acoustic gives a warm background to the nicely scaled performances of choir and orchestra, but it has obviously created problems in the tape transfer. As the opening shows, the recording is not always well focused in fortissimos, and the choral outline is furry. Generally the solo voices are naturally caught and the accompaniment sounds fresh, but the moments of spectacle lack the incisive edge and brilliance that this music ideally needs.

Harnoncourt in his search for authenticity in Bach performance has rarely been more successful than here. It will not be to everyone's taste to have a boy treble and male counter-tenor instead of women soloists, but their purity of sound is most affecting. Above all Harnoncourt in this instance never allows his pursuit of authentic sound to weigh the performance down. It has a lightness of touch which should please everyone. The sound, as usual from this source, is well balanced and full, but the transfer is disappointing. It is made at a comparatively low level and takes little advantage of the use of chrome tape. Although throughout the vocal solos the quality is warmly natural, the choruses have a noticeable lack of range and bite and at times a hint that the texture is not quite secure. For some reason at the beginning of side five the choral immediacy improves, and the opening of Part V, *Glory be to Thee*, has greater impact, which is then more or less maintained until the end of the work.

Magnificat in D major BWV 243 (with Christmas interpolations).
    ** Argo KZRC 854 [id.]. Felicity Palmer, Helen Watts, Robert

Tear, Stephen Roberts, King's College Choir, Academy of St Martin-in-the-Fields, Ledger – VIVALDI: *Magnificat.***

Philip Ledger directs a lovely and dramatic account of the *Magnificat*. The warm acoustic of King's College Chapel creates problems of balance and of clarity in this less than fully successful tape transfer. At the opening, one notices that the bass is rather thick and muddy, and the choral sound lacks the definition and sparkle of the best Argo tapes, even though with careful use of the controls the balance can be made to sound quite acceptable. But undoubtedly the performance is attractive and recommendable if boys' voices are welcome in the chorus. The solo voices sound well here and the women are outstanding, as is the St Martin's Academy. The four Christmas interpolations provide an additional attraction, not found in most recordings of this work.

Mass in B minor, BWV 232.
    *** Philips 7699 076 [id.]. Margaret Marshall, Janet Baker, Robert Tear, Samuel Ramey, Chorus and Academy of St Martin-in-the-Fields, Marriner.
    **(*) Telefunken MH 4.35019. Rohtraud Hansmann, Emiko Iiyama, Helen Watts, Kurt Equiluz, Max van Egmond, Vienna Boys' Choir, Chorus Viennensis, Vienna Concentus Musicus, Harnoncourt.
    ** DG 3371 012 [id.]. Gundula Janowitz, Christa Ludwig, Peter Schreier, Robert Kerns, Karl Ridderbusch, Vienna Singverein, Berlin PO, Karajan.
    * CBS 40-79307. Arleen Auger, Julia Hamari, Adalbert Krauss, Wolfgang Schöne, Siegmund

Nimsgern, Gächinger Kantorei, Stuttgart Bach Collegium, Rilling.

Neville Marriner, in a larger recording project than he had ever undertaken before, rose superbly to the challenge. Predictably many of the tempi are daringly fast: *Et resurrexit*, for example, has the Academy Chorus on its toes, but the rhythms are so resiliently sprung that the result is never hectic, exhilarating rather. An even more remarkable achievement is that in the great moments of contemplation, such as *Et incarnatus* and *Crucifixus*, Marriner finds a degree of inner intensity to match the gravity of Bach's inspiration with tempi often slower than usual. That dedication is matched by the soloists, the superb soprano Margaret Mitchell as much as the longer-established singers. Marriner's is a performance which finds the ideal balance between small-scale authenticity and recognition of massive inspiration, neither too small nor too large, and with good atmospheric recording, not quite as defined as it might be on inner detail, there is currently no finer version on tape or disc. The transfer is made at a characteristically modest level, but the wide amplitude of the choral sound is caught without congestion, and as the work proceeds the quality seems also to gain in incisiveness. One's ear soon adjusts to the warm, pleasingly rich sound image, and the recording's overall perspective is well conveyed. The work is laid out on two cassettes, which fit into plastic wells in the slimline box, so that each tape can be removed in its individual plastic library box complete with liner note giving details of contents. As the accompanying booklet is clearly and boldly printed the overall presentation cannot be faulted.

Harnoncourt has very strictly rationed himself to authentic numbers as well as authentic instruments, and, with boys' voices in the choir, the effect is more of a chamber performance. But Harnoncourt's dedication comes over, and if the work's epic qualities are minimized, the music-making brings much refinement of detail to please the ear, and the baroque nature of the score is certainly realized. The use of trebles gives an exciting edge to the *Sanctus* and *Osanna in excelsis* (finely recorded here), which offers compensation for the lack of expressive weight. There is good solo singing throughout, particularly from Helen Watts, and the solo voices are naturally caught. Indeed the recording on chrome tape is generally refined, although some smoothing of the bright treble is advantageous. The level of transfer is comparatively low on the first three sides, then rises strikingly on side four to bring an increase of body and projection. However, the frequency range is wide and there is only occasionally the hint that textures are not absolutely secure in the score's quiet sustained music. There is an excellent bilingual booklet with full notes.

Karajan's performance is marked by his characteristic smoothness of Bach style. He conveys intensity, even religious fervour, but the sharp contours of Bach's majestic writing are often missing. The very opening brings an impressive first entry of the choir on *Kyrie*, but then after the instrumental fugue the contrapuntal entries are sung in a self-consciously softened tone. But for all this there is a strong sense of the work's architecture, and the highly polished surfaces do not obscure the depths of this music.

On CBS, Helmuth Rilling takes the opening *Kyrie* with its fugue very slowly and reverently. If that is acceptable, then this somewhat safe performance has much to recommend it, though most Bach-lovers will almost certainly prefer a performance with more rhythmic resilience. Rilling begins the *Gloria*, for example, with admirably sprung rhythms, but quickly he lets the music trip over itself, and the recording of the chorus throughout is dull, even muddy, the definition not improved by the tape format. The team of soloists is excellent and rather better recorded, but this could not be recommended with any great degree of enthusiasm.

Missa (*Short Mass*; Kyrie and *Gloria* from *Mass in B minor, BWV 232*).

*(*) Telefunken CX 4.41135 [id.]. Rohtraud Hansmann, Emiko Iiyama, Helen Watts, Kurt Equiluz, Max van Egmond, Vienna Boys' Choir, Chorus Viennensis, Vienna Concentus Musicus, Harnoncourt.

Modern research has revealed that Bach composed the *Mass in B minor* in sections, the *Missa* or *Short Mass* (consisting of the *Kyrie* and *Gloria*) being written first (in 1733, some fifteen years before the completion of the work as a whole). The short Mass was suitable for performance either at a Lutheran service or at the Dresden Catholic court. The earlier section stands up well on its own, and this issue (taken from the complete Telefunken version above) will make a useful one-tape sampler of the Harnoncourt style for those unwilling to invest in the whole work. The transfer to chrome tape is smoothly done, if at rather a low level, and though the sound has not quite the clarity of the complete set, the focus is pleasing; both solo voices and chorus emerge satisfactorily from the speakers. The quality of the sound on side two, however, is not as substantial as side one.

Masses: in F major, BWV 233; in A major, BWV 234.

**(*) Argo KZRC 873 [id.]. Wendy Eathorne, Paul Esswood, Neil Jenkins, Richard Hickox Singers and Orch., Hickox.

Following the success of their earlier recording of the two 'short' Lutheran Masses, BWV 235/6 (not yet available on cassette), Richard Hickox has now turned to the others. The performances are expressive but always in excellent style, and the soloists bring conviction and fine musicianship to their parts. The *A major Mass*, which draws on Cantata No. 67 for its *Gloria*, is the more inspired of the two, though both offer many beauties. The element of contrast is provided too: the F major work has a robust opening *Kyrie*, whereas the A major has a more restrained, pastoral atmosphere. The recording quality is generally very good. The transfer gives an overall vivid projection (the level is high), and the solo voices and orchestral detail have both fine presence and excellent naturalness of timbre. The louder choruses have a slight coarseness of grain (choral sound of wide amplitude still seems to offer problems on cassette), and this is noticeable in the opening *Kyrie* of BWV 233, but the effect is not serious.

Motets: *Fürchte dich nicht, BWV 228; Jesu meine Freude, BWV 227; Singet dem Herrn, BWV 225*.

** DG Archive 3310 349. Regensburg Cathedral Choir, Schneidt.

Bach's motets include intricate polyphony and are not easy to sing; they also offer interpretative problems of style and emotional response. The longest of them here, *Jesu meine Freude* (which has a whole cassette side to itself), also demands a concern for its overall shape. In fact it is this work which comes off best. Schneidt's manner is direct, and his choir gives an expressive performance, which is helped by good recording, clearly transferred. *Singet dem Herrn*, with its antiphonal effects (well managed), is rather less effective. In the faster rhythmic passages there is a tendency for the music to jog along in rather too robust a way. However, there is no lack of spirit in the singing here. The recording is somewhat less sharply focused on side two than on side one.

St John Passion, BWV 245: highlights (in German): Nos. 1, 12, 13, 16–20, 28–31, 33–47, 49–52, 58, 67.

**(*) Decca KSXC 6778. Elly Ameling, Julia Hamari, Dieter Ellenbeck, Werner Hollweg, Hermann Prey, Walter Berry, Stuttgart Hymnus Boys' Choir, Stuttgart CO, Münchinger.

Münchinger's reading matches his other recordings of Bach choral works, with a superb line-up of soloists, all of them clear-toned and precise, and a fresh, young-sounding tenor, Dieter Ellenbeck, as Evangelist. Though Münchinger does not equal a conductor like Britten in individuality of imagination, he points the musical balance of the score most satisfyingly without idiosyncrasy. For sound scholarly reasons he uses organ continuo with no harpsichord. The selection here is generous and well made, and the transfer is generally good, although the chorus is not quite so well focused as the soloists.

St Matthew Passion, BWV 244.

*(*) DG 3371 007 [id.]. Peter Schreier, Dietrich Fischer-Dieskau, Gundula Janowitz, Christa Ludwig, Anton Diakov, Walter Ludwig, Vienna Singverein, Boys' Choir, German Opera Chorus, Berlin, Berlin PO, Karajan.

St Matthew Passion: excerpts.

** DG 3300 631 (from above set).

Karajan's Bach, always polished, grows smoother still with the years. His account of the *St Matthew Passion* is plainly aimed at devotees – of Karajan as much as of Bach. The result, concentrated in refinement, faithfully reflects the live performances he has given in Berlin. With excellent singing and playing and with reverberant recording moulded to the interpretation, it represents an individual view pursued in the face of the current fashion, and many will

enjoy it. However, on tape the transfer (a relatively early one) produces furry choral sound and no special degree of presence for the soloists. The sound is pleasant but neither clear nor vivid.

The selection of choruses and arias reflects Karajan's polished and smooth approach. Here the tape transfer is fresher than for the complete set; the chorus is still backwardly balanced, but the detail is better, and the soloists sound quite natural.

COLLECTIONS

Arias: *Bist du bei mir.* Cantata arias: *No. 6: Hochgelobter Gottessohn; No. 11: Ach bleibe doch; No. 34: Wohl euch ihr auserwählten Seelen; No. 129: Gelobet sei der Herr; No. 161: Komm, du süsse Todesstunde; No. 190: Lobe, Zion, deinen Gott. Christmas oratorio: Bereite dich. Easter oratorio: Saget, saget mir geschwinde. Magnificat: Et exultavit. St John Passion: Es ist vollbracht.*

*** HMV TC-ASD 3265. Janet Baker (mezzo-soprano), Academy of St Martin-in-the-Fields, Marriner.

Predictably Dame Janet Baker gives beautiful and deeply felt performances of a fine collection of Bach arias. Sweet contemplative arias predominate, and an excellent case is made for including the alternative cantata version, *Ach bleibe doch,* of what became the *Agnus Dei* in the *B minor Mass.* The accompaniments could hardly be more understanding (the gamba solo in *Es ist vollbracht* adding extra poignancy), and the recording is rich and warm. The cassette is of excellent quality; the voice is caught with naturalness, and the accompaniments have excellent life and colour.

Arias: *Mass in B minor: Agnus Dei; Qui sedes. St John Passion: All is ful-*

filled. St Matthew Passion: Grief for sin.

(M) *** Decca KCSP 531. Kathleen Ferrier (contralto), LPO, Boult – HANDEL: *Arias.****

In the early days of stereo Sir Adrian Boult and the LPO with devotion and great skill re-recorded the accompaniments for these arias so that the new sound completely masked the old. It is splendid to hear Kathleen Ferrier's voice (and this was one of her finest records) enhanced by the greater warmth and beauty of the orchestra in stereo, and all who participated are to be congratulated on the complete artistic and technical success of this fine issue. The sound is pleasingly full, with the voice admirably clear, although there is some lack of dynamic contrast caused by the forward projection of the sound picture.

'Favourite composer': (i) *Brandenburg concerto No. 2 in F major, BWV 1047; Suite No. 3 in D major, BWV 1068;* (ii) *Italian concerto in F major, BWV 971;* (iii) *Chorale prelude: Wachet auf, BWV 645;* (iv) *Toccata and fugue in D minor, BWV 565;* (v) *Cantata No. 147: Jesu, joy of man's desiring;* (i; vi; vii) *Christmas oratorio, BWV 248: Part 2;* (i; viii) *Mass in B minor, BWV 232: Sanctus; Osanna;* (i; vi; ix) *St Matthew Passion: Peter's denial.*

(B) ** (*) Decca KDPC 535/6. (i) Stuttgart CO, Münchinger; (ii) George Malcolm (harpsichord); (iii) Simon Preston (organ); (iv) Karl Richter (organ); (v) St John's College Choir, Guest; (vi) Elly Ameling (soprano), Peter Pears (tenor); (vii) Helen Watts (contralto), Tom Krause (bass), Lübecker Kantorei; (viii) Vienna Academy Choir; (ix) Marga

Höffgen (contralto), Stuttgart Hymnus Boys' Choir.

An excellent selection offering performances of a high standard and first-class sound. As this pair of cassettes costs no more than one full-priced tape, it is excellent value, although Decca's single-tape anthology (see below) is even more economically devised. The transfers offer first-class quality throughout – the vocal items are particularly successful – and the overall level and clarity are well managed.

'The glory of Bach': (i) *Brandenburg concerto No. 2 in F major, BWV 1047:* 3rd movt; (ii) *Suite No. 2 in B minor, BWV 1067: Badinerie; Su. No. 3 in D major, BWV 1068: Ai;* (iii) *Cantata No. 147: Jesu, joy of man's desiring;* (iv) *Toccata and fugue in D minor, BWV 565; Chorale prelude: Wachet auf, BWV 645;* (v) *Christmas oratorio, BWV 248: Shepherds' music; Jauchzet, frohlocket; Mass in B minor, BWV 232: Sanctus.*

(M) ** DG Privilege 3335 246. (i) Lucerne Festival Orch., Baumgartner; (ii) Berlin PO, Karajan; (iii) Wilhelm Kempff (piano); (iv) Karl Richter (organ); (v) Munich Bach Choir and Orch., Richter.

A well engineered anthology that will please especially those who admire the German approach to Bach. While the excerpts from the *Suites* under Karajan are hardly pure in style, and Kempff's *Jesu, joy of man's desiring* is uncompromisingly strong, Karl Richter's more sober manner as both organist and conductor is effectively demonstrated. The transfer to tape is a little lacking in range but is impressively free from distortion and has plenty of body and detail. Generally the items make a good compilation, although *Wachet auf* follows a little un-

23

easily after the famous *Air* from the *Suite in D major*.

'The world of Bach': (i) *Brandenburg concerto No. 2 in F major, BWV 1047; Suite No. 2 in B minor, BWV 1067: Badinerie; Suite No. 3 in D major, BWV 1068: Air;* (ii) *Italian concerto, BWV 971:* 1st movt; (iii) *Toccata and fugue in D minor, BWV 565;* (iv) *Cantata No. 147: Jesu, joy of man's desiring;* (v) *Cantata No. 208: Sheep may safely graze;* (i; vi) *Christmas oratorio, BWV 248: Jauchzet, frohlocket;* (vii) *Mass in B minor, BWV 232: Agnus Dei;* (i; viii) *St Matthew Passion, BWV 244: Wir setzen uns mit Tränen nieder* (chorus).

(M) *** Decca KCSP 322. (i) Stuttgart CO, Münchinger; (ii) George Malcolm (harpsichord); (iii) Karl Richter (organ); (iv) St John's College Choir, Guest; (v) Kirsten Flagstad (soprano), LPO, Boult; (vi) Lübecker Kantorei; (vii) Kathleen Ferrier (contralto), LPO, Boult; (viii) Stuttgart Hymnus Boys' Choir.

A characteristically skilful Decca anthology that is even more than the sum of its parts, which itself is considerable. The juxtaposition of pieces is managed with perfect taste so that each seems to follow on spontaneously. The *Second Brandenburg concerto* and the other short orchestral items show the Stuttgart team at their best, but the real highlights here are vocal, notably Kathleen Ferrier's beautiful contribution, and the oratorio excerpts. The recording is consistently good throughout and often very good indeed. The transfer to tape has been well managed and the quality is consistently clear, except for a moment on side two, where the focus slips just a little in the organ *Toccata and fugue in D minor*. This

is a most satisfying concert in its own right but is also one that should tempt inexperienced listeners to explore further.

'Your kind of Bach': (i) *Brandenburg concerto No. 3 in G major, BWV 1048;* (ii; iii) *Double violin concerto in D minor, BWV 1043:* 2nd movt; (iii) *Suite No. 2 in B minor, BWV 1067: Badinerie; Suite No. 3 in D major, BWV 1068: Air;* (iv) *Violin partita No. 3 in E major, BWV 1006: Prelude;* (v) *Italian concerto in F major, BWV 971:* 1st movt; (vi) *Toccata and fugue in D minor, BWV 565;* (vii) *Bist du bei mir;* (viii) *Cantata No. 80: Chorale: Ein feste Burg;* (ix) *Cantata No. 147: Chorale: Jesu, joy of man's desiring;* (x) *Cantata No. 208: Sheep may safely graze.*

** EMI TC-EXES 5011. (i) LPO, Boult; (ii) Yehudi Menuhin, Christian Ferras (violins); (iii) Bath Festival Orch., Menuhin; (iv) Josef Suk (violin); (v) George Malcolm (harpsichord); (vi) Fernando Germani (organ); (vii) Elly Ameling (soprano), Dalton Baldwin (piano); (viii) South German Madrigal Choir, Consortium Musicum, Gonnenwein; (ix) King's College Choir, Academy of St Martin-in-the-Fields, Marriner; (x) Hallé Orch., Barbirolli.

An enjoyable collection; the recording is good on side one and often very good on the second side. The question of varying levels is not always managed too well: the *Italian concerto* excerpt seems to burst in on the listener, but the programme is imaginatively chosen to provide contrast and the performances are all distinguished.

Balakirev, Mily
(1837–1910)

Piano concerto No. 2 in A flat major,
Op. posth (completed by Liapunov).
   (M) * Turnabout KTVC 34645.
   Michael Ponti, Westphalian
   SO, Landau – LIAPUNOV:
   Rhapsody.*

Balakirev was still in his teens when he wrote his *First Concerto*, only one movement of which survives. He began the *Second* in 1861, when he was in his mid-twenties, but could not be persuaded to write down the second and third movements until 1906. Even so he left the finale unfinished, and after his death Liapunov completed the work. The slow movement is the most poetic of the three, and in more persuasive hands it could be effective. Unfortunately the performance is somewhat insensitive and the orchestral playing undistinguished. Moreover the recording is shallow, with lustreless strings, although the piano tone is clear and the transfer to tape is faithful.

Russia (symphonic poem).
   *(*) HMV TC-ASD 3193.
   Bournemouth SO, Brusilow –
   BORODIN: *Symphony No. 2*;
   RIMSKY-KORSAKOV: *Skaz-*
   ka.*(*)

This is the second overture on Russian themes that Balakirev composed. It originally appeared under the title *A Thousand Years* in 1862, but was revised in the 1880s. This is a straightforward performance that will give pleasure, even if one would have welcomed a greater sense of characterization and poetry. The recording is very forward, with the woodwind soloists larger than life, but the sound has plenty of colour, even if the range of dynamic is restricted.

Symphony No. 1 in C major.
   (M) **(*) HMV TC-EXE 193.
   RPO, Beecham – BORODIN:
   Polovtsian dances.***

This is as fine a symphony as ever came from Russia, with a startlingly original first movement, a wonderfully lyrical slow movement, a sparkling scherzo and a breezy finale. It is an extended piece, but Balakirev's material and treatment can easily sustain the length, particularly when the performance is as glowing as Beecham's. Admittedly Karajan was more dynamic and passionate in his old recording, but Beecham offers just as many felicities, and the sound on tape is agreeable, if somewhat lacking in sparkle and glitter.

Barber, Samuel
(born 1910)

Adagio for strings.
   ⊛ *** Argo KZRC 845 [id.].
   Academy of St Martin-in-the-
   Fields, Marriner – COPLAND:
   Quiet City; COWELL: *Hymn*;
   CRESTON: *Rumor*; IVES: *Sym-*
   phony No. 3.***

Samuel Barber's *Adagio for strings* is a transcription of the slow movement of his fine *String quartet*, Op. 11, and brought him international fame in its pioneer recording by Toscanini and the NBC Orchestra. This performance all but matches Toscanini's intensity and has enormous eloquence and conviction. It is arguably the most satisfying version we have had since the war. The quality of the recorded sound is altogether superb, never excessively analytical, but splendidly detailed and rich. The rest of this programme of twentieth-century American music has been chosen with skill. The cassette offers sound of demonstration quality, and the wide dynamic range of the recording is accommodated without stress.

Hermit songs, Op. 29.
> *** Enigma κ 453541. Sandra Browne (mezzo-soprano), Michael Isador (piano) – COPLAND: *Poems of Emily Dickinson.***(*)

Freely lyrical, with the occasional hint of Britten in the piano accompaniments, Barber's settings of poems translated from ancient Irish manuscripts make an appealing cycle, well coupled with Copland, and beautifully sung by Sandra Browne, a warm-toned mezzo. The transfer is of good quality: both vocal and piano timbres are truthful, and the balance is good if characteristically forward.

Barrios, Agustin
(20th century)

Aconquija; Aire de Zamba; La catedral; Choro de suadade; Cueca; Estudio; Una limosna el amor de Dios; Madrigal (Gavota); Maxixa; Mazurka apassionata; Minuet; Preludio; Sueño en la floresta; Valse No. 3; Villancico de Navidad.
> **(*) CBS 40-76662. John Williams (guitar).

Agustin Barrios is a little-known Paraguayan guitarist and composer who had the distinction of making (in 1909) the first known recording of a guitar. His music essentially belongs to the previous century. Its invention is fresh, if sometimes ingenuous, and the pieces here are well varied in style. In the expert hands of John Williams the collection provides a very entertaining recital, ideal for late-evening listening. Try the charming opening *La catedral* (sweet but not sugary) or

spool on to the irresistible *Sueño en la floresta*, which ends the side in a breathtaking haze of fluttering figurations that remind one of Tarrega's *Recuerdos de la Alhambra*. The recording is excellent, lacking only the final degree of upper range, although the balance is characteristically close. (At one point in our copy there was just a suspicion that a very short passage of music was insecure in pitch, but it was only a second or two and is probably not common to all copies.) The liner leaflet, disgracefully, merely lists the music, giving no information about it or the composer.

Bartók, Béla
(1881–1945)

Concerto for orchestra.
> (M) (*) Supraphon 04.50515. Czech PO, Ančerl.

(i) *Concerto for orchestra;* (ii) *Dance suite.*
> *** Decca κsxc 6212. LSO, Solti.
> (M) ** DG Privilege 3335 202. (i) Berlin PO, Karajan; (ii) Hungarian Radio Orch., Lehel.

Solti has become so much a part of the English musical scene one tends to forget his Hungarian upbringing. You could hardly ignore it after hearing this tape, which gives Bartók's last-period lyricism the inflections of genuine Hungarian folk-song. This in effect means that Solti allows himself all sorts of *rubato* effects not strictly marked in the score, but the fire and intensity behind his interpretation come through in magnificent playing by the LSO from first bar to last. The inclusion of a fill-up, particularly one so generous as the *Dance suite*, is most welcome. The title *Dance suite* may suggest something rather trivial, but the beauty of Bartók's inspiration in this product of the early twenties (generally his most dissonant period) lies in the way that one can appreciate it on many different levels. Solti's performance has all the fire and passion one could want. The brilliant recording, outstanding in its day, shows its age a little in the string sound, but in all other respects is of high quality. In spite of Dolby one notices a little tape hiss at the opening of the *Concerto*; otherwise this is one of Decca's finest cassettes. The sound is full, brilliant and clear.

The Berlin Philharmonic, in superb form, gives a performance of the *Concerto* that is rich, romantic and smooth – for some ears perhaps excessively so. Karajan is right in treating Bartók emotionally, but the comparison with Solti immediately points the contrast between Berlin romanticism and earthy red-blooded Hungarian passion. Both conductors allow themselves a fair degree of *rubato*, but Solti's is linked with the Hungarian folk-song idiom where Karajan's moulding of phrases is essentially of the German tradition. The DG transfer offers smooth, natural sound, vivid too in the *Concerto*, but in the *Dance suite* the recording is seriously lacking in detail and presence, and Gyorgy Lehel's performance (although idiomatic) is not given the bite and projection that Decca give to Solti.

Ančerl's performance, warm and understanding rather than especially brilliant, is very reverberantly recorded, and the dim cassette transfer reveals very little detail. In any case at the first string *tutti* the volume level becomes unstable, and this is not acceptable for serious listening.

Concerto for orchestra; Hungarian Pictures.
 *** Decca KSXC 6730 [Lon. 5-6949]. Israel PO, Mehta.

A brilliantly played and superbly recorded account of the *Concerto for orchestra* is coupled to the five *Hungarian Pictures*, which Bartók scored for orchestra in 1931, some twenty years after

their original composition as piano pieces. They have great charm, and the glowing orchestral colours are splendidly realized here. The Israel Philharmonic, recorded in Kingsway Hall, London, sounds far finer than when it faces the microphones on home ground. The sound is rich, and though the performance of the *Concerto* lacks the last degree of bite that you find in Solti's Decca version of ten years earlier, the combination of brilliance and warm expressiveness is very attractive. The finale has a measure of jollity in it (what Bartók called its 'life-assertion') at a tempo which allows the strings to articulate their rushing semiquavers. The recording is in the demonstration class, with translucent woodwind, rich, firmly focused brass, and plenty of sheen on the strings. Furthermore the brilliance, detail and atmosphere on tape (the opening of the *Concerto* is particularly impressive) are the hallmark of one of Decca's best transfers. A slight treble cut is advantageous, but then the richness of the brass and the sheen on the strings are most impressive.

Piano concerto No. 1 in A major; Rhapsody for piano and orchestra, Op. 1.
 **(*) Decca KSXC 6815. Pascal Rogé, LSO, Weller.
Piano concertos Nos. 2 in G major; 3 in E major.
 ** Decca KSXC 6816. Rogé, LSO, Weller.

Pascal Rogé enjoys the advantage of outstandingly good recording: indeed the piano sounds very much as it would in the concert hall, but at the same time orchestral detail is remarkably lucid. The more natural sound picture reduces the percussive, aggressive impact that the *First Concerto* can have, but it must also be admitted that the musical characterization is not so strong here as with Anda (see below). There is an even more noticeable lack of bite and concentration in the outer movements of concertos 2 and 3. Nonetheless this gifted pianist shows genuine feeling for keyboard colour, and there may well be those for whom these readings will have a greater appeal than Anda's more abrasive approach. On tape, as on disc, the recording is extremely vivid, and the cassette containing the *Second* and *Third Concertos* often approaches demonstration standard. The slow movement and finale of No. 2 have splendid brilliance and colour.

Piano concertos Nos. 2 and 3.
　(M) ** DG Privilege 3335 262 [id.]. Géza Anda, Berlin Radio SO, Fricsay.

Anda's performances of the Bartók concertos have acquired something like classic status. In a medium-priced coupling like this they should certainly be considered – refined yet urgent, incisive but red-blooded too. The recording balance unduly favours the piano, but the main snag of this transfer is the lack of absolute crispness of focus in the orchestral picture. The basic resonance is obviously a problem when the upper range is marginally restricted in this way, and the transients are not completely sharp and clean.

(i) *Piano concerto No. 2;* (ii) *Sonata for two pianos and percussion.*
　(M) ** Turnabout KTVC 34036. György Sándor (piano), with (i) Vienna SO, Gielen; (ii) Rolf Reinhardt (piano), Otto Schad, Richard Sohm (percussion).

This is an excellent cassette. The excess reverberation in the *Sonata* has offered no transfer problems, and the *Concerto* sounds very well indeed. This is quite the equal of the equivalent disc. Sandor (who was the first pianist ever to record the *Third Concerto* in the days of 78s) gives a strong, idiomatic account of a concerto which if anything is even more difficult to interpret than No. 1. The coupling, a simi-

larly compelling account of the *Sonata for two pianos and percussion*, is rather let down by the acoustic of the recording, which is too reverberant to allow Bartók's detail to bite properly.

Violin concerto No. 2 in B minor.
　*** Decca KSXC 6802 [Lon. 5-7023]. Kyung-Wha Chung, LSO, Solti.

The combination of Kyung-Wha Chung and Solti brings a fiery, diamond-bright performance in which the Hungarian inflections are sharply brought out. It is a strong, characterful reading, not without a good deal of lyrical feeling, but with no attempt made to smooth out the work's sharper contours. The forward balance means that Miss Chung undoubtedly sounds somewhat larger than life, and the recording in consequence has less dynamic range than some Decca issues. But the sound is admirably vivid and splendidly detailed without loss of warmth, and the image of the solo violin has plenty of body.

The Miraculous Mandarin (ballet): *suite, Op. 19; Music for strings, percussion and celesta.*
　*(*) DG 3300 887 [id.]. Boston SO, Ozawa.

This tape sounds quite different from the equivalent LPs. The reverberant acoustic means that the orchestral detail at the opening of the *The Miraculous Mandarin* is rather fuzzy, and there is a lack of crispness of outline generally. This is even more serious in the *Music for strings, percussion and celesta*, where the sound picture has atmosphere but lacks transient bite and sparkle in the upper range, so necessary in this score. The beauty of tone of the Boston players might be thought to blunt somewhat the aggressive power of *The Miraculous Mandarin*, and this effect is emphasized on tape. The performance of the *Music for strings, percussion and celesta* is less than ideal, with flaws in ensemble, and relatively slack playing in the second and fourth movements.

2 Rumanian dances, Op. 8a.
** Pye ZCPCNHX 3. Orch. of St John's, Smith Square, Lubbock – RAVEL: *Ma Mère l'Oye*; STRAVINSKY: *Pulcinella.**(**)

Though the two Bartók dances are not given quite the bite they demand, they make an attractive fill-up to a tape which admirably displays the talents of one of London's newer chamber orchestras. The transfer is lively and generally offers good sound here, but there is a hint of coarseness in the acoustic that reveals itself more in the couplings.

Sonata for two pianos and percussion.
(***) Philips 7300 644 [id.]. Martha Argerich, Stephen Bishop-Kovacevich (pianos), Willy Goodswaard, Michel de Roo (percussion) – DEBUSSY and MOZART: *Piano duet music.***

A strongly atmospheric and finely characterized performance; this is most imaginative playing, and it is afforded an excellent recording. Unfortunately the transfer is made at an unsatisfactorily low level: the opening is barely audible, there is little percussive bite, and the transients are generally poor.

Bluebeard's Castle (opera): complete (in Hungarian).
*(**) CBS 40-76518. Tatiana Troyanos, Siegmund Nimsgern, BBC SO, Boulez.

Bartók's idea of portraying marital conflict in an opera was as unpromising as could be, but in the event *Bluebeard's Castle* is an enthralling work with its con-

centration on mood, atmosphere and slow development as Bluebeard's wife finds the key to each new door, and the comparative absence of action makes it an ideal work for recording. Here more than ever Boulez reveals what warmth has developed in his character as an interpreter, and the soloists are vibrantly committed. The recording is vivid, and presents the singers in a slightly contrasted acoustic, as though on a separate stage. It has transferred quite well to tape, although side two of our original review copy sounded markedly more brilliant than side one. However, this cassette is issued without a libretto or notes, whereas the equivalent disc comes in a box album with booklet and is obviously a far better investment.

Beethoven, Ludwig van (1770–1827)

Piano concertos Nos. 1–5.
*** Decca K 44 K 43 [Lon. 5-2404]. Vladimir Ashkenazy, Chicago SO, Solti.
*** DG 3371 010 [id.]. Wilhelm Kempff, Berlin PO, Leitner.
Piano concertos Nos. 1–5; (i) *Choral fantasia in C minor, Op. 80.*
⊛ *** Philips 7699 061. Alfred Brendel, LPO, Haitink, (i) with LPO Choir.

Technically the Philips set is superb, and these must be numbered among the best concerto recordings available in cassette form. Given an artist of Brendel's distinction, it would be surprising if this set were not in the first flight artistically, even if there are moments when one's mind returns to his earlier Turnabout recordings, which are often especially characterful and spontaneous. But the orchestral accompaniments in the earlier recordings cannot compare with the new ones, which also show a flowing spontaneity of their own. Indeed these performances are as satisfying as the recording is rich. The perspective between soloist and orchestra is perfectly judged and the piano tone itself is remarkably lifelike, being clean and well focused throughout its register. There is general consent that these performances are among the very finest on the market, and as sound they certainly head the list.

The partnership of Ashkenazy and Solti is fascinating. Where Solti is fiery and intense, Ashkenazy provides an introspective balance. No better example of this can be found than in the slow movement of the *Fourth Concerto*. The 'masculine/feminine' dialogue has rarely been so strongly contrasted on record, Solti strong and commanding, Ashkenazy's reply exquisitely gentle, yet never losing the argument. Ashkenazy brings a hushed, poetic quality to every slow movement, while Solti's urgency maintains a vivid forward impulse in the outer movements. Sometimes, as in the *C minor Concerto*, one feels that the music-making is too intense. Here a more relaxed, lyrical approach can find in the first movement a warmth of humanity that Solti misses. But for the most part the listener is given an overriding impression of vitality and freshness, and the *Emperor* performance, while on the grandest scale, has a marvellously individual moment in the first movement when Ashkenazy lingers over his presentation of the second subject. The Chicago orchestral playing is characteristically brilliant, and the transfer to tape is markedly successful, offering well sustained, truthful piano tone and a bold orchestral image, with brilliant strings and a firm, resonant bass. The sound is brighter and less beautiful than in the Philips Brendel set, but the overall balance certainly matches the character of the performances. The *Emperor*, however, seems drier in quality than the rest of the series and produces a touch of harshness, but it is not serious and responds to the controls.

Kempff's cycle of the Beethoven concertos has never been surpassed for its consistent freshness of imagination. Individually there are weightier readings of each of these concertos, but none – not even Brendel's – more spontaneously captures the eager greatness of this music in its full range of expressiveness. The recordings are getting rather old now, but they do not sound dated and they have transferred to cassette with excellent clarity and bloom, although there is considerably more tape hiss than with the more modern sets. This applies, of course, to the individual issues as well as the box and will trouble young ears more than older ones. The orchestral sound is a little thicker in the *First Concerto* than in the *Third* (these are back to back on a single tape). The *Emperor*, given a tape to itself, is particularly successfully balanced.

Piano concerto No. 1 in C major, Op. 15.

> *** Decca KSXC 6651 [Lon. 5-6853]. Vladimir Ashkenazy, Chicago SO, Solti (with *Sonata No. 8, Pathétique****).

> *** DG 3300 227 [id.]. Wilhelm Kempff, Berlin PO, Leitner.

> (M) **(*) Decca Jubilee KJBC 39. Friedrich Gulda, Vienna PO, Stein (with *Sonata No. 14, Moonlight***(*)).

> (M) **(*) Philips 7317 142. Claudio Arrau, Concertgebouw Orch., Haitink (with *Sonata No. 6****).

> (M) ** DG Privilege 3335 273. Christoph Eschenbach, Berlin PO, Karajan.

(i) *Piano concerto No. 1;* Overture: *Leonora No. 3, Op. 72b.*

> (M) (**) CBS Classics 40-61817. New York PO, Bernstein, (i) with Leonard Bernstein (piano).

Piano concerto No. 1; Rondo in B flat

major (for piano and orchestra), *G.151.*

(M) ** Turnabout KTVC 34205. Alfred Brendel, Vienna Volksoper Orch. or Stuttgart PO, Boettcher.

Ashkenazy has the advantage of a bold, modern recording of considerable depth and power. The sound is notably resonant in the middle range, imparting a slight huskiness to the orchestral image in the first movement. The performance is characteristic of the Ashkenazy/Solti partnership, with a strong large-scale opening *tutti* balanced by the comparative reticence of the soloist's lyricism. Solti, however, ensures that when Ashkenazy is taking the dominating role the woodwind comments have no lack of delicacy. The hushed slow movement is very beautiful, and taken as a whole this is most satisfying. Many will be attracted by the substantial coupling, a major performance indeed, with its calm *Adagio cantabile* and cool, flowing finale making a perfect balance with the opening movement. The transfer of the concerto is of Decca's best quality, the resonance of the recording caught most naturally.

Kempff's sense of repose in this concerto is remarkable. The slow movement is in fact a shade faster than in his earlier version, yet the profundity of his sense of calm creates the illusion of something much slower. In the finale the playing sparkles joyously. The recording is good, with the piano balanced farther back than is common with DG. The transfer to tape offers first-class sound, with a natural overall quality and clean, clear piano timbre.

Gulda gives a strong, direct reading, just a little disappointing in the slow movement (extrovert, with eighteenth-century elements underlined) but otherwise very satisfying. The first movement has Beethoven's third and longest cadenza, and the finale grows in crispness and point as it progresses, a delightful performance. Gulda's way of letting the

music speak for itself also makes for a fresh and enjoyable reading of the *Moonlight sonata*. The recording is excellent, provided the unusual timbre of the piano, a little shallow on top, is acceptable. The transfer is of admirable quality, bright and vivid and generally well focused, though the acoustic is fairly resonant.

Brendel's too is among the most satisfying readings of the *First Concerto* available. His tempi for the outer movements are measured, but such is his rhythmic point (particularly in the dactylic rhythms of the finale) and such is his concentration that the result is never heavy. Similarly in the slow movement his tempo is rather slow for *Largo*, but the natural weight of expression has the immediacy of a live performance. The long cadenza in the first movement is interestingly confected from two of the cadenzas by Beethoven himself. The snag is the playing and recording of the orchestra – rather underpowered, with string tone that often sounds seedy. Brendel's concentration turns the *B flat Rondo*, a lightweight early piece, into something genuinely bright and pointed. Despite the accompaniment, at medium price this is a good bargain; generally the quality of the tape transfer is fresh, with clear piano image, although the orchestral tuttis are not always cleanly detailed. There is one moment in the finale of the concerto where the basses are explosive. But this offers enjoyable listening quality generally, and the background is virtually silent.

Arrau's performance is lightweight, fresh and lithe, essentially early Beethoven, almost Mozartian. The slow movement, however, has depth. The coupling is equally good, and with characteristic Philips Concertgebouw sound this is a strong competitor at medium price. The tape quality is of Philips' best, warm, truthful and musically balanced. The level is quite high; there is some lack of inner detail in the first movement, but those who like the characteristic Philips sound will not be disappointed here, and the hiss level is not a problem.

31

Eschenbach and Karajan choose a slow tempo for the first movement, and though the concentration holds the attention, the result here is closer to a chamber approach. A beautiful performance of the slow movement and a lightweight finale. The performance is attractive and interesting, but in its concentration on refinement (Karajan's doing?) it misses any sort of greatness. The recording is good – more robust than Arrau's, and with truthful piano timbre, although there is a hint of huskiness in the orchestral tuttis.

Bernstein opens the first movement at a very measured tempo (he is much more deliberate than Brendel and even Eschenbach). He plays with excellent vitality and brilliance and directs from the keyboard. There is no playing to the gallery or idle showmanship; the performance is finely shaped and is only let down by the indifferent quality of the recorded sound. In the overture, which is well played, the recording is shallow and coarse. Things are admittedly better in the concerto and the transfer offers acceptable sound overall; the recording is rather dry but quite well balanced, with more apparent range than on some CBS tapes. Our review copy, however, had a hilarious section of music in the slow movement where the performance gradually slows down and the pitch drops correspondingly. For some time the music proceeds at a snail's pace, then it slowly climbs back to correct speed and pitch. The effect is mirrored in the finale, where it is even funnier. Anyone lucky enough to have found a copy from this batch will surely regard it as a collector's item.

Piano concertos Nos. 1 in C major, Op. 15; 2 in B flat major, Op. 19.
(M) *** Decca KCSP 401. Wilhelm Backhaus, Vienna PO, Schmidt-Isserstedt.

The restoration of the Backhaus set of Beethoven concertos to the catalogue at mid-price is most welcome. Backhaus's recording career spanned fifty of the most important years of the gramophone's history. It was he who made the first serious attempt at recording a major piano concerto (the Grieg, issued during the First World War and condensed to two twelve-inch 78 r.p.m. sides), and the evidence of these fine recordings, made at the end of the 1950s, is that his vitality stayed unimpaired. Indeed, it is the sheer vigour of the solo playing that impresses the listener so much, to say nothing of the excellence of the recording, which has come up fresh and sparkling in these new transfers, not in the least dated. Some might feel that the brisk manner Backhaus adopts in the *First Concerto* suggests superficiality, but this is by no means the case, and repeated listenings yield increasing pleasure: the almost brusque way the pianist treats the slow movement falls into place within the reading as a whole. The *Second Concerto* is even finer. Here the soloist is more generous in his variations of touch, and the flowing spontaneity of the music-making brings a feeling of youthful freshness. The finale is particularly successful. The transfers offer what is virtually demonstration quality; the sound is clear, vivid and sparkling, the balance first-class.

Piano concerto No. 2 in B flat major, Op. 19.
*** DG 3300 485 [id.]. Wilhelm Kempff, Berlin PO, Leitner – *Concerto No. 4.****
*** Decca KSXC 6652 [Lon. 5-6854]. Vladimir Ashkenazy, Chicago SO, Solti (with *Sonata No. 21, Waldstein****).
*** Philips 7300 454 [id.]. Stephen Bishop-Kovacevich, BBC SO, Colin Davis – *Concerto No. 4.****
(M) **(*) Philips 7317 145. Claudio Arrau, Concertege-

bouw Orch., Haitink (with *Sonatas Nos. 1* and *20***).

(M) ** Turnabout KTVC 34206. Alfred Brendel, Vienna Volksoper Orch., Wallberg – *Choral fantasia.*(*)

Piano concertos Nos. 2; 3 in C minor, Op. 37.

(M) **(*) Decca Jubilee KJBC 40. Friedrich Gulda, Vienna PO, Stein.

Kempff's account of the *Second Concerto*, attractively coupled with the *Fourth*, has long been a favourite choice. Like No. 4 it is less individual a performance than on Kempff's earlier, mono LP, but his playing is unmistakable in almost every bar and Leitner's conducting is both strong and sympathetic. The tape is splendidly engineered, with excellent orchestral detail and a bright, lucid piano image. The quality is astonishing considering the age of the original recordings, and because one can with advantage cut back the treble slightly, hiss is not a problem.

Those for whom the coupling of the *Waldstein sonata* is suitable need look no further than the splendid Decca recording by Ashkenazy and Solti, which shows this fine partnership at its most rewarding. Here the poetry of the solo playing is perfectly balanced by the orchestral response. The slow movement is particularly beautiful and its hushed close creates a memorable feeling of repose before the sparkling finale. The recording is first-class in every way. Ashkenazy's *Waldstein* is satisfying too, clear and direct. The great tune of the finale does not steal in quite so magically as with Kempff, for instance, but the performance overall is certainly one of the finest recorded. Early copies of the tape were wrongly edited and offered an incomplete *Waldstein*. This has now been corrected, and the overall quality is first-class.

For those who find Kempff's coupling of the same two concertos too personal,

Stephen Bishop-Kovacevich provides the ideal answer in direct, intense, deeply thought readings of both works, with fine accompaniment from Colin Davis and the BBC Orchestra and with refined recording. Apart from a moment of gruffness in the bass in the first *tutti* of the G major *Concerto* the transfers are of first-class quality, fresh and immediate, with clear piano tone. The closing passages of the slow movements of both concertos show just how good this tape is, with secure, sustained piano notes, and a very quiet background.

Arrau's performance has a spontaneity and life not always present in his earlier recordings. Apparently at this set of sessions he was given longer takes than previously was customary, and the resulting gain in continuity and liveliness is readily apparent. This is a fresh, straightforward account, literal but strong, and it is sensitively accompanied by Haitink. The transfer is of characteristic Philips quality. The level is rather low but the sound is truthful in timbre and musical in balance, if lacking the last degree of brilliance. The cassette moreover, besides coupling the *F minor Piano sonata*, Op. 2/1, in an acceptable if slightly mannered version, offers also the *G major Sonata*, Op. 49/2, which is not present on the equivalent LP. It is a cool but rather attractive performance.

Gulda's coupling is generous, and the performances fresh and enjoyable. In No. 2 the finale is lacking in lilt, but the first movement is strong and lively and the hushed close of the slow movement is beautifully done. No. 3 brings a dramatic performance marked by strong contrasts, and the slow movement has an inner concentration from the start. The finale, not too fast, is nicely accented, and the jauntiness of rhythm in the *Presto* coda makes up for any lack of animal excitement (the speed is relatively slow). The recording is excellent, and the transfer is well balanced, but the upper focus of the orchestra is less than ideal. The upper strings are rather 'fluffy' and the sound is not very clean in the opening of the slow movement of No. 3. The piano tone is somewhat dry, sounding rather like a fortepiano at times.

As in his other Beethoven concerto performances Brendel's concentration makes up for indifferent accompaniment thinly recorded (on tape as on disc). Fortunately the quality of the piano recording is far higher, so that Brendel's contribution at least can be appreciated to the full. Wallberg's conducting is lively and sympathetic, but on the reverse Boettcher is unimaginative. As usual with Turnabout issues the quality of the cassette matches the LP fairly closely.

Piano concerto No. 3 in C minor, Op. 37.

   (*) Philips 7300 163 [id.]. Stephen Bishop-Kovacevich, BBC SO, Colin Davis – *Sonata No. 8.***(*)

   (*) Decca KSXC 6653. Vladimir Ashkenazy, Chicago SO, Solti (with *Sonata No. 26, Les Adieux***(*)).

   (*) Decca KSXC 6653. Vladimir Kempff, Berlin PO, Leitner.

   (M) ***(*)** Decca KCSP 402. Wilhelm Backhaus, Vienna PO, Schmidt-Isserstedt (with *Sonata No. 14, Moonlight**(*)).

   (M) ** Turnabout KTVC 34207 [(d) Vox CT 2113]. Alfred Brendel, Vienna Pro Musica Orch., Wallberg (with *Sonata No. 26, Les Adieux****).

   ** HMV TC-ASD 3543. Sviatoslav Richter, Philharmonia Orch., Muti (with *Andante favori* ***).

   (B) ** Classics for Pleasure TC-CFP 40259. John Lill, Scottish National Orch., Gibson.

Piano concerto No. 3; Rondo in B flat major (for piano and orchestra), *G.151.*

(M) *(*) DG Privilege 3335 107 [id.]. Sviatoslav Richter, Vienna SO, Sanderling.

Like the other issues in the series with Bishop-Kovacevich and Davis, this version of the *Third Concerto* is among the most satisfying available. If Bishop-Kovacevich is less idiosyncratic than such rivals as Kempff (or, on disc, Barenboim), his concentration ensures that there is no lack of characterization. The first movement erupts in a superbly intense account of the cadenza, relishing the virtuosity of the conclusion. The central *Largo* is taken very slowly and intensely, and the finale, relatively relaxed, allows Bishop-Kovacevich to display the extraordinary clarity of his fingerwork. The recording of both the concerto and the *Pathétique sonata* is refined, and on tape the piano timbre is particularly natural. The orchestra, however, is not as bright and detailed as one would ideally like, and a slight increase of treble with similar bass cut is advisable. However, there are no real hiss problems.

The one controversial performance in the Ashkenazy/Solti set is created by the almost fierce intensity of the orchestral tuttis of the outer movements. The strength of the playing is in no doubt, but some will want a more relaxed atmosphere. The slow movement is finely done, and the bold performance of the *Les Adieux sonata* makes an appropriate fill-up. The transfer is at a high level; the slow movement sounds especially well. The piano tone is good throughout (of demonstration quality in the sonata), but there is a touch of gruffness in the bass at one or two loud moments in the orchestral tuttis of the outer movements, when the sound is not absolutely clean.

Kempff is here in subdued mood compared with the other performances in his Beethoven cycle. The speed of the first movement is astonishingly slow, though the squareness conveys the architecture of the movement more effectively. For once in a DG studio Kempff was not at his sprightliest. Yet even so the performance has rewards of its own, and the slow movement is most beautiful. The recording is very good and has – like the rest of the Kempff series – transferred realistically to tape.

After the *Emperor*, KCSP 402 is the most obviously attractive performance in the Backhaus canon. The opening *tutti* is magisterial, but the basic mood is essentially classical, and the lyrical flow of the first movement's development section is memorable. The freshness of the sound suits the playing, and the only hint that the recording is not freshly minted is to be found in the upper string tone, which is sparer in texture than one would expect today. The piano tone is attractively bright, but with no lack of depth. In the slow movement Backhaus refuses to yield to any romantic impulses, but his mood of classical restraint is balanced by the vigorous rhythms of the finale. The approach to the first movement of the *Moonlight sonata*, which acts as a filler, is characteristically severe, but, in spite of some technical fluffs in the finale, this is still a performance that obstinately remains in the mind. The transfer to cassette is well balanced and admirably clear.

Brendel's account is among the finest of his Beethoven series, better balanced between piano and orchestra than some of the others, though still with some shrillness in the sound (on tape as well as disc). The interpretation of the soloist is deeply satisfying, with the most delicate tonal and rhythmic control married to intellectual strength. The slow movement has depth as well as poetry and the finale is beautifully jaunty. The sonata is given an equally intense and alert performance.

Richter's HMV performance is consciously wayward, lyrical to a fault. With such a master there is much detail to enjoy, and Muti draws sympathetic accompaniment from the Philharmonia players, but it is a version for Richter devotees, not for general recommenda-

tion. The fill-up is beautifully played. The transfer is of good quality, lacking only the last degree of range and with rich, natural piano tone. The resonance does not impede the orchestral detail.

A characteristically clear, direct account from John Lill and Sir Alexander Gibson. The performance is not without spontaneity and character, but it lacks individuality, although the slow movement has undoubted eloquence. The recording is clear and well balanced, and the transfer to tape offers vivid, well-detailed piano sound.

Richter's DG account is too chilly and detached to be wholly convincing. Like Schnabel, Richter takes the slow movement very slowly indeed, but unlike Schnabel he provides little warmth, and the result is curiously square. The finale is unpleasantly hard-driven. However, the filler is very attractive. Richter's approach to the *Rondo* is effortlessly brilliant, but not to the exclusion of all else: there is subtlety and even a touch of humour, and, above all, complete spontaneity and a sense of enjoyment throughout. This is available with a different coupling: see below.

Piano concerto No. 4 in G major, Op. 58.
   *** DG 3300 485 [id.]. Wilhelm Kempff, Berlin PO, Leitner – *Concerto No. 2.****
   *** Philips 7300 454 [id.]. Stephen Bishop-Kovacevich, BBC SO, Colin Davis – *Concerto No. 2.****
   *** DG 3300 791 [id.]. Maurizio Pollini, Vienna PO, Boehm.
   (M) **(*) HMV TC-EXE 156. Emil Gilels, Philharmonia Orch., Ludwig – MOZART: *Violin concerto No. 3.***(*)
   (*) Decca KSXC 6886. Radu Lupu, Israel PO, Mehta – *Sonatas 19* and *20*; *Variations.**
   (M) ** Turnabout KTVC 34208

[(d) Vox CT 2113]. Alfred Brendel, Vienna Pro Musica Orch., Wallberg (with *Sonata No. 24* and *Andante favori***).

(M) *(*) Philips 7317 101 [7310 106]. Claudio Arrau, Concertgebouw Orch., Haitink (with *Sonata No. 2: Scherzo* *(*)).

(M) *(*) Decca KCSP 403. Wilhelm Backhaus, Vienna PO, Schmidt-Isserstedt (with *Sonata No. 8, Pathétique**(*)).

(i) *Piano concerto No. 4*. Overture: *Leonora No. 3, Op. 72b*.

*** Decca KSXC 6654 [Lon. 5-6856]. Chicago SO, Solti, (i) with Vladimir Ashkenazy.

The Ashkenazy/Solti performance of the *G major Concerto* is one of the finest of their complete series, the contrast between the musical personalities of soloist and conductor bringing new insights to this masterly score. The performance of the overture is fresh and dramatic, and this issue, with an excellent, clear cassette transfer, can be recommended alongside those of Kempff, Bishop-Kovacevich and Pollini.

Although Kempff's delicacy of fingerwork and his shading of tone colour are as effervescent as ever, this is not so personal a reading as on his earlier mono LP. There were moments in that of the purest magic, provided one was ready to accept some waywardness. This later version also allows some speed variation, but the increased sense of unity owes much, it is plain, to the fine control of the conductor, Leitner. The sound of the tape transfer is first-class in every way.

The Bishop-Kovacevich recording is discussed under its coupling.

Pollini's account is a very distinguished one. More aristocratic playing would be hard to find, save perhaps from Gilels. Since Kempff and Bishop-Kovacevich offer the *Second Concerto* as a coupling, this is short measure; but given playing of this stature, in which

classical poise and poetic sensitivity are so delicately balanced, this tape almost leads the field. Boehm is a faithful accompanist, and the sound is of excellent quality. The transfer is admirable, fractionally dry in the bass, but with fine range, body and presence.

Gilels's version, very competitively priced, may be regarded as an equally desirable alternative choice. This is a strong poetic reading of striking authority and eloquence. The poetry of the dialogue in the slow movement is finely realized, and there is a rare combination of strength and sparkle in the finale. The recording is remarkably good: the piano tone is fresh and the orchestra well balanced. The transfer to tape is on the whole successful, with convincing projection of the soloists, but is slightly less refined in the orchestral tuttis.

Radu Lupu is an artist of rare eloquence and he brings an inner serenity and repose to this magical concerto. Had he enjoyed the advantage of more sensitive orchestral support, this would be a very formidable issue indeed. But the opening of the slow movement is distinctly coarse, and at no time does one feel that Mehta's sensibility is a match for his soloist. The recording is distinguished by excellent engineering, and the transfer is beautifully refined, if without a strikingly dramatic dynamic range.

Anyone starting the Turnabout tape expecting the *Fourth Concerto* and receiving as a prelude Brendel's gentle performance of the *Andante favori* will not have his or her anticipatory mood spoiled: if the extra filler (not on the disc) had to be at the beginning of this tape, the choice of music was well made. Brendel's interpretation of the concerto is deeply satisfying, but as in the rest of his series he is hampered by unimaginative accompaniment thinly recorded. The first-movement *tutti*, for example, is rhythmically stodgy, and that detracts from the impact of the soloist in this work more seriously than in the other Beethoven concertos. It is interesting that Brendel uses the second of the cadenzas by Beethoven, not generally heard. The sound on cassette is clear, and the transfer does not disguise the thin upper strings of the orchestra.

Arrau's is an unusually relaxed view of the first movement. But unlike some of the others in his cycle, it seems a relatively mannered performance, sounding unspontaneous.

Backhaus's gruff manner in this most lyrical of concertos will not be to all tastes, yet there is a strength and integrity to the performance which offer some compensation for the starkness of approach. The famous dialogue between piano and orchestra in the slow movement is played in an exceedingly deadpan manner, yet if anything this serves to underline Beethoven's contrasts even more than in a romantic performance. There are moments in the finale when the playing is not as cleanly accurate, but even these can be forgiven, and so can the sound, which is brilliantly clear – to match the music-making – but not as warm as in others of this series. The vivid brilliance of the transfer shows up the upper string tone in the first *tutti* of the concerto, but one adjusts to this early Decca sound, for the acoustic is open and the piano tone boldly convincing. The performance of the sonata, however (which is even more literal than the concerto), is not helped by the dry piano image, especially in the slow movement.

Piano concerto No. 5 in E flat major (Emperor), Op. 73.
> *** DG 923014 [id.]. Wilhelm Kempff, Berlin PO, Leitner.
> (M) *** Philips Festivo 7310 013. Stephen Bishop-Kovacevich, LSO, Colin Davis.
> (M) *** Decca KCSP 452. Wilhelm Backhaus, Vienna PO, Schmidt-Isserstedt.
> (M) **(*) Philips 7317 141 [7310 086]. Claudio Arrau, Concertgebouw Orch., Haitink.

> (M) **(*) HMV TC-SXLP 30223. Emil Gilels, Cleveland Orch., Szell.
> **(*) Philips 7300 542 [id.]. Alfred Brendel, LPO, Haitink.
> (M) **(*) Decca Jubilee KJBC 18. Friedrich Gulda, Vienna PO, Stein.
> (M) **(*) DG Privilege 3335 296 [3300 384]. Christoph Eschenbach, Boston SO, Ozawa.
> **(*) RCA RK 11420. Artur Rubinstein, LPO, Barenboim.
> (B) **(*) DG Heliodor 3348 206. Andor Foldes, Berlin PO, Leitner.
> (M) **(*) CBS Classics 40-61918 [Col. MT 31807]. Rudolf Serkin, New York PO, Bernstein.
> (B) ** Classics for Pleasure TC-CFP 40087. John Lill, Scottish National Orch., Gibson.
> (M) ** Decca KCSP 334. Clifford Curzon, Vienna PO, Knappertsbusch.
> (M) ** Turnabout KTVC 34209. Alfred Brendel, Vienna Pro Musica Orch., Mehta (with *Fantasia*, Op. 77, and *Rondo*, Op. 51/2**).
> (M) ** RCA Gold Seal GK 25014. Rudolf Firkusny, RPO, Kempe.

(i) *Piano concerto No. 5. Overture: Coriolan, Op. 62.*
> *** Decca KSXC 16655 [Lon. 5-6857]. Chicago SO, Solti, (i) with Vladimir Ashkenazy.

Even amid the wealth of fine *Emperor* performances Kempff's version stands out as perhaps the most refreshing and imaginative of all. The interests of the musical argument always take precedence over the demands of virtuosity. Beside less thoughtful pianists Kempff's interpretation may at times sound comparatively small-scale: there is no attempt at the big bow-wow approach. But strength there is in plenty, and excitement too. As ever, Kempff's range of tone colour is extraordinarily wide, from the merest half-tone, as though the fingers were barely brushing the keys, to the crisp impact of a dry *fortissimo*. The transfer to tape has been recently remastered and provides full-bodied orchestral sound and first-class piano timbre. The level is high, and the recording, while not always absolutely clean, has fine life and impact.

Bishop-Kovacevich's is also one of the most deeply satisfying versions of this much-recorded concerto ever made. His is not a brash, extrovert way. With alert, sharp-edged accompaniment from Colin Davis, he gives a clean dynamic performance of the outer movements, then in the central slow movement finds a depth of intensity that completely explodes any idea of this as a lighter central resting point. Even so he avoids weighing the simple plan down with unstylistic mannerisms: he relies simply on natural, unforced concentration in the most delicate, hushed tones. The transfer is successful and quite satisfying. The overall sound is rich and full, with excellent piano tone, although the orchestral balance is improved with a slight bass cut. At Festivo price this is a real bargain.

The Ashkenazy/Solti cassette opens with a brilliant performance of the *Coriolan overture*, vividly recorded and making a considerable impact. The quality changes slightly at the beginning of the concerto, having less weight, and with the reverberation not controlled so cleanly. But the piano tone is clear and crystalline, and the sound is of generally high quality. Ashkenazy and Solti give an excitingly dramatic performance of the concerto, one which is on the largest possible scale, yet is consistently imbued with poetry. Alongside the *Fourth Concerto* this represents the peak of achievement of their complete cycle.

There is absolutely no question about

the power and authority of Backhaus's *Emperor*. The performance is at once vigorous and forthright. It does not lack the grand manner, yet there is lyrical feeling too. There is even a touch of exuberance in the finale. In short, this is the best of both Backhaus and Schmidt-Isserstedt; and what a fine conductor he has proved throughout this series of recordings, providing a firm, yet often mellow strength against which Backhaus's sometimes uncompromising solo playing is set in bold relief. Some might feel that more variety of colour might be appropriate in the slow movement, yet Backhaus's restraint does not stem from insensitivity, and this is undoubtedly a performance to uncover new facets of a much-played masterpiece. The recording is splendidly bold and resonant to match this genuinely large-scale conception, and in spite of its relative age this is one of the best-sounding *Emperor*s on cassette: an excellent bargain.

Arrau's version appeared first as part of a complete cycle, and it is remarkable how much more spontaneous he sounds here than in his previous account of the work (an early Columbia record). The slow movement in particular conveys the tension of a live performance – it sounds as though it might have been done in a single unedited take. Arrau is at his most commanding and authoritative in the outer movements; the finale is most stylishly played. The recording is first-rate, and, even without consideration of its reasonable price, this version is one of the very finest available on all counts. The transfer is at rather a low level (especially in the first movement) and it needs a high volume setting and a slight treble lift to make maximum impact. But the balance is good and the recording is clear.

Of the many other versions available few are more superb than Gilels; here strength is matched with poetry in no small measure. It goes without saying that Szell has tremendous grip and that the playing of the Cleveland Orchestra is beyond reproach. Memories of Gilels's earlier recording with the Philharmonia Orchestra under Leopold Ludwig are not completely banished (it had even greater humanity in some ways) but, make no mistake, this is a performance that must be numbered among the very finest on the market. Listening to it reaffirms one's conviction that Gilels is one of the very greatest Beethoven pianists of the present age. At medium price this is very competitive, even though the dynamic range of the recording (which is admirably full-blooded) is not as wide as on the equivalent disc. There is also a patch of less than completely clear orchestral sound at the opening of the slow movement.

In Brendel's Philips version there is a great deal to admire from the artistic point of view. It is spaciously conceived and the phrasing has no lack of eloquence. But generally the reading is less spontaneous in feeling than Brendel's earlier Turnabout recording with Mehta, although that is not nearly so well recorded. Undoubtedly the new version will give satisfaction, but there is a studied quality about the music-making that keeps this performance from being at the top of the list. Moreover the transfer is a shade disappointing. The sound is truthful, with natural piano tone and a good balance, but the level is low and there is some lack of bite in the upper strings; this is particularly noticeable in the finale.

With its dramatically recorded opening (the tone of the Bösendorfer piano extremely vivid) Gulda's account of the first movement does not lack a robust quality, yet he plays less for excitement than for poetry. The passages in his reading of the *Emperor* that latch in the memory are the gentle ones, whether the half-tones of the second subject in the first movement or the serene phrases of the slow movement, here given with real *Innigkeit*. For some reason the recording focus slips marginally at the opening of side two and the piano timbre becomes less clean, but the finale is splendidly

clear and lively. Although there are more individual performances available, this cassette is not likely to disappoint.

Eschenbach gives a deeply satisfying interpretation, helped by the equally youthful urgency of his accompanist. With thoughtfulness and bravura combined, it stands among the finest versions available, but the recording is reverberant even by Boston standards, which obscures a fair amount of inner detail. The transfer is made at quite a high level (although the slow movement is rather less vivid), but the upper range lacks sparkle and the lack of clarity in the orchestra is more striking on cassette than on disc.

Rubinstein plays with spontaneous inspiration, compelling attention in every phrase, and the Philharmonia under Daniel Barenboim accompanies with keen understanding. The balance, however, is highly contrived, with an excessively forward balance for the piano, which sounds larger than life. The orchestral wind solos are similarly spotlighted, and although the strings are laid out fairly convincingly within a reverberant acoustic, the result is unreal. The transfer is of good quality, giving bold, bright piano tone and no lack of detail.

Foldes's recording dates from 1959, but the sound is fresh, and the piano is truthfully recorded. The reading is clearcut, classical in feeling (not unlike Brendel's, but with obviously better orchestral playing). Foldes is a trifle cool in the slow movement but provides a sparkling finale. The tape transfer is most successful, with a natural piano image and good balance. At Heliodor price this is an excellent bargain.

Serkin gives a characteristically noble and commanding performance, sympathetically supported by Bernstein and the New York Philharmonic. But it is not just the somewhat coarse recording quality which prevents this from being among the most refined as well as the most powerful versions: both soloist and orchestra fall short on occasion. The transfer is made at quite a high level and produces a fierce orchestral image and clear but comparatively bloomless piano timbre. However, the performance triumphs over these impediments and the spirit of the music-making undoubtedly comes over. In spite of the lack of refinement the quality is quite acceptable if the treble is cut back.

John Lill has too often seemed inhibited by the recording process, but here, in the first offering of his Beethoven concerto cycle, his rare combination of power and poetry is captured with seeming spontaneity. The recording is obviously modern and well balanced and sounds well in the slow movement and finale, with notably bold, clear piano timbre. In the first movement, however, the focus is less clean, and the lack of the last degree of refinement in the orchestral tuttis detracts slightly from the appeal of this reasonably-priced issue.

Curzon's is a refined, thoughtful reading of the *Emperor*, almost Mozartian in the delicacy of the finale but with keen intelligence and inner concentration working throughout. The recording, one of Decca's earliest stereo issues, has been revamped well, but on top there is a limited range, and the orchestral quality has moments of slight roughness. Thus the tape transfer has not the lively open sound in the treble that one usually expects from a Decca cassette. But the performance is memorable for the aristocratic account of the slow movement, where Curzon's cool poise creates striking tension and atmosphere. The lyrical finale gives much pleasure too, and the recording seems more open on side two than on side one.

Brendel's Turnabout cassette includes a solo piano item not included on the equivalent disc. Although the *Fantasia*, which begins the tape, shows Brendel's musical personality at its most individual, it seems questionable whether the piece makes the right prelude for the *Emperor*. However, Brendel gives a splendidly bold and vigorous reading of

the concerto, and he is well supported by Zubin Mehta and the Vienna Pro Musica Orchestra. This is a performance without idiosyncrasy, yet strong in style and personality. Brendel's sense of line in the slow movement has a most compelling effect on the listener, so inevitable does his placing of the notes seem. The beginning of the finale is prepared most beautifully, and the main theme emerges vividly with great character. With a good balance between piano and orchestra, this too is recommended, even though the recording acoustic is rather dry. The cassette transfer is faithful in providing an orchestral texture that is clear rather than rich and weighty.

Firkusny's version was recorded in the 1960s for Reader's Digest. It is a commanding, lyrical reading, well recorded. Kempe directs the orchestra with characteristic warmth: the *Adagio* is nobly shaped and the vigorous finale nicely prepared. Some ears find the overall account slightly inflexible compared with rival mid-priced versions, but to others the element of weight and the feeling for the grand manner is distinctly attractive. When the cassette was first issued different copies seemed to produce different quality, with convincing piano timbre but varying degrees of refinement in the orchestra. This is a tape to be sampled before purchase.

(i–ii) *Piano concerto No. 5 in E flat major* (*Emperor*), *Op. 73;* (ii) Overtures: *Egmont, Op. 84; Leonora No. 3, Op. 72b; Symphonies Nos.* (iii) *5 in C minor, Op. 67;* (ii) *6 in F major* (*Pastoral*), *Op. 68;* (iii–iv) *9 in D minor* (*Choral*), *Op. 125;* (v; i) *Violin sonata No. 5 in F major* (*Spring*), *Op. 24;* (vi) *Piano sonatas Nos. 8 in C minor* (*Pathétique*), *Op. 13; 14 in C sharp minor* (*Moonlight*), *Op. 27/2; 23 in F minor* (*Appassionata*), *Op. 57.*

(M) **(*) Decca к 77 к 54. (i) Vladimir Ashkenazy (piano);

(ii) Chicago SO, Solti; (iii) Vienna PO, Schmidt-Isserstedt; (iv) Sutherland, Horne, King, Talvela, Vienna State Opera Chorus; (v) Itzhak Perlman (violin); (vi) Wilhelm Backhaus (piano).

This album was issued to commemorate the 150th anniversary of the death of Beethoven, and the box is rather handsome, with gold lettering on pale maroon. The selection is inevitably an arbitrary one, but while the performances can in varying degrees be criticized subjectively, the spirit of Beethoven is never absent from the music-making. The Ashkenazy/Solti *Emperor* and the Schmidt-Isserstedt performances of the symphonies will certainly give satisfaction, but Solti's view of the *Pastoral* may not be to all tastes. It is curious that the *Spring sonata* (beautifully played as it is) was chosen rather than the *Kreutzer*; but no one will regret having the Backhaus performances of the piano sonatas. They all show his granite-like integrity, and if the *Moonlight* is determinedly unromantic, the *Appassionata* is unforgettable. The piano tone here is first-class, bold and clear, with a richly sonorous bass. Elsewhere the cassette sound is well up to Decca's high standard, except for the very end of the *Choral symphony*, where the bass drum causes the same disturbance as it does on the individual issue of this recording. The *Emperor* is a trifle dry in acoustic, but yields to the controls. The only work needing a side turn in the middle is the *Ninth Symphony*, which turns after the *Adagio*. The two overtures are on side eight on their own.

Violin concerto in D major, Op. 61.
> ⊛ (M) *** Philips 7317 139. Herman Krebbers, Concertgebouw Orch., Haitink.
> **(*) DG 3300 903. Pinchas Zukerman, Chicago SO, Barenboim.

(M) **(*) DG Privilege 3318 015. Wolfgang Schneiderhan, Berlin PO, Jochum.

(M) ** HMV TC-EXE 197. David Oistrakh, French National Radio Orch., Cluytens.

(M) (**) CBS Classics 40-61598. Isaac Stern, New York PO, Bernstein.

(**) RCA Gold Seal GK 25005. Igor Oistrakh, Vienna SO, David Oistrakh.

(**) CBS 40-76477. Isaac Stern, New York PO, Bernstein.

(i) *Violin concerto;* Overture: *Coriolan, Op. 62.*
> **(*) HMV TC-ASD 2667. New Philharmonia Orch., Boult, (i) with Josef Suk.

(i) *Violin concerto;* (ii) *Romances for violin and orchestra Nos. 1 in G major, Op. 40; 2 in F major, Op. 50.*
> (M) *** Philips Festivo 7310 051 [id.]. Arthur Grumiaux, with (i) New Philharmonia Orch., Galliera; (ii) Concertgebouw Orch., Haitink.

There are a number of fine recordings of Beethoven's *Violin concerto*, but we are agreed that there is something very special about the Krebbers Philips issue. As a soloist, Krebbers has not quite the commanding 'star' quality of, for instance, a David Oistrakh, but he plays with a wonderful naturalness and a totally unforced spontaneity. The slow movement has a tender simplicity which is irresistible, and it is followed by a delightfully relaxed and playful reading of the finale. In the first movement Haitink and his soloist form a partnership that brings out the symphonic strength more than any other reading, except perhaps Haitink's version (on disc) with Szeryng. Krebbers is more meticulous than most virtuosi in playing *a tempo*, even in passagework. With a lesser artist that could have meant a dull result, but Krebbers's artistry is magnetic and his technique flawless. Altogether this is a memorable issue and the recording is excellent; the balance of the soloist is a fraction too close, but no matter: the sound itself is first-rate. The transfer is fresh and clear to suit the performance, not spectacular but truthful and well balanced and giving Krebbers's tone a natural projection and bloom.

The restoration of Grumiaux's earlier Philips recording to the catalogue on Festivo, coupled to appealing accounts of the two *Romances*, certainly makes a very competitive issue. The performance of the concerto is imbued throughout with the spirit of classical serenity. The combination of warmth and restraint in the slow movement is refreshing, especially in the beautiful second subject, and Grumiaux's variation on the main theme which follows has a graceful lightness of touch. Galliera accompanies eloquently and is in obvious rapport with his soloist. The recording is rich and full, the solo image truthful. The upper range lacks the last degree of sparkle, but the sound is brighter when the two *Romances* follow on as encores after the concerto. They are admirably played.

Zukerman and Barenboim take a spacious and persuasive view of the concerto, with the great span of the first movement stretched to the limit but still held in complete concentration. If warmth and beauty are the qualities most wanted, then this is almost an ideal version, with the immaculate playing of the Chicago orchestra backing up the soloist splendidly. However, on the cassette the transfer level is not very high (the recording has a wide dynamic range), and the violin image is rather backwardly balanced. Although the sound itself is natural, it is not very vividly projected, especially in the first movement.

Suk's performance is more controversial. The first movement is taken at an unusually slow tempo, and neither E.G.

nor I.M. finds that the playing has the kind of urgency and concentration to sustain the conception. But for R.L., Suk's playing is both noble and spacious. The performance is classical in style, although Suk, like Kreisler, pulls back at the G minor section in the development of the first movement. But it is the breadth and grandeur of design that emerge. Sir Adrian embodies the revisions in the score brought to light in Alan Tyson's edition, and the recording has exceptional body of tone. The eloquence of the slow movement and the lightness and sparkle of the finale are in no doubt. And, though no one buys a recording of the *Violin concerto* for the sake of the *Coriolan overture*, it would almost be worth it for Boult's superbly played account. It is certainly among the finest available at present. The EMI transfer, made at a high level, is extremely vivid, if lacking the last degree of refinement at one or two moments of *fortissimo*.

Schneiderhan's reading on DG's mid-priced label makes a very considerable bargain. The serene spiritual beauty of the slow movement and the playing of the elusive second subject have seldom been surpassed, and the orchestra under Jochum provides a background tapestry of power and dignity. Against it Schneiderhan's small silvery tone and purity of style are so consistently poised and have such an innate sense of classicism that the senses and spirit alike are satisfied. The snag is the recording of the soloist, which makes the violin tone sound thin. But this remains one of the great readings of the greatest of all violin concertos. As an added point of interest Schneiderhan uses the cadenzas provided (by Beethoven?) for the transcription of the work for piano and orchestra. The first-movement cadenza is long and varied in mood and includes a solo part for the timpani. The tape transfer needs some smoothing back in the treble but can be made to sound very well.

David Oistrakh's strong, aristocratic reading on HMV Concert Classics is also a fine one. The HMV recording is undoubtedly superior, with a spacious acoustic and warm, resonant orchestral tone. The balance, however, places the soloist unnaturally forward, although he is beautifully recorded. The reading is characteristically assured, the soloist's phrasing and sense of line impeccable, but for some ears there is a suggestion of aloofness in the slow movement. The tape transfer is made at a high level and the quality is excellent, although the tonal breadth has been achieved at the expense of a wide dynamic range – there are too few pianissimos here.

The reissue of Isaac Stern's earlier performance on CBS Classics shows the intense creative relationship established between Stern and Bernstein. Stern's reading has a tremendous onward flow, his personality projected strongly, yet Bernstein keeps the orchestra well in the picture (in spite of the forward balance of the soloist), and the energy of the music-making is compulsive. The close CBS recording means that a real *pianissimo* in the slow movement is not possible, but the intensity is in no doubt, and the finale is comparably vigorous. The tape transfer, however, is not successful; the soloist is made to sound thin and wiry, and the orchestral textures are fierce, unrefined and not secure in amplitude.

It is David Oistrakh who dominates the account on RCA Gold Seal by his son, Igor. David conducts, and his deliberate manner in the first two movements sets the seal of his personality firmly on the music-making; this in spite of a balance which places the soloist in an unnaturally forward position. Undoubtedly Igor plays with eloquence and feeling, but the first movement refuses to take spiritual flight, and the reprise of the second subject in the slow movement lacks the touch of incandescence that can make this passage so supremely beautiful. The soloist is not helped by the forward orchestral woodwind, which creates an ungainly effect (and is not the fault of the orchestral players).

The copy of the tape we tried was not a successful transfer, with explosive distortion caused by the timpani, muddying the tuttis. Later copies may correct this fault.

On his newest CBS tape Stern gives a characteristically romantic reading, but this is less spontaneous-sounding than his earlier recording, and though the sound is fuller, CBS highlighting gets in the way of ideal balance. Moreover the transfer to tape is not successful, with unacceptable discoloration of the upper partials of the solo violin timbre and a general lack of refinement.

There is also a recording by Christian Ferras with the Berlin Philharmonic Orchestra under Karajan (DG 923026), but although this is well engineered the performance does not seem competitive with the best of the tapes listed above. DG have also issued this version in a box together with the violin concertos of Brahms, Sibelius and Tchaikovsky (3371 021).

Triple concerto for violin, violoncello, piano and orchestra in C major, Op. 56.

> *(**) Philips 7300 604 [id.]. Beaux Arts Trio, LPO, Haitink.
>
> (M) * DG Privilege 3335 153 [922015]. Wolfgang Schneiderhan, Pierre Fournier, Géza Anda, Berlin Radio Orch., Fricsay.

The world's most distinguished regular piano trio makes a natural choice when it comes to soloists for this great but wayward concerto. If the cellist, Bernard Greenhouse, lacks the full vibrant character of a Rostropovich in his first entries on each theme, he is more clearly coordinated with his colleagues, and consistently the joy of this performance – with the soloists projected out in front of the orchestra – is to relish the interplay between the instruments. The result adds up to a really satisfying structure instead of a series of separate memorable passages. Haitink's splendid direction helps too, with powerful tuttis and fine rhythmic pointing in the *polacca* rhythms of the finale. The engineers have found the problems of balance impossible to solve, with the orchestra damped down during solo passages; and with a very low-level transfer there is not the refinement of detail on tape that distinguishes the equivalent disc. For any degree of impact the volume level has to be turned well up, with the consequent increase of background noise. The quality is basically natural, but tends to lack firmness of outline, and one could not describe the sound as full-blooded.

The alternative Privilege cassette offers a performance of breadth and a genuine grasp of structure, with fine contributions from each of the distinguished soloists. Only in the first movement does one sense a slight want of spontaneity, but in all other respects this is fine playing. The recording balance places the soloists well forward, but the orchestra remains in the picture. However, the recording has not transferred very convincingly to cassette. The overall focus is poor and there is a recurring fuzziness in the images of soloists and orchestra alike.

The famous David Oistrakh/Rostropovich/Richter version is available on tape, but only in a rather turgid non-Dolby transfer (HMV TC-ASD 2582).

Overtures
(see also under 'Vocal music', p. 82)

Overtures: *The Consecration of the House, Op. 124; Coriolan, Op. 62; The Creatures of Prometheus, Op. 43* (with ballet music: *Adagio; Finale*); *Egmont, Op. 84; Fidelio, Op. 72c; King Stephen, Op. 117; Leonora Nos. 1–3, Opp. 138; 72a; 72b.*
> (M) (***) HMV TC-SXDW 3032. Philharmonia or New Philharmonia Orchestras, Klemperer.

It was a splendid idea for EMI to recouple Klemperer's performances of the Beethoven overtures in this double-tape format, economically priced. There is some really inspired playing here. Even the comparatively slight *King Stephen* is given strength, and *The Consecration of the House* has seldom sounded so magnificent on record. The second tape collects together Klemperer's performances of the four overtures written for *Fidelio* at various stages. The approach, as one expects with Klemperer, uses measured tempi to bring out the architectural strength – even *Fidelio* is more serious than usual – but such is the conductor's control over tension that no unbiased listener could find the result dull or heavy. *Coriolan* is particularly strong, and Klemperer invests the extra items from the *Prometheus* ballet (included on the first tape) with an unexpected nobility of contour. Recordings of varying vintage come up well, but the cassette transfer has been mismanaged and offers coarse, distorted sound.

Overtures: (i) *The Consecration of the House, Op. 124; Fidelio, Op. 72c;* (ii) *Leonora No. 2, Op. 72a;* (i) *Leonora No. 3, Op. 72b; Namensfeier, Op. 115;* (iii) *The Ruins of Athens, Op. 113.*
> (B) *(*) DG Heliodor 3348 138. (i) Lamoureux Orch., Markevitch; (ii) Berlin PO, Jochum; (iii) Bavarian Radio Orch., Jochum.

Three of Beethoven's four overtures for his only opera, plus three other comparatively rare overtures, make generous measure at Heliodor price. The stylistic contrast between the two conductors is less distracting than one would expect, though naturally the Paris orchestra, with its French *vibrato*, does not always sound idiomatic. Markevitch makes the *Consecration of the House* less weighty than usual, almost frivolous, but generally his interpretations are clean and dramatic. Jochum's two contributions are more clearly in the German tradition (and better recorded), though the Bavarian Radio Orchestra is less polished than its rival. The transfer to tape offers vivid if slightly dry quality, with an unresonant bass. The only exception is *The Ruins of Athens*, where the recording is top-heavy, with shrill strings.

Overtures: (i) *Coriolan, Op. 62; The Creatures of Prometheus, Op. 43; Egmont, Op. 84;* (ii) *Fidelio, Op. 72c; Leonora No. 3, Op. 72b.*
> (M) ** DG Privilege 3335 135. (i) Vienna PO, (ii) Dresden State Orch., Boehm.

These are characteristically civilized performances, without the adrenalin or thrust of Karajan but well played and recorded. *Coriolan* is particularly well characterized and has a noble restraint which is highly effective. *Leonora No. 3,* although not super-brilliant, is enjoyable too, but *Egmont* (which opens the tape) is somewhat bland and underpowered. On tape the sound of the first three overtures, played by the VPO, is first-class, with warmth of sonority nicely balanced with brilliance and no lack of detail; on side two the recording of the Dresden orchestra is less good, with the upper strings less than ideally smooth in *Fidelio*. The focus improves markedly in *Leonora No. 3*.

Overtures: *Coriolan, Op. 62; Fidelio, Op. 72c; Leonora No. 3, Op. 72b.*
> **(*) DG 923057 [id.]. Berlin PO, Karajan – SCHUBERT: *Symphony No. 8.***(*)

Karajan gives characteristically brilliant performances of these three overtures, ending *Fidelio* and *Leonora No. 3* with bravura displays of virtuosity at speed. The recording is reverberant, but the level of transfer is comparatively high and there is no lack of brilliance (although there is a touch of roughness at the climax of *Fidelio*). On our copy (a German-manufactured tape) there was a hiatus near the beginning of *Fidelio*, with a drop-out followed by a momentary, but serious pitch disturbance. However, this is unlikely to stem from the master tape and will probably disappear from later copies.

Romances for violin and orchestra Nos. 1 in G major, Op. 40; 2 in F major, Op. 50.
> (M) ** DG Privilege 3335 109. David Oistrakh, RPO, Goossens – BACH: *Violin concertos Nos. 1–2.***(*)
> ** DG 3300 496 [id.]. Pinchas Zukerman, LPO, Barenboim – SIBELIUS: *Violin concerto.***

(i) *Romances Nos. 1 and 2;* (ii) (Piano) *Andante favori in G major, G.170; Für Elise; Rondo à capriccio in G major (Rage over a lost penny), Op. 129.*
> (B) *** DG 3308 270. (i) Oistrakh (as above); (ii) Wilhelm Kempff (piano).

Oistrakh's performances of the two *Romances* are of outstanding quality. However, in the Privilege transfer to tape the recording has been given a somewhat unromantic edge, and a treble cut is needed to achieve a natural image for the soloist. These performances are also included on a sampler tape issued in association with DG's Beethoven Edition, coupled with some first-class Kempff performances of short piano pieces. The transfer is rather smoother here and clearly focused, but the piano music on side one is transferred at rather a low level because of the wide dynamic range encompassed. However, a slight treble cut is possible to deal with the background hiss.

Zukerman is less forwardly balanced

in the *Romances* than in the Sibelius coupling. These are good, eloquent performances, well recorded, and those who like their Sibelius firmly in the romantic-virtuoso tradition might like to consider this well-transferred tape.

Rondo in B flat major (for piano and orchestra), *G.151.*

*** DG 923059 [id.]. Sviatoslav Richter, Vienna SO, Sanderling – RACHMANINOV: *Piano concerto No. 2.***(*)

Richter's performance, reviewed above under *Piano concerto No. 3*, is here coupled to a recommendable (if full-priced) version of Rachmaninov's *Second Piano Concerto*, to which it makes a strikingly good foil.

Symphonies Nos. 1–9; Overtures: The Consecration of the House; Coriolan; The Creatures of Prometheus; Egmont (with incidental music); *Fidelio; King Stephen; Leonora Nos. 1–3.*

*(*) HMV TC-SLS 788. Philharmonia Orch., Klemperer (with soloists and chorus).

Whereas the equivalent LP set is on nine discs, this tape set is compressed on to five cassettes, and the most obvious advantages of this medium are somewhat diluted. While we are offered symphonies 1, 2 and 4–8 each complete on a single side and No. 9 divided over two, the other music is less readily accessible, and it is a pity that the *Eroica* had to be given a turnover before the finale. Many of the overtures are placed to follow a symphony, and the *Egmont* incidental music comes after *Symphony No. 1*. If one does not switch off quickly at the end of the *Choral symphony* the *Prometheus overture* appears, an admirable little piece in its own right but something of an anticlimax after the closing bars of No. 9. If these incidental items could have been given a cassette to themselves (and there is room in the box) this would have been altogether better planned. In spite of this the set certainly invites dipping into and provides good value for money in showing Klemperer's achievement in Beethoven's orchestral music. There are some disappointments, notably in symphonies 1 (over-careful, with more than a hint of ponderousness), 5 (which obstinately refuses to catch fire, and offers some congestion here in the transfer of the finale), 7 (with slow speeds), 8 (excessively weighty and rather stiff), and an uneven *Choral symphony* with not especially distinguished solo singing. However, the *Choral* is very successfully transferred to tape, as are symphonies 2, 3, 4 and 6 (apart from a tiny slip of pitch in the first movement, which may not be common to all copies). The performances of these works are among the very finest ever recorded, and the overtures too are generally very successful in their magisterial way, although they suffer from occasional patches of roughness in the sound (presumably contributed by the very high level of transfer throughout). *Consecration of the House* sounds rough-hewn at the opening; there is some minor distortion in *Coriolan* and a hint of discoloration at the opening of *King Stephen*, while *Fidelio* has a pitch slip mirroring that in the *Pastoral symphony* at the same point in the tape. In the symphonies the sound is more consistently fresh, although there is some thickness of texture in places. But the main problem is the reduction of dynamic range throughout. The powerful nature of the performances minimizes the harm this does, but the range is, in effect, only from *mezzo-forte* to *forte*; Beethoven's contrasts are diminished and in slow crescendos, e.g. in the first movement of the *Eroica* or the opening of the finale of the *Choral*, the expected tonal climax never arrives.

Symphonies Nos. 1–9; Overtures: *Coriolan; The Creatures of Prometheus; Egmont.*

> ** DG 3378 065. Vienna PO, Boehm (with soloists and chorus).

Boehm directs centrally satisfying readings of all the symphonies, beautifully played and smoothly recorded. What these mature readings may ultimately lack, when considered as a sequence, is the sort of sharp idiosyncrasy which makes for dramatic memorability. Boehm's view of Beethoven tends to be straight and direct, avoiding extreme speeds. It is no accident, therefore, that the *Pastoral* is one of the highlights of the set; and provided that one is not looking for excitement, these performances can be warmly recommended. They are currently available only on tape, and the transfers are well made.

Symphonies Nos. 1–9; Overtures: *Coriolan; Egmont; Leonora No. 3.*

> **(*) Decca K 3 F 10 and 11 (2 boxes) [Lon. 5-9].Chicago SO, Solti (with soloists and chorus).

Solti's epic Beethoven cycle with his own Chicago orchestra has a firm centrality to it. The recording of symphonies 1 to 8 followed on the outstandingly successful version of the *Ninth* with which Solti started his cycle. The performance of the *Eroica* has comparable qualities, with expansive, steady tempi and a dedicated, hushed account of the slow movement. Here and elsewhere Solti shows his new-found ability to relax as well as to press dramatically forward, and there is plenty of sunshine in the even-numbered symphonies, though Nos. 1 and 8 are arguably too weighty in their tone of voice. The recording has Decca's characteristic brilliance and sharpness of focus (best in Nos. 6 and 7, recorded at the Sofiensaal in Vienna), and one powerful point of distinction is that, for the very first time, every single repeat is

observed. On cassettes the set is available in two separate boxes of three. KF 10 includes symphonies 2, 3, 4, 5 and 7, with each symphony given a complete cassette side to itself, except No. 3, which is on two sides with the *Coriolan* and *Egmont* overtures as fillers. KF 11 combines 1 and 8 on a single cassette, but the other two cassettes are much less well arranged. One includes *Leonora No. 3* plus the first movement of the *Ninth* on one side, and the second and third movements of the *Ninth* on side two; the other cassette has the finale of the *Ninth* and first movement of the *Pastoral* on one side, with the remainder of the *Pastoral* on side two. How much clumsier could you get! However, the recording is consistently fine throughout the set, having plenty of weight and excellent detail. The *Eroica* offers no transfer problems here (as it does in the individual issue – see below), but the engineers *almost* set too high a level for the *Seventh*, excitingly vivid though the effect is. KF 11 includes a fourth tape with Solti in conversation with William Mann.

Symphonies Nos. 1–9.

> *** DG 3378 070 [id.]. Berlin PO, Karajan (with Tomowa-Sintow, Baltsa, Schreier, van Dam, Vienna Singverein).
> ** Philips 7699 037. LPO, Haitink (with soloists and chorus).

Some fifteen years after his first Beethoven cycle with the Berlin Philharmonic, Karajan recorded the nine symphonies again for the same company, and once more presented a series of extraordinary consistency, superbly played and recorded. Just as the cycle of 1962 established standards which were hard for any rival to match, let alone outshine, so the 1977 cycle, different in emphasis on certain symphonies, is if anything more satisfying, thanks largely to richer, fuller and more immediate sound.

Interpretatively, Karajan's views on Beethoven have changed relatively little –

consistency has always been one of his most striking qualities, almost to the fault of predictability – but some of the modifications are significant. In the first two symphonies it is partly a question of recording quality, but the earlier feeling of eighteenth-century elegance has given way to genuine Beethovenian strength and urgency, applied even in these early works. The *Eroica* – given a superlative performance in the earlier set – presents the one major disappointment of the new cycle, at least in the outer movements. These are faster than before, with a more brittle, slightly rushed manner, though the *Funeral march* remains very similar, measured and direct. To compensate for that disappointment, the first movement of the *Pastoral*, angular and tense in the earlier cycle, has elegance and joyfulness at a tempo barely any slower, while the other movements too avoid the tense manner of the earlier version. Otherwise the middle symphonies remain very much as they were in the 1962 cycle. Finales tend to be a little faster than before, though not so much as to sound breathless.

Most important of all, the *Ninth* is given a superlative performance. In the first movement the precision of the individual notes of the *tremolo* at the start points the first important change, and the recording, exceptionally rich and forward, underlines an extra toughness and intensity. The scherzo is a fraction slower than before and more lilting, while the slow movement is warmer and more relaxed, less metrical by a tiny but vital margin. As for the finale, it benefits from a more passionate view of the recitatives (both instrumental and vocal), while the two men soloists, Peter Schreier and José van Dam, easily outshine their rivals of 1962. The coda, taken very fast indeed, brings an exciting culmination.

Though the outer movements of the *Eroica* remain a noticeable drawback, and Karajan observes far fewer repeats than is nowadays customary (in expositions only in Nos. 1, 5 and 8), this is a set

which makes an obvious first choice. The tape arrangement is excellent, with symphonies 1 and 2, 4 and 5, and 6 and 7 paired, the *Eroica* having a cassette to itself and 8 and 9 spread conveniently over two cassettes. There is a well-produced booklet. On technical grounds the tapes cannot be faulted, with body and warmth as well as plenty of clarity. The fact that the *pianissimo* string detail seems to recede is an acoustic curiosity which apparently stems from the hall where the recordings were made, and it is not distracting. On our review set there was a tiny pitch slip in the minuet of No. 8, mirrored in the first movement of No. 9, but this is unlikely to be common to all copies.

Haitink's cycle brings superbly resilient performances, generally light of texture. These are readings which, without fuss, without any self-conscious feeling that we are being treated to the Word of God, have a sense of rightness in almost every single movement. If anyone fears that Haitink's will be a lightweight view, the *Eroica* and the *Ninth* should effectively counter that, for with Haitink these are the pinnacles of the cycle, as they must be. In the *Eroica*, the *Funeral march* starts with none of the usual hesitations, for Haitink from the first bar makes clear that even in hushed inner tones this is a march. If in the *Ninth* Haitink's reading seems initially to have less of cataclysm than usual, the consistency is plain, for the work is made to flower as though it is a natural development from the earlier Beethoven symphonies. The sublime slow movement with Haitink suggests perfect peace on earth rather than the cosmic contrast of god and man, such as you find in Solti's reading. The finale brings above all a hymn to joy, not to freedom or fate but to simple happiness. Though Haitink may not be seeking to scale Everests as Solti and Karajan do, he generally has more light and shade, tautening and relaxing as flexibly as in the concert hall. The transfer to tape, however, loses some of the bite and attack present on the discs. The quality is agreeably warm and spacious, but the emphasis on the area of middle frequencies means that inner detail is not ideally clear, and one has a feeling that the upper frequency range is restricted. The pairings include Nos. 1 and 8, and 2 and 4. Nos. 3 and 9 are coupled too, to prevent breaking the slow movement of the *Eroica*; but this introduces two turnovers between movements of No. 9, an unsatisfactory solution of the problem.

Symphonies Nos. 1 in C major, Op. 21; 2 in D major, Op. 36.
    **(*) DG 3301 101 [id.]. Berlin PO, Karajan.
    (M) **(*) Decca Jubilee KJBC 3. Vienna PO, Schmidt-Isserstedt.
    CBS 40-61901. New York PO, Bernstein.
Symphonies Nos. 1; 8 in F major, Op. 93.
    **(*) Decca KSXC 6760 [Lón. 5-6926]. Chicago SO, Solti.
    (B) ** Rediffusion Legend KLGD 005. Czech PO, Meylan.
    (B) * DG Heliodor 3348 224. Bavarian Radio Orch. or Berlin PO, Jochum.

Karajan directs polished and elegant performances whose firm lines give the necessary strength. Where in his 1962 versions Karajan ran the risk of seeming a little lightweight, he avoided this in 1977, but the weighty recording, less naturally balanced, with close-up effects, is less believable. It has transferred to tape with plenty of life, the orchestra having good body and detail. There is a feeling of slight recession of the image in *piano* and *pianissimo* string passages, as noticed in the complete set.

The Schmidt-Isserstedt/VPO recordings were reissued at medium price to launch Decca's Jubilee label. For both symphonies 1 and 2 Schmidt-Isserstedt

adopts unusually slow tempi, giving each movement a hint of ponderousness. In the finales of both symphonies the measured approach is a pure delight, revealing detail normally submerged and with nicely pointed playing from the Vienna Philharmonic. These are natural, unforced performances to give much pleasure, and in a first-class transfer to cassette, with clean, fresh sound throughout, this is excellent value at medium price.

Though both the Solti performances are vigorous and dramatic, this is not the coupling with which to convert anyone to Solti's Beethoven, the conceptions lacking geniality, though Solti's urgency is most persuasive. Bright recording, and an excellent cassette transfer offering both brilliance and weight.

Meylan's performances with the Czech Philharmonic are freshly enjoyable if essentially lightweight. Rhythms are brightly sprung, and the polished playing from strings and wind alike is highly engaging: the finale to the *First Symphony* is particularly successful played like this. The textures of the recordings match the playing, the timpani backwardly balanced so that the sound is brightly incisive but not weighty, although it does not lack body.

On Heliodor, Jochum gives refreshingly unmannered readings of both symphonies. As representative of the German tradition these performances are very enjoyable, and at Heliodor price this would be very competitive were the recording consistent. However, while the recording of No. 8 (by the Berlin Philharmonic) has a pleasing bloom and is naturally balanced, the acoustic for No. 1 (the Bavarian Radio Orchestra) is less readily captured in the transfer, and the dryness of the orchestral timbre produces patches of ugly sound. Here a lower level would certainly have brought more refinement.

Bernstein's tape is ruled out of consideration by the poor quality of the sound, which is fierce and has distortion in the woodwind tone, producing curious fluctuation of tone, like a bad film soundtrack. This is greatly to be regretted for the performances are rewarding. No. 1 receives a well-shaped reading with no lack of momentum and pace, while in No. 2 the orchestra play as if their lives depended on it. Bernstein observes the exposition repeat (as he does also in No. 1) and the movement is wholly free from any mannerisms. The slow movement is sensitively shaped, and the tempo relationships between first and second movements are well judged. Both the other movements are very fast and have a Toscanini-like sense of drive. It is to be hoped that CBS will remaster this tape at a later stage, and perhaps provide some notes too: there are none with any of the Bernstein Beethoven series.

Symphony No. 2 in D major, Op. 36; Overture: *The Consecration of the House, Op. 124.*
   (B) *(*) Rediffusion Legend KLGD 021. Czech PO, Ferencsik.
Symphony No. 2; Overture: *Leonora No. 3, Op. 72b.*
   ** Philips 7300 525 [id.]. BBC SO or LSO, Colin Davis.
Symphonies Nos. 2; 4 in B flat major, Op. 60.
   **(*) Decca KBB2 7042 [Lon. 5-7054]. Chicago SO, Solti.

On tape Decca have coupled Solti's performances of Symphonies 2 and 4, whereas on disc they are issued separately. The timings are close (35 and 37 minutes respectively). The high-level transfers produce orchestral sound of considerable breadth and power, brilliant yet with a strong bass line. Some care has to be taken to balance the controls to get the best results and remove a suspicion of harshness, but the impact and detail of the recording are certainly impressive. Solti's account of No. 2 is a performance of extremes. Though this is early Beet-

hoven, the young composer was intent on writing a symphony on a scale never attempted before, and Solti clearly conveys that absence of apology. The slow introduction is massive and measured, leading to a fast and weighty account of the *Allegro.* The *Larghetto* has spacious refinement, and the last two movements bring performances that are tough, bold and fast. A similar feeling of scale imbues Solti's *Fourth,* a reading that is vigorous, even exuberant, but not strong enough on charm, even if a rather gruff sense of humour does appear in the finale. With Solti the *Fourth* clearly points forward to the *Seventh Symphony,* which its structure so strikingly resembles, on such points as the slow introduction and the extra sections in the scherzo. The Chicago playing is flawless, with a highly polished violin tone sustaining the poised beauty of the *Adagio,* and the finale has superb vitality.

Davis with the BBC Symphony Orchestra presents the *Second* as a large-scale work, yet his rhythmic resilience and refinement of detail prevent the result from becoming heavy. The wit and humour of the scherzo, slower than usual, present an obvious instance. The overture (with the LSO) is equally well played and makes a powerful fill-up. The recording, which is rich and full-blooded, has transferred to tape only moderately well, the balance emphasizing the bass and middle frequencies. The upper strings sound feathery and lightweight, although the woodwind are naturally placed.

The sound of the Czech Philharmonic recording under Ferencsik could hardly be more different from that offered on Philips. It is very bright and crisp, needing a cut-back of treble, but then yielding a lively overall balance to suit the performance, which is stylishly played but rather lacking in depth. The reading is straightforward, not very individual but not dull. The overture makes a good filler, and this tape is quite good value.

Symphony No. 3 in E flat major (*Eroica*), *Op. 55*.

> *** DG 3301 103 [id.]. Berlin PO, Karajan.
>
> (M) *** Decca Jubilee KJBC 6. Vienna PO, Schmidt-Isserstedt.
>
> **(*) CBS 40–76706. Cleveland Orch., Maazel.
>
> **(*) Enigma K 453543. Hallé Orch., Loughran.
>
> (M) *(**) CBS Classics 40-61902 [Col. MT 31822]. New York PO, Bernstein.
>
> (***) Decca KSXC 16829 [Lon. 5-7057]. Chicago SO, Solti – WEBER: *Oberon overture*.**
>
> (B) ** DG Heliodor 3348 278. Rotterdam PO, Decker.
>
> (**) HMV TC-EXE 192 [Angel 4XS 36461]. BBC SO, Barbirolli.
>
> * Symphonica CSYM 5 [Peters PCE 020]. Symphonica of London, Morris.

Symphony No. 3; Overture: *Coriolan, Op. 62*.

> (M) **(*) DG Privilege 3335 101 [id.]. Berlin PO, Boehm.

Symphony No. 3; Overture: *Egmont, Op. 84*.

> *** HMV TC-ASD 3376. LSO, Jochum.
>
> ** DG 3300 486 [id.]. Vienna PO, Boehm.
>
> (B) ** DG Heliodor 3348 088. Berlin PO, Fricsay.

Symphony No. 3; Overture: *Leonora No. 3, Op. 72b*.

> (M) ** Philips 7317 102. Concertgebouw Orch., Monteux.

Not everyone will live comfortably with the fiery intensity of fast tempi in Karajan's outer movements, but in this 1977 performance the contrasts are heightened, with, if anything, an even more intense account of the *Funeral*

march than in his earlier recording. A point to consider is the absence of the exposition repeat in the first movement (until recent years rarely observed in recordings), but this is among the most polished as well as the most dramatic accounts available. The sound is full-blooded, and though there are some intrusive close-up effects the comparatively high level (for DG) of the transfer produces plenty of bite and detail without coarseness. (At the time of going to press Karajan's earlier recording is still available and may suit those who find the newer account too hard-driven; it is lively in sound and offers the bonus of the *Coriolan overture*: DG 923063.)

Jochum's is a magnificent reading, direct in outline and manner but with keen refinement of detail. Tempi are all centrally convincing, and the exposition repeat is observed in the first movement. The glory of the performance lies above all in the dedicated account of the *Funeral march*, never overstated but darkly intense. The sound is among the richest and best-balanced ever given to this symphony, and the tape transfer is first-class, robust in outline, with plenty of inner detail. The overture is also splendidly played and the sound here is only marginally less clean.

Schmidt-Isserstedt on Jubilee may not show quite the same power as in some of the other symphonies in his cycle, but his is a very satisfying, thoughtful reading, not lacking dramatic weight, and very well recorded. This is very much a performance to live with; its qualities become more and more apparent with repetition. The tape transfer is successful in combining fullness with detail. The quality seems marginally brighter on side one than on side two (the opening of the scherzo seems a little subdued in timbre), but the finale offers both weight and brilliance.

Maazel takes a clean-cut, direct view, not just in his relatively uninflected rhythmic style but in sensible middle-of-the-road tempi for all four movements, which he keeps steadier than is common. With the first-movement exposition repeat observed, there is much in this version's favour, but it is a performance which in sum lacks light and shade, with – for example – little sense of inner tension or tenderness in the *Funeral march*. But the discipline of the Cleveland Orchestra is superb, with special praise needed for the lower strings and the tough-toned horns in the trio of the third movement, never troubled for a second by the fast tempo. The recorded sound on disc is rather edgy but this is smoothed in the tape transfer; the comparatively low level brings less bite and range, and while the balance is truthful the overall quality has less presence than the LP.

Loughran began his cycle of Beethoven symphonies with an account of the *Eroica* which has all the rhythmic urgency and sense of spontaneity that makes his Brahms cycle so compelling. This is a performance with minor flaws – the Hallé violins are not always sweet-toned – but it is an exceptionally compelling one, with finely chosen tempi forthrightly maintained and a resilience of pulse in the first movement that is memorable. The recording quality is full, but the closeness of balance in a relatively narrow stereo spectrum hardly does justice to the hushed playing in the *Funeral march*, and occasionally exposes individual instruments. The transfer is somewhat sharp-edged and requires a treble cut and bass lift, but in general it produces clean, satisfying sound, with a natural balance and bloom on the woodwind.

In many ways Boehm's Privilege account is to be preferred to his later reading with the Vienna Philharmonic made in the early 1970s. The Berlin version is a decade earlier, so that the recording is marginally less vivid and detailed, though there is really not a great deal in it. The tape transfer is made at a comparatively low level on side one, but is higher on side two (which also includes the overture), where the sound is correspondingly more vivid. Boehm's Berlin reading has all the sanity and good sense that distinguish his

Vienna recording but has the additional virtue of greater spontaneity. It is unhurried, lyrical, less taut and powerful than Bernstein or Karajan, and has some of the sobriety of his Vienna account.

Bernstein's account of the *Eroica* is electrically intense. He takes the first movement almost as fast as Toscanini, and maintains the tension over a fuller span by including the exposition repeat. The *Funeral march* is darkly tragic, and the reading as a whole has great power. The sound quality here is rather better than on the other CBS tapes of this series, but it is never really congenial, and lacks clarity on side two.

The power and weight of Solti's reading are apparent from the very opening bars. The forward momentum is strong and positive. The tempo is comparatively relaxed, and this is matched by a very slow speed for the *Funeral march*. Yet the concentration creates an electric degree of tension, which is naturally resolved in the sparkling scherzo and the vigorous lyricism of the finale. The drawback here is the level of transfer. Decca have set it too high, and before the end of the slow movement there is a hint of coarseness, while in the finale the sound becomes distinctly rough.

Fricsay's performance is easy to enjoy, particularly when the sound on this cassette is so well balanced, and the impact so impressive. But Fricsay's romantic way with the first movement and his unashamed easing and tightening of the tempo will not appeal to all listeners. Similarly the tension is not consistently maintained in the slow movement, although the climax is well made. The last two movements are less controversial and there is some superb horn-playing in both. The *Egmont overture* is presented very dramatically and becomes a genuine bonus at bargain price, but the performance of the symphony cannot be recommended without reservations.

Barbirolli's account is on one of those EMI cassettes with a limited dynamic range. The sound is bright and forward, but the effect of Beethoven's crescendos is minimized. Barbirolli secures good playing from the BBC Symphony Orchestra, and those who like brisk tempi in the opening movement will doubtless find Sir John insufficiently taut and lacking in tension. There could be more forward drive and sense of momentum, but scarcely more humanity. Both the scherzo and the finale are excellently paced.

Decker's version with the Rotterdam orchestra on Heliodor is very well recorded. The balance is impressively natural, with fine range and weight. This is a direct if not especially imaginative reading. Decker chooses a slow basic tempo for the *Funeral march* and he is not helped in sustaining the tension by a side-break. The horn-playing in the trio of the scherzo is somewhat mannered, but the finale is exciting. Taken as a whole this may be thought to be good value (although the break in the *Funeral march* is a distinct drawback).

Monteux's recording on Philips offers a sizeable bonus in the *Leonora No. 3 overture*. The symphony is well played and recorded but lacks real weight in the *Funeral march*.

Wyn Morris gives a compelling and often individual reading. His tempo for the first movement is as fast as in Karajan's latest version, yet there is no hint of haste, since it regularly acquires a three-in-a-bar dance-like quality. The horn and woodwind playing is excellent, though ensemble is not always perfect; and until the closing bars, when Morris allows a marked slowing, the *Funeral march* lacks something in weight. The scherzo, like the first movement, is exceptionally fast but well sprung. The recording is not as clean on detail as it should be, and it lacks brightness. To make matters worse the tape sounds like a non-Dolby cassette and suffers from a very restricted frequency ceiling. The upper strings lack bite and detail and the opening of the *Funeral march* is subfusc. There is some coarsening at the climax of the scherzo.

The break in the slow movement (before the *fugato*) is another considerable drawback.

Symphonies Nos. 3 in E flat major (Eroica), Op. 55; 7 in A major, Op. 92.
 (B)**(*)Decca Historic KMON2 7053. Vienna PO or Concertgebouw Orch., Erich Kleiber.

Kleiber's performances of both these symphonies are classics of recording. In the *Eroica* (with the VPO) he set the pattern for the observance of the exposition repeat – which Beethoven himself urged – and the weight and gravity of his view have rarely been matched. In the *Seventh* he has an idiosyncratic reading for the closing bars of the *Allegretto* (all pizzicato), but this too is an intense, finely sprung performance. The original cassette transfer of this coupling was not a success, with too little edge to the upper strings and a booming bass, but Decca tried a second time and have produced a much better balance to do justice to the admittedly limited range of sound present on the early LP originals. Indeed No. 7 (which had very thin violins on disc) has been successfully smoothed without losing the life of the performance.

Symphony No. 4 in B flat major, Op. 60.
 *** DG 3301 104 [id.]. Berlin PO, Karajan.
 (M) ** DG Privilege 3335 218. RPO, Dorati.
Symphony No. 4; Overture: The Consecration of the House, Op. 124.
 (M) *** Decca Jubilee KJBC 7. Vienna PO, Schmidt-Isserstedt.
Symphony No. 4; Overture: King Stephen, Op. 117.
 (B) *(*) Rediffusion Legend KLGD 003. Czech PO, Ferencsik.

Symphony No. 4; Overtures: *Leonora Nos. 1, Op. 138; 3, Op. 72b.*
(M) **(*) Philips 7317 161 [7300 002]. Concertgebouw Orch., Jochum.

Symphonies Nos. 4; 8 in F major, Op. 93.
(M) (**) CBS Classics 40-61903. New York PO, Bernstein.

The precision of the Berlin Philharmonic under Karajan – made the more evident by close-up sound which exposes every flicker of *tremolo* – is a thing of wonder, and if anything Karajan in this 1977 performance conveys more weight and strength than before, with more emphasis in the *Adagio*. Only the extremely fast tempo for the finale marks a questionable development, but even there brilliance and excitement are never in doubt. On tape the orchestral image is full-blooded and clear, but again one notices the tendency for the strings to recede in pianissimos.

Hans Schmidt-Isserstedt's thoughtful, poetic style is well suited to the *Fourth* and provides a complete contrast to Solti (see above under the *Second Symphony*) and Karajan. His account of the first movement has more relaxation in it than is common these days, and the very slow *Adagio* he chooses allows Beethoven's lyricism to flower in a comparatively gentle atmosphere. That does not mean that Schmidt-Isserstedt's is too small scale or wayward a reading, but that he finds in this odd-man-out among the symphonies a different range of Beethovenian qualities. Excellent recording, though on tape the opening of the first movement seems less transparent and detailed than is usual from Decca. The recording springs to life at the *Allegro*, and the liveliness is maintained on side two.

Jochum's Concertgebouw version brings a rather less radiantly beautiful account of the *Adagio* than in his earlier Heliodor performance (not yet issued on cassette), but it still stands as a strong, compelling reading. The transfer is successful: the orchestra has plenty of life, although the resonant acoustic means that the inner detail is not sharply defined. The overall balance is good, and this makes a viable alternative to the Jubilee version under Schmidt-Isserstedt.

Dorati's rather deliberate opening sets the style for his performance, which in spite of vigorous outer movements is rhythmically rather square. The *Adagio* is comparatively matter-of-fact and unimaginative, and the third movement lacks any feeling of geniality. This is enjoyable in its purposeful, straightforward way, with good orchestral playing and excellent recording, but even at medium price it is not really competitive, especially now that Schmidt-Isserstedt's version has been reissued on Decca's Jubilee label. The tape transfer is of excellent quality, offering full yet detailed sound within a warmly resonant (but not too resonant) acoustic.

Ferencsik's reading with the Czech Philharmonic is straightforward to the point of routine, and although the orchestral contribution is not lacking in personality, in the last analysis this is not memorable. The recording is well detailed and has more weight than the others in the Czech Beethoven series.

Bernstein's performances of the *Fourth* and the *Eighth* have genuine stature. The *Eighth* is given tremendous sweep and power: indeed, Bernstein has something of the breadth and urgency that inform Kleiber's Beethoven. Tempi are admittedly on the brisk side, particularly in the *Fourth Symphony*: No. 8 gains in tautness and concentration as a result, but there is a certain loss of mystery at the opening of No. 4. The first movement as a whole suffers on this count. But the playing pulsates with highly disciplined energy, and both symphonies have splendid grip. The cassette transfer, however, seems to offer unreliable quality. One copy tried had 'throttled' distortion of the upper partials of the woodwind and general insecurity; another was more successful, and, while not offering wide-ranging sound or any real degree of refinement, was comparable to the disc, but with a somewhat fuller bass.

Symphony No. 5 in C minor, Op. 67.
   *** DG 3300 472 [id.]. Vienna PO, Carlos Kleiber.
   *** DG 3301 105 [id.]. Berlin PO, Karajan.
   *** Enigma K 453544. Hallé Orch., Loughran.
   (M) **(*) Philips 7317 133. Concertgebouw Orch., Szell – MOZART: *Symphony No. 40; Così overture.****
   (M) ** DG Privilege 3335 103 [id.]. Berlin PO, Maazel – SCHUBERT: *Symphony No. 8;* BRAHMS: *Tragic overture.***
   (M) ** DG Privilege 3335 216. RPO, Dorati.
   (M) (**) CBS Classics 40-61904 [Col. MT 31810]. New York PO, Bernstein.
   *(*) CBS 40-76672. Cleveland Orch., Maazel.
   (B) (*) DG Heliodor 3348 028. Berlin PO, Fricsay.
Symphony No. 5; Overture: The Creatures of Prometheus, Op. 43.
   *(*) HMV TC-ASD 2960 [Angel 4xs 36927]. LSO, Previn.
Symphony No. 5; Overture: Fidelio, Op. 72c.
   *** HMV TC-ASD 3484. LSO, Jochum.
   (B) ** DG Heliodor 3348 255. Bavarian Radio Orch., Jochum.
Symphony No. 5; Overture: Leonora No. 3, Op. 72b.
   **(*) Decca KSXC 6762 [Lon. 5-6930]. Chicago SO, Solti.
   (M) ** Philips Festivo 7310 060. Leipzig Gewandhaus Orch., Masur.
Symphonies Nos. 5; 8 in F major, Op. 93.
   (M) *** Decca Jubilee KJBC 5. Vienna PO, Schmidt-Isserstedt.
   (B) ** Classics for Pleasure TC-CFP 40007. Berlin PO, Cluytens.
   ** Philips 7300 252 [id.]. BBC SO, Colin Davis (with *The Creatures of Prometheus overture***).
   (M) * Decca KCSP 326. Suisse Romande Orch., Ansermet.

Beethoven's *Fifth* is strikingly well served on tape, with fine new cassettes from Jochum, Karajan and Loughran to stand alongside the famous recording by Carlos Kleiber. For many the first choice will be the outstanding new version on HMV by Jochum and the LSO, superbly recorded and very successfully trans-ferred to tape. The sound has splendid richness and body, excellent detail, and is most realistically balanced. It is usual enough for a conductor to treat Beet-hoven's *Fifth* as an epic work, but Joch-um's idea of the epic here is massive rather than compressed, and in this he is aided not only by superbly chiselled play-ing from the LSO but by the opulent re-cording. The first movement is strong and central in the German tradition, with big contrasts, but it is the *Andante* which especially marks this newest Jochum reading out. It is spacious and poised yet fresh and unmannered, with no hint of the German band in the brassy fortissi-mos. With Jochum they frame the moments of hushed intensity, so that the *pianissimo* hints at the motto rhythm take on a key importance. The scherzo is taken slower than usual, easy and light at the very start, then weighty; the finale enters as an expression not of bombast but of pure joy. The expansiveness is underlined by Jochum's observance of the exposition repeat. As a coupling Jochum again offers the *Fidelio overture* (as on his earlier Heliodor issue) in a brilliant performance, rather less sumptuously recorded than the symphony.

Carlos Kleiber's *Fifth* stands out among all others as did his father Erich's famous performance two decades earlier. Under Kleiber the first movement is electrifying, but has a hushed intensity too. The slow movement is tender and delicate, with dynamic contrasts underlined but not exaggerated. The horns, like the rest of the VPO, are in superb form, and the finale, even more than usual, releases the music into pure daylight. The graduation of dynamics from the hushed *pianissimo* of the close of the scherzo to the weight of the great opening statement of the finale has not been heard on a recording with such overwhelming effect since Toscanini. The transfer encompasses the wide dynamics without difficulty, although some later copies are not as clean in sound nor as wide-ranging as the original review copy, which came from Germany. However, most listeners will be willing to accept a minor degree of roughness with the impact and excitement of this unique performance.

Karajan's new cassette offers bright, full-bodied sound if not quite so spectacularly wide dynamics as with Kleiber. Whatever reservations may be made about the other performances in Karajan's 1977 cycle of the Beethoven symphonies, his version of the *Fifth* is magnificent in every way, tough and urgently incisive, with fast tempi bringing weight as well as excitement. There is richness but no blatancy in the finale, and this version can be confidently recommended alongside Kleiber's and Jochum's. Karajan's earlier performance was also a fine one, with speeds in the Toscanini tradition, suggesting swaggering extroversion, the hero striding forward. As we go to press it is

available in an excellent tape transfer, full-blooded and brilliant (DG 923011). It has the advantage of offering the *Fidelio* and *Leonora No. 3 overtures* as a very considerable bonus, also excitingly played and brilliantly transferred. They fill most of side one of the cassette. Then comes the first movement of the symphony, with the other three movements on side two, perhaps not an ideal arrangement.

Loughran continues his Beethoven series with an exceptionally vibrant account of the *Fifth*. Compared with Jochum's, his first movement is leonine rather than massive, but by observing the repeats in both outer movements Loughran underlines the scale of the symphony as well as its strength. After a direct yet lyrical *Andante* comes a fast scherzo, with nimble playing from the lower strings; and the release of exultant energy in the finale caps a performance which is notable above all for its vigour and forward impulse. The bright, vivid recording has transferred to tape with admirable presence and detail. It sounds best with a slight treble reduction.

Solti's version opens with the *Leonora overture*, a sensible enough procedure on disc, but less satisfactory on tape, since one needs to spool on to get at the symphony. But the recording itself shows the weight and body characteristic of this series, if a touch of harshness too in the brilliant upper string tone. Solti's is a big, bold reading of the *Fifth*, tense but not neurotic, with a warm, expansive account of the slow movement, a surprisingly measured view of the scherzo, and a really joyful account of the finale. With *Leonora No. 3* dramatically performed as a fill-up it makes a good recommendation for anyone collecting this Decca series.

Szell's Concertgebouw recording has a generous coupling and makes a good medium-priced recommendation with fine playing and good recording. The transfer has no lack of bite and impact, although the level is comparatively low.

On the DG Privilege label Maazel

offers a hard-driven, exciting performance, and the warm playing of the Berlin Philharmonic Orchestra tempers the conductor's impetuosity. Thus although the slow movement is dramatic, with striking contrasts of dynamic, its opening lyrical theme is played with singing tone whenever it dominates the proceedings. The finale could perhaps do with a little more dignity, but those wanting a straightforward, exciting account should find this very acceptable if the main coupling – a fresh but comparatively uneventful reading of Schubert's *Unfinished symphony* – is suitable. On cassette an extra bonus is provided: the tape turns over after the first movement of the Beethoven (which follows the Schubert on side one), and side two includes the rest of the symphony plus Brahms's *Tragic overture*. The sound on cassette is well balanced, not lacking either brilliance or body of tone. Compared with this, Maazel's 1978 CBS recording is distinctly uncompetitive: it offers the *Fifth* only, at full price and with quality which, while perfectly acceptable, is not nearly so vivid as in the older DG recording. In any case this Cleveland performance misses the spontaneous urgency of the earlier account, recorded in Berlin. Even when tempi are fast, the result has a tendency to squareness, and the slow movement is unduly heavy.

In Jochum's earlier recording on Heliodor, after an unexpectedly restrained opening he launches into a finely vigorous reading, unmarred by any romantic exaggerations, gripping in a totally natural, unforced way. The finale is especially fine and beautifully prepared like Kleiber's. The cassette transfer needs a high-level playback to make maximum effect, and the sound has generally less body and detail than in the finest tapes from this source, though it is more than acceptable at bargain price.

Kurt Masur's recordings of the Beethoven symphonies were somewhat underrated when they first appeared. In terms of sheer naturalness of utterance, un-

forced eloquence and superlative discipline, the Leipzig Gewandhaus Orchestra is second to none. Masur's account of the *Fifth* does not match the dramatic fire and intensity of Carlos Kleiber's, nor has he the concentration of Karajan, but at medium price (and given the excellence of the recording) this deserves to be taken seriously. It is perhaps just a shade too 'civilized' to be ideal, but it is certainly too good to be written off. Although it benefits from a bass cut, the sound on tape is full and clear; but side one opens with the overture (not an ideal arrangement on cassette), and on our copy there was minor disturbance of the texture at its beginning.

Dorati's Privilege issue cannot be recommended with any enthusiasm. It is a sound, straightforward account, well played and very well recorded, but the conductor fails to set the adrenalin racing and he misses the full sense of the work's drama, particularly in the finale. This does not compare with Szell or Jochum, who also offer more music; but the quality of the transfer is excellent, clean, open and with plenty of body and weight.

The *Fifth* is one of the finest of the Bernstein cycle, a strong, dramatic reading, not quite so distinguished as his *Eroica* but as concentrated and vital as his *Eighth*. The CBS recording, however, is harsh in its fierceness, although there is only minor woodwind discoloration. Were the recording really distinguished it would warrant a full two-star recommendation.

Previn's is an unexpected reading, the opposite of what some of his admirers will expect. His view of the *Fifth* is essentially weighty and sober. His tempi are consistently slow (hence the extravagant layout), and there is no attempt to whip up excitement, although the fine playing of the LSO brings some striking dramatic moments, notably on the big crescendo from scherzo to finale. But in the last analysis this recording lacks a Beethovenian impact of the kind to make it really memorable.

Fricsay's murky and turgid *Fifth* on Heliodor really will not do. It is undeniably heavy-handed, and although there is some fine detail from the Berlin Philharmonic, there are much better contenders on the market.

The coupling of symphonies 5 and 8 is a happy idea, and on Decca Schmidt-Isserstedt offers strong readings of both; this is a splendid tape with generous sides and first-rate recording. Schmidt-Isserstedt makes no allowances and includes exposition repeats in both the first movements. The first movement of No. 8 is slower than usual in the interests of emphasizing that this is not simply Beethoven's 'Little one' but a powerful, symphonic argument. There is a crisp, light *Allegretto* and a minuet more heavily pointed than usual, with a Brahmsian touch in the trio. But it is the account of the *Fifth* that stands out, with a first movement that has both bite and breathing space, a nicely measured *Andante* and a gloriously triumphant finale. Only the scherzo invites controversy by its slow tempo, but logic plays its part in the choice in that it allows the double-basses in the trio to play their scampering part without either stumbling or having the conductor slow for them. The transfer to tape is markedly successful, the wide dynamic range of the recording accommodated with breadth and clarity.

At bargain price Cluytens's cassette is outstanding value with good sound. The *Fifth* is an admirably refreshing reading, among the finest available, direct and urgent, unforcedly compelling, and it observes the exposition repeat. The Berlin horns in the finale are most exciting. The *Eighth* too is most satisfying: despite a slowish tempo for the first movement, the point of the Berlin playing keeps the performance alert all through. The level of transfer is extraordinarily high, yet there is only a marginal lack of refinement in the quality. The dynamic range has been reduced, but because of the strong character of the playing this is

only really striking in the great crescendo into the finale of the *Fifth*, which does not expand properly. (As we go to press, this tape is being mastered.) The *Eighth* is similar in quality; the inner movements sound very well although the horns in the trio of the third movement seem over-resonant in tone.

Though there is much fine playing in Davis's coupling, the performances rarely take fire. The first movement of the *Fifth* has the disadvantage of omitting the exposition repeat, essential in this movement. The transfer of the *Fifth* is satisfyingly done, with plenty of weight and no lack of bite. The opening of the scherzo, where the horns blaze in, has a hint of roughness, but generally the quality is good. If anything the *Eighth* has an even more vivid sound, with plenty of bite in the strings.

The clear, dry recording for Ansermet matches his cool approach to the *Fifth*, and the warmer acoustic matches his rather more relaxed and genial account of the *Eighth*. (Here the bass is slightly over-resonant.) But Ansermet's performances lack the red-blooded Beethovenian character.

Symphony No. 6 in F major (Pastoral), Op. 68.

*** Enigma κ 453545. Hallé Orch., Loughran.

(B) *** Classics for Pleasure TC-CFP 40017. Berlin PO, Cluytens.

*** HMV TC-ASD 3583. LSO, Jochum.

**(*) HMV TC-ASD 3456. LPO, Boult.

** (*) DG 3301 106 [id.]. Berlin PO, Karajan.

(M) ** DG Privilege 3335 219. RPO, Dorati.

(B) ** DG Heliodor 3348 205. Berlin PO, Maazel.

(B) *(*) Philips Fontana 7328 007. LSO, Dorati.

(M) (**) HMV Greensleeve TC-ESD 7004. Munich PO, Kempe.

(M) * CBS Classics 40-61905. New York PO, Bernstein.

Symphony No. 6; Overture: Coriolan, Op. 62.

*** DG 3300 476 [id.]. Vienna PO, Boehm.

**(*) Decca KSXC 16763 [Lon. 5-7052]. Chicago SO, Solti.

Symphony No. 6; Overture: The Creatures of Prometheus, Op. 43.

** (*) Philips 7300 361 [id.]. BBC SO, Colin Davis.

(M) ** Philips 7317 097. LSO, Colin Davis.

Symphony No. 6; Overture: Egmont, Op. 84.

(M) ** Decca Jubilee KJBC 2. Vienna PO, Schmidt-Isserstedt.

Boehm gives a beautiful, unforced reading of the *Pastoral*, one of the best-played (even if Vienna violins are not quite as splendid on this showing as those of Berlin) and certainly one of the very best-recorded. In the first movement he observes the exposition repeat (not many versions do); and though the dynamic contrasts are never underplayed and the phrasing is affectionate, there is a feeling of inevitable rightness about Boehm's approach, no sense of an interpreter enforcing his will. Only the slow movement with its even stressing raises any reservation, and that very slight. The transfer offers lively, clear sound, with no lack of warmth, and excellent balance. The overture (not present on the disc) is welcome.

Loughran's performance shows him at his most persuasive, conveying the joy of Beethoven's arrival in the countryside with seeming spontaneity, so that the whole performance carries forward in a single sweep. The slow movement is especially fine; in the scherzo the horns sing out exuberantly, so that after the storm the dewy radiance of the finale is the more refreshing. The Hallé is on peak form,

and the recording is rich and bright. The transfer to tape is highly successful, natural in timbre with warm strings, yet excellent inner detail and a fine bloom on the orchestra.

Cluytens's recording is intensely warm-hearted and atmospheric. On analysis alone one might object to the occasional idiosyncrasy, the very affectionate phrasing and a few speed changes. But the obvious spontaneity makes the whole performance most compelling. Each movement has a glow which can only come from complete sympathy between players and conductor, and the final *Shepherds' hymn after the storm* shines out as an apotheosis. In the linking passage after the storm Beethoven's picture of a world freshened by rain is most vivid, and from there to the end the sense of joyous release increases in triumphant crescendo. The transfer to tape richly captures the warmth of the recording, yet there is no lack of upper range or detail. A splendid bargain.

Jochum's HMV version is among the most distinctive. His tempo for the first movement is exceptionally slow (slower than he himself was in his earlier recording for Philips), but the rhythms are so exquisitely sprung that the result has more the flavour of a country dance than usual, with a hint of rustic tone in some of the wind solos (presumably, with these LSO players, that is by intent). There is a dance element too in Jochum's *Scene by the brook*, with the lapping triplet rhythms pointed as delectably as by Klemperer. The scherzo is jaunty and sharp-hitting, the *Storm* is given classical strength, and the *Shepherds' merry-making* is fresh and innocent, again with a persuasive lilt. This will not be everyone's first choice, but with full and finely balanced recording it is a most compelling reading. It has transferred smoothly to tape, the rich warm sound retaining its bloom and a good deal of detail. There is a hint of the refinement slipping just a little in the *Storm* and in the climax at the very end of the *Shepherds' hymn*.

One might compare Sir Adrian Boult's reading of the *Pastoral* with his classic view of Schubert's *Great C major Symphony*. In both by some sleight of hand he disguises every interpretative problem, making it all seem easy and fresh, poised and natural. It is an attractive formula, though some may find the very lack of idiosyncrasy less than completely satisfying, particularly in the slow movement, which lacks the memorability of the Loughran or Cluytens versions. But with full, rich recording, the storm has rarely sounded so magisterial, or for that matter the culminating climax of the finale. The tape transfer offers clear yet full-blooded orchestral textures, with plenty of range as well as warmth. The detail is not always absolutely refined, but the overall vividness suits Boult's directness.

Solti gives a bright, fresh, resilient performance which consistently conveys the high spirits of Beethoven's inspiration. The contrasts are big and bold, with resonant tone from the Chicago orchestra, and they are splendidly caught by the Decca engineers working in their favourite haunt of the Sofiensaal in Vienna. This is a performance about which there is a divergence of views; some ears find Solti not quite relaxed and the orchestral playing marginally too high-powered for the essentially lyrical quality of Beethoven's inspiration. The sound in the symphony is first-class, rich with both weight and plenty of detail, but for some reason the quality in the overture is rather less refined.

Colin Davis has twice recorded the same coupling (the symphony and *Prometheus overture*). His earlier LSO performance is lightweight, agreeably fresh, almost Mozartian in approach. To some ears it sounds understated; others find its unpretentious air attractive. It has certainly transferred splendidly to tape, with a vivid bright-eyed quality that suits the performance admirably. The newer performance with the BBC Symphony Orchestra is broader and warmer, helped by well-balanced, full sound. The controversial point about this account is the very measured reading of the fourth movement, the *Storm*. Though the playing is refined, inevitably it lacks something in excitement. Nonetheless it matches Davis's relaxed approach to the whole work.

In 1962 Karajan's reading of the *Pastoral* was tense and prickly. Here in 1977 his manner was more sympathetic, but it is still an interpretation which is reluctant to relax in Beethoven's countryside, a townsman's highly polished idea of the pastoral. Anyone collecting a set of the Karajan versions separately will be well pleased, but there are better single recommendations. Full, often close-up recording; the transfer seems marginally brighter on side two.

Dorati's way with the *Pastoral* is to take the first movement disconcertingly fast, and he does this in his newer RPO version as well as in the earlier Fontana recording with the LSO. Here the whole performance is endowed with the vigour of a walk on a cold winter's morning. Yet the LSO responds with spirited playing, and the clean, vivid sound projects the music admirably. However, in the newer Privilege tape, while Dorati's manner is still very direct, with few concessions to expressiveness, the RPO playing tends to provide a mellowing effect. Provided one can adjust to Dorati's approach the result is convincing, and the remaining movements are attractively fresh in a less brutal way. But the sound on Privilege seems to become a little clouded by the resonance; detail is not ideally clear, and in the finale the comparatively low level of the transfer reduces the dynamic thrust of the climax. Overall the recording is warm rather than brilliant.

Schmidt-Isserstedt's Decca recording is technically one of the finest tape versions of the *Pastoral*; the sound is admirably clear, yet has no lack of fullness. Yet the performance is in the last analysis disappointing. Schmidt-Isserstedt offers a good, clean, straightforward classical account. But there is somehow a lack of atmosphere and warmth, in the approach rather than the playing, and certainly an absence of charm.

There are no romantic eccentricities in Maazel's reading; indeed he is straightforward almost to a fault. He chooses fairly fast tempi for the first two movements, and although the Berlin Philharmonic Orchestra plays well for him the result is efficient rather than warmhearted. The scherzo bursts into life, but the finale returns to the refined mood of the first two movements. The recording is good, a little husky and unrefined in the more expansive moments.

Kempe's performance, taken from his complete cycle, is one of the most genially satisfying in that set. The sound is basically very good on the cassette, but the limitation of dynamic on the transfer means that in the storm the raindrops patter like hailstones and the thunder is diminished by comparison; also the big swelling climaxes at the end of the first and last movements are much reduced. Elsewhere the character of the playing and its expressiveness carry the music.

As usual in Beethoven, Bernstein is admirably free from undue expressive vehemence here, and there is little of the self-indulgence that mars some of his Mahler symphonies. At the same time there is not the subtlety or richness of detail that one finds in the Boehm and Loughran readings with the Berlin and Hallé Orchestras respectively. The recording faults noticeable in the rest of Bernstein's series are much less insistent here, although the recorded sound is over-brilliant.

Symphony No. 7 in A major, Op. 92.
　**(*) Philips 700 562 [id.]. LSO, Colin Davis.
　(M) **(*) HMV TC-EXE 138. RPO, Colin Davis.
　**(*) DG 3300 706 [id.]. Vienna PO, Carlos Kleiber.

　**(*) Enigma K 453546. Hallé Orch., Loughran.
　**(*) DG 3301 107 [id.]. Berlin PO, Karajan.
　(M) ** DG Privilege 3335 336. RPO, Dorati.
　(M) ** DG Privilege 3335 252. Bavarian Radio SO, Kubelik.
　(M) * CBS Classics 40-61906. New York PO, Bernstein.

Symphony No. 7; Overtures: Coriolan, Op. 62; Egmont, Op. 84.
　**(*) Philips 7300 418 [id.]. LPO, Haitink.

Symphony No. 7; Overture: Egmont, Op. 84.
　*** Decca KSXC 6764 [Lon. 5-7053]. Chicago SO, Solti.
　**(*) Decca KPFC 4342 [Lon. 5-21139]. New Philharmonia Orch., Stokowski.
　*(*) Decca KSXCN 6673. Los Angeles PO, Mehta.

Symphony No. 7; Overtures: Egmont, Op. 84; Leonora No. 3, Op. 72b.
　(M) * Decca KCSP 327. Suisse Romande Orch., Ansermet.

Symphony No. 7; Overture: Fidelio, Op. 72c.
　(M) *** Philips 7317 180 [7300 024]. Concertgebouw Orch., Jochum.
　(B) (**) RCA Camden C4-5026 [RK 1150]. Chicago SO, Reiner.

Symphony No. 7; Overture: Leonora No. 3, Op. 72b.
　(M) *** Decca Jubilee KJBC 4. Vienna PO, Schmidt-Isserstedt.

Beethoven's *Seventh* is extremely well represented on tape in both full and medium price-ranges; indeed several of the finest available versions cost less than full price. Notable among these, on both musical and technical grounds, is Schmidt-Isserstedt's comparatively conventional reading on Decca's Jubilee label. This is a glowing, magnetic performance that compels attention from first bar to last, and with outstandingly vivid recording quality this is one of the very finest Beethoven symphony tapes in the catalogue. Tempi are generally judged with perfect regard for the often conflicting requirements of symphony and dance – not too ponderous, not too hectic. The generous fill-up is most welcome, a splendidly dramatic performance of *Leonora No. 3*. For both symphony and overture the Vienna Philharmonic is in outstanding form. The transfer is notable for its clarity and weight.

No less fine is Jochum's medium-priced Philips recording, which has the advantage of including a brilliantly successful account of the *Fidelio overture*. Under Jochum the playing of the Concertgebouw in the vital dance rhythms of the symphony is superbly enunciated. The skipping rhythms of the first movement – not too fast – have rarely been so crisply pointed. Similarly with the scherzo; and the finale has comparable clarity despite the fast tempo. In the *Allegretto* Jochum's tough, direct manner makes for sharp terracing rather than gentle moulding, and the classical strength is underlined when there is no tempo change for the central section. The recording is very well balanced and the transfer first-class, although one needs a high-level playback and a reduction of bass. (Even so there is no great problem with background hiss.)

Solti is immensely powerful and energetic but always resilient, to bring out the dance-like qualities of the music. The hushed and measured account of the introduction sets the tone of seriousness, but joy is in the skipping rhythms of the *Allegro*, while the lyrical breadth of the *Allegretto* is most persuasive. Solti's observance of all the repeats underlines the massiveness of scale. The recording, made in the Sofiensaal in Vienna, is

among the finest in the Solti cycle, and this is a most exciting tape.

Loughran's Beethoven is rugged and energetic. The energy shines through, even when – as in the outer movements – he chooses basic tempi a degree more relaxed than is common. Like his Brahms performances for CFP, this account of the *Seventh* conveys an immediate spontaneity, with light and shade fully contrasted. Though the playing of the Hallé is not always quite so refined as that on the finest rival versions, this is a powerful contender, with full atmospheric recording. All repeats are observed. The sound on tape is very bright, and the tuttis, although clear, are somewhat lacking in richness. Care with the balance is necessary if the strings are not to seem slightly raw. However, a good sound can be obtained, and the slight lack of refinement of texture in the central climax of the scherzo is not too serious.

Colin Davis, having recorded the *Seventh* with outstanding (and maybe unexpected) success early in his recording career, triumphantly returned to the 'apotheosis of the dance' and directed the LSO in a performance if anything even more electrifying and certainly more refined. Without losing his essential freshness, Davis has here presented his reading in even sharper focus. The slow introduction, now more massive and with refined violin tone, leads again to an account of the first movement exceptionally crisp in rhythm and resilient. This time too all the repeats are observed, a procedure amply justified in so exhilarating a performance. The Philips recording is full-blooded, with plenty of life in the treble but a rather too ample bass which wants cutting back. One or two climaxes (that in the trio of the scherzo, for instance) lack something in refinement, but the transfer level is quite high and the recording has plenty of life and detail.

Davis's earlier recording on HMV has long established itself as a firm recommendation. It may be on medium-price label, but it rivals any performance ever recorded. Here is an ideal illustration of the difference between a studio run-through and a performance that genuinely takes one forward compellingly from bar to bar. Admittedly the opening of the slow introduction is a shade lacking in weight, but from there on there is barely a blemish. The first movement, with delicious pointing of the dotted rhythm, has both stylishness and strength. The slow movement, taken at a measured speed, is beautifully controlled not only in the detailed phrasing but over the architectural span of the whole movement. The scherzo, with all the repeats taken, is wonderfully rumbustious, with some superb woodwind playing. The finale, taken very fast indeed, barely allows one to breathe for excitement. The tape transfer was a relatively early EMI Dolby issue. The copy we heard offered bright, well-balanced sound that was generally most impressive.

Of all the recordings of Beethoven's *Seventh Symphony* that have been issued in recent years none has caused more interest or controversy than the version by the VPO under Carlos Kleiber. By some voices it has been hailed as the finest since Toscanini; others find it unrelenting: like Toscanini, certainly, but with less lyricism – and certainly this is a performance where symphonic argument never yields to the charms of the dance. Kleiber's incisively dramatic approach is marked instead with sharp dynamic contrasts and thrustful rhythms. Another controversial point is that Kleiber, like his father (see under *Symphony No. 3*), maintains the pizzicato for the strings on the final brief phrase of the *Allegretto*, a curious effect. About the recording there is less argument: the quality has a constriction to it and it is much less open than one expects from DG working in Vienna, with little of the bloom that distinguished the Kubelik version with the same orchestra (on disc). Yet even this is not all loss, for the spare, leonine quality of the sound somehow matches the intensity and urgency of the argument. This could not sensibly be suggested as a first recommendation for an only purchase, but it is not a recording to ignore, and many will feel that its interest is such as to constitute an essential supplement to any Beethoven collection. The cassette generally offers a marginally fuller sound than the LP. It has plenty of brilliance and a wide dynamic range. The very first tutti of the first movement's *Allegro* has a touch of coarseness, and there is a tendency in the slow movement for the orchestra to recede slightly in the very quiet passages.

A similar ambivalence must also surround a recommendation for Stokowski's electrifying Decca recording. Stokowski made a famous black-label 78 r.p.m. version of this work in the early days of electric recording, and this later version is every bit as vital and rewarding. Again the comparison with the stature of Toscanini springs to mind, and undoubtedly this is one of the very finest of the recordings Stokowski made in the last decade. The generally fast tempi have a youthful urgency with no breathlessness, and the slow movement is marvellously eloquent. The big snag is that Stokowski omits the second of the three statements of the scherzo, turning Beethoven's ABABA structure into a conventional ABA. But this remains a very exciting, even inspired performance and it has transferred splendidly to cassette, the sound clear, full-bodied yet with plenty of vibrancy.

Karajan gives a tense reading of the *Seventh*, emphasizing its dramatic rather than its dance-like qualities. The slow introduction is tough rather than monumental at a fastish tempo; the main *Allegro* is fresh and bright and not very lilting in its 6/8 rhythm, though it is more sharply pointed in this 1977 performance than in the 1962 version. The *Allegretto* is this time a little weightier, but Karajan's consistency is perhaps the point to emphasize. With brilliant recording – the finale given splendid edge – yet not lacking fullness, this can be recommended to those collecting the Karajan series; but there are more attractive recommendations on tape.

Haitink's view of No. 7 is marked by resilient rhythms in all four movements, so that the skipping 6/8 measure of the first movement has a rare lightness, and the *Allegretto* a gently pointed stylishness. The scherzo is fast and nimble, though with the trio sections controversially slow; the finale, despite a tempo which tests the LPO players to the full, has freshness and exhilaration. This is a satisfying and undistracting reading rather than a strongly characterized one. The cassette ends with the *Egmont overture* and opens with *Coriolan*, which some may consider a disadvantage when they want to get at the symphony. The recording is full and well-balanced and has been generally well transferred to tape, the quality not lacking brightness but yet full-blooded. The finale seems marginally less clean in detail than the rest of the work; both overtures come off effectively.

An excellent performance from Dorati. The first movement, although not taken very fast, has plenty of rhythmic lift, and the inclusion of the exposition repeat increases the feeling of weight. The *Allegretto* is refined yet built to a well-proportioned climax; the scherzo has bite and colour, and the finale plenty of high spirits. The tape transfer, however, is made at an unambitious level, and although the recording is well balanced, full and clear, the playback level necessary for maximum impact brings some hiss, and the quiet opening of the second movement is adversely affected by the poor signal-to-noise ratio.

A lyrical Beethovenian, Kubelik directs a sparkling yet relaxed account at the opposite pole to that of Karajan. With his own Bavarian Radio Orchestra his reading is ever warmer and more spontaneous-sounding than in his Vienna recording made for DG as part of his complete Beethoven cycle (not available on tape). Unfortunately the transfer

seems to have dried out some of the recording's basic warmth and taken away the bloom from the string tone (the violins sound thin). With careful use of the controls, however, an acceptable balance can be achieved.

Apart from a relatively slack performance of the *Egmont overture* as a fill-up, Mehta's is a thoroughly enjoyable tape. The reading of the *Seventh* is marked by fast speeds, which in fact sound slower than they are – sign of acute control. A bright, exciting reading, which falls short only in the company of such interpreters as Davis, Schmidt-Isserstedt and Karajan. The recording is rather larger than life in the Los Angeles manner, and in the transfer the reverberation has produced a lack of internal clarity, though the quality is quite agreeable.

A powerful, understanding performance from Reiner, particularly impressive in the first and third movements, where the power is combined with fine rhythmic lift to confirm Wagner's 'apotheosis of the dance'. The fast tempo for the finale draws unscampering brilliance from the Chicago orchestra. Marginally less impressive are the symphony's slow introduction and the *Allegretto* second movement, where Reiner's manner at fastish speeds is cooler. The atmospheric Chicago recording has been put on to tape quite acceptably, but unfortunately the Dolby process has been mismanaged and in order to achieve an acceptably bright treble response one is forced to leave out the Dolby circuitry on playback.

Ansermet starts well, with a poised introduction (taken rather fast) building up to a fine climax, but his Swiss players just cannot rival other performances in discipline and polish. The result lacks a real sense of style, and although the recording is good this cassette is not really competitive.

Bernstein's performance is characteristically vital, but with fierce sound and unrefined textures this cassette can hardly be recommended, in spite of the undoubted merits of the performance.

Symphonies Nos. 8 in F major, Op. 93
(see also under Symphonies 1, 4 and
5); *9 in D minor (Choral), Op. 125.*
   *** DG 3370 109 [id.]. Tomowa-
   Sintow, Baltsa, Schreier, van
   Dam, Vienna Singverein, Berlin
   PO, Karajan.
Symphony No. 9.
   *** Decca KBB2 7041 [Lon. 5-8].
   Lorengar, Minton, Burrows,
   Talvela, Chicago Symphony
   Chorus, Chicago SO, Solti.
   *** Decca Phase 4 KPFC 4183
   [Lon. 5-21043]. Harper, Watts,
   Young, McIntyre, LSO
   Chorus, LSO, Stokowski.
   (M) *** Decca KCSP 328. Suther-
   land, Suddaby, Dermota, Van
   Mill, Chorale du Brassus and
   Chœur des Jeunes de l'Église
   Nationale Vaudoise, Suisse
   Romande Orch., Ansermet.
   (M) **(*) Decca Jubilee KJBC
   1. Sutherland, Horne, King,
   Talvela, Vienna State Opera
   Chorus, Vienna PO, Schmidt-
   Isserstedt.
   (M) *(*) Philips Festivo 7310 012.
   Tomowa-Sintow, Burmeister,
   Schreier, Adam, Berlin Radio
   Chorus, Leipzig Radio Chorus
   and Gewandhaus Orch., Masur.
   *(*) CBS Classics 40-61907.
   Arroyo, Sarfaty, de Virgilio,
   Scott, Juilliard Chorus, New
   York, PO, Bernstein.
   (*) Philips 7317 021. Stich-
   Randall, Rössl-Majdan, Der-
   mota, Schoeffler, Vienna State
   Opera Chorus, Vienna SO,
   Boehm.
   (M) (*) CBS Classics 40-61747
   [Col. MT 31818]. Amara, Choo-
   kasian, Alexander, Macurdy,
   Mormon Tabernacle Choir,
   Philadelphia Orch., Ormandy.

Fine as Karajan's earlier DG reading
of the *Ninth* was, this 1977 performance
reveals even greater insight, above all in
the *Adagio*, where Karajan conveys spiritual intensity at a slower tempo than
before. In the finale the concluding erup-
tion has an animal excitement rarely
heard from this highly controlled conductor, and the tape transfer gives the
choral sound splendid edge and presence
(finer even than that in the complete set
issue). The soloists make an excellent
team, with contralto, tenor and bass all
better than their predecessors. The recording balance sounds rather more contrived than before, less atmospheric, but
the overall sound picture has transferred
to tape with good body and detail. This is
the finest sounding *Choral symphony* on
tape and wins on just a few points over
the Solti set, which was issued earlier by
Decca and at the time represented the
highest state of the transfer art.

On the fourth side Karajan directs an
electrically tense performance of the
Eighth Symphony, missing some of the
joy of Beethoven's 'Little one' but justi-
fying the brisk tempi by the brilliant
playing of the orchestra. This is also extremely satisfactory as sound and the
two cassettes are offered in an excellently
contrived box, so that they can be removed in their plastic 'library boxes', a
far superior arrangement to having them
naked in a plastic shell as favoured by
Decca and EMI. There are excellent
notes.

The penny-in-the-slot criticism would
be to suggest that Solti and the Chicago
Symphony Orchestra skate over the surface of the *Ninth*, but the whole performance belies any such assumption. If you
regard the sublime slow movement as the
key to this epic work, then Solti clearly is
with you. With spacious measured tempi
he leads the ear on, not only with his
phrasing but with his subtle shading of
dynamic down to whispered *pianissimo*.
Here is *Innigkeit* of a concentration rarely
heard in the recording studio, even in the
Ninth. Solti in the first movement is sear-

ing in his dynamic contrasts, maybe too brutally so, while the precision of the finale, with superb choral work and solo singing, confirms this as one of the very finest *Ninths* available. Superb recording quality, clean yet coordinated, and the transfer to tape is highly sophisticated, with clear, realistic choral sound and excellent presence for the soloists.

Schmidt-Isserstedt, with no exaggeration and few if any high-flown purple passages, gives an intensely satisfying reading of the *Ninth*, which in many ways is easier to live with than more monumental, more obviously great performances. The approach associates the work more readily than most with Beethoven's earlier symphonic achievements – the link with the *Pastoral* at the end of the slow movement, for example – but it is the fine singing of soloists and chorus in the finale that above all makes this one of the keenest current recommendations. All four soloists are in peak form, and no rival version matches the beauty and balance of ensemble. The recording is of first-class quality, matching the disc closely in weight and detail until the coda of the finale, where there is a miscalculation and the entry of the bass drum muddles the texture unattractively and spoils the work's closing pages.

Unmistakably Stokowski's is a great, compelling account of the *Ninth*. There is the sort of tension about this recorded performance which one expects from a great conductor in the concert hall, and that compulsion carries one over all of Stokowski's idiosyncrasies, including a fair amount of touching up in the orchestration. The first movement is strong and dramatic, taken at a Toscanini pace; the scherzo is light and pointed, with timpani cutting through; the slow movement has great depth and *Innigkeit*, and that perhaps more than anything confirms the greatness of the performance, for the finale with some strangely slow tempi is uneven, despite fine singing. Excellent Phase Four recording, and although this was an early Decca tape issue the transfer

is very successful in matching body and detail.

Equally the most remarkable thing about Ansermet's *Ninth* is the quality of the recording; the transfer has been achieved with complete success. The clarity of detail suits the interpretation, which lacks the weight of more traditional readings, but has a freshness which makes it consistently enjoyable and interesting. The first two movements are clear-cut and dramatic, and the slow movement is restrained. The finale, if a little lightweight, gains from the clarity of recording and the quality of the soloists, with Joan Sutherland at her most beautiful. The choir is energetic but not always perfectly disciplined. However, the choral sound on tape is excellent, and the final climax with bass drum and cymbals offers no problems.

Masur gives a spacious, well-proportioned, and often noble account of the *Ninth*, and it is well worth hearing. But competition is stiff, and in spite of first-class orchestral playing this version does not measure up to the finest available; the Schmidt-Isserstedt version (also at medium price) is more strongly characterized besides being much more successfully transferred to tape. On this Philips issue the sound is generally full and clear, but the choral finale does not produce the sophistication of detail and texture of the Decca and DG recordings. Moreover the side turn comes fairly near the opening of the slow movement and is the more irritating because by adding a few more inches of tape it could have been avoided.

From Bernstein a finely shaped first movement which has genuine breadth and eloquence; a frenetic scherzo, which must be the fastest on tape; a slow movement that has considerable warmth but not quite enough inwardness and repose; an often intense and dramatic finale with some fine contributions from the soloists and chorus. The recording is not of the finest quality, but – although it has a poorly managed break in the slow movement – this is one of the most successful of Bernstein's Beethoven series, with the chorus quite well caught in the finale. Yet given the strength of the competition from such artists as Karajan, Solti, Schmidt-Isserstedt and Stokowski, this not unimpressive account must be passed over.

Boehm's performance, similarly, has many merits, but the transfer is not very successful and the result is in no way memorable except for unclear recording with a boomy bass and unrefined sound in the finale which tends to break up somewhat under pressure. The slow-movement break is not well managed either.

The other CBS Classics tape, from Ormandy, also offers only fair, restricted recording. Ormandy, fast and clear even on the opening tremolos, makes it clear that mystery plays no part in his concept of the *Ninth*. Though the resonance of the Philadelphia players, particularly the strings, is as ever impressive, with superb articulation in the scherzo, Beethoven's deeper qualities are smoothed over, above all in the slow movement. Among the soloists the bass is disappointing.

CHAMBER MUSIC

Clarinet trio in B flat major, Op. 11 (for clarinet, piano and cello).

(M) ** Turnabout KTVC 34108. David Glazer (clarinet), Frank Glazer (piano), David Soyer (cello) – BRAHMS: *Clarinet trio.***

This is a successful performance in which good teamwork counts quite as much as the convincing style of the clarinettist, David Glazer. The playing has plenty of life and the finale is particularly spontaneous: it is one of those happy light-hearted inventions that remind one of the *Septet*. The recording is dry but projects the music-making well. The transfer is clean and of good quality.

(i–iii) *Piano trios Nos. 4 in D major (Ghost), Op. 70/1; 6 in B flat major (Archduke), Op. 97;* (iv) *Septet in E flat major, Op. 20;* (v) *Sextet in E flat major, Op. 81b;* (v) *String quartets Nos. 1–4, Op. 18/1–4; 7–9 (Rasumovsky), Op. 59/1–3; 13, Op. 130; 16, Op. 135;* (vii; i) *Violin sonatas Nos. 5 (Spring), Op. 24; 8 in G major, Op. 30/3; 9 (Kreutzer), Op. 47;* (iii; i) *Violoncello sonata No. 2 in G minor, Op. 5/2.*

**(*) DG 3378 052. (i) Wilhelm Kempff (piano); (ii) Henryk Szeryng (violin); (iii) Pierre Fournier (cello); (iv) members of the Berlin Philharmonic Octet; (v) Gerd Seifert, Manfred Klier (horns), Drolc Qt; (vi) Amadeus Qt; (vii) Yehudi Menuhin (violin).

This set is part of DG's Beethoven Edition, which on tape (as distinct from on disc) offers a digest of the Beethoven chamber music repertoire rather than an integral collection. However, there is so little chamber music available on cassette that this generally well-produced box is welcome enough, and the booklet of notes is adequate, if by no means ample in its information. The transfers are nearly all made at a comparatively low level; the sound is smooth and agreeable, and certainly not lacking in detail, although the upper range (while not blunted in any way) is not so obviously wide as on some DG issues. The Amadeus Quartet are at their finest in the four Op. 18 quartets, less riveting in the *Rasumovskys* (recorded at a higher level and with a tendency to over-brightness) but undoubtedly self-assured. The *Piano trios* are effective too, the *Archduke* showing considerable imagination, but not a large-scale reading. The *Violin sonatas* are inspirational performances, Menuhin and Kempff bringing out the best in each other. The *Kreutzer* sounds especially realistic; the *Spring*, transferred at a lower level, has rather less presence. The level of the *Cello sonata* is also low, and this is one of the least immediate recordings. In the *Sextet*, Op. 81b, the horns tend to dominate the texture unduly, the resonance of the recording causing an emphasis on their contribution. The *Septet*, Op. 20, is well balanced.

Piano trio No. 6 in B flat major (Archduke), Op. 97.
 (B) *(*) Rediffusion Legend KLGD 002. Suk Trio.

Quite surprisingly, apart from the DG Beethoven Edition set (see above), this is the only *Archduke* on tape, and it is rather spoiled by the somewhat edgy recorded quality, which makes the two stringed instruments sound 'buzzy'. The performance is excellent, with a spaciously conceived first movement, apt tempi throughout and plenty of life.

Septet in E flat major, Op. 20.
 (M) **(*) Decca Ace of Diamonds KSDC 200. Members of the Vienna Octet.
Septet; Fugue for string quintet, Op. 137.
 *** DG 3300 799. Vienna Philharmonic Chamber Ens.

The Vienna Philharmonic Chamber Ensemble gives a most distinguished account of the *Septet*, which must now replace the Decca Vienna Octet version at the head of the list. It is beautifully played and has the advantage of finely truthful recording. An eminently civilized cassette. The transfer is immaculate, extremely smooth and natural yet with plenty of detail.

The Decca recording of the *Septet* remains competitive at medium price. The spontaneity of the playing helps a great deal, and the stereo is notably realistic and clear, contributing much to the illusion of a live performance. The transfer is of good quality. It is made at a high level

and there is plenty of presence, although there is a degree of edge on the first violin tone which is less than wholly natural.

String quartets Nos. 1 in F major; 2 in G major, Op. 18/1–2.
 (M) *** Decca Ace of Diamonds KSDC 478. Gabrieli Qt.

The Gabrielis are a well-balanced and intelligent team whose readings of both quartets hold their own even against the stiff competition offered by the versions available only on disc. In No. 1 they show consistent vitality and imagination; their phrasing is alive, rhythmic articulation is well-defined, and they are responsive to the overall shape of the structure. There is an appealing freshness about their playing, and the slow movement fares particularly well. It has gentleness and reticence, and its melodic line is most sensitively shaped without the slightest trace of exaggerated expressive feeling. In No. 2 they give a no less impressive account of themselves, and although their rivals on disc are at times more authoritative, the freshness and naturalness of their playing as well as the excellence of the Decca recording make this a most competitive issue. The transfer is first-class, with a virtually silent background, and readily shows the advantages of tape in the field of chamber music.

Violin sonatas Nos. 1–10.
 ⊛ *** Decca K 92 K 53 [Lon. CSA 5-2501]. Itzhak Perlman (violin), Vladimir Ashkenazy (piano).

This most distinguished box undoubtedly offers the finest complete set of the Beethoven *Violin sonatas* to be recorded in stereo. Perlman and Ashkenazy are to the 1970s what Kreisler and Rupp were for the 1930s and 40s, and Grumiaux and Haskil were for the 50s. These performances offer a blend of classical purity and yet spontaneous vitality that is irresistible. Their musicianship and judgement are matched by a poise and elegance that give consistent pleasure. Moreover the strength and perception of the music-making are matched by a recording of striking presence and naturalness. The balance and projection of the two instruments (both of which are recorded with vivid realism and truthfulness of timbre) vary a little between sonatas, but are never less than first-class, and provide a consistent demonstration of how realistic tape reproduction can be. The sonatas are grouped on three tapes: Nos. 2, 3, 5 and 7 are on the first; the *Kreutzer* is given side three to itself, with Nos. 4 and 8 on side four; the final cassette completes the series with Sonatas 1, 6 and 10. This offers the only broken work, for No. 1 begins on side five, after No. 10, and concludes before No. 6, which is a pity, to save a few inches of tape. There is a leaflet but the print, though perfectly readable, is rather small.

Violin sonatas Nos. 1 in D major, Op. 12/1; 10 in G major, Op. 96.
   *** Decca KSXC 6790. Perlman, Ashkenazy.

Perlman and Ashkenazy offer the first and last of the sonatas in performances that could scarcely be improved upon. No phrase is unimaginatively handled or too lovingly caressed; their approach strikes a perfect balance between classical virtue and expressive spontaneity. Excellent recording, with an immaculate transfer.

Violin sonatas Nos. 2 in A major, Op. 12/2; 9 in A major (Kreutzer), Op. 47.
   *** Decca KSXC 6632. Perlman, Ashkenazy.

A superb performance of the *Kreutzer sonata*, undoubtedly the finest available. The strong first movement is followed by a wonderfully eloquent account of the variations. The beauty of Perlman's lyrical playing in the closing pages makes one catch one's breath, and the hushed answering chords from Ashkenazy show how complete is the *rapport* between these two artists. The lilting rhythms of the finale are irresistible. The coupling is no less strongly characterized, and the recording has the truthfulness of timbre and balance characteristic of this admirable series. The tape transfer is extremely vivid, the very high level on side one contributing a slight dryness of texture and needing a careful balance of the controls. But the sound mellows from the second movement onwards, and with a silent background the quality is very impressive.

Violin sonatas Nos. 3 in E flat major, Op. 12/3; 8 in G major, Op. 30/3.
   *** Decca KSXC 6789. Perlman, Ashkenazy.

Perlman and Ashkenazy play the *E flat Sonata* with exemplary warmth and naturalness; tempi are excellently judged and articulation could hardly be more alive. The *G major* is no less finely characterized, and there is plenty of dramatic contrast in the first movement. The Decca recording has immediacy and presence. A winner. The cassette transfer offers excellent, vivid quality, although perhaps the sound is a little dry: side two is marginally fuller in this respect.

Violin sonatas Nos. 4 in A minor, Op. 23; 5 in F major (Spring), Op. 24.
   *** Decca KSXC 6736. Perlman, Ashkenazy.

Sparkling, alert performances full of vitality and imagination. There is no question of virtuoso performers inflating the music or adopting unstylish mannerisms. The manner is youthful, the style classical. The degree of restraint never obstructs the dynamism, and with outstanding recording quality this tape can be warmly recommended, even though it provides rather short value for money. A little judicious smoothing of the treble is needed for a natural violin timbre, but that removes the last vestiges of hiss and then the quality is admirable and the balance excellent.

Violin sonatas Nos. 5 in F major (Spring), Op. 24; 9 in A major (Kreutzer), Op. 47.

> (M) *** HMV TC-EXE 71. Yehudi Menuhin (violin), Hephzibah Menuhin (piano).

Yehudi Menuhin's playing does not always offer absolutely immaculate technique. A slightly sharp note in a cadential phrase, perhaps, or a quick passage not perfectly controlled might catch the ear, but these are lost and forgotten in the warmth of the readings as a whole. The playing has great spontaneity – the flow of the opening pastoral melody of the *Spring sonata*, the sustained tension of the *Adagio* of the same work, or the beautiful closing pages of the variations in the *Kreutzer*: these are high spots in music-making which remains on a consistently high level. We tried a comparatively recent copy of this cassette, which was an early EMI Dolby issue, and found the quality first-class, with clear, sonorous piano timbre and an admirably lifelike violin image. The transfer level is comparatively low, which means a degree of hiss, but the sound itself is refined.

Violin sonatas Nos. 6 in A major; 7 in C minor, Op. 30/1–2.

> *** Decca KSXC 6791. Perlman, Ashkenazy.

These performances by Perlman and Ashkenazy are well up to the standard of the previous issues in this series. Their discernment is matched by their spontaneity, while the recording balance is wholly satisfying. The quality on this tape is perhaps the finest of the series, outstandingly natural in timbre and balance. The rich piano sonority in the *C minor Sonata* is especially satisfying.

Music for mandolin: *Adagio ma non troppo* (for mandolin and harpsichord); *Sonatina in C major; Sonatina in C minor, G.150; Variations in D major.*

> (M) * Turnabout KTVC 34110. Elfriede Kunschak (mandolin), Maria Hinterleitner (harpsichord) – SCHLICK: *Divertimento.**

The interest of this repertoire is diminished here by performances which make the music sound very slight indeed; and the instrumentalists are not helped by a recording which lacks bite and provides little light and shade.

Piano sonatas

Piano sonatas Nos. 1 in F minor; 2 in A major, Op. 2/1–2; 25 in G major, Op. 79.

> (M) **(*) Turnabout KTVC 34120. Alfred Brendel.

From the very start of the little *F minor Sonata* which opens the greatest of all sonata cycles, Brendel makes clear the weight and seriousness of his approach. This is no mere Haydnesque reading, but a determined attempt to present the work as revolutionary in the way it must have struck the first listeners. A little more sparkle might have lightened the reading without any loss of weight, and in the longer Op. 2/2 Brendel does find a deeper imaginative vein. An excellent performance of the elusive *G major Sonata*, and more atmospheric recording than in most of the issues in this cycle. The transfers are of first-class quality; this is a highly recommendable cassette.

Piano sonatas Nos. 1 in F minor, Op. 2/1; 24 in F sharp major, Op. 78; 28 in A major, Op. 101.

> **(*) Enigma K 453525. John Lill.

These are among the finest performances in John Lill's cycle. His deliberation at the opening of *Sonata No. 1* gives the first movement great character, and the slow movement too is most eloquently played. The *Adagio* of No. 28 again shows the keen intelligence of the playing at its most impressive. The piano sound has a touch of hardness at the top but has more warmth and bloom than on some of the cassettes issued earlier in this series.

Piano sonatas Nos. 2 in A major; 3 in C major, Op. 2/2–3.
> *** Decca KSXC 6808 [Lon. 5-7028]. Vladimir Ashkenazy.
> *(*) Enigma K 453524. John Lill.

Ashkenazy brings to these two early sonatas the concentrated unaffected qualities which make his recordings of the *Violin sonatas* with Perlman so eminently convincing. Interpretatively the manner is strong and direct, treating the young Beethoven rightly as a fully mature composer, no imitator of Mozart and Haydn: but the important point is that whether in fast music or slow the pianist conveys the feeling of new discovery and ready communication. The recording captures the piano sound with vivid reality, percussive but not clangorous, and the transfer is of first-class quality.

The Enigma recording has great presence, and the piano tone is admirably secure. John Lill brings a formidable technique to both sonatas and the first movement of Op. 2/2 is crisply articulated, though it could do with greater lightness of touch. Both slow movements are wanting in real poetry, though it must be admitted that the close balance does the pianist a disservice, rendering the *fortissimo* outburst in the slow movement of Op. 2/3 harsh and shallow. There is a directness of utterance here but little real tenderness or charm, and although the transfer is clear it is hard-edged. Alongside Ashkenazy neither performance nor recording really competes.

Piano sonatas Nos. 3 in C major, Op. 2/3; 4 in E flat major, Op. 7.
> (M) **(*) Turnabout KTVC 34121. Brendel.

A good coupling of two of Beethoven's most ambitious early sonatas. In both, Brendel's concentration underlines the strength, and in the orchestral textures of the first movement of Op. 7 his directness is particularly impressive. He is less persuasive in the slow movements, although the *Adagio* of Op. 2/3 has undoubted eloquence and an appealing simplicity. The transfer is vividly made; the sound is marginally crisper on side one but is excellent throughout, easily matching the disc.

Piano sonatas Nos. 5 in C minor; 6 in F major, Op. 10/1–2; 13 in E flat major, Op. 27/1.
> (M) ** Turnabout KTVC 34117. Brendel.

Brendel's coupling spoils the usual arrangement of having all three Op. 10 sonatas coupled together. In these two shorter sonatas from the opus, his clear, direct style suits the pithiness of argument. For the first and less famous of the two Op. 27 *'Fantasy' sonatas* Brendel's concentration makes for satisfying results, though fantasy in a strict sense is not one of his strong suits. The clear recording has transferred well to tape; the piano image is bold and bright, slightly shallow, but not objectionably so.

Piano sonatas Nos. 5 in C minor; 6 in F major, Op. 10/1–2; 15 in D major (Pastoral), Op. 28.
> *** Decca KSXC 6804 [Lon. 5-7024]. Ashkenazy.

An alert and dramatic account of the *C minor Sonata*, Op. 10/1, that is tauter than Brendel's yet no less poetic. The slow movement is direct and unaffected, and totally compelling. The tempo in the finale is expertly judged and Ashkenazy plays with crisp articulation and virtuosity without any egocentric display. The *F minor Sonata* is no less fine, beautifully alert and rhythmic but not neglectful of lyrical feeling. Some may find the tempo in the first movement of the so-called *Pastoral* a little too relaxed, but the glowing warmth and natural flow of the reading carry complete conviction. The slow movement could perhaps have greater concentration, but on the whole this performance is as eloquent as any in the catalogue and it is beautifully recorded. It is to be preferred to its rivals on cassette, though in the *F major Sonata*, Op. 10/2, the Gilels (see below) is in a class of its own. The transfer generally offers first-class quality, with a lovely bloom on the tone in the *Pastoral sonata*. In the outer movements of Op. 10/1 Ashkenazy creates a wide dynamic range, and the bold transients of the *fortissimo* chords are impressively clean.

Piano sonatas Nos. 6 in F major, Op. 10/2; 23 in F minor (Appassionata), Op. 57.
(*) DG 3300 379. Emil Gilels.

Gilels is a supremely great pianist, and his record of the *Appassionata* must rank among the finest ever made. His art is so totally at the service of the composer and his playing is so subtle and poetic that these familiar sonatas emerge as fresh experiences. With artistry of this power and eloquence, criticism is silenced. The DG recording is a fine one, with a genuine sense of presence. The cassette is clearly transferred, but the quality is hard-edged in Op. 57.

Piano sonatas Nos. 7 in D major, Op. 10/3; 9 in E major; 10 in G major, Op. 14/1–2.
(M) **(*) Turnabout KTVC 34118. Brendel.**

Another attractive coupling of early sonatas from Brendel's Turnabout cycle. Op. 10/3 is the most expansive of the early

sonatas, with its orchestral textures in the first movement and its genuine depth in the D minor slow movement. It is well contrasted with the less ambitious but closely argued sonatas of Op. 14, both fine works despite their associations with piano lessons. Except perhaps in the great D minor slow movement Brendel's strong, direct manner is consistently satisfying, and the recording is no more clattery than in most of the others of the series. The cassette transfer is of excellent quality, quite the equal of the disc.

Piano sonatas Nos. 7 in D major, Op. 10/3; 14 in C sharp minor (Moonlight), Op. 27/2; 25 in G major, Op. 79.
*** Philips 7300 303 [id.]. Brendel.

The *D major Sonata*, one of the greatest of Beethoven's early works, here inspires Brendel to his finest playing. It is surprising to find him in his own liner-note using the word 'exquisite' of a work which rightly he makes strong, notably in the visionary *Largo e mesto* slow movement. The *Moonlight* is indeed exquisite, lacking a little of the spontaneity of Brendel's Turnabout version (not yet issued on cassette) but finely poised. The little Op. 79 sonata is a nicely varied makeweight. The sound is excellent, characteristic of the best issues in the Philips Brendel series, clear and full.

Piano sonatas Nos. 7 in D major, Op. 10/3; in F minor (Appassionata), Op. 57.
*** Decca KSXC 6603. Vladimir Ashkenazy.

Ashkenazy's *Appassionata* is superb, and it is linked with a thoughtful and masterly account of the *D major Sonata*, Op. 10/3. However, those who feel strongly about matters of tempo may well find Ashkenazy a little too free in the first movement of the *Appassionata*. The sound is firm and well defined, and the transfer is bold and clear, sonorous in the middle range and richly weighted in the bass. There is a hint of metallic quality in the treble in the fortissimos of the *Appassionata*.

Piano sonata No. 8 in C minor (Pathétique), Op. 13.
  (*) Philips 7300 163 [id.]. Stephen Bishop-Kovacevich – *Piano concerto No. 3*.(*)

Bishop's account of the *Pathétique* is totally unmannered and refreshing, though some will prefer more deliberate expressiveness in the lyrical slow movement. Recording to match that of the coupling.

Piano sonatas Nos. 8 (Pathétique), 11, 14 (Moonlight), 15 (Pastoral), 17 (Tempest), 21 (Waldstein), 23 (Appassionata), 24–5, 26 (Les Adieux), 28, 29 (Hammerklavier), 30–32; Andante favori in F major, G.170; 6 Bagatelles, Op. 126; 6 Ecossaises in E flat major; Für Elise; Rondo à capriccio in G major (Rage over a lost penny), Op. 129; 6 Variations in Paisiello's duet 'Nel cor più' in G major; 2 Rondos, Op. 51/1–2.
  *** DG 3378 053. Wilhelm Kempff.

This box of six generously filled tapes offers nearly half the piano sonatas plus a disarmingly beautiful collection of shorter occasional pieces. The recording is consistently good throughout but seems to improve as the set progresses, with the transfer level becoming more adventurous. In many ways the piano timbre here is more agreeable than on the equivalent discs: it is clear in focus yet has plenty of sonority. The *Waldstein* and *Appassionata* both reproduce strikingly well, and the late sonatas are perhaps finest of all, notable for a very quiet background, whereas some of the earlier

works offer a degree of background hiss stemming from the pre-Dolby era of the master tapes. Kempff's Beethoven has been providing a deeply spiritual experience for record collectors since the twenties, and though there may be argument about his clear and refreshing style in Beethoven, there is no doubt whatever of the inner compulsion which holds all these performances together. Kempff more than any other pianist has the power to make one appreciate and understand Beethoven in a new way, and that remains so however many times one has heard him. It makes a fascinating study to compare these interpretations not only with those of other pianists, but with Kempff's own earlier ones. The performances of the named sonatas have a characteristic directness, yet they have individuality of spirit too. The *Hammerklavier* represents Kempff's interpretative approach to Beethoven at its most extreme and therefore controversial. Here his preference for measured allegros and fastish andantes gives a different weighting to the movements from usual, but in each the concentration of the playing is inescapable, and anyone prepared to hear the music with new ears will find profound enjoyment. The readings of the other late sonatas are comparably intense in the control of structure but with a feeling of rhapsodic freedom too, of new visions emerging. Above all these magnificent recordings never fail to reveal Kempff's own spontaneity in the recording studio, his ability to rethink the reading on each occasion.

Piano sonatas Nos. 8 in C minor (Pathétique), Op. 13; 14 in C sharp minor (Moonlight), Op. 27/2; 21 in C major (Waldstein), Op. 53.
  **(*) Decca KSXC 6576. Radu Lupu.

Radu Lupu has the gift of being able to create a spontaneous performance in the recording studio. Sometimes he is mannered, as in his rather deliberate approach to the famous slow movement of the *Pathétique sonata*, or at the opening of the *Moonlight*, but the playing carries conviction, and the performances of both these works are individual and enjoyable. But Lupu is less successful in holding the concentration of the *Waldstein* finale, after having prepared the opening beautifully, and it is this that lets down an otherwise impressive issue. Decca's recording is first-rate in every way, sonorous and clear, a real piano sound, and this cassette undoubtedly offers demonstration quality.

Piano sonatas Nos. 8 in C minor (Pathétique), Op. 13; 14 in C sharp minor (Moonlight), Op. 27/2; 23 in F minor (Appassionata), Op. 57.

    *** DG 3300 506 [id.] (with *'Nel cor più' variations*). Wilhelm Kempff.

    (M) **(*) Decca KCSP 69. Wilhelm Backhaus.

    ** Enigma K 453520. John Lill.

Kempff's tape shows so well his ability to rethink Beethoven's music within the recording studio. He coupled these three works together in a (no less successful) early stereo LP. Here the slow movement of the *Pathétique*, for example, is slower and more expressively romantic than before, but still restrained. The *Appassionata* is characteristically clear, and if anything more classically 'straight' than it was before. The opening of the *Moonlight* is gently atmospheric, the scherzo is poised, yet there is admirable contrast in the finale. Everything Kempff does has his individual stamp, and above all he never fails to convey the deep intensity of a master in communion with Beethoven. The recording is beautifully crisp and clear, but a little shallow sometimes: one notices this more in a work like the *Pathétique* with a slow movement that makes special use of the piano's sustaining quality. The tape transfer, however, seems

marginally fuller than the LP. It includes a bonus (not present on the disc) of the *'Nel cor più' variations*, played with telling simplicity. This acts as a short prelude to the performance of the *Appassionata* on side two.

Backhaus's performances are less refined, less imaginative than those of Kempff, but they have a rugged authority that remains compelling throughout. It is amazing that an octogenarian could produce such positive, alert playing, but by the standards of Kempff and Brendel his style is wilful, with a touch of heaviness that is not always cancelled out by the electric concentration. The *Appassionata*, however, is a very fine performance, compelling from the first note to the last. The transfers offer excellent piano tone, bold and clearly focused.

John Lill plays the opening of the *Moonlight* evocatively, and the contrast with the finale, which is taken with furious bravura, is striking. The slow movement of the *Pathétique* is thoughtful, but lacks something in poetic feeling. This is strong, intelligent playing, but it is not helped by the close balance, which provides a rather hard piano image, although the timbre is secure and not without depth.

Unfortunately Barenboim's fine performances of this coupling (HMV TC-EXE 23) are not available in Dolby form, although the piano tone is truthful.

Piano sonatas Nos. 8 in C minor (Pathétique), Op. 13; 18 in E flat major, Op. 31/3; 19 in G minor, Op. 49/1; Piano sonata No. 7, Op. 10/3: Rondo.

    *** Philips 7300 478 [id.]. Brendel.

Brendel's *Pathétique* is given a strong, intelligent reading, and the little *G minor Sonata*, Op. 49/1, is beautifully played. His Op. 31/3 is more subtly coloured both in interpretation and recording than Lazar Berman's (see below). An excellent coupling. The cassette is transferred clearly and is truthful in balance, but side one (which contains, in the main, *Sonata No. 8*) offers a touch of hardness to edge the piano image. Side two is freer, and the quality here often reaches demonstration standard. The *Rondo* from Op. 10/3 is added as a filler not present on the disc.

Piano sonatas Nos. 8 in C minor (Pathétique), Op. 13; 21 in C major (Waldstein), Op. 53; 26 in E flat major (Les Adieux), Op. 81a.
    ** (*) Decca KSXC 6706 [Lon. 5-6921]. Ashkenazy.

Taking a broadly lyrical view, Ashkenazy gives a deeply satisfying reading of the *Waldstein sonata*. His degree of restraint, his occasional hesitations, intensify his thoughtful approach, never interrupt the broader span of argument. The *Pathétique*, perhaps understated for so ebulliently youthful a work, with the finale unusually gentle, conveys the underlying power, and *Les Adieux* brings a vehement first movement and memorable concentration. Excellent recording. The cassette transfer is good, but the quality tends to harden and become brittle on side two. (Our copy had a momentary pitch-slip near the very opening, mirrored at the close of the second side, but this is unlikely to be common to all batches.)

Piano sonatas Nos. 11 in B flat major, Op. 22; 15 in D major (Pastoral), Op. 28.
    (M) ** Turnabout KTVC 34119. Brendel.

Brendel gives clean, concentrated performances of two of Beethoven's most imaginative 'in-between' sonatas, which give a clear foretaste of his middle-period strength. The nickname *Pastoral* has not brought Op. 28 the popularity it deserves, perhaps because it provides only a half-truth in describing the work's character. Brendel consistently holds the attention with his unforced straightforward manner, but by his very reticence misses

some of the sparkle of the music, the element of charm which in his more idiosyncratic way a pianist like Barenboim uses to heighten the music's strength. The cassette transfer is excellent, among the best of the Brendel Turnabout series, with a mellow sonority yet plenty of clarity.

Piano sonatas Nos. 12 in A flat major, Op. 26; 16 in G major, Op. 31/1.
    *** DG 3300 654. Gilels.

Gilels has something of the same wisdom and vision that one finds with Solomon. So complete is his identification with Beethoven and so personal is his playing that it seems to bring the listener into direct contact with the composer. The rhythmic articulation in the *G major Sonata* is superbly crisp and the texture is always wonderfully alive. The Gilels Beethoven cycle, if it is ever completed, will be to our age what Schnabel's was to the musical world of the 1930s and 40s. The clear, slightly dry piano tone is securely transferred to tape, although on the cassette the perspective of the image seems to shift slightly: in the quieter music Gilels seems more distant from the listener.

Piano sonatas Nos. 13 in E flat major, Op. 27/1; 17 in D minor (Tempest), Op. 31/2; 19 in G minor, Op. 49/1.
    *(*) Enigma K 453521. Lill.

John Lill's account of Op. 27/1 is thoughtful, but not really imaginative enough, and memories of the marvellous range of colour that Schnabel produced in the first movement flood back. There is no want of fire in Op. 31/2, but it is in no sense a performance of real stature. The piano sound is firm and secure, but rather heavily weighted in the bass, although not beyond correction.

Piano sonatas Nos. 15 in D major (Pastoral), Op. 28; 21 in C major

(*Waldstein*), *Op. 53; 24 in F sharp major, Op. 78; 25 in G major, Op. 79.*

(M) *** DG Privilege 3335 291. Kempff.

Kempff's readings are individual and personal. In the *Waldstein*, for instance, although the opening movement is dramatic, Kempff's preparation for the great theme of the finale is gentle, and when it appears the effect is to give the melody a less joyous quality than we are used to. But there is a compensating spiritual depth, and with the suggestion of a more reserved forward momentum, the finale gains in grandeur what it loses in sheer vivacity. The first movement of the *Pastoral* is imbued with the classical spirit, as if Kempff were anxious not to overplay the mood suggestion of the title, which was provided by the work's publisher, not its composer. The *Andante*, 'ticking' along with soft sombre colouring, is enchanting, and the opening of No. 24 with its almost immediate change of tempo is handled with typical Kempff subtlety. The atmosphere of No. 25 is more matter-of-fact: the performance is admirably fresh and spontaneous. The transfers are of good quality. The *Waldstein* is placed first and has slightly less body to the piano tone (the level is fractionally lower than in the rest of the collection), but it is clean and clear.

Piano sonatas Nos. 15 in D major (Pastoral), Op. 28; 26 in E flat major (Les Adieux), Op. 81a; 27 in E minor, Op. 90.

**Enigma K 453523. Lill.

As sound this cassette is undeniably impressive, and though the sound picture favours the bass end of the instrument the treble has no lack of clarity. John Lill adopts very deliberate tempi in the *Pastoral sonata*, where one feels some want of flow, yet *Les Adieux* is a distinct success, though Brendel's performance has even more character, and at no time is

Gilels challenged in *Les Adieux* or in the E minor work, even though Lill is obviously at home in this sonata too.

Piano sonatas Nos. 16 in G major, Op. 31/1; 18 in E flat major, Op. 31/3; 20 in G major, Op. 49/2.

*(*) Enigma K 453522. Lill.

The first movement of the *G major Sonata*, Op. 31/1, is keenly alive here, and it is cleanly articulated if somewhat aggressive. The slow movement is a little prosaic, though there are some sensitive touches. But Gilels has so much greater humanity and imagination that it would be perverse to recommend the Enigma cassette in preference (although of course the couplings are different). In the *E flat Sonata* there is much to admire, but the cold, analytical recording does not flatter the artist.

Piano sonatas Nos. 17 in D minor (Tempest), Op. 31/2; 21 in C major (Waldstein), Op. 53.

(M) *** Turnabout KTVC 341151. Brendel.

Op. 31/2, with its romantic echoes of Beethoven's improvisation style, produces electrically sharp playing and spontaneity. In the *Waldstein* too, Brendel's fresh straightforward concentration produces a cleanly satisfying version, spontaneous-sounding but controlled. The finale, rippling and gentle, is very satisfying, and this is one of the very finest *Waldstein* performances ever recorded. Recording quality is among the best of the Turnabout series. The cassette transfer is of very good quality, offering bold but not shallow timbre, with the edges of the piano image marginally softer in No. 17 (which comes on side two).

Piano sonata No. 18 in E flat major, Op. 31/3.

⊛*** RCA RK 12397 [ARK 1 2397].

Artur Rubinstein – SCHU-MANN: *Fantasiestücke*.***

Rubinstein, in an enthralling perform-ance recorded in his ninetieth year, plays with the freshest spontaneity as though in the excitement of new discovery. This has always been a favourite sonata with him, and he is fiery and mercurial in the outer movements and the scherzo, searching afresh; the slow movement brings a warm cello-like *legato* with magical phrasing. An individual but unforgettable perfor-mance, marked by light pedalling and sharp clarity of detail. The cassette offers superb quality: this is one of the finest piano tapes from any company, the transfer rich in timbre and clear, yet with the most satisfying tonal body.

Piano sonatas Nos. 18 in E flat major, Op. 31/3; 23 in F minor (Appas-sionata), Op. 57.
   **(*) CBS 40-76533 [Col. MT 34218]. Lazar Berman.

Whether or not you respond to him, there is no denying that Lazar Berman has a strong keyboard personality. His *Appassionata* is a powerfully conceived and gripping performance, though it does not eclipse memories of Richter or Gilels. However, both here and in the *E flat Sonata*, Op. 31/3, it is evident that we are listening to a pianist of stature. There is scrupulous attention to detail and a strong feeling for the architecture of the pieces. Moreover he is accorded a good recording that only just falls short of three-star quality on account of some shallowness. A high-level transfer brings considerable immediacy to the sound on tape, yet encompasses the wide dynamic range comfortably. The timbre is rather clattery on top – where Berman's pres-sure is considerable at fortissimos – but there is no lack of colour in the piano's middle range, and the presence is a strong factor when the playing is so riveting.

Piano sonatas Nos. 19 in G minor; 20 in G major, Op. 49/1–2; 32 Variations
on an original theme in C minor, G. 191.
   *** Decca KSXC 6886. Lupu – *Piano concerto No. 4.***(*)

Radu Lupu is an artist of no mean depth, and his account of these two sona-tas and the *32 Variations* does him justice. They are coupled with a performance of the *G major Concerto* that is a little spoilt by insensitive orchestral support. The recording of the piano music is admirably full and the transfer natural and well focused, showing a wider range of dyn-amics than in the concerto.

Piano sonatas Nos. 19 in G minor; 20 in G major, Op. 49/1–2; 28 in A major, Op. 101; 30 in E major, Op. 109.
   (M) *(*) Turnabout KTVC 34111. Brendel.

Brendel's Op. 109 has no great inten-sity, and the first movement of Op. 101 is disappointingly underplayed. But the measure of music is very generous indeed for a cheap issue, and the recording is fair. The cassette transfer is of rather mixed quality: Op. 109 is hard and clat-tery, but the two Op. 49 sonatas are pleas-ing, although there was a suspicion of unsteadiness on our copy.

Piano sonata No. 21 in C major (Waldstein), Op. 53.
   ** Decca Phase 4 KPFC 4433 [Lon. 5-21183]. Ilana Vered – SCHUBERT: *Wanderer fan-tasy.***

Ilana Vered's account of the *Wald-stein* might be described as sturdy. It is not without poetry (she prepares for the finale beautifully), but her positive, robust manner does not uncover all the secrets this sonata contains. Yet in its way the playing sounds spontaneous. The piano is recorded truthfully, but the balance is very forward in the Phase Four manner, and this seems to emphasize the element of deliberation in the playing.

77

The transfer is admirable, clear and with plenty of body.

Piano sonatas Nos. 21 in C major (Waldstein), Op. 53; 28 in A major, Op. 101.
*** DG 3300 260. Gilels.

Gilels is at his most inspired in both sonatas, playing with the sort of rapt concentration that makes one forget that it is not a live performance. The elusive Op. 101 is given a superb reading, the first movement and the *Adagio* before the elaborate contrapuntal finale both deeply expressive. The *Waldstein* too has poetry in plenty, and the recording is first-rate. The cassette was originally issued in non-Dolbyized form; the newer transfer (with Dolby) is successful, offering a clear piano image with plenty of substance, a trifle dry but certainly lifelike.

Piano sonata No. 23 in F minor (Appassionata), Op. 57.
(M) (*) Saga CA 5430. Berman – LISZT: *Sonata*.(*)

In this Saga issue, which presumably has a Russian source, the recording has a very limited dynamic range. Anyone who has heard Berman live will know just how wide are the dynamic contrasts of his playing, and this is borne out by his CBS recording of this sonata (see above). The piano timbre is acceptable, but this issue cannot be recommended with any confidence, even at medium price.

Piano sonatas Nos. 23 in F minor (Appassionata), Op. 57; 26 in E flat major (Les Adieux), Op. 81a; 27 in E minor, Op. 90.
(M) ** Turnabout KTVC 34116. Brendel.

Brendel's account of the *Appassionata* is one of the less imaginative readings in his earlier Beethoven cycle. The very opening is simply and directly done in a way that would have been satisfying enough in a lesser sonata but here gives little expectation of the great statements to come. The coda is clean and sharp to round the movement off consistently, but the variations sound a little heavy in their squareness. The slow movement of *Les Adieux* too lacks a hushed quality. The finale is strong and direct. There is much more *Innigkeit* in the wayward and elusive opening movement of Op. 90, and Brendel gives a smoothly flowing reading of the haunting second movement. From the sound of the recording, marginally less atmospheric than the best of them, this was one of the first of the series to be recorded. The cassette transfer is faithful, as in the rest of the series, although on our copy there was some minor discoloration on the opening notes of the first movement of *Les Adieux*.

Piano sonatas Nos. 24 in F sharp major, Op. 78; 31 in A flat major, Op. 110; 32 in C minor, Op. 111.
(M) ** Turnabout KTVC 34113. Brendel.

From the evidence of publication and of recording quality it seems that Brendel recorded the late sonatas first, probably a mistake, since these lack something of the depth and inner tension that distinguish the very best performances of his Turnabout cycle. Neither of the last sonatas draws from him quite the *Innigkeit* one expects from such a master pianist (the variations of No. 32 are particularly disappointing), but it is a generous coupling and by most pianists' standards these are certainly distinguished performances. The tape transfer is of excellent quality.

Piano sonatas Nos. 27–32.
*** DG 3371 033 [id.]. Maurizio Pollini.

Here is playing of the highest order of mastery. Pollini's *Hammerklavier* is the best to have been recorded for many years: it has superb rhythmic grip, alert articulation, sensitivity to line and gradation of tone, as well as a masterly control of the long paragraph. Hardly less impressive is his eloquent account of Op. 111, which has a peerless authority and expressive power. Joan Chissell spoke of the 'noble purity' of these performances, and this telling phrase sums them up. The slow movement of Op. 110 may be a trifle fast for some tastes, and in the *A major Sonata* Gilels has greater poetry and humanity. But taken by and large this is a magnificent achievement and as sheer pianism it is quite stunning. The recording has excellent body and transparency and there is little to choose between disc and cassette, so impressive is the latter. This set won the 1977 Gramophone Critics' Award for instrumental music, and rightly so.

Piano sonatas Nos. 28 in A major, Op. 101; 30 in E major, Op. 109.
   *** Decca ᴋsxc 6809 [Lon. 5-7029]. Ashkenazy.

These are distinguished performances of both sonatas, as one would expect, and there is an impressive sense of repose in the slow movement of Op. 109. Perhaps Gilels finds greater depth in Op. 101 (his version is coupled with the *Waldstein*), but this is not to deny that Ashkenazy is searching and masterly too. The sound is of excellent quality, with exceptional dynamic range. The transfer is admirably clear and clean; there is a minor degree of edge on the treble in fortissimos, but this can be softened with the controls.

Piano sonatas Nos. 28 in A major, Op. 101; 32 in C minor, Op. 111.
   *** DG 3300 870. Pollini.

Pollini's account of Op. 101 is finely shaped, and no subtlety of phrasing or dynamic nuance goes unnoticed. His first movement is more tautly held together than with, say, Brendel, who sees this movement in a different light though he is by no means inflexible. Pollini is no less

impressive in the finale, which is superbly fashioned and has an imposing sense of energy and power, yet is never overdriven. Gilels perhaps brings greater wisdom and humanity to the sonata, but Pollini gives an impressive account for all that. So, too, in his Op. 111, even though other pianists have found greater depths in the *Arietta*. But this is by any standards a most searching and masterly account, and the recording is of the same high demonstration standard as in the *Hammerklavier* (below). There is no difference to speak of between disc and cassette versions.

Piano sonata No. 29 in B flat major (Hammerklavier), Op. 106.
   ❇ *** DG 3300 869. Pollini.

This is arguably the finest *Hammerklavier* to have been recorded in stereo. There may be some details more tellingly illuminated by other pianists, but no version currently before the public, on disc or tape, is more perfect. No one quite matches Pollini's stunning finale; its strength and controlled power silence criticism. Moreover the sound is most impressive, wide-ranging and absolutely real, and there is scarcely any difference between disc and cassette.

Piano sonatas Nos. 29 in B flat major (Hammerklavier), Op. 106; 30 in E major, Op. 109.
   (M) *** DG Privilege 3335 329. Kempff.

Something has already been said about Kempff's approach to the late sonatas (see under *Sonata No. 8*). The first two movements of the *Hammerklavier* are far less hectic than usual, but the clarity of texture makes for a sharp, dramatic image, and though the slow movement flows quicker than is common, there is a thoughtfulness of utterance which gives it profundity and prevents it from sounding lightweight. As for the finale, it provides the clearest justification for the approach. Where normally the contrapuntal writing gets muddled, Kempff's clarity of finger-work brings a new freshness that lacks nothing in excitement. The reading of Op. 109 matches Kempff's other performances of the late sonatas in its imaginative intensity and architectural control. The transfer is made at a moderately high level; the piano quality is clear and dry, a little lacking in bloom and inclined to harden at fortissimos.

Piano sonatas Nos. 30 in E major, Op. 109; 31 in A flat major, Op. 110.
**(*) DG 3300 645. Pollini.

Masterly pianism from Pollini. In terms of keyboard control and colour, not to mention commanding intelligence, his art defies criticism. Both sonatas are tautly held together; every phrase is moulded with marmoreal perfection, every detail of articulation and dynamic nuance is perfectly placed, and there is no doubt that these are in every way formidable and thought-provoking readings. But somehow one is left strangely unmoved here. Pollini does not scale the heights or plumb the depths as did Schnabel, who remains in a class of his own in both sonatas, and in Op. 110 both Bishop-Kovacevich (on disc) and Brendel have surpassed Pollini. But given piano-playing of this order, finely recorded, one cannot ignore this remarkable issue. The cassette transfer is clear but slightly dry, without quite the bloom of the LP.

Piano sonatas Nos. 31 in A flat major, Op. 110; 32 in C minor, Op. 111.
*** Decca KSXC 6630 [Lon. 5-6843]. Ashkenazy.

Ashkenazy plays the last two sonatas with a depth and spontaneity which put this issue among the very finest available. In the slow movement of Op. 111 Ashkenazy creates the highest degree of concentration at the slowest possible speed, and there is an element of detachment which brings added refinement. If anything the interpretation of Op. 110 is even more remarkable, consistently revealing. The recording is a little clangorous, but the ear quickly adjusts; the cassette transfer is outstanding, clear and bold and beautifully steady in tone.

Miscellaneous piano music

Andante favori in F major, G.170; Für Elise; Rondo à capriccio in G major (Rage over a lost penny), Op. 129; 2 Rondos, Op. 51/1–2; Piano sonata excerpts: No. 8 (Pathétique): 2nd movt; No. 14 (Moonlight): 1st movt; No. 20 in G major, Op. 49/2 (complete).
(B) ** DG Heliodor 3348 266. Kempff.

The shorter pieces here are presented in Kempff's characteristically spontaneous manner. The inclusion of the sonata movements (although they are beautifully played) seems designed to attract the wider musical public rather than the specialist collector. Nevertheless this tape is well recorded and attractive for what it is. The transfer is clear and clean: side one seems to have a cooler atmosphere and sharper outline than side two, where there is marginally more bloom on the piano tone. But both offer good quality, even if the transfer is made at rather a low level.

Andante favori in F major, G.170; 6 Ecossaises in E flat major; Für Elise; Klavierstück in B flat major; Polonaise in C major, Op. 89; Rondo à capriccio in G major (Rage over a lost penny), Op. 129; 5 Variations on 'Rule Britannia', G.190; 6 Variations on the Turkish march from 'The Ruins of Athens', Op. 76; 7

Variations on 'God Save the King',
G.189.

(M) **(*) Turnabout KTVC 34162.
Brendel.

The simplicity of Beethoven's variations on *God Save the King* is disarming,
and *Rule Britannia* is also without rhetoric. Brendel plays them eloquently but
with the right, unforced manner, and he is
equally at home in the attractive set using
the *Turkish march* as their basis. Both
Für Elise and the charming *Andante
favori* have a gentle romanticism which
Brendel matches exactly in his approach,
and the *Klavierstück* is another pleasant
example of mild Beethoven. The *Rondo
à capriccio* is suitably impulsive, Brendel
marginally less clean-fingered than usual
here, but he throws off the *Ecossaises*
splendidly and the *Polonaise* (not in the
least characteristic) is given the proper
rubato. The piano tone is variable, but
always acceptable. The cassette transfer
is very successful, although varying in
quality. Side one (which opens with the
Rondo à capriccio) is bold and brilliant
within a fairly dry acoustic. On the
second side the recording is more reverberant and transferred at a slightly lower
level. But the sound is clear and the tape
can be made to sound well throughout.

7 Bagatelles, Op. 33; 11 Bagatelles,
Op. 119; 6 Bagatelles, Op. 126.

(M) *** Turnabout KTVC 34077.
Brendel.

Beethoven's *Bagatelles*, particularly
those from Opp. 119 and 126, have often
been dismissed as chips from the
master's workbench. Brendel treats them
as worthwhile miniatures, and he shapes
them with care and precision. His taste
can never be faulted, and he is supported
by mostly excellent recording. The treble
is sometimes on the brittle side, but the
focus is exact in all but the most complicated moments, when there is a slight
excess of reverberation, not in the overall
acoustic but in the piano's basic texture.

If anything the cassette sounds better
than the disc; it is an exemplary transfer,
full-bodied, yet crisp in the upper register. The level is high, so there is no hiss
problem.

15 Variations and fugue on a theme
from 'Prometheus' in E flat major
(Eroica variations), Op. 35.

*** Decca KSXC 6523. Clifford
Curzon – SCHUBERT: *Moments
musicaux.****

Curzon's reading of the *Eroica variations* has commanding character and
great pianistic strength. Its coupling, the
Moments musicaux played with touching
eloquence, is attractive, and the recording is a fine one. The piano image is
undoubtedly realistic and offers warm,
well-focused sound, and this has transferred to tape admirably. A slight cut-
back of bass is needed to improve the balance, but the treble is clear and the
piano's middle range has attractive
colour and sonority.

15 Variations and fugue on a theme
from 'Prometheus' in E flat major
(Eroica variations), Op. 35; 32
Variations on an original theme in C
minor, G.191; 6 Variations in F
major, Op. 34.

(M) **(*) Philips Universo 7317
200. Arrau.

Characteristically strong and intelligent performances from Claudio Arrau,
without quite the individuality of Curzon
but undoubtedly satisfying in their clarity
of purpose. The piano tone is perhaps not
as rich as in Arrau's more recent recordings, but it is well balanced, and the transfer is firm and clear, with no lack of
colour.

33 Variations in C major on a waltz by
Diabelli, Op. 120.

(M) **(*) Turnabout KTVC 34139.
Brendel.

** Symphonica CSYM 9 [Peters PCE 042]. Charles Rosen.

As one would expect, Brendel gives a powerful, commanding account of Beethoven's most taxing piano work. As in his live performances he builds up the variations unerringly, but it is surprising to find to what degree he indulges in little accelerandos in each half of those variations which involve crescendos. Broadly his approach is romantic, with the adagio variation, No. 29, made into a moving lament. Few, if any, performances of this work on record convey its continuity so convincingly. The recording is faithful enough, but not really soft enough in pianissimos. However, the cassette version is exceptionally successful, and in some ways it is preferable to the disc.

Charles Rosen's view of this Everest of piano literature is purposeful and tough, hard to the point of being unrelenting. With clear but not especially rich recording to match, one misses the gentler halftones (as for example in the great adagio variation, No. 29, where Rosen ignores the *mezza voce* marking at a trivially fast tempo); but there is much to enjoy in this formidably intense interpretation. The recording is faithfully transferred to tape. Our copy was non-Dolbyized, but we are assured that by the time this book is in print copies reaching the shops will include Dolby, when no doubt the reverse-labelling will also be corrected.

VOCAL AND CHORAL MUSIC

Vocal music and music for the stage: (i) Overtures: *The Consecration of the House, Op. 124; Coriolan, Op. 62; The Creatures of Prometheus, Op. 43; Egmont, Op. 84; King Stephen, Op. 117; Leonora No. 3, Op. 72b; The Ruins of Athens, Op. 113;* (ii–iv) *Ah perfido!, Op. 65;* (v–vi; iii–iv) *Choral fantasia, Op. 80;* (vii;

vi; iii; viii) *Christus am Ölberge* (*Christ on the Mount of Olives*), *Op. 85;* (ix) *Mass in C major, Op. 86;* (x; vi; i) *Missa solemnis in D major, Op. 123;* (xi) *Fidelio* (opera; complete).

**(*) DG 3378 054. (i) Berlin PO, Karajan; (ii) Birgit Nilsson (soprano); (iii) Vienna SO; (iv) Leitner; (v) Joerg Demus (piano); (vi) Vienna Singverein; (vii) Elizabeth Harwood, James King, Franz Crass; (viii) Klee; (ix) Gundula Janowitz, Julia Hamari, Horst Laubenthal, Ernst Schramm, Munich Bach Choir and Orch., Richter; (x) Gundula Janowitz, Christa Ludwig, Fritz Wunderlich, Walter Berry; (xi) Gwyneth Jones, Edith Mathis, James King, Peter Schreier, Theo Adam, Franz Crass, Dresden State Opera Chorus and Orch., Boehm.

This is an outstandingly attractive set, in many ways the most useful and desirable of DG's tape issues from their Beethoven Edition. All the performances are distinguished, and while some are finer than others they have transferred to tape with such consistent vividness, presence and detail that they can give nothing but satisfaction. The overtures get the set off to an exhilarating start. One cannot but marvel at the superlative playing of the Berlin Philharmonic, which has both brilliance and atmosphere, while the sound quality is first-class. Demus's reading of the *Choral fantasia* is both strong and faithful, and the inclusion of *Christ on the Mount of Olives* is particularly valuable. Beethoven's oratorio is an under-rated work, not sublime as you would hope for from the composer of the *Missa solemnis*, but compellingly dramatic for most of the time. James King as a Heldentenor soloist underlines the operatic quality; the radiance of Elizabeth

Harwood's voice is powerfully caught, and Franz Crass makes a comparably intense partner. Bernhard Klee draws lively playing from the Vienna Symphoniker, and the recording, one or two balances apart, is first-rate. Karajan's 1966 recording of the *Missa solemnis* has transferred remarkably well, considering that the originally choral sound lacked a degree of impact. Here it projects well and with an exceptionally fine team of soloists the beauty and power of the performance are undeniable. Equally, although Richter's account of the *C major Mass* is not noted for its degree of imagination, it is not lacking in authority, and there is no doubt of the effect here with the balance so good. The final work in this tape box is Boehm's version of *Fidelio*, sounding extremely fresh and conveniently fitted on to two cassettes. Here Boehm is returning to an orchestra he directed in the thirties, and he brings maturity and warmth to Beethoven's great score. Unfortunately there are flaws in the cast. Gwyneth Jones produces too many squally notes to be a satisfying Leonora (although it is undoubtedly a strong characterization); James King is an uninspired Florestan, and Theo Adam as Pizarro is no more appealing to the ear. However, the bright quality of the transfer gives plenty of edge and projection to the characters and brings the drama fully alive in a most satisfying way.

Choral fantasia (for piano, chorus and orchestra), *Op. 80.*
>   (M) *(*) Turnabout KTVC 34206. Alfred Brendel, Stuttgart Lehrergesangverein, Stuttgart PO, Boettcher – *Piano concerto No. 2.***

Beethoven's curious hybrid work for piano, chorus and orchestra, which so obviously anticipates the *Choral symphony*, has been very lucky in its recordings, but at present this is the only version available separately on tape. The opening

cadenza is exceedingly well done by Brendel, who makes up for the weakness of his partners. Boettcher is unimaginative in a work that is unusually difficult to hold together. The chorus sings well, but the brief vocal solos are poorly done. Again this is a cassette transfer where side one is better than side two (although later copies may improve), so that the recording of the *Fantasia*, although clear, has noticeably less body than the first part of the *Second Piano concerto* which is the coupling.

Egmont (incidental music), *Op. 84*: complete recording, with narration based on the text by Grillparzer, and melodrama from the play by Goethe.
>   **(*) Decca KSXC 6465 [Lon. 5-6675]. Pilar Lorengar (soprano), Klausjuergen Wussow (speaker), Vienna PO, Szell.

The problem of performing Beethoven's incidental music for Goethe's *Egmont* within the original dramatic context is at least partially solved by using a text by the Austrian poet Franz Grillparzer. The music is interspersed at the appropriate points, including dramatic drum-rolls in Egmont's final peroration, this last scene being from Goethe's original. This presentation, with Klausjuergen Wussow the admirably committed speaker, is dramatic in the extreme. Szell's conducting is superb, the music marvellously characterized, the tension lightened in certain places with subtlety and the whole given a flowing dramatic impact. The snag is that whereas the experience of listening to the music is eminently renewable, one wonders if many will want to have the melodrama repeatedly. The songs are movingly sung by Pilar Lorengar. The transfer to cassette was a relatively early one and the sound, although well balanced, has not the upper range of the best Decca issues. Also our copy has a touch

83

of discoloration once or twice on the upper woodwind partials. This is less likely to be present on newer copies, and certainly the dramatic final climax is accommodated without any distortion.

Folk-song arrangements: *Behold, my love; Come, fill, fill, my good fellow; Duncan Gray; The elfin fairies; Faithful Johnnie; He promised me at parting; Highlander's lament; Highland watch; The Miller of Dee; Music, love and wine; Oh, had my fate been joined with thine; Oh, sweet were the hours; The pulse of an Irishman; Put around the bright wine.*

(M) *** DG Privilege 3335 241. Edith Mathis, Alexander Young, Dietrich Fischer-Dieskau, RIAS Chamber Choir, Andreas Röhn (violin), Georg Donderer (cello), Karl Engel (piano).

This delightful tape comes from the bicentenary set of vocal music that DG issued in 1970. It need hardly be said that the singing is of the highest order, and for those who have not heard any of Beethoven's folk-song arrangements it is a must. Beethoven obviously lavished much attention on them, and this issue is as successful as the delightful compilation Fischer-Dieskau made in the mid-sixties of folk-song settings by Haydn, Beethoven and Weber, surely one of the greatest records of its kind. This deserves a strong and unqualified recommendation, for the transfer is of good quality, well balanced and natural, with good presence for the voices, and lacking only the last degree of upper range. The accompanying leaflet generously unfolds to give all the words of the songs.

(i) *Mass in C major, Op. 86;* (ii) *Missa solemnis in D major, Op. 123.*

**(*) Philips 7699 077 [id.]. LSO Chorus, LSO, Colin Davis, with Patricia Payne, Robert Tear, (i) Christiane Eda-Pierre, Kurt Moll or (ii) Anna Tomowa-Sintow, Robert Lloyd.

Colin Davis directs a fresh and direct performance of the *Missa solemnis*, and couples with it an outstanding account of the earlier *Mass in C*, even sharper and more intense than Giulini's fine version (which is not available on tape). The lesser work is the one which challenges Davis to the finer performance, and the moment of the keenest individuality: the repeated cries of *Passus* ('suffered') in the *Credo* are made agonizingly to reflect Beethoven's own knowledge of suffering, his despair over his deafness, never more intense than in the years leading up to this work of 1807 – written in Heiligenstadt with all its reminders of the despairing Testament of 1802. The recording of the chorus is fresh and bright to match the reading, but in the *Missa solemnis* the voices sound relatively dull and distant. In principle this, like Klemperer's reading, is more symphonic than devotional, but the recording has a hint of mistiness belying that. The soloists' excellent contributions in both works are nicely balanced, placed at a distance like the chorus. The wide dynamic range of the recording is faithfully captured on tape. The massive weight of the choruses is contained with virtually no congestion, even if the resultant overall transfer level is low, which means that the recording's upper range lacks edge. The second tape includes the *Agnus Dei* from the *Missa solemnis* and thus earns a black mark: there was no reason why each work could not have been offered complete on one cassette. Tape 2, moreover, is transferred at a fractionally lower level, so that the soloists sound more backward than in tape 1. The presentation is sophisticated, with removable tape boxes within the slimline album-shell. The multilingual notes are clearly printed.

Missa solemnis in D major, Op. 123.
  *(*) Decca к 87 к 22. Lucia Popp,
    Yvonne Minton, Mallory
    Walker, Gwynne Howell,
    Chicago Symphony Chorus
    and Orch., Solti.
* HMV TC-SLS 989. Heather
    Harper, Janet Baker, Robert
    Tear, Hans Sotin, New
    Philharmonia Chorus, LPO,
    Giulini.

Solti's view of the *Missa solemnis* is
essentially dramatic, hardly at all spiritual. With full-ranging sound, brilliant
and forward, the result might have been
involving, like Solti's Chicago readings
of the Beethoven symphonies, but there is
a series of shortcomings which between
them detract from the impact of the performance. In the first place the ensemble
is far less crisp than one expects from this
source, with some ragged playing in the
orchestra and poor coordination with the
chorus. The choral contribution is variably successful, with some entries
sharply incisive (the tenors, for example,
in *Glorificamus* in the *Gloria*) but others
which are dim. The solo team is not well
matched either, and the discrepancies are
made the more glaring by unnatural forward positioning for the voices. In addition, the women overweigh the men, and
the first entry for the tenor in the *Kyrie* is
so feeble as to make one lose patience at
the very start. He does not improve
much, though Lucia Popp, Yvonne
Minton and Gwynne Howell all have
splendid moments. The tape transfer
contains the weighty choral tone impressively and the sound remains spacious
and uncongested. However, this is made
easy by the narrow dynamics of the recording (on disc as well as tape), with the
forward soloists often creating as much
tonal volume as the choir, thus minimizing the element of contrast. The violin
solos in the *Benedictus* are also made to
sound larger than life. There is a fine overall bloom on the sound but little sense of

spectacle in the climaxes. However, this is
not the fault of the transfer but is inherent
in the recording itself.

EMI's transfer of Giulini's performance is similarly all on one dynamic level,
so that the quartet of soloists creates
nearly as many decibels as the whole
chorus at full stretch. The overall quality
is good rather than excellent (the opening
and closing pages of the work are not too
clear in focus), and one cannot feel that
the overall effect of the music-making
realizes the composer's intentions. There
is virtually no sense of any kind of hushed
tension, an essential quality in this of all
choral works, and the ensemble of the
chorus is far from perfect. The soloists
are excellent.

OPERA

Fidelio: complete.
  *** HMV TC-SLS 5006. Christa
    Ludwig, Jon Vickers, Gottlob
    Frick, Walter Berry, Franz
    Crass, Philharmonia Chorus
    and Orch., Klemperer.
  **(*) DG 3371 039 [id.]. Gundula
    Janowitz, René Kollo, Manfred
    Jungwirth, Hans Sotin, Diet-
    rich Fischer-Dieskau, Vienna
    State Opera Chorus, Vienna
    PO, Bernstein.

Klemperer's great set of *Fidelio* is a
massive performance but one with wonderful incandescence and spiritual
strength, and with a final scene where,
more than in any other performance ever
recorded, the parallel with the finale of
the *Choral symphony* is underlined.
Christa Ludwig was an unexpected
choice as Leonore but proved to be an
inspired one, her richness of tone colour
and her flexibility spanning every register. Vickers and Frick, both singing their
original Covent Garden parts, could
hardly be bettered, and Walter Berry's
Pizarro, although not at all sinister, is
vocally most satisfying. The cassette

issue, like the EMI set of Bizet's *Carmen*, offers somewhat different sound quality on each of the two cassettes. Act 1 on tape one offers full, rich sound with both bloom and presence on the voices; in Act 2 the quality is rather more vibrant and sharply defined because of a higher transfer level, which is effective for the opera's climax.

Bernstein, as one would expect, directs a reading of *Fidelio* full of dramatic flair. The recording was made in conjunction with live performances by the same cast at the Vienna State Opera, and the atmosphere in the domestic scenes at the start might almost come from a predecessor of the stage musical (compliment intended), with Lucia Popp as Marzelline particularly enchanting. The spoken dialogue is splendidly produced too. The Canon Quartet in Act 1 has warmth and humanity rather than monumental qualities; and though Bernstein later rises splendidly to the high drama of Act 2 (the confrontation with Pizarro in the Quartet is as exciting as in Klemperer's classic reading), it remains a drama on a human scale. Gundula Janowitz sings most beautifully as Leonore, shading her phrases in the long opening section of the *Abscheulicher*, coping superbly with the intricacies of the *Allegro* and falling short only at the very end, in a less than triumphant pay-off. Kollo as Florestan is intelligent and musicianly but indulges in too many intrusive aitches, and there is some coarseness of tone. Hans Sotin as Pizarro sings with superb projection, and the size of voice makes up for its not sounding villainous. Manfred Jungwirth makes an engaging Rocco, though his singing is not always perfectly steady. Fischer-Dieskau – once an incomparable Pizarro – here makes a noble Don Fernando in the final scene. In keeping with Bernstein's approach the voices are placed rather close, and the balance is not always quite consistent, though the sound is vivid. The cassette transfer is made at a comparatively modest level, which means that there is some lack of range in the orchestral sound of the overture. As soon as the opera itself begins, however, the refinement of the recording, both of voices and of background orchestral detail, gives much pleasure. The level appears to rise slightly on side two (the scene between Pizarro and Rocco), giving greater presence and impact; the spoken dialogue is certainly projected dramatically. Generally the quality is first-class, with a realistic stage perspective (although the choral sound is not very incisive). The presentation too (in DG's removable plastic boxes) is handsome, but the libretto – clearly printed though it is – is not ideal. The format (three tapes) is the same as on discs, three sides for each act and the Overture *Leonora No. 3* at the end of side five (with no pause) after the duet, *O namenlose Freude*.

COLLECTIONS

Amnesty International concert; Overture: *Leonora No. 3, Op. 72b; Piano concerto No. 4 in G major, Op. 58; Symphony No. 5 in C minor, Op. 67.*

(M) *** DG 3378 074. Claudio Arrau, Bavarian Radio SO, Bernstein (a live concert recorded in Munich, 17 October 1975, in aid of Amnesty International).

There is a lot to be said for recording live concerts if the results are as satisfactory as they are here, for whatever reservations one may have about these readings, they have undoubted electricity and prompt one to applaud immediately after each work. (Applause incidentally is edited out and the audience is admirably unobtrusive.) In the overture tempi are a little exaggerated, as are pianissimos and other details: a trifle self-conscious, but, as is so often the case with Bernstein's Beethoven, curiously convincing. The

Fifth Symphony is not the equal of its most distinguished recorded rivals, but it is eminently worth hearing; and though Arrau is not as polished or considered here as in his Philips recording with Haitink, he has a spontaneity that makes up for it. These performances, whatever one's criticisms on points of detail, have personality, and the recordings are truthful as far as both balance and timbre are concerned.

'*Favourite composer*': (i; ii) *Piano concerto No. 5 in E flat major* (*Emperor*), *Op. 85;* Overtures: (ii) *Egmont, Op. 84;* (iii) *Leonora No. 3, Op. 72b;* (iv) *Symphony No. 6 in F major* (*Pastoral*), *Op. 68;* (v) *Piano sonata No. 14 in C sharp minor* (*Moonlight*), *Op. 27/2.*
(B) *(*) Decca KDPC 529/30. Julius Katchen; (ii) LSO, Gamba; (iii) Israel PO, Maazel; (iv) Suisse Romande Orch., Ansermet; (v) Friedrich Gulda.

These two tapes are generously filled, but are let down by Ansermet's *Pastoral symphony*, which suffers from poor wind intonation, and Maazel's hard-driven account of *Leonora No. 3.* Even in the bargain range this is a disappointing collection, in spite of the excellence of Katchen's *Emperor*. The cassettes are well transferred. The quality in the symphony is exceptionally good – bright and very lively. The concerto is not quite so open in acoustic, but the overtures have plenty of life and the piano tone is natural, if seeming a little confined in range.

'*Your kind of Beethoven*': Symphonies Nos. (i; ii) *5 in C minor, Op. 67:* 1st movt; (iii; iv) *6 in F major* (*Pastoral*), *Op. 68:* finale; (i; iv; v) *9 in D minor* (*Choral*), *Op. 125:* conclusion; (vi) *The Ruins of Athens, Op. 113: Turkish march;* (vii) *Piano sonatas Nos. 8 in C minor* (*Pathéti-*

que), *Op. 13: Adagio; 14 in C sharp minor* (*Moonlight*), *Op. 27/2:* 1st movt; (viii) *Für Elise;* (ix) Irish songs: *He promised me at parting.*
* (*) EMI TC-EXES 5005. (i) LSO; (ii) Previn; (iii) New Philharmonia Orch.; (iv) Giulini; (v) LSO Chorus, soloists; (vi) RPO, Beecham; (vii) Daniel Barenboim; (viii) John Ogdon; (ix) Victoria de los Angeles, Dietrich Fischer-Dieskau.

Beethoven is not the kind of composer to suit a miniature anthology. The selection here is inevitably based on excerpts, which are not satisfying on their own and refuse to gell with the slighter pieces interspersed between them. On side one the slow movement of the *Pathétique sonata* is sandwiched between the first movement of the *Fifth Symphony* and the finale of the *Pastoral symphony*. However, the mixture on side two is rather more successful, with the Los Angeles/Fischer-Dieskau duet a delightful surprise. The two piano items here are enjoyable, as is Beecham's *Turkish march*, although there are some problems about variations of dynamics between the individual recordings. The last ten minutes or so of the finale of the *Choral symphony* are transferred with fair success; elsewhere the sound in the orchestral items is often only moderate.

'*The world of Beethoven*': (i–iii) *Piano concerto No. 5 in E flat major* (*Emperor*), *Op. 73*: finale; (ii; iv) *Egmont overture, Op. 84;* (ii; v) Symphonies Nos. *5 in C minor, Op. 67*: 1st movt; *6 in F major* (*Pastoral*), *Op. 68*: finale; *9 in D minor* (*Choral*), *Op. 125*: finale (excerpt); (vi) *Piano sonatas Nos. 8 in C minor* (*Pathétique*), *Op. 13*: 2nd movt; *14 in C sharp minor* (*Moonlight*), *Op. 27/2*:

1st movt; (ii; vii) *Fidelio: Mir ist so wunderbar* (quartet).

(M) *(*) Decca KCSP 324. (i) Friedrich Gulda; (ii) Vienna PO; (iii) Stein; (iv) Szell; (v) Schmidt-Isserstedt; (vi) Wilhelm Backhaus; (vii) with soloists, cond. Maazel.

Such a collection indisputably shows the range of Beethoven's genius, but in itself does not make a very satisfactory concert. The performances are not even in quality. Szell's *Egmont overture* is a highlight, but the finale from Schmidt-Isserstedt's *Pastoral symphony* (which ends side one) lacks a feeling of spiritual repose. The transfer offers rather variable quality, mostly acceptable but sometimes not very refined.

Bellini, Vincenzo
(1801–35)

Norma (opera): complete.
**(*) Decca K 21 K 32 [Lon. 51394]. Joan Sutherland, Marilyn Horne, John Alexander, Richard Cross, LSO Chorus, LSO, Bonynge.
(M) *(**) HMV TC-SLS 5115. Maria Callas, Ebe Stignani, Mario Filippeschi, Nicola Rossi-Lemeni, Chorus and Orch. of La Scala, Milan, Serafin.

It is a measure of Joan Sutherland's concern for musical values that she deliberately surrounds herself with singers who match her own quality and not (as some divas have done) with singers who stand no chance of detracting from the star's glory. She is here joined by an Adalgisa in Marilyn Horne whose control of florid singing is just as remarkable as Sutherland's own, and who

sometimes even outshines the heroine in musical imaginativeness. But fine as Horne's contribution is, Sutherland's marked a new level of achievement in her recording career. Accepting the need for a dramatic approach very much in the school of Callas, she then ensures at the same time that something as near as possible to musical perfection is achieved. The old trouble of diction with the words masked is occasionally present; but basically this is a most compelling performance, musically and dramatically, and in this Sutherland is helped by the conducting of her husband, Richard Bonynge. On this showing there are few finer Bellini conductors before the public today, for in the many conventional accompaniment figures he manages to keep musical interest alive with sprung rhythm and with the subtlest attention to the vocal line. The other soloists are all very good indeed, John Alexander and Richard Cross both young, clear-voiced singers. The recording, made at Walthamstow, has the usual fine qualities of Decca opera recording. The tape transfer has been made at a high level and generally the sound is vivid and the moments of spectacle are well handled; but Sutherland's voice tends to peak very occasionally on high *fortissimo* notes, and the same thing occurs in the Sutherland/Horne Act 2 duet. The recording is not so completely free in texture as some others from this source.

Callas made her first recording of *Norma* in 1954, and though already there were signs of unsteadiness in the upper register, it caught the full, magnificent character of the voice in all its freshness and vibrancy of imagination. Though later – as illustrated in the (disc) stereo recording of 1960 – there were moments of deeper insight and even deeper expressiveness, this earlier version remains a unique reminder of Callas at her peak, and it is disappointing that much of the rest is flawed. It is good to hear Ebe Stignani as Adalgisa – the role she also took for Callas's Covent Garden début – but its matronliness requires some adjustment in the listener. Filippeschi and Rossi-Lemeni are relatively coarse and unbeautiful, while even with the expert guidance of Serafin the forces of La Scala are far from polished. But with Callas in such form these penalties are worth enduring. The stereo transcription is fair for its period.

The transfer begins well, with attractively smooth sound for the opening scene of Act 1, but when Callas enters there is a hint of discomfort at peaks, and this applies again to a lesser extent when Norma and Adalgisa sing their Act 2 duet. There is a shrillness to the top notes here and in Callas's solos in the latter part of the opera, and this is something that must be accepted as part of the recording. The cassettes are labelled to indicate that the opera consists of two acts only, whereas according to the libretto (printed in very small type) there are four.

I Puritani (opera): complete.

*** Decca κ 25 κ 32 [Lon. 5-13111]. Joan Sutherland, Luciano Pavarotti, Piero Cappuccilli, Nicolai Ghiaurov, Royal Opera House, Covent Garden, Chorus and Orch., Bonynge.

(M) ** HMV TC-SLS 5140. Maria Callas, Giuseppe di Stefano, Rolando Panerai, Nicola Rossi-Lemeni, Chorus and Orch. of La Scala, Milan, Serafin.

Ten years after her first recording of *I Puritani*, made in Florence, Joan Sutherland returned to this limpidly lyrical music. 'Opera must make people weep, shudder, die through the singing,' wrote Bellini to his librettist, and this sharply committed performance – much crisper of ensemble than the earlier one, with Bonynge this time adopting a more urgently expressive style – breathes life into what can seem a rather limp story about Cavaliers and Roundheads. Where the earlier set was recorded when Sutherland had adopted a soft-grained style, with consonants largely eliminated and a tendency to lag behind the beat, this time her singing is fresher and brighter. The lovely aria *Qui la voce* is no longer a wordless melisma, and though the great showpiece *Son vergin vezzosa* is now taken dangerously fast, the extra bite and tautness are exhilarating. Pavarotti, possessor of the most radiantly beautiful of tenor voices, shows himself a remarkable Bellini stylist, rarely if ever coarsening a legato line, unlike so many of his Italian colleagues. Ghiaurov and Cappuccilli make up an impressive cast, and the only disappointing contributor is Anita Caminada in the small role of Enrichette – Queen Henrietta Maria in disguise. Vivid, atmospheric recording. The tape transfer is of very high quality in Acts 1 and 3, with fine detail and an attractive bloom on the voices, but it is slightly less perfect in focus in Act 2. Act 3 (on side four) offers demonstration sound, with voices splendidly free.

Those who complain that this opera represents Bellini at his least compelling dramatically should certainly hear Callas. Though the bite of the voice itself is slightly dulled by the stereo transcription, the compulsion of her singing is irresistible. In 1953, when she made the recording, her voice was already afflicted with hardness on top and some unsteadiness, and for sheer beauty of sound Sutherland is consistently preferable, whether in *Qui la voce* or in the exhilarating *Son vergin vezzosa*; but Callas, once heard, is unforgettable, and this reissue is welcome. None of the other soloists is ideally stylish, though most of the singing is acceptable. As can be heard at the very opening, the upper range of the sound is restricted and both orchestra and chorus are muffled, although later the sound opens up, with brighter treble detail in places. The level is well judged, and the solo voices are quite kindly treated, so that they have a fair degree of bloom and reasonable presence. The opera is admirably laid out on two cassettes, with Act 1 complete on the first, Acts 2 and 3 given a side each on the second. The libretto is clearly printed.

La Sonnambula (opera): complete.
(M) **(*) HMV TC-SLS 5134 [Angel 4x2G 6108]. Maria Callas, Nicola Monti, Fiorenza Cossotto, Nicola Zaccaria, Eugenia Ratti, Chorus and Orch. of La `Scala, Milan, Votto.

Of Callas's recorded Bellini performances this is arguably the best, more full of surprises than her early versions of *Norma* and *I Puritani*. From the moment she starts her first recitative you have a perfect picture of an innocent girl: fresh-sounding as well as sparkling, every phrase reflects the magnetic Callas imagination. Nicola Monti is a light-weight but elegant tenor, and the rest of the cast provides good support. The recording, made in 1957, is altogether more sophisticated than the sound in the earlier sets, and it has come up well in the new stereo transcription. The tape transfer is generally successful. The date of the recording is obvious from the choral sound, but the solo voices are mostly fresh and clear and the overall quality is bright: indeed a slight treble cut may be found useful to take a touch of shrillness from Callas's voice. There is only the occasional hint of peaking, and the level has been well judged to give maximum presence. The libretto is clearly printed and easy to read.

Berg, Alban
(1885–1935)

Lyric suite.
** CBS 40-76305. New York PO, Boulez – SCHOENBERG: *Verklaerte Nacht.***

The transcription for string orchestra of the three inner movements of Berg's *Lyric suite* takes fifteen minutes, which is short measure for a whole side. It is expressively played by the New York Philharmonic under Boulez, even if his reading is not quite so subtle or refined as that recorded (on disc only) by Karajan and the Berlin Philharmonic, whose *pianissimo* tone is not matched by the New Yorkers. Comparisons apart, however, this is fine playing (dodecaphony with a human face), and the recording is perfectly acceptable. On tape the sound is quite well balanced; the transfer level here is rather higher than for the Schoenberg coupling, and the upper range, in consequence, has rather more detail and bite. In fact the quality is quite vivid.

Lulu (opera): complete.
*** Decca K 48 K 32. Anja Silja, Brigitte Fassbaender, Walter Berry, Josef Hopferweiser, Kurt Moll, Werner Krenn, Vienna PO, Dohnányi.

It is a revelation to hear what has long been thought an exceptionally difficult score performed with such urgency and refinement and recorded with such richness and clarity. Previous recordings on disc were made during live performances, which means that Dohnányi is the first to achieve anything like precision. Not only that, the sheer beauty of the orchestral sound is ravishing and goes with the fine sharpness of the characterization. The pity is that Dohnányi was still not able to record the completed Act 3, for which Pierre Boulez – who directed the Paris premiere – had first recording rights. As previously on record, two movements of the *Lulu symphony* are used as a replacement.

Anja Silja is vividly in character, attacking the stratospheric top notes with ease, always singing with power and rarely falling into her usual hardness. Walter Berry too is exceptionally strong as Dr Schön, aptly sinister, and even the small roles are cast from strength. The Vienna Philharmonic plays ravishingly, underlining the opera's status – whatever the formal patterns behind the notes, and whatever the subject – as an offshoot of romanticism. The cassettes, like the discs, set new standards, with sound of amazing vividness and depth. The layout, placing one act on each of the two tapes, offers a superior presentation to the three LPs. The libretto booklet is clearly printed.

Berkeley, Lennox
(born 1903)

Guitar concerto.
   (*) RCA RK 11734 [ARK 1 1181]. Julian Bream, Monteverdi Orch., Gardiner – RODRIGO: *Concierto de Aranjuez.**

When it was originally performed as part of the City of London Festival of 1974, this concertante work for Julian Bream was described as a concertino. Though the orchestral writing was light, that diminutive title was unfair to an extended work which presents a serious as well as an attractive argument, with elegant architecture and a stylish brand of guitar-writing that never leans barrenly on Spanish models. Bream's performance is superb, and the recording vivid. An attractive if out-of-the-way coupling for the most popular of all guitar concertos. On tape the recording is vivid, but the close balance of the soloist produces a comparatively limited dynamic range.

Berlioz, Hector
(1803–69)

Harold in Italy, Op. 16.
   **(*) HMV TC-ASD 3389 [Angel 4xs 37413]. Donald McInnes (viola), Orchestre National de France, Bernstein.
   **(*) Decca KSXC 6873. Robert Vernon (viola), Cleveland Orch., Maazel.
   ** Decca KSXC 16732 [(d) Lon. 5-6951]. Daniel Benyamini (viola), Israel PO, Mehta (with BEETHOVEN: *The Creatures of Prometheus overture***).

Although by no means outstanding the HMV cassette transfer of *Harold in Italy* is good. The resonant sound picture is not always captured without smudging of detail (notably in the first movement, where there is a touch of glassiness in the upper string tone); but the solo viola is warmly portrayed and the image well integrated with the overall texture. Side two seems transferred at a fractionally lower level than side one, and the *Orgy of Brigands* sounds spacious and atmospheric, although a little more sparkle and range in the treble would have been welcome. With the understanding players of the Orchestre National, Bernstein gives a performance that is both exciting and introspective. It has warmth too. His earlier account with the New York Philharmonic was sharper-focused than this, thanks in part to the CBS recording (not yet available on tape), and its tauter discipline made for a performance at once fiercer and more purposeful. But in some ways, with French players Bernstein's slightly more relaxed manner is more authentic, so that the galloping rhythms of the first and third movements are more lilting, if fractionally less precise. Donald McInnes is a violist with a superb rich and even tone, one who responds at all times to the conductor but who has plenty of individuality.

A well-recorded and excellently played account comes from Robert Vernon and the Cleveland Orchestra under Maazel. In terms of imagination and insight, however, it does not displace the Bernstein version; but technically it is the most impressive tape of this work yet to appear. The transfer is refined, with excellent detail and a rich overall sound picture, yet with good transients, the percussion and brass vividly outlined. Compared to the disc the final orgy seems marginally less expansive in the matter of dynamic range, but in all other respects there is no perceptible difference between LP and tape.

Mehta draws sonorous playing from the Israel Philharmonic, and the recording has a beefy large-scale quality that does not always suit the music, particularly when the solo viola is balanced too close. Though this is enjoyable, some of Berlioz's subtlety is missing. The cassette version offers sound of generally good quality, but it lacks the sparkle we are used to from the best Decca issues. The Beethoven overture which acts as coupling on tape but not LP is well done and emerges more vividly than the main work.

Collections of overtures etc.

Overtures: *Béatrice et Bénédict; Benvenuto Cellini, Op. 23; Le Carnaval romain, Op. 9; Le Corsaire, Op. 21. La Damnation de Faust: Hungarian march; Dance of the Sylphs; Minuet of the Will-o'-the-Wisps.*
  ** Decca KSXC 6165. Suisse Romande Orch., Ansermet.

Overtures: *Béatrice et Bénédict; Benvenuto Cellini; Le Carnaval romain; Le Corsaire; Les Francs-juges, Op. 3.*
  (**) HMV TC-ASD 3212. LSO, Previn.

The Decca Ansermet collection offers bright, well-balanced sound, full-blooded and not without sparkle. The performances too are idiomatic, and it is a pity that the SRO does not quite com-

mand the virtuosity and *élan* this music calls for. There is much that is attractive about Previn's collection (his version of *Les Francs-juges* is particularly winning), but the snag with this HMV cassette is its severely restricted dynamic range.

Symphonie fantastique, Op. 14.
  *** DG 3300 498 [id.]. Berlin PO, Karajan.
  *** HMV TC-ASD 3263 [Angel 4XS 37138]. ORTF National Orch., Martinon.
  ** (*) HMV TC-ASD 3397 [Angel 4XS 37414]. Orchestre National de France, Bernstein.
  **(*) Philips 7300 313 [id.]. Concertgebouw Orch., Colin Davis.
  **(*) Decca Phase 4 KPFC 4160. New Philharmonia Orch., Stokowski.
  (B) ** DG Heliodor 3348 172. Lamoureux Orch., Markevitch.
  (M) ** Philips 7317 156 [7310 031]. LSO, Colin Davis.
  ** HMV TC-ASD 3496. LSO, Previn.
  * (*) DG 3300 316 [id.]. Boston SO, Ozawa.
  (M) * DG Privilege 3335 256 [923113]. Berlin PO, Karajan.
  (B) (*) Pye ZCCCB 15010. Hallé Orch., Barbirolli.

Symphonie fantastique; Overture: *Les Francs-juges, Op. 3.*
  * Decca KSXC 16571 [(d) Lon. 5-6790]. Chicago SO, Solti.

The *Symphonie fantastique* is well served on cassette, and Karajan's new recording (not to be confused with his old one, reissued on Privilege) must head the list. Although he omits the repeat in the first movement (both Martinon and Davis show that its inclusion balances the movement's structure), this reading is first-class, and the DG tape is outstandingly well engineered, the sound having brilliance and atmosphere and often providing demonstration quality. The very opening reveals the greater depth (compared to Karajan's earlier account), the extra intensity in hushed *pianissimo*; and the beautiful DG recording brings out every nuance of the Berlin orchestra's unusually subtle tone colours. The immensely dramatic finale too sends the adrenalin racing, and in most respects this issue is unrivalled despite the drawback mentioned above. There is little doubt, however, that French musicians working under a French conductor show a unique seductiveness in Martinon's version. In its way this is as magically compelling as Beecham's ancient version with the same orchestra. Martinon provides the extra brass parts normally omitted, and though the result is brilliant, he never presses on too frenetically. The *March to the scaffold* is aptly menacing, rather than merely jaunty. But most of all the reading is outstanding for its warm shaping of phrase, so that the slow movement – which can so easily fall apart in fragments – is here compellingly moulded from beginning to end. The transfer is not so dramatically vivid in projection as Karajan's DG tape, but the quality is spacious and warm to match the conductor's approach.

Bernstein directs a brilliant and understanding performance which captures more than most the wild, volatile quality of Berlioz's inspiration. Others like Martinon and Davis may give a clearer idea of the symphonic logic of the piece, but Bernstein (unlike them, omitting the exposition repeat) has more urgency, and his reading culminates in superb accounts of the *March to the scaffold* and the *Witches' sabbath*, full of rhythmic swagger and natural flair. The recording is rich and opulent, and pleasingly spacious; but on tape the first-movement climax lacks any kind of detail, and this lack of internal focus

remains to some extent throughout, although the resonance of the acoustic is well caught and the orchestra has plenty of body and impact.

Colin Davis chose the *Symphonie fantastique* for his first recording with the Amsterdam Concertgebouw Orchestra. The interpretation is very similar to his earlier account with the LSO (see below), only the performance has even more energy, life and colour. The slow movement too is more atmospheric than before, if not quite as fine as Martinon's outstanding performance. It is not helped by Philips's crude side-break. Moreover the sound is rather lacking in sparkle. The quality on side two is generally impressive, but on the first side the strings lack life in their upper range. The recording is otherwise well balanced.

Stokowski's Decca recording was a comparatively early Decca issue on tape, but the transfer is highly spectacular, well detailed and vividly catching the reverberant acoustic. It is an idiosyncratic performance that by some Stokowskian magic manages to convey complete warm-hearted conviction. Stokowski's warmth of phrasing is aptly romantic, but generally the surprising thing is his meticulous concern for markings. The hairpin dynamic marks are even exaggerated, but unlike many less flamboyant conductors, he refuses to whip up codas into a frenzy, and some may be disappointed at his comparatively relaxed tempo for the finale. This tape, incidentally, remains in the catalogue at full price, although the disc has been reissued on Ace of Diamonds. There is a break in the slow movement.

Markevitch's DG recording was also technically among the best available, and in the tape issue the sound is remarkably good, rich and clear and with plenty of bloom. The strings in the slow movement can be made to sound particularly fresh and pleasing. The performance is impulsive, and if the reading falls short of the highest standards it is still convincing, and the orchestral playing is excellent.

93

Davis's earlier recording has been re-issued in an admirably fresh transfer on Philips's medium-priced label. The first movement begins with a fine sense of atmosphere, but the tension is not always maintained throughout the movement, and the *Adagio*, although beautifully played, is a little detached. The two final movements are very exciting. In the *March to the scaffold* Davis gives the rhythm exactly the right spring, and by doing the rarely heard repeat he adds to our pleasure. The finale is compelling to the last bar, with really taut orchestral playing and clear projection from the recording. The transfer is admirably clear and clean, with vivid brass and string detail. The sound is slightly dry and gives a less massive, less atmospheric sound picture than in Davis's re-recording with the Concertgebouw Orchestra.

Previn's performance, although the interpretation is an individual one and has its insights and moments of great intensity, is in the last analysis disappointing. The first movement is undoubtedly exciting, but its fluctuations of tempi do not always convince, though there is a fine sense of apotheosis at the close. The second movement is curiously lacking in lilt, and the slowly paced *March to the scaffold* sounds heavy rather than powerful. The finale is successful, and with brilliant orchestral playing and fine rich recording Previn's admirers may find this version rewarding. The transfer to tape is not as richly resonant in the bass as the disc, but has plenty of impact and bright detail.

Ozawa's account is not without excitement, and the clipped rhythms of the *March to the scaffold*, taken at a fairly brisk tempo, make this movement sound especially characterful. But as a whole the reading shows no special insights, and the reverberant Boston acoustic tends to blunt the cutting edge of the orchestra. The level of transfer is comparatively low, and the quality is atmospheric rather than vivid, which matches the soft-centred nature of Ozawa's conception.

Karajan's earlier recording of the *Symphonie fantastique*, now available on Privilege, was altogether too erratic to be entirely convincing. The first movement *allegro*, after the slow introduction, charges off at full speed in a most wilful and unspontaneous fashion, and Karajan's tempo fluctuations throughout are not only overtly personal but tend to interfere with the music's structure. The waltz is played with splendid panache, but Karajan's wilfulness is apparent at the end. This is a performance that different ears react to differently, but all will agree that the low-level Privilege transfer is lacking in definition, range and sparkle but not hiss.

Solti's tape opens with a hard-driven but extremely vivid account of the *Francs-juges overture*, with superbrilliant sound which continues in the first two movements of the symphony. The tape is marginally less open on side two, and the blaze of sound in the fourth and fifth movements lacks the last degree of freshness and sparkle in the treble, but remains nevertheless of good Decca quality. The level of the transfer is high. But – although hardly a semiquaver is out of place – somehow, for once, the spirit of the music eludes the conductor. The work sounds over-rehearsed.

Barbirolli's LP is still very competitive in spite of the age of the recording, the performance having both excitement and breadth. However, the transfer to tape irons out all the climaxes and the music never rises above *mezzo forte*. The way the volume fades at the climax of the waltz movement is particularly grotesque.

VOCAL MUSIC AND OPERA

L'Enfance du Christ, Op. 25 (complete).
**(*) Philips 7699 058. Janet Baker, Eric Tappy, Philip

Langridge, Thomas Allen, Raimund Herincx, Joseph Rouleau, Jules Bastin, John Alldis Choir, LSO, Colin Davis.

Davis characteristically directs a fresh and refined reading of one of Berlioz's most directly appealing works. The beautifully balanced recording intensifies the colour and atmosphere of the writing, so that the *Nocturnal march*, for example, in the first part, is wonderfully mysterious. There is a fine complement of soloists, and although Eric Tappy's tone as narrator is not always sweet, his sense of style is immaculate. Janet Baker and Thomas Allen as ever both sing beautifully. The transfer to tape has been made at an almost incredibly low level, and although background hiss remains minimal, and the score's more delicate pages (the *Shepherds' carol* and final chorus and the delightful scoring for flutes and harp at the opening of side four) are well caught, the more robust moments tend to lack projection. The solo voices are natural. The booklet provided with the set is clearly printed but isolates the translations, so that each language is printed independently – a curiously inept idea.

Les Nuits d'été (song cycle), *Op. 7.*
  (M) *** Decca Jubilee KJBC 15. Régine Crespin (mezzo-soprano), Suisse Romande Orch., Ansermet – RAVEL: *Shéhérazade.****

Crespin's sheer richness of tone and a style which has an operatic basis do not prevent her from bringing out the subtlety of Berlioz's writing. *Le spectre de la rose* (a wonderful song), for instance, has a bigness of style and colouring and an immediate sense of drama that immediately conjure up the opera house. But this is not a criticism. With Ansermet brilliantly directing the accompaniment, this glowing performance is a *tour de force*. Decca's sound too is vividly clear, the voice dramatically projected.

Requiem mass (*Grande messe des morts*), *Op. 5.*
  *(*) Philips 7699 008 [id.]. Ronald Dowd (tenor), Wandsworth School Boys' Choir, LSO, Colin Davis.
  *(*) HMV TC-SLS 982. Robert Tear (tenor), CBSO Chorus, City of Birmingham SO, Frémaux.

Neither the Davis nor the Frémaux set really encompasses this spectacular score without signs of strain. The wide dynamic range of the Philips transfer has led to obtrusive tape hiss in the quieter moments. The HMV set has a more compressed dynamic range, generally sounds more comfortable, and successfully manages all but the very loudest moments.

Davis went to Westminster Cathedral for his recording sessions, which should have been atmospheric enough, but then the engineers were allowed to produce a sound which minimizes the massiveness of forces in anything but the loudest fortissimos, thanks to the closeness of the microphones. In many passages one can hear individual voices in the choir. Once that is said, the performance itself is a fine one, though still not as full of mystery as it might be. The large-scale brass sound is well caught, and the choral fortissimos are helped by the fresh cutting edge of the Wandsworth Boys' Choir. It was Davis's idea not Berlioz's to have boys included, but it is entirely in character. Their brilliance rather shows up the adult singers. The LSO provides finely incisive accompaniment.

It is disappointing that for Frémaux's performance the EMI engineers fell into the same trap as the Philips ones in the Davis set, only rather more so. The choir and orchestra are recorded relatively closely, making the result seem too small-scale for such a work. Detail is clarified, and there is a typical bloom on the sound, but the absence of true pianissimos is just as serious as the failure to expand in the big climaxes, making a potentially fine performance far less effective than it might have been. The chorus work is surprisingly variable.

Roméo et Juliette, Op. 17: orchestral music only.
*** Decca KSXC 6800. Vienna PO, Maazel.

Maazel's excellent complete performance is available on disc only, but this set of excerpts shows the vividness and detail of its source. The transfer is admirably done.

Roméo et Juliette, Op. 17: Love scene.
*** DG 3300 284 [id.]. San Francisco SO, Ozawa – PROKOFIEV: *Romeo and Juliet suite;* TCHAIKOVSKY: *Romeo and Juliet.****
(M) *(*) Philips 7320 045. Concertgebouw Orch., Colin Davis – TCHAIKOVSKY: *Romeo and Juliet.*(*)

Ozawa presents an attractive coupling of three very contrasted views of Shakespeare's lovers. The Berlioz has all the warmth and glow required in this vision of the great love scene. The opulent recording has transferred very well to tape, and this is a most attractive issue.

Davis's excerpt is finely played, but the recording, although good, lacks brilliance. This is offered on a mid-priced tape, but the more generous Ozawa coupling is a much better investment.

Les Troyens (opera): highlights.
*** Philips 7300 050. Josephine Veasey, Jon Vickers, Berit Lindholm, Peter Glossop, Roger Soyer, Ian Partridge,

Wandsworth School Boys' Choir, Royal Opera House, Covent Garden, Chorus and Orch., Colin Davis.

Choosing excerpts from so wide-ranging a work as *Les Troyens* is impossibly difficult. Any choice inevitably leaves out favourite items – the immolation of the women at the end of Act 1 and the great love duet, *O nuit d'ivresse*, are both omitted here – but what is included provides a superb sampler of the five-disc complete set, with the magnificent drama of the Trojan horse scene, the *Royal hunt and storm* with choral comment, Aeneas's magnificent Act 5 aria and Dido's death aria. The transfer is faithful to the excellent recording of the complete set, if lacking the last degree of brilliance, with the distance effects in the march scene not very crisp in focus. The *Royal hunt and storm*, however, has impressive spaciousness and impact.

(i) *Les Troyens, Act 5, Scenes 2 and 3. La Mort de Cléopâtre* (lyric scene for voice and orchestra).
(M) *** HMV TC-SXLP 30248. Janet Baker (soprano), (i) with Bernadette Greevy (contralto), Keith Erwen (tenor), Gwynne Howell (baritone), Ambrosian Opera Chorus; LSO, Gibson.

Janet Baker's deeply moving rendering of the concluding scenes of Berlioz's epic opera makes an essential supplement to the complete recording for any devoted Berliozian and may conversely work towards persuading others to try the complete opera. Baker, helped by the warm, sympathetic accompaniment under Gibson's direction, allows herself a range of tone-colour and a depth of expressiveness not matched by Josephine Veasey, the Dido in the Philips set. This is a more intimate, more personally agonized portrayal of Dido's tragedy, in many ways more moving. It is a pity that the reverse does not provide more music from *Les Troyens*; but Berlioz's early scena on the death of another classical heroine is a fine piece, beautifully performed. The transfer is of good quality, one of EMI's best, with a fine bloom on the voice in *Les Troyens* and the chorus convincingly caught, if without the last degree of sharpness of projection. In *La Mort de Cléopâtre* the voice has a degree of edge not noticeable on side one and a treble cut is necessary, but the detail and projection are good.

Les Troyens: Trojan march; Royal hunt and storm.

(M) **(*) HMV TC-SXLP 30260. Beecham Choral Society, RPO, Beecham – BIZET: *Symphony***; DELIBES: *Le Roi s'amuse.***(*)

Beecham's version of the *Royal hunt and storm* has splendid panache and atmosphere, and the *Trojan march* is characteristically ebullient. The recordings are good (though the focus of the chorus in the former piece is less than exact), and they have transferred to tape with good impact and detail, the level well calculated.

COLLECTION

'Favourite composer': (i) Overtures: *Le Carnaval romain, Op. 9; Le Corsaire, Op. 21. La Damnation de Faust: Hungarian march.* (ii) *Symphonie fantastique, Op. 14.* (iii) *L'Enfance du Christ:* Part 2, Scene 1. (iv; i) *Nuits d'été: Le spectre de la rose.* (v) *Les Troyens à Carthage: Je vais mourir.*

(B) ** Decca KDPC 613/4. (i) Suisse Romande Orch., Ansermet; (ii) Vienna PO, Monteux; (iii) Peter Pears, St Anthony Singers, Goldsbrough Orch., Colin Davis; (iv) Régine Crespin; (v) Josephine Veasey, Orch. of the Royal Opera House, Covent Garden, Kubelik.

These recordings, though not new, make up a generous cross-section of Berlioz's music for about the cost of one full-priced issue. Josephine Veasey sings eloquently in the excerpt from *Les Troyens*, and the substantial excerpt from *The Childhood of Christ* (including the delightful *Shepherds' farewell*) is most welcome. Monteux's version of the *Symphonie fantastique* is among the best of the medium-priced issues, with a thrilling finale, and it is given here without a break in the slow movement. The recording is admirably vivid throughout, although in the symphony the upper strings have not quite the richness one would find in a modern recording; and the Ansermet sound balance is a little brittle in the upper register. But the transfers are sophisticated, and there is much to enjoy here.

Bernstein, Leonard (born 1918)

Candide: overture.

*** Decca KSXC 6811 [Lon. 5-7031]. Los Angeles PO, Mehta – COPLAND: *Appalachian Spring*; GERSHWIN: *American in Paris.****

Bernstein's witty little overture makes a splendid curtain-raiser for a finely planned coupling of Copland and Gershwin, distinguished by excellent performances and glowing recording. The cassette is brilliantly transferred. The level is high; there seems a marginal lack of body in the middle frequencies, and for best results a slight increase of bass and decrease of treble are useful.

97

(i) *Candide: overture; Fancy Free:* complete; *On the Town: Three dances (1, The great lover displays himself; 2, Lonely town; 3, Times Square);* (ii) *Prelude, fugue and riffs.*
> (M) ** CBS 40-61816. (i) New York PO, the composer; (ii) Benny Goodman and Columbia Jazz Combo.

Candide: overture; Fancy Free: excerpts; *On the Town:* Finale, Act 1; *Times Square; On the Waterfront: Symphonic suite; West Side Story: Symphonic dances.*
> *(*) Decca Phase 4 KPFC 4211. RPO, Rogers.

The CBS collection of some of Leonard Bernstein's most approachable works, most of them with jazz overtones, and including both of the sailor-based dramatic pieces, makes an excellent mid-price issue. The overture to *Candide* is one of the most exhilarating of the century, an equivalent to Rossini. These performances are irrepressible, and the recording is cleanly transferred. There is some lack of range in the treble, however, which makes the resonance tend to tire the ear in the overture and the *Prelude, fugue and riffs.* The quality is otherwise good.

Eric Rogers directs his performances with gusto and obvious enjoyment, as his somewhat naïve sleeve-note confirms. The recording is vivid, but very close, and this allows only a limited dynamic range. The overall effect combines with the conductor's relative lack of subtlety to present the music in an unsatisfactorily deadpan manner, though there is no lack of excitement.

West Side Story: Symphonic dances.
> (M) **(*) DG Privilege 3335 210. San Francisco SO, Ozawa –
> GERSHWIN: *Piano concerto.***(*)

Ozawa's performance, helped by DG's rich atmospheric recording, is more seductive than the composer's own (on disc). The result is vivid and attractive, and Bernstein's cunningly made selection of dances emerges as a very successful concert piece in its own right, particularly with this approach, which innocently conceals any sentimentality. The cassette transfer is of good quality but has not quite the upper range of the disc, which means that the basic resonance is not as cleanly handled as on the LP. But it still makes enjoyable listening.

Berwald, Franz (1796–1868)

Grand septet in B flat major.
> *** CRD CRDC 4044. Nash Ens.
> – HUMMEL: *Septet.****

Berwald's only *Septet* is a work of genuine quality and deserves a secure place in the repertory instead of on its periphery. It dates from 1828 and is for the same forces as the Beethoven *Septet*; the invention is lively and the ideas have charm. It is eminently well played by the Nash Ensemble and finely recorded. The transfer offers sound that is warm, yet clean in detail; it is altogether excellent, and this issue joins the slender rank of chamber-music tapes that can be recommended unreservedly.

Bizet, Georges (1838–75)

L'Arlésienne: Suites Nos. 1 and 2; Carmen: Suites Nos. 1 and 2.
> *(**) CBS 40-76857 [Col. XMT 34503] (omits *Intermezzo* in

L'Arlésienne Suite No. 2).
National PO, Stokowski.

L'Arlésienne: Suites Nos. 1 and 2;
Carmen: Suite No. 1.
- (M) *** HMV TC-SXLP 30276.
  French National Radio Orch.,
  Beecham.
- ** DG 3300 182 [id.]. Berlin PO,
  Karajan.

L'Arlésienne: Suites Nos. 1 and 2;
Carmen: Suite No. 1; Suite No. 2: La
garde montante; Danse bohème
(only).
- (B) ** DG Heliodor 3348 173.
  Hague Resident Orch.,
  Otterloo.

L'Arlésienne: Suite No. 1; Suite No.
2: Farandole (only); Carmen: Suites
Nos. 1 and 2.
- (M) **(*) Decca Ace of Diamonds KSDC 492. New Philharmonia Orch., Munch.

L'Arlésienne: Suite No. 1; Carmen:
Suites Nos. 1 and 2.
- (M) *(*) Philips 7317 095.
  Lamoureux Orch., Marke-
  vitch.

The characteristic Beecham swagger in
the opening *Prélude* to *Carmen* is unique;
and his use of the cymbals too is marvellously telling. But it is the glowing woodwind detail that shows the Beecham
magic at its most individual. Sonically the
recordings are not as rich as the best of
recent versions, but the sound is undoubtedly vivid and there is no lack of sparkle
in the upper range. These performances
are incomparable in many ways, and
the bright clean cassette transfer recom-
mends this issue above all others in this
repertoire.

Munch's recording was originally
issued in Decca's Phase Four series, and
there is no doubt that the sound is extraordinarily vivid. Although the last
degree of refinement is missing in favour
of bright colours and forward projection,

this remains a very attractive issue. There
is plenty of orchestral brilliance, and the
many felicitous details of woodwind scoring, for which Bizet is justly famous, are
projected without undue exaggeration.
Generally the readings are stylish, and if
the last ounce of swagger is missing, the
playing is still infectiously lively.

Although different copies seem to vary
slightly in their degree of refinement, the
Stokowski tape is one of CBS's better
issues. The resonance of the recording brings a lack of absolute clarity
in Stokowski's swaggering *Carmen
Prélude*, but generally the sound has both
clarity and bloom. On the *L'Arlésienne*
side the higher level of transfer brings
plenty of projection, although on one
copy tried there was a hint of coarseness
too. These performances were certainly
among the finest that Stokowski
recorded shortly before his death. The
polish and vitality of the playing are striking, from the opening bar of the *Carmen
Prélude*, taken at a cracking pace but
never sounding rushed. The liner leaflet
says ominously 'Bizet–Stokowski', but
in the event the conductor leaves the
scores virtually intact, except for the
omission of the *Intermezzo* from
L'Arlésienne Suite No. 2. His obviously
romantic approach to the lyrical music of
both works never becomes too indulgent,
and the panache of the music-making is
headily enjoyable.

Karajan's Berlin Philharmonic performance of the *L'Arlésienne* incidental
music is more idiomatic than his earlier
set with the Philharmonia; indeed the
playing is splendidly alive throughout,
with plenty of character and bite. The
recording of the *First Suite* (alone on the
first side of the cassette) is especially attractive, warm and atmospheric but not
lacking immediacy. Side two is good too,
but the *Carmen suite*, although brilliantly
played, has been transferred with less
than ideal sparkle – the percussive effects
do not come through with quite the glitter they really need. Even so, this makes
enjoyable listening.

The Hague Heliodor coupling offers a suite from *L'Arlésienne* to each side and fills up with the *Carmen* excerpts. Generally the orchestral playing is good and the sound vivid. The playing is crisply projected and enjoyable for its bright-eyed spontaneity. There is a touch of brashness occasionally, as in the *Carmen Prélude* and the *Danse bohème*, but generally the recording has been transferred skilfully on to cassette. At Heliodor price, this is certainly competitive.

Markevitch's selection is well played and vividly characterized. However, the rich, reverberant recording has provided some transfer problems and the tuttis tend to be clouded, although the music's gentler moments have plenty of glow and bloom.

Jeux d'enfants (Children's Games): Suite.
> (M) ** HMV TC-EXE 69. Philharmonia Orch., Giulini – DVOŘÁK: *Symphony No. 9; Carnaval overture.***

A brightly played and brilliantly recorded account of Bizet's charming suite makes a sizeable extra bonus for Giulini's recording of the *New World*, especially as the tape includes the *Carnaval overture* too.

Symphony in C major.
> *** Argo KZRC 719 [id.]. Academy of St Martin-in-the-Fields, Marriner – PROKOFIEV: *Symphony No. 1.****
> (M) *** HMV TC-SXLP 30260. French National Radio Orch., Beecham – BERLIOZ: *Les Troyens excerpts*; DELIBES: *Le Roi s'amuse.***(*)

Symphony in C major; L'Arlésienne: Suite No. 1; Suite No. 2: Menuet; Farandole.
> ** Decca KSXC 6350. Suisse Romande Orch., Gibson.

Symphony in C major; Jeux d'enfants: Suite; La Jolie Fille de Perth: Suite.
> (M) **(*) DG Privilege 3335 238. ORTF Orch., Martinon.

Marriner's performance is beautifully played and richly recorded, in a warm, resonant acoustic. Perhaps there is a trifle too much reverberation, but it is easy to adjust, and the wit of the finale is not blunted: this is irrepressibly gay and high-spirited. With an equally successful coupling this is a very desirable tape; the transfer offers demonstration quality throughout.

No one has ever matched Sir Thomas Beecham in the way he brought out the spring-like qualities in Bizet's youthful symphony. The playing of the French orchestra is not quite so polished as that of Marriner's group, but Sir Thomas's panache more than makes amends, and the slow movement is delightful. The recording is even more reverberant than the Argo version, which gives a bigness of scale to the performance, if posing problems of slight excess of resonance in the transfer. However, this has been skilfully managed and the sound is rich, with no lack of sparkle or detail.

Although Martinon's performance of the *Symphony* has not quite the magic of the Marriner or Beecham accounts, it is still very good indeed. The reading is crisp and fresh-sounding, if somewhat lightweight. Martinon favours brisk tempi, not only in the *Symphony* but also in the faster movements of the two suites. The *Galop* which ends *Jeux d'enfants* is taken at almost breakneck speed. However, the *Symphony*'s slow movement is nicely turned, and the little march which opens *Jeux d'enfants* is most felicitous in its dainty pointing. The sparkle of the music-making is well conveyed by the cassette transfer, which is clear and truthful.

Gibson's performance is given a first-rate Decca recording, but in the last analysis the music's presentation (like the generous coupling) is a little faceless.

Carmen (opera): complete.

*** Decca K 11 K 33 [Lon. 5-13115]. Tatiana Troyanos, Placido Domingo, José van Dam, Kiri te Kanawa, John Alldis Choir, LPO, Solti.

*** DG 3371 040 [id.]. Teresa Berganza, Placido Domingo, Sherrill Milnes, Ileana Cotrubas, Ambrosian Singers, LSO, Abbado.

*** HMV TC-SLS 5021. Victoria de los Angeles, Nicolai Gedda, Ernest Blanc, Janine Micheau, Chorus and Orch. of Radio-diffusion Française, Petits Chanteurs de Versailles, Beecham.

(***) DG 3371 006 [id.]. Marilyn Horne, James McCracken, Tom Krause, Adriana Maliponte, Manhattan Opera Chorus, Children's Chorus, Metropolitan Opera Orch., Bernstein.

(***) RCA RK 40004 [ARK 3 2542]. Leontyne Price, Franco Corelli, Robert Merrill, Mirella Freni, Vienna State Opera Chorus, Vienna Boys' Choir, Vienna PO, Karajan.

Few operas have been more successfully recorded over the years than *Carmen*, and the five finest issues have all been issued in tape form. Unfortunately two of them, the DG Horne/Bernstein and RCA Price/Karajan sets, have been muffed in their transfers, though it seems likely that improved copies of this DG version may filter through eventually.

Quite apart from superb playing and singing, stunningly brilliant recording and arguably the most satisfying solution yet to the vexed question of text, Solti's Decca version is remarkable for its new illumination of characters everyone thinks they know inside out. Tatiana Troyanos is quite simply the subtlest Carmen on record. The blatant sexuality which is so often accepted as the essential ingredient in Carmen's character is here replaced by a far more insidious fascination, for there is a degree of vulnerability in this heroine. You can understand why she falls in love and then out again. Escamillo too is more readily sympathetic, not just the flashy matador who steals the hero's girl, in some ways the custodian of rationality; whereas Don José is revealed as weak rather than just a victim. Troyanos's singing is delicately seductive too, with no hint of vulgarity, while the others make up the most consistent singing cast recorded to date. Solti like Bernstein and Abbado uses spoken dialogue and a modification of the Oeser edition, deciding in each individual instance whether to accept amendments to Bizet's first thoughts. Fine as other versions of this much-recorded opera are, Solti's dramatic and sensitive account must take first place. The cassette transfer is outstanding, losing little if any of the tingling immediacy and drama of the discs.

Superbly disciplined, Abbado's performance nails its colours to the mast at the very start in a breathtakingly fast account of the opening prelude. Through the four acts there are other examples of idiosyncratic tempi, but the whole entertainment hangs together with keen compulsion, reflecting the fact that these same performers – Sherrill Milnes as Escamillo excepted – took part in the Edinburgh Festival production directly associated with this recording project. Conductor and orchestra can take a large share of credit for the performance's success, for though the singing is never less than enjoyable, it is on the whole less characterful than on some rival sets. Teresa Berganza is a seductive if somewhat unsmiling Carmen – not without sensuality, and producing consistently beautiful tone, but lacking some of the flair which makes for a three-dimensional portrait. If you want a restrained and thoughtful view, then Tatiana Troyanos in Solti's set, also opposite the admirably consistent Placido Domingo, is preferable. Ileana Cotrubas as Micaela is not always as sweetly steady as she can be; Milnes makes a heroic matador. The spoken dialogue is excellently produced, and the sound is vivid, betraying not at all that the sessions took place in different studios (in London as well as Edinburgh). The transfer level is – as usual with DG – moderate, and the wide dynamic range of the recording means that some of the detail is not as sharply focused as it might be. The choruses too sound atmospheric rather than crystal-clear, and there is not the vivid projection of the Solti Decca set, although the solo voices are natural, and the rich, somewhat mellow sound matches the Berganza/Abbado conception quite effectively. The recording has good perspective: the distant crowd in the finale registers dramatically. The set is handsomely presented, with removable tape boxes, following the disc format in layout; but the print of the slim four-language libretto is very small.

Beecham's approach to Bizet's well-worn score is no less fresh and revealing. Like Bernstein's, his speeds are not always conventional but they always *sound* right. And unlike so many strong-willed conductors in opera Beecham allows his singers room to breathe and to expand their characterizations. It seems he specially chose de los Angeles to be his Carmen although she had never sung the part on the stage before making the recording. He conceived the *femme fatale* not as the usual glad-eyed character, but as someone far more subtly seductive, winning her admirers not so much by direct assault and high voltage as by genuine charm and real femininity. De los Angeles suits this conception perfectly; her characterization of Carmen is absolutely bewitching, and when in the Quintet scene she says *Je suis amoureuse* one believes her absolutely. Naturally

the other singers are not nearly so dominant as this, but they make admirable foils: Gedda is pleasantly light-voiced as ever, Janine Micheau is a sweet Micaela, and Ernest Blanc makes an attractive Escamillo. The stereo recording does not add to things in the way that the best Decca opera recordings do, and there seems to have been little attempt at stage production, but the sound is warm yet suitably brilliant, and the recording does not show its age. The cassette transfer is also successful, although with early copies of the first cassette (not the second) some taming of an over-fierce treble was needed. Later copies seem to be more uniform in quality, which is certainly vivid throughout.

It was bold of DG to choose the USA for the Bernstein set; this was the first major opera recording undertaken there for many years. It was based on the Metropolitan Opera's spectacular production of *Carmen* with Bernstein conducting the same cast, and the sessions clearly gained from being interleaved with live performances. Bizet scholars may argue about details of the text used in the performances: Bernstein adopted the original version of 1875 with spoken dialogue but with variations designed to suit a stage production. Some of his slow tempi will be questioned too, but what really matters is the authentic tingle of dramatic tension which impregnates the whole entertainment. Never before, not even in Beecham's classic set, had the full theatrical flavour of Bizet's score been conveyed, and Marilyn Horne – occasionally coarse in expression – gives a most fully satisfying reading of the heroine's role, a great vivid characterization, warts and all. The rest of the cast similarly works to Bernstein's consistent overall plan. The singing is not all perfect, but it is always vigorous and colourful, and so (despite often poor French accents) is the spoken dialogue. A presentation hard to resist, with generally atmospheric recording. Unfortunately the DG cassette transfer was a very early one and severely

lacks brilliance and life. It is only acceptable at all if the Dolby circuitry is left
unused.

With Karajan's version much depends
on the listener's reaction to the conductor's tempi and to Leontyne Price's
smoky-toned Carmen. Comparing other
recordings of the regular version with
sung recitative, the Beecham set remains
the most magical, but if you are looking
for a heroine who is a sexual threat as well
as a charmer, Price is the more convincing. Corelli has moments of coarseness,
but his is still a heroic performance.
Robert Merrill sings with gloriously firm
tone, while Freni is, as ever, an enchanting Micaela. As a performance this set
remains a keen competitor, with Karajan
always inspired in his fresh look at a
much-played score. Unfortunately the
RCA cassette version is of poor quality.
The very opening is aggressive, with
little bloom; moreover side breaks are
disfigured by quick fades (the one at
the end of the first side is particularly
inept).

Carmen: highlights.
  *** Decca KCET 621 (from above
    set with Troyanos; Solti).
  *** DG 3300 478 [id.] (from
    above set with Horne;
    Bernstein).
  (M) *(**) HMV Greensleeve TC-
    ESD 7047 (from above set with
    de los Angeles; Beecham).
  **(*) Decca KCET 622 (from
    above set with Troyanos; Solti)
    – BORODIN: *Prince Igor:
    Polovtsian dances***; TCHAI-
    KOVSKY: *Eugene Onegin* ex-
    cerpts.**(*)

The generous selection from Solti's set
on KCET 621 has transferred to tape
admirably. The wide reverberation of the
recording offers no problems, and the
level is high. The solo voices have fine
presence and naturalness, and the recording is rich and weighty, though per-

haps lacking the last degree of sharp-
edged presence in the big choral
numbers.

With Micaela completely omitted, the
selection from the Bernstein set is hardly
fair to Bizet, but if anything it underlines
the idiosyncratic quality of that Met.
performance, with the forceful, vibrant
contribution of Marilyn Horne well to
the fore. Preludes, entractes, Quintet and
Card scene are all welcome inclusions.
The transfer has an admirably dramatic,
vivid quality. Both voices and orchestra
are given striking clarity and projection, and the closing scene between Don
José and Carmen, with the chorus
coming from a distance, is a demonstration of just how much detail and
atmosphere a modern tape transfer can
provide. What a pity that the complete
set was not managed with the same
skill.

The Beecham/los Angeles tape offers
a delightful collection of plums from
Bizet's masterly score, and anyone who,
for whatever reason, decides to get one of
the other complete sets might consider
this as a supplement. The recording retains the lively qualities of the original,
but the tape transfer has moments when
the refinement slips at peaks, especially
on side two, which is transferred at marginally higher level than side one.
However, this is not too serious.

The collection on KCET 622 is centred
around Solti and includes an attractive
selection of colourful and atmospheric
opera excerpts taken from several Solti
recordings, notably *Carmen* and *Eugene
Onegin*. The sound in the items from
Carmen (including the *Prelude,
Habañera, Gypsy song, Toreador march*
and chorus, plus various entractes) is
marginally less vivid than in the complete
set but remains atmospheric in a characteristically Decca way. However, at premium price, some might question the
value of this reissue.

Carmen: highlights: *Prelude; Habañera; Seguidilla and Duet; Gypsy song; Quintet; Card trio; Duet and Finale.*

**(*) Decca Phase 4 KPFC 4204. Marilyn Horne, Michele Molese, soloists, Royal Philharmonic Chorus and Orch., Henry Lewis.

Perhaps the most fascinating tape of *Carmen* excerpts is the Decca Phase Four issue with Marilyn Horne, made some years before her complete New York recording. She it was who was the singing voice behind Dorothy Dandridge in the film *Carmen Jones*; and here, with a decade more of experience, she is even more searingly compelling as the fire-eating heroine. There is not only dramatic presence but musical control too, and the flair of the performance is well matched by the spread of Phase Four sound. The side-lengths are not generous, but the sparkle of the recording makes some amends, and Henry Lewis's conducting has no lack of flair. This was an early Decca transfer, but it was well managed.

Les Pêcheurs de perles (The Pearl Fishers; opera): complete.

** HMV TC-SLS 5113. Ileana Cotrubas, Alain Vanzo, Guillermo Sarabia, Roger Soyer, Paris Opera Chorus and Orch., Prêtre.

A modern version of this most atmospheric opera was certainly needed, but Prêtre's set is a mixed success. Ileana Cotrubas is superb as the High Priestess, Leila, projecting character as well as singing beautifully. The tenor, Alain Vanzo, is also most stylish, but after that the snags begin, not just with the singing (Sarabia a variably focused baritone) but with the conducting (Prêtre generally fast, unlilting and unfeeling) and the recording (not sufficiently atmospheric). In

principle it may seem a positive gain to have the original 1863 score reinstated, but it is hard not to feel disappointed when the great duet for the pearl fishers culminates not in a rich reprise of the big melody but in a tinkly little waltz theme. The transfer is smooth, with generally good detail and the perspectives of distance well managed.

COLLECTION

'Favourite composer': (i) *L'Arlésienne: Suites Nos. 1–2; Jeux d'enfants: Suite; La Jolie Fille de Perth: Suite; Symphony in C major;* (ii) *Carmen:* highlights.

(B) *** Decca KDPC 559/60. (i) Suisse Romande Orch., Ansermet; (ii) Resnik, del Monaco, Krause; Schippers.

An excellent two-tape set at little more than the cost of one premium-priced cassette offers a first-class anthology of some of Bizet's finest music. The performances of the *Symphony* and orchestral suites are first-class, and the recording is warm and vivid throughout, although the selection from *Carmen* does not supply as much presence to the voices as one might expect. In this respect the tape set is to be preferred to the discs, as generally the cassette sound is marginally sharper-edged. Musically the items from the opera come up surprisingly well, with Resnik projecting convincingly, the *Toreador song* of Tom Krause suitably forthright and the Don José of Mario del Monaco dramatically convincing with its plebeian lack of refinement.

Bliss, Arthur
(1891–1975)

A Colour symphony; Things to Come
(incidental music for H. G. Wells
film).
> *(**) HMV TC-ASD 3416. RPO,
> Groves.

Bliss's *Colour symphony* comes from
1922, and this is its first recording since
the composer's own, made in the mid-
1950s. Inspired by a chance encounter
with a book on heraldry, Bliss conceived
this series of mood pictures on the theme
of the symbolic meanings associated with
the primary colours. The work is too episodic to be truly symphonic but it is nonetheless highly effective and is expertly
scored. It comes into its own in this sympathetic performance. *Things to Come* is
given in an extended form admirably
assembled by Christopher Palmer, who
has also scored the opening *Prologue*,
since the full score and parts do not sur-
vive. This work dates more than the
Symphony and its style is at times somewhat eclectic. But its invention is often
attractive, and the splendid *March* offers
what is perhaps the single most memorable idea to come from the pen of its composer. Unfortunately the resonant recording has not transferred well to tape. In
the *Colour symphony* there are rough
edges to the sound and in fact no real
sophistication of timbre, while the finale
becomes turgid at its climax. *Things to
Come* fares slightly better (the *March*
comes off relatively unscathed) but again
in the finale the reverberation proves difficult to contain.

Concerto for two pianos (arr.
Phillips).
> (M) *** HMV Greensleeve TC-
> ESD 7065. Cyril Smith, Phyllis
> Sellick (pianos), City of Birm-

ingham SO, Arnold – ARNOLD
and JACOB: *Concertos*.***

Bliss worked with Clifford Phillips to arrange his *Two-piano concerto* in
a three-handed version for Cyril Smith
and Phyllis Sellick to play. That was the
work's second transformation: it had
started life as a concerto for piano, tenor
strings and percussion in 1921, and was
turned into a double piano concerto three
years later. The vigour of early Bliss
makes for attractive results, with echoes
of *Petrushka* and Debussy nicely worked
in. If you think Bliss cribbed from the
Ravel *Piano concerto* in his finale, you are
wrong: Bliss wrote his concerto well
before the Ravel appeared. Superbly
played and richly recorded, it makes a
delightful companion piece for the other
two works on this cassette. The warmly
resonant recording has transferred
vividly, and the sound has plenty of life
and presence.

(i) *Violoncello concerto. Miracle in
the Gorbals* (ballet): *suite*.
> *(**) HMV TC-ASD 3342.
> Bournemouth SO, Berglund, (i)
> with Arto Noras (cello).

Bliss originally called his *Cello concerto* a concertino. He wrote it for
Rostropovich, who first played it at the
1970 Aldeburgh Festival, and it was
Britten who persuaded the composer to
change the diminutive title. With a passionate opening of Brahmsian eloquence,
the first movement is one of the most inspired that Bliss ever wrote. The slow
movement, with its rhapsodic style and
elegiac atmosphere, is not so sharply
memorable, but the finale has splendid
vigour and momentum. Arto Noras
is the superbly eloquent soloist, and
Berglund's accompaniment, pulsing
with life, is little short of inspired. The
coupling, an extended selection from the
Miracle in the Gorbals ballet, also shows
Bliss at his most imaginative; the invention is of consistently high quality. Again

the orchestral playing is full of life and spontaneity, and the recording is highly spectacular. The cassette is often vivid, but it has an element of coarseness at the climaxes of the ballet music and never reaches the demonstration standard of the equivalent LP. The transfer of the *Concerto* is acceptable. The recording is well balanced but lacks range and detail.

Kenilworth: suite.
*** Decca KSXC 6820. Grimethorpe Colliery Band, Howarth – ELGAR: *Severn suite* **(*); HOLST: *Moorside suite;* IRELAND: *Comedy overture.****

Bliss's *Kenilworth suite* shows him at his most colourful (the music conjures up the pageantry that accompanied the visit of Queen Elizabeth I to Kenilworth Castle in 1575). This performance is brilliantly played and recorded with admirable clarity and sparkle. The inner detail has notable refinement and bloom, and the couplings, no less finely played and recorded, make this issue a very attractive anthology.

(i) *Pastoral* (*Lie strewn the white flocks*); (ii) *A Knot of Riddles.*
** Pye ZCP 507. (i) Sybil Michelow (mezzo-soprano), Bruckner-Mahler Choir of London; (ii) John Shirley-Quirk (bar.); both with London CO, Morris.

Bliss's eightieth year produced a good crop of first recordings of his work. These are two attractive song cycles that show his art at its least demanding. He conceived the *Pastoral* as a classical fantasy, linking verse from widely different sources, and using mezzo-soprano, chorus, flute (beautifully played here by Norman Knight), timpani and strings. *A Knot of Riddles* is just as easy on the ear – arguably too easy – with English riddles

translated from the Anglo-Saxon and provided with a solution by the soloist after each one. This is a much later work, written for the Cheltenham Festival in 1963. It is here sung with fine point by John Shirley-Quirk. The recording is good, but this was a very early Pye cassette, and the transfer, although smooth, is not striking in presence.

Bloch, Ernest (1880–1959)

Schelomo: Hebrew rhapsody (for cello and orchestra).
(M) ** DG Privilege 3335 201 [id.]. Pierre Fournier, Berlin PO, Wallenstein – ELGAR: *Cello concerto.***
(***) HMV TC-ASD 3334 [Angel 4xs 37256]. Mstislav Rostropovich, French National Radio Orch., Bernstein – SCHUMANN: *Cello concerto.*(*)

(i) *Schelomo*; (ii) *Suite for viola and orchestra.*
(M) ** Turnabout KTVC 34622. (i) Laszlo Varga, Westphalian SO, Landau; (ii) Milton Katims, Seattle SO, Siegle.

Fournier's fervent advocacy is impressive, and although his coupling with Elgar is somewhat let down by the recording balance – the cello is far too close and orchestral detail is not fully revealed – the sound is otherwise excellent and the transfer well managed.

Unfortunately the HMV tape cannot be recommended, even though the collaboration of Rostropovich and Bernstein produced a superb performance, the rhapsodic flow of the music-making conveying total concentration from the deeply meditative opening phrases (*con somma espressione*) onwards. The recording, rich and pleasing on LP, has been given unrefined sound on tape; the upper register of the recording is fuzzy and unfocused, especially at climaxes. Under these circumstances the Turnabout cassette is well worth considering. Varga's performance is totally committed, and although Rostropovich brings a degree of ecstasy and fervour to *Schelomo* that Varga does not match, this is still fine playing. The recording of the *Suite for viola and orchestra* is the only one available at present. The work dates from 1919 and was originally written for viola and piano. The music is highly atmospheric and colourful, though at times just a little diffuse. Katims plays eloquently. The viola is forwardly balanced and at times the evocative orchestral score is masked. But the orchestra itself is admirably balanced and the acoustic warm and open. The sound on tape is bold and clear, with plenty of atmosphere, both soloists projected well forward, but with plenty of body to their tone. An excellent cassette.

Boccherini, Luigi (1743–1805)

Violoncello concerto No. 2 in D major.

 *** DG 3300 974 [id.]. Mstislav Rostropovich, Zurich Collegium Musicum, Sacher – TARTINI and VIVALDI: *Concertos*.***

Although essentially a performance in the grand manner (with Rostropovich providing his own cadenzas), this music-making also has tremendous vitality, with extremely lively outer movements to balance the eloquence of the *Adagio*. The forceful nature of the performance is short on charm and so perhaps a little out of character for an essentially elegant

composer like Boccherini; but Rostropovich is so compelling that reservations are swept aside. He is given an alert accompaniment by Sacher, and the recording has fine body and presence. The tape transfer too has excellent range and detail.

String quintets in E major, Op. 13/5; in A minor, Op. 47/1.

 (M) ** Turnabout KTVC 34094. Günter Kehr Quintet.

The *E major Quintet* is the source of the famous 'Boccherini Minuet'. It is beautifully played here, with delicacy and restraint, and one feels it deserves its fame. The work as a whole is attractive, particularly the opening movement, which is harmonically rich, to remind the listener almost of Mozart. It is played here with warmth and gives much pleasure. Only in the finale does one feel that the players miscalculate, but it is partly Boccherini's fault for writing yet another *galant* movement instead of a rondo with more fire to it. This tendency to blandness is felt throughout the A minor work, which is pleasant but less distinguished. But here the players could have helped with more bite to the outer movements. The recording is warm-toned but with the microphones very near the players, which exaggerates their reluctance to make contrasts of both style and dynamic. The cassette transfer is a good one, reflecting the LP quality faithfully.

Boieldieu, François Adrien (1775–1834)

(i) *Harp concerto in C major;* (ii) *Piano concerto in F major.*

 (M) ** Turnabout KTVC 34148.
 (i) Marie-Claire Jamet, Paul

Kuentz CO of Paris, Kuentz; (ii) Martin Galling, Innsbruck SO, Wagner.

Marie-Claire Jamet plays the *Harp concerto* with style and refinement, and she is especially good in the engaging closing rondo. The balance is well managed and Paul Kuentz sees that the tuttis have plenty of life. The *Piano concerto* is a two-movement work with an attractive set of variations on a pastoral theme as its second section, which ends rather abruptly. It is played here with character and makes a good coupling, even if it is not as memorable as the work for harp. The cassette transfer is clear but a trifle hard-toned. The level is

Boismortier, Joseph
(1691–1775)

Bassoon concerto in D major.
   (M) ** Turnabout KTVC 134039. George Zukerman, Württemberg CO, Faerber – MOZART: *Bassoon concerto*; WEBER: *Andante* etc.**

In order to provide equal measure on the Turnabout cassette of bassoon concertos by Mozart and Weber, this short bonus has been added which is not present on the equivalent LP. It is not great music, perhaps, but very pleasant withal, and the transfer is of good quality. Zukerman is a persuasive soloist and he is well accompanied. His attractively 'woody' tone production is well caught by the recording here.

Boito, Arrigo
(1842–1918)

Mefistofele (opera): Prologue.
   (**) DG 3370 022 [id.]. Nicolai Ghiaurov, Vienna State Opera Chorus, Vienna PO, Bernstein – LISZT: *Faust symphony.****

Although there are two recordings of the complete opera (neither of them available on cassette), the only other complete version of the Prologue is Toscanini's classic account from 1954 (now long deleted on disc). Bernstein thus has the field to himself both in disc and cassette formats. This recording was made in Vienna and finds Ghiaurov in excellent form. The sound is wide in range but could generally be described as acceptable rather than distinguished. Moreover, unusually for DG, the level of the transfer has been miscalculated, so that the cataclysmic effects at the opening offer severe distortion, though the quality improves later.

Bolcom, William
(born 1938)

Frescoes.
   *** Advent F 1036 (see p. xxiii) [id.]. Bruce Mather (piano and harmonium), Pierrette LePage (piano and harpsichord) – MILHAUD: *La Création du monde*; WEILL: *Kleine Dreigroschenmusik.****

William Bolcom's *Frescoes* provides an unintimidating avant-garde work to be linked with music by Milhaud and Kurt Weill. The piece divides into two sections (*War in Heaven* and *The Caves of*

Orcus) but the illustrative technique is similar in both, creating kaleidoscopic changes of mood by the use of piano (or pianos), sustained writing for the harmonium and delicate harpsichord embroidery. The recording makes great use of spatial effects, forward and back as well as left and right; the impressive realism of the sound (at times the grand piano seems right in the room) helps to create considerable atmosphere. But the performance itself has a nagging tension (although the music lightens almost to the point of humour at times). A fascinating and worthwhile expedition for the adventurous listener: there is nothing wildly outlandish here, but much that is imaginative.

Borodin, Alexander
(1833–87)

(i) *In the Steppes of Central Asia*; (ii) *Prince Igor: Polovtsian dances.*
- (B) ** Decca KDPC 2 7055. Suisse Romande Orch., Ansermet, (ii) with chorus – MUSSORGSKY: *Night on the Bare Mountain**(*); RIMSKY-KORSAKOV: *Scheherazade* etc.***

Ansermet's performance of *In the Steppes of Central Asia* could do with more of a sense of blossoming romanticism, but the piece is clearly laid out and vividly recorded. The *Polovtsian dances* (also available differently coupled; see below) are equally reliably done, and the excitement of the closing pages is helped by the excellent recording, with a clearly focused chorus.

Symphony No. 2 in B minor.
- *(*) HMV TC-ASD 3193. Bournemouth SO, Brusilow – BALA-

KIREV: *Russia*; RIMSKY-KORSAKOV: *Skazka.**(*)

Symphony No. 2; (i) Prince Igor: Polovtsian dances.
- (M) *(*) Supraphon 041126. Czech PO, Smetáček, (i) with chorus.

Smetáček's performance of Borodin's masterly *Second Symphony* is a fine one, with plenty of drama in the first movement, and a strong, throbbing scherzo. The slow movement has genuine Slavic character, and the finale has sparkle and a lightness of touch without sounding insubstantial. The *Polovtsian dances* are excitingly done too. The recording is good, well balanced, with plenty of life and detail, and the transfer to tape, if lacking the last degree of brilliance, is serviceable. This is on the whole preferable to the HMV alternative. Brusilow's opening is emphatic to the point of being portentous, and the overall shape of the first movement is not very tautly held together. The scherzo sparkles, and there are moments of excitement in the development of the first movement; but for the most part the performance is not really distinguished, although this cassette offers unusual and attractive couplings which may be a decisive factor for some collectors. However, the sound on tape is somewhat inflated. The massed strings at the end of the slow movement are undoubtedly rich and full, but the quality is not always completely refined and the dynamic range is not very wide.

Symphony No. 3 in A minor (Unfinished).
- (M) *** Philips 7317 032. LPO, Lloyd-Jones – *Concert of Russian music.****

Lloyd-Jones's recording of the incomplete *Third Symphony* is part of a highly recommendable medium-priced anthology of Russian music: see our Concerts section below. The transfer is admirably vivid.

Prince Igor: Polovtsian dances.
- *** Decca KCET 622. LSO Chorus, LSO, Solti – BIZET: *Carmen* excerpts; TCHAIKOVSKY: *Eugene Onegin* excerpts.
- (M) *** Decca KCSP 127. Solti (as above) – *Concert.****
- (M) *** HMV TC-EXE 193. Beecham Choral Society, RPO, Beecham – BALAKIREV: *Symphony No. 1.***(*)
- **(*) DG 3336 379 [id.]. Chicago SO, Barenboim – MUSSORGSKY: *Night on the Bare Mountain****; RIMSKY-KORSAKOV: *Capriccio espagnol*; *Russian Easter Festival overture.***(*)
- ** Decca KSXC 2268. Radio Lausanne Choir, Chœur des Jeunes, Suisse Romande Orch., Ansermet – RIMSKY-KORSAKOV: *Scheherazade.***

Decca have reissued Solti's fine account coupled to excerpts from *Carmen* and *Eugene Onegin*. The new transfer is stunningly vivid, of demonstration quality from first bar to last, and the couplings are undoubtedly attractive. But the premium price for this reissue is questionable, and Solti's version is also available on KCSP 127, the anthology called *Georg Solti conducts*, a most attractive tape at medium price (discussed in detail below, in our Concerts section), while Ansermet's account is also included in an excellent double compilation of Russian music (see above).

The transfer of Beecham's performance is very successful, with vivid detail and plenty of impact. Beecham misses out the percussion-led opening dance, but plays the remainder of the score with a charismatic mixture of lyricism and sparkle. He builds a splendid final climax, and with remarkably good recording this can certainly

be recommended if the coupling is suitable.

Barenboim's version is splendidly played and has plenty of life and impetus. Indeed one hardly misses the chorus, so lively is the orchestral playing. However, at the very opening there is an absence of sheer glitter in the percussion-led opening dance and a slight lack of upper range in the transfer (our review copy was a British-manufactured one). Later, however, the sound expands spectacularly – the bass drum is caught with aplomb – and the colour and detail of the orchestra are impressive.

Ansermet's performance is a reliably good one, though the tension tends to sag in the passages where the choir – which is not outstanding – is expected to carry the music with only slight support from the orchestra. The end goes well. The recording is bright and clear.

Boyce, William
(1710–79)

Symphonies Nos. 1 in B flat major; 2 in A major; 3 in C major; 4 in F major; 5 in D major; 6 in F major; 7 in B flat major; 8 in D minor.
- *** Argo KZRC 874. Academy of St Martin-in-the-Fields, Marriner.
- (M) ** Turnabout KTVC 34133. Württemberg CO, Faerber.

The eight symphonies recorded here are wonderfully inventive and entertaining. The orchestration is nicely varied; No. 5, for instance, opens with trumpets in a most regal manner, and in the diversity of its melodic and rhythmic patterns evokes the spirit of Handel, as do the broad opening of No. 1, the jollier No. 4 and the slow movement of No. 6.

Marriner provides exhilarating performances in which the rhythmic subtleties, both in fast music and slow, are guaranteed to enchant. The recording, which is characteristically sophisticated, was made in the ample acoustic of St John's, Smith Square. The tape transfer has been rebalanced and is slightly dry in timbre: an increase of bass plus a comparable treble reduction improves the textural warmth without impairing the clarity and detail.

Faerber too is always alive and spirited, so that the vigour and weight of the Württemberg approach are well in keeping with symphonic style. The recording is lively and forward (a trifle thinner on side one than on side two, but always clean). The tape transfer is very well done, bright and clear, and this issue remains competitive at medium price.

(i) *Organ voluntaries Nos. 1, 2, 4 and 10;* (ii) Anthems: *By the waters of Babylon; I have surely built thee a house; O where shall wisdom be found; Turn unto me, O Lord.*

 (M) (***) Saga CA 5440. (i) Arthur Wills (organ); (ii) Ely Cathedral Choir, Wills; Gerald Gifford (organ).

It may seem strange to hear formal eighteenth-century settings of words set dramatically in our century by Sir William Walton, but the music of Boyce is most compelling. The anthems in particular make this an interesting issue, not least because it comes at medium price. The organ voluntaries come as a welcome addition and are used as interludes between the choral items. However, one needs a fairly tolerant ear to enjoy this tape, for the upper focus is fluffy and the texture of the sound insecure.

Brahms, Johannes (1833–97)

Piano concerto No. 1 in D minor, Op. 15.

 *** Decca KSXC 6023. Clifford Curzon, LSO, Szell.
 *** DG 3300 264. Emil Gilels, Berlin PO, Jochum.
 *** Decca KSXC 6728 [Lon. 5-6947]. Radu Lupu, LPO, de Waart.
 **(*) Enigma K 453570. John Lill, Hallé Orch., Loughran.
 (M) *(**) HMV TC-SXLP 30283. Daniel Barenboim, New Philharmonia Orch., Barbirolli.
 ** Advent E 1052 (see p. xxiii) [id.]. Bruno-Leonardo Gelber, Munich PO, Decker.
 (M) *(*) Philips 7317 201. Claudio Arrau, Concertgebouw Orch., Haitink.
 *(*) Decca KSXC 6797 [Lon. 5-7018]. Artur Rubinstein, Israel PO, Mehta.

Curzon has a leonine power that fully matches Brahms's keyboard style and penetrates both the reflective inner world of the slow movement and the abundantly vital and massive opening movement. This is still among the very best versions available, though the recording gives evidence of close-microphone techniques, used within a reverberant acoustic. The strings have a tendency to fierceness, especially in the powerful opening tutti of the first movement, and the piano image spreads a little. Having said this, one must comment with pleasure on the range and body of the cassette sound. The one great blot is that Decca have made their break in the middle of the slow movement.

Among the most recent accounts, that

of Gilels stands out as being to the 1970s what the Curzon was to the 1960s. It has a magisterial strength blended with a warmth, humanity and depth that are altogether inspiring. Jochum is a superb accompanist, and the only reservation is the recording, which though warm does not focus the piano and orchestra in truthful proportion. For all that, however, this remains an altogether outstanding performance artistically, and it has transferred extremely well to tape. In spite of the reverberant acoustic the sound is excellent. (Unfortunately this cassette has been withdrawn in the UK just as we go to press.)

Radu Lupu eschews *Sturm und Drang*, and his is not a reading that compares with the thrilling, dramatic account Szell and Curzon gave us; that remains a classic. Lupu approaches the work through the eyes of a decade when the piano was not the leonine monster it was to become later on in the century. His is a deeply reflective and intelligent performance, full of masterly touches and an affecting poetry that falls short of the thrusting combative power we expect from a Serkin or Curzon. De Waart provides sensitive support and matches Lupu's approach admirably. The reading is a valuable corrective to the accepted view of this masterpiece. Decca produce a particularly truthful sound picture. The acoustic is fresh and open, yet every detail registers its presence, while the relationship of piano and orchestra is ideal. The soloist is not too sharply in focus but sounds as he might in the concert hall with the sound not being unnaturally channelled in the listener's direction. Wide-ranging and full-bodied recording helps too. Not a first choice: Curzon and Gilels are not displaced, but this is an immensely rewarding performance and may be recommended enthusiastically to those who want a second, alternative view.

John Lill and the Hallé Orchestra under James Loughran take a somewhat serious view of Brahms's concerto. The first movement is measured and power-ful, thoughtful rather than extrovert. The slow movement is eloquently shaped and the finale vigorous, but the atmosphere remains comparatively restrained. In its way this is a sturdily satisfying account, and not without poetic feeling, even if the colouring is sometimes sombre. The opening strings lack something in richness of timbre, but the Hallé playing is accomplished. The transfer is of first-rate quality; the opening timpani roll seems for a moment to overwhelm the listener, but that is the only fault. The piano is realistically balanced; the timbre clear and bold rather than warm in quality. The orchestral detail is excellent and the overall sound has plenty of realism and impact.

Barenboim and Barbirolli are superbly recorded on disc, but the tape transfer is not one of EMI's best. The opening tutti is ill-focused, and the upper orchestral detail is not very clean throughout. The piano tone is good, if not outstanding, but the whole sound balance lacks warmth, which is exactly what the performance, heroic and marvellously spacious, needs if it it to make its full effect. Tempi are broad, but the interpretation is sustained by its intensity of concentration. The sound seems marginally richer in the finale.

Bruno-Leonardo Gelber is a young virtuoso from Buenos Aires, and so strong and accomplished a performance of this demanding work is a remarkable achievement. Since Brahms himself was emerging as a young musical lion at the time he wrote the work, there is much to be said for youthful bravura. The Munich Philharmonic Orchestra under Franz Decker provides a sympathetic accompaniment, but the recording dates from 1967 and the wide range of the chrome tape transfer shows its age in the rather fizzy focus of the upper strings. Otherwise the sound is full, and the piano timbre is admirably natural, with plenty of bloom. The balance is good. However, compared with Curzon or Gilels, the result is a little faceless.

Haitink's opening tutti for Arrau is measured, and the forward impulse of the music is rather sluggish. The reading tends to be idiosyncratic and not wholly convincing, although the slow movement undoubtedly has atmosphere and moments of poetry. The recording lacks clarity of inner detail and though the strings have life and the piano timbre is not unnatural the balance is less than ideal. The transfer is well managed (apart from a lapse near the beginning of the first movement when the timpani cause a momentary loss of textural steadiness).

With more than a sprinkling of wrong notes, Rubinstein's Israel recording may not provide a general recommendation, but the character and drive of the man in his late eighties emerge vividly. To hear such a performance once in the concert hall one would readily pay far more. Unfortunately the recording balances the piano far too forwardly, so that the orchestral sound, clean enough on its own, becomes submerged even behind Rubinstein's most casual passagework. The transfer offers vivid quality, the piano timbre bright rather than sonorous.

Piano concerto No. 2 in B flat major, Op. 83.
   *** Advent E 1053 (see p. xxiii) [id.]. Bruno-Leonardo Gelber, RPO, Kempe.
   *** DG 3300 790 [id.]. Maurizio Pollini, Vienna PO, Abbado.
   (***) DG 3300 265. Emil Gilels, Berlin PO, Jochum.
   (M) **(*) RCA Gold Seal GK 11267 [AGK 1 1267]. Sviatoslav Richter, Chicago SO, Leinsdorf.
   ** Decca KSXC 6309. Vladimir Ashkenazy, LSO, Mehta.
   (M) ** DG Privilege 3335 263. Géza Anda, Berlin PO, Karajan.
   (M) *(*) Philips Festivo 7310 052.

   Claudio Arrau, Concertgebouw Orch., Haitink.
   *(*) Decca Phase 4 KPFC 4428. Ilana Vered, RPO, Fistoulari.
(i) *Piano concerto No. 2; Hungarian dances Nos. 1 and 3.*
   ** Philips 7300 293 [id.]. Concertgebouw Orch., Haintink, (i) with Alfred Brendel.

The Advent cassette of the Gelber/Kempe recording of Brahms's *Second Concerto* is superbly full-blooded in the sound picture it presents to the listener. The high-level chrome transfer produces the widest amplitude and range of sound: the bottom octaves of the piano carry a satisfying weight of sonority, yet the upper range has fine presence and bloom. The bass is very slightly over-resonant and needs cutting back just a little; but generally this is magnificent quality. It presents the music-making in the most persuasive light possible and it is a performance that we have previously underestimated on disc. It has striking spontaneity of feeling. The first movement is especially fine, spacious yet powerful, the tension held consistently. The *Andante* is comparably eloquent; the finale has a rippling lightness at the opening which is highly engaging, but develops a degree of lyrical fervour to match the earlier movements yet without ever losing its *grazioso* feeling.

Pollini's account is powerful and impressive, in many ways more classical in feeling than Gilels. He has the measure of the concerto's scale and breadth, and is given excellent support by the Vienna Philharmonic under Abbado. Pollini may not possess the rich humanity of Gilels or create the degree of intensity which distinguished the Barenboim/Barbirolli partnership, but he has unfailing perception and never invests detail with excessive significance. This is among the finest versions now in the catalogue and is excellently recorded. The transfer to cassette, although not at the highest level, is immaculate, with realistic piano timbre.

Gilels's partnership with Jochum produces music-making of rare magic and it is only the want of a sharp focus and more natural balance in the recording that prevents it from sweeping the board altogether. Moreover it was originally issued on cassette in non-Dolby form, as was Barenboim's on HMV. DG's policy, however, is to make Dolby transfers available as stocks of the pre-Dolby transfers become depleted. So it is important to check for the Dolby logo when making a purchase. Backhaus's Decca recording (KSXC 6322) also remains in the catalogue as a non-Dolby issue and the sound of the original transfer was not always clear.

The reissue of Richter's 1961 recording with Leinsdorf is most welcome. The performance has all the intensity of a live occasion and finds Richter in splendid form. It is a wayward account, mannered in places, but with impressive weight and authority; it is far more spontaneous and dashing than Richter's later recording with Maazel and the Orchestre de Paris (now deleted in the UK). This reading catches fire, and although the quality of the recorded sound calls for some tolerance, it has been greatly improved in the remastering. Indeed the transfer is excellent; the piano timbre is truthful, and the orchestra has quite good detail and no lack of warmth and bloom.

Brendel's is a finely recorded account, but the performance falls a little below expectations. He seems too judicious and adopts a deliberately restrained approach, so keen is he to eschew the grand manner. The results, though always commanding respect, are not wholly convincing; but the engineers produce first-rate sound, and the transfer is strikingly more vivid and immediate than Brendel's cassette of the *First Concerto*.

Ashkenazy's version was recorded in conjunction with a live performance at the Royal Festival Hall, the sessions taking place (at Kingsway Hall) imme-

diately after the concert. That being so, it is surprising to find that the chief shortcoming of the account, compared with the main rival versions, is a lack of tension. With much beautiful detail and some wonderfully poetic playing from Ashkenazy the performance still fails to come alive as it should. Naturally Ashkenazy is most successful in the lighter moments, but one is continually left uninvolved. The recording quality is outstandingly good, and the cassette transfer is very sophisticated, full-bodied with a most realistic piano image.

The partnership of Anda with the Berlin Philharmonic Orchestra provides much beautiful playing from soloist and orchestra alike. The performance is rhapsodically wayward, and the freely expansive treatment of the first movement does not always sound completely spontaneous. The slow movement is often richly eloquent, and the finale has a persuasive lyrical charm. There is much to admire and enjoy here, even if, taken as a whole, the reading is not entirely convincing. The recording is appropriately fullblooded, and the balance is good, even though the internal detail is not always transparently clear. But the tape transfer is well managed and as sound this makes satisfying listening.

Arrau's view of Brahms is at times a somewhat mannered one and his control of tempo does not always sound convincing, particularly in the first movement, where the long span of the structure needs more of a constant forward thrust than it receives here. The slow movement has undoubted eloquence and the finale plenty of spirit. The recording is excellent, and the tape transfer offers good quality, full yet with an agreeably bright and open treble. The piano timbre is clean and realistic.

Ilana Vered, a characterful pianist in other Phase Four issues, is overparted in this concerto. In the first movement and the scherzo the playing is laboured, and in the finale – where Miss Vered begins to sparkle – the recording balance changes and the piano, hitherto very forward, moves further back in relation to the orchestra. The tape quality is good, fresher on side two than side one, where a degree of cut-back in the bass is necessary.

Violin concerto in D major, Op. 77.
> (M) **(*) HMV TC-SXLP 30264. David Oistrakh, French National Radio Orch., Klemperer.
> **(*) DG 3300 592 [id.]. Nathan Milstein, Vienna PO, Jochum.
> *(**) HMV TC-ASD 3385 [Angel 4xs 37286]. Itzhak Perlman, Chicago SO, Giulini.
> (***) HMV TC-ASD 2525 [Angel 4xs 36033]. David Oistrakh, Cleveland Orch., Szell.
> (B) *(*) DG Heliodor 3348 263. Andrei Korsakov, Belgian Radio Orch., Defossez.

(i) *Violin concerto; Hungarian dances Nos. 1 and 3.*
> (M) *** Philips 7317 149. Concertgebouw Orch., Haitink, (i) with Herman Krebbers.

Krebbers, concertmaster of the Concertgebouw and a master violinist of the first order in his own right, gives one of the most deeply satisfying readings of Brahms's *Violin concerto* ever recorded, strong and urgent yet tenderly poetic too, and always full of spontaneous imagination. The total commitment behind the performance is not only the work of the soloist but that of his colleagues and their conductor, who perform as at a live concert. The recording, with the violin slightly forward but not obtrusively so, is full and immediate, and it has transferred well to tape, lacking only the very last degree of range in the upper partials of the timbre of the soloist.

The conjunction of two such positive artists as Oistrakh and Klemperer made for a reading characteful to the point of idiosyncrasy, monumental and strong rather than sweetly lyrical; the opening of the first movement has a feeling of engulfing power. The slow movement is particularly fine, and the French oboist plays beautifully. Oistrakh sounds superbly poised and confident, and in the finale, if the tempo is a shade deliberate, the total effect is one of clear gain. The sound is good and the transfer fullbodied yet clear; it needs a little treble cut but then produces a realistic balance. On one copy tried the upper focus was marginally less clean than on the review tape, which was first-rate.

To praise Milstein's version for the refinement and beauty of the accompaniment may sound like a backhanded compliment, and so perhaps it is, when for all the beauty and brilliance of the playing this is not quite the flawless Milstein reading of the Brahms that he had put on record for other companies. The hint of unease in the soloist is only relative, and those who want to hear him in the finest possible recorded sound can be safely directed here. Jochum secures playing of great warmth and distinction from the Vienna Philharmonic. Moreover the transfer is of very high quality, offering a most natural balance.

A distinguished account of the solo part from Perlman, finely supported by Giulini and the Chicago Symphony Orchestra, a reading of darker hue than is customary, with a thoughtful, searching slow movement rather than the autumnal rhapsody which it so often becomes. Giulini could be tauter, perhaps, in the first movement but the songful playing of Perlman always holds the listener. The recording places the soloist rather too forward, and while the sound on tape is full-blooded, it lacks refinement in the upper frequencies. On our copy the upper harmonics of the soloist's tone were not always absolutely pure, and the orchestral wind was marginally affected in places.

Oistrakh's version with Szell is full of controlled feeling and disciplined vitality, and it is a pity that the quality of the transfer is unreliable. We tried two copies and neither produced refined sound; the warmth and body of the disc version are missing and the timbres are meagre and lacking in refinement.

The recording by Andrei Korsakov was made in front of an audience on the occasion of the Concours Musical International Reine Elisabeth, held in Belgium in 1971. The audience betrays its presence only by an occasional muffled cough until the very end, when the applause explodes into the listener's room and quite spoils the effect of the music by making one jump. Certainly the account of the finale is brilliant enough, and indeed the soloist plays with strong feeling throughout. His timbre, however, is small and thin as recorded, and the upper partials of the recording are not always absolutely clean. The orchestral contribution is vigorous and has plenty of impact, so it might be thought that this is fair value at Heliodor price.

Double concerto for violin, violoncello and orchestra in A minor, Op. 102.
  (*) HMV TC-ASD 3312 [(d) Angel 4xs 36032]. David Oistrakh, Mstislav Rostropovich, Cleveland Orch., Szell – DVOŘÁK: *Slavonic dances Nos. 3 and 10.*(*)
(i) *Double concerto; Tragic overture, Op. 81.*
  (M) *(*) Supraphon 045573. Czech PO, Ančerl, (i) with Josef Suk and André Navarra.

The performance by Oistrakh and Rostropovich with the Cleveland Orchestra under Szell must be considered the most powerful and eloquent version of the *Double concerto* to be recorded since the days of Heifetz and Feuermann or Thibaud and Casals, and it deserves the strongest recommendation. Originally the tape transfer was made at too high a level and produced severe distortion at peaks; but current copies show a

considerable improvement, though some lack of refinement remains on side two.

The old Supraphon account by Suk and Navarra makes a more than acceptable medium-priced recommendation. The orchestral sound is lively, the soloists are smoothly recorded and there is no lack of detail. When one turns over for the finale the level of the transfer rises markedly and the first orchestral tutti shows some lack of refinement. But the sound is vivid in the overture, without congestion. The solo playing is undoubtedly eloquent (Navarra outstanding) and though Ančerl is not the most imaginative of Brahms conductors (the slow movement is rather square), this is certainly a satisfying performance.

Hungarian dances Nos. 1–3; 5–6; 10–21.
  (M) * Supraphon 041206. Prague SO, Dixon.

Stylish and warmly played performances of more than three quarters of the *Hungarian dances*. There is some felicitous woodwind detail and nicely turned string phrasing. The recording sounds pleasant, but the transfer lacks sparkle in the treble; so this tape is best used for background listening, for which it serves agreeably.

Hungarian dances Nos. 1 in G minor; 5 in G minor; 6 in D major; 7 in A major; 12 in D minor; 13 in D major; 19 in B minor; 21 in E minor.
  (M) **(*) Decca KCSP 377. Vienna PO, Reiner – DVOŘÁK: *Slavonic dances.***(*)

Reiner's recording is in Decca's highest class, and the playing is lively and polished. Reiner treats the dances as conductor's display pieces, and he indulges in *rubato* and effects of his own (witness No. 12); but his affection is obvious. The transfers are brilliant and sparkling and the level is high. There is a touch of glare on the upper string tone, but this can be minimized with the controls.

Hungarian dances Nos. 1 in G minor; 3 in F major; 5 in G minor; 6 in D major.
> (M) ** DG Privilege 3318 005 [(d) 923001]. Berlin PO, Karajan – LISZT: *Hungarian fantasia* etc.**(*)

The combination of Brahms *Hungarian dances* and Karajan would seem irresistible; but if these performances are not without the expected panache, they offer brilliance rather than affection, and there is not the warmth that some conductors find. The recording too is almost over-bright. But the selection offers four favourites, excellent orchestral playing and an unusual coupling, so most should be satisfied. The cassette transfer is well managed, smooth yet lively.

Serenades Nos. 1 in D major, Op. 11; 2 in A major, Op. 16; Variations on a theme of Haydn, Op. 56a.
> **(*) HMV TC-SLS 5137. LPO, Boult.

Sir Adrian's warmly lyrical approach to the two *Serenades* gives great pleasure. With excellent orchestral playing he produces ripe, spontaneous performances, glowing and fresh. Tempi are not always conventional, but Boult's way with these delightful scores is engaging enough to blunt any criticism of detail. The *Variations* too are vividly presented and strongly characterized. The warmly reverberant acoustic produces transfers of generally good quality, although in the tuttis the last degree of refinement of focus is missing in the upper range. This is not seriously detrimental: the sound remains pleasing. The recording of the *Variations* seems appropriately more lively, and the somewhat higher level of the transfer here gives the orchestra greater presence and impact.

Serenade No. 1 in D major, Op. 11; Tragic overture, Op. 81.
> **(*) Philips 7300 584 [id.]. Concertgebouw Orch., Haitink.

A finely proportioned, relaxed yet vital account of the delightful *Serenade No. 1* from Haitink and the Concertgebouw Orchestra. The wind-playing is particularly distinguished, and while the players obviously relish the many delights of this much under-rated score, the architecture is firmly held together without the slightest trace of expressive indulgence. The balance places the listener fairly well back, but the perspective is true to life and the sound blends admirably. There is a taut account of the *Tragic overture* (on tape only) as a makeweight. The original transfer lacked inner clarity and detail, with the bass smudged and over-full in relation to the treble. However, Philips have now made a new transfer which has been agreeably rebalanced and has characteristic warmth and refinement of detail. A highly recommendable issue.

Serenade No. 2 in A major, Op. 16.
> **(*) Decca KSXC 6368. LSO, Kertesz – DVOŘÁK: *Serenade.**(*)

'I was in a perfectly blissful mood. I have rarely written music with such delight,' wrote Brahms to Joachim when arranging this delectable *Serenade* for piano duet. The work has surprisingly autumnal colourings, and one would not be surprised to learn that it was a late rather than an early work. It was in fact begun before Brahms had finished work on the *D major Serenade* and thus dates from his mid-twenties. Kertesz gives an alert yet at the same time relaxed account of it. Moreover he offers excellent value in giving the Dvořák *Wind serenade* in an altogether admirable reading. The cassette issue offers admirable sound in the Brahms, but less clarity in the coupling.

Symphonies Nos. 1–4.
> *** DG 3371 015 [id.]. Berlin PO, Karajan.
> ** DG 3371 023 [id.]. Vienna PO, Boehm.

Symphonies Nos. 1–4; Academic Festival overture, Op. 80; Tragic overture, Op. 81; (i) *Alto rhapsody, Op. 53.*

> (***) HMV TC-SLS 5009. LPO or LSO, Boult, (i) with Janet Baker (mezzo-soprano), John Alldis Choir.

Symphonies Nos. 1–4; Academic Festival overture; Tragic overture.

> *(**) HMV TC-SLS 5093. LPO, Jochum.

Symphonies Nos. 1–4; Academic Festival overture; Tragic overture; Variations on a theme of Haydn, Op. 56a.

> ** Decca K 39 K 44 [Lon. 5-2405]. Cleveland Orch., Maazel.

Symphonies Nos. 1–4; Tragic overture.

> **(*) DG 3371 041 [id.]. Berlin PO, Karajan.

Karajan's first cycle (3371 015) dates from 1964, but the sound is still fresh and warm, while the performances are no less vivid. This may soon be deleted (the separate issues from this cycle have already disappeared), and as a box it is over-priced, but the orchestral playing is of such superlative quality that reservations are quickly eroded. The *First* and *Fourth Symphonies* are particularly powerful in these readings, although the *Second* is also impressive, a beautifully shaped reading, full of warmth and radiance. Perhaps there are one or two self-conscious moments, but in general this is playing of great mastery. The transfer tends, in places, to have an over-ample bass response, but when this is cut back a fine balance can be achieved, for there is no lack of life and range in the treble. The layout of the music is satisfactory.

Broadly, Karajan's 1978 cycle (3371 041) shows that his readings of the Brahms symphonies, with lyrical and dramatic elements finely balanced, have changed little over the years, though it is

worth noting that in the later set his approach to No. 3 is stronger and more direct, with less mannered phrasing in the third movement. The playing of the Berlin Philharmonic remains uniquely sweet, and the ensemble is finely polished. If the results are not always as incisively alert or as warm in texture as Karajan's earlier Berlin performances, that is partly due to less flattering recorded sound. Balance and top response are not always kind to the exposed violins, though in this the cassette version is preferable to the discs. The transfers throughout are fresh and clean, though there is the merest hint that the steadiness of texture is ruffled by the repeated drum beats at the opening of *Symphony No. 1.* Essentially the sound is dry: the strings lack the resonance they have in the earlier recordings, yet there is no lack of body, and the internal clarity is matched by the brightly lit upper strings. The bass is not expansive but it does not lack sonority. The *Second* and *Fourth Symphonies* are back to back and are thus heard without a turnover break. No. 3 uses the *Tragic overture* as fill-up. As we go to press, these new performances are being issued separately as follows: *Symphony No. 1* 3301 131; *Symphony No. 2* 3301 132; *Symphony No. 3* and the *Tragic overture* 3301 133; *Symphony No. 4* 3301 134.

Jochum's Brahms is akin to his Bruckner, comparably inspirational and compelling. In these richly enjoyable performances one may start by noting the idiosyncrasies – the hectic (and thrilling) tempo for the finale of No. 2 or the warmly coaxing manner in that of No. 4 – but as in Furtwängler performances of Brahms the points of individuality find their place undistractingly overall. Like Furtwängler, his mentor among conductors, Jochum builds massively, yet the freshness of inspiration remains, and there are few cycles of these symphonies that can match this one in the compelling illusion of live communication, so that the passionate accelerandi seem totally natural. The precision of the LPO ensemble, even more meticulously drilled than in the fine Boult performances, underpins this spontaneity and, like Boult, Jochum observes the exposition repeats. The tape transfer offers satisfyingly rich textures; the ripeness of the sound is right for Brahms and the string tone has bite as well as body. The orchestral balance does not produce the widest dynamic range, and wind solos are often forward, but this is not necessarily a disadvantage in Brahms. There is a touch of shrillness in No. 2, and at the opening of No. 1 the hammering timpani strokes disturb the texture slightly. At other times there is a lack of refinement in the upper partials of the woodwind. If it were not for these technical faults the set would be worthy of a rosette.

Boehm's cycle will to most Brahmsians seem idiosyncratic, though the conductor himself might point to the fact that he learnt his Brahms interpretation from the composer's friend, Eusebius Mandyczewski. Slow movements in particular are unusually slow, which in live performances from Boehm can be most affecting, but here the tension is relatively low and the string sound relatively thin. An expensive set with no fill-ups.

With all but one of the individual performances in the Boult cycle awarded three full stars, the merits of the set can be taken for granted: noble, straightforward readings that always come up fresh. It is ironic to remember that the whole cycle was started by accident, when Boult – in his crisp efficiency – had completed his schedule with two sessions to spare, and elected to do Brahms's *Third* as an unplanned extra. With Janet Baker in the *Alto rhapsody* the fill-up items are welcome, but note that the Brahms *Haydn variations* are not included. Unfortunately the transfer to tape was made at the time when EMI were experimenting with restricting the dynamic range in order to provide a transfer at the highest level. This has had disastrous effects on recordings where the balance originally

tended to provide not as wide a dynamic contrast as in some versions. The sound at the opening of No. 1 is fierce, while the quality at the beginning of No. 3 is almost explosive in its vigour. The prevailing *mezzo forte* means that in the first movements the second subjects tend to arrive with almost no reduction in the music's sonic impact, and the ebb and flow of tension are altered accordingly. In the *Alto rhapsody* the recording provides a glorious stream of vocal tone, but no light and shade.

The brilliant sound picture which Decca provide for Maazel certainly helps to bring out the brazen qualities of his interpretations. Unfortunately they are not uniformly satisfying, often detached to the point of being chilly, lacking the sort of tensions and communicated warmth one expects in live performances. But the orchestral playing (with one or two exceptions) is superlatively good, as one would expect from the Clevelanders. The fill-ups are more generous than in some rival sets, but Maazel does not observe the exposition repeats in Nos. 1, 2 and 3. The transfers to tape offer dry, clean sound, neither especially warm nor expansive, but clear and well balanced to suit the spirit of the music-making. There is the faintest ripple in the steadiness of texture at the hammered timpani strokes in the introduction of the *First Symphony*.

Haitink's performances of the symphonies were issued in the UK in a box (and although now withdrawn here they remain available in the USA: 7699 011). The performances are on the whole very satisfying, Nos. 1 and 3 first-class, No. 2 enjoyable and only No. 4 marginally disappointing. Throughout the orchestral playing of the Concertgebouw is of very high quality. The recording too is fresh and naturally balanced, but the set is ruined by an exceedingly inept layout, with all the symphonies split clumsily to fit them on three tapes, when they could easily have been placed back to back on two.

Symphony No. 1 in C minor, Op. 68.
*** DG 3301 131 [id.]. Berlin PO, Karajan.

(B) **(*) Classics for Pleasure TC-CFP 40096. Hallé Orch., Loughran.

**(*) Decca Phase 4 KPFC 4305. LSO, Stokowski.

(M) *(**) HMV TC-SXLP 30217. Philharmonia Orch., Klemperer.

**(*) DG 3300 889. Boston SO, Ozawa.

(M) ** DG Privilege 3335 102. Berlin PO, Boehm.

** DG 3300 959. Vienna PO, Boehm.

** Decca KSXC 6783 [Lon. 5-7007]. Cleveland Orch., Maazel.

(M) (**) RCA Gold Seal GK 25001. LSO, Horenstein.

Karajan's new version makes an impressive first choice, with richer sound than in the boxed set. But Loughran provides a recommendable bargain version, the first to observe the exposition repeat in the first movement. The reading from first to last is as refreshing as Boult's HMV recording (no longer available on tape). The second and third movements both have a spring-like quality, and the slow movement is less sweet than usual, while the 6/8 trio of the third movement is taken for once at a speed which allows the climax not to sound breathless. The introduction to the finale is unusually slow, weighty and concentrated, while the great string melody is not smoothed over at all. The entry of the chorale at the end finds Loughran characteristically refusing to slow down to half speed. Though some of the woodwind playing is not ideally responsive, the whole orchestra, particularly the strings, shows a natural feeling for Brahms's style. The transfer is generally a good one, with pleasing sound if no special freshness. There is no

lack of warmth and the balance is good. The dynamic range is somewhat restricted but not seriously.

The Stokowski version is taken from live recordings of his sixtieth-anniversary concerts with the LSO. The Phase Four engineers had to marry up recordings taken at two performances, one at the Royal Festival Hall, one at the Royal Albert Hall, which led to the sound being less expansive than it might be. The spontaneous sense of flow, the urgency of Stokowski's Brahms style, are nonetheless well conveyed in an exciting performance. It may lack a degree of polish compared with the finest studio-made versions, but it has its place. The recording is not ideal, not so much on account of the close balance on the wind (this is tastefully managed) but because of the lack of clarity at climaxes. But the performance has transferred well to tape, with a high level and a good balance.

Klemperer's is a tremendously compelling reading. From the first bar of the introduction, with its thundering, relentless timpani strokes, Klemperer's conception moves with a single momentum to the final C major chord of the last movement. The greatness of the performance is in no doubt, but the sound on tape is somewhat coarse-grained, although the dynamic range is left unaltered.

An unexpectedly heavyweight manner weighs down sections of the first and last movements in Ozawa's Boston version, with the famous main theme of the finale presented slowly, so that inconsistencies inevitably follow. Even so the performance does not lack warmth and spirit, and the Boston playing is finely polished (with a notably beautiful contribution from the first oboe). Untraditional as it is in control of tempo, this interpretation undoubtedly has spontaneity; the recording is first-class, and the transfer, made at a quite high level for DG, is rich and full, with excellent detail. This is one of the best-sounding Brahms *Firsts* on tape.

It is fascinating to compare Boehm's

earlier Berlin version of No. 1 with the reading in his 1976 Vienna cycle. In the sixties Boehm's preference for slow tempi was not so extreme, and the result – with more polished playing from the Berliners – is more centrally recommendable. The recording is well balanced and the transfer satisfactorily full-bodied and clear. There is a hint at the very opening that the timpani strokes are disturbing the texture, but this is marginal and the sound soon settles down.

With its relatively slow tempi Boehm's Vienna version has a certain massive quality. The interpretation is very much in the German tradition, and many will find the rhythmic pulse too robust and deliberate. The violin sound is not so refined and sweet as one normally expects from the Viennese orchestra, and the transfer (which is clear and well balanced) does nothing to hide the thinness of the upper string sound.

With generally spacious tempi and a moulded style, Maazel draws from his superb Cleveland Orchestra a reading that might be described as like Karajan with an American accent. If expressive conductors can be divided into those who naturally urge the music onwards and those who lovingly hold it back, Maazel here belongs to the latter category. That is until the great main melody of the finale, where he adopts a tempo far faster than usual, making the music almost breathless in its energy. Brilliant recording; technically this tape is impressive.

The refinement of Horenstein's reading comes out incomparably at the start of the *Andante*, wonderfully delicate in lyricism at a really hushed *pianissimo*. Horenstein was a Brahmsian who, with a broadly expressive style from phrase to phrase, yet preferred to keep a basically steady pulse through a movement. The LSO was at its peak when this recording was made in the sixties (the horn-playing is magnificent). Unfortunately the sound on tape, although clear, is fierce and without tonal bloom.

Symphony No. 2 in D major, Op. 73.
 *** DG 3301 132 [id.]. Berlin PO, Karajan.
 (B) **(*) Classics for Pleasure TC-CFP 40219. Hallé Orch., Loughran.

Symphony No. 2; Tragic overture, Op. 81.
 (M) **(*) HMV TC-SXLP 30238. Philharmonia Orch., Klemperer.
 *(*) Decca KSXC 6834. Cleveland Orch., Maazel.

Symphony No. 2; Variations on a theme of Haydn, Op. 56a.
 ** DG 3300 960. Vienna PO, Boehm.

Symphony No. 2; (i) Alto rhapsody, Op. 53.
 **(*) HMV TC-ASD 2746. LPO, Boult, (i) with Janet Baker (mezzo-soprano), John Alldis Choir.

Karajan's new performance sounds superb here – much richer than in the boxed set. A demonstration tape. But Boult's version still has a special place of honour. It has warmth, dignity and nobility and offers playing of great expressive power which scores over the reissued Klemperer recording in having slightly more sense of spontaneity. It is superlatively recorded, and as the fill-up is the memorable account of the *Alto rhapsody* from Janet Baker, its claims are indeed strong. It has transferred quite well to tape, although the sound varies from side to side: on side two the range of the sound is noticeably less fresh although textures are warmer.

As a Brahmsian James Loughran is a master of transition, and his account of No. 2, like those in the rest of his excellent Brahms cycle with the Hallé, has a natural, warm flow, carrying the listener on, even while the basic approach is direct and unfussy. On interpretation his reading (with exposition repeat included) matches and even outshines any in the catalogue, at whatever price, and the modern CFP recording is warm and naturally balanced, though there are one or two noticeable tape-joins. The Hallé ensemble and string tone are not always quite as polished as in the versions from metropolitan orchestras, but the sense of spontaneity is ample compensation. The sound of the tape transfer is pleasingly fresh, and the woodwind (forwardly balanced) have an attractive colouring in the slow movement; the string tone is rich and expansive here too. However, the recording's dynamics do not expand to the fullest possible extent in the biggest climaxes.

Klemperer's is a great performance, the product of a strong and vital intelligence. By the side of Boult, for example, he may seem a trifle severe and uncompromising, but he underlines the power of the symphony without diminishing its lyrical eloquence in any way. The *Tragic overture* is done with equal strength, and this mid-priced cassette can be made to sound well. The quality is somewhat fierce, but has no lack of body and responds to the controls. The woodwind have plenty of bloom, and the recording has a wide dynamic range.

The distinctive point about Boehm's reading is the very slow tempo for the second-movement *Adagio*. There the conductor's moulded style rivets the attention and one quickly accepts the extra spaciousness. The first and third movements too are both on the slow side, but the real disappointment of the issue is that the Vienna strings are not nearly so sweet in tone as one expects. The fill-up is generous but disappointing, an ungratiating, heavyweight account of the *Variations*. The transfer is made at a low level, but the treble is bright, and hiss is therefore not a problem. Without some cut-back the upper strings sound excessively thin, and there is shrillness too in the *Variations*.

Starting with a horn solo decidedly on

the flat side of the note, Maazel's account of the *Second* never really recovers, despite some beautiful playing from all sections. In the first movement the evenly stressed rhythm contradicts the expressive phrasing; the slow movement is big and rich but has little forward pulse, while the finale ends with blaring vulgarity. Rich Decca recording of good Cleveland vintage and a clear, clean transfer. Technically this is a very good tape.

Symphony No. 3 in F major, Op. 90; Academic Festival overture, Op. 80.
> (M) **(*) HMV TC-SXLP 30255. Philharmonia Orch., Klemperer.

Symphony No. 3; Hungarian dances Nos. 1 in G minor; 3 in F major; 19 in B minor.
> (B) **(*) Classics for Pleasure TC-CFP 40237. Hallé Orch., Loughran.

Symphony No. 3; Tragic overture, Op. 81.
> *** Philips 7300 139. Concertgebouw Orch., Haitink.
> *** DG 3301 133 [id.]. Berlin PO, Karajan.
> (B) ** DG Heliodor 3348 192. Berlin PO, Maazel.

Symphony No. 3; Variations on a theme of Haydn, Op. 56a.
> ** Decca KSXC 6835. Cleveland Orch., Maazel.

Symphony No. 3; (i) Alto rhapsody, Op. 53.
> ** DG 3300 992. Vienna PO, Boehm, (i) with Christa Ludwig (mezzo-soprano), Vienna Singverein.

The orchestral playing of the Concertgebouw for Haitink is distinguished by unanimity of attack and chording, wonderfully true intonation and homogeneity of tone. The transfer, though not made at a very high level, is a very good one, with clean, incisive string tone and a warmly natural balance. Haitink's firmness of grip makes this issue a first choice in the absence of Boult's performance from the catalogue. However, Karajan's new tape with the same coupling is no less recommendable, with a higher level and full, clear sound.

Klemperer's account of the *Third* is even more individual than his other Brahms symphony performances. With slow speeds and all repeats taken his timing is much more extended than usual. But for all his expansiveness Klemperer does not make the music sound opulent. There is a severity about his approach which may at first seem unappealing, but which comes to underline the strength of the architecture. The transfer has been made with a different level on each side. Side one (with the first two movements) is the higher, and there is hint of coarseness in the opening *tutti* (although it may be more obvious on some copies than others). This is noticeable again at the repeat of the first movement's exposition, but the quality tends to settle down after that, although there is a touch of rawness to the upper strings. Side two is altogether smoother.

Loughran, so urgently spontaneous in the other three Brahms symphonies, takes an unexpectedly measured view of No. 3. Though initially his slow tempi for all four movements may seem to undermine tension, on repetition this emerges as an unusually satisfying reading, presenting the *Third* as an autumnal work with lighter scoring than in the other symphonies. The total impression is of toughness and restraint set alongside flowing lyricism. As is habitual with Loughran, the exposition repeat is observed in the first movement, an important point in this of all the Brahms symphonies. The recording is extremely vivid, but the transfer has ironed out its dynamic contrast to the detriment of the playing. In all other respects the sound is excellent.

Maazel's version is refreshingly forthright, with fine ensemble from the Cleveland players. The slow movement is beautifully done, but ultimately, like the other performances in Maazel's cycle, this lacks the tensions which simulate a live rendering. The same applies to the generous fill-up (achieved at the expense of an exposition repeat in the symphony). The recording quality is outstandingly full and clear; the transfer is extremely brilliant, and although it does not lack body the upper strings sound very bright and somewhat wanting in bloom. A degree of treble cut is essential.

Boehm's reading is on the whole disappointing, the reins held comparatively slackly until the finale, which at last acquires the sort of momentum essential in this symphony. The merit of the tape lies far more in the expansive account of the *Alto rhapsody* provided as fill-up, with Christa Ludwig singing radiantly and the Vienna Philharmonic playing with an intensity not achieved in the symphony. The transfer to tape is certainly successful: the symphony's outer movements have striking bite and detail, with fresh upper strings. Only in the slow movement does the lack of textural warmth (which affects the wind timbres too) become a drawback, and this is a feature of the master recording. In the *Alto rhapsody* Ludwig's voice is truthfully caught and the choral sound is convincing too, the male voices warm in tone and well balanced with the soloist.

Maazel's view is the very opposite of staid – even with this most illustrious of German orchestras. It is all most exciting and vigorous, and the orchestra obviously enjoys its night out, but for repetition as a recording one has to be very careful indeed before recommending a decidedly wilful performance like this (which might be 'fresh' and exhilarating in the concert hall). One thinks of the frenzy of excitement in the first-movement coda, followed by complete relaxation for the final bars; the leisurely, free rhythm for the slow movement and the almost dead halt at the middle section with its chorale-like chords (very mannered this). The *Tragic overture* has been called one of Brahms's dullest pieces, but that is the last adjective one could apply to Maazel's reading. The transfer is generally very good. There is a hint of roughness at the very opening and the resonance seems marginally uncontrolled at times in the finale, but at Heliodor price this is good value, and the overture is certainly brilliantly recorded.

Symphony No. 4 in E minor, Op. 98.
   *** DG 3301 134 [id.]. Berlin PO, Karajan.
   (M) *** HMV TC-EXE 196. Philharmonia Orch., Klemperer.
   *** Decca KSXC 6890. Chicago SO, Solti.
   (B) *** Classics for Pleasure TC-CFP 40084. Hallé Orch., Loughran.
   (M) **(*) RCA Gold Seal GK 11961. RPO, Reiner.
   (B) * RCA Camden C4-5032. Boston SO, Munch.
Symphony No. 4; Tragic overture, Op. 81.
   **(*) DG 3300 894. Vienna PO, Boehm.

Karajan's fine performance is outstandingly well transferred, with splendid body of string tone and excellent detail. A clear first choice.

Klemperer's granite strength, coupled with his ability to clarify thick textures and his feeling for Brahmsian lyricism, makes his version one of the most satisfying ever recorded. The finale may lack something in sheer excitement, but the gravity of Klemperer's tone of voice, natural and unforced, in this movement as in the others, makes for a compelling result. As in the rest of the cycle, recorded in the late fifties, Klemperer was at his peak here. The recording, warm and spa-

cious, has been well transferred to make a good mid-price recommendation. The sound is smooth yet vivid, and there is no reduction in the dynamic range in the latest batch of cassettes sampled.

After a full twenty-five years recording for Decca, Solti at last came round to Brahms, and this account of No. 4 was the first result of that project. The most distinctive point about the reading, after a very direct, fast and steady first movement, is that the *Andante moderato* of the second movement is very slow indeed, more an *adagio*. It is not just that it starts slowly, as in some other versions; Solti characteristically maintains that speed with complete concentration. Not everyone will like the result, but it is unfailingly pure and strong, not only in the slow movement but throughout. The playing of the Chicago orchestra is magnificent – note the cellos in the second subject of the first movement, and the articulation of the anapaestic rhythms in the scherzo – and the recording is full and precise. The transfer is made at the highest level and gives the orchestra a massive richness of texture. The richly resonant bass needs cutting back if it is not to cause imbalance (and disturbance), but the treble is remarkably free and wide-ranging.

Loughran's account, like Barbirolli's before him with the same orchestra (not available on cassette), is outstanding. At bargain price and with excellent sound it should not be missed. Loughran's approach is unobtrusively direct. He is rarely if ever concerned to underline interpretative points, yet as the concentration grows after the deceptively gentle start, so one more and more appreciates the satisfying assurance with which he solves every problem. His tempi – except perhaps for a relatively slow account of the scherzo – are unexceptionable, and like Barbirolli he believes in adopting expressive phrasing within a basically steady tempo. The Hallé strings are in excellent form, and so for that matter are all the sections of the orchestra. The sound quality is lively, with brightly lit upper strings. The bass is a little dry but responds to the controls to make a convincing overall balance.

Boehm's account of No. 4 is the most successful performance in his Vienna cycle, with a spacious and noble reading of the first movement and a finely contrasted view of the final passacaglia, lyrical and dramatic elements sharply defined. There is heavy underlining in the great string melody of the slow movement, but this and other idiosyncrasies never interfere with the consistency of the reading. It may lack a little in weight and incisiveness, but with a dramatic performance of the *Tragic overture* as fill-up it is well worth considering. The sound on tape has plenty of life (the middle strings in the slow movement not lacking in warmth), and there are both body and detail, although in the opening movement one notices a slight recession of the orchestral image in the *pianissimo* passages. The overture is even brighter in quality than the symphony, and a touch of fierceness in the upper strings needs some control.

Reiner's version with the RPO, made in the early 1960s, is strongly competitive. Indeed it is one of the tautest readings currently available, without any loss of warmth. The RPO made this recording with Beecham personnel still present, and the incisive playing brings strength as well as polish. The first movement may strike some readers as too fast and its opening not sufficiently spacious, but few would question its sense of flow and urgency. Excellent recording for its period and a clear if rather fierce transfer (especially in the slow movement). However, the sound yields to the controls and a satisfying balance can be achieved.

Munch has some fine moments. His speed for the opening movement is slow, and the shaping is finely conceived and carefully executed. The slow movement shows the orchestra at its most affectionate, but the last two movements rather let down the standard: the impression is of a distinct slackening of tension, so that the fragmentary construction of the finale becomes too apparent. Unfortunately the tape transfer is lustreless, and the Dolby treatment seems to have been mismanaged so that if one cuts out the hiss one loses any vestige of brilliance in the orchestral sound.

Tragic overture, Op. 81.
(M) ** DG Privilege 3335 103. Berlin PO, Maazel – BEETHOVEN: *Symphony No. 5*; SCHUBERT: *Symphony No. 8.***

This lively performance makes a bonus for the coupling of Beethoven's *Fifth* and Schubert's *Unfinished*. The sound in the Brahms is not quite so clean in detail as in the symphonies, but it is still good.

Tragic overture, Op. 81; Variations on a theme of Haydn, Op. 56a; (i) *Alto rhapsody, Op. 53.*
*(**) DG 3336 396. Vienna PO, Boehm, (i) with Christa Ludwig (mezzo-soprano), Vienna Singverein.

The spacious account of the *Alto rhapsody* is the gem of Boehm's collection of shorter Brahms pieces. Christa Ludwig is wonderfully intense in her illumination of both words and music, producing glorious tone-colours despite the extra strain on breath-control from the slow tempi. The *Tragic overture* is given a strong traditional reading; but, with the violin section unflatteringly recorded, the *Variations* have their disappointments, very much in the heavyweight German tradition and with generally slow tempi made heavier by even stressing. Note too that no room was found for the *Academic Festival overture*. Those wanting the surpassingly beautiful account of the *Alto rhapsody* might prefer this mixed collection to the alternative coupling with the *Third Symphony*; but the transfer of the overture and the *Variations* is made at only a modest level, and the string tone is rather thin and lacking body, although

125

the recording is clear and fills out satisfactorily at climaxes. Unusually and inexusably for DG, the side-turn comes after Variation VI (before the *Grazioso*), an ill-positioned break. On side two the level drops further for the *Alto rhapsody*, and Christa Ludwig's voice seems relatively distant.

Variations on a theme of Haydn (St Anthony chorale), Op. 56a.
  (M) **(*) HMV TC-SXLP 30278. Philharmonia Orch., Giulini – SCHUBERT: *Symphony No. 8.****
  **(*) DG 3300 586. LPO, Jochum – ELGAR: *Enigma variations*.*(**)
  (M) **(*) Decca KCSP 121. LSO, Monteux – ELGAR: *Enigma variations*.*(**)

Giulini's 1962 recording of the *St Anthony variations* coupled to Schubert was one of the outstanding issues in the early stereo catalogue. It still sounds well, and it is a pity that the tape transfer is over-brilliant. The bright upper strings may approach shrillness on some machines, but a reduction of treble improves things considerably without losing the inner detail. The challenge of variation form obviously suited Giulini and it certainly demonstrates the superb quality of the Philharmonia Orchestra of the early sixties. The freshness of the performance is matched by Giulini's control of the overall structure: the finale has a memorable culminating inevitability.

Jochum is as naturally a Brahmsian as he is a Brucknerian, and his account of the *St Anthony variations* has a natural freshness which disguises the subtlety of detail. This is an ideal coupling for his superb reading of *Enigma*. Monteux offers a fresh, enjoyable performance to match his *Enigma variations* on the reverse. The orchestral playing is excellent, and the vigorous style gives the music a splendid forward impulse. The bright

recording still sounds well, and these cassette transfers are both acceptable, though neither is among its respective company's best. The Decca sound in the Brahms is marginally preferable to the DG, where there is a slight lack of refinement, but neither is entirely successful in containing the Elgar.

CHAMBER MUSIC

Clarinet trio in A minor, Op. 114.
  ** Enigma K 453533. Keith Puddy (clarinet), John Streets (piano), Keith Harvey (cello) – WEBER: *Grand duo concertante*.**
  (M) ** Turnabout KTVC 34108. David Glazer (clarinet), Frank Glazer (piano), David Soyer (cello) – BEETHOVEN: *Clarinet trio*.**

Brahms's *Clarinet trio* is one of his most attractive chamber works, but in recordings it has proved elusive. Keith Puddy and his colleagues give a straight and freshly attractive performance, well recorded, but some of Brahms's autumnal overtones are missing. The tape transfer is pleasant, and although the balance is close, the outline is soft-grained; ideally one would have liked a sharper definition.

The Turnabout performance is well played too, although it is not preferable to the Enigma issue. However, this is a case where the cassette transfer is notably successful. There is a most natural overall balance and the sound is pleasing, so that the performance here comes alive more readily than it does on disc.

Horn trio in E flat major, Op. 40.
  (*) Decca KSXC 6408. Barry Tuckwell (horn), Itzhak Perlman (violin), Vladimir Ashkenazy (piano) – FRANCK: *Violin sonata*.(*)

A superb performance of Brahms's marvellous *Horn trio* from Tuckwell, Perlman and Ashkenazy. They realize to the full the music's passionate impulse, and the performance moves forward from the gentle opening, through the sparkling scherzo (a typical Brahmsian inspiration, broad in manner as well as vivacious, with a heart-warming trio), the more introspective but still outgiving *Adagio* and the gay, spirited finale. The recording is worthy of the playing, although the cassette transfer is disappointing by Decca's usually high standards. The level is rather low and this seems to adversely affect the recording balance in favour of the solo horn.

String quartet No. 3 in B flat major, Op. 67.

(M) *** Decca Ace of Diamonds KSDC 510. Musikverein (Küchl) Qt – SCHUMANN: *String quartet No. 1.****

There have been some fine accounts of the Op. 67 quartet in the LP catalogue, notably those by the Italian and Melos Quartets (neither available on cassette). This version by the Musikverein Quartet, formerly known as the Küchl Quartet (after the first violin), is arguably the finest of them all. Their playing is effortlessly natural and has both warmth and finesse, and they are most truthfully recorded. These artists made a great impression with their finely poised Mozart quartets (K.575 and 590), also available on cassette, and their excellence is equalled here by a clean, bright recording which has transferred to tape with fine presence and detail. The naturalness of the string timbre is matched by an agreeable ambient warmth.

String sextet in No. 1 in B flat major, Op. 18.

*** CRD CRDC 4034. Augmented Alberni Qt – SCHUBERT: *String quartet No. 12 (Quartettsatz).****

Brahms's *B flat major String sextet* makes an unexpected early début in the tape catalogue, and Brahms-lovers who normally fight shy of his chamber music are urged to try this work (scored for two violins, two violas and two cellos) with its richly orchestral textures. The second-movement theme and variations is immediately attractive, while the *Ländler*-like trio of the scherzo will surely find a ready response in any lover of Viennese-styled melody. In short this is a most rewarding piece, especially when it is played as eloquently as it is here, with a ripely blended recording to match the warmth of the playing. At times one might feel a degree more fire would be welcome, but the performance does not lack spontaneity. The transfer is immaculate and beautifully balanced, and there are good notes, clearly printed.

String sextet No. 2 in G major, Op. 36.

*** CRD CRDC 4046. Augmented Alberni Qt – BRUCKNER: *Intermezzo and Trio.****

A splendid account of the *Second String sextet* to match the excellence of the *First* by this same group. Both works have proved elusive in the recording studio, but now we have thoroughly recommendable versions on tape and disc. The playing is splendidly alive and succeeds in matching expressive feeling with vigour. The finale is especially spirited. On tape the sound is full-blooded, with a fresh, clean treble. The richness of texture is not allowed to congeal, and a nice balance is achieved between blend and detail.

Viola sonatas Nos. 1 in F minor; 2 in E flat major, Op. 120/1–2.

**(*) DG 3300 722. Pinchas Zukerman (viola), Daniel Barenboim (piano).

These works of Brahms's last years are not generously represented in the catalogue in either their viola or clarinet form. Zukerman's playing is marked by an unfailing polish and a persuasive sweetness of tone. There is none of the expressive exaggeration that occasionally marks his playing (the Sibelius concerto is an example), while Barenboim is at his very best and conveys an evident sense of pleasure and enjoyment. Some listeners may find the readings a trifle suave (both players take pleasure in the shaping and polishing of a phrase), but the dominant impression left by these accounts is of an unforced naturalness and effortless musicality. The balance between the two players is impeccable, and the timbre of both instruments is truthfully captured. The cassette transfer is smooth but a little lacking in range; the sound is otherwise natural.

Violoncello sonatas Nos. 1 in E minor, Op. 38; 2 in F major, Op. 99.
  *(*) HMV TC-ASD 3612. Paul Tortelier (cello), Maria de la Pau (piano).

Tortelier and Maria de la Pau give a less intensely emotional and more classical account of these sonatas than is usual. Their playing is undoubtedly eloquent, but could not be described as romantically ardent in the way of the Du Pré/Barenboim readings (also on HMV, but not issued in cassette form). The tape transfer lacks the last degree of range. The richly resonant, forwardly placed cello has a very broad image and the focus is not sharp. The piano is given plenty of weight too, but the balance emphasizes that this is a recording rather than creating the effect of the two artists realistically distanced as in a live recital.

PIANO MUSIC

4 Ballades, Op. 10: Nos. 1 in D minor (Edward); 2 in D major; 3 in B minor; 4 in B major; 7 Fantasias, Op. 116.
  **(*) DG 3300 655. Emil Gilels.

Gilels offers artistry of an order that silences criticism. In terms of imaginative vitality and musical insight it would be difficult to surpass these readings. It goes without saying that at no time is one's attention drawn to Gilels's keyboard mastery, for so complete is his identification with the musical inspiration that one thinks only of Brahms. The *Ballades* have never been so marvellously played on record. The recording is a good one, but there is a touch of hardness to the piano image, and the sound on the cassette has not quite the bloom of the equivalent disc.

Ballade in G minor, Op. 118/3; Intermezzi: in E major, Op. 116/6; in E flat major, Op. 117/1; Rhapsody in G minor, Op. 79/2; Romance in F major, Op. 118/5; Variations and fugue on a theme by Handel, Op. 24; Waltzes, Op. 39, Nos. 1, 2, 4, 6, 9–11, 13–15.
  (M) *** Turnabout KTVC 34165. Walter Klien.

This collection is cleverly planned and superbly played. It has all the excitement and spontaneity of a live recital: there are few more enjoyable collections of Brahms's piano music at any price. The piano tone is a trifle hard – some machines will react to it more kindly than others – but it has plenty of brilliance, a wide dynamic range and a firm bass. This is very necessary to encompass Klien's range of dynamic and timbre, from the *sotto voce* of some of the *Handel variations* and *Waltzes* to the stormy passions of the *Rhapsody in G minor*, which begins side two superbly. After the extremely fine and varied reading of the *Variations*, side one closes with a melting performance of the *Intermezzo in E flat*, and side two ends equally memorably with the most famous of the Brahms *Waltzes*. Whether in the fully flowering lyricism of the *Romance in F*, the staccato forcefulness of the *G minor Ballade*, or the contrasting legato of the *Intermezzo in E major*, this is pianism of the very first rank. The cassette transfer is very well done, offering rather mellower sound than the equivalent LP and with a slightly softer outline on side two than side one.

7 Fantasias, Op. 116; Variations and fugue on a theme by Handel, Op. 24.
*** Decca KSXC 6786. Pascal Rogé.

A splendidly bold and alive account of the *Handel variations* from Pascal Rogé. The variety of keyboard colouring he commands brings great diversity to the individual variations, yet the account has a flowing spontaneity that is wholly compelling. The readings of the *Op. 116 Fantasias* are no less perceptive, and their often sombre atmosphere is lightened by the imagination of the playing. As in the *Variations*, Rogé's technical command is put entirely at the service of the composer, and this is most distinguished playing. The recording too is first-class, full-bodied yet bright, and the cassette transfer is admirably clear, the variety of timbre truthfully caught, with excellent weight and presence.

Hungarian dances Nos. 1–21 (for piano duet).
*** DG 3300 710 [id.]. Alfons and Aloys Kontarsky.
(M) ** Turnabout KTVC 34068. Walter and Beatrice Klien.
(M) (**) HMV TC-HQS 1380. Michel Béroff and Jean-Philippe Collard.

The Kontarsky duo are given a crisp, modern DG recording, and their performances are brilliant and full of character. The transfer is of high quality, with crisp, secure piano tone. There is just a touch of hardness, but no lack of atmosphere. The level is not particularly high, but hiss is not a problem.

Undoubtedly the Klien cassette makes

a worthy companion to the fine Turnabout collection of the Dvořák *Slavonic dances*. The playing here is splendid, with plenty of rhythmic nuance and an excellent sense of style. It must be admitted that in some cases the Brahms pieces are not quite so effective on the piano as on the orchestra. But this is the way they were conceived (Brahms, in fact, orchestrated only three of them himself), and it is unlikely we shall have a jollier performance of them. The Turnabout transfer is clean but rather brittle, and even a bass lift and a treble reduction still leave an edge on the piano timbre. However, this cassette costs a good deal less than the DG issue.

Béroff and Collard are crisp and unlingering in a characteristically French way: these are sparkling performances which are freshly convincing rather than charming. Some Brahmsians may prefer a more relaxed approach, but the urgency of these brilliant young French pianists is infectious. The recording is bright, but the tape is put out of court by the too high level of the transfer, which brings an unacceptable amount of distortion.

VOCAL AND CHORAL MUSIC

(i) *Alto rhapsody, Op. 53;* (ii) *A German requiem, Op. 45.*
(**) CBS 40-79211. New Philharmonia Orch., Maazel, with (i) Ileana Cotrubas (soprano), Hermann Prey (bar.), New Philharmonia Chorus; (ii) Yvonne Minton (contralto), Ambrosian Male Singers.
(i) *A German requiem. Tragic overture, Op. 81; Variations on a theme of Haydn, Op. 56a.*
*(*) HMV TC-SLS 996 [Angel 4x2s 3838]. Berlin PO, Karajan, (i) with Anna Tomowa-Sintow

(soprano), José van Dam (bass), Vienna Singverein.

There is no really recommendable tape version of the Brahms *Requiem*. Karajan gives a characteristically smooth and moulded reading with excellent soloists. Anna Tomowa-Sintow sings with rich, creamy tone colour, and José van Dam is equally expressive, with smooth firm tone. The choral singing is excellent but the recording, lacking the last degree of definition on disc, is even more poorly focused on tape and the climaxes lack refinement. The fill-ups are given excellent performances, well worthy of Karajan.

Maazel directs a strong unaffected performance of the *Requiem*, most impressive in the great choral climaxes such as *Denn alles Fleisch*. But the fuzzy choral focus of the CBS tape transfer gives little satisfaction. There is more of a sense of spontaneity here than in Maazel's Cleveland recordings of the Brahms symphonies, and the soloists are both good, though Cotrubas's beautiful tone has a hint of unsteadiness, exaggerated by the recording. Yvonne Minton sings with gloriously full tone and expansive phrasing. Our copy had pitch unsteadiness to add to its unattractiveness (this may not be present on all copies), and the CBS box is not very robustly made.

4 Serious songs, Op. 121. (i) *2 Songs with viola, Op. 91.* Songs: *Auf dem Kirchhofe; Der Jäger; Regenlied; Sapphische Ode; Ständchen; Therese; Vergebliches Ständchen; Wie Melodien zieht es mir.*

> ****(*) HMV TC-ASD 3605.** Janet Baker (mezzo-soprano), André Previn (piano), (i) with Cecil Aronowitz (viola).

The gravity and nobility of Janet Baker's singing in the *Four Serious songs* underlines the weight of the biblical words while presenting them with a far wider and more beautiful range of tone-colour than is common. André Previn's accompaniment is placed rather backwardly, but his rhythmic control provides fine support, and in the more varied songs on the reverse the partnership blossoms still further, best of all in the two *Viola songs*, which are ravishingly sung and played, with the late Cecil Aronowitz making his last appearance on record. The witty *Vergebliches Ständchen* is taken more slowly than usual, with pauses exaggerated, but like the other performances it emerges warm and compelling. Apart from the piano balance the recording is excellent. The tape transfer has plenty of presence, but the vocal projection is rather fierce in fortissimos (slightly less so in the miscellaneous songs than in Op. 121), and one has to take care with the controls if the sound is to be naturally smoothed.

COLLECTIONS

'Favourite composer': (i) *Academic Festival overture, Op. 80;* (ii; iii) *Hungarian dances Nos. 1 in G minor; 5 in G minor; 6 in D major; 12 in D minor; 13 in D major; 19 in B minor; 21 in E minor;* (ii; iv) *Symphony No. 1 in C minor, Op. 68;* (v) *Variations on a theme of Haydn, Op. 56a;* (vi) *Intermezzo in B flat minor, Op. 117/2; Rhapsody No. 2 in G minor, Op. 79/2;* (vi) *Waltz in A flat major, Op. 39/15;* (vii; i) *Alto rhapsody, Op. 53.*

> (B) ****** Decca KDPC 553/4. (i) Suisse Romande Orch., Ansermet; (ii) Vienna PO; (iii) Reiner; (iv) Krips; (v) LSO, Monteux; (vi) Julius Katchen (piano); (vii) Helen Watts (contralto), Chœurs de la Radio Suisse Romande.

Unlike *The world of Brahms* (see below) this set concentrates on complete works, and the two tapes may be considered fair value at the price asked. Helen Watts's account of the *Alto rhapsody* is boldly direct rather than melting. The main orchestral works (some of which have been considered separately above) make an enjoyable, if not distinctive concert. The transfers are well managed.

'The world of Brahms': (i) *Academic Festival overture, Op. 80;* (ii; iii) *Piano concerto No. 2 in B flat major, Op. 83:* finale; (ii; iv) *Hungarian dance No. 5 in G minor;* (ii; v) *Symphony No. 2 in D major, Op. 73:* 3rd movt; (ii; vi) *Symphony No. 3 in F major, Op. 90:* 3rd movt; (vii) *Clarinet quintet in B minor, Op. 115:* 3rd movt; (viii) *Intermezzo in B flat minor, Op. 117/2; Rhapsody No. 2 in G minor, Op. 79/2;* (ix) *Waltz No. 15 in A flat major, Op. 39;* (x; i) *A German requiem, Op. 45: How lovely are Thy dwellings* (in German); (xi) *Wiegenlied, Op. 49/4.*

   (M) ** Decca KCSP 315. (i) Suisse Romande Orch., Ansermet; (ii) Vienna PO; (iii) Boehm, with Wilhelm Backhaus (piano); (iv) Reiner; (v) Kertesz; (vi) Karajan; (vii) Alfred Boskovsky (clarinet), members of the Vienna Octet; (viii) Julius Katchen (piano); (ix) Bracha Eden and Alexander Tamir (piano duet); (x) Swiss Radio Choir and Lausanne Pro Arte Choir; (xi) Renata Tebaldi (soprano), New Philharmonia Orch., Guadagno.

Although skilfully put together to make an agreeable overall concert, this collection does not gell as successfully as some in this series. It was a mistake to open with the *Hungarian dance*, certainly part of Brahms's world but surely not of prime importance. The *Academic Festival overture*, which begins side two, would

have been a better choice. But the instrumental items here are notably successful, with Julius Katchen on top form, and the lovely *Andantino* from the *Clarinet quintet* should surely tempt many into investigating the complete work. It was a happy idea to include the finale from the Backhaus version of the *Second Concerto*, a movement for which he has always been famous since his early 78 recording. The recording is generally good throughout, though the quality on tape tends to vary a little between items.

Brian, Havergal (1876–1972)

Symphonies Nos. 8 in B flat minor; 9 in A minor.

   *** HMV TC-ASD 3486. Royal Liverpool PO, Groves.

It is astonishing that Havergal Brian's music has been so shamefully neglected by the recording companies in favour of avant-garde scores of much more dubious merit. But following on Lyrita's recording of the *Sixth* and *Sixteenth Symphonies* (not yet available on tape) this enterprising coupling from HMV undoubtedly deserves support. Groves gives a splendid account of the *Ninth*, a work of undoubted power and atmosphere. No. 8 is a rather more complex and enigmatic piece, and the performance is marginally less assured. But there is fine orchestral playing throughout and the coupling merits the strongest recommendation, for the music's harmonic language is not too 'difficult' for anyone who enjoys Mahler to come to terms with. The recording is first-class and the transfer has excellent presence and detail, crisp brass and plenty of atmosphere.

Britten, Benjamin
(1913–76)

(i) *Piano concerto in D major, Op. 13;*
(ii) *Violin concerto in D minor, Op. 15.*

> *** Decca KSXC 6512. ECO, the composer, with (i) Sviatoslav Richter; (ii) Mark Lubotsky.

Both these works come from early in Britten's career, but as the performances here amply confirm there is nothing immature or superficial about them. Richter – a regular visitor to Aldeburgh – is incomparable in interpreting the *Piano concerto*, not only the thoughtful introspective moments but the Liszt-like bravura passages (many of them surprising from this composer). The *Violin concerto* is constructed in three movements, but the manner and idiom are subtler. With its highly original violin sonorities it makes a splendid vehicle for another Soviet artist, the young violinist Mark Lubotsky, whose Soviet-made recording (not available in the West) persuaded Britten that here was his ideal interpreter. Recorded in the Maltings, the playing of the ECO under the composer's direction matches the inspiration of the soloists. The excellent recording is matched by the cassette transfer, which is bold and clear with plenty of body and detail throughout both sides, the resonance of the recording well caught.

Violin concerto in D minor, Op. 15.

> ⊛ *** HMV TC-ASD 3483. Ida Haendel, Bournemouth SO, Berglund – WALTON: *Violin concerto.****
>
> (M) * RCA Gold Seal GK 25096. Paul Kling, Louisville Orch., Whitney – RUBBRA: *Improvisations.**

It is quite astonishing that the cassette catalogue should provide three different recordings of the Britten *Violin concerto*. Ida Haendel's performance is a worthy challenger to Mark Lubotsky's account coupled with the *Piano concerto* (see above). Miss Haendel's ravishing playing places the work firmly in the European tradition. She brings great panache and brilliance to the music as well as a great expressive warmth. This is a reading very much in the grand manner, and it finds Paavo Berglund in excellent form. His support is sensitive in matters of detail and full of atmosphere. The recording is the richest and most successfully realistic of all, with a beautifully spacious perspective and warm, velvety string tone that is positively Mediterranean in feeling. The soloist is balanced a little close, but generally the security of her technique can stand up to such a revealing spotlight. If the Lubotsky version has the authority of the composer's direction, the Haendel has no less conviction and spirit. The tape transfer must be accounted one of the most successful now on the market: it is difficult to tell much difference between it and the LP.

The RCA recording is far from recent and the Louisville Orchestra not in the first flight. Yet the performance communicates a genuine enjoyment of the concerto. Paul Kling is an assured player and his approach is distinguished by an evident affection for the score. The first movement is eloquently played, and it is only in the *Vivace* that the limitations of the orchestra are revealed and their technique strained. The upper strings are not always clean (take fig. 43 in the finale) and the playing is a little scrappy. There is no real challenge to the Lubotsky or Haendel versions, particularly in terms of the virtuosity of the players or the quality of the recorded sound, but this performance does nonetheless convey a real commitment to the score. The coupling is of interest and makes it well worth considering. The cassette transfer is acceptable, though no one could call the sound distinguished by modern-day standards. The sound is smoother than in the coupling, but the soloist is projected well forward and the orchestral balance is poor.

Prelude and fugue for eighteen-part string orchestra, Op. 29 (see also under *Phaedra* below); *Simple symphony (for strings), Op. 4; Variations on a theme of Frank Bridge, Op. 10.*
    **(*) RCA RK 25146. Bournemouth Sinfonietta, Ronald Thomas.

Though inevitably comparisons with Britten's own recordings of these three string works reveal felicities that are missing here, the coupling is most attractive, the performances have a natural expressive warmth which is most engaging, and, not least, the recording has a ripeness and resonance which are most satisfying, particularly in the bass registers. For some reason the left channel is weak in the transfer of the *Variations* on side one, throwing the sound image over to the right. However, the quality itself is good and even more vivid on side two, with excellent detail. Some treble cut is advisable, or the climax of the slow movement of the *Simple symphony* becomes unnaturally bright.

Simple symphony (for strings), Op. 4.
    ** Pye Ensayo ZCNEL 2012. ECO, Asensio – HINDEMITH: *5 Pieces;* RESPIGHI: *Ancient airs and dances: Suite No. 3.***

Britten's own infectious and beautifully recorded performance of the *Simple symphony* (in an anthology of music by Bridge, Delius, Elgar and Purcell: KSXC 6405) was an early Decca tape issue and is not Dolbyized. Enrique Asensio's approach is rather serious in tone although the music is well played. There is no hint of humour in the approach to Britten's youthful score (the *Playful pizzicato* and *Frolicsome finale* are worthy of a young

Mozart) but there is no condescension either, and the closing movement is brilliantly done. The tape is well engineered throughout, with excellent string tone.

Variations on a theme of Frank Bridge, Op. 10.
    (*) Argo KZRC 860 [id.]. Academy of St Martin-in-the-Fields, Marriner – BUTTERWORTH: *Banks of Green Willow* etc.(*)

Variations on a theme of Frank Bridge; The Young Person's Guide to the Orchestra (Variations and fugue on a theme of Purcell), Op. 34.
    *** Decca KSXC 6450. ECO or LSO, the composer.

Britten's set of *Variations on a theme of Frank Bridge* was conceived as a brilliant display piece for the Boyd Neel Orchestra. Although his performance (and recording) has no lack of robust qualities, Britten goes for half-tones much more often than other conductors in this work, and he achieves an almost circumspect coolness in the waltz-parody of the *Romance*. In the Viennese waltz section later Britten is again subtly atmospheric, and in the *Funeral march* he is more solemn than Ronald Thomas, showing here, as in the finale, that this is music to be taken seriously for all the lighthearted mood of the opening sections of the work. With its superb sound, this is another example of Britten at his most convincing and spontaneous in the recording studio. His view of his *Young Person's Guide* is, by contrast, very brisk – so brisk that even the LSO players cannot always quite match him. But every bar has a vigour which makes the music sound even more youthful than usual, and the headlong, uninhibited account of the final fugue (trombones as vulgar as you like) is an absolute joy. A marvellous coupling for young and old alike. Outstanding recording which transferred brilliantly to tape, even though this was an early Decca cassette issue.

Though not even Marriner quite matches the natural warmth of expression of the composer himself in the *Bridge Variations* – compare the *Funeral march*, for example – his is a superb performance, if anything even more polished, and recorded with a vividness that sets new standards. With the beautiful Butterworth pieces it is a warmly attractive coupling. The cassette transfer is vivid but slightly hard-edged. The brilliance suits the Britten better than the Butterworth couplings.

The Young Person's Guide to the Orchestra (Variations and fugue on a theme of Purcell), Op. 34.

(*) HMV TC-ASD 2935 [Angel 4XS 36962]. André Previn (narrator), LSO, Previn – PROKOFIEV: *Peter and the Wolf.*(*)

(M) **(*) Decca KCSP 520. Sean Connery (narrator), RPO, Dorati – PROKOFIEV: *Peter and the Wolf.****

(B) **(*) Classics for Pleasure TC-CFP 185. Richard Baker (narrator), New Philharmonia Orch., Leppard – PROKOFIEV: *Peter and the Wolf.***

(M) **(*) Philips 7317 093 (without narration). Concertgebouw Orch., Haitink – PROKOFIEV: *Peter and the Wolf**; RAVEL: *Ma Mère l'Oye.****

** HMV TC-ASD 3417 (without narration). Royal Liverpool PO, Groves – ELGAR: *Enigma variations.***

*(*) RCA RK 12743 [ARK 1 2743] (without narration). Philadelphia Orch., Ormandy – PROKOFIEV: *Peter and the Wolf.****

Quite apart from the brilliance of the LSO's playing and the ripe warmth of the recording, Previn's account of the *Young Person's Guide* is characterized by his own dry microphone manner in the narration. This is obviously directed at older children than those to whom Mia Farrow is talking in *Peter and the Wolf*, but it still makes a delightful coupling. The transfer has plenty of body, and detail is quite good. The refinement only slips momentarily at the sumptuous opening statement and the final climax of the fugue.

The Sean Connery/Dorati version is obviously aimed at the listener whose knowledge of the orchestra is minimal. Connery's easy style is attractive, and this version should go down well with young people, even if some of the points are made rather heavily. The orchestral playing is first-rate (although there is a momentary lapse of ensemble from one of the percussion players at the beginning), and Phase Four techniques have been used to bring forward solo instruments and sections of the orchestra, which seems justifiable in this instance. The transfer has one or two moments of slight blurring of the focus during Britten's ample scoring of Purcell's great tune at the opening, but generally the quality here is extremely vivid and clear. This is perhaps not a version for everyone, but many will like it very much, for it has an attractive spontaneous quality, to which Connery contributes not a little.

Otherwise, the most successful cassette transfer of the *Young Person's Guide* is the Classics for Pleasure issue, and it is a pity that the rather cosy narration by Richard Baker tends to hold up the flow of the music. The orchestral playing is lively and the recording vivid, but one feels that there are too many words here. However, the sound is undoubtedly first-class.

Haitink's is a comparatively straightforward performance, with no special imaginative insight or sparkle. Partly because of the acoustic, the climax of the fugue at the end lacks refinement, but taken as a whole the account, which is well played, is quite compelling. The transfer is of very good quality after a hint of minor overloading at the very opening. The couplings are generous and well done.

Groves's recording of the Britten *Variations* is imaginatively coupled with the other most popular set of orchestral variations by a British composer, and it is opulently recorded. The performance is lively; if it lacks the last degree of finesse it has both high spirits and a sense of humour, with the trumpet variation taken at a spanking pace, and the flute and clarinet variations delightfully extrovert. The resonance of the recording clouds the broad opening statement, but elsewhere the sound is agreeably rich and vivid, if not always ideally clear.

Ormandy's performance is straightforward and very well played. It has no special individuality, and the recording has an element of harshness in *tutti*. The reverberation offers problems at the opening and close of the work, when the focus of the climaxes tends to blur.

The Young Person's Guide to the Orchestra (*Variations and fugue on a theme of Purcell*), *Op. 34; Peter Grimes: 4 Sea interludes.*
> (M) *(**) HMV TC-SXLP 30240 (without narration). Philharmonia Orch., Giulini.

The sound here is astonishingly rich for a recording dating from the mid-sixties, with excellent bloom and atmosphere. Giulini's manner is rather literal and detached, and the first three *Peter Grimes Interludes* do not quite come to life. But the Philharmonia playing is superb, and in the final storm interlude there is no lack of excitement. Similarly the *Variations* take a little while to warm up, but with the Philharmonia in fine form there is much to enjoy; the bassoon and harp variations are especially mem-

orable. The transfer is acceptable, but the climaxes lack the refinement found on the LP and the inner detail is less clear.

CHAMBER MUSIC

Suite: *The Courtly Dances from Gloriana* (arr. Bream).
> **(*) RCA RK 11673 [RK 1052]. Julian Bream Consort – RODRIGO: *Concierto de Aranjuez***(*); VIVALDI: *Lute concerto.***

Like all Britten's operas, *Gloriana*, with its moving portrayal of the ageing Queen and the fall of her ex-lover Essex, is reliably gripping in the theatre. One of the highlights of the score is this group of Elizabethan dances, originally played by a small stage orchestra. The freshness of invention contains only a suggestion of pastiche, and although the emotional depth of the deceptively simple yet eloquent *Pavan* suggests a later century, somehow there is no feeling of anachronism. Bream's arrangement for his six players is brilliantly done, and the music's wit emerges as strongly as its variety of melodic invention. The playing and recording bring over all the spontaneity and warmth of a live performance. The transfer is of quite good quality, although it does not match the refinement of the LP.

VOCAL AND CHORAL MUSIC

A Ceremony of Carols, Op. 28.
> (M) *** Argo KCSP 164. St John's College Choir, Guest; Marisa Robles (harp) – Collection: 'The world of Christmas', Vol. 2.***

(i) *A Ceremony of Carols. Missa brevis in D major, Op. 63; The Golden Vanity.*

(M) ** Pye ZCTPL 13065. Winchester Cathedral Choir, Neary, (i) with Marisa Robles (harp).

Argo have provided us with a definitive recording of the *Ceremony of Carols*, one of Britten's freshest and most spontaneous works. This St John's performance has tingling vitality, spacious sound, and a superb contribution from Marisa Robles, who plays with masterly sensitivity, especially in her solo *Interlude*. On Argo's medium-price label, it is coupled to a delectable selection of traditional carols and modern settings. This is one of the finest collections of Christmas music in the catalogue, and the transfer is admirably smooth and secure.

At medium price the Pye coupling of three of Britten's most imaginative works for treble voices is welcome, but none of the performances can quite match those on the finest recordings. In particular Britten made a sharper, more dramatic impact in *The Golden Vanity* (not available on cassette); and partly because of a lack of bite in the recording quality the performances never quite spring to life as they should. Even so, this issue clearly shows the Winchester choir as one of the finest and truest-tuned among cathedral choirs today. Unfortunately the cassette is spoilt by a very low-level transfer, which has virtually no impact and lots of hiss.

(i–iii) *Phaedra, Op. 93;* (iv) *Sacred and Profane* (*8 medieval lyrics*), *Op. 91; Shepherd's carol; Sweet was the song; The sycamore tree; Wealden trio* (*Christmas song*)*;* (ii; v) *Prelude and fugue for eighteen-part string orchestra, Op. 29.*

   *** Decca KSXC 6847. (i) Janet Baker (mezzo-soprano); (ii) ECO; (iii) cond. Bedford; (iv) Wilbye Consort, Pears; (v) cond. the composer.

Phaedra is the work Britten wrote at the very end of his life for Janet Baker. Setting words from Robert Lowell's fine translation of Racine's play, the composer encapsulated the character of the tragic heroine, and provided vocal writing which brings out every glorious facet of Janet Baker's voice. The use of harpsichord in the recitatives linking the sections of this scena is no mere neo-classical device but a sharply atmospheric and dramatic stroke. *Sacred and Profane*, a collection of settings of medieval words that are curiously ironic in some of their overtones, is another highly imaginative product of Britten's last period, while the *Prelude and fugue* provides a welcome example, previously unissued, of Britten's own conducting. The ingenuity of this tribute to the Boyd Neel Orchestra is submerged by the music's energy as the composer interprets it. A fine collection with superb performances. The transfer is of outstanding, demonstration quality. The opening *Prelude and fugue* is beautifully recorded, and the voices are most natural throughout. In particular the sound in the recordings by the Wilbye Consort is delightfully fresh, while Janet Baker's voice is admirably caught.

Spring symphony, Op. 44.

   *** HMV TC-ASD 3650. Sheila Armstrong, Janet Baker, Robert Tear, St Clement Dane's School Boys' Choir, LSO Chorus, LSO, Previn.

Just as Colin Davis's interpretation of *Peter Grimes* provides a strikingly new view of a work of which the composer seems the natural interpreter, so André Previn's reading of the *Spring symphony* is valuably distinctive. Like Britten (whose electrifying recording is not available on cassette), Previn makes this above all a work of exultation, a genuine celebration of spring; but here more than with Britten the kernel of what the work has to say comes out in the longest of the solo settings, using

Auden's poem *Out on the lawn I lie in bed*. With Janet Baker as soloist it rises above the lazily atmospheric mood of the opening to evoke the threat of war and darkness. Perhaps surprisingly, it is Britten who generally adopts faster tempi and a sharper rhythmic style, whereas Previn is generally the more atmospheric and mysterious, grading the climaxes and shading the tones over longer spans. He also takes more care over pointing Britten's pay-offs, often with the help of Robert Tear's sense of timing, as at the very end on *I cease*. The recording is atmospheric, and the transfer is excellent, with good clarity and warmth though not quite the glorious richness of bass resonance that distinguishes the disc.

War requiem, Op. 66.

⊛ *** Decca K 27 K 22 [Lon. 5-1255]. Galina Vishnevskaya, Peter Pears, Dietrich Fischer-Dieskau, Bach Choir, LSO Chorus, Highgate School Choir, Melos Ens., LSO, the composer.

This most successful project hardly needs recommendation. With the composer's own choice of forces under his direction, and with all the technical care of the Decca engineers, it has deserved all its success, and it is worth noting that in an important respect recording techniques were able to fulfil the composer's directions even more completely than any live performance. Britten pointed the contrast between the full choir and orchestra in the settings of the *Requiem* and the tenor, baritone and chamber orchestra in the intervening settings of the Wilfred Owen poems. What a recording can do that is impossible in a cathedral or concert hall is to modify the acoustic for each, and this has been done most sensitively and effectively by the Decca engineers. The Owen settings strike one more sharply than the Latin settings, but gradually as the work progresses the pro-

cess of integration is accomplished, and the way the soloists' cries of *Let us sleep now* fade into the final chorus is almost unbearably moving on tape as in performance. The recorded performance comes near to the ideal, but it is a pity that Britten insisted on Vishnevskaya for the soprano solos. Having a Russian singer was emotionally right, but musically Heather Harper would have been so much better still.

The cassette issue – like Decca's *Ring* on tape – offers sound of amazing depth and clarity. The work's closing pages are wonderfully effective heard against an almost silent background, with no possible danger of intrusive clicks and pops.

OPERA

The Little Sweep: complete.

**(*) HMV TC-ASD 3608. Robert Lloyd, Robert Tear, Sam Monck, Heather Begg, Catherine Benson, Mary Wells, Finchley Children's Music Group, Choral Scholars of King's College, Medici Qt, two pianos, percussion, Ledger.

The composer's own recording of *The Little Sweep* – the operatic second half of the entertainment *Let's Make an Opera* – was in mono only, and one principal gain in this recording directed by Britten's longtime collaborator at the Aldeburgh Festival is the vividness of atmosphere. The game of hide-and-seek sounds much more real, and though the words are not always ideally clear, there is a good illusion of having an audience and not a trained choir singing them. In the cast Sam Monck as the little sweep himself is delightfully fresh-toned and artless – less expressive than the star-to-be, David Hemmings, on Britten's record but just as appealing – and among the others the outstanding contributor is Heather Begg as the dragon-like Miss Baggott, bringing out the occasional likenesses with Gilbert and Sullivan in some of the patter ensembles. Apart from the cast of grown-ups, the solos are taken by members of the Finchley Children's Music Group, and Ledger's direction follows very much in the tradition set by the composer himself without lacking impetus. The transients, as can be heard at the very opening, are not absolutely crisp on the high-level transfer. But the ambience is well caught, and if the sound is not quite as refined as the disc, it is certainly vividly enjoyable.

Peter Grimes: complete.

⊛ *** Decca κ 71 κ 33. Peter Pears, Claire Watson, James Pease, Jean Watson, Raymond Nilsson, Owen Brannigan, Geraint Evans, Chorus and Orch. of Royal Opera House, Covent Garden, the composer.

*** Philips 7699 089. Jon Vickers, Heather Harper, Jonathan Summers, Elizabeth Bainbridge, Thomas Allen, Forbes Robinson, Chorus and Orch. of Royal Opera House, Covent Garden, Colin Davis.

The Decca recording of *Peter Grimes* was one of the first great achievements of the stereo era. Few opera recordings can claim to be so definitive, with Peter Pears, for whom it was written, in the name part, Owen Brannigan (another member of the original team) and a first-rate cast. One was a little apprehensive about Claire Watson as Ellen Orford, a part which Joan Cross made her own, but in the event Miss Watson gives a most sympathetic performance, and her voice records beautifully. Another member of the cast from across the Atlantic, James Pease, as the understanding Captain Balstrode, is brilliantly incisive musically and dramatically; but beyond that it becomes increasingly unfair to single out individual performances. Britten con-

ducts brilliantly and secures splendidly incisive playing, with the whole orchestra on its toes throughout. The recording, superbly atmospheric, has so many felicities that it would be hard to enumerate them, and the Decca engineers have done wonders in making up aurally for the lack of visual effects. The tape transfer is marvellously sophisticated, with fine detail and atmosphere. The big choral climax of Act 3 has a slightly grainy focus, but in all other respects the quality is demonstration-worthy, with a splendid overall bloom and richness.

Colin Davis takes a fundamentally darker, tougher view of *Peter Grimes* than the composer himself. In some ways the result is even more powerful if less varied and atmospheric, with the Borough turned into a dark place full of Strindbergian tensions and Grimes himself, powerful physically (no intellectual misplaced), turned into a Hardy-like figure. It was Jon Vickers's heroic interpretation in the Met. production in New York which first prompted Davis to press for a new recording, and the result brings keen new illumination on what arguably remains the greatest of Britten's operas. In no way can it be said to supplant the composer's own unique recording; and Peter Pears's richly detailed and keenly sensitive performance in the name part remains unique too, even though Vickers is so plainly closer in frame and spirit to Crabbe's rough fisherman. Slow-spoken and weighty, Vickers is frighteningly intense.

On the Davis set Heather Harper as Ellen Orford is far more moving than her opposite number, and generally the Philips cast is younger-voiced and fresher, with specially fine contributions from Jonathan Summers as Balstrode (a late choice) and Thomas Allen as Ned Keene. It is a pity the recording producer did not favour the sort of atmospheric effects which set the seal on the Decca version as a riveting experience, but in a way that reinforces Davis's point about the actual notes needing no outside aid.

The recording, made at All Saints, Tooting Graveney (not the ideal venue), is rich and vivid, with fine balancing. The Philips transfer is of excellent quality, warmly atmospheric and with natural vocal timbre, although it by no means supersedes the Decca set as recorded sound, notably in its upper range, which is somewhat less free and clear. The presentation is handsome, with a triple-language libretto.

Brouwer, Leo
(born 1939)

Guitar concerto.
(*) CBS 40-76715. John Williams, London Sinfonietta, Howarth – ARNOLD: *Guitar concerto.*(*)

Leo Brouwer, born in Cuba, has established quite a following for himself in avant-garde circles. He draws widely on modern techniques but always with artistic motivation and taste. This concerto makes imaginative use of unusual sonorities (one is reminded of the whisperings of a tropical forest and the flight of exotic birds) and is throughout compelling. John Williams plays with authority and virtuosity, and Elgar Howarth and the London Sinfonietta give convinced support. The guitar sounds a little larger than life but not unacceptably so. The stereo is wide in spread and reasonably well detailed. The transfer is smooth, but ideally one wants a degree more range in the upper register and more sparkle in the transients for this kind of score. In this respect the tape is no match for the disc, which has striking internal clarity.

Bruch, Max
(1838–1920)

Violin concerto No. 1 in G minor, Op. 26.
(M) *** Decca KCSP 88. Ruggiero Ricci, LSO, Gamba – MENDELSSOHN: *Concerto.****
(*) HMV TC-ASD 2926 [Angel 4xs 36963]. Itzhak Perlman, LSO, Previn – MENDELSSOHN: *Concerto.*(*)
(*) CBS 40-76726. Pinchas Zukerman, Los Angeles PO, Mehta – LALO: *Symphonie espagnole.(**)
(M) ** Supraphon 045546. Josef Suk, Czech PO, Ančerl – MENDELSSOHN: *Concerto.***
(B) ** DG Heliodor 3348 170. Erica Morini, Berlin Radio Orch., Fricsay – GLAZOUNOV: *Concerto.***
(M) ** Philips 7317 107. Arthur Grumiaux, Concertgebouw Orch., Haitink – MENDELSSOHN: *Concerto.***
(M) *(*) DG Privilege 3335 294. Yong Uck Kim, Bamberg SO, Kamu – MENDELSSOHN: *Concerto.**(*)
(M) (**) HMV TC-SXLP 30245. Nathan Milstein, Philharmonia Orch., Barzin – MENDELSSOHN: *Concerto.*(**)

In discussing individual performances of Bruch's *First Violin concerto*, Kyung-Wha Chung's, coupled to the *Scottish fantasia*, must be considered among the very finest. It is reviewed below. Of the others, probably the most richly recorded is Perlman's; but there is perhaps the faintest reservation about this reading, a glowing, powerful account that is almost too sure of itself. With Previn and the LSO backing him up, Perlman's is a strong, confident interpretation, forthrightly masculine – the contrast with Kyung-Wha Chung's inner qualities is very striking. The opulent, full recording suits the performance, and the coupling is outstanding among the many fine versions of the Mendelssohn concerto. Unfortunately the cassette transfer (which is certainly vivid) has a restricted dynamic range.

Undoubtedly the most successful cassette version from all points of view is Ricci's. Although this was an early transfer, it is in every way first-class, admirably clear and clean. Ricci has an outstanding technique and he has also a very characteristic tone, which alongside Perlman's rich sound, for instance, is more open and uncovered. But the performance here has a fine intensity and there is a natural warmth which brings out the music's temperament without indulging it. The stereo recording matches the playing with well defined quality and plenty of depth.

Zukerman's account is splendidly eloquent, and the slow movement is played most beautifully. The recording is good too and the balance convincing within a fairly resonant acoustic. The transfer is on the whole successful, with good range, and there is more refinement here than in the generous Lalo coupling.

Suk's Supraphon version is surprisingly successful. The warmly resonant recording has transferred well, and the solo image is clearly projected against a substantial orchestral backcloth. The reading sounds freshly sympathetic, and although the finale is taken rather slowly it is not without sparkle. With a good coupling this is certainly enjoyable.

Erica Morini's account with Ferenc Fricsay is really very competitive at its bargain price. It dates from the late 1950s, but still sounds remarkably fresh and has the attraction of Glazounov's concerto as a coupling. Erica Morini's tender performance of the famous slow movement is particularly memorable. The recording has transferred well, and the cassette can be strongly recommended.

Grumiaux's thoughtful approach, although tasteful and enjoyable in its way, is on the cool side for such a red-blooded work, but with well-balanced recording this may well suit some, and the Mendelssohn coupling shows Grumiaux at his elegant best.

Yong Uck Kim is a player of sensitivity and refinement, and his accounts of both the Bruch and the Mendelssohn concertos impress by their purity of style and understated feeling. However, such an approach is rather less successful in this ripely romantic work than in the coupling, which readily responds to such delicacy of feeling. Unfortunately the orchestral accompaniment does not match the solo playing in finesse, but the recording is good and well balanced. The transfer, made at a fairly high level, provides full-blooded sound and quite good detail, although the orchestra sounds a trifle thick in texture.

Milstein's aristocratic and lyrical playing undoubtedly gives pleasure, but the recording could be fresher and more expansive. In the cassette transfer the upper partials of the violin are not entirely natural and the sound is edgy, with unrefined orchestral tuttis.

Violin concertos Nos. 1 in G minor, Op. 26; 2 in D minor, Op. 44.
**(*) HMV TC-ASD 2852. Yehudi Menuhin, LSO, Boult.

Were not the Bruch *First Violin concerto* such a striking masterpiece the *Second* might be better known. Its melodies have less individuality, but its romanticism is unforced and attractive and it is strong in atmosphere. Menuhin is persuasive in the warmth and obvious affection of his interpretation, but he tends to be somewhat sketchy in the detail of the solo part, and the intonation and focus of his playing are far from exact. Yet it says a great deal for the strength of his musical personality that, in spite of the technical lapses, the performance is so enjoyable. Boult's accompaniment is equally sympathetic and many will feel this a worthwhile addition to the catalogue. With the *G minor Concerto*, Menuhin is on familiar ground, but there is no sign of over-familiarity, and the lovely slow movement is given a performance of great warmth and spiritual beauty. The orchestra accompanies admirably, and the recording has transferred well to tape, with the soloist clearly focused. There is some muddiness in the orchestra in the finale of the *First Concerto*, but otherwise there is little to fault.

Violin concerto No. 1 in G minor, Op. 26; Scottish fantasia for violin and orchestra, Op. 46.

*** Decca KSXC 6573. Kyung-Wha Chung, RPO, Kempe.

The magic of Kyung-Wha Chung, a spontaneously inspired violinist if ever there was one, comes over beguilingly in this very desirable Bruch coupling. There may be more glossily perfect accounts of the famous *G minor Concerto*, but Kyung-Wha Chung goes straight to the heart, finding mystery and fantasy as well as more extrovert qualities. Just as strikingly in the *Scottish fantasia* she transcends the episodic nature of the writing to give the music a genuine depth and concentration, above all in the lovely slow movement. Kempe and the Royal Philharmonic, not always perfectly polished, give sympathetic accompaniment, well caught in a glowing recording. The tape transfer is of very good quality if not quite so rich as the LP, with the sharpness of the solo violin image emphasized by a degree of edge in the treble.

Violin concerto No. 2 in D minor, Op. 44; Scottish fantasia for violin and orchestra, Op. 46.

(***) HMV TC-ASD 3310.

Itzhak Perlman, New Philharmonia Orch., Lopez-Cobós.

Superlative playing from Perlman invests the first movement of the *Second Violin concerto* with such warmth that it compares favourably with the more famous G minor work. In Perlman's hands both the main themes are given a soaring memorability, and the coda is exquisitely managed. If the rest of the work has a lower level of inspiration, it is still richly enjoyable, and Perlman's account of the delightful *Scottish fantasia* is wholly delectable, showing the same degree of stylish lyricism and eloquence of phrasing. For those who already have a record of the *First Concerto* this coupling will be ideal, and the EMI recording is fully worthy of the performances. Unfortunately it has not transferred well to tape. There is a lack of refinement at orchestral tuttis, and the sound is poorly detailed.

Bruckner, Anton (1824–96)

Symphony No. 3 in D minor.

(M) *** DG Privilege 3335 265. Bavarian Radio Orch., Jochum.

** Decca KSXC 6505. Vienna PO, Boehm.

Now that Jochum's atmospheric and deeply felt account is available on Privilege it may be counted a clear first choice, indeed one of the most successful Bruckner recordings on cassette. Although the sound has not the very widest range it is rich and spacious with seldom any suggestion that the acoustic is not free. An excellent issue in every way. Boehm, like Jochum, uses the Nowak edition. His is the more recently recorded version and the performance is admirably free from eccentricity. However, this is not one of Decca's more refined transfers: at tuttis in the outer movements there is a hint of coarseness in the bass. The upper register is fresh and pleasing and the recording has a wider range than the DG Privilege issue, but the latter makes the more consistently agreeable listening.

Symphony No. 4 in E flat major (Romantic).

*** Decca KBB2 7039. Vienna PO, Boehm.

**(*) DG 3300 674 [id.]. Berlin PO, Karajan.

**(*) Decca KSXC 6227. LSO, Kertesz.

(M) (**) HMV TC-EXE 75. Philharmonia Orch., Klemperer.

*(*) DG 3300 328 [id.]. Chicago SO, Barenboim.

(M) * Turnabout KTVC 34107. Bamberg SO, Hollreiser.

The advantage of Boehm's compelling account in its disc version is that it accommodates each movement on a side, thus using two LPs instead of one. The tape, however, very sensibly fits the work on two sides, without any mid-movement breaks. Boehm's performance is splendidly free from eccentricity, beautifully shaped and finely played, and it deserves a strong recommendation, for the transfer is exceptionally sophisticated, spectacular in range if slightly dry in the bass. But it is issued as a 'double tape' to match the discs and is therefore expensive.

Karajan's DG recording is dramatically taut and more crisply disciplined than his HMV version (issued five years earlier on disc but not available on tape). Yet he retains all the qualities of strength and mystery. In the slow movement Karajan's lyricism is simpler and more natural, less consciously expressive than before, and the DG recording is refined and well detailed. On tape, however, its

lightness in the bass makes the balance sound somewhat top-heavy, and in the loudest climaxes this emphasis on the treble is not easy to rebalance satisfactorily with the controls.

Kertesz's issue was a comparatively early Decca one and the tape remains at full price, though the disc has been issued on Ace of Diamonds. It is a fine performance: Kertesz shows himself the master of the long crescendo, so that, with the widest dynamic range and beautifully controlled speeds, this is a vividly dramatic reading. In the first two movements, in particular, Kertesz even outshines Klemperer in the feeling of architectural strength, and though he misses some of the boisterous humour that Klemperer finds in the last two movements, this remains among the finest versions. The transfer is admirably clear and detailed, and although the transfer level is high there is absolutely no congestion. However, to achieve this the bass has been lightened and the balance is distinctly top-heavy throughout, although not shrill.

Klemperer's magisterial performance is only moderately well transferred to tape. Early copies offered different quality on each side, with side two brighter than side one. But a recent tape showed a poor degree of impact and generally unrefined sound quality, with congestion in the final climax. The reading has an impressive weight and cogency, but it needs better projection and detail than this.

The Chicago orchestra plays magnificently for Barenboim, and the recording is a fine one, but the reading is mannered and its insights confined to the surface. Hollreiser's performance too – even at Turnabout price – must be regretfully passed over. The reading lacks impact and character, and although the recording is acceptable it is by no means outstanding.

Symphony No. 5 in B flat major.
*** DG 3370 025 [id.]. Berlin PO, Karajan.

**(*) Decca KSXC2 7061. Vienna PO, Maazel.

Karajan's reading is not just poised and polished; it is superbly structured on every level, clear on detail as well as on overall architecture. Maybe the slow movement lacks some of the simple dedication which makes Jochum's reading with the same orchestra (available on disc only) so compelling, but here as in his other Bruckner performances for DG, Karajan takes a patrician view of this great and individual symphonist. The playing of the Berlin Philharmonic is magnificent and the recording rich and opulent to match, more spacious than some other recent offerings from this source. The transfer is sophisticated, refined in detail (although, as usual in Karajan DG recordings, the perspective changes slightly in the pianissimos), full-blooded but slightly dry in the bass. The second movement and finale have a slightly lower transfer level than sides one and three to accommodate the climaxes, and the range is, in consequence, fractionally less wide; but overall the sound is impressively clear.

Maazel's performance of the *Fifth* has a great deal to commend it. It is beautifully played and recorded: it has fine detail and body, and Maazel's control of tempo-changes is masterly, combining flexibility with firmness of grip. Yet ultimately the impression it leaves is curiously clinical. There is too little sense of atmosphere and of awareness of the spiritual dimensions of this composer. The transfer, however, has splendid richness, weight and detail, with biting brass and a natural sheen to the strings. The woodwind colour is luminous, and there is an agreeable spaciousness. The wide dynamic and frequency range is encompassed without any hint of congestion.

Symphony No. 6 in A major.
*(**) Decca KSXC 6682. Vienna PO, Stein.

Horst Stein gives a nobly-wrought performance with the Vienna Philharmonic. The slow movement has a genuine eloquence and gravity; and the performance of the other three is refreshingly free of eccentricity and strikes the right degree of breadth and dignity. Stein brings both imagination and feeling to this score and is excellently recorded. The cassette transfer is generally good, but the sound is a little turgid in the loudest climaxes. Thus the heavy brass scoring is not always congenial in the outer movements, although overall the quality is spacious, with plenty of bloom on the orchestra.

Symphony No. 7 in E major.
*** DG 3370 023 [id.]. Berlin PO, Karajan – WAGNER: *Siegfried idyll.****
(M) **(*) Philips 7431 125. Concertgebouw Orch., Haitink.
** Decca KCET2 7046. Vienna PO, Solti – WAGNER: *Siegfried idyll.****
*(*) RCA RK 31347. Leipzig Gewandhaus Orch., Masur.
(***) HMV TC-SLS 5086. Berlin PO, Karajan (with WAGNER: *Preludes to Parsifal and Tristan*(***)).

As with Bruckner's *Fourth*, Karajan recorded the *Seventh* for HMV five years before his DG version. The HMV recording was originally coupled to the *Fourth* but was later also issued in this coupling with some finely played Wagner excerpts. In the HMV performance of the *Seventh*, Karajan showed a superb feeling for the work's architecture, and the playing of the Berlin Philharmonic is gorgeous. However, the sound provided by the HMV tape transfer cannot claim this epithet. The final climax of the first movement is coarse, and the slow movement too loses its tonal beauty at peaks, where the sonority is lacking.

The DG recording earns no such strictures. This is undoubtedly a great performance: Karajan draws superb playing from the Berlin Philharmonic, and his newer interpretation shows even greater power and nobility. The richly textured string-playing in the slow movement is matched by brass timbres of comparable sonority. The scherzo's lyricism is beautifully caught, and the finale, like the reading as a whole, has strength without bombast. The transfer to tape is on the whole very successful. There are moments when the refinement slips a little (for example in the cymbal-topped climax of the slow movement) and there is a hint of roughness at the very loudest tuttis; but generally the body and detail of the sound are impressive, and this makes a clear first choice on tape.

Haitink's reading, originally coupled to the *Te Deum*, has been reissued and, complete on two sides, is a bargain in the medium price-range, even though there is a (well-placed) turnover break in the *Adagio*. The performance is eminently committed, finely played and well recorded. The slow movement lacks a degree of expansive warmth – the climax is not quite so overwhelming as with Karajan – but the reading as a whole spans the overall architecture impressively. The tape transfer is of excellent quality; the sound is less sumptuous than the DG Karajan set, but the big climaxes are captured without congestion, and there is good balance and inner detail.

We have somewhat mixed views about the Solti performance. R.L. admires it rather more than do E.G. or I.M. Certainly the orchestral playing does not lack intensity, but the string-playing in the *Adagio* has a certain febrile quality that is not wholly sympathetic; and the timing of the great climax does not produce the sense of architectural inevitability that Karajan conveys. The Decca tape transfer is undoubtedly admirable. The textures have excellent detail, while the brass sonorities are captured realistically. The slow movement's peak is managed with

much more clarity than on the DG version, and the closing pages of the first and last movements are accommodated with barely a hint of strain.

Masur's performance opens with impressively romantic atmosphere: the climbing theme of the first movement has a genuine feeling of mystery and anticipation. But although the orchestra plays eloquently the performance as a whole lacks the sense of architectural inevitability, and the placing of the slow movement climax (the cymbal clash omitted) is not wholly convincing. The recording is generally good, but the strings tend to lack bloom in the upper register, and this fault is emphasized by the balance on tape, which also has moments when at lower levels the orchestral textures lack a degree of security. The break in the slow movement is clumsily managed, with the sound cut off suddenly.

Symphonies Nos. 7 in E major; 8 in C minor.
   *(*) DG 3371 027 [id.]. Vienna PO, Boehm.

Boehm's account of No. 7 comes in harness with No. 8. It goes without saying that the playing of the Vienna Philharmonic is of the highest order, but the performances taken as a whole are plain to the point of being dour. There is a fine sense of architecture and the music is firmly held together, but Boehm's phrasing is often prosaic and lacking in magic. The recording is admirably vivid and clear, and the tape transfers are up to DG's usual high standard: No. 8 is especially good and Bruckner's heavy brass scoring is carefully balanced so that the textures do not become congested.

Symphony No. 8 in C minor.
   *** DG 3370 019 [id.]. Berlin PO, Karajan.
   *(*) Decca KSXC2 7023. Los Angeles PO, Mehta.

Karajan has recorded the *Eighth* in

stereo twice, first for HMV in 1958 and again for DG in 1976. The newer DG set has greater richness and refinement of recording, and the performance is noble and searching, the approach consistent with the earlier version (which is not available on tape), although the later reading has perhaps the greater depth. It is majestic, massive in scale, and immaculate in detail, and the tape transfer is one of DG's very best, with an extremely wide dynamic range, yet no lack of detail at *pianissimo* levels. The recording expands massively to the huge climaxes, with great weight and amplitude in the third movement (where the level rises slightly) and finale. There is a warmth in the sound and a beautiful sheen on the high strings which gives special distinction here. At the closing climax of the finale the refinement slips fractionally, but for the most part this is of demonstration quality.

The Los Angeles orchestra plays well for Mehta, but the Decca engineers did not match their colleagues who made Solti's Bruckner recordings in Vienna. And, technically impressive as the playing is, there is something too glossy, not searching enough, in the results, and the sublime slow movement tends to be vulgarized. The sound of the tape transfer is impressively rich, although just occasionally the heavy brass strain the engineers' resources and there is a hint of congestion.

Symphony No. 9 in D minor.
   *** DG 3300 828 [id.]. Berlin PO, Karajan.
   **(*) Decca KSXC 6202. Vienna PO, Mehta.
   (B) **(*) Philips 7327 058. Concertgebouw Orch., van Beinum.
   *(*) HMV TC-ASD 3382. Chicago SO, Giulini.

Eight years separated Karajan's two recordings of Bruckner's *Ninth*, both made with the Berlin Philharmonic for DG. The earlier version was available on cassette (923078) although in the UK not in Dolbyized form. Good though that earlier tape was, it is in any case superseded on technical grounds by this new one, and the closer recording quality has proved suitable for cassette transfer. The differences between the two performances are relatively small. The earlier version brings natural gravity and profound contemplation in greater measure, with manners a degree more affectionate; the new one concentrates on strength and impact. As before, the playing of the Berlin Philharmonic is immaculate, and the music is allowed to speak for itself, yet the overall architecture is firmly shaped. A most impressive issue.

Mehta's reading has moments of considerable power and orchestral playing of great splendour. In overall cogency it does not match Karajan's versions, and the somewhat febrile, oversweet *vibrato* on the strings at the opening of the finale is rather tiresome on repetition. Nonetheless this is not to be dismissed out of hand, and Decca's recording is up to the high standards of the house. Not a first recommendation, maybe, but a much better performance than one had expected, and the transfer has an impressively wide dynamic range and is generally well detailed. The sound is less dramatically incisive than the German transfer of Karajan's DG issue (although some later copies of the DG tape are not so sharply focused), but it has richer, more glowing string tone than the DG recording. Moreover the Decca recording offers two movements on each side (leaving a run-off of 9½ minutes on side two), whereas the DG tape makes a break in the middle of the scherzo.

Eduard van Beinum's splendid performance dates from the mid-1950s, but the sound is remarkably fresh and eminently well balanced. Only in the most massive climaxes does one feel the absence of stereo and the need for the texture to open out. Van Beinum's reading has superb control and feeling for proportion, and the playing of the Concertgebouw Orchestra is beyond praise. This *Ninth* has breadth and majesty; in magic and atmosphere as well as the quality of the recording, it is surpassed by Karajan and Jochum (the latter not available on cassette) but in all other respects it holds its own. The cassette serves as a reminder of the high standards of engineering achieved by the Dutch engineers in the 1950s; the aural perspective is natural and the sound is truthful in timbre and clean in focus. At the price this is highly competitive and it is to be preferred to the Giulini.

Giulini's version of the *Ninth* is a good deal less persuasive than its rivals. There is no lack of power or grandeur, and predictably Giulini expends enormous care over detail, fashioning each phrase with care and thought. Indeed this may lie at the heart of the problem, for in some ways the sheer mystery of this noble score seems to elude him, even if he uncovers much beauty of detail. The transfer generally reproduces well and has a spacious sound, but readers should be warned that something goes awry in the horn parts in the first movement (bars 551 onwards). This cassette offers no serious challenge to its competitors.

Intermezzo and trio for string quintet.
*** CRD CRDC 4046. Augmented Alberni Qt – BRAHMS: *Sextet No. 2.****

Bruckner wrote this attractive *Intermezzo and trio* as an alternative movement for the scherzo of his *Quintet in F major*, which was considered 'too difficult'. Following on after the vigorous finale of the Brahms *Sextet* the autumnal feeling of the Bruckner with its lighter (but still rich) textures makes a most pleasing 'encore'. The recording is excellent and the transfer freshly vivid, with fine range and detail.

Helgoland.
*** Symphonica CSYM 11. Ambrosian Male-Voice Chorus, Symphonica of London, Morris – WAGNER: *Das Liebesmahl der Apostel.***(*)

Helgoland was written during the long-delayed composition of Bruckner's *Ninth Symphony*, and might be regarded as a secular counterpart to the *Te Deum*. It is as well to ignore the banal words of Dr August Silberstein about the North Sea island which in succession was under the crowns of Denmark and Great Britain before being ceded to Germany. Though latterly the work has been underprized, early responses were more enthusiastic than was common with Bruckner, and this recording, well conducted by Wyn Morris, helps to explain why. The sound is atmospheric and spacious, and although, as in the Wagner coupling, the chorus is backwardly balanced, the final climax has splendid breadth. It is extremely well captured in this excellent tape transfer.

Mass No. 2 in E minor; Te Deum.
*(*) Decca KSXC 6837. Judith Blegen, Margarita Lilove, Claes Haaken Ahnsjö, Peter Meven, Vienna State Opera Chorus, Vienna PO, Mehta; Josef Bock (organ).
Te Deum.
(*) DG 3300 704 [id.]. Anna Tomowa-Sintow, Agnes Baltsa, Werner Krenn, Peter Schreier, José van Dam, Vienna Singverein, Berlin PO, Karajan – MOZART: *Mass No. 16.*(*)

Karajan's account of the *Te Deum* is spacious and strong, bringing out the score's breadth and drama. This is very satisfying, and if the coupling is suitable this is self-recommending. The transfer to tape has an impressive breadth. The level is high for DG, and there is occasionally a hint that it is fractionally too high, but the vividness of the sound is striking.

The Mehta issue is much less attractive. The Decca transfer is good on the whole, though one does feel the need for a more open quality in the choral sound. But it is not that the recording is essentially lacking in projection or realism, but rather that the performances are not really idiomatic. Mehta is a shade too expressive and his chorus a little too operatic in character as well as name.

Butterworth, George (1885–1916)

The Banks of Green Willow (*idyll*); *2 English idylls; A Shropshire Lad* (*rhapsody*).
> ****(*)** Argo KZRC 860 [id.]. Academy of St Martin-in-the-Fields, Marriner – BRITTEN: *Variations on a theme of Frank Bridge.*****(*)**

These appealing pieces are given beautiful performances by Marriner and the Academy. Boult's recording of the same works (on a Lyrita LP) brings perhaps an even greater degree of finesse, but these are very fine indeed. The recording is vivid and wide-ranging, but the quality of the transfer seems to tighten its upper register and the violins are given added edge. This music needs atmosphere in preference to such brightly lit timbres, and one has to take care with the controls to restore the warmth of the recording. Even so, by the standard of some other companies' tape issues this is still an attractive cassette.

Byrd, William (1543–1623)

Ave verum; Domine, salva nos; Gaudeamus omnes; Haec dies; Ne irascaris; Vide, domine.
> ******* HMV TC-CSD 3779. The King's Singers – TALLIS: *Lamentations.********

With a small consort of voices these great Byrd motets lose little or none of their intensity of expression, and with its fine coupling this is a refreshing tape. As ever, the ensemble of the King's Singers is immaculate, and the quality of the transfer is excellent too. The voices are caught with absolute naturalness, and the resonance of the acoustic provides warmth and bloom without loss of refinement or detail.

Mass for four voices; Mass for five voices.
> ******* Argo KZRC 858 [id.]. Christ Church Cathedral Choir, Oxford, Preston.

Though the couplings are different, it is fascinating to compare the Christ Church performances of both *Masses* with those of King's College Choir, recorded over a decade earlier and not yet issued on tape. In the four-part *Mass* the Oxford choir's more forthright, less moulded style is most refreshing, but sounds relatively square in rhythm. In the five-part *Mass*, on the other hand, the Christ Church choristers outshine their Cambridge rivals with a sharper, more dramatic performance, which is superbly resilient in the often complex cross-rhythms. The recording is gloriously clear and atmospheric, with the voices sharply distinguished across the stereo spectrum. The tape transfer is absolutely immaculate, beautifully focused.

Canteloube, Marie-Joseph (1879–1957)

Chants d'Auvergne (arrangements):
*Baïlero; 3 Bourées; L'Aio dè rotso;
Ound' onorèn gorda; Obal din lou
Limouzi; La delaïssádo; Lo fiolaire;
Passo pel prat; Brezairola; Chut
chut.*

*** HMV TC-ASD 2826. Victoria
de los Angeles (soprano), Lamoureux Orch., Jacquillat –
CHAUSSON: *Poème de l'amour
et de la mer.***(*)

Canteloube, pupil of Vincent d'Indy,
made a collection of charming folk-songs
from the Auvergne which he then presented with seductive opulence. Some
might prefer an edgier, more French-
sounding voice, but the warmth of Victoria de los Angeles's tone matches exactly the allure of the settings of this
selection of ten songs. The transfer is distinctly successful with both sparkle and
warmth given to the voice as well as the
accompaniment; the Chausson coupling
was rather less clearly focused on our
copy.

*Chants d'Auvergne: L'Antouèno;
Pastourelle; L'Aio dè rotso; Baïlèro;
Passo pel prat; Malurous qu'o uno
fenno; Brezairola.*

(**) RCA RK 42006. Anna Moffo
(soprano), American SO,
Stokowski – RACHMANINOV:
Vocalise; VILLA-LOBOS: *Bachianas Brasilieras No. 5.*(**)

Moffo too gives radiant performances,
helped by the sumptuous accompaniment which Stokowski provides. The
result is sweet, seductively so, but unfortunately the sound on the cassette is shrill
(one needs a strong treble cut to make the
quality comfortable), and there is little
weight at the bass end.

Carter, Elliot (born 1908)

String quartets Nos. 1 and 2.
** Advent D 1007 (see p. xxiii)
[id.]. Composers Qt.

Tough scores that repay study but
whose idiom will doubtless prove too
rebarbative to the general listener.
Carter's mind is complex and his textures
are densely argued and impenetrable.
The sound tends to be a little aggressive
but the performances have authority and
it would be difficult to improve on them.
Carter is a highly respected figure, and
this is a valuable addition to the repertory.

Castelnuovo-Tedesco, Mario (1895–1968)

Guitar concerto in D major, Op. 99.
**(*) DG 3300 718 [id.]. Narciso
Yepes, LSO, Navarro – VILLA-
LOBOS: *Concerto.***(*)
** CBS 40-76634. John Williams,
ECO, Groves – ARNOLD: *Sere-
nade**; DODGSON: *Concerto
No. 2.***(*)

Castelnuovo-Tedesco's *Guitar concerto* is a work of considerable charm
with its gently lyrical first movement and
an *Andantino* with a 'lollipop' tune that
reminds one of something else. It is very
well played by Yepes, who is attentively
accompanied by Navarro and the LSO.
The DG transfer is of excellent quality,
lacking only the last degree of range and
sparkle.

John Williams has recorded the concerto before, with Ormandy, but that version is no longer available. It was fresher and had more pace than the new recording with Groves. Here Williams is placed far forward, with the result that it is not always possible to locate him in relation to his colleagues. But if the sound is untruthful as far as perspective is concerned (and there are few concertante guitar records that do not suffer from this fault in some degree) it is by no means unpleasing. These artists make the most of the slow movement's poetry, and the work has considerable melodic appeal. The attractions of this cassette are the accompanying works, particularly Stephen Dodgson's *Second Concerto*.

Chabrier, Emmanuel (1841–94)

España (rhapsody).
  (M) *** Decca Eclipse KECC 797. LSO, Argenta – *Concert.***(*)

Argenta's account is brilliant and sparkling, the finest in the present catalogues, and it is vivaciously recorded. The couplings, Spanish dances by Granados and Moszkowski and Rimsky-Korsakov's *Capriccio espagnol*, are no less attractively presented. This tape is discussed in more detail in our Concerts section below. The transfer offers vivid quality in the Chabrier.

España (rhapsody); *Habañera; Marche joyeuse; Suite pastorale; Le Roi malgré lui* (opera): *Danse slave; Fête polonaise.*
  (M) *(*) HMV Greensleeve TC-ESD 7046. Paris Opera Orch., Mari.
España (rhapsody); *Marche joyeuse; Suite pastorale; Le Roi malgré lui* (opera): *Danse slave; Fête polonaise.*

  (M) **(*) Decca Jubilee KJBC 10. Suisse Romande Orch., Ansermet.

Ansermet's tape offers extremely brilliant recording, typical of Decca's best in terms of amplitude (and percussion and bass drum) but with rather more edge to the treble than on some recordings from this source. The performances are all good, with a certain Gallic accent coming through in places, but *España* lacks the uninhibited exuberance that Beecham, for instance, brought to it. Those who like this touch of reserve will also like the *Suite pastorale*, which is rather contained, especially in the third movement, *Sous Bois*. However, the *Marche joyeuse* certainly offers its measure of high spirits; the *Danse slave* has an agreeable panache, and the *Fête polonaise* goes splendidly. With all one's reservations, as a whole this tape offers an enjoyable selection of Chabrier's most attractive music, and the transfer is first-class, with plenty of sparkle in the percussion and the bass drum accommodated impressively.

The Opera Orchestra is not among the finest ensembles Paris can offer and the playing on the HMV tape does not match the standards of finish and elegance one would expect from the Orchestre National. Jean-Baptiste Mari's performance of *España* is lively and direct, but in the last analysis it lacks *élan*. It is well played, as is the rest of the programme here, although the conductor's *rubato* in *Fête polonaise* is not wholly convincing. The charming *Suite pastorale* is effective. The sound is certainly bright and clear. But it lacks sumptuousness, and the tape transfer emphasizes this lack of richness in the middle frequencies, and hardens the treble noticeably in both *España* and the *Suite*. One can adjust the controls, of course, but undoubtedly the Decca cassette offers a better quality, even though the recording is obviously not so modern.

149

Chaminade, Cécile
(1857–1944)

Concertino for flute and orchestra,
Op. 107.
   *** RCA RK 25109. James
   Galway, RPO, Dutoit –
   FAURÉ: *Fantaisie*; IBERT: *Con-*
   certo; POULENC: *Sonata*.***

The Chaminade *Concertino* undoubtedly has great charm. The principal
theme of the first movement is of the kind
that insinuates itself irresistibly into the
subconscious, and the work has a delightful period atmosphere. It is splendidly
played by James Galway, who is given
excellent support by the RPO under
Charles Dutoit. The recording is admirably spacious and finely detailed, and it
has transferred to cassette with excellent
presence and no lack of bloom. Altogether this is a most desirable and enjoyable anthology.

Charpentier, Marc-Antoine
(1634–1704)

Magnificat; Te Deum.
   **(*) HMV TC-ASD 3482. Felicity
   Lott, Eiddwen Harrhy, Charles
   Brett, Ian Partridge, Stephen
   Roberts, King's College Choir,
   Academy of St Martin-in-the-
   Fields, Ledger.

This is the best-known of Marc-
Antoine Charpentier's *Te Deum* settings
written for the Sainte-Chapelle. There is a
mixture of choruses, solo numbers and
concertante movements, for which Charpentier provides invention of no mean
distinction. The *Magnificat* is in D minor,
for double choir, and has a good deal of

antiphonal writing. Although none of
this music has the depth of Purcell, it has
a *douceur* and a freshness that make it
highly appealing. The performances have
vitality and boldness, and the singing is
stylish. The sound on tape is of pleasing
quality. The choral detail lacks the last
degree of freshness (this is more noticeable in the *Magnificat* on side two), and
the forwardly balanced soloists are not
quite as clearly defined as they might be;
but the overall balance is effective and the
orchestra generally sounds well.

Chausson, Ernest
(1855–99)

Poème for violin and orchestra, Op.
25.
   (M) *** HMV TC-EXE 73. Nathan
   Milstein, Philharmonia Orch.,
   Fistoulari – SAINT-SAËNS: *Con-*
   certo No. 3 etc.**(*)
   ** CBS 40-76530 [Col. MT 34550].
   Isaac Stern, Orchestre de Paris,
   Barenboim – FAURÉ: *Berceuse*;
   SAINT-SAËNS: *Concerto No.*
   3.*(*)
   (B) * DG Heliodor 3348 264.
   Miriam Fried (violin), Gisele
   Demoulin (piano) – SIBELIUS:
   Concerto.*

Chausson's beautiful *Poème* is
brought off successfully on the medium-
priced HMV cassette. Milstein's account
is still among the best on the market;
though not new it sounds remarkably
fresh and is excellently balanced. The
transfer is vivid, with a believable image
for the soloist.

In Stern's fine reading the *Poème* has
strength and no sentimentality, and the
CBS recording has good detail, with a
strong forward projection for the soloist.

But the transfer of the Fauré and Saint-Saëns couplings is rather less distinguished. Miriam Fried hardly competes: her version is recorded with piano, and the keyboard makes a very monochrome substitute for Chausson's evocative scoring. The transfer is of good quality.

Poème de l'amour et de la mer (song cycle), *Op. 19*.
   *** HMV TC-ASD 3455. Janet Baker (mezzo-soprano), LSO, Previn – DUPARC: *Mélodies*.***
   (*) HMV TC-ASD 2826. Victoria de los Angeles (soprano), Lamoureux Orch., Jacquillat – CANTELOUBE: *Chants d'Auvergne*.*
   (**) Symphonica CSYM 6 [Peters PCE 021]. Montserrat Caballé (soprano), Symphonica of London, Morris – DEBUSSY: *La Damoiselle élue*.(**)

Dame Janet Baker, always at her most inspired in French music, gives a glorious, heartfelt performance of the *Poème de l'amour et de la mer*, both radiant and searching, so that this picture of love in two aspects, first emergent, then past, has a sharpness of focus often denied it. The singer is superbly reinforced by the accompaniment of Previn and the LSO, with clarity and warmth combined. The transfer is very kind to the voice and provides a glowingly atmospheric orchestral backcloth, even if the upper range of the orchestral sound lacks something in detail and definition.

The voice of Victoria de los Angeles is also well suited to Chausson's warm and evocative piece. Coupled with Canteloube's charming folk-song settings, it can certainly be recommended, although on tape the sound is less clearly focused than in the coupling, and occasionally the texture seems marginally insecure.

Montserrat Caballé, singing a role often taken by a mezzo-soprano, gives a warmly expressive reading, but next to the versions by Dame Janet Baker and Los Angeles it lacks a specific understanding of either the words or the music. But anyone attracted to the rare Debussy coupling will find much that is beautiful here, including the atmospheric orchestral backing provided by Wyn Morris. Unfortunately the tape transfer, although slightly fresher than in the Debussy coupling, is very restricted in range and the voice tends to harden in climaxes.

Cherubini, Luigi (1760–1842)

Requiem in D minor (for male voices and orchestra).
   *** HMV TC-ASD 3073. Ambrosian Singers, New Philharmonia Orch., Muti.

The darkness of colour in Cherubini's *D minor Requiem* using male voices goes with much solemn minor-key music (a little inflated by Beethovenian standards) and some striking anticipations of Verdi. In this fine, committed performance under Muti, one forgets the scarcity of really memorable melodies and relishes the drama and distinctive textures, particularly when the recording is so good. Moreover it has been successfully transferred at a high level, so that the full body of the choral tone is given eloquent projection, while the *piano* passages have both detail and substance.

Chopin, Frédéric
(1810–49)

CONCERTANTE AND
ORCHESTRAL MUSIC

Andante spianato and Grande polonaise brillante, Op. 22; Krakowiak (concert rondo), Op. 14.

(M) *** Turnabout KTVC 137015. Peter Frankl, Innsbruck SO, Wagner – LISZT: *Hungarian fantasia; Mephisto waltz.****

Peter Frankl's sensitive performances of the *Andante spianato* and the *Krakowiak* (which has a couple of fetching tunes, one at the opening and one later on) have much to commend them. The Turnabout recording is good, if a little reverberant, and the cassette version is outstanding, in many ways preferable to the disc. Also it includes a makeweight, not on the disc, Brendel's performance of Liszt's *Mephisto waltz*. The piano tone in the latter piece is less real than elsewhere (reflecting the early date of the recording), but in general this tape offers quality which is demonstration-worthy in its sparkle and naturalness.

Piano concerto No. 1 in E minor, Op. 11.

*** DG 3301 125. Krystian Zimerman, Los Angeles PO, Giulini.

(*) DG 923083 [id.]. Martha Argerich, LSO, Abbado – LISZT: *Concerto No. 1.*(*)

Piano concerto No. 1; Krakowiak, Op. 14.

(B) *(*) DG Heliodor 3348 066. Stefan Askenase, Hague Residentie Orch., Otterloo.

Piano concerto No. 1; Mazurkas Nos. 5 in B flat major, Op. 7/1; 46 in C

major, Op. 67/3; 47 in A minor, Op. 68/2; 54 in D major, Op. posth.

(M) ** DG Privilege 3335 206. Tamás Vásáry, Berlin, PO, Semkow.

Piano concerto No. 1; Piano sonata No. 2 in B flat minor (Funeral march), Op. 35.

*(*) Decca Phase 4 KPFC 4311. Israela Margalit, New Philharmonia Orch., Maazel.

Pollini's famous recording of Chopin's *E minor Concerto* was available for a brief span on an HMV cassette (TC-EXE 66) but was then withdrawn. However, Zimerman's is arguably the finest version of the concerto to have appeared in the 1970s, and is worthy to stand alongside Pollini's classic account and Gilels's famous recording from the mid-sixties. He is fresh, poetic and individual in his approach, and is afforded a cleanly detailed recording by the DG engineers. A sparkling, beautifully characterized reading which differs in many details from Zimerman's concert performances that we have heard broadcast, but which remains spontaneous and freshly elegant. The transfer is first-class – of DG's best quality.

The distinction of the Argerich/Abbado performance is immediately apparent in the opening orchestral *ritornello* with Abbado's flexible approach. Martha Argerich follows his lead and her affectionate phrasing provides some lovely playing, especially in the slow movement. Perhaps in the passage-work she is sometimes rather too intense, giving the music a toccata-like effect, but this is far preferable to the rambling style we are sometimes offered. With excellent recording this is, after Pollini's, one of the most satisfactory versions of this elusive concerto available on tape or disc.

The Privilege transfer of Vásáry's performance sounds well, with a good balance and excellent piano tone. Vásáry's manner is somewhat self-effacing: the gentle poetry of the solo playing is in distinct contrast with the much more extrovert orchestral contribution under Semkow. But soloist and orchestra match their styles in the slow movement, which is beautifully done, and the finale has no lack of vivacity and sparkle.

Askenase on Heliodor still offers good value in the bargain field, though there is a certain pallor about his playing. It is refined, stylish and neat but he is not as strongly characterful as Argerich or Vásáry in No. 1, at any rate, though he is well served by the Hague Residentie Orchestra under Willem van Otterloo (and by the DG engineers). The sound is still remarkably fresh for its period and there is a nice, aristocratic feel to the solo playing. The transfer is of excellent quality.

On Decca husband and wife as conductor and soloist, Maazel and Margalit, produce a harmonious, enjoyable reading of the concerto; but with indifferent orchestral playing and idiosyncratic sound it is not one of the most recommendable versions. Nor can this version of the sonata quite compare with the finest available.

Piano concerto No. 2 in F minor, Op. 21.

*** Decca KSXC 16528. Alicia de Larrocha, Suisse Romande Orch., Comissiona – FALLA: *Nights in the Gardens of Spain.***(*)

(***) Decca KSXC 6174 [Lon. 5-6440]. Vladimir Ashkenazy, LSO, Zinman – BACH: *Harpsichord concerto No. 1.*(**)

** DG 3301 042 [id.]. Martha Argerich, National SO of Washington, Rostropovich – SCHUMANN: *Piano concerto.***

Piano concerto No. 2; Polonaises Nos. 3 in A major, Op. 40/1; 6 in A flat major, Op. 53.

(B) *(*) DG Heliodor 3348 124.

Stefan Askenase, Berlin PO, Ludwig.

Ashkenazy's sympathy with the music is very obvious and his sophisticated use of light and shade in the opening movement, and the subtlety of phrasing and *rubato*, are a constant source of pleasure. The recitativo section in the *Larghetto*, which can often sound merely rhetorical, is here shaped with mastery, and there is a delicious lightness of touch in the finale. David Zinman and the players of the LSO are obviously in full contact with the soloist. Unfortunately the transfer to tape has been made at fractionally too high a level and there is a lack of refinement in the orchestral sound, rare for Decca. Moreover the Bach coupling offers real coarseness.

Larrocha's account is attractive and poetic. It is beautifully played, and matches her excellent performance of the Falla coupling. There is much to admire here, including the fine Decca engineering. The transfer of the Chopin offers first-rate quality, rich and smooth, yet with no lack of presence.

A strong but not always very romantic performance from Argerich and Rostropovich. Although the slow movement has an eloquent central climax, its full poetry does not emerge until the closing pages, and the finale, though vivacious, is not really memorable. Excellent recording and a lively, well-detailed transfer, but the wide dynamic range brings some recession of imagery in the score's quieter passages.

Askenase's playing seems somewhat slack and lacking in character. His sensibility asserts itself in the slow movement, but in the last analysis this cannot be strongly recommended, even at Heliodor price; the *Polonaises* which act as a filler are disappointing too. The transfer is of first-rate quality, fresh, natural and well balanced, with excellent piano tone.

(i) *A Month in the Country* (ballet; arr. John Lanchbery); *Barcarolle,*

153

Op. 60; Waltz in E major, Op. posth.
(M) *(*) HMV Greensleeve TC-ESD 7037. Philip Gammon (piano), (i) with Royal Opera House, Covent Garden, Orch., Lanchbery.

John Lanchbery's score for Frederick Ashton's ballet, based on Turgenev's *A Month in the Country*, is constructed from concertante works that Chopin wrote in his late teens, the *Fantasy on Polish airs*, the *Grande polonaise brillante* (which the composer joined to the *Andante spianato* years later) and the *Là ci darem variations* (using Mozart's air from *Don Giovanni*). Lanchbery comments – not unfairly – that Chopin's scoring is 'slender and at times sketchy', and so he has added his own touching up (although it does not seem to make a great deal of difference). The result is a very lightweight score which needs a pianist like Rubinstein to bring it fully to life. Philip Gammon's playing is musical and accomplished, and the orchestral accompaniment is tasteful. The transfer to tape is acceptable but more suitable for a modest player than for wide-range reproduction. The orchestral sound lacks inner detail, although the piano timbre is pleasant enough, especially in the solo items provided as a makeweight.

Les Sylphides (ballet; orchestrated by Roy Douglas).
(M) *** DG Privilege 3335 189. Berlin PO, Karajan – DELIBES: *Coppélia.****
(M) ** Decca Eclipse KECC 809. Paris Conservatoire Orch., Maag – DELIBES: *La Source.***

Karajan has the advantage of limpid and svelte playing from the Berlin Philharmonic Orchestra and he evokes a delicacy of texture which consistently delights the ear. The woodwind solos are played gently and lovingly and one can feel the conductor's touch on the phrasing. The recording is warm and vivid, the upper register not lacking sparkle, but it is slightly less smooth than the sound on disc.

The Paris Conservatoire plays sensitively under the musical baton of Peter Maag, and the French wind-playing has plenty of character. The transfer to tape is vivid without lacking warmth, and the rather bright, pithy string tone of the recording is agreeably mellowed.

PIANO MUSIC

Ballades Nos. 1 in G minor, Op. 23; 2 in F major, Op. 38; 3 in A flat major, Op. 47; 4 in F minor, Op. 52; 3 Nouvelles études, Op. posth.
*** Decca KSXC 6143. Vladimir Ashkenazy.

Ballades Nos. 1–4; Fantaisie in F minor, Op. 49.
*** Philips 7300 605. Claudio Arrau.
(M) *(*) Turnabout KTVC 34271. Peter Frankl.

Ballades Nos. 1–4; Fantaisie-impromptu in C sharp minor, Op. 66; Impromptus Nos. 1–3.
(M) ** DG Privilege 3335 284. Tamás Vásáry.

Ballades Nos. 1–4; Fantaisie-impromptu in C sharp minor, Op. 66; Polonaise No. 6 in A flat major, Op. 53.
**(*) HMV TC-ASD 3552. Cristina Ortiz.

There is no technical reservation about Ashkenazy's finely recorded Decca tape. Indeed the recording here is admirably natural and clear, although on our copy the sound on side two seemed marginally crisper in focus. The readings are thoughtful and essentially unflashy. The *rubato* arises naturally from Ashkenazy's personal approach to the music. The intimacy of the recording allows him to share this with the listener. The openings of the *First* and *Fourth Ballades* show this quality well; the music unfolds naturally and without emphasis. All in all this is a most satisfying tape, with beautiful performances of the *Nouvelles études* thrown in for good measure.

Arrau's coupling of the four *Ballades* with the *Fantaisie in F minor* is characteristically individual. The playing has Arrau's usual command and technical control, but here there is a searching quality and a spontaneity too which he does not always find in the recording studio. His seriousness of purpose is heightened by the freshness of the *rubato* (immediately noticeable in the *Ballade in G minor*). It is as though Arrau were seeking to present Chopin not just as a romantic composer but within the broad classical tradition with Schubert and Schumann, even as a successor to Beethoven. The rich colouring and bold, weighty tonal production help to sustain this conception. The *Fantaisie* is undoubtedly compelling played in this way, thoughtful yet with great strength. Superb piano recording, richly and clearly transferred. A first-rate cassette in every way.

Cristina Ortiz aims at a popular recital. She plays simply and eloquently and her phrasing is thoroughly musical, the *rubato* natural. If the last degree of lyric fervour is sometimes missing, this is still very enjoyable, and the recording is very well balanced. The tape transfer too is excellent, full and vivid with no hardness in the treble and there is both colour and resonance to give the timbre body and character.

Vásáry's coupling is generous and on the whole attractive. He is rather matter-of-fact in the *Impromptus*, but the performances have excellent detail and are not insensitive. The *Ballades* are imaginatively played, and these readings, although personal, offer poetry as well as bravura. The *G minor Ballade* is outstanding, with a fine romantic sweep, but

the other three are each individual and rewarding. The piano tone is on the dry side, although bolder and slightly fuller in the *Ballades*. The transfers are of excellent quality throughout.

Peter Frankl shows himself a Chopin player of remarkable sensitivity and flair. There is a most affecting intimacy in his gentle opening of the *F major* and *F minor Ballades* to show that his approach is not that of the barnstorming virtuoso; yet there is romantic exuberance in plenty in the eloquent phrases of the *G minor* and *A flat major* works. The feeling of impetuosity which a youthful player can bring to this music is here tempered by the intelligence with which the mood and atmosphere of these contrasted pieces are so surely caught. The serious opening of the *Fantaisie* is particularly well managed. Unfortunately the recording is not outstanding; it is on the hard side, and the quality of the Turnabout cassette is rather shallow, acceptable but not excellent: in the louder passages one notices the lack of deep sonority in the bass.

Études, Op. 10/1–12; Op. 25/1–12.

> **(*)** DG 3300 287 [id.]. Maurizio Pollini.
> **(*)** Decca KSXC 6710 [Lon. 5-6844]. Vladimir Ashkenazy.
> (M) ** Philips 7317 184. Nikita Magaloff.
> (M) ** DG Privilege 3335 266. Tamás Vásáry.
> ** Advent E 1018 (see p. xxiii) [id.]. Ilana Vered.

Pollini's electrifying account is masterly. He won the Warsaw Chopin Prize in 1959 when he was only eighteen and his playing of the Polish master has not declined in the meantime. These must be given a strong recommendation in spite of the recording, which is clear but rather shallow, and sometimes verges on the brittle. The ample brightness means that one can readily cut back the treble and remove any vestiges of tape hiss, but the tendency for the timbre to sound hard-edged can make the recording sound over-emphatic, especially on a smaller player.

Ashkenazy's Decca issue completely supersedes his earlier recording on Melodiya imports or *Chant du Monde*. Playing of total mastery and excellently recorded, this can safely be recommended alongside Pollini's, and the choice left to individual taste. The Decca transfer – made at a high level – generally sounds more congenial than the DG tape. The piano tone, however, is a trifle metallic and not wholly natural.

Assured performances from Magaloff, offering very accomplished and certainly characterful playing. If occasionally the last touch of individuality is missing, the studies flow attractively from one to another giving the spontaneous feeling of live music-making. The piano tone is convincingly rich and firm, but lacks something in sparkle. The transfer level is only moderately high, but as the upper range of the recording is mellow anyway, one can cut back any remaining hiss without affecting the timbre greatly.

Vásáry's performances are boldly confident and in general his technique is equal to the considerable demands of the music. But the playing is not as imaginative as that offered by either Ashkenazy or Pollini, and the lyrical studies do not always blossom as they might. Nevertheless with clear piano timbre (not richly coloured) and a consistently clean transfer this may be considered good value in the medium price-range.

Ilana Vered plays with great fluency and often impresses with her flair. There are, however, some self-indulgent touches and some wilful *rubato* that does not fully convince. The recording is somewhat bottom-heavy and not always clean, so that this does not in any sense challenge the recommendations above.

Impromptus Nos. 1 in A flat major, Op. 29; 2 in F sharp major, Op. 36; 3 in G flat major, Op. 51; Fantaisie-impromptu in C sharp minor, Op. 66; Scherzi Nos. 1 in B minor, Op. 20; 2 in B flat minor, Op. 31; 3 in C sharp minor, Op. 39; 4 in E major, Op. 54.

*(*) DG 3336 378. Roberto Szidon.

Roberto Szidon is a strong player but he is more convincing in the *Impromptus*, which are given an appropriate improvisatory quality, than in the *Scherzi*. Here his playing is distinguished by an impressive dexterity and attack, and its brilliance and power are never in doubt; yet, although there are sensitive touches, one would welcome greater poetic feeling in some of the more reflective moments. Szidon is not helped by the DG recording, which (although comparatively mellow in the *Impromptus*) is rather hard and shallow-sounding in the *Scherzi*.

Nocturnes Nos. 1–21.

(M) *** CBS 40-61827 (Nos. 1–8; 19–21); 40-61828 (Nos. 9–18). Fou Ts'ong.

Fou Ts'ong plays the melting *Nocturnes in B major*, Op. 9/3, and *D flat major*, Op. 27/2, quite magically, reminding one of Solomon – and there can surely be no higher tribute. He is at his very best in the gentle poetic pieces; in the more robust *Nocturnes* his *rubato* is less subtle, the style not so relaxed. But this is undoubtedly distinguished playing and there is much to delight the ear, not least the very good CBS recording and secure transfers, which provide a most realistic piano image, mellow yet clear in outline. There are excellent, readable notes too. The layout is unconventional, with tape one opening with the three posthumous works and then returning to the beginning and presenting the rest in numerical order. At medium price, this set can be strongly recommended.

Polonaises Nos. 1–16.

(M) *(*) Turnabout KTVC 34254/5. Peter Frankl.

Polonaises Nos. 1–7.
  *(**) DG 3300 659 [id.]. Maurizio
    Pollini.
  (M) ** DG Privilege 3335 258.
    Shura Cherkassky.

Pollini offers outstanding mastery as
well as subtle poetry. This playing is
spellbinding and easily leads the field.
Unfortunately the cassette transfer is not
one of DG's best: the piano timbre is disappointingly hard and shallow.

Frankl approaches the music with a
pleasing freshness. He eschews the grand
manner and thus the two most famous
pieces fit into the cycle naturally and dramatically, without being show-off war-
horses. Elsewhere the pianist finds much
that is reflective and poetic, and reveals
the complete set of *Polonaises* as much
wider in musical range and less rhetorical, overall, than the better-known
works suggest. The cassettes are comparatively inexpensive, and decently presented, with good notes. The cassette transfers are clear and secure, but the piano
timbre lacks sparkle and bloom. The
slightly 'dead' quality can be improved
by care in balancing the controls, but the
quality is not really distinguished, although it offers rather more body than
the recording DG manage for Pollini.

Shura Cherkassky is sometimes an
idiosyncratic artist, and his playing here
has certain eccentricities of style and
tempo. Compared with Pollini or Frankl
this sometimes sounds wilful, but it has a
redeeming spontaneity. The recording is
generally truthful although not distinguished; there is some lack of range,
which brings a touch of hardness in the
treble. However, the hint of shallowness
of timbre can be helped by careful balance of the controls, and this tape can be
made to produce a fuller sound than
either the Pollini or the Frankl issues.

*24 Preludes, Op. 28; Preludes Nos. 25
in C sharp minor, Op. 45; 26 in A flat
major, Op. posth.*

*** DG 3300 550 [id.] (Nos. 1–24
  only). Maurizio Pollini.
*** CBS 40-76422. Murray Per-
  ahia.
**(*) DG 3300 721 [id.]. Martha
  Argerich.
**(*) Philips 7300 335 [id.]. Clau-
  dio Arrau.
*(*) Advent E 1024 (see p. xxiii)
  [id.] (Nos. 1–24 only). Ivan
  Moravec.

*24 Preludes, Op. 28; Polonaise No. 6
in A flat major, Op. 53.*

  (M) ** DG Privilege 3335 154
    [id.]. Géza Anda.

We are eminently well-served in this
repertoire, and as is so often the case,
choice will be a matter of personal predilection. It goes without saying that all
these pianists are masters of the keyboard, but some are artists of such strong
personality that criticism is altogether
silenced. Such is the case with Maurizio
Pollini, whose reading evinces an
effortless and complete mastery. While
listening to him, one has difficulty in
imagining that there can be any alternative interpretation. He has impeccable
taste in handling *rubato*, the firmest sense
of line and form, and no trace of excess
sentiment. His recording is a good one,
though the sound – slightly dry in timbre
– is not quite as natural or as fresh as the
balance that DG provide for Argerich.
Even so, one would be tempted to make
Pollini first choice were one to possess
only one version.

Murray Perahia brings a remarkable
freshness to the *Preludes*. There are no
routine expressive gestures; everything
radiates a spontaneity tempered with
impeccable control. Indeed, he inflects
certain phrases (in the *A flat Prelude*, for
example) with a subtlety and poetic feeling second to none. Unfortunately the
CBS recording does not do full justice to
him, although this is one of those curious
instances when the cassette seems to offer
more body and bloom in the piano timbre

than the disc, in spite of a restricted range.

But undoubtedly those looking for the finest *recording* of the *Preludes* on tape must turn to Martha Argerich's DG version. Her playing, moreover, is of the highest quality, spontaneous and inspirational, although its impetuosity will not appeal to all tastes. But her instinct is sure, and the exciting onward surge of the cycle is balanced by strong emotional contrasts and undoubted poetry when the writing is reflective. The recording is first-class, with a richly resonant bass and splendid colour in the piano's middle register. Because of the amplitude of the sound the level of the transfer is not unduly high, so that the background is not absolutely silent, but this remains a very impressive issue.

The Arrau set is much admired, and he certainly receives an opulent, full-bodied recording that has plenty of detail and presence and does justice to his subtle nuances of tone. Every prelude bears the imprint of a strong personality, to which not all listeners respond. Arrau can sometimes sound a shade calculated (his *rubato* seeming arbitrary and contrived), but there is little evidence of this here. His *Preludes* appear to spring from an inner conviction, even if the outer results will not be universally liked. The recording is of excellent quality, the piano tone rich and weighty in the bass, although its texture seems to add a Schumannesque flavour to the music-making at times.

Anda comes in the medium-price category and his playing is undoubtedly distinguished, showing its own special insights. He is accorded satisfactory sound. The fact remains, however, that whether you choose Pollini or Perahia, Argerich or Arrau, all are well worth the extra outlay if (like most collectors) you can afford only one version.

We have heard some distinguished Mozart and Debussy playing from Ivan Moravec, and it is surprising to find him curiously unpoetic in some of these wonderful miniatures. In terms of polish he does not match rivals such as Pollini or Perahia. The recording is good and well transferred, but this is not one of Advent's finer issues.

Scherzi Nos. 1 in B minor, Op. 20; 2 in B flat minor, Op. 31; 3 in C sharp minor, Op. 39; 4 in E major, Op. 54; Barcarolle in F sharp major, Op. 60; Prelude in C sharp minor, Op. 45.
    *** Decca KSXC 6334. Vladimir Ashkenazy.
Scherzi Nos. 1–4; Barcarolle in F sharp major, Op. 60; Berceuse in D flat major, Op. 57.
    (M) * Philips 7317 187. Nikita Magaloff.

Chopin's *Scherzi* are a long way from the original derivation of the genre as essentially light-hearted and humorous. Ashkenazy offers dazzling playing of the highest order, and the Decca recording is first-rate. The cassette offers strong, bold, secure tone and a virtually silent background (although on our copy side two sounded marginally less bright than side one). The two substantial bonus items are played equally beautifully.

After this Magaloff's performances sound dull. He is not helped by the Philips recording, which is diffuse and over-resonant (the *Barcarolle*, on side two, has the detail clouded), and the softness of the focus does not suit the *Scherzi*, limiting their brilliance of projection. Even the lovely *Berceuse* sounds relatively lack-lustre.

Piano sonatas Nos. 2 in B flat minor (Funeral march), Op. 35; 3 in B minor, Op. 58.
    *(**) CBS 40-76242. Murray Perahia.
    (M) *(*) Philips 7317 188. Nikita Magaloff.
Piano sonata No. 2; Fantasia in F minor, Op. 49; Funeral march in C

minor, Op. 72/2; 3 Nouvelles études, Op. posth.

(M) ** CBS 40-61857. Fou Ts'ong.

Piano sonata No. 2; Mazurka in A flat major, Op. 59/2; Nocturnes: in F major, Op. 15/1; in F sharp major, Op. 15/2; Grande valse brillante, Op. 18.

*** Decca KSXC 6575. Vladimir Ashkenazy.

Piano sonata No. 3; Ballade No. 4 in F minor, Op. 52; Mazurkas: in B flat major, Op. 7/1; in A minor, Op. 17/4; Nocturne No. 15 in F minor, Op. 55/1; Polonaise No. 3 in A major (Military), Op. 41/1; Waltz No. 3 in A minor, Op. 34/2.

*** Decca Phase 4 KPFC 4313. Ilana Vered.

Murray Perahia seems naturally attuned to working in the recording studio. Like his first recording of Schumann this one shows a spontaneous imagination at work, questing onwards. The technique is remarkable even by today's standards, but it is so natural to the player that he never uses it for mere display, and always there is an underlying sense of structural purpose. The dry, unrushed account of the finale of the *B flat minor Sonata* is typical of Perahia's freshness, and the only pity is that the recording of the piano is rather clattery and limited in range.

Magaloff's Philips recording is rich and resonant, the balance in favour of the piano's middle range giving (especially in the *B flat minor Sonata*) a Schumannesque quality. The playing too seems heavy in style, although the central episode in the *Funeral march* achieves an arresting atmosphere of repose – the tempo slow and deliberate – that makes a striking poetic contrast with the outer sections. On the whole the performance of the *Third Sonata* is the more successful, and the textures seem lighter. The

tape transfer is successful in other respects, marginally brighter on side two.

Ashkenazy's must rank as the finest among recorded performances of the *B flat minor Sonata*. It was made during a live recital at Essex University, and the concert was also filmed. Decca made sure that the sound suffered no loss from the circumstances; indeed the quality is outstandingly natural: the piano has splendid resonance and realism. The opening (and closing) applause is an irritant, but in all other respects this tape earns the highest praise. The performance of the *Sonata* is of the highest distinction, of great power and eloquence, yet with the music's poetry fully realized – the playing of the middle section of the slow movement is exquisite. The rest of the programme has a comparable spontaneity, and if the final *Presto* of the *Sonata* is not absolutely immaculate, who will cavil, with music-making of this quality. The cassette transfer is of excellent quality, and those wanting recommendable versions of both *Piano sonatas* might consider the purchase of this tape and Vered's Phase Four collection.

Fou Ts'ong is in good form in his recital. These are strong, boldly varied performances, with the lyrical contrasts (the middle section of the *Funeral march* of Op. 35 is meltingly expressive) serving to heighten the eloquence and power of the reading as a whole. The finale of the *Sonata* is well brought off. The alternative *Funeral march* dates from 1827 and is less memorable, although Fou Ts'ong makes a good case for it. The programme overall is interestingly chosen, and this tape makes an excellent medium-priced supplement to Fou Ts'ong's set of the *Nocturnes*. The recording is clear and full and has on the whole been cleanly and realistically transferred.

The recital from Ilana Vered featuring the *Third Sonata* within a well-balanced programme is highly rewarding. The playing is unfailingly poetic, often inspirational, notably in the meltingly lovely performance of the *Largo* of the *B minor Sonata*. Equally distinctive are the accounts of the *Nocturne in F minor* and the deliciously rhythmic *Mazurka in B flat major*. The style is wayward (the *Ballade* is a deeply felt and very individual performance) but it is never less than compelling, and one often has the sensation of being at a live recital. The recording is excellent, with no Phase Four exaggerations, and the cassette transfer is outstanding: the piano tone has splendid presence and sonority. This is demonstration quality.

Waltzes Nos. 1–19.
   *** DG 3300 965 (Nos. 1–14 only). Krystian Zimerman.
   (B) *** DG Heliodor 3348 146 (Nos. 1–14 only). Stefan Askenase.
   (M) **(*) Decca KCSP 486 (Nos. 1–15; 19). Peter Katin.
   (M) **(*) Philips 7317 185. Nikita Magaloff.
   (M) ** CBS Embassy 40-30096 (Nos. 1–14 only). Philippe Entremont.
   (B) ** Philips Fontana 7327 042 (Nos. 1–14 only). György Cziffra.
   (**) RCA RK 11705 [RK 1071] (Nos. 1–14 only). Artur Rubinstein.
   (M) ** DG Privilege 3335 267 (Nos. 1–17). Tamás Vásáry.
   *(*) Advent E 1006 (see p. xxiii) [id.] (Nos. 1–14 only). Antonio Barbosa.

Very distinguished playing from the young Polish pianist Krystian Zimerman, who won the 1975 Warsaw competition at the age of eighteen. He is in the same line as Pollini and Argerich (who also record for DG), and his account of the *Waltzes* is uncommonly mature. Rubinstein and Lipatti have been mentioned by others in discussing

these performances, and rightly so: this artist is in a special class. Excellent recording; the transfer is truthful and well balanced, but made at an almost unbelievably low level. Yet the detail is good, although there is a slight lack of presence unless one turns the volume well up. Nonetheless this is a most desirable issue.

Askenase's set also offers playing of the utmost distinction. These performances show a most natural *rubato*, every bar illuminated by Askenase's natural feeling for the Chopin line and phrase. The extrovert waltzes have a sparkling precision, while the more intimate pieces have an unmatched poetic sensibility. Yet the playing is not introvert but outgiving, making a direct contact with the listener. Do not judge the recording quality by the opening *Waltz in A flat*, which sounds rather dry in timbre. The sound (both on tape and disc) is not especially rich but it is clear and natural, and the ear can soon adjust to the lack of resonance when the playing is so masterly.

Peter Katin's tape is superbly recorded. This is demonstration quality, with the piano naturally balanced yet no want of sparkle. Katin plays the *Waltzes* not in numerical order, as is customary, but in chronological sequence, which seems more sensible. The playing is musical, thoughtful and affectionate, and if the last degree of extrovert bravura is missing in the more vivid pieces, this is still a very enjoyable collection, and certainly has its measure of poetry.

Magaloff too is beautifully recorded, the piano tone rich, with no suggestion of plumminess, the treble bright yet never hard-edged. The performances too are most enjoyable, lacking the last degree of individuality, perhaps, but well characterized and communicative. The *rubato* is nicely judged, never wilful, and there are continual contrasts between intimacy and bravura (the *Grande valse brillante* is notably successful). Perhaps the most attractive feature about this set is the spontaneous onward flow, each waltz seen within the context of the complete cycle.

Entremont is on good form and at his very best in the bravura of the more brilliant *Waltzes*; nevertheless he shows a proper sense of nuance in graduating his tone in the gentler pieces. There is no lack of sensibility here or of intelligence. The recording is clear and forward in the American manner, bright but not without bloom. The transfer is first-class and the tape sound is virtually identical with the disc.

Cziffra's *rubato* sometimes seems a little calculated, but these are enjoyable performances, essentially extrovert but not lacking in sensibility. He is boldly recorded; the sound has more substance than on Askenase's Heliodor issue, even if Cziffra's playing is less memorable. The transfer is fresh and clean, virtually indistinguishable from the equivalent LP.

The chiselled perfection of Rubinstein's collection, each waltz glittering like a finely polished diamond, with much subtlety of colour and *rubato*, is set at naught by the RCA transfer, which offers flutter and discoloration of the piano timbre. However, RCA are now offering greatly improved sound on their newest issues, so it is possible that the latest copies of this tape will be more secure in tone and pitch.

Vásáry's tempi are fast and his manner sometimes seems unnecessarily brisk. He is more persuasive in the relaxed, lyrical pieces, and elsewhere there is the occasional flash of poetry, but for the most part the performances, although not lacking style, are without individuality, and they seldom charm the ear. The recording is crisp and cleanly transferred, but the piano quality is rather dry.

Antonio Barbosa establishes himself from the first bar as a virtuoso of great accomplishment; but his sheer technical brilliance outstrips his artistry. In terms of subtlety and sensitivity, he is no match for Zimerman or Askenase. By that comparison he seems superficial, and he is unflatteringly recorded in what sounds like a smallish studio with added echo.

Miscellaneous recitals

Ballade No. 1 in G minor, Op. 23; Barcarolle in F sharp major, Op. 60; Étude in E major, Op. 10/3; Fantaisie-impromptu in C sharp minor, Op. 66; Nocturne in D flat major, Op. 27/2; Scherzo No. 3 in C sharp minor, Op. 39; Waltzes: in D flat major (Minute); in C sharp minor, Op. 64/1–2.

** Decca Phase 4 KPFC 4262. Ivan Davis.

Despite unnaturally close recording (the effect is something like having one's ear inside the piano lid) this is an impressive recital, with Ivan Davis's mercurial imagination given full rein. It is a great pity the recording was not made by Decca's standard techniques; however, the cassette transfer is a good one.

'Popular Chopin': Ballade No. 1 in G minor, Op. 23; Études Nos. 3 in E major, Op. 10/3; 12 in C minor (Revolutionary), Op. 10/12; Fantaisie-impromptu in C sharp minor, Op. 66; Mazurkas Nos. 5 in B flat major, Op. 7/1; 23 in D major, Op. 33/2; Nocturnes Nos. 2 in E flat major, Op. 9/2; 5 in C sharp major, Op. 15/2; Polonaises Nos. 3 in A major, Op. 40/1; 6 in A flat major, Op. 53; Preludes Nos. 7 in A major, Op. 28/7; 15 in D flat major (Raindrop), Op. 28/15; Waltzes Nos. 6 in D flat major (Minute); 7 in C sharp minor, Op. 64/1–2.

(M) ** HMV TC-HQS 1189. John Ogdon.

This is playing of strong character, but it is a little uneven in penetrating the core of the music. Highlights include the two *Polonaises*, which open the tape boldly,

161

and the *Ballade*, which provides a melting, romantic conclusion. The *Nocturnes* too are successful, the *rubato* personal but convincing. The *Mazurkas* seem less sure in style, and in the *Fantaisie-impromptu*, although the slow middle theme is beautiful, there is some flurry in the outer sections. But taken as a whole this recital is successful, even if its title suggests a more out-and-out popular selection than Ogdon provides. The transfer is of good quality, the sound rather dry on side one, richer on side two, and often very good indeed in this latter part of the recital.

'The Chopin I love', Vol. 1: Ballade No. 1 in G minor, Op. 23; Fantaisie-impromptu in C sharp minor, Op. 66; Mazurka in D major, Op. 33/2; Nocturnes: in E flat major, Op. 9/2; in F sharp major, Op. 15/2; in D flat major, Op. 27/2; Polonaises: in A major, Op. 40/1; in A flat major, Op. 53; Waltzes: in A flat major, Op. 34/1; in D flat major, Op. 64/1; in C sharp minor, Op. 64/2.

(***) RCA RK 11664 [RK 1172]. Artur Rubinstein.

Rubinstein opens with the *Polonaise in A flat major*, and the rather dry recorded quality is a shade disconcerting in so bold a work. Indeed on tape the sound is aggressively hard in tone, although the timbre becomes richer in the *Waltz in C sharp minor*, which follows the *Polonaise*. But on the whole the transfers here are well managed, clear and with a degree of sparkle when required. However, our copy was not entirely free from wow. The performances are incomparable and gain from the care with which the selection has been made and arranged into a rewarding recital.

Ballade No. 1 in G minor, Op. 23; Mazurkas Nos. 19 in B minor; 20 in D flat major, Op. 30/2 and 3; 22 in G

sharp minor; 25 in B minor, Op. 33/1 and 4; 34 in C major, Op. 56/2; 43 in G minor, Op. 67/2; 45 in A minor, Op. 67/4; 46 in C major; 47 in A minor; 49 in F minor, Op. 68/1, 2 and 4; Prelude No. 25 in C sharp minor, Op. 45; Scherzo No. 2 in B flat minor, Op. 31.

*** DG 3300 349. Arturo Benedetti Michelangeli.

Although this recital does not seem to quite add up as a whole, the performances are highly distinguished. Michelangeli's individuality comes out especially in the *Ballade*, a very free rhapsodic performance, which nevertheless holds together by the very compulsion of the playing. Michelangeli's special brand of poetry is again felt in the *Mazurkas*, which show a wide range of mood and dynamic; and the *Scherzo* is extremely brilliant, yet without any suggestion whatsoever of superficiality. The piano tone is real and lifelike, agreeably mellow as transferred to tape and admirably secure.

Ballade No. 2 in F major, Op. 38; Études: in A flat major; in F minor, Op. 25/1–2; Impromptu No. 2 in F sharp major, Op. 36; Mazurkas Nos. 44 in C major, Op. 67/3; 47 in A minor, Op. 68/2; Nocturnes Nos. 15 in F minor, Op. 55/1; 20 in C sharp minor, Op. posth.; Scherzo No. 2 in B flat minor, Op. 31; Piano sonata No. 2 in B flat minor, Op. 35: Funeral march (only); Waltz No. 3 in A major (Grande valse brillante), Op. 34/2.

(M) *** DG Privilege 3335 211. Tamás Vásáry.

Among arbitrarily arranged Chopin collections made from older recordings, this stands out for its balance and for the attractive arrangement of items, so that each sets off the character of the pieces before and after it. The recital opens with the two *Études* and then comes a splendidly brilliant account of the *Scherzo in B flat minor*, followed by the *Nocturne in C sharp minor*, the *Impromptu* and two diverse *Mazurkas*. Side two opens with the famous slow movement from the *Sonata*, Op. 35, moves on to the *Ballade in F major*, which is beautifully played, and the *Grande valse brillante*. The tape closes nostalgically with the *Nocturne in F minor*. Vásáry is on top form throughout, and the recording is excellent, varying a little in level between items, but firm and secure, and naturally balanced. A first-rate issue in every way.

Ballade No. 3 in A flat major, Op. 47; Fantaisie-impromptu in C sharp minor, Op. 66; Impromptus Nos. 1 in A flat major, Op. 29; 2 in F sharp major, Op. 36; 3 in G flat major, Op. 51; Mazurkas, Op. 41: Nos. 1 in C sharp minor; 2 in E minor; 3 in B major; 4 in A flat major; Scherzo No. 3 in C sharp minor, Op. 39.

(B) *** DG Heliodor 3348 215.
Stefan Askenase.

This is marvellously positive playing, full of personality and character. The recording too is bold and full, better than many of DG's more recent (and more expensive) piano recordings. Askenase always compels the attention, and his vigorous romantic style here makes a very attractive recital. The transfer is very good, offering a natural piano image, full and well balanced rather than especially brilliant.

Barcarolle in F sharp major, Op. 60; Berceuse in D flat major, Op. 57; Fantaisie-impromptu in C sharp minor, Op. 66; Polonaise No. 3 in A major, Op. 40/1; Scherzo No. 2 in B flat minor, Op. 31; Waltzes Nos. 1 in E flat major (Grande valse brillante), Op. 18; 3 in A minor, Op. 34/2; 14 in E minor, Op. posth.

(B) *(*) DG Heliodor 3348 276.
Stefan Askenase.

Askenase is at his best here in the *Berceuse* and the *Waltzes*; the *Grande valse brillante* is especially good. Elsewhere the effect of the music-making is less magical (the opening *Polonaise in A major* seems to lack grandeur), but the pianist is not helped by the dry recording, clear but rather lacking in timbre and inner colour.

Barcarolle in F sharp major, Op. 60; Mazurkas: in B major; in F minor; in C sharp minor, Op. 63/1–3; in G minor; in A minor, Op. 67/2 and 4; in F minor, Op. 68/4; Nocturnes: in B major; in E major, Op. 62/1–2; Polonaise (Fantaisie) in A flat major, Op. 61; Waltzes: in D flat major (Minute); in C sharp minor; in A flat major, Op 64/1–3.

*** Decca KSXC 6801 [Lon. 5-7022]. Vladimir Ashkenazy.

Ashkenazy is recording the complete Chopin piano music, but instead of adopting the usual generic approach he is compiling a series of mixed programmes that have the benefit of musical contrast and show something of Chopin's development. This issue brings us music from 1845–6 to the end of Chopin's life. The sound quality is impressively lifelike and has considerable depth in the bass. (The recording was made at All Saints' Church, Petersham.) The performances have strong personality and an aristocratic poise, even if one takes issue with the odd tempo: the *Waltzes* are a bit fast. This is in every way impressive and, in spite of some bass heaviness, beautifully recorded. The transfer to tape is first-class, clear, secure and naturally balanced.

Berceuse in D flat major, Op. 57; Mazurkas: in A minor; in A flat major; in F sharp minor, Op. 59/1–5;

163

Nocturnes: in F minor; in E flat major, Op. 55/1 and 2; Piano sonata No. 3 in B minor, Op. 58.
*** Decca KSXC 6810. Vladimir Ashkenazy.

This issue continues Ashkenazy's distinguished series with a memorable performance of the *B minor Sonata* (some might not like the accelerando treatment of the finale, but it is undoubtedly exciting), set within a beautifully arranged programme. The *Berceuse* is played gently, but the *Mazurkas* bring a splendid element of contrast. Ashkenazy's flexible, poetic phrasing is always a joy. The naturally balanced piano timbre has transferred well, with plenty of depth and an agreeably warm colouring of the middle register of the keyboard.

Arrangements by Leopold Godowsky: *Études: Op. 10, Nos. 1, 3, 5 (2 versions), 6–7; Op. 25, No. 1; Trois Nouvelles Etudes: No. 1, Op. posth.; Waltzes: in D flat major (Minute); in A flat major, Op. 64/1 and 3; in A flat major, Op. 69/1; in F minor; in D flat major, Op. 70/2 and 3; in E flat major, Op. 18* (concert paraphrase).
** Oiseau-Lyre KDSLC 26. Jorge Bolet.

It seems remarkable today that anyone should want to try to 'improve' on Chopin, yet Leopold Godowsky (1870–1938) made transcriptions of a great deal of Chopin's music, elaborating the textures in such a way as to place the new versions beyond the reach of all but the bravest virtuosi. It must be said that these performances by Jorge Bolet show the most remarkable technical command of Godowsky's complexities, but what he fails to do is to convince the listener that the prodigious effort is really worth while. A degree more audacity of manner might have helped, but, brilliant as the playing is, one is not per-

suaded to enjoy oneself in spite of all preconceptions. The recording is of good quality and the transfer is clean and bold, a trifle metallic in the treble.

COLLECTIONS

'Favourite composer': (i) *Ballade No. 3 in A flat major, Op. 47; Barcarolle in F sharp major, Op. 60; Berceuse in D flat major, Op. 57;* (ii) *Études, Op. 10, Nos. 3 in E major; 5 in G flat major; Op. 25, Nos. 1 in A flat major; 2 in F minor; 9 in B flat major;* (i) *Fantaisie-impromptu in C sharp minor, Op. 66; Impromptu No. 1 in A flat major, Op. 29;* (iii) *Mazurka No. 23 in D major, Op. 33/2;* (iv) *Nocturnes Nos. 2 in E flat major, Op. 9/2; 5 in F sharp major, Op. 15/2; 8 in D flat major, Op. 27/2; Polonaises Nos.* (v) *3 in A major, Op. 40/1;* (vi) *6 in A flat major, Op. 53;* (vii) *Prelude No. 15 in D flat major (Raindrop), Op. 28;* (i) *Piano sonata No. 2 in B flat minor (Funeral march), Op. 35; Scherzo No. 3 in C sharp minor, Op. 39;* (iv) *Waltzes Nos. 1 in E flat major (Grande valse brillante), Op. 18; 6 in D flat major (Minute); 7 in C sharp minor, Op. 64/1–2; 11 in G flat major, Op. 70/1.*

(B) ** Decca KDPC 563/4. (i) Wilhelm Kempff; (ii) Wilhelm Backhaus; (iii) Nikita Magaloff; (iv) Peter Katin; (v) Ilana Vered; (vi) Julius Katchen; (vii) Friedrich Gulda.

This is a pretty formidable set of Chopin favourites, but it is less attractive as a collection than some others in the *Favourite composer* series. The music is not laid out in the order above but in well arranged groups. The first tape is given over to the distinctive but not always idiomatic playing of Kempff, and is let down a little by the piano recording, which in terms of colour has a certain pallor. The sound immediately perks up on side three with the performances by Peter Katin of some of the *Nocturnes*, and one is surprised to find that these are not true stereo, but transcriptions from mono. The uninformed ear would be easily taken in. Side four includes Ilana Vered's *Polonaise in A major*, and a selection of *Waltzes* nicely played by Katin, and here the recording is excellent. The transfers are of immaculate quality, and there is virtually no difference in sound between disc and tape.

'Your kind of Chopin': Études: (i) *Op. 10, Nos. 3 in E major; 5 in G flat major; 12 in C minor (Revolutionary);* (ii) *in G flat major, Op. 25/9;* (iii) *Fantaisie-impromptu in C sharp minor, Op. 66; Nocturnes Nos. 1 in E flat major, Op. 9/2;* (ii) *10 in A flat major, Op. 32/2;* (iv) *Polonaises Nos. 3 in A major, Op. 40/1;* (v) *6 in A flat major (Heroic), Op. 53;* (vi) *Preludes, Op. 28, Nos. 7 in A major; 20 in C minor;* (vii) *Waltzes Nos. 1 in E flat major (Grande valse brillante), Op. 18; 6 in D flat major (Minute); 7 in C sharp minor, Op. 64/1–2.*

(M) *** HMV TC-EXES 5003. (i) Agustin Anievas; (ii) Daniel Adni; (iii) John Ogdon; (iv) Garrick Ohlsson; (v) Maurizio Pollini; (vi) Rafael Orozco; (vii) Witold Malcuzynski.

EMI has an excellent roster of pianists and the programme here includes many favourites. The compilation has been made with skill; each side opens with bravura, and the 'recital' closes with Pollini's splendid version of the *Heroic polonaise in A flat*. Malcuzynski's *Grande valse brillante* has a characteristic glitter, and other attractive performances include the *Sylphides Nocturne in A flat* and Daniel Adni's *'Butterfly' Study*,

which takes wing with charming grace. The transfers offer very good quality and very little hiss.

Coates, Eric
(1886–1958)

Calling all Workers march; The Jester at the Wedding: suite; The Merrymakers; overture; Miniature suite; The Three Elizabeths: suite.

(M) *(**) HMV Greensleeve TC-ESD 7005. City of Birmingham SO, Kilbey.

This reissue of the finest collection of Eric Coates's music in the present catalogues on HMV Greensleeve is most welcome. Most of the items offer very good sound, only *The Three Elizabeths* having slightly less sparkle and body than the rest of the programme. Reginald Kilbey unexpectedly proves himself the ideal Coates conductor, with a real flair for catching the sparkle of Coates's leaping allegro figurations. His shaping of the secondary theme of the lovely slow movement of the *Three Elizabeths suite* has an affectionate grace. Equally the *Scène de bal*, with its delightful evocation of porcelain china dancing figures, is done with superb point and style. The marches are splendidly alive and vigorous, and the first movement of the *Three Elizabeths* is sustained with a consistent throbbing forward momentum, in spite of the fact that the recording's comparative lack of middle frequencies gives less internal support than intended by the composer. One cannot recommend this tuneful and entertaining music too highly, and it is a pity that the otherwise vivid cassette version is one of those EMI issues with a narrowed dynamic range. However, the effect is not too serious, and the main reduction of contrast comes in the slow movements of the *Three Elizabeths* and the *Miniature suite*. The sound is otherwise pleasing, crisper and more brilliant on side two than side one.

Dancing Nights (concert valse); *The Enchanted Garden* (ballet); *London Calling* (march); *The Selfish Giant* (phantasy for orchestra); *The Seven Seas* (march); *The Three Men* (suite).

> (M) **(*) HMV Greensleeve TC-ESD 7062. Sydney SO, Lanchbery.

A welcome collection, even though only *The Three Men* could be called vintage Eric Coates. The last movement, in particular, is irresistible, with its affectionate interpolation of *Johnny Comes down to Hilo*, which wittily turns into *Three Blind Mice*. Neither *The Enchanted Garden* nor *The Selfish Giant* (inspired by Oscar Wilde's children's story) shows Coates's invention at its most memorable. Both are expertly constructed, however, and display the composer's characteristic orchestral flair, while the writing undoubtedly sounds spontaneous. The *Seven Seas* march (used as a TV theme) has a jolly main tune; the waltz *Dancing Nights* is agreeable and includes a surprisingly pointed allusion to Ravel's *La Valse*. The performances here are vigorous and spirited. They are very well played too (and Coates demands a good deal of instrumental virtuosity to sound as crisp in ensemble as this). The recording is spacious and lively; the acoustic is just right for the music, although the resonance means that the tape transfer (otherwise excellent) lacks a degree of sharpness of focus.

Copland, Aaron
(born 1900)

Appalachian Spring (ballet).
> *** Decca KSXC 6811 [Lon. 5-7031]. Los Angeles PO, Mehta – BERNSTEIN: *Candide overture*; GERSHWIN: *American in Paris*.***

This collection is attractively planned, and Mehta's performance of *Appalachian Spring* is second to none and beautifully recorded. If the couplings are suitable this is an excellent investment. The cassette transfer is excellent too, if anything clearer and brighter than the disc, if not quite so ample in sound.

Appalachian Spring; Fanfare for the Common Man; (i) *Lincoln Portrait* (for speaker and orchestra).
> (***) CBS 40-72872. LSO, the composer, (i) with Henry Fonda (narrator).

There is an innocence, a fresh purity, about Copland's London reading of *Appalachian Spring* which is most appealing, especially since the LSO is in such good form – the hushed string-playing is most beautiful. The recording is agreeably atmospheric both here and in the *Fanfare for the Common Man*, which is the more effective for being slightly underplayed. However, the *Lincoln Portrait* is unconvincing, with a narration that sounds too stagey. For non-Americans Copland should devise a version without narrative. The transfer to tape is not very successful, and the lack of clean transients means that the sharper detail of *Appalachian Spring* is blunted and the *Fanfare* tends to blur badly. Although the warmth and atmosphere of the recording are generally well caught there are patches of roughness and moments of distortion which show that the transfer level was set a shade too high.

Appalachian Spring; The Tender Land (opera): *orchestral suite*.
> (M) (**) RCA Gold Seal GK 42705. Boston SO, the composer.

Copland's early Boston recording of *Appalachian Spring* has an appealing breadth and warmth of humanity, helped by the resonance of the RCA recording. *The Tender Land* suite comes from an opera dating from 1954: we are given the love duet, virtually complete (without singers, of course), the Party music from Act 2, and the quintet *The promise of living* which forms the first-act finale. This is very typical Copland, if not as memorable as the coupling. One can imagine how effective the chorale-like quintet would be with voices; one is also reminded how near the American 'musical' is in style to Copland's conception of American opera. Unfortunately the transfer has been made at marginally too high a level. At the climaxes of *Appalachian Spring* there is overloading distortion, and there are patches of coarseness in the opera suite too; here the sound seems very forward, with a limited range of dynamic.

Billy the Kid (ballet); *Fanfare for the Common Man; Rodeo* (ballet): *4 Dance episodes.*
  (M) **(*) Turnabout KTVC 34169. Dallas SO, Johanos.

The Dallas orchestra does not provide the incisive discipline of, say, the New York Philharmonic under Bernstein, but – being Texans – they know what cowboy music is about, and the playing is both idiomatic and spontaneous. The barndance rhythmic style also comes naturally, and the gun battles are done with the percussive effectiveness of familiarity. The recording is suitably atmospheric. The transfer, made at a high level, is extraordinarily vivid. One has to cut back the bass at the opening of the *Fanfare* or the bass drum is too reverberant, but the resonant brass textures are sonorously caught, and in the ballet music the percussive transients are splendidly alive and clear. A most enjoyable tape and a very good bargain.

Dance symphony.
  (M) **(*) Turnabout KTVC 34670. Boston MIT SO, Epstein – PISTON: *The Incredible Flutist.***(*)

Written in the late 1920s, Copland's *Dance symphony* is a most likeable score, deriving its material (as does the coupling) from the ballet. What the playing here lacks in polish it makes up for by vitality, but at the same time it would be idle to pretend that the orchestra of the Massachusetts Institute of Technology is a virtuoso body (there is some less than accurate intonation). Nor is the recording first-class. However, readers may well overlook that for the sake of acquiring this rarity, whose robust vigour will give much pleasure. The transfer to tape is of high quality. The resonant acoustic blunts the sharpness of focus a little, but the sound is agreeably atmospheric and the orchestral textures are vivid and truthfully balanced.

Fanfare for the Common Man.
  (M) *** Decca KCSP 525. Los Angeles PO, Mehta – GERSHWIN: *American in Paris* etc.***

The use of Copland's *Fanfare* on TV has made it specially popular, and the dramatic presentation here should satisfy all tastes. The opening on the drums is highly spectacular, and the brass has splendid sonority too in this vivid transfer. With attractive couplings this is a highly recommendable issue on all counts.

Quiet City.
  *** Argo KZRC 845 [id.]. Academy of St Martin-in-the-Fields, Marriner – BARBER: *Adagio* ⊛; COWELL: *Hymn*; CRESTON: *Rumor*; IVES: *Symphony No. 3.***

A most poetic and evocative account of Copland's *Quiet City*. It is splendidly recorded, and the playing of both trumpet and cor anglais soloists is of the highest order. Superb recording and valuable couplings make this a most attractive proposition. The tape transfer has been managed impeccably, and the quality has fine atmosphere and detail.

El Salón México.
(B) ** Classics for Pleasure TC-CFP 40240. LPO, Pritchard – GERSHWIN: *American in Paris* etc.**

A budget-priced version of Copland's vivacious picture of a Mexican dance-hall salon is most welcome, and if John Pritchard's account is too lacking in rhythmic incisiveness to be entirely satisfactory, the score's atmosphere and colouring are very well caught. The recording is good and the cassette version seems even more vivid and full-blooded than the disc, the orchestral colours glowing and the presentation bright and immediate.

12 Poems of Emily Dickinson.
(*) Enigma K 453541. Sandra Browne (mezzo-soprano), Michael Isador (piano) – BARBER: *Hermit songs.***

Sandra Browne's mezzo tone is rich and attractive, and she sings Copland's settings of Emily Dickinson with warm understanding, if without the final degree of imagination and variety of mood that would make the performances really distinctive. But this is unusual repertoire for cassette issue and it is worthy of support. Provided one accepts the forward balance, characteristic of this label, the sound on tape is truthful and kind to both voice and piano.

Corelli, Arcangelo (1653–1713)

Concerti grossi, Op. 6, Nos. 2 in F major; 3 in C minor; 8 in G minor (Christmas concerto); 12 in F major.
*** Argo KZRC 15016. Academy of St Martin-in-the-Fields, Marriner.

Corelli has never enjoyed a boom comparable with that of Vivaldi in the 1950s, and this is currently the only tape available of the masterly Op. 6 concertos. They are rich in melodic invention and harmonic resource, and one wonders why they have been neglected for so long at a time when much lesser music of this period has been duplicated. The set from which this tape is drawn is available complete on three LPs, and this selection of four of the most attractive works is available in a special cassette-only issue. With expert playing, vital yet sympathetic, and with beautiful sound – the transfer is of demonstration quality – this is one of the most desirable tapes over the whole range of baroque music.

Corrette, Michel (1709–95)

Organ concerto in D minor, Op. 26/6.
(M) (**) Turnabout KTVC 34135. Helmuth Rilling, Württemberg CO, Faerber – ALBINONI: *Adagio* **; HANDEL: *Organ concerto*; MOZART: *Sonata.*(**)

This *Concerto* is charmingly slight, and the performance here is successful in catching the baroque miniaturism. But the transfer is below Decca's best quality and the sound lacks range and sparkle at the top.

Couperin, François (1668–1733)

(i) *Les Goûts-réunis: No. 8 in G major (Dans le goût théâtral;* arr. Oubradous); (ii) *Pièces en concerto* (arr. Bazelaire).
> (**) HMV TC-ASD 3321. Scottish CO, (i) with John Wilbraham (trumpet), cond. Paul Tortelier; (ii) with Tortelier (cello) – BACH: *Suite No. 3.*(**)

Oubradous's arrangement of the eighth of this set of *Concerts royaux* is quite tasteful in the matter of instrumentation, but the feeling of the music as played here seems slightly out of period, though charming enough. The *Pièces*, mainly for cello and strings (although there is a nimble harpsichord solo in the middle to offer agreeable contrast), are lively in invention and altogether effective. The recording is atmospheric but has a rough patch near the beginning caused by a miscalculation in the transfer. The layout of the music follows the LP, including the overture of the *Concert* on side one immediately after the Bach suite, where it suffers from the roughness of sound which spoils the transfer of that work.

Cowell, Henry (1897–1965)

Hymn and fuguing tune No. 10 for oboe and strings.
> *** Argo KZRC 845 [id.]. Celia Nicklin (oboe), Academy of St Martin-in-the-Fields, Marriner –BARBER: *Adagio* ❀; COPLAND: *Quiet City*; CRESTON: *Rumor*; IVES: *Symphony No. 3.****

Henry Cowell attracted a good deal of attention in the 1920s with his iconoclastic piano music (it was he who invented 'tone clusters') and he was a prolific symphonist. He also wrote a pioneering study of Ives. This likeable *Hymn and fuguing tune* is well worth having and is expertly played and recorded here. The cassette transfer is of immaculate quality.

Creston, Paul (born 1906)

A Rumor.
> *** Argo KZRC 845 [id.]. Academy of St Martin-in-the-Fields, Marriner – BARBER: *Adagio* ❀; COPLAND: *Quiet City*; COWELL: *Hymn*; IVES: *Symphony No. 3.****

At one time Creston was represented in the catalogue by his *Second* and *Third Symphonies*, and his current neglect seems unjust. *A Rumor* is a thoroughly witty and engaging piece and is played here with plenty of character by the Academy under Neville Marriner. It completes a thoroughly rewarding and approachable tape of twentieth-century American music that deserves the widest currency. The cassette transfer offers demonstration-quality sound throughout.

Crumb, George (born 1926)

Ancient Voices of Children (song cycle).
> *** Advent F 1035 (see p. xxiii) [id.]. Jan DeGaetani (mezzo-soprano), Michael Dash

169

(treble), Contemporary Chamber Ens., Weisberg – SCHOENBERG: *Pierrot Lunaire*.***

Crumb, like many other composers today, whether in America or in Europe, creates weird effects on conventional instruments ('preparing' piano, harp and mandolin in various unexpected ways) as well as using unconventional percussion instruments such as a toy piano. The wonder is that this setting of extracts from Lorca's poems shows genuine imagination. Whatever the means, the words are enhanced, and this brilliant performance gives one all the dynamism needed if one is to surmount the difficulties of such music. The recording is both lively and atmospheric, and the high-level Advent chrome transfer is of excellent quality. This issue intelligently couples Crumb's work with an outstanding performance of Schoenberg's *Pierrot Lunaire* by the same artists (both were originally issued on two separate Nonesuch LPs).

Davis, Carl
(20th century)

Music for television: *The Long Search; Marie Curie (A portrait in music); The Mayor of Casterbridge; Our Mutual Friend; The Snow Goose; Wuthering Heights.*
> *** EMI TC-INS 3021. RPO, the composer.

Carl Davis is a master of the special technique – essential for TV incidental music – of encapsulating atmospheric and musical feeling within short musical paragraphs. His penchant for orchestral colour undoubtedly carries an individual stamp, particularly his use of solo stringed instruments to focus the inten-

sity of his themes. Davis is usually called on to provide background scores for serious productions, and so a good deal of the writing here has a sombre atmosphere; but the tender music for *The Snow Goose* (which opens the collection) shows that he can lighten his style without becoming in the least trivial. All the excerpts are worth having, but probably the most welcome items will be the *Portrait* based on the poignantly strong *Marie Curie* and the memorable title music for *Wuthering Heights*, with its fierce intensity and eloquent scoring (Jack Brymer the clarinet soloist). The orchestral playing under the composer is highly expressive and beautifully recorded, and the cassette transfer is one of EMI's best.

Debussy, Claude
(1862–1918)

(i) *Danses sacrée et profane* (for harp and orchestra). *Images for orchestra (Gigues; Ibéria; Rondes de printemps).*
> **(*) Philips 7300 669 [id.]. Concertgebouw Orch., Haitink, (i) with Vera Badings (harp).

Issued as a celebration of Haitink's fiftieth birthday, this coupling of the *Images* with the *Danses sacrée et profane* shows orchestra and conductor on top form. This is repertoire in which the great Dutch orchestra is completely at home, and the performances combine warm, expressive playing with vividness of detail and meticulously balanced textures. On disc the recording is outstandingly rich, yet has no lack of transparency; the tape transfer – made at quite a high level for Philips – is less satisfactory in the *Images*, where the lower range of the orchestra is clouded and there is some lack of freedom at the top. The quality in the more lightly scored *Danses sacrée et profane* is beautifully fresh and glowing. The layout, however, is curiously clumsy, with *Ibéria* on side one and *Gigues* and *Rondes de Printemps* on side two followed by the *Danses*.

Images for orchestra (Gigues; Ibéria; Rondes de printemps); Le Martyre de Saint Sébastien (symphonic fragments).
(M) *** Philips 7317 199. LSO, Monteux.

The restoration of Monteux's classic coupling to the catalogue is most welcome, and it makes a splendid addition to the Debussy cassettography, particularly as the transfer – made at a high level – has fine immediacy and detail. Indeed one would hardly suspect that the recording dates from the mid-sixties, for the woodwind colouring is deliciously translucent and there is a fine sheen of sensuousness to the string tone (especially in *Les parfums de la nuit*). Monteux's performance of the *Images* was notable for its freshness and impetus (although this is achieved by the electricity of the playing rather than fast tempi). There is a vivid yet refined feeling for colour which is carried through into the orchestral sections from *Le Martyre* (in its fuller form a cantata written to a text by D'Annunzio). The delicacy of texture of Debussy's exquisite scoring is marvellously balanced by Monteux and he never lets the music become static.

(i) *Images: Ibéria; Rondes de printemps* (only); (ii) *Jeux;* (i) *La Mer;* (i; iii) *Nocturnes;* (ii) *Prélude à l'après-midi d'un faune; Rhapsody No. 1 for clarinet and orchestra.*
(B) ** Rediffusion Legend KLGDD 102. Czech PO, (i) Fournet, (ii) Baudo; (iii) with chorus – RAVEL: *Alborada* etc.**

The extraordinarily clear recording in these transfers brings a pointillist detail to Debussy's scores. The wind textures are particularly appealing and although the string tone lacks body and warmth (which is a serious drawback in *La Mer*) the ear tends to adjust very quickly. One is reminded of Ansermet's early mono LPs by the sharpness and vividness of the orchestral images and the dry quality of the violins, although the stereo brings a sense of atmosphere. The fine playing of the Czech Philharmonic is able to withstand the scrutiny such clarity provides. *Jeux*, in particular, has an iridescent clarity that is quite irresistible. The lack of sensuous warmth, however, detracts from other performances (notably the *Prélude*), but at bargain price this is certainly to be sampled. Some of the performances are still available in their original Supraphon transfers (see below), where they are made to sound quite different.

Images: Ibéria; Rondes de Printemps (only).
(M) (*) Supraphon 0450614. Czech PO, Fournet – FALLA: *Three-cornered Hat.*(*)
Images: Ibéria (only); *Nocturnes (Nuages; Fêtes;* (i) *Sirènes).*
**(*) Decca KSXC 6742 [Lon. 5-6968]. Washington National SO, Dorati, (i) with Washington Oratorio Society Chorus.
Images: Ibéria (only).
(M) **(*) HMV TC-SXLP 30263 [Angel 4XG 60102]. French National Radio Orch., Stokowski – IBERT: *Escales* ***; RAVEL: *Alborada.***(*)

Dorati's performances are vividly direct, not without atmosphere and enjoyable for the splendid Decca recording and for the conductor's sense of the dramatic. The playing is very good if not offering the last degree of polish; perhaps to compensate, the orchestral colours are bold and the transfer is of excellent quality, only lacking the last degree of transparency.

The HMV collection is vintage Stokowski, and although the forwardly balanced recording robs the performance of *Ibéria* of some of its mystery, the playing is extremely vivid. The exhilarating pace of the opening section is matched by the languorous sensualityy of *Les parfums de la nuit*, while the finale has tremendous vitality and rhythmic grip. The RTF orchestra responds with good discipline as well as enthusiasm, and although the recording perspectives are not always natural, the sound has warmth as well as sparkle. The transfer is of excellent quality; it offers splendid detail and glitter yet has body too. In many ways this approaches demonstration sound.

After the brilliance of the Decca and HMV recordings the Supraphon transfer of Fournet's early Czech performances of *Ibéria* and the *Rondes de Printemps* sound impossibly restricted in range. The playing has undoubted atmosphere, but the lack of sparkle in the treble takes the life out of the music-making.

Jeux; Nocturnes (*Nuages; Fêtes;* (i) *Sirènes*); *Tarantelle styrienne* (*Danse*).
  (M) **(*) Decca Eclipse KECC 816. Suisse Romande Orch., Ansermet, (i) with chorus.

Ansermet's account of *Jeux* has plenty of atmosphere: it is in fact one of his finest Debussy recordings. The *Nocturnes* too are not wanting an evocative quality and have characteristic detail. *Sirènes* is the least successful; the chorus is balanced rather forwardly and the singing lacks a sense of mystery. The *Danse* (*Tarantelle styrienne*) is vividly done. At medium price this tape is well worth considering, and the recording is agreeably warm and smooth, if without quite the transparency of the disc. The upper string sound is notably free from the degree of edginess one might expect in a recording dating from the late 50s–early 60s.

Le Martyre de Saint Sébastien (symphonic fragments); *Printemps*.
  *** DG 3300 879 [id.]. Orchestre de Paris, Barenboim.

One of Barenboim's very finest recordings, this couples two Debussy rarities, the early *Printemps* and the fragments from *Le Martyre de Saint Sébastien*. In *Le Martyre* Barenboim succeeds in distilling an intense, rapt quality and brings to life the evocative atmosphere of this score in a way that has not been matched since Cantelli's mono HMV record. If Barenboim does not suffuse the score with quite the same delicacy of feeling that Cantelli secured, he still refrains from any expressive indulgence and allows the music to speak for itself. He is no less persuasive in *Printemps*, which receives as good a performance as any in the LP catalogue (much more convincing than Ansermet's). The recording is spacious and well-balanced, with good stereo definition and range. It is most successfully transferred to cassette, which yields excellent quality. This enterprising and not particularly popular coupling deserves the widest circulation, for it will give much pleasure.

La Mer.
  (B) ** Pye ZCCCB 15013. Hallé Orch., Barbirolli – RAVEL: *Daphnis* etc.**
  (B) *(*) RCA Camden C4-5039. Boston SO, Munch – RAVEL: *Rapsodie espagnole.*(*)
La Mer; Marche écossaise; Prélude à l'après-midi d'un faune; (i) *Rhapsody for clarinet and orchestra.*
  **(*) Philips 7300 586 [id.]. Concertgebouw Orch., Haitink, (i) with George Pieterson (clarinet).
La Mer; Nocturnes (*Nuages; Fêtes;* (i) *Sirènes*).
  *** DG 3301 056. Orchestre de

Paris, Barenboim, (i) with chorus.

(M) ** HMV TC-EXE 185. Philharmonia Orch., Giulini, (i) with chorus.

(M) ** Philips 7317 194 [7310 089]. Concertgebouw Orch., Inbal, (i) with chorus.

(M) ** Supraphon 045575. Czech PO, Fournet, (i) with chorus.

(B) ** Philips Fontana 7327 044. Concertgebouw Orch., van Beinum.

La Mer; Prélude à l'après-midi d'un faune.
*** DG 923075 [id.]. Berlin PO, Karajan – RAVEL: *Daphnis.****
** Decca KSXC 6813 [Lon. 5-7033]. Chicago SO, Solti – RAVEL: *Boléro.***
*(*) HMV TC-ASD 3431. Berlin PO, Karajan – RAVEL: *Boléro.***

As far as *La Mer* is concerned, Karajan's 1965 DG recording with the Berlin Philharmonic is still first choice. It has total commitment and a fastidious care for detail, and it evokes the spirit of the work as effectively as it observes the letter. The performance of the *Prélude à l'après-midi d'un faune* is no less outstanding, the cool perfection of the opening flute solo matched by ravishing string-playing in the central section. The sound remains fresh and well-detailed. The cassette was originally issued in non-Dolbyized form; it always sounded well, but in the new transfer with Dolby the quality is first-class, with fine body of tone and excellent range and detail. Care must be taken with the controls to get the upper string tone exactly right, for the sound has remarkable range and brilliance and needs a little softening, especially in the *Prélude*.

Karajan's 1978 re-recording of *La Mer* for HMV may not have the supreme refinement of this earlier version – partly a question of the warmer, vaguer recording – but it has a comparable concentration, with the structure persuasively and inevitably built. At the very opening of the work the extremes of dynamic and tempo may seem exaggerated, and at times there is a suggestion of the pursuit of beauty of sound for its own sake, but there is never any doubt about the brilliance and virtuosity of the Berlin orchestra. These are qualities that it commands in abundance. The *Prélude* has an appropriate languor and poetry, and there is a persuasive warmth about this performance, beautifully moulded; but again the earlier performance distilled greater atmosphere and magic. The new recording is well engineered, although the cassette is not quite the equal of the disc, particularly in climaxes, and the sound lacks the range and detail of the DG German-manufactured tape.

Barenboim's coupling certainly offers first-rate recording, and the performances, although highly individual in their control of tempo, have great electricity. For some ears the effect (with the wind balanced rather forward) may lack the subtlety that distinguishes the Karajan or Giulini versions, but there is a fervour that more than compensates: *Sirènes* develops a feeling of soaring ecstasy, and the closing pages with the chorus are very beautiful. Similarly Barenboim creates a superb climax in the *Jeux de vagues* of *La Mer*, and the finale is no less exciting. The recording has a wide dynamic range and the tape transfer is not made at a very high level, but detail is good and the climaxes expand most impressively. If all copies are as good as the one sent for review, this can be recommended very highly on sonic terms.

Haitink's reading of *La Mer* is altogether tauter than Karajan's, though both pay great attention to dynamic gradations, and both secure playing of great sensitivity and virtuosity from their respective orchestras. Haitink, oddly enough, is much closer to Karajan's tempo in his 1965 recording than to the recent EMI version. *De l'aube à midi sur la mer* has real atmosphere in Haitink's hands. The *Jeux de vagues* is no less fresh; the *Dialogue du vent et de la mer* is both fast and exciting. An interesting point is that the brief fanfares that Debussy removed eight bars before fig. 60 are restored (as they were by Ansermet), but Haitink gives them to horns. Karajan, who omitted them in the DG version, now restores them, but on trumpets. The *Prélude à l'après-midi d'un faune* and the undervalued *Clarinet rhapsody* are atmospherically played too, though the former is less languorous than under Karajan. The recording is truthful, natural in perspective and realistic in colour. The cassette is marginally less refined in detail than the disc version (although it has more realism than the EMI Karajan). The level of transfer is not as low as on some Philips issues, but the upper frequencies are not completely fresh and sparkling. However, the ear readily adjusts to the warmly reverberant acoustic of the Concertgebouw and the sound is undoubtedly spacious and pleasing.

Giulini's account of *La Mer* is very distinguished, and it is given the benefit of good EMI recording. It would be difficult to fault this reading, and at its competitive price this tape comes near to the top of the recommended list. The Philharmonia are in splendid form. Under Giulini the *Nocturnes* are played with great delicacy of feeling and refinement of detail. *Nuages* is perhaps a little too dreamy but nonetheless full of atmosphere. *Sirènes* is all too wanting in a sense of movement: it is slow to the point of sluggishness. The transfer offers vivid sound but some lack of range and refinement in the treble. Even so the quality is acceptable.

Inbal secures some first-rate playing from the Concertgebouw Orchestra, and his readings are not lacking in atmosphere. The overall structure of *La Mer* is sensitively controlled, and the final climax is impressively powerful. However, the wide range of the recording has meant a comparatively low transfer level, and the orchestral detail is not ideally clear (although it is better than on the van Beinum tape). The overall focus is sharper in the *Nocturnes*, which come off well. Without losing the music's atmosphere Inbal creates more of a feeling of momentum than Giulini, and *Sirènes* has a sense of rapture missing in the HMV performance. The transfer is undoubtedly smoother than the HMV Giulini tape, with richer string sound.

Fournet's performances have undoubted warmth and atmosphere and the Supraphon tape offers a richer sound than Giulini's HMV issue. Indeed the quality is at times extremely vivid and the warmth of the string textures does not bring any loss of detail. The orchestral playing is extremely good, with luminous colouring in the first of the *Nocturnes* and a processional in *Fêtes* which is made very effective by Fournet's aptly chosen tempo. There are moments when the refinement of the transfer slips (notably at the choral entry in *Sirènes*), but generally this is a rewarding coupling.

The performances by Eduard van Beinum and the Concertgebouw Orchestra must date from the earliest days of stereo. The recording, although warmly atmospheric, is not very detailed (although it is not restricted or muffled). The orchestral playing is superb and this is undoubtedly highly distinguished music-making; the final section of *La Mer* has unforgettable vigour and precision of ensemble. There is not quite the degree of languor and delicacy that Karajan finds in his DG coupling, but there is no want of feeling and this makes an excellent bargain-priced issue.

Whether or not influenced by the character of the Ravel coupling, Solti treats the two evocative Debussy works as virtuoso showpieces. That works very well in the two fast movements of *La Mer* (helped by brightly analytical recording), but much of the poetry is lost in the opening movement, not to mention *L'Après-midi*. The transfer has plenty of range and detail, and as on the disc the sound is brightly lit, verging on fierceness at climaxes.

Barbirolli's early recording of *La Mer* for Pye must not be forgotten. It is an atmospheric performance which becomes especially exciting in its closing pages, and it has transferred quite well to tape. The upper register of the strings has a degree of fizziness but responds to the controls without losing the recording's inner detail (but reducing the hiss). This cannot be recommended above van Beinum's Fontana coupling, but it is preferable to Munch's RCA Camden issue, where the playing is first-class but the conductor tends to drive too hard. The Camden transfer is goodish, with the Dolby process slightly more effectively applied than on some issues from this source.

La Mer; Petite suite; Prélude à l'après-midi d'un faune; Suite bergamasque: Clair de lune; Tarantelle styrienne (Danse).
> (M) ** Decca KCSP 231. Suisse Romande Orch., Ansermet.

This anthology provides a comparatively inexpensive way of sampling Ansermet's individual and often rewarding approach to the music of Debussy. It includes the second of his three LP versions of *La Mer*, which was made in 1957; the performance is direct and unmannered, with vivid detail. The *Petite suite*, heard in Büsser's charming orchestration, is more controversial: some ears find the phrasing charmless and the weakness of intonation distracting. Others unrepentantly find this performance characterful and spontaneous. The other fill-ups are attractively played, and, given the price tag, the collection may be considered good value. However, the tape transfer of *La Mer* tends to reveal the early date of the recording and one has to take care to rebalance the controls between items. There is no lack of brilliance in the other pieces, and the *Petite*

suite has plenty of colour. The bass needs some control, both here and in *Clair de lune*.

CHAMBER MUSIC

String quartet in G minor.
> (M) *(*) Argo KZKC 46. Aeolian Qt – RAVEL: Quartet.*

This is the only performance of the Debussy *String quartet* available on cassette, and it must be given a qualified welcome. The recording is good and the transfer has body and impressive transparency. The performance is good rather than outstanding: more polish and finesse would be welcome, but the slow movement is played with considerable warmth (and given glowing sound by the engineers).

PIANO MUSIC

2 Arabesques; Children's Corner; Estampes: Jardins sous la pluie; L'Isle joyeuse; La Plus que lente; Suite bergamasque: Clair de lune.
> (M) *** Turnabout KTVC 34166. Peter Frankl.

This is an excellent collection. Turnabout recordings often seem to sound better on tape than on disc and this is no exception. The piano tone is clear and bold, and the high level of the transfer means that background hiss is very minimal indeed. Peter Frankl is a highly sensitive Debussyian: whether in the delicate filigree of the *Arabesques* or in the simple charm of *Children's Corner* (especially successfully transferred), his touch is as sure as his sense of style; *Jardins sous la pluie* is particularly evocative.

2 Arabesques; Danse bohèmienne; Estampes (Pagodes; La soirée dans

Grenade; Jardins sous la pluie); Mazurka; Pour le piano; Rêverie; Suite bergamasque (Prélude; Menuet; Clair de lune; Passepied).

*** Decca KSXC 6855. Pascal Rogé.

An excellent performance of the *Suite bergamasque*, with crisp, well articulated playing in the *Passepied* 'and genuine poetry in the famous *Clair de lune. Pour le piano* is no less effective, and only in *La soirée dans Grenade* does one perhaps feel that a little more atmosphere would not be out of place. But this is a minor quibble, and there is much else to admire here: Rogé is both vital and sensitive, and his intelligence and fine technique are always in evidence. The sound is superbly well defined and eminently secure and firm. The bottom end of the piano reproduces in a most lifelike fashion, and only in the last degree of sparkle is missing at the top compared to the disc. Otherwise there is very little to choose between them: one has to balance the disadvantage of the slight surface on the disc against the slight loss of top on the tape.

2 Arabesques; L'Isle joyeuse; Images, Book 1: Reflets dans l'eau; Préludes, Book 1: Danseuses de Delphes; La sérénade interrompue; La cathédrale engloutie; La danse de Puck; Minstrels; Book 2: La puerta del vino; General Lavine – eccentric; Feux d'artifice; La Plus que lente; Suite bergamasque: Clair de lune.

(M) * CBS 40-61068. Philippe Entremont.

These are clean, robust performances, not showing much delicacy of feeling and wanting in the kind of atmosphere this music ideally demands. It is difficult to recommend this issue with any great degree of enthusiasm, even though the piano timbre is clean and clear. It is also rather hard in the transatlantic manner, and somewhat lacking in bloom, but the transfer to tape reflects the image provided by the equivalent LP.

Children's Corner; Images, Sets 1 and 2.

*** DG 3300 226. Arturo Benedetti Michelangeli.

Michelangeli's collection is outstanding here. It is a magical recital, and the transfer to tape is clear, slightly mellow in outline but secure and well balanced. Michelangeli enters the recording studio much too rarely, and this tape offers some of the most distinguished Debussy playing in the catalogue.

Children's Corner. Préludes, Book 1: 4, Les sons et les parfums; 5, Les collines d'Anacapri; 10, La cathédrale engloutie; Book 2: 7, La terrasse des audiences; 2, Feux d'artifice. Suite bergamasque: Clair de lune.

*** Advent E 1029 (see p. xxiii) [id.]. Ivan Moravec.

The Czech pianist Ivan Moravec possesses formidable technique and considerable imagination. *Les collines d'Anacapri* and *Les sons et les parfums tournent dans l'air du soir* (and for that matter the other preludes) are most sensitively played. He gives great attention to details of colour and evokes atmosphere with much skill (*La terrasse* receives one of the most poetic recorded performances we have heard). The recording is well-balanced and clean. Interesting performances, far more successful than Moravec's set of Chopin *Preludes*, and worthy to stand alongside Pascal Rogé's Decca anthology.

En blanc et noir.

** Philips 7300 644 [id.]. Martha Argerich, Stephen Bishop-Kovacevich – BARTÓK: *Sonata for 2 pianos and percussion* (***); MOZART: *Andante and variations.***

An intensely vital and imaginative reading of one of Debussy's most neglected yet rewarding scores. *En blanc et noir* comes from the last years of his life and is full of unexpected touches. This is the finest account available on disc or tape, and it is a pity that the transfer is made at a low level; the piano tone itself is natural, but the focus is not very sharp and immediate.

Préludes, Books 1 and 2.
  (M) ** DG Privilege 3335 260/1. Dino Ciani.

This set marks the début of the complete *Préludes* in the tape catalogue. Dino Ciani has a fine technique and plays with intelligence, taste and a fine sense of atmosphere. This is helped by the transfer, which is lacking in the last degree of range (the original recording is impeccable) and tends, with the help of the basic resonance, to fractionally blur the piano image. But the sound remains pleasing and does not lack body and timbre. Incidentally, for those who admire *La cathédrale engloutie*, it is given a particularly strong and imaginative performance.

Préludes, Book 1.
  **(*) DG 3301 200 [id.]. Arturo Benedetti Michelangeli.
  (M) ** Saga CA 5391. Livia Rev.

It goes without saying that Michelangeli's account of the *Préludes* reveals the highest pianistic distinction. It is in many ways a wholly compelling and masterful reading of these miniature tone poems, with hardly a note or dynamic out of place, and it can be confidently recommended. Yet it remains for the most part remote and cool: authoritative playing that is somehow wanting in mystery and humanity. Clean, detailed recording, and the tape transfer is natural and secure in timbre; the production copy proved softer in outline, with marginally less presence, than the original review copy sent from Hanover.

Livia Rev is a most sensitive artist who has never received her due. She has a real feeling for atmosphere and plays with consummate artistry. Unfortunately the recording, though adequate, is not distinguished. The cassette transfer is fair; the quality is smooth and reasonably secure. This is in the medium price-range and may well be thought competitive, for the quality of the music-making is not in doubt.

Préludes, Book 1: 1, Danseuses de Delphes; 2, Voiles; 3, Le vent dans la plaine; 5, Les collines d'Anacapri; 8, La fille aux cheveux de lin; 9, La sérénade interrompue; 10, La cathédrale engloutie; 11, La danse de Puck; Book 2: 3, La puerta del vino; 4, Les fées sont d'exquises danseuses; 6, General Lavine – eccentric, 7, La terrasse des audiences; 8, Ondine; 9, Homage à S. Pickwick Esq. P.P.M.P.C.; 11, Les tierces alternée; 12, Feux d'artifice.
  (B) **(*) DG Heliodor 3348 285. Monique Haas.

Monique Haas's collection of *Préludes* is generous, with eight items from each book, and at Heliodor price this is likely to prove an attractive anthology for those with a limited budget. Refined classical playing, well if somewhat dryly recorded; Monique Haas is a trifle cool, perhaps – she is not so imaginative or atmospheric as Richter – but eminently sound and recommendable. The more extrovert items come off especially well: *La cathédral engloutie* is vividly imaginative, and *Feux d'artifice* really sparkles, helped by the clear clean transfer.

Préludes, Book 2.
  (M) **(*) Turnabout KTVC 34360. Sviatoslav Richter.

Richter's recording of the second book of *Préludes* was made at a public recital, and the soft outlines of the piano

177

image seem ideal for spinning the magic of most of these pieces, creating a mood and texture exactly like a French impressionist painting. Perhaps in *General Lavine – eccentric* one would ideally ask for more bite, but the superb virtuosity of *Les tierces alternées* comes over unscathed, and the fiery cascades and splutters of *Feux d'artifice* are projected by the sheer bravura of the pianism. Elsewhere the gentle haze over the piano (the articulation itself is clear enough) suits Richter's musing, introvert style, and *Brouillards, Feuilles mortes* and especially *Bruyères* are wonderfully atmospheric. The audience for the most part listen in silence, but there is an intrusive neighbouring church bell at the opening. The cassette transfer is of high quality and matches the disc.

VOCAL MUSIC

La Damoiselle élue.
(**) Symphonica CSYM 6 [Peters PCE 021]. Montserrat Caballé, Janet Coster, Ambrosian Ladies' Chorus, Symphonica of London, Morris – CHAUSSON: *Poème de l'amour et de la mer.*(**)

Debussy's early cantata *La Damoiselle élue* has been seriously neglected by the recording companies. It is a highly evocative setting of Rossetti in translation, using a soprano women's chorus and mezzo-soprano solo as well as a soprano for the central role of the Blessed Damozel. This rich and expressive performance is focused, predictably enough, on Caballé's radiant assumption of the principal role; her timbre sometimes suggests her compatriot Victoria de los Angeles. She produces ecstatic high pianissimos, but at times she allows scooping up to notes, and her French pronunciation is idiosyncratic. Warm recording which brings out some of the

unexpected *Parsifal* echoes. Unfortunately the poor quality of the transfer precludes a recommendation; the treble is woolly with the lack of any kind of detail, while the upper range of the sound is very restricted.

COLLECTION

'*Favourite composer*': (i) *Images: Ibéria* (only). *La Mer.* (i; ii) *Nocturnes.* (i) *Prélude à l'après-midi d'un faune.* (iii) *Images: Reflets dans l'eau. L'Isle joyeuse.* (iv) *Petite suite: En bateau. Préludes, Book 1:* (v) *La fille aux cheveux de lin;* (vi) *La cathédrale engloutie.* (v) *Suite bergamasque: Clair de lune.*
(B) ** Decca KDPC 619/20. (i) Suisse Romande Orch., Ansermet; (ii) with female chorus; (iii) Friedrich Gulda (piano); (iv) Bracha Eden, Alexander Tamir (piano duet); (v) Joseph Cooper (piano); (vi) Jean-Rodolphe Kars (piano).

This compilation, which includes Ansermet's *La Mer*, *Ibéria* and the *Nocturnes*, is an attractive one, for although the SRO is not the finest of orchestras Ansermet's readings will not fail to give pleasure. The version of *La Mer* included here, however, is the 1965 recording (as distinct from the second, 1957 account, which appears on KCSP 231), and the intonation (in the horns, for instance, and the cor anglais and cello melody in *De l'aube à midi*) is sometimes less than impressive, although the orchestral sound is faithfully captured by the more modern and sophisticated microphones. The piano music on the second tape is all well played. The opening *En bateau* (from the *Petite suite*), heard in its original piano duet version, is highly engaging, and the two Gulda performances, although impulsive, are full of character.

The recording throughout is bright and well detailed and the range of the tape transfer is impressive, with the percussive transients strikingly crisp. The orchestral sound is very brightly lit but responds to a cut-back of 'top'. *Ibéria* is especially vivid, although the *Prélude à l'après-midi d'un faune* is somewhat fierce.

Delibes, Léo
(1836–91)

Coppélia (ballet): complete.
(***) HMV TC-SLS 5091 [Angel 4XS 2-3843]. Paris Opera Orch., Mari.
(**) Decca KDPC 2 7045. Suisse Romande Orch., Ansermet.

Delibes's masterpiece makes admirable cassette listening. The impression *Coppélia* gives in the theatre is of an unending succession of colour and memorable tunes. Tchaikovsky admired the score, and rightly so, for there is not one dull bar. The HMV recording under Jean-Baptiste Mari is in every way worthy of the score. The elegant and sensitive playing conjures up a marvellous theatrical atmosphere, and the stage scene is readily re-created in the mind's eye. Mari uses danceable tempi throughout, yet there is never any loss of momentum, and the long-breathed string phrasing is a source of continual pleasure. The telling musical characterization, from the robust peasantry to the delicately pointed *Dance of the Automatons*, is vividly memorable. The sound is most naturally balanced within a perfectly chosen acoustic, and on disc this is one of the finest ballet recordings ever made. Unfortunately the tape quality does not match that of the LPs. It is generally acceptable, and side four (most of Act 3) is good, but elsewhere there is not the refinement and transparency of texture that is found on

the discs; also some of the wind solos (notably the clarinet) were disfigured by discoloration of the upper partials on our copy.

The Decca transfer of the classic Ansermet set is, alas, no more readily recommendable. The sound on disc has been most agreeably remastered, but on tape the strings are dry and lustreless and there is some congestion in Act 1 where the bass drum muddies the orchestral texture. The performance itself is full of character. The orchestral playing is always good and sometimes very good, but one must accept the French quality of the woodwind: the oboe and clarinet soloists sound a little reedy. Ansermet's authoritative hand is always apparent, and his power of evocation (especially in the first scenes of Act 2) makes some delightful effects. The *Dance of the Automatons* sparkles like a music-box, and, as might be expected, the passage (at the beginning of side three) where Swanhilda pretends to be Coppélia coming to life and dances her stiff little waltz is pointed with loving care. The whole of the *Divertissement* is brilliantly played.

Coppélia (ballet): highlights; *Sylvia* (ballet): highlights.
**(*) Decca KSXC 6776. Suisse Romande or New Philharmonia Orch., Bonynge.
Coppélia: highlights; *Sylvia*: suite.
(M) (**) Decca KCSP 314. Suisse Romande Orch., Ansermet.
Coppélia: suite.
(M) *** DG Privilege 3335 189. Berlin PO, Karajan – CHOPIN: *Les Sylphides*.***
Coppélia: suite; *Sylvia*: suite.
**(*) Decca Phase 4 KPFC 4358 [Lon. 5-21147]. LPO, Black.

Bonynge would seem an obvious choice here (although Stanley Black's cassette is unexpectedly attractive). Bonynge's selection from *Sylvia* is particularly enjoyable. He mixes a couple of unfamiliar items in with the usual suite and is served with most beautiful playing from the New, Philharmonia. The *Coppélia* selection is less imaginative. Most of the music is taken from Act 1 and too little comes from the two succeeding acts. The omission of the *Automatons* number is regrettable (that was even included in the very first extensive selection from this ballet on 78 r.p.m. discs, conducted by Constant Lambert). Also the orchestral playing in Geneva is not as polished as that in London, for all Bonynge's obvious care. But having made one's reservations, this is still a very enjoyable tape; the quality throughout is vividly robust, the wind detail colourful and pleasing.

Karajan secures some wonderfully elegant playing from the Berlin Philharmonic Orchestra, and his lightness of touch is delightful. The *Valse de la Poupée* is beautifully pointed and the variations which follow have a suave panache which is captivating. The *Czárdás* is played very slowly and heavily, and its curiously studied tempo may spoil the tape for some. The recording is even better than on the reverse and can be made to sound very impressive. The cassette transfer offers sparkling quality.

Stanley Black produces some fetching playing from the LPO. In *Coppélia* the vivacious accounts of the *Danse de fête* and final galop are very enjoyable. Earlier, in the *Scène* and *Valse de la Poupée*, the musical characterization has not the distinction that a conductor like Ansermet brings to it. But in *Sylvia* there is plenty of life and vigour, and the *Valse lente* is beautifully done. With absolutely top-class recording, brilliant and sparkling, yet not lacking ripeness, this is very attractive indeed; and the cassette is in the demonstration class, lively yet full-blooded and with plenty of resilience and range.

Ansermet's selection from *Coppélia* is balanced with an equally vivacious suite from *Sylvia*, not taken from a complete recording but originally recorded as just a suite. The sound is first-rate here, but in *Coppélia* the problems with the bass drum remain and the sound is congested in places.

Le Roi s'amuse: ballet music.
(M) **(*) HMV TC-SXLP 30260. RPO, Beecham – BIZET: *Symphony***; BERLIOZ: *Les Troyens excerpts.***(*)

Delibes's ballet music for *Le Roi s'amuse* is not an independent work, but was written for a revival of Victor Hugo's play in 1882. The music has an element of pastiche and its grace and elegance are superbly realized under Beecham's baton. Indeed the orchestral playing is a constant source of delight. The recording is very good too and has transferred well to tape apart from a little thickness of texture in the broader tuttis. This is a delightful compilation.

La Source (ballet): excerpts.
(M) ** Decca Eclipse KECC 809. Paris Conservatoire Orch., Maag – CHOPIN: *Les Sylphides.***

La Source (1866) was the earliest of the Delibes ballets. It was written in collaboration with Leon Minkus (each wrote half the music) and the success of the Delibes section of the score (Act 2 and the first part of Act 3) did much to establish his reputation as a composer. He used his own sections again (with more music added) for a later ballet called *Naïla*. Peter Maag's account is charchterful and stylish: the pointed string tunes are especially well done. There is some excellent wind-playing too, and both the solo flautist and the principal horn are given opportunities to distinguish themselves. The recording is clear and vivid and has transferred most convincingly to tape, with plenty of life and detail.

Sylvia (ballet): complete.

   *** HMV TC-SLS 5126 [Angel 4x2s 3860]. Paris Opera Orch., Mari.

The ballet *Sylvia* appeared five years after *Coppélia* and was first produced at the Paris Opera in 1875. While confirming the success of the earlier work, *Sylvia* has never displaced it in the affections of the public, and understandably so. It is an attractive score with some memorable tunes, but to be honest nearly all of these are contained in the suite, and in the full score we hear them more than once. But if the work is not as consistently inspired as *Coppélia*, it contains some delightful music and characteristically felicitous scoring. Mari's natural sympathy and warmth make the very most of this, and he is supported throughout by beautiful orchestral playing and rich, glowing recording. The transfer offers EMI's best quality, full yet clear, with bloom on woodwind and strings alike.

Delius, Frederick
(1862–1934)

Air and dance; Fennimore and Gerda: Intermezzo; Hassan: Intermezzo and Serenade; Koanga: La Calinda; On Hearing the First Cuckoo in Spring; A Song before Sunrise; Summer Night on the River; A Village Romeo and Juliet: The Walk to the Paradise Garden.

   *** Argo KZRC 875. Academy of St Martin-in-the-Fields, Marriner.

No grumbles here: these are lovely performances, warm, tender and eloquent. They are beautifully played and recorded in a splendid acoustic. There is no need for any collector to hesitate here. The transfers are generally up to Argo's high standard, with admirable detail. The massed upper strings have not quite the bloom of the LP, and a slight treble reduction is useful.

2 Aquarelles (arr. Fenby); *Fennimore and Gerda: Intermezzo* (arr. Beecham); *Hassan: Intermezzo and Serenade* (arr. Beecham); *Irmelin: Prelude; Late Swallows* (arr. Fenby); *On Hearing the First Cuckoo in Spring; A Song before Sunrise; Summer Night on the River.*

   *** RCA RK 25079. Bournemouth Sinfonietta, Del Mar.

There are few finer interpreters of Delius today than Del Mar, once a protégé of Beecham, and this nicely balanced collection of miniatures is among the most broadly recommendable of Delius collections available. The performances are just as warm and atmospheric as Barbirolli's in a collection (see below) which overlaps this one, and if anything have a stronger sense of line. Warm, modern recording to match, and a highly successful transfer, the sound fresh yet with an excellent overall bloom and a high level to minimize background noise.

2 Aquarelles; Fennimore and Gerda: Intermezzo; On Hearing the First Cuckoo in Spring; Summer Night on the River.

   *** DG 3300 500 [id.]. ECO, Barenboim – *Concert.****

Barenboim's luxuriant performances have a gorgeous sensuousness and a warm, sleepy atmosphere to seduce even those normally resistant to Delius's pastoralism. The couplings are no less enticing. This tape is discussed fully in our Concerts section.

Brigg Fair; On Hearing the First Cuckoo in Spring; A Song of

Summer; A Village Romeo and Juliet: The Walk to the Paradise Garden.

(M) ** Decca Eclipse KECC 633. LSO, Collins.

These lovely performances, very much in the Beecham tradition, were one of the highlights of the early Decca LP catalogue and showed, alongside Anthony Collins's recordings of the Sibelius symphonies, that he was a great conductor. The delicacy of texture is emphasized by a recording of wide dynamic range, and there is some lack of substance in the gentle woodwind sounds at the opening of *Brigg Fair*. But the ear soon adjusts, and though the orchestral climaxes have a touch of hardness, considering the age of the original recordings the quality is really very good indeed.

Violin concerto; (i) *Double concerto for violin, violoncello and orchestra.*

*(**) HMV TC-ASD 3343. Yehudi Menuhin, RPO, Meredith Davies, (i) with Paul Tortelier.

Both these masterly concertos refute in their superbly balanced one-movement structures the idea that Delius had no grasp of musical logic. Deryck Cooke published an intensive analysis of the *Violin concerto* showing the inter-relationship of almost every bar, and the same can readily be done for the even more neglected *Double concerto*. They make the ideal Delius coupling, and it is good to have the works presented by two master musicians in warm, wide-ranging recordings. As a performance the more successful is the *Double concerto*, where Tortelier's example was plainly a challenge to Menuhin. Theirs is a somewhat lighter view of the work than that of the soloists in the earlier Pye version (on disc only), in which Norman Del Mar drew more richly expressive playing from the RPO than Meredith Davies does. But the four-square power of the work is never in doubt here. In the *Violin concerto*

Menuhin does not always produce his sweetest tone, but he gives a heartfelt performance, and the writing above the stave is eloquently played. The transfer is generally of good quality, but the timbre of the solo violin seems excessively bright. The quality is short of being edgy but the treble balance is not ideal, as any softening of the solo image tends to interfere with the orchestral detail. Different tape decks will react differently to this problem, and the volume level of playback is also critical.

In a Summer Garden; Koanga: La Calinda (dance); *Late Swallows* (arr. Fenby); *On Hearing the First Cuckoo in Spring; A Song before Sunrise; Summer Night on the River; Hassan* (incidental music): *Intermezzo;* (i) *Serenade.*

*** HMV TC-ASD 2477. Hallé Orch., Barbirolli, (i) with Robert Tear (tenor).

Atmospheric and loving performances of these colourful scores. Sir John shows an admirable feeling for the sense of light Delius conjures up and for the luxuriance of texture his music possesses. At times he dwells a little too affectionately over details and one wants the music to move on, but for the most part reservations on this score are few. The recording is admirably rich and detailed, but there are times when one could wish for a slightly more backward woodwind balance. The transfer has been beautifully managed; this is one of EMI's best cassettes.

Dodgson, Stephen (born 1924)

Guitar concerto No. 2 (for guitar and chamber orchestra).

(*) CBS 40-76634. John Williams, ECO, Groves – ARNOLD: *Serenade*; CASTELNUOVO-TEDESCO: *Concerto.***

John Williams has consistently championed the music of Stephen Dodgson, who composed this work expressly for him. Written in 1972, the concerto has both charm and substance. Its ideas hold the listener, its textures are both varied and imaginative and its sound world is fresh and luminous. The performance is expert, and though the sound picture is not perfectly natural (the guitar is closely observed and looms too large in the aural canvas), no one will object. The overall timbre is faithful and orchestral detail is vivid and in good perspective. More bloom and expansiveness in the top register and this tape would rate a full three stars. But this is a rewarding work, authoritatively played.

Dohnányi, Ernst von (1877–1960)

Variations on a nursery tune (for piano and orchestra), *Op. 25*.
> *** HMV TC-ASD 3197. Cristina Ortiz, New Philharmonia Orch., Koizumi – RACHMANINOV: *Rhapsody*.

A superb coupling by Cristina Ortiz and the young Japanese conductor Kazuhiro Koizumi. They are helped by a splendrous recording of truly demonstration quality, but the performance itself is equally memorable. Dohnányi's score is characterized with feeling and wit; every point is made with telling skill, from the melodrama of the opening and the innocent piano entry through to the beautifully managed coda. The music-making has flair, humour, spontaneity and conveyed enjoyment; and the coupling is first-class too. The cassette transfer offers

outstanding quality and is demonstration-worthy in its own right.

(i) *Variations on a nursery tune, Op. 25. Suite* (for orchestra) *in F sharp minor, Op. 19*.
> (M) ** Turnabout KTVC 34623. Seattle SO, Katims, (i) with Béla Siki (piano).

The main interest here is the *Suite in F sharp minor*, an eclectic but agreeably entertaining work, diverse in mood and style and (like the *Variations*) scored with a nice feeling for the orchestral palette. It is given a lively and accomplished performance and is well recorded. The performance of the *Variations*, with its distinguished soloist, is impressively bold and direct (with plenty of brilliance from Béla Siki) but lacks something in geniality. There is wit here without the feeling of conveyed enjoyment that Ortiz manages alongside her bravura. The recording is not as opulent as the HMV issue, but is still good, and those interested in the *Suite* will find this a worthwhile tape. The sound on the cassette is slightly dry, and somewhat hard-edged in the *Suite*, which is transferred at a marginally higher level.

Donizetti, Gaetano (1797–1848)

String quartet in D major (arr. for string orchestra).
> *** Argo KZRC 603 [id.]. Academy of St Martin-in-the-Fields, Marriner – ROSSINI: *String sonatas Nos. 2 and 4.****

This delightful 'prentice work has sunny lyricism and a melodic freshness that speaks of youthful genius. The composer's craftsmanship is obvious and the writing is such that (like Verdi's *String quartet*) it lends itself readily to performance by a string orchestra, especially when the playing is as warm-hearted and polished as on this immaculately recorded Argo tape. Most enjoyable. The transfer offers rather more edge on the sound than in the Rossini coupling, but the quality is clean and lifelike.

OPERA

L'Elisir d'amore: complete.
　　*(**) CBS 40-79210. Ileana Cotrubas, Placido Domingo, Geraint Evans, Ingvar Wixell, Lillian Watson, Chorus and Orch. of Royal Opera House, Covent Garden, Pritchard.

Geared to a successful Covent Garden production, this CBS issue presents a strong and enjoyable performance, well sung and well characterized. Delight centres very much round the delectable Adina of Ileana Cotrubas. Quite apart from the delicacy of her singing, she presents a sparkling flirtatious character to underline the point of the whole story. Placido Domingo, by contrast, is less the world's fool that Nemorino should be, more a conventional hero. It is a large voice for the role, and *Una furtiva lagrima* is not pure enough in its legato; but otherwise his singing is stylish and vigorous. Sir Geraint Evans gives a vivid characterization of Dr Dulcamara, though the microphone sometimes brings out roughness of tone. Ingvar Wixell is an upstanding Belcore. The sound on the tape is generally acceptable if not distinguished, with the stage atmosphere quite well conveyed; but our review copy every now and then produced gurgling discoloration of the woodwind, and occasionally the voices too (*Una furtiva lagrima* was not completely free from it). Later copies may well offer more secure sound, but the box CBS provides is not very robust and the collector who buys this set on tape is asked to send away for the libretto!

La Favorita: complete.
　　**(*) Decca K 96 K 33 [Lon. 5-13113]. Luciano Pavarotti, Fiorenza Cossotto, Gabriel Bacquier, Nicolai Ghiaurov, Ileana Cotrubas, Chorus and Orch. of Teatro Comunale, Bologna, Bonynge.

No opera of Donizetti shows more clearly than *La Favorita* just how deeply he influenced the development of Verdi. Almost every scene brings anticipations not just of early Verdi but of the middle operas and even of such mature masterpieces as *Don Carlo* and *La Forza del destino*. *La Favorita* may not have so many headily memorable tunes as the finest Donizetti operas, but red-blooded drama provides ample compensation. Set in Spain in the early fourteenth century, the story revolves round the predicament of Fernando – strongly and imaginatively sung here by Pavarotti – torn between religious devotion and love for the beautiful Leonora, who (unknown to him) is the mistress of the king.

This new recording made in Bologna is not ideal – showing signs that the sessions were not easy – but the colour and vigour of the writing are never in doubt. The mezzo role of the heroine is taken by Cossotto, formidably powerful if not quite at her finest, while Ileana Cotrubas comparably is imaginative as her confidant Ines, but not quite at her peak. Bacquier and Ghiaurov make up a team which should have been even better, but which will still give much satisfaction. Bright Decca recording, again not quite out of the top drawer. The transfer is generally well managed. There seems to be some lack of sparkle in the overture, but the voices are naturally projected (the Act 2 Alfonso/Leonora duet at the beginning of side three has a very striking immediacy). The chorus is not as sharply focused as in some Decca opera sets, but this is caused by the rather reverberant sound picture. The opera is well laid out (although not every act concludes at a side-end), and the libretto is admirably clear.

La Fille du régiment: complete.

 ⚝ *** Decca K 23 K 22 [Lon. 5-1273]. Joan Sutherland, Luciano Pavarotti, Monica Sinclair, Spiro Malas, Edith Coates, Chorus and Orch. of Royal Opera House, Covent Garden, Bonynge.

This is a fizzing performance of a delightful Donizetti romp that can be confidently recommended for both comedy and fine singing. It was with this cast that the piece was revived at Covent Garden in the 1960s, and Sutherland immediately showed how naturally she took to the role of tomboy. Marie is a *vivandière* in the army of Napoleon, and the jolly, almost Gilbertian, plot involves her translation back to a noble background from which as an infant she was lost. This original French version favoured by Richard Bonynge is fuller than the Italian revision, and with a cast that at the time of the recording sessions was also appearing in the theatre the performance could hardly achieve higher spirits with keener assurance. Sutherland is in turn brilliantly comic and pathetically affecting, and no better sampler of the whole set need be suggested than part of the last side, where Marie is reunited with her army friends (including the hero). Pavarotti makes an engaging hero, Monica Sinclair a formidable Countess, and even if the French accents are often suspect it is a small price to pay for such a brilliant, happy opera set. The tape transfer is of Decca's best quality, bright and sparkling, yet (as the overture immediately shows) offering plenty of warmth and bloom. The voices project splendidly but without any artificial edge: a demonstration set. The libretto is clearly printed and easy to read.

Linda di Chamounix: Ah! tardai troppo ... O luce di quest anima. Lucia di Lammermoor: Ancor non giunse! ... Regnava nel silenzio; Mad scene (complete).

 (M) **(*) Decca Ace of Diamonds KSDC 146. Joan Sutherland, Paris Conservatoire Orch., Santi – VERDI: *Arias.***(*)

No rave notice could really exaggerate the quality of this singing, and in many ways this first recording made by Joan Sutherland of the *Lucia* Mad scene has not been surpassed by either of her complete recordings of the opera (1961 and 1971). In fact this recital must be set on a pedestal as one of the finest and most dramatically thrilling displays of coloratura ever recorded. It is not just that Sutherland shows here a Tetrazzini-like perfection, but that she makes these stylized tunes and florid passages into something intensely moving. The youthful freshness of the voice is extremely appealing, and the tonal beauty is often quite magical. With an excellent stereo recording this remains one of the great recitals. The transfer to tape was a relatively early Decca issue and, as current copies show, the focus in the orchestra sometimes lacks the last degree of crispness. The voice for the most part sounds deliciously limpid and fresh, although the famous duet with the flute in the *Lucia di Lammermoor* Mad scene brings a few peaking notes.

Lucia di Lammermoor: complete.

 *** Decca K 2 L 22 [Lon. 5-13103]. Joan Sutherland, Luciano Pavarotti, Sherrill Milnes, Nicolai Ghiaurov, Chorus and Orch. of Royal Opera House, Covent Garden, Bonynge.

 **(*) Philips 7699 056 [id.]. Montserrat Caballé, José Carreras, Vicente Sardinero, Samuel Ramey, Ambrosian Singers,

New Philharmonia Orch., López Cobos.

(***) HMV TC-SLS 5056. Maria Callas, Giuseppe di Stefano, Tito Gobbi, Chorus and Orch. of Maggio Musicale Fiorentino, Serafin.

It was hardly surprising that after ten years Decca should want to re-record Sutherland in the role with which she is inseparably associated. Though some of the girlish freshness of voice which marked the 1961 recording has disappeared in the 1971 set, the detailed understanding has been intensified, and the mooning manner which in 1961 was just emerging has been counteracted. Really there is no one today to outshine Sutherland in this opera; and rightly for this recording she insisted on doing the whole of the Mad scene in a single session, making sure it was consistent from beginning to end. Power is there as well as delicacy, and the rest of the cast is first-rate. Pavarotti, through much of the opera not so sensitive as he can be, proves magnificent in his final scene. The recording quality is superb, though choral interjections are not always forward enough. In this set, unlike Sutherland's earlier one, the text is absolutely complete. On tape the sound is first-class, the transfer level nicely calculated to give both presence and bloom to the solo voices, while the ensembles are spacious.

The idea behind the Philips set with Caballé is fascinating, a return to what the conductor, Jesús López Cobos, believes is Donizetti's original concept, an opera for dramatic soprano, not a light coloratura. Compared with the text we know, transpositions paradoxically are for the most part upwards (made possible when no stratospheric coloratura additions are needed), but Cobos's direction hardly compensates for the lack of brilliance, and, José Carreras apart, the singing is not especially persuasive, even that of Caballé. With a comparatively high-level transfer by Philips's standards the

sound has plenty of presence; indeed the brilliance of the choral scenes carries with it a hint of hardness. But this remains a first-class example of the immediacy possible in transferring a modern opera recording to cassette tape.

It was Callas, some years before Sutherland emerged as the Lucia of our time, who established this as a vividly dramatic role, not just an excuse for pretty coloratura. Hers, needless to say, is not the portrait of a sweet girl, wronged and wilting, but a formidably tragic characterization. This recording is taken from Callas's earlier mono set, with the diva vocally better controlled (indeed some of the coloratura is brilliant in its own right) and with memorable, if not always perfectly stylish, contributions from di Stefano and Gobbi. The text used – unlike recent recordings – has the usual stage cuts, but Callas's irresistible musical imagination, her ability to turn a well-known phrase with unforgettable inflection, supremely justifies the preservation of a historic recording. Different machines (and ears) will judge the excellence of the transfer individually. Certainly the acoustic is confined and the chorus poorly focused and muddy. The solo voices are on the whole well caught, though occasionally the patina of Callas's tone is discoloured at peaks.

Maria Stuarda: complete.

*** Decca K 2 A 33 [Lon. 5-13117]. Joan Sutherland, Huguette Tourangeau, Luciano Pavarotti, Chorus and Orch. of Teatro Comunale, Bologna, Bonynge.

Among the fictional versions of English history which attracted Italian opera composers of the last century, Donizetti's opera on the conflict of Elizabeth I and Mary Queen of Scots stands out as one of the most tellingly dramatic. The confrontation between the two Queens is so brilliantly effective that one regrets that history did not actually manage such a meeting between the royal cousins. In presenting the opera on record, Richard Bonynge and the Decca producers have vividly captured the feeling of a stage performance. Unusually for Decca, the text is slightly cut, but only the extreme purist will be worried. The contrast between the full soprano Maria and the dark mezzo Elisabetta is underlined by some transpositions, with Tourangeau emerging as a powerful villainess in this slanted version of the story. Pavarotti turns Leicester into a passionate Italian lover, not at all an Elizabethan gentleman. As for Sutherland she is at her most fully dramatic too, and the great moment when she flings the insult *Vil bastarda* at her cousin brings a superb snarl. In the lovely prayer before the Queen's execution with its glorious melody, Sutherland is richly forthright but does not quite efface memories of Janet Baker's stage performances at the Coliseum (involving different transpositions). Otherwise Sutherland remains the most commanding of Donizetti sopranos, and Bonynge directs an urgent account of an unfailingly enjoyable opera. The recording is bright and full; the tape transfer offers splendid presence, and the background detail is good too. It sounds best with a very slight treble cut and matching bass increase. The libretto is exceptionally clear, printed in bold, black type; the synopsis is in smaller type but is still readable.

Dowland, John
(1563–1626)

Consort music: *Alman a 2; Can she excuse galliard; Captain Piper's pavan and galliard; Dowland's first galliard; Fortune my foe; Frog galliard; Katherine Darcie's galliard; Lachrimae antiquae novae pavan and galliard; Lachrimae pavan; Lady, if you so spite me; La Mia Barbara pavan and galliard; Mistress Nichol's alman; Mistress Nichol's alman a 2; Mistress Nichol's alman a 5; M. John Langton's pavan and galliard; Pavan a 4; Round battell galliard; Susanna fair galliard; Tarleton's jigge; Volta a 4; Were every thought an eye.*

*** Oiseau-Lyre KDSLC 533.
Consort of Musicke, Anthony Rooley (lute).

It is by no means certain that all the music recorded here is authentic Dowland, but this anthology does serve to remind us how widely his music was admired and arranged during his lifetime. Three of the *Pavans* and *Galliards* come from Thomas Simpson's *Opusculum* (1610) and two of the *Pavans* are direct recompositions of Dowland's *Lachrimae*. Four of the settings are from Morley's *Consort Lessons*, and there are five pieces from the Cambridge MS. that are performed most attractively here. Marvellous playing comes in the pieces from Simpson's *Taffel-consort* (1621). The recording maintains the high standard of this Oiseau-Lyre series, although the forward balance brings a comparatively limited dynamic range. In all other respects the sound is first-class and the transfer quality sophisticated in detail and timbre.

Lute music: *Captain Digorie Piper's galliard; 2 Fancies (Nos. 5 and 73); Farewell; Forlorn hope fancy; Galliard to Lachrimae; Mr Langton's galliard; My Lord Chamberlain, his galliard; My Lord Willoughby's welcome home; Piper's pavan; Resolution; Sir John Souche's galliard.*

*** RCA RK 11491 [ARK 1 1491].
Julian Bream (lute).

An impeccably played recital, as might be expected from this fine artist. Bream captures the dolorous colouring of Dowland's galliards with uncanny insight, and the music is full of atmosphere. The recording is well nigh perfect. It needs to be reproduced at a relatively low level, perhaps with a slight treble reduction, and then the illusion is complete. The transfer is immaculate and the background is silent.

Dukas, Paul
(1865–1935)

L'Apprenti sorcier (The Sorcerer's Apprentice).
- (M) *** Decca Jubilee KJBC 36. Suisse Romande Orch., Ansermet – HONEGGER: *Pacific 231*; RAVEL: *Boléro* etc.***
- **(*) HMV TC-ASD 3008. City of Birmingham SO, Frémaux – *Concert.***(*)
- (M) ** Decca KCSP 376. Israel PO, Solti – ROSSINI: *La Boutique fantasque.***
- (B) (*) RCA Camden C4-5031. Boston SO, Munch – IBERT: *Escales**; RAVEL: *Boléro* etc.(*)

It is perhaps strange that the current catalogue does not contain an outstanding modern recording of *L'Apprenti sorcier* to provide for the seventies the equivalent of Stokowski's memorable 78 set. Ansermet's account is easily the best recommendation. The recording perhaps lacks the last degree of brilliance, but it is still a fine one. The performance too is slightly relaxed, yet it has a cumulative effect: one has the feeling of real calamity before the magician hurriedly returns at the end to put right the mischief his apprentice has wrought.

The Frémaux version (a vividly atmospheric one, lacking something in sheer élan) is also part of an enjoyable if not distinctive concert of French music, which is discussed in our Concerts section. Recorded in the Great Hall of Birmingham University, this has transferred well to cassette and can be recommended if the couplings are suitable.

Solti's natural intensity suits the music and his tempi are very well chosen: the first entry of the main tune is immediately right. The recording is spacious, and the strings swirl nicely in their watery descriptive passages. The clear cassette transfer has no lack of brilliance but is slightly dry.

Munch's performance is a lively one and – particularly with the attractive coupling of Ibert's *Escales* – it would be very competitive if the transfer had been a success. As it is, the treble response is minimal and one has to dispense with the Dolby circuitry to get any kind of sparkle out of the recording.

La Péri (including Fanfare) – poème dansé.
- *(*) CBS 40-76519 [Col. MT 34201]. New York PO, Boulez – ROUSSEL: *Symphony No. 3.*(**)

Dukas's *La Péri*, written for Diaghilev in 1912, is based on a tale from ancient Persian mythology. The King Iskander discovers the Péri asleep and steals her lotus blossom with its power of immortal youth. The Péri awakens and stimulates the King's desire with an erotic dance (hints of *Salome* in the music). The King succumbs and returns the flower, whereupon the object of his passion promptly vanishes, leaving him to reflect that he has been caught out by the oldest trick of all. The opening *Fanfare* is reminiscent of the brass writing of Gabrieli, but the rest of the score, while imaginatively orchestrated, contains what to some ears seems relatively unmemorable thematic material. Boulez gives a most sensitive and atmospheric account. It is imaginative and poetic, and the orchestral playing is of the highest quality. Even those who do not normally respond to this conductor will find their reservations swept aside. The recording has too much resonance for comfort, and the detail does not register as clearly as it might. However, the transfer is reasonably bright and sounds quite well. Unfortunately the coupling is, technically speaking, much less successful.

Duparc, Henri
(1848–1933)

Mélodies: *Au pays où se fait la guerre; L'Invitation au voyage; Le Manoir de Rosemonde; Phidylé; La Vie antérieure.*

*** HMV TC-ASD 3455. Janet Baker (mezzo-soprano), LSO, Previn – CHAUSSON: *Poème de l'amour et de la mer.****

Duparc, most sparing of composers, actually dared to orchestrate some of the handful of songs he wrote in his early career. Purist lovers of French *mélodie* will no doubt prefer the original piano accompaniments, but this record will triumphantly prove to non-specialists that the extra richness and colour of the orchestral versions add to the depth and intensity of these exceptionally sensitive word-settings, above all in the greatest of all, *Phidylé*. But as Dame Janet Baker and André Previn present them, each one of these songs is a jewelled miniature of breathtaking beauty, and the clear, ripe, beautifully balanced recording is fully worthy of the performances. The transfer to tape is spaciously atmospheric, the acoustic well caught even if the detail is less clear than on the LP.

Dussek (Dusik), Jan
(1760–1812)

Double piano concerto in B flat major.

(M) *(*) Turnabout KTVC 34204. Toni and Rosi Grünschlag (pianos), Vienna Volksoper Orch., Angerer – SCHUMANN: *Andante and variations.***(*)

It is something of a tradition for double piano concertos to be genial works, and Dussek's is no exception. Above all such a piece needs spontaneity and conveyed enjoyment from the performers, and the Grünschlag duo offers this quality in abundance. They are experts both as a partnership and in matters of technique, and they play with such *brio* that a relatively slight work is made very enjoyable indeed. The lyricism of the slow movement and the gay chatter of the finale are especially enjoyable, and the first-rate recording balances the personalities of the solo team against a lively orchestral accompaniment. This is highly infectious. A good coupling too. The transfer offers well-balanced, generally pleasing sound, although the resonance obscures some detail. But this is a cassette where the quality differs on each side: the above comments apply to side one; when one turns over to side two for the finale, there is a lack of sparkle, and the Schumann coupling is similarly affected.

Dvořák, Antonin
(1841–1904)

Overtures: (i; ii) *Carnaval, Op. 92; Hussite, Op. 67; In Nature's Realm, Op. 91; My Home, Op. 62; Othello,*

Op. 93. Symphonic poems: (i; iii) *The Golden Spinning Wheel, Op. 109;* (iv) *A Hero's Song, Op. 111;* (i; iii) *The Noonday Witch, Op. 108; The Water Goblin, Op. 107; The Wild Dove, Op. 110*. (i; v) *Symphonic variations, Op. 78*.

(B) (**) Rediffusion Legend KLGDD 101. (i) Czech PO; (ii) Ančerl; (iii) Chalabala; (iv) Prague Radio Orch., Klíma; (v) Neumann.

This immensely valuable collection of Dvořák's orchestral music (including the rare *Hero's Song*) has the particular interest of showing the special qualities of orchestral colour and rhythmic inflection, to say nothing of atmosphere, a Czech group can bring to this repertoire. The performances are splendidly played and have plenty of life and spontaneity; and basically the recordings are all good, some very good. Unfortunately the transfers are a mixed success. In order to produce a high-level transfer without too many problems the body of the orchestral sound has been thinned out, so that the string tone is papery and lacking in realism. Often the treble is fierce, but even so, minor congestion is not avoided, especially where Dvořák uses the timpani strongly (when the texture is disturbed). *The Golden Spinning Wheel* is badly affected in this way. The last two tapes seem the most successful technically, one containing the three linked overtures, Opp. 91–3, and the other combining the *Symphonic variations* with *A Hero's Song*. Elsewhere one has to accept very mixed quality, although the woodwind seems to escape without too much loss of bloom. The notes are adequate and these tapes are very reasonably priced, but it is a great pity that more care was not taken in their remastering for cassette issue.

Piano concerto in G minor, Op. 33.
  (***) HMV TC-ASD 3371.
Sviatoslav Richter, Bavarian State Orch., Carlos Kleiber.

The *Piano concerto* comes from a vintage period which also saw the completion of the *F major Symphony*. Richter plays the solo part in its original form (and not the more 'pianistically effective' revision), and his judgement is triumphantly vindicated. This is the most persuasive and masterly account of the concerto ever recorded; its ideas emerge with an engaging freshness and warmth, while the greater simplicity of Dvořák's own keyboard writing proves in Richter's hands to be the more telling and profound. Never has the slow movement sounded as moving as it does here. Kleiber secures excellent results from the Bavarian orchestra. The recording, though not in the demonstration class, is basically good, but it has been transferred to tape at too high a level. The opening orchestral *tutti* is coarse and unrefined, and one is not tempted to continue listening. No doubt an improved transfer will appear in due course.

Violin concerto in A minor, Op. 53.
  (M) ** Decca KCSP 398. Ruggiero Ricci, LSO, Sargent – SIBELIUS: *Concerto*.**(*)
Violin concerto; Romance in F minor (for violin and orchestra), *Op. 11.*
  (M) (**) Supraphon 045181. Josef Suk, Czech PO, Ančerl.

Ruggiero Ricci has fire and dash, and he receives fine support from Sargent and the LSO. But perhaps, by the side of Suk, one feels there is a want of inner warmth and purity of spirit. The recording belies its age (it first appeared in 1960) and is clear and well balanced. The very opening of the concerto on tape seems to lack the last degree of refinement, but generally the transfer is bold and clear, with a wide range.

Suk's performance is lyrical in the simplest possible way, and its eloquence is endearing, in spite of the somewhat dated

Supraphon sound. The bonus is the charming *Romance* that Dvořák adopted from the slow movement of his *F minor String quartet*. This is played to perfection by Suk, who realizes its simple charm with skill and affection. The glowing orchestral part is equally enjoyable. Unfortunately the current Supraphon transfer is not really recommendable. On side one there is a very limited treble response; if one cuts the bass right back, the quality is acceptable but seriously lacks sparkle. Side two offers curiously exaggerated high frequencies, giving a 'comb and paper' effect to the upper range which is difficult to smooth out.

Violoncello concerto in B minor, Op. 104.

(*) DG 923098 [id.]. Mstislav Rostropovich, Berlin PO, Karajan – TCHAIKOVSKY: *Variations on a rococo theme.*(*)

(M) ** HMV TC-EXE 158. Paul Tortelier, Philharmonia Orch., Sargent.

*(*) HMV TC-ASD 3452. Rostropovich, LPO, Giulini – SAINT-SAËNS: *Concerto No. 1.***

(B) *(*) DG Heliodor 3348 134. Anja Thauer, Czech PO, Madal – MUSSORGSKY: *Night on the Bare Mountain.**(*)

Violoncello concerto; Rondo in G minor, Op. 94; Waldesruhe (*Silent Woods*), *Op. 68* (both for cello and orchestra).

(M) *** Philips 7317 162. Maurice Gendron, LPO, Haitink.

(M) *(*) Turnabout KTVC 37099. Zara Nelsova, St Louis SO, Susskind.

(i) *Violoncello concerto. Slavonic dances Nos. 1 and 7, Op. 46/1 and 7; 16, Op. 72/8.*

(M) (***) DG Privilege 3335 106. Berlin PO, Szell or Karajan, (i) with Pierre Fournier.

Gendron's is the finest available tape of Dvořák's *Cello concerto*. The sound is rich and full-bodied, and the orchestral tuttis have plenty of bite. With excellent balance, this is a most satisfying cassette. The performance is marvellously fresh and lyrical, and has the advantage of impeccable orchestral support from the LPO under Haitink. There is a real spontaneity about this playing, and its warmth is splendidly captured by the Philips engineers. There are two engaging fill-ups.

The collaboration of Rostropovich and Karajan makes for superb results, warm as well as refined in reflection of the finest qualities in each of the two principals. If Rostropovich can sometimes sound self-indulgent in this most romantic of cello concertos, the degree of control provided by the conductor here gives a firm yet supple base, and there have been few recorded accounts so deeply satisfying. The result is unashamedly romantic, with many moments of dalliance, but the concentration is never in doubt. Superb playing by the Berliners, and a bonus (not to be taken for granted with this concerto) in the shape of Tchaikovsky's glorious variations. The cassette transfer has long been in the catalogue in non-Dolbyized form but has recently appeared suitably remastered. However, while the new transfer gives the orchestral tuttis plenty of life, the solo cello – which is naturally balanced – seems less well defined and tends to lack body and substance, particularly when Rostropovich is playing *piano* and *pianissimo*. But the quality is free and quite refined, whereas the newer HMV tape, where Rostropovich is partnered by Giulini, has one or two moments of roughness at the peaks of orchestral tuttis. The solo cello is given a stronger image here, and the overall sound is agreeably warm if lacking detail and an extended range. But this newest interpretation is the least successful of Rostropovich's three recordings of the concerto. He makes heavy weather of much of it, and his unrelieved emotional intensity is matched by Giulini, who focuses attention on beauty of detail rather than structural cohesion. Of course there are many subtleties that compel admiration, and the engineering is impressive.

The Tortelier performance on HMV has all the rich, romantic concentration one expects from this great cellist. There are minor technical blemishes in the finale (so there always were with Casals), but this is a performance that hangs together and reveals new facets in the work every time one hears it. With the genuine tension of a live performance (in the first two movements at least) it is one of the most enjoyable and warm-hearted versions ever recorded. The stereo gives an excellent sense of atmosphere but does not always provide absolute inner clarity. Generally the transfer offers warm, vivid sound, and the level is high. There are one or two short patches where the sound roughens slightly, but none is very serious.

Fournier's reading has a sweep of conception and richness of tone and phrasing which carry along the melodic lines with exactly the mixture of nobility and tension that the work demands. Fournier can relax and beguile the ear in the lyrical passages, and yet catch up the listener in his exuberance in the exciting finale. The phrasing in the slow movement is ravishing, and the interpretation as a whole balances beautifully. DG's recording, however, is marred by the quality of the transfer. The upper orchestral strings are made to sound poorly focused, and the solo cello image is surrounded with a 'buzzy' halo. With a treble cut-back or filter one can smooth the upper register, but the stridency in the orchestral strings is not easy to tame without losing the recording's detail.

Zara Nelsova is an admirable soloist,

and her performance is a fine one. Moreover she is well supported by the St Louis orchestra under Walter Susskind. The recording has plenty of body and is firmly focused, but the orchestral detail is not always well revealed, although this is not the fault of the tape transfer, which is secure and clean. With Gendron's Philips tape offering exactly the same programme, this Turnabout issue is not well enough balanced to compete; Gendron offers every bit as much warmth and the sound of his cello is richer and more beautiful.

Anja Thauer is an eloquent cellist, but the tone she produces is rather lightweight for this concerto, which ideally needs rich, full-blooded timbre. Miss Thauer plays the slow movement with considerable feeling and is at her best in the finale, where she shows both imagination and vigour. The orchestral support is good, but (like the soloist) it is not notable here for body and weight of tone, which suggests that much of the fault may lie with the recording itself. The transfer is clear and clean. What a curiously chosen coupling!

The Golden Spinning Wheel, Op. 100; Symphonic variations, Op. 78.
　** Decca KSXC 6510. LSO, Kertesz.
Hussite overture, Op. 67; The Noonday Witch, Op. 108; The Water Goblin, Op. 107.
　(M) (**) Supraphon 045455. Czech PO, Ančerl or Chalabala.

Dvořák has a cheerfully extrovert way of looking at the morbid national legends on which he bases his symphonic poems. It would be difficult to guess, from hearing the music without pre-knowledge of the programmes, the amount of unpleasant sudden death that goes on within. The heroine of the charming *Golden Spinning Wheel* (a just favourite of Sir Thomas Beecham's) is killed and mutilated by her stepmother; *The Noonday Witch* is the traditional ogress threatened to erring children by distraught mothers, and here she gets her prey; *The Water Goblin*, having ensnared his maiden, dashes their green-haired child, decapitated, at her feet when she escapes back to mother. The music is colourful, with attractive invention and characteristically imaginative orchestration. The Decca coupling of *The Golden Spinning Wheel*, with its magical horn calls, and a fine performance of the *Symphonic variations* makes a desirable issue, with playing well up to the high standard Kertesz and the LSO consistently achieved in their Dvořák series. The transfer to tape, however, was an early Decca issue and in *The Golden Spinning Wheel* there is a hint of over-modulation at peaks, although otherwise the quality is good. Side two offers a smooth rather than sparkling balance, which tends to give the *Variations* a Brahmsian flavour.

The *Hussite overture* (which includes themes based on the Hussite hymn and St Wenceslas plain chant) is also patriotic in inspiration, if rather less successful than *My Home*. The Supraphon tape coupling it with two symphonic poems has plenty to recommend it on the musical side (the orchestral playing is often vividly atmospheric, and the readings are imaginative); but unfortunately the transfer is unacceptable. The sound has a very limited range, and while never refined becomes markedly less so at the opening of *The Noonday Witch* in the middle of side one. There is a turnover break in this work, and the sound is faded down and up again. To complete the clumsiness, the music is quickly cut off on the finale chord before the reverberation has died away naturally, and this happens again at the end of the *Hussite overture*.

Serenade for strings in E major, Op. 22.

*** Philips 7300 532 [id.]. ECO, Leppard – TCHAIKOVSKY: *String serenade*.***

*** Argo KZRC 848 [id.]. Academy of St Martin-in-the-Fields, Marriner – TCHAIKOVSKY: *String serenade*.***

*** Argo KZRC 670 [id.] (as above, cond. Marriner) – GRIEG: *Holberg suite*.***

(M) *** DG Privilege 3318 047. ECO, Kubelik – SMETANA: *Má Vlast excerpts*.**(*)

(B) *** DG Heliodor 3348 121. North-West German Radio SO, Schmidt-Isserstedt – TCHAIKOVSKY: *String serenade*.*(*)

(*) Advent E 1047 (see p. xxiii) [id.]. RPO, Stokowski – PURCELL: *Dido's lament(*); VAUGHAN WILLIAMS: *Tallis fantasia*.**(*)

(M) ** Decca KCSP 375. Israel PO, Kubelik – TCHAIKOVSKY: *String serenade*.**

Dvořák's *String serenade* is exceptionally well represented on tape, and the top five listings all provide most sophisticated sound. Both Argo tapes offer rich, well-defined string timbre, and there is a choice of coupling, which is unusual on cassette. Whether the Grieg or Tchaikovsky is chosen they will give great satisfaction. In the Dvořák work some ears might find the textures created by the Academy strings almost too rich for the innocent simplicity of the composer's invention (although the balance of timbre is slightly more leonine on tape than on disc). Yet such beguiling playing is difficult to resist, especially when the recording is so clear and glowing.

The English Chamber Orchestra seem to have made a speciality of recording Dvořák's *Serenade*; they are shown here in two of their recordings, each substantially different in character. On Leppard's Philips tape the orchestra is given superb recording, wide in range and natural in timbre. Leppard's approach is direct, even robust, perhaps not quite as refined as Marriner, but without that overtly expressive quality which – for instance at the very opening of the Argo performance – verges on indulgence. The tempi of the allegros have a strong momentum, but Leppard's natural flexibility prevents the brisk manner from losing its resilience. The finale is wonderfully bright and invigorating.

Kubelik's Privilege tape, too, is notably successful, a performance that is beautifully lyrical, yet strong in impulse. The recording is brightly lit but of very good quality. With its attractive couplings this is a genuine bargain at medium price. This too has a tape transfer of demonstration quality: the string tone is brilliant, yet has richness and depth too.

A lyrical account from Schmidt-Isserstedt, truthfully recorded. This was originally coupled to an indifferent account of the Brahms *Serenade No. 2* but is now paired with an attractive account of the Tchaikovsky. The recording too is first-class, clean and clear, yet with no lack of body. The snag is that the Tchaikovsky coupling is much less clear, although acceptable.

The Stokowskian magic is very much apparent in the Advent/Desmar recording, not only in the ripeness of the string playing but in the masterly control of tension. Thus the opening is slow and affectionate, without dragging or sounding too overtly expressive. There is concentration in every bar, and the lyrical flow is highly engaging. In the second movement Stokowski's delicacy at a quick tempo is exhilarating, and the trio is beautifully managed, with less variation of tempo than in the Leppard version. The lilting scherzo is matched by the warmth of the *Larghetto*, and the finale is superbly resilient. The RPO are kept on their toes throughout, and the wide-range recording is faithfully transferred (on chrome tape), though there is slight featheriness at times in the focus of the upper strings.

Although it opens persuasively,

Kubelik's earlier performance on Decca relies on virility rather than charm to make its appeal. It is certainly splendidly alive, and the finale gains from such treatment. But the third movement is very fast indeed. The recording is wide in range, with a very bright treble, and the transfer is rather grainy in texture.

(i) *Serenade for strings in E major, Op. 22;* (ii) *Serenade in D minor* (for 10 wind instruments, cello and double-bass), *Op. 44.*

(M) ** Supraphon 0450760. (i) Czech CO, Vlach; (ii) Prague Chamber Harmony, Turnovsky.

(M) * CBS Classics 40-61811. (i) Munich PO, Kempe; (ii) Marlboro Woodwind Ens., Moyse.

Serenade in D minor, Op. 44.
*(*) Decca KSXC 6368. Members of the LSO, Kertesz – BRAHMS: *Serenade No. 2.***(*)

The Czech issue repeats a coupling that Supraphon made famous as an early mono LP. Then Talich gave a magical account of the *String serenade*, and it was coupled to a wonderfully earthy performance of the companion work for wind by a group of professors from the Prague Conservatoire. As so often happens in recording, this remake does not quite equal that earlier success. Czech chamber-music playing is justly renowned, but Josef Vlach does not find the incandescence that illuminated the Talich performance; and the wind group, although it has attractive moments of lightness and humour, has not quite the earthy grace those professors found. But having said that, this coupling is still most enjoyable. It is full and clear as a recording, and the playing in the *String serenade* has an easy, unforced way with it that suits Dvořák's ingenuous mood. The middle movements are especially warm and beautiful. The character of the wind-playing too has a robust colouring that non-Czech players find difficult to match. This is certainly an attractive mid-priced cassette, a little lacking in range, but with an attractively warm middle register that gives plenty of character to the wind instruments and is not lost on the string-playing either.

The CBS version of the same coupling is well played, but the muffled recording takes all the sparkle out of the work for strings, while the *Wind serenade* has not the character here which makes the other versions so attractive.

Kertesz gives a delightfully idiomatic account of the enchanting *Wind serenade*, and the Decca recording is basically excellent. However, this is another of those tapes with different quality on each side. The Brahms coupling has plenty of sparkle, but the Dvořák has been given a more restricted range, and the sound is rather plummy.

Slavonic dances Nos. 1–8, Op. 46/1–8; 9–16, Op. 72/1–8.
  *(**) Decca Phase 4 KPFC 4396. Czech PO, Neumann.
Slavonic dances Nos. 1–8.
  (B) ** Rediffusion Legend KLGD 015. Czech PO, Sejna.
Slavonic dances Nos. 1–8; Scherzo capriccioso, Op. 66.
  *** DG 3300 422 [id.]. Bavarian Radio SO, Kubelik.
Slavonic dances Nos. 9–16.
  (B) ** Rediffusion Legend KLGD 039. Czech PO, Sejna.
Slavonic dances Nos. 1, 3, 8, Op. 46/1, 3, 8; 9–10, Op. 72/1–2.
  (M) **(*) Decca KCSP 377. Vienna PO, Reiner – BRAHMS: *Hungarian dances.***(*)
Slavonic dances Nos. 1, 3, 8, Op. 46/1, 3, 8; 10, 13, 15, Op. 72/2, 5, 7.
  ** Advent E 1025 (see p. xxiii) [id.]. LSO, Kosler – MOZART: *Symphony No. 38.***

Slavonic dances Nos. 3, Op. 46/3; 10, Op. 72/2.
  (*) HMV TC-ASD 3312. Cleveland Orch., Szell – BRAHMS: *Double concerto.*(*)
Slavonic dance No. 10, Op. 72/2.
  ** Decca Phase 4 KPFC 4333 [Lon. 5-21117]. Czech PO, Stokowski – RIMSKY-KORSA-KOV: *Capriccio espagnol***(*); SCRIABIN: *Poème de l'extase.****

The complete set of the *Slavonic dances* by Neumann and the Czech Philharmonic Orchestra was originally a Telefunken issue, but Decca have remastered the recording and added artificial Phase Four brilliance. As the recording tended to be very brightly lit anyway, the effect is to make the sound aggressive, and this tape needs considerable treble control to become amenable listening. DG issued all sixteen dances on two cassettes (the second, 3300 593, coupling the Op. 72 dances with the *My Home overture*), but then they deleted the second tape in the UK (though it is still available in the USA). Although the format is uneconomical, the playing is first-class, polished and sparkling, and the sound is very good too, provided one cuts back the bass a little. However, taking price into consideration, the best buy here would seem to be the two Legend tapes offering all sixteen dances. The Czech Philharmonic have something special to contribute in this repertoire, and they do not disappoint, with felicitous wind solos and lilting string-playing. Both tapes offer bright, well-balanced sound quality, and undoubtedly the music-making is vivacious and idiomatic. (On our copy of KLGD 039 there were two curious patches of increased background noise towards the end of side two.)

Reiner's readings are polished and enjoyable, if not penetrating too far below the surface in the lyrical music, where he is inclined to be mannered. But the overall effect has plenty of sparkle, and one's reservations are soon forgotten. The transfers are brilliant and sparkling, and the level is high. There is a touch of glare on the upper strings, but this can be minimized with careful setting of the controls. The Brahms coupling is good too.

Zdenek Kosler's readings are warmly enjoyable, and the LSO plays vivaciously. But the performances, although vivid and colourful, lack something in sheer élan: these dances sound lively but not irrepressibly exuberant. The recording is excellent, and the bright transfers have weight to balance the extended upper range of the chrome tape. The upper focus lacks only the last degree of sharpness.

Szell's HMV performances are brilliant and polished, yet have no lack of warmth. They make an excellent fill-up for the finest available performance of Brahms's *Double concerto*. The tape transfer is generally excellent, although the focus of the upper strings is just a little feathery at times.

Stokowski gives an idiosyncratic reading of the E minor dance, slow and smoochy, a memorable fill-up to the major works. The sound is good.

Symphonies Nos. 5–9.
  ⊛ *** Decca κ 67 κ 53. LSO, Kertesz.

Kertesz's idiomatic and exciting performances of the last five symphonies are coupled together in a box of three cassettes. No. 5 is paired with No. 9; No. 7 with No. 8 (a side to each work), and No. 6 is alone on the third cassette. The transfers are of excellent quality: the sound is a trifle dry in No. 5, but elsewhere the ambience is well managed. No. 6 is especially bright and sparkling, while Nos. 7 and 8 and especially No. 9 have fine body and clarity, with a pleasing bloom on the woodwind. A most desirable box.

Symphony No. 5 in F major (originally Op. 24 (1875); published as Op. 76); Overtures: *Carnaval, Op. 92; My Home, Op. 62.*
  *** Decca κsxc 16273. LSO, Kertesz.

Even more than most Dvořák, this is a work to make one share, if only for a moment, in the happy emotions of a saint; and what could be more welcome in modern nerve-racked life? The feeling of joy is here expressed so intensely that it provokes tears rather than laughter, and it is hard to understand why this marvellous work has been neglected for so long. It used to be called the *Pastoral*, but although it shares Beethoven's key and uses the flute a great deal (a Dvořákian characteristic) the nickname is not specially apt. What initially strikes one are the echoes of Wagner – forest murmurs (Bohemian ones) in the opening pages, a direct lift from *Siegfried's Rhine Journey* in the second theme and so on – but by the time he wrote the work, 1875, Dvořák's individuality as a musician was well established, and the composer's signature is in effect written on every bar. The slow movement is as beautiful as any in the symphonies, the scherzo is a gloriously bouncing piece with themes squandered generously, and the finale, though long, is intensely original in structure and argument. Kertesz's performance is straight and dramatic, with tempi very well chosen to allow for infectious rhythmic pointing. Excellent recording and first-class transfers – of Decca's highest standard. In the *Carnaval overture* (which is not on the equivalent disc) the recording is especially brilliant.

Symphony No. 6; Carnaval overture, Op. 92.
  *** Decca κsxc 6253. LSO, Kertesz.

If the three immediately preceding Dvořák symphonies reflect the influence of Wagner, this one just as clearly reflects that of Brahms, and particularly of the Brahms *Second Symphony*. Not only the shape of themes but the actual layout in the first movement have strong affinities with the Brahmsian model, but Kertesz's performance effectively underlines the individuality of the writing as well. This is a marvellous work that with the *Fifth* and *Seventh* forms the backbone of the Dvořák cycle, and that is hardly an idea we should have been likely to advance before Kertesz gave us fresh insight into these vividly inspired works. Kertesz's reading is fresh, literal and dramatic in his characteristic Dvořák manner, and his tempi are eminently well chosen. The recording too is excellent, and the transfer offers plenty of body and clarity, although the level is not as high as on some Decca tapes. The *Carnaval overture* does not sound as crisp and sparkling here as on the cassette that couples it with the *Fifth Symphony*.

Symphony No. 7 in D minor, Op. 70.
*** Philips 7300 535 [id.]. Concertgebouw Orch., Colin Davis.
(M) *** Decca Eclipse KECC 779. LSO, Monteux.
**(*) Decca KSXC 6115. LSO, Kertesz.
(B) ** Rediffusion Legend KLGD 007. Czech PO, Kosler.
(M) *(*) CBS Classics 40-61732. Cleveland Orch., Szell.
(**) HMV TC-ASD 3325. LPO, Giulini.

The *Seventh Symphony* is well represented on tape, and there is a clear first choice. The Philips transfer of the Colin Davis version is unusually brilliant for this company, yet without any loss of depth. Davis's view is wonderfully refreshing and the typically refined Philips sound balance matches his clean, urgent approach. In the scherzo, with its cross-rhythms, Davis marks the sforzandos more sharply than usual. There is tough-

ness and fierceness in the outer movements, yet the music-making never becomes aggressive, and the slow movement brings the most distinctive performance of all, less sweet than usual, almost Brucknerian in its hushed nobility and sharply terraced contrasts.

Compared to the Davis approach Monteux sounds strikingly warm-hearted, and this cassette is undoubtedly a strong contender at medium price. Monteux's performance has always been a favourite: it is exciting, idiomatic, and pleasingly tinged with geniality. The orchestral playing is first-rate, and the Decca recording has withstood the test of time. The beautiful opening and closing pages of the *Poco adagio* and the brilliant finale are highlights of a reading which, if it has a slightly mannered effect here and there, is satisfying overall. The transfer has been well managed, although the level needs to be brought up: then the tuttis expand splendidly and are vivid. The quieter passages, however, lack something in sharpness, but the overall quality is rich and satisfying.

Kertesz offers a relaxed reading, beautifully recorded. There is much to give pleasure here, especially the warm orchestral playing. There is no lack of tension, yet somehow the excitement of the climaxes does not always completely catch fire and the last degree of spontaneity is missing, although the finale is especially successful. The transfer is first-class, with a fractionally lower level of impact on side two.

Kosler's performance, which dates from the mid-1960s, is eminently well played. The first movement is measured and weighty, but the added breadth will undoubtedly appeal to some tastes. It lacks the drama and concentration of Colin Davis's much tauter reading, but Czech orchestras bring a special lyrical intensity to Dvořák, and even if Kosler's reading lacks the individuality of those by Davis, Monteux and Kertesz, the orchestral sound works in his favour. It is brightly transferred to tape with good detail and no feeling of shallowness.

Szell's performance has a strong forward impulse, and though it may lack the geniality of Monteux, the slow movement is genuinely moving and there is no lack of sparkle in the playing, which has vitality as well as discipline. However, the CBS tape transfer has a comparatively limited range (although side two is brighter than side one, because of an increase in the transfer level). The overall quality is agreeable and mellow, and the forward balance of the wind means that detail is satisfactory.

Giulini is a conductor who believes in making Dvořák sing, and even in the darkest of his symphonies Dvořákian sunshine keeps bursting out. The ripe recording encourages Giulini to produce rounded textures and rounded phrases, but it is not in any way a self-indulgent performance, and the concentration from first to last makes for buoyancy instead of the more usual biting qualities. This would be much higher up the list of recommendations if the HMV transfer were a success. But it was made at too high a level, which brings unacceptable coarseness at fortissimos.

Symphony No. 8 in G major, Op. 88.
  (M) ** Supraphon 0401203. Czech PO, Neumann.
  (M) *(*) CBS Classics 40-61274. Columbia SO, Walter.
  (M) *(*) Rediffusion Royale KROY 2003. Slovak PO, Kosler.
Symphony No. 8; Scherzo capriccioso, Op. 66.
  *** Decca KSXC 6044. LSO, Kertesz.
Symphony No. 8; Slavonic dances Nos. 2, 4, 6, Op. 46/2, 4 and 6.
  (M) *(*) Philips 7317 157 [7310 078]. Concertgebouw Orch., Haitink.
Symphony No. 8; The Wood Dove, Op. 110.

*(*) Decca KSXC 6750 [Lon. 5-6979]. Los Angeles PO, Mehta.

Kertesz's coupling is a happy choice and helps to place his performance of the symphony at the top of the list. The reading is fresh, spontaneous and exciting. The slow movement is affectionate and captures well the pastoral quality of the writing, and the tempo for the *Allegretto grazioso* is particularly well judged. The Decca recording is extremely brilliant but is notable also for warmth in the middle and lower strings. The cassette is of demonstration standard, with sparkling, full-blooded sound that achieves striking richness in the slow movement.

The Czech Philharmonic Orchestra always have something special to contribute to a performance of a Dvořák symphony, partly the combination of warmth and lyrical fervour but also the colouring provided by strings and wind soloists. Neumann's performance is direct, without idiosyncrasy, spontaneous without being earth-shaking. The Supraphon transfer is well balanced but made at rather a low level. However, with the volume up it can be made to sound well, and this is the best recommendation for the symphony in the mid-priced area at present.

Bruno Walter gives a strong yet lyrical reading, warm and full of affection. But the overall lyricism never takes the place of virility, and the fine orchestral playing means that there is no lack of impetus and vigour. Walter finds a stature in the finale that eludes some other conductors, and if the CBS transfer were more distinguished this would be rated very highly indeed. As it is, the sound has a mellow warmth but lacks range and bite. As usual with CBS, the wind is given a forward balance, so that the score's detail is not covered up, but the ears crave a more vivid projection of the upper strings (especially after sampling the Kertesz Decca cassette).

Although the Slovak orchestra is not on a par with the Czech Philharmonic, it plays with a refreshing and natural sympathy for Dvořák's score. This is not a performance of outstanding personality, but it has a genuine sense of momentum and a feeling for the overall shape of the symphony. The transfer is much more vivid than that provided by CBS for Walter. Indeed at times the upper strings are a trifle too bright. However, this is not beyond control; the orchestra timbres blend well, and there is no lack of the warmth which this symphony must have if it is to make its full effect.

Haitink's account is rather underpowered, an agreeable but not really a memorable performance. The recording does not help, having some lack of brilliance and bite, and in the *Dances* the lack of sparkle in the sound itself is a serious handicap. Mehta's is a version big and bold but almost totally lacking in tenderness and charm, essential qualities even in this ebullient symphony. The shortcomings are made the clearer when *The Wood Dove*, an attractive fill-up, is so affectionately and delicately performed. Big, bold recording to match; the transfer is clean and bright.

Symphony No. 9 in E minor (From the New World), Op. 95.

(M) *** Decca Jubilee KJBC 37. New Philharmonia Orch., Dorati.

*** Philips 7300 671 [id.]. Concertgebouw Orch., Colin Davis.

**(*) DG 923008 [id.]. Berlin PO, Karajan (with *Slavonic dance No. 1, Op. 46/1*).

(M) **(*) Philips 7317 193. LSO, Rowicki.

**(*) Enigma K 453530. New Philharmonia Orch., Handley.

(*) Double Decca KDPC 2 7054. Vienna PO, Kertesz – TCHAIKOVSKY: *Symphony No. 6.*

**(*) DG 3300 881 [id.]. Chicago SO, Giulini.

*(**) HMV TC-ASD 3407 [Angel 4xs 37437]. Berlin PO, Karajan – SMETANA: *Vltava.*(**)*

(M) **(*) RCA GK 25060. RPO, Horenstein.

** HMV TC-ASD 3285 [Angel 4xs 37230]. New Philharmonia Orch., Muti.

** Advent E 1054 (see p. xxiii) [id.]. Orchestre de Paris, Prêtre.

(M) *(*) Decca KCSP 87 (as above, cond. Kertesz).

(M) *(*) CBS Classics 40-61234. Columbia SO, Walter.

(M) (**) DG Privilege 3318 007. Berlin PO, Fricsay.

* Philips 7300 419 [id.]. San Francisco SO, Ozawa.

Symphony No. 9; Carnaval overture, Op. 92.

(M) ** HMV TC-EXE 69. Philharmonia Orch., Giulini – BIZET: *Jeux d'enfants.***

(B) ** Classics for Pleasure TC-CFP 104. Philharmonia Orch., Sawallisch.

*(*) Decca KSXC 6751 [Lon. 5-6980]. Los Angeles PO, Mehta.

Symphony No. 9; Othello overture, Op. 93.

*** Decca KSXC 6291. LSO, Kertesz.

The great popularity of the *New World symphony* is in no doubt, with some two thirds of all the available recordings of Dvořák's masterpiece issued on cassette. Of these, two contrasted issues from Decca stand out.

Kertesz made his earlier recording in 1961 with the Vienna Philharmonic, but to make his cycle of the symphonies really uniform, Decca sponsored an entirely new version with the London Symphony Orchestra. In the seven years which separated the two, Kertesz had matured enormously, so that the later version is one of the finest ever recorded and on many counts the most completely recommendable of all. Above all Kertesz had learnt to cover his interpretative tracks, so that the tempo changes in the first movement – almost inevitable and certainly desirable – are achieved with utmost subtlety. This time, too, Kertesz takes the exposition repeat, so giving the first movement – otherwise very short – its proper stature. But it is in the slow movement that Kertesz's sensitivity emerges most vividly. In essence his approach is as simple and straightforward as could be, yet the hushed intensity of the playing conveys a depth of feeling that makes one hear the music with new ears. Tempi in the last two movements are also perfectly judged – not too fast in the finale – and the recording quality is outstanding, among the best this symphony has had. The LSO tape was originally issued by Decca in non-Dolbyized form and had the honour to be the very first tape from this source to be especially reissued in a new transfer with the Dolby process included. The sound is most beautiful, the transfer highly sophisticated in all respects. However, the packaging remains the same, and though there are not likely to be many copies of the earlier issue still left in shops it is well to check that the Dolby logo is on the cassette front.

The Dorati performance makes a perfect foil to Kertesz. Contrasting with Kertesz's simple lyricism Dorati is immediate and direct, with bold primary colours heightening the drama throughout. Rarely have the Decca Phase Four techniques been used to better artistic effect, and the recording is extremely vivid, without loss of warmth. This cassette is also one of Decca's finest, clear and sonorous, although slightly dry in timbre, to reflect the Phase Four microphone techniques. The new Jubilee transfer is brightly lit but responds well to a slight reduction of treble, which improves the naturalness of the upper strings. This reissue is an outstanding bargain.

Davis's Concertgebouw recording is splendidly played and recorded. His view is nothing if not straightforward, and

some might feel that the interpretation is too literal. The cor anglais solo in the *Largo*, for instance, is beautifully played but the effect is not very resilient, and later, when the horns echo the theme at the end of the opening section, the impression is positive rather than poetic. The finale too opens a little stolidly. But when this is said there is a great deal to enjoy here. The performance as a whole has undoubted spontaneity, and when the reading has such a feeling of momentum Dvořák's lyrical inspiration readily blossoms. The tape transfer is one of Philips's very best, the level higher than usual, giving clarity as well as weight and richness to the orchestral sound. A most enjoyable tape if not the obvious first choice.

Rowicki is fresh and direct, somewhat lightweight in the first movement, although he observes the exposition repeat. The *Largo* is not as memorable as in some other versions, but the finale is particularly successful, and the relaxed mood at the centre of the scherzo brings out the rustic colouring of the scoring. The recording is first-rate, bright and very well balanced, and it has transferred to tape admirably, with no lack of projection and detail in spite of the comparatively modest level. The sound of the upper strings is especially convincing.

The Enigma issue is also technically one of the best *New World* cassettes, with clear, forward sound, the violins perhaps a shade over-bright, but not lacking sheen (the opening of the finale sounds especially well). Vernon Handley's sharply energetic performance carries an attractive rhythmic spring throughout (the lilting woodwind in the scherzo are particularly engaging, clearly projected by the close balance). As a whole the reading is sensitive and understanding and carries spontaneity, but some might find the slow movement not as sensuously beautiful as in some versions (the clear recorded patina and comparatively unresonant bass contribute to this).

Decca have reissued Kertesz's earlier

Vienna performance twice. It is available separately on a mid-priced cassette, where the recording is clear but slightly over-modulated (causing a degree of roughness in the peaks of the outer movements and in the climax of the *Largo*), and on a 'Double Decca' issue (costing only slightly more than a single full-priced tape) coupled to Martinon's impetuous account of Tchaikovsky's *Pathétique symphony*. Here the level has been cut back a little, and although the loudest climaxes remain a trifle fierce, they yield to the controls; and otherwise the sound is bright and well detailed, if without the bloom of Kertesz's full-priced cassette. The Vienna performance is enjoyable and agreeably fresh, not without its occasional idiosyncrasy – the gentle treatment of the first movement's second subject is less convincingly prepared than in Kertesz's later LSO version, and there is a sudden quickening of tempo after its reprise at the end. There is plenty of excitement, and the Vienna Philharmonic plays the *Largo* beautifully.

Giulini first recorded the *New World* for HMV, when the old Philharmonia was at its peak. The result has a refinement, coupled with a degree of detachment, which for some will make it an ideal reading. This is emotion observed from outside rather than experienced direct, and the result, with its beautiful moulding of phrase, is very refreshing. For a general recommendation this may well be too cool a reading, but with vivid recording quality, excellent for its period, this clearly has a place in the catalogue. The transfer is bright and clear, if at times rather sharp-edged, with touches of stridency, although none very serious. The cassette, however, generously provides a second bonus besides the *Carnaval overture*: an excellent account of Bizet's *Children's Games suite*. Giulini's second recording was made in Chicago for DG, and as before he takes a sympathetic but slightly detached view. The high polish of the Chicago playing ensures that this newer version is most enjoyable; but by

the highest standards the DG performance is slightly over-refined and lacking the last degree of spontaneity, with the last two movements biting less sharply than before. However, on tape the transfer (which is smooth to suit the performance), although made at rather a low level generally, has slightly more projection and bite on side two.

Karajan offers two different performances on tape of the *New World*. The DG recording dates from 1959, and the transfer to tape was one of DG's earliest Dolby issues with slightly different sound quality on each side. The first two movements sound natural and pleasing, with no lack of body, but the sound on side two has rather more sparkle, which suits the scherzo and finale rather well. Throughout, the transfer copes admirably with a wide dynamic range. The *Slavonic dance* filler is exceptionally brilliant; in the slow movement of the symphony there is an effect of recession of the orchestral image in *pianissimos*. The performance itself is first-class. Karajan's emphasis here is on lyricism, and in spite of the exciting build-up of power in the first movement it is the lovingly phrased second subject group that remains in the memory. In the great *Largo*, Karajan achieves a kind of detached repose which lets the music speak for itself, and in the scherzo the rustic qualities in the second strain of the first section as well as the trio are evoked gently to captivating effect. The finale begins boldly and conveys a feeling of sheer high spirits, yet the composer's backward glances to earlier material are handled with an evocative nostalgia before the music sweeps away again to its exhilarating conclusion.

We are not wholly agreed on whether Karajan's 1977 re-recording for HMV is finer than the DG version. Certainly the HMV transfer is less completely successful. The sound is rich and full, but not always perfectly refined in texture (the cor anglais solo in the slow movement has discoloration in its upper harmonics), and the inner detail is not ideally clear. The new performance offers splendidly vigorous and sympathetic orchestral playing, and the reading as a whole is direct and has no lack of freshness. However, for I.M. the HMV version of the *Largo* has less poetic feeling than the earlier account, where the orchestral playing is so expressive, with very little conscious moulding from Karajan. The advantage of the newer issue is the substantial bonus of a good performance of Smetana's *Vltava*.

Horenstein's is a superb version, freshly revealing in an unforced way, with a steady tempo maintained far more than usual in the first movement and solo work by the wind-players suggesting that this was the RPO Beecham-vintage. In the slow movement the great cor anglais solo is sweetly folk-like, and Horenstein brings out the high dynamic contrasts, helped by excellent recording which has transferred to tape quite successfully. The sound lacks something in bloom but is clean and clear and has a good dynamic range.

Muti's is a sweet and amiable performance, unsensationally attractive but ignoring the minor textual points raised by Czech scholars which a true Dvořákian would have observed. Rich, smooth recording, making the great cor anglais melody of the slow movement sound a little bland in simplicity. The transfer is of good quality, bold and vivid, with plenty of warmth and a fairly wide dynamic range.

The main interest of the Advent recording by the Orchestre de Paris under Georges Prêtre is that the symphony is given complete on one cassette side, side two being left blank. The performance is atmospheric, warmly responsive but not strikingly dramatic. It is not helped by the recessed recording, copied at a lower level than is usual for this source. Even with chrome tape, the detail is not very crisp, and in the slow movement the cor anglais solo is distant. Prêtre does not observe the first-movement exposition repeat,

and although this version is enjoyable and not without character, it is hardly competitive, since this work is so well represented on tape.

Walter's recording dates from 1960, being one of the products of this great conductor's Indian summer in the recording studios not long before he died. It is an essentially lyrical reading, and the conductor finds great richness of detail in Dvořák's score. The expressive power of the *Largo* is matched by Walter's lilting way with the rhythms of the scherzo. The finale, taken slower than usual, has great dignity and an underlying nobility. This would be near the top of the list were the recording fully acceptable. But the very opening of the symphony offers muffled strings, and the lack of range and detail throughout is a serious drawback.

The DG Privilege transfer is disappointing, with tuttis not entirely free from discoloration. Fricsay's characteristically romantic performance, with its wilful changes of tempo, needs a full-blooded romantic sound, but only in the slow movement, which is beautiful, is the sound entirely worthy of the strength of the interpretation.

Sawallisch's approach is straightforward and without mannerisms. There is more poetry in the slow movement than he finds, but overall the orchestral playing is sensitive, and the conductor's conception consistent and well integrated. The stereo recording is excellent, and with a brilliant and idiomatic performance of *Carnaval* thrown in, this is good value in the lowest price-range. The transfer is vivid and has plenty of range, although the bright upper register needs a little smoothing with the controls to produce the maximum possible refinement.

Mehta's is a brilliant extrovert reading, crisply disciplined and recorded massively to match; it misses most of Dvořák's subtler shadings, lacking grace and charm. The transfer offers brilliant full-blooded sound, and this is certainly preferable to Ozawa's disappointing version; where the close, boxy recording underlines the shortcomings of the performance, surprisingly square from this conductor.

String quartets Nos. (i) *8 in E major, Op. 80;* (ii) *9 in D minor, Op. 34;* (iii) *10 in E flat major, Op. 51;* (iv) *11 in C major, Op. 61;* (v) *12 in F major* (*American*), *Op. 96; 13 in G major, Op. 106; 14 in A flat major, Op. 105.*

(B) *(*) Rediffusion Legend KLGDD 103. (i) Dvořák Qt; (ii) Smetana Qt; (iii) Vlach Qt; (iv) Novák Qt; (v) Prague Qt.

Czech musicians have an understandable affinity with the chamber music of Dvořák, and these distinguished performances dating from the sixties are very welcome indeed, especially when the four tapes are so reasonably priced. All the performances are splendidly played and there is admirable life and feeling. The recording is impeccably clear and with a high-level transfer there is virtually no background noise. The snag is the recording balance itself, which although admirably detailed is dry in timbre and lacks warmth and bloom. There is a noticeable lack of resonance in the bass, and comparison with the discs reveals an agreeable ambient glow on LP which seems largely to evaporate in the tape transfer. However, with some smoothing of the treble and a bass lift acceptable quality can be achieved, even if the lack of richness of texture remains a drawback. The sound is clean and undistorted.

String quintet in E flat major, Op. 97; (i) *Bagatelles for string trio and harmonium, Op. 47.*

(M) *** Decca Ace of Diamonds KSDC 487. Vienna Philharmonic Quintet, (i) with Peter Planyavsky (harmonium).

The Vienna Philharmonic performance of the splendid *E flat Quintet*, one of the greatest works of Dvořák's American period, is as cultured as one would

expect from these players, and it is beautifully recorded. The delicious *Bagatelles* are also very well done. The transfer is of outstanding quality, offering beautiful sound, warm and clear. With such refined textures this is another demonstration of how good chamber music can sound on tape.

Slavonic dances Nos. 1–8, Op. 46/1–8; 9–16, Op. 72/1–8.

(M) **(*) Turnabout KTVC 34060. Alfred Brendel, Walter Klien (piano duet).

This is polished and affectionate playing. Both pianists show a real feeling for the style of the music and there will be many who find that the dances sound fresher on the piano than on the orchestra. This is not a tape to be played all at once, but taken in sections it is very enjoyable indeed. The acoustic here is a little over-reverberant but the sound itself is good. The transfer is satisfactory and copes with the reverberant piano image without loss of quality.

'Favourite composer': (i; ii) *Carnaval overture, Op. 92; Scherzo capriccioso, Op. 66;* (iii; iv) *Serenade for strings in E major, Op. 22;* (v; vi) *Slavonic dances Nos. 1 in C major; 8 in G minor, Op. 46/1 and 8; 10 in E minor, Op. 72/2;* (v; ii) *Symphony No. 9 in E minor* (*From the New World*), *Op. 95;* (vii) *Rusalka: Invocation to the moon.*

(B) *** Decca KDPC 539/40. (i) LSO; (ii) Kertesz; (iii) Israel PO; (iv) Kubelik; (v) Vienna PO; (vi) Reiner; (vii) Pilar Lorengar (soprano), Orch. of St Cecilia Academy, Rome, Patané.

An outstanding collection which is more than the sum of its parts. The selection has been well and generously made, and there is not a performance here that can be seriously faulted; most are first-rate. The order of the programme has been intelligently planned for tape issue. We are given the symphony complete on the first side of cassette one (and most vividly transferred) coupled with the *Serenade* and *Scherzo capriccioso*, while the second cassette includes the shorter pieces. The *Carnaval overture*, like the *Scherzo*, is given demonstration sound, and the quality is generally brilliant, though there is a touch of glare on the first *Slavonic dance*.

Electronic music

BERIO. Luciano: *Visage* (for magnetic tape, based on the voice of Cathy Berberian and electronic sounds). CAGE, John: *Fontana Mix* (a realization of the version for magnetic tape alone). MIMAROGLU, Ilhan: *Agony* (visual study No. 4, after Arshile Gorky).

(M) ** Turnabout KTVC 34046.

Cornelius Cardew, our own British avant-gardiste, is quoted as saying that there seems to be a sense of logic and cohesion in Cage's indeterminate music. 'The logic', Cage replied, 'was not put there by me.' He can say that again! Even so, a tape like this of highly experimental music does give the average listener an excellent chance to work hard at this apparently impossible music. Whether in fact with indeterminate music there is any purpose in having an utterly fixed recorded performance is a question that the avant-gardistes will have to sort out, but that philosophical point need hardly worry anyone else. The Cage is the most interesting of the pieces here, a sort of musical equivalent of a *collage*, with voices, whistling, dog-barking superimposed in wild array. What it all means

is anyone's guess, but perhaps one should not take it too seriously. The transfer is atmospheric rather than sharply focused.

Elgar, Edward (1857–1934)

3 Bavarian dances, Op. 27. Caracta-cus, Op. 35: Woodland interludes. Chanson de matin; Chanson de nuit, Op. 15/1 and 2. Contrasts, Op. 10/3. Dream children, Op. 43. Falstaff, Op. 68: 2 Interludes. Salut d'amour. Serenade lyrique. (i) *Soliloquy for oboe* (orch. Jacob).

*** RCA RK 11746. Bournemouth Sinfonietta, Del Mar, (i) with Leon Goossens (oboe).

The real treasure in this superb collection of Elgar miniatures is the *Soliloquy* which Elgar wrote right at the end of his life for Leon Goossens. It was the only movement completed of a projected suite, a wayward improvisatory piece which yet has a character of its own. Here the dedicatee plays it with his long-recognizable tone colour and feeling for phrase in an orchestration by Gordon Jacob. Most of the other pieces are well-known, but they come up with new warmth and commitment in splendid performances under Del Mar. The rich, glowing recording had transferred splendidly to tape in the high-level transfer we sampled. The notes are generous, but one needs a magnifying glass to read them.

'The miniature Elgar': Bavarian dance No. 2. Beau Brummel: Minuet. Chanson de matin. Dream Children, Op. 43/1 and 2. Nursery suite. The Serious Doll. The Starlight Express: (i) *Organ Grinder's songs: My Old Tunes; To the Children. The Wand of*

Youth suites: excerpts: *Serenade; Sun dance; The Tame Bear.*

(M) *** HMV Greensleeve TC-ESD 7068. RPO, Collingwood, (i) with Frederick Harvey (bar.).

Inspired by the BBC TV *Monitor* film on Elgar's life, this wholly delightful anthology collects together some of the com poser's most attractive contributions in the lighter field, including several of those fragile and nostalgic little portraits which give the *Nursery* and *Wand of Youth* suites their special character. Frederick Harvey joins the orchestra for two *Organ Grinder's songs* written as incidental music for *The Starlight Express.* These are splendidly alive, with as much interest in the orchestra as in the stirringly melodic vocal line. Throughout this very well recorded collection the orchestral playing under Lawrance Collingwood is especially sympathetic, and the programme as a whole has been cleverly planned to make a highly enjoyable concert in itself. The transfer is immaculate, first-class in every way.

'Miniatures': Carissima. Chanson de matin; Chanson de nuit, Op. 15/1 and 2. Elegy for strings, Op. 58. (i) Romance for bassoon and orchestra, Op. 62. Rosemary (That's for remembrance). Salut d'amour, Op. 12. Serenade for strings in E minor, Op. 20. Sospiri, Op. 70.

*(*) CBS 40-76423. ECO, Barenboim, (i) with Martin Gatt (bassoon).

Barenboim tends to dwell too affectionately on detail and the results are frankly schmaltzy. The recording is not the most natural in balance, though it is by no means unpleasing. The transfer is acceptable, but no more; the sound lacks sparkle, the acoustic sounding slightly hollow because of the restricted frequency range.

'The lighter Elgar': Carissima. Contrasts, Op. 10/3. May song. Mazurka, Op. 10/1. Mina. Minuet, Op. 21. (i) Romance for bassoon and orchestra. Rosemary (That's for remembrance). Sérénade lyrique. Sérénade mauresque, Op. 10/2. Sevillana, Op. 7.

(M) *** HMV Greensleeve TC-ESD 7009. Northern Sinfonia Orch., Marriner, (i) with Michael Chapman (bassoon).

The best of Elgar's light music has a gentle delicacy of texture, and as often as not a touch of melancholy, which is irresistible to nearly all Elgarians. Not everything here is on the very highest level of invention, but all the music is pleasing and a good deal of it is delightful for its tender moods and restrained scoring, favouring flute, bassoon, and the clarinet in middle or lower register. A boisterous piece like *Sevillana* may be rather conventional, but it has Elgar's characteristic exuberance, which represents the other side of the coin. The most distinguished item here is the rhapsodic *Romance for bassoon and orchestra,* but the whole programme offers quiet enjoyment and is just the thing for the late evening. It is played with style and affection by the Northern Sinfonia under Neville Marriner, and HMV have provided that warm, glowing orchestral sound that is their special province for Elgar's music. The transfer is of outstanding, demonstration quality. An A/B comparison with the disc revealed no perceptible difference. Unfortunately no notes are provided, a distinct loss for a collection of this kind.

Chanson de matin; Chanson de nuit, Op. 15/1 and 2; Cockaigne overture, Op. 40; Pomp and Circumstance marches Nos. 1 and 4, Op. 39; Serenade for strings in E minor, Op. 20.

(B) **(*) Pye ZCCOB 654. RPO or Pro Arte Orch., Weldon.

It is strange to see EMI-sourced material appearing on a Pye Precision tape, but these recordings (dating from the mid-sixties) originally appeared on disc from World Record Club, and Pye later appropriated the tape rights. They are all excellent performances, thoroughly musical and well made. George Weldon was often more successful with his recordings than in the concert hall; in the studio he was unfailingly sympathetic and was able to retain a genuine feeling of spontaneity. Perhaps *Cockaigne* and the *Pomp and Circumstance marches* fall a little short on flair, but the *String serenade* is warmly affectionate, and it is beautifully recorded. The transfers lack the last degree of range and sparkle, but they are well balanced and the textures have both richness and fair detail. This is a genuine bargain.

Cockaigne overture, Op. 40; Crown of India suite, Op. 66; Pomp and Circumstance marches, Op. 39/1–5.
**(*) RCA RK 25158. Scottish National Orch., Gibson.

Cockaigne overture; Froissart (concert overture), Op. 19; In the South (Alassio), Op. 50; HANDEL (arr. Elgar): Overture in D minor.
(***) HMV TC-ASD 2822. LPO, Boult.

Cockaigne overture; Pomp and Circumstance marches, Op. 39/1–5; National anthem (arr. Elgar).
**(*) Decca KSXC 6848 [Lon. 5-7072]. LPO, Solti.

Cockaigne overture; Variations on an original theme (Enigma), Op. 36.
**(*) Decca KSXC 6795 [(d) Lon. 5-6984]. LPO or Chicago SO, Solti.
(M) ** Philips 7317 198. LSO, Colin Davis.

Boult's unique insight into the problems of Elgar interpretation is characteristically illustrated in his programme of overtures. Though other Elgarians may be more ripely romantic, Boult with his incisiveness is both dramatic and noble. The recording – not quite consistent between items – is rich and atmospheric, and it is good to have the Handel arrangement included as a makeweight. The recording has been vividly transferred to tape and the level is high. Unfortunately, however, this has been achieved by a narrowing of the dynamic range, so that the opening of *Cockaigne*, for instance, is very forward, and the big brassy climaxes fail to expand properly. The unknowing ear is readily deceived on first hearing, but after a time the effect is unsatisfying.

Gibson directs vigorously sympathetic performances of an attractive programme, well recorded and brilliantly transferred to cassette. *Cockaigne* is attractively spirited, and although the Scottish orchestra misses something of the music's opulence, this is undoubtedly enjoyable. The *Pomp and Circumstance marches* are taken at a spanking pace, but with no lack of swagger, and there is a strong feeling of pageantry too. The music has great forward thrust, and the recording acoustic provides vivid colour, yet not too much resonance.

With Solti the *Enigma variations* become a dazzling showpiece. Though the charm of the work is given short measure, the structure emerges the more sharply, with the fast variations taken at breakneck speed and with the Chicago orchestra challenged to supreme virtuosity. The disappointment is *Nimrod*, where from a basic tempo faster than usual Solti allows himself to get faster and faster still, in a style that misses the feeling of *nobilmente*. Solti's view of *Cockaigne* is similarly one of extremes, but here, with the LPO, recorded more richly and just as brilliantly, there is more sparkle, a mercurial element. The transfer is of Decca's best quality throughout and offers a demonstration standard in *Cockaigne*. The *Variations* are offered complete, without a break on side one, and the overture on side two with a 14½-minute run-off. Why not an extra work here for the cassette issue? The notes, however, are generous.

Many will be glad that Decca have also issued Solti's fine account of *Cockaigne* recoupled to a complete set of the *Pomp and Circumstance marches*. Solti's view of the *Marches* is vigorous yet refined, with sharp pointing of the outer sections, spaciousness in the great melodies, and a real sense of pageantry. The quality of the sound on tape is thrilling, with splendid weight and breadth. Indeed the bass response at the climax of the first march has marginally too much amplitude, with the bass drum accentuated. But this is the only miscalculation of balance; generally the effect makes a thrilling impact and the recording gives a bloom to the performances which few Elgarians will resist.

Davis's coupling has transferred well to tape, the quality sounding fresher than on the original full-priced LP, even though the last degree of range is absent. His reading of the *Enigma variations* is in the main a traditional one, with each variation carefully shaped, and undoubtedly first-class playing from the LSO throughout. The manner is a shade circumspect, but it is not without spontaneity. In *Cockaigne*, however, the conductor is more wilful in his choice of tempi and some may resist the broadening in the big brassy climax (consistent each time it appears). However, there is no doubt that the reading has plenty of life.

Violin concerto in B minor, Op. 61.
    (***) CBS 40-76528. Pinchas Zukerman, LPO, Barenboim.
    *(**) Decca KSXC 6842. Kyung-Wha Chung, LPO, Solti.
    (M)**(*) World Records TC-SH 288. Albert Sammons, New Queen's Hall Orch., Sir Henry Wood (recorded 1929).
    ** HMV TC-ASD 3598. Ida Haendel, LPO, Boult.

Zukerman, coming fresh to the Elgar *Violin concerto* (the most difficult concerto he had ever attempted, so he said), was inspired to give a reading which gloriously combines the virtuoso swagger of a Heifetz with the tender, heartfelt warmth of the young Menuhin, plus much of individual responsiveness. In the first movement, with the command and the warmth superbly established, Zukerman gives a breathtaking account of the third theme, hushed and inner as though in personal meditation. The slow movement is altogether simpler, rather less involved, while the finale in its many sections is masterfully held together, brilliant but never breathless in the main *Allegro* and culminating in a deeply felt rendering of the long accompanied cadenza, freely expansive yet concentrated. With rich recording (the violin a shade on the close side) this represents the version of a masterpiece that many Elgarians have been waiting for over decades. When first issued the CBS tape offered very poor quality, although brighter on side two than side one. Later copies are more acceptable, though the orchestral sound has much more brilliance and range on the second side. Indeed the marvellous last movement sounds well. Perhaps in due course the factory will manage to increase the range on side one too.

Kyung-Wha Chung's is an intense and deeply committed reading which rises to great heights in the heartfelt account of the slow movement – made the more affecting by its vein of melancholy – and the wide-ranging performance of the finale. At the start of that third movement Chung at a fast tempo finds a rare vein of fantasy, a mercurial quality, and the great accompanied cadenza is commandingly done, ending on an achingly beautiful phrase from the third subject of the first movement. The third movement itself brings much beautiful playing too, but there are one or two tiny flaws of intonation, and there Solti's accompaniment does not have quite so firm a grasp. But as an illuminating alternative to the

Zukerman performance, this is certainly refreshing. The high-level transfer is admirably clear and is not lacking weight and body in the orchestra. An extreme treble cut-back is necessary, however, if the soloist's tone is not to prove uncomfortably sharp-edged. Such a cut produces a more than acceptable sound, but it also means that the recording's upper frequencies are removed, with a consequent reduction of the subtleties of the orchestral detail.

The pioneering 1929 recording shows what a magnificent artist Albert Sammons was. His tone was big, his technique effortless and his phrasing pregnant with meaning. Although the youthful Menuhin recording (not available on tape) falls into a special category, it is a pity that it overshadowed this earlier version. Menuhin's was an angelic performance and this is seraphic, and there is room for them both. The orchestral playing is remarkably vital and sensitive, and given the fact that the recording is half a century old, it reproduces with astonishing vividness. The transfer is admirably clear and well balanced, but the printed notes are in impossibly small type.

Ida Haendel adopts tempi so consistently spacious that they will amaze most Elgarians. She plays with feeling and all her usual firmness of tone, and with the most stylish of all Elgar conductors beside her the result is never less than interesting. The slow movement is richly expressive. However, the finale lacks the tension of a live performance, and other versions are preferable to this. The recording is admirably full and clear, and the tape transfer is of excellent quality, brilliant yet with plenty of body; the solo violin is cleanly focused but warm in tone.

Menuhin's 1966 performance with Boult is also available on tape (HMV TC-ASD 2259) and although it is not Dolbyized the over-bright transfer lends itself to cutting back, so that the hiss can be minimized. But side two (which includes *The Kingdom Prelude*) is not without roughness.

Violoncello concerto in E minor, Op. 85.
> **(*)** HMV TC-ASD 655. Jacqueline du Pré, LSO, Barbirolli – *Sea Pictures.***(*)**
> (M) ** DG Privilege 3335 201 [id.]. Pierre Fournier, Berlin PO, Wallenstein – BLOCH: *Schelomo.* **

(i) *Violoncello concerto. Introduction and allegro for strings, Op. 47; Serenade for strings in E minor, Op. 20.*
> **(*)** HMV TC-ASD 2906. LPO, Boult, (i) with Paul Tortelier.

(i) *Violoncello concerto;* (ii) *Variations on an original theme* (*Enigma*), Op. 36.
> *(**)** CBS 40-76529 [Col. MT 34530]. (i) Jacqueline du Pré, Philadelphia Orch.; (ii) LPO; both cond. Barenboim.

It was in the Elgar *Cello concerto* that Jacqueline du Pré first won world recognition, and the HMV recording gives a wonderful idea of how so young a girl captured such attention and even persuaded the Americans to listen enraptured to Elgar. Du Pré is essentially a spontaneous artist. No two performances by her were exactly alike, and wisely Barbirolli at the recording sessions encouraged her above all to express emotion through the notes. The style is freely rhapsodic. The tempi, long-breathed in first and third movements, are allowed still more elbow-room when du Pré's expressiveness requires it, and in the slow movement, brief and concentrated, her 'inner' intensity conveys a depth of expressiveness rarely achieved by any cellist on record. Brilliant virtuoso playing too in scherzo and finale. The recording gives plenty of presence to the soloist, and the transfer is vivid, if with an apparent reduction of light and shade.

Jacqueline du Pré's second recording of the Elgar concerto was taken from live performances in Philadelphia in November 1970, and whatever the slight blemishes (questionable balances, some coughing) this is a superb picture of an artist in full flight. Here on CBS you have the romantic view of Elgar at its most compelling, and though some Elgarians will fairly enough prefer more restraint in this autumnal work, the mastery of du Pré lies not just in her total commitment from phrase to phrase but in the feeling for the whole. More than in any other account on record, even her own with Barbirolli, this one sets sights on the moment in the Epilogue where the slow-movement theme returns, the work's innermost sanctuary of repose. In the finale, at a cracking basic tempo, the ensemble is not flawless, but all through the Philadelphia Orchestra plays with commanding virtuosity, and Daniel Barenboim is the most understanding of accompanists. His view of *Enigma* is full of fantasy, and its most distinctive point is its concern for the miniature element. Without belittling the delicate variations, Barenboim both makes them sparkle and gives them emotional point, while the big variations have full weight; and the finale brings extra fierceness at a fast tempo. On its original issue the quality of the CBS cassette was unacceptable. A more recent copy showed improvement; the recorded range is not very wide, but the sound balance is fairly good, with more detail in the *Cello concerto* than the *Variations*, where the tuttis fail to open out and lack freshness of timbre.

Tortelier gives a noble and restrained performance which will appeal to those who feel that Jacqueline du Pré wears her heart a little too much on her sleeve in this work, marvellous though her playing is. Boult accompanies with splendid tact and on the reverse side gives committed and finely recorded accounts of the *Introduction and allegro* and the *Serenade for strings*. The recording has breadth, and the transfer is of good quality, full and rich, if lacking bite in the treble. But the overall balance is good, especially in the concerto.

Fournier's account has both fervour and conviction, but unfortunately he suffers from a close microphone balance, and the result (besides reducing the dynamic contrast of the solo playing) obscures some of the orchestral detail. Even so this is a moving and eloquent account that might well be thought competitive if the coupling is suitable. The transfer is of good quality, reflecting the balance and timbre shown on the disc faithfully enough.

Crown of India suite, Op. 66; Imperial march, Op. 32; Pomp and Circumstance marches, Op. 39/1–5.
  *(*) CBS 40-77248 [Col. MT 32936]. LPO, Barenboim.

Barenboim is never less than interesting in these readings of Elgar's ceremonial music, well coupled, but his judgement is not infallible. His tempi are surprisingly fast (though Elgar's own tended to be fast too), and not all Elgarians will approve of his updating of Edwardian majesty. If only the recording were richer, the interpretations would emerge more convincingly than they do. The transfer offers variable sound. The *Marches* are generally bright, but taken as a whole the somewhat restricted frequency range will suit smaller machines better than large ones.

Elegy for strings, Op. 58; Froissart overture, Op. 19; Pomp and Circumstance marches, Op. 39/1–5; Sospiri, Op. 70.
  **(*) HMV TC-ASD 2292. New Philharmonia or Philharmonia Orch., Barbirolli.

The five *Pomp and Circumstance marches* make a very good suite, with plenty of contrast in Nos. 2 and 3 to offset the Edwardian bombast of 1 and 4. The splendid *nobilmente* of No. 5 closes the set in rousing fashion. Barbirolli is obviously determined not to overdo the patriotism, and the studio recording suits this fresh approach. The sound is bright, but one notices that the recording of the string pieces offers more warmth in the middle range. The *Elegy* shows Barbirolli at his gentle best; *Sospiri* is contrastingly passionate, and the collection concludes with the early overture *Froissart*. Here the orchestral links with Brahms are strong, but the fingerprints of the Elgar to emerge later are everywhere, and if the piece is loose in structure it has a striking main theme. Generally the transfers are good, and well balanced. The *Elegy* sounds especially rich, with most natural strings; *Froissart* too is lively, but the *Pomp and Circumstance marches* on side one could have used a touch more sparkle in the treble, although there is plenty of weight, and the organ is accommodated without stress.

Elegy for strings, Op. 58; Introduction and allegro for strings, Op. 47; Serenade for strings in E minor, Op. 20; Sospiri, Op. 70; The Spanish Lady: suite (ed. Young).

> *** Argo KZRC 573 [id.]. Academy of St Martin-in-the-Fields, Marriner.

At first hearing Marriner's interpretations of these Elgar works sound strangely unidiomatic. They grow on one – even the somewhat stiff manner of the *Introduction and allegro* – and the subtlety and strength of Marriner's unique band of string players are never in doubt. The tape is valuable for Elgarians in including the brief snippets arranged by Percy Young from Elgar's unfinished opera *The Spanish Lady*, but musically they have little substance. But what musical riches in all the rest – reflection of the composer's lifelong understanding of string tone. Argo cassettes are notable for their natural quality, and the string timbre here is beautiful: the *Serenade* which opens side one is of demonstration standard. Side two is marginally less open in the treble, but still excellent.

(i) *Falstaff* (symphonic study), *Op. 68;* (ii) *Froissart overture, Op. 19;* (iii) *Introduction and allegro for strings, Op. 47.*

> (M) *(**) HMV TC-SXLP 30279. (i) Hallé Orch.; (ii) New Philharmonia Orch.; (iii) Sinfonia of London, Allegri Qt; all cond. Barbirolli.

Barbirolli's ripely expansive view of *Falstaff* is not helped in this tape transfer by a recording that is anything but ripe. The detail is clear and the orchestral wind timbres do not lack luminosity; but the absence of richness in the string timbre is a distinct drawback here, and also in the *Froissart overture,* which is otherwise vivid enough (but sounds better on TC-ASD 2292 – see above). Barbirolli's passionate lyricism plus exceptionally fine string playing from the London Sinfonia produce an outstanding and definitive account of the *Introduction and allegro,* and here the recording has more warmth and resonance in the lower frequencies; but even so it does not match the amplitude of the disc version.

In the South (Alassio) (concert overture), Op. 50.

> (M) *** HMV Greensleeve TC-ESD 7013. Bournemouth SO, Silvestri – VAUGHAN WILLIAMS: *Tallis fantasia* etc.**(*)
> *(*) CBS 40-76579. LPO, Barenboim – *Sea Pictures.***

On HMV a really stunning performance of *In the South,* given one of EMI's most spectacular recordings. Silvestri knits the work's structure together more convincingly than one would have believed possible, and the strong forward momentum does not prevent the Italian sunshine (seen through English eyes) bringing a Mediterranean glow to the gentler, atmospheric pages of the score. But it is the virile opening and closing sections which Silvestri makes especially compelling, and at the same time he shows the music's parallel with the style of Richard Strauss. It was not a coincidence that the composer of *Don Juan* found an affinity with the bursting melodic fervour which was a dominant part of Elgar's musical personality, and which is so exhilarating here. The Bournemouth orchestra offers playing of a virtuoso order and the same absolute commitment which distinguishes Silvestri's direction. The cassette transfer is extremely successful, brilliant yet with plenty of orchestral weight and good detail.

In the concert-hall Barenboim has directed performances of *In the South* full of his usual passionate commitment, but this recording – given sound of limited range on tape – disappointingly presents a performance which fails to add up the sum of its parts, lacking concentration and impetus.

Introduction and allegro for strings, Op. 47; Serenade for strings in E minor, Op. 20.
> (M) ** Pye ZCTPL 13069. Orch. of St John's, Smith Square, Lubbock – TIPPETT: *Fantasia concertante* etc.*(*)

Introduction and allegro; Variations on an original theme (Enigma), Op. 36.
> (B) *(*) Classics for Pleasure TC-CFP 40022. LPO, Boult.

Boult's earlier stereo version of the *Enigma variations* dates from the 1960s, and the recording, although vivid and clear, lacks the richness and body of string tone which one expects in this work. The tape transfer is of first-class quality on side one, which takes the listener to the end of Variation No. 13, but when one turns over the level rises and with it the degree of brilliance in the treble, hitherto controllable but now difficult to tame. Thus the climaxes of the *Introduction and allegro* have a thinness in the upper range that ill suits the music.

Boult's performances are well made (there is some fine playing in both works) but not as fine as his later re-recordings for HMV.

John Lubbock and his St John's Orchestra on their generously filled tape provide strong if not distinctive performances. The recording is good, but the collection is let down a little by the failure of the orchestra to come completely to grips with the technical complexities of the Tippett *Corelli Fantasia*, which is one of the couplings. The transfer offers a natural balance, with more presence for Elgar than Tippett.

Pomp and Circumstance marches, Op. 39/1–5; Empire march.
> **(*) HMV TC-ASD 3388. [Angel 4xs 37436]. LPO, Boult – WALTON: *Crown Imperial* etc.**(*)

Pomp and Circumstance marches, Op. 39/1–5; Variations on an original theme (Enigma), Op. 36.
> (M) *** DG Privilege 3335 217. RPO, Del Mar.

Boult's approach to the *Pomp and Circumstance marches* is brisk and direct, with almost a no-nonsense manner in places. There is not a hint of vulgarity, and the freshness is most attractive, though it is a pity Boult omits the repeats in the Dvořák-like No. 2. The *Empire march*, written for the 1924 Wembley Exhibition, has not been recorded again since then, but makes a good bonus for the more characteristic pieces. The recording is warm and immediate and the coupling surely an ideal one. The tape transfer is made at a very high level, and although the sound quality is rich and full-blooded, the wide amplitude of the recording brings some lack of focus in the bass. However, it is easy to accept this slight muddying of texture when the sound has such a feeling of pageantry.

In the *Enigma variations* Del Mar comes closer than any other conductor to the responsive *rubato* style of Elgar himself, who directed an unforgettable performance on record in 1926. Like the composer, Del Mar uses the fluctuations to point the emotional message of the work with wonderful power and spontaneity, and the RPO plays superbly. Recorded in Guildford Cathedral with plentiful reverberation, this version has the advantage of a splendid contribution from the organ at the end. The five *Pomp and Circumstance marches* on the reverse are given Prom-style performances full of flair and urgency, although some might feel that the chosen speeds are a trifle fast and Del Mar's approach not relaxed enough to bring out the *nobilmente*. The reverberant sound here adds something of an aggressive edge to the music-making. Even so, at medium price this is a very competitive issue. The cassette transfer is of the highest quality, minimizing the edge in the *Marches* without robbing them of bite and offering splendid sound in the *Variations* – perhaps the best available from any source, although Solti's Decca recording (see under *Cockaigne*) is very good too.

Severn suite, Op. 87 (original version for brass band).

> *** RCA RK 25078. Black Dyke Mills Band, Newsome – *Concert*.***
> **(*) Decca KSXC 6820. Grimethorpe Colliery Band, Howarth – BLISS: *Kenilworth;* HOLST: *Moorside suite;* IRELAND: *Comedy overture*.***

The Black Dyke Mills Band was in superlative form when their recording was made; the playing reaches almost unbelievable standards of expertise and panache. Roy Newsome conducts a splendid performance of Elgar's *Severn suite*; the opening theme is given a swagger and feeling of pageantry that remain obstinately in the memory, and the rest of the piece is no less impressive, though the quality of the music itself is uneven.

The RCA recording is excellent, but the couplings, though played with similar expertise and sympathy, are much less interesting than the works on the alternative Decca collection. Rubbra's *Variations on 'The Shining River'* are atmospheric but not really memorable; the Fletcher *Epic symphony* has an appealing slow movement, but otherwise, like Eric Ball's *Sinfonietta*, it shows facility rather than inspiration in its invention. The tape transfer is very good, but though brilliant it has rather less richness of sonority than the Decca cassette, which is of demonstration standard. The Grimethorpe performance of the Elgar, recorded with outstanding clarity and bloom, is admirably direct, but Elgar Howarth's reading shows less eloquence and atmosphere than Roy Newsome's. Nevertheless the vigour of the playing of the Grimethorpe colliers gives pleasure, and the other works (especially the Holst) are presented with comparable brilliance.

Symphony No. 1 in A flat major, Op. 55.

> *** Decca KSXC 6569. LPO, Solti.
> *** HMV TC-ASD 3330. LPO, Boult.
> (M) **(*) HMV TC-SXLP 30268. Philharmonia Orch., Barbirolli.

No work of Elgar's more completely captures the atmosphere of uninhibited opulence which his generation of composers was the last to enjoy. Elgar, unlike composers after him, did not have to apologize for writing a symphony nearly an hour long, nor for writing tunes of a warmth and memorability that are strikingly his.

Before Solti recorded the *First* he made a searching study of Elgar's own 78 recording, and the modifications of detailed markings implicit in that are reproduced here, not with a sense of calculation but with very much the same rich, committed qualities that mark out the Elgar performance. Solti, even more than in Mahler, here seems freed from emotional inhibition, with every climax superbly thrust home and the hushed intensity of the glorious slow movement captured with commanding eloquence. The cassette is not quite so sumptuous as the LP, but it is of high quality by any standards, clear with a strong, rich bass. It is vital to get the volume setting right at the opening or there is a tendency for the bass to be too ample. One needs a high level of playback; then the balance is excellent.

If Solti, following the composer, underlines the passionate dedication of the *First Symphony*, Boult on HMV more clearly presents it as a close counterpart of the *Second*, with hints of reflective nostalgia amid the triumph. Until this final version, made when Sir Adrian was eighty-seven, his recordings of the *First* had been among his less riveting Elgar performances. But the HMV issue, recorded with an opulence to outshine even the Decca sound for Solti, contains a radiantly beautiful performance, less thrustful than Solti's, with speeds less extreme in both directions: richly paced in the first movement, swaggering in the syncopated march-rhythms of the scherzo and similarly bouncing in the Brahmsian rhythms of the finale. Most clearly distinctive is the lovely slow movement, presented as a seamless flow of melody, faster, less 'inner' than with Solti and above all glowing with untroubled sweetness. The transfer is rich and full-blooded. Although the level is quite high it nevertheless needs a high-volume replay to bring out the full detail and impact. It can be made to sound very well indeed.

Barbirolli's HMV reissue is disappointing. The transfer has produced thin and papery string tone in the climaxes of the first movement; on side two the quality improves, but the sound of the upper strings cannot be described as rich, though the Philharmonia Orchestra plays eloquently enough. There is a lack of weight and substance in the bass too.

Barbirolli's tempi are controversial; apart from the very slow speed chosen for the slow movement, there is a hint of heaviness in the first movement too, where after the slow march introduction the music should surge along.

Symphony No. 2 in E flat major, Op. 63.
> *** HMV TC-ASD 3266. LPO, Boult.
> *** Decca KSXC 6723. LPO, Solti (with WAGNER: *Die Meistersinger Prelude***(*)).

For his fifth recording of the *Second Symphony* Sir Adrian Boult, incomparable Elgarian, drew from the LPO the most richly satisfying performance of all. Over the years Sir Adrian's view of the glorious nobility of the first movement has mellowed a degree. The tempo is a shade slower than before (and much slower than Solti's or the composer's own in the great leaping 12/8 theme), but the pointing of climaxes is unrivalled. With Boult more than anyone else the architecture is clearly and strongly established, with tempo changes less exaggerated than usual. The peak comes in the great *Funeral march*, where the concentration of the performance is irresistible. The LPO strings play gloriously, with the great swooping violin phrases at the climaxes inspiring a frisson as in a live performance. The scherzo has lightness and delicacy, with Boult very little slower than Solti but giving more room to breathe. In the finale, firm and strong, Boult cleverly conceals the repetitiveness of the main theme, and gives a radiant account of the lovely epilogue. With superb, opulent recording, this is a version to convert new listeners to a love of Elgar. The tape transfer is admirably rich, yet with good detail, one of EMI's best cassettes.

Solti's incandescent performance is modelled closely on Elgar's own surprisingly clipped and urgent reading, but benefits from virtuoso playing by the LPO and superbly balanced sound. Fast tempi bring searing concentration and an account of the finale that for once presents a true climax. This is a fitting companion to Solti's magnificent account of No. 1. The tape transfer is of very high quality, splendidly rich and opulent, yet admirably clear. Because of the wide dynamic range of the recording, the basic level is lower than usual with Decca, so, even with Dolby, a certain amount of hiss remains. But the quality is frequently demonstration-worthy. The Wagner overture is a bonus (not on the equivalent disc). The recording is reverberant but the massive sound is well contained, although the reverberation masks some detail: this is not quite as clear as the Elgar.

Variations on an original theme (Enigma), Op. 36 (see also under *Cockaigne; Cello concerto; Pomp and Circumstance marches*).

*(**) DG 3300 586. LPO, Jochum – BRAHMS: *Variations on a theme of Haydn.***(*)

(M) *(**) Decca KCSP 121. LSO, Monteux – BRAHMS: *Variations on a theme of Haydn.***(*)

(*) Decca KSXC 6592. Los Angeles PO, Mehta – IVES: *Symphony No. 1.*(*)

** HMV TC-ASD 3417. Royal Liverpool PO, Groves – BRITTEN: *Young Person's Guide to the Orchestra.***

(M) (**) HMV TC-EXE 39. Philharmonia Orch., Sargent – VAUGHAN WILLIAMS: *Tallis fantasia.*(***)

*(*) Philips 7300 344. Concertgebouw Orch., Haitink – R. STRAUSS: *Don Juan.**(*)

The amplitude of Elgar's climaxes in the *Enigma variations* obviously offers transfer problems, and these are most

successfully overcome on the DG Privilege cassette conducted by Norman Del Mar (see above under the *Pomp and Circumstance marches*). Boult's HMV recording, coupled to music of Vaughan Williams, is unfortunately available only in non-Dolby form, and the sound (although agreeable) is not brilliant enough for one to be able to cut back the all too prevalent hiss. Neither the Jochum tape nor the Monteux is technically immaculate. The Monteux Decca issue is generally vivid, but there is a hint of congestion at the major climaxes. There is undoubtedly a marvellous freshness about Monteux's approach – what a remarkably versatile musician he was – and the music is obviously deeply felt. He secures a real *pianissimo* at the beginning of *Nimrod*, the playing hardly above a whisper, yet the tension electric. Slowly the great tune is built up in elegiac fashion, and the superb climax is the more effective in consequence. Differences from traditional tempi elsewhere are marginal, and add to rather than detract from one's enjoyment. Readers interested in Monteux's performance on tape will also find it included in a *Favourite composer* compilation in an excellent new transfer (see below).

When Jochum recorded *Enigma*, he had not conducted it for several decades, but his thoughtful insight in fresh study produced an outstanding reading, arguably the most satisfying of all. The key to the whole work as Jochum sees it is *Nimrod*. Like others – including Elgar himself – Jochum sets a very slow *adagio* at the start, slower than the metronome marking in the score, but unlike others he maintains that measured tempo, and with the subtlest gradations builds an even bigger, nobler climax than you find in *accelerando* readings. It is like a Bruckner slow movement in microcosm, around which revolve the other variations, all of them delicately detailed, with a natural feeling for Elgarian *rubato*. The finale has a degree of restraint in its nobility, no vulgarity whatever. The playing of the LSO is both strong and refined, but the DG transfer lacks this latter quality and the climax of *Nimrod* is coarsened by a momentary overload, rare from this company.

Mehta, born and brought up in India, has evidently not rejected all sympathy for the British Raj and its associations. (He even claims that cricket is his favourite sport.) Certainly he is a strong and sensitive interpreter of Elgar if this highly enjoyable account is anything to go by. There are no special revelations, but with spectacular recording quality and fine playing it can be warmly recommended to those who fancy the Ives coupling. The transfer, although a comparatively early Decca issue on tape, has been well managed, offering a wide dynamic range and missing only the last degree of brilliance. It is well balanced and accommodates the organ in the closing pages without congestion.

Groves offers a straightforward version, with comparatively slow tempi throughout. Some ears may find his manner staid, but others will respond to his warmth, and this reading certainly does not seek to distort the music with interpretative quirks. *Nimrod* is characteristic of the whole: there is no hushed *pianissimo* at the beginning; rather the climax is allowed to unfold simply, but with undoubted eloquence, and then fall away again with a natural ebb and flow. There is some rich orchestral tone which compensates for the occasional less-than-crisp ensemble. The finale has real *nobilmente*. The transfer offers warm, resonant and not very detailed sound. There is plenty of weight for the final variation, which comes after the side-turn. An agreeable but not a refined cassette.

Sargent's recording is impressive in sonority (if not always in clarity). The performance is a traditional one and makes much of the *nobilmente* character of the score. The transfer was a very early EMI Dolby issue and the range of the recording is limited, so that very little detail emerges, especially from the

strings. The texture too is insecure; the amplitude of the sound seems to widen and retract, while the climaxes are harsh and burst on the listener. In *Nimrod* there is that curious pulsing effect that seems to affect some early transfers (and we tried a recent shop copy to check that things had not improved).

Haitink's reading, thoughtfully direct and beautifully played, yet lacks the dynamism which welds the variations into a unity. The blood never tingles, as it does in the Strauss coupling. The transfer, made at a low level, lacks brilliance; it has weight but seriously lacks sparkle.

VOCAL AND CHORAL MUSIC

The Apostles (oratorio), *Op. 49*. Talk: *The Apostles and the Kingdom* (written by Michael Kennedy; read by Sir Adrian Boult).
**(*) HMV TC-SLS 976. Sheila Armstrong, Helen Watts, Robert Tear, Benjamin Luxon, Clifford Grant, John Carol Case, Downe House School Choir, LPO Choir, LPO, Boult.

Sir Adrian Boult at eighty-five directed one of his most inspired recordings, an account of Elgar's long-neglected oratorio (the first of a projected trilogy; *The Kingdom* was the second) which must warm the heart of any Elgarian. That the work failed earlier to make the impact it deserves stands as a condemnation of fashion. It may not have quite such memorable melodies as *Gerontius* or *The Kingdom*, but many of the set numbers, like the setting of the Beatitudes, *By the Wayside*, show Elgar at his most inspired, and the characters of Mary Magdalene and Judas are unexpectedly rounded and sympathetic. Generally fine singing – notably from Sheila Armstrong and Helen Watts – and a recording as rich and faithful as anyone could want. The cassette transfer is of good quality, although the level is rather low. But the climaxes expand without congestion.

Caractacus (cantata), *Op. 35:* complete.
  *(**) HMV TC-SLS 998. Sheila Armstrong, Robert Tear, Peter Glossop, Brian Rayner Cook, Malcolm King, Richard Stuart, Liverpool Philharmonic Choir, Royal Liverpool PO, Groves.

Caractacus, based on the story of the ancient British hero pardoned by the Emperor Claudius, dropped out of the regular repertory long ago, forgotten except for the rousing *Triumphal march* and some notorious lines about the nations standing to 'hymn the praise of Britain like brothers hand in hand'. In fact only a tiny proportion of the piece is at all jingoistic, and such passages as the duet between Caractacus's daughter and her lover are as tenderly beautiful as anything Elgar wrote before *Enigma*. This is a fine performance which with ripe recording brings out all the Elgarian atmosphere (even if it does not manage a clear projection of the words); but it partly explains the neglect. The dramatic interest is limited, and the melodies are generally not as memorable as they might be. But *Caractacus* gives a rich insight into the happy Elgar early in his career, a composer still limited but delightfully approachable. The early transfers to tape were only moderately successful, and a current copy, tried just before this book went to press, still showed a coarsening of the sound at times in choral climaxes, noticeable in the opening scene. There are moments where the refinement slips elsewhere, although, surprisingly, the score's ample closing section (with the famous march) comes off with comparatively little loss of focus. The text is not easy to read in the small type of the condensed-size booklet.

Coronation ode, Op. 44; National anthem (arr. Elgar).
  (***) HMV TC-ASD 3345. Felicity Lott, Alfreda Hodgson, Richard Morton, Stephen Roberts, Cambridge University Music Society, King's College Choir, New Philharmonia Orch., Band of Royal Military School of Music, Ledger –
  PARRY: *I was glad.*(***)

Elgar's *Coronation ode* is far more than a jingoistic occasional piece, though it was indeed the work which first featured *Land of Hope and Glory*. The most tender moment of all is reserved for the first faint flickerings of that second national anthem, introduced gently on the harp to clarinet accompaniment. All told, the work contains much Elgarian treasure, and Ledger is superb in capturing the necessary swagger and panache, flouting all thought of potentially bad taste. With extra brass bands, it presents a glorious experience. Excellent singing and playing, though the male soloists do not quite match their female colleagues. Unfortunately the tape transfer, with coarse, crumbling sound quality, cannot be recommended, but it is to be hoped that later copies will be remastered.

The Dream of Gerontius (oratorio), *Op. 38.*
  (***) HMV TC-SLS 987. Helen Watts, Nicolai Gedda, Robert Lloyd, John Alldis Choir, LPO Choir, New Philharmonia Orch., Boult.

Boult provides the performance of *The Dream of Gerontius* for which Elgarians have been waiting since the advent of stereo recording. Listening to this wonderful set one feels that this is the culmination of a long history of partial or complete recordings of this great masterpiece which stretches far back into the days of acoustic 78 r.p.m. discs. Here

Boult's total dedication is matched by a sense both of wonder and of drama. The spiritual feeling is intense, but the human qualities of the narrative are fully realized, and the glorious closing pages are so beautiful that Elgar's vision is made to become one of the most unforgettable moments in all musical literature. Boult's unexpected choice of Gedda in the role of Gerontius brings a new dimension to this characterization, which is perfectly matched by Helen Watts as the Angel. The dialogues between the two have a natural spontaneity as Gerontius's questions and doubts find a response which is at once gently understanding and nobly authoritative. It is a fascinating vocal partnership, and it is matched by the commanding manner which Robert Lloyd finds for both his roles. The orchestral playing is always responsive and often, like the choral singing, very beautiful. The lovely wind-playing at the opening of Part 2 is matched by the luminosity of tone of the choral pianissimos, while the dramatic passages bring splendid incisiveness and bold assurance from the singers. The recording was originally one of EMI's first great successes in tape-transferring. The dynamic range of the disc recording was slightly narrowed, but the presentation of the soloists was strikingly vivid and dramatic and – apart from a degree of sibilance – the choral tone was very impressive. Unfortunately the original standard seems not to have been maintained; a recent copy showed that unpleasant 'pulsing' unsteadiness of tone which affects some transfers, while the sound itself was often edgy and uncongenial.

Sea Pictures (song cycle), *Op. 37.*
    (*) HMV TC-ASD 655. Janet Baker (mezzo-soprano), LSO, Barbirolli – *Cello concerto.*(*)
    ** CBS 40-76579. Yvonne Minton (mezzo-soprano), LPO, Barenboim – *In the South.**(*)

Sea Pictures hardly matches the mature inspiration of the *Cello concerto,* with which it is coupled on the HMV tape, but it is heartwarming here nonetheless. Like Jacqueline du Pré, Janet Baker is an artist who has the power to evoke in the recording studio the vividness of a live performance. With the help of Barbirolli she makes the cycle far more convincing than it usually seems, with words that are often trite clothed in music that seems to transform them. Warm recording. The cassette transfer projects the soloist well forward and treats the voice kindly, even if there is marginally less refinement of detail than on the equivalent LP.

Yvonne Minton uses her rich tone sensitively, but at few points does this performance match that of Janet Baker, a model for all others. The recording produces a warm orchestral sound, and although the range is limited, the vocal timbre is natural.

COLLECTION

'Favourite composer': (i) *Chanson de matin; Chanson de nuit, Op. 15/1 and 2;* (ii) *Introduction and allegro for strings, Op. 47;* (iii; iv) *Pomp and Circumstance marches, Op. 39/1–5;* (v) *Serenade for strings in E minor, Op. 20;* (iii; vi) *Variations on an original theme (Enigma). Op. 36.*
    (B) *** Decca KDPC 537/8. (i) LPO, Boult; (ii) Academy of St Martin-in-the-Fields, Marriner; (iii) LSO; (iv) Bliss; (v) RPO, Cox; (vi) Monteux.

A successful set, with Bliss's *Pomp and Circumstance marches* and Monteux's *Enigma* the highlights. Boult's two *Chansons* are stereo transcriptions of good mono recordings, but they sound well, and the only performance here that is slightly under-characterized is the *Serenade.* The transfers are of very good quality indeed: the *Enigma variations* (complete on one side with the five *Pomp and Circumstance marches* on the reverse) sound freshly minted – in many ways the sound here is preferable to the equivalent disc. The *Chansons* lean heavily towards the right channel but the sound itself is excellent.

Ewald, Victor
(1860–1935)

Brass quintets Nos. 1 in B flat major, Op. 5; 2 in E flat major, Op. 6; 3 in D flat major.
*** Advent E 1066 (see p. xxiii) [id.]. Empire Brass Quintet.

Victor Vladimirovich Ewald was born in St Petersburg, where he earned a living as a civil engineer. He was a keen cellist and played at the soirées held by Belayev every Friday. In the 1893 competition organized by the St Petesburg Quartet Society he won third prize with his Op. 1, though Rimsky-Korsakov, who was on the jury, thought the piece was 'written in a well-ordered manner, but nothing beyond that'. Belayev published Op. 1 and a number of other pieces by Ewald over the years, including the Op. 5 quintet recorded here. The ideas are conventionally post-nationalist, the opening of Op. 5 having a slight resemblance to Borodin's *Third Symphony*, and there are touches of Schumann and Dvořák. Pleasant, albeit insubstantial music, superbly crafted but of no great individuality. The playing here is absolutely first-class, with excellent ensemble, attack and blend. The recording too is firmly focused, wide in range and full-blodied. Excellent.

Falla, Manuel de
(1876–1946)

(i) *Harpsichord concerto;* (ii; iii) *Nights in the Gardens of Spain;* (ii) *Fantasia Baetica.*
(M) ** Turnabout KTVC 34588. (i) Martin Galling (harpsichord) with Chamber Ens.; (ii) György Sándor (piano); (iii) Radio Luxembourg Orch., Froment.

This makes a useful anthology, with a lively account of the *Harpsichord concerto* matched to a reading of *Nights in the Gardens of Spain* which has atmosphere as well as brilliance. The recording places the piano well forward in the latter work, and in the former all the instruments of the accompanying chamber group are closely microphoned, so that the possibilities of light and shade are somewhat reduced. Nevertheless the recording is otherwise good, and these are performances of character. The tape transfer is exceptionally well done, every bit the equal of the disc.

El amor brujo (*Love, the Magician*; ballet): complete.
(M) *** Decca Jubilee KJBC 50. Nati Mistral (mezzo-soprano), New Philharmonia Orch., Frühbeck de Burgos – GRANADOS: *Goyescas;* RAVEL: *Alborada* etc.***
** DG 3370 028 [id.]. Teresa Berganza (mezzo-soprano), LSO, Navarra – *La vida breve.***(*)
(i) *El amor brujo;* (ii) *The Three-cornered Hat* (*El sombrero de tres picos;* ballet): complete.
(***) RCA RK 12387 [ARK 1 2387]. LSO, Mata, with (i) Nati Mistral; (ii) Maria Luisa Salinas (mezzo-sopranos).

Frühbeck de Burgos provides us with a completely recommendable version of *El amor brujo*. His superbly graduated crescendo after the spiky opening is immediately compelling, and the control of atmosphere in the quieter music is masterly. Equally the *Ritual fire dance* is blazingly brilliant. Nati Mistral has the vibrant open-throated production of the real flamenco singer. She is less polished than Los Angeles in her HMV version (not yet available on tape), but if anything the music sounds more authentic this way. Brilliant sound, a trifle light in the bass, but offering luminous textures in the quieter sections. The cassette transfer, made at a high level, is admirably vivid.

El amor brujo makes an ideal coupling for Falla's compact opera *La vida breve*. However, the performance by the LSO under Garcia Navarra, with Teresa Berganza as soloist, is not so compelling as that of the principal work, and the recording is less atmospheric. As in the opera coupling, the transfer level is low, and the opening fanfare does not have the glittering impact it ideally needs. The orchestral detail is quite refined and Berganza's contribution is well projected, but the orchestral tuttis lack bite and projection. However, this should deter no one from sampling the opera.

The RCA issue is an obvious and certainly a generous coupling. The performances are vividly atmospheric, with much spirited and refined orchestral playing and excellent contributions from the soloists. Unfortunately the tape transfer is excessively bright, with a harsh glare on the string tone, little bloom on the orchestra generally, and a tendency to shrillness. The lack of warmth and glow is serious in scores which depend so much on the ambient effect of the orchestral sound.

(i) *Nights in the Gardens of Spain;* (ii) *The Three-cornered Hat (El sombrero de tres picos;* ballet): *suite.*
(M) ** DG Privilege 3335 268. (i)
Margrit Weber (piano), Bavarian Radio SO, Kubelik; (ii) Berlin Radio SO, Maazel.
(i) *Nights in the Gardens of Spain. The Three-cornered Hat: 3 Dances.*
(*) Decca KSXC 16528. Alicia de Larrocha (piano), (i) with Suisse Romande Orch., Comissiona – CHOPIN: *Piano concerto No. 2.**

Alicia de Larrocha is in just as fine form in the *Nights in the Gardens of Spain* as she is in the Chopin coupling. She brings plenty of poetry and vitality to this evocative score, and she receives admirable support from Comissiona and the engineers. This is one of the finest versions of the work now available. The cassette opens with the bonus item (not on the equivalent LP), the three dances from *The Three-cornered Hat*, vividly played as a piano solo. The opening of the main work which follows is almost too brilliantly recorded, and the brightly lit sound picture needs subduing with the controls if the music's full atmosphere is to evolve.

The DG Privilege transfer also offers extremely vivid sound, but here there is less edge on the treble, and indeed the quality is very impressive, with fine piano tone. It is just right for the performance, which is rather more robust than the Decca version. Margrit Weber gives a brilliant account of the solo part, and Kubelik is equally direct, although the music-making is certainly not without atmosphere. This is highly enjoyable with a sparkling, even exhilarating quality matched by the brightness of the transfer. Maazel's selection from *The Three-cornered Hat* has much less charisma. The music is well played, but the performances are not distinctive, lacking the last degree of colour and vigour. The transfer too offers less bite and presence than its coupling and the reverberation helps to take some of the edge off the sound.

219

The Three-cornered Hat (El sombrero de tres picos; ballet): complete.

*** DG 3300 823 [id.]. Teresa Berganza (mezzo-soprano), Boston SO, Ozawa.

(M) **(*) HMV TC-EXE 188. Victoria de los Angeles (soprano), Philharmonia Orch., Frühbeck de Burgos.

Arguably the Ozawa is now the best version of *The Three-cornered Hat* in its complete form on the market. Berganza was also the soloist in Ansermet's recording (not currently available on cassette), though the quality of the orchestral playing in the Boston version is superior to that of the Suisse Romande. The playing too is altogether more idiomatic in feeling than that of the New York orchestra under Pierre Boulez, but this latter performance, originally issued on tape by CBS, has been withdrawn in the UK, although it remains available in the USA (MT 33970). Choice resides between the highly colourful account under Ozawa and the atmospherically recorded version on HMV with Victoria de los Angeles as the (slightly sedate) soloist. The DG recording is vividly alive and has admirable presence without distorting perspectives, though Berganza is not located off-stage as directed. If the choral opening sounds somewhat self-conscious on DG, the opening 'Olés' on the HMV tape are no more convincing. The DG transfer has a wide dynamic range and is realistically balanced; the balance on the HMV tape is much more forward, and the acoustic is reverberant. However, the projection of the sound is undoubtedly vivid, and it certainly gives Frühbeck de Burgos's account exciting presence, even if the overall effect is less refined, and this HMV tape is excellent value.

The Three-cornered Hat: 3 Dances.

(M) (*) Supraphon 0450614.

Czech PO, Fournet – DEBUSSY: *Images.*(*)

The dim Supraphon transfer takes all the life out of these performances. The original LP certainly did not lack brilliance, but this cassette has none at all.

La vida breve (opera): complete.

(*) DG 3370 028 [id.]. Teresa Berganza, Alicia Nafé, José Carreras, LSO, Navarra – *El amor brujo.*

La vida breve is a kind of Spanish *Cavalleria Rusticana* without the melodrama and with a conspicuously weak plot. The heroine dies of a broken heart when her lover deserts her for another, and it is hard to make her role sound convincing. Teresa Berganza may not have the light-of-eye expressiveness of her compatriot Victoria de los Angeles, who made two earlier recordings, but hers is a strong, earthy account which helps to compensate for Falla's dramatic weaknesses; and it is good to have so fine a singer as José Carreras in the relatively small tenor role of Paco. Reliant as the piece is on atmosphere above all, it makes an excellent subject for recording, and with vivid performances from the LSO and Ambrosian Singers, idiomatically directed, the result here is a convincing success. Recording balance is not always ideal, and DG's transfer is made at a rather low level. The quality is refined, with the voices clear and some lovely translucent sounds from the woodwind, but some of the background detail (the recessed choruses, for instance) is slightly less vivid on tape than on disc. The famous orchestral dance (which comes at the end of side two) lacks something in range and glitter; but at the opening of side three the level rises slightly and gives the quality a little more edge. The tapes are in DG's removable box format, and the libretto, though printed in small type, is clear enough.

Fauré, Gabriel
(1845–1924)

Berceuse in D major (for violin and orchestra), *Op. 16.*
*(*) CBS 40-76530 [Col. MT 34550]. Isaac Stern, Orchestre de Paris, Barenboim – CHAUSSON: *Poème***; SAINT-SAËNS: *Concerto No. 3.**(*)

The lovely *Berceuse*, unaffectedly played, makes a charming fill-up for the two longer concertante works. The transfer offers pleasant rather than distinguished quality, lacking crispness of outline and detail.

Fantaisie for flute and orchestra (arr. Galway).
*** RCA RK 25109. James Galway (flute), RPO, Dutoit – CHAMINADE: *Concertino*; IBERT: *Concerto*; POULENC: *Sonata.****

James Galway's arrangement of a *Fantaisie for flute and piano* that Fauré composed in the late 1890s makes an appealing fill-up to an enterprising collection of concertante flute works impeccably played and finely recorded. There are two genuine flute concertos here (Ibert and Chaminade) and two arrangements, this and Lennox Berkeley's expert orchestration of Poulenc's *Flute sonata*. A well-transferred tape that will give great pleasure.

Masques et Bergamasques: suite, Op. 112.
(B) * Pye ZCCCB 15020. French CO, Lizzio – SAINT-SAËNS: *Carnival of Animals.**

The orchestral playing of the French Chamber Orchestra is not very distinguished and the violins are given a thin tonal patina by the transfer. Otherwise the sound is bright until towards the end, when the refinement slips because of marginal over-modulation. Fauré's music is delightfully fresh, and its spirit and personality are certainly conveyed here.

Pelléas et Mélisande: suite, Op. 80.
(**) CBS 40-76526 [Col. MT 34506]. New Philharmonia Orch., Andrew Davis – FRANCK: *Symphony.*(**)

Fauré's *Pelléas et Mélisande* music makes an unexpected but attractive coupling for the Franck *Symphony*, particularly when Andrew Davis's performance of these atmospheric pieces is so freshly responsive. The transfer to tape, however, has not been a success, with unrefined textures and coarsening at climaxes.

Impromptu No. 5 in F minor, Op. 102; Nocturne No. 13 in B minor, Op. 119.
*** RCA RK 12548 [ARK 1 2548]. Vladimir Horowitz (piano) – LISZT: *Sonata.****

These two beautiful Fauré pieces complete the second side of Horowitz's Liszt *Sonata*, which is unaccountably spread over a side and a half. Fauré is not a composer that we associate with Horowitz, but these pieces are in impeccable style. Excellent sound, clear and bold, and an immaculate transfer.

Requiem, Op. 48.
(B) *** Classics for Pleasure TC-CFP 40234. Victoria de los Angeles (soprano), Dietrich Fischer-Dieskau (bar.), Elisabeth Brasseur Choir, Paris Conservatoire Orch., Cluytens.
(M) ** Decca KCSP 504. Suzanne Danco (soprano), Gérard

Souzay (bar.), L'Union Chorale de la Tour de Peilz, Suisse Romande Orch., Ansermet.

Requiem; Cantique de Jean Racine, Op. 11.

*** Argo KZRC 841 [id.]. Jonathan Bond (treble), Benjamin Luxon (bar.), St John's College Choir, Academy of St Martin-in-the-Fields, Guest; Stephen Cleobury (organ).

**(*) HMV TC-ASD 3501. Norma Burrowes (soprano), Brian Rayner Cook (bar.), City of Birmingham SO and Chorus, Frémaux.

(i) *Requiem. Pavane, Op. 50.*

*** CBS 40-76734. Ambrosian Singers, Philharmonia Orch., Andrew Davis, (i) with Lucia Popp (soprano), Siegmund Nimsgern (bar.).

The directness and clarity of Andrew Davis's reading go with a concentrated, dedicated manner and a masterly control of texture to bring out the purity and beauty of Fauré's orchestration to the full. Moreover the fresh vigour of the choral singing achieves an admirable balance between ecstasy and restraint in this most elusive of requiem settings. The style of the phrasing is not so openly expressive as in some other versions, but that is in character with the intimacy of the reading, culminating in a wonderfully measured and intense account of the final *In Paradisum*. Lucia Popp is both rich and pure, and Siegmund Nimsgern (if less memorable) is refined in tone and detailed in his pointing. The recording, made in a church, matches the intimate manner, and the transfer is the finest we have yet heard from CBS, the choral sound atmospheric yet clear and the overall balance excellent in every way. The *Pavane*, heard in its choral version, makes an attractive fill-up.

However the Los Angeles/Fischer-Dieskau version made under the late André Cluytens in the early 1960s is available at bargain price, and its claims on the collector's pocket are almost irresistible. It has always been a good-sounding version, with great expressive eloquence in its favour, even if the choir is not as fine as St John's. The transfer to tape is of excellent quality, with plenty of atmosphere and good detail. Los Angeles's solo on side two sounds particularly fresh and natural.

George Guest's performance is on a smaller scale than the CFP version. The excellence of both is not in question, but in these matters tastes differ, although undoubtedly the St John's set has a magic that works from the opening bars onwards. The Argo recording is wide-ranging and exceptionally truthful, but the smaller scale of the conception may not enjoy universal appeal. The King's College Choir recording (on HMV TC-ASD 2358) is unfortunately not available in Dolbyized form, and the transfer is not very distinguished. In any case admirers of Fauré may find its Anglican accents unidiomatic, but the treble soloist is far purer in tone than his opposite number from St John's, and many may feel that the King's performance is the finer of the two.

Frémaux's version is attractively atmospheric, the recording comparatively recessed. Frémaux has a moulded style which does not spill over in too much expressiveness, and there is a natural warmth about this performance that is highly persuasive. Norma Burrowes sings beautifully, her innocent style most engaging. On tape the backward balance means that the focus is not as clear as on the CBS version, but the slight blurring of detail is by no means a serious drawback in this work when the music-making is so sympathetic. The soloists are naturally caught and the orchestral balance is good.

The excellent Decca transfer of Ansermet's version offers uniformly good quality with a wide dynamic range. But the detail of the sound picture only serves to emphasize the rather thin-toned contribution of the chorus. However, there is no doubt that this performance has character, and the solo singing is good (even if Danco is no match for Los Angeles in sheer spiritual beauty).

Franck, César
(1822–90)

Symphonic variations for piano and orchestra.
*** Decca KSXC 2173. Clifford Curzon, LSO, Boult – GRIEG: *Piano concerto;* LITOLFF: *Scherzo.****
** Decca KSXC 6599. Alicia de Larrocha, LPO, Frühbeck de Burgos – KHACHATURIAN: *Piano concerto.***
** Advent E 1051 (see p. xxiii) [id.]. György Cziffra, Budapest SO, György Cziffra Jnr – GRIEG: *Piano concerto.***(*)

Curzon's performance has stood the test of time. It is a deliciously fresh reading without idiosyncrasy, and can be recommended unreservedly, particularly with the coupling equally brilliantly done. The recording is beautifully clean and clear, and the cassette transfer is of matching quality.

The Spanish interpreters, Alicia de Larrocha and Frühbeck de Burgos, give a reading that more than usual brings out the French delicacy of the variations. Good recording quality: an unexpected coupling for a variable account of the Khachaturian *Concerto.* The transfer is good, but this is not one of Decca's most brilliant tapes.

The Cziffras offer the same coupling as Curzon but without his attractive Litolff bonus. Although the transfer is of

Advent's usual high standard, the EMI Pathé recording is not particularly distinguished; the orchestral sound has a somewhat cavernous quality, and the sound overall lacks sparkle and refined detail. The essentially romantic performance offers much to please, and Cziffra is on good form, but in the work's closing pages there is a lack of rhythmic sparkle in the orchestra. However, this is still enjoyable and will be acceptable for those interested in the coupling.

(i) *Symphonic variations for piano and orchestra. Symphony in D minor.*
**(*) Decca KSXC 6823 [Lon. 5-7044]. Cleveland Orch., Maazel, (i) with Pascal Rogé.
** HMV TC-ASD 3308. Bournemouth SO, Berglund, (i) with Sylvia Kersenbaum.

It is curious that this coupling was not more often used in the past, for its attractions are obvious. Then both Decca and HMV made virtually simultaneous issues on tape and disc.

The execution on the Maazel tape is far crisper than on Berglund's, and the performances are exciting, but a lack of lyrical tenderness robs the *Symphony* of some of its more appealing qualities. The rich melody of the second subject finds Maazel introducing tenutos, which in so clipped and precise a performance seem obtrusive. Maazel's earlier account on Privilege (see below) was more moving and impressive. In the *Variations* Pascal Rogé shows himself particularly sensitive to dynamic shadings and reveals a fine blend of intelligence and technique, even if his playing is a trifle reticent at times. Excellent recording, and the Decca cassette transfer is outstandingly brilliant and detailed, with splendid impact.

Berglund directs a rugged performance of a symphony which is usually regarded as a product of the hot-house. There are even hints of Sibelius. It is an approach which to some ears grows the more attractive with repetition, strong and expressive in style of phrasing, with tempi evenly maintained. However, the comparatively slow speeds chosen in the outer movements do bring a loss of romantic urgency, and some will find this lack of impulse a serious drawback. The playing is not always perfectly polished, but with a warm-blooded performance of the *Variations*, full of fantasy and poetry from the soloist, it makes an attractive coupling. The HMV transfer is of quite good quality but does not match the Decca in brilliance and refinement of detail.

Symphony in D minor.
- (M) **(*) HMV TC-SXLP 30256. French National Radio Orch., Beecham.
- (M) *** DG Privilege 3335 156. Berlin Radio SO, Maazel.
- (M) *(**) RCA Gold Seal GK 25004. RCA Victor SO, Boult.
- (**) CBS 40-76526 [Col. MT 34506]. New Philharmonia Orch., Andrew Davis – FAURÉ: *Pelléas et Mélisande.*(**)

Beecham's splendidly vigorous account of the César Franck *Symphony* has been too long out of the catalogue. The sheer gusto of the outer movements is exhilarating, and even though Sir Thomas's treatment of the second subject of the first movement is somewhat indulgent, the interpretation remains highly convincing. There are expressive mannerisms in the slow movement too, but Beecham conjures eloquent playing from the orchestra and maintains a high level of tension. In some ways Maazel's straighter version is more effective (and the tape transfer is preferable), but Beecham's magnetism is compelling, and this version – however idiosyncratic – will be first choice for all those who admire his special feeling for French music. The tape transfer is admirably robust, and the full-blooded orchestral tone suits the fervour of Beecham's advocacy. There is some lack of refinement in tuttis, but a cut-back of treble mitigates this considerably. The effect is immensely vivid, and the detail is good too, so that the ear adjusts to the absence of overall smoothness, for the sound does not lack body.

Maazel's account too is outstanding, beautifully shaped both in its overall structure and in incidental details. Yet though each phrase is sensitively moulded, there is no sense of self-conscious striving for beauty of effect. Maazel adopts a fairly brisk tempo in the slow movement, which, surprisingly enough, greatly enhances its poetry and dignity; his finale is also splendidly vital and succeeds in filtering out the excesses of grandiose sentiment and vulgarity that disfigure this edifice. The work gains enormously from the strong control and deliberate understatement as well as the refinement of tone and phrasing that mark this reading. (Paray also used to be particularly impressive in this way.) The recording is admirably well-blended and musically balanced. The cassette transfer is splendid. (Unfortunately this tape has been withdrawn just as we go to press.)

Sir Adrian's freshly incisive reading was recorded for the Reader's Digest record club in the early sixties, and the pseudonymous orchestra is almost certainly the Philharmonia at its peak. Sir Adrian's manner after the rapt and dedicated account of the slow introduction is brisk, urgent and direct, with crisply pointed rhythms preventing any feeling of breathlessness and with all sentimentality and vulgarity completely removed. Much of this music might almost be by Elgar – at least Sir Adrian seems to tell us so, with nobility one of the elements. The playing is superb: the woodwind is outstandingly fine, and the horn solos suggest that Alan Civil was on the roster. The recording is basically excellent for its period, but the RCA transfer has an element of coarseness in the upper string tone which detracts from the refinement of the music-making.

Though Andrew Davis's reading is attractively fresh and direct, with much fine playing (the opening of the finale is superbly incisive), here is another studio performance from this conductor which in the end adds up to less than the sum of its parts, lacking the ebb and flow of tension. Moreover the tape transfer is of poor quality, with patches of unacceptable coarseness in the climaxes of all three movements.

Violin sonata in A major.
(*) Decca KSXC 6408. Itzhak Perlman (violin), Vladimir Ashkenazy (piano) – BRAHMS: *Horn trio.*(*)

A superb account of the *Violin sonata.* The first movement catches the listener by the ears with its tremendous forward impulse, and the whole performance has the kind of spontaneity which is too rare in recordings. The passionate commitment of the playing in no way swamps the work's lyrical flow, and it is difficult to imagine the music being more convincingly presented. The transfer is of good quality (the Franck is more pleasing than the Brahms coupling), but the level is low and by Decca standards this is disappointing.

Flute sonata in A major (transcription of the *Violin sonata*).
*** RCA RK 25029 [LRK 1 5095]. James Galway (flute), Martha Argerich (piano) – PROKOFIEV: *Flute sonata.****

Although the prospect of hearing the Franck *Violin sonata* arranged for flute may strike you as unappealing, the actual experience strangely belies expectation, thanks to the expert advocacy of these artists. Of course, in the scherzo the flute cannot match the character and bite of the violin, but elsewhere it is surprising how well this music responds to Mr Galway's transcription and his sweet-toned virtuosity. Argerich is absolutely

superb here, and the recording is truthful in quality and wide-ranging. The balance is just a trifle close but is thoroughly musical, and if it is played at a slightly lower level setting than usual it yields a sound that is pleasingly fresh and well defined. The cassette transfer is first-class. The balance is a forward one, but there is no lack of light and shade, and the flute timbre is faithfully captured.

Gay, John
(1685–1732)

The Beggar's Opera (arr. Austin).
(M) *** HMV TC 2-ESDW 704. Elsie Morison, John Cameron, Monica Sinclair, Ian Wallace, Owen Brannigan, Constance Shacklock, Alexander Young, Pro Arte Chorus and Orch., Sargent.

The Beggar's Opera was the eighteenth-century equivalent of the modern American musical. It was first produced in 1728 and caused a sensation with audiences used to the stylized Italian opera favoured by Handel. Its impact produced a whole series of inferior ballad operas, culminating a century later in works like *Maritana* and *The Bohemian Girl* which are far removed from Gay's piece in spirit as well as social content. The performance under Sargent is in every way first-class, with soloists who could hardly be bettered and with linking dialogue, spoken by actors, to make the result most dramatic. The chorus is no less effective; EMI chose *Let us take the road* for inclusion on their original stereo demonstration disc. Indeed the sense of presence and atmosphere throughout is highly compelling, and the demonstration quality of the tape is obvious throughout, with remarkable immediacy for both the spoken drama and the music itself. A very successful issue that gives much pleasure.

German, Edward
(1862–1936)

Welsh rhapsody.
(***) HMV TC-ASD 2400. Scottish National Orch., Gibson – HARTY: *With the Wild Geese;* MacCUNN: *Land of Mountain and Flood;* SMYTH: *The Wreckers overture.*(***)

Edward German's *Welsh rhapsody,* written for the Cardiff Festival of 1904, makes a colourful and exciting finale for this enterprising collection of genre British tone pictures. German is content not to interfere with the traditional melodies he uses, and he relies on his orchestral skill to retain the listener's interest, in which he is very successful. The closing pages, based on *Men of Harlech,* are prepared in an almost Tchaikovskian manner to provide a rousing conclusion. This is a good example of a tune with an inbuilt eloquence that cannot be improved upon. Unfortunately the transfer was made during the period when EMI were experimenting with a narrowed dynamic range. The orchestra is pushed right forward with unattractively congealed textures and an absence of light and shade.

Gershwin, George
(1898–1937)

An American in Paris.
*** Decca KSXC 6811 [Lon. 5-7031]. Los Angeles PO, Mehta – BERNSTEIN: *Candide overture;* COPLAND: *Appalachian Spring.****
** DG 3300 788 [id.] San Francisco SO, Ozawa – RUSSO: *Street music.***

An American in Paris; Cuban overture; Rhapsody in Blue.
** Decca KSXC 16727 [Lon. 5-6946], Ivan Davis (piano), Cleveland Orch., Maazel (with GOTTSCHALK: *Le Bananier; The Banjo****).

An American in Paris; Porgy and Bess: Symphonic picture (arr. Robert Russell Bennett).
(B) ** Classics for Pleasure TC-CFP 40240. LPO, Pritchard – COPLAND: *El Salón México.***

(i) *An American in Paris;* (ii) *Rhapsody in Blue.*
**(*) CBS 40-76509. (i) New York PO; (ii) the composer (piano; from 1925 piano roll), Columbia Jazz Band; both cond. Tilson Thomas.
(M) *** Decca KCSP 525. (i) Los Angeles PO, Mehta; (ii) Julius Katchen (piano), LSO, Kertesz – COPLAND: *Fanfare.****

Piano concerto in F major.
(M) **(*) DG Privilege 3335 210. Roberto Szidon (piano), LPO, Downes – BERNSTEIN: *West Side Story: Symphonic dances.***(*)

Piano concerto in F major; Rhapsody in Blue. Piano solo: *3 Preludes.*
(M) ** Turnabout KTVC 34457. Eugene List (piano), Berlin SO, Adler.

Rhapsody in Blue.
(*) Decca KSXC 6411. Julius Katchen (piano), LSO, Kertesz – PROKOFIEV: *Piano concerto No. 3;* RAVEL: *Piano concerto in D major.**

In 1925 George Gershwin made a piano roll recording of *Rhapsody in Blue,* providing both the piano part and a reduction of the orchestration, so that the work was in essence complete. In 1976

Thomas Shepard conceived the idea of a modern recording using the composer's own performance, but deleting the orchestral sections from the roll and substituting a modern re-creation of the original instrumentation as scored by Ferde Grofé for Paul Whiteman's orchestral jazz band. With loving care Tom Shepard and the record's producer, Andrew Kazdin, covered every hole on the roll which did not relate to the piano part and then assembled in the recording studio a group of eminent musicians to play Grofé's scoring, which featured mostly wind, including a variety of saxophones, clarinets and brass, plus eight violins. Gershwin's performance was recorded from the pianola and the tape was then used by Michael Tilson Thomas and his 'Columbia Jazz Band' who fitted the accompaniment round it. The spontaneity of the finished performance is quite riveting. Gershwin's tempi are sometimes disconcertingly fast (the first big tutti for the band makes one really sit up) but when one adjusts there is no question that the music-making has an irresistible flavour of the twenties, the rhythms exhilaratingly rooty-tooty. The actual instrumental playing demands and receives extreme bravura from the accompanying musicians, although when the big tune arrives it is introduced slowly and graciously, heightening the contrast with the infectiously brilliant outer sections. This is surely a definitive account that makes one rethink the work, so often heard in its more sober symphonic dress (later the orchestration was filled out more conventionally). There is room for both versions, of course, but this one has a unique authenticity. Fortunately the coupling is equally good, a quite marvellous performance of *An American in Paris*, with the NYPO, where the episodic nature of the writing is drawn together in a most satisfying way. The recording is brilliant, and the tape transfer is excellent, slightly more mellow than the disc and in some ways more enjoyable because of this. However, it must be

admitted that the sound does not have quite the upper range of the LP.

Mehta's splendidly alive account of *An American in Paris* is available on a medium-price tape where if anything the sound has an even better balance between sparkle and richness than on the full-priced issue (KSXC 6811). The Copland coupling is first-rate too, and if Katchen's *Rhapsody* is less idiomatic it has crisp and detailed sound. However, the full-price tape offers the only first-class transfer of Copland's *Appalachian Spring* in the current catalogue.

There is a softness of focus in Ozawa's view of the Gershwin work which takes away the necessary bite, and though the recording quality is full and close it lacks something in glitter in the transfer to tape.

Maazel's performances (with Ivan Davis both brilliant and sophisticated in the *Rhapsody*) are in the last analysis disappointing. The recording does not help, being very brightly lit to the point of brashness. This makes the *Cuban overture* sound emptier and noisier than usual, and one feels also that the kernel of the two main works is missing. The great blues melody at the centre of *An American in Paris* sounds undernourished; it surely needs to be more sensuous than this. However, the tape transfer is of high quality, brilliant and clear, and the two Gottschalk encores make an attractive bonus (not on the equivalent disc).

André Previn makes a very attractive coupling of *American in Paris*, the *Piano concerto* and *Rhapsody in Blue* (HMV TC-ASD 2754), but unfortunately the transfers, although of good quality, are not Dolbyized, and the *Concerto* lacks something in upper range, so there is no possibility of minimizing the hiss.

Pritchard's account of *An American in Paris* is agreeable but lightweight and not very idiomatic. He comes into his own in the *Porgy and Bess Symphonic picture*, which he treats very much operatically, rather than as a glossy orchestral paraphrase. The lyrical numbers are played tenderly and there is a lack of the kind of extrovert bravura we usually get with American performances of this cleverly dovetailed selection. The recording is good, not sumptuous but truthful. The cassette transfer is vivid, although in *Porgy and Bess* one notices that the contrasts in dynamic (very much part of the arranger's 'symphonic' conception) are narrowed.

Eugene List's Turnabout tape uses the original scoring in the *Rhapsody*, but the effect is shallow compared with the CBS recording which uses the composer's own piano roll. The range of the Turnabout transfer is wider, but this only serves to emphasize the thin recorded quality, which makes the brass sound brash. In spite of the crisp precision of the solo playing one cannot recommend this without some reservation. The *Concerto* fares better, although the quality is never rich. But what redeems this cassette is the distinguished solo performances, always brilliant but never hard. The three piano *Preludes* are particularly valuable.

Roberto Szidon on Privilege treats the *Concerto* as he would any other romantic piano concerto, and with rhythms superbly lithe and tonal colouring enchantingly subtle in its range, the result brings freshness and stature to the music. The jazz idiom is seen here as an essential but not overwhelmingly dominant element. Downes and the LPO match the soloist in understanding and virtuosity. As can be heard at the opening solo for percussion, the range of the recording lacks the last degree of transient sparkle, but remains good, and although the resonance of the recording is not quite as clearly focused as on the disc, this tape is still very recommendable.

Julius Katchen made an early stereo record, coupling the *Concerto* and the *Rhapsody*, with Mantovani, but the partnership was not a particularly fruitful one. Katchen re-recorded the *Rhapsody* with Kertesz not long before he died, and listening to this vivid and exciting playing no one would suspect that his health was

anything other than robust. The Ravel and Prokofiev couplings are both splendid, but the *Rhapsody* lacks that elusive idiomatic quality it needs to spring fully to life. The transfer on the full-priced tape (KSXC 6411) is excellent, but the recording sounds even crisper on the KCSP reissue.

Broadway overtures: *Funny Face; Girl Crazy; Let 'Em Eat Cake; Of Thee I Sing; Oh, Kay; Strike Up the Band*.
*** CBS 40–76632. Buffalo PO, Tilson Thomas.

These Broadway overtures are given expert and idiomatic performances by Michael Tilson Thomas and the Buffalo orchestra. After the success of his coupling of the *Rhapsody in Blue* and *An American in Paris* one would expect no less from this brilliant conductor. Oddly enough, there is no alternative compilation on cassette, but any newcomer will have to be very good indeed to beat this. The recording is well detailed, with good stereo definition and wide range. Balance and perspective are perfectly truthful, and the strings reproduce cleanly and smoothly at the top of the aural spectrum. A first-class issue that will give wide pleasure.

Clap yo' hands; Do, do, do; Do it again; Fascinating rhythm; I got rhythm; I'll build a stairway to paradise; Impromptu in two keys; Liza; The man I love; Merry Andrew; My one and only; Nobody but you; Oh, lady be good; Piano playin' Jazzbo Brown; 3 Preludes; Promenade; Rialto ripples; Somebody loves me; Strike up the band; Swanee; Sweet and low down; 'S wonderful; That certain feeling; Three-quarter blues; Who cares.
**(*) Advent D 1034 (see p. xxiii) [id.]. William Bolcom (piano).

A useful collection including a group of famous Gershwin songs in their piano-only arrangements. William Bolcom conveys his enthusiam for the music, but sometimes the vigorous rhythmic style he employes seems over-emphatic: with a more relaxed approach this delightfully tuneful and spontaneous writing could be left to speak for itself. The second side of the tape offers a valuable recital of Gershwin's non-vocal piano music, again played with much sympathy but sometimes a lack of incandescence. The Advent transfer is splendidly realistic, although the recording is rather close.

Rhapsody in Blue (solo piano version); *Do it again; I got rhythm; I'll build a stairway to paradise; Liza; The man I love; Nobody but you; Oh, lady be good; 3 Preludes; Somebody loves me; Swanee; Sweet and low down; 'S wonderful; That certain feeling; Who cares.*
** CBS 40-76508 [Col. MT 34221]. André Watts (piano).

Only the keenest Gershwin collector is likely to want the solo piano version of the *Rhapsody in Blue*, even though André Watts's performance is thoughtful as well as brilliant. However, the songs are ever attractive, even without the vocals, and these assured if sometimes wilful performances have plenty of life. The recording is somewhat hard in the American manner, and in some ways the mellower cassette is preferable to the disc.

Porgy and Bess (opera): complete.
*** Decca K 3 Q 23 [Lon. 5-13116]. Willard White, Leona Mitchell, McHenry Boatwright, Florence Quivar, Barbara Henricks, François Clemmons, Arthur Thompson, Cleveland Chorus, Children's Chorus and Orch., Maazel.
**(*) RCA RK 02109 [ARK 3 2109]. Donnie Ray Albert, Clamma Dale, Andrew Smith, Wilma Shakesnider, Larry Marschall, Children's Chorus, Houston Grand Opera Chorus and Orch., DeMain.

If anyone was ever in doubt whether Gershwin in *Porgy and Bess* had really written an opera as opposed to a jumped-up musical, this superb recording with Cleveland forces conducted by Maazel establishes the work's formidable status beyond question. For one thing Maazel includes the complete text, which was in fact cut even before the first stage presentation. Some half-hour of virtually unknown music, including many highly evocative passages and some striking choruses, reinforces the consistency of Gershwin's inspiration. It is not just a question of the big numbers presenting some of the most memorable melodies of the twentieth century, but of a grand dramatic design which triumphs superbly over the almost impossible conjunction of conventions – opera and the American musical.

With a cast that makes up an excellent team, there is no attempt to glamorize characters who are far from conventional, and the story is the more moving for that, with moments potentially embarrassing ('I's the only woman Porgy ever had,' says Bess to Crown in Act 2) given genuine dramatic force à la Puccini. The vigour and colour are irresistible, and the recording is one of the most vivid that even Decca has produced. Willard White is a magnificent Porgy, dark of tone, while Leona Mitchell's vibrant Bess has a moving streak of vulnerability, and François Clemmons as Sportin' Life achieves the near-impossible by actually singing the role and making one forget Cab Calloway. But it is above all Maazel's triumph, a tremendous first complete recording with dazzling playing from the Cleveland Orchestra. The cassette set is only marginally less brilliant than the discs, with excellent

229

projection of the soloists and plenty of atmosphere.

The distinction is readily drawn between Maazel's Cleveland performance and John DeMain's equally complete and authoritative account on RCA. Where Maazel easily and naturally demonstrates the operatic qualities of Gershwin's masterpiece, DeMain – with a cast which had a riotous success with the piece on Broadway and elsewhere in the United States – presents a performance clearly in the tradition of the Broadway musical. There is much to be said for both views, and it is worth noting that American listeners tend to prefer the less operatic manner of the RCA set. The casts are equally impressive vocally, with the RCA singers a degree more characterful. Donnie Ray Albert, as Porgy, uses his bass-like resonance impressively, though not everyone will like the suspicion of hamming, which works less well in a recording than on stage. That underlining of expressiveness is a characteristic of the performance, so that the climax of the key duet, *Bess, you is my woman now*, has a less natural, more stagey manner, producing, for some ears, less of a frisson than the more delicate Cleveland version. For others the more robust Houston approach has a degree of dramatic immediacy, associated with the tradition of the American popular theatre, which is irresistible. This basic contrast will decide most listeners' approach, and although the RCA recording has not quite the Decca richness it is strikingly vivid and alive. The RCA tape transfer is not quite so sophisticated as the Decca, but it matches the records in presence, giving fine projection of the solo voices, although the chorus is sometimes less well focused. The spectacle is only moderately well managed – the storm scene at the end of Act 2, with the special effects in full flight, could do with sharper detail and there is a moment of blasting at the end of side four at the climax of the duet *I loves you, Porgy*, but otherwise there is little to complain of except the badly produced libretto, printed on poor-quality paper in incredibly small type.

Gibbons, Orlando (1583–1625)

First song of Moses; Second preces; Psalm 145; Voluntary; Te Deum; Voluntary; Jubilate; This is the record of John; See, see, the word is incarnate; Glorious and powerful God.

(M) ** Argo KZKC 8. King's College Choir, Jacobean Consort of Viols, Simon Preston (organ), Willcocks.

This is an early Argo stereo recording, and the attempt to simulate antiphonal alternation in the *Psalm* is not wholly clear. But generally the sound is very good, although not perhaps ideally intimate for the verse anthems. The programme is imaginatively chosen and the music all of high quality. The consort of viols is not too well balanced, however, and makes less than its full effect. The cassette transfer is of good quality, reflecting the fact that the original recording is not as clear as Argo's more modern ventures in this field.

Giuliani, Mauro (1781–1828)

Guitar concerto No.1 in A major, Op. 30.

⊛ *** Philips 7300 369 [id.]. Pepe Romero, Academy of St Martin-in-the-Fields, Marriner – RODRIGO: *Concierto madrigal*.***

What makes this performance so distinctive is the splendid accompaniment provided by the Academy of St Martin-in-the-Fields under Marriner, matched by superb recording. The shaping of the naïf contours of Giuliani's orchestral *ritornello* is deliciously judged, and throughout there are many delightful touches from the orchestra. Romero is a first-rate player, and with such a backing the performance as a whole has an irresistible, smiling quality; the finale is marvellously vivacious, the sparkling orchestral rhythms a constant joy. The cassette transfer is of demonstration quality, matching the disc in its refinement and bloom.

The version by Karl Scheit on Turnabout (KTVC 34123), is let down by a somewhat dim recording, This tape is discussed in our Concerts section below.

Guitar concertos Nos. 2 in A major, Op. 36; 3 in F major, Op. 70.
**(*) Philips 7300 598 [id.]. Pepe Romero, Academy of St Martin-in-the-Fields, Marriner.

The *F major Concerto* is a delightful work, quite the equal of Op. 30 and in some ways even more fetching. It is attractively scored, using the timpani effectively, as can be heard near the very opening, as well as adding wind parts (the coupled *A major Concerto* is for strings alone). The first movement begins with an engaging little march theme whose dotted rhythms remind one of Hummel (the two composers were almost exact contemporaries), and the simple development has plenty of charm. The amiable *Siciliano* which forms the *Andantino* is matched by an unforceful closing *Polonaise*. Here perhaps Marriner is too rhythmically gentle, but the performance as a whole is very enjoyable and beautifully recorded. The Op. 36 work is pleasant but less memorable. The smiling warmth of the orchestral introduction tempts Marriner into leaving too slack a rein,

and the work does not seem to attain its full sparkle until the closing rondo. However, this is still agreeable, and playing and recording are excellent. The transfer of both concertos is of Philips' best quality: No. 3 approaches demonstration standard.

Introduction, theme, variation and polonaise (for guitar and orchestra), *Op. 65.*
*** Philips 7300 442 [id.]. Pepe Romero, Academy of St Martin-in-the-Fields, Marriner
– RODRIGO: *Fantasia.****

Giuliani's set of variations is an agreeable work, and if its invention only just rises above the trivial, it is redeemed here by a performance of great vitality and charm, with a splendid orchestral backing for the soloist and first-rate recording both on tape and disc. The other virtue of this issue is its excellent coupling.

Le Rossiniane, Opp. 119 and 121.
(***) RCA RK 1 0711 [ARK 1 0711]. Julian Bream (guitar)
SOR: *Grand sonata.*(***)

Giuliani's six *Rossiniane* were, as the title suggests, based on the operas of Rossini. One might expect the music to be witty and memorably tuneful, but that is not so. Even the accompanying notes admit that some of the music is boring, and indeed it is difficult to sustain one's interest here. The playing is first-class, of course, and the recording immaculate.

Sonata for violin and guitar.
*** CBS 40-76525 [Col. MT 34508]. Itzhak Perlman (violin), John Williams (guitar) – PAGANINI: *Cantabile* etc.***

Giuliani's *Sonata* is amiable enough though hardly substantial fare; but it is played with such artistry here that it appears better music than it is. The record-

231

ing is in need of more ambience, but sound is invariably a matter of taste, and there is no reason to withhold a strong recommendation. The tape transfer is of excellent quality.

Variations on a theme by Handel, Op. 107.
> *** CBS 40-73745. John Williams (guitar) – PAGANINI: *Caprice; Sonata* etc.**(*)

The *Variations* are on the theme known as *The Harmonious Blacksmith*. Their construction is guileless but agreeable, and they are expertly played and well recorded. This is only a very small part of a collection mostly devoted to music of Paganini. The transfer is clear, with no lack of immediacy.

Glazounov, Alexander (1865–1936)

Chant du ménestrel (for cello and orchestra). *Op. 71.*
> *** DG 3300 653 [id.]. Mstislav Rostropovich, Boston SO, Ozawa – SHOSTAKOVICH: *Cello concerto. No. 2.****

Glazounov's *Chant du ménestrel*, which dates from 1900, is an amiable four-minute piece and serves as an excellent fill-up to the *Second Concerto* of Shostakovich, which it precedes on Rostropovich's recording. The cassette transfer is of good quality, if lacking the last degree of immediacy of focus.

Violin concerto in A minor, Op. 82.
> (B) ** DG Heliodor 3348 170. Erica Morini, Berlin Radio Orch., Fricsay – BRUCH: *Concerto No. 1.***

Erica Morini's sweetly lyrical account of the Glazounov *Concerto* is eminently acceptable, even if it is no challenge to Heifetz's incomparable version (not available on tape). However, this is in every respect a pleasing and well-recorded performance which wears its years lightly (it was made in the late 1950s). There is an audible edit with a drop in pitch at one point, but otherwise there are no serious reservations. The transfer is first-class, clear and clean, with a natural image for the soloist and plenty of body and clarity in the orchestra.

The Seasons (ballet), *Op. 67; Concert waltzes Nos. 1 in D major, Op. 57; 2 in F major, Op. 51.*
> **(*) HMV TC-ASD 3601. Philharmonia Orch., Svetlanov.

Apart from the charming *Violin concerto*, *The Seasons* would seem to be Glazounov's strongest claim to the attention of posterity. It is an early work, first performed at St Petersburg in 1900, the choreography being by the famous Petipa. With colourful orchestration, a generous sprinkling of distinctive melody, and, at the opening of *Autumn*, one of the most virile and memorable tunes Glazounov ever penned, the ballet surely deserves to return to the repertoire. Svetlanov's account is most beautifully played and recorded. His approach is engagingly affectionate; he caresses the lyrical melodies persuasively, so that if the big tune of the *Bacchanale* has slightly less thrust than usual it fits readily into the overall conception. The richly glowing HMV recording has for the most part transferred well, wanting only the last degree of transient sparkle (the opening of the finale lacks absolute clarity of focus). The two *Waltzes* make a beguiling and elegant encore.

Gluck, Christoph
(1714–87)

Arias: *Alceste: Divinités du Styx.*
Armide: Le perfide Renaud. Iphigénie
en Aulide: Vous essayez . . . Par la
crainte; Adieu, conservez dans votre
âme. Iphigénie en Tauride: Non,
cet affreux devoir. Orfeo ed Euridice:
Che puro ciel; Che farò senza Euri-
dice. Paride ed Elena: Spiagge
amate; Oh, del mio dolce ardor; Le
belle immagini; Di te scordarmi. La
Rencontre imprévue: Bel inconnu; Je
cherche à vous faire.
> *** Philips 7300 440 [id.]. Janet
> Baker (mezzo-soprano), ECO,
> Leppard.

Helped by alert and sensitive accompaniments from Raymond Leppard and
the ECO, Janet Baker's singing of Gluck
is a revelation, completely undermining
any idea of something square or dull in
his inspiration. The most famous arias
bring unconventional readings – *Divin-*
ités du Styx deliberately less commanding, more thoughtful than usual – but the
rarities are what inspire Dame Janet most
keenly: the four arias from *Paride ed*
Elena, for example, are vividly contrasted
in their sharply compact form. Outstandingly beautiful recording, and the tape
quality is good too. The transfer has
plenty of life, but the high level of modulation has added a touch of hardness
to the voice and the overall quality is
marginally lacking in refinement. It may
well be that some copies (and some reproducers) will show this more than
others.

Goldmark, Karl
(1830–1915)

Violin concerto No. 1 in A minor, Op.
28.
> ** HMV TC-ASD 3408 [Angel
> 4XS 37445]. Itzhak Perlman,
> Pittsburgh SO, Previn – SARA-
> SATE: *Zigeunerweisen.***

Like Goldmark's *Rustic Wedding*
symphony, this, the first of his two violin
concertos, maintains a peripheral position in the catalogue. It is a pleasing and
warm-hearted concerto in the romantic
tradition that deserves to be better
known. It could not be more beautifully
played than it is here by Itzhak Perlman,
whose effortless virtuosity and lyrical
poise even challenge Milstein's aristocratic recording of the late 1950s. The
latter (not available on cassette) was
better balanced, for here the EMI engineers have placed Perlman very much in
the foreground, so much so that orchestral detail does not always register as it
should. The cassette produces warm, full-
blooded sound (even if the perspective is
no better than on the disc). The soloist is
clearly focused, but the climaxes could
reproduce more smoothly. This is very
charming and likeable music, however,
and Perlman plays it most winningly.

Gottschalk, Louis
(1829–69)

(i; ii) *Grande Fantaisie triomphale sur*
l'Hymne Nationale Brésilien, Op. 69
(arr. Adler); (i; iii) *Grande tarantelle*
(arr. Kay); *'The Union': Concert*
paraphrase on national airs, Op. 48
(arr. Adler); *Variations on the Por-*

tuguese national hymn (ed. List); (i; iv or i; v) *5 pieces for piano, four hands.*
(M) *** Turnabout KTVC 37034.
(i) Eugene List (piano); (ii) Berlin SO, Adler; (iii) Vienna State Opera Orch., Buketoff; (iv) Cary Lewis (piano); (v) Brady Millican (piano).

Louis Gottschalk was born in New Orleans of mixed German and French parentage. He studied music in Paris under Charles Hallé and then launched himself on a hugely successful career as composer/conductor/virtuoso pianist. He travelled widely (constantly moving thoughout Europe and the USA), appealing to a society whose musical taste was without pretensions. As a touring star (perhaps comparable in many ways to the pop stars of today) he was to some extent an isolated figure, cut off from serious musical influences. His subservience to public taste led to a continual infusion of national and patriotic airs into his scores, and his music retained a refreshing naïvety to the last.

This tape offers a distinguished anthology with obvious dedication from editors and executants alike. Fortunately the recording is of high quality, not rich, perhaps, but always vivid and sparkling. Eugene List (as we know from his Gershwin recordings) was just the man to choose as soloist: he is marvellously deadpan. Whether tongue-in-cheek or not he manages to sound stylish throughout and in *The Union concert paraphrase*, which is outrageous, he is superb. There is no space here to dwell on the felicities of Gottschalk's elegant vulgarity: if you fancy Lisztian bravura flavoured with an ingenuous period manner try this cassette. The transfer is notably clean and clear, catching the slightly brittle brilliance of the original recording admirably. Highly recommended.

Piano pieces: *Le Bananier* (chanson nègre); *The Banjo* (Grotesque fan-

tasie); *The Dying Poet* (méditation); *Grand scherzo; Le Mancenillier* (sérénade); *Manchega* (Étude de concert); *O ma charmante* (caprice); *Souvenirs d'Andalousie; Souvenir de Porto Rico; Suis moi; Tournament galop.*
**(*) Decca KSXC 6725 [Lon. 5-6943]. Ivan Davis.

Ivan Davis's collection of Gottschalk pieces is irresistible, for he is a fun pianist who warmly relishes – with just a hint of tongue-in-cheek – a consciously sentimental piece like *The Dying Poet*, and whose rhythmic pointing in *The Banjo* has fine wit. The result is that the composer's genuine imagination comes through far more keenly than in oversolemn performances. The recording is basically excellent, but in the transfer to tape the sound on side one (particularly in the opening piece) has become artificially bright and seems shallow and clattery, with a very dry bass. Side two is much better balanced yet retains its sparkle.

Gounod, Charles
(1818–93)

Faust: Ballet suite; Waltz.
(M) **(*) HMV TC-SXLP 30224 (without *Waltz*). Philharmonia Orch., Karajan – OFFENBACH: *Gaîté Parisienne****; WALDTEUFEL: *Les Patineurs.*⊛***
** DG 3300 215 [id.]. Berlin PO, Karajan – OFFENBACH: *Gaîté Parisienne.***
(M) ** Decca Jubilee KJBC 12 [Lon. 5-6780] (without *Waltz*). Orch. of the Royal Opera

House, Covent Garden, Solti – OFFENBACH: *Gaîté Parisienne.***

Although the HMV tape omits the *Waltz*, it includes instead an incomparable account of Waldteufel's *Skaters' waltz*. The HMV recording is not so sumptuous as the DG, but it is smooth and well balanced, and it matches Karajan's urbane approach to the music. The Philharmonia provide elegant, almost too polished playing, but the music's vitality is not lost. The transfer is most successful, crisp and clean. The recording is a trifle dry but has a compensating freshness.

On the DG tape the score is even more streamlined and the *Waltz* rather hard-driven. But the effect is vivid enough, for the transfer offers brilliant sound.

Bright, intense playing under Solti. There is some lack of poise and elegance, but the music-making certainly has sparkle and excitement. The transfer to tape offers admirably lively sound.

Gowers, Patrick
(20th century)

(i) *Chamber concerto for guitar;* (ii) *Rhapsody for guitar, electric guitars and organ.*

> (M) ** CBS Classics 40-61790. John Williams (guitar, (ii) and electric guitar), with (i) Chamber Ens., the composer (organ), Salmon; (ii) the composer (electric organ).

This coupling of two works previously available separately seems eminently sensible. Patrick Gowers is a highly intelligent and resourceful musician, and as long as you do not take it too seriously his *Chamber concerto* is crisp, enjoyable

music. It is complete with parts for alto saxophone, bass guitar, electric organ and drums, as well as string trio. The *Rhapsody* too has many imaginative effects, although it will not automatically enjoy universal appeal. Both are made to sound far more persuasive by the artistry of John Williams, a superb advocate. The recording is rather close, but that apart, the coupling can be recommended. On tape the sound is restricted in range, but pleasingly intimate and well balanced. The guitar reproduces naturally in spite of the lack of really crisp transients.

Grainger, Percy
(1882–1961)

Duke of Marlborough fanfare; Lisbon; My Robin is to Greenwood Gone; Shepherd's Hey; Piano duet: *Let's Dance Gay in Green Meadow;* Vocal and choral: *Bold William Taylor; I'm Seventeen come Sunday; Lord Maxwell's Goodnight; The Lost Lady Found; The Pretty Maid Milkin' her Cow; Scotch strathspey and reel; Shallow Brown; The Sprig of Thyme; There Was a Pig Went out to Dig; Willow Willow.*

> *** Decca KSXC 6410. Peter Pears (tenor), John Shirley-Quirk (bar.), Ambrosian Singers, ECO, Britten; Britten and Viola Tunnard (pianos).

This is an altogether delightful anthology, beautifully recorded and played by these distinguished artists. Grainger's talent was a smaller one than his more fervent advocates would have us believe, but his imagination in the art of arranging folk-song was prodigious. The *Willow song* is a touching and indeed haunting piece and shows the quality of

Grainger's harmonic resource. The opening fanfare too is strikingly original and so is *Shallow Brown*. Indeed each of the items here, with one or two exceptions, is obstinately memorable, and the recording is an extremely good one. The cassette transfer is smooth and truthful.

Granados, Enrique
(1867–1916)

Goyescas: Intermezzo.
(M) *** Decca Jubilee KJBC 50. New Philharmonia Orch., Frühbeck de Burgos – FALLA: *El amor brujo;* RAVEL: *Alborada* etc.***

A lusciously brilliant performance, superbly recorded by Decca, and the transfer is first-class.

12 Danzas españolas, Op. 37.
*** CRD CRDC 4021. Thomas Rajna (piano).

Granados's *Spanish dances* are by no means all lightweight. Their invention is of high quality, and their colour and atmosphere are persuasively revealed in these fine performances by Thomas Rajna. Some of them are familiar in transcriptions for orchestra or guitar, but the sensitive playing here shows that they truly belong to the piano. The recording is well balanced, and the transfer is clear if at times lacking in bloom at the top. But with adjustment of the controls a fully acceptable sound can be obtained. The slight hardening of tone is noticeable only at fortissimos.

Goyescas: complete.
*** Decca KSXC 6785 [Lon. 5-7009]. Alicia de Larrocha (piano).

A most distinguished issue: Alicia de Larrocha brings a special authority and sympathy to the *Goyescas*. Her playing has the crisp articulation and rhythmic vitality that these pieces call for, and the overall impression could hardly be more idiomatic in flavour. These performances are now the finest in the catalogue (displacing the disc-only recordings by Rajna on CRD and Mario Miranda on Saga). The sound is remarkably firm and secure, with a sonorous bass, rich and resonant. However, there is a slightly metallic tinge to the treble, bringing a hardening of timbre on fortissimos on the tape which is less apparent on disc. This may not be discernible on some machines.

Gregorian chant

Music for Lent and Easter: Sexagesima Sunday: *Introit* (Mode 1); *Tract* (Mode 8). 2nd Sunday in Lent: *Communion* (Mode 5). Palm Sunday: *Offertory* (Mode 8). Maundy Thursday: *Gradual* (Mode 5); *Offertory* (Mode 2). Easter Sunday: *Introit* (Mode 4); *Gradual* (Mode 2); *Alleluia* (Mode 7); *Sequence* (Mode 1). Easter Sunday: *Offertory* (Mode 4); *Communion* (Mode 6); *Antiphon* (Mode 6). Ascension: *Introit* (Mode 7); *Offertory* (Mode 1). Pentecost Sunday: *Introit* (Mode 8); *Sequence* (Mode 1). Corpus Christi Day: *Communion* (Mode 7).
(M) *** Turnabout KTVC 34070. Vienna Hofburgkapelle Choir, Schabasser.

The singing of this Viennese choir is strikingly beautiful. The mellifluous lines and positive phrasing afford the ear constant pleasure, especially when the style chosen discreetly varies the rhythmic flow and does not insist on an unending stream of even notes. The recording is very good indeed, and a selection from the liturgy surrounding Holy Week is a sensible idea for a single-tape issue. At medium price this cassette – which is well transferred – makes an excellent introduction to Gregorian music for the small collection.

Grieg, Edvard (1843–1907)

Piano concerto in A minor, Op. 16.
*** Decca KSXC 2173. Clifford Curzon, LPO, Fjeldstad – FRANCK: *Symphonic variations;* LITOLFF: *Scherzo.****
(*) Philips 7300 113 [id.]. Stephen Bishop-Kovacevich, BBC SO, Colin Davis – SCHUMANN: *Concerto.*(*)
*** Decca KSXC 6624. Radu Lupu, LSO, Previn – SCHUMANN: *Concerto.***(*)
*** Enigma K 453564. Judit Jaimes, LSO, Mata – SCHUMANN: *Concerto.***(*)
(*) Advent E 1051 (see p. xxiii) [id.]. György Cziffra, Budapest SO, György Cziffra Jnr – FRANCK: *Symphonic variations.*
(B) **(*) Pye ZCCOB 656. Shura Cherkassky, LPO, Boult – SCHUMANN: *Concerto.***(*)
(M) ** CBS Classics 40-61697. Nelson Freire, Munich PO, Kempe – TCHAIKOVSKY: *Concerto No. 1.***
** DG 923016 [id.]. Géza Anda, Berlin PO, Kubelik – SCHUMANN: *Concerto.***

** HMV TC-ASD 3521. Horacio Gutiérrez, LPO, Tennstedt – SCHUMANN: *Concerto.***
*(*) HMV TC-ASD 3133 [Angel 4xs 36899]. Sviatoslav Richter, Monte Carlo Opera Orch., Matačić – SCHUMANN: *Concerto.*(*)

The sensitivity of Clifford Curzon in the recording studio is never in doubt, and his has been a favourite performance of the Grieg *Concerto* over a long period. The couplings include the finest available account of Franck's *Symphonic variations.* Curzon's approach to the Grieg is not as individual as Bishop-Kovacevich's – there is a suggestion of self-effacement – but the performance has strength and power as well as freshness. The quality of the recording in this tape transfer entirely belies its age. The piano tone is splendidly rich and full-bodied, and the orchestra has fine detail and impact.

Stephen Bishop-Kovacevich and Colin Davis had already proved how fruitful is their recording collaboration in the music of Beethoven. Turning to two of the great romantic concertos they show an equal freshness and imagination. Whether in the clarity of virtuoso fingerwork or the shading of half-tone, Bishop-Kovacevich is among the most illuminating of the many great pianists who have recorded the Grieg *Concerto.* This is Grieg presented with bravura and refinement, the spontaneity of the music-making bringing a sparkle throughout. With excellent recording, this tape would have been first choice if the quality of the transfer were more lively. The sound is pleasingly warm and musical and the piano tone is good, but the low level of this early Philips transfer reveals comparatively little detail in the orchestra, although the sound here is fresher than in the Schumann coupling.

Radu Lupu is given a bold, brightly lit recording (one of Decca's very best, in fact) and his performance is enjoyable.

There is both warmth and poetry in the slow movement: the hushed opening is particularly telling. There is a hint of calculation at the coda of the first movement, but the performance – if without quite the individuality of Bishop-Kovacevich's – does not lack spontaneity, and the orchestral contribution under Previn is a strong one. The Schumann coupling is rather less attractive. However, the tape transfer is of demonstration quality, strikingly fresh and immediate, with an excellent balance and truthful piano timbre.

Judit Jaimes and the LSO under Eduardo Mata make a first-class partnership and provide a reading that is as sympathetic as it is strong and brilliant. The expressive playing from the soloist is matched by the orchestra; the slow movement is eloquent and the lyrical side of the finale is sensitively brought out. The recording is crisp and vivid, a little dry perhaps, but the piano timbre is full and natural. The transfer is excellent in every way. This is undoubtedly one of very finest available versions, and the coupling is only slightly less attractive.

György Cziffra recorded the Grieg *Concerto* on disc in the early days of stereo for HMV (ASD 301, coupled to the Liszt *Second Concerto*). This newer Advent recording also has an EMI (Pathé Marconi) source, but here, instead of the Philharmonia, an Eastern European orchestra is used, a step backwards, for the playing does not match that of the earlier version. The recording too is not particularly distinguished: the orchestral detail is unrefined and the piano tone bold but slightly brittle on top. That said, this is a fascinating and immensely rewarding performance. As before, Cziffra's reading is individual to the point of wilfulness, yet it never fails to be interesting and enjoyable. Moreover, the individuality is fully reflected in the imaginative orchestral accompaniment under Cziffra Junior; like the solo playing it is full of poetic touches, for example the hushed *pianissimo* just before the coda of the first

movement. The music comes vividly to life and both the slow movement and the lyrical episode of the finale carry moments of memorably expressive beauty to balance the impulsive bravura (heard at its most impressively extrovert in the first-movement cadenza). The Advent transfer is full-blooded and clear and makes the most of the recording's best points.

Cherkassky's account on Pye has an EMI source. It was originally issued on World Record Club and later on Music for Pleasure. Both are deleted now and at present this fine performance is not available on disc. It is coupled to a wonderfully poetic account of the Schumann *Concerto*. Cherkassky's reading of the Grieg is bold and extrovert: he is particularly commanding in the slow movement, which has considerable depth. The transfer to tape is generally clear, with plenty of warmth in the orchestral strings. The last degree of bloom is missing from the upper range, but the balance is good and this is an undoubted bargain.

The CBS reissue of the Nelson Freire/Kempe performance is unexpectedly attractive. The recording balance gives plenty of brilliance to the piano yet an agreeable ambient warmth to the orchestra. The orchestral playing itself is virile to match the degree of impetuosity shown by the soloist, and this is altogether a fresh, spontaneous account, essentially extrovert but not lacking a feeling for the score's gentler sensibilities. The tape transfer gives a bold piano image and a generally satisfactory orchestral balance, although a timpani roll does bring slight disturbance of the texture, because of the high transfer level.

Anda's performance is a fresh one, sometimes slightly mannered but in a quite agreeable way. The orchestral playing has plenty of life. The DG sound is well balanced, perhaps a trifle opaque in *tutti*, but with no lack of brightness in the treble. The piano timbre has real sparkle, notably in the finale, which is most attractively done.

Though Gutiérrez's Grieg is slightly better than the Schumann coupling, it is not competitive. There are some felicitous touches, but in terms of poetry and artistic finesse he offers no challenge to the finest of his rivals. The recording is good and the transfer of excellent quality, but not finer than the Enigma or Decca issues.

Richter is disappointingly wilful, drawing out many passages self-indulgently. With indifferent sound, this is not a competitive version.

(i) *Piano concerto in A minor, Op. 16;* (ii) *Peer Gynt* (incidental music): *Suite No. 1, Op. 46* (complete).

(M) ** Decca KCSP 170. (i) Peter Katin, LPO, Colin Davis; (ii) LSO, Fjeldstad – LITOLFF: *Scherzo.***

Peter Katin's early Decca performance has character and is completely unhackneyed. Katin seems to have reacted deliberately against the frequently made criticism that his performances are lightweight: there is no question of that comment applying here. If anything he seems loath to colour his playing with halftones, The outer movements are the most successful, with Davis's brisk and masterly conducting adding to the feeling of a new work. The slow movement does not relax quite enough, but there is the compensation that this is utterly unsentimental. With Fjeldstad's fine account of the *First Peer Gynt suite* (extracted from his Ace of Diamonds tape) and the Litolff *Scherzo*, this must be counted a keen competitor for its very positive qualities. The recording is excellent, and the cassette transfer, although an early issue, is a good one.

(i) *Piano concerto in A minor, Op. 16. Peer Gynt* (incidental music), *Op. 23: Morning; Anitra's dance; In the Hall of the Mountain King; Arab dance; Solveig's song.*

(B) *(*) Classics for Pleasure TC-

CFP 160. LPO, Pritchard, (i) with Peter Katin.

This is a modern recording and well transferred. Katin's approach to the *Concerto* is fresh, but this performance is somehow unmemorable, and the *Peer Gynt* music seems equally matter-of-fact.

2 Elegiac melodies, Op. 34; Holberg suite, Op. 40; 2 Norwegian melodies (In the style of a folksong; Cowkeeper's tune and Country dance), Op. 63; Peer Gynt (incidental music), *Op. 46: Death of Aase; Sigurd Jorsalfar* (suite), *Op. 56: Homage march.*

** Decca KSXC 6766. National PO, Boskovsky.

Though Willi Boskovsky presents an attractive Grieg coupling and the recording is both rich and brilliant, the actual performances are undistinguished, lacking the point and refinement one expects of this orchestra, formed largely for recording. Boskovsky's rhythmic flair is less apparent here than in his home repertory. The tape transfer is of excellent, lively quality.

2 Elegiac melodies, Op. 34; Norwegian melodies, Op. 63, No. 2: Cowkeeper's tune and Country dance; Wedding Day at Troldhaugen, Op. 65/6.

(M) *** Decca KCSP 91. London Proms Orch., Mackerras – SIBELIUS: *Finlandia* etc.***

Mackerras offers here a most pleasant selection of Grieg miniatures played with sympathy and taste. The *Cowkeeper's tune and Country dance* (which end one side of the tape) are particularly enjoyable, the gentle eloquence of the opening delightfully offset by the rustic pizzicatos of the dance. The *Elegiac melodies* too are played most beautifully, although the recording here is bright and clear rather than especially rich. Mackerras has arranged the programme to intersperse the Grieg items with some little-known but attractive music of Sibelius. This enjoyable lightweight cassette is a good deal more than the sum of its component parts. The tape transfer was one of Decca's early successes; the sound has plenty of life and colour. Recommended.

Holberg suite, Op. 40.

 *** Argo KZRC 670 [id.]. Academy of St Martin-in-the Fields, Marriner – DVOŘÁK: *Serenade.****

Marriner's richly lyrical account of the *Holberg suite* is very enjoyable indeed. The *Air* has a pleasing graciousness and the final *Rigaudon* plenty of sparkle, and with first-class sound and a good coupling this can be recommended, particularly as the tape transfer is of Argo's demonstration quality.

(i) *Holberg suite, Op. 40;* (ii) *Norwegian melodies, Op. 63, No. 2: Cowkeeper's tune and Country dance;* (iii) *Peer Gynt* (incidental music): *Suite No. 1, Op. 46; Suite No. 2, Op. 55: Solveig's song; Sigurd Jorsalfar* (suite), *Op. 56.*

 (M) **(*) Decca KCSP 421. (i) Stuttgart CO, Münchinger; (ii) London Proms Orch., Mackerras; (iii) LSO, Fjeldstad.

Fjeldstad's *Peer Gynt* items (taken from his fuller selection on KSDC 111) are distinguished by freshly refined playing and very good recording that seldom betrays its age in any way. The climax of *In the Hall of the Mountain King* is superb, and *Solveig's song* is phrased with disarming eloquence. The *Sigurd Jorsalfar suite* is equally fine, beautifully played and finely recorded. After this Münchinger's *Holberg suite* seems a trifle dour, though it is well played, and the recording is thinner here in the matter of string texture.

However, the *Cowkeeper's tune* is richly done and the *Country dance* makes an infectious close to the concert. Here the sound is first-rate. The cassette transfer is of the highest quality (slightly brighter than the LP).

Lyric suite, Op. 54: 4 Norwegian dances, Op. 35; Peer Gynt (incidental music), *Op. 23: Overture; Dance of the Mountain King's daughter; Norwegian bridal procession; Sigurd Jorsalfar* (suite), *Op. 56: Homage march.*

 (M) *** HMV TC-SXLP 30254. Hallé Orch., Barbirolli.

There are many characteristic touches in Barbirolli's Grieg anthology, and great warmth throughout. The *Lyric suite* is especially fine, and the complete set of *Norwegian dances* is also valuable. The Hallé were on good form when this compilation was recorded, and it is most welcome back in the catalogue at mid-price. Incidentally readers who already have recordings of the two *Peer Gynt suites* will notice that these excerpts are not included in them, which makes this issue doubly useful for filling in the gaps in a smaller collection. The transfer to tape is highly successful; the *Lyric suite* and *Peer Gynt* items offer demonstration quality, with a lovely bloom on the strings and a most agreeable warmth and bloom on the woodwind. There is ultimately some lack of brilliance in the *Homage march*, but this is nevertheless an excellent cassette. The *Norwegian dances* sound splendidly bright and vivid.

Lyric suite, Op. 54; Norwegian dance No. 2, Op. 35; Peer Gynt (incidental music), *Op. 23; Morning; Death of Aase; Anitra's dance; Ingrid's lament; In the Hall of the Mountain King.*

 **(*) Decca Phase 4 KPFC 4206. LSO, Black.

Stanley Black's performance of the *Peer Gynt* incidental music is generally lithe and pleasing. He sets a too careful tempo for *Morning* and does not quite solve the *accelerando* problems of *In the Hall of the Mountain King* with complete spontaneity; on the other hand the *Death of Aase* is shaped eloquently and *Ingrid's lament* has a fine passionate lyricism. The *Lyric suite* is especially successful: Black shows a feeling for line and colour, and again the listener has a feeling of the music's spring-like freshness. The best-known *Norwegian dance* makes an attractive bonus. The sound is rich and vivid, with sparkle as well as atmosphere, and generally the stereo is of Decca's superior quality, with a good cassette transfer (an early tape issue, but well done).

Lyric suite, Op. 54; Peer Gynt: Suites Nos. 1, Op. 46; 2, Op. 55.
(M) *(*) Supraphon 045374, Prague SO,. Neumann.

Neumann's approach is fresh but comparatively unromantic. He takes *Morning*, from the first *Peer Gynt suite*, faster than usual, and there is a distinct loss of atmosphere. However, the rest of the music is strongly characterized, even if the end result lacks individuality. The *Lyric suite* too is a vivid rather than a melting performance. Undoubtedly part of this effect is caused by the bright immediacy of the recording, which some may like for its presence and detail. However, a fairly strong treble cut is needed to prevent the upper strings from being fierce.

Peer Gynt (incidental music), *Op. 23:* complete.
(B) **(*) Pye ZCCOB 655. April Cantelo (soprano), RPO, Gibson.
(M) ** Philips 7317 009 [7310 017] (without *Overture* and *Dance of the Mountain King's Daughter*).

Adele Stolte (soprano), Leipzig Gewandhaus Orch., Neumann.

The Pye tape offers a recording originally issued by World Record Club and later reissued (on disc only) on Music for Pleasure's short-lived classical Fanfare label. Gibson's selection is complete and although he does not have the advantage of a chorus, April Cantelo's contribution is a striking one (she sings both *Solveig's song* and the *Cradle song* with appealing freshness). The performances generally show Gibson at his very best; they are spontaneous and full of character. The recording too offers rich string textures and brings out the warmth of the music-making. Although it lacks the very last degree of range and sparkle the transfer is well balanced and makes very agreeable listening. One single drum roll causes a moment where the refinement slips, but otherwise the quality is consistently excellent. This is a real bargain.

The Leipzig performances are warmly attractive, with a good soloist in Adele Stolte. The recording is over-reverberant, but pleasantly so. The cassette transfer is bass-heavy but can be successfully rebalanced with the controls. Readers will note that this selection omits two items. Barbirolli's cassette (EMI Studio 2 TC-TWO 269) is absolutely complete but is not Dolbyized.

Peer Gynt (incidental music): *Suites Nos. 1, Op. 46; 2, Op. 55; Prelude; Dance of the Mountain King's Daughter.*
(M) **(*) Decca Ace of Diamonds KSDC 111. LSO, Fjeldstad.

In its original form Fjeldstad's record was one of the really outstanding early Decca stereo LPs, and its reissue on an Ace of Diamonds tape makes an attractive purchase in spite of some over-modulation and a general tightening up of the treble. The LSO is very sensitive, and the tender string playing in *Solveig's song* is quite lovely. The conductor begins *In the*

Hall of the Mountain King rather slowly but builds up a blaze of excitement at the end and quite justifies his conception. The cassette is brilliantly transferred throughout and matches the LP in the rather tart upper-string timbre. But even so this is a vividly recommendable selection.

Peer Gynt: Suites Nos. 1, Op. 46; 2, Op. 55; 4 Norwegian dances, Op. 35.
   **(*) Philips 7300 513 [id.]. ECO, Leppard.

Leppard's tape is beautifully recorded, the sound at once spacious and sparkling. The music-making is fresh and has an air of thoughfulness which will appeal to many, especially as the orchestral playing is so good. However, there is occasionally just a hint of a lack of vitality: *In the Hall of the Mountain King*, for instance, opens slowly and atmospherically, then does not build up quite the head of steam one expects. The *Four Norwegian dances* are splendidly done, with playing of vigour and showing a fine sense of colour. The cassette transfer is of good quality but is marginally less refined than the equivalent LP.

Peer Gynt: Suites Nos. 1, Op. 46; 2, Op. 55; Sigurd Jorsalfar (suite), Op. 56.
   **(*) DG 3300 314 [id.]. Berlin PO, Karajan.

Highly expressive performances played with superlative skill and polish. Some may even feel that they are a little too expressive and that the simplicity and freshness of Grieg are somewhat lost to view. However, most people will merely be lost in admiration for the superb playing. The recording is extremely fine, and the transfer generally of superior quality. There is just a touch of muddiness with the entry of the bass drum at the climax of *In the Hall of the Mountain King*, and a hint of brashness in the *Sigurd Jorsalfar Homage march*.

(i) *Peer Gynt: Suites Nos. 1, Op. 46; 2, Op. 55;* (ii) *Sigurd Jorsalfar* (suite), *Op. 56: Homage march; Wedding Day at Troldhaugen, Op. 65/6.*
   (M) ** DG Privilege 3318 041. (i) Bamberg SO, Kraus; (ii) Nordmark SO, Steiner.

These performances are sensitive and well characterized. The orchestral playing is excellent, and the warm, slightly reverberant acoustic suits the music particularly well. On disc this coupling is somewhat marred by steely upper-string tone, but the cassette transfer is mellower. The focus of the muted strings in the *Death of Aase* is a little hazy, but otherwise the sound is agreeably smooth without the loss of inner detail, although the transients in the *Sigurd Jorsalfar march* are not very crisp. The music is attractively laid out, with one suite complete on each side and the extra item in each case acting as an encore. The quality seems slightly crisper on side two.

Peer Gynt: Suites Nos. 1, Op. 46; 2, Op. 55; 4 Symphonic dances, Op. 64.
   (M) ** HMV TC-EXE 190. Philharmonia Orch., Susskind.

Susskind's performances of the *Peer Gynt suites* are beautifully shaped and spaciously recorded. Both *Morning* and *Solveig's song* offer first-class string-playing. At the very beginning of the *Arab dance* the bass drum is only just audible, but this is the only miscalculation in an outstanding set of performances. The recording is somewhat less full in the *Symphonic dances* but still vivid, and Susskind's performances are very well characterized. He finds plenty of colour in Nos. 2 and 3 and the contrasts in No. 4 are made with the subtlety only possible with an orchestra of the calibre of the Philharmonia. The cassette transfer is particularly smooth and agreeable in *Peer Gynt*, a little less refined in the *Symphonic dances*.

Peer Gynt: Suites Nos. 1, Op. 46; 2, Op. 55. Songs: From Monte Pincio; Ich liebe dich; Lauf der Welt; The Princess; The Swan.

(***) CBS 40-76527 [Col. MT 34531]. Elisabeth Söderström (soprano), New Philharmonia Orch., Andrew Davis.

Bright, immediate recording goes with freshly thought performances of some of Grieg's most familiar music. A special attraction is the singing of Elisabeth Söderström, not only in *Solveig's song* but in the orchestral songs (some of them with Davis's instrumentation), which make a delightful and original fill-up. Unfortunately it is impossible to recommend the cassette transfer with any confidence. The copy we tried was coarse in orchestral tuttis and generally unrefined.

Peer Gynt: Suite No. 1, Op. 46; Suite No. 2, Op. 55: Ingrid's lament; Solveig's song.

(M) *** Decca Jubilee KJBC 16 [Lon. 5-6420]. Vienna PO, Karajan – TCHAIKOVSKY: *Nutcracker suite.****

Peer Gynt: Suite No. 1; Suite No. 2: Solveig's song.

*** Decca Phase 4 KPFC 4352 [Lon. 5-21142]. Boston Pops Orch., Fiedler – TCHAIKOVSKY: *Nutcracker suite.****

Karajan's selection is beautifully played, and the rich, clear recording is outstanding. The readings are broad in style, less individual perhaps than Fjeldstad's in his complete set, but not lacking in freshness. *Solveig's song* is particularly beautiful. The new Jubilee transfer is most successful, with plenty of sparkle and colour. With a slight treble reduction it approaches demonstration standard.

Fiedler's performance is direct, alive and spontaneous. It is recorded with ex-

ceptional life and vividness and is very enjoyable indeed. There are more tender accounts of *Solveig's song* available, but that is the only reservation, and the Tchaikovsky coupling is equally good. The cassette faithfully reflects the disc.

Violoncello sonata in A minor. Op. 36.

(M) (**) HMV TC-HQS 1398. Paul Tortelier (cello), Robert Weisz (piano) – SCHUBERT: *Arpeggione sonata.*(**)

Paul Tortelier's eloquent performance of Grieg's little-known *Cello sonata* is spoilt here by a miscalculated transfer. Immediately at the opening there is a degree of coarse harmonic distortion which is quite unacceptable.

Ballade, Op. 24; Holberg suite, Op. 40; Lyric pieces, Op. 43.

(M) ** Turnabout KTVC 34365. Walter Klien (piano).

For those who want to represent Grieg's piano music in their collection, this is an inviting recital. True the *Ballade* is a bit discursive at times, but Walter Klien plays most sensitively, and the recording, although not by any means outstanding, is acceptable. The transfer is clear and secure, but the treble response hardens under pressure (this is especially noticeable in the first and last movements of the *Holberg suite* and in the *Ballade*, which is more shallowly recorded than the rest of the music). Klien, however, finds ample colour in the piano's middle register.

Lyric pieces: Op. 12/1; Op. 38/1; Op. 43/1 and 2; Op. 47/2–4; Op. 54/4 and 5; Op. 57/6; Op. 62/4 and 6; Op. 65/5; Op. 68/2, 3 and 5; Op. 71/1, 3, 6 and 7.

⊛ *** DG 3300 499 [id.]. Emil Gilels (piano).

A generous selection of Grieg's *Lyric pieces*, from the well-known *Papillon*, Op. 43/1, to the less often heard and highly poetic set Op. 71, written at the turn of the century. On disc this excellently recorded survey is an alternative to Daniel Adni's complete box (not available on cassette), but Gilels's playing is of a wholly different order. Good though Mr Adni is, with Gilels we are in the presence of a great keyboard master whose characterization and control of colour and articulation are wholly remarkable. An altogether outstanding collection, which has transferred successfully to tape. The piano quality is admirably natural, although the level is not quite as high as it might be.

'Favourite composer': (i) *Piano concerto in A minor, Op. 16;* (ii) *Holberg suite, Op. 40;* (iii; iv) *Lyric suite, Op. 54;* (iii; v) *Peer Gynt: Suites Nos. 1, Op. 46; 2, Op. 55; Prelude; Dance of the Mountain King's Daughter; Sigurd Jorsalfar* (suite), *Op. 56.*
> (B) **(*) Decca KDPC 567/8. (i) Julius Katchen, Israel PO, Kertesz; (ii) Stuttgart CO, Münchinger; (iii) LSO; (iv) Black; (v) Fjeldstad.

All these performances are discussed above under their original couplings. They make an outstanding anthology. The only item below the remarkably high overall standard is Münchinger's rather unsmiling account of the *Holberg suite*. But this can be forgiven when the tapes are generously full and the *Peer Gynt* and *Lyric suites* are so successful; indeed Stanley Black's performance of the latter work is one of the more memorable items. On tape the sound matches the excellence of the discs (its imagery slightly brighter) except in the *Piano concerto*, where, for some reason, the treble seems accentuated, giving a slightly brash effect to the orchestral tuttis.

'Your kind of Grieg': (i–iii) *Piano concerto in A minor, Op. 16:* 1st movt; (iv) *Elegiac melody No. 2: The last spring, Op. 34; Holberg suite, Op. 40: Prelude;* (v) *Norwegian dance No. 2, Op. 35;* (vi; iii) *Peer Gynt suite No. 1, Op. 46: Morning; In the Hall of the Mountain King;* (v) *Sigurd Jorsalfar* (suite), *Op. 56: Homage march;* (i) *Lyric pieces: Wedding Day at Troldhaugen, Op. 65/6;* (vii) *Ich liebe dich.*
> (M) *(*) HMV TC-EXES 5006. (i) John Ogdon (piano); (ii) New Philharmonia Orch.; (iii) Berglund; (iv) Northern Sinfonia Orch., Tortelier; (v) Hallé Orch., Barbirolli; (vi) Bournemouth SO; (vii) Elly Ameling (soprano), Dalton Baldwin (piano).

Grieg was above all else a miniaturist, and his music easily fits into an anthology of this kind. It has been skilfully chosen, and all the performances except the first movement of the *Piano concerto* are distinctive. The recording, however, is only moderately good, not always as bright and fresh in quality as it should be. The transfer (on our copy) also showed a degree of pulsing unsteadiness of tone in two places, but this may not be common to later copies. Of course none of this is very noticeable in the car, where this sort of tape can be very useful.

Handel, George Frederick (1685–1759)

Concerti grossi, Op. 3/1–6.
> **(*) Enigma K 453551. Northern Sinfonia, Malcolm.
> (M) ** Turnabout KTVC 34103. Mainz CO, Kehr.

George Malcolm's performances are spirited and stylish and not lacking polish. The recording is vivid, but the forward balance of the oboes makes them sound rather larger than life and tends to reduce the dynamic range, although the contrasts of light and shade within the strings are effective. Rhythms are sometimes jogging rather than sprightly, but this is enjoyable music-making, and the transfer has plenty of life and detail.

Admirably stylish performances too from Kehr, with appropriate ornamentation not overdone, and excellent wind-playing to match the contribution from the strings. The recording is fresh yet full. A most successful cassette, and one that costs considerably less than the Enigma issue, which has slightly more refined sound, but is not preferable on every count.

Concerti grossi, Op. 6/1–12.
* CBS 40-79306. La Grande Écurie et la Chambre du Roy, Malgoire.

On the whole this is a disappointing set. Although the playing is often lively, at other times the phrasing is heavy and weighs down the music's impulse. The use of oboes in the earlier concertos adds colour but seems not to represent the composer's final intention. Much of the style here errs towards French elegance and for some reason the very famous melody in No. 12 is turned into a minuet. The decorations are not always convincing, but it is the lack of freshness in the overall presentation which is the greatest drawback. The grandeur of Handel's overall conception is only hinted at. On the tape the sound is very variable. One set tried was more consistent than another, where on each cassette side two seemed more vivid (but also harsher) than side one. The high level at times brings coarseness of grain to the sound, which is somewhat bass-heavy. The resonant acoustic tends to reduce the dynamic contrast.

(i) Concerti grossi, Op. 6, Nos. 3 in E minor; 4 in A minor; 8 in C minor; (ii) Music for the Royal Fireworks.
(M) ** DG Privilege 3335 269. Berlin PO, cond. (i) Karajan, (ii) Kubelik.

Karajan directs the performances of the Op. 6 Concerti grossi from the keyboard and so, while a large body of strings has been used in a reverberant acoustic, the continuo comes through very clearly, because the recording engineers have made it do so. The playing of the Berlin orchestra, it need hardly be said, is lively and polished, but the spirit of these great baroque concertos is not fully revealed, although there is much to admire. The recording is good but does not conceal the fact that the string tone is not of the most modern. Kubelik's Royal Fireworks music also uses a large orchestra, although the low-level transfer prevents the full body and presence of the original sound from coming over. Nevertheless if one turns the volume well up (which brings up the background hiss too), one achieves a fair impact, and the playing is again polished and spirited, although, like the Karajan Concerti grossi, it tends to add a nineteenth-century veneer to Handel's original intentions.

Harp concerto in F major, Op. 4/5; Concerto for lute and harp in B flat major, Op. 4/6; Concerto grosso in C major (Alexander's Feast); Water music: suites Nos. 1–3 (complete).
(B) **(*) Oiseau-Lyre KDPC 2 7056. Philomusica of London, Granville Jones or Dart, with Osian Ellis (harp), Desmond Dupré (lute), Thurston Dart (organ).

This cassette conveniently couples the contents of two highly recommended LPs. The recording is admirably fresh and only blots its copy-book in the most minor way at the very end of the Water

245

music, where in the third suite the high-level transfer produces a slipping of the overall refinement when the trumpets enter in one of Handel's more ambitious tuttis. Otherwise the robust yet clear quality gives much pleasure, and the stylish playing is matched by the scholarship of the preparation. The *Harp concerto* and the *Concerto for lute and harp* both come from the Op. 4 set of works for organ, but they are no less attractive in this alternative form, particularly as the recording of the soloists is so clearly focused. The balance is first-class. The sound in the *Alexander's Feast* concerto grosso is not quite so refined as in the concertos, but much of this enjoyable tape offers demonstration quality.

(i) *Oboe concertos Nos. 1 in B flat major; 2 in B flat major; Variant of No. 2 in B flat major; 3 in G minor. Solomon* (oratorio): *Arrival of the Queen of Sheba; Berenice* (opera): Overture.

> (M) **(*) Argo KZKC 2. Academy of St Martin-in-the-Fields, Marriner, (i) with Roger Lord (oboe).

This is an attractively planned collection, stylishly played. The *Berenice overture* is best-known for its famous minuet tune, but it is all attractive, and the *Oboe concertos* have a similar immediate appeal, their style predominantly lyrical. The cassette transfer is beautifully clear but benefits from a reduction of treble, which also restores the warmth to the orchestral tone. With such an adjustment it is possible to get a very sophisticated sound from this tape.

Oboe concertos Nos. 1–3; Concerto grosso in G major, Op. 3/3; (i) *Sonata a cinque in B flat major* (for violin, oboe and strings).

> ** Philips 7300 450. Heinz Holliger, ECO, Leppard, (i) with Kenneth Sillito (violin).

Holliger, being a creative artist as well as a masterly interpreter, does not hesitate to embellish repeats, and his ornamentation may overstep the boundaries some listeners are prepared to accept. His playing and that of the other artists in this recording is exquisite, and the Philips engineers produce a smooth and well-detailed recording. However, for the *Oboe concertos* many readers may prefer Roger Lord (see above), who eschews the exaggerated ornamentation in which Holliger indulges. The transfer is of high quality, smooth and natural in tone and balance, if a little lacking in transparency and sparkle.

Oboe concerto No. 3 in G minor; Organ concerto No. 7 in F major (The Cuckoo and the Nightingale); Concerto in D major for flute, violin and cello; Concerto in D minor for 2 violins and cello: Trio sonata in F major for oboe, bassoon and continuo.

> *** Telefunken CX 4.41270 [id.]. Vienna Concentus Musicus, Harnoncourt.

An entirely delightful collection of lightweight Handel, felicitously played and very well recorded, that will give great pleasure to any Handelian. The variety of the instrumentation is matched by the diversity of the composer's invention. The cassette transfer (made on chrome tape) is of first-class quality, producing most sophisticated sound, natural in balance.

Organ concertos Nos. 1 in G minor; 2 in B flat major; 3 in G minor; 4 and 5 in F major; 6 in B flat major, Op. 4/1–6; 13 in B flat major; 14 in A major; 15 in B flat major; 16 in D minor; 17 in G minor; 18 in B flat major, Op. 7/1–6.

> **(*) Telefunken MH 4.35282 [id.]. Herbert Tachezi (organ), Vienna Concentus Musicus, Harnoncourt.

Herbert Tachezi offers the Op. 4 and Op. 7 concertos complete, and the transfer is of high quality, using chrome tape. We are told in the accompanying booklet (which devotes a three-and-a-half-page essay to the problems of interpretation and performance but says nothing about the concertos themselves) that the ornamentation involved in these performances was essentially spontaneous and even varied from take to take. This may have made the accompanying orchestral group over-cautious, for they sometimes seem rather square. The scale of the music-making is relatively modest, creating an agreeable chamber-music atmosphere. However, at times one feels that the more robust and grander qualities of Handel's inspiration are played down. Tachezi's registration and decorative flourishes give consistent cause for pleasure; his unnamed organ is a splendid instrument and obviously well chosen for this repertoire. It makes a strong contrast with the 'authentic' string group, which at times produces a rather sombre colouring. Their rhythmic pointing can sometimes be agreeably lively too. The use of chrome tape brings a wide frequency range, refined detail and an open, spacious feeling to the sound itself. A treble cut will almost certainly be useful, and this smooths the occasional hint that the upper harmonics of this wide-ranging sound picture lack the last degree of purity. But when this is done the recording sounds very sophisticated and the background is virtually silent. The layout on two tapes does not seem quite ideal; if three had been used it would have been possible to have two works to each side.

Organ concerto No. 7 in F major (The Cuckoo and the Nightingale).
> (M) (**) Turnabout KTVC 34135. Helmuth Rilling (organ), Württemberg CO, Faerber – ALBINONI: *Adagio***; CORRETTE: *Concerto*; MOZART: *Sonata.*(**)

It is useful to have a medium-price version of *The Cuckoo and the Nightingale*, although the bird effects are played rather literally and without any special charm. The performance throughout is accurate and musical rather than imaginative. The cassette transfer is not one of Decca's best. The balance is rather lacklustre and the treble is not very bright.

Overtures: *Agrippina; Alcina; Belshazzar; Deidamia; Jephtha; Radamisto; Rinaldo; Rodelinda; Susanna.*
> (M) *** DG Privilege 3335 242. LPO, Karl Richter.

Richter is weighty, but his broadness of style is tempered by brilliantly alert orchestral playing, with allegros taken exhilaratingly fast. At the opening of *Alcina* one wonders if the sound is going to lack freshness, but the weightiness soon gives way to sparkling detail, and on side two this cassette often reaches demonstration standard. Those who admire the German tradition in Handel will find this partnership with a British orchestra fruitful and rewarding.

Music for the Royal Fireworks; Concerti grossi, Op. 3, Nos. 2 in B flat major; 5 in D major.
> (B) **(*) Classics for Pleasure TC-CFP 103. Virtuosi of London, Davison.

Music for the Royal Fireworks (original wind scoring); *Concertos Nos. 1 in F major; 3 in D major; Concerto a due cori No. 2 in F major.*
> **(*) HMV TC-ASD 3395 [Angel 4xs 37404]. LSO, Mackerras.

Music for the Royal Fireworks; Water music: suites Nos. 1–3 (complete).
> *** Argo KZRC 697 [id.]. Academy of St Martin-in-the-Fields, Marriner.

Music for the Royal Fireworks;

Water music: suite (original versions).

  (B) *(*) DG Heliodor 3348 169. Schola Cantorum Basiliensis, Wenzinger.

Royal Fireworks music: suite.

  (B) ** Philips Fontana 7328 612. Berlin Radio SO, Maazel – J. C. BACH: *Harp concerto;* HAYDN: *Symphony No. 101.***

Royal Fireworks music: suite; Water music: suite (both arr. Harty).

  (M) ** HMV TC-EXE 137. RPO, Weldon.

Royal Fireworks music: suite; Water music: suite (arr. Harty and Szell); *The Faithful Shepherd* (suite, arr. and ed. Beecham)*: Minuet; Xerxes: Largo* (arr. Reinhardt).

  (M) **(*) Decca KCSP 120 [Lon. 5-6236]. LSO, Szell.

Water music: suites Nos. 1–3 (complete).

  **(*) Oiseau-Lyre KDSLC 543. Academy of Ancient Music, dir. Hogwood (harpsichord).

  **(*) Philips 7300 060. ECO, Leppard.

  (B) **(*) Philips Fontana 7327 027. Concertgebouw Orch., van Beinum.

  ** HMV TC-ASD 3597 [Angel 4xs 37532] Prague CO, Mackerras.

  (M) ** DG Privilege 3335 137. Berlin PO, Kubelik.

Water music: suite (arr. Harty).

  (M) ** HMV TC-EXE 67 [(d) Angel 4xs 35948]. Berlin PO, Karajan – LEOPOLD MOZART: *Toy symphony* *(*); MOZART: *Ave verum; Serenade No. 13; German dance, K.605/3.***

Among the many fine cassettes of the *Royal Fireworks* and *Water music*, there are three that stand out from the others.

For those wanting a first-class tape combining both scores complete, the Argo issue by the Academy of St Martin-in-the-Fields in an obvious choice. Marriner directs the most sparkling account of the complete *Water music* yet to appear. All the well-loved movements we knew in the Harty suite come out even more refreshed than usual, and the rest is similarly stylish. Scholars may argue about some textual points, but even before the Leppard/ECO version this account by the Academy must stand at the head of the list. It is a substantial advantage that the cassette – unlike its rivals – also includes the complete *Fireworks music*. There Marriner's interpretation is more obviously controversial, for he deliberately avoids a weighty manner, even in the magisterial opening of the overture. But with superb, resonant recording this generous coupling makes very sound sense. The tape transfer has been very successfully managed at a high level, offering excellent detail and presence without loss of bloom.

Having purchased this admirable issue one can make a worthwhile supplement to it with the Mackerras recordings of the original wind score of the *Fireworks music*. Here is the work as Handel first conceived it. Mackerras originally recorded this version for Pye on the 200th anniversary of Handel's death, using an enormous band including twenty-four oboes, twelve bassoons and contra-bassoons, nine horns, nine trumpets, side-drums and three pairs of kettle-drums. Now HMV has attempted to present a comparable recording with the benefit of modern stereo. Once again the martial music is formidably impressive (even if the LSO horns are not here quite as thrilling as in that famous original recording – not available on tape). Although the HMV sound has a closer acoustic, the impact of this unique ensemble is vividly and powerfully caught. The *Concerto a due cori No. 2* is also impressive with its antiphonal wind effects, and the two other concertos with their anticipations of the *Fireworks music* make an apt fill-up. These massive sounds transfer to tape surprisingly well. The side-drums lack crispness of transients (a common fault with EMI tapes), but generally the quality is vivid with very little hint of strain, and there is some attractively fresh string and wind sound in the concertos on the second side.

The third special recommendation is a highly enjoyable account of the two Handel–Harty suites under George Szell, with Handel's *Largo* and the *Minuet* from Beecham's *Faithful Shepherd suite* thrown in for good measure. The orchestral playing throughout this tape is quite outstanding, and the strings are wonderfully expressive in the slower pieces. The horns too excel, and this makes a good bargain in the medium price-range. Apart from a hint of too high modulation at the very opening of the *Water music* and a similar short patch in the *Fireworks music*, neither of which is serious, this cassette offers outstandingly vivid quality and a high transfer level.

Of the other cassettes, the Classics for Pleasure coupling is crisply immediate, if slightly wanting in resonance. The playing is fresh and stylish but lacks weight in the *Fireworks music*. Even so this is very enjoyable, and the sound on the Classics for Pleasure cassette is fresh and clean, perhaps a little light in bass, but otherwise realistic. The dynamic range is not as wide as it might be, but there is no lack of light and shade, and side two often offers demonstration quality. This is certainly excellent value.

The playing of the Schola Cantorum Basiliensis, on Heliodor, shows a splendid feeling for the open-air style of the music, with crisp, buoyant rhythms. The use of original instruments in the *Fireworks music* brings a suitably robust effect (complete with less-than-perfect intonation), while a fuller version is used for the *Water music*. There is some stridency in the sound itself, added by the transfer, which the comparatively dry acoustic reveals only too readily, and on

side one there are one or two patches of congestion which a slightly lower transfer level would have avoided.

Maazel's *Suite* is attractively coupled. His tempi, however, are very brisk, and some may feel that the main allegro of the *Overture* is too fast. But with lively recording this tape certainly projects a feeling of animation.

Weldon's HMV coupling of the *Suites* is also strong in character. The RPO play persuasively, and the transfer is vivid and clear – although there are some curiously long silent spaces between some of the items, and there is a touch of over-modulation at the beginning of the *Water music*. The Szell tape offers more music than Weldon's and is preferable on grounds of performance too.

We turn now to cassettes of the *Water music* heard complete but uncoupled. The Academy of Ancient Music has made many recordings for Oiseau-Lyre but few more striking than this account of music well-known in less authentic renderings. Though it may come as a surprise to hear the familiar *Air* taken so fast – like a minuet – the sparkle and airiness of the invention are arrestingly caught. The timbres of original instruments are here aurally fascinating, with *vibrato*-less string tone never squeezed too painfully. It was with this work that the Academy made its Prom début in the summer of 1978, and the spirit of that occasion is matched by this performance, in which scholarship and imagination are happily joined. The transfer, however, is somewhat astringent in quality, and the upper partials are not always absolutely clean, which slightly affects the trumpets in the *Third Suite*.

Raymond Leppard and the ECO give elegant, beautifully-turned and stylish performances, with well-judged and truthful recording. The transfer to tape is generally smooth and pleasing, although on our copy there was some slight overloading when the horns were playing full out. This may have been cured in later copies. One must also not forget

249

Thurston Dart's admirable performance, available very reasonably priced
on a Double Decca tape (see above under
the *Harp concerto*).

Both the Kubelik and the van Beinum
versions use a full orchestra. With the
Berlin Philharmonic the playing is predictably fine, but Kubelik's manner is
sometimes a trifle stiff. The recording has
been freshened but is still rather thick in
texture, and on the rare occasions when
the harpsichord appears it is mouse-
sized. The cassette transfer is of generally
good quality, but it is not as successful as
the cheaper Fontana tape by Eduard van
Beinum and the Concertgebouw Orchestra. The Fontana recording, if resonant,
is splendidly warm and spacious, the orchestral soloists showing a strong sense
of personality. The balance allows the
harpsicord to come through without
making it sound ridiculous. There are not
many van Beinum recordings in the catalogue, but this one shows again what a
splendid conductor he was, finding
vigour and colour in Handel's allegros
and graciousness in the lyrical tunes. This
is most enjoyable and reasonably priced
too; and the cassette is a real bargain.

Mackerras is a lively Handelian, as
many recordings, including his HMV
version of the complete *Firework music*,
have shown; and his version of the *Water
music* is often elegant and gracious in its
phrasing, with spirited playing from the
wind. But there is a heavy quality in the
string tone (not only a question of the
resonant recording) which – especially
when heard in comparison with the version by the Academy of Ancient Music –
weighs the music down somewhat. The
sound, however, is rich and vivid, and the
HMV transfer is smooth and generally
well focused, so that some ears may
prefer this balance to the more astringent
qualities of the Oiseau-Lyre set. The
music is played in three suites, but the
sequence, with the G major suite coming
last, is less effective than when the D
major culmination (including trumpets)
is used.

Karajan favours a big-orchestra
sound, and originally the recording was
rich but slightly woolly. The face-lift has
made the strings sound rather out of
focus in the loudest moments, but the
performance is good of its kind and
should suit those who want the concert as
a whole. The transfer is of good quality
throughout.

VOCAL AND CHORAL MUSIC

Acis and Galatea (masque).
*** Argo к 114 к 22, Jill Gomez,
  Robert Tear, Philip Langridge,
  Benjamin Luxon, Chorus and
  Academy of St Martin-in-the-
  Fields, Marriner.
*** DG Archive 3375 004, Norma
  Burrowes, Anthony Rolfe
  Johnson, Martyn Hill, Paul
  Elliot, Willard White, English
  Baroque Soloists, Gardiner;
  Nicholas Kraemer (harpsi-
  chord).

The refinement and rhythmic lift of
the Academy's playing under Marriner
makes for a lively and highly engaging
performance of *Acis and Galatea*, marked
by characterful solo singing from a
strong team. The choruses are sung by a
vocal quartet (not the same singers) and
with warmly atmospheric recording the
result is a sparkling entertainment.
Robert Tear's tone is not always ideally
mellifluous (for instance in *Love in her
eyes sits playing*), but like the others he
has a good feeling for Handel style, and
the sweetness of Jill Gomez's contribution is a delight. The transfer, made at a
characteristically high level, has plenty of
range and detail, capturing the resonant
acoustic faithfully and placing soloists
and chorus in realistic perspective. There
is a slight lack of smoothness in the extreme treble, but this is marginal. Generally the sound is vivid and sophisticated
in quality. The layout is the same as on

the Archive set, two tapes with one act on each. The Decca leaflet, however, is much inferior to the DG booklet.

Some of John Eliot Gardiner's tempi are idiosyncratic (some too fast, some too slow), but the scale of performance, using original instruments, is beautifully judged to simulate domestic conditions such as there might have been in the first performance for the Duke of Chandos, with the vocal soloists banding together for the choruses. The acoustic is far drier than in the Argo version, and the soloists are less characterful, though more consistently sweet of tone. The authentic sounds of the English Baroque Soloists are finely controlled so as not to offend unprepared ears too blatantly, and those who prefer *vibrato*-less string tone for music of this period should certainly select this. The DG transfer is made at a somewhat lower level than the Argo, producing an extra smoothness in the treble, although there is no lack of life to the voices. The orchestra, in particular, has splendid presence and detail. The soloists are balanced well forward and the perspective in this sense less suggestive of a concert (or stage) performance than the Argo balance. But the overall effect is undoubtedly sophisticated, as is the presentation, with a handsome booklet and each tape in its own removable plastic box and a particularly attractive design on the liner leaflet.

Anthem for the Foundling Hospital; Ode for the birthday of Queen Anne.
 *** Oiseau-Lyre KDSLC 541. Judith Nelson, Emma Kirkby, Shirley Minty, James Bowman, Martyn Hill, Daivd Thomas, Choir of Christ Church Cathedral, Oxford, Academy of Ancient Music, Preston.

Two splendid examples of Handel's occasional music make an excellent coupling, superbly performed and recorded. The *Ode* is an early work, written soon after Handel arrived in England. It has its

Italianate attractions, but it is the much later *Foundling Hospital Anthem* on the reverse which is much the more memorable, not just because it concludes with an alternative version of the *Hallelujah chorus* (sounding delightfully fresh on this scale with the Christ Church Choir) but because the other borrowed numbers are superb too. An extra tang is given by the accompaniment on original instruments. The transfer is of excellent quality, with plenty of bloom as well as clarity and a very good choral focus, considering the degree of resonance. There is plenty of body too, as the *Hallelujah chorus* readily shows. A highly recommendable issue in every way.

Coronation anthems (for the coronation of King George II and Queen Caroline): 1, *Zadok the Priest;* 2, *The King shall Rejoice;* 3, *My Heart is Inditing;* 4, *Let Thy Hand be Strengthened.*
 **(*) Argo KZRC 5369. King's College Choir, ECO, Willcocks; Thurston Dart (harpsichord).
 ** Enigma K 453542. Huddersfield Choral Society, Northern Sinfonia Orch., Pritchard; Keith Rhodes (organ).

The King's performances on Argo have transferred very well to tape, the resonance satisfactorily controlled with plenty of bloom on the sound. The relatively lightweight effect of the choir may not be to all tastes: the texture is bright rather than massive, but has an agreeable cutting edge which brings out the words incisively. Although the large-scale ceremonial element is not emphasized, these performances have held an honoured place in the disc catalogue for some years and the cassette seems likely to provide equal enjoyment.

For those who like these anthems sung by a big choir the Enigma performances are attractively crisp and direct, and the transfer to tape produces bright sound, the orchestral strings perhaps needing a little taming. The choral tone has plenty of weight and attack in fortissimos, but at more modest volume levels the detail and outline are less clearly focused. But the balance is good.

'Great choruses': Coronation anthem: Zadok the Priest. Israel in Egypt: But as for his people; Sing ye to the Lord. Judas Maccabaeus: See, the conquering hero comes; Sing unto God; Hallelujah, amen. Messiah: For unto us a Child is born; Hallelujah. Samson: Awake the trumpet's lofty sound; Let their celestial concerts all unite. Saul: Welcome, welcome, mighty King; David his ten thousands slew; How excellent Thy name. Xerxes: Holy art Thou (Largo).

(M) ** CBS 40-61139. Mormon Tabernacle Choir, Philadelphia Orch., Ormandy.

There is only one Mormon Tabernacle Choir and they sing Handel with a unique fervour. With Ormandy in charge these performances are extremely vivid; *See, the conquering hero* and the *Messiah* items are especially good. The religiose version of the *Largo* (with totally different words from the original) is acceptable when the presentation is so eloquently sincere. Considering the amplitude of the sound, the CBS transfer is surprisingly good; the choral focus is never crisp, but it is quite adequate and only becomes fuzzy at the opening of *Zadok the Priest*.

Judas Maccabaeus (oratorio): complete.

*** DG 3376 011 [id.]. Felicity Palmer, Janet Baker, Paul Esswood, Ryland Davies, John Shirley-Quirk, Christopher Keyte, Wandsworth School Choir, ECO, Mackerras.

Judas Maccabaeus may have a lopsided story, with a high proportion of the finest music given to the anonymous soprano and contralto roles, Israelitish Woman (Felicity Palmer) and Israelitish Man (Janet Baker), but the sequence of Handelian gems is irresistible, the more so in a performance as sparkling as this one under Charles Mackerras. Unlike many, particularly those which in scholarly fashion attempt to restore Handel's original proportions, this holds together with no let-up of intensity, and though not everyone will approve of the use of boys' voices in the choir (inevitably the tone and intonation are not flawless) it gives an extra bite of character. Hearing even so hackneyed a number as *See, the conquering hero* in its true scale is a delightful surprise. The orchestral group and continuo sound splendidly crisp, and when the trumpets come in at *Sound an alarm* the impact is considerable, just as it must have been for the original Handelian audience. Though some may regret the passing of the old-style fruity singing in the great tenor and bass arias, Ryland Davies and John Shirley-Quirk are most stylish, while both Felicity Palmer and Dame Janet crown the whole set with glorious singing, not least in a delectable sequence on the subject of liberty towards the end of Act 1. The recording quality is outstanding, ideally fresh, vivid and clear, and the tape transfer is of demonstration quality, indistinguishable from the discs, with the solo voices sounding particularly natural and the upper range of the spectrum spacious and free.

Arias: *Judas Maccabaeus: Father of Heaven. Messiah: He was despised; O thou that tellest. Samson: Return, O God of hosts.*

(M) *** Decca KCSP 531. Kathleen Ferrier (contralto), LPO, Boult – BACH: *Arias.****

The tape issue of Kathleen Ferrier's outstanding recital of Bach and Handel arias, where the new stereo-recorded accompaniment was lovingly superimposed over the old mono orchestral contribution, is most welcome. The transfer to tape has been well done; the voice is naturally caught, although there is some lack of dynamic range.

Lucrezia (cantata). Arias: *Ariodante: Dopo notte. Atalanta: Care selve. Hercules: Where shall I fly? Joshua: O had I Jubal's lyre. Rodelinda: Dove sei, amato bene? Xerxes: Ombra mai fù (Largo)*.

   *** Philips 7300 345. Janet Baker (mezzo-soprano), ECO, Leppard.

Even among Janet Baker's recordings this Handel recital marks a special contribution, ranging as it does from the pure gravity of *Ombra mai fù* to the passionate commitment and supreme coloratura virtuosity in *Dopo notte* from *Ariodante*. Leppard gives sparkling support, and the whole is recorded with natural and refined balance. The tape transfer is first-class in every way.

Messiah (oratorio): complete.

   (M) *** HMV TC-SLS 774. Elizabeth Harwood, Janet Baker, Paul Esswood, Robert Tear, Raimund Herincx, Ambrosian Singers, ECO, Mackerras.

   **(*) Philips 7699 009 [id.]. Heather Harper, Helen Watts, John Wakefield, John Shirley-Quirk, Chorus, LSO, Colin Davis.

   **(*) Argo K 18 K 32 [id.]. Elly Ameling, Anna Reynolds, Philip Langridge, Gwynne Howell, Chorus, Academy of St Martin-in-the Fields, Marriner.

   (M) ** Decca K 104 K 33. Joan Sutherland, Grace Bumbry, Kenneth McKellar, David Ward, LSO Chorus, LSO, Boult.

   ** Advent EE 1061 (see p. xxiii) [id.]. Diana Hoagland, Barbara Wallace, Pamela Gore, George Livings, David Evitts, Handel and Haydn Society Chorus and Orch., Dunn.

   *(*) DG 3371 009 [id.]. Helen Donath, Anna Reynolds, Stuart Burrows, Donald McIntyre, John Alldis Choir, LPO, Karl Richter.

Few recordings of much-repeated works have made such an impact as Colin Davis's account of *Messiah*. With the help of the recording manager, Harold Lawrence, he took a completely new look at the score, attempted to give an authentic reading, and as a result made everyone hear the music with new ears. Initially the traditionalist may be worried by the very fast speeds Davis tends to adopt for choruses, but a fine professional body (unnamed) surmounts every technical difficulty with ease. The chorus is always fresh, and, thanks to Davis, the rhythmic bounce of such choruses as *For unto us* is really infectious. Even *Hallelujah* loses little and gains much from being performed by an authentic-sized chorus, and the incisive choral singing makes amends at every point for lack of 'Huddersfield-style' massiveness. Excellent contributions from all four soloists, particularly Helen Watts, who following early precedent is given *For He is like a refiner's fire* to sing instead of the bass, and produces a glorious chest register. With Davis's briskness there is everything to be said for the inclusion of all the numbers traditionally omitted. Unfortunately the transfer is of somewhat uneven quality. The upper strings have a tendency to lack body and need a degree of filtering if they are not to sound papery. The choruses at times also have too great a ratio of consonant articulation to richness of tone. However with care the controls can be used to take the edge off the sound and produce a good balance. Parts of the set provide excellent quality, notably the *Hallelujah chorus.*

When the HMV version under Mackerras was first issued, only a month or two after the Davis set, it seemed to come into direct competition, to its disadvantage. But relistening confirms that the Mackerras view can give equal pleasure, and on tape it is preferable. The choruses on HMV have not the same vitality as on Philips, but they have a compensating body and richness. There is indeed much to commend in the Ambrosian/ECO set, not least the modest price. One could well argue that Basil Lam's edition of the score goes deeper than Davis's in pursuing the authentic approach, but for the layman the main difference will be that, more than Davis, Mackerras adopts Handel's generally forgotten alternative versions. So the soprano aria *Rejoice greatly* is given in its optional 12/8 version, with compound time adding a skip to the rhythm. A male alto is also included among the soloists, and he is given some of the bass arias as well as some of the regular alto passages. Among the soloists Janet Baker is outstanding. Her intense, slow account of *He was despised* – with decorations on the reprise – is sung with profound feeling. Good recording, rather warmer and less bright than the rival Philips. Like Davis, Mackerras includes all the numbers traditionally omitted. The HMV tape transfer is undoubtedly more successful than the Philips set; the sound is somewhat variable but is always good and often very good indeed.

The finest *recording* of *Messiah* on tape, perhaps not surprisingly, is the Argo set. The idea behind Neville Marriner's attractive version was to present *Messiah* as nearly as possible in the text followed in its first London performance in 1743. So the refiner's fire 'of the contralto has no rushing to it, for that graphic passage was introduced later in Handel's revisions, and as in the Mackerras set on HMV the skipping 12/8 version of *Rejoice greatly* is followed

instead of the usual one. The losses are as great as the gains, but the result has unusual unity, thanks also to Marriner's direction. His tempi in fast choruses can hardly be counted as authentic in any way, for with a small professional chorus he has gone even further than Colin Davis in lightening them, and has thus made possible speeds that almost pass belief. Purist doubts tend to be dissipated by the overall sense of fantasy, and though Anna Reynolds's contralto is not ideally suited to recording, it is otherwise an excellent band of soloists, and in any case Miss Reynolds sings *He was despised* most movingly on a thread of sound. Vivid recording, and the tape transfer is of demonstration quality.

Boult's Decca set dates from 1961 but does not sound its age. Indeed the extremely vivid tape transfer projects the performance with admirable detail and bloom, and only very occasionally does the refinement slip marginally in the choral focus. (Side one seems fractionally less clean than the rest of the set: this is most noticeable in *And He shall purify.*) However, in featuring Joan Sutherland in the soprano role the producer created problems. She alone pays any attention to the question of whether or not to use ornamentation in the repeats of the *da capo* arias. What she does is mostly in good taste, and her sense of style usually saves the situation when there is any doubt; but none of the other singers does anything more than give us the notes as they stand in the score. Grace Bumbry produces a pleasant but somewhat invariable timbre, not always too secure in intonation. McKellar's tenor contribution lacks something in dramatic vitality, and the same may be said of Ward (who is a better Handel singer than McKellar). Chorus and orchestra sound well under Boult's distinguished baton; but *Messiah*, for all the importance of its choruses, ultimately stands or falls by its soloists.

The Advent recording is spaced over two tapes, with the first hour and a half on one (all of Part 1 and the first eleven numbers of Part 2) and the final fifty-five minutes on the second. The transfer is of good quality, wholly without distortion, but the level is fairly modest and does not bring with it the widest upper range possible with chrome tape. However, with a slight bass cut the balance is excellent and the sound rich (solo voices and orchestral strings are pleasingly natural) and sonorous. There is, however, little feeling of spectacle. Both orchestrally and vocally the performance is conceived on concerto grosso lines, with a small chamber group to accompany the vocal solos, and a fuller ripieno for the choruses. The soprano role is shared by two quite different voices, one lighter and more attractive than the other, and it must be said that although all the solo singing is quite accomplished (the contralto is weakest) the male soloists are stronger than the ladies. *He was despised*, for instance, is eloquent, but not memorable, and *I know that my Redeemer liveth* (which, like *Rejoice greatly,* is rather backwardly balanced) is light in manner, paced slightly quicker than is traditional, although pleasantly decorated. All the soloists provide a certain amount of ornamentation (near the very opening the tenor gives a rather nice flourish on *Comfort ye*), and for the most part it is judicious and effective. The chorus is small and sings with an attractive purity of style; but the results are neither incisive nor very robust (and are not helped by the recording, which is rather flabby at times). The over-riding impression is cosy, although pleasing. The edition used (prepared by Dr Alfred Mann) seeks to create the scale and authenticity of the composer's original intentions (*For He is like a refiner's fire* is given to the contralto), but because of the fairly complacent tempi and the warm resonance of the recording, the overall effect is warmly traditional, although the overture opens with an unexpected lightly dotted rhythm. A booklet prepared for use with the recording, including libretto and notes (which we have not seen), is available from the publishers for an extra $2.

For their English recording of *Messiah* DG chose one of Germany's favourite conductors. Maybe it is a comment on national preferences, but to English ears Richter's direction is unrelievedly dull, and the fine singing of the choir and soloists hardly has a chance to make its point. The transfer – made at a comparatively low level – does not help to add life to the music-making; it is acceptable but not one of DG's best.

Messiah: highlights.
>   *** Argo KZRC 879 (from above set cond. Marriner).
>   ** Decca KSXC 6540. Joan Sutherland, Dermot Coleman, Huguette Tourangeau, Werner Krenn, Tom Krause, Ambrosian Singers, ECO, Bonynge.
>   ** DG 3300 643 (from above set cond. Richter).
>   (B) * Classics for Pleasure TC-CFP 40020. Elsie Morison, Marjorie Thomas, Richard Lewis, Huddersfield Choral Society, Royal Liverpool PO, Sargent.

Messiah: choruses.
>   ** HMV TC-CSD 3778. King's College Choir, Academy of St Martin-in-the-Fields, Willcocks.
>   ** Argo KZRC 872 (from above set cond. Marriner).

A highlights tape is perhaps the best way to sample the Marriner performance with its fresh sound, splendid solo and choral singing, and superb recording. The tape transfer is first-class and only wants a slight trimming of the treble to produce a most realistic balance. The selection is generous.

Bonynge's complete recording is not available on cassette, so his selection too is valuable as a sampler of his exuberant way with Handel's masterpiece. As in the Davis complete set the tempi of the choruses are often very fast, and the overall result is most refreshing. Among the soloists the one disappointment is Huguette Tourangeau. Hers is a most remarkable voice for opera, but it is less well suited here. Werner Krenn and Tom Krause sing musically and with plenty of vigour when required. The ornamentation is striking throughout, although Sutherland – sounding fresher than in her earlier 1961 recording – sings *I know that my Redeemer liveth* with no trills at all. The cassette transfer is very good on side one, but lacks the last degree of refinement in the more strenuous moments on side two, although the quality remains fully acceptable.

Even though it seems perverse to recommend a selection from a performance where the overall direction lacks vitality to English ears, the high-level transfer of the highlights from Richter's set produces admirably vivid sound, much more successful than the complete version. The choruses in particular are given plenty of freshness and bite.

Many will undoubtedly want a sampler of Sir Malcolm Sargent's traditional account of *Messiah*. This contains some fine solo singing, notably from Elsie Morison and Richard Lewis, but the choruses are disappointing, heavy in style and recorded in a curiously muffled way which cannot entirely be the fault of the singing itself. Moreover the tape transfer is not a success, with fuzzy choral sound and examples of the unsteady pulsing in the texture which afflicted some early transfers.

One wonders what Handel would have thought of the idea of listening to his *Messiah* choruses without the contrasting arias in between. Of course the choruses themselves are not without variety of style, as is well shown by the King's collection, recorded within their famous acoustic, which brings special colour to the choral sound yet allows the words to remain clear. The music-making on this tape lacks the sheer zest of the Marriner recording but is enjoyable in a different way. The cassette transfer is of good qual-

ity, catching the acoustic without clouding the detail, although side one seems marginally crisper in focus than side two.

KZRC 872 offers a most generous selection, with some twenty-five items. Although choruses predominate, various solo recitatives and one or two duets are also included to provide introductions and a degree of contrast. The light choral textures and the pace of the music-making are emphasized in a collection of this kind, and it is a pity that the tape transfer has not a crisper focus. The quality is perfectly acceptable, but the choral tone lacks incisive freshness and that is certainly not the fault of the singing, for the sound on both the complete set and the highlights tape (KZRC 879) is preferable.

OPERA

Rinaldo: complete.
*(**) CBS 40-79308. Carolyn Watkinson, Ileana Cotrubas, Jeanette Scovotti, Paul Esswood, Charles Brett, Ulrik Cold, Le Grande Écurie et la Chambre du Roy, Malgoire.

The vigour of Malgoire's direction of an opera which plainly for him is very much alive, no museum-piece, will attract many who normally steer clear of Handel opera, particularly in performances like this which use authentic instruments. The elaborate decorations on *da capo* arias are imaginatively done; but, most effectively, the famous *Cara sposa* is left without ornamentation, sung beautifully by the contralto Rinaldo, Carolyn Watkinson. The finest singing comes from Ileana Cotrubas, but under Malgoire the whole team is convincing. The recording is basically bright and spacious, and this adds to the impression of vigour; the magic sounds associated with the sorceress Armida are well conveyed, as in the arrival of her airborne chariot. Needless to say, the story about the crusader Rinaldo hardly matters at all, Handel's invention is such a delight. The CBS transfer is fresher and has more range than some recordings from this source. The continuo detail is clearly focused and the voices have plenty of life. However, at times the high loud notes produce a peaking effect, and the upper register of the recording is not always clean. When the trumpets enter towards the end of the opera, they are not very comfortably recorded and in the work's closing sections the orchestral sound coarsens generally. The box provided with the tapes has a flimsy cardboard inner shell which soon disintegrates, and no libretto is included: instead the purchaser is invited to write to Paris for one.

Vocal collection

Arias: *Acis and Galatea: I rage . . . O ruddier than the cherry. Alexander's Feast: Bacchus ever fair and young. Orlando: O how dark the path we follow. Samson: Honour and arms. Theodora: Go, my faithful soldier.*

(M) ** HMV Greensleeve TC-ESD 7059. Owen Brannigan (bass), Handel Opera Society Chorus, Philomusica of London, Farncombe – MOZART: *Opera arias.***

Owen Brannigan's style, both in Handel and in Mozart, can readily be criticized (intrusive aitches in florid divisions and so on), but the positive character of this singer who was one of the most endearing of his generation comes out well in this lively collection, the genial nature of the vocal personality readily projected. The vivid, high-level transfer gives the voice plenty of presence and body, although the choral sound is not always completely refined.

COLLECTIONS

'*Favourite composer*': (i) *Organ concerto No. 2 in B flat major, Op. 4/2.* (ii) *Royal Fireworks music: suite; Water music: suite* (arr. Harty and Szell). *The Faithful Shepherd: Minuet* (arr. Beecham). (iii; iv) *Solomon: Arrival of the Queen of Sheba.* (ii) *Xerxes: Largo* (arr. Reinhardt). (v) *Coronation anthem: Zadok the Priest. Messiah:* highlights: (vi) *Ev'ry valley;* (vii) *O thou that tellest;* (vi) *For unto us a child is born; I know that my Redeemer liveth; The trumpet shall sound; Hallelujah chorus.* (iii; viii) *Rodelinda: Dove sei (Art thou troubled).*

(B) *** Decca KDPC 551/2. (i) Karl Richter (organ), CO; (ii) LSO, Szell; (iii) Academy of St Martin-in-the-Fields; (iv) Marriner; (v) King's College Choir, ECO, Willcocks; (vi) Joan Sutherland (soprano), Kenneth McKellar (tenor), David Ward (bass), LSO Chorus, LSO, Boult; (vii) Kathleen Ferrier (contralto), LPO, Boult; (viii) Bernadette Greevy (contralto), cond. Leppard.

'*The world of Handel*': (i; ii) *Music for the Royal Fireworks: Overture. Water music: Air; Hornpipe. Solomon: Arrival of the Queen of Sheba.* (iii) *Coronation anthem: Zadok the Priest. Judas Maccabaeus: See, the conquering hero comes. Messiah:* (iv) *He was despised;* (v) *Hallelujah chorus.* (vi) *Samson: Let the bright Seraphim.* (i; vii) *Acis and Galatea: I rage . . . O ruddier than the cherry.* (i; viii) *Rodelinda: Dove sei (Art thou troubled).* (ix) *Xerxes: Ombra mai fù (Largo).*

(M) *** Decca KCSP 448. (i) Academy of St Martin-in-the-Fields; (ii) Marriner; (iii) Handel Opera Society Chorus and Orch., Farncombe; (iv) Kathleen Ferrier (contralto), LPO, Boult; (v) LSO Chorus, LSO, Boult; (vi) Joan Sutherland (soprano); (vii) Forbes Robinson (bass), dir. Ledger; (viii) Bernadette Greevy (contralto), cond. Leppard; (ix) Kenneth McKellar (tenor), Royal Opera House, Covent Garden, Orch., Boult.

These are both excellent anthologies, selected with skill, and to some extent, but not entirely, covering the same ground. The performances are matched by the excellence of the recording, and whether the double- or single-tape format is chosen the investment will be worthwhile. The transfers are of excellent quality.

'The glory of Handel': (i; ii) Concerto grosso in B minor, Op. 6/6: Musette. (i; iii) Royal Fireworks music: Overture. (iv) Saul: Dead march. (i; iii) Water music: Overture; Hornpipe. (v) Harpsichord suite No. 5 in E minor: Air and variations (Harmonious Blacksmith). (iv: vi) Judas Maccabaeus: See, the conquering hero comes. (vii) Messiah: Hallelujah chorus; I know that my Redeemer liveth.
(M) ** DG Privilege 3335 247. (i) Berlin PO; (ii) Karajan; (iii) Kubelik; (iv) ECO, Mackerras; (v) Li Stadelmann (harpsichord); (vi) Wandsworth School Choir; (vii) Helen Donath (soprano), John Alldis Choir, LPO, Karl Richter.

A well-balanced collection on this DG Privilege tape, showing not just the German way with Handel but the British view too. The selection is well made, and the generally excellent performances are matched by good recording, although the choruses lack something in sharpness of focus.

'The popular Mr Handel': Alcina: Entrée; Il ballo. Ariodante: Dream music. Berenice: Overture. Faramondo: Overture. Messiah: Overture; Pastoral symphony. Saul: Dead march. Scipione: March. Solomon: Arrival of the Queen of Sheba. Water music: Lento; Hornpipe; Air.
(M) ** HMV Greensleeve TC-ESD 7031. Bournemouth Sinfonietta, Montgomery.

A somewhat cosy mélange of Handelian tit-bits, all attractively tuneful and smoothly played if without the alert stylishness the St Martin's Academy bring to this repertoire. The approach has more in common with Sir Thomas Beecham's lollipops, although the playing displays affection rather than wit. The lack of crisp pointing in the Arrival of the Queen of Sheba is characteristic of the approach; on the other hand the Dead march from Saul has charm in the scoring presented here. The recording is warm, and as the transfer has not a very striking range in the treble this tape makes agreeable background listening.

'Your kind of Handel': (i; ii) Organ concerto No. 7 in F major (The Cuckoo and the Nightingale); (iii) Royal Fireworks music: Minuet. Water music: Allegro deciso. (iv; v) Coronation anthem: Zadok the Priest. (vi) Joshua: O had I Jubal's lyre. Messiah: (vii; viii) O thou that tellest; (ix; viii) I know that my Redeemer liveth; (x) Pastoral symphony; (iv; viii) Hallelujah chorus. *Solomon:* (xi) *Arrival of the Queen of Sheba;* (iv; v) *From the Censer curling rising.* (xii) *Xerxes: Ombra mai fù (Largo).*

(**) HMV TC-EXES 5007. (i) Simon Preston (organ); (ii) Bath Festival Orch., Menuhin; (iii) RPO, Weldon; (iv) Ambrosian Singers; (v) Menuhin Festival Orch., Menuhin; (vi) Lucia Popp (soprano), ECO, Fischer; (vii) Janet Baker (contralto); (viii) ECO, Mackerras; (ix) Elizabeth Harwood (soprano); (x) Academy of St Martin-in-the-Fields, Willcocks; (xi) RPO, Beecham; (xii) Fritz Wunderlich (tenor), Bavarian State Opera Orch., Muller-Kray.

An attractive collection – the roster of artists indicates that the musical quality is never in doubt – is let down by the variable technical competence of the transfers. The choruses tend to be rough and poorly focused (*Hallelujah*, which ends the collection, is the best of them). The vocal solos, however, come off well, and one especially welcomes the inclusion of Fritz Wunderlich to sing the famous *Largo* and Sir Thomas Beecham to direct *The Arrival of the Queen of Sheba*.

Harty, Hamilton
(1879–1941)

With the Wild Geese (symphonic poem).
(***) HMV TC-ASD 2400. Scottish National Orch., Gibson – GERMAN: *Welsh rhapsody*; MacCUNN: *Land of Mountain and Flood*; SMYTH: *The Wreckers overture.*(***)

With the Wild Geese, written in 1910 for the Cardiff Festival, is a melodramatic piece about the Irish soldiers fighting on the French side in the Battle of Fontenoy. The ingredients – a gay Irish theme and a call to arms among them – are effectively deployed, and although the music does not reveal a strong individual personality, it is carried by a romantic sweep which is well exploited here. Unfortunately this was one of EMI's transfers where a high level was achieved by narrowing the dynamic range, and the orchestral textures are unrefined as well.

Haslam, David
(20th century)

Juanita, the Spanish lobster.
** CRD CRD 4032. Johnny Morris (narrator), Northern Sinfonia Orch., the composer – PROKOFIEV: *Peter and the Wolf.***

Johnny Morris's tale of how Juanita, the Spanish lobster, gets caught and rescued in the nick of time has more narrative detail than story-line. It is supported by a colourful and undoubtedly tuneful score by David Haslam, but the music is not really distinguished enough for re-hearing by way of a recording, although it is not without charm. The narrator is given some songs to provide variety within the spoken text, and they have something of an *Alice in Wonderland* flavour. Johnny Morris's personality is well projected by an excellent recording and the performance is first-rate. The transfer too is immaculate.

Haydn, Josef
(1732–1809)

(i) *Fortepiano concertinos: in C major, H.XIV/3; in C major, H.XIV/11; in C major, H.XIV/12; in G major, H.XIV/13; in F major, H.XVIII/F2; Fortepiano concerto in C major, H.XVIII/10.* (ii) *Organ concertos Nos. 1 in C major, H.XVIII/1; 2 in C major, H.XVIII/8; 3 in C major, H.XVIII/5.* (i) *Divertimentos: in C major, H.XIV/C2; in C major, H.XIV/7; in C major, H.XIV/8; in C major, H.XIV/9.* (i) *Sonata in E flat major for violin, cello, 2 horns and fortepiano.*

(M) ** Turnabout KTVC 37103/5 (available separately). (i) Ilse von Alpenheim (fortepiano), Instrumental Ens.; (ii) Franz Lehrndorfer (organ), Württemberg CO, Faerber.

It is curious that such an ambitious set of early – and frankly immature – Haydn should be issued on cassette when there is so much of his later music still not available. These are competent, spirited performances of essentially lightweight music, which taken in small doses is agreeable enough. The tinkly fortepiano is well balanced, and the recordings are good if not distinguished. The three organ concertos are certainly successful and Franz Lehrndorfer is quite a persuasive soloist, although the sound is clear rather than rich. The most interesting work here is the *Sonata in E flat*, a kind of piano trio with ad lib horns – and they are by no means always conventional horn parts – which is given an extremely vigorous performance (although the sound is two-dimensional). The transfers are quite vivid and perhaps cover some of the rough edges of the original recording.

(i) *Horn concerto No. 2 in D major;* (ii) *Oboe concerto in C major;* (iii) *Trumpet concerto in E flat major.*

(M) *(*) Turnabout KTVC 34031. Stuttgart Pro Musica Orch., Reinhardt, with (i) Karl Arnold; (ii) Friedrich Milde; (iii) Walter Gleisle.

A good performance of the *Trumpet concerto* from Gleisle, strong and bold and played with obvious technical confidence. The acoustic of the recording is a trifle over-blown, and in the *Horn concerto*, which is a much less impressive performance, the rather coarse horn tone tends to boom reverberantly. However, the inclusion of the *Oboe concerto* to some extent restores the balance. This is most beautifully played by Friedrich Milde, who is nicely recorded; but here the upper strings of the orchestra are not too cleanly caught by the engineers. In other respects the accompaniments are good throughout.

Piano concerto in D major.

(M) ** Turnabout KTVC 34073. Alfred Brendel, Vienna CO, Angerer – HUMMEL: *Piano concerto in B minor.***(*)

Piano concertos in D major; in G major.

*(*) HMV TC-ASD 3128. Arturo Benedetti Michelangeli, Zurich CO, de Stoutz.

Curiously detached playing from Michelangeli diminishes the appeal of this issue. The great pianist adds to the range of the keyboard and thickens various chords. The piano tone could be fresher, and despite the contribution of the Zurich orchestra under Edmond de Stoutz, which is lively enough, this issue cannot be accounted an unreserved success. The transfer of side one – at a high level – is first-class, in spite of the curiously reverberant piano image, but at the beginning of side two the acoustic blurs into marginal distortion at the beginning, tending to clear up as the tape progresses.

Brendel's performance of the D major work is a neat small-scale reading, with crisp enunciation from the pianist and an attentive accompaniment. The recording is bright and fresh, and it has transferred well to cassette.

(i) *Trumpet concerto in E flat major.*
6 Allemandes (for small orchestra).
  ** Argo KZRC 543 [id.]. Academy of St Martin-in-the-Fields, Marriner, (i) with Alan Stringer – M. HAYDN: *Horn concerto* etc.**

Alan Stringer favours a forthright, open tone, and no doubt there is a conscious attempt to simulate the primitive instrument Haydn would have known. The orchestral accompaniment has a contrasting finesse and reminds us that there is an elegant side of this concerto, particularly in the gracious slow movement. The transfer is of good quality, both in the *Concerto* and in the six beautifully played dances which Argo offer as a bonus. However, the range of the recording is not quite so open at the top as in the Michael Haydn coupling.

Violin concerto No. 1 in C major; Sinfonia concertante in B flat major (for oboe, bassoon, violin, cello and orchestra).
  ** DG 3300 907. Pinchas Zukerman (violin), with the Los Angeles PO.

A useful cassette coupling since neither the *Concerto* nor the magnificent *Sinfonia concertante* is otherwise obtainable in this format. Zukerman gives suave readings of both works, and in his hands the *Sinfonia concertante* seems a trifle bland. The recordings are eminently serviceable, and the tape transfer is smooth

and well balanced, if lacking the last degree of range and sparkle.

Violoncello concerto in D major.
  (M) **(*) HMV TC-SXLP 30273. Jacqueline du Pré, LSO, Barbirolli – MONN: *Concerto.***(*)
Violoncello concertos (i) *in C major;* (ii) *in D major.*
  (M) ** Philips 7317 115. Maurice Gendron, with (i) LSO, Leppard; (ii) Lamoureux Orch., Casals.

It is a pity that HMV did not couple Jacqueline du Pré's performances of the two Haydn *Cello concertos* together for this reissue. She recorded the C major work – by now well accepted in the canon after its exciting rediscovery – rather earlier with her husband, Daniel Barenboim, and this is not available on cassette. With Barbirolli to partner her, the style here is even more romantic, and though purists may object, the conviction and flair of the playing are extraordinarily compelling. The recording is full and well balanced, but the high-level transfer has produced some minor lack of refinement, most noticeable in the orchestral upper strings. However, this is not serious and can be smoothed, for the recording has plenty of range.

Gendron's account of the C *major Concerto* is highly musical and is sensitively accompanied. In the D *major Concerto* he is right on form, and the stylishness of his phrasing, coupled to complete security of intonation, makes for an admirable performance of this attractive concerto, which can be recommended very highly. Pablo Casals's sympathetic handling of the orchestral contribution plays no little part in making this performance the success it undoubtedly is. The transfer is lively but the orchestral sound has rather 'tizzy' strings, and the upper partials of the solo cello seem similarly emphasized.

261

The Seven Last Words of Christ (original orchestral version).

 *** HMV TC-ASD 3451. Academy of St Martin-in-the-Fields, Marriner.

Marriner directs performances of Haydn's great sequence of slow movements in the orchestral version which completely give the lie to the idea that consistently slow tempi make for lack of variety. Marriner's way is both deeply felt and stylish, while the Academy plays with customary warmth and polish. Excellent, full recording too. Marriner with his finely chosen tempi makes a formidable case for regarding this original version of the score as even finer than those for string quartet, piano and accompanied chorus. The transfer is sophisticated, with plenty of detail and glowing wind and string textures.

Symphonies Nos. 22 in E flat major (Philosopher); 23 in A major; 24 in D major.

 *** DG 3300 885. Prague SO, Klee.

Numerically consecutive but sharply contrasted, this group of early symphonies is particularly attractive, with the *Philosopher* leading the way in the sharpest originality. The concertante flute in the slow movement of No. 24 is most attractive. Klee is particularly successful in the brilliant finales, and the string playing is superbly refined throughout. The transfers are very successful; the quality is good on side one but at the side-turn the level rises, increasing the presence and liveliness of the sound still further. The minuet of No. 23 sounds splendid, and the finale has remarkable presence: the sound here is of outstanding quality, demonstrating just how good a cassette can be. This same vividness is retained in No. 24, and the concertante section in the slow movement featuring the solo flute is superbly recorded.

Symphonies Nos. 22 in E flat major (Philosopher); 55 in E flat major (Schoolmaster).

 **(*) Philips 7300 560. Academy of St Martin-in-the-Fields, Marriner.

Very good performances, generally well recorded. The *Philosopher* comes off very well but is not to be preferred to Klee's DG version, which has the advantage of more brilliant sound in its tape version. The *Schoolmaster* is nicely characterized; there is a hint of blandness in the second movement, but the performance as a whole gives undoubted pleasure. However, the level of transfer is low here, and the openings of both works are somewhat subfusc. The recording is basically well balanced and natural, but loses some of its life and inner detail compared with the disc, which is fresher in the treble.

Symphonies Nos. 25 in C major; 26 in D minor (Lamentatione); 27 in G major; 28 in A major.

 (M) *** Decca Ace of Diamonds KSDC 457. Philharmonia Hungarica, Dorati.

Four delectable, exhilarating symphonies, including one masterpiece, *Lamentatione*, later than the others (1768 as against 1764–5, a formidable interval when Haydn was developing so fast). The D minor darkness of *Lamentatione* has one thinking back as well as forward, with Bachian chorale-like echoes in the first two movements, 'No Haydn symphony is more telling in its violent expression', says H. C. Robbins Landon. No. 28 brings an extraordinary slow movement with fanfares on high muted violins interrupting a rich G-string melody. Infectiously energetic performances, and the first-class cassette transfer is every bit the equal of the disc.

(i) *Symphonies Nos. 43 in E flat major (Mercury); 59 in A major (Fire);* (ii)

String quartet No. 17 in F major, Op. 3/5: Serenade.
*** Philips 7300 524 [id.]. (i) Academy of St Martin-in-the-Fields, Marriner; (ii) Italian Qt.

No. 59 is the earlier of the two symphonies, dating from the late 1760s. No. 43 receives an elegant, fresh performance, with polished string playing and a splendid feeling of vitality. The recording is musically balanced and detail nicely transparent. The transfer is a good one, with fresh upper strings and a general bloom on the orchestral textures. The harpsichord comes through without being too insistent. The famous *Serenade* (not really by Haydn at all) makes a delightful encore piece, agreeably following the end of Symphony No. 59.

Symphonies Nos. 44 in E minor (Trauer-symphonie); 49 in F minor (La Passione).
⊛ *** Philips 7300 561 [id.]. Academy of St Martin-in-the Fields, Marriner.
Symphonies Nos. 44 and 49; Overture: Armida.
**(*) DG 3300 708 [id.]. ECO, Barenboim.

Superlative playing from Marriner and the Academy: even amongst their many fine Haydn couplings this stands out. The wonderfully expressive string phrasing of the opening *Adagio* of No. 49 is superbly contrasted with the genial and buoyant rhythms of the second movement *Allegro*. There is some excellent horn-playing in both works, almost self-effacing in its delicacy. But perhaps the highlight of this splendid coupling is the tender way Marriner shapes the radiantly elegiac slow movement of No. 44, which Haydn is reported to have chosen for performance at his funeral (hence the title). A discreet harpsichord continuo is used in both symphonies. The contrast between

repose and restless vitality which is at the heart of both these works is the hallmark of the performances, which are recorded with characteristic Philips naturalness and glow. The cassette transfer, made at quite a high level, is very well judged and is of outstanding quality, and there are excellent notes. The tape cannot be too highly recommended.

Barenboim's performances are beautifully played but are perhaps a little soft-centred. The expressive quality of the opening *Adagio* of No. 49 is richly caught, and the *Allegro di molto* which follows is vigorously pointed; but the overall impression of over-refinement persists. The recording is of DG's finest quality and the transfers are good, offering warm sound and fine detail. There is very little difference in sound between this and the equivalent LP.

Symphonies Nos. 48 in C major (Maria Theresia); 85 in B flat major (La Reine).
**(*) Philips 7300 536. Academy of St Martin-in-the-Fields, Marriner.

Both these symphonies have regal titles; the festive C major work is perhaps the more stately. Marriner gives fresh and in every way lively performances that have many sensitive touches, yet are not free from a certain blandness. The slow movement of *La Reine*, for example, is just a shade too fast and undercharacterized to grip the listener, and the trio of the minuet could do with more personality. Much the same can be said of the *Maria Theresia symphony*, but there is no denying the musicianship of the playing and the refined quality of the Philips recording. The sound quality has a pleasingly warm acoustic and a totally realistic perspective. Despite the reservations these are eminently enjoyable performances, and the cassette sound is almost indistinguishable from the disc.

263

Symphonies Nos. 82 in C major (The Bear); 83 in G minor (La Poule).
- (M) *** Decca Ace of Diamonds KSDC 482. Philharmonia Hungarica, Dorati.

Symphonies Nos. 84 in E flat major; 85 in B flat major (La Reine).
- (M) *** Decca Ace of Diamonds KSDC 483. Philharmonia Hungarica, Dorati.

Symphonies Nos. 86 in D major; 87 in A major.
- (M) *** Decca Ace of Diamonds KSDC 484. Philharmonia Hungarica, Dorati.

These splendid performances of the *Paris symphonies* are most welcome on cassette, particularly as the transfers are highly sophisticated. The level is high and if there is a slight edge at times on the upper strings, a treble reduction and comparable increase of bass soon restore the bloom to the sound, and the woodwind detail is delightful. The performances themselves almost always outshine their direct rivals on disc, the playing consistently fresh and stylish, the recording balance always vivid. Even the least-known of these symphonies, No. 84, has a first movement of the most delicate fantasy, and the whole set can be warmly recommended.

Symphonies Nos. 87 in A major; 103 in E flat major (Drum Roll).
- **(*) Philips 7300 589 [id.]. Concertgebouw Orch., Colin Davis.

Ten years separate these two symphonies, and although No. 103 is deservedly a favourite, a special interest of this issue is the earlier work, written in 1785 and intended by Haydn to preface his *Paris* set. The imaginative structure of the first movement, in which repeats are marked not only for the exposition but for the development too, is matched by the songful cantilena of the *Adagio* with its concertante woodwind, operatic in style. Then after the minuet (with an attractive oboe solo in the trio) comes a finale of great vitality and formal compression. The work obviously fires Davis's imagination, and he secures most refined string playing in the first movement, robust and delicate by turns, and deliciously balanced wind solos in the *Adagio*. The finale is splendidly alert. The account of No. 103 is hardly less persuasive. Davis's conception is of the highest order of sensitivity and imagination, almost in the Beecham tradition. Phrasing is the soul of music-making and Davis draws from the great Dutch orchestra playing that exhibits both delicacy and vitality and phrasing that breathes naturally. The mysterious opening drum roll is followed by genially growling lower strings, and the conductor's obvious feeling for the work's atmosphere is matched by his lilting treatment of the second subject of the allegro. The variations which form the slow movement are spaciously and imaginatively done, and altogether this is one of the finest accounts ever recorded of this popular work. The sound is rich and detailed and it is a pity that the tape transfer (very good indeed in No. 87) produces some clouding of texture in the tuttis of the *Drum Roll*. But for most listeners this will not be serious enough to interfere with enjoyment and we cannot disallow a third star.

Symphonies Nos. 88 in G major; 96 in D major (Miracle).
- **(*) HMV TC-ASD 3328. LSO, Previn.

Sparkling performances from Previn of both symphonies; the pointing and attention to detail, matched by the genial atmosphere, bring in No. 96 a Beechamesque touch to the music-making. The finales have real wit, and the concertante element of No. 96 is delightfully brought out. The broad, expressive style in the glorious *Adagio* of No. 88 brings warmth without self-indulgence. Originally the cassette transfer produced coarse sound in the climaxes caused by too high a level of modulation. Recent copies have shown considerable improvement, the sound generally warm and vivid, the refinement slipping only marginally. Two different copies sampled were not absolutely consistent in this respect.

Symphonies Nos. 88 in G major; 99 in E flat major.
**(*) Philips 7300 534 [id.]. Concertgebouw Orch., Colin Davis.

Davis secures wonderfully precise ensemble from the Concertgebouw players, and in spite of the ample acoustic (which tends to present a comparatively large-scale view of Haydn) the clarity of the playing brings a remarkable degree of inner detail. The manner is direct and fresh in both symphonies, and the one disappointment here is the slow movement of No. 88. Davis's moulding seems too calculated, and he rarely allows his players to go below *mezzo forte*, so that the music's expressive richness tends to elude the performers. The recording is rich but has no lack of brightness, and the transfer is generally successful, though weighted rather heavily in the bass.

Symphonies Nos. 91 in E flat major; 103 in E flat major (Drum Roll).
(B) *** DG Heliodor 3348 147. Bavarian Radio SO, Jochum.

Jochum, coupling No. 91 with the *Drum Roll* in an excellent recording at bargain price, offers warmth, humanity and vitality. The Bavarian orchestra plays superbly, and those wanting either symphony need really look no further. The recording has remarkable detail and freshness, and the transfer to tape is of very high quality, perhaps a trifle dry in the bass but with no lack of bloom on the strings and wind. This is highly recommendable.

Symphonies Nos. 92 in G major (Oxford); 104 in D major (London).
**(*) Philips 7300 593 [id.]. Academy of St Martin-in-the-Fields, Marriner.

Alert, intelligent and musicianly performances of the *Oxford* and *London symphonies*, reflecting the generally high standard of this series and its continuing freshness. The recorded sound is natural and well balanced too, and this is thoroughly recommendable. The transfer is smooth, with good detail in *piano* passages and a fine bloom on the wood-wind. The level is modest and in *tutti* the orchestra is slightly less crisp than on the equivalent LP, but the difference is marginal.

Symphonies Nos. 93 in D major; 94 in G major (Surprise); 95 in C minor; 96 in D major (Miracle); 97 in C major; 98 in B flat major; 99 in E flat major; 100 in G major (Military); 101 in D major (Clock); 102 in B flat major; 103 in E flat major (Drum Roll); 104 in D major (London).
(M) *** Decca K 89 K 64. Philharmonia Hungarica, Dorati.

Dorati and the Philharmonia Hungarica, working in comparative isolation in Marl in West Germany, carried through their monumental project of recording the complete Haydn symphonies with not a suspicion of routine. These final masterpieces are performed with a glowing sense of commitment, and Dorati, no doubt taking his cue from the editor, H. C. Robbins Landon, generally chooses rather relaxed tempi for the first movements – as in No. 93, which is just as deliciously lilting as in Szell's masterly version (not available on cassette). In slow movements Dorati's tempi are on the fast side, but only in No. 94, the *Surprise*, is the result really controversial. Though an extra desk of strings has been added to each section, the results are authentically in scale, with individual solos emerging unforcedly against the glowing acoustic, and with intimacy comes extra dramatic force in sforzandos. A magnificent set in almost every way. On tape the sound is highly sophisticated in its detail and bloom, with fresh, resilient string sound and glowing woodwind. The body of the recording is matched by its transparency, which only slips a fraction momentarily in the 'military' sections of No. 100. The only snag is the ham-fisted presentation, which apportions three symphonies to each cassette, so that in each case the middle symphony is split between the two sides. The booklet too could have used a larger type-face to advantage.

Symphonies Nos. 94 in G major (Surprise); 96 in D major (Miracle).

**(*) Philips 7300 594 [id.]. Academy of St Martin-in-the-Fields, Marriner.

Another splendid issue in the remarkably satisfying Academy series of the mature Haydn symphonies. The freshness of the playing is matched by the natural warmth of the recordings. There is most delightful woodwind detail in No. 96 (the oboe solo in the trio of the minuet is a joy) and the genially resilient rhythms in the first movements are matched by the lightness of the finale. No. 94 has a particularly fine performance of the variations which form the slow movement (the 'surprise' itself most effective). The recording is well up to Philips' high standard and the transfers are of generally excellent quality with fractionally less refinement in No. 94 than 96.

Symphonies Nos. 94 in G major (Surprise); 101 in D major (Clock).

*** DG 3300 628. LPO, Jochum.

(M) *** Decca KCSP 494. Philharmonia Hungarica, Dorati.

(M) ** DG Privilege 3335 289 [923033]. Berlin PO, Richter.

Jochum's performances derive from the complete set of *London symphonies* that DG released here on disc in 1973, the *Surprise* having appeared the previous year as a trailer. These are marvellously fresh, crisp accounts of both symphonies, well recorded. The transfers are smooth and warm, with vivid string tone and the woodwind detail nicely delineated, yet with the bloom on the sound remaining fresh.

In Decca's cheapest price-range, the coupling of Dorati's versions of the *Surprise* and the *Clock* makes an attractive sampler for his series, though, as mentioned above, the *Surprise* with its brisk slow movement is one of his more controversial readings. The cassette transfer is of first-class quality, the sound slightly crisper in Symphony No. 94, slightly warmer and richer (if with marginally less sparkle) in No. 101.

Karl Richter's Privilege coupling is more sober. The playing is first-class, of course, but the direction is rather straitlaced. The recording is excellent and the transfer, made at a fairly high level, is full-bodied and lively, if sometimes a little thick in the bass.

Symphonies Nos. 96 in D major (Miracle); 98 in B flat major; 99 in E flat major; 104 in D major (London).

** Advent F 1003 (see p. xxiii) [id.]. Little Orch. of London, Leslie Jones.

Leslie Jones was among the pioneers in recording Haydn symphonies in their proper scale and featuring a harpsichord continuo. Although at some points this may be distracting, the recording balance does not exaggerate the harpsichord. Jones's interpretations are sound and understanding, and if the playing of the Little Orchestra of London is sometimes not as polished as it might be, it is almost always lively and enthusiastic. The recording quality is bright and reasonably fresh, although it seems a little dated now. It has to be admitted that these (originally Nonesuch) recordings of the late sixties have been rather superseded; the Dorati versions are immensely superior. The transfers are clear and clean, although there are one or two disturbing examples of pre- and post-echo at the beginnings and ends of movements. All four symphonies are placed on a double tape, two on each side, with a decent pause between each work.

Symphonies No. 99 in E flat major; 100 in G major (Military).
*** DG 3300 402 [id.]. LPO, Jochum.

Fast as Jochum is in outer movements, the rhythm is superbly controlled, above all in the final *Presto* of No. 100, where the triplets are miraculously well defined. In the spacious *Adagio* of No. 99 Jochum inspires radiant playing in the reprise. Excellent recording and an outstanding cassette transfer, fresh and clear.

Symphonies Nos. 100 in G major (Military); 103 in E flat major (Drum Roll).
**(*) Philips 7300 543 [id.]. Academy of St Martin-in-the-Fields, Marriner.

These are first-class performances, with beautifully sprung rhythms and excellent detail. The atmosphere at the opening of the *Drum Roll* is wonderfully caught, and the first movement's second subject shows the fine pointing and lightness of touch which distinguish the music-making throughout. The recording is sophisticated in balance and natural in timbre, although the moments of percussive spectacle in the *Military symphony* are not very crisp in definition.

Symphony No. 101 in D major (Clock).
(B) ** Philips Fontana 7328 612. Vienna SO, Sawallisch – J. C. BACH: *Harp concerto*; HANDEL: *Royal Fireworks suite.***

Sawallisch's account of the *Clock Symphony* is characteristically direct and straightforward, and with its unexpected couplings this tape is quite attractive at bargain price. The transfer is lively, with plenty of detail and generally vivid sound.

Symphonies Nos. 101 in D major (Clock); 102 in B flat major.
(M) *** HMV TC-SXLP 30265. RPO, Beecham.

These performances are in a class of their own. Phrasing is the soul of music, and these artists shape each phrase as naturally as they breathe. Perhaps not every detail is perfect: the chording in the introduction to No. 102 is not beyond reproach; but these performances penetrate the spirit of the music as do few others. Like the companion recordings of Symphonies Nos. 103 and 104, these were made before H. C. Robbins Landon's editions came into general currency. There is a drop of pitch in the slow movement of No. 102 caused by an edit of the master tape; but none of these small reservations detract from the magic of these performances. The sound balance is an object lesson of its kind, even if the frequency range is a little limited by modern standards. The transfer is made at a high level, and generally the quality is fresh and well detailed. Just occasionally in the outer movements the texture clouds a little at fortissimos, but not seriously.

Symphonies Nos. 103 in E flat major (Drum Roll); 104 in D major (London).
(M) *** HMV TC-SXLP 30257. RPO, Beecham.
(M) **(*) Decca Ace of Diamonds KSDC 362. Vienna PO, Karajan.
Symphony No. 104 in D major (London).

* HMV TC-ASD 3203. Berlin PO, Karajan – SCHUBERT: *Symphony No. 8.***

Beecham's coupling is self-recommending. Haydn's last two symphonies have rarely, if ever, sounded so captivating and sparkling as they do here. Beecham does not use authentic texts – he was a law unto himself in such matters – but the spirit of Haydn is superbly caught, whether in the affectionately measured (but never mannered) slow movements or in the exhilarating rhythmic spring of the outer movements. The recording is warmly attractive, and the transfer is admirably managed. The balance is most natural, and the level has been calculated to achieve refinement of detail as well as plenty of warmth. Though the quality has not the brilliance of a more modern recording it does not sound in the least dated, and the body of string tone is particularly impressive.

Karajan's Decca performances date from the early sixties, but the recording still sounds warm and fresh. Karajan's account of No. 103 is polished and well made, but there is some lack of warmth and humanity in the reading, although the tempi are sensible and the balance is good. The reading of No. 104 is more direct, with plenty of earthy vigour in the outer movements and a beautifully shaped slow movement. The tape transfers are generally excellent, although No. 103 on side one is marginally cleaner in focus than its companion on side two.

In the *London symphony* on HMV, Karajan does not match his earlier Vienna recording; the newer Berlin version is richly recorded but the performance is distinctly ponderous.

String quartets Nos. 77 in C major (Emperor); 78 in B flat major (Sunrise), Op. 76/3–4.
*** Philips 7300 523 [id.]. Italian Qt.

(M) **(*) Argo KZKC 16. Aeolian Qt.

The Italian performances are beautifully shaped and keenly alert. The playing too has much warmth, and the group is beautifully recorded. The transfer is of first-rate quality; made at a comparatively high level, it has fine body and detail and is admirably natural in balance and focus. A little bass cut may be necessary on some machines, although the treble is free and clear. By the side of the Italians the Aeolians' playing is less refined, but these too are most enjoyable accounts. The slow movement of the *Emperor* is played in rather a measured fashion but with considerable eloquence, and the fresh, crisp articulation in the first movement of Op. 76/4 is very attractive. In short, while the Italians remain first choice, this is an admirable medium-priced alternative and the cassette transfer offers demonstration quality throughout.

Piano sonatas Nos. 33 (in the Universal Edition; H.20) in C minor; 35 (43) in A flat major; 38 (23) in F major; 47 (32) in B minor.
*(*) Advent E 1068 (see p. xxiii) [id.]. Malcolm Bilson (piano).

Haydn keyboard sonatas are so underrepresented on cassette that one cannot afford to look any gift-horse in the mouth. Professor Bilson records these sonatas on a period instrument, a replica of a fortepiano of the 1780s made by Philip Belt of Stonington, Connecticut. He is rather forwardly recorded, though reducing the level helps a little to diminish the impression that he is playing thunderously. These are well-shaped, scholarly readings, but not perhaps as imaginative or sensitive as they might be. Only limited pleasure can be found here.

Piano sonatas Nos. 48 (H.35) in C major; 49 (36) in C sharp minor; 50 (37) in D major; 53 (34) in E minor.
*** DG 3300 736. Christoph Eschenbach.

This tape offers a quite exceptionally realistic image of the piano, with remarkable presence; one can imagine Eschenbach at the end of the room. The performances are of the highest quality. Eschenbach's touch is extremely crisp: he is obviously thinking of the piano's ancestor in producing such clear articulation, yet there is no lack of depth to the music-making, which is eminently civilized. A most distinguished collection.

The Creation (Die Schöpfung; oratorio): complete (in German).
*** Decca K 50 K 22 [Lon. 5-12108]. Lucia Popp, Helena Döse, Werner Hollweg, Benjamin Luxon, Kurt Moll, Brighton Festival Chorus, RPO, Dorati.
*** DG 3370 005 [id.]. Gundula Janowitz, Christa Ludwig, Fritz Wunderlich, Werner Krenn, Dietrich Fischer-Dieskau, Walter Berry, Vienna Singverein, Berlin PO, Karajan.
**(*) HMV TC-SLS 5125. Helen Donath, Robert Tear, José van Dam, Philharmonia Chorus and Orch., Frühbeck de Burgos.

This is a case where choice between the best available performances is reversed in the LP and tape versions. The Decca recording has been transferred with great skill. The sound is marvellously spacious, with the most natural bloom on the solo voices, and the orchestral detail (especially the woodwind) is wonderfully vivid. The chorus is less well defined (as it is on disc) but still sounds well. Dorati, as one

would expect, directs a lively and well-sprung account of Haydn's great oratorio. In crispness of ensemble it does not match the Karajan set, and the solo singing here is less reliable, but it remains very enjoyable and Part 1 is enchanting. Here Lucia Popp sings radiantly and the orchestra is at its peak (the accompaniment to *On mighty pens* is deliciously brought off). Helena Döse, who takes the part of Eve, is less reliable, and Part 2 is generally less distinguished in consequence. But the performance conveys such a feeling of joy throughout that with such splendid sound it must be first choice.

Karajan produces one of his most rapt choral performances. His concentration on refinement and polish might in principle seem out of place in a work which tells of religious faith in the directest terms. In fact the result is outstanding. The combination of the Berlin Philharmonic at its most intense and the great Viennese choir makes for a performance that is not only polished but warm and dramatically strong too. The soloists are an extraordinarily fine team, more consistent in quality than those on any rival version. This was one of the last recordings made by the incomparable Fritz Wunderlich, and fortunately his magnificent contribution extended to all the arias, leaving Werner Krenn to fill in the gaps of recitative left unrecorded. The recording quality has a wide dynamic range, and even though the transfer level is high it needs the volume fairly well up for maximum impact. Then the solo voices have ample presence and the balance is natural. The choruses lack the last degree of refinement of focus but in all other respects the sound is excellent, if without quite the bloom of the Decca set.

Rafael Frühbeck de Burgos directs a genial performance, recorded with richness and immediacy. Though the Karajan version has even crisper ensemble in both chorus and orchestra, the easier pacing of Frühbeck provides an alternative which for many will be more sympathetic. The soloists are all excellent, and though Helen Donath is not so pure-toned as her rivals on DG and Decca, with a hint of flutter in the voice, she is wonderfully agile in ornamentation, as in the bird-like quality she gives to the aria *On mighty pens*. The chorus might gain from a rather more forward balance. The transfer is made at a high level and it brings a hint of congestion at one or two peaks. The choruses are full-bodied, but the lack of a clean upper focus prevents any sense of incisiveness. The solo voices sound well, and the general perspective is good; but the quality lacks the overall refinement of the Decca set and is not as clear as the DG transfer.

Masses Nos. (i) *1 in F major* (*Missa brevis*); (ii) *4 in G major* (*Missa Sancti Nicolai*.
>   **(*)** Oiseau-Lyre KDSLC 538. Judith Nelson, Choir of Christ Church Cathedral, Oxford, Academy of Ancient Music, Preston, with (i) Emma Kirkby; (ii) Shirley Minty, Roger Covey-Crump, David Thomas.

Haydn wrote the early *Missa brevis* when he was seventeen. The setting is engagingly unpretentious; some of its sections last for under two minutes and none takes more than three and a half. The two soprano soloists here match their voices admirably and the effect is delightful. The *Missa Sancti Nicolai* dates from 1772 but has a comparable freshness of inspiration. The unconventional time-signature of the *Kyrie* establishes the composer's individuality, and the deeply expressive central section of the *Credo* is matched by the characterful opening of the *Sanctus* and the touch of melancholy in the *Agnus Dei*. This performance is first-rate in every way, beautifully sung, with spontaneity in every bar, and a highly characterful accompaniment. The transfer does not catch the reverberant acoustic without some blurring of the choral passages,

but the soloists are naturally focused and the balance is excellent. Highly recommended.

Masses Nos. 5 in B flat major (*Little organ Mass*): *Missa brevis Sancti Joannis de Deo; 6 in C major* (*Missa Cellensis*): *Mariazeller Mass. Mechanical organ pieces Nos. 3, 6–8.*
>   ******* Argo KZRC 867. Jennifer Smith, Helen Watts, Robert Tear, Benjamin Luxon, St John's College Choir, Academy of St Martin-in-the-Fields, Guest; John Scott (organ).

The *Little organ Mass*, which dates from 1775, fares extremely well in this fine performance. There is some excellent invention in this piece, though it is not by any means the equal of the *Mariazeller Mass* of 1782, which H. C. Robbins Landon called 'the most perfect large-scale work Haydn achieved' in this particular period. The singing here is of admirable quality, and so too is the orchestral playing. Excellent recording and a good balance make this a desirable issue for all Haydn lovers; the *Mechanical organ pieces* are piquantly registered and make an enjoyable bonus. The transfers are of first-class quality; the choral tone is generally well focused, and there is an excellent overall perspective. The *Little organ Mass* is of demonstration standard.

Mass No. 9 in D minor (*Nelson Mass*): *Missa in angustiis.*
>   ******* Argo KZRC 5325. Sylvia Stahlman, Helen Watts, Wilfred Brown, Tom Krause, King's College Choir, LSO, Willcocks.

Haydn's *Nelson Mass* is a tremendous work and clearly among his greatest music. Its impact in this splendid performance and recording is breathtaking. The solo singing is uniformly good, Sylvia Stahlman negotiating her florid music with great skill, and David Willcocks maintains quite remarkable tension throughout. The recording manages the many exciting and very loud climaxes without any difficulty and transfers the King's acoustic with complete success to tape. The massed trebles of the choir are given a fine attack without unnatural edge or peaking.

The Seasons (*Die Jahreszeiten;* oratorio): complete (in German).
   *** DG 3371 028. Gundula Janowitz, Peter Schreier, Martti Talvela, Vienna SO, Boehm.
   *** Decca κ 88 κ 32. Ileana Cotrubas, Werner Krenn, Hans Sotin, Brighton Festival Chorus, RPO, Dorati.

The Seasons shows Haydn in the innocent pictorial vein of the Adam and Eve music of *The Creation*, and the imagery is brilliantly realized. The atmospheric orchestral writing describing the character of the seasons; the pictures of birds and animals; the storm; the hunt; the chorus in praise of the pleasures of the cup: these are among the many imaginative delights. Haydn shows here, as often in the works of his maturity, that his eye sees with the freshness of youth, while his genius can record with the skill and experience that can only come from many years of apprenticeship to a beloved art. The work, essentially genial, ends with the composer looking towards heaven and after-life. It is an expression of a simple faith and of a human being to whom life on the whole has been kind, and who was duly grateful to record the many earthly pleasures he had enjoyed. Boehm's performance fully enters into the spirit of the music. The soloists are excellent and characterize the music fully; the chorus sing enthusiastically and are well recorded. But it is Boehm's set. He secures fine orchestral playing throughout, an excellent overall musical balance and a real spontaneity in music that needs

this above all else. As with many of DG's more recent tape transfers one is struck by the realism of the solo voices. There is a slight edge here, but when it is removed the presence still remains, against a virtually silent background. Gundula Janowitz is particularly well caught, but then so are her companions. The spectacular *Hunting chorus* is a highlight of the set, with splendid bite; elsewhere the choral focus is marginally less clean but still very good. A wholly recommendable issue.

Dorati brings to Haydn's last oratorio an innocent dedication, at times pointing to a folk-like inspiration, which is most compelling. This is not always so polished an account as others available on disc and tape, but with excellent solo singing and bright chorus work it is just as enjoyable. The choruses of peasants in Part 3, for instance, are strikingly robust, with accented rhythms to give a boisterous jollity. Textually there is the important advantage that, with the encouragement of H. C. Robbins Landon (who provides the excellent album notes), Dorati has restored the original version, notably the cuts in the introductions to *Autumn* and *Winter*, the latter with some wonderfully adventurous harmonies. The gains are marginal but important, and the recording quality is of outstanding vividness. The balance places the soloists well forward (they are made to sound somewhat larger than life); but the choral climaxes expand excitingly so that there is no lack of dynamic contrast. The orchestral detail too is well realized; the pictorial effects towards the end of Part 2 are highly effective. The performance as a whole is splendidly animated. With Dorati this is above all a happy work, a point made all the more telling by the immediacy of the sound. Dorati's directness is sometimes less engaging than Boehm's smiling geniality, but the Decca recording has transferred splendidly to tape, with a fine bloom on singers and orchestra alike. The level is high, which brings plenty of range and colour (the hunting horns in Part 3 are superb), and undoubtedly the Decca reproduces more spectacularly than the DG recording. Also (unlike the DG set, which follows the disc layout) the Decca set – on two cassettes – allots each of the four seasons a single side to itself. The libretto is admirably clear.

'*Favourite composer*': (i) *Trumpet concerto in E flat major;* (ii; iii) *Symphonies Nos. 94 in G major* (*Surprise*)*; 101 in D major* (*Clock*)*;* (iv) *String quartet No. 77 in C major* (*Emperor*)*, Op. 76/3:* 2nd movt; (v) *Andante with variations in F minor;* (vi; ii) *The Creation:* highlights.

  (B) ** Decca KDPC 611/2.
      (i) Alan Stringer, Academy of St Martin-in-the-Fields, Marriner; (ii) Vienna PO; (iii) Monteux; (iv) Aeolian Qt; (v) Wilhelm Backhaus (piano); (vi) Elly Ameling, Erna Spoorenberg, Werner Krenn, Tom Krause, Robin Fairhurst, Vienna State Opera Chorus, Münchinger.

Monteux's genial coupling of the *Surprise* and *Clock symphonies* is not otherwise available on cassette. These are captivating performances, with polished playing and many a turn of phrase to delight the ear. The recordings are excellent, do not sound in the least dated, and have transferred to tape with fine bloom and no lack of presence. The sound on the second tape, however, is less refined. Alan Stringer's open trumpet tone and the accompanying orchestral group are given an element of coarseness by the high-level transfer, and the excerpt from the *Emperor quartet* provides an almost overwhelmingly forward balance. The generous excerpts from Münchinger's distinguished account of *The Creation* (of which the accompanying notes, unusually for Decca, give no details) are also transferred at marginally too high a level and the sound roughens somewhat at peaks.

Haydn, Michael (1737–1806)

(i) *Horn concerto in D major. 6 Minuets* (for small orchestra).
  ** Argo KZRC 543 [id.]. Academy of St Martin-in-the-Fields, Marriner, (i) with Barry Tuckwell – J. HAYDN: *Trumpet concerto* etc.**

Another interesting but not memorable addition to the virtuoso horn repertory serves to show what masterpieces were the four Mozart concertos (and indeed the one by Josef Haydn, to a lesser extent). The writing here is clumsier, but this impression is not helped by the performance, which is vigorous but slightly square. The *Minuets*, a most attractive bonus, are beautifully played, and are almost worthy of Josef! The transfer is of first-class quality in every way, with more range and detail here than in the coupling.

Hely-Hutchinson, Victor (1901–47)

A carol symphony.
  (M) (**) HMV Greensleeve TC-ESD 7021. Pro Arte Orch., Rose – VAUGHAN WILLIAMS: *Fantasia; Carols.***

Hely-Hutchinson's *Carol symphony* dates from the late 1920s, when it was still fashionable to regard the 'symphony' as an appropriate formal design for even a light-hearted piece. The snag is that carols, if they are good ones, are outstanding little works of art in their own right and don't admit improvement by 'symphonic' treatment. All you can do with them is to alter their orchestral dress.

their harmony (which is seldom an improvement) or, as Constant Lambert observed about the symphonic treatment of folk-songs, play them again louder. Hely-Hutchinson does all these things and in the slow movement introduces Mahlerian harmonies for the *Coventry carol*. But he also creates a deliciously imaginative effect where the solo harp embroiders *Nowell*, even if the climax which follows goes on too long. The first movement too could do with judicious cuts; the scherzo is quite effective and in the finale the composer gathers all the strands together very engagingly. But without a Beecham at the helm the work as a whole tends to outstay its welcome. The performance is sensitive and competent, but Guildford Cathedral was not the proper venue for a piece of this intimate nature. Unfortunately the transfer of the *Carol symphony* offers sound which is disappointingly shallow, with a papery upper string quality, poorly focused. The balance is shrill and topheavy. The Vaughan Williams work and the carols have more substance and are altogether more successful.

*** Decca Phase 4 KPFC 4354 [Lon. 5-21143]. Kingsway Chorus and SO, Camarata.

Victor Herbert's musical plays may seem irretrievably dated now, but in their day they made theatrical history with their lavish costumes, ingenious stage effects and productions offering a degree of spectacle not seen before. But without good tunes no musical show stays in the public favour for very long. As we all know, Victor Herbert wrote some splendid tunes, and many of the best of them are here, presented with enthusiasm and much feeling for the music's style, within an appropriately resonant acoustic. The excellent chorus sings with considerable spirit and unashamed romanticism, and the orchestra produces a vivid backcloth. *Every day is ladies' day* is a highlight (recalling in the mind's eye the Hollywoodian imagery of Busby Berkeley, who would have been an ideal Herbert producer). The *March of the toys* has a touched-up orchestration but still comes over as a genuinely inspired piece. The whole programme seems apt for the somewhat artificial Phase Four balancing, and the tape transfer has admirable life and breadth. An exhilarating collection.

Herbert, Victor
(1859–1924)

'Operetta spectacular': Babes in Toyland: *Overture; March of the toys; Toyland* (finale). *Mademoiselle Modiste: Kiss me again; Want what I want. Naughty Marietta: Tramp, tramp; Italian street song; Ah sweet mystery of life. The Red Mill: Moonbeams; Every day is ladies' day. Sweethearts: Sweetheart medley; Sweethearts.* Songs: *When you're away; Streets of New York; A kiss in the dark.*

Hérold, Ferdinand
(1791–1833)

La Fille mal gardée (ballet, arr. John Lanchbery): extended excerpts.
*** Decca KSXC 2313. Orch. of Royal Opera House, Covent Garden, Lanchbery.

The ballet *La Fille mal gardée* dates originally from 1789 and has had a long and chequered history. The tale is a simple one of thwarted rustic love which comes right in the end, and the original score was made up from folk melodies and 'pop' songs of the time. Since 1789 it has been revised and rewritten by Hérold (1828), Hertel (1864) and Feldt (1937). The present score, commissioned by Frederick Ashton for a Royal Ballet revival, was prepared and exceedingly skilfully scored by John Lanchbery, who drew in the main on Hérold's version. However, Lanchbery also interpolates a single Hertel number, a gorgeously vulgar *Clog Dance* for Simone (who as a character is one of the ancestors of our pantomime Dame). Hérold's score also included tunes from Rossini's *Barber of Seville* and *Cenerentola*, together with a Donizetti selection (mainly from *L'Elisir d'amore*). That the ballet is therefore a complete hotch-potch does not prevent it from being marvellously entertaining. The music is popular in appeal but, being French, is witty too and of course it is tuneful from beginning to end. The performance here is brilliantly played, displaying both affection and sparkle in ample quantity. The transfer is generally very good indeed. The basic reverberation of the recording does offer a few cloudy moments (more often on side one than side two), but much of the sound is vivid and sparkling in Decca's best manner and often reaches demonstration standards in its delicious colour and the fine detail of the wind solos.

Herrmann, Bernard (1911–75)

Film music: *Citizen Kane: Overture; The Devil and Daniel Webster: Sleigh-ride; Gulliver's Travels: The King's March; Jason and the Argonauts: Prelude; Journey to the Centre of the Earth: Atlantis; The Mysterious Island: Prelude; The Balloon; North by Northwest: Overture; Psycho: A narrative for orchestra; The Seventh Voyage of Sinbad: Over-*

ture; The Snows of Kilimanjaro: Memory waltz; Vertigo: Scène d'amour.
*** Decca Phase 4 KPFC 4365, LPO or National PO, the composer.

Bernard Herrmann's first and perhaps his finest film-score was written for *Citizen Kane*, and this entertaining anthology of his work in this field appropriately opens with the vivacious *Overture*. The other items here show Herrmann's vivid imagination constantly at work, from the spectacle of *The Mysterious Island* and *Journey to the Centre of the Earth* to the viciousness of the chilling musical background for the murder scene in Hitchcock's *Psycho*. Herrmann's command of the orchestra was masterly and the quality of his invention far above that of the average film background music. The music is splendidly played and brilliantly recorded; the cassette transfer equals the demonstration quality of the disc.

Film music: *Gulliver's Travels: suite; Jason and the Argonauts: suite; The Mysterious Island: suite.*
*** Decca Phase 4 KPFC 4337. National PO, the composer.

These more extended selections from Herrmann's film-scores show even more strikingly his feeling for orchestral colour and sonorities. He can readily create a feeling of power or menace with quite simple harmonic devices, thanks to the skill with which the music is scored. This is not to decry the quality of the invention, which is especially delightful in the lightweight suite from *Gulliver's Travels*, full of felicitous detail, and tuneful in an easy-going way. The descriptive writing too is impressively realized: *The giant bee* in *The Mysterious Island* makes Rimsky-Korsakov's sound picture seem tame by comparison. Collectors of film music will find that this issue is among the finest of the genre. The recording is spectacular throughout, and like its companion has transferred splendidly to tape. There is a fine sense of spectacle in the music for *Jason* and *The Mysterious Island*, and the charming lightweight scoring of *Gulliver's Travels* has plenty of sparkle.

Hindemith, Paul
(1895–1963)

Mathis der Maler (*Symphony*).
   (*) Advent D 1043 (see p. xxiii) [id.]. LSO, Horenstein – R. STRAUSS: *Death and Transfiguration*.

Horenstein's account of *Mathis der Maler* was the last recording he made and has the merit of breadth and weight. The recording lacks the last degree of sumptuousness and warmth, but the strings and brass are truthful in timbre and Advent's transfer faithfully reflects the detail and body of the LP version. The coupling is not a welcome one (Karajan's account of *Death and Transfiguration* eclipses this version), but Horenstein's admirers will probably want this issue nonetheless.

5 Pieces for strings (*Fünf Stücke*), *Op. 44/4*.
   ** Pye Ensayo ZCNEL 2012. ECO, Asensio – BRITTEN: *Simple symphony*; RESPIGHI: *Ancient airs and dances*.**

Asensio gives a straight-faced account of Hindemith's *Five Pieces*, with no attempt to charm. But the composer would surely have approved; the effect is very like a German performance, and the individual movements are effectively characterized. The recording is good and the cassette is well engineered, with a fine body of string tone and good detail.

Hoffmann, Ernst
(1776–1822)

Mandolin concerto in D major.
   (M) ** Turnabout KTVC 34003. Elfriede Kunschak, Vienna Pro Musica Orch., Hladky – HUMMEL: *Mandolin concerto*.**

This work is of considerably less musical interest than the Hummel concerto on the other side, but the playing of Elfriede Kunschak is lively enough. By no means a masterpiece, but of interest to mandolin enthusiasts. The cassette transfer is beautifully managed, with a lifelike timbre for the solo mandolin and a most pleasing orchestral image. This is one of Turnabout's best cassettes.

Hoffmeister, Franz
(1754–1812)

Flute concerto in G major.
   ** Enigma K 453538. Ingrid Dingfelder (flute), ECO, Leonard – TELEMANN: *Suite in A minor*.**

Franz Hoffmeister, publisher as well as musician, earns posterity's gratitude for coming to Mozart's financial aid more than once when he was in dire financial straits. But Hoffmeister is worth remembering also for this comely flute concerto, which has more than a little Mozartian flavour if none of his genius. The lyrical secondary theme of the first movement has an attractive grace, and there is a lively finale. The work is impeccably played here, and the recording, forwardly balanced in the Enigma manner, is first-class. The tape transfer is of exemplary quality. Take a little off the top and one is reminded of the kind of clean, crisp sound Argo produce for baroque music –

275

and one can pay no higher compliment. The notes provided with the cassette, however, are printed in grotesquely small type and are impossible to read comfortably, even with a magnifying glass.

Holst, Gustav
(1874–1934)

(i) *Egdon Heath, Op. 47; The Perfect Fool* (opera): *ballet suite, Op. 39;* (ii) *Hymn of Jesus, Op. 37.*

(M) *** Decca Jubilee KJBC 49. (i) LPO; (ii) BBC SO and Chorus; all cond. Boult.

Fine performances of the *Hymn of Jesus* and *Egdon Heath* are suitably leavened here with a brilliant and flashingly colourful account of the *Perfect Fool ballet suite* – Holst at his most vividly extrovert and colourful. Boult's performance of the *Hymn of Jesus* is undoubtedly a fine one, bringing out its mystical element as well as its atmosphere. The recording has a wide dynamic range and the work's climaxes are dramatically made. The bleak, sombre evocation of *Egdon Heath* is hauntingly conveyed and provides yet another contrast. Although the account of the *Hymn of Jesus* is perhaps not quite so penetrating as Groves's on HMV (see below), there will be many who prefer the couplings on this excellent Decca tape. The transfer is marvellously vivid, with a wide dynamic range and plenty of atmosphere in the *Hymn of Jesus* yet offering the most refined detail. In *The Perfect Fool* the brass (especially the trombones) have an exhilarating bite. A demonstration issue.

A Moorside suite (original version for brass band).

*** Decca KSXC 6820. Grimethorpe Colliery Band, Howarth – BLISS: *Kenilworth****;

ELGAR: *Severn suite***(*); IRELAND: *Comedy overture.****

Holst's *Moorside suite* sounds splendid in its original brass-band form (it was written for the national championship contest at Crystal Palace in 1928), and it is superbly played here, with great vigour and refinement of detail. The Decca recording too is outstanding, and the tape transfer is of demonstration quality. This is the finest of the four performances in this attractive anthology; it is genuinely memorable.

The Planets (suite), *Op. 32.*

*** HMV TC-ASD 3649. LPO, Geoffrey Mitchell Choir, Boult.

(M) *** Decca Jubilee KJBC 30. Vienna PO, Vienna State Opera Chorus, Karajan.

**(*) HMV TC-ASD 3002 [Angel 4xs. 36991]. LSO, Ambrosian Singers, Previn.

*** Decca KCET 628. LPO and Choir, Solti.

*** Philips 7300 643 [id.]. Concertgebouw Orch., Ambrosian Singers, Marriner.

*** CBS 40-73001 [Col. MT 33125]. New York PO and Chorus, Bernstein.

*** Decca KSXC 6529 [Lon. 5-6734]. Los Angeles PO and Chorus, Mehta.

(B) **(*) Classics for Pleasure TC-CFP 175. BBC SO and Chorus, Sargent.

*(**) RCA RK 11797 [ARK 11797]. Philadelphia Orch. and Chorus, Ormandy.

** Philips 7300 058 [id.]. LPO, John Alldis Choir, Haitink.

(B) ** Classics for Pleasure TC-CFP 40343. Hallé Orch. and Chorus, Loughran.

(M) *(*) Decca Eclipse ECS 600. LSO and Chorus, Sargent.

(M) *(*) Turnabout KTVC 34598 [CT 2153] Ronald Arnatt Chorale and Missouri Singers, St Louis SO, Susskind.

It was Sir Adrian Boult who, over sixty years ago, first 'made *The Planets* shine', as the composer put it, and now in his ninetieth year he has recorded it for the last time. It sets the seal on a magnificent Indian summer in the recording studio, a performance at once intense and beautifully played, spacious and dramatic, rapt and pointed. If the opening of *Mars* – noticeably slower than in Boult's previous recordings – suggests a slackening, the opposite proves true: that movement gains greater weight at a slower tempo. *Mercury* has lift and clarity, not just rushing brilliance, and it is striking that in Holst's syncopations – as in the introduction to *Jupiter* – Boult allows himself a jaunty, even jazzy freedom which adds an infectious sparkle. The great melody of *Jupiter* is calculatedly less resonant and more flowing than previously but is more moving, and *Uranus* as well as *Jupiter* has its measure of jollity, with the lolloping 6/8 rhythms delectably pointed. The spacious slow movements are finely poised and the recording is of demonstration quality, gloriously full and opulent, with the tape measuring up well to the disc. The focus slips a little in *Mars*.

Previn's is an outstandingly attractive version and the recording, transferred at a high level, is exceptionally clear and vivid, revealing excellent detail, almost matching the equivalent LP, which is of demonstration quality. However, there is some roughness in *Mars* and at the climax of *Saturn* to show that a fractionally lower level would have produced even more sophisticated results. Even so with translucent strings and plenty of bite and sonority from the brass this remains for the most part a very good tape, and the gently receding vocal contribution in *Neptune* is certainly successful.

The alternative choice must lie next with the richly atmospheric Karajan set, which undoubtedly offers demonstration quality throughout much of the cassette. Decca have used an ambitiously high transfer level and have taken care with the balance, so that the range of the sound is very striking, with splendid presence and detail. But it is the performance itself which is so fascinating. Here we have a conductor of world reputation turning his attention to a work which one has tended to think of as essentially English and transforming it into an international score. Karajan's reading is a revelation. The terrifying impact of *Mars* with those whining Wagnerian tubas we have never heard before like this. Boult found a purity of texture in *Venus* that Karajan transmutes into a more sensuous sheen – this is the Venus of ardour rather than mysticism – but in *Mercury* the gossamer textures at the end of the piece are as striking as the impact of the central climax. *Jupiter* is bucolic and breezy, the Vienna strings bringing their own characteristic tone colour to the big central tune, and *Saturn* and *Uranus* are outstanding. Here the Vienna Philharmonic brass comes completely into its own: the slow, sad march of *Saturn* is wonderfully cumulative in its emotional effect. The wordless chorus too at the end of *Neptune* is strikingly atmospheric.

With *Mars* opening with a brilliant cutting edge and at the fastest possible tempo, Solti's version could not be more contrasted with Boult's new recording, which arrived simultaneously. Solti's pacing is exhilarating to the point of fieceness in the vigorous movements, and undoubtedly his direct manner is refreshing, the rhythms clipped and precise, sometimes at the expense of resilience. His directness in *Jupiter* (with the trumpets coming through splendidly) is certainly riveting, the big tune taken literally rather than affectionately. In *Saturn* the spareness of texture is finely sustained; here the tempo is slow, the detail precise, while in *Neptune* the coolness is even more striking when the pianissimos are achieved with such a high degree of tension. The recording has remarkable clarity and detail, and Solti's clear-headed intensity undoubtedly shows refreshing new insights into this multi-faceted score, even if some will prefer a more atmospheric viewpoint. The recording gives the orchestra great presence and on technical grounds this Decca tape is very impressive, clearly detailed yet with plenty of atmosphere and striking weight and sonority in the bass. The climax of *Uranus* is riveting. In *Mars* there is just a touch of roughness.

Marriner's account is marked by splendid orchestral playing and richly spacious recording. The opulence and beauty of the sound here are very strik-ing, but in the tape transfer the balance is rather too heavily weighted in the bass and lacks the last degree of range and sparkle in the treble. Even so, if one cuts back the bass and uses a high-level play-back the sound remains very impressive. The performance is full of individual touches, which some will warm to more readily than others. At the very opening of *Mars* – taken more slowly than usual – a sudden crescendo on the timpani gives a sense of underlying menace, and the flamboyant use of the tam-tam increases the feeling of spectacle. The orchestral playing in *Venus* is richly refined (a ravishing horn solo and translucent flutes). Marriner's tempo is relatively fast, and the music's sensuousness is only hinted at: here the essential mood is one of innocence. The big tune in *Jupiter* is given a slow but gloriously rich presenta-tion, but for some Marriner might seem too weighty. *Uranus* has a skittish quality (particularly its middle section) and is vividly coloured. There is beautiful sing-ing from the Ambrosians in *Neptune*, although the final fade is not so distantly ethereal as in some versions. But even with the reservations about the sound balance, this performance has many re-freshing features.

Bernstein's version is on one of the very best tapes we have had from CBS. The recording is beautifully detailed,

with an excellent range and fine body of tone as well as glitter. The original LP was similarly clear but lacked substance in the bass to compensate the over-bright treble. Here the balance is first-class, and indeed the deep bass pedals in *Saturn* are most subtle in effect. The choral singing in *Neptune* is most refined and the closing *diminuendo* is very beautiful. In *Jupiter* Bernstein takes the big tune rather de-liberately but this is effective when the body of string tone is so well focused. A most enjoyable issue and certainly among the best available.

Among the finest cassettes of all, tech-nically speaking, is the Mehta version. This Los Angeles Decca recording set a new standard of sonic splendour for a work which since the 78 days has put re-cording engineers on their mettle. The power and impact of *Mars* are impressive indeed; the strings in *Venus* are richly sensuous; and the brass and timpani in *Uranus* have superb body, colour and bite. One has a few reservations about the performance, which has not the indivi-duality of those of Karajan, Previn or Boult. Mehta's approach is literal, but not without character and impulse. As sheer sound (and Holst's score depends a good deal on the orchestral sound itself) this is very exciting indeed.

The Classics for Pleasure engineers have freshened the quality of Sargent's early stereo recording, especially on side two, where *Uranus* has splendid clarity and bite, and the organ pedals come through well in *Saturn*. Sargent's perfor-mance is full of character, with a sombre *Saturn* and the central tune in *Jupiter* given special dignity. The tape transfer is admirably clear and vivid.

Ormandy's recording has some fine moments, notably *Uranus* and the closing pages of both *Saturn* and *Neptune*. Here the performance is helped by the sophisti-cation of the recording, whereas at the opening of *Mars* the rather glassy string tone is less attractive. In the famous cen-tral tune of *Jupiter* Ormandy takes a slow pace and emphasizes the accents rather stolidly. Taken as a whole this version (although it will have obvious appeal in the USA) is less idiomatic than the finest British versions, while the interpretation lacks the individuality and power of Karajan's magnificent account on Decca. The transfer is rather harsh, with an accentuated treble not balanced by a comparably rich bass. Everything is too brightly lit, to the point of glare, and though by cutting the 'top' well back an acceptable sound can be achieved there are much more recommendable tapes available.

Haitink starts off *Mars* at a very slow tempo, and dissects the texture almost as though he were putting it under a musical microscope. The hairpin dynamic marks, for example, are very precise, but the result hardly sweeps one away. *Venus* here is certainly the bringer of peace but not of love, *Mercury* brings reminders of Strauss and Rimsky-Korsakov. *Jupiter* sounds the more noble for restrained treatment. And so on. It is all very different from usual, and with fine playing and unobtrusively clean recording it will please many. But it is plainly not for those who want excitement from this colourful work. The transfer is made at a modest level, and although well balanced the sound is reverberant and lacks sparkle and crisp detail.

Loughran, whose recorded performances with the Hallé Orchestra have consistently conveyed alertness and spontaneity, is not at his best here. He finds plenty of atmosphere in Holst's score, but the music-making is relatively pedestrian, even though the playing itself is often very fine. The compensating factor is the recording, which is ripely vivid and marvellously refined in detail. The brass are given splendid bite and sonority and as sound this is among the very finest cassettes of *The Planets*. Although there is some remarkably good quality in places (notably *Saturn* and *Uranus*) there seems little point in recommending Sargent's earlier Decca Eclipse version, for the recording – good

though it is – is not real stereo and the performance has no special merits to recommend it above the Classics for Pleasure issue. The strings sound glassy in *Mars*; elsewhere the range is comparatively restricted and there are hints of tonal insecurity in the transfer, notably in *Venus* and *Neptune*. Even so, anyone coming upon this tape will be surprised how well it sounds.

Walter Susskind's performance is alert and well played and is basically well recorded. The sound is both vivid and atmospheric, but the hall in which the recording was made is very resonant and this blurs the rhythms in *Mars* and tends to create an ugliness of effect not intended by the composer. The blurring adds to the sensuousness of *Venus* and the brass is enriched in *Saturn*. But in the faster music the reverberation causes an unwanted muddiness, and *Uranus* loses much of its edge. This is a great pity, since the music-making is sympathetic and spontaneous. The transfer to tape is of high quality.

Suites for military band Nos. 1 in E flat major, Op. 28/1; 2 in F major, Op. 28/2; Hammersmith: Prelude and scherzo, Op. 52.
*** Enigma K 453565. London Wind Orch., Wick – VAUGHAN WILLIAMS: *English folk-songs suite; Toccata.****

The two Holst *Military band suites* make an exhilarating listening experience when they are played so brilliantly and with such obvious pleasure as by this group of wind soloists drawn from the LSO. The performances have great spontaneity, even if they are essentially lightweight. Denis Wick, the musical director, says in his notes that some of the music on this tape 'has not been recorded before, using the composer's original scoring'. He is obviously not aware of the famous 1960 recordings by the Eastman Wind Ensemble under Frederick

Fennell (available in the UK on disc but unfortunately deleted on tape). Fennell paced the great *Chaconne* of the *First Suite* slightly more slowly and created a marvellous climax, with some frisson-making whacks on the bass drum at its peak. Here the effect is less monumental, but the performances generally are attractively volatile. *Hammersmith* (which gives the tape its rather off-putting title, '*By tram from Hammersmith*') is well done, though lacking something in atmospheric poetry. A most enjoyable issue, splendidly recorded and given a transfer of the most vivid, demonstration quality.

Choral hymns from the Rig-Veda, Op. 26/4 (Second group); Festival Te Deum; Hymn of Jesus, Op. 37; Ode to Death, Op. 38.
> ****(*) HMV** TC-ASD 3435. LSO Chorus, Choristers of St Paul's Cathedral, LPO, Groves.

This recording of the *Hymn of Jesus* is basically finer than Boult's account (see above under *Egdon Heath*), which has served collectors well over the years. Sir Charles Groves brings great sympathy and conviction to this beautiful and moving score, whose visionary quality has never paled. He is moreover given a recording of great clarity and presence. Like *Hymn of Jesus*, the Short *Festival Te Deum* comes from 1919 but takes only a little over four minutes and is an 'occasional' piece, less original than the *Hymn*. The *Ode to Death* is from the same period, written in memory of Holst's friends killed in the 1914–18 war. A setting of Whitman, it must be accounted one of Holst's most inspired and haunting scores, comparable in quality with the *Choral fantasia*, and it is eloquently performed here. Its neglect is unaccountable; this is its first recording. The second group of *Rig-Veda hymns* are less of a revelation: they were written in the immediate wake of Holst's Algerian visit of 1909, which also produced *Beni Mora*. These are on familiar Holstian lines, though they make considerable demands on the singers. A most welcome issue. We find copies of the cassette tend to produce varying quality, though always good. One copy tried offered demonstration sound, clear and clean in the loudest climaxes, whereas another produced a lack of refinement in the most expansive moments.

Honegger, Arthur (1892–1955)

Pacific 231.
> (M) ******* Decca Jubilee KJBC 36. Suisse Romande Orch., Ansermet – DUKAS: *L'Apprenti sorcier;* RAVEL: *Boléro* etc.*******
> (**) HMV TC-ASD 2989. City of Birmingham SO, Frémaux – IBERT: *Divertissement;* POULENC: *Les Biches* (**); SATIE: *Gymnopédies.********

The polyphonic climax of Honegger's orchestral portrayal of a railway locomotive needs reasonable clarity of recording to achieve its maximum impact. The reverberation is perhaps not quite perfectly judged on Ansermet's tape, but the power of the mighty engine is marvellously conveyed and its surging lyricism too, while the grinding tension of the final braking gives this mechanical monster an almost human personality. This is much preferable to the HMV version, which is almost oppressively reverberant and has a tape transfer with a very restricted upper frequency response. On Decca the wide amplitude of the sound is impressively contained.

Hsien Hsing-hai
(and others)
(20th century)

Piano concerto (Yellow River) (communally adapted from cantata by Central Philharmonic Society).
*(**) Decca Phase 4 KPFC 4299. Ilana Vered, National PO, Howarth – MOZART: *Piano concerto No. 21.**

The *Yellow River concerto*, written by a committee of Chinese musicians rather than by a single composer, is as crude a piece as you would expect from such a source. Echoes of Tchaikovsky, Rachmaninov, Dvořák and Hollywood filmscores, not to mention Negro spirituals and *The Sound of Music*, make an extraordinary mixture, which just conceivably might acquire unthinking popularity with a Royal Albert Hall audience. It is undeniably tuneful and for all its outrageous vulgarity (or perhaps because of it) one member of the reviewing team finds it all rather exhilarating, if perhaps a shade too long. It is spectacularly recorded in a suitably blown-up way, and the transfer to tape is admirably vivid.

Hummel, Johann
(1778–1837)

(i) *Bassoon concerto in F major;* (ii) *Concertino in G major for piano and orchestra, Op. 73* (arr. of *Mandolin concerto); 'La Galante' Rondeau for piano, Op. 120.*
(M) *** Turnabout KTVC 34348. (i) George Zukerman, Württemberg CO, Faerber; (ii) Martin Galling, Berlin SO, Bünte.

Hummel's *Bassoon concerto* is a winner, with all the charm, if perhaps not quite the depth, of the famous work by Mozart. It is played with real appreciation of its genial humour by George Zukerman, who shows himself also an uncommonly good musician in matters of technique and phrasing. The *Concertino*, with its immediately catchy dotted melody in the first movement, has an equally *galant* quality and its amiable chatter is never empty. Again good playing, and an excellent recording throughout; the clicks you hear on side two, incidentally, are not transfer faults but the bassoonist's busy keys. The outstanding cassette transfer offers demonstration quality, with beautifully focused images of the solo piano and solo bassoon and a most realistic orchestral balance.

Mandolin concerto in G major.
(M) ** Turnabout KTVC 34003. Edith Bauer-Slais, Vienna Pro Musica Orch., Hladky – HOFFMANN: *Mandolin concerto.***

Mandolin enthusiasts will be glad to have this coupling; others might find the limitation of tone colour a drawback, although Hummel exploits the instrument's possibilities skilfully. The invention is attractive if not memorable. The soloist here makes the most of the work, and the accompaniment is sound. The cassette transfer is of excellent quality to match the equally well-managed coupling.

(i) *Piano concerto in A minor, Op. 85;* (i; ii) *Double concerto in G major for piano, violin and orchestra, Op. 17.*
(M) *(*) Turnabout KTVC 34028. Stuttgart PO, Paulmüller, with (i) Martin Galling (piano); (ii) Susanne Lautenbacher (violin).

Hummel's *A minor Piano concerto* is conventional structurally but uses attractive melodic material, operatic in style.

The work is well played and recorded here, and the tape transfer is nicely managed. Lovers of the early-nineteenth-century piano concerto will find this an agreeable addition to the repertory. The *Double concerto* is a less interesting work, not improved by a highly modulated recording which places the soloists rather on top of the listener. The transfer is not very clean, and the solo violin sounds somewhat rough and spiky in timbre.

Piano concerto in B minor, Op. 89.
(M) **(*) Turnabout KTVC 34073. Martin Galling, Innsbruck SO, Robert Wagner – HAYDN: *Piano concerto in D major.***

Hummel's *B minor Concerto* has some good tunes and is well made. There is some adventurous writing for the horns in the slow movement, but the playing here (as of the orchestra generally) is not especially refined. The soloist, however, is excellent, and the cassette transfer is also of the highest quality; the glowing sound at the very least matches the LP. This is not a great concerto, perhaps, but it has great charm and spontaneity and a number of original touches. With such attractive recording Hummel's melodies spring to life and the flow of invention tickles the ear readily.

Septet in D minor, Op. 74.
*** CRD CRDC 4044. Nash Ens. – BERWALD: *Grand septet.****

An enchanting and inventive work with a virtuoso piano part, expertly dispatched here by Clifford Benson. The *Septet* is full of vitality, and its scherzo in particular has enormous charm and individuality. A fine performance and excellent recording make this a desirable issue, particularly in view of the enterprising coupling, which is not otherwise available. The transfer is up to the usual high standard of CRD chamber-music tapes: the sound has warmth and bloom, with good detail.

Humperdinck, Engelbert (1854–1921)

Hänsel und Gretel (opera): complete.
⊛ *** HMV TC-SLS 5145. Elisabeth Schwarzkopf, Elisabeth Grümmer, Josef Metternich, Maria von Ilosvay, Else Schürhoff, Anny Felbermayer, Choirs of Loughton High School for Girls and Bancroft's School, Philharmonia Orch., Karajan.
**(*) Decca K 131 K 22. Brigitte Fassbaender, Lucia Popp, Walter Berry, Julia Hamari, Anny Schlemm, Norma Burrowes, Edita Gruberova, Vienna Boys' Choir, Vienna PO, Solti.

Karajan's classic set of Humperdinck's children's opera with Schwarzkopf and Grümmer peerless in the name parts is enchanting. This was an instance where everything in the recording went right. No other version begins to match it in polish and flair, or indeed in its magical feeling of ambience. The original mono LP set was already extremely atmospheric – the cuckoos in the wood, for example – but the stereo transcription adds an irresistible further bloom without losing the inner focus. One notices that the main image stays fairly centrally situated between the speakers, but in all other respects the sound has a clarity and warmth that rival recordings made in the 1970s. There is much to delight here; the smaller parts are beautifully done and Else Schürhoff's Witch is memorable. The tape transfer is splendid: one can only marvel at its smooth vividness of vocal detail and the translucent quality of the woodwind. The libretto is in EMI's usual small print, but the English words are printed in a bold typeface and can be read easily enough.

Solti with the Vienna Philharmonic directs a strong, spectacular version, emphasizing the Wagnerian associations of the score. It is well sung – both principals are engaging – but just a little short on charm. The solo singing is not so steady in tone as on the EMI set, and the lack of geniality in the atmosphere is a drawback in a work of this nature. Needless to say, Solti does the *Witch's ride* excitingly, and the VPO are throughout encouraged to play with consistent fervour. Edita Gruberova is an excellent Dew Fairy and Walter Berry is first-rate as Peter. Anny Schlemm's Witch is a very strong characterization indeed, and there are some imaginative touches of stereo production associated with *Hocus pocus* and her other moments of magic. The recording is admirably vivid, but its sense of spectacle does not erase one's memory of the Karajan version. The transfer is characteristically brilliant, with vivid detail but not a great deal of warmth.

Ibert, Jacques
(1890–1962)

Flute concerto.
*** RCA RK 25109. James Galway (flute), RPO, Dutoit – CHAMINADE: *Concertino*; FAURÉ: *Fantaisie*; POULENC: *Sonata*.***

Ibert's high-spirited and inventive concerto deserves the widest currency; it has no lack of charm and lyrical appeal, particularly when it is as well performed as it is here by James Galway and the RPO under Charles Dutoit. Moreover it has the distinct advantage of highly attractive couplings. There is no alternative on cassette, but it will be difficult to supersede this version, which enjoys a clear, spacious recording and has been skilfully transferred.

Divertissement for chamber orchestra.
(**) HMV TC-ASD 2989. City of Birmingham SO, Frémaux – HONEGGER: *Pacific 231*; POULENC: *Les Biches* (**); SATIE: *Gymnopédies*.***

The reverberant acoustic of the recording here is less than ideal for Ibert's witty piece, and although the performance is vigorous and warm-hearted it suffers from the restricted range of the cassette transfer, which, while quite well balanced, has a total absence of sparkle in the treble.

Escales (symphonic pieces).
(M) *** HMV TC-SXLP 30263 [Angel 4xG 60102]. French National Radio Orch., Stokowski – DEBUSSY: *Ibéria*; RAVEL: *Alborada*.**(*)
(B) * RCA Camden c4-5031. Boston SO, Munch – DUKAS: *L'Apprenti sorcier*; RAVEL: *Boléro* etc.(*)

Ibert's evocative *Escales* (*Ports of Call*) is given a memorable performance on the HMV tape. Stokowski is on top form, conjuring the most vivid colours from the French orchestra. The gorgeously rich string patina in the opening Italian vista is matched by the seductive sounds of the North African snake-charmer, while the closing section has the most compelling animation. The recording is very vivid indeed, and if there is an element of glare this only emphasizes the presence of the Mediterranean sunshine. The sound on cassette is first-class. One needs just a little treble cut to restore the sheen on the upper strings (Stokowski creates some gorgeous sounds), but the richly coloured score has splendidly robust detail.

Munch's performance has transferred more successfully than the other items on this cassette. But the treble is still dim and there is a curious 'bubbling' disturbance at the opening (on our review copy).

d'Indy, Vincent (1851–1931)

Symphonie sur un chant montagnard français (Symphony on a French mountain air), Op. 25.

** HMV TC-ASD 3480. Aldo Ciccolini (piano), Orchestre de Paris, Baudo – SAINT-SAËNS: *Piano concerto No. 5.***

The *Symphonie sur un chant montagnard français* is the work by which d'Indy is known in this country, though the *Second Symphony* and *Istar* are occasionally heard. Aldo Ciccolini gives a good account of himself in the demanding solo part and the Orchestre de Paris under Serge Baudo give sympathetic support. The mountaineer's song may be too much of a good thing for some listeners (it recurs in all three movements) but d'Indy's music is both charming and resourceful, and the work has genuine warmth to commend it. The transfer is of pleasing quality, with a feeling of atmosphere and good piano tone. At climaxes the recording is somewhat opaque but it does not coarsen.

Ireland, John (1879–1962)

A Comedy overture.

*** Decca KSXC 6820. Grimethorpe Colliery Band, Howarth – BLISS: *Kenilworth* ***; ELGAR: *Severn suite* **(*); HOLST: *Moorside suite.****

Ireland's *Comedy overture* was later transcribed for orchestra and retitled *A London overture*. Perhaps the pithy main theme (*Piccadilly*) is rather more effective on strings, but it is always interesting to hear a composer's first thoughts. The precision of the playing of the Grimethorpe band and the detail and bloom of the Decca recording make this account extremely attractive. The cassette transfer is of excellent quality.

Ives, Charles (1874–1954)

Symphony No. 1 in D minor.

(*) Decca KSXC 6592. Los Angeles PO, Mehta – ELGAR: *Enigma variations.*(*)

Ives's charming *First Symphony*, a student work much influenced by Dvořák and Tchaikovsky but still with touches of individuality, is given a superb performance by Mehta, beautifully recorded. The pity is that he makes a substantial cut in the finale, to make it 'more compact and convincing'. One is inevitably suspicious of such claims, yet the symphony seems to stand up very well in this performance, which has transferred to tape with the recording's wide dynamic range successfully encompassed. The disc has marginally more brilliance and sharpness of detail, yet the cassette is admirably balanced and the sound has plenty of body.

Symphony No. 3.

*** Argo KZRC 845 [id.]. Academy of St Martin-in-the-Fields, Marriner – BARBER: *Adagio* ❀; COPLAND: *Quiet City;* COWELL: *Hymn;* CRESTON: *Rumor.****

The *Third Symphony* is one of Ives's better works, and Marriner's version comes in an anthology of unusual interest and merit. The performance of the symphony is impressive, and is faithfully recorded; the tape transfer is in every way first-class.

Jacob, Gordon
(born 1895)

Concerto for three hands on one or two pianos.
>   (M) *** HMV Greensleeve TC-ESD 7065. Cyril Smith and Phyllis Sellick (pianos), City of Birmingham SO, Arnold – ARNOLD and BLISS: *Concertos.****

Gordon Jacob has been seriously neglected in the recording studio. His keen professionalism, his willingness to stay within comparatively modest bounds, make for highly enjoyable results. This work is longer than the other two on the tape, taking up one whole side, but with its memorable ideas it is a worthy companion piece for Arnold and Bliss. The second of the four movements is particularly attractive in its easy lyricism, and so is the finale – a tarantella, ending with a brassy flourish. The electricity of the soloists is again splendidly matched by the ebullient conducting of Malcolm Arnold. Outstanding recording quality and a vivid transfer to tape.

5 Pieces.
>   *** Argo KZRC 856. Tommy Reilly (harmonica), Academy of St Martin-in-the-Fields, Marriner – MOODY: *Little suite;* TAUSKY: *Concertino;* VAUGHAN WILLIAMS: *Romance.****

The *Five Pieces* are delightful, and the invention is of a consistently high standard; the *Cradle song* and *Threnody* are particularly charming. The scoring is

extremely felicitous, and with such beautiful playing and recording this is a rewarding collection. The tape transfer is of excellent quality, the harmonica cleanly focused and the orchestral balance warm and natural.

Janáček, Leoš
(1854–1928)

Sinfonietta; Taras Bulba (rhapsody for orchestra).
>   (M) ** Supraphon 045380. Czech PO, Ančerl.

Janáček's *Sinfonietta*, with its sonorous opening fanfare (using twelve trumpets), is a splendidly spontaneous work, richly inspired throughout, and the *Taras Bulba* rhapsody is hardly less imaginative. The story on which this three-movement piece is based is full of cruelty and bloodthirsty detail, but Janáček's inspiration was fired by the underlying theme of heroism and the survival of the human spirit. *Taras Bulba* is not just another melodramatic tone poem but, like the *Sinfonietta*, is full of original orchestral effects, and the quality of its invention is high. Both performances here have vitality and atmosphere and the excellent Supraphon transfer manages the reverberant recording skilfully – the massive brass sonorities in the *Sinfonietta* sound rich and full, as do the climaxes of *Taras Bulba*.

String quartets Nos. 1 (Kreutzer sonata); 2 (Intimate pages).
>   (M) *** Decca Ace of Diamonds KSDC 527. Gabrieli Qt.

Janáček's two string quartets come from his last years and are among his most deeply individual and profoundly impassioned utterances. The Gabrieli

285

Quartet have the measure of this highly original music and give every bit as idiomatic an account of these masterpieces as did the Janáček Quartet in the 1960s. They have the advantage of a finely focused and beautifully balanced recording which has maximum clarity and blend as well as considerable warmth. The cassette quality is first-class, most natural in timbre, without edginess, and lacking only the minutest degree of upper range compared with the LP. In every way this is a most rewarding issue.

Glagolitic Mass.
   ** Decca KSXC 6600. Teresa Kubiak, Anne Collins, Robert Tear, Wolfgang Schone, Brighton Festival Chorus, RPO, Kempe.
   (M) *(*) Supraphon 0450519. Libuse Domaninská, Vera Soukupová, Beno Blachut, Eduard Haken, Czech Philharmonic Chorus and Orch., Ančerl.

Written when Janáček was over seventy, this is one of his most important and most exciting works, full of those strikingly fresh uses of sound that make his music so distinctive. The opening instrumental movement has much in common with the opening fanfare of the *Sinfonietta*, and all the other movements reveal an original approach to the church service. The text is taken from native Croatian variations of the Latin text, and Janáček himself said that he had village services in mind when he wrote the work. Not that this complex and often advanced music could be performed in any ordinary village church, but its vitality bespeaks a folk inspiration. Though Kempe's interpretation and the singing of the Brighton Festival Chorus do not always have the snapping authenticity of the Supraphon performance, it is an important advantage to have recording of such realism, and the playing of the

Royal Philharmonic is wonderfully committed and vivid. First-rate solo singing, with Teresa Kubiak particularly impressive. The transfer is satisfactory, if not one of Decca's best. It is made at a comparatively low level and the sound seems fresher on side two than side one.

The Czech performance remains a classic account and the recording is atmospheric, if not as clear and vivid as the Decca. The Supraphon transfer is quite successful, though not outstandingly sharp in focus. There is not the widest range, but the soloists and chorus sound natural. A certain lack of refinement is apparent at times, notably in the work's closing pages.

Kátya Kabanová (opera): complete.
   ⊛ *** Decca K 51 K 22 [Lon. 5-12109]. Elisabeth Söderström, DaliborJedlička,PeterDvorský, Libuše Márová, Naděžda Kniplová, Zdeněk Svehla, Vienna State Opera Chorus, Vienna PO, Mackerras.

An altogether superb issue on all counts and a triumphant success for Charles Mackerras, who draws playing of great eloquence from the Vienna Philharmonic. *Kátya Kabanová* is based on Ostrovsky's play *The Storm*, which has inspired other operas as well as Tchaikovsky's overture, and was his first stage work after the First World War. (It is worth adding that this is the first recording of a Janáček opera ever made outside Czechoslovakia.) Elisabeth Söderström dominates the cast as the tragic heroine and gives a performance of great insight and sensitivity; she touches the listener far more deeply than did her predecessor on Supraphon (disc only), and is supported by Mackerras with an imaginative grip and flair that outstrip his Czech colleagues. The plot (very briefly) centres on Kátya, a person of unusual goodness whose marriage is loveless, and her husband, dominated by his mother. Her infatuation with Boris (Peter Dvorský), her subsequent confession of adultery and her ultimate suicide are pictured with music of the most powerful and atmospheric kind. The other soloists are all Czech and their characterizations suitably authentic. But it is the superb orchestral playing and the inspired performance of Söderström that make this set so memorable. The recording has a realism and truthfulness that do full justice to Janáček's marvellous score. The difference between disc and cassette is minimal.

Joplin, Scott
(1868–1917)

ORCHESTRAL COLLECTIONS

Bethena; Elite syncopations; Euphonic sounds; Gladiolus rag; Magnetic rag; Original rags; Palm Leaf rags; Peacherine rag; Pineapple rag; Scott Joplin's new rag: Solace (A Mexican serenade); Wall Street rag.
  ** London KHCU 5009. New England Conservatory Ragtime Ens., Schuller.
The Cascades; The Chrysanthemum; The Easy Winners; The Entertainer (2 versions); Maple Leaf rag; Ragtime dance; Sugar Cane; Sunflower slow drag (2 versions).
  *(**) EMI TC-EMD 5503 [Angel 4xs 36060]. New England Conservatory Ragtime Ens., Schuller; Myron Romanul (piano).

Scott Joplin wrote fifty-one piano rags (some in conjunction with other composers) and it is not clear how much hand he had in the orchestrations: probably little,

the arrangements being fitted to the instrumentation available. Joplin's talent was narrow in range but strong in personality, so that almost any of his compositions is instantly recognizable, not only by the fairly rigid rhythmic straitjacket, but also by its melodic and harmonic individuality. The orchestral versions, however, with their unsophisticated scoring, add little to the music's impact, and purists will undoubtedly prefer the piano anthologies. Günther Schuller's New England group has quite striking projection. There is plenty of atmosphere and spontaneity, and the playing is rhythmically convincing. The second issue (KHCU 5009) seems to have a crisper rhythmic point, helped by the brighter focus of the London recording. The cassette too is crisply transferred, and the level is high. TC-EMD 5503 offers alternative piano and orchestral versions of two favourite items. The transfer is made at a very low level, and unfortunately besides having a lack of range and sparkle in the treble it tends to over-emphasize the large drum in the rhythm section unrealistically. With a bass cut and a treble lift a fairly acceptable sound can be obtained.

Elite syncopations (ballet).
  **(*) CRD CRDC 4029. Philip Gammon (piano), members of the Royal Ballet Orch.

These are authentic arrangements, many of them by Günther Schuller, and they are played with a fine sense of style. Most of the favourite rags are included (though not *The Entertainer*), plus some novelties, and the orchestrations are nicely varied, with the solo piano often left to play alone. The recording is really first-class, and Joplin fans will find this very enjoyable, although some might feel the approach is *too* sophisticated. The tape transfer is admirably crisp and well balanced, and this is agreeable background music, the sophistication of the presentation lending itself to such a use.

The Prodigal Son (ballet; orch. and arr. Grant Hossack).

** CBS 40-73363. London Festival Ballet Orch., Hossack.

Grant Hossack's ballet compiled from the music of Joplin follows an honourable tradition which includes *Pineapple Poll* and Lanchbery's *Tales of Beatrix Potter*. The arranger has tried to use the instrumental traditions of both symphonic and popular idioms, and his score is considerably more vivid than the original orchestrations used in Joplin's own time. But in the last analysis Joplin's music is not varied enough for this kind of treatment, although one can imagine that when the eye is absorbed with the stage action it would be effective enough. Good performances and recording; in fact this makes a pleasant background tape. The sound is rather more vivid on side two than side one.

Scott Joplin (film musical; arr. Dick Hyman): includes *Maple Leaf rag; Solace; Pleasant Moments; Heliotrope Bouquet; Elite syncopations; Peachtime rag; The Entertainer; Weeping Willow; Wall Street rag; Gladiolus rag*.

** MCA TC-MCF 2801. Various artists, orch., Hyman.

This cannot be regarded as a general recommendation; its association with the film scenario is indelible. But with Dick Hyman (who recorded a most distinguished set of the Joplin piano rags for RCA – now, alas, deleted in the UK) as director, the music-making is bound to have interest. Most of the more famous rags are here, either played straight or adapted as incidental music to accompany the film narrative. One of the highlights is an orchestral arrangement of *Solace*, with superb trumpet and alto saxophone solo contributions from Ray Crisara and Phil Bodner, and there is an exhilarating piano duo sequence (*Cutting Contest*; *Maple Leaf rag*) where Dick Hyman is joined by Hank Jones on a second keyboard. Earlier some of the pianistic bravura – exploiting the stratospheric regions of the piano – may seem overdone, but Joplin's music hardly exists within a purist tradition. The orchestrations are well managed, and the bright, lively recording is clearly transferred.

The Sting (incidental music for film; arr. Marvin Hamlisch): includes *The Entertainer; Solace; The Easy Winners; Pineapple rag; Gladiolus rag; Merry-go-round; Listen to the Mocking Bird; Darling Nellie Gray; Turkey in the Straw; Ragtime dance*.

*** MCA TC-MCF 2537. Marvin Hamlisch (piano), orch., Hamlisch.

Although listed as a 'film soundtrack recording' this was obviously recorded *for* rather than from the soundtrack, and the technical quality is excellent. The piano timbre seems particularly well balanced and just right for the music with plenty of point yet not shallow. The small orchestral group too is nicely judged and plays with stylish enthusiasm. There is also a small selection of melodies played on what sounds like a Gavioli fairground organ (or a good imitation). *The Entertainer* is used as a motto theme throughout, but few will object to the regular reprise of this famous piece; it sounds especially well in concertante form on its final appearance. The recording has transferred well to tape and is crisp and clear.

Rags (arr. Perlman): *Bethena; The Easy Winners; Elite syncopations; The Entertainer; Magnetic rag; Pineapple rag; Ragtime dance; Solace; The Strenuous Life; Sugar Cane rag*.

*(**) HMV TC-ASD 3075 [Angel 4xs 37113]. Itzhak Perlman (violin), André Previn (piano).

Perlman and Previn letting their hair down present a winning combination in a whole sequence of Joplin's most naggingly haunting rags. This is very much Previn's country, and his rhythmic zest infects his brilliant partner. Originally this was very well transferred to tape, but a recent copy we tried showed a higher-level transfer, with a fizzy, distorted violin image. This is a tape to sample before purchase.

PIANO COLLECTIONS

Bethena; Elite syncopations; Eugenia; Leola; Paragon rag; Pineapple rag; Rose leaf rag; Solace (A Mexican serenade).
> (M) **(*) Nonesuch N5 71264. Joshua Rifkin (piano).

The Cascades; The Chrysanthemum; Country Club; The Nonpareil; Original rags; Stoptime rag; Sugar Cane; Weeping Willow.
> (M) **(*) Nonesuch N5 71305. Joshua Rifkin (piano).

16 Piano rags (as in above two collections).
> *** Advent F 1042 (see p. xxiii) [id.]. Joshua Rifkin (as above).

The Entertainer; Euphonic sounds; Fig Leaf rag; Gladiolus rag; Magnetic rag; Maple Leaf rag; Ragtime dance; Scott Joplin's new rag.
> (M) **(*) Nonesuch N5 71248. Joshua Rifkin (piano).

> *** Advent E 1013 (see p. xxiii) [id.]. Joshua Rifkin (as above; with *Collection of rags* by Turpin, Joplin, Lamb, Scott, Roberts, Bolcom, Albright, played by William Bolcom, piano***).

Bethena; Harmony Club waltz; Magnetic rag; Maple Leaf rag; Paragon rag; Pineapple rag; Scott Joplin's new rag; Solace (A Mexican serenade); Swipesy cake walk.
> *(*) Decca Phase 4 KPFC 4292. Eric Rogers (piano).

Cleopha; Easy Winners; Elite syncopations; The Entertainer; Gladiolus rag; Maple Leaf rag; Original rags; Pineapple rag; Rag-time dance; Scott Joplin's new rag; Solace (A Mexican serenade); Sunflower slow drag.
> (M) *(*) CBS Embassy 40-31043. Ronnie Price (piano), with rhythm.

Joshua Rifkin is the pianist whose name has been indelibly associated with the recent Scott Joplin cult, stimulated by the soundtrack background music of the very successful film *The Sting*. There is no question that, of the pianists represented here, his contribution is the most distinguished. His relaxed, cool style, rhythms not too exact, and more than a hint of monochrome in the tone colour, is distinctive. Perhaps the playing is a trifle too studied – a little more obvious joy in the music would be attractive – but there is no doubt that this playing has style. However, if it is taken a whole tape at a time (and one assumes that Mr Rifkin will eventually work his way through all fifty-one pieces) the danger of monotony is real, when the basic approach is comparatively rigid. The Nonesuch recording is excellent, slightly more mellow on the first tape (N5 71248), to match the playing itself. The transfers are natural. The last degree of range is missing in the treble, but with a bass cut the balance can be made to sound very convincing, as the piano's treble is never muffled. On tape as on disc, N5 71264 and N5 71305 are slightly crisper than the first issue.

Joshua Rifkin's recordings are also available in first-class chrome transfers on the Advent label. The contents of the first two Nonesuch collections are offered back to back, and the third is coupled with a fascinating cross-section of music by other ragtime composers.

William Bolcom, the pianist in this group, is altogether more percussive in his approach, the style jazzily rhythmic. The opening *Ragtime nightmare* is particularly arresting; the programme has no lack of contrast, and this makes an excellent appendix to the Joplin items. The transfers are characteristic of Advent's superb technical quality (apart from one or two moments of pre-echo), and the sound obviously has more range than the Nonesuch transfers.

Eric Rogers plays his opening number, *Maple Leaf rag*, on a very old upright Bechstein, slightly twangy in the treble and not quite in tune. It sounds marvellous. He appears to use several pianos on his record, including a Steinway grand for one item, but unfortunately we are not given more details. This issue has plenty of personality but the playing itself is not really distinctive. The transfer is admirably crisp on side one, slightly less so on side two.

For those wanting a budget-priced tape including both *The Entertainer* (of *The Sting* fame) and *Maple Leaf rag*, Ronnie Price's CBS Embassy cassette may serve. The recording is bold and forward, the rhythm group unostentatious but not unstylish; the playing is alive and spontaneous, and the selection generous. The tape transfer is good, though not sparkling. The level on playback needs to be well up for maximum impact, but then the piano and rhythm are quite convincingly balanced.

Ketèlbey, Albert
(1875–1959)

Bells across the Meadow; Chal Romano (*Gypsy Lad*)*; The Clock and the Dresden Figures; In a Chinese Temple Garden; In a Monastery Garden; In a Persian Market; In the Moonlight; In the Mystic Land of Egypt; Sanctuary of the Heart.*
> ****(*)**HMV TC-ASD 3542. Vernon Midgley, Jean Temperley, Ambrosian Singers, Leslie Pearson (piano), Philharmonia Orch., Lanchbery.

A splendid collection in every way. John Lanchbery plainly has a very soft spot for Ketèlbey's tuneful music (and there are some very good tunes here), and he uses every possible resource to ensure that when the composer demands spectacle he gets it. *In the Mystic Land of Egypt*, for instance, uses soloist and chorus in canon in the principal tune (and very fetching too). *The Clock and the Dresden Figures* is deliciously done, with Leslie Pearson playing the concertante piano part in scintillating fashion. Perhaps in the *Monastery Garden* the distant monks are a shade too realistically distant, but in *Sanctuary of the Heart* there is no mistaking that the heart is worn firmly on the sleeve. The orchestral playing throughout is not only polished but warm-hearted – the middle section of *Bells across the Meadow*, which has a delightful melodic contour, is played most tenderly and loses any hint of vulgarity. Yet when vulgarity is called for it is not shirked – only it's a stylish kind of vulgarity! The *Chal Romano* has an unexpectedly vigorous melodic impulse, reminding the listener of Eric Coates. The recording is excellent, but the transfer, generally full and brilliant, is not absolutely refined throughout. There is some over-resonant bass, for instance, in the opening work, *In a Persian Market*.

Khachaturian, Aram
(1903–78)

Piano concerto in D flat major.
> ****** Decca KSXC 6599. Alicia de Larrocha, LPO, Frühbeck de

Burgos – FRANCK: *Symphonic variations.***

The slow movement of Khachaturian's colourful concerto as interpreted by a Spanish pianist and a Spanish conductor sounds evocatively like Falla, and the finale too is infectiously jaunty. Not so in the first movement, which is disappointingly slack in rhythm at a dangerously slow tempo. The transfer is full but lacks something in sparkle; side two has less refined definition than side one, and this suits the Franck *Variations* better than the Khachaturian finale.

Gayaneh (ballet): excerpts; *Masquerade: suite.*
(M) *** Supraphon 0401226. Brno State PO, Belohlávek.

A first-class coupling of an extended selection from *Gayaneh* and the suite from *Masquerade*, which is less indelible but still enjoyable in its lightweight way. The orchestral playing is full of verve and spirit and most sympathetic to the genuinely inspired lyrical music of *Gayaneh*. The recording is vivid and the acoustic has just the right degree of reverberation. The transfer is one of Supraphon's very best, lively and sparkling but with plenty of tonal fullness.

Gayaneh (ballet): excerpts; *Spartacus* (ballet): excerpts.
*** Decca KSXC 6000. Vienna PO, the composer.
(***) HMV TC-ASD 3347. LSO, the composer.

The Decca and HMV selections are not identical, but both include the items likely to be of principal interest. The HMV recording is immensely spectacular; it is also very resonant and has not transferred to tape very comfortably. The reverberation coarsens the sound notably in the opening *Lezghinka* and the *Adagio of Spartacus and Phrygia* (with its *Onedin Line* associations), which is almost ex-

cessively sumptuous. The Decca cassette was an early issue and originally not a very successful transfer, the sound turgid and muddled. But it has been remastered, and the recording now sounds wonderfully fresh and colourful, the reverberation well controlled and with vivid colour and detail throughout. The famous *Onedin Line* tune emerges with splendid richness on the strings, and the freshening of the quality throughout both sides often brings a demonstration standard of vividness.

Kodály, Zoltán
(1882–1967)

Háry János: suite.
*** Decca Phase 4 KPFC 4355 [Lon. 5-21146]. Netherlands Radio Orch., Dorati – PROKOFIEV: *Lieutenant Kijé.****
(M) **(*) RCA Gold Seal GK 42698. Boston SO, Leinsdorf – PROKOFIEV: *Lieutenant Kijé.***(*)

The Netherlands orchestra is by no means one of the world's most polished ensembles, but the Decca recording is exceptionally vivid and Dorati's direct manner produces strong musical characterization. The Phase Four techniques are not exaggerated and they do no harm to Kodály's bright orchestral colours. The transfer to tape is admirably clear and vivid.

Leinsdorf draws brilliant, colourful playing from the Boston orchestra. The recording – mid-sixties vintage – is excellent, but the transfer is made at a comparably modest level and the acoustic is reverberant, so that the transients are not so crisp, and the sound not as refined and clear, as on Dorati's Decca tape. However, this is still an enjoyable tape.

Háry János: suite and two arias:
*Poor I am still; Once I had a brood of
chicks. Dances of Galánta.*

(M) *** Decca Jubilee KJBC 55.
Olga Szönyi (soprano), LSO,
Kertesz.

Háry János is superbly played and recorded. This has always been something
of a demonstration piece, and once again
The battle and defeat of Napoleon proves
an example of how much modern recording can offer in realism and clarity. In the
Viennese musical clock the percussion
balance might ideally have achieved a crisper effect, especially from the side-drum,
but some will be glad not to have the kit-
chen department exaggerated as it sometimes is. One certainly could not fault the
balance of the cimbalom, which emerges
as soloist in the *Intermezzo* without
drowning everything. Throughout, the
orchestral playing has great élan, something which the *Dances of Galánta* share;
indeed they are so well played they almost
rise to the stature of *János.* The two arias
are short but attractive, and Miss Szönyi
sings with such character that her Slavonic wobbles can be quite forgiven. The
transfer, made at the highest level, is
stunningly vivid – one of Decca's very
best. The bloom and detail in *Háry János*
are remarkable (the horns sound especially rich), and the *Dances of Galánta* are
hardly less spectacular.

Lalo, Édouard
(1823–92)

(i) *Violoncello concerto in D minor;*
(ii) *Symphonie espagnole* (for violin
and orchestra), *Op. 21.*

*(**) HMV TC-ASD 3209. City
of Birmingham SO, Frémaux,
with (i) Paul Tortelier (cello),
(ii) Yan Pascal Tortelier
(violin).

Tortelier father and son appear in an
attractive coupling of Lalo concertante
pieces, particularly apt when the *Cello
concerto,* like the *Symphonie espagnole,*
has at least two striking ideas that
directly echo the dance music of Spain. It
is the *Cello concerto* that brings the more
impressive performance, with Tortelier
inspired by relatively uninventive music
to give a superbly expressive reading, full
of imaginative phrasing. The violin work,
warmly played by Tortelier junior, is
given its full five-movement form. The
transfer of the *Symphonie espagnole* is of
admirable quality, with a most realistic
projection of the soloist and plenty of
weight and detail in the orchestra. There
is a momentary hint of overmodulation
from the deep brass in the slow movement but the finale has splendid sparkle.
The transfer of the *Cello concerto* has less
sparkle and the detail is not so clear. But
the quality is still good, smoother but well
balanced if somewhat sombre in colouring.

Symphonie espagnole (for violin and
orchesta), *Op. 21.*

(M) *** HMV TC-SXLP 30277.
Yehudi Menuhin, Philhar-
monia Orch., Goossens–SAINT-
SAËNS: *Havanaise* etc.***

*(**) CBS 40-76726. Pinchas
Zukerman, Los Angeles PO,
Mehta – BRUCH: *Violin con-
certo No. 1.***(*)

(M) ** RCA Gold Seal GK 11329.
Itzhak Perlman, LSO, Previn –
RAVEL: *Tzigane.**(*)

Menuhin's recording of the *Symphonie espagnole* dates from the earliest
years of stereo. It is a scintillating performance, matched by clean sound and
excellent balance (the woodwind detail at
the opening of the finale is a joy). Menuhin was on top form when the recording
was made, and his control of colour is
matched by his feeling for the music's
rhythmic character. The way he shapes

the sinuous secondary theme of the first movement is wonderfully engaging. The accompaniment too is first-class and the recording admirably bright and clear. On disc it seems a shade too brightly lit, but the tape transfer needs only the slightest reduction of treble. The overall effect is irresistibly vivid.

Zukerman's account is first-class in every way. The playing has real panache, and Mehta accompanies vividly. The recording is basically excellent, but the high level of the transfer has brought moments where the refinement slips, and the upper partials of the solo violin are not always clean.

Perlman plays the *Symphonie* brilliantly, sparkling in the bravura and relishing the expressive melodies without over-indulging them. He is ably supported by Previn, but the snag is the recording balance, which places the violin much too far forward. This aural spotlight is obtained at the orchestra's expense, and accompanying detail is sometimes all but masked, although Previn ensures that the tuttis have plenty of impact. The transfer to tape tends to smooth the touch of harshness on Perlman's tone, although the orchestra still lacks bloom. However, the performance is so infectiously spirited that it is easy to enjoy it in spite of the faults.

Lanchbery, John
(born 1923)

Tales of Beatrix Potter (ballet arranged from popular tunes of the Victorian era).
**(*) HMV TC-CSD 3690. Orch. of the Royal Opera House, Covent Garden, Lanchbery.

Here is a companion score for John Lanchbery's arrangement of *La Fille mal gardée*. The music is not as distinguished melodically as the compilation of Hérold

tunes, but the colourful and witty orchestration is a source of delight and this is really top-drawer EMI sound, as the opening bars readily show. The composer-arranger used Victorian tunes (including some by Sullivan) of the period of the Beatrix Potter stories, and they are so skilfully linked that one would think the score was 'composed' as original music. The film of the ballet was a great success and this recording deserves to be too. The musicassette sound is of high quality, although the treble is not as sharply defined as on the disc. But at the other end of the spectrum the recording has weight and sonority, with the bass drum nicely caught. With a wider dynamic range this would have been first-class.

Langford, Gordon
(20th century)

Prelude and fugue. (i) *Rhapsody for trombone. Sinfonietta*. Arrangements: FAURÉ: *Pavane. A Sullivan fantasy*. TRAD.: *Billy Boy; Irish Washerwoman; Waltzing Matilda*.
(M) *** RCA MPK 253. Black Dyke Mills Band, Newsome, (i) with Don Lusher (trombone).

Gordon Langford is a British composer of modest pretensions, best-known for his witty arrangements of traditional airs, some of which are included on this cassette. They are splendidly played and very enjoyable; so is the arrangement of Fauré's *Pavane*, not a piece one associates with brass bands. The *Rhapsody for trombone* is cleverly written, and with its syncopated rhythms in its lively outer sections it occupies musical territory between the 'classical' and 'popular' traditions rather effectively. It is an extended piece but does not outstay its welcome, particularly as the soloist, Don Lusher, besides displaying appropriate bravura, is obviously completely at home with the idiom. The *Sinfonietta* is a good-humoured, lightweight piece, of no great moment but effectively scored, obviously rewarding to play, and undoubtedly entertaining. The Black Dyke Mills Band displays characteristic virtuosity and understanding throughout, and as the recording is superb (the warmly reverberant acoustic is perfect for the music) and the tape transfer of demonstration quality, this can be recommended with all possible enthusiasm to brass band buffs.

Lanner, Joseph
(1801–43)

Bruder Halt! (galop), *Op. 16; Dampf-walzer und Galopp, Op. 94; Hofball-tanz* (waltz), *Op. 161; Marienwalzer, Op. 143; Neujahrsgalopp, Op. 61/2; Pesther-Walzer, Op. 93; Tarantel-Galopp, Op. 125; Die Werber Waltz, Op. 103.*
(M) (**) HMV Greensleeve TC-ESD 7045. Johann Strauss Orch. of Vienna, Boskovsky.

This Lanner selection offers lively invention and shows us the musical background from which the masterpieces of Johann Strauss emerged. Lanner's music is vivacious and elegant but lacks the memorability of invention of the famous Strauss dance music. It is all presented most agreeably, but the recording lacks crispness of focus – the side-drum (the essential condiment in this kind of music) is fizzy and ill-defined. The sound is acceptable on a small player.

Lehár, Franz
(1870–1948)

The Land of Smiles (Das Land des Lächelns; operetta): complete.
(M) *** HMV TC2–SXDW 3044. Elisabeth Schwarzkopf, Nicolai Gedda, Erich Kunz, Emmy Loose, Otakar Kraus, Philharmonia Chorus and Orch., Ackermann.

Even by the standards of Viennese operetta *Land of Smiles* has an offbeat plot, with its uncomfortable clash of East and West. Coming to it after hearing Johann Strauss, one cannot help being struck by the seriousness of emotion. These are real characters, not machinery in an elaborate charade, even if the situation comes dangerously close to the sentimental. Completed in 1929, this was relatively late Lehár, and some of his writing seems to have reflected serious models, though fascinatingly the parallels with Richard Strauss's *Arabella* (both musical and dramatic) are in Lehár's favour, for *Land of Smiles* came four years before the opera.

Though Gedda does not have quite the passionate flair of Tauber in his famous *Dein ist mein ganzes herz*, his thoughtful artistry matches a performance which effortlessly brings out the serious parallels without weighing the work down. Schwarzkopf and Kunz sing delectably and the stereo transcription brings out the ravishing sounds of Lehár's often Puccini-like invention. The transfer to tape is very lively, almost too lively: one needs a strong treble cut if the voices are not to sound edgy and their aura of microphone resonance overemphasized, so that consonants become exaggerated. The orchestral strings too, as one notices in the overture, are inclined to sound grainy in texture. However, if the top is cut back the recording's basic kernel of warmth and atmosphere remains without the quality sounding damped, and the bloom on the voices of Gedda and Kunz, especially, is striking.

The Merry Widow (*Die lustige Witwe*; operetta): complete.
  ⊛ (M) *** HMV TC2-SXDW 3045. Elisabeth Schwarzkopf, Nicolai Gedda, Erich Kunz, Emmy Loose, Otakar Kraus, Philharmonia Chorus and Orch., Ackermann.
  (**) DG 3370 003 [id.]. Elizabeth Harwood, René Kollo, Zoltan Kelemen, Teresa Stratas, Werner Hollweg, Donald Grobe, Chorus of German Opera, Berlin, Berlin PO, Karajan.

Curiously, EMI have not made the classic stereo Schwarzkopf *Merry Widow* available on tape; instead they have reissued the earlier mono version, conducted by Otto Ackermann. It was this set of the early 1950s which established a new pattern in recording operetta. Some were even scandalized when Schwarzkopf insisted on treating the *Viljalied* very seriously indeed at an unusually slow tempo, but the big step forward was that an operetta was treated with all the care for detail normally lavished on grand opera, and the result had heightened character, both dramatic and musical, with high polish and sharp focus the order of the day. Ten years later in stereo Schwarzkopf was to record the role again, if anything with even greater point and perception, but here she has extra youthful vivacity and the *Viljalied* – ecstatically drawn out – is unique. The set also includes the heavyweight (Richard) Straussian overture which Lehár appended to the score (omitted in the stereo version). Some may be troubled that Kunz as Danilo sounds older than the Baron, but it is still a superbly characterful cast, and the transfer from mono has been well done; indeed

the atmospheric effect of the recording in the first-class tape version is so striking that at times one almost thinks this is real stereo. The transfer is very kind to the solo voices, the choruses and ensembles are well-focused, with an agreeable warmth, and there is a pleasing ambient glow over the whole proceedings. Indeed this need make no apologies at all technically, and is preferable in every way to the Karajan set.

'Brahms's *Requiem* performed to the tunes of Lehár' was how one wit described the Karajan version, with its carefully measured tempi and absence of sparkle. Though Harwood is an appealing Widow, she seems colourless beside Schwarzkopf. The recording has religious reverberation, and the tape transfer – one of DG's earliest Dolby transfers – was mismanaged, so that the treble response is muffled. It is to be hoped that better-quality copies will have appeared by the time we are in print.

The Merry Widow: highlights.
  *(*) DG 3300 729 [id.] (from above recording cond. Karajan).
  (M) (*) Saga CA 5365. Mimi Coertse, Friedl Loor, Karl Terkal, Vienna Volksoper Chorus and Orch., Hagen.

Karajan's highlights have been more successfully transferred than the complete set from which they come, although the sound is not really refined and the left-hand channel is weak in relation to the right.

On Saga, with Mimi Coertse a vivacious Widow and excellent support from the other soloists, the selection is undoubtedly spirited, with plenty of style and sparkle. The snag is the recording, originally on Vox and made in the late fifties. It is poorly focused and gritty in the treble, tolerable only to indulgent ears. Side one is rather fluffy in focus; side two is brighter (and grittier).

The Merry Widow (in an English version by Sheldon Harnick): abridged recording.

** HMV TC-ASD 3500 [complete set on Angel 4xs 37500]. Beverly Sills, Alan Titus, Glenys Fowles, Henry Price, David Rae Smith, New York City Opera Chorus and Orch., Redel.

Based on a new production given at the New York City Opera in 1978, this HMV recording has much to recommend it. The selection is generous (there is more than an hour of music), the translation is spirited and in good taste, and the musical direction first-class. Julius Redel's easy Viennese-styled *rubato* is highly engaging and generally produces more sparkling results than Bonynge's somewhat more forced brilliance. The cast is uniformly good. Alan Titus is a persuasive Danilo; his tender way with the waltz at the end is touching. Glenys Fowles is no less pleasing as Valencienne, fresh of voice and vivacious. But not everyone will respond to the quick, intense *vibrato* of Beverly Sills in the name part, which, of course, dominates the proceedings. One can adjust to it, but Lehár's music needs the kind of smiling vocal lyricism which Schwarzkopf alone provides. The HMV recording is excellent, warm and atmospheric; the transfer is agreeably kind in sound but does not lack brightness, although it has not the obvious range and sparkle of the Decca highlights selection (see below).

The Merry Widow (in an English version by Christopher Hassall): concise recording.

** HMV TC-CSD 1259. Sadler's Wells Opera Company and Orch., Reid.

(B) ** Classics for Pleasure TC-CFP 40276. Catherine Wilson, Jonny Blanc, Patricia Hay, David Hillman, William McCue, Gordon Sandison, Scottish Opera Chorus, Scottish Philharmonia Orch., Gibson.

The performance on HMV does not always have an *echt*-Viennese flavour; nevertheless it says much for the achievement of the Sadler's Wells production that their concise version is so successful. For many, the deciding factor will be the English words, sung in an admirable translation, but one is not sure that this is so important on a recording. The Sadler's Wells cast is strongly characterized: only in Howell Glynne's approach is there a suspicion of Gilbert and Sullivan. Thomas Round is an appropriately raffish Danilo, though it is a pity the recording tends to exaggerate the unevenness in his voice. William McAlpine as the second tenor, Camille de Rosillon, comes over much better, and his *Red as the rose* is exquisitely sung. The chorus is outstandingly good (especially the men) in the big scenes. The transfer offers clear, brilliant sound with plenty of glitter but with a touch of hardness on the voices. But the recording is not a new one and there is no lack of impact or sparkle here, even if the acoustic is not as open as one would ideally like.

The Scottish production is also enjoyable. The singers make an excellent team (the ensembles go especially well) and Gibson conducts throughout in an attractively spirited way. The solo singing is agreeable rather than memorable (*Vilja*, for instance, is hardly melting) but the atmosphere of the music comes over readily. The recording is vivid but the reverberation has provided some problems; the snares on the oft-used side-drum (in the orchestral percussion) are fizzily focused, and this lack of absolute sharpness of outline is present in climaxes. However, the solo voices are clear and natural and there is plenty of bloom on the sound. This is good value.

The Merry Widow (in an English version by Richard Bonynge): highlights.

** Decca KCET 629. Joan Sutherland, Werner Krenn, Regina Resnik, Graeme Ewer, National PO, Bonynge.

Although not everyone will take to Sutherland's Widow, this is generally an attractive English version. The exuberantly breezy overture (arranged by Douglas Gamley) sets the mood of the proceedings, and the slightly brash recording (the sheen on the strings sounding artificially bright) is determinedly effervescent. The chorus sings with great zest and the ensembles are infectious. The whole of the closing part of the tape – the finale of Act 2; Njegus's aria (nicely done by Graeme Ewer); the introduction of the girls from Maxims and the famous Waltz duet – is certainly vivacious; the Parisian atmosphere is a trifle overdone, but enjoyably so. Earlier Sutherland's *Vilja* loses out on charm because of her wide *vibrato*, but the Waltz duet with Krenn is engaging.

The Merry Widow (ballet; arr. John Lanchbery): highlights.

(**) HMV TC-CSD 3772 [Angel 4xs 37092]. Adelaide Singers, Adelaide SO, Lanchbery.

This is much less successful as a score than Lanchbery's other ballets; it sounds for all the world like a theatrical selection with the chorus joining in now and then. The orchestral playing here is far from sophisticated, but the recording is good. Unfortunately the reverberant acoustic has brought problems to the tape transfer, and the tuttis lose their refinement of focus.

Paganini (operetta): complete.

*** HMV TC-SLS 5122. Nicolai Gedda, Anneliese Rothenberger, Friedrich Lenz, Benno Kusche, Bavarian State Opera Chorus, Bavarian SO, Boskovsky.

By 1925, when he completed the operetta *Paganini*, Lehár had begun to look for his subjects to romanticized biography of the kind which the infant cinema was already appropriating. Lehár shrewdly saw that his audience would welcome a similar trend, and so he enthusiastically took over a libretto (originally sent to him anonymously) involving the early life of the demon violinist and a love affair (unsubstantiated by history) with the princess of the state where Paganini was court violinist. This subject gave Lehár a chance to exploit the vein of seriousness he was favouring. *Paganini* is an operetta with symphonic aspirations, as carefully calculated on its way as a Puccini opera. After failure in Vienna, it was a wild success in Berlin with Tauber as hero. What is missing is the wealth of memorable tunes which mark earlier Lehár, but this red-blooded performance under Willi Boskovsky makes an excellent case for the piece, with generally first-rate singing and Ulf Hoelscher taking the important violin solos. Warm and resonant recording but bad close balance for the speaking voices. However, the recording has been very skilfully transferred. The chorus is not crystal-clear and the degree of projection of the solo voices varies a little (the opening of side three is notably vivid). But the ambient glow of the sound is striking from the opening, and this makes very agreeable listening.

'*The world of Lehár*': (i) *Giuditta: Meine Lippen, sie küssen.* (i; ii) *Der Graf von Luxemburg: Sind sie von sinnen . . . Lieber Freund . . .* Waltz: *Bist du's lachendes Gluck.* (iii; iv) *Das Land des Lächelns: Dein ist mein ganzes Herz; Wer hat die Liebe uns ins Herz gesenkt.* (i; v) *Die lustige Witwe: Dance; Vilja;* Waltz: *Lippen*

Schweigen; Finale: *Ja, das Studium der Weiber ist schwer.* (iv) *Paganini: Gern hab' ich die Frau'n gekusst.* (iii) *Schön ist die Welt: Ich bin verliebt.* (i; ii) *Der Zarewitsch: Volgalied: Allein wieder allein! Kosende Wellen;* Finale. (i) *Zigeunerliebe: Hör ich Cymbalklänge.*

> (M) **(*) Decca KCSP 517. (i-iv) Vienna Volksoper Chorus and Orch., various conductors; (i) Hilde Gueden; (ii) Waldemar Kmentt; (iii) Renate Holm; (iv) Werner Krenn; (v) Per Grunden, Vienna State Opera Chorus and Orch., Stolz.

An excellent anthology, the best collection of Lehár's music on a single tape or disc. The compiler has drawn heavily on a stylish operetta duet recital of Renate Holm and Werner Krenn (his opening *Dein ist mein ganzes Herz* is splendid) and also on Hilde Gueden's vintage recordings from the late fifties and early sixties. Highlights include the delicious *Ich bin verliebt* (Renate Holm) from *Schön ist die Welt* and Hilde Gueden's enchanting waltz song from *Giuditta, Meine Lippen, sie küssen so heiss.* The excerpt from *Der Zarewitsch* has a splendidly atmospheric gypsy accompaniment. On side two there are some lively items from Decca's 1958 *Merry Widow.* The recordings come up surprisingly well, and the tape transfers are generally vivid (the percussion is pleasingly crisp in the excerpt from *Schön ist die Welt);* but in the excerpts from *The Merry Widow* on side two the reverberant acoustic brings a slipping in the clarity of focus.

Leoncavallo, Ruggiero
(1858–1919)

I Pagliacci (opera): complete.
> **(*) DG 3371 011 [id.]. Joan

Carlyle, Carlo Bergonzi, Ugo Benelli, Giuseppe Taddei, Rolando Panerai, Chorus and Orch. of La Scala, Milan, Karajan – MASCAGNI: *Cavalleria Rusticana.****

> (M) **(*) HMV TC-SLS 819. Maria Callas, Giuseppe di Stefano, Tito Gobbi, Chorus and Orch. of La Scala, Milan, Serafin – MASCAGNI: *Cavalleria Rusticana.*(**)

I Pagliacci: complete. Arias: *La Bohème: Ed ora, conoscetela; Musette svarie sulla bocca; Non parlate così; Io non ho; Scuoti o vento. Zazà: Mamma, io non l'ho avuta mai; Zazà, piccola zingara. Chatterton: Non saria meglio.*

> (***) RCA RK 40003. Montserrat Caballé, Placido Domingo, Sherrill Milnes, John Alldis Choir, LSO, Santi.

The Italian opera traditionalists may jib at Karajan's treatment of Leoncavallo's melodrama – and for that matter its companion piece. He does nothing less than refine them, with longbreathed, expansive tempi and the minimum exaggeration. One would expect such a process to take the guts out of the drama, but with Karajan – as in *Carmen, Tosca, Aïda,* etc. – the result is superb. One is made to hear the beauty of the music first and foremost, and that somehow makes one understand the drama more. Passions are no longer torn to tatters, Italian-style – and Karajan's choice of soloists was clearly aimed to help that – but the passions are still there, and rarely if ever on record has the Scala Orchestra played with such beautiful feeling for tone colour. Bergonzi is among the most sensitive of Italian tenors of heroic quality, and it is good to have Joan Carlyle doing a major operatic role on record, touching if often rather cool. Taddei is magnificently strong, and Benelli and Panerai could hardly be bettered in the roles of Beppe and Silvio. The recording is good but needs to be reproduced at a high volume level if it is to have full immediacy. The transfer to tape is smoothly done, the quality always agreeable, but the choral detail rather soft-grained. If only the level had been marginally higher this would have been first-class. It is still good. The booklet offered with this set is comparatively meagre and there is no libretto, which seems particularly perverse with a *verismo* opera, where the narrative detail is important for full enjoyment.

The combination of Callas and Gobbi in *I Pagliacci* makes for thrilling drama, even if the characterization is not entirely conventional (a flashing-eyed Nedda this). There are many points at which Callas finds extra intensity, extra meaning, so that the performance is well worth hearing for her alone, particularly when she is also the principal attraction in the companion version of *Cavalleria Rusticana*. Serafin's direction is strong and direct. The transfer seems more successful than the coupling in catching the presence of the original set: the voices and therefore the drama project more readily than in *Cavalleria Rusticana*. The choral and orchestral detail is blurred but not unacceptably so, while the voices of Callas and Gobbi have an unforgettably vibrant quality.

For those who do not want the obvious coupling with *Cavalleria Rusticana*, the RCA performance would seem to be a first-rate recommendation, with fine singing from all three principals, vivid playing and recording, and one or two extra passages not normally performed – as in the Nedda–Silvio duet. Milnes is superb in the Prologue, and though Caballé does not always suggest a young girl this is technically the most beautifully recorded account of the role of Nedda available. The fill-up of six rare Leoncavallo arias sung by the three principals is particulary attractive. However, unfortunately the transfer offers unrefined

quality (and, on our set, wow) and as this particular issue is available on two LPs, whereas the tape box comes at the same price as the others in the series, which in all cases are the equivalent of three LPs, it seems singularly poor value.

I Pagliacci: highlights.

> (M) *** DG Privilege 3335 199 [922012] (from above set cond. Karajan) – MASCAGNI: *Cavalleria Rusticana* highlights.***
> *(*) Decca KCET 490. Pilar Lorengar, James McCracken, Robert Merrill, Tom Krause, Chorus and Orch. of St Cecilia Academy, Rome, Gardelli – MASCAGNI: *Cavalleria Rusticana* highlights.*(*)

Both these selections are coupled to highlights from *Cavalleria Rusticana* (the Gardelli to another Decca recording under Varviso). Karajan's, with all the advantages of his complete set, is easily the finer and at Privilege price is an obvious 'best buy'. As with the complete set the transfer of the *Pagliacci* excerpts has rather less presence than the coupling but is still very good. The overall balance and warmth of the sound are impressive. On the more expensive Decca issue McCracken is disappointingly coarse, although Lorengar and Krause sing well in the Nedda–Silvio duet. The transfer is of good quality.

Leoni, Franco
(1884–1949)

(i) *L'Oracolo* (opera): complete. *Reminiscences of the music from James Bernard Fagan's play 'The Prayer of the Sword'.*

> *** Decca K 34 K 22 [Lon. 5-12107]. National PO, Bonynge,

(i) with Joan Sutherland, Tito Gobbi, Huguette Tourangeau, Richard Van Allan, Ryland Davies, John Alldis Choir, Finchley Children's Music Group.

L'Oracolo, heard first at Covent Garden in 1905, the work of a contemporary of Puccini who settled in London, tells the lurid story of the wicked Chim-Fen, who finally gets strangled, to the delight of everyone, with his own pigtail. In the meantime the heroine goes mad after the murder of her beloved, and the whole drama is set against sound-effects which are superbly caught in this brilliant first recording. The very opening – three bangs on the bass drum, two crowings of a cockerel and a great jabber in Chinese from the chorus – might be a hi-fi demonstration, and Decca engineers have certainly seized their chance. The transfer throughout is of the highest quality, immensely vivid yet with fine atmosphere and bloom on the voices.

The piece gives marvellous opportunities not only to the veteran Tito Gobbi (relishing the character's wickedness) but to Sutherland, specialist in mad scenes, and to Richard Van Allan as the doctor who finally dispatches Chim-Fen. Though Leoni's actual idiom is rather bland for so dark a story, and his melodies never quite come up to Puccini standard, it makes a fine, compact entertainment in such a performance as this, directed with passionate conviction by Richard Bonynge and with superb playing from the National Philharmonic. The fill-up presents some innocuously sweet incidental music, and this too is beautifully recorded.

Liapunov, Sergei (1859–1924)

Rhapsody on Ukrainian themes for piano and orchestra, Op. 28.
  (M) * Turnabout KTVC 34645. Michael Ponti, Westphalian SO, Landau – BALAKIREV: *Piano concerto No. 2.**

Liapunov is probably best known for his set of *Transcendental studies*, but he composed a good deal of other music as well, including two symphonies, two piano concertos, a violin concerto and some tone poems. He also completed the finale of the Balakirev concerto with which this *Rhapsody* is coupled. The work dates from 1908 and is dedicated to no less an artist than Busoni. The score has much charm; but, though Michael Ponti copes manfully, the orchestral playing is lacklustre and the tape transfer offers thin-sounding strings and a dry acoustic with a rather contrived balance. Generally the sound has slightly more bloom than in the Balakirev coupling, and the piano tone is clear.

Liszt, Franz (1811–86)

Piano concerto No. 1 in E flat major, G.124.
  (*) DG 923083 [id.]. Martha Argerich, LSO, Abbado – CHOPIN: *Concerto No. 1.(*)
  ** HMV TC-ASD 3262 [Angel 4xs 37177]. Horacio Gutierrez, LSO, Previn – TCHAIKOVSKY: *Concerto No. 1.**
Piano concertos Nos. 1 in E flat major, G.124; 2 in A major, G.125.

*** DG 3300 770 [id.]. Lazar Berman, Vienna SO, Giulini.

(M) *** Philips 7328 028. Byron Janis, Moscow PO, Kondrashin, or Moscow Radio Orch., Rozhdestvensky.

**(*) Pye ZCPNH 7. Michele Campanella, LPO, Soudant.

**(*) Decca Phase 4 KPFC 4252. Ivan Davis, RPO, Downes.

(M) ** Turnabout KTVC 34215. Alfred Brendel, Vienna Pro Musica Orch., Gielen.

(B) *(*) RCA Camden C4-5047. Leonard Pennario, LSO, Leibowitz.

Piano concertos Nos. 1 and 2; Totentanz (for piano and orchestra), G.126.

*** Philips 7300 229 [id.]. Alfred Brendel, LPO, Haitink.

(i) *Piano concertos Nos. 1 and 2. Hungarian rhapsody No. 12 in C sharp minor, G.244; Mephisto waltz No. 1, G.514.*

(M) **(*) Decca KCSP 318. Julius Katchen, (i) with LSO, Argenta.

Among a number of fine tapes coupling the Liszt concertos, three stand out, even above the high standards set by the others. Brendel's Philips issue must take pride of place, particularly as the Philips transfer is bold and clear and lacks only the last degree of glitter (the triangle in the scherzo of the *First Concerto* is somewhat reticent). This cassette also offers an extra work, the *Totentanz*, and the performances are as poetic as they are brilliant; those who doubt the musical substance of No. 2 will find their reservations melt away.

Lazar Berman has the advantage of Giulini's sensitive and masterly accompaniment with the Vienna Symphony, and even if you feel that these scores hold no surprises for you, try to hear his recordings. Berman's playing is consistently poetic and he illuminates detail in a way that has the power to touch the listener. Some of his rapt, quiet tone would probably not register without the tactful assistance of the DG engineers, who enable all the detail to 'tell', but the balance is most musical and well judged. A very thoughtful account of No. 1 and a poetic reading of the *A major* make this a most desirable issue. Giulini keeps a strong grip on the proceedings and secures an excellent response from his players. These performances do not eclipse Brendel's but they are among the best currently available. The cassette transfer is of immaculate quality, a trifle dry perhaps (the orchestral strings have not a great deal of resonance) but with the piano timbre clear and truthful.

The other Philips tape is also a distinguished one, and brilliantly transferred too, even if the balance is somewhat less natural than on Brendel's issue. In both works the partnership between soloist (Byron Janis) and conductor (Kondrashin in No. 1, Rozhdestvensky in No. 2) is unusually close. In the slow movement of No. 1 Janis offers most poetic playing, and the scherzo is deliciously light, while the clipped martial rhythms of the finale are almost over-characterized. The reflective opening of the *Second Concerto* is another superb moment, and Rozhdestvensky's contribution throughout has an appealing lyrical feeling. The finale, as in the *First Concerto*, has an unashamed touch of melodrama about it, and there is an exhilarating dash in the pianism at the closing pages. The Mercury-sourced recording was notable for its sparkle, and this comes out very attractively in the famous 'Triangle scherzo' of the *First Concerto*, while the piano timbre is given fine presence throughout. At medium price this issue is an excellent bargain.

The Pye recording for Campanella and Soudant is also impressively spectacular, with spacious orchestral sound, resonant brass and a large-scale piano image. The performances combine thoughtfulness with brilliance, and although bravura is to the fore there is poetry here too. Michele Campanella displays a formidable technique to match his sensibility. The LPO playing too is refined and altogether this is most enjoyable, with a vivid, high-level transfer bringing out all the detail. In the last analysis this has not the distinction of Brendel or Berman, but it matches Janis in panache (if not in economy). The *Second Concerto* is especially sympathetic.

Ivan Davis's performances are vividly characterized and they show real poetic feeling. Those to whom the vivid spotlighting of Phase Four techniques appeals will not be disappointed with this record on musical grounds, and certainly the recording is demonstration-worthy, in its way. Davis points the close of the first movement of No. 1 with both humour and magic, a delectable moment. The resonant recording means that on tape the orchestral image sometimes loses its sharpness of detail (more in the *A major* than in the *E flat Concerto*), but this is being very critical. The overall sound has fine body and the forwardly projected piano is rich in timbre, the treble clean and sparkling yet never hard.

Katchen is superb in the *E flat Concerto*, slightly less successful with the changes of mood of the *Second*. But by any standards these are commanding performances, showing Katchen in his best light. They are well recorded too, and many will feel that at the price, with characteristically strong accounts of the *Twelfth Hungarian rhapsody* and the *Mephisto waltz* thrown in for good measure, this is very competitive in the medium-price range. The transfer (an early Decca issue) misses the last degree of brilliance (and the early recording brings some hiss too), but it is well balanced.

Brendel's earlier performances for Turnabout are perhaps not entirely superseded by his newer Philips issue.

The orchestral support, particularly in No. 2, is not very polished, and the balance, with a tendency to spotlight orchestral solos, is rather artificial against the reverberant acoustic chosen. But the playing has a striking freshness and spontaneity. Brendel brings a musing, improvisatory quality to the A major work, and his control of bravura in both concertos is illuminating as well as exciting. On tape the longer *Second Concerto* has been placed on side one. Here the sound is brilliant but the strings are thin; side two with the *First Concerto* is mellower and one notices the reverberation more. One wonders why Decca did not even up the two sides with one of Brendel's solo recordings and make this Turnabout issue more competitive.

Pennario gives extremely brilliant, virtuoso performances, with vivid stereo to bring everything forward. The result is highly effective, with some superb, glittering bravura from the pianist, and plenty of excitement from the orchestra too. The closing pages of the *A major Concerto* are splendidly exhilarating, with the brashness put to the service of the music. The transfer is rather better than one is usually offered by this series; it is quite well balanced, if lacking the last degree of sparkle.

Turning now to recordings of the *E flat Concerto* not paired with the *Second*, one finds a clear, direct, sometimes even fastidious approach from Martha Argerich (who couples the *First Concerto* to Chopin's *First*). She plays the *Larghetto* meltingly, and there is an excellent partnership between pianist and conductor. Both are agreed to minimize the work's flamboyance without reducing the voltage. This is very much a performance to live with and many should find it exactly to their taste, even if Liszt himself might have thought it a trifle too sophisticated.

The partnership between Horacio Gutierrez and Previn is in the last analysis disappointing. In the *E flat Concerto* Gutierrez, for all his prodigious technique, is no barnstormer and indeed it is the work's reflective passages which tell most readily. But the music's drama is less well caught, and the sumptuous recording seems almost to detract from the sparkle of the music.

A Faust symphony, G.108.
> *** DG 3370 022 [id.]. Kenneth Riegel (tenor), Tanglewood Festival Chorus, Boston SO, Bernstein – BOITO: *Mefistofele: Prologue.*(**)

Bernstein recorded this symphony in the mid-1960s, but this new version, made in Boston, is both more sensitive and more brilliant. It is the first modern recording to offer a serious challenge to Beecham's classic account made in the late 1950s (which is not, alas, available on cassette). The *Gretchen* movement is most beautifully played here, with finely delineated detail and refined texture. The tenor soloist in the finale is excellent, and the Boston orchestra produce some exciting and atmospheric playing. The cassette transfer is extremely vivid, with the forward balance of the violins made to seem only just behind the speakers. The brass has splendid presence too, and the woodwind detail registers well. In the finale the singers are well focused and realistically placed.

Symphonic poems: *Festklänge, G.101; Les Préludes, G.97; Prometheus, G.99.*
> *** Decca KSXC 6863 [Lon. 5-7084]. LPO, Solti.

Solti is just the conductor for Liszt's symphonic poems: he finds the right kind of intensity so that *Les Préludes* is exciting, without vulgarity, yet does not lose its flamboyant character. The closing pages are superbly rousing, but are not without dignity. There is plenty of drama in *Prometheus* and some beautifully refined orchestral playing in *Festklänge*, yet the tension is strongly held. The re-

cording is splendidly vivid and the cassette transfer has superb life and colour.

(i) *Hungarian fantasia for piano and orchestra, G.123;* (ii) *Mephisto waltz No. 1, G.514.*
> (M) *** Turnabout KTVC 137015 (i) Peter Frankl, Innsbruck SO, Wagner; (ii) Alfred Brendel (piano) – CHOPIN: *Andante spianato* etc.***

(i) *Hungarian fantasia for piano and orchestra. Hungarian rhapsodies* (for orchestra) *Nos. 4 and 5, G.359.*
> (M) **(*) DG Privilege 3318 005 [(d) 923086]. Berlin PO, Karajan, (i) with Shura Cherkassky – BRAHMS: *Hungarian dances.***

Peter Frankl is less concerned with bravura than some other interpreters are, but he is spontaneous and thoroughly musical. The cassette transfer is exceptionally successful, offering demonstration quality in the *Hungarian fantasia.* The piano tone in the *Mephisto waltz* (admirably played by Alfred Brendel) is marginally less real, but that is a faithful reflection of the original, early recording. (This bonus is not present on the equivalent LP.)

Cherkassky plays the *Hungarian fantasia* affectionately, with glittering fingerwork, and there are some delightful touches from the orchestra; a little more panache from the soloist would have made the performance irresistible. The recording throughout is first-rate and this is a highly competitive version of this piece. Of the two *Rhapsodies,* No. 5 is less known. It is a fine work, not in the least superficial, and Karajan's memorable performance, passionate yet with a touch of restraint, raises its deep melancholy to the level of grand tragedy. This is most moving. No. 4 is more quixotic in style but its flashes of orchestral colour and changes of mood are well managed. Again the recording is excellent, and the cassette transfer has plenty of life. The sound has fine body yet no lack of clarity and sparkle.

Hungarian rhapsodies (orch. Liszt and Doppler), *G.359: Nos. 1 in F major; 4 in D minor; 8 in D major (Carnival in Pest); Rákóczy march (No. 15 for piano). Hungarian battle march, G.119.*

(M) *(*) HMV Greensleeve TC-ESD 7039. Philharmonia Hungarica, Boskovsky.

Boskovsky shows no special feeling for the Hungarian folk idiom which was the basis of Liszt's inspiration. He misses the mercurial element, the sudden changes of mood, which are a feature of these works. However, the performances are well played, fresh and not unspontaneous, if never grippingly exciting. The little-known *Hungarian battle march* does not emerge here as a lost masterpiece. The music has transferred quite well to tape, although the sound (while still vivid) falls short of the degree of sparkle and presence on the equivalent LP.

Hungarian rhapsodies, G.359: Nos. 2 in C minor (orch. Müller-Berghaus); *3 in D major; 5 in E minor* (both orch. Doppler); *Mephisto waltz No. 1, G.110/2.*

(M) ** HMV Greensleeve TC-ESD 7058 [Angel 4xs 37278]. LPO, Boskovsky.

This is more successful than Boskovsky's first collection of *Hungarian rhapsodies* (see above). The famous No. 2 is sumptuously done, and No. 3 with its effective use of the cimbalom has plenty of colour. The gypsy element too is quite well managed, and with excellent orchestral playing the *Mephisto waltz* (using the less often heard alternative version, with its more poetic ending) is suitably atmospheric. The rich recording has on the whole been well transferred, although

the focus is not absolutely crisp; but the reverberant accoustic suits the music.

Hungarian rhapsody No. 2, G.359; Les Préludes (symphonic poem), *G.97.*

(*) DG 923049 [id.]. Berlin PO, Karajan – SMETANA: *Vltava* etc.(*)

Karajan certainly plays *Les Préludes* with plenty of gusto, but his approach is also bombastic in the outer sections and he does not find all the underlying dignity in the music that Furtwängler (for instance) did. This is undoubtedly exciting; the contrast in the pastoral section is well made, and the orchestral playing is first-rate, but something is missing in this reading. Karajan tends to over-sophisticize the *Hungarian rhapsody*, but this is very enjoyable – it can hardly fail to be when so well played. The recording has transferred very successfully to tape, and some of the brashness of the orchestral balance seems tempered in the symphonic poem.

Hungarian rhapsodies Nos. 2 and 4, G.359; Symphonic poems: Mazeppa, G.100; Les Préludes, G.97.

(M) ** DG Privilege 3335 110. Berlin PO, Karajan.

This collection of reissues exists only in cassette form. It is notable for Karajan's inspired performance of what is perhaps Liszt's greatest symphonic poem, *Mazeppa*. It is superbly played, and the distant brass effects at the final climax are well managed by the engineers. On tape, however, the sound does not have quite the ambient richness of the original LP (now deleted). The other items sound well enough (*Les Préludes* a trifle brash as on disc and in the collection above), although the recording here is good rather than sparkling in detail and lustre. But the tape is worth having for *Mazeppa*.

Hungarian rhapsodies Nos. 4 and 5, G.359; Tasso, lamento e trionfo (symphonic poem), *G.96.*

> *** DG 3300 698 [id.]. Berlin PO, Karajan.

Before hearing this magnificent collection one might wonder why Karajan wanted to record the *Fourth* and *Fifth Hungarian rhapsodies* again, when his earlier recording (coupled to the *Hungarian fantasia*) is so successful. But the new performances are quite marvellous, Karajan and his players clearly revelling in each turn of phrase in the quixotic No. 4, and producing their gravest manner for No. 5. Equally the sound is stunningly realistic. The performance of *Tasso* does not have the electric tension of Solti's version (not available on tape), but again the power and refinement of the orchestral playing are a continual delight. The very end is a trifle bombastic, but throughout the middle section we are offered music-making of the very highest calibre. This is one of Karajan's most impressive recent recordings. The transfer to tape – made at a high level – is hardly less impressive than the disc, the wide dynamic range producing some thrilling contrasts, with a superb sheen on the upper strings. The closing pages of *Tasso* on our production copy lack something in refinement, but otherwise the sound is in the demonstration class. This issue is very highly recommended.

Symphonic poems: *Orpheus, G.98; Les Préludes, G.97; Tasso, lamento e trionfo, G.96.*

> (M) **(*) Philips Festivo 7310 056. LPO, Haitink.

The finest performance here is that of *Orpheus*, which is most sympathetically played. The music of *Les Préludes* and *Tasso* creates its scenic backgrounds with bold strokes of the brush, and the vividness of the transfer, made at an unusually high level for Philips, helps to add a rumbustious quality to Haitink's performances. The recording certainly sounds more lively here than on the original full-priced LP issue, and while Haitink's approach is not wholly successful – he tends to produce melodramatic effects in the more vigorous music – these are enjoyable and well characterized performances. The tape quality perhaps lacks the last degree of refinement at fortissimos but is full-blooded, with plenty of warmth and impact.

(i) *Totentanz* (for piano and orchestra), *G.126. Csárdás macabre, G.224.* (i) SCHUBERT–LISZT: *Wanderer fantasia* (for piano and orchestra).

> (M) **(*) Turnabout KTVC 34265. Alfred Brendel (piano), (i) with Vienna Volksoper Orch., Gielen.

As Brendel suggested in his sleeve-note for this issue, Liszt's transcription for piano and orchestra of Schubert's *Wanderer fantasia* must be thought of not as an attempt to improve on Schubert but rather as an interesting example of stylistic contrast. Certainly Liszt's flamboyant opening gets the piece off to a good start, and so convincing is the orchestration that – without preconceptions – it does not sound any more like a transcription than, say, Liszt's *Hungarian fantasia*. The present performance is characteristically spontaneous, and if neither the orchestral playing nor the recording is refined, the reverberant acoustic suits the ambience of the music. The *Totentanz* is another vivid Brendel performance, and the *Csárdás macabre* makes an interesting bonus for a most enjoyable collection. The transfer is quite successful: the piano tone is generally good and there is some attractive orchestral detail. The element of crudeness in the tuttis is common to disc and tape.

Piano music

Années de pèlerinage, 2nd year, G.161: Sonetto del Petrarca Nos. 47, 104, 123; Tarantella. Études d'exécution transcendante d'après Paganini, G.140, Nos. 1–6.

(M) *(**) Turnabout KTVC 34353. Alfred Brendel.

Brendel is on top form in the *Paganini studies*. Characteristically there is little extrovert flamboyance. But the mixture of delicacy and brilliance which informs the playing still captures the Lisztian spirit, and Brendel's subtlety adds an extra dimension. The recording is excellent, better than most of Brendel's Turnabout issues. The *Années de pèlerinage* are thoughtfully played, evoking the classical spirit of their inspiration. The tape transfer is basically good, but side one is adversely affected by either pre-echo or print-through, which can be heard in the quieter music.

Années de pèlerinage, Book 2, Supplement: Venezia e Napoli (Gondoliera; Canzone; Tarantella), G.162. Mephisto waltz No. 1, G.514. Piano sonata in B minor, G.178.

*(**) HMV TC-ASD 3228. Lazar Berman.

Berman, lately acclaimed as a Soviet wonder pianist to be bracketed with Richter, demands to be judged by almost superhuman standards. The performance of the *Sonata* creates an electrifying tension from the first bars, but taken as a whole it is perhaps less spontaneous-sounding than Berman's earlier account on Saga (see below). Nevertheless this is still fabulous playing, and if the pieces from the *Supplement* to *Les Années de pèlerinage* are presented almost too boldly, there are still dozens of examples of magical pianism, and the *Mephisto waltz* has seldom been played with more demonic panache. The record-

ing is bold to match and a trifle hard too. The cassette is secure but tends to exaggerate the clattery quality of the piano tone at peaks.

Apparitions No. 1, G.155; Harmonies poétiques et religieuses, G.154; Harmonies poétiques et religieuses, G.173: Bénédiction de Dieu dans la solitude; 5 Hungarian folk-songs, G.245; 4 Little pieces, G.192; En rêve, G.207; Valse à capriccio sur deux motifs de Lucia et Parisina, G.401.

(M) *** Turnabout KTVC 34310. Louis Kentner.

Among Kentner's Liszt recordings this collection stands out. The performance of the early fantasy version of the *Harmonies poétiques et religieuses* has real power, and the same combination of strength and poetry infuses the *Bénédiction de Dieu dans la solitude*, one of Liszt's most atmospheric tone paintings. Equally the restrained romanticism in *Apparitions* is just right. The recording is good and the transfer naturally balanced if a little lacking in brilliance.

Concert paraphrases: *Bénédiction et serment, deux motifs de Benvenuto Cellini* (Berlioz), *G.396; Isolde's Liebestod from Tristan und Isolde* (Wagner), *G.447; Miserere du Trovatore* (Verdi), *G.433; Oberon overture* (Weber), *G.574; Pilgrims' chorus from Tannhäuser* (Wagner), *G.443; Réminiscences de Lucia di Lammermoor* (Donizetti), *G.397; Réminiscences de Norma* (Bellini), *G.394.*

(M) *(*) Turnabout KTVC 34352. Alfred Brendel.

On the evidence of this tape, operatic style (especially in Donizetti, Bellini and early Verdi) is not Alfred Brendel's special métier. He plays strongly and emotionally but does not easily catch the spirit of the music. The most enjoyable performance here is the transcription of the *Oberon overture* of Weber, which is played with appealing delicacy and lightness of touch. Elsewhere the reverberant and rather clangy piano tone does not help with the louder climaxes. The tape transfer matches the quality of the equivalent LP, though the sound is clearer on side one, richer on side two (which includes the Weber overture).

Wagner concert paraphrases: *Der fliegende Holländer: Spinning song, G.440; Lohengrin: Bridal march, G.445; Parsifal: Feierlicher Marsch, G.450; Der Ring des Nibelungen: Valhalla, G.449; Tannhäuser overture, G.442; Tristan und Isolde: Liebestod, G.447.*

**(*) Pye ZCPNH 2. Michele Campanella.

As we know from his record of the concertos Michele Campanella is an uncommonly fine Liszt player, and although he does not quite solve the problems of the swirling accompaniment to the *Pilgrims' chorus* theme in the *Tannhäuser overture*, this remains a powerful reading. Here as elsewhere Campanella shows a splendid feeling not only for Wagner's musical line but also for the orchestral colour expressed in Liszt's pianistic terms. The *Spinning song* is most attractive, and the *Parsifal* music both eloquent and beautiful. The *Tristan Liebestod* could perhaps be more directly passionate, but there is no lack of underlying expressive feeling. Generally the transfer is very successful, offering body and bloom as well as clarity to the piano image. Just occasionally there is a hint of unsteadiness in the sustained tone, but for the most part the quality is secure.

Concert paraphrases: for 2 pianos: *Réminiscences de Don Juan* (Mozart), *G.656; Réminiscences de*

Norma (Bellini), *G.655;* for piano, 4 hands: *La Sonnambula fantasia* (Bellini), *G.627; Tscherkessenmarsch from Glinka's Russlan and Ludmilla, G.629.*

*(*) Advent E 1027 (see p. xxiii) [id.]. Richard and John Contiguglia.

Most of Liszt's concert paraphrases are for solo piano, but these are either for two pianos or one piano, four hands; they are re-creations rather than transcriptions, and are of more than passing interest. Richard and John Contiguglia are accomplished players, but the recording, like so many from this source, tends to be closely balanced, so that the action is often audible. The sound needs to expand a little, and prolonged listening proves tiring on the ear. In terms of quality the image is remarkably firm and vivid, but artistically this issue is not a distinguished one.

(i) *Concerto pathétique in E minor, G.258* (for 2 pianos). *Rapsodie espagnole, G.254; Rhapsody on Hungarian songs in A minor, G.242; Rumanian rhapsody, G.242.*

(M) ** Turnabout KTVC 34444. Louis Kentner, (i) with Joan Havill (pianos).

The *Concerto pathétique* is a difficult work to bring off: it needs a partnership in virtuosity, yet both participants must share overall control. Louis Kentner and Joan Havill are successful with the rhapsodic flow, and, with Kentner clearly dominating, they make a good team. But the Turnabout recording is inclined to smudge with resonance. The rest of Kentner's programme is an attractive one, but the playing, if sometimes powerful in manner, lacks incandescence. The cassette transfer, however, is undoubtedly successful. The sound on side one, which includes the Spanish and Rumanian rhapsodies, glitters attractively, although there is a touch of hardness. On side two the *Concerto pathétique* is rather less clear because of the reverberation, but the quality remains good.

Études d'exécution transcendante, *G.139* (complete).
*(*) Advent E 1010 (see p. xxiii) [id.]. Russell Sherman.
Études d'exécution transcendante, *G.139* (complete); *Études de concert Nos. 1–3, G.145.*
*** Philips 7505 081 [id.]. Claudio Arrau.

A formidable achievement for an artist in his seventies. Arrau plays always with great panache and musical insight, which more than compensate for the occasional smudginess of the recorded sound (common to disc and tape). On record both Lazar Berman and Cziffra (the latter now deleted) brought greater obvious virtuosity to these pieces, but both are much younger men. Arrau's playing is most masterly and poetic, and the recording, if too reverberant, is admirably truthful. The *Études de concert* are no less successful. The cassette survives the most rigorous A/B comparison with the disc: there is virtually no difference between them.

The Advent tape offers an excellently transferred and firmly focused sound, even if it tends to be bottom-heavy. Russell Sherman is a fine pianist but he does not command the panache of a great virtuoso like Arrau or Berman, and neither in terms of technique nor for imagination can he match Arrau.

Harmonies poétiques et religieuses, *G.173: Nos. 3, Bénédiction de Dieu dans la solitude; 4, Pensées de morts; Prelude and fugue on the name BACH, G.260; Variations on Bach's 'Weinen, Klagen, Sorgen, Zagen', G.673.*
*** Philips 7300 565. Alfred Brendel.

The *Prelude and fugue on the name BACH* and the *Variations on 'Weinen, Klagen, Sorgen, Zagen'* are better known in their organ versions but sound no less impressive on the piano, particularly when they are played as masterfully as they are here by Brendel. This is a magnificent recital, and the recording is wide-ranging and realistic. The transfer, made at a high level, is strikingly rich and full. Indeed the sound quality of the cassette yields little if anything to that of the disc, which is high praise indeed.

Piano sonata in B minor, G.178.
(*) RCA RK 12548 [ARK 1 2548]. Vladimir Horowitz – FAURÉ: *Impromptu; Nocturne.**
** Decca KSXC 6756 [Lon. 5-6989]. Alicia de Larrocha – SCHUMANN: *Fantasia in C.***
(M) (*) Saga CA 5430. Lazar Berman – BEETHOVEN: *Piano sonata No. 23.(*)*

There need be no doubt about the electricity that Horowitz engenders. This is playing of such high voltage as to hold the listener from the first bar to the last. At the risk of sounding tiresome, the performance does not quite possess the freshness or virtuosity of Horowitz's famous pre-war 78 r.p.m. recording; perhaps one should say that its magic is of a totally different kind. The recording is full and wide-ranging and the sonorities occasionally even sound orchestral. The tape transfer is of high quality, comparing well with the disc. However, the break in continuity – on cassette as well as LP the sonata is spread over two sides – is unfortunate to say the least, even if it is well placed. That may disqualify this issue for some listeners, particularly as the Fauré coupling is not generous.

There is some formidable piano playing from Miss de Larrocha too and she has the advantage of an unbroken performance recorded in a pleasing, open acoustic. There need be no reservation on the count of recording quality, and her coupling is a worthwhile one. Yet for all the many perceptive touches, her view of the sonata is a little too idiosyncratic to be placed in the first flight of available recorded performances.

With its restricted dynamic range Berman's Saga issue provides only a half-picture of his interpretation of the sonata. The piano tone is acceptably mellow but entirely lacks projection and dramatic bite.

Readers are reminded that Pascal Rogé's outstanding performance is available in Decca's *Favourite composer* collection (see below).

Piano sonata in B minor, G.178; Années de pèlerinage, 2nd year, G.161: Dante sonata; Bagatelle without tonality (1885); Hungarian rhapsody No. 11, G.244; Unstern, G.208.
(M) ** Turnabout KTVC 134232. Alfred Brendel.

This is another example of a Turnabout issue where the tape sounds more congenial than the equivalent LP. Brendel's performance of the sonata is as emotionally strong as it is structurally convincing, and while the piano tone here remains on the hard side the projection of the performance is effectively bold and dramatic. The other pieces are also finely played. *Unstern* is offered as a bonus not included on the equivalent LP, but is a stereo transcription of a mono recording. However, the mellow, slightly husky piano image is not unpleasing.

Piano sonata in B minor, G.178; Polonaise in E minor, G.223; Réminiscences de Don Juan (Mozart), G.148.
(M) **(*) DG Privilege 3335 270. Tamás Vásáry.

Vásáry's performance of the sonata is undoubtedly distinguished, not without romantic feeling, but thoughtful rather than flamboyant. It has genuine poetry, however, and there is no lack of power. The couplings are attractive, the *Polonaise*, a fine piece, boldly played and recorded, and the *Don Juan* fantasia has undoubted panache. The recording is a little dry in the sonata but clear and well balanced; the sound seems rather fuller on side two. The transfers are faithful, but the modest level brings some background hiss.

Organ music

Fantasia and fugue on 'Ad nos, ad salutarem undam', G.259; Prelude and fugue on the name BACH, G.260; Variations on Bach's 'Weinen, Klagen, Sorgen, Zagen', G.673.
**(*) Enigma K 453559. Jennifer Bate (organ of the Royal Albert Hall, London).

To put the huge organ at the Albert Hall on cassette would seem a daunting prospect, but the transfers of this flamboyant music have been managed with surprising aplomb. The balance does not make too much of the very deep bass, but in all other respects the sound is convincing: it is certainly overwhelming at the spectacular climaxes. Miss Bate gives impetuous performances, and her bravura carries the listener. To focus such massive keyboard tuttis within a small listening area is an achievement in itself, even if this is a cassette to listen to one side at a time!

COLLECTION

'Favourite composer': (i) *Piano concertos Nos. 1 in E flat major, G.124; 2 in A major, G.125.* (ii) *Les Préludes, G.97.* (Piano) (iii) *Hungarian rhapsody No. 2, G.244; Liebestraum No. 3 in A flat major, G.541;* (iv) *Piano*

sonata in B minor, G.178; (v) Valse
oubliée No. 1, G.215. (Organ) (iv)
Prelude and fugue on the name
BACH, G.260.

(B) **(*) Decca KDPC 621/2. (i)
Ivan Davis, RPO, Downes; (ii)
LPO, Herrmann; (iii) Ilana
Vered; (iv) Pascal Rogé; (v)
Joseph Cooper; (vi) Simon Pres-
ton (organ of Hull City Hall).

Pascal Rogé gives a brilliant and
commanding performance of the sonata,
very well recorded indeed, and Ivan
Davis's performances of the two concertos can certainly be recommended if one
can accept the forward balance (see
above). Joseph Cooper's Valse oubliée is
stylish, and Simon Preston's version of
the Prelude and fugue on BACH is undoubtedly distinguished. All are vividly
transferred, at a high level, and the only
disappointing item here is Bernard Herrmann's rather heavy version of Les Préludes, where the recording also roughens
somewhat at the final climax.

Litolff, Henri
(1818–91)

Concerto symphonique No. 4 in D
minor, Op. 102: Scherzo (only).
*** Decca KSXC 2173. Clifford
Curzon, LPO, Boult – GRIEG:
Concerto; FRANCK: Symphonic
variations.***

(B) *** Classics for Pleasure TC-
CFP 115. Peter Katin, LPO,
Pritchard – TCHAIKOVSKY:
Concerto No. 1.*(*)

(M) ** Decca KCSP 170. Peter
Katin, LPO, Colin Davis –
GRIEG: Concerto; Peer Gynt
suite No. 1.**

(B) ** Pye ZCCOB 652. Shura

Cherkassky, LPO, Boult –
TCHAIKOVSKY: Concerto No.
1.*

Curzon provides all the sparkle
Litolff's infectious Scherzo requires, and
this is a delightful makeweight to excellent performances of the Grieg and the
Franck. The recording has the same fine
qualities as the rest of the issue, and the
cassette transfer has a fine sparkle.

On Classics for Pleasure too a scintillating performance, brilliantly recorded;
if only the concerto which forms the
coupling had the same kind of panache
this tape would be a world-beater. The
transfer is of demonstration quality.

On Decca KCSP the Scherzo is rattled
off at hair-raising speed. One might
prefer something more infectiously gay,
but Katin and Davis still manage something of a skipping lilt, and as a fill-up for
an excellent Grieg coupling it is welcome
enough. Like the coupling it is very well
transferred.

Like Katin's performance with Pritchard, Cherkassky's is coupled to an
unconvincing account of the Tchaikovsky B flat minor Piano concerto (made
even less attractive on tape by a clumsy
turnover break in the middle of the slow
movement). However, the performance
of the Litolff is undoubtedly attractive,
including repeats and without cuts. Cherkassky is on top form and his playing is
crisp and clear as well as vivacious. Boult
accompanies nimbly, and the recording
balance is natural. The transfer is of very
good quality too.

Lloyd Webber, Andrew
(born 1948)

Variations.
*(**) MCA TC-MCF 2824. Julian
Lloyd Webber (cello), Don
Airey, Rod Argent (key-
boards), Jon Hiseman (drums

and percussion), John Mole (bass guitar), Gary Moore (guitar), Barbara Thompson (wind instruments), dir. the composer.

This fascinating hybrid work inhabits the world of 'pop' music of the late seventies yet draws inspiration from the classical mainstream of variations on Paganini's ubiquitous theme, which has inspired so many diverse compositions over the past century and a half. Andrew Lloyd Webber's piece began life as a comparatively short twenty-minute work, composed with his brother's brilliant cello-playing very much in mind. It was then expanded to the format here recorded, lasting about half an hour, and has since been blown up to even greater proportions for a concert performance at the Royal Festival Hall, which received a very mixed press. The vulgarity of the ambience of its 'pop' sections will exasperate many listeners, yet its sheer vitality cannot be ignored and the lyrical variations, featuring the flute and solo cello, are genuinely memorable. A good tape to try in the car; the quality of the transfer is acceptable but hardly worthy of wide-range equipment.

MacCunn, Hamish (1868–1916)

Overture: Land of the Mountain and the Flood.
(***) HMV TC-ASD 2400. Scottish National Orch., Gibson – HARTY: *With the Wild Geese;* GERMAN: *Welsh rhapsody;* SMYTH: *The Wreckers overture.*(***)

MacCunn's descriptive overture is no masterpiece, but it is attractively atmospheric and effectively constructed. It

makes a more than agreeable Scottish contribution to this anthology of music from the four countries of the United Kingdom. Performance and recording are both excellent, but the cassette transfer has a very restricted dynamic range and the orchestral sound is thick and turgid.

Machaut, Guillaume de (*c.* 1300–1377)

Amours me fait desirer (ballade); *Dame se vous m'estes* (bagpipe solo); *De bon espoir – Puis que la douce* (motet); *De toutes flours* (ballade); *Douce dame jolie* (virelai); *Hareu! hareu! – Helas! ou sera pris cònfors* (motet); *Ma fin est mon commencement* (rondeau); *Mes esperie se combat* (ballade); *Phyton, le mervilleus serpent* (ballade); *Quant j'ay l'espart* (rondeau); *Quant je sui mis* (virelai); *Quant Theseus – Ne quier veoir* (double ballade); *Se je souspir* (virelai); *Trop plus est belle – Biauté paree – Je ne sui* (motet). (Also includes LESCUREL: *A vous douce debonaire;* MOLLINS: *Amis tous dous;* ANON: *La Septime;* ANDRIEU: *Armes amours; O flour des flours.*)
*** HMV TC-ASD 3454. Early Music Consort of London, Munrow.

David Munrow's gift for bringing medieval music fully back to life was seldom shown more surely than here, with superb singing and instrumental playing (even a bagpipe solo!). Tape collectors interested in venturing as far back as the fourteenth century will not be disappointed with this enterprising collection, full of spontaneity and immaculately transferred.

Mahler, Gustav
(1860–1911)

Symphony No. 1 in D major (Titan).
*** Decca KSXC 6113. LSO, Solti.
*** Advent D 1019 (see p. xxiii) [id.]. LSO, Horenstein.
**(*) RCA RK 10894 [ARK 1 0894]. LSO, Levine.
**(*) DG 3300 993 [id.]. Boston SO, Ozawa.
**(*) Decca Phase 4 KPFC 4402 [Lon. 5-21167]. RPO, Paita.
(M) **(*) Decca KCSP 521. RPO, Leinsdorf.
(M) **(*) DG Privilege 3335 172 [923070]. Bavarian Radio Orch., Kubelik.
**(*) Philips 7300 397 [id.]. Concertgebouw Orch., Haitink.
**(*) HMV TC-ASD 3541. LPO, Tennstedt.
(B) ** DG Heliodor 3348 123. Dresden State Orch., Suitner.
*(*) Decca KSXC 6779 [Lon. 5-7004]. Israel PO, Mehta.
(*) Supraphon 045067. Czech PO, Ančerl.
Symphony No. 1 (original 1893 version, including *Blumine*).
* Pye Virtuoso ZCPC 506. New Philharmonia Orch., Morris.

Among the top half-dozen or so tapes it is very difficult to suggest a clear first recommendation. Each represents conductor and orchestra on top form, and the final choice will be personal and subjective. The LSO play Mahler's *First* like no other orchestra. Under Solti they catch the magical writing at the opening with a singular evocative quality, at least partly related to the peculiarly characteristic blend of wind timbres. Solti gives the orchestra its full head and coaxes some magnificent playing from the brass in the finale and wonderfully warm string tone throughout. His tendency to drive hard is felt only in the second movement, which is pressed a little too much, although he relaxes beautifully in the central section. Specially memorable is the poignancy of the introduction of the *Frère Jacques* theme in the slow movement, and the exultant brilliance of the closing pages. The cassette transfer has recently been remastered. Made at a high level, it has plenty of weight and impact. Considering the degree of reverberation (which is naturally captured) the detail is excellent and only becomes slightly less sharply focused at the most expansive climaxes.

The distinguishing feature of the Advent Horenstein issue is that the symphony is presented without a break on one side, side two being left blank. The gain in intensity when the listener's concentration is not broken is remarkable, and the chrome transfer, although (because of the very wide dynamic range of the recording) it is not made at the highest level, brings refinement of *pianissimo* detail, with the most beautiful translucent sounds from strings and woodwind in the slow movement. The result is a freshness and concentration which puts this version in a very special category among the many rival accounts. Solti provides a sharper experience (and the Decca sound is impressive too); he is more immediately exciting in virtuosity; but with measured tempi and a manner which conceals much art Horenstein links the work more clearly with the later Mahler symphonies. Fine recording, though the timpani is balanced rather close and this brings a slight disturbance to the tape transfer at the opening of the finale.

Like Solti and Horenstein, James Levine has the LSO, and arguably he draws from it the most exciting playing of all. It is a reading of high contrasts, with extremes of tempo and dynamic brought out with total conviction. In that emphasis on drama Levine provides a very individual and strong performance, and the result is highly compelling. The RCA recording is appropriately brilliant, but the tape transfer, made at a high level, is garishly lit, with an excess of fizzy treble in the strings. The sound is not too difficult to control (a filter is a help), for it has plenty of ambient warmth, although the bass is light. Generally side two is smoother than side one, where at the climax of the first movement the quality breaks up a little. However, with all its faults, the cassette undoubtedly projects the music-making with thrilling effect, and there will be many collectors who are willing to accept the lack of refinement for the totally compelling nature of the performance. There is no mid-movement break: there are two movements complete on each side.

Ozawa brings out the youthful exhilaration of Mahler's inspiration. The first movement is fleet and resilient, lightly referring to the *Wayfaring Lad* theme, and the freshness as well as the polish of the Boston playing make for a result both electrifying and beautiful. In the second movement Ozawa is relaxed and lilting, while in the slow movement his shading of dynamic is wonderfully poised, and the double-bass soloist is outstandingly pure in tone. This is a performance which leans towards a consciously expressive style – maybe too much so in the great melody of the finale – but which still maintains its freshness. The recording has great warmth, while the high-level DG transfer is strikingly wide in range. However, the balance of the upper string timbre is over-bright and the treble needs cutting back if the sheen is not to sound edgily focused. When this is done the detail remains and the sound is rich and full, with an agreeable bloom on the orchestra in the central movements. The closing pages of the finale are very spectacular.

Carlos Paita's Latin view of Mahler is striking for its spontaneous qualities. This is a most enjoyable performance in spite of its extremes of tempo (par-

ticularly in the first movement, where there are some expressive lunges, whether in sudden rubatos or tenutos). The coda produces some scrambled ensemble, but otherwise the playing of the RPO is very good indeed, notably so in a beautiful account of the long-drawn melody in the finale. The recording is full and immediate and the transfer to tape highly sophisticated. Indeed technically this cassette is outstanding: the detail and atmosphere at the opening of the first movement are especially delightful, and the spectacle of the finale is managed with aplomb. No less congenial is the warmth in the slow movement.

Taking sound quality as well as interpretation into account, Leinsdorf's version must probably be considered best buy in the budget price-range. This was originally a Phase Four issue, and Phase Four recordings usually transfer well to tape, with plenty of sparkle and clarity. This is no exception, and although Leinsdorf may not be as poetic as Kubelik, his is a strong and colourful version, finely controlled and built with sustained concentration. The recording, with brass well forward, is one of the best made in Decca's Phase Four system. The transfer to tape is highly sophisticated, among the cleanest available of this symphony. It is a trifle over-bright but has plenty of warmth too (the middle strings have a most natural richness of texture). The first-movement climax makes a great impact, with its brilliance well supported in the brass, and there is much subtlety of colour in the slow movement. Perhaps the refinement slips very marginally in the exuberant closing bars of the finale but surely no more than the slight fall-off in quality one gets (even with the best of pick-ups) at the very end of a long LP side. An impressive achievement. There is no mid-movement break.

Kubelik gives an intensively poetic reading. He is here at his finest in Mahler, and though, as in later symphonies, he is sometimes tempted to choose a tempo on the fast side, the result here could hardly be more glowing. The *rubato* in the slow funeral march is most subtly handled. In its Privilege reissue the sound is a little dry in the bass (but still excellent); the cassette transfer, however, has a tendency to be over-bright and the upper strings lack body. But if the controls are used with care this can yield satisfactory results.

When Philips gathered together Haitink's recordings of Mahler symphonies, they took the trouble to make a new version of No. 1; and not only is it far more refined as a recording, the reading is if anything even more thoughtfully idiomatic than before in Haitink's unexaggerated Mahler style. The transfer is of first-class quality, a trifle dry, but clear and clean with natural string timbre and no lack of range in the upper register.

Tennstedt's manner in Mahler is somewhat severe, with textures fresh and neat and the style of phrasing generally less moulded than we have come to expect. This concentration on precision and directness means that when the conductor does indulge in *rubato* or speed-changes it does not sound quite consistent and comes as a surprise, as in the big string melody of the finale. Most Mahlerians will prefer a more felt performance than this, but for some it could be a good choice; its rich warm recording has transferred surprisingly well to cassette, considering the resonance and the wide amplitude of the sound. There is a slight loss of focus at both ends of the spectrum but the sumptuousness is well retained.

Suitner's is a lightweight performance – in the interpretative sense – but spontaneous and enjoyable. Like Ančerl, Suitner does not always show a feeling for the overall structure, but he certainly creates a sense of atmosphere, and in this he is helped by the DG recording, which also has a wide dynamic range. The slow movement is not very sombre, but the mood created fits well into the extrovert nature of the performance overall, with its jubilant conclusion. With a clear, well-balanced transfer this makes an excellent bargain recommendation, although Leinsdorf's KCSP issue does not cost very much more and offers a much more modern recording.

Mehta's version is brilliantly recorded, but the hard-driving, frenetic quality of the outer movements is unattractive and the warmth of the slow movement offers insufficient compensation. The transfer is first-class, but this cannot be recommended except to those seeking an approach to Mahler which is essentially outside the European tradition.

Ančerl's performance is well characterized. The control of tension in the first movement is unconventional but the inner movements are undoubtedly successful and the finale is compelling. Unfortunately the sound on the Supraphon tape is muddy and the volume pulls back at the first real climax of the first movement. Even with such restricted dynamics the quality does not manage to avoid congestion in places. Not recommended.

Wyn Morris adds to the usual four movements of the *First Symphony* the recently unveiled movement, *Blumine*, which came second in Mahler's original scheme; and in the other four movements Morris adopts the original scoring instead of Mahler's revision. The result is a curiosity well worth investigating, if with less polished playing than in the best rival versions. Fair recording; the transfer was an early one and offers acceptable quality only.

Symphony No. 2 in C minor (Resurrection).

  *** DG 3370 015 [id.]. Carol Neblett (soprano), Marilyn Horne (mezzo-soprano), Chicago Symphony Chorus and Orch., Abbado.

  *** Decca KCET 2 7002 [Lon. 5-2217]. Heather Harper (soprano), Helen Watts (contralto), LSO Chorus, LSO, Solti.

*** Decca KSXC 2 7037 [Lon. 5-2242]. Ileana Cotrubas (soprano), Christa Ludwig (mezzo-soprano), Vienna State Opera Chorus, Vienna PO, Mehta.

*(*) Symphonica CSYM 7/8. Elizabeth Ander (soprano), Alfreda Hodgson (contralto), Ambrosian Singers, Symphonica of London, Morris.

If on occasion in the past Abbado has seemed to be a little too controlled in the recording studio, his collaboration with the Chicago orchestra in this, his first recording of a Mahler symphony, combines almost miraculous precision with electrifying urgency. The total conviction of the performance establishes itself in the very first bars, weighty yet marvellously precise on detail, with dotted rhythms sharply brought out. It proves a performance of extremes, with variations of tempo more confidently marked than is common, but with concentration so intense there is no hint of self-indulgence. The delicacy of the Chicago orchestra in the second and third movements is as remarkable as its precision – the second movement is relatively fast, like an elegant minuet – while the great contrasts of the later movements prove a challenge not only to the performers but to the DG engineers, who produce sound of superlative quality – even if the actual range of dynamic may prove a problem to those anxious not to annoy the neighbours. Generally the singing is as splendid as the playing, but if there is even a minor disappointment, it lies in the closing pages. Other versions – such as Klemperer's (not yet available on tape) or Mehta's – there convey a more overwhelming emotional involvement, the triumph of Judgement Day itself, whereas Abbado keeps his sharpness of focus to the very end The transfer level is on the low side and though this leaves room for a marvellous

expansion of sound in the finale, and a generally refined (though not a sharply detailed) sound picture elsewhere, it does bring up a degree of background hiss. Also there is some lack of orchestral presence, although the voices are beautifully caught. It is a pity a turnover was necessary in the middle of the fifth movement.

Solti's account is one of his most impressive Mahler performances, superbly tense in the first movement to match and even outshine the heroic model of Klemperer. In the slow *Ländler* of the second movement Solti brings superb refinement of detail and a precise control of dynamic, and again in the third movement he concentrates with hushed intensity on precise control of dynamic and atmosphere. In the fourth movement, the setting of *Urlicht* from *Des Knaben Wunderhorn*, Solti's contralto, Helen Watts, is even more expressive than her recorded rivals, with real 'inner' feeling conveyed in the chorale. For the first four movements Solti's is on balance the most completely satisfying performance, but when he comes to the massive finale with its expansive picture of Judgement Day, he falls a little short of the spiritual nobility that Klemperer for one brings to the music. The LPs are famous for their outstanding technical quality, and the cassette is equally praiseworthy, with clear detail and rich, clearly projected stereo. The brass is particularly effective and the choral recording in the finale is most convincing. With the double-length tape format, only one turnover is necessary.

Zubin Mehta sounds a different conductor, not at all like his Los Angeles self, when he is drawing so sympathetic a Mahler performance as this from the Vienna Philharmonic. The refinement of the playing, recorded with glorious richness and clarity, puts this among the finest versions of the symphony. At the very start Mehta's fast tempo brings resilience, not aggressiveness, and the *espressivo* lyricism is equally persuasive. The second movement has *grazioso* delicacy, and though the third movement begins with the sharpest possible timpani strokes, there is no hint of brutality, and the *Wunderhorn* rhythms have a delightful lilt. After that, without a side-break, comes *Urlicht, pianissimo* in D flat after the scherzo's final cadence in C minor, and Christa Ludwig is in superb form. The enormous span of the finale brings clarity as well as magnificence, with fine placing of soloists and chorus and glorious atmosphere in such moments as the evocation of birdsong over distant horns, as heavenly a moment as Mahler ever conceived. The transfer is of very high quality. The distant brass effects and indeed the full panoply of *fortissimo* brass is superbly caught. The first quiet choral entry is magical, heard against a background of virtual silence. Some of the *pianissimo* string detail is perhaps mellowed here, but the complete security of the transfer, from the quietest moments to the huge final climax, is very impressive indeed.

Wyn Morris's version is uneven. In the first two movements the lack of bite in the ensemble (with some obvious exceptions, for instance in the brassy start of the recapitulation in the first movement) puts it well behind its rivals, but from the third movement onwards the whole concept is tauter, and though the choir is somewhat small to represent the Heavenly Host on Judgement Day, the dramatic urgency reflects Morris's Walter-like concept of Mahler. The soloists are well-matched, but the recording is not ideally clear, and has a limited top. The transfer to tape is not very successful. Although it is warm-textured, the outer movements convey a limited dynamic range and there is a feeling in the first movement of the climaxes being pulled back. Even so the textures are not always free from moments of clouding at times, and there are odd spots of minor congestion. The cassette numbering is misleading: in fact the symphony is spaced out over two sides of one tape.

Symphony No. 3 in D minor.
**(*) Advent F 1009 (see p. xxiii) [id.]. Norma Procter (contralto), Wandsworth School Boys' Choir, Ambrosian Singers, LSO, Horenstein.
*(**) RCA RK 01757. Marilyn Horne (mezzo-soprano), Glen Ellyn Children's Chorus, Chicago Symphony Chorus and Orch., Levine.

More than other issues in Advent's excellent series of Horenstein's Unicorn recordings of Mahler, Hindemith and Nielsen, this account of the Mahler *Third* shows the conductor at his most intensely committed. The manner is still very consistent in its simple dedication to the authority of the score and its rejection of romantic indulgence, but here there is an extra intensity, and the result has the sort of frisson-making quality one remembers from live Horenstein performances. Above all the restraint of the finale is intensely compelling. Though the strings are rather backwardly balanced and the timpani are too prominent, the brass sounds splendid and the recording has transferred with excellent detail. Fine vocal contributions from Norma Procter, the Ambrosian Singers and the Wandsworth Choir, although side two of the transfer brings a lower level and the singers are not given as much presence as might be ideal. The post-horn solos, however, are beautifully focused, the effect strikingly atmospheric. The chrome-tape quality is undoubtedly sophisticated; there is some lack of warmth in the middle frequencies, but admirable overall clarity.

James Levine directs a superb rhythmic account of the *Third Symphony*, with splendidly judged tempi which allow extra swagger (most important in the first movement), more lilt and more sense of atmosphere. The choral contributions too are outstandingly fine. In the radiant finale Levine's tempo is daringly slow, but he sustains it superbly, though in that movement the recording has some congestion at climaxes. Otherwise the RCA sound on tape is brilliant to the point of brashness, and rather shallow too. It is clearly detailed, but not rich enough for Mahler. Also there is some flutter (mostly slight), and the trombone solo in the first movement is disfigured in this way. With manipulation of the controls the quality can be made acceptable, for there is no real distortion in spite of the high transfer level, and everything has a proper immediacy (except the post-horn solos, which are agreeably diffuse and distant). The voices too are quite well caught. It is a pity a break had to be made in the long first movement, but it is well chosen, and the notes are clearly printed.

Symphony No. 4 in G major.
(***) RCA RK 11733 [ARK 1 0895]. Judith Blegen (soprano), Chicago SO, Levine.
(M) *** DG Privilege 3335 119 [923082]. Elsie Morison (soprano), Bavarian Radio SO, Kubelik.
** DG 3300 966 [id.]. Frederica von Stade (mezzo-soprano), Vienna PO, Abbado.
** Philips 7300 209 [18230 CAA]. Elly Ameling (soprano), Concertgebouw Orch., Haitink.
(B) ** Classics for Pleasure TC-CFP 159 [Mon. 55001]. Margaret Price (soprano), LPO, Horenstein.

Unfortunately the CBS cassette of Szell's outstanding Cleveland performance is not really recommendable, for the sound is poor and the tape is a non-Dolby transfer. Levine's tape is also very disappointing, but in the medium price-range the Kubelik Privilege issue can be readily recommended, and the transfer is of high quality, offering well-detailed and refined sound with plenty of body and impact. The Bavarian orchestra phrase

beautifully, and their playing has great vitality. With generally faster tempi than are common the effect is light and luminous, with a charming, boyish account of the final song from Elsie Morison.

James Levine draws a superlative performance from the Chicago orchestra, one which stands comparison with the very finest versions ever recorded, bringing out not just the charm but the deeper emotions too. The subtlety of his control of tempo, so vital in Mahler, is superbly demonstrated, and he has the advantage of Blegen as a freshly attractive soloist. Unfortunately the transfer pulls back the volume on all fortissimos, and the great climax of the slow movement goes for naught. The sound is otherwise clear but the close-microphoning of the wind further reduces the effect of dynamic contrast. To make matters worse our review copy had discoloration in the upper partials of the woodwind timbres. It may be that by the time we are in print RCA will have withdrawn this and issued a remastered version.

After Abbado's superb performance of Mahler's *Second* with the Chicago orchestra, his recording of the *Fourth* is disappointing, above all in the self-consciously expressive reading of the slow movement. There is much beauty in detail, but the Vienna Philharmonic has played and has been recorded better than this.

Haitink's version is predictably well played and recorded, but the performance is rather sober and lacking in imaginative detail and fire. The transfer is of good quality, fresh and pleasing, but this remains disappointing.

Horenstein's characteristic simplicity of approach seems too deliberate (the rhythms of the second movement, for instance, are curiously precise) and even the great slow movement sounds didactic, though it is not without atmosphere. Margaret Price's singing in the finale is beautiful but cool, in line with the rest of the interpretation. The recording is forwardly balanced so the tape transfer has excellent detail, and certainly the sound throughout is extremely vivid (if rather dry in acoustic), with agreeably rich yet transparent string textures.

Symphony No. 5 in C sharp minor.
> *** HMV TC-SLS 785. New Philharmonia Orch., Barbirolli – *5 Rückert Lieder.****
> **(*) Decca KCET 2 7001 [Lon. 5-2228]. Chicago SO, Solti – *Des Knaben Wunderhorn.***(*)

Symphony No. 5; (i) Kindertotenlieder.
> *** DG 3370 006. Berlin PO, Karajan, (i) with Christa Ludwig (mezzo-soprano).

Symphony No. 5; (i) Lieder eines fahrenden Gesellen.
> *** Philips 7505 069 [id.]. Concertgebouw Orch., Haitink, (i) with Hermann Prey (bar.).
> *(*) Symphonica CSYM 3/4. Symphonica of London, Morris, (i) with Roland Hermann (bar.).

Symphony No. 5; Symphony No. 10 in F sharp major (Unfinished): Adagio.
> ** Decca KSXC 2 7048 [Lon. 5-2248]. Los Angeles PO, Mehta.

Barbirolli's recording of Mahler's *Fifth* provides a unique experience. On any count it is one of the greatest, most warmly affecting performances he ever recorded, and it brings on the fourth side a performance of the *5 Rückert Lieder* with Janet Baker as soloist that achieves a degree of poetic intensity rarely heard in the recording studio, even from these superlative artists. The *Fifth* saw Barbirolli as ever an expansive Mahlerian, yet far more than in his recording of the *Sixth* (made a year earlier) his concentration convinces one that his tempi are right. Though the very opening may lose something in sheer dramatic bite there is always a sense of power in reserve, and when the main *Funeral march* emerges

there is a frisson such as one experiences in the concert hall but rarely from a recording. A classic performance, given a ripe recording which has transferred well to tape. There is perhaps a slight lack of crispness of focus at the beginning of the work, with its dramatic fanfare, but in general the richness of the strings and brass comes over gloriously, and the finale has plenty of weight and impact.

Karajan's characteristic emphasis on polish and refinement goes with sharpness of focus. His is at once the most beautiful as well as the most intense version available, starting with an account of the first movement which brings more biting funeral-march rhythms than any rival. Resplendent recording, rich and refined, to match the radiant playing of the Berlin Philharmonic. Christa Ludwig's warm singing in *Kindertotenlieder* marks out a valuable fill-up. The cassette version is of excellent quality, clear and clean.

Those who resist Barbirolli's expansiveness and Karajan's refinement will probably find the ideal alternative in Haitink's fresh and direct reading, with finely judged tempi, unexaggerated observance of Mahler's markings, and refined playing from the Concertgebouw. The famous *Adagietto* is relatively cool, but its beauty is as intense as ever. Good, well-balanced Philips recording, and a first-class transfer to tape. At the very opening tutti there is a hint that the wide range of sound encompassed by the recording lacks absolute clarity of focus, but this is momentary, and the transfer throughout is of the very highest standard, offering splendid weight and richness and excellent clarity and detail. The tape is differently coupled from the LPs, but Hermann Prey's performance of the *Lieder eines fahrenden Gesellen* is most welcome.

The opening *Funeral march* sets the tone of Solti's reading. At a tempo faster than usual, it is wistful rather than deeply tragic, even though the dynamic contrasts are superbly pointed, and the string tone could hardly be more resonant. In the pivotal *Adagietto* too Solti secures intensely beautiful playing, but the result lacks the 'inner' quality one finds so abundantly in Barbirolli's interpretation. Gloriously rich if slightly over-reverberant recording, and the cassette transfer is characteristically brilliant. However, it was an early Decca tape issue and the sound is not quite so free and open as the disc quality, with a suggestion of strain once or twice. But the detail is clear and the effect admirably full-blooded.

Brilliant as the recording is of Mehta's Los Angeles version, and the playing too, it misses the natural warmth of expression which the same conductor found in his reading of No. 2 with the Vienna Philharmonic. Most impressive is the virtuoso scherzo, but in their different ways both the opening *Funeral march* and the beautiful *Adagietto* lack the inner quality which is essential if the faster movements are to be aptly framed. The brilliance of the finale is exaggerated by Mehta's very fast tempo, missing the *Wunderhorn* overtones of this most optimistic of Mahler's conclusions. The *Adagio* from the unfinished *Tenth* is spaciously played, and throughout the set the recording is admirably clear and vividly detailed (the opening trumpet of the first movement of the *Fifth* is dramatically projected to set the mood of the performance immediately). There is no lack of body and weight and one is struck by the translucent string quality and excellent focus in the *Adagio* from the *Tenth*.

Wyn Morris starts with a strikingly commanding account of the *Funeral march*, but then the second movement is a little cautious, lacking bite, with the ensemble less crisp than elsewhere. In the third movement Morris captures the Viennese lilt very winningly; he takes the *Adagietto* at a flowing tempo and the finale in a broad expansive sweep, not quite as sharply focused as it might be. It is a sympathetic reading, but not consistent in its success. Fair atmospheric recording, but a transfer of uneven qua-

lity. There is a degree of congestion at the opening of the first movement and then intermittently throughout; in the scherzo the lack of refinement is more marginal and on side two the sound is generally clear and unblemished. The quality is good for the fill-up, and Roland Hermann's performance of the *Lieder eines fahrenden Gesellen* is fresh and intelligent, though his baritone is sometimes too gritty, and at times expressiveness is underlined too heavily.

Symphony No. 6 in A minor.
*** DG 3370 026 [id.]. Berlin PO, Karajan.

With superlative playing from the Berlin Philharmonic, Karajan's reading of the *Sixth* is a revelation, above all in the slow movement, which here becomes far more than a lyrical interlude. With this *Andante moderato* made to flower in poignant melancholy and with a simpler lyrical style than Karajan usually adopts, it emerges as one of the greatest of Mahler's slow movements. The whole balance of the symphony is altered. Though the outer movements firmly make this the darkest of the Mahler symphonies, their sharp focus in Karajan's reading – with contrasts of light and shade heightened – make them both compelling and refreshing. Significantly, in his care for tonal colouring Karajan brings out a number of overtones related to Wagner's *Ring*. The superb DG recording, with its wide dynamics, adds enormously to the impact. It is given a characteristically sophisticated transfer, although on tape the bass response is a little dry and (especially noticeable at the opening) the upper strings are very bright and will need just a little smoothing. But when this is done the detail remains admirably refined. The packaging, with the two plastic library boxes containing the cassettes removable from their wells in the album, is ideal, and the notes are clearly printed.

Symphony No. 8 in E flat major (Symphony of 1000).
> ⊛ *** Decca KCET 2 7006 [Lon. 5-1295]. Heather Harper, Lucia Popp, Yvonne Minton, Helen Watts, René Kollo, John Shirley-Quirk, Martti Talvela, Vienna Boys' Choir, Vienna State Opera Chorus and Singverein, Chicago SO, Solti.
> *(**) Symphonica CSYM 1/2 [RCA CRK 2 0359]. Josie Barker, Elizabeth Simon, Joyce Blackham, Alfreda Hodgson, John Mitchinson, Raymond Myers, Gwynne Howell, Choruses and Symphonica of London, Morris.

Solti's is a classic recording. Challenged by the tightest possible recording schedule, the American orchestra and European singers responded to Solti at his most inspired with a performance that vividly captures the atmosphere of a great occasion – essential in this of all works. There is nothing cautious about the surging dynamism of the first movement, the electrifying hymn, *Veni Creator spiritus*; and the long second movement setting the final scene of Goethe's *Faust* proceeds through its contrasted sections with unrelenting intensity. The hushed prelude in Solti's hands is sharp-edged in *pianissimo*, not at all comforting, while the magnificent recording copes superbly with every strand of texture and the fullest range of dynamic – spectacularly so in the great final crescendo to the words *Alles vergängliche*. A triumph for everyone concerned, and the quality of the cassette transfer is little short of astonishing, carrying the extraordinarily wide dynamic range with remarkable richness and detail.

Wyn Morris's version, recorded like Solti's in conjunction with a live performance, has its flaws of detail but triumphantly conveys a sense of occasion against a warm atmospheric acoustic. However,

the degree of reverberation brings with it an element of congestion at peaks in the first movement. Morris's approach to Mahler is consciously expressive, more in the style of Bruno Walter than Solti. With dedicated singing from soloists and choirs and first-rate playing from the pick-up orchestra this account has much to commend it, not least its obvious forward impulse and spontaneity, which make one forgive the patches of vocal inadequacy. The transfer offers excellent detail and (in the latter part of the work especially) some really refined textures, but one has also to accept the patches of roughness at peaks, noticeable, for instance, at the work's very opening. As a full-priced issue this is much less competitive than it was when it was issued at medium price.

Symphony No. 9 in D major.
> **(*) DG 3370 018 [id.]. Chicago SO, Giulini.
> (***) Decca KCET 2 7003. LSO, Solti.

Giulini's much admired version provides more satisfactory quality on cassette than Solti's set; but when Decca remaster their tapes the latter will revert to first choice. Giulini's performance opens atmospherically, but the warmth engendered is not evenly sustained. The very quality one expects of him, dedication, is lacking. He sets tempi that are a shade too measured for a sense of impetus to assert itself. The orchestral playing is of the highest standard and the reading contains many insights, but in the last analysis the listener senses that the concentration does not hold consistently, even though there are some fine moments. The transfer is clear and generally impressive, although there is some lack of body and bloom to the upper strings in *fortissimo*. The finale, however, sounds strikingly vivid. The packaging is sophisticated.

Solti's is a brilliant, dramatic performance, but one which finally falls just a little short of being a great performance in its extrovert approach to the spiritual beauty of the finale. In the middle two movements it would be hard to match Solti for the point and precision of the playing. The tempo for the second-movement *Ländler* may be slow, but with such pointing the slowness is amply justified – quite apart from following Mahler's marking. The third movement is given the most brilliant account ever recorded; but in the outer movements one feels that Solti is not penetrating deeply enough. He allows the composer's passionate utterances to emerge too readily. He makes Mahler wear his heart on his sleeve, and although there may be justifications for that, it leaves something out that we have come to expect. The recording quality is superb, with a fantastic range of dynamic, confidently handled by the engineers, but unfortunately something seems to have gone wrong with this transfer. It is muddy, bass-heavy and ill-defined at the opening of the first movement and later produces unrefined detail and coarseness at climaxes uncharacteristic of Decca. We remembered this as being a good tape when first issued, but current copies are not satisfactory.

Symphony No. 10 in F sharp major (Unfinished): completed by Deryck Cooke.
  (M) ** CBS 40-61447. Philadelphia Orch., Ormandy.

Deryck Cooke described the score he prepared of Mahler's *Tenth Symphony* as a 'performing version', for the composer sketched the outline of all five movements to the last bar. The precise proportions were clear, and the harmony and much of the instrumentation could be inferred, while the first movement and the central *Purgatorio* movement were complete. In this earlier version recorded by Ormandy, Cooke left the last two movements relatively bald in their scoring and the finale, in particular, does not sound as authentically Mahlerian as

Cooke's final version (recorded on Philips but not available on tape). Ormandy's tempi, particularly for the fateful slow finale with its hammer blows, are on the fast side, but the fine playing of the Philadelphia strings helps to sustain the intensity even if the last degree of tragic weight is missing. The bright recording has transferred acceptably to cassette, although the reverberation brings some lack of refinement in climaxes. The string timbre is faithfully caught, however, and the opening and closing sections of the symphony are effective here.

(i) *Symphony No. 10 in F sharp major (Unfinished): Adagio.* (ii) *Kindertotenlieder.*
  ** CBS 40-76475. (ii) New York PO, Bernstein; (ii) Janet Baker (mezzo-soprano), Israel PO, Bernstein.

In the *Adagio* from the *Tenth Symphony* Bernstein uses the old, fallible edition, but the passionate commitment of his performance is hard to resist, with contrasts underlined between the sharpness of the *Andante* passages and the free expressiveness of the main *Adagio*. Janet Baker's CBS recording of *Kindertotenlieder* was made after a series of performances in Israel with Bernstein conducting. Comparison with her earlier HMV set under Barbirolli (not yet available on tape) shows a darker colouring, a less tender, tougher approach. The closeness of the CBS recording sometimes exaggerates a slight beat in Dame Janet's voice, never there before, but it is a gloriously involving performance. In the fifth song the storm music is wonderfully sharp and biting, with the cradle-song resolutions beautifully poised and steady. The Israel recording has less atmosphere than the New York one. The transfer to tape is of fair quality, not very refined in detail and range, but generally kind to the voice.

321

LIEDER AND SONG CYCLES

Kindertotenlieder: see above under Symphonies Nos. 5 and 10.

Des Knaben Wunderhorn.
   *** Philips 7300 572 [id.]. Jessye Norman (soprano), John Shirley-Quirk (bar.), Concertgebouw Orch., Haitink.

Though some may prefer a more sharply characterful reading of these keenly imagined songs than this, the results here are most refined and satisfying. With the help of superb recording – as impressive in the cassette version as on disc – the singing of both Jessye Norman and John Shirley-Quirk brings out the purely musical imaginations of Mahler at his finest, while Haitink draws superbly clean and polished playing from his own Concertgebouw Orchestra. Although the comparatively low-level transfer does not have quite the upper range of the disc, the balance is excellent. Both the voices and the orchestral tapestry have been beautifully caught within an ambience of great warmth: there are some lovely sounds on this tape which should give great satisfaction.

Des Knaben Wunderhorn: excerpts (*Das irdische Leben; Verlor'ne Müh; Wo die schönen Trompeten blasen; Rheinlegendchen*).
   (*) Decca KCET 2 7001 [Lon. 5-2228]. Yvonne Minton (contralto), Chicago SO, Solti – *Symphony No. 5.*(*)

Yvonne Minton, a singer whom Solti encouraged enormously in her career at Covent Garden, makes a splendid soloist in these colourful songs from *Des Knaben Wunderhorn.* A pity that as a fill-up they make rather short measure. Fine recording, as in the symphony, and the cassette transfer is of excellent Decca quality.

Das Lied von der Erde.
   *** Philips 7300 362 [id.]. Janet Baker (mezzo-soprano), James King (tenor), Concertgebouw Orch., Haitink.
   *** Decca KCET 555 [Lon. 5-26292]. Yvonne Minton (contralto), René Kollo (tenor), Chicago SO, Solti.
   (M) **(*) Decca Jubilee KJBC 13. James King (tenor), Dietrich Fischer-Dieskau (bar.), Vienna PO, Bernstein.

(i) *Das Lied von der Erde. 5 Rückert Lieder.*
   *** DG 3370 007 [id.]. Christa Ludwig (mezzo-soprano), Berlin PO, Karajan, (i) with René Kollo (tenor).
   (B) **(*) Decca KMON 2 7050. Kathleen Ferrier (contralto), Vienna PO, Walter, (i) with Julius Patzak (tenor).

The combination of Haitink, the most thoughtfully dedicated of Mahler conductors, and Janet Baker, the most deeply committed of Mahler singers, produces radiantly beautiful and moving results, helped by superbly refined and atmospheric recording. If usually these songs reflect a degree of oriental reticence, Dame Janet more clearly relates them to Mahler's other great orchestral songs, so complete is the sense of involvement, with the conductor matching his soloist's mood. The concentration over the long final *Abschied* has never been surpassed on record (amost all of it was recorded in a single take). Haitink impressively opens the cycle with an account of the first tenor song which subtly confirms its symphonic shape, less free in tempo than usual but presenting unusually strong contrasts between the main stanzas and the tender refrain, *Dunkel ist das Leben.* James King cannot match his solo partner, often failing to find fantasy, but his singing is intelligent and more sympathetic than it was on the Bernstein Decca set (see below). The balance with the tenor is admirably realistic, but Dame Janet's voice is brought a shade closer. Although not as brilliantly clear as the Solti version (as is noticeable at the exuberant opening) this Philips transfer has fine atmosphere and warmth and is very kind to the voices. It is for the most part demonstration-worthy in a different way from the Decca.

In sheer beauty of sound and precision of texture, few versions match Solti's with the Chicago orchestra, helped by brilliant but refined recording. As an interpretation it may lose something in mystery from this very precision, but the concentration of Solti in a consciously less romantic style than Walter or Bernstein adopt is highly compelling, above all in the final *Abschied*, slower than usual and bringing in the final section an unusually close observance of Mahler's *pianissimo* markings. Minton exactly matches Solti's style, consistently at her most perceptive and sensitive, while Kollo presents Heldentenor strength combined with sensitivity. The recording has no need to give the tenor an unnaturally close balance, and the result is the more exciting. The tape transfer is outstandingly brilliant and clear, if perhaps not quite as atmospheric as the Haitink/Philips issue.

If Haitink presents *Das Lied* as a great symphonic masterpiece (Mahler himself called it a symphony, but for superstitious reasons failed to number it), Karajan presents it as the most seductive sequence of atmospheric songs. It may seem strange that so central a conductor has generally avoided Mahler until late in his career, but the result here is everything one could have hoped for, combining Karajan's characteristic refinement and polish with a deep sense of melancholy. The balancing of textures, the weaving of separate strands into a transparent tapestry, has never been so flawlessly achieved as here, and Karajan's way of presenting Mahler's orchestration in the subtlest tones rather than in full colours is arguably more apt. In any case what matters is that, along with his characteristic refinement, Karajan conveys the ebb and flow of tension as in a live performance. He is helped enormously by the soloists, both of whom have recorded this work several times, but never more richly than here. This is a two-tape set, and though that may seem extravagant, Christa Ludwig's singing of the *Rückert Lieder* is far more than a mere makeweight, for these are fine, positive performances. The DG cassette transfer offers sound which is crystal-clear but rather lacking in bloom. The dynamic range is very wide, and the quieter music seems not as immediate as the climaxes, which have a tendency to sound slightly aggressive (in orchestral timbre) because of the edge on the recorded quality.

The reissue of the classic Ferrier/Walter version of *Das Lied* restores in this cassette version its original coupling when it first appeared on a two-disc set. Patzak as well as Ferrier bring keen insight, and Walter draws even more affectionate playing from the Vienna Philharmonic than he did from his American orchestras; but one cannot help noticing that Mahler performances have grown more sophisticated since the early fifties when these recordings were made (the *Rückert Lieder* as well as *Das Lied*) and Ferrier, for all her gorgeous tone colours, sometimes sounds a little stiff of phrase. The transfer is on the whole very successful. It is very kind to Kathleen Ferrier's voice and the orchestral tapestry is given bloom and atmosphere. There is only a hint of restricted range, more than compensated for by the warmth of the string tone (the edginess characteristic of Decca recordings of this period is not noticeable). There is sometimes a touch of hardness on the tenor voice, and very occasionally a hint of insecurity of texture. It is perhaps a pity that the tape opens with the *Rückert* songs and makes a break in *Das Lied*.

Bernstein's version stands on its own

in using a baritone instead of a contralto voice in partnership with the tenor, and even though Fischer-Dieskau is as sensitive as ever, it is doubtful whether even he can match the finest contralto in the role, for one needs a lightening of tone in the even-numbered songs rather than – as here – a darkening. Nor can a baritone voice give quite such precision to the notes as Mahler's rounded melodies clearly need. James King is a strong-voiced tenor, but his phrasing and word-pointing sound comparatively stiff. However, Bernstein's tempi are aptly chosen for the music and this helps to make the tenor songs sparkle as they should, and though the final *Abschied*, taken at a very slow tempo indeed, puts extra strain on everyone, Bernstein's intensity carries the performance through. The high-level transfer is admirably vivid, with good projection of the voices, but the orchestral bass is dry and there is a lack of glow and richness in the upper strings, although there is plenty of clarity and detail.

Lieder eines fahrenden Gesellen: see above under *Symphony No. 5.*

5 Rückert Lieder (see also under *Das Lied von der Erde*).

*** HMV TC-SLS 785. Janet Baker (mezzo-soprano), New Philharmonia Orch., Barbirolli – *Symphony No. 5*.***

Few more lovely Mahler recordings have ever been made than this collection of the *Five Rückert Lieder* used as a fill-up for Barbirolli's ripe and expansive account of the *Fifth Symphony*. The range of tone colour used by Janet Baker in these subtly contrasted songs is ravishing, and it is matched by dedicated playing from the New Philharmonia. No Mahlerian should miss hearing this. The recording is one of the finest ever produced by EMI, and it has been smoothly transferred, so that the solo voice sounds

natural against a rich orchestral back-cloth.

COLLECTION

'The world of Mahler': Symphonies Nos. (i) *1 in D major:* 2nd movt; (ii) *4 in G major:* 1st movt; (iii) *5 in C sharp minor: Adagietto;* (iii; iv) *8 in E flat major:* finale. (iii; v) *Des Knaben Wunderhorn: Rheinlegendchen. Lieder eines fahrenden Gesellen: Ging heut' morgen über's Feld.*

(M) ** Decca KCSP 15362. (i) LSO; (ii) Concertgebouw Orch.; (iii) Chicago SO; (iv) René Kollo (tenor), and choruses; (v) Yvonne Minton (contralto); all cond. Solti.

It is not certain that a collection of odd movements of this kind serves Mahler's cause. The *Adagietto* from the *Fifth Symphony*, which opens side two, stands well on its own (as we remember from 78 days), but in general this is a sampler for public libraries rather than a rewarding disc for regular use in even the small private collection. It is a pity that the tape opens with the first movement of the *Fourth*, which (attractive though it is) is not one of Solti's most convincing Mahler performances. The transfers are of good quality, and the cassette offers an extra item from *Des Knaben Wunderhorn* not included on the equivalent LP.

Mascagni, Pietro
(1863–1945)

L'Amico Fritz (opera): complete.

(M) *** HMV TC-SLS 5107. Luciano Pavarotti, Mirella Freni, Vincenzo Sardinero,

Chorus and Orch. of the Royal Opera House, Covent Garden, Gavazzeni.

The haunting *Cherry duet* from this opera whets the appetite for more, and it is good to hear so rare and charming a piece, one that is not likely to enter the repertory of our British opera houses. Even so enthusiasm has to be tempered a little, because no other number in the opera approaches the famous duet in its memorability. The libretto too is delicate to the point of feebleness. This performance could be more refined, though Freni and Pavarotti are most attractive artists, and this was recorded in 1969 when they were both at their freshest. The Covent Garden Orchestra responds loyally; the recording is warm and atmospheric, and it has transferred very successfully to tape, Mascagni's lightweight orchestration sounding pleasingly luminous and the voices natural and well focused. While the dramatic conception is at the opposite end of the scale from *Cavalleria Rusticana*, one is easily beguiled by the music's charm, and the Puccinian influences are by no means a disadvantage. The opera is well laid out on tape, and the printing of the libretto is bold and clear.

Cavalleria Rusticana (opera): complete.
*** DG 3371 011 [id.]. Fiorenza Cossotto, Carlo Bergonzi, Giangiacomo Guelfi, Chorus and Orch. of La Scala, Milan, Karajan – LEONCAVALLO: *I Pagliacci*.**(*)
(M) *(**) HMV TC-SLS 819. Maria Callas, Giuseppe di Stefano, Rolando Panerei, Chorus and Orch. of La Scala, Milan, Serafin – LEONCAVALLO: *I Pagliacci*.**(*)
(M) ** CBS 40-61640. Margaret Harshaw, Richard Tucker, Mildred Miller, Frank Guarrera,

Chorus and Orch. of Metropolitan Opera, New York, Cleva.

Karajan's coupling of *Cavalleria Rusticana* and *I Pagliacci* is an excellent demonstration of how much the actual level of a transfer to cassette tape affects the recording quality. The first two sides of *Cavalleria Rusticana* are transferred at a comparatively ambitious level for DG and the quality often approaches demonstration standard and easily matches the discs. It is clear, and has excellent impact yet retains its bloom. On side three the volume drops marginally and the focus softens, the voices, chorus and orchestra all slightly less crisp (but still good). Karajan pays Mascagni the tribute of taking his markings literally, so that well-worn melodies come out with new purity and freshness, and the singers have been chosen to match that. Cossotto quite as much as Bergonzi keeps a pure, firm line that is all too rare in this much-abused music. Together they show that much of the vulgarity lies in interpretations rather than in Mascagni's inspiration. Not that there is any lack of dramatic bite (except marginally, because of the recording balance in some of the chorus work). There is no libretto provided with this set.

Despite the sympathetic direction of Serafin (although he is less characterful than usual), the other Scala performance lacks much in atmosphere – almost inevitable in a stereo transcription of an original mono recording, however well balanced. The justification of the performance lies above all else in the searing characterization of Santuzza from Maria Callas, apt to the role or not. With Callas providing the central focus the performance seems to centre round the aria *Voi lo sapete*, wonderfully dark and intense. Challenged by the heroine, di Stefano and Panerai generally sing well, if hardly with comparable point and detail. There is nothing whatever of sentimentality here, rather passionate intensity, even if the supporting cast cannot begin to match Callas in this quality, and the performance as a whole provides a refreshingly new look at a work which here is far more than just sweetly lyrical. The restricted frequency range means that the opera's opening choruses sound rather mushy, but the solo voices are on the whole well treated, although the sound is not entirely without peaking. The quality has less presence here than in *Pagliacci*.

The CBS recording has the singular advantage of fitting the opera comfortably on two sides of a mid-priced cassette. The recording dates from 1955, and considering its age the quality is quite astonishingly good, much clearer in focus than the EMI set and with such conveyed atmosphere that at times one has the impression of listening to real stereo rather than a transcription. The performance has plenty of spontaneity, and if Margaret Harshaw as Santuzza does not project a large-sized personality she sings musically and not without drama, and there are no squally notes as so often happens in this role. Mildred Miller makes a charming Lola (her music is stylishly accompanied by Cleva) but the star of the set is undoubtedly Richard Tucker, whose lusty portrayal of Turiddu is red-blooded without being coarse.

Cavalleria Rusticana: highlights.
(M) *** DG Privilege 3335 199 [922012] (from above set cond. Karajan) – LEONCAVALLO: *I Pagliacci* highlights.***
*(*) Decca KCET 490. Elena Suliotis, Mario del Monaco, Tito Gobbi, Rome Opera Chorus and Orch., Varviso – LEONCAVALLO: *I Pagliacci* highlights.*(*)

Karajan's set of highlights, with its refinement of direction as well as the fresh sophistication of the solo singing, is easily preferable to the full-priced Decca issue. Suliotis's contribution is not always fully controlled vocally, and del

Monaco is not at his best either. Both are well transferred to tape; the DG selection has marginally less bite and sparkle than its coupling, but is still good.

Massenet, Jules (1842–1912)

Scènes pittoresques; Le Cid: ballet music; *La Vierge: The Last Sleep of the Virgin.*
(M) *** HMV Greensleeve TC-ESD 7040. City of Birmingham SO, Frémaux.

This is a most delightful tape. The performances both of the wittily tuneful ballet music and of the charming 'picture-postcard' *Scènes pittoresques* are highly effective. *The Last Sleep of the Virgin* was a favourite piece of Sir Thomas Beecham's and Frémaux presents it lovingly. The string playing here is quite beautiful, but the orchestra throughout is on its toes. The sound is superbly vivid and rich, and the *Aubade* in the ballet suite is a demonstration item *par excellence*. The tape transfer is admirably managed, skilfully catching the rich ambience of the Great Hall of Birmingham University, where the recordings were made. The bass drum seems to offer no problems and the castanets in *Le Cid* are projected in the most lively fashion.

Le Cid: ballet music; *Ariane: Lamento d'Ariane.*
*** Decca KSXC 6812 [Lon. 5-7032]. National PO, Bonynge – MEYERBEER: *Les Patineurs.***

Decca have, over the years, made a house speciality of recording the ballet music from *Le Cid* and coupling it with Constant Lambert's arrangement of Meyerbeer. Bonynge's new version is the finest ever, with the most seductive orchestral playing, superbly recorded. The bonus item, the *Lament* from *Ariane*, is pleasing but not distinctive. The transfer produces agreeably warm, resonant sound, perhaps a trifle over-rich in bass and middle compared to the upper range, but still very enjoyable. With careful setting of the controls the quality can be very impressive. The strings are most natural.

Manon (opera): complete.
(M) *** HMV TC-SLS 5119. Victoria de los Angeles, Henri Legay, Michel Dens, Jean Borthaye (baritones), Chorus and Orch. of the Paris Opéra-Comique, Monteux.

It is strange that despite the increase of interest in Massenet's music, there has been no fully recommendable version of this most popular of his operas – and arguably the finest – since this superb mono set from the mid-sixties. Pierre Monteux (who had still some years of active career before him) never recorded a more glowing opera performance, and he was aided by the most radiant of heroines, Victoria de los Angeles at her very peak, the voice meltingly beautiful and finely poised, the characterization unfailingly endearing. In the aria *Je suis encore tout étourdie*, it is not just that she convinces one totally of her emotional involvement and phrases magically but that the fluttering phrases at the end of each section are breathtakingly delicate. Try as sample the scene where des Grieux first meets Manon: Henri Legay conveys the wonderment of the moment and Monteux's conducting ensures an authentic frisson. The stereo transcription has transferred quite admirably to tape. The recording has splendid presence, and the lightness of orchestral texture suits the French ambience of the opera. The string tone is not especially rich (arguably thinner violins than in the original discs), but the tape transfer does not emphasize this and the sound is clean and never edgy.

The voices are faithfully caught (especially los Angeles and Henri Legay's deliciously light tenor), and the orchestral detail is a constant pleasure in this truly magical account of a most moving opera.

Werther (opera): complete. (Also includes recital by Gedda: arias from ADAM: *Le Postillon de Longjumeau;* MASSENET: *Manon;* THOMAS: *Mignon;* GOUNOD: *Mireille;* LALO: *Le Roi d'Ys.*)
(M) *** HMV TC-SLS 5105. Victoria de los Angeles, Nicolai Gedda, Mady Mesplé, Roger Soyer, Jean-Christophe Benoît, Children's chorus from La Maîtrise de l'O.R.T.F., Orchestre de Paris, Prêtre.

Here is a classic instance where the cassette medium works far more conveniently than disc. EMI fits each of the acts of this subtlest of Massenet's operas without break on to a single cassette side, whereas on disc each act is broken. The disc fill-up, an attractive French opera recital from Gedda, then remains separate on the fourth side. There is an excellently produced libretto, clearly printed (though it indicates six side-breaks, as on LP, and not four as on tape). Prêtre, more passionate and committed than is common with him in the recording studio, inspires Gedda to give one of his finest and most searching performances as Goethe's romantic hero, while Victoria de los Angeles is here at her most tenderly affecting. Already in 1969, when the recording was made, the voice was not flawless, but the character and imagination of her singing are compelling. Mesplé is a somewhat shrill Sophie, but reservations are of little moment. The recorded quality is warmly vivid and it is well transferred if lacking the last degree of range in the treble. The sound is free from blemishes, and both los Angeles and Mesplé are treated well by the recording.

There is plenty of life in the Gedda recital and the balance generally has more sparkle here.

Maunder, John
(1858–1920)

Olivet to Calvary (cantata).
> (M) **(*) HMV TC-ESD 7051. John Mitchinson (tenor), Frederick Harvey (bar.), Guildford Cathedral Choir, Barry Rose; Peter Moorse (organ).

It is easy to be patronizing about music like this. Its melodic and harmonic flavour will for many tastes seem too highly coloured and sugary for the subject, but provided one accepts the conventions of style in which it is composed the music is effective and often moving. The performance has an attractive simplicity and genuine eloquence. Just occasionally the soloists overdo the drama in their enunciation, but for the most part they are sensitive to the text and the obvious dedication of the music. Frederick Harvey is particularly moving at the actual moment of Christ's death: in a passage that, insensitively handled, could be positively embarrassing, he creates a magical, hushed intensity. The choir sing beautifully, and in the gentler, lyrical writing (the semi-chorus *O Thou whose sweet compassion*, for example) sentimentality is skilfully avoided. The HMV recording is first-class in every way and the tape quality is equally fine for the most part, with splendid projection for the soloists. The quieter choral passages sound very beautiful, made the more so by the recording's atmospheric warmth. On our review copy there was a slip in refinement at a couple of choral peaks on side one and at the big choral climax just before the end of the work.

Mendelssohn, Felix
(1809–47)

Piano concertos Nos. 1 in G minor, Op. 25; 2 in D minor, Op. 40.
> ** CBS 40-76376. Murray Perahia, Academy of St Martin-in-the-Fields, Marriner.

Perahia's performances are highly rewarding, but the CBS sound leaves something to be desired. The acoustic of the recording is somewhat confined, but the piano tone is clear and agreeable. The orchestral sound lacks brilliance in the treble but is not muffled. Perahia's playing catches the Mendelssohnian spirit with admirable perception. There is sensibility and sparkle, the slow movements are shaped most beautifully, and obviously the partnership with Marriner is very successful, for the Academy give a most sensitive backing.

Violin concerto in D minor, Op. posth.; Violin concerto in E minor, Op. 64.
> **(*) Philips 7300 522. Salvatore Accardo, LPO, Dutoit.
> ** HMV TC-ASD 2809. Yehudi Menuhin, LSO, Frühbeck de Burgos.
> *(*) Philips 7300 248 [id.]. Arthur Grumiaux, New Philharmonia Orch., Krenz (with BEETHOVEN: *Minuet in G major*).

Mendelssohn's early *D minor Violin concerto* was completed when he was thirteen, after he had written the first five *Symphonies for strings*. As a structure it is amazingly accomplished, but only the finale has memorable themes. The best-recorded of these three tapes is Accardo's, which is naturally balanced and well detailed. Accardo has made a considerable reputation in the baroque field (his recordings of the concertos of

Vivaldi are of outstanding quality). The freshness of his style here is most appealing. In the *E minor Concerto* the outer movements are lithe and sparkling, and the slow movement, taken slower than usual, is expressive in a natural, unforced way. But some ears will find his refined phrasing too restrained to capture Mendelssohn's romantic inspiration in its full bloom. This comparative lack of romantic ripeness is more suitable for the juvenile work, but tends to disguise any foreshadowing of the later Mendelssohn. Even so these are distinctive performances, in some ways more memorable than those of Grumiaux, who is more conventional in approach. Certainly the sensibility of Accardo's playing gives much pleasure.

Menuhin plays the early concerto with obvious devotion. In the famous *E minor Concerto* his performance has its moments of roughness but it has a magic too – at the appearance of the first movement's second subject and in the slow movement, where Grumiaux (who is undoubtedly more polished) plays beautifully but is very slightly bland. The HMV transfer is of acceptable but not outstanding quality, but the Philips tape of the Grumiaux performance is disappointing. The backward balance of the soloist in the *E minor Concerto* is exaggerated by the low level of the recording; the *D minor Concerto* is slightly more vivid, but neither has a great deal of impact. Beethoven's *Minuet in G major*, which acts as a bonus (with the piano accompaniment played by Istvan Hajdu), comes at the end of side two, and its mood seems totally inappropriate at the end of the concerto.

Violin concerto in D minor, Op. posth.; (i) *Double concerto in D minor for violin, piano and string orchestra.*
(M) *** Turnabout KTVC 34662. Susanne Lautenbacher (violin), Württemberg CO, Faerber, (i) with Marylene Dosse (piano).

Mendelssohn wrote the delightful *Double concerto for violin and piano* when he was fourteen, and it is another example of his extraordinary youthful precocity. It is not just that the invention is attractive; the young composer's natural feeling for the difficult medium of the duet concerto is matched by the substance of his musical arguments. Admittedly here the work has been cut (from forty minutes to just under thirty), but the result is an astonishingly well-made piece, enjoyable from the first bar to the last. Both soloists are in excellent form, and they are well accompanied. The recording too is good, even if the balance is somewhat artificial, with the violin and the piano placed forward and separated clearly. As a coupling Susanne Lautenbacher provides a well-made and sensitive performance of the early *D minor Violin concerto*. This is a thoroughly worthwhile issue, and all Mendelssohnians should try it. The transfer is first-class in every way, crisp and clear and with splendid definition and body – a real demonstration tape.

Violin concerto in E minor, Op. 64.
*** Decca Phase 4 KPFC 4345 [Lon. 5-21116]. Ruggiero Ricci, Netherlands Radio Orch., Fournet – TCHAIKOVSKY: *Violin concerto.****

(*) HMV TC-ASD 2926 [Angel 4XS 36963]. Itzhak Perlman, LSO, Previn – BRUCH: *Concerto No. 1.*(*)

(M) *** Decca KCSP 88. Ruggiero Ricci, LSO, Gamba – BRUCH: *Concerto No. 1.****

(M) ** Philips 7317 107. Arthur Grumiaux, Concertgebouw Orch., Haitink – BRUCH: *Concerto No. 1.***

(M) ** Supraphon 045546. Josef Suk, Czech PO, Ančerl – BRUCH: *Concerto No. 1.***

(M) *(*) DG Privilege 3335 294.

Yong Uck Kim, Bamberg SO, Kamu – BRUCH: *Concerto No. 1.**(*)

(M) (**) HMV TC-SXLP 30245. Nathan Milstein, Philharmonia Orch., Barzin – BRUCH: *Concerto No. 1.*(**)

Violin concerto in E minor; A Midsummer Night's Dream: Incidental music, Op. 61: Nocturne.

*(*) Philips 7300 853. Henryk Szeryng, Concertgebouw Orch., Haitink – TCHAIKOVSKY: *Concerto.**(*)

(i) *Violin concerto in E minor;* (ii) *Symphony No. 4 in A major (Italian), Op. 90.*

(B) ** Philips Fontana 7327 001. (i) Michèle Auclair, Innsbruck SO, Wagner; (ii) Vienna SO, Sawallisch.

Ricci's Phase Four performance of the Mendelssohn is even finer than his successful earlier version with Gamba. The balance places him well forward and reveals plenty of orchestral detail by the close microphoning of the woodwind. In the finale the listener's pleasure is enhanced by Fournet's precision in matching the solo line with the accompaniment, which adds considerable extra sparkle. The slow movement has a disarming simple eloquence, and the reading as a whole is undoubtedly distinguished. The vivid recording is admirably transferred to the cassette, which is of demonstration quality.

Perlman gives a performance as full of flair as any available, and he is superbly matched by the LSO under Previn, always an illuminating interpreter of Mendelssohn. With ripe recording quality, this must stand among the first recommendations for a deservedly much-recorded work. Unfortunately the vivid cassette transfer suffers from a restricted dynamic range, although in all other respects the sound is excellent.

Ricci's earlier performance is clean and sympathetic, and technically brilliant. There is perhaps some lack of repose and depth of feeling in the slow movement, but Ricci is far from being one of the virtuosi who ride roughshod over a work. Gamba too conducts with vigour and sympathy. For those who need a cheaper tape, and who particularly want the very fine Bruch coupling, this is a good recommendation, with an excellent cassette transfer, clear and clean, and with no lack of fullness.

Grumiaux's performance is characteristically assured and graceful. There is a suggestion of reticence in the slow movement which some will like more than others, but the finale has a compensating brilliance. Haitink accompanies convincingly, and the balance and recorded sound are both good.

A sympathetic account from Suk, whose tone and intonation are always congenial. There is plenty of sparkle in the finale, which gains from not being rushed off its feet. The slow movement is straightforwardly lyrical, and the warm, reverberant recording is effectively balanced. The Supraphon transfer is fresh and pleasing, with the soloist naturally projected, and the overall sound picture clear yet with no lack of bloom.

The Privilege performance by Yong Uck Kim is genuinely touching, with an unforced eloquence that carries conviction. Unfortunately the soloist is handicapped by less than first-class orchestral support, and as a whole the coupling does not challenge the finest of its rivals. However, this is a rewarding performance which was underrated on its first appearance; those who investigate it may well feel that the rewards of Yong's playing outweigh the drawback of the orchestral support. The recording is eminently satisfactory, but the transfer level is marginally lower here than in the Bruch coupling: although the sound is pleasing, there is ultimately a lack of range and transparency.

Milstein is not at his most fervently

lyrical or totally committed in his performance. There is some patchy intonation at one point in the first movement, but that is not enough in itself to cause more than a passing raised eyebrow. But there is a certain quality of detachment here, and in a highly competitive field this, for all its fine musicianship (there is some good orchestral playing), is not as memorable as the very finest on tape. Moreover the transfer is not very refined, and the upper partials of the solo violin timbre are edgy and discoloured.

Szeryng's performance is sensitive and lyrical, but it has no specially individual qualities either from the soloist or in the accompaniment. It is not helped by the transfer, which is made at a very low level and provides only woolly orchestral detail. The *Nocturne* from *A Midsummer Night's Dream* makes a pleasant bonus after the concerto.

Michèle Auclair gives a rich, romantic performance. The slow movement is a little on the heavy side – Mendelssohn's sweet lyricism benefits from gentler treatment than this – but the outer movements are splendid, with plenty of flair and 'temperament'. The recording is excellent and the transfer is full-blooded and clear. The coupling of the *Italian symphony* has rather less lustre; the transfer does not lack freshness, but the age of the recording is more apparent here. The performance is lively and at bargain price this coupling is more than acceptable.

Overtures: *Athalie, Op. 74; Calm Sea and Prosperous Voyage (Meeresstille und glückliche Fahrt), Op. 27; The Hebrides (Fingal's Cave), Op. 26; Ruy Blas, Op. 95; Son and Stranger (Die Heimkehr aus der Fremde), Op. 89.*

(M) (***) HMV Greensleeve TC-ESD 7003. New Philharmonia Orch., Atzmon.

Moshe Atzmon directs an outstanding collection of Mendelssohn overtures, including two favourites and three rela-tively rare offerings, all beautifully played and recorded on the mid-price Greensleeve label. Unfortunately the cassette version is spoilt by a restricted dynamic range. This makes nonsense of the climaxes in *Fingal's Cave*, and the opening of *Calm Sea and Prosperous Voyage* is far too loud.

Overtures: *Calm Sea and Prosperous Voyage (Meeresstille und glückliche Fahrt), Op. 27; Fair Melusina (Die schöne Melusine), Op. 32; The Hebrides (Fingal's Cave), Op. 26; A Midsummer Night's Dream, Op. 21; Ruy Blas, Op. 95.*

** DG 3300 782. LSO, Chmura.

Gabriel Chmura is clearly a talent to watch. He has won both the Cantelli and the Karajan competitions and is still only in his early thirties. He is obviously on guard against the impetuosity of youth, and these performances tend towards the other extreme: he errs on the side of excessive caution in *The Hebrides*, where his tempo is a bit too measured. This could have more lightness of touch, and *Ruy Blas*, too, needs more zest if it is to be really exciting. Yet he pays scrupulous attention to detail and is plainly both conscientious in his approach and deeply musical. The orchestral playing is obviously well prepared and has real finish, while the recording is clean, well focused and bright without being over-lit. There is impressive range, and the transfer matches the disc in its truthfulness of timbre and balance. The tuttis are fresh. The detail is a little less positive in the pianissimos, but there are no hiss problems.

Overtures: *The Hebrides (Fingal's Cave), Op. 26; A Midsummer Night's Dream, Op. 21.*

(M) ** Decca KCSP 92. LSO, Maag – ROSSINI: *Overtures.***

These performances are well-known in other couplings (see below). They are both first-rate; *Fingal's Cave* is especially exciting, colourful, and vividly transferred.

Symphonies for string orchestra Nos. 9 in C major; 10 in B minor; 12 in G minor.

(M) *** Argo KZKC 7. Academy of St Martin-in-the-Fields, Marriner.

Hans Keller has argued that Mendelssohn wrote more finished masterpieces as a boy than even Mozart, and the magnificent set of twelve string symphonies that he wrote for family concerts in Berlin from the age of eleven shows just what a naturally fertile imagination the child had. Though the influences – J. S. Bach, C. P. E. Bach, Mozart and even Beethoven – are obvious enough, the genuine individuality is what makes most of the works, and certainly the three offered here, a consistent delight. The opening of No. 9 (the most extended piece here) hints at the later oratorio style until its seriousness dissolves into an attractive walking pizzicato that might remind one of the second movement of the *Italian symphony*. The writing throughout is masterly, with some fine individual movements, especially the *Poco adagio* of No. 9 and the flowing tranquillity of the *Andante* of No. 12. All the music is splendidly brought to life here by committed, vivacious playing and excellent recording. The transfer to tape offers fresh and lively string timbre with fine presence, although for some reason there seems rather more body to the tone on side two (Nos. 10 and 12).

Symphonies Nos. 1 in C minor, Op. 11; (i) 2 in B flat major (Hymn of Praise), Op. 52; 3 in A minor (Scottish), Op. 56; 4 in A major (Italian), Op. 90; 5 in D minor (Reformation), Op. 107.

**(*) DG 3371 020 [id.]. Berlin PO, Karajan, (i) with soloists and chorus.

Karajan's set of the Mendelssohn symphonies is a generally safe recommendation. The solo singing in the *Hymn of Praise* is capable rather than inspired and the choral tone here is rather dry, but the recording is otherwise faithful. The *Scottish symphony* is a particularly remarkable account (at the time of going to print the individual issue, coupled to *Fingal's Cave* on 3300 181, is not available in Dolby form) and so too is the early *C minor*. The *Italian symphony* is predictably brilliant, and while there is some minor reservations to be made about the *Reformation symphony*, the outstanding orchestral playing and well-balanced recording offer much to admire. Our tape set, however, showed some transfer faults, with pitch slips on the first two sides, and the high level has brought one or two moments of coarseness (the trombones distort in the finale of the *Second Symphony*, and there is some discoloration at the opening of No. 5). However, this was a comparatively early DG box issue and it is likely that later copies will have cured these faults.

Symphonies Nos. 1 in C minor, Op. 11; 5 in D minor (Reformation), Op. 107.

**(*) Decca KSXC 6818. Vienna PO, Dohnányi.

Christoph von Dohnányi directs crisp, electric performances of an excellent Mendelssohn coupling. The recording is outstandingly faithful, and only occasionally does one miss a lighter touch, some sign that these are Viennese players: the early symphony should really convey more charm. The cassette transfer is extremely successful, full-blooded yet refined in detail.

Symphony No. 3 in A minor (Scottish), Op. 56; Overture: Calm Sea and Prosperous Voyage (Meeresstille und glückliche Fahrt), Op. 27.

(***) HMV TC-ASD 3184. New Philharmonia Orch., Muti.

Symphony No. 3; Overture: *The Hebrides (Fingal's Cave), Op. 26.*
- (***) DG 3300 181 [id.]. Berlin PO, Karajan.
- (M) *** Decca KCSP 503. LSO, Maag.

Symphonies Nos. 3; 4 in A major (Italian), Op. 90.
- *** Decca KSXC 6363. LSO, Abbado.

Choice here resides between Abbado and Maag. Abbado has the advantage of a highly competitive coupling. His *Scottish* is beautifully played, each phrase sensitively moulded, and the LSO responds to his direction throughout with the greatest lightness of tone and delicacy of feeling. The Decca engineers also provide first-rate recording, and the transfer is of matching quality, rich and detailed with a fine overall bloom.

Under Maag too the *Scottish symphony* is played most beautifully, and its pastoral character, occasioned by Mendelssohn's considerable use of the strings throughout, is amplified by a recording of great warmth. The opening string cantilena is poised and very gracious and thus sets the mood for what is to follow. The stereo is excellent. One small complaint: Maag is too ponderous in the final *Maestoso*, but there is a compensating breadth and the effect is almost Klempererian. The transfer is absolutely first-class, quite disguising the age of the original recording, and with bright, natural strings and glowing woodwind detail. The bass is warm yet never clouds the texture. *Fingal's Cave* is no less successful and this remains one of the most satisfying accounts of this evocative overture in the catalogue.

Karajan's coupling is very fine indeed. There are some slight eccentricities of tempo: the opening of the *Symphony* is rather measured, while the closing pages of the finale are taken with exuberant brilliance. But the orchestral playing is superb, the conductor's warmth comes

over readily, and the direct eloquence of the reading, with no fussiness, is irresistible. The scherzo is marvellously done and becomes a real highlight of the performance, while there is no doubt that Karajan's final coda has a splendid buoyancy and power. With bright, clear recording, and a characterful account of *Fingal's Cave*, this would rate very highly indeed, but the tape – at the time of going to press – is still available only in non-Dolby form. The transfer is well balanced, so when DG finally issue a Dolby version it should be worth waiting for.

Muti's is a smiling performance, but one which also gives Mendelssohn his due weight. Muti emerges as a natural interpreter of this composer with his delicate rhythmic pointing. In the first movement he sustains concentration even at a slowish tempo, with the big exposition repeat for once observed. It is typical of Muti that the swinging 6/8 rhythms of the final coda, which can easily seem pompous, bring a natural, easy expansion. The overture is successful too. Recorded in vivid sound, this would make an excellent alternative to Abbado's fine reading, which is more generously coupled, but unfortunately the cassette transfer has a limited range of dynamics, unlike the equivalent disc, which is notable for its enormous dynamic breadth.

Symphony No. 4 in A major (Italian), Op. 90.
- (M) *** World Records TC-SH 290. Philharmonia Orch., Cantelli – SCHUBERT: *Symphony No. 8.*⊛***
- (***) HMV TC-ASD 3365. New Philharmonia Orch., Muti – SCHUMANN: *Symphony No. 4.*(***)

Symphony No. 4; Overture: *The Hebrides (Fingal's Cave), Op. 26.*
- (M) ** CBS Classics 40-61019 [(d) Col. MT 6975]. Cleveland

Orch., Szell – WEBER: *Oberon overture.***

(i) *Symphony No. 4;* (ii) *A Midsummer Night's Dream: Overture, Op. 21; Incidental music, Op. 61; Scherzo; Nocturne; Wedding march.*
(M) ** Philips 7317 140. Concertgebouw Orch., cond. (i) Haitink; (ii) Szell.
** Philips 7300 480 [id.]. Boston SO, Colin Davis.

Symphonies Nos. 4; 5 in D minor (Reformation), Op. 107.
(B) (*) RCA Camden c4-5035. Boston SO, Munch.

What is it that makes Guido Cantelli's performances so memorable? There are no personal touches of the kind we are used to from Furtwängler, Koussevitzky or Toscanini. In many ways he was a self-effacing conductor, concerned largely with perfection of detail, ensemble and balance, yet never at the expense of the overall impression. He was an artist with a highly developed sense of proportion; the part never detracts from the beauty of the whole, yet no single detail fails to tell. Remarkably few allowances need be made for the sound quality here, even though it is almost a quarter of a century old. The Schubert symphony with which it is coupled is genuinely stereo, but this is mono. Nonetheless, it sounds as fresh and alive as do the performances themselves. The transfer is clear, warm-toned and well balanced, but the small type used for the liner notes is virtually unreadable.

Haitink's account of the symphony offers generally fast tempi in the opening two movements, but the third movement has something of the poise which Mendelssohn in his civilized way requires, and the orchestral playing is superb throughout. In the transfer the recording sounds well, with a fine, open acoustic. Szell's performances of the items from *A Midsummer Night's Dream* also have plenty of character and colour, and again the

sound is open and bright, although not as pleasingly full as in the symphony. The orchestral playing is first-rate, especially the violins in the overture. The transfer is very successful indeed, offering fresh, clear orchestral sound with no lack of bloom or body. Only in the *Wedding march* does the resonance produce a less than refined image, and even here the sound is good. Elsewhere it is often demonstration-worthy and belies the age of the recording.

Davis provides a delightful Mendelssohn coupling, an exhilarating but never breathless account of the *Italian symphony* (complete with exposition repeat), coupled with the four most important items from the *Midsummer Night's Dream* music. Unlike so many versions of this symphony, this is not one which insists on brilliance at all costs, and the recording is warm and refined. One recognizes that the Philips engineers are working in Boston. Again there have been more delicate readings of the *Midsummer Night's Dream* pieces, but the ripeness of the Boston playing is most persuasive. The transfer is basically of good quality, offering warm yet vivid orchestral balance. But there is occasionally a lack of ultimate refinement in the tuttis; it is only marginal, but the overall sound has not quite the freedom of the equivalent LP.

Muti's is a glowing exhilarating performance of the *Italian symphony*. With well-chosen tempi – not rushed in the finely articulated first movement – his is among the finest accounts available. If his relatively fast view of the third movement (marked *con moto*) allows less shaping, he takes a strikingly effective view of the finale, underlining a diabolic quality in the tarantella (*Saltarello*) rather than giving the movement wit. Rich, warm recording, but unfortunately the transfer has been made at a level that is marginally too high, and there is roughness and constriction in the tuttis of the outer movements, plus a lack of general refinement of detail.

Szell's mid-priced CBS tape offers rather short measure, but the transfer is of excellent quality, with very good detail in the symphony, plenty of body, and bright yet not over-lit string timbre. The gleamingly resilient performance has plenty of sparkle. The outer movements are taken briskly, but the nimble orchestral playing prevents any feeling of glossiness, and the observance of the exposition repeat in the first movement with its extended leadback is a strong point in favour. Apart from the clean articulation in the fast movements the wind players distinguish themselves again with delightful solo playing in the central movements. While some ears may find this account as a whole does not relax enough, this remains a performance of considerable character. The reading of *The Hebrides* is lively but tends to lack atmosphere.

Disappointing performances from Munch, over-driven and charmless, and not helped by a lacklustre transfer where the Dolby treatment makes little effect. Moreover the *Reformation symphony* is coarsened by the reverberation, which produces severe congestion in the transfer.

Octet (for strings) *in E flat major, Op. 20.*

  (M) ** Decca Ace of Diamonds KSDC 389. Members of the Vienna Octet – RIMSKY-KORSAKOV: *Quintet.****

This is a highly enjoyable version of the *Octet*, happily accommodated complete on one side, and with an entertaining coupling. The Decca recording is well detailed, and the performance is intense and well integrated, with a quietly beautiful account of the *Andante*, a splendidly vivacious scherzo and a busy, crisp finale. The transfer is very bright, and taming of the upper string sound is necessary or the timbre is unnaturally pithy. However, the recording has no lack of body and the Rimsky-Korsakov coupling offers a very good sound balance.

A Midsummer Night's Dream: Overture, Op. 21; Incidental music, Op. 61 (1, Scherzo; 2, Melodrama; 2a, Fairy march; 3, You spotted snakes; 4, Melodrama; 5, Intermezzo; 6, Melodrama; 7, Nocturne; 8, Melodrama; 9, Wedding march; 10, Melodrama; 10a, Funeral march; 11, Dance of the clowns; 12, Melodrama; 13, Finale).

  **(*) HMV TC-ASD 3377 [Angel 4xs 37268] (complete). Lilian Watson, Delia Wallis, Finchley Children's Music Group, LSO, Previn.

  (M) **(*) Philips Festivo 7310 021 [id.] (omitting Nos. 2, 4, 6, 8, 10, 12). Rae Woodland, Helen Watts, Chorus, Concertgebouw Orch., Haitink.

  *(**) RCA RK 12084 [ARK 1-2084] (omitting Nos. 4, 10, 12; sung in German), Judith Blegen, Frederica von Stade, women's voices of the Mendelssohn Club of Philadelphia, Philadelphia Orch., Ormandy.

  (M) **(*) Decca KCSP 451 (omitting Nos. 2, 2a, 4, 6, 8, 10, 10a, 12). Jennifer Vyvyan, Marion Lowe, Female Chorus of the Royal Opera House, Covent Garden, LSO, Maag.

  (M) **(*) HMV TC-EXE 186 (omitting Nos. 2, 4, 6, 8, 10, 12). Heather Harper, Janet Baker, Chorus, Philharmonia Orch., Klemperer.

Previn offers a wonderfully refreshing account of the complete score; the veiled *pianissimo* of the violins at the beginning of the *Overture* and the delicious woodwind detail in the *Scherzo* certainly bring Mendelssohn's fairies into the orchestra. Even the little melodramas which come between the main items sound spontaneous here, and the contribution of the soloists and chorus is first-class. The *Nocturne* (taken slowly) is serenely romantic and the *Wedding march* resplendent. The recording is rich and naturally balanced and has much refinement of detail. The transfer to tape has generally been well managed, although the absolute refinement of texture seems to vary a little between different copies.

The playing on Haitink's Festivo tape is also wonderfully felicitous, the musical characterization sensitive. The violins in the *Overture* play with great delicacy, and everywhere the woodwind solos offer the listener continual pleasure. The grace of the ensemble in the *Intermezzo* gives this less-inspired piece an unusual lightness, and the little *Funeral march* is memorable too. The horn playing in the *Nocturne* is excellent, and the *Wedding march* has fine dignity and panache. Here, however, the recording is blurred a little by the resonance. In their stereo recordings of the mid-sixties the Philips engineers had trouble with the acoustic of Concertgebouw, and they have not avoided a degree of muddiness in the tuttis of the *Overture*, while the focus of the choruses is not entirely clean. But the transfer is of generally good quality, controlling the reverberant bass acceptably, and this undoubtedly makes enjoyable listening. On our copy there was a slight disturbance in the upper partials of the woodwind in Mendelssohn's magical opening and closing chords.

The distinctive point about Ormandy's version is that it uses the German translation of Shakespeare (which is of course what Mendelssohn originally set), so that *You spotted snakes* has a straight quaver rhythm when it becomes *Bunte Schlagen*. The Philadelphia Orchestra's playing is light and brilliant if not quite so infectiously pointed as in some versions. Ormandy includes most of the extra melodramas, but not in the usual order. The recording is among RCA's best from this source, but the transfer has rather too much treble and the violins need a strong cutback of 'top'

if they are to sound natural. The woodwind detail has plenty of colour but on side two there is a touch of harshness in the recording of the *Wedding march*.

Maag's recording dates from the early days of stereo, and although his selection is less complete than the others, at budget price it makes a more than serviceable collection. The fairy string music is beautifully played. Maag's treatment of the *Overture*'s forthright second subject strikes the ear as curiously mannered, and the recording includes a strong contribution from a fruity bass wind instrument that might possibly be Mendelssohn's ophicleide, but is probably a well-played tuba. The horn soloist in the *Nocturne* is perhaps over-careful, but the tranquil mood is nicely contrasted with the short *agitato* middle section. The vocal contributions are excellent. The recording is clean and well projected, and the transfer is excellent, clear and fresh. A little treble cut will smooth the upper strings; then there is a fine overall bloom.

Klemperer's recording (which dates from 1961) also sounds remarkably fresh in this transfer. The recording was made when the Philharmonia was at its peak and the orchestral playing is superb, the wind solos so nimble that even the *Scherzo*, taken slower than usual, has a light touch. The contribution of soloists and chorus is first-class, and the tape has the advantage of including Nos. 2a and 10a, omitted by Maag. On balance the Decca performance has a marginally lighter touch; the HMV offers the more distinguished playing and singing. The transfer is of excellent quality, fresh and clear, although our copy had some minor discoloration in the upper partials of the opening woodwind chords. Nevertheless this is a very good tape.

'Favourite composer': (i; ii) *Violin concerto in E minor, Op. 64;* (ii; iii) Overture: *The Hebrides (Fingal's Cave), Op. 26;* (iv) *A Midsummer*

Night's Dream: Overture, Op. 21; Incidental music, Op. 61: Scherzo; Nocturne; Wedding march; Symphony No. 4 in A major (Italian), Op. 90; (v) *Songs without words Nos. 30 in A major (Spring song), Op. 62/6; 34 in C major (Bees' wedding), Op. 67/4;* (vi) *Hear my prayer (O for the wings of a dove).*

(B) ** Decca KDPC 557/8. (i) Ruggiero Ricci (violin), Gamba; (ii) LSO; (iii) Maag; (iv) Suisse Romande Orch., Ansermet; (v) Wilhelm Backhaus (piano); (vi) Alastair Roberts (treble), St John's College, Cambridge, Choir, Guest; Peter White (organ).

'The world of Mendelssohn': (i; ii) *Violin concerto in E minor, Op. 64:* 2nd movt; (ii; iii) Overture: *The Hebrides (Fingal's Cave), Op. 26;* (iv) *A Midsummer Night's Dream: Overture, Op. 21; Symphony No. 4 in A major (Italian), Op. 90:* 1st movt; (vi) *Octet in E flat major, Op. 20: Scherzo;* (v) *Songs without words Nos. 30 in A major (Spring song), Op. 62/6; 34 in C major (Bees' wedding), Op. 67/4;* (vii) *Auf Flügeln des Gesanges (On wings of song);* (viii) *Elijah: O rest in the Lord;* (ix) *Hear my prayer (O for the wings of a dove).*

(M) ** Decca KCSP 433. (i)–(v) as above tape; (vi) Vienna Octet; (vii) Joan Sutherland (soprano), New Philharmonia Orch., Bonynge; (viii) Kathleen Ferrier (contralto), Boyd Neel Orch.; (ix) Alastair Roberts etc. (as above tape).

Of these collections the double-tape *Favourite composer* anthology is perhaps the better value, as all the performances are complete. Ricci's account of the *Violin concerto* is first-class, and Ansermet's *Italian symphony* is more than serviceable. The same conductor's account of the *Midsummer Night's Dream* music is not one of his finest performances, but it is well recorded. Backhaus's rather brittle *Songs without words* and the slightly self-conscious account of the choral piece are also in the single-tape collection. This is on the whole satisfactorily balanced but inevitably suffers a little from bittiness. However, Mendelssohn is a composer whose music can readily subdivide into separate movements without too much loss. The transfers of both anthologies to tape are well managed, although there is more noticeable variation of quality in the single-tape selection.

Messager, André (1853–1929)

Les Deux Pigeons (ballet): suite; *Isoline* (ballet): suite.

(M) *** HMV Greensleeve TC-ESD 7048. Orchestre de Paris, Jacquillat – *Concert.****

What an enchanting score is Messager's *Two Pigeons* ballet; and there is some lovely music in *Isoline* too. Part of a wholly recommendable concert of French music, this can be welcomed with the utmost enthusiasm. The transfer is most successful, offering plenty of warmth and colour as well as sparkle.

Messiaen, Olivier (born 1908)

Turangalîla symphony.

*** HMV TC-SLS 5117. Michel Béroff (piano), Jeanne Loriod

(ondes martenot), LSO, Previn.

Messiaen's *Turangalîla symphony* was written at a time (1946–8) when – Shostakovich notwithstanding – the symphonic tradition seemed at its lowest ebb. Yet it is unquestionably a masterpiece: an uneven masterpiece perhaps, but a work of great magnetism and imaginative power. Its characteristic mysticism is balanced by its strongly communicative nature – even at a first hearing it evokes a direct and immediate response in its audience. Messiaen's conception is on an epic scale, to embrace almost the totality of human experience. This is immediately implied in the Sanskrit title, a complex word suggesting the interplay of life forces, creation and dissolution, but which is also divisible: *Turanga* is Time and also implies rhythmic movement; *Lîla* is Love; and with a strong inspiration from the Tristan and Isolde legend Messiaen's love music dominates his conception of human existence. The actual love sequences feature the ondes martenot with its 'velvety glissandi'. This fascinating texture is a truly twentieth-century sound, and at times it has an unearthly quality suggesting Man looking out into a universe which is almost his to grasp. The piano obbligato is also a strong feature of the score, and the balance here is skilfully managed so that it is integrated within the orchestral tapestry yet provides a dominating decorative influence. The spirit of Debussy hovers over the piano writing, while the Stravinsky of *Le Sacre* is clearly an influence elsewhere. But this is by no means an eclectic work; it is wholly original and its themes (with their element of vulgarity as well as mysticism) are undoubtedly haunting.

The essence of the symphony is more readily captured in the concert hall than in the recording studio, but Previn's vividly direct approach, helped by recording of spectacular amplitude and dynamic range, certainly creates tingling electricity from the first bar to the last. Perhaps the music's atmospheric qualities are marginally less well captured here than in Ozawa's earlier RCA set (now long deleted), which was softer-grained. Previn is at his very best in the work's more robust moments, for instance the jazzy fifth movement, and he catches the wit at the beginning of *Chant d'amour 2*. The idyllic *Garden of the sleep of love* is both serene and poetically sensuous, and the mysterious opening of the third movement is highly evocative. The apotheosis of the love theme in the closing pages is jubilant and life-enhancing. The bright, vivid detail of the recording is captured extraordinarily well on tape, which on an A/B comparison with the discs reveals fractionally more sharpness of detail, but, correspondingly, there is marginally less depth. However, the differences are minimal. The transfer is of demonstration quality, one of EMI's finest cassette achievements. The accompanying leaflet has rather small print but is quite readable.

Meyerbeer, Giacomo (1791–1864)

Les Patineurs (ballet suite, orch. Lambert).
*** Decca KSXC 6812 [Lon. 5-7032]. National PO, Bonynge – MASSENET: *Le Cid ballet* etc.***

Les Patineurs was arranged by Constant Lambert using excerpts from two of Meyerbeer's operas, *Le Prophète* and *L'Étoile du Nord*. Bonynge's approach is warm and elegant; he is comparatively easy-going, but the rich recording, with its ample bass line, matches the music-making admirably. With such polished orchestral playing and obvious dedication from conductor and players alike this Decca tape – transferred brightly and smoothly – is very beguiling.

Milhaud, Darius
(1892–1974)

Le Bœuf sur le toit (ballet); *La Création du monde* (ballet); *Saudades do Brazil Nos. 7–9 and 11.*

**(*) HMV TC-ASD 3444 [Angel 4xs 37442]. Orchestre National de France, Bernstein.

An attractive coupling not otherwise available, either on cassette or disc. Milhaud was essentially a Mediterranean composer whose scores radiate a sunny, relaxed charm that is irresistible. The *Saudades do Brazil* come from the period when he served as Claudel's secretary in Rio de Janeiro, while the two ballet scores come from the 1920s. As one would expect, Bernstein finds this repertoire thoroughly congenial, though his performance of *La Création du monde* disappoints slightly: the French orchestra do not respond with the verve and virtuosity that the Boston orchestra gave Munch in a now deleted RCA recording. Nor does *Le Bœuf sur le toit* have quite the sparkle and infectious gaiety that the music ideally demands. This is not to deny that these are good performances and well worth acquiring, particularly as the recordings are well balanced and vividly detailed. On tape the sound has agreeable warmth and atmosphere, and the overall quality is good even though the upper transients are not ideally crisp and clean. Also the string tone could be smoother and richer.

Le Carnaval d'Aix (fantasy for piano and orchestra).

(B) **(*) DG Heliodor 3348 284. Claude Helffer, Monte Carlo Opera Orch., Frémaux – TUR-INA: *Danzas fantásticas*** (with BRITTEN: *Young Person's Guide**).

Milhaud's delightful *Carnaval d'Aix* was written for a visit to America in 1927. It was an arrangement of an earlier work, the ballet *Salade*, which he had composed for Massine three years previously. Although very French in flavour the score also shows influences of Stravinsky's *Pulcinella*. It is wittily good-natured throughout and is in essence a set of variations, producing twelve delightfully vivacious miniatures. The performance here is spirited and stylish; Claude Helffer is an excellent soloist, and the orchestral playing has such verve that one is hardly aware that the Monte Carlo orchestra is not one of the outstanding orchestras of Europe. The playing is much less distinguished in Britten's *Young Person's Guide to the Orchestra*, which acts as the main coupling (the oboes and middle strings are particularly vulnerable here), but the Turina *Dances* are attractively played and this modestly priced tape, which is vividly transferred, is well worth having for two works out of the three.

La Création du monde.

*** Advent F 1036 (see p. xxiii) [id.]. Contemporary Chamber Ens., Weisberg – BOLCOM: *Frescoes;* WEILL: *Kleine Dreigroschenmusik.****

A splendid, atmospheric account of this sinuously rhythmic score. Milhaud wrote it in 1923 after a visit to the United States, and this performance makes the most of its transatlantic associations, drawing parallels with Gershwin as well as acknowledging the jazz derivations. The recording is good and the transfer wide in range.

Monn, Georg Matthias
(1717–50)

Violoncello concerto in G minor.
(M) **(*) HMV TC-SXLP 30273.
Jacqueline du Pré (cello), LSO,
Barbirolli – HAYDN: *Concerto
in D major.***(*)

Monn's attractive *Cello concerto* has
the distinction of arriving in an edition
prepared by Arnold Schoenberg (though
the harpsichord continuo player, Valda
Aveling, has modified what he wrote).
The work very much follows the traditions established in the preceding generation by J. S. Bach and Vivaldi, with
alternating ritornelli and solo passages in
the outer movements and a siciliano-like
Adagio for slow movement. Positive
playing from du Pré, sympathetically
accompanied by Barbirolli and the LSO.
The sound is full and clear; the transfer is
smoother and fresher than in the Haydn
coupling.

Monteverdi, Claudio
(1567–1643)

(i) Madrigals: *Amor che deggio far;
Con che soavita; Tempro la cetra.* (ii)
*Il Combattimento di Tancredi e Clor-
inda.*
(M) *(*) Turnabout KTVC 34018.
Rodolfo Malacarne (tenor),
Laerte Malaguti (bass), Mainz
CO, Kehr, with (i) Annelies
Monkewitz (soprano), Karl-
heinz Peters (bass); (ii) Elisa-
beth Speiser (soprano).

This is an area of music as yet ill-served
on tape and it is a pity one cannot be
more enthusiastic about the performances on this extremely well-recorded

cassette. The vocal and orchestral quality
is first-rate throughout, both natural
and 'live'; but the main burden of the
performances falls on the shoulders of
Rodolfo Malacarne, who has a very pleasing tenor voice but whose style is lyrical
to the point of being flaccid. Thus *Il
Combattimento* lacks realism and drama,
while of the madrigals, the most effective
here, *Amor* (for vocal quartet), is not
complete. Even so the singing is enjoyable, in spite of its lack of fire and sparkle,
when the sound is so persuasive.

*Vespro della Beata Vergine
(Vespers).*
(**) HMV TC-SLS 5064. Elly
Ameling, Norma Burrowes,
Charles Brett, Anthony Rolfe
Johnson, Robert Tear, Martyn
Hill, Peter Knapp, John Noble,
King's College Choir, Early
Music Consort of London,
Ledger.
*Vespro della Beata Vergine
(Vespers); Missa in illo tempore;
Magnificat.*
⊛ *** DG Archive 3376. 010.
Paul Esswood, Kevin Smith,
Ian Partridge, John Elwes,
David Thomas, Christopher
Keyte, Instrumental Soloists,
Regensburg Cathedral Choir,
Schneidt.

Schneidt's is the most dedicated and
beautiful performance of Monteverdi's
choral masterpiece yet recorded. With
male voices alone – soloists as well as
choir – and a small authentic band of instrumentalists (the cornetti squealing delightfully), its intimacy is set against a
gloriously free church acoustic, which yet
allows clarity. The Regensburg Choir
uses young voices, and the tenor and bass
singing is not always as incisive as it
might be, but the rest is superbly sensitive, not just the bright-sounding trebles
but the excellent team of soloists, all of

them from Britain. In live performance it may not be possible for two male altos to take the solo parts in *Pulchra es*, but here Paul Esswood and Kevin Smith sing radiantly, while Ian Partridge in *Nigra sum* excels even his standards of expressiveness and beautiful tone colour. Not the least attraction is that for a price very little higher than that of the rival set, DG also includes the alternative and scarcely less elaborate setting of the *Magnificat*, as well as the superb *Missa in illo tempore*. The tape transfer is of outstanding quality; the choral sound is free and clear, the resonant acoustic and sense of spaciousness truthfully caught. The perspectives of distance from front to back are admirable, and the soloists are given a natural bloom on their voices which is particularly appealing. The recording has a wide dynamic range but it is encompassed without strain and the pianissimos do not lose their immediacy.

The HMV King's version is given a most disappointing transfer. At the very beginning there is an unbearable passage of what appears to be intermodulation distortion, confusing the texture unpleasantly; and generally the narrowed dynamic range, which means that soloists and chorus are all presented on the same dynamic plane, makes listening very dull and the performance sound uninspired. The tempi are often disturbingly fast, yet lacking the rhythmic resilience which makes the rival version on DG so compelling. The solo singing is good, but there is a perfunctory element which prevents this glorious music from flowering as it should.

L'Incoronazione di Poppea, Act 1: *Disprezzata Regina* (Ottavia's lament); Act 3: *Addio Roma* (Ottavia's farewell). *L'Arianna: Lasciatemi morire* (Ariadne's lament).

(M) *** HMV TC-SXLP 30280. Janet Baker (contralto), ECO,

Leppard – A. and D. SCARLATTI: *Cantatas*.***

In the operatic field Leppard's approach to Monteverdi and his school has sometimes raised scholarly temperatures, but the general listener can revel in the richness and elaboration. In any case, in these extended Monteverdi offerings the artistry of Janet Baker provides the cornerstone, and the flowing *arioso* of these classically inspired scenas inspires her to bring out the living, human intensity of each situation. There is not quite the variety of expression one finds in Monteverdi's madrigals – inevitably so with operatic *arioso* – but the range of emotion is if anything greater. The recording is admirably vivid, and the high-level transfer gives the voice splendid presence and the orchestra excellent weight and detail. There is no peaking, though occasionally there is the slightest hint that the level is approaching the upper limits: but not enough to prevent a strong recommendation.

Montsalvatge, Xavier (born 1912)

Concerto breve for piano and orchestra.

*** Decca KSXC 6757 [Lon. 5-6990]. Alicia de Larrocha, RPO, Frühbeck de Burgos – SURINACH: *Piano concerto*.**(*)

Xavier Montsalvatge's *Concerto breve* is dedicated to Alicia de Larrocha, who plays it here with authority and conviction. She is sympathetically accompanied by the RPO under Frühbeck de Burgos and is given excellent Decca engineering. The work itself has facility and good workmanship to commend it, but it would be idle to pretend that its thematic

341

substance was particularly memorable or distinguished (or for that matter that the work evinced strong personality). However, the tape transfer is spectacularly brilliant (as the opening chord immediately demonstrates), with strikingly crisp transients and sparkling, bold piano tone.

Moody, James
(20th century)

Little suite.

*** Argo KZRC 856. Tommy Reilly (harmonica), Academy of St Martin-in-the-Fields, Marriner – JACOB: *5 Pieces;* TAUSKY: *Concertino;* VAUGHAN WILLIAMS: *Romance.****

James Moody's *Little suite* consists of five miniatures, beautifully written and expertly scored. Their diversity of mood and colour gives great pleasure, especially when they are so immaculately played and recorded. The cassette transfer is of high quality, clean and clear; this is altogether a most attractive anthology.

Mozart, Leopold
(1719–87)

Musical Sleighride (Schlittenfahrt); Toy symphony (attrib. Haydn).

(M) ** Turnabout KTVC 34134. Württemberg CO, Faerber – MOZART: *Musical Joke.***

Toy symphony.

(M) *(*) HMV TC-EXE 67. Philharmonia Orch., Karajan –

HANDEL: *Water music;* MOZART: *Ave verum; Serenade No. 13; German dance, K.605/3.***

Quite whether the *Toy symphony* and *Musical Sleighride* fit the title on the Turnabout tape, *Humour in music*, one is not sure, but both pieces are brightly played and well recorded. The transfers too are fresh and pleasing. This issue is inexpensive, and whether or not one agrees with the title, the collection is convenient enough. Karajan is gracious, but plodding and totally devoid of humour. However, the rest of his concert is quite attractive, and the transfers are generally of good quality (though once or twice there is a touch of pre-echo).

Mozart, Wolfgang
(1756–91)

Adagio and fugue in C minor, K.546; Divertimento for strings No. 1 in D major, K.136; Serenades Nos. 6 in D major (Serenata notturna), K.239; 13 in G major (Eine kleine Nachtmusik), K.525.

(M) ** Philips Universo 7317 123. I Musici.

The performances here are very relaxed (the central movements of K.525 especially so) but the breadth of the sound and warmth of the playing generally carry the day. The *Adagio and fugue* lacks cumulative tension, and the *Serenata notturna* is played steadily; but if one accepts the approach, there is much to enjoy. The cassette transfer is exceptionally successful, made at a high level and offering very natural string tone. The opening of the *Serenata notturna* is rather less clear than the rest of the programme, but generally the sound is of demonstration quality.

*Adagio and fugue in C minor, K.546;
Divertimento for strings No. 1 in D
major, K.136; Serenade No. 13 in G
major (Eine kleine Nachtmusik),
K.525.*

(M) *(*) Supraphon 045190. Czech
CO, Vlach.

The Czech Chamber Orchestra give
what is best described as a sturdy account
of the *Adagio and fugue*, and they play the
best-known of the string *Divertimenti*
with plenty of spirit. Unfortunately *Eine
kleine Nachtmusik* is clumsily split, with
the first movement on side one and the
other three on side two. This also is a
vigorous performance, well played and
with a strongly expressive *Andante*. The
acoustic is reverberant and it gives the
strings plenty of body. The transfer is
quite well managed although on our copy
the textures of the first movement of the
Divertimento, which opens the tape, were
not completely secure. The sound settles
down later and is good on side two.

(i) *Bassoon concerto in B flat major,
K.191; Clarinet concerto in A major,
K.622; Flute concerto No. 1 in G
major, K.313; Flute and harp concerto in C major, K.299; Horn concertos Nos. 1–4; Concerto rondo for
horn and orchestra in E flat major,
K.371; Oboe concerto in C major,
K.314;* (ii) *Violin concertos Nos. 3–5;
Adagio for violin and orchestra in E
major, K.261.*

(M) *** Philips 7699 048. (i) Aca-
demy of St Martin-in-the-
Fields, Marriner, with Michael
Chapman (bassoon), Jack
Brymer (clarinet), Claude Mon-
teux (flute), Osian Ellis (harp),
Alan Civil (horn) or Neil Black
(oboe); (ii) Henryk Szeryng
(violin), New Philharmonia
Orch., Gibson.

An outstanding collection. The performances of the *Bassoon, Clarinet* and
Oboe concertos are as fine as any available, and the three *Violin concertos* too
are played with splendid style and spirit.
The recording is always good and generally excellent (notably so in the works for
bassoon, clarinet and oboe, though
sometimes the balance makes the solo
instrument sound larger than life). The
orchestral detail is slightly less fresh in
sound in the *Flute concertos*, but delicately textured in the *Flute and harp concerto*. Alan Civil's image tends to dominate the *Horn concertos*, and in K.371 the
resonance spreads the tone somewhat,
but the focus in the *Violin concertos* is
admirably managed. The music is accommodated on six sides, so that there are
usually two concertos to a side, ideal for
the car, but less convenient if one wants
to get at the second concerto quickly. The
works for violin are on the third tape, and
K.218 breaks for turnover after the slow
movement. There are excellent, clearly
printed notes.

*Bassoon concerto in B flat major,
K.191.*

(M) ** Turnabout KTVC 134039.
George Zukerman, Württem-
berg CO, Faerber – BOIS-
MORTIER: *Concerto;* WEBER:
*Andante; Concerto.***

George Zukerman is the principal bassoonist of the CBC Radio Orchestra, and
he is a soloist of the very front rank. His
flexible phrasing and sweetness of tone
are a constant source of pleasure, and if
he emphasizes the lyrical side of the bassoon's character rather at the expense of
its secondary humorous role, there is no
lack of high spirits in the finale. The only
reservation about this otherwise admirable performance is Zukerman's decision to add fairly long cadenzas to each
movement, which would be more sensible
in a concert performance than for repeated recorded listening. The recording

is excellent, and the transfer is a good one, giving a truthful projection of the soloist and a clear yet full orchestral texture. Moreover this cassette offers as a bonus a miniature concerto by Boismortier not present on the equivalent LP.

(i) *Bassoon concerto in B flat major, K.191;* (ii) *Clarinet concerto in A major, K.622.*
    *** DG 3300 383. Vienna PO, Boehm, with (i) Dietmar Zeman; (ii) Alfred Prinz.
(i) *Bassoon concerto in B flat major;* (ii) *Clarinet concerto in A major;* (iii) *Adagio and Rondo in C minor for glass harmonica, K.617.*
    (M) ** DG Privilege 3335 188. (i) Maurice Allard, Lamoureux Orch. of Paris, Markevitch; (ii) Karl Leister, Berlin PO, Kubelik; (iii) Nicanor Zabaleta (harp), members of the Paul Kuentz CO.
(i) *Bassoon concerto in B flat major;* (ii) *Clarinet concerto in A major. March in D major, K.249; Thamos, King of Egypt* (incidental music), *K.345: Entr'acte No. 2.*
    (M) **(*) HMV TC-SXLP 30246. RPO, Beecham, with (i) Gwydion Brooke; (ii) Jack Brymer.

The early HMV coupling of the *Bassoon* and *Clarinet concertos* is one of Beecham's most beguiling recordings. Both his soloists play with great character and beauty, and the affectionate accompaniment is wonderfully gracious. Some listeners, however, might resist these blandishments and find the approach too richly indulgent, lacking momentum and vitality. For them Karl Boehm's tape provides an admirable alternative, even if Boehm's cultured approach seems slightly dour after Beecham's warmth. The HMV transfers seem a little variable from copy to copy.

The *Clarinet concerto* is generally well managed, with a smooth, warm orchestral sound and a faithful image of the soloist. The *Bassoon concerto* is at a slightly higher level, and the forward balancing of the soloist produces a larger-than-life effect. There is less refinement in the overall sound here and this applies also to the two attractive bonus items, which on one copy tried produced a certain amount of coarseness.

Zeman gives a highly competitive account of the *Bassoon concerto*, a distinguished performance by any standards. Prinz's account of the *Clarinet concerto* too is beautifully turned; both deserve a position of honour in the field. The recording is truthful and well balanced, and the cassette transfer is of good quality, reflecting the different acoustics of the two recordings: the *Clarinet concerto* is rather light in texture, with a gently defined bass, the *Bassoon concerto* much more resonant and ample in tone, making the orchestra image comparatively expansive.

On the Privilege tape Karl Leister gives a thoughtfully sensitive and musical performance of the *Clarinet concerto*, but with his gentle, introvert style and lack of a forceful personality the effect is rather too self-effacing. However, Kubelik's attention to detail and gracious phrasing mean that the orchestral contribution gives special pleasure. The recording is first-class and it has transferred freshly. When one turns over for the *Bassoon concerto* the orchestral quality is fiercer, without much bloom on the upper strings. But Maurice Allard plays a characterful bassoon; his timbre is attractively woody (it suggests a French instrument, certainly) and his reading shows imagination and humour. The transcription of Mozart's *Adagio and Rondo*, K.617, for harp with flute, oboe, viola and cello is most engaging. It is beautifully played and recorded, and the sound on tape is excellent.

(i; ii) *Clarinet concerto in A major,*

K.622; (ii; iii) *Flute and harp concerto in C major, K.299;* (iv–vi) *Flute concerto No. 2 in D major, K.314;* (vii; v; viii) *Horn concertos Nos. 2 and 4 in E flat major, K.417 and 495.*

(B) **(*) Decca KDPC 521/2. (i) Alfred Prinz (clarinet); (ii) Vienna PO, Münchinger; (iii) Werner Tripp (flute), Hubert Jellinek (harp); (iv) Claude Monteux (flute); (v) LSO; (vi) Pierre Monteux; (vii) Barry Tuckwell (horn); (viii) Maag.

These are all first-class performances and this twin-tape set is competitively priced. The snag is that by including only two of the *Horn concertos* this anthology cuts across all the issues offering the complete set. The cassette transfers are generally good, lacking only the very last degree of refinement and clarity in the *Clarinet* and *Flute and harp concertos.* The orchestral bass seems rather heavy and clumsy in the *Flute concerto* and is not quite clean in the works for horn, but the solo instruments are very well caught and Claude Monteux's nimble account of the *Flute concerto* is one of the highlights of this collection.

(i) *Clarinet concerto in A major, K.622;* (ii) *Flute and harp concerto in C major, K.299.*

*** Philips 7300 301 [id.]. Academy of St Martin-in-the-Fields, Marriner, with (i) Jack Brymer; (ii) Claude Monteux, Osian Ellis.

(M) **(*) Decca KCSP 495. Vienna PO, Münchinger, with (i) Alfred Prinz; (ii) Werner Tripp, Hubert Jellinek.

The recording of the *Clarinet concerto* on Philips is the third that Jack Brymer has made. In some ways it is the best, for he plays with deepened insight and feeling. Only in the balance of the recording must we enter a reservation: Brymer plays a jumbo clarinet and is thus out of proportion to the excellent Academy. However, the recording is otherwise realistic and eminently truthful in timbre, and the performance is altogether outstanding. The pairing with the *Flute and harp concerto* is unique to tape; these performances are differently coupled on disc. Marriner's account of the latter work is also handicapped by larger-than-life soloists, but the performance is so songful and elegant that it carries all before it, and both recordings are smoothly transferred.

The Decca recording, warm and resonant, has on the whole transferred well to tape, although the detail and focus (notably in the *Clarinet concerto*) miss the very last degree of refinement. The balance between the soloists in the *Flute and harp concerto* is finely calculated, and the overall imagery is more realistic than on the Philips tape. Beauty of tone and phrase are a hallmark of the solo playing throughout, and Münchinger provides most sensitive accompaniments. This is an enjoyable coupling and good value.

(i) *Clarinet concerto in A major, K.622;* (ii) *Sinfonia concertante for violin and viola in E flat major, K.364.*

(M) **(*) Decca Jubilee KJBC 48. (i) Gervase de Peyer, LSO, Maag; (ii) Igor Oistrakh (violin), David Oistrakh (viola), Moscow PO, Kondrashin.

Gervase de Peyer's performance of the *Clarinet concerto* is as fine as any available, fluent and lively, with masterly phrasing in the slow movement and a vivacious finale. It was a happy idea to recouple it on Jubilee with the Oistrakhs' version of the *Sinfonia concertante.* This performance also offers distinguished solo playing and is notable for its relaxed manner. Everything is shaped most musically, but sometimes the listener might

345

feel that the performers, in their care for detail, are less involved with the music itself. However, the outer movements have plenty of vitality, and the sound is basically very good, although the tape transfer tends to show the age of the recording (1964) by the lack of sharpness in the focus of the upper orchestral strings. This can be tidied up satisfactorily with the controls, and the quality in the *Clarinet concerto* is generally excellent.

Flute concertos Nos. 1 in G major, K.313; 2 in D major, K.314; Andante in C major for flute and orchestra, K.315.

(M) *** Philips 7317 195 [7310 091]. Hubert Barwahser, LSO, Colin Davis.

**(*) RCA RK 11732. James Galway, Lucerne Festival Strings, Baumgartner.

(M) *(*) HMV TC-EXE 164. Elaine Shaffer, Philharmonia Orch., Kurtz.

The Barwahser versions date from the mid-sixties, but the recording sounds astonishingly full and fresh. The solo flute is quite beautifully caught and no less convincingly balanced in this excellent tape transfer (made at a higher level than is usual for Philips). The performances are consistently polished and elegant, helped by the warmth of the recording. Barwahser's phrasing is unfailingly beautiful; his playing of the slow movement of the *G major Concerto* recalls Gluck in its delicacy of line. Some might feel that the style of the soloist has too much of a French classical feeling, that it is too cool. But though his manner is slightly detached at times – in the *Andante* of K.314, for instance – this certainly does not reflect any lack of sensibility, and the finale of that same D major work has splendid lightness and sparkle. In the separate *Andante* (originally an alternative slow movement for the *First Concerto*) James Galway's playing has slightly more character, but

in general this medium-priced Philips tape remains first choice, taking into account the superior recording.

Galway's performances can be recommended with no reservations whatsoever, and without modifying one's admiration for Barwahser. Galway's playing has spontaneity, virtuosity, charm and refinement, and he is well supported by the Lucerne orchestra. Originally the RCA tape was of poor technical quality, but current copies show considerable improvement and are reliably secure in matters of pitch. The recording balance, however, remains top-heavy; Galway's famous silver flute is made to sound exaggeratedly metallic, but modification of the flute timbre comes when the treble is cut well back (and this is necessary if the strings are not to sound thin). Generally the orchestral tone lacks the body of the equivalent disc, although an acceptable balance can be obtained by juggling with the controls. There is no lack of clarity and detail. Incidentally there are excellent musical notes with both the above issues. Philips have a high reputation in this respect, and one is glad to see that RCA are following suit.

Shaffer's performances are not strong in personality, and although the playing itself is nimble and musically phrased this issue can only be given a qualified recommendation. The transfer of side one rather lacks refinement and range in the treble and there are hints of coarseness at the end of the side. Side two has a very high level of transfer, making the recording sound very forward. The upper range improves and often the quality is excellent, but one sometimes has the feeling that the sound is on the verge of overloading. The fade at the end of the slow movement of K.314 is rather too quick and the natural reverberation of the last chord is cut fractionally short. The sound in the lovely *Andante in C*, however, is particularly pleasing.

(i) *Flute and harp concerto in C major, K.299. Flute concerto in G* major, K.622G (arrangement of Clarinet concerto, ed. Galway).

**(*) RCA RK 25171. James Galway (flute), LSO, Mata, (i) with Marisa Robles (harp). .

The *Flute and harp concerto* has seldom sounded so lively in a recording as it does here, with an engaging element of fantasy in the music-making, a radiant slow movement, and an irrepressibly spirited finale. Marisa Robles makes a characterful match for the ubiquitous Galway. The balance of the soloists is forward, but not unrealistically so. The *Flute concerto* arranged from Mozart's masterpiece for clarinet is more controversial; the key of G major as well as Galway's silvery flute timbre make for even lighter results than one might have anticipated. The scintillating finale is especially successful. The recording is good; the transfer misses the last degree of refinement in the orchestral detail. The strings sound marginally fresher in the *Flute concerto* than in K.299.

(i) *Flute and harp concerto in C major, K.299;* (ii) *Piano concerto No. 21 in C major, K.467.*

(M) ** Turnabout KTVC 134087. (i) Jean Patéro (flute), Helga Storck (harp), Württemberg CO, Faerber; (ii) Walter Klien (piano), Mainz CO, Kehr.

This coupling is unique to cassette; both performances are differently coupled on LP. The transfer is very positive and vivid, and to get the best results a treble cut is needed to soften the upper strings; and for the proper delicacy of timbre it is best not to reproduce the *Flute and harp concerto* at a high level, or the tendency to harshness in the orchestral strings is emphasized. But with care in setting the controls one can achieve acceptable quality, very much the equal of the recordings on disc; the solo instruments in both works, although forwardly placed, are truthfully caught. Both per-

formances are attractive and Klien's expressive and stylish account of K.467 gives much pleasure. If the strings in the poetic cantilena in the concerto's famous *Andante* are not as richly immaculate as in some full-priced versions, the finale is extremely vivacious, with some spirited playing from the orchestra's wind soloists.

(i) *Flute and harp concerto in C major, K.299. Sinfonia concertante for oboe, clarinet, horn and bassoon in E flat major, K.297b.*

**(*) DG 3300 715 [id.]. Vienna PO, Boehm, (i) with Wolfgang Schulz (flute), Nicanor Zabaleta (harp).

These are superlative performances, and this version of the *Flute and harp concerto* is better balanced, as far as the relationship between soloists and orchestra is concerned, than the Philips issue (see above), though the Philips engineers have cleaner detail. Indeed this transfer is not one of DG's best: there is some lack of refinement of texture, and this is music which calls for that above all else. The performance of the *Sinfonia concertante* sounds amazingly idiomatic and well blended, and it is a pity that the overall effect is not technically as sophisticated as the playing of the Vienna orchestra.

Horn concertos Nos. 1 in D major, K.412; 2 in E flat major, K.417; 3 in E flat major, K.447; 4 in E flat major, K.495.

*(**) HMV TC-ASD 1140. Dennis Brain, Philharmonia Orch., Karajan.

*** DG 923091 [id.]. Gerd Seifert, Berlin PO, Karajan.

*** Telefunken CX4.41272 [id.]. Hermann Baumann (natural hand-horn), Vienna Concentus Musicus, Harnoncourt.

(B) **(*) Classics for Pleasure TC-

CFP 148. James Brown, Virtuosi of London, Davison.

(B) *(*) Philips Fontana 7327 059. Erich Penzel, Vienna SO, Paumgartner.

Horn concertos Nos. 1–4; Fragment of Horn concerto No. 5 in E major, K.App.98a.

(M) *** Decca Jubilee KJBC 70. Barry Tuckwell, LSO, Maag.

Horn concertos Nos. 1–4; Concert rondo for horn and orchestra in E flat major, K.371 (ed. Civil).

*** Philips 7300 199 [id.]. Alan Civil, Academy of St Martin-in-the-Fields, Marriner.

(B) *(*) Pye ZCCOB 651. Alan Civil, RPO, Kempe.

All recordings of the Mozart *Horn concertos* stand to be judged by the set recorded by Dennis Brain in mono and reissued in a stereo transcription. Boyd Neel once said that Brain, besides being a superb horn-player, was also the finest Mozartian of his generation. Certainly his accounts of these marvellous concertos have a unique combination of poetry and exuberance of spirit. Unfortunately the transfer to tape has not been well managed. Dennis Brain made a beautifully clear, precisely articulated sound, but here the timbre is made to spread unnaturally. The transfer level is high but the dynamic range is very limited. One needs a treble lift (which brings up the noticeable background hiss) and a bass cut, and even then the orchestra seems dim and recessed and the fine touches of detail Karajan secures in the accompaniment are all but lost. Juggling with the controls produces some improvement but this cannot be compared with the equivalent LP.

Barry Tuckwell was the first 'natural successor' to the Brain mantle. His easy technique, smooth, warm tone and obvious musicianship command attention and give immediate pleasure. His actual tone is broader than that of Brain and he spreads his phrases widely. His HMV tape (TC-ASD 2720 [Angel 4xs 36840]) conveniently collects together all Mozart's concertante music for horn, but unfortunately this issue is not Dolbyized and although the sound is otherwise excellent, the hiss level is unacceptable. The performances are vigorous, rich in phrase, with beautifully managed accompaniments, but the approach is straightforward rather than providing special moments of magic or new illumination. Tuckwell's earlier collection on Decca is generally preferable. Here Peter Maag's accompaniments are admirably crisp as well as elegant, giving an attractive buoyancy to the orchestra. With first-rate Decca sound, admirably fresh and detailed, this is highly enjoyable, and the Decca transfer is of excellent quality.

Gerd Seifert has been principal horn of the Berlin Philharmonic since 1964, and his warm, rich tone is familiar on many records. His approach to the Mozart concertos has an attractive, simple eloquence based on the absolute technical mastery of his difficult instrument. His phrasing and control of light and shade give particular pleasure and he shows here a special feeling for Mozart's lyrical flow, so that the slow movement of the *Second Concerto* and the first movement of the *Third* are memorable. His nimbleness brings an effective lightness to the gay rondos of all three works, the agility of his tongue giving the production of the notes themselves a Mozartian delicacy. Yet there is no lack of robust quality to the music-making, as is shown in the rondo of the *First Concerto*. As a soloist Seifert has slightly less personality than some players, but the strong directing force of Karajan's beautifully polished accompaniments compensates. A most enjoyable tape, smoothly transferred and realistically balanced.

Alan Civil's performances on Philips are his third integral recording of these concertos. He includes the *Concert rondo* as a bonus; it is an attractive piece and well worth having. The playing is characteristically fresh and enjoyable, and Civil has the advantage of Marriner's elegant and lively accompaniments. The balance (as in other Philips recordings of Mozart's wind concertos) has the effect of making the horn sound somewhat larger than life, and the orchestral sound is somewhat 'plushy' and lacking in bite, although very agreeable.

The bargain-priced Pye tape offers one of Alan Civil's earlier sets of the Mozart horn concertos, which was originally recorded for World Record Club. In many ways this is the finest of his three integral recordings. The playing is flexible in line, lyrical in feeling yet essentially genial, with Kempe providing smiling accompaniments. The soloist's touches of rubato and his subtle control of light and shade are matched by phrasing of the highest order, and he is beautifully recorded. The horn timbre has transferred well to tape, but the orchestral sound is unrefined in texture and the recording has a limited upper range. In spite of the excellence of the playing this cannot be counted a high recommendation until Pye freshen the quality of the transfer.

Hermann Baumann on Telefunken uses the original hand-horn, without valves, for which the concertos were written. This implies at least some alteration in timbre, as certain notes have to be 'stopped', with the hand in the bell of the instrument, if they are to be in tune. But Herr Baumann is not in the least intimidated by this problem: he plays throughout with consummate tonal smoothness and a totally relaxed manner. He only lets the listener hear the stopped effect when he decides that the tonal change can be put to good artistic effect, as for instance in the rondo of No. 2 or his own cadenza for No. 3. Here also he uses horn chords (where several notes are produced simultaneously by resonating the instrument's harmonics), but as a complement to the music rather than as a gimmick. (Alan Civil uses the same device in his recording of the *Concert rondo*.) The slow

movement of No. 3 has one of Mozart's richest melodies and its touch of chromaticism is managed with superb flexibility and smoothness, so that one can only wonder at Baumann's artistry and skill. In short these are remarkably satisfying performances, by any standards. Baumann's execution in the gay rondos is a delight and his tone is particularly characterful. It is splendid to have such a successful representation of the horn sound that Mozart would have recognized, and which indeed all nineteenth-century composers would have expected. The cassette transfer is on chrome tape and offers good quality, although the level of transfer does not take full advantage of the possibilities of this medium.

On Classics for Pleasure James Brown's performances have plenty of life and spirit and are enjoyably spontaneous. Arthur Davison's contribution is a major one. Using a small group of genuine Mozartian dimensions, he achieves crisply sprung accompaniments and he is always attentive to the soloist's style. This is straightforward and musical. The cassette transfer offers extremely good sound, the soloist naturally caught and the balance well managed, so it is a pity that the dynamic range is comparatively restricted, tempering the music's light and shade and giving little or no contrast between the solo horn and the orchestral *tutti*.

Erich Penzel is a very capable player, but his phrasing is on the square side and his timbre rather open, lacking the richness and refinement of colour of the English tradition of horn-playing. The accompaniments under Paumgartner are alert and spirited, but neither orchestra nor soloist is helped by the forward projection, which tends to reduce the amount of dynamic contrast available, for the strings as well as the solo horn. If you want straightforward, robust performances, this is fair value and the transfer matches the disc faithfully, providing vivid sound, reasonably well detailed.

Oboe concerto in C major, K.314;
Oboe concerto in E flat major,
K.App.294b (attrib. Mozart and ed.
Jensen-Maedel).
> ****(*) HMV** TC-ASD 3553. Han
> de Vries (oboe), Prague CO,
> Kersjes.

The oboe sound that Han de Vries
creates is small and neat, light in timbre
and texture, but beautifully articulated.
If the slender image lacks a degree of
tonal opulence, the playing is consistently
alert, at once expressive and delicate, the
phrasing and style above all classical in
manner. This certainly works well in
Mozart, particularly as the accompaniment is crisp and in scale. The *E flat Concerto*, at best a Mozart attribution, is a
pleasant, sprightly, but uninspired *galant*
work, more Weberian than Mozartian
and with a hint of Hummel. Han de
Vries plays it nimbly and eloquently.
The recording is fresh and clean and has
transferred to tape with excellent presence and detail.

Piano concertos

Piano concertos Nos. 1 in F major,
K.37; 2 in B flat major, K.39; 3 in D
major, K.40; 4 in G major, K.41.
> ****(*) HMV** TC-ASD 3218. Daniel
> Barenboim, ECO.

Mozart composed these concertos in
Salzburg at the tender age of eleven. He
apparently borrowed much of the music
from three minor contemporaries, Johan
Schobert, Leontzi Honnauer, and Hermann Raupach (the originals were discovered in 1908). Even so, if none of the
works is a masterpiece, Mozart somehow
put an overriding stamp of personality on
the music, which is not without interest.
One of the more striking movements is
the *Andante* of K.37 (probably based on
Schobert), with its 'Scottish snap' rhythmic feature, which obviously caught the
young composer's fancy. Barenboim

gives sensitive accounts, admirably recorded. The tape transfer offers very
natural piano tone, but the orchestra
sound lacks something in refinement and
transparency, although the ear tends to
adjust as the music unfolds.

(i) *Piano concertos Nos. 5 in D major,*
K.175; 9 in E flat major, K.271; (ii)
Harpsichord concerto in D major,
K.107 (arr. of a sonata by J. C.
Bach).
> (M) ******* Turnabout KTVC 134313.
> (i) Peter Frankl (piano), Vienna
> Volksoper Orch., Fischer; (ii)
> Martin Galling (harpsichord),
> Stuttgart Soloists.

Peter Frankl has given us fine Mozart-
playing on Turnabout before, but this
splendid account of K.271 is outstanding
among all mid-priced Mozart concerto
performances. As a work K.175 is less
remarkable, but again the life and style of
the playing give immense pleasure, particularly in the finale. The recording,
generally excellent in K.271, is slightly
drier here. Martin Galling's performance of the little *Harpsichord concerto in D major* is an attractive bonus
(not included on the equivalent disc). It is
splendidly played and very well recorded
to match the first-class transfers of the
two piano concertos.

Piano concertos Nos. 6 in B flat
major, K.238; 20 in D minor, K.466.
> ****(*) Decca** KSXC 6353. Vladimir
> Ashkenazy, LSO, Schmidt-
> Isserstedt.

K.238 brings an eloquent performance
of a charming work, beautifully accompanied, and an altogether worthy companion to Ashkenazy's other tape of
early Mozart concertos (see below). Unfortunately the great *D minor Concerto* is
too well regulated in emotional temperature and is a little lacking in spontaneity
and sparkle. The recording is excellent,

and the cassette transfer offers outstanding sound, clear and transparent with fine body.

Piano concertos Nos. 8 in C major, K.246; 9 in E flat major, K.271; Concert rondo (for piano and orchestra) No. 2 in A major, K.386.

⊛ *** Decca KSXC 6259. Vladimir Ashkenazy, LSO, Kertesz.

Magnificent performances and recording. Ashkenazy has the requisite sparkle, humanity and command of keyboard tone, and his readings can only be called inspired. Both concertos are underrepresented in the catalogue, but with playing of this order further duplication is rendered unnecessary. Ashkenazy is well supported by the LSO under Kertesz, and the recording is superb. The cassette offers demonstration quality.

Piano concertos Nos. 9 in E flat major, K.271; 11 in F major, K.413; 14 in E flat major, K.449; 20 in D minor, K.466; 21 in C major, K. 467; 24 in C minor, K.491.

*** CBS 40-79317. Murray Perahia, ECO.

These are among the most distinguished Mozart performances in the catalogue. They are not unblemished (there is some less than perfect intonation from the wind in K.271 and K.466), but Perahia offers playing of a consistent excellence and distinction. He has the power to draw from the keyboard a quality of sound that few of his rivals can begin to approach. In K.413 and K.466 the recording does justice to the quality and range of colour that he commands, and elsewhere the sound is eminently satisfactory. These are searching and poetic performances that only gain by repetition, and the reservations mentioned in the individual reviews below melt away as one gets to know these beautiful readings more closely.

Perahia's blend of sensuousness and spirituality is very special. This set earns a rosette in its disc format, and the cassette transfers are among the best to come from CBS. They are slightly variable in level, and the orchestral quality is not always as rich and detailed as on disc (the upper strings noticeably lack bloom in K.271); but the piano timbre is consistently natural and with slight adjustments of the controls these tapes yield satisfactory results. They are individually packed in plastic library boxes within a sturdy album, and the notes are clearly printed.

Piano concertos Nos. (i) 9 in E flat major, K.271; 17 in G major, K.453; 19 in F major, K.459; (ii) 20 in D minor, K.466; (i) 21 in C major, K.467; 23 in A major, K.488; 26 in D major (Coronation), K.537; (ii) 27 in B flat major, K.595; Concert rondos (for piano and orchestra) Nos. 1 in D major, K.382; 2 in A major, K.386.

(M) ** Philips 7699 047. Ingrid Haebler, LSO, cond. (i) Rowicki; (ii) Galliera.

Ingrid Haebler's readings of the Mozart piano concertos are distinguished by a singular poise, meticulous finger control and great delicacy of touch. Unfortunately bite and dramatic intensity are seldom much in evidence, but within her carefully delineated boundaries she undoubtedly gives pleasure by her restrained sensibility and musicianship. She is helped by finely judged recordings, warm and spacious yet crystal-clear, and the orchestral response is most sympathetic, particularly in the concertos conducted by Rowicki. She is at her most characteristic in the early masterpiece K.371, with a clean, classical approach; moreover the recording is in the demonstration class. It would be difficult to imagine a more poised account of No. 17 in G major; the playing may lack the ultimate in sparkle and forward drive, but Miss Haebler plays lovingly and with great poetry. Her tempi in the *D minor Concerto* are warmly relaxed and on the leisurely side. She takes 34′ 35″ for the performance, which gives some idea of just how slow she is. She displays much delicate colouring, but more forward movement throughout and greater tautness in the finale would have been welcome. She is just a bit *too* relaxed for comfort, and matters are not helped by Galliera, who keeps his players on too slack a rein. Rowicki directs the *A major Concerto*, and this is an enjoyable performance (though both Kempff and Barenboim are to be preferred). Comments about the other readings are given below under the appropriate single couplings. What can be emphasized about this set as a whole is the uniform excellence of the tape transfers, wholly natural in timbre, beautifully balanced, with a clean orchestra focus and a totally believable piano image. Some might feel, however, that the layout is not ideal, for Nos. 9, 17 and 19 are on the first of three cassettes, with a turnover after the first movement of K.453; a similar arrangement applies to Nos. 20, 21 and 23 (the turnover break coming after the first movement of K.488). The *Coronation concerto* and K.595 have a side each, with one of the two *Rondos* following in each instance.

Piano concertos Nos. 9 in E flat major, K.271; 21 in C major, K.467.
**(*) CBS 40-76584 [Col. MT 34562]. Murray Perahia, ECO.
*(*) Pye ZCPNH 1. Nina Milkina, Orch. of St John's, Smith Square, Lubbock.

Perahia's reading of K.271 is wonderfully refreshing, delicate, with diamond-bright articulation, urgently youthful in its resilience. In the C minor slow movement, beautifully poised, Perahia finds gravity without weighing the music down. The famous *C major Concerto* is given a more variable, though still highly imaginative, performance. If the first movement is given charm rather than

strength, it is the opposite with the slow movement and finale. Faithful, well-balanced recording; the tape transfer offers realistic piano tone, but the orchestral quality is rather amorphous.

Nina Milkina is a much admired artist and a highly sensitive Mozartian. Tempi are well judged and passagework immaculate. She is eminently stylish throughout, though she does limit her dynamic range (not without reason, of course) and her playing sounds a shade small-scale as a result. The orchestral playing is better in K.467 than in K.271, where more polish would not come amiss. The acoustic is a little too reverberant and the piano not perfectly in focus in the first movement of K.271; this is more noticeable on tape than on disc. All in all, given its price, it does not displace Perahia.

Piano concertos Nos. 11 in F major, K.413; 15 in B flat major, K.450.
(M) ** Turnabout KTVC 34027. Peter Frankl, Württemberg CO, Faerber.

Peter Frankl gives sensitive and assured accounts of both works, and he plays the slow movement of the *F major Concerto* beautifully. The Württemberg orchestra provides excellent accompaniments, and the recording of both piano and orchestra is pleasingly full. The cassette is admirably transferred; this is another Turnabout issue which generally sounds finer on tape than disc. The quality is smooth, yet has fine life and presence. There is an agreeable overall warmth, and the piano tone is most natural. A most enjoyable coupling.

Piano concertos Nos. 11 in F major, K.413; 20 in D minor, K.466.
*** CBS 40-76651. Murray Perahia, ECO.

This is the most impressive of Perahia's Mozart concerto issues so far. He plays both works with abundant artistry and imagination, and is well served by the CBS engineers. These are finely integrated readings: the solo entry in the first movement of K.413 could hardly emerge more organically from the texture, and in the slow movement Perahia is more withdrawn, more private than many of his competitors. In K.466 he brings less dramatic fire than in some rival versions, but there is a strong case for so doing. Too many artists view this work merely from the vantagepoint of *Don Giovanni* rather than seeing it in terms of its own unique sensibility. Here none of the disturbing undercurrents go unnoted, but at the same time the work's spiritual dimensions remain within the period: not the only way of looking at this concerto, but a most convincing one. Although the upper range is not very extended this remains a most enjoyable tape; the piano timbre is natural, as is the balance, and the orchestral sound is not without detail yet has plenty of body.

Piano concertos Nos. 12 in A major, K.414; 21 in C major, K.467.
**(*) Decca KSXC 6698. Radu Lupu, ECO, Segal.

There is much that is beautiful here, including really lovely sounds from the orchestra, and hushed playing from Radu Lupu in the slow movements of both concertos. The music-making has life and sensibility, and both performances are very enjoyable, only lacking the last degree of distinction. The recording quality calls for no reservations whatsoever, and the transfer to tape is of superb quality, balanced most naturally.

Piano concertos Nos. 14 in E flat major, K.449; 24 in C minor, K.491.
**(*) CBS 40-76481 [Col. MT 34219]. Murray Perahia, ECO.

Very distinguished playing from Perahia. His reading of K.449 is immensely civilized and full of grace. This artist has the power to make each phrase sound freshly experienced and vibrant, though greater robustness might not be out of place. All the same, this is one of the best accounts of the concerto to have appeared recently. The slow movement of the *C minor* is exquisitely played, and Perahia's control of keyboard colour and his sensitivity in matters of tonal nuance excite unstinted admiration. He also conducts and secures from the ECO excellent results and responsive phrasing (though less than impeccable wind intonation in one place). His is an inward reading, not so full of dramatic intensity as some rivals, but enormously rewarding. The transfer offers pleasing piano timbre and is technically secure, but the detail and focus of the orchestra are rather less impressive.

Piano concertos Nos. 15 in B flat major, K.450; 25 in C major, K.503.
(B) ** DG Heliodor 3348 193. Andor Foldes, Berlin PO, Ludwig.

We hear too little of Andor Foldes in the recording studio. Although neither of these performances is in the very top flight, they are both thoroughly musical and give genuine pleasure. Foldes always phrases elegantly: he is particularly good in the first movement of K.503, and in both finales his lightness of touch has both charm and sparkle. The slow movement of K.450 shows Leopold Ludwig at his best, but everywhere he makes sure that the orchestral detail comes through. He is helped by excellent recording, which is well detailed and gives a natural piano image. The tape transfer is immaculate; this is an excellent bargain.

Piano concertos Nos. (i) 16 in D major, K.451; (ii) 23 in A major, K.488.
(M) ** Turnabout KTVC 34286. Walter Klien, Vienna Volksoper Orch., cond. (i) Angerer, (ii) Maag.

Klien's approach is essentially simple, but the lyrical flow is well sustained in K.488 by both soloist and orchestra, and the beauty of the slow movement gives much pleasure. The sound too is excellent. The coupling is rather less successful. The recording of the orchestra here is very forward and communicates a touch of aggressiveness. Angerer is not so stylish a Mozartian as Maag, but both he and Klien are not helped by the recording, which also spreads the piano image unrealistically. The cassette is fairly good: No. 23 on side one is cleanly transferred, and the sound here is of a high standard; side two is not quite so clean – just a hint of coarsening occasionally in the tuttis. But generally this is up to Turnabout standard.

Piano concertos Nos. (i) *17 in G major, K.453;* (ii) *19 in F major, K.459.*

(M) ** Turnabout KTVC 34080. Alfred Brendel, Vienna Volksoper Orch., cond. (i) Angerer, (ii) Boettcher.

Brendel is a reliable Mozartian, and this coupling is helped by a vivacious orchestral contribution. In No. 17 the recording is on the thin side in the orchestra, but at Brendel's entry one forgets this slight fault. His phrasing in the second subject of the first movement and throughout the *Andante* is a constant source of pleasure, whereas both soloist and orchestra share in the high spirits of the finale. In No. 19 the sound is immediately fuller and richer, generally very satisfying, with excellent quality and a good balance for the piano. Again the genial touch which soloist and orchestra show in the shaping of the melodic line is immediately felt from the opening. The cassette offers characteristic Turnabout sound, the orchestral acoustic not very refined, the piano tone clear and realistic. The woodwind too are nicely projected and they play an important part in both

works. The overall quality is bright, and there are no hiss problems.

Piano concertos Nos. 17 in G major, K.453; 21 in C major, K.467.

** DG 923052. Géza Anda, Camerata Academica of the Salzburg Mozarteum.

In the *G major* Anda, who is soloist and conductor, errs a little on the side of heaviness of style. But the Salzburg performance has strength and poetry, while the DG recording is excellent in both balance and clarity. Anda continues with a successful performance of K.467, notably for a beautifully poised orchestral introduction to the slow movement. One notices a certain rhythmic rigidity, and a lighter touch in the finale would have been acceptable; but on the whole this is a satisfying reading, very well recorded. The cassette transfers are of good quality. There is plenty of life in the strings in K.467; indeed there is a touch of fizziness, but the orchestra sounds admirably rich in the famous slow movement.

Piano concertos Nos. 17 in G major, K.453; 24 in C minor, K.491.

**(*) HMV TC-ASD 2951. André Previn, LSO, Boult.

André Previn is a stylish Mozartian at the keyboard, presenting a sparkling and resilient account of K.453 and a somewhat cooler one of the great *C minor*. In K.491 Boult seems to discipline the performance a degree too much (one suspects that Previn alone would have produced more sparkle), but K.453 is as fine a version as any, and is beautifully recorded. The tape transfer is rather lacking in sparkle, but the recording is otherwise excellent, and certainly a smooth image, as presented here, can be very persuasive in Mozart.

Piano concertos Nos. 17 in G major, K.453; 26 in D major (Coronation), K.537.

(M) ** Philips 7317 137. Ingrid Haebler, LSO, Rowicki.

In the *G major Concerto*, it is difficult not to admire Ingrid Haebler's elegant, cool style and her meticulously clean articulation, even if one regrets a certain want of temperament and intensity. Rowicki and the LSO give excellent support and the engineers produce a warm, spacious sound in which detail tells without any loss of natural perspective. Whatever reservations one may have, there is no denying that Miss Haebler plays lovingly and with great poetry. Her account of the first movement of the *Coronation concerto* is straightforward and dignified, but in the main theme of the slow movement she exaggerates staccato markings and even plays the top A of the theme staccato, which seems to trivialize it. (Her earlier version with Colin Davis and the LSO was more judiciously pedalled.) Casadesus (see below) pedals it throughout and underlines its shape, lending it an almost legato character. Despite the excellent balance, with admirably clean detail, this version is not to be preferred to the less well recorded Casadesus/Szell reading, also at mid-price. However, on tape the sound is very pleasing; the orchestra lacks something in brilliance and detail but the piano tone is very good, and the sound suits the slightly cosy but enjoyable performances.

Piano concertos Nos. 18 in B flat major, K.456; 27 in B flat major, K.595.
   *** Philips 7300 383 [id.]. Alfred Brendel, Academy of St Martin-in-the-Fields, Marriner.

These are enchanting performances, most beautifully recorded, on tape as well as disc. There is immaculate and supremely intelligent playing in both concertos from Brendel and the Academy of St Martin-in-the-Fields. The slow movement of K.595 has not quite the breadth of Gilels' (see below), which remains in a

class of its own. However, those collecting Brendel's cycle will need no prompting to add these splendid performances. Everything is deeply thought out, but retains its spontaneity. On cassette the piano tone is particularly natural, with glowing detail from the orchestra.

Piano concertos Nos. 19 in F major, K.459; 23 in A major, K. 488.
   *** DG 3300 716 [id.]. Maurizio Pollini, Vienna PO, Boehm.
   *** Philips 7300 227 [id.]. Alfred Brendel, Academy of St Martin-in-the-Fields, Marriner.

The DG issue is very distinguished indeed. Pollini is sparkling in the *F major*, and in the *A major* has a superbly poised, vibrant sense of line. Every phrase here seems to speak, and he is given excellent support from Boehm and the Vienna orchestra. There is no sense of haste in the outer movements; everything is admirably paced. Good, well-detailed and finely balanced sound make this one of the finest Mozart concerto recordings DG have given us. Among the K.488s, this must be ranked second to none. The transfer to cassette is immaculate, beautifully refined and natural in balance.

With Brendel the first movement of K.459 is played at a slightly quicker tempo than usual, but the performance sparkles throughout, and the playing of the Academy of St Martin-in-the-Fields could hardly be improved upon. The slow movement is quite magical, and the finale again has great zest and brilliance. Brendel's account of K.488 is among the best in the catalogue. It is more spontaneous in feeling than Curzon's (masterly though that is), in better taste than Barenboim's (he indulges in some marvellously sensuous but out-of-style phrasing and rushes the finale), and is impeccably played. The decoration of the solo part in the slow movement is never obtrusive, always in style, and the playing exhibits

355

throughout a sensibility that is at one with the composer's world. The recording is a fine one, with truthful balance and wide range. The tape transfer offers a refined and realistic sound balance, mellower and warmer in acoustic than the DG Pollini recording, to match the sunny qualities of the playing here.

Piano concertos Nos. 19 in F major, K.459; 27 in B flat major, K.595.
  (M) **(*) DG Privilege 3335 244. Géza Anda, Camerata Academica of the Salzburg Mozarteum.

Anda's performance of K.595 is one of the very finest accounts of this work now before the public, and it is beautifully recorded, with fresh clear sound and a wholly natural image of the piano. This is demonstration quality. The sound is rather less clear and free on the second side – although still good – and the piano tone (as on the equivalent LP) is less well focused here. But, as always, Anda's playing is deft and lively, and this tape can certainly be recommended.

Piano concertos Nos. 20 in D minor, K.466; 21 in C major, K.467.
  *** DG 3300 492. Friedrich Gulda, Vienna PO, Abbado.

This cassette was issued at about the same time as a TV programme showing Gulda and Abbado rehearsing and playing together. On television Gulda used a Bösendorfer piano (which he has favoured previously in the recording studio), and one suspects that this instrument was used here. The piano tone is clean, crisp and clear, with just a hint of the character of a fortepiano about it. The quality of the tone colour is admirably suited to these readings, which have an element of classical restraint yet at the same time are committed and have no lack of warmth. Abbado's introduction for the *C major Concerto* shows him immediately a first-class Mozartian, and the

orchestral wind-playing is delightful. The famous slow-movement melody too is simply phrased, without excess romanticism, and the gay finale makes a perfect foil. The *D minor* is equally well proportioned and only marginally less memorable. The recording is first-class even by DG standards, and the cassette transfer is splendid. An outstanding coupling in every way.

Piano concertos Nos. 20 in D minor, K.466; 23 in A major, K.488.
  *** HMV TC-ASD 2318. Daniel Barenboim, ECO.

An enchanting coupling from Barenboim. This was the first of his Mozart concerto series with the ECO, and his playing has all the sparkle and sensitivity one could ask for. There are times when his delicacy of fingerwork comes close to preciosity, as at the end of the opening of the theme in the slow movement of the *A major*, but it never goes over the edge. The orchestral accompaniment is admirably alive, and one's only serious reservation concerns the somewhat fast tempi in the finales. The stereo sound is spacious and truthful and the whole production is a distinguished one. The transfer is of excellent quality: although a comparatively early HMV Dolby issue, it offers natural piano tone and plenty of life and bloom in the orchestral sound.

Piano concertos Nos. 20 in D minor, K. 466; 24 in C minor, K.491.
  (M) **(*) DG Privilege 3335 226. Géza Anda, Camerata Academica of the Salzburg Mozarteum.

For this Privilege reissue DG have recoupled two of Anda's stronger performances. There are more distinguished recordings of both concertos, but Anda is a stylish and spontaneous artist, and the sound quality, though not in the first class, is eminently acceptable. K.491 is the finer of the two performances, with notable polish and sparkle throughout. The transfer is of generally good quality, with truthful piano tone and excellent woodwind detail in the orchestra. There is a lack of bloom on the upper strings, and although a slight treble cut provides an acceptable smoothing without spoiling the overall clarity, the thinness of the violin timbre remains noticeable.

Piano concerto No. 20 in D minor, K.466; (i) *Double piano concerto in E flat major, K.365.*
>   *(*) HMV TC-ASD 3337. André Previn, LSO, Previn, (i) with Radu Lupu.

With the best will in the world, Previn's reading of the solo part in the great *D minor Concerto* cannot be said to match those of Ashkenazy, Brendel, Barenboim or Perahia. Needless to say, everything is musical enough, but the performance as a whole lacks real personality. It is fluent, intelligent and far from unenjoyable, yet ultimately bland. The recording is admirably detailed and well balanced, as is also the case in the *Double concerto.* Again this version with Lupu does not possess the sparkle and distinction of Gilels and *fille* on DG, or the less well-engineered Brendel/Klien account on Turnabout (see below). In a cruelly competitive field this issue, for all its merits, does not stand out. The tape transfer, although rather dry, is of good quality.

Piano concerto No. 21 in C major, K.467.
>   * Decca Phase 4 KPFC 4299. Ilana Vered, RPO, Foster – HSIEN HSING-HAI: *Yellow River concerto.**(**)

Ilana Vered, an imaginative pianist in romantic music, gives a sticky account of the *C major Concerto,* coarsely recorded – an unappealing coupling for the strange *Yellow River concerto.* The tape transfer faithfully reflects the rather over-

blown quality of the Phase Four recording. The piano timbre is good.

Piano concertos Nos. 21 in C major, K.467; 22 in E flat major, K.482.
>   (M) *** HMV TC-EXE 99. Annie Fischer, Philharmonia Orch., Sawallisch.

This coupling was very highly regarded when it first appeared in 1959. The general style of performance of Mozart concertos in recent years has tended to become more robust, but even so Miss Fischer's gentle, limpid touch, with its frequent use of half tones, gives a great deal of pleasure. The slow movements of both concertos are beautifully done, and the pianist's intimate manner is often shared by the Philharmonia's wind soloists, who offer playing of polish and delicacy. Sawallisch's contribution too is considerable, and his firm directing hand ensures that neither performance becomes effete. These are essentially small-scale readings, and the refined approach does reduce the opportunities for displaying sparkle and wit. But the coupling is convenient and Miss Fischer's silken touch is highly persuasive. The recording is nicely balanced, full in tone, and does not sound dated. The cassette offers most natural sound, beautiful piano tone, and an excellent balance.

Piano concertos Nos. 21 in C major, K.467; 23 in A major, K.488.
>   **(*) Decca Phase 4 KPFC 4340 [Lon. 5-21138]. Ilana Vered, LPO, Segal.
>   ** HMV TC-ASD 3596. Christoph Eschenbach, LPO.

Ilana Vered plays with the spontaneity of youth, phrasing most persuasively. In K.488 she takes a dangerously slow tempo for the central *Adagio* and does not avoid heaviness, but that is an exception. The opening of the famous slow movement of K.467 is played most delicately by the orchestral strings. Close-up recording; the transfer is immaculate, with fine piano tone and a warm, clear orchestral image. This is a most enjoyable tape and the coupling is undoubtedly attractive: it is a pity that the slow tempo for the *Adagio* of K.488 is exaggerated.

Eschenbach is a stylist and he gives fine-grained accounts of these concertos, directing proceedings from the keyboard. Not even Edwin Fischer secured impeccable ensemble in this repertoire, and one wonders whether the presence of a well-matched conductor of equal sensitivity might not have secured more strongly characterized results. The slow movement of K.488 is finely judged, without any of the expressive over-refinements that worry some listeners in Barenboim's version, and every phrase is sensitively shaped. But in this concerto Eschenbach is outshone by the crisp elegance of Pollini, and in K.467 he does not match the blend of sensuousness and spirituality that distinguishes Perahia. Excellent recording and a fresh, clear transfer.

(i) *Piano concertos Nos. 21 in C major, K.467; 25 in C major, K.503;* (ii) *Le Nozze di Figaro: Overture.*
 *** Philips 7300 250 [id.]. (i) Stephen Bishop-Kovacevich, LSO; (ii) BBC SO; all cond. Colin Davis.

This is among the most searching and satisfying couplings of Mozart piano concertos available. The partnership of Bishop-Kovacevich and Davis almost invariably produces inspired performances, and here their equal dedication to Mozart, their balancing of strength and charm, drama and tenderness, make for performances which retain their sense of spontaneity but plainly result from deep thought. Never has the famous slow movement of K.467 sounded so ethereally beautiful as here, with superb LSO string tone, and the weight of both these great C major works is formidably conveyed. The sound is beautifully balanced and refined. The cassette is good too, but

the transfer level is rather low. The recording is naturally balanced and clean, although the overture (a bonus not on the equivalent disc) is duller in sound than the concertos.

Piano concertos Nos. 21 in C major, K.467; 27 in B flat major, K.595.
 **(*) HMV TC-ASD 2465 [(d) Angel 4xs 36814]. Daniel Barenboim, ECO.

There need be no reservations about Barenboim's account of K.467, which is accomplished in every way. His version of K.595 will be more controversial. He indulges in great refinements of touch, and his reading of the slow movement in particular is overtly romantic. Anda (see above under No. 19) was more successful in obtaining the right perspective and holding the balance between detail and structure. The cassette transfer is smooth, clear and warm – one of EMI's best. It lacks something in immediacy but makes very pleasing listening.

Piano concerto No. 21 in C major, K.467; (i) *Double piano concerto in E flat major, K.365.*
 (M) ** Philips 7317 112. Ingrid Haebler, LSO, Rowicki, (i) with Ludwig Hoffmann.

The first movement of Haebler's K.467 is a little straitlaced, without the breadth and dignity that some artists have brought to it or the urgency that one has from the others. Neither soloist nor conductor can wholly escape the charge of prettifying the music. Haebler plays her own cadenzas – and very good they are – but in the heavenly slow movement she is not as imaginative as either Casadesus or Annie Fischer. (Alas, Miss Fischer uses Busoni's somewhat inappropriate cadenzas.) Rowicki's direction is on the whole excellent and the sound beautifully clean. The *Double concerto* is given a fresh and unaffected reading, very well recorded, and Haebler and

Hoffmann play splendidly; but other versions (see below) have more personality and inner life. On cassette the sound in K.467 is particularly crisp and fresh and suits the precise playing admirably. The level is high; it is fractionally lower in the *Double concerto* but the quality remains vivid, with very realistic piano tone.

(i; ii) *Piano concerto No. 21 in C major, K.467;* (ii) *Serenade No. 13 in G major* (*Eine kleine Nachtmusik*); (iii) *Oboe quartet in F major, K.370.*
(B) **(*) Classics for Pleasure TC-CFP 40009. (i) Moura Lympany; (ii) Virtuosi of London, Davison; (iii) Ian Wilson (oboe), Gabrieli Qt.

Although this issue was obviously inspired by the *Elvira Madigan* film, the performance of the concerto is in no way over-romanticized. It is of authentic Mozartian proportions, neat, small in scale, but with plenty of character. The account of *Eine kleine Nachtmusik* is first-rate. It is robust yet elegant, not polished to the final degree but crisply articulated, with a beautifully judged *Romanze*, spontaneous and graceful. The recording is clear and vivid to suit the performance. On cassette there is a delightful bonus, a first-class performance of the *Oboe quartet* from Ian Wilson and the Gabrieli Quartet. The recording is wonderfully fresh and greatly increases the attraction of this tape issue. In the concerto it is generally refined, with truthful piano timbre, although the dynamic range is not especially wide. In the *Serenade* the dynamics are narrowed still further, with the music tending to stay on a *mezzo forte* level, although the playing itself has no lack of light and shade.

Piano concerto No. 22 in E flat major, K.482; Concert rondos (for piano and orchestra) *Nos. 1 in D major, K.382; 2 in A major, K.386.* (Solo piano) *Adagio in B minor, K.540.*

*** Philips 7300 521 [id.]. Alfred Brendel, Academy of St Martin-in-the-Fields, Marriner.

A very distinguished account of the *E flat Concerto* from Brendel and the Academy, beautifully recorded by the Philips engineers. Brendel's earlier account with Angerer (see below), like his K.503, enjoyed a well-deserved celebrity in its day, but the new version has more sparkle and greater depth and is infinitely better recorded. Brendel's first movement has breadth and grandeur as well as sensitivity, while the slow movement has great poetry. There have been some impressive accounts of this concerto in recent years but it is fair to say that there is none finer than this, nor any that is more beautifully recorded. The two *Concert rondos* – the first (K.382) is the Viennese alternative to the *Salzburg concerto* (K.175) – are no less elegantly performed. On tape the sound is of characteristically smooth Philips quality, with warm orchestral textures and fine piano tone. The bass is rather resonant, and some might crave a little more brilliance, but the overall effect is natural. For some reason the level of transfer is lower in the two *Rondos* than in the *Concerto*, which brings more hiss than necessary. The *Adagio in B minor* is a finely played and recorded bonus not present on the equivalent LP.

Piano concerto No. 22 in E flat major, K.482; Concert rondo (for piano and orchestra) *No. 1 in D major, K.382.*
(M) *(*) Turnabout KTVC 34233. Alfred Brendel, Vienna CO or Pro Musica Orch., Angerer.

In the concerto the orchestra plays with plenty of character and there is some excellent wind-playing in the slow movement and finale. The snag is the string tone, which is thin and whiskery. But the recording is basically well balanced. Brendel plays the first movement with

MOZART

authority, the *Andante* very beautifully, and the finale quite enchantingly. His limpid, silken tone contrasts with the pithy orchestra at his first entry in the opening movement, and his gentle sound for the opening of the closing *Allegro* is most beautiful, as is the contrasting middle section. The attractive *Rondo*, K.382, is given a scaled-down performance that suits its intimate atmosphere perfectly. The cassette transfer generally offers smoother sound than the disc and is to be preferred, but the smoothing of the upper frequencies on tape does not entirely disguise the thinness of the upper string tone (although the piano timbre is pleasing). The *Rondo* sounds fuller than the *Concerto* in this respect.

Piano concertos Nos. 23 in A major, K.488; 24 in C minor, K.491.

(M) *** DG Privilege 3335 204 [id.]. Wilhelm Kempff, Bamberg SO, Leitner.

Kempff's is a truly outstanding coupling of two of Mozart's greatest concertos. The sunny mood of the outer movements of the *A major Concerto* is perfectly contrasted here with the darker colouring of the *Adagio* (a wonderfully expressive performance), and the sombre yet dramatic atmosphere of the opening of the C minor work is perceptively caught by Leitner, who provides distinguished accompaniments to both works. The poetry of Kempff's playing is a constant joy, and with excellent recording this remains very highly recommendable. The cassette transfer is good but rather too bright in the treble, producing fizzy strings.

Clifford Curzon has also recorded this coupling (Decca KSXC 6354), but although the performances are distinguished the tape is not Dolbyized and cannot be recommended.

Piano concerto No. 24 in C minor, K.491; (i) *Triple piano concerto in F*

major, K.242. (Solo piano) *Fantasy in D minor, K.397.*

(M) *(*) Philips 7317 158. Ingrid Haebler, LSO, Colin Davis, (i) with Ludwig Hoffmann, Sas Bunge.

Haebler does not quite compete in the *C minor Concerto*, for although she is well recorded she lacks the tragic intensity and dramatic power the score needs. The *Triple concerto* is given a fresh, well-made performance, without any special distinction, though the moderate price and fine recording must be noted in its favour. The transfer is of high quality, smooth and warm, yet well detailed with natural piano quality. The *Fantasy in D minor* offered at the end of side two (it is not on the equivalent LP) is a considerable bonus. It is beautifully played and superbly recorded.

Piano concerto No. 24 in C minor, K.491. (Solo piano) *Fantasy in C minor, K.475; Piano sonata No. 14 in C minor, K.457.*

(M) **(*) Turnabout KTVC 34178. Walter Klien, Vienna Volksoper Orch., Maag.

In the concerto Maag's strong opening tutti has plenty of character, and at his first entry Klien's piano image seeks to contrast the meek with the powerful. But although the possibilities of contrast are fully exploited, during the movement the soloist's contribution expands to match that of the orchestra. The slow movement again shows the felicity of the partnership, and the finale is particularly successful. All in all this is a satisfying performance, and if the string-playing is not immaculate, Maag's direction is distinguished and the wind-playing in the *Larghetto* is nicely pointed. What puts this tape into the three-star class are the outstandingly fine performances of the *C minor Sonata* and *Fantasy*: this is most sensitive Mozart playing and beautifully

360

recorded. The cassette transfer is highly successful. The level in the concerto is high; the quality is full-bodied as well as clear and the treble has plenty of sparkle. The piano timbre for the solo works on side two is marginally less bright but the balance is realistic.

Piano concertos Nos. 25 in C major, K.503; 27 in B flat major, K.595.
   ** DG 3300 642 [id.]. Friedrich Gulda, Vienna PO, Abbado.
   (M) ** Turnabout KTVC 34129. Alfred Brendel, Vienna Pro Musica or Volksoper Orchestras, Angerer.

Gulda is a strangely cool pianist at times. Both in the *C major* and in the valedictory *B flat Concerto* he disciplines his responses splendidly, though there is no want of finesse or feeling. Abbado provides appropriately sensitive and well-shaped accompaniments with the Vienna Philharmonic. Excellent recording from the DG engineers makes this a worthwhile issue, even if it does not displace Gilels in K.595 or Bishop-Kovacevich in K.503. The cassette transfer is of excellent quality.

The transfer of Brendel's K.503 throws into bold relief the orchestral upper strings. Such emphasis of playing which is not altogether immaculate is not entirely desirable, but Brendel's contribution is eminently stylish: his phrasing of the lyrical secondary themes of the outer movements gives much pleasure. The recording of No. 27 is different again, with the soloist recorded backwardly in a curiously reverberant acoustic and the orchestra brightly forward. But the ear adjusts to a balance in antithesis to concert-hall procedure, and the ear is soon taken with Brendel's sure phrasing and natural feeling for nuance and tempo. With any reservations this remains good value, offering as it does a full hour of Mozart. The cassette transfer is clear, but otherwise is acceptable rather than outstanding.

Piano concertos Nos. 26 in D major (Coronation), K.537; 27 in B flat major, K.595.
   (M) **(*) CBS Classics 40-61597. Robert Casadesus, Cleveland SO, Szell.

Mozart's last piano concertos inspire Casadesus and Szell to two intensely memorable performances, each of them underlining the dramatic contrast of soloist and orchestra, almost as a meeting of heroine and hero. Casadesus's Mozart may at first seem understated, but the imagination behind his readings is apparent in every phrase, and though the balance favours the soloist, the accompaniment too could hardly be more stylish. Strongly recommended at medium price, even though the cassette transfer is only of moderate quality. At the opening of No. 26 one notices immediately that the orchestral textures are rather thick and lacking transparency, but the piano tone is natural and the ear soon adjusts to this relative lack of refinement of detail.

Piano concerto No. 26 in D major (Coronation), K.537. (Solo piano) Fantasy in D minor, K.397; Piano sonata No. 17 in D major, K.576; 12 Variations on 'Ah, vous dirai-je, maman', K.265.
   (M) ** Turnabout KTVC 34194. Walter Klien, Vienna Volksoper Orch., Maag.

This is another Turnabout cassette that is preferable to the equivalent LP, where the orchestral sound is unattractively thin in the upper register. Here, for the most part, the orchestral picture is smoother, and it is certainly vivid and detailed, while the piano tone is first-class, especially on side two, where it offers demonstration quality in the delightful *Variations* (which are not included on the equivalent LP). In the *Concerto*, Peter Maag manages a nice Mozartian balance, even though his orchestra is not of the top flight, and he makes a good partner for Klien, whose approach is coolly classical, although not without life and elegance. The slow movement is phrased nicely and the finale is gay. When playing alone Klien tends to be rhythmically impulsive, and this shows up even more in his solo performances, which are all splendidly alive.

Piano concerto No. 27 in B flat major, K.595; (i) *Double piano concerto in E flat major, K.365.*

⊛ *** DG 3300 406 [id.]. Emil Gilels, Vienna PO, Boehm, (i) with Elena Gilels.

Gilels playing Mozart is in a class of his own. His is supremely lyrical playing that evinces all the classical virtues. No detail is allowed to detract from the picture as a whole; the pace is totally unhurried and superbly controlled. There is no point-making by means of agogic distortion or sudden rapt *pianissimo*; all the points are made by means of articulation and tone and each phrase is marvellously alive. The slow-movement theme, for example, is played with a simplicity that is not arch as it is in some performances; nor is it over-refined in tone, and the result gives added depth and spirituality. This is playing of the highest order of artistic integrity and poetic insight, while Boehm and the Vienna Philharmonic provide excellent support. The performance of the marvellous *Double concerto* is no less enjoyable. Its mood is rather more serious than the Brendel/Klien version (see below), but this is not to suggest that the music's sunny qualities are not brought out, and the interplay of phrasing between the two soloists is beautifully conveyed by the recording. On tape as on disc the quality is first-class, and this is certainly one of the very finest Mozart piano concerto couplings in the catalogue. The separation between the two soloists in K.365 is managed with exceptional sophistication, so that the instruments make a homogeneous partnership

yet the listener has the pleasure of hearing phrases pass from one side of the audio spectrum to the other.

Double piano concerto in E flat major, K.365.

(M) **(*) Turnabout KTVC 34064. Alfred Brendel, Walter Klien, Vienna Volksoper Orch., Angerer – *Fugue and Sonata for 2 pianos.***(*)

It is a pity that this cassette – because of uneven side lengths – is programmed to start with the solo piano pieces, where the piano tone is clear but slightly hard. The stereo separation is very impressive, as it is in the concerto, which (with a top cut and bass boost) is often of very good quality, even though the recording is obviously an old one. Brendel and Klien give an entirely delightful performance of the concerto, and if the orchestral contribution is not especially polished it is lively and spirited. One's enjoyment is enhanced by the rapport between the two soloists, who readily convey their pleasure in Mozart's skilful antiphonal writing. The opening *tutti* is light in bass and there is a slight tendency for the left channel to be stronger than the right, but the overall stereo effect remains convincing. Both couplings are attractive, again displaying Mozart's genial preoccupation with the antiphonal possibilities of his medium.

Violin concertos

Adagio in E major (for violin and orchestra), *K.261; Violin concertos Nos. 1–5.* (i) *Concertone in C major* (for 2 violins, oboe, cello and orchestra), *K.190. Rondos* (for violin and orchestra) *Nos. 1 in B flat major (Rondo concertante), K.269; 2 in C major, K.373.* (i) *Sinfonia concertante for violin and viola in E flat major, K.364.*

(M) ** HMV TC-SLS 828. David Oistrakh (violin or viola), Berlin PO, Oistrakh, (i) with Igor Oistrakh (violin).

Oistrakh is predictably strong and positive as a Mozartian, and he is well accompanied by the Berlin Philharmonic; but there are too many touches of unwanted heaviness to make this an ideal cycle. Needless to say, the performances have their fine moments. The slow movements of the *G major* (K.216) and *D major* (K.218) *Concertos* are memorably expressive and the *Rondo concertante* is played with real sparkle. On the other hand the *Sinfonia concertante* is disappointingly unimaginative, and the *Concertone* too is given a pedestrian reading. The recordings are consistently lively in their tape format. The transfer level is high and although there are occasional patches where the refinement of orchestral texture slips (usually caused by the horns) the sound is generally bright and clear. The soloist is balanced well forward in something of a spotlight, which of course reduces the dynamic contrast between the solo instrument and the accompaniment. For some reason the *Third Concerto* throws the balance markedly over to the right channel.

Violin concertos Nos. 2 in D major, K.211; 4 in D major, K.218.
(M) **(*) Philips 7317 148. Herman Krebbers, Netherlands CO, Zinman.

With his immaculate intonation and subtle rhythmic sense Krebbers gives splendid performances, brightly recorded with the soloist well forward, and with crisply alert accompaniments from the excellent Netherlands Chamber Orchestra. The earlier *D major Concerto* brings the most beautiful high-floated solo entries in the central slow movement and relaxed tempi, beautifully sprung, in the outer movements. The transfer is very brightly lit (both soloist and orchestra)

and the upper range has rather less body than usual with Philips. The tape sounds best with a fair amount of treble cut.

Violin concerto No. 3 in G major, K.216.
(M) **(*) HMV TC-EXE 156. David Oistrakh, Philharmonia Orch.
 – BEETHOVEN: *Piano concerto No. 4.***(*)

David Oistrakh was at his finest in this beautiful performance of Mozart's *G major Concerto*. His supple, richly toned yet essentially classical style suits the melodic line of this youthful work and gives it the stature of maturity. The orchestral contribution is directed by the soloist himself and is surprisingly polished. EMI provide a vivid sound, and with its unexpected but highly successful coupling this cassette is certainly a fine bargain. The sound on tape is brightly lit and clear. On one copy we tried, the upper partials of the solo violin had a hint of discoloration.

Violin concertos Nos. 3 in G major, K.216; 4 in D major, K.218.
*** CRD CRDC 4041. Ronald Thomas, New London Soloists Ens.

These are extremely stylish performances, with alert accompaniments. The presentation is crisply small-scale (a continuo is used in the orchestra) and is strictly in period, yet one of the pleasures of the coupling is the gracious phrasing, by soloist and orchestra alike, in both slow movements. Ronald Thomas has a warm, clear tone and plays very sensitively, with no romantic indulgence yet plenty of feeling. The spirited finales provide excellent contrast. The transfer is of very high quality, beautifully fresh and clean. A small top cut is useful to soften the treble a little, but the sound is undoubtedly realistically balanced, even if the soloist is forwardly placed. Besides directing the orchestra Ronald Thomas plays his own admirable cadenzas, so this is very much his cassette; but Roy Carter and Bob Auger (producer and balance engineer) deserve praise for an issue worthy to stand beside those made by much larger companies.

Violin concertos Nos. 3 in G major, K.216; 5 in A major (Turkish), K.219.
   **(*) DG 3301 049 [id.]. Anne-Sophie Mutter, Berlin PO, Karajan.
   (M) (**) Rediffusion Royale KROY 2012. José Asensio, ECO.

Extraordinarily mature and accomplished playing from Anne-Sophie Mutter, who was a mere fourteen years of age when this recording was made. Her playing has polish but artistry too, and it goes without saying that she receives the most superb orchestral support from the Berlin Philharmonic and Karajan. With a well-balanced and finely detailed recording this is an eminently recommendable issue; but in the cassette transfer the forward placing of the soloist means that, although the timbre and detail of the violin are admirably clear (if very bright), the recessed orchestral detail is less clean, notably in the finale of No. 5. However, overall the sound is good.

Light, well-sprung performances from Asensio (better-known under his other surname, García, as leader of the ECO) with natural, well-chosen tempi. Though the violinist directs the orchestra himself, tricky entries and tempo changes (as in the finale of K.219) are well disciplined, and there is some attractively expressive playing from soloist and orchestra alike in both slow movements. The snag is the over-blown quality of the tape transfer. The acoustic is reverberant and the high level makes everything seem larger than life. The grain of the solo violin timbre too is slightly coarse, but the feeling of everything being on top of the listener seems to persist even when the volume level is cut back.

(i) *Violin concerto No. 3 in G major, K.216;* (ii) *Sinfonia concertante for violin and viola in E flat major, K.364.*
   (M) ** CBS Classics 40-61810. Isaac Stern, with (i) Cleveland Orch., Szell; (ii) Walter Trampler (viola), LSO.

Stern's interpretation of the *G major Concerto* has always displayed his qualities of sparkling stylishness at their most intense. With beautifully poised and pointed accompaniment from Szell and the Cleveland Orchestra it is a most satisfying reading. The coupling – with Stern himself directing – is less assured. Though the outer movements bring spirited playing, the slow movement sounds too tense, and (thanks in part to the recording) the light and shade of this masterpiece are not fully conveyed. The transfer is bright and lively, the timbre of the soloists well focused. The orchestral detail is not ideally refined, but with a treble cut an acceptable balance can be obtained. The beauty of Stern's account of K.216 easily triumphs over the comparatively undistinguished sound.

Violin concertos Nos. 4 in D major, K.218; 5 in A major (Turkish), K.219.
   (M) *(*) Turnabout KTVC 34186. György Pauk, Württemberg CO, Faerber.

Although smoothed a little by the tape transfer the recorded tone of this Turnabout coupling is very thin in the treble. However, the orchestra is not without body, and the soloist's timbre and classical line are acceptable. The performances are neat, quite stylish and accurate in intonation, but they do not compare with the best.

Divertimenti

3 Divertimenti for strings (Nos. 1 in D major; 2 in B flat major; 3 in F major), K.136–8; Symphony No. 13 in F major, K.112.

(M) *(*) Rediffusion Royale KROY 2014. ECO, López Cobós.

Lively, positive performances from Jesús López Cobós and the ECO, lacking real distinction but with plenty of spirit and in proper scale. The recording has great vividness and immediacy, but the high-level tape transfer wants a degree of taming if it is not to sound strident.

3 Divertimenti for strings, K.136–8; Serenades Nos. 6 in D major (Serenata notturna), K.239; 13 in G major (Eine kleine Nachtmusik), K.525.

(M) ** DG Privilege 3335 259. Berlin PO, Karajan.

Karajan's DG version of *Eine kleine Nachtmusik* dates from the mid-sixties. It is admirably robust, yet has no want of elegance. Lithe playing in the first movement is matched by a *Romanze* which is not dragged yet not over-indulgent; and the last two movements, though a little lacking in bite, fit well into the spacious conception, using a full body of strings. The recording is full, well balanced and clean. After this the quality in the *Serenata notturna* seems distinctly dated, without lustre, although the spatial effects are quite well made. The sound recovers for the three *String divertimenti*, which are beautifully played and prompt the liveliest admiration. Cultured and effortless readings, they are perhaps fractionally too spick and span, although the finale of K.138 demonstrates the wonderful ensemble of the Berlin orchestra to perfection.

Divertimenti for strings Nos. 2 in B flat major; 3 in F major, K.137–8;

Divertimento No. 10 in F major (for 2 horns and strings), K.247.

**(*) HMV TC-ASD 3465. Polish CO, Maksymiuk.

The *String divertimenti* are played here most winningly, with expressive slow movements and crisp, alert allegros that have exhilarating rhythmic bounce. The Polish Chamber Orchestra provides a full body of tone and their ensemble is generally polished. It needs to be in the six-movement *F major Divertimento*, K.247, which is easier to bring off on a small chamber group with one instrument to each part. The first violin line, concertante in style, requires complete unanimity, and here the playing is pretty impressive, if not quite immaculate. This performance as a whole is gracious but has not quite the degree of sparkle of the *String divertimenti*, though it is very enjoyable. The recording is full and well balanced, and the tape transfer is generally well managed. A little top cut helps to retain the bloom in the upper register.

Divertimento No. 17 in D major, K.334.

*** Decca KSXC 6724. Vienna Mozart Ens., Boskovsky.

The K.334 *Divertimento* is a captivating piece scored for string quintet (including double-bass) and two horns (used sparingly but effectively). It has a famous minuet which everyone knows, but the whole work offers Mozartian melody at its most attractive. Boskovsky's performance is outstanding. It is superbly recorded and offers sparkling, unaffected playing of great spontaneity. Even by Decca standards this is an outstanding cassette. The quality is quite beautiful, with rich, clean string tone and splendid sparkle in the finale.

A Musical Joke (Ein Musikalischer Spass), K.522.

(M) ** Turnabout KTVC 34134. Württemberg CO, Faerber –

LEOPOLD MOZART: *Musical Sleighride.***

The best way to bring off the *Musical Joke* in a recording is to do what the ensemble does here and play it absolutely deadpan. The outrageously wrong notes for the horns in the minuet sound grotesque, and the ridiculous coda lets the piece grind effectively to its close. The music is well played, and the recording is generally good. However, on tape the horns seem to have an excessively forward balance and sometimes tend to almost overwhelm the sound picture.

Overtures: *Apollo et Hyacinthus; Ascanio in Alba; Bastien und Bastienne; La Clemenza di Tito; Idomeneo; Der Schauspieldirektor (The Impresario); Lucio Silla; Mitridate; Il Re pastore; Il Sogno di Scipione.*
(M) **(*) Turnabout KTVC 34628. Württemberg CO, Faerber.

Faerber draws brisk and enjoyable performances from his Württemberg orchestra of a generous list of rare Mozart opera overtures, most of them early, but all of them with endearing ideas. The performances are not always perfectly polished, but at budget price this is well worth investigating, especially as the sound on tape is so successful. The transfer is of very good quality, with plenty of body to the orchestra and a clean upper string sound. The wind balance is well managed, and this cassette makes an excellent bargain.

Overtures: *Così fan tutte; Don Giovanni; Die Entführung aus dem Serail; Le Nozze di Figaro; Der Schauspieldirektor; Die Zauberflöte. Symphony No. 32 in G major, K.318.*
(M) **(*) DG Privilege 3335 229 [id.]. Various orchestras, Boehm.

These performances are nearly all taken from Boehm's complete opera sets, which sometimes means that, without the concert ending, the music cuts off disconcertingly. On the credit side the performances are of very high quality, with plenty of life and sparkle, and the recording (if varying a little in character between items) is generally excellent. The inclusion of the little *G major Symphony* (itself structured in the three-part style of an Italian overture) was a happy idea. The cassette transfer is lively, though it tends to have an over-bright treble response on the second side. Nevertheless the sound can be rebalanced satisfactorily.

Serenades

Serenade No. 1 in D major, K.100; A Musical Joke (Ein musikalischer Spass), K.522.
(M) *** Decca Jubilee KJBC 51. Vienna Mozart Ens., Boskovsky.
Serenades Nos. 3 in D major, K.185; 13 in G major (Eine kleine Nachtmusik), K.525.
⊛ (M) *** Decca Jubilee KJBC 19. Vienna Mozart Ens., Boskovsky.

The reissue of Boskovsky's admirable Mozart series of *Serenades* and *Divertimenti* can do nothing but enhance the value of the excellent mid-priced Jubilee label. Given playing of such elegance and sparkle and recording quality of the highest Decca standard, it is unlikely that confidence in this series will be misplaced. Boskovsky and his ensemble can even succeed with a piece like *The Musical Joke,* making it appear as an almost unqualified masterpiece. KJBC 19 is notable for offering what is in many ways the freshest account of *Eine kleine Nachtmusik* available on cassette or disc, and the sound quality on the tape is superb – the illusion that this modest, perfectly sized, perfectly balanced string group is playing at the end of one's room is very real. The

Serenade in D major is only marginally less believable, and in the miniature violin concerto which forms its centrepiece the balance and timbre of the solo violin are beautifully managed. The transfer on KJBC 51 is also successful, although the string tone in the *Serenade* is slightly lacking in bloom in the upper range and needs smoothing with the controls. But *The Musical Joke* on side two has plenty of warmth and sounds very well indeed. Incidentally readers may be surprised to discover that the finale of this work contains a very well-known TV signature tune.

Serenade No. 4 in D major (Colloredo), K.203; (i) *Concerto rondo in E flat major for horn and orchestra, K.371* (arr. Smith).
> (M) **(*) Decca Jubilee KJBC 54.
> Vienna Mozart Ens., Boskovsky, (i) with Roland Berger (horn).

This *Serenade* dates in all probability from the year 1774, when Mozart was eighteen, and the suggestion by Mozart's first biographer that it was written for the name-day of Archbishop Colloredo has resulted in it being called the *Colloredo serenade*. Like many of the other serenades, the work embraces a violin concerto (preceding the independent concertos by several months), the solo part being played here with great distinction by Alfred Staar. The music – in particular the *Night music* for muted strings – is altogether delightful. The *Rondo*, K.371, is the earliest of Mozart's horn pieces. It survives in a fragmentary condition, and the arrangement here is by the producer of the Decca Mozart series, Erik Smith. The transfer is clear and clean, but as with the other cassettes in this series the orchestral quality is a little dry and there is some lack of bloom on the upper register of the strings.

(i) *Serenades Nos. 5 in D major, K.204; 6 in D major (Serenata not-*

turna), K.239; 7 in D major (Haffner), K.250; 9 in D major (Posthorn), K.320; (ii) *10 in B flat major for 13 wind instruments, K.361; 12 in C minor, K.388;* (iii) *13 in G major (Eine kleine Nachtmusik), K.525;* (i) *Notturno in D major for 4 orchestras, K.286.*
> (M) *** Philips 7699 049. (i) Dresden State Orch., de Waart or Suitner; (ii) Netherlands Wind Ens., de Waart; (iii) Berlin Philharmonic Octet.

A most desirable collection. The performance of the K.204 *Serenade* (with its miniature violin concerto beautifully played by Uto Ughi) is matched by those of the *Haffner* and the *Posthorn*, full of sparkle and elegance, with admirable phrasing and detail under Edo de Waart, who also directs superb versions of the two *Wind serenades*. The recording is both warm and clean and has very striking body and bloom in the great *B flat major Serenade*, K.361. Suitner directs the *Serenata notturna* and the *Notturno*, where the placing of the four orchestral groups is well caught by the recording, which has notable richness and depth of acoustic.

Serenades Nos. 6 in D major (Serenata notturna), K.239; 13 in G major (Eine kleine Nachtmusik), K.525; Symphony No. 29 in A major, K.201.
> *(*) CRD CRD 4040. New London Soloists Ens., Ronald Thomas.

This CRD cassette offers totally different transfer levels on each side, and in consequence there is a complete contrast in the sound itself. It is also unique in using a harpsichord continuo in *Eine kleine Nachtmusik*, not very prominently, to be sure, but it is distinctly audible at times. This is a pleasing, gracious performance, warmly yet not very incisively recorded. Side one continues with the first movement of the *Serenata notturna*; and when one turns over the difference is startling! It is like the sun coming out from behind the clouds. The level shoots up and the orchestral textures are splendidly bright and resilient, with excellent detail and bloom. The music springs to life and one can only lament that K.239 was split between the sides. The *Symphony* is given an alert, genial performance of considerable character. The orchestral playing is excellent and it is quite splendidly recorded, the resonance perfectly calculated, as it is not in the Argo coupling of this work with the *Symphony No. 25* (see below).

Serenade No. 7 in D major (Haffner), K.250.
(M) *** Decca Jubilee KJBC 31. Vienna Mozart Ens., Boskovsky.
(M) **(*) DG Privilege 3335 139. Bavarian Radio Orch., Kubelik.

Boskovsky's performance of the delightful *Haffner serenade* is marvellously alive, full of sparkle and elegance, with admirable phrasing and feeling for detail. The Decca Jubilee transfer is admirably clean and crisp, but it is a little lacking in warmth, and needs a slight treble cut (and perhaps some increase in bass). It can be made to sound well, but by the best Decca standards is just a shade disappointing. Undoubtedly Kubelik's version (also at mid-price) is well worth the money. The performance has warmth and is well enough recorded to be competitive. The transfer is a little dry in the bass (the Decca has rather more bloom), and the treble needs a little smoothing, especially in the section featuring the solo violin.

Serenade No. 9 in D major (Posthorn), K.320.
(M) *** Decca Jubilee KJBC 34. Adolf Holler (posthorn), Vienna Mozart Ens., Boskovsky.

The Decca cassette upholds the fine tradition set by this series. None of its competitors on disc matches its natural musicality and sparkle. Tape collectors, who are not offered an alternative separate version at present, can rest content; Boskovsky's performance of this marvellous work is without question the best, and it has the advantage of superb Decca recording. The transfer is a little dry in the matter of string tone, which is not so rich as on some Decca tapes. But its crispness of detail suits the music, and there is plenty of bloom on the wind. The posthorn solos of Adolf Holler are splendidly clear.

Serenade No. 10 in B flat major for 13 wind instruments, K.361 (original version).
*** HMV TC-ASD 3426. Members of the ECO, Barenboim.

The Barenboim/ECO recording of Mozart's great *B flat Serenade* must be the most stylish of recent years. Here we have expertly blended wind tone and keenly alive playing, free from any traces of the self-indulgence that occasionally mars Barenboim's music-making. Tempi are a little on the brisk side but none the worse for that, and the quality of the recorded sound is fresh and firmly focused, with no want of body and definition. This is the first real challenge to the eminently stylish and crisp performance recorded on Philips by the Netherlands Wind Ensemble under Edo de Waart, made in the early seventies. This is available only as part of a larger package (see above), and in single cassette form Barenboim's version must be accounted an unqualified success. Only the old Furtwängler account (on disc only, and interpretatively very similar) surpasses it in terms of warmth and humanity. The sound on tape is admirably fresh and truthful in timbre. The transfer level is high, yet there is no coarseness. The blend in *tutti* is homogeneous and rich, but the detail is good. Indeed there is little to choose between the quality of tape and disc.

Serenade No. 13 in G major (Eine kleine Nachtmusik), K.525 (see also under Piano concerto No. 21; 3 Divertimenti for strings; Serenades Nos. 3, 5 and 6).

> **(*) DG 3300 731. Vienna PO, Boehm – SAINT-SAËNS: *Carnival of the Animals*.*****

Serenade No. 13 (Eine kleine Nachtmusik); German dance, K.605/3: Sleighride.

> (M) ** HMV TC-EXE 67. Berlin PO, Karajan – *Ave verum*; HANDEL: *Water music***; LEOPOLD MOZART: *Toy symphony*.*(*)

There are of course many other excellent versions of Mozart's famous *Night music*, notably Boskovsky's (coupled to the *Serenade No. 3*), Karajan's later DG version (with the *String divertimenti* and *Serenata notturna*) and Davison's on bargain label (with the *Piano concerto No. 21* and the *Oboe quartet*). But the Boehm performance is among the finest, polished and spacious, with a neat, lightly pointed finale. The cassette transfer is made at a high level and the sound is rich and detailed. Although this performance is given a whole side to itself and is therefore uneconomical, if the excellent (and unexpected) coupling is suitable this issue can be strongly recommended.

Karajan's earlier EMI performance, characteristically smooth but beautifully played and not without spirit, is attractive enough, again if the couplings are right. The transfer is well managed and the sound is not too dated. The favourite *German dance* is well done too.

Serenade No. 13 in G major (Eine kleine Nachtmusik), K.525. (i) Sinfonia concertante for violin and viola in E flat major, K.364. Symphony No. 32 in G major, K.318.

> **(*) Argo KZRC 679 [id.]. Academy of St Martin-in-the-Fields, Marriner, (i) with Ian Loveday (violin), Stephen Shingles (viola).

An attractive Mozart coupling stylishly played by the St Martin's Academy, with refined, atmospheric recording. The performance of the *Sinfonia concertante* with two regular members of the Academy as soloists goes for elegance rather than any stronger Mozartian qualities. Rival versions may make the outer movements sound more searingly inspired, and the slow movement here is wistfully refined rather than tragic, but there is a clear case for this approach. Both the brief exuberant *Symphony* and *Eine kleine Nachtmusik* are delightfully played. Versions of this most popular serenade which have such fresh, unaffected refinement are rare. The cassette transfer, however, is disappointing. The horns give trouble in the transfer of the *Sinfonia concertante*, tending to overload slightly, and the string tone generally lacks bloom. On side two the quality is splendid at the beginning, rich and open, but later on there are moments when the clarity of focus blurs slightly.

Serenade No. 13 in G major (Eine kleine Nachtmusik), K.525; Symphony No. 40 in G minor, K.550.

> ** Decca KSXC 6844 [Lon. 5-7066]. Israel PO, Mehta.

Mehta directs a refined and athletic reading of the *G minor Symphony*, with rhythms well sprung in the outer movements at tempi marginally slower than usual. With exposition repeats observed in both, the weight of argument is reinforced, while Mehta uses the sparer version of the score, without clarinets. The recording is among the best that Decca has made with the Israel orchestra, but *Eine kleine Nachtmusik*, attractive as a coupling, is not nearly so recommendable. The phrasing of the Israel strings is not so refined, although the reading is strong and stylish enough. On tape, however, the recording of the *Serenade* is full and pleasing, and as the transfer of the *Symphony* is also vivid and clear, this makes quite an attractive coupling.

(i) *Sinfonia concertante for violin and viola in E flat major, K.364* (see also under *Clarinet concerto; Adagio in E; Violin concerto No. 3; Serenade No. 13*); (ii) *Concertone in C major* (for 2 violins, oboe, cello and orchestra), *K.190.*

> (M) * Turnabout KTVC 34098. Susanne Lautenbacher (violin), Stuttgart Bach Collegium, Rilling, with (i) Ulrich Koch (viola); (ii) Werner Keltsch (violin).

The chief attraction of this issue is the suitability of the coupling, the rare *C major Concertone*, with its unexpected collection of solo instruments. It is not the most memorable of Mozart's works, but it is interesting to hear. The *Sinfonia concertante* is given a less polished account than one would normally ask for, with intonation by the soloists that is not always very sweet. The recording balance pushes the soloists forward and the transfer produces wiry tone for both violin and viola.

Sonata for organ and orchestra No. 4 in D major, K.144.

> (M) (**) Turnabout KTVC 34135. Helmuth Rilling (organ), Württemberg CO, Faerber –
> ALBINONI: *Adagio **;* COR-
> RETTE: *Concerto;* HANDEL:
> *Cuckoo and the Nightingale concerto.(**)*

Helmuth Rilling gives a sturdy if unsubtle account of K.144, but the tape is not likely to be chosen for this piece among its varied contents. The recording on tape is only fair, bright but with a degree of coarseness.

Symphonies

Symphonies Nos. 1 in E flat major, K.16; 4 in D major, K.19; 5 in B flat major, K.22; 6 in F major, K.43.

> (M) *** Turnabout KTVC 37087. Mainz CO, Kehr.

These recordings date from the 1960s but in many respects remain superior to later rivals: they have a spontaneity and vitality that make them preferable to the Boehm complete set (of which the first tape box, containing the early symphonies, is currently not available in the UK) and the recordings are no less fresh and detailed. No. 1 dates from Mozart's London visit, when he was only eight, and like the companion works here it is lightly scored: strings, two oboes and two horns. No. 5 in B flat was composed in the Netherlands and like all these symphonies is modelled on the Italian sinfonia or overture. The transfer to tape is most successful, although it may require some smoothing at the top.

Symphonies Nos. 7 in D major, K.45; 8 in D major, K.48; in G major, K.45a (Anhang 221); in B flat major, K.45b (Anhang 214).

> (M) *** Turnabout KTVC 37088. Mainz CO, Kehr.

Another delightful tape in the Kehr series of Mozart symphonies. The *Symphony No. 7 in D major* was composed in January 1768, a few days before Mozart's thirteenth birthday, and makes use of trumpet and timpani. Its successor has no lack of drama or charm. The *Lambacher Sinfonia, K.45a,* is so called because Leopold Mozart is supposed to have presented the autograph to the

Benedictine monastery at Lambach on the Mozarts' visit in 1769. The transfer is vividly managed, although the treble needs cutting back somewhat.

Symphonies Nos. 9 in C major, K.73; 10 in G major, K.74; 42 in F major, K.75; 43 in F major, K.76.
(M) *** Turnabout KTVC 37089. Mainz CO, Kehr.

These performances continue to have a charm which eludes many subsequent rivals. Günter Kehr produces stylish and vital performances from his Mainz orchestra, who are eminently well recorded. The earliest of these symphonies is *No. 43 in F* (K.76 or 42a), whose finale draws on a Rameau *Gavotte*, and which dates from about 1766. The others come from 1770-71, though the editors of the latest Köchel give *No. 9 in C*, K.73, an earlier date. The transfers are clean and firm, although the timbre of the upper strings needs smoothing to give a natural effect.

Symphonies Nos. 13 in F major, K.112; 14 in A major, K.114; 15 in F major, K.124; 16 in C major, K.128.
*** Argo KZRC 594 [id.]. Academy of St Martin-in-the-Fields, Marriner.

Brisk, fresh performances of four early Mozart symphonies to extend the high reputation of this fine group. These symphonies come from the period after Mozart's initial essays, when he was beginning to imitate rather than to express his own untrammelled if immature genius. They are smoother than the very first symphonies but not more interesting. Marriner's directness refuses to compromise, and with bright, clean recording they give much pleasure. The tape transfer is admirably clean; the treble is marginally sharp-edged, and the violins need softening a little and the bass bringing up with the controls.

Symphonies Nos. 18 in F major, K.130; 19 in E flat major, K.132; 24 in B flat major, K.182 (EK.166e).
(M) *** Turnabout KTVC 34038. Mainz CO, Kehr.

This tape continues Kehr's excellent series. The playing is crisp and clean, and not without warmth. The alertness of the ensemble gives special pleasure; the recording maintains the standard of the earlier symphonies, and the tape transfer is of high quality. This can be cordially recommended.

Symphonies Nos. 25–41 (complete).
**(*) DG 3378 066. Berlin PO, Boehm.

Boehm has recorded all the Mozart symphonies for DG, but only the second box of tapes is available in the UK. Although there are some very fine performances here, the set is let down at times by a certain stiffness and want of sparkle. Of course the orchestral playing from the Berlin Philharmonic is a joy in itself; phrasing is immaculate and ensemble beautifully disciplined. Boehm's seriousness is not without a compensating dignity and eloquence. Many collectors will undoubtedly be attracted by the sophistication of the presentation here. The works are spaced out over six tapes, and undoubtedly a box of this kind is an ideal medium for exploration of the lesser-known works. The quality of the transfers is superb, immaculately clear and splendidly balanced.

Symphonies Nos. 25 in G minor, K.183; 29 in A major, K.201.
*** Decca KSXC 6879. ECO, Britten.
*(**) Argo KZRC 706 [id.]. Academy of St Martin-in-the-Fields, Marriner.
(**) HMV TC-ASD 3326. New Philharmonia Orch., Muti.

Several years before his untimely death Benjamin Britten recorded these exhilarating performances of the two greatest of Mozart's early symphonies; but inexplicably the recording remained unissued, finally providing a superb codicil to Britten's recording career. It is striking that in many movements Britten's tempi and even his approach are very close to those of Neville Marriner on his excellent Argo coupling, but it is Britten's genius, along with his crisp articulation and sprung rhythms, which provides the occasional touch of pure individual magic. Britten's slow movements give a clear contrast, rather weightier than Marriner's, particularly in the 'little' *G minor*, where Britten, with a slower speed and more expressive phrasing, underlines the elegiac quality of the music. The rich, well-balanced recording has been given a first-class transfer, with excellent detail and range. The spacious acoustic is well caught and both strings and woodwind have a most pleasing bloom.

The Argo performances have splendid life and detail. The pointing of the phrases of the *G minor* is done with a superb sense of style, and the scale of No. 29 is broad and forward-looking. However, the transfer to tape is not entirely successful. The resonance, coupled to a fairly high level of transfer, offers some problems in the finale of No. 29 and a considerable lack of refinement in No. 25 on side two. The high-placed horn parts characteristic of Mozart's A major symphonies, which ring out exuberantly in these performances, tend to roughen here. Otherwise the sound is gloriously rich with splendid strings.

On HMV the opening of No. 25, with its commanding octave passage, seems well upholstered rather than tough and incisive. Muti and what sounds like a relatively large Mozart orchestra cannot match Britten or Marriner, whose performances are altogether sharper, at a faster tempo. In No. 29 the contrast is not so extreme, but there again some will prefer a warmer, larger-scale view of early Mozart. The recording, basically good, rich and atmospheric, has been spoiled in

the tape transfer by too high a modulation, bringing coarseness in tuttis.

Symphonies Nos. 29 in A major, K.201; 33 in B flat major, K.319.
(M) **(*) DG Privilege 3335 155. Berlin PO, Karajan.

A lively account of the *A major Symphony* from Karajan, but one which may be a trifle too smooth for some tastes. The orchestral playing is, of course, superlative, and the DG sound is warm and velvety. Much the same comments apply to the *B flat Symphony*. On tape the quality is generally excellent, appropriately slightly more robust in No. 33 than in No. 29 (which is fractionally lower in level, and marginally less refined in detail). But in both symphonies the strings have fine body and the overall sound has a natural bloom and resonance.

Symphonies Nos. 31 in D major (Paris), K.297; 36 in C major (Linz), K.425; Les Petits Riens, K.299b: Overture.
(B) ** DG Heliodor 3348 220. Bavarian Radio SO, Leitner.

Ferdinand Leitner is best known as the excellent conductor of Kempff's recordings of the Beethoven concertos. In Mozart he shows some predilection for slow tempi, as in the introduction to the *Linz symphony*. But the orchestral playing here is first-class, and these readings are fresh, unmannered and thoroughly musical. The conductor's personality does not emerge strongly, but Mozart's does, and with lively sound this is an excellent bargain, even if the *Overture* does not sparkle quite as it might. The transfer to tape is of excellent quality.

Symphonies Nos. 32 in G major, K.318; 35 in D major (Haffner), K.385; 36 in C major (Linz), K.425; 38 in D major (Prague), K.504; 39 in E flat major, K.543; 40 in G minor,

K.550; 41 in C major (Jupiter), K.551.

*** DG 3371 038 [id.]. Berlin PO, Karajan. Also available separately: 3301 136 (Nos. 32, 35, 36); 3301 137 (Nos. 38, 39); 3301 138 (Nos. 40, 41).

It is difficult to conceive of better big-band Mozart than these beautifully played and vitally alert readings. There are details about which some may have reservations: the minuet and trio of the *Linz* may seem too slow, and the opening of the *G minor*, which is a shade faster than in Karajan's Vienna performance, may not be quite dark enough for some tastes. In general, however, these are such finely proportioned readings, so exquisitely paced and shaped, that it is hard to see how they could be surpassed. As recordings they are well balanced, alive and yet smooth. Either as a complete set or as individual issues, these hold their own with the best, and the cassette transfers are altogether excellent. The level is generally quite high (although Nos. 38 and 39, on tape 2, are slightly lower than the others, with a fractional reduction of brilliance and detail). No. 40 and (especially) the *Jupiter* sound superb.

Symphonies Nos. 34 in C major, K.338; 39 in E flat major, K.543.

* Decca KSXC [Lon. 5-7055]. Israel PO, Mehta.

A disappointing coupling. Neither performance is distinguished, and there is far too much emphasis on surface brilliance. This is exaggerated by the recording, which is very close and brightly lit. The upper string tone is almost totally without bloom, an effect exacerbated by the cassette transfer, which gives the strings a thin, feathery texture. The inflexible performance of No. 39 is particularly unbeguiling, especially the last two movements, taken fast but sounding rushed rather than offering a sense of exhilaration.

Symphonies Nos. 35 in D major (Haffner), K.385; 40 in G minor, K.550; March in D major, K. 385a.

(M) **(*) Philips Festivo 7310 022 [7300 086]. Academy of St Martin-in-the-Fields, Marriner.

Marriner's stylish coupling uses original scorings of both works – minus flutes and clarinets in the *Haffner*, minus clarinets in No. 40. The *March* is included as a makeweight following after the *Haffner*, since (having the same K. number) it has long been associated with this symphony. Marriner's readings are finely detailed but dynamic too, nicely scaled against warm, refined recording. The sound on tape is particularly good in K.550, but in the *Haffner* there is some excessive bass resonance which brings a degree of roughness to the tuttis, although this is not too serious.

Symphonies Nos. 35 in D major (Haffner), K.385; 41 in C major (Jupiter), K.551.

(M) *(*) Decca KCSP 336. Israel PO, Josef Krips.

* HMV TC-ASD 3158. LPO, Boult.

Krips's performances, which date from 1960, are still serviceable, although the *Haffner* is more successful than the *Jupiter*. But the layout of the cassette is unfortunate, with the first three movements of the *Jupiter* on side one, and the finale on side two with the *Haffner*. The latter performance shows Krips on top form. The outer movements have plenty of zest; there is a pert yet gracious *Andante* and a notably elegant minuet. The sound is good too, although it has noticeably less body in the *Jupiter*. Here Krips holds the tension much more slackly. The transfers are well managed but do not disguise the fact that the recordings are nearly twenty years old.

Boult's coupling is not one of his more successful issues. The performances are somewhat stolid and Sir Adrian did not draw the most sensitive playing from the LPO on this occasion. Neither performance is at all distinguished; moreover the resonance clouds the opening of the *Jupiter*, and the transfer to tape is generally muddy in the bass, with little brilliance in the string timbre.

Symphony No. 38 in D major (Prague), K.504.
    (*) Decca KSXC 6539. ECO, Britten – SCHUBERT: *Symphony No. 8.***(*)*
    ** Advent E 1025 (see p. xxiii) [id.]. LSO, Kosler – DVOŘÁK: *Slavonic dances.***

Britten conveys a real sense of occasion, from the weighty introduction through a glowing and resilient account of the *Allegro* to a full, flowing reading of the *Andante*. The *Giovanni* overtones are very clear indeed. The resonant Maltings recording has on the whole transferred well to tape. There is a moment of congestion in the bass at the very opening, and some smoothing of the upper strings may be useful; but the sound is otherwise spacious and free, with plenty of bloom.

Kosler secures infectiously alert playing from the LSO in the outer movements; the woodwind articulation in the finale is a joy. But the slow movement is rather less imaginative, and an element of routine creeps in here. The recording is splendid, and the transfer is of Advent's highest quality, crisp and bright with plenty of depth and resonance. This is demonstration sound.

Symphonies Nos. 39 in E flat major, K.543; 40 in G minor, K.550; Symphony No. 14 in A major, K.114: excerpt.
    (M) *** Philips 7317 100. LSO, Colin Davis.

Strong, straightforward performances from Davis, refreshingly stylish and alive.

The vivacious finale of No. 39 and the slow movement of the *G minor Symphony* have splendid character. A rehearing of this issue confirms its very special qualities, and inclines us to place it as first choice for these symphonies. The cassette transfer is very successful, although in reproduction it is essential to cut back an excessive bass response. Once this is done the quality is first-rate, with lively violin tone and a rich overall bloom on the sound. An insubstantial bonus, not on the equivalent disc, is included on the tape – a movement from the early *A major Symphony*.

(i) *Symphony No. 40 in G minor, K.550;* (ii) *Così fan tutte: overture.*
    (M) *** Philips 7317 133. (i) LSO, Colin Davis; (ii) Vienna SO, Paumgartner – BEETHOVEN: *Symphony No. 5.***(*)*

Whether coupled with Mozart's *Symphony No. 39* (see above) or with George Szell's impressive account of Beethoven's *Fifth* Davis's version of No. 40 is one of the most recommendable ever issued, with its direct, alert interpretation, stylish from first bar to last. The transfer here is particularly fine, and the recording approaches demonstration quality. The overture is a bonus not included on the equivalent disc.

Symphony No. 40 in G minor, K.550; Serenade No. 6 in D major (Serenata notturna), K.239.
    (*) Decca KSXC 6372. ECO, Britten.

Britten takes all repeats in the symphony (the slow movement here is longer than that of the *Eroica*) but is almost totally convincing, with the rich Maltings sound to give added weight. The *Serenata notturna* is enchanting. The transfer has been made at a high level, and the rich reverberant sound is thickened slightly by the horns in *tutti*. The cassette turns over after the first two movements of the symphony, and the textures in the serenade are strikingly fresh.

Symphonies Nos. 40 in G minor, K.550; 41 in C major (Jupiter), K.551.

*** DG 3300 780 [id.]. Vienna PO, Boehm.

(M) **(*) Decca Ace of Diamonds KSDC 361. Vienna PO, Karajan.

(B) (***) Classics for Pleasure TC-CFP 40253. LPO, Mackerras.

(M) ** Decca Jubilee KJBC 8. New Philharmonia Orch., Giulini.

(B) *(*) Philips Fontana 7328 006. LSO, Dorati or Schmidt-Isserstedt.

Boehm recorded this same coupling earlier with the Berlin Philharmonic as part of his complete Mozart cycle, but his Vienna versions, as well as being more vividly and immediately recorded, also present more alert, more spontaneous-sounding performances, with the octogenarian conductor sounding more youthful than before. Boehm takes a relatively measured view of the outer movements of No. 40, but the resilience of the playing rivets the attention and avoids any sort of squareness. Excellent recommendations for both symphonies, though in No. 41 the equivalent LP issue (using a single side for each work) prevented the observance of exposition repeats which many count desirable in Mozart's most massive symphony. The transfers are of excellent quality, clear and clean and with no lack of body and bloom on the orchestra. The focus seems fractionally sharper in the *Jupiter*.

Karajan's Ace of Diamonds coupling remains good value. In the *G minor* every detail is beautifully in place, each phrase nicely shaped and in perspective. The exposition repeat in the first movement is observed, though the chords linking it to the development are prominent at a slightly higher level, and the balance

thereafter appears to be closer. Beautifully articulate and suave, this performance has a genuine dramatic power, even though one feels that it all moves within carefully regulated emotional limits. Karajan does tend to beautify detail without adding corresponding stature. The reading of the *Jupiter* is a strong one, one of the best things Karajan did in his short period in the Decca studios. The performance is direct and has breadth as well as warmth. The orchestral playing is excellent, and with first-rate sound this is certainly enjoyable. The cassette transfer is good, but on the copy tried the quality was crisper in the *Jupiter* than in No. 40.

Mackerras directs excellent clean-cut performances which stand comparison with any at whatever price. He observes exposition repeats in the outer movements of the *G minor*, but not in the *Jupiter*, which is a pity in so majestic a work. Some may prefer a more affectionate style in slow movements, but at half the price of the Boehm tape and cheaper than the Karajan, and with clean modern recording, this would seem an outstanding bargain. Unfortunately the cassette transfer has a very limited dynamic range indeed; Mozart's intended contrasts are minimized and the performances made to sound bland. It is hoped that Classics for Pleasure will remaster this issue.

The Decca Jubilee reissue was Giulini's first recording for Decca with the New Philharmonia. They play well for him and the recording is warm and detailed, of Decca's finest quality. However, the performances, although they offer beautifully polished playing, are curiously lacking in vitality, neither classically poised nor romantically charged. However, the tape transfer is exceptionally successful, the quality splendidly fresh, clean, brightly lit yet without any suggestion of glare.

The Fontana issue offers a fine performance of the *Jupiter* under Schmidt-Isserstedt, with an impressively shaped *Andante* and a vigorous and strong finale. Dorati's account of the *G minor*, however, is less sympathetic; its rhythmic articulation tends to interfere with the lyrical flow of the first movement, while the minuet is almost staccato in its crisp enunciation. The recording is good, and the transfer crisp and clean.

CHAMBER AND INSTRUMENTAL MUSIC

(i; ii) *Clarinet quintet in A major, K.581;* (iii) *Clarinet trio in E flat major, K.498;* (iv) *Divertimento in E flat major for string trio, K.563;* (ii; v) *Oboe quartet in F major, K.370;* (vi) *Piano trio in E major, K.542;* (vii) *String quartets Nos. 17 in B flat major (Hunt), K.458; 19 in C major (Dissonance), K.465;* (viii) *String quintet No. 4 in G minor, K.516;* (ix) *Violin sonatas Nos. 32 in B flat major, K.454; 34 in A major, K.526.*

(M) *** Philips 7699 051. (i) George Pieterson (clarinet); (ii) Grumiaux Ens.; (iii) Jack Brymer (clarinet), Stephen Bishop-Kovacevich (piano), Patrick Ireland (viola); (iv) Grumiaux Trio; (v) Pierre Pierlot (oboe); (vi) Beaux Arts Trio; (vii) Italian Qt; (viii) Grumiaux Quintet; (ix) Henryk Szeryng (violin), Ingrid Haebler (piano).

Here is another extremely useful box in the Philips Mozart edition, offering the tape collector a good deal of music that is otherwise not available. The *Clarinet quintet* is persuasively played by George Pieterson, perhaps not the finest available recorded account but a very enjoyable one. The sound has plenty of life, whereas in the *Clarinet trio* the quality is almost over-smooth. However, this too is a warmly musical performance. With the *Divertimento in E flat for string trio* we come to one of the very finest of all

Mozart chamber-music recordings, and it has transferred to tape with immaculate realism; the sound is in the demonstration class. Grumiaux has long been remarkable, even among the most outstanding virtuosi of his day, for his purity of intonation, and here he is joined by two players (George Janzer, viola, and Eva Szabo, cello) with a similarly refined and classical style. This may be only an *ad hoc* group but their unanimity is most striking, and Grumiaux's individual artistry gives the interpretation great distinction. The title 'Divertimento' is of course a monumental misnomer; this is one of the richest of Mozart's last-period chamber works, far too rarely heard in the concert hall. Pierre Pierlot's account of the *Oboe quartet* is pert and lively, but his bright tone is emphasized by the recording balance and the sound seems a little top-heavy. The Italians play Mozart's two most famous string quartets in impeccable style, the playing polished yet unfailingly perceptive. The recording has a touch of edge on the leader's tone which needs smoothing, and this applies also to the two violin sonatas contributed by Szeryng and Haebler. Otherwise the balance is lifelike. Szeryng's playing is altogether masterly and Miss Haebler brings an admirable vitality and robustness to her part: her playing has sparkle and great spontaneity. The piano timbre is a trifle dry but is otherwise very realistic. No reservations either about the Grumiaux Quintet's performance of the famous *G minor String quintet*, a civilized reading combining sensibility and vitality and most convincingly balanced in this transfer to tape. The general layout on the three cassettes is satisfactory, and the notes are more than adequate.

Clarinet quintet in A major, K.581.
(M) *(**) HMV TC-HQS 1395. Gervase de Peyer (clarinet), members of the Melos Ens. – WEBER: *Clarinet quintet.* (***)

Gervase de Peyer's earlier recording of the *Clarinet quintet* for HMV has not quite the vitality of his newer DG version (coupled to the *Oboe quartet* – see below), but its limpid warmth is very attractive. Coupled to the Weber *Quintet* this makes an attractive medium-price reissue. Unfortunately the transfer, though well balanced, is poorly focused in the treble, and the lack of smoothness and security seriously mars this issue at present.

(i) *Clarinet quintet in A major, K.581. Divertimento in D major, K.136* (quartet version).
(M) (***) Saga CA 5291. Aeolian Qt, (i) with Thea King (clarinet).

Thea King is a fine Mozartian. She plays the *Quintet* in a classical manner, but with great refinement in matters of tonal shading, and her phrasing is most beautiful. There is, it is true, a touch of coolness in the first two movements, but the music still glows, and Miss King's articulation in the third-movement solos and in the delightfully pointed finale is a joy to hear. The closing pages of the work are especially beautiful. This is all helped by excellent support from the Aeolian Quartet and good recording from Saga. The filler is bright and breezy, with very fast tempi for the outer movements and a graceful, if matter-of-fact, account of the *Andante*. The cassette transfer unfortunately offers only fair quality. The upper partials of the transfer are not clean and the clarinet focus is 'fluffy'.

(i) *Clarinet quintet in A major, K.581;*
(ii) *Oboe quartet in F major, K.370.*
*** DG 3300 720. Amadeus Qt, with (i) Gervase de Peyer (clarinet); (ii) Lothar Koch (oboe).
(M) **(*) DG Privilege 3335 287. Members of the Berlin PO, with (i) Karl Leistrer; (ii) Lothar Koch.

The Amadeus coupling is splendid. Gervase de Peyer gives a warm, smiling account of the *Clarinet quintet*, with a sunny opening movement, a gently expressive *Larghetto* and a delightfully genial finale. The performance is matched by the refinement of Koch in the *Oboe quartet*. With creamy tone and wonderfully stylish phrasing he is superb. The Amadeus accompany with sensitivity, and the recording is flawless. So is the cassette transfer, a demonstration tape with strikingly natural quality for both the wind soloists and the strings.

The Privilege reissue offers fine playing but a somewhat suave atmosphere in the central movements of the *Clarinet quintet*. Karl Leister, the clarinettist, does not emerge as a strong individual personality, but he plays most musically and this performance undoubtedly gives pleasure. Lothar Koch shows a sweetly pointed timbre and a most sensitive feeling for the style of the *Oboe quartet*, though this is not quite so distinguished as his later Amadeus version. The Privilege transfers are of excellent quality; the *Clarinet quintet* is especially vivid, the level unusually high for DG.

Flute quartets Nos. 1 in D major, K.285; 2 in G major, K.285a; 3 in C major, K.285c; 4 in A major, K. 298.
*** DG 3300 983. Andreas Blau (flute), Amadeus Qt.
** Enigma K 453554. Richard Adeney (flute), Hugh Maguire (violin), Cecil Aronowitz (viola), Terence Weill (cello).

Mozart professed an aversion for the flute (partly because at the time its intonation was suspect), yet he wrote some delightful music for it, none more so than these delicious lightweight quartets. Both the playing and the recording balance on the DG tape bring out their delicacy of texture. The solo wind instrument is beautifully integrated with the strings, and though the flute dominates, the other instruments are in no way over-weighed. The phrasing throughout breathes naturally. The enchanting slow movement of K.285, where the flute cantilena is floated over a pizzicato accompaniment, is very beautifully done, and the ear is caught by the gracious shaping of the *galant* themes used as the basis for variations in the second movement of K.285c or the no less charming opening movement of K.298. Andreas Blau is a splendid artist and the Amadeus accompany him with subtlety and distinction. The transfer is immaculate, the level not especially high, but the detail quite refined.

The performance by Richard Adeney and members of the Melos Ensemble is totally different in character. The music-making is essentially extrovert, fresh and enjoyable, even pert in the vivacious allegros. The balance treats the flute much more in a solo capacity and is generally far closer and more vivid than the the DG version. The level of transfer is higher and the string group has more edge, but less transparency and delicacy. The effect is undoubtedly spontaneous but the playing has not quite the imaginative insight (or indeed the persuasive charm) of the DG set.

(i) *Horn quintet in E flat major, K.407;* (ii) *Oboe quartet in F major, K.370;* (iii) *Clarinet trio in E flat major, K.498.*

(M) ** Turnabout KTVC 34035. Members of the Endres Qt, with (i) Sebastian Huber (horn); (ii) Alfred Sous (oboe); (iii) Walter Triebskorn (clarinet).

An excellent transfer – smoother than the equivalent LP but clean and clear. The oboe tone sounds particularly fresh and sweet, and the upper register of the clarinet is caught without discoloration. The performances are all characterful, and they are well balanced and recorded. In the last analysis the music-making here

is not really distinctive, but it represents good value.

Oboe quartet in F major, K.370; Oboe quintet in C minor, K.406 (arr. of *Serenade No. 12 in C minor, K.388); Adagio and Rondo in C minor/major for glass harmonica, flute, oboe, viola and cello, K.617.*

*** Philips 7300 607 [id.]. Heinz Holliger (oboe), Aurèle Nicolet (flute), Herman Krebbers (violin), Karl Schouten, Judith de Munk-Gerö (violas), Jean Decross (cello), Bruno Hoffmann (glass harmonica).

With such a distinguished roster it is not surprising that these performances are first-class. Moreover they are beautifully recorded, and the tape transfer, made at quite a high level, has splendid immediacy; Holliger's oboe is given a bright clear timbre to dominate the strings without too forward a balance. The curiosity here is Mozart's own arrangement of his *Wind serenade*, K.388, which some might feel sounds best in its original format. However, undoubtedly the playing here is persuasive, and of course the account of the *Oboe quartet* is peerless. Finally and certainly not least is the work for glass harmonica played on Bruno Hoffmann's set of drinking glasses (with moistened fingers). It is an indelibly piquant sound and the result is delightful (for the piece does not outstay its welcome).

String quartets and quintets

String quartets Nos. 14 in G major, K.387; 15 in D minor, K.421 (*Haydn quartets*).

*(*) DG 3300 898. Melos Qt of Stuttgart.

Well-shaped and finely proportioned readings, played with good ensemble and internal balance. At times one feels the Melos could play with greater spontaneity: the outer movements of the *D minor Quartet* come close to being square, and more could be made of the slow movement, which is wanting in repose and is just a little prosaic. The *G major Quartet* is finely played, but here and there one feels the need of greater freshness and imagination. In short, the players fail to project a feeling of joy in the music, and the sobriety of approach undoubtedly makes its mark on the listener. Technically the recording is secure. There is warm, natural string quality here, perhaps a trifle bland, but completely without edge, though also perhaps lacking the final degree of range in the treble.

String quartets Nos. 16 in E flat major, K.428; 17 in B flat major (Hunt), K.458.

   *** DG 3300 800. Melos Qt of Stuttgart.

The Melos Quartet plays with genuine spirit and commitment here, offering alert, keenly poised readings that are totally free from egocentric mannerisms. The recording is eminently fresh and firmly focused. For some reason the quality on tape is more vivid, with greater presence and range in the *Hunt quartet* than in K.428, where the sound, although warm and pleasing, has rather less sparkle. But this is an excellent issue and the balance is good.

String quartets Nos. 21 in D major (Prussian No. 1), K.575; 23 in F major (Prussian No. 3), K.590.

   (M) *** Decca Ace of Diamonds KSDC 509. Küchl Qt.

The Küchl Quartet are all members of the Vienna Philharmonic, and their performances compare favourably with any available. There is a marvellously unforced, relaxed and natural musicianship in evidence: nothing is rushed, yet one never gets the feeling that tempi are too leisurely. Nothing is over-emphatic, yet at the same time ideas are beautifully characterized. Every phrase is nicely turned but never self-consciously so. They sound as if they are playing chamber music in the home and not as if they are addressing a concert public. The playing is polished yet unassuming, and they are superbly recorded. The cassette transfer is marvellously refined, exceptionally clear and lifelike: a slight treble cut and a balanced bass lift may be useful on some players, but this is a very sophisticated tape indeed.

String quintet No. 3 in C major, K.515.

   (M) * Argo KZKC 17. Augmented Aeolian Qt.

The *C major Quintet* is an unquestioned masterpiece and is not generously represented in the recording catalogues. The Aeolian Quartet, with Kenneth Essex as the second viola, give a spirited but unsubtle reading of this great work. They do not make the most of dynamic contrasts, nor do the phrases breathe with the natural spontaneity that the music demands, while in terms of tonal beauty they do not command the finesse of Grumiaux's team (who in any case do not include this work in the Philips chamber-music box). Thus in the tape field this deserves a qualified recommendation *faute de mieux*, but it is not a distinguished performance. The recording is of high quality, completely natural in texture and with plenty of warmth. The level is high, which means a silent background, but the very forward balance tends to exaggerate the lack of dynamic contrast in the playing itself.

String quintet No. 4 in G minor, K.516.

   (M) * Argo KZKC 35. Augmented Aeolian Qt.

A most disappointing performance of Mozart's most famous string quintet.

379

The approach is altogether too literal; it has too little finesse and absolutely no magic. As in the performance of the companion *C major Quintet*, it is the finale which comes off best, but the rest is obstinately unmemorable. The recording is good and the transfer clear, although in the first movement the leader's tone seems somewhat fierce.

Piano music

Andante and variations, K.501.
   ** Philips 7300 644 [id.]. Martha Argerich, Stephen Bishop-Kovacevich (piano duet) – BARTÓK: *Sonata for 2 pianos and percussion* (***); DEBUSSY: *En blanc et noir.***

The charming *Andante and variations* is taken at a rather brisker tempo than usual, but the playing of this duo is unfailingly sensitive and vital. The sound is much better here than in the Bartók coupling; but the level remains low, so that, although the piano tone is natural, the performance lacks projection.

Fugue in C minor for 2 pianos, K.426; Double piano sonata in D major, K.448.
   (M) **(*) Turnabout KTVC 34064. Alfred Brendel, Walter Klien (pianos) – *Double concerto.***(*)

No musician composed more naturally for the stereo medium than Mozart. The way he dovetails the writing for the two players so that the musical argument is deftly handed to and fro commands wonder as well as pleasure. Brendel and Klien present this music with a splendid combination of alertness and spontaneity. They convey their enjoyment readily to the listener and it is a pity the rather hard piano recording on this Turnabout cassette detracts a little from

the overall effect. This remains a recommendable coupling, as careful rebalancing of the controls can improve matters.

Fantasies: in C minor, K.475; in D minor, K.397; Piano sonatas Nos. 8 in A minor, K.310; 11 in A major, K. 331.
   (M) *** DG Privilege 3335 168. Wilhelm Kempff.

Kempff's disarming simplicity of style hides great art. This is a wonderful recital, in a class of its own and not to be missed on any account. The performance of the mature *Fantasy*, K.475, is surely one of the most beautiful pieces of Mozart-playing ever recorded. The recording is good, and the high-level transfer is first-class, clear, clean, natural and secure.

Piano sonatas Nos. 2 in F major, K.280; 3 in B flat major, K.281; 9 in D major, K.311; 10 in C major, K.330.
   *** DG 3301 052 [id.]. Krystian Zimerman.

Marvellous playing. Krystian Zimerman makes no pretences of playing a fortepiano, using a wide range of tonal shading and phrases delicately echoed in the baroque manner. Yet the playing is essentially robust, and the slow movements of K.311 and K.330 are played with great eloquence, without ever taking the music outside the period of its natural sensibility. The recording is flawless, absolutely natural in balance, and the (German-made) tape we listened to offered superbly realistic piano tone, rich, clear in detail, and perfectly focused.

Organ music

Fantasia in F minor, K.594; Fantasia in F minor, K. 608.
   (M) *** Argo KZKC 13. Simon Preston (organ of Westminster

Abbey) – BACH: *Schübler chorales.****

These two *Fantasias* were originally written for mechanical clock, and not everyone will approve Simon Preston's display performances which convincingly bring out unexpected power. But with opulent organ sound and a most attractive coupling this is recommended even for those who resist recordings of the organ. The transfer is of immaculate quality and quite distortion-free.

VOCAL AND CHORAL MUSIC

Lieder: *Abendempfindung; Als Luise die Briefe ihres Ungetreuen Liebhabers verbrannte; An die Einsamkeit; An die Freundschaft; An die Hoffnung; Dans un bois solitaire; Eine kleine deutsche Kantate; Gesellenreise; Die grossmütige Gelassenheit; Die kleine Spinnerin; Das Lied der Trennung; Oiseaux, si tous les ans; Ridente la calma; Sehnsucht nach dem Frühling; Das Veilchen; Der Zauberer; Die Zufriedenheit.*

(M) (***) Saga CA 5441. Jill ·Gomez (soprano), John Constable (piano).

Jill Gomez sings a delightful selection of Mozart songs very charmingly, and she is well accompanied by John Constable. On the Saga budget label, that should be recommendation enough. On side one the recording is admirably clear – much clearer than on many Saga tapes – but the level is just a shade too high and the voice peaks at fortissimos. Side two has a much lower level and the quality gives less presence to the artists, but it is mellow and without distortion, until towards the end of the recital, when the peaking on high notes returns.

Sacred music: (i–iii) *Ave verum corpus, K.618;* (ii–iv) *Exsultate jubilate, K.165;* (i–iii) *Kyrie in D minor, K.431. Masses Nos.* (v) *10 in C major (Spatzenmesse), K.220 (Missa brevis);* (ii; iii; vi–viii) *11 in C major (Credo), K. 257;* (v) *16 in C major (Coronation), K.317;* (i–iii; vi; ix) *18 in C minor (Great), K.427;* (iii; vi; viii; x) *Requiem Mass (No. 19) in D minor, K.626.* (i–iv; xi) *Vesperae solennes de confessore in C major, K.339.*

**(*) Philips 7699 052. (i) LSO Chorus; (ii) LSO; (iii) Colin Davis; (iv) Kiri Te Kanawa; (v) Soloists, Vienna Boys' Choir, Chorus Viennensis, Vienna Cathedral Orch., Grossman; (vi) Helen Donath, Ryland Davies; (vii) Gillian Knight, Clifford Grant; (viii) John Alldis Choir; (ix) Heather Harper, Stafford Dean; (x) Yvonne Minton, Gerd Nienstedt, BBC SO; (xi) Elizabeth Bainbridge, Ryland Davies, Gwynne Howell.

This Mozart Edition box is especially useful because some of these works are not otherwise available on tape. The transfers are remarkably successful. Often the acoustic is necessarily reverberant, yet this has seemed to offer no problems. The choral and orchestral sound has fine body and no lack of focus, yet there is plenty of atmosphere. The *Missa brevis*, K.220, which follows the *Coronation Mass* on the first cassette, is especially fine and these two Vienna performances have plenty of life, with good solo contributions. Colin Davis obviously relishes the vigorous qualities of the *Credo Mass*, and this dramatic, often secular-sounding music is splendidly sung, played and recorded. In the *C minor Mass* Davis follows the trend today by rejecting the accretions which were formerly used to turn this incomplete torso of a work into a full setting of the liturgy. Robbins Landon's edition prompts him to a strong and intense performance which brings out the darkness of tragedy behind Mozart's use of the minor key, helped by fine singing from Helen Donath and Heather Harper, whose voices sound freshly beautiful here. Davis's *Requiem Mass* is discussed below under its separate issue: sufficient to say that the transfer here belies the age of the original recording and is admirably balanced. The shorter works range from the early soprano cantata *Exsultate jubilate*, with its famous setting of *Alleluia*, to the equally popular *Ave verum*. Kiri Te Kanawa is the brilliant soloist in the cantata and her radiant account of the lovely *Laudate Dominum* is one of the highspots of the *Solemn Vespers*. That work, with its dramatic choruses, is among Mozart's most inspired of his Salzburg period, and is given a fine responsive performance. The *Kyrie in D minor*, K.341, written in Munich in 1781, is also a very impressive work. Its long-breathed *Andante maestoso* has considerable strength of feeling, and the work features an unusually large orchestra, including four horns. A first-class set, well laid out on three cassettes, with excellent notes. Our review copy developed a touch of discoloration of the high woodwind partials near the ends of sides three and five, but this seems unlikely to be common to all copies, for the recording generally is admirably clean.

Ave verum corpus, K.618.

(M) ** HMV TC-EXE 67. Vienna Singverein, Philharmonia Orch., Karajan – *Serenade No. 13; German dance, K.605/3**;* LEOPOLD MOZART: *Toy symphony* *(*); HANDEL: *Water music.***

This is part of a quite attractive anthology, and if Karajan's account of the *Ave verum* is rather suave, it is well sung and smoothly transferred.

Benedictus sit Deus (offertory), *K.117; Exsultate jubilate, K.165.*

(M) * Turnabout KTVC 34029. Marguerita Lavergne (soprano), Vienna Oratorio Choir, Vienna Pro Musica Orch., Grossman – VIVALDI: *Gloria.**(*)

There is far too much swooping here to make the vocal line really enjoyable; and in any event the accompaniment is not up to standard. Not recommended, as the Vivaldi coupling (which is quite well done) is also available on a superior Argo cassette.

Mass No. 4 in C minor (Weisenhausmesse), K.139.

*** DG 3300 777 [id.]. Gundula Janowitz, Frederica von Stade, Wieslaw Ochman, Kurt Moll, Vienna State Opera Chorus, Vienna PO, Abbado.

The thirteen-year-old Mozart did not respond to the key of C minor in the way that he came to do later, or for that matter in the way that the teenage Beethoven did in choral music. (His way was quickly to turn to C major instead.) But by any standards this is a remarkably sustained example of the young composer's powers, with bustling allegros in the *Kyrie, Gloria* and *Credo* as well as at the end of the *Agnus Dei*, while the *Gloria* and *Credo* end with full-scale fugues. This far from negligible piece sounds its very best in Abbado's persuasive hands. The DG recording is lively, and the tape transfer is fresh and spacious. The balance of the solists seems a trifle backward, but their relationship with chorus and orchestra is not unrealistic in terms of a live performance.

Mass No. 16 in C major (Coronation), K.317.

**(*) DG 3300 704 [id.]. Anna Tomowa-Sintow, Agnes Baltsa,

Werner Krenn, José van Dam, Vienna Singverein, Berlin PO, Karajan – BRUCKNER: *Te Deum.***(*)

(i) *Mass No. 16;* (ii) *Et incarnatus est* (from *Mass No. 18 in C minor, K.427); Exsultate jubilate, K.165.*

(M) *** DG Privilege 3335 148 [id.]. (i) Maria Stader, Oralia Dominguez, Ernst Haefliger, Michel Roux, Elisabeth Brasseur Choir, Lamoureux Orch., Markevitch; (ii) Maria Stader (soprano), Berlin Radio SO, Fricsay.

Mass No. 16; Vesperae solennes de confessore in C major, K.339.

*(*) HMV TC-ASD 3373. Edda Moser, Julia Hamari, Nicolai Gedda, Dietrich Fischer-Dieskau, Bavarian Radio Chorus and SO, Jochum.

Markevitch's performance of the delightful *Coronation Mass* is incisively brilliant, and its sheer vigour is irresistible. That is not to say that its lyrical moments are not equally successful. He has a splendid team of soloists, and they are well matched in ensemble as well as providing very good individual contributions. The *Agnus Dei* is especially fine. Having sung so well in the *Mass* Maria Stader gives excellent performances on side two. The recording has plenty of life and detail, and the cassette transfer has almost an excess of brilliance, with an edge on the choral sound which gives it splendid life. The solo voices are well caught, and the tape offers fine presence and naturalness for Maria Stader's solo items on side two.

If the Bruckner coupling is attractive, then Karajan's version offers a great deal to enjoy. It is a dramatic reading, lacking something perhaps in rhythmic resilience, but with excellent solo singing as well as a sharply defined contribution from the chorus. There is no lack of

strength, and the score's lyrical elements are sensitively managed. Unfortunately the cassette suffers from recession of image in the music's gentler pages and is a trifle fierce otherwise, although the vividness of the overall sound picture is in no doubt.

The lack of clarity in the recording and the questionable balance put the HMV version out of account. Having the *Vespers* for coupling is particularly attractive, though the fruity-toned Edda Moser is hardly the right choice for the heavenly *Laudate Dominum*. Gedda is below form too. The transfer to tape has brought a not very successful attempt to brighten and clarify the rather mushy sound of the disc. In consequence the opening of the *Coronation Mass* is distinctly rough, and one needs a cut-back of treble if the solo voices are not to sound edgy. The *Solemn Vespers* sounds rather smoother and here the soloists are more naturally caught.

Mass No. 18 in C minor (Great), K.427.

(M) ** Turnabout KTVC 34174. Wilma Lipp, Christa Ludwig, Murray Dickie, Walter Berry, Vienna Oratorio Choir, Vienna Pro Musica Orch., Grossman.

An enjoyable rather than an outstanding performance. Wilma Lipp tends to let the side down with her lack of poise at times; her part in the proceedings is a dominant one, so the good contribution from the other soloists does not entirely compensate, particularly as the recording balance is only fair. However, the life and spontaneity of the performance make considerable amends, and the music-making is vividly transferred to tape.

Requiem Mass (No. 19) in D minor, K.626.

*** DG 3300 705 [id.]. Anna Tomowa-Sintow, Agnes Baltsa, Werner Krenn, José van Dam,

Vienna Singverein, Berlin PO, Karajan.

**(*) Philips 7300 993 [id.]. Helen Donath, Yvonne Minton, Ryland Davies, Gerd Nienstedt, John Alldis Choir, BBC SO, Colin Davis.

**(*) Argo KZRC 876 [id.]. Ileana Cotrubas, Helen Watts, Robert Tear, John Shirley-Quirk, Chorus, Academy of St Martin-in-the-Fields, Marriner.

(M) **(*) Decca KCSP 476. Elly Ameling, Marilyn Horne, Ugo Benelli, Tugomir Franc, Vienna State Opera Chorus, Vienna PO, Kertesz.

(M) **(*) HMV TC-SXLP 30237. Edith Mathis, Grace Bumbry, George Shirley, Marius Rintzler, New Philharmonia Chorus and Orch., Frühbeck de Burgos.

** HMV TC-ASD 2788. Sheila Armstrong, Janet Baker, Nicolai Gedda, Dietrich Fischer-Dieskau, John Alldis Choir, ECO, Barenboim.

** DG 3300 296 [id.]. Edith Mathis, Julia Hamari, Wieslaw Ochman, Karl Ridderbusch, Vienna State Opera Chorus, Vienna PO, Boehm.

(M) ** DG Privilege 3335 257 [923066]. Wilma Lipp, Hilde Rössl-Majdan, Anton Dermota, Walter Berry, Vienna Singverein, Berlin PO, Karajan.

In contrast to his earlier recording of the *Requiem* (now on DG Privilege), Karajan's later version is outstandingly fine, more deeply committed than one has come to expect from this conductor in Mozart. The toughness of Karajan's approach is established from the start with incisive playing and clean-focused

singing from the chorus, not too large and set a little behind. The fine quartet of soloists too is beautifully blended, and through everything – whatever the creative source, Süssmayr or Mozart – the conductor superbly establishes a sense of unity. The reading has its moments of romantic expressiveness, but nothing is smoothed over, and with superbly vivid recording such a passage as the *Dies irae* has exceptional freshness and intensity. On the whole this is the finest current recording, and generally the transfer is of excellent quality. Some of the massed choral sound is rather more opaque than on the equivalent LP, but the orchestra has plenty of life and the solo voices sound natural and are convincingly balanced; indeed the overall perspective is realistically conveyed.

Colin Davis, with a smaller choir, gives a more intimate performance than is common, and with his natural sense of style he finds much beauty of detail. In principle the performance should have given the sort of 'new look' to the Mozart *Requiem* that was such a striking success in Handel's *Messiah*, but Davis does not provide the same sort of 'bite' that in performances on this scale should compensate for sheer massiveness of tone. The BBC Symphony Orchestra is in good form and the soloists – although varying in quality – keep up a laudably high standard. Anyone wanting a version on this authentic scale need not hesitate, but this is plainly not the definitive version. The recording is good but neither as sweet nor as crystal-clear as it might be. The balance of the sound on tape is pleasingly natural (although a slight treble lift and matching bass cut is useful), and there is a bloom on the solo voices. The orchestra is not without presence, and if the choruses are not incisive, they are not woolly either; on side two the quality seems just marginally brighter and crisper. However, because of the lack of brightness there is obviously more of a problem with tape hiss than usual.

Marriner, who can usually be relied on to produce vigorous and sympathetic performances in the recording studio, generates less electricity than usual in the *Requiem*. It is interesting to have a version which uses the Beyer edition and aims at removing the faults of Süssmayr's completion, amending points in the harmony and instrumentation, but few will register any significant differences except in such instances as the extension of the *Osanna*. Solo singing is good, but the chorus could be more alert. The transfer, however, is very sophisticated, perhaps the best available of this work, with incisive choral tone and very clear projection of the soloists. It sounds best with a very slight treble reduction but then is most impressively balanced, with little loss of atmosphere.

Kertesz takes a large-scale view of Mozart's last work, but unfortunately he cannot rely on a really first-rate chorus. Much of the choral singing here is rather wild and smudgy, enthusiastic but not stylish enough for Mozart, and the impression is made worse by the forward balance of the singers against the orchestra. Kertesz goes further than usual towards a romantic view of the work. The recording has the usual Decca brilliance, and the cassette transfer is admirably clear and crisp. This is good value at medium price.

The glory of Frühbeck's HMV is the singing of the New Philharmonia Chorus, and with the choral music very much the centre of interest, that gives it an edge over Davis on Philips and Kertesz on Decca. This is unashamedly big-scale Mozart, and that is perhaps apt for a work that has less need for apology than was once thought. (Research suggests that Süssmayr's contribution was smaller than was once believed, and certainly the aesthetic test is clear: very little indeed falls below what one would expect of a Mozart masterpiece and much is of supreme greatness.) Frühbeck does not have a very subtle Mozart style, and on detail some of his rivals outshine him; for

instance, Davis's *Recordare* is much more relaxed and refined. But as an interpretation it stands well in the middle of the road, not too romantic, not too frigidly classic, and quite apart from the choral singing – recorded with beautiful balance and richness – the soloists are all first-rate, rather better than Kertesz's. However, the transfer has produced some loss of refinement in the larger choral climaxes, but real congestion is avoided and the spaciousness of the recording is retained. The solo voices sound well.

As in his recording of Bach's *Magnificat*, Barenboim's exuberance may raise a few eyebrows. Mozart's *Dies irae*, for instance, has such zest that one senses the chorus galloping towards the Day of Judgement with enthusiasm. Yet the underlying drama and musicality of the performance as a whole disarm criticism. The intensity of Barenboim's feeling comes over from the opening bar, and the *Kyrie eleison* is stirring indeed. The lyricism of the score is beautifully calculated; the operatic-styled quartet which closes the *Tuba mirum* is particularly lovely. So too is the closing section of *Confutatis maledictis*, which creates a gentle mood for the opening of the *Lacrimosa*. Here Barenboim's emotional contrasts dramatize the words superbly. The *Sanctus* is gloriously forthright. With a good solo team, excellent choral singing and fine orchestral playing (the opening of the *Lacrimosa* is beautifully managed), this is a splendidly alive performance, and HMV's sound is very good. The cassette transfer, however, is rather confined in sound. The solo voices and ensembles come over quite well, but the massively recorded choruses fail to open up as they should. This was a very early HMV Dolby issue, and it may be that later copies will improve in this respect.

Boehm's is a spacious and solemn view of the work, with good solo singing and fine choral and orchestral response. It is not as incisive and dramatic an account as Karajan's later version, or Davis's with more modest forces; nor is it quite as lively in expressive detail as the Frühbeck de Burgos. An immensely polished performance in every way, it is not as fully satisfying as the best of its rivals.

Karajan's earlier recording has been reissued on Privilege in an acceptable new transfer. There is some lack of range and the choral tone lacks edge and detail. Karajan here takes a typically suave view of the work. The chief objection to this version is that detail tends to be sacrificed in favour of warmth and atmosphere. The solo quartet are wonderfully blended, so rare an occurrence in this work above all, and although the chorus lack firmness of line they are helped out by the spirited playing of the Berlin Philharmonic.

Thamos, King of Egypt (incidental music), *K.345*.
(M) ** Turnabout KTVC 34679. Charlotte Lehmann, Rose Scheible, Oly Pfaff, Bruce Abel, Heilbronn Vocal Ens., Württemberg CO, Faerber.

The music for the play *Thamos, King of Egypt* is now thought to come from 1776–7 (rather than two years later on). Joerg Faerber's version is welcome as the only representation of this delightful score on cassette. The singing is fully acceptable; the orchestral playing is thoroughly musical, and the performance as a whole has life and spontaneity. The textures are not ideally transparent on this recording (the string quality above the stave is wanting in freshness, and the sound fails to expand) but the transfer is lively and vivid, and the choral focus good. Given the interest of the music and the modest price, this issue is worth investigating.

OPERA

Bastien und Bastienne: complete.
*** DG 3306 038. Edith Mathis, Claes Haaken Ahnsjö, Walter Berry, Salzburg Mozarteum Orch., Hager.

The one-act opera *Bastien und Bastienne* is mainly famous because its overture contains a theme which might or might not have prompted Beethoven for the opening theme of the *Eroica symphony*. Otherwise nothing in Mozart's little *Singspiel* comes anywhere near epic scale. As William Mann says in his comprehensive survey of the Mozart operas, it makes an attractive piece for students or the marionette theatre, but nonetheless it provides delightful material too for singers as accomplished as those on this DG recording. Conducted by Leopold Hager, the performance is at once lively and scholarly, though many will count the extra recitatives (completed by Hager) a move in the wrong direction when such a *Singspiel* in German is well served with spoken dialogue. Fresh, well-balanced recording and a clear, clean transfer to match the LP very closely.

La Clemenza di Tito: complete.
*** Philips 7699 038 [id.]. Janet Baker, Yvonne Minton, Stuart Burrows, Frederica von Stade, Lucia Popp, Robert Lloyd, Chorus and Orch. of the Royal Opera House, Covent Garden, Colin Davis.

It was a revelation, even to dedicated Mozartians, to find in the Covent Garden production that *La Clemenza di Tito* had so much to offer. This superb set, among the finest of Colin Davis's many Mozart recordings, sums up the achievement of the stage production and adds still more, for, above all, the performance of Dame Janet Baker in the key role of Vitellia has deepened and intensified. Not only is her singing formidably brilliant, with every roulade and exposed leap flawlessly attacked; she actually makes one believe in the emotional development of an impossible character, one who develops from villainy to virtue with the scantiest preparation. Whereas earlier Dame Janet found the evil hard to convey on stage, here the venom as well as the transformation are commandingly convincing. The two other mezzo-sopranos, Minton as Sesto and von Stade in the small role of Annio, are superb too, while Burrows has rarely if ever sung so stylishly on a recording as here; he makes the forgiving emperor a rounded and sympathetic character, not just a bore. The recitatives add to the compulsion of the drama – here they are far more than mere formal links – while Davis's swaggering manner in the pageant music heightens the genuine feeling conveyed in much of the rest, transforming what used to be dismissed as a dry *opera seria*. Excellent recording; the transfer is smooth and pleasant, if made at rather a low level. However, the detail is quite good and the voices have no lack of bloom, though a high volume setting is necessary to give them full presence. The chorus lacks clarity in its upper register but is better focused in Act 2 than in Act 1. Considering the level the overall effect is remarkably good.

Così fan tutte: complete.

(M) **(*) HMV TC-SLS 5028. Elisabeth Schwarzkopf, Christa Ludwig, Hanny Steffek, Alfredo Kraus, Giuseppe Taddei, Walter Berry, Philharmonia Chorus and Orch., Boehm.

(M) **(*) Philips 7699 055. Montserrat Caballé, Janet Baker, Ileana Cotrubas, Nicolai Gedda, Wladimiro Ganzarolli, Richard van Allan, Chorus and Orch. of the Royal Opera House, Covent Garden, Colin Davis.

** DG 3371 019 [id.]. Gundula Janowitz, Brigitte Fassbaender, Reri Grist, Hermann Prey, Peter Schreier, Rolando Panerai, Vienna State Opera Chorus, Vienna PO, Boehm.

Boehm's HMV set (unlike some of its rivals on disc) presents a discreetly tailored text, with cuts in the long recitatives and two brief cuts in the finales. But once that is said (and there is a case for not regarding it as a disadvantage), there is everything in favour of this classic set, which presents Boehm at his most genially perceptive and with glorious solo singing, headed by the incomparable Fiordiligi of Schwarzkopf and the equally moving Dorabella of Ludwig. With sound that remains sparklingly atmospheric, vividly creating the illusion of a stage performance, and production that remains a superb memento of Walter Legge's artistic finesse, it would stand almost any comparison at full price. In this reissue it offers a bargain without parallel. Listen to Schwarzkopf's commanding account of *Come scoglio*, more perfect in detail than any since, and you are not likely to hesitate.

The cassette transfer is generally good, but has slight problems with the recording's extremes of dynamic: the distant effects seem slightly too distant, while there is occasional slight peaking on the ladies' voices at fortissimos (in *Come scoglio*, for instance). One would not want to exaggerate this; the recording is lively, with good presence, yet has a good deal of atmosphere and warmth. However, on our set the level rose on side four and brought with it a degree of fierceness. Even so, the sound has more body than the Philips version. Both are conveniently laid out on two cassettes, with each of the two acts given a tape to itself. The EMI libretto is printed in very small type, but at least it is bold; the Philips libretto offers a similar typeface, but is much fainter.

Colin Davis has rarely if ever made a more captivating recording than his magical set of *Così fan tutte*. His energy and sparkle are here set against inspired and characterful singing from the three women soloists. Montserrat Caballé and Janet Baker prove a winning partnership, each one challenging and abetting the other all the time. Cotrubas equally is a vivid Despina, never merely arch. The men too make a strong team. Though Gedda has moments of rough tone, his account of *Una aura amorosa* is honeyed and delicate, and though Ganzarolli falls short in one of his prominent arias, it is a spirited, incisive performance, while Richard van Allan here naturally assumes the status of an international recording artist with flair and imagination. Sparkling recitatives (complete) and recording which has you riveted by the play of the action. However, the transfer to tape sometimes has a distinctly edgy quality (noticeable on the male voices immediately after the overture). The female voices are less affected by this, and with a treble cut the sound can be smoothed. But although it has good presence the recording has not as much warmth and body as the EMI set.

Boehm's DG recording makes a delightful memento. It was recorded live during the Salzburg Festival performance on the conductor's eightieth birthday, and though the zest and sparkle of the occasion come over delightfully, with as splendid a cast as you could gather, the ensemble is not quite crisp enough to sustain repeated listening. Quite apart from occasional mishaps (remarkably few) the balance favours the voices, with stage noises made the more prominent. There is certainly a place for this set, but hardly in competition with Boehm's own HMV version or Colin Davis's account. The cassette transfer is lively, with good presence.

Così fan tutte: highlights.
 ** Decca KCET 595. Pilar Lorengar, Teresa Berganza, Jane Berbié, Ryland Davies, Tom Krause, Gabriel Bacquier, Chorus of the Royal Opera House, Covent Garden, LPO, Solti.

Solti's complete set (not available on tape) will please only those who want high voltage at all costs even in this most genial of Mozartian comedies. There is little relaxation and little charm, which underlines the shortcomings of the singing cast, notably of Pilar Lorengar, whose grainy voice is not well treated by the microphone, and who here in places conveys uncertainty. It is a pity that the crackling wit of Solti's Covent Garden performances was not more magically captured on record. This selection is generous and sensitively chosen. However, the complete recording has now been reissued at medium price on disc; so this top-price tape, even though it is cleanly transferred and reflects the brilliance of the original recording, seems an expensive way to sample a flawed set.

Don Giovanni: complete.
 ⊛ (M) *** HMV TC-SLS 5083. Eberhard Waechter, Elisabeth Schwarzkopf, Joan Sutherland, Graziella Sciutti, Luigi Alva, Giuseppe Taddei, Philharmonia Chorus and Orch., Giulini.
 (M) **(*) Philips 7699 054. Ingvar Wixell, Martina Arroyo, Kiri Te Kanawa, Mirella Freni, Stuart Burrows, Wladimiro Ganzarolli, Chorus and Orch. of the Royal Opera House, Covent Garden, Colin Davis.
 **(*) DG 3371 042 [id.]. 1977 Salzburg Festival production: Sherrill Milnes, Anna Tomowa-Sintow, Teresa Zylis-Gara, Edith Mathis, Peter Schreier, Walter Berry, Vienna State Opera Chorus, Vienna PO, Boehm.
 *(*) DG 3371 014 [id.]. Dietrich

Fischer-Dieskau, Martina Arroyo, Birgit Nilsson, Reri Grist, Peter Schreier, Ezio Flagello, Prague National Theatre Chorus and Orch., Boehm.

The return of the classic Giulini HMV set to the LP catalogue brought out vividly just what had been lacking in rival versions. Not only is the singing cast more consistent than any other; the direction of Giulini and the playing of the vintage Philharmonia Orchestra give this performance an athletic vigour which carries all before it. The whole production owes much to the work of Walter Legge, uncredited in the original issue but the prime mover behind this and so many other Philharmonia issues. Legge's wife, Elisabeth Schwarzkopf, as Elvira, emerges as a dominant figure to give a distinctive but totally apt slant to this endlessly invigorating drama. No wilting sufferer this but the most formidable of women, who flies at the Don with such cries as *Perfido mostro!* unforgettably sung. The young Sutherland may be relatively reticent as Anna, but with such technical ease and consistent beauty of tone, she makes a superb foil. Taddei is a delightful Leporello, and each member of the cast – including the young Cappuccilli as Masetto – combines fine singing with keen dramatic sense. Recitatives are scintillating, and only the occasional exaggerated snarl from the Don of Eberhard Waechter mars the superb vocal standards. Even that goes well with his fresh and youthful portrait of the central character. The reissue sounds excellent, bright and well balanced, and the transfer is generally successful, missing only the last degree of refinement (most noticeably in the Act 1 finale, but this is not serious enough to prevent the strongest recommendation). A slight treble reduction smooths the sound without spoiling its immediacy. Each act is complete on one of the two cassettes, but the small print of the libretto, though clear, is not ideal.

The final test of a recording of this most searching of operas is whether it adds up to more than the sum of its parts. Colin Davis's certainly does, with a singing cast that has fewer shortcomings than almost any other on tape and much positive strength. For once one can listen untroubled by vocal blemishes. Martina Arroyo controls her massive dramatic voice more completely than one would think possible, and she is strongly and imaginatively contrasted with the sweetly expressive Elvira of Kiri Te Kanawa and the sparkling Zerlina of Freni. As in the Davis *Figaro*, Ingvar Wixell and Wladimiro Ganzarolli make a formidable master/servant team, with excellent vocal acting, while Stuart Burrows sings gloriously as Don Ottavio, and Richard van Allan is a characterful Masetto. Davis draws a fresh and immediate performance from his team, riveting from beginning to end. The Philips transfer is not always as sharply focused as it might be, and sometimes lacks the last degree of body and richness. However, the level is quite high, and there is no lack of presence and atmosphere. The opera is admirably laid out on two cassettes with one act complete on each, but the libretto offers extremely fine print that will seem elusive to all but the youngest eyes.

Recorded in 1977 at a sequence of live performances in the Kleines Festspielhaus at Salzburg, Karl Boehm's second recording of this opera has an engaging vigour. The tempi are sometimes on the slow side, but the concentration is unfailing, and the whole reading centres round an assumption of the role of the Don which is richly heroic and far more sympathetic in characterization than is common. Sherrill Milnes sings with a richness and commitment which match his swaggering stage presence. Anna Tomowa-Sintow as Donna Anna is generally creamy-toned, only occasionally betraying a flutter, while Teresa Zylis-Gara as Elvira controls her warm voice with delicacy. These are stylish performances without being deeply memorable. Edith Mathis sings with her usual intelligence, but the tone is not always perfectly focused. Firm reliable performances from the men. Unlike Boehm's Salzburg *Così fan tutte*, where the ensembles were distractingly ragged, this live *Giovanni* presents a strong and consistently enjoyable experience distinct from that on any other set. The recording – favouring the voices but amazingly good under the conditions – is especially vivid in the culminating scene. This set has one savouring the unique flavour of Mozart opera in Salzburg with remarkable realism and with few distractions. The transfer, made at a fairly high level for DG, has plenty of immediacy, but the upper range is not too cleanly focused (affecting both voices and upper strings in the orchestra). However, a treble cut or filter tidies this well enough. The level rises further in the finale, adding extra edge to the opera's dramatic close. The layout follows the discs, with three sides to each act; the small-print libretto is clear.

In the mid-sixties DG opted to go to Prague – scene of the opera's original production – for the second set it had made within six years with Fischer-Dieskau as the Don. Sadly that was a mistake. The orchestra of the Prague National Theatre was just not polished enough to play for a Mozart opera recording, even with Karl Boehm in charge, and that alone effectively prevents this set from offering a really keen challenge in the *Don Giovanni* race. Fischer-Dieskau here avoids the leering, overpointed manner that had marred his earlier version under Fricsay, but except in the *Serenade*, which sounds as though it was recorded on a separate day, the voice is in astonishingly rough condition, the *vibrato* not just gritty but sometimes even wobbly. The dramatic partnership with Ezio Flagello as Leporello is still most appealing, but the cast of women hardly matches Giulini's or Davis's. Birgit Nilsson's Donna Anna is at least commanding, but the tone is too raw for

Mozart. Martina Arroyo here has a rich tone but little dramatic presence, which leaves Reri Grist as the most convincing of the women singers. The recording is somewhat reverberant (as can be heard at once in the overture, where the detail is not very crisp), and the transfer produces less refined quality than is usual in DG taped opera sets. The recitatives are clear enough, but the ensembles are not always cleanly focused, and there is the occasional moment of peaking on climaxes. Much of the time the quality is good, however, and none of the points we have mentioned seriously mars enjoyment of the music; but Boehm's later Salzburg set is clearly preferable.

Idomeneo: complete.
  *** DG 3371 043. Edith Mathis, Julia Varady, Wieslaw Ochman, Peter Schreier, Hermann Winkler, Leipzig Radio Choir, Dresden State Orch., Boehm.

DG's recording of *Idomeneo* is admirably set out on three cassettes (as against the equivalent of four LPs), with each of the three acts complete on a single tape. The transfer level is high and the quality is first-class in every way. This is one of DG's very best opera issues, and the libretto is clearly printed, even though the type is small. Textually, however, Karl Boehm's version gives grounds for regrets. The score is snipped about in the interests of a staged production, and, like previous accounts on disc, it opts for a tenor in the role of Idamante. But once that is said, this is an enormously successful and richly enjoyable set, completing Boehm's incomparable series of Mozart's operatic masterpieces with a version of this *opera seria* which as a dramatic experience outshines all previous ones. Boehm's conducting is a delight, often spacious but never heavy in the wrong way, with lightened textures and sprung rhythms which have one relishing Mozartian felicities as never before. Even where the tempi are unconventional, as in the hectic speed for the final chorus, Boehm conveys fresh delight, and his singing cast is generally the best ever recorded. As Idomeneo, Wieslaw Ochman, with tenor tone often too tight, is a relatively dull dog, but the other principals are generally excellent. Peter Schreier as Idamante too might have sounded more consistently sweet, but the imagination is irresistible. Edith Mathis is at her most beguiling as Ilia, but it is Julia Varady as Elettra who gives the most compelling performance of all, sharply incisive in her dramatic outbursts but at the same time precise and pure-toned, a Mozartian stylist through and through. Hermann Winkler as Arbace is squarely Germanic, and it is a pity that the *secco* recitatives are heavily done, but whatever incidental reservations have to be made this is a superbly compelling set which leaves one in no doubt of the work's status as a masterpiece.

Le Nozze di Figaro (The Marriage of Figaro): complete.

⊛ (M) *** Decca K 79 K 32. Hilde Gueden, Suzanne Danco, Lisa della Casa, Alfred Poell, Cesare Siepi, Murray Dickie, Fernando Corena, Vienna State Opera Chorus, Vienna PO, Erich Kleiber.

(M) *** Philips 7699 053. Mirella Freni, Jessye Norman, Yvonne Minton, Ingvar Wixell, Wladimiro Ganzarolli, Clifford Grant, Robert Tear, BBC Chorus and SO, Colin Davis.

*** DG 3371 005 [id.]. Edith Mathis, Gundula Janowitz, Tatiana Troyanos, Dietrich Fischer-Dieskau, Hermann Prey, Peter Lagger, German Opera Chorus and Orch., Berlin, Boehm.

The Kleiber cassette box of *The Marriage of Figaro* is one of the great achievements of the tape catalogue. The expertly managed transfer gives new life to an old recording (unbelievably, the set was one of the Mozart bicentenary recordings of the mid-1950s), and indeed it brings a completely new dimension to the performance as a whole, by presenting each act, unbroken, on one of its four cassette sides. With no interruption the compelling onward flow of Kleiber's shaping of each act (and especially the miraculous Act 2) becomes apparent as never before, and the warm, honeyed quality of the sound gives consistent pleasure. The age of the original occasionally shows in the string tone (the overture is a trifle shrill) and in the stereo placing of the singers (sometimes the projection is not quite as vivid as it might be), but the smiling ambience of the acoustic is perfectly judged for this most lyrically vivacious of all operas. There is much fine singing throughout, and few if any sets have since matched its constant stylishness. Gueden's Susanna might be criticized, but her golden tones are certainly characterful, and Danco and Della Casa are both at their finest. A dark-toned Figaro in Siepi brings added contrast, and if the pace of the recitatives is rather slow, this is not inconsistent within the context of Kleiber's overall view. There is an admirably clear libretto, printed in large easy-to-read type. This set cannot be too highly recommended – for I.M. it is desert-island fare.

Colin Davis produces generally the most enjoyable of the more recent versions of this much recorded opera. His pacing of the recitatives has a sparkle that directly reflects experience in the opera house, and his tempi generally are beautifully chosen to make their dramatic points. Vocally the cast is exceptionally consistent. Mirella Freni (Susanna) is the least satisfying, but these are all steady voices which take to recording well, and it is good to have so ravishingly beautiful a voice as Jessye Norman's for the Countess. The Figaro of Wladimiro Ganzarolli and the Count of Ingvar Wixell project with exceptional clarity and vigour, and there is fine singing too from Yvonne Minton as Cherubino, Clifford Grant as Bartolo and Robert Tear as Basilio.

The recording, though not so clean and precisely focused as Kleiber's outstanding Decca set (it has more reverberation than many will like for this opera), is commendably atmospheric and offers much the most congenial sound of the three Davis recordings of Mozart operas which Philips have reissued as volumes 8 10 of their Mozart Edition. The ensembles have fine presence, and the stereo detail remains clear, the resonance not causing blurring. Figaro's voice seems to have its upper partials slightly over-balanced at times, but generally the balance is natural. As in the Decca set each act is complete on one of the four cassette sides, and the gain in the second act is no less striking here. The libretto has the small print characteristic of the series but is readable.

Boehm's DG version of *Figaro* gives a complete text, with Marcellina's and Basilio's Act 4 arias included. (Kleiber rivals him in that completeness, though his Susanna has to sing the Barbarina number.) In many ways Boehm's is the most consistently assured performance. The women all sing beautifully, with Janowitz's Countess, Mathis's Susanna and Troyanos's Cherubino all ravishing the ear in contrasted ways. Prey is an intelligent if not very jolly-sounding Figaro, and Fischer-Dieskau gives his dark, sharply defined reading of the Count's role. All told, a great success, with fine playing and recording. But at medium price Kleiber and Davis offer versions with at least equal merit, and the DG transfer has been made at rather a low level, at times lacking something in body. But with the level up there is plenty of detail and presence, for the overall quality is characteristically smooth and the vocal colour is pleasingly natural.

Le Nozze di Figaro: highlights.
(M) *** Decca KCSP 514. Lisa

della Casa, Roberta Peters, Rosalind Elias, George London, Giorgio Tozzi, Vienna State Opera Chorus, Vienna PO, Leinsdorf.

This excellent and thoroughly enjoyable sampler reminds us of the many qualities of Leinsdorf's *Figaro* recording. The selection is generous (52 minutes); it is subtitled 'Scenes and arias', and thus makes no attempt to provide a potted opera, which is impossible with a work so teeming with highlights. It rightly concentrates on the contributions of the ladies, who stand out in a generally good cast, Roberta Peters a sparkling Susanna, and Lisa della Casa characteristically fine as the Countess. Their famous *Letter duet* (*Cosa mi narri?*) shows how delightfully the voices match, but the beauty of Della Casa's *Porgi amor* and *Dove sono* are matched by Susanna's charming *Deh vieni*, while Rosalind Elias as Cherubino provides a no less memorable *Voi che sapete*. But there are fourteen numbers here and they give an excellent sampler of the fresh, alert qualities of the performance as a whole. The recording needs some smoothing of the treble (the transfer does not disguise the slightly dated string tone) but is then excellent, with plenty of atmosphere and bloom on the voices.

Die Zauberflöte (*The Magic Flute*): complete.
*** DG 3371 002 [id.]. Evelyn Lear, Roberta Peters, Lisa Otto, Fritz Wunderlich, Dietrich Fischer-Dieskau, Hans Hotter, Franz Crass, Berlin RIAS Chamber Choir, Berlin PO, Boehm.
**(*) Decca K 2 A 4. Pilar Lorengar, Cristina Deutekom, Stuart Burrows, Dietrich Fischer-Dieskau, Hermann Prey, Martti Talvela, Vienna State

Opera Chorus, Vienna PO, Solti.

One of the glories of Boehm's DG set is the singing of Fritz Wunderlich as Tamino, a wonderful memorial to a singer much missed. Passages that normally seem merely incidental come alive thanks to his beautiful, intense singing. Fischer-Dieskau, with characteristic word-pointing, makes a sparkling Papageno on record (he is too big of frame, he says, to do the role on stage) and Franz Crass is a satisfyingly straightforward Sarastro. The team of women is well below this standard – Lear taxed cruelly in *Ach, ich fühl's*, Peters shrill in the upper register (although the effect is exciting), and the Three Ladies do not blend well – but the direction of Boehm is superb, light and lyrical, but weighty where necessary to make a glowing, compelling experience. For a long time this set (one of DG's first operas issued on tape) was available only in non-Dolby form, but as we go to press Dolbyized sets have become available. The very wide amplitude and dynamic range of the recording have offered some transfer problems. The level might seem low at first (the overture lacks something in projection), but the transfer has needed to leave a margin for the dynamic peaks of the recording – the chorus at the end of Act 2, for instance, or the Queen of the Night's most famous aria. The quality is a little uneven, though generally sophisticated. The ladies' voices sometimes give a hint of peaking, but this is not serious, and generally the sound is clean and natural, while the balance with the orchestra is excellent. The libretto is readable but far from ideal: this is a problem DG have not solved.

If one is looking for Mozartian charm in this most monumental of Mozart's operas, then plainly Solti's reading must be rejected. It is tough, strong and brilliant, and it is arguable that in this opera those are the required qualities above all; but even so the absence of charm has a

cumulative effect. The drama may be consistently vital, but ultimately the full variety of Mozart's inspiration is not achieved. On the male side the cast is very strong indeed, with Stuart Burrows assuming his international mantle easily with stylish and rich-toned singing. Martti Talvela and Fischer-Dieskau as Sarastro and the Speaker respectively provide a stronger contrast than usual, each superb in his way, and Hermann Prey rounds out the character of Papageno with intelligent pointing of words. The cast of women is less consistent. Pilar Lorengar's Pamina is sweetly attractive as long as your ear is not worried by her obtrusive *vibrato*, while Cristina Deutekom's Queen of the Night is technically impressive, though marred by a curious warbling quality in the coloratura, almost like an intrusive 'w' where you sometimes have the intrusive 'h'. The Three Ladies make a strong team (Yvonne Minton in the middle), and it was a good idea to give the parts of the Three Boys to genuine trebles. Fine recording quality, and a good transfer.

Die Zauberflöte: highlights.
> ** DG 922014 [id.] (from above set cond. Boehm).
> ** Decca KCET 527 (from above set cond. Solti).

The selection from the DG *Zauberflöte* is a generous one but obviously not directed towards bringing out the special qualities of Boehm's performance. Much of the least impressive singing with the Three Ladies, Pamina and the Queen of Night gets chosen; conversely one would like more of Wunderlich's Tamino, the great glory of the set. Including the overture in such a tape also seems a waste. The Solti highlights tape makes a fair sampler for those who want to try his strong Mozartian approach but not to invest in the complete set.

OPERA RECITAL

Arias: *Don Giovanni: One moment
. . . Pray allow me. The Magic Flute:
O hear us, Isis and Osiris!; We know
no thought of vengeance. The Marriage of Figaro: Now for vengeance.
The Seraglio; When a maiden takes
your fancy; Ha! my pretty brace of
fellows. Zäide: The hungry man who
dines in state.*

> (M) ** HMV Greensleeve TC-ESD
> 7059. Owen Brannigan (bass),
> Philomusica of London, Farn-
> combe – HANDEL: *Arias.***

In Mozart – rarely sung in English in
the recording studio – one's reservations
about Brannigan's style seem less important than in Handel. Here is a singer
whose whole being comes alive in everything he sings: this is not an ideal memorial but it is one to cherish. The transfers
are of excellent quality, the voice given a
vivid presence.

COLLECTIONS

'Favourite composer': (i; ii) *Clarinet
concerto in A major, K.622;* (iii)
*Piano concerto No. 21 in C major,
K.467;* (iv) *German dance, K.605/3:
Sleighride;* (ii; v) Overture: *Le Nozze
di Figaro;* (ii; vi) *Serenade No. 13 in G
major (Eine kleine Nachtmusik),
K.525;* (vii) *Symphony No. 40 in G
minor, K.550.*

> (B) **(*) Decca KDPC 541/2. (i)
> Alfred Prinz (clarinet), Münch-
> inger; (ii) Vienna PO; (iii) Ilana
> Vered (piano), LPO, Segal; (iv)
> Vienna Mozart Ens., Boskov-
> sky; (v) Erich Kleiber; (vii) New
> Philharmonia Orch., Giulini.

These are in general recommendable
performances, although Giulini's account of the *G minor Symphony* is not one

of his finest recordings. But with excellent
sound this would make a good start for
any Mozart collection. Excellent transfers too: the only recording which sounds
a little dated is Kleiber's *Marriage of
Figaro overture*, which is a bit fierce.
Apart from this, the quality has plenty of
warmth, body and life; *Eine kleine Nachtmusik* is especially vivid.

'An hour with Mozart': (i) *Adagio
and fugue in C minor, K. 546;* (ii)
*Piano concerto No. 23 in A major,
K.488:* finale; (iii–v) *Piano concerto
No. 25 in C major, K.503:* 1st movt;
(vi) *Violin concerto No. 4 in D major,
K.218: Andante;* (i) *Serenade No. 13
in G major (Eine kleine Nachtmusik),
K.525: Rondo;* (iv; vii) *Symphony
No. 40 in G minor, K.550:* 1st movt;
(iii) *Piano sonata No. 11 in A major,
K.331:* finale *(Alla turca); Le Nozze
di Figaro:* (viii; vii) *Overture;* (vii–ix)
Voi che sapete.

> (M) ** Philips 7431 111. (i) I
> Musici; (ii) Alfred Brendel
> (piano), Academy of St Martin-
> in-the-Fields, Marriner; (iii)
> Ingrid Haebler (piano); (iv)
> LSO; (v) Galliera; (vi) Michèle
> Auclair (violin), Stuttgart PO,
> Couraud; (vii) Colin Davis;
> (viii) BBC SO; (ix) Elly Amel-
> ing (soprano).

With only one vocal contribution,
albeit a charming one, this is primarily an
orchestral collection, and it is not as imaginatively chosen as the HMV or Decca
tapes, although there is a somewhat
longer playing time. The inclusion of the
Adagio and fugue was a curious choice
(and the performance is rather static), but
taken as a whole the programme is suitably diverse and quite well balanced,
and generally this selection makes agreeable listening. The transfers are of good
quality until the closing item, the excerpt
from the *A major Piano concerto*, which

for some reason is thick-textured and muffled. This tape was issued as a kind of bargain sampler to go with the Philips series of Mozart boxes.

'A Mozart Prom': Overture: *Le Nozze di Figaro.* (i) *Horn concerto No. 4 in E flat major, K.495. Symphony No. 40 in G minor, K.550.*
  (M) ** Decca KCSP 522. RPO, Foster, (i) with Alan Civil (horn).

While this is a highly agreeable concert one is not sure whether this kind of arrangement is ideal for a collector, as it inevitably cuts across other couplings. But it would perhaps be an acceptable gift for someone whose collection only occupies the fringe areas of classical music. The performance of the overture is alert and spirited and Alan Civil is on top form in the concerto. The symphony is given a warmly spontaneous reading, not really distinguished but quite eloquent and well played. The transfer is of excellent Decca quality, rich and detailed, although the bass in the symphony is over-resonant and needs controlling.

'The world of Mozart': (i) *Clarinet concerto in A major, K.622:* 2nd movt; (ii) *Horn concerto No. 4 in E flat major, K.495:* finale; (iii) *Piano concerto No. 20 in D minor, K.466:* 2nd movt; (iv) *German dance, K.605/3: Sleighride; Serenade No. 13 in G major (Eine kleine Nachtmusik), K.525:* 1st movt; (v) *Symphony No. 40 in G minor, K.550:* 1st movt; (vi) *Piano sonata No. 11 in A major, K.331:* finale *(Alla Turca);* (vii) *Ave verum corpus, K.618;* (viii) *Exsultate jubilate, K.165: Alleluia;* (ix) *Così fan tutte: Soave sia il vento* (trio); (x) *Don Giovanni: Deh vieni alla finestra* (serenade); (xi) *Le Nozze di Figaro: Voi che sapete;* (xii) *Die Zauberflöte: Der Vogelfanger.*

(M) *** Decca KCSP 251. (i) Gervase de Peyer (clarinet), (ii) Barry Tuckwell (horn), both with LSO, Maag; (iii) Julius Katchen (piano), Stuttgart CO, Münchinger; (iv) Vienna Mozart Ens., Boskovsky; (v) New Philharmonia Orch., Giulini; (vi) Wilhelm Backhaus (piano); (vii) Choir of St John's College, Cambridge; (viii) Erna Spoorenberg (soprano); (ix) Lucia Popp (soprano), Brigitte Fassbaender (contralto), Tom Krause (bass), Vienna Opera Orch., Kertesz; (x) Gabriel Bacquier (bar.); (xi) Teresa Berganza (mezzo-soprano); (xii) Geraint Evans (bar.) (with orch.).

A really outstanding collection, brilliantly compiled so that each excerpt makes the right kind of contrast with what has gone before. The performances are all of high quality and this should tempt many to explore further, while for the confirmed Mozartian it makes a glorious concert of favourites. Highly recommended, although the quality of the tape transfer is just a little variable.

'Your kind of Mozart': (i) *Horn concerto No. 4 in E flat major, K. 495:* finale; (ii) *Piano concerto No. 21 in C major, K.467: Andante;* (iii) *German dance, K.605/3: Sleighride;* (ii) *Serenade No. 13 in G major (Eine kleine Nachtmusik), K.525: Rondo;* (iv) *Sinfonia concertante for violin and viola in E flat major, K.364:* 3rd movt; (ii) *Symphony No. 40 in G minor, K.550:* 1st movt; (iii; v) *Ave verum corpus, K.618;* (vi) *Exsultate jubilate, K.165: Alleluia;* (vii) *Così fan tutte: Soave sia il vento* (trio); *Don Giovanni:* (viii–x) *Là ci darem*

la mano; (ix; x) *Champagne aria;* (x; xi) *Le Nozze di Figaro: Non più andrai.*

(M) *** HMV TC-EXES 5002. (i) Barry Tuckwell (horn), Academy of St Martin-in-the-Fields, Marriner; (ii) Daniel Barenboim, ECO; (iii) Berlin PO, Karajan; (iv) Norbert Brainin (violin), Peter Schidlof (viola), Netherlands CO, Zinman; (v) Vienna Singverein; (vi) Lucia Popp (soprano), ECO, Fischer; (vii) Elisabeth Schwarzkopf, Walter Berry, Christa Ludwig, Philharmonia Orch., Boehm; (viii) Graziella Sciutti (soprano); (ix) Eberhard Waechter (bar.); (x) Philharmonia Orch., Giulini; (xi) Giuseppe Taddei (bar.).

Mozart is a composer whose every individual movement is so perfect in itself that it readily stands alone. Such a collection as this (as Decca have already shown with their *World of Mozart* tape) cannot fail, and if anything this HMV anthology is even more winning than the Decca one. Its special strength lies in the vocal performances. Lucia Popp gives a ravishing account of the *Alleluia,* and the excerpts from *Così fan tutte* and *Don Giovanni* show the peerless excellence of the sets from which they are taken. Barenboim directs a fine performance of the first movement of the *G minor Symphony* (the complete recording is only available in non-Dolby form), and he is equally sympathetic in the excerpt from Mozart's *Night music.* But for many the richly romantic account of the famous slow movement from the *'Elvira Madigan Piano concerto'* (a little out of period but not essentially unstylish) will be very much a highlight. The concert ends with Barry Tuckwell's bright-eyed *Rondo,* where his perkiness recalls Dennis Brain. The transfers are generally good throughout,

though not ultra-brilliant (side one is improved by a slight bass cut). An especially enjoyable collection for use in the car.

Mussorgsky, Modest (1839–81)

Night on the Bare Mountain (original version).

(M) *** Philips 7317 032. LPO, Lloyd-Jones – Concert.***

Night on the Bare Mountain (arr. Rimsky-Korsakov).

*** DG 3336 379 [id.]. Chicago SO, Barenboim – BORODIN: *Polovtsian dances*; RIMSKY-KORSAKOV: *Capriccio espagnol* etc.**(*)

(B) ** DG Heliodor 3348 267. Berlin PO, Maazel – RESPIGHI: *Pines of Rome***; RIMSKY-KORSAKOV: *Capriccio espagnol.***(*)

(B) ** DG Heliodor 3348 267. Maazel (as above) – DVOŘÁK: *Cello concerto.**(*)

(B) *(*) Decca KDPC 2 7055. Suisse Romande Orch., Ansermet – BORODIN: *In the Steppes* etc.**; RIMSKY-KORSAKOV: *Scheherazade* etc.***

Night on the Bare Mountain; Khovantschina: Prelude.

*** Decca KSXC 6263. LSO, Solti – Concert.***

Night on the Bare Mountain; Khovantschina: Prelude; Dance of the Persian slaves.

(M) *** Decca KCSP 257. Berlin PO, Solti – Concert.***

Mussorgsky wrote his *Night on the Bare Mountain* in 1867 but never heard it played. The piece we know, although it uses some of Mussorgsky's basic material, is much more the work of Rimsky-Korsakov, who added much music of his own, including the contrasting lyrical section at the end. The original has undoubted power and fascination, but its construction is a good deal less polished, and there are few who would argue that Rimsky's piece is not more telling and vividly dramatic, even if it is so little like the original. But David Lloyd-Jones's performance is first-class and Mussorgsky's own score is well worth having when so vividly played and recorded. The transfer too is first-class, and this attractive anthology is one of Philips' best medium-priced tapes. It is discussed more fully in our Concerts section.

Turning now to performances of the Rimsky-Korsakov arrangement, there is a clear first choice on cassette. Solti's LSO performance has tremendous electricity, and the sound of the tape transfer is superb, with impressive weight and detail. This is part of an equally recommendable concert of Russian music. Surprisingly the second choice is also conducted by Solti, this time using the Berlin Philharmonic Orchestra. Once again the collection includes also the beautiful *Khovantschina Prelude*, and it adds the *Persian dance* for good measure. The performance of the *Prelude* is particularly atmospheric, and this tape has the advantage of economy. The sound is excellent.

Barenboim's account of *Night on the Bare Mountain* is also a powerful one, vividly and weightily recorded. The transfer is of excellent quality, well balanced and with good presence. By its side the much older Maazel version, which dates from the earliest days of stereo, is less richly expansive as sound; the main interest of this tape is the couplings by Rimsky-Korsakov and (especially) Respighi. This performance is also available coupled to Dvořák's *Cello concerto*, but the transfer here has less body and range.

Ansermet's performance is straightforward and quite strong. The wide-ranging recording is impressive generally, but the transfer is a little spoiled by an over-recorded bass drum which disturbs the texture once or twice.

Night on the Bare Mountain; Pictures at an Exhibition (orch. Ravel).
  (M) **(*) Turnabout KTVC 34633. St Louis SO, Slatkin.
  (M) ** RCA Gold Seal GK 42702. Chicago SO, Ozawa.

The quality of the Turnabout recording of *Pictures at an Exhibition*, on cassette as on disc, is remarkably fine, often approaching demonstration standard. The acoustic is spacious, the detail clear, and the *Great gate of Kiev* has both majesty and a feeling of spectacle. The performance offers orchestral playing of excellent quality, even if the characterization is less sharply defined than with Karajan. *Night on the Bare Mountain* has plenty of colour and impact, and on tape seems also to have more weight and power than on disc. In the *Pictures* there are no transfer problems with the climax of the *Great gate of Kiev*.

Above all Ozawa shows his feeling for orchestral colour in his undoubtedly successful version of *Pictures at an Exhibition*. Moreover the orchestra is on top form; yet the virtuosity is always put to the service of the music's pictorialism and atmosphere. Ozawa does not force the pace or make unnecessary underlining; he lets the work unfold naturally, though with excellent incidental detail. The coupling is strikingly vivid, with plenty of electricity, and the recording is full and atmospheric, lacking only the last degree of clarity. The transfer, however, because of the resonance, lacks transient crispness at climaxes, and the *Great gate of Kiev* is not as cleanly focused as in the best competing versions on tape. There are no comparable problems in *Night on the Bare Mountain*, where the outline is clean and secure.

Pictures at an Exhibition (orch. Ravel).

⊛ *** H M V TC-ASD 3645. Philadelphia Orch., Muti – STRAVINSKY‡ *Firebird suite.****

*** DG 923018 [id.]. Berlin PO, Karajan – RAVEL: *Boléro.*** (*)

*** DG 3300 783 [id.]. Chicago SO, Giulini – PROKOFIEV: *Symphony No. 1.****

(*) Decca Phase 4 KPFC 4255 [Lon. 5-21079]. New Philharmonia Orch., Maazel – PROKOFIEV: *Piano concerto No. 3.*(*)

Muti's riveting new version of *Pictures at an Exhibition* is the first recording to do full justice to the Philadelphia sound. Here is a far richer and full-blooded quality than has been previously captured on disc or tape. The lower strings in *Samuel Goldenberg* have extraordinary body and presence, and *Baba-Yaga* has an unsurpassed virtuosity and attack as well as being of demonstration standard as a recording. The glorious orchestral tone, the richly glowing colours, the sheer homogeneity of the strings and perfection of ensemble are a consistent source of pleasure. Muti's reading is second to none, and the orchestral playing is altogether breathtaking. Any comparison is only with the finest of partnerships on record (Toscanini and the NBC, Koussevitzky and the Boston Symphony, Karajan and the Berlin Philharmonic), and, given the excellent recorded sound and well-managed transfer – the tape only marginally less clean than the LP – this more than holds its own with previous versions. The coupling is no less thrilling.

Karajan's version, like so many of his best issues, makes one feel that he has re-thought the score. One fascinating feature of his reading is that the *Promenades* are often slower than usual, suggesting that the 'visitor to the exhibition' is taking a more leisurely stroll between the exhibits. It is the remarkable sophistication of the orchestral playing that makes this issue so distinguished. The brass in particular are superb, and especially so in the famous *Catacombs* sequence, where the aural sonority has a unique majesty. The lightly pointed tuba-playing in *The hut on fowl's legs* is a delicious example of the subtlety of this performance, which is again shown in the restraint of *The old castle*. Even though this was an early issue the DG transfer is strikingly successful, and the range and clarity of the sound are impressive, especially in the final climax.

It is fascinating that Giulini's equally successful account should use the Chicago orchestra, thus repeating Reiner's success of the early days of stereo. The modern recording, however, is noticeably more refined and detailed, with brilliant percussive effects (a superb bass drum in *The hut on fowl's legs*). With superlative orchestral playing and strong characterization this is highly recommendable, and the transfer is generally of excellent quality. There is no difficulty in encompassing the final climax of the *Great gate of Kiev*. The recording's transients, however, are not always absolutely clean, so that some of the percussive effects are not as sharply focused as they might be (the side-drum snares are not absolutely crisp).

Though the characterization is less subtle than in the best rival versions, Maazel's is an immensely vivid reading. The coupling is attractive, the recording is good, and the cassette transfer is strikingly brilliant and clearly focused, if lacking the last degree of warmth.

Pictures at an Exhibition (arr. for brass ensemble by Elgar Howarth).

*** Argo KZRC 885. Philip Jones Brass Ens., Howarth.

There is no reason why Mussorgsky's famous piano work should not be transcribed for brass as effectively as for a full symphony orchestra, and Elgar

Howarth's inspired arrangement fully justifies the experiment. There is never any feeling of limited colour; indeed the pictures of the unhatched chicks and the market place at Limoges have great pictorial vividness, and the evocation of the dead has an almost cinematic element of fantasy. The final *Great gate of Kiev* is as thrilling here as in any orchestral recording, and elsewhere the deep brass effects are superbly sonorous. The disc version has already acquired 'collector' status as a demonstration record, and the tape transfer is hardly less impressive. Made at the highest level, it lacks nothing in depth and immediacy and is only marginally less open than the marvellous disc. Either will give great satisfaction.

Pictures at an Exhibition: (i) orch. Ravel; (ii) original piano version.
> **(*)** Decca KSXC 6328 [Lon. 5-6559]. (i) Los Angeles PO, Mehta; (ii) Vladimir Ashkenazy.
> (M) *(*) HMV TC-SXLP 30233. (i) Philharmonia Orch., Maazel; (ii) Gina Bachauer.

Pictures at an Exhibition (original piano version).
> *** DG 3301 096 [id.]. Lazar Berman – SHOSTAKOVICH: *Preludes.******
> **(*)** Decca KSXC 6840. Vladimir Ashkenazy – TCHAIKOVSKY: *Piano concerto No. 1.******
> (M) ** DG Privilege 3335 272 [id.]. Rudolf Firkusny – RACHMANINOV: *Preludes.***(*)

The original piano version of *Pictures at an Exhibition* and Ravel's orchestration make an obvious coupling, and if Mehta's performance is less imaginative than the best rivals, the Decca recording is quite vivid, warm and atmospheric. It is well transferred to tape, though this is not one of Decca's very best issues. Ashkenazy's account of the original piano

score is distinguished by poetic feeling, but lacks something of the extrovert flair with which pianists like Richter or Berman can make one forget all about the orchestral transcription. Decca have also recoupled Ashkenazy's piano version with the Tchaikovsky *B flat minor Piano concerto* and have taken the opportunity to improve the sound still further. If this coupling is attractive, the tape cannot be faulted on technical grounds.

By comparison the HMV issue is distinctly second-best. Maazel's performance is brilliant in the extreme and offers superb orchestral virtuosity from the Philharmonia in peak form. But the characterization is not notable for subtlety; the conductor obviously regards the work as an orchestral showpiece. Also Gina Bachauer, although she plays gamely (and weightily), has neither the technical command nor the sensibility of Berman or Ashkenazy. The piano recording is rather dated, but the orchestral recording is brilliant.

Lazar Berman opens his account of the original piano version with an uncompromisingly fast pacing of the *Promenade*. One can picture him striding round the exhibition brusquely, hands behind his back, only stopping to admire those pictures which take his fancy. The ox-wagon (*Bydlo*) certainly does, and undoubtedly *Catacombs* and *Cum mortuis* make a very direct communication, for the playing here has arresting power and atmosphere. On the other hand the *Ballet of the unhatched chicks* finds him more concerned with articulation (the playing is superb) than evocation. The *Great gate of Kiev* makes a riveting (if not overwhelming) climax, and with splendid sound this is undoubtedly the most compelling account of the work to have been recorded in recent years. The coupling too is first-rate and the transfer is of DG's finest quality: the piano tone is completely natural, with splendid resonance and depth.

At medium price, Firkusny's account

deserves to be considered. The playing is spontaneous, and the music sounds fresh and well characterized, even if there is some lack of extrovert bravura at the end. The piano tone on tape is firm and realistic, lacking something in brilliance, but well balanced.

Boris Godunov (opera; original version): complete.

**(*) HMV TC-SLS 1000 [Angel 4x4x 3844]. Martti Talvela, Bożena Kinasz, Bohdan Paprocki, Nicolai Gedda, Leonard Mróz, Andrzej Hiolski, Aage Haugland, Cracow Philharmonic Boys' Chorus, Polish Radio Chorus, Polish Radio National SO, Semkow.

Boris Godunov (arr. Rimsky-Korsakov and Ippolitov-Ivanov): complete.

⊛ *** Decca K 81 K 43. Nicolai Ghiaurov, Galina Vishnevskaya, Aleksei Maslennikov, Ludovico Spiess, Martti Talvela, Zoltan Kelemen, Anton Diakov, Vienna Boys' Choir, Sofia Radio Chorus, Vienna State Opera Chorus, Vienna PO, Karajan.

The Decca set marks one of this company's finest achievements in the tape field. Its success comes nearer than previous recordings to conveying the rugged greatness of Mussorgsky's masterpiece, partly because of the superb control of Karajan, partly because of the outstanding sound quality, incomparably more vivid than other versions. The depth, clarity and resonance of the big choral scenes of the Prologue and Act 4 are truly astonishing, while the recording's perspectives of distance are most convincing. If Ghiaurov in the title role lacks some of the dramatic intensity of Christoff, he is more accurate in singing the notes rather than indulging in evocative sing-speech.

Not everyone will like the baritonal tinge that results, but ultimately this is exceedingly satisfying for repeated hearings, especially when the tape transfer has caught the voice so beautifully, with natural colour and great presence. Indeed all the solo voices here are admirably natural, and the rich colours of Rimsky-Korsakov's orchestration are glowingly presented. That Karajan – as in his Salzburg performances, on which this is based – opted for the Rimsky-Korsakov version is disappointing for collectors who prefer the darker, earthier original, but this version matches Karajan's qualities. Only the coronation scene lacks something of the weight and momentum one ideally wants. For the rest the chorus is finely intense. The only serious disappointment vocally is the Marina of Vishnevskaya, too squally for Western ears. The opera is well laid out on three cassettes (in place of four discs), with the Prologue and Act 1, Scene 1, on side one; Act 1, Scene 2, on side two; Act 2 on side three; Act 3 beginning on side four and concluding on side five, which then continues with the opening of Act 4, this act terminating on side six. The booklet with libretto is admirably compiled and clearly printed.

It is sad that Semkow's version, the first-ever complete recording of Mussorgsky's original score, lacks the sort of rugged, intense qualities which are essential if this balder, less colourful edition of the opera is to make its full impact. The recording balance is partly at fault, for the relative closeness of sound works against any feeling of grandeur, with the orchestra somewhat distanced behind the voices. The result is lacking in weight and atmosphere, though the performance still boasts some distinguished singing, not least from the excellent Polish Radio Chorus. Martti Talvela sings most beautifully, making the role of the Tsar more lyrical than usual, and the firm darkness of tone is most impressive. Otherwise a good, generally reliable set, which remains somewhat uninspired by the measured direction of Semkow. The transfer is of excellent quality, but lacks the sense of spectacle of the Decca set.

Nicolai, Otto
(1810–49)

Die lustigen Weiber von Windsor (*The Merry Wives of Windsor;* opera): complete.
*** DG 3371 026 [id.]. Helen Donath, Kurt Moll, Edith Mathis, Hanna Schwarz, Bernd Weikl, Peter Schreier, Siegfried Vogel, German State Opera Chorus, Berlin State Orch., Klee.
*** Decca κ 86 κ 33 [Lon. 5-13127]. Helen Donath, Karl Ridderbusch, Trudeliese Schmidt, Wolfgang Brendel, Alexander Malta, Claes Haaken Ahnsjö, Bavarian Radio Chorus and SO, Kubelik.

Bernhard Klee directs a scintillating performance in which the comedy lifts off from the moment the first number starts. It would be hard to assemble a cast better than this, with Kurt Moll a gloriously firm-toned Falstaff, and no weak link at all. The patter passages are delectably done, and Nicolai's tenderness is beautifully caught too. As an opera this may not have the brilliant insight of Verdi or all the atmosphere of Vaughan Williams, but it has its own brand of effervescence which is equally endearing in a performance such as this. The German dialogue has been tailored to length, but the device of having a chuckling waiter from the Garter Inn to provide necessary links is not always successful. For some reason the first of the three DG tapes is transferred at a strikingly lower level (on both sides) than the remaining two. The sound

is notable throughout for its crisp, sparkling detail and presence, but undoubtedly Act 1 sounds marginally less effective than the rest of the set, and to get full impact in the overture one has to accept a little hiss. The libretto is readable, better than some DG booklets but not ideal.

Kubelik's performance may not have quite the dramatic ebullience which makes the DG recording so exhilarating an experience, but in many ways his extra subtlety brings more perceptive results – in the entry of Falstaff in Act 1, for example, where Kubelik conveys the tongue-in-cheek quality of Nicolai's *pomposo* writing and Klee takes it seriously. In quality of singing there is little to choose between this cast and the outstanding one on DG, though Ridderbusch as Falstaff is straighter and nobler, Moll on DG more sparkling. The dialogue here is more crisply edited, without the device of the Garter Inn waiter. The Decca recording is rather more resonant and warmer in acoustic than the DG. The focus is marginally less clean at times, although Act 3 sounds especially vivid. The Decca acoustic, however, undoubtedly has more atmosphere, and another point in favour of the Decca set is the beautifully produced libretto, which is much easier to read and use than the DG booklet.

Nielsen, Carl
(1865–1931)

(i) *Symphony No. 2* (*The Four Temperaments*), *Op. 16; Little suite for string orchestra, Op. 1;* (ii) *Serenata in vano.*
(м) (**) Turnabout κτvc 34049. (i) Tivoli Concert SO, Garaguly; (ii) Nielsen Quintet.

The *Second Symphony* is one of Nielsen's most attractive works; compact in

401

layout, direct in utterance, it is an admirable example of his early style at its very best. It first made its appearance on record in the late forties on Danish 78s conducted by the late Thomas Jensen, and this has never been surpassed since. The Garaguly performance is brisk but has plenty of fire and attack. It has not the breadth or majesty of Jensen's 78s and the second movement is too fast. The recording is not ideal, rather dry in the bass and with a tendency to shrillness in the treble, but for all that the tape is fairly enjoyable and the reading as a whole has a certain dignity. The *Little suite* is an enchanting piece and an incredibly assured work for so young a composer. The recording is good though a little lacking in warmth. Garaguly, a Hungarian, has a distinct feeling for this music – sympathies no doubt fostered by his long residence in Scandinavia. The *Serenata in vano* is a slight work, not the best Nielsen by any means, but enjoyable nonetheless. It receives a thoroughly idiomatic reading here. On tape the sound in both the symphony and the *Little suite* is unattractively dry and lacking in body. There is no actual distortion, but the quality is fierce under pressure. The *Serenata* fares better, and has more warmth and substance.

Symphony No. 5, Op. 50; Helios overture, Op. 17.
*(*) RCA RK 25148. Scottish National Orch., Gibson.

Symphony No. 5; En Sagadroøm, Op. 39.
*(**) Advent D 1005 (see p. xxiii) [id.]. New Philharmonia Orch., Horenstein.

Horenstein gives a dignified but slightly detached account of the *Fifth*. His feeling for the overall structure of the work is strong, but poetic detail is not always savoured to the full. This version restores Nielsen's original text and omits some of the accretions to be found in earlier performances; and the string-playing of the New Philharmonia is extremely fine, though sometimes the last degree of lyric fervour is missing. The balance in the symphony gives far too great a prominence to the percussion, and this brings problems with the tape transfer at the climax of the first movement, which is confused, while later the timpani bring a moment of overloading. Not quite enough weight is given to the massed violins, but the range of the chrome transfer brings excellent *pianissimo* string detail. *En Sagadroøm*, which is poetically done, is beautifully recorded and well transferred, but the patches of roughness in the main work prevent this from being one of Advent's most recommendable issues, even though all the music is presented complete on side one of the tape.

On RCA a likeable performance of the *Fifth Symphony* brings some idiomatic orchestral playing from Gibson and the Scottish National Orchestra. The approach is fresh and enthusiastic, and the music unfolds organically and naturally. One bar before figure 3 in the first movement there is a B flat instead of a natural, which will worry many collectors on repetition; but this is a small blemish to put in the balance sheet against some imaginative and committed playing. There is a poetic and eloquent account of the *Helios overture* as a fill-up. The recording is well balanced, though just a little lacking in transparency. The tape transfer is not without bloom and atmosphere, but the quality harshens in the climaxes.

Offenbach, Jacques (1819–80)

Gaîté Parisienne (ballet music, arr. Rosenthal): complete; *La Fille du tambour-major:* overture.

** HMV TC-ASD 3311 [Angel 4xs 37209]. Monte Carlo Opera Orch., Rosenthal.

Manuel Rosenthal's account of *Gaîté Parisienne* is absolutely complete, and this issue has the added fascination (provided by the notes) of giving the sources for all the music in the score. The performance itself, however, has not the verve and glamour of those by Paul Strauss and Karajan (see below). The music is presented with warmth and well played, but the lack of bubbling effervescence is often apparent. The overture is an attractive bonus, and Rosenthal directs this with rather more élan than his own score. The reverberant recording is not quite as clean on the tape as on the equivalent disc: the ear senses a marginal lack of refinement on tape, although the overall quality is pleasing and does not lack brilliance.

Gaîté Parisienne (ballet music, arr. Rosenthal): extended excerpts.
(B) *** DG Heliodor 3348 248. Berlin Radio Orch., Paul Strauss – J. STRAUSS: *Beau Danube*.***
(M) *** HMV TC-SXLP 30224. Philharmonia Orch., Karajan – GOUNOD: *Faust ballet* **(*); WALDTEUFEL: *Les Patineurs*.⊛ ***
** DG 3300 215 [id.]. Berlin PO, Karajan – GOUNOD: *Faust ballet*.**
(M) ** Decca Jubilee KJBC 12 [Lon. 5-6780]. Orch. of the Royal Opera House, Covent Garden, Solti – GOUNOD: *Faust ballet*.**

Paul Strauss's account is irresistibly vivacious. Try the exuberant opening brass fanfares to sample the sheer vitality. There is sparkle from beginning to end, and the score's lyrical moments are played with panache: the *Barcarolle*, for instance, is beautifully done. The recording, which dates from the earliest days of stereo (when the performance was first issued on two sides of a ten-inch disc), is, astonishingly, still demonstration-worthy with its colour and brilliantly managed resonant (but not too resonant) acoustic. The cassette is of the same high quality as the LP; they are virtually indistinguishable.

Karajan's Philharmonia recording dates from the late fifties, but it too does not show its age. The quality is a little dry (and the piccolo sometimes adds a hint of edge to the texture), but it matches the witty, polished playing – the Philharmonia on top form and obviously enjoying their unforced bravura. The transfer is sparkling, with no lack of weight. Indeed the quality often approaches demonstration standard.

Karajan's DG selection is brilliantly played and vividly recorded. It lacks something in charm but nothing in boisterousness. The tape transfer is full-blooded and there is a rather intrusive bass drum (often a problem on an older recording). On the whole the earlier Philharmonia version is to be preferred.

Solti drives *Gaîté Parisienne* hard and misses the essential geniality of the music. The orchestra gives a virtuoso performance and their bravura is certainly infectious (even if sometimes a little breathless). The sound is both brilliant and sumptuous and Decca have managed to transfer the wide reverberation and amplitude to cassette with remarkable aplomb.

Overtures: *Barbe-Bleue; La Belle Hélène; La Grande-Duchesse de Gérolstein; Orpheus in the Underworld; La Vie Parisienne.*
(M)(**) HMV Greensleeve TC-ESD 7034. City of Birmingham SO, Frémaux.

Vividly recorded, the performances on this reissue are enjoyable enough, with good orchestral playing throughout. But although the music-making is lively there is a lack of subtlety and wit. One has only to listen to the introduction of the waltz in *La Belle Hélène* to realize that just a touch more delicacy would have given the tune much more lift. The best performance here is *La Vie Parisienne*; the famous *Orpheus in the Underworld*, comparatively robust, is enjoyably vigorous. The transfer to tape is not very well managed. There is a general lack of refinement, and the side-drum is poorly focused, indicating that the transients are blurred.

Le Papillon (ballet-pantomime): complete.
*** Decca KSXC 6588. LSO, Bonynge.

Le Papillon is Offenbach's only full-length ballet and it dates from 1860. The quality of the invention is high, the music sparkles from beginning to end, and in such a sympathetic performance, vividly recorded, it cannot fail to give pleasure. Highly recommended to all lovers of ballet and Offenbach. The tape transfer is of properly brilliant quality.

Les Contes d'Hoffmann (*The Tales of Hoffmann*; opera): complete.
⊛ *** Decca K 109 K 32. Joan Sutherland, Placido Domingo, Huguette Tourangeau, Gabriel Bacquier, Radio Suisse Romande and Lausanne Pro Arte Choruses, Suisse Romande Orch., Bonynge.

Joan Sutherland gives a virtuoso performance in four heroine roles here, not only as Olympia, Giulietta and Antonia but as Stella in the Epilogue. Bonynge's direction is unfailingly sympathetic, while Sutherland is impressive in each role, notably as the doll Olympia and in the pathos of the Antonia scene. As Giulietta she hardly sounds like a *femme fatale*, but still produces beautiful sing-

ing. Domingo gives one of his finest recorded performances, and so does Gabriel Bacquier. This version – very close to the one prepared by Tom Hammond for the English National Opera – is given greater weight by the inclusion in the Epilogue of the quartet previously inserted into the Venice scene as a septet, a magnificent climax. Bonynge opts for spoken dialogue and puts the Antonia scene last as being the more substantial. With superb, atmospheric recording quality and a clear yet sumptuous tape transfer, this is a memorable set in every way, far more than the sum of its parts.

Les Contes d'Hoffmann: highlights.
*** Decca KCET 569 [Lon. 5-22639] (from above set).

This splendid highlights tape is outstandingly generous. One of the finest compilations of its kind from any opera, it gives a superbly managed distillation of nearly all the finest items, and it is edited most skilfully. The cassette transfer is of demonstration quality.

Orpheus in the Underworld (operetta): abridged version (in English).
**(*) HMV TC-CSD 1316. June Bronhill, Eric Shilling, Kevin Miller, Jon Weaving, Susanne Steele, Margaret Nisbett, Deirdre Thurlow, Alan Crofoot, Sadler's Wells Opera Chorus and Orch., Faris.

With a single reservation only, this is an enchanting selection. Without visual help the recording manages to convey the high spirits and genuine gaiety of the piece, plus – and this is an achievement for a non-Parisian company – the sense of French poise and precision. June Bronhill in the *Concerto duet* is infectiously provocative about her poor suitor's music. One's only complaint is that Alan Crofoot's King of the Boeotians is needlessly cruel vocally. The sound is full and brilliant, with plenty of atmosphere, and the transfer is vivid and sparkling. There is just a hint of peaking on one or two female high notes, but this is not too serious. The balance produces a fair amount of forward projection, and while this reduces the dynamic range somewhat it increases the presence of the soloists.

'The world of Offenbach': Overtures: (i; ii) *La Belle Hélène;* (iii; iv) *La Fille du tambour-major;* (i; ii) *Orpheus in the Underworld.* (iii; iv) *Le Papillon: Valse des rayons. Les Contes d'Hoffmann:* (v; i; iv) *Ballad of Kleinzach;* (vi; i; iv) *Doll's song;* (vi; vii; i; iv) *Barcarolle. La Grande-Duchesse de Gérolstein:* (viii; i; ix) *Piff-paff-puff;* (x–xii) *Portez armes . . . J'aime les militaires. La Périchole:* (x; i; xii) *Air de lettre; Ah! quel dîner.*

(M) *** Decca KCSP 512. (i) Suisse Romande Orch.; (ii) Ansermet; (iii) LSO; (iv) Bonynge; (v) Placido Domingo; (vi) Joan Sutherland; (vii) Huguette Tourangeau; (viii) Fernando Corena; (ix) Walker; (x) Régine Crespin; (xi) Vienna Volksoper Orch.; (xii) Lombard.

A characteristically felicitous Decca anthology, as generous as it is wide-ranging. The performances cannot be faulted; Ansermet and Bonynge offer much character in the overtures, and the vocal numbers – which come from a wide variety of sources – are no less colourful. The recording throughout is immensely vivid, and the high-level transfer offers a wide range and striking presence. The opening of side two (*La Fille du tambour-major*) has a touch of fierceness, but yields to rebalancing; indeed care with the balance of treble and bass can yield demonstration results through much of the tape. Ansermet incidentally takes the final *Can-can* of the *Orpheus overture* (which closes the concert) slower than usual, but invests it with such rhythmic vigour that the music sounds freshly minted.

Orff, Carl
(born 1895)

Carmina Burana (*cantiones profanae*).

*** HMV TC-ASD 3117 [Angel 4XS 37117]. Sheila Armstrong, Gerald English, Thomas Allen, St Clement Danes Grammar School Boys' Choir, LSO, Previn.

*** DG 923062 [id.]. Gundula Janowitz, Gerhard Stolze, Dietrich Fischer-Dieskau, Schoneberger Boys' Choir, Chorus and Orch. of German Opera, Berlin, Jochum.

(B) **(*) Pye Collector ZCCCB 15001. Gerda Hartmann, Richard Brunner, Rudolf Knoll, Salzburg Mozarteum Choir and Orch., Prestel.

**(*) Philips 7300 444 [id.]. Celestina Casapietra, Horst Heistermann, Karl-Heinz Stryczek, Dresden Kapelknaben, Leipzig Radio Chorus and SO, Kegel.

(M) **(*) Supraphon 0450409. Milada Šubrtová, Jaroslav Tomanek, Teodor Šrubar, Czech Philharmonic Chorus and Orch., Smetáček.

(M) **(*) Decca Jubilee KJBC 78 [Lon. 5-21153]. Norma Burrowes, Louis Devos, John Shirley-Quirk, Brighton Festival Chorus, Southern Boys' Choir, RPO, Dorati.

(B) ** DG Heliodor 3348 194. Jutta Vulpius, Hans-Joachim Rotzsch, Kurt Rehm, Kurt Hubenthal, Leipzig Radio and Children's Choirs and Radio SO, Kegel.

Previn's version, richly recorded, is strong on humour and rhythmic point. Thomas Allen's contribution is one of the glories of the performance, and in their lesser roles the soprano and tenor are equally stylish. The chorus sings vigorously, the men often using an aptly rough tone. The main point of contrast between Previn and his rivals lies in his pointing of rhythm, more sprung, less mechanistic. He goes nowhere near self-indulgence, but he gives a resilience to rhythms which brings out a strain not just of humour but of real wit. This is a performance which swaggers along and makes you smile. The recording captures the antiphonal effects brilliantly, better in the orchestra than the chorus. Although the tape was originally unreliable, current copies are of sophisticated quality, giving plenty of detail and atmosphere, a refined projection of the soloists and plenty of weight and detail to the choir.

The DG production under Jochum too is highly distinguished but until recently was not available in the UK in Dolby form. Dolby copies arrived just as we were going to print, and the remastering is impressive, with a slightly higher level (and noticeably more edge to the chorus) on side two than side one. However, the sound is excellent throughout, and although the chorus are heard at their best when the music blazes, there is much refinement of detail, and the closing scene is moulded by Jochum with a wonderful control, Klemperer-like in its restrained power. The very wide dynamic range of the recording, however, means that when the choral singing is gentle it is in danger of losing presence and impact, an effect common to both disc and tape. Fischer-Dieskau's contribution is characteristically refined, but not too much so, and

his first solo, *Omnia Sol temperat*, and later *Dies, nox et omnia* are both very beautiful, with the kind of tonal shading that a great Lieder singer can bring. Perhaps *Estuans interius* needs a heavier voice, but Fischer-Dieskau is suitably gruff in the Abbot's song – so much so that for the moment the voice is unrecognizable. Gerhard Stolze too is very stylish in his falsetto *Song of the roasted swan*. The soprano, Gundula Janowitz, finds a quiet ecstasy for her contribution, which is beautifully sung.

On bargain label there is an excellent case for Kurt Prestel's version (a favourite of I.M.'s). This is amiably earthy and direct, in a reading which favours rather slow speeds but does not lose forward momentum. By the standards of more expensive versions the imprecisions of ensemble may irritate some ears, but there is a vitality about the performance that matches Orff's prose well. The cassette is of such outstanding quality, with fine sparkle and edge, that it must be considered among the best buys on tape.

On Philips Herbert Kegel secures very fine singing from the superb Leipzig choir, but the lightness of his touch produces some lack of tension in places, in spite of the variety of colour he finds in Orff's score. The very opening of the work, for instance, lacks the last degree of exuberance, and there is certainly a lack of electricity in the closing section of *Cours d'amours*. The soloists make a good team, and project well, notably the tenor, Horst Heistermann. The recording is of the highest quality, both natural and vivid, and the tape is technically the most impressive available issue of this work.

The Supraphon performance is most exhilarating: Orff's primitive rhythms come over with splendid impact. This is all superbly colourful and exciting. But the soloists are uneven. Milada Šubrtová is the most striking, but Teodor Šrubar has a very wide *vibrato* which may not appeal to all ears. Even so the power and exuberance of this account are in no doubt, and the recording is both atmospheric and vivid. The transfer is of good quality.

Dorati's Jubilee version was originally recorded in Phase Four. It is a beefy, vibrant account with good singing and playing. Despite some eccentric speeds, Dorati shows a fine rhythmic sense, but the performance cannot quite match the best available. The tape transfer reflects the LP both in its vividness and in the hints of congestion at peaks.

On his earlier DG recording, reissued on Heliodor, Kegel directs a literal, largely unpointed reading which conveys little of the fun of the extrovert numbers or the tenderness of the first spring chorus. The ensemble of the magnificent Leipzig choir is superb, sounding relatively small in a very clean acoustic. The recording is nicely balanced and immediate.

Pachelbel, Johann
(1653–1706)

Canon and Gigue in D major (arr. for strings by Seiffert).
   *** DG 3300 317 [id.]. Berlin PO, Karajan – *Concert.****
Canon (arr. Münchinger).
   (M) **(*) Decca Ace of Diamonds KSDC 411 [Lon. 5-6206]. Stuttgart CO, Münchinger – *Concert.****

Pachelbel's *Canon* is justly famous, one of those short pieces like Purcell's *Chaconne* that are simple in structure, short, but totally memorable. Karajan adds the *Gigue* with which the piece was paired in its original form (for three violins and continuo). His performance is totally out of period, but the gorgeous playing of the Berlin Philharmonic is utterly persuasive and the other items in this collection (called *Adagio*) include Albinoni's famous piece and music by Boccherini, Vivaldi and Respighi. Those requiring a

more severe (and stylish) presentation of the *Canon* will find that Münchinger's Ace of Diamonds tape best meets their needs. Both recordings are well transferred; more details can be found in our Concerts section.

Paganini, Niccolò
(1782–1840)

Violin concertos Nos. 1 in D major, Op. 6; 2 in B minor, Op. 7; 3 in E major; 4 in D minor; 5 in A minor; 6 in E minor, Op. posth.; Le Streghe (Witches' dance): Variations on a theme by Süssmayr, Op. 8.
   **(*) DG 3378 067 [id.]. Salvatore Accardo, LPO, Dutoit.

Paganini's concertos can all too often seem sensationally boring, and it is a tribute to the virtuosity and artistry of Salvatore Accardo that they reveal so much musical interest in his hands. Accardo has a formidable technique, marvellously true intonation and impeccable good taste and style, and it is a blend of all these that makes these performances so satisfying and enjoyable. He is moreover beautifully accompanied by the LPO and Charles Dutoit, and the recording is exemplary. The transfers are of high DG quality but have some problems with the very reverberant acoustic, which means that the focus of the orchestra is not as clear-cut as it might be. The focus of the soloist is admirable, however, and frequently the overall sound picture is very convincing (notably so in the *Sixth Concerto*). At the opening of the *Second Concerto* (coupled to the *Fourth* on the second cassette) there is a curious gremlin – a high-pitched piping rhythmic figure, like some kind of celestial piccolo, which can be heard above the music for a couple of minutes then disappears. This concerto also offers a degree of discoloration of the upper harmonics of the solo violin timbre.

Violin concerto No. 1 in D major, Op. 6.

*** Decca KSXC 6798. Boris Belkin, Israel PO, Mehta.

Violin concerto No. 1; Le Streghe (Witches' dance): Variations on a theme by Süssmayr, Op. 8.

**(*) DG 3300 714 [id.]. Salvatore Accardo, LPO, Dutoit.

Both Accardo and Belkin (unlike some of their competitors on LP) play this concerto complete. Accardo offers a fill-up into the bargain and his playing has a poise and effortless virtuosity that carry all before it. The cassette transfer, however, is disappointing; the orchestra is poorly focused because of the reverberation, and the upper transients are 'fizzy'. The solo violin on the whole reproduces naturally.

Belkin also plays splendidly. He too has a marvellous command of his instrument plus a sweet and appealing tone. He is well accompanied, although some might find Mehta's way with the tuttis a trifle overpowering. However, the sumptuous Decca recording has transferred very impressively to tape; provided the over-ample bass is cut back a little, this approaches demonstration quality, with the solo violin naturally projected.

Violin concertos Nos. 1 in D major, Op. 6; 2 in B minor, Op. 7.

(M) *** DG Privilege 3335 207 [923097]. Shmuel Ashkenasi, Vienna SO, Esser.

With Shmuel Ashkenasi the many technical difficulties are surmounted in an easy, confident style. The accompaniment too is nicely made, and the slightly dry recording focuses everything exactly, with the soloist spotlighted in the foreground. Some might feel a lack of nineteenth-century flamboyance, but most

will sense Ashkenasi's natural sympathy. The close microphone may seem to some ears to be too close in some of the more fiendish tessitura, but the bravura displayed by the soloist generally, and especially in the *La Campanella* finale of No. 2, shows how completely he is in control, and this is one of the highlights of a good medium-priced coupling. The transfer is fresh and immediate and loses nothing on the LP quality; indeed it gains slightly by smoothing the upper partials of the soloist's tone marginally, without losing the freshness and immediacy of the overall sound picture.

Violin concerto No. 2 in B minor, Op. 7; La Primavera (Sonata for violin and orchestra in A major); Introduction and Variations on 'Non più mesta' from Rossini's 'La Cenerentola', Op. 12.

*** DG 3300 900 [id.]. Salvatore Accardo, LPO, Dutoit.

The *Second Concerto* takes its nickname, *La Campanella*, from the obbligato bell in the rondo (which Paganini himself sometimes played as a separate piece). The *Second* is a shorter work than its predecessor, occupying one side only. The fill-ups, *La Primavera*, a late work, and the variations on *Non più mesta*, are both played with effortless wizardry by the virtuoso soloist, beautifully accompanied and naturally recorded. On tape the sound is generally fresh and well balanced, although some might feel the opening tutti of the concerto a little dry. The soloist is truthfully caught and generally this tape offers sophisticated quality.

Violin concerto No. 3 in E major.

** Philips 7300 103. Henryk Szeryng, LSO, Gibson.

Paganini kept for himself the prerogative of performing his own violin concertos, and took strict security precautions to ensure that the orchestral parts could not fall into other hands. His two best-known works were not published until after his death, and the secrets of his *Fourth Concerto* were successfully kept until 1954, when the lost score came to light and the work was recorded by Grumiaux. The Paganini family then made available the orchestral parts of the *Third Concerto*, and with a good deal of publicity Henryk Szeryng gave its first posthumous performances and made the present recording. The performance is dazzling technically. The first movement, however, is not of great musical interest, and the best movement is undoubtedly the *Adagio*, a brief aria-like format, eloquent in shape and marked by the composer *Cantabile spianato*. The work would have fitted comfortably on to a single side, so is rather expensive in its present form. The tape transfer is made at a low level and the overall focus is not very clean, because of the reverberant recording.

Violin concerto No. 6 in E minor, Op. posth.

   *** DG 3300 412 [id.]. Salvatore Accardo, LPO, Dutoit.

This further newly discovered concerto (one wonders how many more will be unearthed) is entirely characteristic, tuneful and bristling with bravura. Salvatore Accardo gives a fine performance, with warmly romantic phrasing in the slow movement and much brilliance in the finale. The cassette is beautifully recorded, with clean, warm sound and a natural image for the soloist.

I Palpiti; Maestosa sonata sentimentale; Perpetuela; Sonata con variazioni su un tema di Joseph Weigl; Sonata Napoleone.

   *** DG 3336 376. Salvatore Accardo, LPO, Dutoit.

An admirable supplement to the dazzling box of concertos that Salvatore Accardo has already recorded. This col-

lection assembles five works, four of which are not otherwise available on disc or tape. They are all frankly display pieces that Accardo turns into music. The measure of his achievement is that one almost forgets his virtuosity, so effortless does it all seem, and listens to the music as such. It is all highly enjoyable and the playing of the LPO under Charles Dutoit altogether exemplary. Ideas from Rossini (*Di tanti palpiti, di tante pene* from Act 1 of *Tancredi*) and Haydn turn up in *I Palpiti* and the *Maestosa sonata sentimentale* respectively. The stunning playing is supported by remarkably well balanced and cleanly focused recording, and the cassette is every bit as good as the disc. A hugely enjoyable issue.

Violin and guitar: *Cantabile; Centone di sonate No. 1 in A major; Sonata in E minor, Op. 3/6; Sonata concertata in A major.*

   *** CBS 40-76525 [Col. MT 34508]. Itzhak Perlman (violin), John Williams (guitar) – GIULIANI: *Sonata.****

Superb playing from both Perlman and John Williams captures the listener's attention throughout this slight but very agreeable music. With a good balance, the music-making here gives much pleasure, and this tape will be very suitable for late-evening listening. The transfer is of very good quality.

Caprices, Op. 1, Nos. 1–24 (for solo violin).

   *** HMV TC-ASD 3384. Itzhak Perlman (violin).

These two dozen *Caprices* probably represent the peak of violinistic difficulty, even though more than a century has gone by since their composition, and many new works continue to exploit the extraordinary range of effects possible on one four-stringed instrument. Perlman's playing is of the utmost virtuosity, superbly assured and polished. The

HMV transfer is generally good, though slightly crisper in focus on side two, where the quality is often very good indeed. On side one it is more noticeable that the upper range of the recording is not far-reaching.

Guitar: *Caprice, Op. 1/24; Sonata in A major.* (i) *Terzetto in D major for violin, violoncello and guitar.*

   (*) CBS 40-73745. John Williams (guitar), (i) with Alan Loveday (violin), Amaryllis Fleming (cello) – GIULIANI: *Variations.**

Both the main works here are attractive. The *Terzetto* is small-scale but very charming; the *Romanza* of the *Sonata* is especially fetching, and John Williams's skill brings the music fully to life. The transfers are good, but in the *Terzetto* the cello is backwardly balanced and the string instruments reveal the comparatively limited range in the treble, although the quality is pleasant.

Palestrina, Giovanni da (*c.* 1525–1594)

Hodie Beata Virgo; Litaniae de Beata Virgine Maria in 8 parts; Magnificat in 8 parts (Primi Toni); Senex puerum portabat; Stabat Mater.

   (M) *** Argo KZKC 4. King's College Choir, Willcocks.

This is an exceptionally fine collection. The flowing melodic lines and serene beauty which are the unique features of Palestrina's music are apparent throughout this programme, and the dedication and accomplishment of the performance are beyond question. Argo's recording is no less successful, and this may be highly recommended, especially in this medium-

priced reissue. The transfer is beautifully natural, although the level is high and there are one or two climaxes in the *Stabat Mater* on side one when there is a fractional hint that it is nearing the upper limit. But one must not over-state this; the effect is marginal, and generally this is a tape of demonstration quality.

Missa: Hodie Christus natus est. Motets: *Ave Maria; Canite tuba; Hodie Christus natus est; Jubilate Deo; O magnum mysterium; Tui sunt caeli.*

   *** HMV TC-ASD 3559. King's College Choir, Ledger.

One of the best recordings to come from King's recently, this issue assembles the motet *Hodie Christus natus est* as well as the Mass, plus a handful of motets of which two are new to the catalogue. The performances are very persuasive indeed, admirably expressive without being in the least unstylish. The boys' voices are well focused and do not suffer from the hooting King's quality that worries some listeners. There is a genuine warmth too about these performances. They are spaciously recorded, and the transfer, although not made at the highest level, is of excellent quality; the recording focus is secure, and the atmosphere is naturally conveyed.

Missa Papae Marcelli. Alma redemptoris Mater (antiphon). Motets: *Dominus Jesus in qua nocte; Peccantem me quotidie. Stabat Mater.*

   ** Enigma K 453560. Pro Cantione Antiqua, Turner.

The *Missa Papae Marcelli*, Palestrina's most famous Mass and a key work in the history of the Roman liturgy, seems unlucky in the recording studio. This performance by the Pro Cantione Antiqua under Bruno Turner is certainly expressive, the lines of the music clear yet well blended. There is a lack of fervour, but no absence of musical accomplishment; the singing is of first-class quality, technically speaking. The drawback is the clear, precise acoustic, which robs the music of atmosphere and a sense of mystery; a warmer, more reverberant ambience is surely needed. These comments might generally apply to the collection as a whole (and there is undoubtedly some splendid music here), but the recording is technically immaculate, beautifully truthful and clear in detail; and the tape transfer catches every nuance of colour and is perfectly focused throughout. As with most Enigma cassettes, one needs a magnifying glass to read the notes comfortably.

Parry, Hubert
(1848–1918)

I was glad (from Psalm 122).
(***) HMV TC-ASD 3345. Cambridge University Music Society, King's College Choir, New Philharmonia Orch., Ledger – ELGAR: *Coronation ode* etc.(***)

This expansive version of Parry's most popular church anthem makes an excellent coupling for Elgar's magnificent *Ode*. The recording is basically of splendid quality, but the transfer has been made at too high a level, which has unacceptably coarsened the sound.

Pergolesi, Giovanni
(1710–36)

Magnificat.
**(*) Argo KZRC 505. Elizabeth Vaughan, Janet Baker, Ian

Partridge, Christopher Keyte, King's College Choir, Academy of St Martin-in-the-Fields, Willcocks – VIVALDI : *Gloria.***(*)

This Pergolesi *Magnificat* – doubtfully attributed, like so much that goes under this composer's name – is a comparatively pale piece to go with the great Vivaldi *Gloria*. But King's Choir gives a beautiful performance, and the recording matches it in intensity of atmosphere. The transfer is characteristically sophisticated and catches the King's resonance very satisfactorily.

Piston, Walter
(1894–1976)

The Incredible Flutist (ballet): suite.
(M) **(*) Turnabout KTVC 34670. MIT SO, Epstein – COPLAND: *Dance symphony.***(*)

Walter Piston's ballet *The Incredible Flutist* is probably his best-known work and has reached a wider public than any of his eight symphonies. It was written in the 1930s after his studies with Nadia Boulanger in Paris, and some of the episodes are distinctly Gallic in atmosphere. *The Incredible Flutist* is a highly attractive score that deserves wide popularity, and this performance by the orchestra of the Massachusetts Institute of Technology, though not of the highest order of virtuosity, is eminently acceptable; and there is no current alternative. This score would suit Bernstein and we must hope that he will record it some day; he was a pupil of Piston in the 1940s. The recording could be warmer and richer but on the whole this is more successful than the Copland side. The transfer is of excellent quality, vividly atmospheric and with plenty of body and detail.

411

Poulenc, Francis
(1889–1963)

Babar, le petit éléphant.
(***) EMI Bronze TC-BRNA 502
(original version). Eleanor
Bron (narrator), Susan Brad-
shaw (piano) – SAINT-SAËNS:
Carnival of the Animals.(*)
(M) ** HMV Greensleeve TC-ESD
7020 [Angel 4xs 36644] (orch.
Françaix). Peter Ustinov (nar-
rator), Paris Conservatoire
Orch., Prêtre – SAINT-SAËNS:
Carnival of the Animals.***

Babar, an entertainment for children,
was originally for narrator and piano.
The music is unambitious but has a gentle
charm, notably in the expressions of
unforced melancholy when things are
not turning out quite as Babar expected. Eleanor Bron's version uses the
original piano score, which (for all the
skill of Jean Françaix's orchestration, favoured by Ustinov) is altogether
fresher and more subtle in its illustrative
detail. Susan Bradshaw is superb; her
playing shows splendid bravura and
great sympathy and style. Miss Bron too
seems wholly involved in the narrative,
and she makes telling use of contrasts of
dynamic as well as vocal timbre. The recording is excellent and well balanced,
but unfortunately the tape transfer is very
poorly managed. There is pre- and post-
echo, and Miss Bron's voice is balanced
forwardly and her consonants exaggerated, at times to the point of ugliness
(with moments of roughness at climactic
points). The piano tone is hard, unglam-
orous and brittle, and unnaturally
edged.
　Ustinov's avuncular narration is attractive, and the orchestra do their bit persuasively, but the piece seems rather
drawn out, and ideally one needs the

book too with its charming illustrations.
The cassette transfer is clear.

Les Biches (ballet): suite.
(**) HMV TC-ASD 2989. City
of Birmingham SO, Frémaux –
IBERT: *Divertissement;* HONEG-
GER: *Pacific 231*(**); SATIE:
Gymnopédies.***

The reverberation of the Great Hall
of Birmingham University, where this
recording was made, does not have such
an adverse effect on Poulenc's *Les Biches*
as it does on the Ibert and Honegger
scores. The performance is a jolly one,
even if the tempo for the opening trumpet
tune seems too fast. The transfer has a
limited range, and although the colour of
Poulenc's charming score is still conveyed the lack of bite and sparkle seriously blunts the wit.

*Concert champêtre for harpsichord
and orchestra; Concerto in G minor
for organ, strings and timpani.*
*(**) HMV TC-ASD 3489. Simon
Preston (harpsichord or organ),
LSO, Previn.

Each of these recordings is realistically
balanced, and Simon Preston, who plays
the solo parts in both concertos (the only
artist to have done so in the recording
studio), produces readings of great fluency
and authority. Previn, too, has a genuine
feeling for the music, though in the finale of
the *Concert champêtre* there are odd
moments when the phrasing might be
more characterful. But there need be no
real reservations here; the playing is
always musical, often sparkling, and the
recording is undoubtedly realistic. The
transfer of the *Concert champêtre* is
beautifully managed, clear and clean,
with everything natural and in perspective. However, much less care has been
taken with the *Organ concerto*, and there
is a hint of discomfort when the organ is
playing a loud solo passage, whereas in

concertante tuttis the texture tends to become muddled.

(i) *Piano concerto;* (ii) *Gloria.*
**(*) HMV TC-ASD 3299. City of Birmingham SO, Frémaux, with (i) Cristina Ortiz (piano); (ii) Norma Burrowes (soprano), CBSO Chorus.

Cristina Ortiz gives an alert and stylish account of the disarming *Piano concerto,* and is given splendid support by Louis Frémaux with the Birmingham orchestra. His account of the *Gloria* competes with Prêtre's superb version (which is not available on tape); Frémaux secures excellent results too, and the recording is spectacular. The tape transfer of the *Concerto* is good, bright and detailed, although the last degree of refinement is missing. The opening of the *Gloria* has a hint of roughness, but the quality generally has plenty of life.

Sonata for flute and orchestra (orch. Berkeley).
*** RCA RK 25109. James Galway, RPO, Dutoit – CHAMINADE: *Concertino*; FAURÉ: *Fantaisie*; IBERT: *Concerto.***

Poulenc's *Flute sonata,* composed in the mid-1950s towards the end of his life, deserves to be widely popular, so beguiling is its delightful opening theme. Yet so far it remains relatively neglected in the British catalogue (though not the American one) and this is the only version currently available. Let us hope that Sir Lennox Berkeley's delightful arrangement and James Galway's persuasive advocacy will bring it to a larger public. The performance is elegant and polished and the orchestration highly successful. The recording is admirably spacious and well detailed and the tape transfer is clear and clean.

Prokofiev, Serge (1891–1953)

Autumnal (In Autumn): see under *Piano concertos.*

Chout (The Buffoon; ballet): *Suite, Op. 21; Romeo and Juliet* (ballet): *Suite, Op. 64.*
(M) ******* Decca Jubilee KJBC 56. LSO, Abbado.

It is difficult to see why a well-selected suite from *Chout* should not be as popular as any of Prokofiev's other ballet scores. It is marvellously inventive music which shows Prokofiev's harmonic resource at its most delicious. Abbado's version with the LSO offers a generous part of the score, including some of the loosely-written connecting tissue, and Abbado reveals a sensitive ear for balance of texture. The excerpts from *Romeo and Juliet* are well chosen: they include some of the most delightful numbers that are normally omitted from the suites, such as the *Dance with mandolins,* the *Aubade* and so on. The *Dance of the girls* is very sensuous but too slow, far slower than on Prokofiev's own 78s. However, Abbado shows here a delicacy and lightness of touch that are most captivating. The recording is a model of its kind, with a beautifully balanced perspective and no lack of stereo presence. Moreover the transfer is of Decca's top quality, splendidly vivid and detailed. Highly recommended.

Cinderella (ballet), *Op. 87:* excerpts; *Romeo and Juliet* (ballet), *Op. 64:* excerpts.
(M) ***(*) Decca** KCSP 226. Suisse Romande Orch., Ansermet.

These excerpts are taken from a double album, providing extended selections from both ballets, which Ansermet recorded in 1962. The condensed version is

413

fair value for money, as Ansermet's Pro-kofiev is nearly always characterful. But the orchestral playing is less than distin-guished, and Ansermet's directing hand seems less assured than usual in matters of style. The recording is vivid but at the loudest moments it is not as open and free from congestion as the best recordings from this source, and this is reflected in the tape transfer.

(i–iii) *Piano concertos Nos. 1–5;* (ii; iv) *In Autumn (Autumnal), Op. 8; Symphony No. 1 in D major (Classi-cal), Op. 25;* (i; v) *Overture on Hebrew themes, Op. 34.*

(M) *** Decca к 3 н 14 [Lon. 5-2314]. (i) Vladimir Ashkenazy (piano); (ii) LSO; (iii) Previn; (iv) cond. Ashkenazy; (v) Keith Puddy (clarinet), Gabrieli Qt.

Ashkenazy's virtuosity is staggering and he plays all the concertos masterfully here. The bottom-heavy balance which was noticed on the discs has been cor-rected in the tape transfer, which is admir-ably balanced. There are certain agogic mannerisms (in the first movement of No. 2 and the slow movement of No. 3), but Ashkenazy has marvellous panache, and Previn is a sensitive accompanist throughout. The performances are dis-cussed in more detail below under their separate issues, but it can be said that the transfers generally represent Decca's very highest standard, offering extremely vivid and brilliant sound, with excellent balance and a high transfer level.

(i) *Piano concertos Nos. 1 in D flat major, Op. 10; 2 in G minor, Op. 16;* (ii) *Overture on Hebrew themes for clarinet, string quartet and piano, Op. 34.*

*** Decca KSXC 6767 [Lon. 5-7062]. Vladimir Ashkenazy, with (i) LSO, Previn, (ii) Keith Puddy (clarinet), Gabrieli Qt.

Ashkenazy is a commanding soloist in both concertos, and his virtuosity in the *First* is quite dazzling. He is curiously wayward in the opening of the *Second*, where he indulges in excessive *rubato*, but there is no question that this is a masterly performance. The piano is very for-wardly placed. The accompaniments are splendidly idiomatic, and apart from the reticent balance, the string tone is beauti-fully fresh in quality. The transfers are extremely vivid and the brilliance of the recording tends to recommend the tape even above the equivalent disc, although there is a touch of harshness caused by resonance in the first move-ment of the *Second Concerto* (which begins at the end of side one). The record-ing of the *Overture* is rather less immed-iate, and the inner string detail is smooth rather than especially well defined.

(i) *Piano concerto No. 1 in D flat major, Op. 10. Romeo and Juliet: Scene and dance of the young girls* (arr. for piano by the composer).

(*) HMV TC-ASD 3571. Andrei Gavrilov, (i) with LSO, Rattle – RAVEL: *Concerto for left hand; Pavane.*(*)

A dazzling account of the *First Con-certo* from the young Soviet pianist Andrei Gavrilov, who replaced Richter at Salzburg in 1975 and has astonished audiences wherever he has appeared. This version is second to none for virtuo-sity or for sensitivity: it is no exaggeration to say that this exhilarating account is the equal of any we have ever heard and superior to most. Apart from its brilli-ance, this performance scores on all other fronts too; Simon Rattle provides an ex-cellent orchestral support and the EMI engineers offer vivid recording. An out-standing issue which commands a rosette in its LP issue. On tape, as the opening *tutti* shows, the reverberation causes some blurring in the orchestral focus, but the piano quality is excellent and the general detail of the recording is good in all but the most expansive fortissimos. Even though this is not technically perfect it must receive the strongest recommendation.

Piano concerto No. 3 in C major, Op. 26.
>   *** Decca KSXC 6411. Julius Katchen, LSO, Kertesz – GERSHWIN: *Rhapsody in Blue***(*); RAVEL: *Piano concerto in D major.****
>   **(*) Decca Phase 4 KPFC 4255 [Lon. 5-21079]. Israela Margalit, New Philharmonia Orch., Maazel – MUSSORGSKY: *Pictures.***(*)
>   (M) * Rediffusion Royale KROY 2007. Marian Lapsansky, Slovak PO, Slovak – RACHMANINOV: *Rhapsody on a theme of Paganini.**

Julius Katchen gives a first-class performance of the solo part and is well accompanied by the LSO under Kertesz. It goes without saying that the recording is of fine quality, with an excellent cassette transfer, natural in timbre and balance, yet with plenty of presence.

The performance by Israela Margalit and Maazel is not the most poised available, but it has a splendid feeling of spontaneity and enjoyment. The recording balance is far from natural, the resonance of the acoustic competing with the microphone spotlighting, but the end result is unfailingly vivid. It is not unlikely that those who buy this for the Mussorgsky coupling may find themselves turning just as readily to the concerto, for the personality and colour of the score emerge strongly here. The cassette transfer offers demonstration quality.

On cassette the Supraphon-source Royale recording is brightly lit to the point of glare, and even with a treble cut the sound remains extremely bold and open, without any real body to the strings. Certainly there is no lack of clarity, and the piano, forwardly projected, is singularly clear. There is no doubt about the intensity of the performance, but coupled to the sound the effect becomes aggressive, and the work's astringency is emphasized at the expense of its lyricism.

(i) *Piano concerto No. 3 in C major, Op. 26;* (ii) *In Autumn (Autumnal), Op. 8; Symphony No. 1 in D major (Classical), Op. 25.*
>   **(*) Decca KSXC 6768 [(d) Lon. 5-6964]. LSO, (i) with Vladimir Ashkenazy (piano), Previn; (ii) cond. Ashkenazy.

This is the least attractive of the three tapes from the Prokofiev concerto box. Ashkenazy's account of the *Third Concerto* is keen-edged and crisply articulated, and he is sympathetically supported by Previn and the LSO. One's reservation concerns the slow movement: Ashkenazy's entry immediately after the theme is uncharacteristically mannered. Good recording. The early *In Autumn* is eminently worth having, and the *Classical symphony* receives a neat and well-turned reading. This sounds especially well on tape.

Piano concertos Nos. 4 in B flat major for left hand, Op. 53; 5 in G major. Op. 55.
>   *** Decca KSXC 6969 [(d) Lon. 5-6964]. Vladimir Ashkenazy, LSO, Previn.

Ashkenazy gives an admirable account of No. 5; every detail of phrasing and articulation is well thought out, and yet there is no want of spontaneity or any hint of calculation. Richter (see below) is wittier and more glittering in the second movement, where Ashkenazy adopts the more measured tempo. In No. 4 he is no less authoritative, though his choice of tempo at figure 51 is puzzling. As in the companion issues, the accompaniment is sensitively played. The quality of sound here is on a demonstration level, with splendid body and sparkle, and a most realistic balance between soloist and orchestra.

Piano concerto No. 5 in G major, Op. 55.

(B) *** DG Heliodor 3348 109. Sviatoslav Richter, Warsaw PO, Rowicki – RAVEL: *Piano concerto in G major.* (*) (*)

Richter's account of the *Fifth Concerto* comes from the early days of LP and is a classic recording. It has virtuosity, panache and brilliance and as a performance outclasses all comers. The newly transferred Heliodor tape has dazzling clarity and brilliance (it is very clean at the top), though on some machines the upper register may sound a trifle brittle. However, whatever other versions of the Prokofiev concertos you may have, this one should not be overlooked.

Violin concertos Nos. 1 in D major, Op. 19; 2 in G minor, Op. 63.

(M) **(*) HMV TC-SXLP 30235. Nathan Milstein, Philharmonia Orch., Giulini or Frühbeck de Burgos.

(M) **(*) CBS 40-61796. Isaac Stern, Philadelphia Orch., Ormandy.

(***) Decca KSXC 6773. Kyung-Wha Chung, LSO, Previn.

Milstein's cassette is clearly preferable to the disappointing Decca tape. The HMV transfer has a more open sound quality, with a more natural bloom and warmth for both soloist and orchestra. There is no lack of presence for Milstein: the opening of the *First Concerto* sounds much fresher here than on Decca and the soloist's timbre is realistic. Milstein's performances have a patrician dis-

tinction, with an element of reserve – emotion implied rather than expressed overtly. This is music of such richness that an approach of this kind brings special rewards.

Stern is extrovert in his romanticism, holding little back. These are superb, deeply perceptive performances, revelling in and bringing out the lyricism in these fine concertos. Ormandy as usual is a first-rate accompanist, providing an immaculate orchestral texture that is faithfully matched to the needs of the soloist yet has a strong personality of its own. The recording balance provides an unnatural spotlight for the solo violin, but otherwise the transfer offers vivid, brightly lit detail. There is plenty of range and only a marginal lack of refinement, more noticeable in No. 2.

Kyung-Wha Chung gives performances of these two gloriously lyrical concertos that are both warm and strong, tender and full of fantasy. Not since David Oistrakh's mono discs of the fifties has the full range of expression in these works been so richly brought out in recordings, thanks to the deeply understanding accompaniment from Previn and the LSO. The lovely melody which opens the slow movement of No. 2 – almost Bellinian, as has often been said – finds Chung playing with an inner, hushed quality, as though the emotion is too deep to be uttered out loud, and the ravishing modulation from E flat to B a page or so later brings an ecstatic *frisson*. Unfortunately on tape the Decca recording is too brightly lit, giving a very aggressive edge to the solo violin tone, and there is an absence of bloom on the orchestra. One needs a strong treble reduction and extra bass, and even then the basic fierceness remains. A disappointing issue.

Lieutenant Kijé (incidental music for a film): *Suite, Op. 60.*

*** Decca Phase 4 KPFC 4355 [Lon. 5-21146]. Netherlands

Radio PO, Dorati – KODÁLY: *Háry János suite*.***

(*) HMV TC-ASD 3029. LSO, Previn – SHOSTAKOVICH: *Symphony No. 6*. (*)

(M) **(*) RCA Gold Seal GK 42698. David Clatworthy (bar.), Boston SO, Leinsdorf – KODÁLY: *Háry János*.**(*)

Dorati is characteristically direct, with everything boldly characterized in this extremely vivid Phase Four recording (not unnaturally balanced, but ensuring that every detail is clear). He secures excellent playing from the Netherlands Orchestra, and with a good coupling this is a most enjoyable cassette; the transfer is of Decca's best quality.

Lieutenant Kijé is given a colourful, swaggering performance by Previn and the LSO, an excellent fill-up for their fine account of Shostakovich's *Sixth Symphony*. The recording is admirably vivid but at times lacks the last degree of crispness of focus in the otherwise well-balanced transfer.

Leinsdorf, always a sharp and stylish interpreter of Prokofiev, directs a sparkling performance of *Lieutenant Kijé* complete with the part for baritone. The late-sixties recording remains one of the finest from this source, and the coupling is ideal. The tape transfer lacks the clean sharpness of outline of the equivalent disc, but the sound remains attractively vivid.

Lieutenant Kijé: Suite, Op. 60; Scythian suite, Op. 20.

*** DG 3300 967 [id.]. Chicago SO, Abbado.

This cassette offers a fine account of *Lieutenant Kijé* coupled with what is probably the best version of the *Scythian suite* to have appeared for many years. Previn has slightly more character in his version of *Kijé*, but Abbado gets wonderfully clean playing from the Chicago orchestra and he is accorded excellent engineering. The *Scythian suite* has drive and fire: in the finale – and even in the second movement – Abbado could bring greater savagery and brilliance than he does, but given the power that the Chicago orchestra do bring to this score, and the refined colouring that Abbado achieves in the atmospheric *Night* movement, there need be no real reservation in recommending this. There is very little to choose between the recordings in cassette or disc form, although the low level of the transfer brings slightly less upper range on tape (in the *Scythian suite* the transients do not quite have the same sparkle as on disc).

Peter and the Wolf, Op. 67.

*** DG 3300 588 [id.]. Hermione Gingold (narrator), Vienna PO, Boehm – SAINT-SAËNS: *Carnival of the Animals*.***

*** Enigma K 453553. Angela Rippon (narrator), RPO, Hughes – SAINT-SAËNS: *Carnival of the Animals*.***

*** CRD CRD 4032 (extended text). Johnny Morris (narrator), Northern Sinfonia, Haslam – HASLAM: *Juanita, the Spanish lobster*.**

(M) *** Decca KCSP 520. Sean Connery (narrator), RPO, Dorati – BRITTEN: *Young Person's Guide*.**(*)

(*) HMV TC-ASD 2935 [Angel 4xs 36962]. Mia Farrow (narrator), LSO, Previn – BRITTEN: *Young Person's Guide*.(*)

**(*) RCA RK 12743 [ARK 1 2743]. David Bowie (narrator), Philadelphia Orch., Ormandy – BRITTEN: *Young Person's Guide*.*(*)

(B) ** Classics for Pleasure TC-CFP 185. Richard Baker (narrator), New Philharmonia Orch.,

417

Leppard – BRITTEN: *Young Person's Guide*.**(*)

(M) ** Philips 7317 093. Alec McCowen (narrator), Concertgebouw Orch., Haitink – BRITTEN: *Young Person's Guide***(*); RAVEL: *Ma Mère l'oye*.***

(M) * CBS Classics 40-61814 [(d) Col. MT 31806]. Leonard Bernstein (narrator and cond.), New York PO – SAINT-SAËNS: *Carnival of the Animals*.*

There are a great many recordings of *Peter and the Wolf*. Finest of all is Sir Ralph Richardson's highly spontaneous account (see below), although Hermione Gingold's narration is equally memorable, and the orchestral playing on the DG tape is of a superlative standard. Some might find Miss Gingold a trifle too camp in her presentation of the text (which was amended and embellished by Edward Greenfield, so comment on our part is perhaps inappropriate). But it is difficult to resist the strength of Miss Gingold's personality and her obvious identification with the events of the tale. Boehm gives a straightforward accompaniment, but is attentive to every detail, and the performance is beautifully characterized. The orchestral recording is quite remarkably transparent and truthful on tape as on disc: the transfer offers stunning realism. The voice itself is a bit larger than life, but has such presence and such a well-judged background ambience that one cannot quibble.

Angela Rippon narrates with charm yet is never in the least coy; indeed she is thoroughly involved in the tale and thus involves the listener too. The accompaniment is equally spirited, with excellent orchestral playing, and the recording is splendidly clear, yet not lacking atmosphere. Anyone wanting this coupling without the verses attached to the Saint-Saëns *Carnival* (as on DG) will find this a first-class investment.

Johnny Morris provides a completely new and extended text. The narration continues with the music far more than in the standard version, the characterizations are filled out and the narrator becomes more integrated with the story. For instance Grandfather wears slippers and they go 'Sl-ip, sl-op' beautifully to Prokofiev's music. At the very end it is suggested that the tale does not end happily ever after for everyone: the Wolf is now in the zoo and the Duck (in spite of the ghostly 'Quack') is almost certain not to see the light of day again. It is all very vivid and convincing, and although obviously aimed at younger children it is never arch. The wind players add to the effect of the new version by superb musical characterization, and they are beautifully recorded; indeed the tape is breathtakingly natural. It is a pity that the coupling is less recommendable, for undoubtedly this 'new-look' *Peter and the Wolf* is a great success.

Sean Connery uses a modern revision of the narrative by Gabrielle Hilton. This exchanges economy of words for a certain colloquial friendliness and invites the narrator to participate more than usual in the narrative. Sean Connery does this very well. His relaxed style, the vocal colour like brown sugar, is certainly attractive from the very beginning (if you can accept such extensions as a 'dumb duck' and a pussy-cat who is 'smooth, but greedy and vain') and when the tale reaches its climax he joins in the fray most enthusiastically. Dorati supports him well and the pace of the orchestral contribution quickens appropriately (in tension rather than tempo). The recording, originally Phase Four, is clear, brilliant and colourful, the spotlighting well used. Children of all ages who have no preconceived notions about the words of the narrative will enjoy this. Both sides of the tape start attractively with the orchestra tuning-up noise, and here the introductory matter is entirely fresh and informal. The transfer is admirably crisp and clear.

Mia Farrow treats *Peter and the Wolf*

as a bed-time story, admirably unmannered and direct. This is almost certainly one of the best versions for younger children. It is an advantage too having the narrator in the same acoustic as the orchestra, which under Previn's direction produces playing both rich and jaunty, with some superb solo work. The transfer offers warm, pleasing sound, with only slight clouding of orchestral detail by the reverberation; the voice is clear and well projected.

David Bowie's narration has undoubted presence and individuality. He makes a few additions to the text, and colours his voice effectively for the different characters. He has the face to say 'Are you sitting comfortably?' before he begins, and on the whole the narration seems aimed at a younger age-group. The manner is direct and slightly deadpan, but definitely attractive. Ormandy accompanies imaginatively, and the orchestral players enter fully into the spirit of the tale. The recording is generally excellent (David Bowie's voice is very close, but admirably real), although once or twice the reverberation brings a little blurring of focus in the percussion.

Richard Baker, balanced well forward in a different acoustic from the orchestra, provides an extra introductory paragraph which might become tedious on repetition. But he conveys the spirit of the story well enough and is only occasionally too coy. Leppard provides an excellent account of the orchestral score and the recording is vivid. But in the last analysis one's reaction depends on how one takes to the narration, and there will be mixed views on this. However, this tape offers excellent value and is admirably clear.

Alec McCowen uses a new text by Erik Smith which is intelligently prepared to give a fresh look at the story. However, the addition of bird imitations, including the duck quacking in the wolf's stomach at the end, is rather twee and seems designed to appeal to the youngest of listeners. McCowen is recorded closely, in a

different acoustic from the orchestra. Taken as a whole the presentation is vivid and undoubtedly children will enjoy its liveliness. The tape transfer is good rather than brilliant, but quite acceptable.

Bernstein introduces *Peter and the Wolf* with a kind of quiz about the characters. The effect is patronizing and certainly unattractive for repeated listening, though the story itself is quite well told and the orchestral playing is excellent. The coupling, for rather similar reasons, cannot be recommended. The tape transfer offers an agreeable sound, but a limited range.

(i) *Peter and the Wolf, Op. 67. Symphony No. 1 in D major* (*Classical*), *Op. 25.*

(M) *** Decca KCSP 90. LSO, Sargent, (i) with Sir Ralph Richardson (narrator).

Sir Ralph Richardson's account is superbly recorded in the very best Decca manner, sumptuous and colourful. Sir Malcolm's direction of the orchestral contribution shows his professionalism at its very best, with very finely prepared orchestral playing, and many imaginative little touches of detail brought to one's attention, yet with the forward momentum of the action perfectly sustained. Sir Ralph brings an actor's feeling for words to the narrative. He dwells lovingly on their sound as well as their meaning, and this preoccupation with the manner in which the story is told matches Sargent's feeling exactly. There are some delicious moments when that sonorous voice delights in its own coloration, none more taking than Grandfather's very reasonable moral: 'and if Peter had not caught the wolf . . . what then?' But of course he did, and in this account it was surely inevitable. The *Symphony* too is superbly played and recorded. All the tempi, except perhaps the finale, are slow, but Sir Malcolm's self-assurance carries its own spontaneity, and this is one of the richest recorded offerings he gave us. The

419

transfer is well managed, full-blooded yet clear. See also *'Favourite composer'*, pp. 423–4.

Romeo and Juliet (ballet), *Op. 64:* complete.

⊛ *** Decca K 20 K 32 [Lon. 5-2312]. Cleveland Orch., Maazel.

This is another of those superb Decca tape sets where the sound is so vivid that one cannot but be astonished at the achievement. The recording is one of Decca's most spectacular, searingly detailed but atmospheric, and the quality on tape is outstandingly brilliant, with lustrous warmth in the lyrical moments, while the weight and power of the climaxes is something to be marvelled at. Maazel's approach is sharply incisive, rhythms consciously metrical; and the precision of ensemble of the Cleveland Orchestra is little short of miraculous. Yet there is no suggestion of rigidity and a feeling of great passion underlies the work's tragic climax.

Romeo and Juliet, Op. 64: excerpts.
*** Decca KSXC 6668 (from above set).

This selection has been chosen to follow through the action of each of the acts of the ballet, and besides giving a bird's-eye picture of the complete work, it shows marvellously the diversity of Prokofiev's inspiration. The cassette transfer is of very high quality.

Romeo and Juliet, Op. 64: Suite No. 1: excerpts (*Masks; Romeo and Juliet; Tybalt's death*); *Suite No. 2* (complete).
(M) ** Supraphon 0450104. Czech PO, Ančerl.

This highly praised recording dates from 1961 but still sounds astonishingly vivid. The Czech Philharmonic Orchestra are in superb form and they display not only the utmost bravura but also great

sympathy for Prokofiev's angular lyricism. The strings play with a memorable fervour, yet Ančerl's reading shows a degree of restraint too, and the full nobility of Prokofiev's masterly score is revealed here. There is some delightful wind-playing, delicately textured and subtly coloured. The recording has plenty of atmosphere and is well transferred generally; only in the most complex climaxes does the resonance generate a degree of coarseness. For the most part the quality is fully acceptable, and this tape has much to commend it.

Romeo and Juliet, Op. 64: Suite No. 1: excerpts.
*** DG 3300 284 [id.]. San Francisco SO, Ozawa – BERLIOZ: *Roméo et Juliette: Love scene;* TCHAIKOVSKY: *Romeo and Juliet*.***

The Prokofiev items make an attractive contrast to the other two very romantic evocations of Shakespeare on the same theme. Ozawa draws from his 'other' orchestra warmly committed playing, helped by rich recording quality. The tape transfer is first-class and the quality is strikingly beautiful.

(i) *Sinfonia concertante (Symphony-Concerto) for violoncello and orchestra, Op. 125;* (ii) *Symphony No. 1 in D major (Classical), Op. 25.*
(M) *** HMV TC-SXLP 30266. (i) Mstislav Rostropovich (cello), RPO, Sargent; (ii) Philharmonia Orch., Kurtz.

The *Sinfonia concertante for cello and orchestra* (1950–52) was originally to have been called *Cello concerto No. 2*, in spite of the fact that it drew on the *E minor Cello concerto* from the pre-war years for much of its thematic substance. In fact the present work, which is dedicated to Rostropovich, is much more of a detailed reworking of the earlier concerto, and as in some of his other later works Prokofiev's second thoughts are not always improvements. However, there is a good deal of marvellous invention here and the playing of the distinguished soloist and the RPO under Sargent is exemplary. The recorded sound rarely betrays its age (it dates from the late 1950s) and only occasionally does one feel the want of greater freshness or richness in the strings. This is a magnificent performance, and there is no current alternative. Kurtz's effervescent version of the *Classical symphony* still sounds delightfully vivid and takes its place among the best on the market. The transfer is of excellent quality, clean and clear and well balanced. In the symphony there is an agreeable bloom on the orchestra; a tendency to shrillness (inherent in the recording itself) is easily smoothed with the controls.

Sinfonietta, Op. 48.
> *** HMV TC-SLS 5110. Philharmonia Orch., Muti – *Ivan the Terrible.****

This excellent performance of a first-class work makes a good bonus for a first-rate account of *Ivan the Terrible.* The transfer is very well done, the sound rich and beautifully detailed.

(i) *Summer Day* (children's suite for small orchestra), *Op. 65a;* (ii) *A Winter Camp-fire* (suite), *Op. 122.*
> (M) *** Supraphon 0450773. (i) Prague CO (without conductor); (ii) Prague Radio SO and Children's Chorus, Klima.

A wholly delightful and unexpected coupling to appear on cassette which will give great pleasure to all those who love *Peter and the Wolf.* The *Summer Day* suite has seven short characteristic movements of great charm. Each sets the other off: the opening *Morning*, lazily atmospheric, is contrasted with *Tag*, which shows the composer at his wittiest, and is played and recorded with irresistible crispness; then comes a beguilingly gentle miniature waltz, and so on. The alert playing of the Prague Chamber Orchestra (without conductor) is a joy. Side two offers a work obviously primarily aimed at boys, with its opening and closing patrol and an enchanting central chorus round the camp-fire, infectiously sung here. The music is presented with great affection; the recording is excellent throughout, and the transfer admirably clean and vivid.

Symphony No. 1 in D major (Classical), Op. 25 (see also above).
> *** Argo KZRC 719 [id.]. Academy of St Martin-in-the-Fields, Marriner – BIZET: *Symphony.****
> *** DG 3300 783 [id.]. Chicago SO, Giulini – MUSSORGSKY: *Pictures.****

This symphony is well served on tape. Marriner is beautifully recorded, in a warm, resonant acoustic. The sound has a quite splendid bloom, but, perhaps partly because of the resonance, Marriner's tempi are comparatively leisurely. The detail is deliciously pointed (the bassoon solo in the first movement is a joy), and the finale, if not as irrepressible as under some conductors, has no lack of vivacity and wit. The transfer offers superb quality, of a demonstration standard.

A refined and spacious account from Giulini, the tempo of the first movement rather measured but not lacking momentum, the slow movement ethereally beautiful, and the finale comparatively easy-going and gracious. Only in the *Gavotte* is the ensemble marginally less than immaculate. With first-class recording to match, this is an attractively different view of the symphony. The transfer is of excellent quality.

PROKOFIEV

Symphonies Nos. 1 in D major (Classical), Op. 25; 7 in C sharp minor, Op. 131.
(*) HMV TC-ASD 3556. LSO, Previn.

In both symphonies (a popular coupling since the earliest days of LP) Previn is highly successful. He produces much inner vitality and warmth, and the EMI engineers provide a strikingly realistic and integrated sound. The *Classical symphony* is more successful here than in Previn's earlier (disc) version on RCA; it is genuinely sunlit and vivacious, and the ripe recording is entirely appropriate. Previn is obviously persuaded of the merits of the underrated and often beguiling *Seventh Symphony*. Here the reverberant acoustic sometimes robs the transfer of the last degree of crispness (the percussion transients are not as sharp as on disc), but the quality remains warmly attractive.

Symphony No. 5 in B flat major, Op. 100.
*** HMV TC-ASD 3115. LSO, Previn.
(*) Decca KSXC 6787. LSO, Weller.

Previn takes a weighty view of a wide-spanning symphony. His first-movement tempo is spacious, and the contrasts are strongly underlined, with Prokofiev's characteristic use of heavy brass, notably the tuba, superbly brought out by the LSO players, not to mention the EMI engineers. The slow movement too is firmly placed in the grand tradition of Russian symphonies. The scherzo and later the finale have fractionally less brilliance than one expects from this source, but with rich recording the result is still formidably powerful. The transfer is impressively full-bodied (the breadth of the climax of the first movement has remarkable weight and amplitude), but the upper strings need control if the violin

timbre is not to sound somewhat shrill. Nevertheless this tape yields very sophisticated detail at times, especially in the scherzo.

Walter Weller's performance has undoubted merits, even if there is a tendency to beautify textures, but his reading is let down by a slow movement which lacks real bite and forward impetus (it is much slower than the metronome marking). Weller makes too much of the *l'istesso tempo* in the scherzo. There is a welcome sense of space, and a genuine finesse, but Previn's reading has much greater concentration. However, Weller gets even better playing than Previn from the LSO, and he is better recorded. The transfer is generally good, but the level seems to have been slightly too ambitious in the first movement, and there is a bass drum contribution that is not comfortably caught. The rest of the symphony is satisfactory.

Flute sonata in D major, Op. 94.
*** RCA RK 25029 [LRK 1 5095]. James Galway (flute), Martha Argerich (piano) – FRANCK: *Flute sonata.****

Prokofiev's *Flute sonata* is more familiar in the transcription he made for violin in collaboration with David Oistrakh. Written in the summer of 1943, it was rightly hailed by Nestyev as Prokofiev's sunniest and most serene wartime composition. It is indeed an enchanting work, and it is difficult to imagine a more beautiful performance than this one. There is a combination of effortless virtuosity and spontaneity of feeling; every detail falls naturally into place. Martha Argerich is at her most sensitive and imaginative, and James Galway at his most virtuosic and lyrical. Throughout, Galway produces the greatest variety of tone colour, and so does his partner; yet in the end one is left admiring the music and not the artistry of the performers, which is as it should be. They are most sympathetically recorded, and the cassette transfer is well made; the flute is truthfully caught, the piano timbre a little dry, but a good balance is achieved between them, even if the spotlight tends to be on Mr Galway.

Violin sonata No. 1 in F minor, Op. 80.
   *** Advent E 1069 (see p. xxiii) [id.]. Emanuel Borok (violin), Tatiana Yampolsky (piano) – SHOSTAKOVICH: *Violin sonata.****

The *First Violin sonata* is one of Prokofiev's finest instrumental works and at the time of writing is otherwise unrepresented in the catalogue either on disc or cassette (the Oistrakh/Richter and Perlman/Ashkenazy versions are both deleted). Emanuel Borok, a Russian violinist who emigrated first to Israel and then to the USA, is at present Assistant Concertmaster (Deputy Leader) of the Boston Symphony, and it is evident from this account that he is a formidable player. He does not obliterate memories of Menuhin's pioneering record of the sonata or of Oistrakh's mono LP with Vladimir Yampolsky, made in the 1950s, but this version is impeccably played (the slow movement is most beautifully done), and it is excellently recorded. The sound is firmly focused (the piano a trifle bottom-heavy) and vividly lifelike. The acoustic is warm and the balance natural. A distinguished issue.

Piano sonata No. 8 in B flat major, Op. 84.
   (*) DG 3300 678 [id.]. Lazar Berman – RACHMANINOV: *Moments musicaux.**

Berman is somewhat wilful here. The first movement is robbed of its forward momentum, and in the middle section of the last movement he even sounds unidiomatic, so wayward is his approach. Masterly piano-playing, needless to say,

and extremely well recorded; the transfer is first-class.

Ivan the Terrible, Op. 116 (film music arr. in oratorio form by Stasevich).
   *** HMV TC-SLS 5110. Irina Arkhipova (mezzo-soprano), Anatoly Mokrenko (bar.), Boris Morgunov (narrator), Ambrosian Chorus, Philharmonia Orch., Muti – *Sinfonietta.****

This oratorio was put together long after Prokofiev's death by the scholar Abram Stasevich, and it lacks the crisp sense of drama which made the comparable cantata *Alexander Nevsky* so strikingly successful. That work, which the composer himself arranged from earlier film music, is crisply dramatic, but with Prokofiev/Stasevich the result is diffuse, and the device of adding a spoken narration (in Russian) could well prove irritating on repetition.

Nevertheless Riccardo Muti's enthusiasm for the piece is hardly misplaced, for, with fine playing and choral singing, there are many imaginative ideas here to relish, not least those using broad, folk-like melodies (including one which also served for Kutuzov's great aria in the opera *War and Peace*). The recording is rich and spacious, and though the histrionic style of the narrator, Morgunov, is unappealing, the two other soloists are both excellent in their limited roles. The *Sinfonietta* makes a highly welcome filler for side four. The transfer is generally very successful. The recording is reverberant, but the detail and sense of spectacle are extremely well caught and the focus is good. Moreover the distanced effects are very well managed. The (very necessary) libretto is beautifully printed in bold, clear black type.

'Favourite composer': (i–iii) *Piano concerto No. 3 in C major, Op. 26;* (iv) *Lieutenant Kijé: Suite, Op. 60;*

(v) *The Love of Three Oranges: March; Scherzo;* (vi; ii; vii) *Peter and the Wolf, Op. 67;* (ii; viii) *Romeo and Juliet, Op. 64: extended suite;* (ii; vii) *Symphony No. 1 in D major (Classical), Op. 25.*

⊛(B) *** Decca KDPC 617/8. (i) Julius Katchen (piano); (ii) LSO; (iii) Kertesz; (iv) Paris Conservatoire Orch., Boult; (v) Suisse Romande Orch., Ansermet; (vi) Sir Ralph Richardson (narrator); (vii) Sargent; (viii) Abbado.

A truly outstanding set which would make an admirable basis for a cassette collection of Prokofiev's music. The performances are all highly recommendable. Sir Malcolm Sargent's account of the *Classical symphony* may not be the most brilliant available, but it is full of character and the recording is remarkably vivid and clear. So too is the transfer of the Richardson/Sargent *Peter and the Wolf.* Katchen's version of the *Third Concerto* has also been praised earlier, and no less welcome is Sir Adrian Boult's witty and atmospheric account of *Lieutenant Kijé*, the recording hardly showing its age (1958) except for the inclusion of rather more background noise than usual. The surprise bonus is Abbado's selection from *Romeo and Juliet*, which includes some of the most delightful numbers that are normally omitted from the suites, such as the *Dance with mandolins*, the *Aubade* and so on. Despite a slight want of intensity and fire, there is an admirable lightness and delicacy of touch here that are most captivating. The recording – warm and rather softgrained – has a beautifully balanced overall perspective and suits the style of the music-making.

Puccini, Giacomo
(1858–1924)

La Bohème (opera): complete.
> *** Decca K 2 B 5 [Lon. 5-1299]. Mirella Freni, Luciano Pavarotti, Rolando Panerai, Nicolai Ghiaurov, Elizabeth Harwood, German Opera Chorus, Berlin, Berlin PO, Karajan.
> *** HMV TC-SLS 896 [Angel 4x2G 6099]. Victoria de los Angeles, Jussi Bjoerling, Robert Merrill, John Reardon, Giorgio Tozzi, Lucine Amara, RCA Victor Chorus and Orch., Columbia Boychoir, Beecham.
> (M) **(*) Decca K 5 K 22. Renata Tebaldi, Carlo Bergonzi, Ettore Bastianini, Cesare Siepi, Fernando Corena, Gianna d'Angelo, Chorus and Orch. of St Cecilia Academy, Rome, Serafin.
> (M) **(*) HMV TC-SLS 5059. Maria Callas, Giuseppe di Stefano, Rolando Panerai, Nicola Zaccaria, Anna Moffo, Chorus and Orch. of La Scala, Milan, Votto.

Karajan takes a characteristically spacious view of *Bohème*, but there is an electric intensity which holds the whole score together as in a live performance – a reflection no doubt of the speed with which the recording was made (long takes were the rule). Karajan unerringly points the climaxes with full force, highlighting them against prevailing pianissimos. Pavarotti is an inspired Rodolfo, with comic flair and expressive passion, while Freni is just as seductive a Mimi as she was in the Schippers recording ten years earlier. Elizabeth Harwood is a charming Musetta, even if her voice is not so sharply contrasted with Freni's as it might be. Fine singing throughout the set. The reverberant Berlin acoustic is glowing and brilliant in superb Decca recording, and the tape transfer is both sumptuous and brilliant, at times of demonstration standard, but a little inconsistent: side four, for instance, is not too vivid at the opening, and benefits from a slight volume increase. The libretto is admirably clear.

Beecham recorded his classic interpretation of *Bohème* in 1956 in sessions in New York that were arranged at the last minute. It was a gamble getting it completed, but the result was incandescent, a unique performance with two favourite singers, Victoria de los Angeles and Jussi Bjoerling, challenged to their utmost in loving, expansive singing. It was always rumoured that three of the four acts had been recorded in stereo, and though this reissue claims only that this is 'transcription stereo' it sound remarkably like the real thing, with the voices made more vivid. The tape transfer has plenty of life, but perhaps not quite as much bloom as the discs: Bjoerling and Los Angeles are well caught but there is some edge on the ensembles. There is no lack of vividness. The libretto uses rather small print.

The earlier Decca set with Tebaldi and Bergonzi was technically an outstanding recording in its day. The depth of the stereo is very striking (at times one might feel that the resonant sound picture detracts a little from the reality). A feature of the original recording was the brightly lit upper strings, and here the very lively transfer reflects that balance, with moments when the sheen of the violins is not natural in its balance of upper partials. But the voices have no lack of bloom (the love scene in Act 1 is notably beautiful). The climax of Act 2, however, is rather fierce. The set is admirably laid out with one act to a side and a splendid libretto clearly printed in large type.

Vocally the performance achieves a consistently high standard, Tebaldi as Mimi the most affecting: she offers some superbly controlled singing, but the individuality of the heroine is not so indelibly conveyed as with Los Angeles or Freni. Carlo Bergonzi is a fine Rodolfo; Bastianini and Siepi are both superb as Marcello and Colline, and even the small parts of Benoit and Alcindoro (as usual taken by a single artist) have the benefit of Corena's magnificent voice. The veteran Serafin was more vital here than on some of his recordings.

Callas, flashing-eyed and formidable, may seem even less suited to the role of Mimi than to that of Butterfly, but characteristically her insights make for an unforgettable performance. The set is worth getting for Act 3 alone, where the predicament of Mimi has never been more heartrendingly conveyed in the recording studio. Though Giuseppe di Stefano is not the subtlest of Rodolfos, he is in excellent voice here, and Moffo and Panerai make a strong partnership as the second pair of lovers. Votto occasionally coarsens Puccini's score – as in the crude crescendo in the closing bars of Act 3 – but he directs with energy. The stereo transcription captures the voices well and the tape transfer is of very high quality. The comparatively restricted dynamic range means that the singers appear to be 'front stage', and there is no lack of light and shade in Act 2. The orchestra sounds gloriously warm (hardly any suggestion of a stereo transcription here) and the voices are clearly and vividly caught; Act 3 seems mellower in sound than the rest but this is very suitable for Puccini's 'slow movement'.

La Bohème: highlights.
*** Decca KCET 579 [Lon. 5-26399] (from above set cond. Karajan).
(M) **(*) Decca Jubilee KJBC 11 (from above set cond. Serafin).
(M) (**) HMV Greensleeve TC-

425

ESD 7023 (from above set cond. Beecham).

It is a pity to cut anything from so taut a score as *Bohème*, but those who need a single tape instead of two will find the selection from the Karajan set ideal. For collectors who want a reminder of Tebaldi with Bergonzi in *Bohème*, the Decca Jubilee selection is well chosen; the recording reflects the qualities of the complete set, with a degree of thinness in the upper register of the orchestra needing a careful balance of the controls. The overall sound, however, has plenty of resonance and warmth. The Beecham selection is clumsily edited. The very opening (*Al quartiere Latin*) begins in mid-air, and the excerpts from Act 2 are faded in and out very ineptly. The quality of the transfer is unrefined, and to add to the lack of focus there was a degree of pulsing (a rhythmic unsteadiness of texture) on our review copy.

La Fanciulla del West (*The Girl of the Golden West;* opera): complete.

⊛ *** DG 3371 031 [id.]. Carol Neblett, Placido Domingo, Sherrill Milnes, Chorus and Orch. of the Royal Opera House, Covent Garden, Mehta.

(M) ** HMV TC-SLS 5079. Birgit Nilsson, Joao Gibin, Andrea Mongelli, Giuseppe Morresi, Chorus and Orch. of La Scala, Milan, Matačić.

Like *Madama Butterfly*, 'The Girl', as Puccini called it in his correspondence, was based on a play by the American David Belasco. The composer wrote the work with all his usual care for detailed planning, both of libretto and of music. In idiom the music marks the halfway stage between *Butterfly* and *Turandot*, and the first audience must have been astonished at the opening of an Italian opera dependent on the whole-tone scale

in a way Debussy would have recognized as akin to his own practice. Nevertheless it produces an effect wildly un-Debussian and entirely Puccinian. DG took the opportunity of recording the opera at the time when Covent Garden was staging a spectacular production in 1977. With one exception the cast remained the same as in the theatre and, as so often in such associated projects, the cohesion of the performance in the recording is enormously intensified. The result is magnificent, underlining the point that – whatever doubts may remain over the subject with its weeping goldminers – Puccini's score is masterly, culminating in a happy ending which brings one of the most telling emotional coups that he ever achieved.

Mehta's manner – as he makes clear at the very start – is on the brisk side, not just in the cakewalk rhythms but even in refusing to let the first great melody, the nostalgic *Che faranno i viecchi miei*, linger into sentimentality. Mehta's tautness then consistently makes up for intrinsic dramatic weaknesses (as, for example, the delayed entries of both heroine and hero in the first act). Sherrill Milnes as Jack Rance was the newcomer to the cast for the recording, and he makes the villain into far more than a small-town Scarpia, giving nobility and understanding to the first act *arioso*. Domingo, as in the theatre, sings heroically, disappointing only in his reluctance to produce soft tone in the great aria *Ch'ella mi creda*. The rest of the Covent Garden team is excellent, not least Gwynne Howell as the minstrel who sings *Che faranno i viecchi miei*; but the crowning glory of a masterly set is the singing of Carol Neblett as the Girl of the Golden West herself, gloriously rich and true and with formidable attack on the exposed high notes. Rich atmospheric recording to match, essential in an opera full of evocative offstage effects. These very distant effects have only fractionally less sharpness of focus on tape than on disc, and this represents one of DG's very finest opera recordings in this medium. The recording has the widest dynamic range, and it opens up thrillingly at climaxes. The close of Act 3 is superbly projected, and the moments of spectacle in the third act (the chorus superbly vivid and clear) are riveting. Besides the detail the sound has great warmth, and the bloom on the solo voices in no way detracts from the feeling of presence. The opera is well laid out on three cassettes, which lift out of their plastic shell complete in their library boxes. Act 1 is complete on the first three sides; Act 2 is on sides four and five; and Act 3 is on side six. The libretto is printed horizontally in four languages and is bold and clear, even though the type size remains rather too small. DG still have not solved this problem.

Matačić's conception is full of drama and passion, and he indulges in strong *rubato*. The EMI sound balance is close and vividly projected, with excellent directional qualities, if not always especially refined in conveying atmosphere. Nilsson makes a formidable Minnie, thrilling as a budding Brünnhilde was bound to be (she recorded this in 1959). On occasion she can sound shrill – imperfectly controlled *vibrato* being the main trouble – but when she is called on to give her full power in the highest register the effect is certainly exciting. Gibin has a good, distinctive timbre and his confessional monologue in Act 2 is imaginatively done. Mongelli's Rance is a splendid characterization. One or two brief passages are omitted, but the cuts are not substantial. The tape transfer is acceptable rather than outstanding, quite atmospheric but lacking refinement of detail.

Madama Butterfly (opera): complete.

   *** Decca K 2 A 1 [Lon. 5-13110]. Mirella Freni, Luciano Pavarotti, Christa Ludwig, Robert Kerns, Vienna State Opera Chorus, Vienna PO, Karajan.

(M) **(*) HMV TC-SLS 5128 [Angel 4x3s 3604]. Victoria de los Angeles, Jussi Bjoerling, Miriam Pirazzini, Mario Sereni, Rome Opera Chorus and Orch., Santini.

*(**) CBS 40-79313. Renata Scotto, Placido Domingo, Gillian Knight, Ingvar Wixell, Malcolm King, Ambrosian Opera Chorus, Philharmonia Orch., Maazel.

(M) *(**) HMV TC-SLS 5015. Maria Callas, Nicolai Gedda, Lucia Danielli, Mario Borriello, Chorus and Orch. of La Scala, Milan, Karajan.

Karajan inspires singers and orchestra to a radiant performance on Decca which brings out all the beauty and intensity of Puccini's score, sweet but not sentimental, powerfully dramatic but not vulgar. He pays the composer the compliment of presenting each climax with precise dynamics, fortissimos surprisingly rare but those few presented with cracking impact. Freni is an enchanting Butterfly, consistently growing in stature from the young girl to the victim of tragedy, sweeter of voice than any recorded rival. Pavarotti is an intensely imaginative Pinkerton, actually inspiring understanding for this thoughtless character, while Christa Ludwig is a splendid Suzuki. The recording is one of Decca's most resplendent, with the Vienna strings producing glowing tone. The transfer is extremely vivid and sparkling, with only marginally less body and warmth than the discs. The sound varies very slightly from side to side but is never less than excellent.

In the late fifties and early sixties Victoria de los Angeles was incomparable in the role of Butterfly, and her 1960 recording displays her art at its most endearing, her range of golden tone colour lovingly exploited, with the voice well recorded for the period, though rather close. Opposite her Jussi Bjoerling was making one of his very last recordings and though he shows few special insights, he produces a flow of rich tone to compare with that of the heroine. Mario Sereni is a full-voiced Sharpless, but Miriam Pirazzini a disappointingly wobbly Suzuki, while Santini is a reliable, generally rather square and unimaginative conductor who rarely gets in the way. With recording quality very acceptable this is an excellent mid-priced recommendation. There is a tiny accidental cut at the start of the suicide aria, eliminating three of the heroine's cries of *Tu*. The transfer is excellent, clear in detail yet with plenty of body, and the voices are naturally projected within an attractively atmospheric ambience. There is a most pleasing bloom on Victoria de los Angeles's contribution, and the upper range is smooth yet not lacking vividness. The libretto is clearly and boldly printed.

Eleven years after her recording with Barbirolli (not currently available on tape), Renata Scotto recorded this role again with Maazel, and the years brought nothing but benefit. The voice – always inclined to spread a little on top at climaxes – had acquired extra richness and was recorded with a warmer tonal bloom. In perception too Scotto's singing is far deeper, most strikingly in Butterfly's *Un bel dì*, where the narrative leads to special intensity on the words *Chiamerà Butterfly dalla lontana*. Maazel is warmly expressive without losing his architectural sense; he has not quite the imaginative individuality of a Karajan or a Barbirolli, but this is both powerful and unsentimental, with a fine feeling for Puccini's subtle orchestration. Other contributors are incidental, even Placido Domingo, who sings heroically as Pinkerton but arguably makes him too genuine a character for such a cad. Wixell's voice is not ideally rounded as Sharpless, but he sings most sensitively, and Gillian Knight makes an expressive Suzuki. Among the others Malcolm King as the Bonze is outstanding in a good team. The recording is rich and warm without having the

bloom of Karajan's Decca set, and the voices are balanced relatively, though not uncomfortably, close. The CBS transfer, however, while clear and immediate, is disappointingly lacking in warmth, and there is little bloom on either voices or orchestra. The level is high and there is seldom any peaking, yet the ear craves greater richness of middle frequencies. The score is robbed of its lifeblood by such a sound balance. There is a clearly printed libretto, and the box is more robust than some earlier CBS album issues.

The idea of the flashing-eyed Maria Callas playing the fifteen-year-old Butterfly may not sound convincing, and certainly this performance will not satisfy those who insist that Puccini's heroine is a totally sweet and innocent character. But Callas's view, aided by superbly imaginative and spacious conducting from Karajan, gives extra dimension to the Puccinian little woman, and with some keenly intelligent singing from Gedda as Pinkerton (a less caddish and more thoughtful characterization than usual) this is a set which has special compulsion. The opera is well presented with a clear easy-to-read libretto, but the spacing out on the three tapes could have been better managed – there is an unnecessarily bad break between sides three and four, and a long run-off at the end of side six suggests that better planning could have avoided this. The recording is of course a transcription from mono, and while it has an agreeable atmospheric resonance the lack of range in the treble produces a degree of muffling, particularly where the chorus is concerned; and the dramatic scene with the Bonze in Act 1 brings some congestion. In spite of the thickness of texture the ear adjusts, and the solo voices are generally well caught, with only the occasional hint of strain at peaks.

Madama Butterfly: highlights.
*** Decca KCET 605 [Lon. 5-62455] (from above Decca set cond. Karajan).

(M) **(*) Decca Jubilee KJBC 32. Renata Tebaldi, Carlo Bergonzi, Chorus and Orch. of St Cecilia Academy, Rome, Serafin.

The obvious first choice for a highlights tape from *Butterfly* (if the purchase of the complete set is impossible) is the generous selection (it includes the *Humming chorus*, omitted from the Jubilee issue) from Karajan's outstanding version. The transfer is quite as rich and naturally managed as the complete set from which it comes, offering first-class Decca quality throughout. There are many beautiful moments too in Tebaldi's performance, even if here she rarely shows the creative insight of characterization that Freni brings to the part.

Serafin's conducting is restrained but sympathetic. The recording has transferred very vividly, and although its age is betrayed by the upper string tone this by no means interferes with the dramatic projection of the singing, for the sound has plenty of body and warmth. With Serafin's complete set not available on tape this makes a fine reminder of a recording which – vocally, at least – represented one of Tebaldi's finest achievements. Few sopranos can float a soft note with such apparent ease, and her rich creamy tone is often all-enveloping in its beauty.

Madam Butterfly: abridged (in English): *Opening and duet; Love duet; One fine day; Telescope duet; Flower duet; Trio and Pinkerton's farewell; Death scene.*

(M) ** HMV Greensleeve TC-ESD 7030. Marie Collier, Charles Craig, Ann Robson, Gwyn Griffiths, Sadler's Wells Chorus and Orch., Balkwill.

There are few better examples than this of opera recorded in English: the clear recording lets the listener hear almost every word, and this is achieved without balancing things excessively in favour of the voices. Marie Collier got inside the part very well, and she had a big, full voice. Some may be troubled by her pronounced *vibrato*; others may find the *vibrato* nothing more than a natural colouring of the voice. As to the choice of extracts, the one omission which is at all serious is the entry of Butterfly. As it is, the duet of Pinkerton and Sharpless cuts off just as she is about to come in. But Craig is a splendid Pinkerton and he was in particularly fresh voice when this record was made. The cassette transfer is extremely vivid and atmospheric; just occasionally there is a touch of peakiness in the vocal climaxes, caused by the high level of transfer.

Tosca (opera): complete.
⊗ (M) *** HMV TC-SLS 825. Maria Callas, Giuseppe di Stefano, Tito Gobbi, Chorus and Orch. of La Scala, Milan, de Sabata.
(M) *** Decca K 59 K 22. Leontyne Price, Giuseppe di Stefano, Giuseppe Taddei, Vienna State Opera Chorus, Vienna PO, Karajan.
*** Philips 7699 034 [id.]. Montserrat Caballé, José Carreras, Ingvar Wixell, Chorus and Orch. of the Royal Opera House, Covent Garden, Colin Davis.

There has never been a finer recorded performance of *Tosca* than Callas's first, with Victor de Sabata conducting and Tito Gobbi as Scarpia. One mentions the prima donna first, because in this of all roles she was able to identify totally with the heroine and turn her into a great tragic figure, not merely the cipher of Sardou's original melodrama. Tito Gobbi too makes the unbelievably villainous police chief into a genuinely three-dimensional character, and Giuseppe di Stefano as the hero, Cavaradossi, was here at his finest. The conducting of Victor de Sabata is spaciously lyrical as well as sharply dramatic, and though the recording (originally mono, here stereo transcription) is obviously limited, it is superbly balanced in Walter Legge's fine production. The transfer is very successful, smooth yet not lacking vividness: the death of Scarpia and the atmospheric opening of Act 3 are both memorable in different ways. The libretto is clearly printed in reasonable-sized type. The opera is well laid out, with Act 1 on side one, Act 2 on sides two and three, and the last act complete on side four.

For those wanting the full advantages of stereo in this most atmospheric of operas the Decca set makes an obvious first choice. Karajan deserves equal credit with his principal singers for his vital, imaginative performance, recorded in Vienna. Some idea of its quality may be gained from the passage at the end of Act 1, just before Scarpia's *Te Deum*. Karajan takes a speed far slower than usual, but there is an intensity which both links one vividly to the Church of San Andrea and builds the necessary tension for depicting Scarpia's villainy. Taddei himself has a marvellously wide range of tone colour, and though he cannot quite match the Gobbi snarl, he has almost every other weapon in his armoury. Leontyne Price is at the peak of her form and di Stefano sings most sensitively. The sound of the Vienna orchestra is enthralling – both more refined and richer than usual in a Puccini opera – and the recording is splendidly vivid in this current transfer, which has been made at the highest possible level and has great warmth and atmosphere to bring a lovely bloom to the voices. Occasionally in the moments of spectacle (the *Te Deum* at the end of side one; and the scene between Scarpia and Tosca at the beginning of side three) the focus of the recording spreads, and at times the orchestra seems larger than

life; but generally the ripeness of the sound is irresistible (the opening of Act 4 is especially impressive), even if generally it has less immediacy and projection than the Davis Philips set, which is drier in acoustic. The Decca libretto is clear but uses rather small print.

Pacing the music naturally and sympathetically, Colin Davis proves a superb Puccinian, one who not only presents Puccini's drama with richness and force, but gives the score the musical strength of a great symphony. Davis rarely if ever chooses idiosyncratic tempi, and his manner is relatively straight, but it remains a strong and understanding reading as well as a refreshing one. In this the quality of the singing from a cast of unusual consistency plays an important part. Caballé may not be so sharply jealous a heroine as her keenest rivals, but with the purity of *Vissi d'arte* coming as a key element in her interpretation, she still presents Tosca as a formidable siren-figure (*mia sirena* being Cavaradossi's expression of endearment). Carreras reinforces his reputation as a tenor of unusual artistry as well as of superb vocal powers. Though Wixell is not ideally well-focused as Scarpia, not at all Italianate of tone, he presents a completely credible lover-figure, not just the lusting ogre of convention. The recording is gloriously rich as well as refined, bringing out the beauties of Puccini's scoring more vividly than any previous set. The cassette transfer too is outstandingly good, one of the best of all Philips' opera issues on tape. The *Te Deum* is spectacular, with hardly any feeling of strain, and the solo voices are given a vivid presence and a fine balance with the orchestra.

Tosca (opera): highlights.
** DG 3306 044. Galina Vishnevskaya, Franco Bonisolli, Matteo Manuguerra, French Radio Chorus and Children's Chorus, French National Orch., Rostropovich.

The complete Rostropovich *Tosca* with Vishnevskaya in the name part has been withdrawn in the UK in its tape format, although it is still available in Europe and the USA [3370 008]. These highlights are therefore welcome, though it is a great pity that the selection, by moving straight from *Vissi d'arte* to *E lucevan le stelle*, omits the electrifying scene where Scarpia is murdered. Reflecting stage performances in Paris the reading is vitally alive, not just in the portrayal of the heroine but in the conducting too, wilful in its rhythmic nudgings but memorably characterful. Vishnevskaya has her squally moments, but her dramatic intensity is most compelling. After hints of sobbing in *Recondita armonia*, Franco Bonisolli proves a fine Cavaradossi, airily youthful of tone, while the Scarpia of Matteo Manuguerra, equally young-sounding and virile, is a magnificently compelling and fresh characterization which in some ways makes Scarpia less double-dyed and more believable as a villain-lover. The transfer is refined in detail and faithful to voices and orchestra, but the level is low and (apart from minor hiss problems) the action sometimes seems rather distant.

Il Trittico: Il Tabarro; Suor Angelica; Gianni Schicchi.
> (M) *** HMV TC-SLS 5066. Victoria de los Angeles, Fedora Barbieri, Tito Gobbi, Giacinto Prandelli, Rome Opera Chorus and Orch., Bellezza, Serafin or Santini.

Only *Gianni Schicchi* is in genuine stereo as opposed to stereo transcription, but these are classic sets which should not be missed by any opera-lover. This vividly atmospheric and brilliantly contrasted group of one-acters has never been more richly and characterfully presented on record, with Tito Gobbi giving two of his ripest characterizations. The role of the deceived bargemaster in *Il*

Tabarro inspires him to one of his very finest recorded performances. Victoria de los Angeles makes a most affecting Angelica in the still underrated central leaf of the triptych, and reappears, charmingly girlish, as Lauretta in *Gianni Schicchi*, where the high comedy has never fizzed so deliciously in a recording as it does here. The tape transfer is particularly successful, disguising the age of the mid-fifties recordings and kind to the voices. Los Angeles's voice in particular has a very pleasing bloom on it, and one is struck throughout by the natural quality of the sound.

Turandot (opera): complete.
> *** Decca K 2 A 2 [Lon. 5-13018]. Joan Sutherland, Luciano Pavarotti, Montserrat Caballé, Peter Pears, Nicolai Ghiaurov, John Alldis Choir, Wandsworth School Boys' Choir, LPO, Mehta.
> **(*) HMV TC-SLS 5135. Montserrat Caballé, José Carreras, Mirella Freni, Michel Sénéchal, Maîtrise de la Cathédrale, Chorus of L'Opéra du Rhin, Strasbourg PO, Lombard.

The role of Turandot, the icy princess, is not one that you would expect to be in Joan Sutherland's repertory, but here she gives an intensely revealing and appealing interpretation, making the character far more human and sympathetic than ever before. This is a character, armoured and unyielding in *In questa reggia*, whose final capitulation to love is a natural development, not an incomprehensible switch. Sutherland's singing is strong and beautiful, while Pavarotti gives a performance equally imaginative, beautiful in sound, strong on detail. To set Caballé against Sutherland was a daring idea, and it works superbly well; Pears as the Emperor is another imaginative choice. Mehta directs a gloriously rich and dramatic performance, superlatively recorded, and on tape the sound is richly atmospheric and deals with the moments of spectacle without strain. The quality is only marginally less open than on the discs. The printing of the libretto is admirably clear.

Having sung Liù opposite Joan Sutherland for Decca, Caballé went on to assume the more taxing role of Turandot. With Mirella Freni as Liù, there is again a powerful confrontation, not between black and white but between subtler, less fixed characters. So from the very start Caballé conveys an element of mystery, while Freni underlines the dramatic rather than the lyrical side of Liù's role. The pity is that the recording is unflattering to the voices – allowing Caballé less warmth and body of tone than usual while setting Freni so close that a flutter keeps intruding. Lombard, so alert and imaginative in French music, proves a stiff and unsympathetic Puccinian, so that the tenor, José Carreras, for example, is prevented from expanding as he should in the big arias. Nor is the Strasbourg Philharmonic a match for the LPO on Decca. The cassette transfer is generally well managed, and it opens vividly, but the sound has less obvious range than on the Decca set. The level drops on the second tape, which reduces the impact of the finale. The opera is well laid out on two cassettes, with Acts 1 and 2 each complete on one side and Act 3 spaced over the remaining two sides. The libretto, however, is in very small print.

Turandot: highlights.
**(*) Decca KCET 573 [Lon. 5-26377] (from above set cond. Mehta).

A very generous and shrewdly chosen collection of excerpts from Mehta's glorious *Turandot*. *Nessun dorma*, with Pavarotti at his finest, is here given a closing cadence for neatness. The opening item, the chorus *Gira la cote*, is faded in, however, which some may find distracting.

The recording is good, but the spectacle is smoothly handled rather than providing the last degree of vividness, and the transfer generally is slightly below Decca's very best quality.

COLLECTIONS

'Favourite composer': Arias, duets and ensembles: (i–v) *La Bohème: Che gelida manina; Sì, mi chiamano Mimì; O soave fanciulla; La commedia è stupenda; Quando men vo; In un coupé; O Mimì, tu più non torni.* (i–ii; v–vi) *Madama Butterfly: Love duet; Flower duet; Humming chorus.* (i; vii–viii; ix) *Tosca: Sante ampolle; Recondita armonia; Te Deum; Vissi d'arte; E lucevan le stelle.* (i; vii; ix) *Manon Lescaut: In quelle trine morbide; Oh, sarò la più bella; Tu, tu amore.* (i; vii; x–xi) *Turandot: Signore, ascolta; Non piangere, Liù; Ah! per l'ultima volta; In questa reggia; Nessun dorma; Tu che di gel sei cinta.* (xii–xiii; xi) *La Fanciulla del West: Ch'ella mi creda.* (i; xiii–xiv) *Gianni Schicchi: O mio babbino caro.*

(B) *** Decca KDPC 533/4. (i–xi) Chorus and Orch. of St Cecilia Academy, Rome; (i) Renata Tebaldi; (ii) Carlo Bergonzi; (iii) Gianna d'Angelo; (iv) Ettore Bastianini; (v) Serafin; (vi) Fiorenza Cossotto; (vii) Mario del Monaco; (viii) George London; (ix) Molinari-Pradelli; (x) Inge Borkh; (xi) Erede; (xii) Jussi Bjoerling; (xiii) Orch. of Maggio Musicale Fiorentino; (xiv) Gardelli.

Now that the first generation of Decca's Puccini recordings has in the main been superseded by later versions, this two-tape anthology is especially valuable in reminding us how high the overall standards were, both of artistry and of recording, and in particular the superb contribution made by Tebaldi, one of the richest voices of our time, or indeed any other time. The selection is made and edited with characteristic Decca skill and provides an enriching experience, containing as it does some of the greatest lyric opera ever written. The set makes a real bargain, and the tape transfers are consistently well done.

'The world of Puccini': (i–iii) La Bohème: Che gelida manina; Sì, mi chiamano Mimì; O soave fanciulla; In un coupé; O Mimì, tu più non torni. (i; ii; iv) Tosca: Te Deum; Vissi d'arte; E lucevan le stelle. (i; ii) Madama Butterfly: Love duet; Un bel dì; Humming chorus. (i; v) Turandot: Signore, ascolta!; Non piangere, Liù!; Ah! per l'ultima volta!; (vi) Nessun dorma.

(M) *** Decca KCSP 365. (i) Renata Tebaldi (soprano); (ii) Carlo Bergonzi (tenor); (iii) Ettore Bastianini (bar.); (iv) George London (bar.); (v) Mario del Monaco (tenor); (vi) Giuseppe di Stefano (tenor); various orchestras and conductors.

This is a splendid anthology. It has been arranged with great skill so that we do not get a string of purple passages, yet many favourites are included. The scene from Act 1 of La Bohème has Tebaldi and Bergonzi on top form and also shows the fine atmospheric sound for which these recordings have been justly famous. After the Love duet and Un bel dì from Butterfly we are given the magical Humming chorus, and side two includes a scene from the early Turandot to show Tebaldi in ravishing voice as Liù. To finish the concert, Giuseppe di Stefano sings Nessun dorma. This is taken from a recital

disc: a cunning idea, as Mario del Monaco's version from the complete set is considerably less stylish. Sometimes the age of the originals shows in the string tone, but for the most part the sound is as vivid as the performances. Highly recommended and very generous too; the transfers are admirably managed throughout.

'Your kind of Puccini': (i; ii) La Bohème: Che gelida manina; Sì, mi chiamano Mimì. (iii) Gianni Schicchi: O mio babbino caro. Madama Butterfly: (iv) Un bel dì; (v) Humming chorus. Manon Lescaut: (i) Donna non vidi mai; (vi) Intermezzo. Tosca: (i) Recondita armonia; (vii) Vissi d'arte; (i) E lucevan le stelle. Turandot: (viii; ix) In questa reggia; (ix) Nessun dorma.

(M) ** HMV TC-EXES 5009. (i) Nicolai Gedda; (ii) Mirella Freni; (iii) Victoria de los Angeles; (iv) Renata Scotto; (v) Rome Opera Chorus, Barbirolli; (vi) New Philharmonia Orch., Bartoletti; (vii) Maria Callas; (viii) Birgit Nilsson; (ix) Franco Corelli; various orchestras and conductors.

Unlike the Decca Puccini collections, this EMI cassette selects favourite purple patches and in so doing does the composer an injustice. Puccini's operas were carefully constructed so that the set pieces were separated by longish sections of 'speaking-style' music, sometimes lyrical, sometimes dramatic. He was a supreme master of the control of dramatic tension, and his emotional climaxes are made the more forceful for being so carefully placed within each score as a whole. Undoubtedly the performances here are individually first-rate, and among the highlights are the Gianni Schicchi and Turandot excerpts, with Barbirolli's marvellously atmospheric account

433

of the *Humming chorus* from *Butterfly* providing a welcome moment of repose. The sound too is consistent, warm rather than brilliant, but it was a pity to end the collection so arbitrarily by cutting off the *Turandot* excerpt in mid-air.

'Famous operatic duets': La *Bohème:* (i; ii) *O soave fanciulla;* (ii; iii) *O Mimì, tu più non torni.* *Madama Butterfly:* (i; ii) *Love duet;* (i; iv) *Flower duet.* Tosca: (i; v) *Mario, Mario!*

> (M) **(*) Decca KCSP 496. (i) Renata Tebaldi (soprano); (ii) Carlo Bergonzi (tenor); (ii) Ettore Bastianini (bar.); (iv) Fiorenza Cossotto (mezzo-soprano); (v) Mario del Monaco (tenor); various orchestras and conductors – VERDI: *La Forza del destino* excerpt.**(*)

Although it opens with *Solenne in quest'ora* from Verdi's *Forza del destino*, this is primarily a collection based on the Tebaldi recordings of the three key Puccini operas. Decca are understandably proud of these recordings, and indeed most of the excerpts are already available in other anthologies (see above). However, the present re-jigging works well enough, and in the current transfer the voices have admirable presence and freshness and the age of the recordings shows only in the string tone. The one small snag is that the final item – the *Flower duet* from *Madama Butterfly* – ends cadentially in the air, and makes an unsatisfactory close to the recital. This could surely have been avoided by re-arrangement of the excerpts.

Purcell, Henry
(1658–95)

Chacony in G minor. Anthems: *Blow up the trumpet in Zion; My heart is inditing; O God, Thou art my God; O God, Thou hast cast us out; Rejoice in the Lord always; Remember not, Lord, our offences.*

> *** Telefunken CX 4.41123. King's College Choir, Willcocks; Leonhardt Consort, Leonhardt.

An attractive concert which happily blends scholarship and spontaneity. The instrumental ensemble uses period instruments and playing style, and the character of the sound is very distinctive. Not all the anthems have instrumental accompaniments but they are all well sung with the characteristic King's penchant for tonal breadth and beauty. Excellent sound. This is a splendid demonstration of the quality possible using CrO_2 tape. The sound is admirably smooth and realistic, and background noise is simply not a problem. Very highly recommended.

(i) *Funeral music for Queen Mary.* Anthems and verse anthems: *Blessed are they that fear the Lord; Hear my prayer, O Lord; My beloved spake; Rejoice in the Lord always; Remember not, Lord, our offences.*

> ** HMV TC-ASD 3316. Soloists, King's College Choir, Ledger, (i) with Philip Jones Brass Ens.

Philip Ledger has the benefit of atmospheric sound for his darkly memorable performance of the *March* from the *Funeral music for Queen Mary*, but the funeral anthems are given less alert performances. However, the choice of three of Purcell's great verse anthems for coupling makes amends. The soloists are from the choir. Although the sound is not quite as open and free on tape as on the LP, the transfer is generally good. The brass at the beginning is clear rather than richly resonant, but the voices on the whole are naturally caught.

Bonduca: Overture and suite. Circe: suite. Sir Anthony Love: Overture and suite.
> **(*)** Oiseau-Lyre KDSLC 527. Judith Nelson, Elizabeth Lane, Prudence Lloyd, James Bowman, Martyn Hill, Paul Elliott, Alan Byers, Peter Bamber, Christopher Keyte, Taverner Choir, Academy of Ancient Music, Hogwood.

Purcell's theatre music, virtually buried along with the plays for which it was written, comes up with wonderful freshness in these performances using authentic instruments. As well as the charming dances and overtures, this tape contains songs and more extended scenes with soloists and chorus, which provide the meatiest items. Tastes may differ on style of baroque performances, but the vigour of Hogwood and his team is hard to resist. However the somewhat astringent timbres of the early stringed instruments need absolutely clean upper partials if the sound is to reach the ears agreeably. The tape transfer is less than perfectly clean (the trumpets are blurred slightly, too, on one occasion), but yields to the controls. The voices, however, are treated very naturally, and the music from *Sir Anthony Love* and (especially) *Circe* is most effective. The technical faults here are minimal, and tape collectors are urged to explore this collection for its freshness of inspiration.

Don Quixote: Overture and incidental music.
> ******* Oiseau-Lyre KDSLC 534. Judith Nelson, Emma Kirkby, James Bowman, Martyn Hill, David Thomas, Academy of Ancient Music, dir. Hogwood (harpsichord and organ).

Purcell was one of the contributors of incidental music to the three plays which Thomas D'Urfey based on Cervantes's famous novel. The music was written at high speed, but, as this charming recording demonstrates, much of it was attractively lively and it richly deserves to be resurrected in such stylish and brightly recorded performances as these. This is one of the most successful of Hogwood's enjoyable series; there is some quite enchanting singing from both the soprano soloists, and the instrumental contribution has splendid bite. The quality of the transfer is first-class, especially crisp on side two, with the most natural projection of the solo voices. Highly recommended.

Dido and Aeneas (opera): complete.
> ******* Decca KCET 615. Janet Baker, Peter Pears, Norma Burrowes, Anna Reynolds, London Opera Chorus, Aldeburgh Festival Strings, Bedford.
> **(M) **** HMV TC-SXLP 30275. Victoria de los Angeles, Peter Glossop, Heather Harper, Patricia Johnson, Ambrosian Singers, ECO, Barbirolli.

With many individual touches in sharp pointing and unexpected tempi that suggest earlier consultation with Benjamin Britten, the Decca version is the recording that Britten himself should have made. Steuart Bedford proves an admirable deputy, and the Britten/Holst edition, with its extra items completing Act 2, is most effective. With Norma Burrowes a touchingly youthful Belinda, with Peter Pears using Lieder style in the unexpected role (for him) of Aeneas, with Anna Reynolds an admirable Sorceress and other star singers even in supporting roles, there is hardly a weak link, and the London Opera Chorus relishes the often unusual tempi.

As for Dame Janet Baker, here returning to the area of her earliest success in the recording studio, the portrait of Dido is even fuller and richer than before, with more daring tonal colouring and challengingly slow tempi for the two big arias. Some will still prefer the heartfelt spontaneity of the youthful performance (not available on tape), but the range of expression on the newer version is unparalleled, and the rich modern recording quality adds to the vividness of the experience. The transfer is generally of high quality, with plenty of presence to the voices and the atmosphere of the recording admirably caught. There is just a suggestion at times that the upper range is not as clean as on the disc; the choral focus slips a little. But this is not enough to qualify a strong recommendation.

Barbirolli – not the most likely conductor for this opera – took some trouble with his text, using the Neville Boyling edition. But on questions of authenticity he is less secure, and there are fewer moments than one would expect of such high emotional intensity as to justify a 'personality' reading. The tempi are generally perverse, with slow speeds predominating – sometimes grotesquely slow – but with Dido's *When I am laid in earth* taken equivalently fast. Victoria de los Angeles makes an appealing Dido, but she does not have anything like the dramatic weight of Janet Baker, and the tone sometimes loses its bloom on top. The other singers are good, and the transfer is successful, crisp and clear with good choral detail; but this version earns only a qualified recommendation.

Dido and Aeneas: Dido's lament (arr. Stokowski).

*(*) Advent E 1047 (see p. xxiii) [id.]. RPO, Stokowski –
DVOŘÁK: *String serenade;*
VAUGHAN WILLIAMS: *Tallis fantasia.***(*)

Stokowski's highly indulgent arrangement of Purcell's famous *Lament* is certainly not for purists, but it is richly played and recorded, and it takes up only a few minutes of an otherwise highly recommendable tape. The transfer is first-class.

Rachmaninov, Sergei (1873–1943)

Piano concertos Nos. 1–4; Rhapsody on a theme of Paganini, Op. 43.
  ⊛ *** Decca K 43 K 33 [Lon. 5-2311]. Vladimir Ashkenazy, LSO, Previn.
  **(*) DG 3371 034 [id.]. Tamás Vásáry, LSO, Ahronovitch.

Ashkenazy's recording of the Rachmaninov concertos and the *Rhapsody on a theme of Paganini* stands out as a major achievement. The individuality and imagination of the playing, and its poetic feeling, provide special rewards, and if sometimes one might ask for a more commanding style, Previn's accompaniments are sympathetic and perceptive to match Ashkenazy's sometimes withdrawn manner. The *Second Concerto* is an outstanding success, notable for perhaps the most beautiful performance of the slow movement currently available. The *Third* is more controversial in its waywardness, but undoubtedly has inspired moments, while the *Rhapsody* has received more brilliant, more boldly extrovert performances from other hands (notably Katchen's). Michelangeli's account of the *Fourth Concerto* (not available on tape) is uniquely magical, but Ashkenazy is very fine too. The Decca sound casts a warm glow over the music-making. Sometimes it is not ideally clear and sometimes one misses an element of glitter, but generally it matches the rhapsodic, musing lyricism of the performances admirably. The cassette box offers extremely sophisticated transfers. In many ways the sound in the *Rhapsody* is preferable in its sparkle and detail to the equivalent LP, and the *Fourth Concerto* too offers impressive demonstration quality. Elsewhere the sound matches that of the discs: it is warm in ambience and naturally balanced.

The Vásáry/Ahronovitch set could not possibly be recommended above that of Ashkenazy and Previn, but their combination of impetuosity and poetry shows a certain consistency when the performances are heard together. The recordings are clear and well balanced, the overall effect vivid. The transfers too are consistently well managed, and even though the level is unambitious the internal detail remains clear. The *Third Concerto* sounds especially well (better-focused than Ashkenazy's Decca version) and its romantic atmosphere is attractively projected. But the low overall transfers may worry younger ears with a degree of background hiss. The individual tapes are in removable boxes, and the booklet of notes is clearly printed.

Piano concertos Nos. 1 in F sharp minor, Op. 1; 2 in C minor, Op. 18.
*** Decca KSXC 6554 [Lon. 5-6774]. Vladimir Ashkenazy, LSO, Previn.
** DG 3300 717 [id.]. Tamás Vásáry, LSO, Ahronovitch.
(M) *(*) Decca KCSP 169. Peter Katin, LPO or New SO, Colin Davis.

In the opening movement of the *First Concerto* Ashkenazy's light, rhapsodic approach minimizes the drama: other accounts have provided more pointed music-making here, but the poetry of the slow movement and the sparkling lilt of the finale (the secondary lyrical theme played with just the right touch of restraint) are irresistible. Again in the *Second Concerto* it is the warm lyricism of the playing which is so compelling. The opening tempo, like Richter's, is slow, but the tension is finely graduated towards the great climax, and the gentle, introspective mood of the *Adagio* is very beautiful indeed. The finale is broad and spacious rather than electrically exciting, but the scintillating, unforced bravura provides all the sparkle necessary. The recording is richly spacious, the piano tone slightly brighter in the *First Concerto*. The transfer is of high quality.

Ahronovitch's direction is nothing if not impetuous, and this performance of the *First Concerto* is full of vigour, with bursts of vivid romanticism. Vásáry's more introvert manner seems to fit well within this dashing framework, and there is no doubt about the freshness of this performance. Moreover the memorable theme of the finale is affectionately shaped, yet not indulged. The *Second Concerto* is also effective, with a fine climax in the first movement. But after that the tension is allowed to drop, and the languorous *Adagio* does not distil the degree of poetry which makes the Ashkenazy/Previn performance so beautiful. The DG recording is bold and colourful, and the transfer is of good quality, although one needs a fairly high volume setting to get the best results.

Boult brings a sympathetic freshness to the *First Concerto*, and his conducting is matched by Katin's spirited playing. The pianist does not attempt a conventional bravura style, and some may be disappointed on this account, but in this shortest of Rachmaninov's concertos the added clarity and point given to so many passages more than make amends (if indeed amends need to be made). The orchestra responds well but does not always play with perfect precision. The stereo is excellent, with good definition and balance. Unfortunately the performance of the *Second Concerto* is underpowered. Katin takes the opening chords in a brisk, matter-of-fact way, and although the lyricism of the first movement is nicely managed, the performance as a whole is not as exciting as the best available. Nevertheless the cassette transfer of this work is very successful and better balanced than the equivalent LP, with splendidly rich piano tone. The sound in the *First Concerto* is only marginally less good.

Piano concerto No. 2 in C minor, Op. 18.

> ****(*)** DG 923059 [id.]. Sviatoslav Richter, Warsaw PO, Wislocki – BEETHOVEN: *Rondo in B flat.****
>
> ****(*)** Decca Phase 4 KPFC 2 7004. Ivan Davis, RPO, Henry Lewis – TCHAIKOVSKY: *Piano concerto No. 1.***(*)
>
> ****(*)** HMV TC-ASD 3457. Dmitri Alexeev, RPO, Fedoseyev – *Preludes.***(*)
>
> (B) ****** Classics for Pleasure TC-CFP 167. Moura Lympany, RPO, Sargent – *Preludes.***

> (i) *Piano concerto No. 2. Études-Tableaux, Op. 39/1, 2 and 5.*
>
> (M) ****** Decca Jubilee KJBC 52. Vladimir Ashkenazy, (i) with Moscow PO, Kondrashin.

Richter has strong, even controversial ideas about speeds in this concerto. The long opening melody of the first movement is taken abnormally slowly, and it is only the sense of mastery which Richter conveys in every note which prevents one from complaining. One ends by admitting how convincing that speed can be in Richter's hands, but away from the magic one realizes that this is not quite the way Rachmaninov himself intended it. The slow movement too is spacious – with complete justification this time – and the opening of the finale lets the floodgates open the other way, for Richter chooses a hair-raisingly fast allegro, which has the Polish players scampering after him as fast as they are able. Richter

does not, however, let himself be rushed in the great secondary melody, so this is a reading of vivid contrasts. Good recording of the piano, less firm of the orchestra, but an atmospheric acoustic adds bloom overall. The transfer is good but (like the disc) lacks the last degree of sharpness of focus of the orchestra.

Though the names of the participants on the Phase Four issue are less imposing, this is a splendid tape, given a full-blooded, rich recording, the piano image large and forward, but not distractingly so. The interpretation is spaciously conceived, the tempo and control of tension in the first movement broad: not as slow as Richter, nor as exuberant as Katchen's (see below). Thus the style of the interpretation falls somewhere between these two alternative recommendations. The sound is excellent in every way. However, being treated as a 'double tape' (on disc, each of the coupled performances was given a whole LP to itself), it is not very economically priced.

The young Soviet pianist Dmitri Alexeev undoubtedly provides a thoroughly enjoyable performance. He has the gift of creating an effect of spontaneity in the recording studio, and the fresh, romantic warmth of his playing is highly engaging. The accompaniment is sympathetic and the RPO are on top form; the string playing in the slow movement matches the gentle eloquence of the wind solos. Fedoseyev paces the first-movement climax admirably, and the close of the movement is especially attractive: the tension is not allowed to drop, yet the relaxed lyrical feeling persists. The finale, however, is rather underpowered. Its lightweight quality is not at odds with the reading as a whole, but compared to, say, Richter, there is some lack of really compelling bravura. Nevertheless this remains a considerable performance, and although the coupling is not generous, the recording is first-class, rich yet detailed. The transfer is very slightly overweighted in the bass but this can easily be corrected, and the quality is otherwise refined and full.

Moura Lympany gives a thoroughly engaging, straightforward reading, helped by first-class recording, with full, rich piano tone and excellent balance. There are many little touches of phrasing and dynamic shading to distinguish the orchestral playing, and the slow movement is notably beautiful. Just occasionally there is the feeling that the tension is *too* much under control, but this is only momentary, for clearly both conductor and soloist are in great sympathy with Rachmaninov's melodic inspiration. The three *Preludes* are admirably chosen and are very effective indeed. The transfer is of excellent quality, clear, secure and well balanced.

Ashkenazy's earlier recording with Kondrashin is disappointing. It is a relaxed, lyrical reading which rises to the climaxes but is seldom as compelling as the best versions. The *Études-tableaux* make an attractive bonus and are, needless to say, very well played. The sound is generally excellent, although the massed string tone here is not as convincing as on Ashkenazy's later Decca recording (coupled to the *First Concerto*), which is well worth the extra cost. The transfer is bold and vivid, with first-class piano tone, although the focus of the upper strings is not always quite clean.

There is also an Advent cassette (E 1055) of an unbelievably indulgent performance by György Cziffra. He opens the first movement very slowly, pulls the tempo about unmercifully and then accelerates grotesquely to the climax. The recording is undistinguished, and the couplings (the *Prelude in G minor* and some transcriptions) offer no compensation.

(i) *Piano concerto No. 2 in C minor, Op. 18;* (ii) *Rhapsody on a theme of Paganini, Op. 43.*

> (M) *** Decca KCSP 505. Julius Katchen, with (i) LSO, Solti; (ii) LPO, Boult.
> (M) ** Philips Festivo 7310 046.

Rafael Orozco, RPO, de Waart.

> (M) *(*) CBS 40-61802 [Col. MT 31813]. Gary Graffman, New York PO, Bernstein.

Katchen gives a dramatic and exciting account of the *C minor Concerto* such as we would expect from this pianist. He had a fabulous technique and was always at pains to demonstrate it at its most spectacular. Generally in this recording that leads to the highest pitch of excitement, but there are a number of passages – notably the big climax as well as the coda of the first movement – where he plays almost too fast. Miraculously he gets round the notes somehow but the result inevitably seems breathless, however exciting it is. The stereo recording is in Decca's best manner and manages to be brilliant and well co-ordinated at the same time. The *Rhapsody* dates from 1934 and thus belongs to the same period as the *Third Symphony*. In many ways it is the most satisfying work Rachmaninov wrote for piano and orchestra, its invention consistently inspired. By virtue of the famous eighteenth variation, which turns Paganini's tune upside-down and imbues it with a lyrical intensity seldom surpassed in the composer's music, the work has remained high in public favour. The impact of this famous section tends to separate the rest of the music into two parts on either side of it, and this factor can sometimes throw a performance out of balance. But the Katchen performance with Boult is superbly shaped and is notable not only for its romantic flair and excitement but for the diversity and wit displayed in the earlier variations. There is no question of anti-climax after the eighteenth, for the forward impetus of the playing has tremendous power and excitement. The transfer of both works is bold and clear and vividly coloured. The piano tone is particularly rich and firm, and detail is excellent. The timbre of the upper strings is not as soft-grained as one would expect in a very modern recording, but the focus is clean and the sound is rich, with a fine overall bloom. Certainly this coupling is splendid value for money.

Rafael Orozco is a fine player and an understanding Rachmaninovian, and he is sympathetically accompanied by the RPO under Edo de Waart. The *Rhapsody* is vividly characterized and the slow movement of the concerto is eloquently expressive. The recording too is good. But Katchen's performances are even more exciting, the Decca recording wears its years lightly, and the Decca tape transfer has far more range and detail than the Festivo issue. Here the orchestral timbres in the concerto sound rather mushy and ill-defined, with comparatively poor transient response in the finale.

Graffman's coupling dates from the mid-sixties and the recording (the piano balanced absurdly forward, so that the orchestra is very much in the background in the *Concerto*), although quite agreeable in timbre, lacks range. There is rather more brilliance in the *Rhapsody*, which is quite successful. But this tape, with its comparatively limited sound, can hardly be compared with Katchen's issue, and Graffman does not show an instinctive feel for Rachmaninov's winding melodic phrases in the *Concerto*.

(i) *Piano concerto No. 2 in C minor, Op. 18;* (ii) *Rhapsody on a theme of Paganini, Op. 43.* (Piano) *Prelude in C sharp minor, Op. 3/2;* CHOPIN: *Mazurkas: in B flat major, Op. 7/1; in A minor, Op. 17/4.*

  *(*) Decca Phase 4 KPFC 14327 [Lon. 5-21099]. Ilana Vered, with (i) New Philharmonia Orch., Andrew Davis; (ii) LSO, Vonk.

Ilana Vered is a naturally expressive interpreter of Rachmaninov, but these performances are put out of court by absurd balance, with the orchestra heard faintly behind elephantine piano tone. In interpretation the *Variations* are more sharply

pointed than the concerto, where Miss Vered's style comes to sound mannered. The tape transfer is of good quality, and for an unexpected bonus throws in two Chopin *Mazurkas* (not on the equivalent disc); they are very well played too.

Piano concerto No. 3 in D minor, Op. 30.

  **(*) RCA RK 12633 [CRK 1 2633]. Vladimir Horowitz, New York PO, Ormandy.

  (M) *** Decca Jubilee KJBC 53. Vladimir Ashenazy, LSO, Fistoulari.

  **(*) Decca KSXC 6555 [Lon. 5-6775]. Ashkenazy, LSO, Previn.

  **(*) CBS 40-76597 [Col. MT 34540]. Lazar Berman, LSO, Abbado.

  *(**) RCA RX 11324 [ARK 1 1324]. Ashkenazy, Philadelphia Orch., Ormandy.

  (M) *(**) HMV Greensleeve TC-ESD 7032. Andrei Gavrilov, USSR SO, Lazarev.

  (B) ** DG Heliodor 3348 262. Joseph Alfidi, Orchestre National de Belgique, Defossez.

  ** DG 3300 859. Tamás Vásáry, LSO, Ahronovitch.

The new Horowitz/Ormandy performance (recorded in Carnegie Hall in January 1978) must certainly go to the top of the list. Horowitz's legendary association with this work daunted even the composer himself, and undoubtedly this new version is masterly. Inevitably, perhaps, with rosy memories of the famous 78 r.p.m. recording, there is a slight element of disappointment. Some of the old magic seems to be missing; this is partly due to the clear, clinical recorded sound. Every detail of the piano part is revealed, and the dryness of timbre is matched by the orchestral texture, which has little expansive richness. All the more credit to Ormandy for creating a genuinely expansive romanticism in the great slow movement. The outer movements have undoubted electricity, but it is the fascination of the detail that makes one want to return to this remarkable recorded document. Not quite all the playing is immaculate, and there is some rhythmic eccentricity in the finale; but for those who can accept the 'bare bones' of the recorded sound (impeccably transferred and if anything slightly smoother and warmer on cassette) this issue will be indispensable.

Ashkenazy's reading with Previn of the *Third Concerto*, played absolutely complete, is the controversial performance in his complete set. In some ways his earlier account with Fistoulari is fresher, and in its Jubilee reissue it is superbly recorded and transferred immaculately. The newer reading has moments of imaginative insight and touches of sheer magic, but in the last analysis it remains not quite satisfying. On tape the warm, Kingsway Hall acoustic seems to cast a glowing haze over parts of this recording, and although much of it sounds beautiful there are moments when the detail falters. The more direct and full-blooded romanticism of the earlier version (with its rich, immediate sound) offers greater satisfaction.

For all the undoubted eloquence and authority of Lazar Berman's playing, his performance is in the last analysis disappointing. In spite of the English venue the recording is comparatively shallow: not only does the piano lack the richness of sonority one would like, but the orchestra, notably at the climax of the slow movement, also lacks body and depth. It is thus in the work's reflective moments (as at the end of the cadenza in the first movement) that Berman's playing is at its most appealing, although the undoubtedly exciting finale has great force and bravura. Abbado accompanies attentively but is let down by the thin-textured recorded sound. The balance on the cassette is generally preferable to the disc. The recording has less range and refinement of detail but is mellower and more sympathetic in tonal quality.

After recording his complete Rachmaninov cycle with Previn for Decca, Ashkenazy made another version of No. 3 in Philadelphia, and though the performance brings exuberant virtuosity, the sound is a disgrace, with some of the most wooden recorded piano tone heard in years.

Had the HMV Melodiya recording (issued on the Greensleeve label) been more transparent and refined in detail the splendid performance by the young Russian virtuoso Andrei Gavrilov would have been first choice, with its bold piano tone. Certainly this is a memorable reading, strong and passionate, yet poetic too. Gavrilov uses the longer, more complex first-movement cadenza and plays it most excitingly; then he relaxes beautifully at the end to create a feeling of repose for the comparatively gentle beginning of the recapitulation. The slow movement is richly eloquent and the (uncut) finale offers a thrilling display of bravura, where Gavrilov's articulation is marvellously clear. The cassette, however, is unrefined at climaxes, and not very agreeable to listen to at these moments of coarseness.

The Heliodor recording was made at a live concert. Although it does not give a very detailed picture of the somewhat recessed orchestra, the piano is naturally recorded, and this version is enjoyable and good value. Joseph Alfidi can be an exciting player, as he shows in the first-movement cadenza and the finale, but the impression the performance leaves is essentially an intimate one (partly because of the recording balance), and the music's lyrical flow is sensitively managed. The audience does not make its presence too apparent, except at the very end with loud applause. The cassette transfer is faithful enough and well balanced.

Vásáry uses the longer version of the first-movement cadenza, but with less spontaneity than Gavrilov. The slow movement is indulgent . and lacks momentum. Vásáry's playing itself is clean, often gentle in style, but the conductor's extremes of tempi are less appropriate here than in the *First Concerto*. Taken as a whole the performance is not without its poetry or excitement (especially in the finale), but in the last analysis its impetuosity of mood remains unsatisfying. The tape transfer is good, but not outstanding. With some adjustment of the controls the overall balance can be made satisfactory (the piano timbre is clean, if a trifle hard), although there is a touch of thickness in the orchestral tuttis.

Piano concerto No. 4 in G minor, Op. 40; Rhapsody on a theme of Paganini, Op. 43.

> *** Decca KSXC 6556 [Lon. 5-6776]. Vladimir Ashkenazy, LSO, Previn.
> **(*) DG 3300 905 [id.]. Tamás Vásáry, LSO, Ahronovitch.

Ashkenazy's special quality of poetry, searchingly individual, is at its most illuminating in this coupling. The performance of the *Fourth Concerto* is the finest since Michelangeli's (not available on cassette), and in the first movement the richness of the recording and its detail (the tuba making a striking contribution to the first movement) is very impressive indeed. The *Largo* is played with a disarmingly simple eloquence and the finale is characteristically assured. The *Rhapsody* too is highly imaginative, not without sparkle or bravura, but with a wider range of feeling than one usually expects in this work. Yet there is no lack of ripeness in the famous eighteenth variation, and the closing variations too are very satisfying. The transfer is exceptionally sophisticated, detailed and with a fine overall bloom and natural balance. The livelier variations in particular offer real demonstration sound quality.

It is perhaps possible to underestimate the qualities of the series of recordings by Vásáry and Ahronovitch. The impetuous style certainly carries excitement with it, and the forward sweep of the *Rhapsody* (the opening faster than usual and with strong contrasts of tempo and mood between brilliant and lyrical variations) certainly does not lack adrenalin. The first movement of the *Concerto* too has a strong forward thrust, with relaxation of tempo for the lyrical music. There is poetry in the slow movement, even if the brilliance of the finale carries also a lack of poise. Both these performances are highly involving and they are well recorded, with a good transfer bringing a convincing overall balance and clear piano timbre. Yet the Decca Ashkenazy tape inevitably remains first choice.

The Isle of the Dead (symphonic poem), *Op. 29; Symphonic dances, Op. 45.*

> *** HMV TC-ASD 3259. LSO, Previn.

The shorter work here, *The Isle of the Dead*, emerges almost as the major offering, with the dark relentless progress of Rachmaninov's scene-painting after Boecklin building up formidably. The *Symphonic dances* bring generally fast tempi and sharp rhythms to underline the dance-like energy (and in the middle movement the dance-like flexibility) rather than the weightier symphonic qualities. With rich, wide-ranging recording the coupling can be recommended. The tape transfer is very well managed. The climaxes of *The Isle of the Dead* and the third *Symphonic dance* are marginally less open than on disc, but the sound is still impressively rich, and the detail generally good.

Rhapsody on a theme of Paganini, Op. 43 (see also under *Piano concertos Nos. 2 and 4*).

> *** HMV TC-ASD 3197. Cristina Ortiz (piano), New Philharmo-

nia Orch., Koizumi – DOH-NÁNYI: *Nursery variations.****

(M) * Rediffusion Royale KROY 2007. Marian Lapsansky (piano), Slovak PO, Slovak – PROKOFIEV: *Piano concerto No. 3.**

The brilliantly vivid account of the *Rhapsody* by Ortiz and her Japanese partner now heads a distinguished list. The balance of the variations is beautifully calculated; there is sparkle and power, and the great romantic blossoming at No. 18 will surely disappoint no one. The recording is outstanding and the demonstration-worthy cassette can be highly recommended.

The Supraphon-source Royale tape offers an unusual coupling, but the performance is too intense and lacking in light and shade to offer much repeated pleasure. The very bold, clear recording is artificially lit (the string tone in the eighteenth variation is fierce), and although the overall effect is undoubtedly vivid its aggressive qualities do not fit Rachmaninov's spirit of romantic sophistication.

Symphonies Nos. (i) *1 in D minor, Op. 13;* (ii) *2 in E minor, Op. 27; 3 in A minor, Op. 44; The Crag (The Rock; fantasia for orchestra), Op. 7.*

(M) *** Decca K 9 K 33. (i) Suisse Romande Orch.; (ii) LPO; Weller.

Walter Weller's performances are not as lushly intense as some, but their romanticism is engaging, and with superb sound from Decca they give real satisfaction. The Suisse Romande Orchestra in No. 1 do not provide such fine playing as the LPO in the other works, but this is a marginal point when the overall achievement is considerable. On tape the sound is vivid and brilliant, with splendid detail and sparkle, achieved at the expense of some small loss of body in the middle frequen-

cies compared to the equivalent discs. However, with a slight bass boost and treble cut a superior quality can be achieved, although the recording is not quite so warm and glowing in No. 1 as in the other symphonies (which are especially fine). The sound in *The Crag* is demonstration-worthy.

Symphony No. 1 in D minor, Op. 13.
**(*) Decca KSXC 6583. Suisse Romande Orch., Weller.
(***) HMV TC-ASD 3137. LSO, Previn.

The *First Symphony* was a failure when it first appeared, and the composer suffered so keenly that he suppressed the work, which only came to light after his death. Its merits are now well-known, and high among them must be the sheer originality and lyrical power of the eloquent slow movement. The finale too, famous once as a television signature tune, has memorable ideas. Weller's version is undoubtedly distinguished but suffers from the fact that the Suisse Romande Orchestra is unable to produce the body and richness of tone that the slow movement ideally demands. The performance has a fine feeling for the music's atmosphere (both inner movements show this readily). The recording is quite splendid, the finest available; its range and impact tell in the outer movements and never more vividly than in the work's dramatic closing pages. The Decca transfer is of excellent quality, and the tape holds the climaxes of the finale with aplomb.

Previn gives a forthright, clean-cut performance, beautifully played and well recorded. It may lack some of the animal vitality that one recognizes in Russian performances (or for that matter Previn's own performances of the later Rachmaninov symphonies), but this is still a richly enjoyable account. Unfortunately a recently tried copy of the HMV tape produced a variable orchestral focus, especially on side one.

Symphony No. 2 in E minor, Op. 27.
- **(*) Philips 7300 653. Rotterdam PO, de Waart.
- **(*) HMV TC-ASD 3606 [Angel 4xs 36954]. RPO, Temirkanov.
- (B) *(**) Classics for Pleasure TC-CFP 40065. Hallé Orch., Loughran.
- **(*) RCA RK 11150 [ARK 1 1150]. Philadelphia Orch., Ormandy.
- ** Enigma K 453568. Philharmonia Orch., Ling Tung.

Unfortunately Previn's outstanding HMV recording of the *Second Symphony* (TC-ASD 2889; USA: Angel 4xs 36954) is available only in non-Dolby form. The symphony is well represented on tape, however, although there is not a clear-cut first recommendation. Edo de Waart's reading is attractively volatile, bringing out the music's freshness. With generally fast tempi the effect is emotionally lightweight, although the slow movement is very beautiful and the refined orchestral playing is naturally expressive throughout. The recording is full and well balanced. The modest level of transfer brings a rich tonal patina without the clearest detail, and for maximum impact a high-level playback is needed. Nevertheless the overall effect is certainly full-blooded, even if there is a lack of sheer brilliance in the upper range.

Yuri Temirkanov regularly adopts a free *rubato* style that is not always completely convincing, even though in the outer movements it gives his reading an attractive expressive warmth. He carries this style a fraction too far in the big melody of the scherzo's first episode, making the effect soupy. The slow movement, taken relatively fast, tends to get even faster, and though it reaches a passionate climax the result lacks breadth. The playing is generally excellent, and the music-making is compulsively exciting in its way, but it does miss some of the work's romantic ripeness. The recording has brilliance and excellent detail, and the tape transfer reflects this, although the sheen on the massed violins has a touch of artificial brightness and there is a slight lack of breadth to their tone in the upper register.

Undoubtedly the most convincing sound is provided by the Enigma tape, which sets a first-class balance between amplitude and brilliance. The detail is excellent and the transients have sparkle without adding an edge to the strings. Ling Tung directs a warm and generally understanding reading, but he is not really memorable, and the playing does not match the standards of the other versions. Notably the violins do not produce the body of tone that this symphony ideally demands. But the quality of the transfer is a considerable compensating factor, and in most ways this tape sounds more attractive than the equivalent disc.

Loughran's account is in the bargain range and could make an excellent alternative recommendation. Although the performance takes a little while to warm up, this is a more intense reading than Weller's (not available separately on tape), with a fine slow movement, and the orchestral playing is excellent. The recording too is vivid and refined in detail. The tape transfer is impressively wide in range and has plenty of dynamic contrast. Our original review tape was first-class, but current copies show too high a level of modulation, producing a break-up of the sound at climaxes, especially in the slow movement.

In his fourth recorded performance Ormandy – no doubt prodded by rivals on record – opened out the old disfiguring cuts, and, with refined string tone and rich recording, produced a characteristically full-blown performance. But next to the finest available it lacks subtlety in its expressiveness, for Ormandy in this music tends to pull out all the emotional stops too soon.

Symphony No. 3 in A minor, Op. 44;
Aleko (opera): *Intermezzo and*
Women's dance.

> *** HMV TC-ASD 3369 [Angel 4xs 37260]. LSO, Previn.

Symphony No. 3; The Crag (The
Rock; fantasia for orchestra*), Op. 7.*

> ** Philips 7300 596 [id.]. Rotterdam PO, de Waart.

Symphony No. 3; Vocalise, Op. 34/
14.

> **(*) Advent E 1046 (see p. xxiii) [id.]. National PO, Stokowski.

Previn's HMV recording of the *Third Symphony* brings a stunning performance. There is much that is elusive in this highly original structure, and Previn conveys the purposefulness of the writing at every point, revelling in the richness but clarifying textures. The LSO has rarely displayed its virtuosity more brilliantly in the recording studio (reflecting the fact that the recording was made immediately after a series of performances of the work in America), and the recording is ample to match. The original copies we tried of this cassette were put out of court by the over-modulated transfer, but EMI have cured this fault and recently sampled copies show an adjusted level with rich sound, considerable sophistication of detail and refined string quality.

An admirably shaped and well-played, if rather lightweight, account comes from Edo de Waart and the Rotterdam Philharmonic, which in his hands is developing into a first-class orchestra. The tension is not very strongly held in the first movement. Here de Waart omits the exposition repeat, whereas both Previn and Weller observe it. He is at his most persuasive in the outer sections of the slow movement, with some tender playing from the strings, but elsewhere there is a lack of fervour. The Philips recording is beautifully spacious and the balance finely integrated. The transfer offers good detail and plenty of weight in the finale, but its comparative lack of robustness in the matter of massed violin tone is a drawback. Nevertheless this is a recommendable account, even if it cannot be said to outclass its competitors.

It was Stokowski who in 1936 in Philadelphia conducted the first performances of Rachmaninov's last symphony. Nearly forty years later in London he recorded it with Sydney Sax's fine group of selected orchestral players, and the result is rewarding and exciting. There are idiosyncrasies in plenty, not least a tempo for the finale that whirls one along in exhilarating danger; but this is a splendid example of Stokowski's energy in old age, his ability to inspire players to a totally individual and riveting performance, not directly comparable with others. The recording has a wide dynamic range, and the Advent transfer catches its detail and range. But the comparatively modest level seems to have taken away some of the richness of the sound: the massed strings, both in the upper and middle ranges, lack the glowing warmth this symphony needs.

6 Moments musicaux, Op. 16.

> *** DG 3300 678 [id.]. Lazar Berman (piano) – PROKOFIEV: *Piano sonata No. 8.***(*)

Masterly and authoritative accounts of this Rachmaninov rarity, beautifully recorded by the DG engineers. The coupling is a somewhat idiosyncratic account of Prokofiev's *Eighth Sonata*, which is wayward and wilful. No such reservations about this fine Rachmaninov, however, which should be heard by all who care for this composer. The transfer is realistically clear and bold, with good sonority and plenty of resonance in the bravura passages.

24 Preludes (complete).

> *** Decca KSXC 2 7038 [Lon. 5-2241]. Vladimir Ashkenazy (piano).

Considering his popularity and their quality, it is odd that Rachmaninov's *Preludes* have not been recorded complete more often. There is no competitor on tape, but Ashkenazy's set is in a class of its own both as performances and as recording. There is superb panache and flair about this playing. The tape transfer is good, but just short of being one of Decca's very best.

Preludes Nos. 3 in B flat major, Op. 23/2; 5 in D major, Op. 23/4; 6 in G minor, Op. 23/5; 8 in C minor, Op. 23/7; 12 in C major, Op. 32/1; 13 in B flat minor, Op. 32/2.
> (M) **(*) DG Privilege 3335 272 [id.]. Sviatoslav Richter (piano) – MUSSORGSKY: *Pictures at an Exhibition.***

Preludes Nos. 4 in D minor, Op. 23/3; 7 in E flat major, Op. 23/6; 23 in G sharp minor, Op. 32/12.
> **(*) HMV TC-ASD 3457. Dmitri Alexeev – *Piano concerto No. 2.***(*)

Preludes Nos. 5 in D major, Op. 23/4; 16 in G major, Op. 32/5; 23 in G sharp minor, Op. 32/12.
> (B) ** Classics for Pleasure TC-CFP 167. Moura Lympany – *Piano concerto No. 2.***

Richter's marvellous performances make one hope that one day we shall have a complete set from him on tape. The transfer on this Privilege cassette offers a quite well-balanced piano image, but the sound could do with a shade more range and brilliance to match Richter's bravura, and the piano's middle register is somewhat lacking in colour.

The freshness of Dmitri Alexeev's playing is notable here, as in the concerto coupling. His characterization is persuasive, if not so commanding as Richter's. But there is undoubted spontaneity, and the *G sharp minor Prelude* comes off especially well. The recording is first-class and the transfer admirably faithful.

Moura Lympany's collection, which is well transferred, is discussed under its coupling.

Suites for 2 pianos Nos. 1 (Fantasy), Op. 5; 2, Op. 17.
> *** Decca KSXC 6697 [Lon. 5-6893]. Vladimir Ashkenazy, André Previn (pianos).

A delectable coupling of the two fine *Piano suites*, beautifully recorded. The colour and flair of Rachmaninov's writing are captured with wonderful imagination – reflection of a live performance by Ashkenazy and Previn at London's South Bank Summer Music in the summer of 1974. The cassette transfer is superbly managed and offers demonstration quality.

(i) The Bells (cantata), Op. 35. Vocalise, Op. 34/14.
> *** HMV TC-ASD 3284. Sheila Armstrong, LSO, Previn, (i) with Robert Tear, John Shirley-Quirk, LSO Chorus.

In *The Bells* the LSO Chorus sings convincingly in the original language. The timbre may not be entirely Russian-sounding (cleaner and fresher in fact), but in what amounts to a choral symphony Previn's concentration on purely musical values as much as on evocation of atmosphere produces powerful results, particularly when the recording is of demonstration standard, rich and vivid. All the soloists are very good, and Sheila Armstrong, tenderly beautiful in the lovely second movement, depicting Poe's *Wedding Bells*, is more than a match for any rival. The transfer has been generally well managed and the sound is undoubtedly vivid, although the chorus lacks the last degree of sharpness of focus.

Liturgy of St John Chrysostom, Op. 31.
> *** HMV TC-SLS 5130. Emilia Maximova, Veselina Zorova,

Yassil Stoytsov, Yordan Vidov, Ivan Petrov, Chorus of Bulgarian Radio (Sofia), Milkov.

The *Liturgy of St John Chrysostom* is the most frequently used liturgy of the Russian Orthodox Church. Rachmaninov's setting is modelled on Tchaikovsky's (1878) and was composed in 1910, three years before *The Bells*. There are twenty movements in all, unified by certain motivic links, and the work is so designed tonally that it can be satisfactorily performed in a concert hall context. It is performed here with striking conviction and feeling, and its rich sonorities are splendidly captured by the engineers in an ample and generous acoustic. This is music of great atmosphere and though perhaps not as consistently individual as the *Vespers* of 1915, it is immensely rewarding and can be warmly recommended. The transfer is highly successful, often of demonstration quality; considering the wide reverberation of the recording there is remarkably little blurring of the choral focus.

Vocalise, Op. 34/14 (arr. Dubensky).
 (**) RCA RK 42006. Anna Moffo (soprano), American SO, Stokowski – CANTELOUBE: *Songs of the Auvergne;* VILLA-LOBOS: *Bachianas Brasileiras No. 5.*(**)

Rachmaninov's *Vocalise* was a favourite showpiece of Stokowski, usually in a purely orchestral arrangement, but here with Moffo at her warmest it is good to have the vocal version so persuasively matching the accompaniment. An attractive coupling for those with a sweet tooth. Unfortunately the transfer is shrill (one needs a very strong treble cut to make the quality comfortable) and there is little compensating weight at the bass end of the recording.

COLLECTIONS

'Favourite composer': (i; ii) *Piano concerto No. 2 in C minor, Op. 18;* (ii–iv) *Rhapsody on a theme of Paganini, Op. 43;* (v) *Symphony No. 2 in E minor, Op. 27;* (iii) *Prelude No. 1 in C sharp minor, Op. 3/2;* (vi) *Vocalise, Op. 34/14.*
 (B) *(*) Decca KDPC 565/6. (i) Julius Katchen, Solti; (ii) LSO; (iii) Ilana Vered (piano); (iv) Vonk; (v) LPO, Boult; (vi) Elisabeth Söderström (soprano), Vladimir Ashkenazy (piano).

Katchen's performance of the *Second Concerto* is a brilliant one and it is a pity that Decca did not stay with this artist instead of choosing Ilana Vered's less successful recording of the *Rhapsody*. Boult's performance of the *Second Symphony* has come up with surprising freshness here, but taken as a whole this is not one of Decca's finest *Favourite composer* anthologies. The sound on the first tape (with the *Concerto* and the *Rhapsody*) is not as clean in the treble as is usual with Decca. The symphony, however, emerges freshly.

'The world of Rachmaninov': (i; ii) *Piano concerto No. 2 in C minor, Op. 18:* 1st movt; 3rd movt (abridged); (i; iii) *Piano concerto No. 3 in D minor, Op. 30:* 3rd movt; (iv; v) *Rhapsody on a theme of Paganini, Op. 43:* Variations 16–18; (vi) *Symphony No. 1 in D minor, Op. 13:* 4th movt (excerpts); (v) *Symphony No. 2 in E minor, Op. 27:* 3rd movt; *Preludes:* (vii) *No. 1 in C sharp minor, Op. 3/2;* (viii) *No. 6 in G minor, Op. 23/5.*
 (M) *** Decca KCSP 310. (i) Vladimir Ashkenazy; (ii)

Moscow PO, Kondrashin; (iii) LSO, Fistoulari; (iv) Julius Katchen (piano); (v) LPO, Boult; (vi) Suisse Romande Orch., Weller; (vii) Bracha Eden, Alexander Tamir (pianos); (viii) Moura Lympany (piano).

This is another of those Decca anthologies that succeed by clever arrangement of items. All the performances are first-rate, although the surprise is how well this transfer of the slow movement of Boult's performance of the *Second Symphony* sounds. Boult conducts the *Rhapsody on a theme of Paganini* too, and it was a happy idea to prepare for the famous eighteenth variation by including the two that come immediately before it. This is followed by (only) part of the finale of the *Second Concerto*, but the transition is painless. We have already had the first movement on side one. With generally excellent sound this makes enjoyable listening for any Rachmaninov-lover and avoids being just a selection of purple patches. Moura Lympany's performance of the *G minor Prelude* is a stereo transcription, but it sounds well. The transfers are excellent, the quality on the first side of the tape approaching a demonstration standard.

Ravel, Maurice (1875–1937)

Alborada del gracioso.

(M) **(*) HMV TC-SXLP 30263 [Angel 4XG 60102]. French National Radio Orch., Stokowski – DEBUSSY: *Ibéria***(*); IBERT: *Escales.****

Stokowski's *Alborada* has tremendous panache. The balance (as throughout this collection) has an element of crudity, with woodwind zooming forward for their solos; but the vivid orchestral playing is highly exhilarating, and the vitality of the music-making is never in question from the first note to the last. The transfer is crisp yet full-bodied: as sheer sound, this is undoubtedly one of the most exciting *Alborada*s on tape.

(i) *Alborada del gracioso; Boléro; Daphnis et Chloé: Suite No. 1;* (ii) *Ma Mère l'Oye (Mother Goose): suite; Pavane pour une infante défunte;* (i) *La Valse.*

(B) ** Rediffusion Legend KLGDD 102. Czech PO, (i) Baudo, (ii) Pedrotti – DEBUSSY: *Images* etc.**

The clear, often translucent sound, offering very refined detail but a lack of sensuous richness to the string tone, is generally less effective in Ravel's music than in the Debussy coupling. The *Alborada* is extremely vivid and sparkling, and *Mother Goose* too offers some delightful wind textures, although the strings in *The fairy garden* are much too bright in timbre to create the full atmosphere of this magical piece. *Boléro* lacks weight at the final climax and the *Pavane* needs more of a feeling of elegant warmth. But when all this is said, there is much to admire in the orchestral playing itself, and with the balance controls adjusted the sound is always more than acceptable. Certainly at the bargain price at which it is offered this set is worth considering.

Alborada del gracioso; Boléro; Pavane pour une infante défunte; La Valse.
> (B) *(**) Classics for Pleasure TC-CFP 40036. Paris Conservatoire Orch., Cluytens.

Cluytens gives a brilliant account of the *Alborada*, although his orchestral playing lacks something in precision; the *Pavane*, however, with its French french horn is slightly less appealing. In *Boléro* Cluytens maintains a consistent tempo: this is vivid and unaffected but in the last analysis not as exciting as some. *La Valse*, on the other hand, is most successful, rising to a climax of considerable intensity. The recording does not date; it is atmospheric, with no lack of body or sparkle. Unfortunately the almost complete absence of dynamic expansion in *Boléro* (the piece starts nearly as loudly as it finishes!) minimizes the appeal of the cassette; but otherwise the sound is very effective, glowing and clear. The *Alborada* has plenty of glitter, and *La Valse* has a reasonable degree of light and shade.

Alborada del gracioso; Boléro; La Valse.
> *(**) CBS 40-76513 [Col. XMT 35103]. Orchestre National de France, Bernstein.

There is no cause for complaint here on grounds of performance. Bernstein secures a first-class response from the Orchestre National (the old Orchestre National de l'ORTF). *La Valse* has a genuine intoxicating quality, and there is no doubt about the success of its companions. Yet given the competition in this repertoire, this issue offers short measure: *Boléro* takes 15′ 35″, and the other side only just exceeds twenty minutes. Moreover the reverberant re-

cording has not been very adequately transferred to tape. The side-drum at the opening of *Boléro* is indistinctly focused, and the climax lacks a really vivid projection because of the relatively low transfer level. The *Alborada* has more sparkle, but the sound in *La Valse* lacks lustre and detail.

Alborada del gracioso; Daphnis et Chloé: Suite No. 2; Pavane pour une infante défunte; Rapsodie espagnole; La Valse.
> (M) ** Decca KCSP 230. Suisse Romande Orch., Ansermet.

Decca's collection, issued as part of 'The world of great classics' series, gives generous value. The *Daphnis* suite is not as well played nor as sensuous as one might ideally ask (the latter being partly the fault of the clinical sound balance of the recording), and the *Alborada* is less vivid than Stokowski's. But Ansermet's coolness suits the *Pavane*, and the *Rapsodie* is quite effective. *La Valse*, always a piece Ansermet did well, is spectacular and atmospheric. The cassette transfers vary a little in quality from piece to piece, but generally offer brilliant sound, with plenty of glitter from the percussion. *Daphnis et Chloé* is notably successful and the balance throughout has good range and clarity. The cataclysmic end of *La Valse* is accommodated with skill.

Alborada del gracioso; Pavane pour une infante défunte.
> (M) *** Decca Jubilee KJBC 50. New Philharmonia Orch., Frühbeck de Burgos – FALLA: *El amor brujo;* GRANADOS: *Goyescas.****

Frühbeck de Burgos's *Alborada* is glitteringly brilliant, helped by one of Decca's best and most transparent recordings. The lovely *Pavane* is hardly less attractive, but this piece almost always seems to come off well in the recording studio. The transfer is characteristically vivid and clear.

Boléro.

(*) DG 923018 [id.]. Berlin PO, Karajan – MUSSORGSKY: *Pictures*.*

** HMV TC-ASD 3431. Berlin PO, Karajan – DEBUSSY: *La Mer; Prélude*.*(*)

** Decca KSXC 6813 [Lon. 5-7033]. Chicago SO, Solti – DEBUSSY: *La Mer; Prélude*.**

Karajan's DG version is contained, but one feels the forward pulse, and the impression is of quickening; yet a check reveals that the tempo at the end has hardly varied from the opening bars (as the composer intended). The orchestral playing is very sophisticated; the trombone *glissandi* in the famous solo are thrown off without a wink and the overall crescendo is beautifully balanced. The DG sound is expansive at the climax although (as so often happens with this piece on tape) the opening is somewhat subfusc. The later HMV account is also superbly played, with sumptuous quality if rather less refinement of detail. On the whole the DG performance has more character.

Metrically rigorous, Solti builds up the nagging climax with superb relentlessness. Though it lacks seductive touches, the performance is beautifully poised and pointed. Brightly analytical recording, and a faithful cassette transfer giving the clearest sound of all three tapes listed here.

Boléro; Daphnis et Chloé: Suite No. 2; Ma Mère l'Oye (Mother Goose): suite; La Valse.

**(*) Decca KSXC 16488. Los Angeles PO, Mehta.

The emphasis here is very much on excitement, although there is no lack of finesse in the *Mother Goose suite*, which is beautifully played. *Boléro* has a strong forward pulse to set the adrenalin racing as the climax approaches, and *La Valse* has a similar spectacular bravura, although the sophistication of both playing and recording avoids any feeling of brashness. Mehta and his orchestra are also very much at home in the music from *Daphnis et Chloé*. The tape transfer has a suitable brilliance to match the performances and is admirably vivid. The muted string timbre is not perhaps quite as truthful as it might be, and the bass drum offers a rather explosive effect in *La Valse*, but generally the quality is superior, if not of Decca's very best.

Boléro; Pavane pour une infante défunte; Le Tombeau de Couperin; La Valse.

*(*) Philips 7300 571 [id.]. Concertgebouw Orch., Haitink.

Fine performances, distinguished by instinctive good judgement and taste. The orchestral playing has characteristic refinement and finish. Yet in *La Valse* Haitink fails to enchant and captivate the listener as does Cluytens (whose Classics for Pleasure recording (see above) sounds every bit as vivid as this); and there is not enough atmosphere in *Le Tombeau de Couperin*. The quality of the cassette transfer is disappointing. The opening of *Boléro* is distant, and the reverberation confuses both the climax of this piece and that of *La Valse*. The lighter textures of *Le Tombeau de Couperin* are more successfully caught, but the low level of transfer brings a certain amount of hiss.

Boléro; Rapsodie espagnole; La Valse.
> ** DG 3300 459 [id.]. Boston SO, Ozawa.

The transfers of these performances are first-rate, with a clear side-drum at the opening of *Boléro*, a splendidly expansive and brilliant climax and equally spectacular demonstration sound (with an impressive bass drum) in the *Rapsodie* and at the close of *La Valse*. The performances themselves, however, although played with distinction, do not display a very high voltage. *Boléro* lacks a compelling forward thrust and *La Valse*, although it has atmosphere, lacks exuberance. The *Rapsodie* too is rather undercharacterized, though it is excitingly recorded: the sound has splendid glitter.

Boléro; La Valse.
> (M) *** Decca Jubilee KJBC 36. Suisse Romande Orch., Ansermet – DUKAS: *L'Apprenti sorcier;* HONEGGER: *Pacific 231.****
> (B) (*) RCA Camden C4-5031. Boston SO, Munch – DUKAS: *L'Apprenti sorcier* (*); IBERT: *Escales.**

Outstanding performances from Ansermet and vivid recording. The couplings too are highly recommendable, and this medium-priced Jubilee tape is a top recommendation in this repertoire. Readers will notice, however, that the two Ravel performances are also available on *The world of Ravel* (see under 'Collections' below).

Munch's performances are vivid enough, although neither *Boléro* nor *La Valse* is in the first class. The transfer has a very restricted dynamic range (*Boléro* hardly gets any louder at the end) and very little treble response.

Piano concerto in G major.
> (B) *(*) DG Heliodor 3348 109. Monique Haas, National Orch.

of Paris, Paray – PROKOFIEV: *Piano concerto No. 5.****

Monique Haas's performance of the *G major Concerto* is neat and nicely turned. It lacks sparkle in the finale, perhaps, but the only serious reservation to be made concerns an awkward change of perspective and aural ambience in the slow movement during the course of the solo preamble. The transfer is of good quality; the recording is rather recessed in comparison with the vivid Prokofiev coupling, with the inner detail less sharply defined, but there is a compensating atmospheric quality which suits the performance.

Piano concerto for the left hand in D major.
> *** Decca KSXC 6411. Julius Katchen, LSO, Kertesz – PROKOFIEV: *Piano concerto No. 3***;* GERSHWIN: *Rhapsody in Blue.**(*)
> (i) *Piano concerto for the left hand. Pavane pour une infante défunte.*
> **(*) HMV TC-ASD 3571. Andrei Gavrilov, LSO, Rattle – PROKOFIEV: *Piano concerto No. 1* etc.**(*)

Katchen gives a brilliant account of the concerto and is most expertly accompanied by the LSO under Kertesz, and no less brilliantly served by the Decca engineers. This was his last recording, alas, and a splendid achievement. It is without doubt among the best versions of the work currently available in the LP catalogue, and the excellent transfer produces natural, splendidly balanced sound, with plenty of sparkle and detail.

Gavrilov's recording of the concerto is altogether dazzling. He plays with effortless virtuosity and brilliance, and, when required, great sensitivity. This performance is the equal of any previous version: it yields to none of the classic accounts of the concerto (either on 78s or LP), and the recording is of high quality. The *Pavane* completes a very distinguished side; apart from the strangely impulsive closing bars, this too is beautiful playing. Gavrilov has superb dash and impeccable style. As in the Prokofiev coupling the upper focus of the tape transfer loses its sharpness in the orchestral tuttis (particularly in the main climax of the concerto), but overall the sound is good and the piano is naturally balanced.

Daphnis et Chloé (ballet): complete.
*** Decca KSXC 6703 [Lon. 5-6898]. Cleveland Orch. with Chorus, Maazel.
(M) *(*) CBS Classics 40-61816. New York PO with Chorus, Bernstein.

Maazel directs a finely moulded performance of Ravel's most magical score. His tempi in the brilliant numbers are fast, the precision of ensemble phenomenal, but elsewhere he indulges in a far more flexible style than is common with him. The result, helped by brilliant recording (more atmospheric than CBS used to produce with this orchestra), is most impressive. The transfer is outstandingly sophisticated, brilliant, and clear in detail. With the Monteux tape on Decca Ace of Diamonds and Boulez's fine version on CBS both withdrawn in the UK, this must receive a strong recommendation *faute de mieux*.

Bernstein's performance dates from the 1960s but has not been issued in the UK until recently. Though well played and sympathetically conducted it does not effectively challenge Maazel (to say nothing of Monteux and Boulez), and the recording is inclined to become shrill in climaxes in the (otherwise acceptable) tape transfer.

(i) *Daphnis et Chloé: Suites Nos. 1 and 2. Ma Mère l'Oye* (*Mother Goose;* ballet): complete.
(M) *** Turnabout KTVC 34603

[CT 2131]. Minnesota Orch., Skrowaczewski, (i) with St Olaf Choir.

The first *Daphnis suite* is absolutely magical in Skrowaczewski's hands, and in terms of sheer atmosphere and imaginative vitality these performances can compare with any of their more prestigious rivals. Though the Minnesota Orchestra is not as superlative an ensemble as the Amsterdam Concertgebouw Orchestra, there is nothing second-rate about its playing, and the recording is beautifully balanced and wide-ranging. Skrowaczewski conveys every subtlety of texture and colour, and he shapes phrases with not merely the good taste and fine musical judgement that Haitink gives us in his Philips recordings, but with a genuine feel for the sensuous, sumptuous qualities of these scores. His *Ma Mère l'Oye* is complete, and can stand comparison with the finest performances on disc. There are finer accounts of the second *Daphnis et Chloé* suite at full price – Karajan's, for instance (see below) – but since Monteux's complete version is not available on tape, and the two suites include almost all the really important music, Skrowaczewski's coupling must rate very highly indeed among the cassettes of Ravel's music. The transfer is extremely sophisticated, smooth and clear with a richness and depth of string tone that are quite unexpected on a recording from a Turnabout source.

Daphnis et Chloé: Suite No. 2.
*** DG 923075 [id.]. Berlin PO, Karajan – DEBUSSY: *La Mer; Prélude.****
(M) ** RCA Gold Seal GK 42701. Chicago SO, Martinon – ROUSSEL: *Bacchus et Ariane.***

Karajan's performance is outstanding among all others; it is one of the very best recordings he has ever made. He has the advantage of the Berlin Philharmonic Orchestra on top form, and it would be difficult to imagine better or more atmospheric playing, which is provided with a superb DG recording. Originally issued in non-Dolby form, the tape transfer has recently been remastered, and, as in the Debussy coupling, the recording has been given a highly sophisticated sound balance with plenty of range and detail.

Martinon demonstrates formidably that the Chicago orchestra in the early sixties was, as now, a hot contender for the title of top orchestra. This is an urgently involving performance of the *Second Suite*, not just brilliant in *Daybreak* and the *Danse finale* but idiomatically expressive. With excellent recording and an apt and unusual coupling it makes an outstanding mid-price recommendation. The transfer is vivid, lacking the last degree of range, but with a fine bloom on the strings and no lack of detail.

Daphnis et Chloé: Suite No. 2; La Valse.
> (B) ** Pye ZCCCB 15013. Hallé Orch. and Chorus, Barbirolli – DEBUSSY: *La Mer.***

The Pye recording here is much more immediate than on the reverse. In *Daphnis et Chloé* Sir John uses a choir as well as orchestra, and his shaping of the great yearning string tune is characteristically sensuous. Perhaps the *Danse générale* has sometimes exploded with greater abandon in a live performance, but this is still very exciting. The performances have transferred successfully to tape. The sound has not the body of the most modern recordings, and the fizzy treble needs cutting back, but this reduces the hiss too, so that it is not a problem. The transfer is not at a very high level, but it has fine detail and sparkle and is free from discoloration. *La Valse* sounds particularly well; *Daphnis et Chloé* could have used more richness to the string tone, but this is more due to the early Pye stereo than to any inadequacy in the transfer. An enjoyable issue.

Ma Mère l'Oye (Mother Goose; ballet; see also above): *suite.*
> *(**) Pye ZCPCNHX 3. Orch. of St John's, Smith Square, Lubbock – BARTÓK: *Rumanian dances***; STRAVINSKY: *Pulcinella suite.*(**)

Lubbock relates Ravel's evocative fairy-tale score more to Stravinsky than usual, less to impressionistic evocation. It seems almost neoclassical, with even the bird noises kept firmly in time. Excellent refined recording, made in the hall from which the orchestra takes its name, but unfortunately some of this refinement has slipped in the tape transfer, with minor discoloration of the upper partials of the orchestral woodwind. It is to be hoped that later copies may have cured this fault.

Ma Mère l'Oye: excerpts.
> (M) *** Philips 7317 093. Concertgebouw Orch., Haitink – BRITTEN: *Young Person's Guide **(*)* ; PROKOFIEV: *Peter and the Wolf.***

These excerpts are an unexpected bonus for a coupling of Britten and Prokofiev. The items included are the *Prélude; Danse du rouet et scène; Interlude;* and the *Pavane de la Belle au bois dormant.* As these luminous and beautifully recorded performances are not otherwise available on tape and the transfer is of very high quality, this is welcome indeed!

Rapsodie espagnole.
> (B) *(*) RCA Camden C4-5039. Boston SO, Munch – DEBUSSY: *La Mer.*(*)

Munch's performance of the *Rapsodie espagnole* emerges here quite vividly and although the transfer could hardly be called sophisticated or wide in range, the coupling is convenient and this is inexpensive.

Tzigane (for violin and orchestra).
>(M) *(*) RCA Gold Seal GK 11329. Itzhak Perlman (violin), LSO, Previn – LALO: *Symphonie espagnole.***

Perlman's performance is a brilliant one and Previn accompanies imaginatively, but the exaggeratedly close balance of the soloist robs the music of subtlety and atmosphere in spite of the fine playing.

Introduction and allegro for harp, flute, clarinet and string quartet.
>(M) *(*) Turnabout KTVC 34161. Helga Storck (harp), Gerd Starke (clarinet), Conrad Hampe (flute), Endres Qt – ROUSSEL: *Serenade*(*) (with DEBUSSY: *Sonata*(*)).

Medium-price issues of this kind of repertoire are more than welcome. But it must be admitted that this performance comes under the category of sound but undistinguished, and the recording is unappealingly balanced. However, the tape is of excellent quality, with good projection of the performance. But the Melos Ensemble's incomparable performance of this work is available on *The world of Ravel* (see under 'Collections' below).

String quartet in F major, Op. 10.
>(M) * Argo KZKC 46. Aeolian Qt – DEBUSSY: *Quartet.*(*)

Neither the Ravel nor the Debussy quartet is otherwise available on tape, and the performances here are well transferred so must be accepted *faute de mieux*, even though neither work receives from the Aeolian Quartet the subtlety and polish they both need. On the whole the Ravel is less successful than the coupling.

The sound is warm and generally well detailed.

Shéhérazade (song cycle).
>(M) *** Decca Jubilee KJBC 15 [Lon. 5-25821]. Régine Crespin (mezzo-soprano), Suisse Romande Orch., Ansermet – BERLIOZ: *Nuits d'été.****

Crespin finds a special sympathy for Ravel's magically sensuous writing, and she is superbly supported by Ansermet. As in the Berlioz coupling her style has distinct echoes of the opera house, but the sheer richness of the singer's tone does not prevent this fine artist achieving the delicate languor demanded by an exquisite song like *The enchanted flute*. Indeed her operatic sense of drama brings almost a sense of self-identification to the listener as the slave-girl sings to the distant sound of her lover's flute (while her master sleeps). This is ravishing. The warm sheen of the glorious Decca recording spins a tonal web around the listener which is quite irresistible. Reissued at medium price this is outstandingly attractive, and the tape transfer is clear, catching most (if not quite all) of the warmth and atmosphere of the disc.

COLLECTIONS

'*Favourite composer*': (i) *Alborada del gracioso; Boléro; Daphnis et Chloé: Suite No. 2; Ma Mère l'Oye: suite; Pavane pour une infante défunte; Rapsodie espagnole; La Valse;* (ii) *Introduction and allegro for harp, flute, clarinet and string quartet.*
>(B) *(*) Decca KDPC 561/2. (i) Suisse Romande Orch., Ansermet; (ii) Osian Ellis (harp), Melos Ens.

Decca's collection here is based on the recordings of Ansermet. This makes a useful anthology (and includes the splendid Melos version of the *Introduction and allegro*), but the transfers are of mixed quality. The *Boléro* and the *Introduction and allegro* are vivid but not too refined; *Ma Mère l'Oye* and the *Rapsodie* suffer from thin upper strings (especially when muted). The rest of the programme has plenty of life and brilliance.

'The world of Ravel': (i) *Boléro;* (ii–iv) *Piano concerto in G major:* finale; (iii–v) *Daphnis et Chloé: Daybreak;* (iii; iv) *Pavane pour une infante défunte; Rapsodie espagnole: Habanera;* (i) *La Valse;* (vi) *Introduction and allegro for harp, flute, clarinet and string quartet;* (vii; i) *Shéhérazade: La flûte enchantée.*

> (M) **(*) Decca KCSP 392. (i) Suisse Romande Orch., Ansermet; (ii) Julius Kätchen (piano); (iii) LSO; (iv) Monteux; (v) Chorus of the Royal Opera House, Covent Garden; (vi) Osian Ellis (harp), Melos Ens.; (vii) Régine Crespin (mezzo-soprano).

This ingenious Ravel anthology, which was assembled by Ray Crick of Decca, has two small drawbacks. It begins, understandably, with Monteux's gorgeous opening to *Daphnis et Chloé,* but because this is taken from a complete set and not a suite, it has to be faded. Also there is a slight miscalculation in including Katchen's brilliant account of the *Piano concerto* finale at the end of side one, immediately following the wonderful sense of stillness of the closing bars of the *Introduction and allegro.* Although the idea of complete contrast is good in theory, in practice this jars on the listener's sensibility. Having said that, one must add that the collection is a marvellous bargain, including as it does Ansermet's two best Ravel performances, *Boléro* and *La Valse,* Monteux's beautiful *Pavane,* the incomparable

Melos account of the *Introduction and allegro,* and a reminder of Crespin's dramatic account of the song cycle *Shéhérazade.* The sound on the tape is remarkably consistent, considering the variety of sources, and is nearly always excellent.

Respighi, Ottorino (1879–1936)

Ancient airs and dances for lute (arr. for orchestra): *Suites Nos. 1–3.*

> (M) *** Philips 7321 022. Philharmonia Hungarica, Dorati (with BARTÓK: *Rumanian folkdances* **).
> **(*) HMV TC-ASD 3188 [Angel 4XS 37301]. Los Angeles CO, Marriner.

Dorati's famous recording, one of the first made by this group of Hungarian expatriates based in Vienna, dates from the early 1960s. The performance is of the utmost distinction: the playing combines brilliance with sensitivity to produce a remarkable feeling for the colour and ambience of the Renaissance dances on which Respighi's three suites (the last for strings alone) are based. Marriner's newer version has the advantage of freshly minted sound and a first-class modern chamber group in Los Angeles. His approach is essentially sunny, bringing out the bright colours and charm of the orchestration. The refinement of the playing (and of the sound) is very striking, and never more so than at the opening of the *Third Suite,* where the string textures are very beautiful. Many will prefer the HMV tape for its fresh charm, but Dorati finds in this music an often sombre dignity and a combination of dark colouring and graciousness that is obstinately memorable. The Philips recording is remarkably lively, and the cassette transfer is outstanding, virtually indistinguishable in quality from the LP. Moreover it throws in as a bonus (not on the disc) an excellent performance by I Musici of Bartók's *Rumanian folkdances*, which are also well transferred. The HMV tape offers rich but rather less refined sound. After the turnover (in the middle of the *Third Suite*) the level rises and the quality is not so clean.

Ancient airs and dances for lute (arr. for orchestra): *Suite No. 3*.

    ** Pye Ensayo ZCNEL 2012. ECO, Asensio – BRITTEN: *Simple symphony;* HINDEMITH: *5 Pieces*.**

This is perhaps the most striking of the three performances on this quite attractive Pye issue. The conductor's approach is rather literal in manner, but the playing is vivid and the slightly pungent sound projects the music well. The cassette transfer is of good quality.

The Birds (suite); *3 Botticelli pictures* (*Trittico Botticelliano*).

    *** HMV TC-ASD 3327. Academy of St Martin-in-the-Fields, Marriner.

The Birds is delightfully played by Marriner and the Academy and beautifully recorded. The score for the *Three Botticelli pictures* is less well known, but it is an enchanting work when presented with such delicacy and refined feeling. Indeed the third Botticelli picture, *The birth of Venus*, has something of the magic of the Ravel of *Ma Mère l'Oye*. The transfer has one or two short passages where the focus coarsens slightly, but for the most part the marvellously translucent recording makes a good deal of its effect on tape. One hopes that by the time we are in print later copies will have cured the lapses of quality noticeable, for instance, at the opening tutti of *The Birds*.

Symphonic poems: *Feste romane; The Pines of Rome*.

    *** Decca KSXC 6822 [Lon. 5-7043]. Cleveland Orch., Maazel.

Maazel's account of *Feste romane* (musically the least interesting of Respighi's three symphonic poems inspired by the capital city) is something of a revelation. The Decca recording is extremely sophisticated in its colour and detail, and Respighi's vividly evocative sound pictures are brought glitteringly to life. The orchestral playing shows matching virtuosity, and the final festival scene (*The night before Epiphany in the Piazza Navona*), with its gaudy clamour of trumpets and snatches of melody from the local organ-grinder, is given a kaleidoscopic imagery exactly as the composer intended. Elsewhere the superbly stylish playing has an almost baroque colouring, so wittily is it pointed. *The Pines of Rome* is given a strong, direct characterization, undoubtedly memorable, but without quite the subtlety or electricity of Maazel's earlier DG Heliodor version (see below). The extraordinary range and detail of *Feste romane* have been transferred to cassette with skill, and the quality is only marginally less sophisticated than that of the disc. In *The Pines* the sound, although still impressive, is not quite on this level. The opening lacks the last degree of crispness to the transients, and the score's closing section, though massively powerful, has not quite the open quality that distinguishes the LP. Even so this remains a remarkable tape.

Symphonic poems: *The Fountains of Rome; The Pines of Rome*.

    *** DG 3301 055 [id.]. Berlin PO, Karajan.

    (M) **(*) Decca Ace of Diamonds KSDC 494 [Lon. 5-21024]. New Philharmonia Orch., Munch.

The Fountains of Rome; The Pines of Rome; Belfagor overture.

** HMV TC-ASD 3372 [Angel 4XS 37402]. LSO, Gardelli.

Karajan's magnificent new coupling tends to sweep the field in this repertoire. The performance of *The Pines of Rome* repeats the success of the famous early stereo version by the same orchestra, conducted by Maazel (see below), but now the lustre of the finest modern recording adds extra richness and depth to the music-making. The playing of the Berlin Philharmonic is wonderfully refined, and the atmosphere of the two middle sections is unforgettable. A superbly distanced and magically haunting trumpet solo is matched by the principal clarinet, who is hardly less evocative. This is all projected against a ravishingly sensuous background of string tone, and when the nightingale begins his song the effect is uncannily real. To set the scene of *The pines of the Appian Way* Karajan creates a riveting pianissimo and slowly builds a climax of tremendous grandeur.

In *The Fountains of Rome* the tension is rather less tautly held, but the broader approach is undoubtedly effective, with stabbing horns at the turning on of the Triton fountain and a massively conceived picture of the triumphal procession of Neptune's chariot which forms the centrepiece of the Trevi fountain. The translucent watery imagery is the more effective in the opening and closing sections when the orchestral playing is so refined in its detail and atmosphere. The transfer is extremely sophisticated. Not made at the very highest level, it lacks the transient glitter (and touch of crudeness) of Munch's Decca cassette, but the sound is superbly rich and full-blooded, and there was no hint of distortion on our copy (a German-manufactured tape).

Munch's version, originally made in Phase Four, is extremely vivid and spectacular. The instrumental spotlighting is undoubtedly done with panache,

and those who regard these scores as 'picture-postcard music' will find that view reinforced. Yet the sense of spectacle is impressive and to a considerable extent redeems the comparative lack of subtlety in the presentation. The cassette transfer is brilliant; although the high level means that the quality is not exactly refined, there is an exciting glitter and phosphorescent brightness to the orchestral colouring.

Gardelli's are atmospheric performances, sympathetic and beautifully played, with much atmospheric warmth if less of a feeling of drama. There are some lustrous sounds here and the tape accommodates them agreeably, if without quite the refined detail of the LP. The climaxes are on the whole well managed. The *Belfagor overture*, a dramatic and lively piece, is strongly characterized and comes off with the utmost vividness.

The Pines of Rome (symphonic poem).

(B) *** DG Heliodor 3348 267. Berlin PO, Maazel – RIMSKY-KORSAKOV: *Capriccio espagnol***(*); MUSSORGSKY: *Night on the Bare Mountain.***

It is good to see this outstanding Berlin Philharmonic compilation of the very early sixties restored to the catalogue. It was this issue, together with Maazel's coupling of Stravinsky's *Firebird suite* and *Chant du rossignol*, which endorsed this conductor's international reputation. The Berlin Philharmonic plays here with breathtaking virtuosity in *The pines of the Villa Borghese*, balanced by wonderfully tender playing in the two middle movements. Then comes the gripping and tautly built crescendo to the exultant climax of the triumphant procession along the Appian Way. The brass is magnificent here, and the atmospheric stereo throughout, which made it one of DG's finest early issues in this medium, is still riveting. The transfer to tape offers first-class sound – clear, translucent and vivid.

Rossiniana (suite arr. from piano pieces by Rossini: *Quelques riens pour album*).
(*) Decca Phase 4 KPFC 4407 [Lon. 5-21172]. RPO, Dorati – ROSSINI: *La Boutique fantasque.*(*)

It is perhaps curious that this work is usually catalogued under Respighi, whereas *La Boutique fantasque*, which Respighi also based on Rossini's music, is more often found under Rossini. *Rossiniana* is not so inspired a score as *La Boutique fantasque*, but it is beautifully played here and Dorati's affection is most persuasive. The recording has more atmosphere than in the coupling (although on cassette the difference is rather less striking than on disc).

Rimsky-Korsakov, Nikolas (1844–1908)

Capriccio espagnol, Op. 34.
(B) **(*) DG Heliodor 3348 267. Berlin PO, Maazel – MUSSORGSKY: *Night on the Bare Mountain***; RESPIGHI: *Pines of Rome.****
(M) **(*) Decca Eclipse KECC 797. LSO, Argenta – *Concert.****
(*) Decca Phase 4 KPFC 4333 [Lon. 5-21117]. New Philharmonia Orch., Stokowski – DVOŘÁK: *Slavonic dance No. 10*; SCRIABIN: *Poème de l'extase.****

Capriccio espagnol; Mlada: Procession of the nobles.
*(**) HMV TC-ASD 3093 [Angel 4xS 37227]. LPO, Boult – TCHAIKOVSKY: *Capriccio italien* etc.*(**)

Capriccio espagnol; Russian Easter Festival overture, Op. 36.
(*) DG 3336 379 [id.]. Chicago SO, Barenboim – BORODIN: *Polovtsian dances*(*); MUSSORGSKY: *Night on the Bare Mountain.****

Maazel's Heliodor tape is an outstanding bargain, with its memorable account of Respighi's *Pines of Rome*. The playing in the *Capriccio espagnol* is almost equally fine, and the relaxed virtuosity in the *Scena e canto gitano* is a delight to the ear after the gorgeous strings and horns in the earlier variations. No less impressive is the breathtaking virtuosity of the closing pages, with every note in its place. The cassette transfer is brilliant but slightly dry in texture (not as expansive as the LP).

Argenta's LSO concert, originally called *España* (it includes a fine account of Chabrier's piece of that name), has also been reissued, on Eclipse, and at its new price it remains very competitive. It is very well recorded, and if the performance of the *Capriccio* has not quite the urgency of Maazel's, it has splendid warmth and detail; the glittering *Scena e canto gitano* is superbly done. On tape the sound lacks something in richness, and the upper range needs a little smoothing, but the quality is certainly vivid.

Stokowski's reading of the *Capriccio* – recorded, unlike the rest of this issue, conventionally in the studio – brings surprisingly relaxed tempi, with jaunty gypsy rhythms deliciously underlined. This is a memorable if idiosyncratic account, slightly cut and rearranged by the conductor. Full-blown recording, well transferred. The Dvořák *Dance* follows on after the *Capriccio* very naturally.

There is a degree of disappointment in Sir Adrian Boult's Rimsky-Korsakov/ Tchaikovsky coupling. He is not helped by the reverberant acoustic, noticeable immediately at the opening *Procession of the nobles.* The *Capriccio espagnol* lacks something in crispness of articulation, and the necessary exuberance is missing in the closing pages. The reverberation does not seem to help the tape transfer, which is on the muddy side.

Barenboim's account of the *Capriccio espagnol,* after a good start, tends to adopt a rather leisurely pace in the variations, and although the orchestral solo playing is first-class, this is not a performance to set the adrenalin racing. It has no lack of colour, and the transfer is very well managed. The *Russian Easter Festival overture* is splendidly dramatic, and full of atmosphere: there is no better performance in the catalogue, on tape or disc, and the transfer is spectacular, with very effective percussion.

Le Coq d'or: suite.
   (M) *(*) RCA Gold Seal GK 42700 [AGK 1 1528]. Boston SO, Leinsdorf – STRAVINSKY: *Firebird suite.*(*)

Rimsky-Korsakov's exotic and attractive orchestral suite from *Le Coq d'or* is currently represented in the tape catalogue by Leinsdorf's version alone. The playing is atmospheric and quite sensuous, but the end effect lacks glitter, mainly because the resonant recording acoustic tends to cloud the transients. As it happens, the tape sounds rather more vivid than the disc, although the quality breaks up a little towards the end of the *Wedding march.*

The Invisible City of Kitezh: suite; May Night: overture; Mlada: suite.
   (M) * Turnabout KTVC 34689. Philharmonia Hungarica, Kapp.

Like the orchestral suite from *Le Coq d'or,* the four tableaux from *The Invisible City of Kitezh* chronicle the main events of the opera, and they contain some char-

acteristically attractive music. The excerpts from *Mlada* include dance and processional music; the *Cortege* or *Procession of the nobles* is one of Rimsky's more familiar occasional pieces. Unfortunately none of the performances here is very sophisticated, and the recording is coarse-grained, with an unrealistically forward balance, most noticeable on side two (*Mlada* and the *May Night overture*). The high-level transfer reflects the lack of refinement, and although the repertoire is attractive, this is a disappointing issue.

Scheherazade (symphonic suite), *Op. 35.*
   *** Philips 7300 226 [id.]. LPO, Haitink.
   (M) *** HMV TC-SXLP 30253 [Angel 4xs 35505]. RPO, Beecham.
   (M) *** Decca KCSP 89 [Lon. 5-15158]. LSO, Monteux.
   **(*) DG 3300 972 [id.]. Boston SO, Ozawa.
   **(*) Decca KSXC 6731 [Lon. 5-6950]. Los Angeles PO, Mehta.
   **(*) Decca KSXC 6874 [Lon. 5-7098]. Cleveland Orch., Maazel.
   (B) ** Classics for Pleasure TC-SIT 60042. Philharmonia Orch., Matačić.
   *(**) RCA RK 11182 [ARK 1 1182]. RPO, Stokowski.
   ** Decca KSXC 2268. Suisse Romande Orch., Ansermet – BORODIN: *Polovtsian dances.***
   (B) * Philips Fontana 7328 009. Minneapolis SO, Dorati.

Scheherazade; May Night: overture.
   (B) *** Decca KDPC 2 7055. Suisse Romande Orch., Ansermet – BORODIN: *In the Steppes* etc.**; MUSSORGSKY: *Night on the Bare Mountain.*(*)

Scheherazade; Tsar Saltan: Flight of the bumble bee; March.

(M) **(*) RCA Gold Seal GK 42703 [AGK 1 1330]. LSO, Previn.

Haitink's Philips recording is the finest account of *Scheherazade* to appear for more than a decade. The playing of the LPO is both sensitive and alert, the interpretation wholly unaffected and totally fresh in impact. The pleasure it affords is greatly enhanced by the quality of the sound, which is exceptionally truthful in both timbre and perspective. It is a relief to hear a solo violin sounding its natural size in relation to the orchestra as a whole. Yet Rodney Friend, who plays the solos subtly, dominates the performance with his richly sinuous picture of Scheherazade herself as narrator of each episode. The cassette transfer is of impressive technical quality. The sound has both richness and weight, and the very wide dynamic range is easily accommodated, though this has meant a low level of transfer. The treble needs boosting a bit, so hiss must be expected. But the overall sound is first-class.

The sumptuousness and glamour of Beecham's performance of *Scheherazade* have transferred to tape with remarkable breadth and detail. Sir Thomas's reading has fine panache, and the solo violin-playing of Steven Staryk is superb and beautifully recorded. Other versions perhaps have more drama and bite, but Sir Thomas's breadth and warm sensuousness have a matching elegance in the orchestral playing and the rich well-balanced sound.

Monteux is even more vivid, helped by the Decca recording, at once brilliant, sparkling, and full-blooded. The orchestral playing is not quite as polished as under Beecham (or indeed Haitink), and the performance, although it does not lack romantic richness in the slow movement, is not especially sensuous. But it has tremendous zest and spontaneity. In the finale Monteux holds back the climax until the last minute and then unleashes the storm with devastating effect. The cassette transfer is first-class, brightly projected to match the music-making. Its penetrating upper range, however, means that the strings reveal the early recording date (1959), although the quality is very good for this period.

Ozawa's is an attractive performance, richly recorded. The first movement is strikingly spacious, building to a fine climax, and if the last degree of vitality is missing from the central movements the orchestral playing is warmly vivid. The finale is lively enough if not earthshaking in its excitement; but the reading as a whole has plenty of colour and atmosphere, and it is certainly enjoyable. The transfer is sophisticated; the dynamic range is wide and the climaxes expand freely, with general refinement of quality, the treble smooth rather than glittering.

At expansive tempi Previn's view of the first three movements is unexpectedly cool, the very opposite of vulgar. With rhythmic pointing which is characteristically crisp the result grows attractive on repetition, while the finale brings one of the most dramatic and brilliant performances ever recorded of that showpiece. The fill-ups provide a charming makeweight, particularly the *Tsar Saltan march* with its reminders of Walton's *Henry V* and Vaughan Williams's *Wasps*. The recording is outstanding for its late-sixties vintage, making this an attractive mid-price issue. The tape transfer fully conveys the richness and warmth of the recording; it has some slight lack of range in the treble, but this is not serious, and the only real blemish is the minor disturbance caused by the bass drum at the climax of the finale.

Ansermet's recording with the Suisse Romande Orchestra was one of Decca's earliest tape issues (KSXC 2268). This recording has been reissued on disc at Ace of Diamonds price, but the tape remains at full price. As the transfer, while perfectly acceptable, has no special qualities, this can hardly be recommended as an economical purchase, in spite of the coupling. However, Decca's reissue in double-length cassette format (coupled to music of Borodin and Mussorgsky and Rimsky-Korsakov's own *May Night overture*) is a different matter. The new transfer has been managed with the utmost sophistication. The original recording on LP was famous for its clarity, bloom and sparkle, but suffered from a slight edge on the string tone. Here that has been smoothed, without any loss of bite, and the strings have striking body and breadth of timbre throughout. The woodwind colours and brass sonorities are superbly caught, and the outer movements are very exciting. There is a slight problem with the bass drum in the overwhelming final climax; but with a reduction of bass this minor disturbance can be minimized, and the recording is otherwise of demonstration quality. The *May Night overture* opens the miscellaneous collection on side two, and one is struck immediately by the presence of the orchestral wind soloists.

Probably the finest cassette of *Scheherazade*, technically speaking, is Mehta's Los Angeles recording, which has consistently rich, resplendent sound and plenty of sparkle. The solo violin is beautifully caught and the orchestral leader, Sidney Harth, offers a sinuously seductive image for Scheherazade's musical narrative. The conductor's approach is affectionate, sometimes slightly mannered, and if the performance has not quite the distinction of its rivals listed above, it is still very enjoyable.

Maazel's straightness, his reluctance to indulge in conventional expressiveness, sharpens the attention on purely musical matters in what is normally treated as a colour piece. But Haitink for one among the many rivals gets the best of both worlds, where Maazel sounds stiff and relatively unsympathetic. The recording is vivid and brilliant but its very clarity detracts from the music's atmospheric qualities. The tape

transfer is of first-class quality, and providing one accepts the forward balance this is technically one of the most impressive cassette versions.

Matačić's performance is in the lowest possible price-range and as such it is a bargain. The Philharmonia playing is of high quality; the finale is really exciting, and if elsewhere the reading lacks the sparkle of the very best versions, it is by no means dull. The transfer is first-class: the recording is admirably rich and lustrous, with glowing woodwind, and it sounds not in the least dated. The forward balance of the wind means that there is less light and shade than in some performances, but the big climaxes expand well (notably in the finale).

The RCA tape of Stokowski's performance is over-brilliant to the point of shrillness, with a dry bass offering little warmth or compensating weight. Even so, an over-prominent bass drum in the finale manages to muddle the orchestral texture. The sensuously beautiful sounds produced by the RPO, with Erich Gruenberg providing a sweet-toned solo commentary, are here robbed of a good deal of their richness and lustre. Stokowski is at his most characteristic in the slow movement, and his nudgings of *rubato* are not always spontaneous in spite of the ample sheen of orchestral tone he creates. There is plenty of drama, but with such a lack of glow in the transfer this does not make very congenial listening.

There is little to recommend Dorati, and in particular the dry and lustreless sound is unappealing. In this price-range Matačić is much to be preferred.

Skazka (fairy tale for orchestra).
  *(*)HMV TC-ASD 3193. Bournemouth SO, Brusilow – BALAKIREV: *Russia*; BORODIN: *Symphony No. 2.*(*)

Skazka is a work of great charm and originality that deserves more than an occasional airing. But Brusilow brings relatively little atmosphere or poetry to this score, and although the recording is good, it is not very impressively transferred.

Piano and wind quintet in B flat major.

(M)***Decca Ace of Diamonds KSDC 389. Walter Panhoffer (piano), members of the Vienna Octet – MENDELSSOHN: *Octet.***

Making an unexpected appearance on cassette, the Rimsky-Korsakov *Quintet* is no masterpiece, but it is thoroughly diverting. Some of its ideas outstay their welcome, but even this does not seriously detract from the pleasure it gives. The piece is like a garrulous but endearing friend whose loquacity is easily borne for the sake of the accompanying charm and good nature. Sparkling performance and excellent recording; the transfer is of very good quality, with a nice bloom on the wind instruments (given a fairly forward balance) and a most realistic piano image. The overall blend of texture is very satisfactory.

Rodrigo, Joaquín
(born 1902)

Concierto de Aranjuez (for guitar and orchestra).

RCA RK 11734 [ARK 1 1181]. Julian Bream, Monteverdi Orch., Gardiner – BERKELEY: *Concerto.(*)

(*)CBS 76369 [Col. MT 33208]. John Williams, ECO, Barenboim – VILLA-LOBOS: *Concerto.**

**(*) RCA RK 11673 [RK 1052]. Julian Bream, Melos Ens., Colin Davis – BRITTEN: *Courtly*

*dances***(*);* VIVALDI: *Lute concerto.***

(B)**Classics for Pleasure TC-CFP 40012. John Zaradin, Philomusica of London, Barbier – *Recital.***

Consideration of the multitude of fine recordings of Rodrigo's delectable and justly popular guitar concerto (its slow movement is probably the most frequently heard excerpt from *any* concerto written in the twentieth century) must take into account the coupling as a prime factor; this work seems to bring out the most imaginative qualities in both soloist and conductor whenever it is played, and almost every recorded performance can be recommended with few if any reservations.

John Williams's newer recording with Barenboim is superior to his earlier version with Ormandy. The playing has marvellous point and spontaneity; the famous *Adagio* has rarely been played with this degree of poetic feeling. There is a hint of rhythmic over-emphasis in the articulation of the finale, but in general this is outstanding as a performance. The balance is good, and on tape the forward placing of the soloist seems rather less exaggerated than on disc. However, the sound, while pleasing, has a low frequency ceiling, and the lack of sparkle and crispness of inner detail must be considered a disadvantage in such a work.

The differences between Bream's two versions are almost too subtle to analyse. Maybe he had a little extra dash in the first one (RK 11673), but here Colin Davis's overall direction has a few moments of slackness. The newer account has the benefit of really modern recording, and the Berkeley *Concerto*, written for Bream, is an elegant and extended piece that makes light of the composer's technical problems. The transfer of this coupling is particularly vivid, although the forward placing of the soloist reduces the dynamic contrast between guitar and orchestra.

Zaradin's performance is bright-eyed and straightforward, with a crisp, immediate recording. The orchestral outline is clear-cut in the somewhat dry manner favoured by John Boyden, who produced many of the Classics for Pleasure original recordings. This is coupled with a recital of solo guitar pieces, discussed below in our Recitals section. Although the dynamic range of the recording of the concerto is limited by the close balance of the solo guitar, the recording conveys an attractive intimacy, and there is plenty of bloom on the sound.

Concierto de Aranjuez; Fantasia para un gentilhombre (both for guitar and orchestra).

*** HMV TC-ASD 3415 [Angel 4XS 37440]. Angel Romero, LSO, Previn.

(M)*** Decca KCSP 233 [Lon. 5-15199]. Narciso Yepes, Spanish National Orch., Argenta or Frühbeck de Burgos.

*(*) DG 3300 172 [id.]. Narciso Yepes, Spanish Radio and TV Orch., Alonso.

Rodrigo's *Fantasia para un gentilhombre* (1954) is neoclassical in atmosphere, with a strong baroque flavour (it has much in common with Respighi's suites of *Ancient airs and dances*, though Rodrigo's treatment of his material is more personal). It is a splendid work and makes perhaps the perfect coupling with the more famous *Concierto de Aranjuez*. The Previn/Romero issue is undoubtedly very successful: Romero does not emerge as a strong personality, but the skill and sensibility of his playing are in no doubt, and Previn is obviously so delighted with the orchestral scores that he communicates his enthusiasm with loving care for detail. Thus, although the solo guitar is slightly larger than life in relation to the orchestra, Previn is still able to bring out the delightful woodwind chatter in the outer movements of the concerto. The famous slow movement is very beautifully played indeed; the opening is especially memorable. The approach to the *Fantasia* is vividly direct, missing some of the essentially Spanish graciousness that marks the Marriner version (the finest available; see below), but its infectious quality is more than enough compensation. The warmly spacious recording has transferred well to tape (the short patch of less than perfectly focused *tutti* at the end of the concerto's slow movement is common to tape and disc).

The Decca tape is very brightly and crisply recorded. It has less obvious warmth than the Previn HMV version, but its bright-eyed quality is pleasing in a quite different way. The concerto is a most attractive performance: the first movement is deliciously pointed, the wind entries made doubly effective by the more subtly atmospheric recording acoustic; the *Adagio* has a thoughtful improvisatory quality, and the finale a lively spontaneity. With a Spanish orchestra the effect is, not surprisingly, more idiomatic than most versions. The recording is a little tight in the upper strings, but the soloist is beautifully recorded; the balance is excellent, and the coupling has comparable personality and style. This is a splendid bargain at medium price.

Yepes's DG coupling is disappointing, for the playing is almost entirely without sparkle. The artists have been recorded in a studio with a dry acoustic which seems to have damped the spontaneity out of the performances, except in the slow movement of the concerto, which seems indestructible.

(i) *Concierto de Aranjuez* (for guitar and orchestra); (ii) *Concierto serenata* (for harp and orchestra).

(M)*** DG Privilege 3318 016. (i) Siegfried Behrend, Berlin PO, Peters; (ii) Nicanor Zabaleta, Berlin Radio Orch., Märzendorfer.

This is an outstanding coupling. Rodrigo's charming *Concierto de Aranjuez* receives here a first-rate modern recording, projected well, bright as a button, and with an excellent balance between soloist and orchestra. Behrend's approach is alive and strong in personality, and the effect is to make this fine work sound less insubstantial than it sometimes does. Most enjoyable, with the players' pleasure in such rewarding music readily conveyed. The delicious harp concerto displays a similar piquancy and charm of melody. In the outer movements especially, the delicate yet colourful orchestration tickles the ear in delightful contrast to the beautifully focused timbre of the harp. Both performance and recording are immaculate. This enjoyable tape cannot be too highly recommended, and the transfer matches the excellence of the recordings. The sound in the harp concerto is particularly transparent.

Concierto madrigal (for 2 guitars and orchestra).

⊛ *** Philips 7300 369 [id.]. Pepe and Angel Romero, Academy of St Martin-in-the-Fields, Marriner – GIULIANI: *Guitar concerto.****

Rodrigo's *Concierto madrigal* is in fact a suite in ten movements, the first seven being miniatures of great charm and diversity (within the characteristically limited range of the composer's style), the last three increasingly ambitious. This is strongly recommended to those who enjoy Rodrigo's other works and who want to hear more of his felicitous invention. The two soloists play splendidly and the accompaniment under Marriner is first-rate. Moreover the balance (although perhaps not absolutely truthful in its imagery of the soloists, who are somewhat larger than life) is superbly managed, so that the orchestral detail is expertly fitted around the solo contribu-

tion. The tape transfer is immaculate – of demonstration quality.

Concierto pastoral (for flute and orchestra); *Fantasia para un gentilhombre* (arr. Galway for flute and orchestra).

*** RCA RK 25193. James Galway (flute), Philharmonia Orch., Mata.

The *Concierto pastoral* was composed for James Galway in 1978. Its spikily brilliant introduction is far from pastoral in feeling, but the mood of the work soon settles down. At first hearing the material seems thinner than usual but Rodrigo's fragmented melodies and rhythmic ostinatos soon insinuate themselves into the listener's memory. The slow movement is especially effective, with a witty scherzando centrepiece framed by the *Adagio* outer sections. James Galway's performance is truly superlative, showing the utmost bravura and matching refinement. He is beautifully recorded (and the tape transfer is immaculately truthful), and the small accompanying chamber orchestra is well balanced. The arrangement of the *Fantasia* is a very free one, necessitating re-orchestration, exchanging clarinet and horn instrumentation for the original scoring for trumpet and piccolo. The solo part too has been rewritten and even extended, apparently with the composer's blessing. The result is, to be honest, not an improvement on the original. But Galway is very persuasive, even if there is a persistent feeling of inflation.

Fantasia para un gentilhombre (for guitar and orchestra).

*** Philips 7300 442 [id.]. Pepe Romero, Academy of St Martin-in-the-Fields, Marriner – GIULIANI: *Introduction, theme, variation and polonaise.****

A warm, gracious account of the *Fantasia*, with the Academy of St Martin-in-the-Fields contributing quite as much as the soloist to the success of the performance. The beauty of the orchestral textures adds much colour to Rodrigo's simple but attractive score, and the recording is splendid, both on disc and on the tape, which is immaculately transferred. Highly recommended.

Rosetti, Francesco (né Rössler, Franz) (1746–92)

Horn concerto in D major.
(M) *(*) Turnabout KTVC 34078. Erich Penzel, Württemberg CO, Faerber – TELEMANN: *Suite*(*); VIVALDI: *Double concerto.*(***)

Francesco Rosetti provided here a quite characterful little concerto, with a well-laid-out first movement, requiring spurts of virtuosity and receiving them here from the soloist, Erich Penzel. The slow movement has a romantic flair, and the finale is jolly. A fairly useful addition to the repertoire, but the transfer to tape is not very refined, though it is the most successful of the three recordings on this cassette, and the solo horn sounds bold and clear.

Rossini, Gioacchino (1792–1868)

La Boutique fantasque (ballet music; arr. Respighi).
(*)Decca Phase 4 KPFC 4407 [Lon. 5-21172]. RPO, Dorati – RESPIGHI: *Rossiniana.*(*)

(M)**Decca KCSP 376. Israel PO, Solti – DUKAS: *L'Apprenti sorcier.***

Dorati's performance has plenty of life and colour, but the recording acoustic is a little lacking in atmosphere: the very opening of *La Boutique fantasque* is made to sound rather dry and unevocative by the relative lack of ambient glow. However, it is easy to make too much of this. The vivacity and point of the orchestral playing are often exhilarating, and on cassette, where the sound is slightly mellower than the equivalent LP, the dryness is much less obvious.

Solti is more intense than Dorati, and his opening is even more precise and matter-of-fact. But as the music continues the listener is caught up in the vitality of the playing, particularly of the Israeli strings. The recording is clear and brilliant and the transfer clean.

String sonatas (Sonate a quattro) Nos. 1 in G major; 2 in A major; 3 in C major; 4 in B flat major; 5 in E flat major; 6 in D major.
***Argo KZRC 506 [id.] (Sonatas 1, 3, 5, 6). Academy of St Martin-in-the-Fields, Marriner.
Argo KZRC 603 [id.] (Nos. 2 and 4). Academy of St Martin-in-the-Fields, Marriner – DONIZETTI: *String quartet.*
String sonatas Nos. 1–4.
(B) ** Rediffusion Legend KLGD 022. ECO, Ros-Marbá.
String sonatas Nos. 1–3 and 6.
(M) ** DG Privilege 3335 187. Berlin PO, Karajan.
String sonatas Nos. 2–5.
**(*)HMV TC-ASD 3464. Polish CO, Maksymiuk.

Unbelievably, these sonatas were written when Rossini was only twelve, yet their invention is consistently on the highest level, bubbling over with humour and infectious spontaneity. The playing of the St Martin's group under Marriner is marvellously fresh and polished, the youthful high spirits of the writing presented with glowing affection and sparkle. KZRC 506 was an early Argo cassette issue and while the quality is generally very good, with plenty of detail and warmth, it has not quite the tonal refinement of the LP. On side two the treble has a hint of grittiness which needs filtering out. However, the recording is responsive to the controls and can be made to yield excellent results. KZRC 603, a later issue, offers superb sound, smooth, rich and refined, with plenty of sparkle.

Generally fine playing from the Polish chamber group, with some impressive scalic bravura and warm phrasing in the slow movements. There is plenty of character here, but in the last analysis the ensemble does not show the immaculate ease of execution of Marriner's Academy, and though the allegros are spirited, with the rhythms nicely pointed, they have not the effervescent wit of the Argo set. The recording is agreeably warm and rich (it is somewhat bass-heavy here, but that is easily corrected), but the textures are at times a little thick because of the resonant acoustic. The transfer, however, is of EMI's highest quality.

Though not as polished as the Argo performances, the selection by the ECO under Antonio Ros-Marbá has plenty of life and spirit, and the playing has genuine sparkle. This bargain-priced tape may in some ways be the best buy in this repertoire for those not wanting the full-priced Marriner set. The recording is resonant but clear, and the high-level tape transfer is admirably open and clear.

Excellent sound from the Karajan cassette. The string tone has admirable freshness and range (the level is high) and only a very slight lack of body suggests that the recording is not brand-new; however, in some ways this is advantageous in preventing the textures from becoming too sumptuous for the good of the music. Alongside Marriner, Karajan's performances sound a little suave. The music cannot help but be effective when it is so beautifully played, but there is much less sparkle and wit here than on the two Argo tapes.

Overtures: *Il Barbiere di Siviglia; La Cambiale di matrimonio; L'Inganno felice; L'Italiana in Algeri; La Scala di seta; Il Signor Bruschino; Tancredi; Il Turco in Italia.*

**(*) Philips 7300 368 [id.]. Academy of St Martin-in-the-Fields, Marriner.

This may seem a strange area of repertory for Neville Marriner and the Academy to explore, but with characteristic concern for interesting points of scholarship Marriner has resurrected the original and lighter orchestrations of these mainly well-known overtures (minus heavy brass and bass drum). They emerge the more sparkling, not just the well-known overtures but also the rarities like *L'Inganno felice. Il Signor Bruschino* brings the tapping of a triangle-stick, not the usual bows. A generous collection, beautifully recorded, although the tape transfer is rather too ample in bass. When this is cut back the sound comes into balance, for the recording's upper range is rich and well focused.

Overtures: *Il Barbiere di Siviglia; La Cenerentola; La Gazza ladra; L'Italiana in Algeri; La Scala di seta; Il Signor Bruschino.*

(B) ** Rediffusion Legend KLGD 023. ECO, Asensio.

These performances use a comparatively small ensemble, and the chamber quality is especially attractive in *La Scala di seta,* where the neat string playing gives much pleasure. Other overtures benefit from the crispness of ensemble, notably *Il Signor Bruschino* and *L'Italiana in*

Algeri. In a piece like *La Gazza ladra* the lack of a sense of robust drama (the opening side-drum too reticent) may be considered a disadvantage, but these are performances of character and they have transferred well to tape. The upper focus is not absolutely clean, but the balance is good and there is a pervading feeling of freshness. On our copy, however, there was now and then a fractional suspicion of wow, a momentary impression that never lasted more than a split second.

Overtures: *Il Barbiere di Siviglia; La Cenerentola; La Gazza ladra; L'Italiana in Algeri; Le Siège de Corinthe; Il Signor Bruschino.*
　*** DG 3300 497 [id.]. LSO, Abbado.

Brilliant, sparkling playing, with splendid discipline, vibrant rhythms and finely articulated phrasing – altogether invigorating and bracing. Once or twice one feels Abbado could smile a little more, but these are superb performances and recorded with great fidelity, wide range and firm body. The cassette transfer is of outstanding quality, with a fine sparkle and bloom on the sound. However, on tape the orchestral image seems to recede somewhat in the pianissimos. Even so, this remains one of the very finest collections of Rossini overtures in the tape catalogue.

Overtures: *Il Barbiere di Siviglia; La Gazza ladra; L'Italiana in Algeri; La Scala di seta; Semiramide; William Tell.*
　*(**) DG 3300 186 [id.]. Berlin PO, Karajan.
　(M) (**) HMV TC-SXLP 30203. Philharmonia Orch., Karajan.

Superbly made performances on DG, offering polish and sheer bravura rather than any special individuality. Karajan takes the main allegro of *La Scala di seta* very fast indeed, but the playing is beauti-

fully light and assured, the oboist managing felicitous control of the phrasing without any suggestion of breathlessness. The oboe solo in *L'Italiana in Algeri* is played with similar poise and assurance. Of their kind these performances are beautifully shaped and the recording is first-class. The cassette transfer offers acceptable rather than outstanding sound, with a lack of refinement in places, notably in *La Gazza ladra* (where the focus loses its crispness) and in the storm sequence and finale of *William Tell.*

The reissue of Karajan's Philharmonia performances of the same set of overtures is even less successful. The recording acoustic is somewhat over-resonant, and the performances have bravura but little finesse, in spite of some excellent orchestral playing. The cassette transfer has a grotesquely reduced dynamic range, so that the opening cellos in *William Tell* sound as loud as the storm sequence.

Overture and Storm music: *Il Barbiere di Siviglia.* Overtures: *La Gazza ladra; La Scala di seta; Semiramide; William Tell.*
　(B) ** DG Heliodor 3348 171. Rome Opera House Orch., Serafin.

Serafin's performances are small in scale, affectionate and relaxed; *La Scala di seta* responds particularly well to this almost chamber-music style of presentation. For some reason we are given extra measure in *La Gazza ladra*, where there is a repeat of the second subject. The recording is good on cassette as on disc, and in the bargain range this is certainly good value.

Overtures: *Il Barbiere di Siviglia; La Gazza ladra; La Scala di seta; Semiramide; William Tell.*
　(M)**(*)Decca Jubilee KJBC 33. LSO, Gamba.

467

This is a very good collection. The performances are taut and exciting and the orchestral playing splendidly alive and polished, even at the very fast speeds sometimes chosen for the allegros. A strong disciplining force – not unlike Toscanini's style – is felt in every piece, and care in phrasing is noticeable at every turn. Particularly captivating is the string cantilena at the introduction of *The Barber of Seville*, which is phrased with a wonderful sense of line. Decca's recording is very good. The only quality perhaps missing is a touch of geniality. The tape transfer, made at a high level, tends to be somewhat fierce in the treble, and although the sound responds to the controls the upper focus is not ideally clean.

Overtures: *La Cenerentola; La Gazza ladra; Le Siège de Corinthe; Semiramide; Il Viaggio a Reims; William Tell.*
*** Philips 7300 595 [id.]. Academy of St Martin-in-the-Fields, Marriner.

A splendid companion anthology for Marriner's earlier collection of Rossini overtures, offering similarly stylish, light-weight performances. The playing is sparkling and lively, and the two less well-known pieces, *The Siege of Corinth* and *The Journey to Rheims*, are particularly delectable. On tape the latter performance is most felicitously balanced, with fine detail, and similarly the strings in *Semiramide* are beautifully clean and crisp. The transfer manages the focus of the side-drum solos at the beginning of the *Thieving Magpie* better than most tapes of this piece. On side one the sound has marginally less brightness, and the galop in *William Tell* lacks something in sheer sonic brilliance. But taken as a whole this is certainly among the most recommendable anthologies of Rossini overtures on cassette.

Overtures: *La Gazza ladra; L'Italiana in Algeri; Semiramide; Il Signor Bruschino; William Tell.*
(B)(***)Classics for Pleasure TC-CFP 40077. RPO, Colin Davis.

Colin Davis is rather more relaxed than Gamba on Decca (see above), but these performances are admirably stylish, with an excellent sense of nuance. The orchestral playing is splendid, and *Semiramide*, which opens side two, is a superb performance, wonderfully crisp and vivid. In *Il Signor Bruschino*, which comes next, it sounds as if the bow-tapping device is done by the leader only. On tape the opening cellos in *William Tell* are very forward and larger than life-size, revealing that this is one of EMI's inflated transfers with limited dynamics. The character of the playing achieves contrast in the typical Rossinian crescendos, but the actual volume level rises comparatively little. The sound is very live and vivid, but the lack of dynamic range is serious in this music.

Overtures: *La Gazza ladra; William Tell.*
(M)**Decca KCSP 92. Paris Conservatoire Orch., Maag – MENDELSSOHN: *Overtures.***

Peter Maag brings a classical restraint to these performances, and perhaps the opening of *William Tell*, given a comparatively dry acoustic, lacks something in romantic flair. But there is plenty of colour in the final galop, and the excitement, if controlled, is real enough. The sense of discipline is even more effective in *La Gazza ladra*, where the crisp pointing gives much pleasure. The recording is clear and clean in Decca's best manner.

Il Barbiere di Siviglia: Overture and highlights. Overtures: *Corradino; L'Italiana in Algeri; Semiramide* (arr. for wind by Wenzel Sedlak).

** Philips 7300 599. Netherlands
Wind Ens.

Marvellously polished playing and
beautiful recorded sound (which has
transferred most naturally to tape)
ensure undoubted enjoyment here. But
not all the wit of the *Barber of Seville*
vocal numbers comes over; one keeps
waiting for the voices to come in. The
overtures on side two are the most rewarding items, particularly *Corradino*.

Petite Messe solennelle.
** Argo K 118 K 22. Margaret
Marshall, Alfreda Hodgson,
Robert Tear, Malcolm King,
London Chamber Choir, Syl-
via Holford, John Constable
(pianos), John Birch (harmo-
nium).

Rossini's *Petite Messe solennelle* must
be the most genial contribution to the
church liturgy in the history of music.
The description *Petite* does not refer to
size, for the piece is comparable in length
to Verdi's *Requiem*; rather it is the composer's modest evaluation of the work's
'significance'. But what a spontaneous
and infectious piece of writing it is, bubbling over with characteristic melodic,
harmonic and rhythmic invention. The
composer never overreaches himself. 'I
was born for *opera buffa*, as well Thou
knowest,' Rossini writes touchingly on
the score. 'Little skill, a little heart, and
that is all. So be Thou blessed and admit
me to paradise.' There is an outstanding
RCA disc version of this work under
Wolfgang Sawallisch, and this new Argo
performance is not its match. The recording is of the highest quality and it has
been transferred with great vividness and
presence (the choral entry at the opening
of the *Gloria* is arresting in its realism);
but the reading is much too literal and
lacks geniality. Both Margaret Marshall
and Alfreda Hodgson sing eloquently;
there is some finely shaped and expressive
choral singing, and good support from

the two pianists, with John Birch on the
harmonium; and the clean well-balanced
sound is a constant source of pleasure.
But the music-making fails to catch the
music's spirit and can give only limited
satisfaction.

Il Barbiere di Siviglia (opera): com-
plete.
*** DG 3371 003 [id.]. Teresa
Berganza, Luigi Alva, Paolo
Montarsolo, Hermann Prey,
Enzo Dara, Ambrosian Opera
Chorus, LSO, Abbado.

Abbado's set has been transferred to
tape with characteristic DG sophistication. The recording was one of this company's very first opera issues on cassette
and was originally in non-Dolby form, so
it is important to check for the Dolby
logo on the box. The re-transfer has been
most successful, with plenty of sparkle
and detail yet no lack of weight. Abbado
directs a clean and satisfying performance that seems to emerge here with more
life than in the LP version. Berganza's
interpretation of the role of Rosina remains very consistent with her earlier
performance on Decca (not yet available
on tape); but the Figaro here, Hermann
Prey, is more reliable, and the playing
and recording have an extra degree of
polish. The text is not so complete as the
Decca (omitting the tenor's Act 2 aria,
for example).

Il Turco in Italia (opera): complete.
(M) ** HMV TC-SLS 5148. Maria
Callas, Nicolai Gedda, Nicola
Rossi-Lemeni, Franco Cala-
brese, Chorus and Orch. of La
Scala, Milan, Gavazzeni.

Callas was at her peak when she
recorded this rare Rossini opera in the
mid-1950s. As ever, there are lumpy
moments vocally, but she gives a sharply
characterful performance as the capri-
cious Fiorilla, married to an elderly, jeal-

ous husband and bored with it. Nicola Rossi-Lemeni as the Turk of the title is characterful too, but not the firmest of singers, and it is left to Nicolai Gedda as the young lover and Franco Calabrese as the jealous husband to match Callas in stylishness. It is good too to have the veteran Mariano Stabile singing the role of the Poet in search of a plot. Walter Legge's production has plainly added to the sparkle, and the stereo transcription recording sounds well for its period. The transfer is smooth and quite well balanced, although the sound reflects the limited range of the discs. The libretto is clear and easy to read.

'The world of Rossini': (i–ii) Overtures: *La Gazza ladra; William Tell.* (i; iii) *Stabat Mater: Inflammatus. Il Barbiere di Siviglia:* (iv) *Largo al factotum;* (v) *Una voce poco fa. La Cenerentola:* (vi) *Zitto, zitto, piano, piano;* (v) *Non più mesta. L'Italiana in Algeri:* (v; vii) *Pria di dividerci da voi. Semiramide:* (v) *Bel raggio lusinghier.*

- (M) **(*) Decca KCSP 445. (i) LSO; (ii) Gamba; (iii) Pilar Lorengar, LSO Chorus, Kertesz; (iv) Ettore Bastianini; (v) Teresa Berganza; (vi) Ugo Benelli, Sesto Bruscantini; (vii) Alva, Corena, Panerai, Tavolaccini, Pace, Montarsolo, Maggio Musicale Fiorentino, Varviso.

On the whole this anthology has been adroitly made. Each side opens with an overture, and the obvious thought comes to mind that a collector interested in this tape might already possess recordings of these very familiar pieces. Nevertheless they are very well played, and the singing here is generally distinguished. Berganza's items are especially fine (although it is perhaps a pity that only the *Non più mesta* section was included from

her *Cenerentola* aria). The ensembles are vivacious, and the programme ends on a more serious note with the *Inflammatus* from the *Stabat Mater,* dramatically sung by Pilar Lorengar. The cassette transfer is very well managed, and this is the sort of collection that can be useful on a car journey.

Roussel, Albert (1869–1937)

Bacchus et Ariane (ballet): *Suite No. 2.*
- (M)**RCA Gold Seal GK 42701. Chicago SO, Martinon – RAVEL: *Daphnis et Chloé.***

As musical director of the Chicago orchestra in the early sixties Martinon made some scintillating recordings of French music, and this is one of them. Other versions of this work on disc may bring out some extra points of expressiveness, but with superb ensemble and fine recording this is a richly enjoyable coupling for an outstanding version of the Ravel. As in the Ravel, the transfer provides a full, rich sound with good detail. The forward balance reduces the dynamic range somewhat, and the upper frequencies lack something in sparkle.

Symphony No. 3 in G minor, Op. 42.
- (**) CBS 40-76519 [Col. MT 34201]. New York PO, Boulez – DUKAS: *La Péri.*(*)

Boulez's first movement is surprisingly slow, but the slow movement itself has great warmth and humanity. Unfortunately the recording is not as excellent as the performance: the acoustic is reverberant and the upper strings are shrill. Moreover the CBS cassette transfer is not a success: the sound is disappointingly lacking in range and sparkle.

Serenade for flute, violin, viola, violoncello and harp, Op. 30.
　(M) *(*) Turnabout KTVC 34161. Wilhelm Schwegler (flute), Helga Storck (harp), members of the Endres Qt – RAVEL: *Introduction and allegro* *(*) (with DEBUSSY: *Sonata* *(*)).

This is a good, workmanlike performance, well if not very subtly recorded. The tape transfer is of excellent quality, in many ways preferable to the equivalent disc.

Rubbra, Edmund
(born 1901)

Improvisations for violin and orchestra, Op. 89.
　(M)*RCA Gold Seal GK 25096. Sidney Harth, Louisville Orch., Whitney – BRITTEN: *Violin concerto.**

Making an unexpected appearance on cassette, Rubbra's *Improvisations* is a work of greater substance than the title suggests. It dates from 1956 and was commissioned by the Louisville Orchestra. Though it bears an adjacent opus number to the *Seventh Symphony* (Op. 88), it draws on material that Rubbra had used in a *Fantasia for violin and orchestra* written in the mid-1930s. It is a work of great serenity and searching beauty, and the playing of Sidney Harth and the orchestra has commitment and eloquence. However, the recording was originally in mono and although it has been refurbished for stereo the tape transfer is unattractively balanced. The sound of the solo violin is very edgy and the or-

chestral strings are fizzy, while the backward positioning of the orchestra gives an unrealistic sound picture with poor detail.

Russo, William
(born 1928)

Street music, Op. 65.
　** DG 3300 788 [id.]. Corky Siegel (harmonica), the composer (piano), San Francisco SO, Ozawa – GERSHWIN: *An American in Paris.***

William Russo has been an assiduous advocate of mixing jazz and blues traditions with the symphony orchestra, and *Street music* has its attractive side. But despite Corky Siegel on harmonica, it is no more successful at achieving genuine integration than other pieces of its kind, and its half-hour span is far too long for the material it contains. Excellent recording and a transfer of good quality, though the close focus for the harmonica makes for some unattractive sound from Mr Siegel. On tape the work begins at the end of side one (after the Gershwin) and turns over after the first movement.

Saint-Saëns, Camille
(1835–1921)

Allegro appassionato for violoncello and orchestra, Op. 43; Caprice in D major for violin and orchestra (arr. Ysaÿe); *Carnival of the Animals: Le cygne; Violoncello concerto No. 1 in A minor, Op. 33; Wedding Cake (Caprice-valse) for piano and strings, Op. 76; Le Déluge: Prelude, Op. 45.*

*(**)HMV TC-ASD 3058. Yan Pascal Tortelier (violin), Maria de la Pau (piano), Paul Tortelier (cello), City of Birmingham SO, Frémaux.

Paul Tortelier gives an assured account of the *A minor Cello concerto*, but fails to make much of the busy but uninspired *Allegro appassionato*. Yan Pascal Tortelier plays with charm in the *Caprice* and catches the *salon* element in the music without vulgarizing it. He plays with pleasing simplicity in the *Prelude* to the oratorio *Le Déluge*, which has a concertante part for the solo violin. The *Wedding Cake caprice* is also nicely done, even though Maria de la Pau does not reveal a strong personality. With *Le cygne* (Paul Tortelier accompanied by a harp) thrown in as a bonus, this is quite an attractive anthology, well recorded; but the transfer, though smooth, is seriously lacking in range and sparkle.

Carnival of the Animals.
*** DG 3300 731. Alfons and Aloys Kontarsky (pianos), Vienna PO, Boehm – MOZART: *Serenade No. 13.***(*)
(M) *** HMV Greensleeve TC-ESD 7020. Aldo Ciccolini, Alexis Weissenberg (pianos), Paris Conservatoire Orch., Prêtre – POULENC: *Babar.***
*** Enigma K 453553. Anthony Goldstone, Ian Brown (pianos), RPO, Hughes – PROKOFIEV: *Peter and the Wolf.***
(M)*CBS 40-61814 [(d) Col. MT 31808]. Leonard Bernstein (narrator and cond.), New York PO – PROKOFIEV: *Peter and the Wolf.**
Carnival of the Animals (with verses by Ogden Nash).
DG 3300 588 [id.]. Hermione Gingold (narrator), Alfons and Aloys Kontarsky (as above) – PROKOFIEV: *Peter and the Wolf.
Carnival of the Animals (with verses by Eleanor Bron).
(*) EMI Bronze TC-BRNA 502. Eleanor Bron (narrator), Susan Bradshaw, Richard Rodney Bennett (pianos), Vesuvius Ens. – POULENC: *Babar.*(***)

Marvellous playing from the Kontarskys and the Vienna Philharmonic and superb recording. Not everyone will care for the inclusion of Ogden Nash's verses (Saint-Saëns's music stands up admirably without them) but those who do will find Miss Gingold's narration is splendidly done – every inflection of that superb voice is to be relished. The alternative is a coupling without text harnessed to an excellent perrformance of *Eine kleine Nachtmusik*. Both sides are thus relatively short and may not seem good value at full price, but the transfer is of demonstration quality, with marvellously clear detail. It is no less good in the version with narration, where the voice, the pianists and the orchestra are all caught in perfect focus and natural sound.

The Paris recording with Ciccolini and Weissenberg (who make a contribution of some distinction) offers a refreshingly brilliant account of Saint-Saëns's *jeu d'esprit*. It opens a little heavily, but the characterization is nicely managed, with some very good orchestral playing. This is thoroughly competitive at bargain price. The cassette transfer is of good quality, marginally drier than the LP.

The two pianists on Enigma play with both style and affection, and the accompaniment has plenty of spirit and spontaneity. The work opens a little heavily, and *The swan* is perhaps a trifle self-effacing, but otherwise this is very enjoyable, the humour appreciated without being underlined. The transfer to tape is admirably clear yet not too dry in ambience.

With its really first-class coupling this tape can be given a strong recommendation.

After Eleanor Bron's imaginative performance of Poulenc's *Babar* her somewhat pretentious verses for the *Carnival of the Animals* are a great disappointment. They are too intellectually intense for Saint-Saëns's whimsical inspiration, and many will strongly resist the 'women's lib' hens ('only the eggless cock is really free-ranging') and the 'welfare state' cuckoo. There is little to commend in this performance with its dry acoustic and poor balance; and the tape transfer produces thin piano timbre and edgy violins, and generally sounds unattractive.

Bernstein also provides a narration and tells us the derivations of Saint-Saëns's orchestral jokes. This might be all very well on a TV programme but is not attractive for repeated listening, interesting as it may be. Young musicians play the solos within the orchestra (*The swan* is played on a double-bass) and are effusively introduced; however well-meaning the conductor is, the effect is patronizing to say the least. The sound is acceptable but has a limited frequency spectrum.

(i) *Carnival of the Animals;* (ii) *Septet in E flat major for trumpet, strings and piano, Op. 65.*
*(*) HMV TC-ASD 3448. Instrumental Ens., Jean-Philippe Collard (piano), with (i) Michel Béroff (piano); (ii) Maurice André (trumpet).

The acoustic of the French EMI recording is unattractively dry in the *Carnival of the Animals*; the piano timbre is rather hard and bloomless. This makes the humour of the piece sound forced, and there is little effect of charm. The *Septet* is similarly unexpansive although clear, and the curious instrumentation of trumpet, strings and piano does not seem to gell, although the performance is lively enough. The tape transfer offers no problems except for a touch of muddiness at the very opening of the *Carnival*, and it is certainly brightly focused.

Piano concertos Nos. 1 in D major, Op. 17; 2 in G minor, Op. 22.
(M)**(*)Turnabout KTVC 37106. Gabriel Tacchino, Radio Luxembourg Orch., Froment.

Piano concertos Nos. 3 in E flat major, Op. 29; 4 in C minor, Op. 44.
(M)**(*)Turnabout KTVC 37107. Tacchino, Radio Luxembourg Orch., Froment.

Piano concerto No. 5 in F major (Egyptian), Op. 103; Africa fantasy, Op. 89; Rapsodie d'Auvergne, Op. 73; Wedding Cake (Caprice-valse), Op. 76 (all for piano and orchestra).
(M)**(*)Turnabout KTVC 37108. Tacchino, Radio Luxembourg Orch., Froment.

Gabriel Tacchino is very good indeed; he has the appropriate keyboard presence and plays with great flair. There is vivid orchestral support, and if the orchestral playing itself lacks the last degree of distinction the performances have such spirit and spontaneity that reservations need not be serious. The transfers are of excellent quality, crisp and clear and with bold, firmly focused piano tone and plenty of detail. There tends to be a touch of hardness on the string tone at times, and the quality in the *Fourth Concerto* has rather more edge than in the rest of the series. But these are sophisticated transfers throughout. The bonus items on the third tape are all well worth having: the *Wedding Cake caprice* is given a most agreeable lightness of texture.

Piano concertos Nos. 1 in D major, Op. 17; 5 in F major (Egyptian), Op. 103.

473

*(*) CBS 40-76532 [Col. MT 34512]. Philippe Entremont, Orchestre du Capitole, Toulouse, Plasson.

Entremont is a vigorously persuasive interpreter of French music, but here the CBS recording does less than justice to his gentler qualities. The piano tone is too clattery and aggressive and the dynamic range too limited for this elegant music. The cassette transfer is reasonably successful, matching the LP in character, but this cannot compete with the Tacchino series (see above).

Piano concerto No. 5 in F major (Egyptian), Op. 103.
** HMV TC-ASD 3480. Aldo Ciccolini, Orchestre de Paris, Baudo – D'INDY: *Symphonie.***

Choice between this and Tacchino's version will probably depend on couplings. The Orchestre de Paris is, of course, a finer body than their rivals from Luxembourg, and undoubtedly Ciccolini's performance is a fine one. The d'Indy rarity makes an attractive partner, and if that work appeals there need be no real hesitation, though the transfer here is not quite as judiciously managed as in the coupling; at the loudest climaxes the refinement slips a little. However, the atmosphere of the recording is well captured (the sound is warmer and fuller than in the Turnabout series and certainly less aggressive than in the Entremont tape); and the piano timbre is natural.

(i) *Violin concertos Nos. 1 in A minor, Op. 20; 2 in C major, Op. 58; 3 in B minor, Op. 61; Caprice andalou, Op. 122; Le Déluge, Op. 45: Prélude; Havanaise, Op. 83; Introduction and rondo capriccioso, Op. 28; Morceau de concert, Op. 62; Romances: in D flat major, Op. 37; in C major, Op.*

48. (ii) *La Muse et le poète, Op. 132* (duo). (Also includes: (i) YSAŸE: *Caprice after the Study in the form of a waltz by Saint-Saëns, Op. 52.*)
(***)HMV TC-SLS 5103. Ulf Hoelscher (violin), with (i) New Philharmonia Orch., Dervaux; (ii) Ralph Kirshbaum (cello).

It is good to see a revival in Saint-Saëns's fortunes. This tape box collects all his music for violin and orchestra (with a short bonus from Ysaÿe) in performances of excellent quality. Ulf Hoelscher is an extremely accomplished soloist who plays with artistry as well as virtuosity, and he uncovers music of genuine worth and much charm, which is not as well known as the second and third *Violin concertos.* Pierre Dervaux directs excellent accompaniments, and the recording is lifelike and natural. The cassette version cannot be recommended at present, for it suffers from distortion on climaxes. The solo violin image is clear and generally well focused, but although the recording is quite well detailed, there is not the bloom that distinguishes the discs. When these problems are rectified this box will be a most desirable addition to the tape catalogue.

Violin concerto No. 3 in B minor, Op. 61.
*** Decca KSXC 6759 [Lon. 5-6992]. Kyung-Wha Chung, LSO, Foster – VIEUXTEMPS: *Violin concerto No. 5.***
*(*) CBS 40-76530 [Col. MT 34550]. Isaac Stern, Orchestre de Paris, Barenboim – CHAUSSON: *Poème**; FAURÉ: *Berceuse.*(*)

Kyung-Wha Chung gives a characteristically passionate account of the finest of the Saint-Saëns concertos, so intense that even a sceptical listener will find it hard not to be convinced that this is a great work. Such music needs this kind of advocacy, and Miss Chung is splendidly backed up by the LSO under Foster. Rich, clear recording, and an excellent tape transfer: the quality is generally first-class, the soloist naturally caught and given a sweet, silky tone, and the orchestral sound not lacking detail and presence.

Stern's violin is for once balanced naturally against the orchestra, and paradoxically it gives his fine performance of the Saint-Saëns more strength than close-up sound does. Though this is not so persuasively affectionate as Kyung-Wha Chung's reading, it makes a fair alternative for those who prefer this coupling. The CBS transfer is acceptable rather than outstanding; the quality is pleasant but it lacks distinctive crispness of outline and internal detail.

(i) *Violin concerto No. 3 in B minor, Op. 61;* (ii) *Introduction and rondo capriccioso* (for violin and orchestra), *Op. 28.*
   (M) **(*) HMV TC-EXE 73. Nathan Milstein, with (i) Philharmonia Orch., Fistoulari; (ii) Concert Arts Orch., Susskind – CHAUSSON: *Poème.*****

Milstein's strong, imperious style adds stature to the first movement of the concerto, and Fistoulari provides a matching strong accompaniment throughout. His presentation of the brass chorale in the finale creates an effect of considerable power. The solo playing is both beautiful and assured, although it does not perhaps have quite the degree of charm that some soloists find in this work. Milstein is glitteringly assured in the *Introduction and rondo capriccioso*, and his effortless bravura is easy to enjoy. His tone is fractionally hardened here by the brightly lit recording, whereas in the concerto the sound is natural. But in both works the overall quality is good, and the cassette transfer is vivid, with excellent reproduction of the soloist.

Violoncello concerto No. 1 in A minor, Op. 33.
   ** HMV TC-ASD 3452. Mstislav Rostropovich, LPO, Giulini – DVOŘÁK: *Cello concerto.*(*)

This serves as a fill-up for the Dvořák concerto, and comes off more successfully than its coupling, though it is not as impressive as Rostropovich's earlier version with Sargent (now deleted). There is less rhetorical intensity here than in the Dvořák, and the performance is nicely recorded. The quality of the transfer seems marginally clearer on side two, so that the Saint-Saëns concerto has rather better detail than the Dvořák. The sound is agreeably warm but lacks the range and sparkle of the finest cassette transfers.

(i; ii) *Danse macabre, Op. 40;* (iii) *Havanaise, Op. 83; Introduction and rondo capriccioso, Op. 28* (both for violin and orchestra); (i; ii) *Le Rouet d'Omphale, Op. 31. Samson et Dalila* (opera): (iv) *Mon cœur s'ouvre à ta voix (Softly awakes my heart);* (i; v) *Bacchanale.*
   (M) **(*) Decca KECC 808. (i) Paris Conservatoire Orch.; (ii) Martinon; (iii) Ruggiero Ricci (violin), LSO, Gamba; (iv) Regina Resnik (contralto); (v) Fistoulari.

This is a characteristically well-made Decca anthology. The Martinon performances of *Danse macabre* and *Le Rouet d'Omphale* are notably successful, and Ricci shows splendid form and plenty of personality in the works featuring the solo violin. Regina Resnik's performance of *Softly awakes my heart* is splendidly rich and resonant, and the collection ends vividly with Fistoulari's account of the *Bacchanale.* Until this point the sound has been first-class in every way, but in the closing bars of the *Bacchanale* the tape transfer has been

475

miscalculated and the bass drum muddies the texture of the final climax. Many will feel, however, that the cassette is still a good investment; it is excellent for use in the car, where the technical mishap is less noticeable.

Havanaise, Op. 83; Introduction and rondo capriccioso, Op. 28 (both for violin and orchestra).

> (M) *** HMV TC-SXLP 30277. Yehudi Menuhin, Philharmonia Orch., Goossens – LALO: *Symphonie espagnole.****

Menuhin is in superb form in these highly engaging performances, and although the recordings date from the late 1950s they still sound freshly vivid. Whether in the lyrical introductions, played with warmth yet not a trace of self-indulgence, or in the *spiccato* bravura at the end of the *Rondo capriccioso*, Menuhin shows consistent panache, and his shaping of the coda to the *Havanaise* is delightful. Goossens accompanies with considerable flair, and the brilliant recordings have been admirably transferred.

Symphony No. 3 in C minor, Op. 78.

> *** DG 3300 619 [id.]. Chicago SO, Barenboim.
> *** Decca KSXC 6482 [Lon. 5-6680]. Los Angeles PO, Mehta.
> (M)(***) HMV Greensleeve TC-ESD 7038. City of Birmingham SO, Frémaux.
> (**) CBS 40-76653 [Col. MT 34573]. New York PO, Bernstein.

Symphony No. 3; (i) *Wedding Cake (Caprice-valse) for piano and strings, Op. 76.*

> *(*) Philips 7300 597 [id.]. Rotterdam PO, de Waart, (i) with Daniel Chorzempa (piano).

This once neglected but now popular symphony is well served by the gramophone, and there are two clear recommendations on tape. Barenboim's is a superlative performance which glows with warmth from beginning to end. In the opening 6/8 section the galloping rhythms are irresistibly pointed, while the linked slow section has a poised stillness in its soaring lyricism which completely avoids any suspicion of sweetness or sentimentality. A brilliant account of the scherzo leads into a magnificent energetic conclusion, with every section of the Chicago orchestra excelling itself in radiant playing. It was a bold idea to record the organ part (played by Gaston Litaize) separately in Chartres Cathedral and marry it with the Chicago performance. The clear benefit is that the organ sound is made more specific instead of washing round every section of the orchestra. It is particularly impressive in its biting entries in the finale, but it also adds to the glow of sound in the slow section without muddying the texture. Not often on a single recording do so many excellences coincide; and this cassette was one of DG's first triumphs in this medium. The quality is fully demonstration-worthy and only very marginally less refined than the outstanding LP.

On Decca the playing of the Los Angeles orchestra is first-class and Mehta draws a well-disciplined and exuberant response from all departments. The recording too is extremely fine, with good detail and a well-lit texture. Again the cassette transfer is first-class.

Frémaux's account with the CBSO is superbly played, and it too is given the benefit of excellent recording which effectively reveals detail without any obtrusive effects and which has plenty of impact. The richness of the slow movement is impressive, and the finale has a good-humoured exhilaration which is very enjoyable indeed. Unfortunately the Greensleeve cassette transfer cannot be recommended. The first two movements are acceptable, although the organ entry in the *Poco adagio* hardly produces a refined sound balance; but in the spectacular finale the recording becomes congested. The opening piano figurations are poorly focused, and the organ climaxes are coarsely unattractive to the ear.

Polished as the playing of the Rotterdam orchestra is, helped by refined Philips recording, the de Waart performance cannot compare in excitement with the finest accounts. Some may be swayed by the attractive fill-up, though after the organ glories at the end of the symphony, few will want to go on at once to such a lightweight piece. The Philips cassette transfer is made at a very low level, and the sound lacks projection and bite.

Bernstein's account is disappointingly slack, and lacks the character one expects in this conductor's recordings. The finale is especially disappointing, with nothing like the electricity of the best versions. The problem is compounded on tape by serious distortion when the organ enters in the last movement. It sounds rather 'boomy' elsewhere and the general recording quality is lack-lustre.

Sarasate, Pablo
(1844–1908)

Zigeunerweisen, Op. 20/1.
HMV TC-ASD 3408 [Angel 4xs 37445]. Itzhak Perlman (violin), Pittsburgh SO, Previn – GOLD-MARK: *Violin concerto.***

The breathtaking account of the *Zigeunerweisen* by Aaron Rosand is not available on cassette, but in any event Perlman's is no less virtuosic and idiomatic. The engineers have placed the distinguished soloist rather too close to the microphone, but Perlman survives any amount of scrutiny and the results are in no way disturbing. This makes an attractive fill-up for Goldmark's charming

concerto (where this version again has the cassette field to itself). In spite of the spotlight on the soloist the transfer provides full-blooded orchestral sound.

Satie, Erik
(1866–1925)

Gymnopédies Nos. 1 and 3 (orch. Debussy).
***HMV TC-ASD 2989. City of Birmingham SO, Frémaux – IBERT: *Divertissement*; HON-EGGER: *Pacific 231*; POULENC: *Les Biches.* (**)

Beautiful orchestral playing and rich resonant recording which suit Debussy's indulgent scoring perfectly. The quality of Satie's inspiration is in no doubt in this beautiful music. The transfer is smooth and rich and of excellent quality, although the couplings fare less well in this reverberant acoustic.

Monotones (ballet, arr. Lanchbery); *Jack in the Box* (orch. Milhaud); *Deux Préludes posthumes* (orch. Poulenc); *Trois Morceaux en forme de poire* (orch. Désormière).
(M) *(*) HMV Greensleeve TC-ESD 7069. Orch. of the Royal Opera House, Covent Garden, Lanchbery.

Sir Frederick Ashton's ballet *Monotones* is principally based on the *Gnossiennes* and *Gymnopédies*. The music is fairly static, and although it is gracefully played there is a lack of momentum here: the best-known third *Gymnopédie* is extended by repetition and at Lanchbery's slow, stately pace almost outlasts its welcome. The arrival of the more lively *Jack in the Box* comes as a relief, but side two returns to the somewhat languid mood of the opening, and the two posthumous *Préludes* seem almost totally lacking in vitality. No doubt this issue will be sought after by balletomanes but it cannot be generally recommended with any enthusiasm. The recording is suitably atmospheric, although on tape the sound is not especially refined in detail, and *Jack in the Box* could do with more glitter.

Gnossiennes Nos. 1, 4 and 5; Trois Gymnopédies; Nocturne No. 1; Passacaille; Six Pièces (Désespoir agréable; Effronterie; Poésie; Prélude canin; Profondeur; Songe creux); Ragtime (from Parade, arr. Ourdine); Sarabandes Nos. 1 and 3; Sonatine bureaucratique; Sports et divertissements; Véritables préludes flasques; Vieux sequins et vieilles cuirasses.

(M)(**) Saga CA 5387. John McCabe (piano).

Although Satie is often overrated by his admirers there is a desperate melancholy and a rich poetic feeling about much of this music which are altogether unique. The *Gymnopédies* show such flashes of innocence and purity of inspiration that criticism is disarmed. John McCabe's performances are cool, even deliberate, but they are not heavy, and his sympathy is never in doubt. He is quite well recorded, but the transfer is of uneven quality. Side one is rather bright, even tinkly in the treble; side two is fuller and better balanced. The piano tone itself is not always absolutely steady. But this tape is in the budget price-range and there is no competition in this repertoire.

Scarlatti, Alessandro (1660–1725)

Cantata pastorale per la Natività di Nostro Signore Gesù Cristo.

(M) *** HMV TC-SXLP 30280. Janet Baker (contralto), ECO, Leppard – MONTEVERDI: *L'Incoronazione di Poppea excerpts;* D. SCARLATTI: *Salve Regina.****

The cooler enchantments of Alessandro Scarlatti make an admirable foil for the intense Monteverdi offerings on this tape, and Janet Baker's depth of expression brings vividness to this *Cantata pastorale* written for Christmas. The recording is transferred with great presence.

Scarlatti, Domenico (1685–1757)

Keyboard sonatas (arr. for guitar), Kk. 159, 175, 208, 213, 380, 448.

*** CBS 40-73545 [Col. MT 34198]. John Williams (guitar) – VILLA-LOBOS: *5 Preludes.****

Guitar arrangements of Scarlatti sonatas have their charms when played by an artist as imaginative as John Williams. The recording is faithful, though rather close and somewhat larger than life, but the cassette transfer is very well managed.

Keyboard sonatas, Kk. 2, 6, 9, 10, 13, 17, 28, 87, 125, 141, 145, 159, 203, 268, 371, 417, 430, 436, 444–6, 517, 533.

* Advent G 1014 (see p. xxiii) [id.]. Anthony di Bonaventura (piano).

Scarlatti on the piano is a relative rarity nowadays, which is a pity since the elegant, delicate accounts of the sonatas recorded by Horowitz, Michelangeli and Casadesus are treasured possessions. In any event, on harpsichord or piano, Scarlatti is not generously represented on cassette and it would be a pleasure to welcome this unreservedly. Anthony di Bonaventura plays with plenty of rhythmic vitality, but he is far too closely recorded and there is little dynamic contrast. His playing is not quite elegant or sensitive enough to dynamic nuances to do full justice to this repertoire. There are numerous musical touches, but the recital does not fully satisfy.

Keyboard sonatas, Kk. 206, 212, 222, 364–5, 370–71, 481, 501–2, 513, 524–5, 532.
> (M) **(*) Argo KZKC 5. Colin Tilney (harpsichord).

Colin Tilney plays a 1782 single-manual instrument by Schudi, strung throughout in brass. The instrument lacks something of the brightness of other harpsichords, but it is good to hear this repertoire without fussy changes in registration. Tilney provides scholarly and authoritative performances, sometimes a little wanting in spontaneity but never in musicality. He is excellently recorded, and the tape transfer is of demonstration quality, with excellent life and presence.

Salve Regina (arr. Leppard).
> (M) *** HMV TC-SXLP 30280. Janet Baker (contralto), ECO, Leppard – MONTEVERDI: *L'Incoronazione di Poppea excerpts;* A. SCARLATTI: *Cantata pastorale.****

This *Salve Regina* has conventional passages, but Janet Baker and Leppard together hardly let you appreciate any weakness, so intense is the performance. There is a hint of edge on the extremely

vivid sound, but it is easily smoothed, and the vocal presence adds to the drama of the presentation.

Schlick, Johann (*c.* 1759–1825)

Divertimento in D major for 2 mandolins and basso continuo.
> (M) * Turnabout KTVC 34110. Elfriede Kunschak, Vinzenz Hladky (mandolins), Maria Hinterleitner (harpsichord) – BEETHOVEN: *Music for mandolin.**

The main interest of this tape is the mandolin music of Beethoven; the Schlick piece is particularly slight and inconsequential. The performance is adequate, and the recording, which is without much dynamic contrast and not very sharply focused, is acceptable only.

Schoenberg, Arnold (1874–1951)

Variations for orchestra, Op. 31; Verklaerte Nacht (orchestral version), *Op. 4.*
> ***DG 3300 627 [id.]. Berlin PO, Karajan.

Karajan's version of *Verklaerte Nacht* is by far the most sensitive and imaginative as well as the most beautifully played that has ever been on the market. A magical reading and beautifully recorded too. The *Variations for orchestra* are also made to sound far more atmospheric and sensuous than they have under less gifted hands. The cassette transfer is well managed, but the orchestral textures here sound marginally less rich and secure than on disc.

Verklaerte Nacht (orchestral version), *Op. 4.*
   ** CBS 40-76305. New York PO, Boulez – BERG: *Lyric suite.***

Boulez secures responsive playing from the strings of the New York Philharmonic and has the measure of Schoenberg's poetic essay. But this performance is no match for Karajan's superbly fashioned and sensitive account and is not as richly recorded, though on tape the sound is well balanced and quite full in texture, so that the absence of the widest spectrum of frequencies is only a marginal drawback.

Pierrot Lunaire (song cycle), *Op. 21.*
   *** Advent F 1035 (see p. xxiii) [id.]. Jan DeGaetani (soprano), Contemporary Chamber Ens., Weisberg – CRUMB: *Ancient Voices.***

This New York performance of Schoenberg's cycle (originally a Nonesuch recording) steers a splendidly confident course between all the many problematic points of interpretation. Jan DeGaetani is a superbly precise soloist, but there is no feeling whatever of pedantry in this music-making, which allows a welcome degree of expressiveness while keeping a sharp focus. The recording is excellent, Advent's transfer is of demonstration quality, and the coupling (by the same artists, from another Nonesuch recording of considerable interest) is happily planned.

Schubert, Franz
(1797–1828)

Overtures: *Fierrabras, D.796;* in the *Italian style in C major, D. 591; Des Teufels Lustschloss, D.84.*
   (*) Decca KSXC 6090. Vienna PO, Kertesz – *Symphony No. 8.**

These overtures make an enterprising coupling for a first-rate account of the *Unfinished symphony. Des Teufels Lustschloss* is a juvenile work, and its bright-eyed freshness shows much in common with the music of the young Mendelssohn. *Fierrabras* is more melodramatic but lively in invention; and Schubert's Rossini-imitation nearly comes off here with such neat, sparkling playing. Excellent recording too, although on our review copy of the tape the sound for the overtures had rather less brilliance and refinement of detail than the symphony.

(i) *Marche militaire in D major, D.733/1;* (ii) *Rosamunde: Overture (Die Zauberharfe, D.644);* incidental music: *Entr'acte in B flat major; Ballet music Nos. 1 and 2, D.797;* (iii) *Symphony No. 8 in B minor (Unfinished), D.759.*
   (M) ** Decca KCSP 225. Vienna PO, cond. (i) Knappertsbusch; (ii) Monteux; (iii) Schuricht.

Carl Schuricht's performance of the *Unfinished* dates from 1957 and was admired in its day. It is an affectionate reading, warmly played, with a strong forward impulse but some lack of drama. This latter aspect is emphasized by the stereo, which, while glowing and natural, has a very limited dynamic range. The *Marche militaire* is played with lots of character by Knappertsbusch and vividly recorded. Monteux's *Rosamunde* excerpts (another early stereo recording, and a good one on all counts) are distinctive, with striking characterization and good playing. In spite of the reduced dynamics in the *Unfinished*, this makes an excellent anthology at medium price. The cassette transfer faithfully reflects the character of all of these recordings and with each provides a satisfactory balance. The sound in the *Unfinished* has not the presence of more recent versions, but is well detailed and has no lack of body.

Symphonies Nos. 1–6 and 8–9; Rosamunde: Overture (Die Zauberharfe, D.644); incidental music: Ballet music Nos. 1 and 2, D.797.
> **(*)** DG 3378 021. Berlin PO, Boehm.
> **(*)** HMV TC-SLS 5127. Berlin PO, Karajan.

Boehm's set of Schubert cassettes is presented in DG's newest packaging so that each of the five tapes can be removed from its own well in the album complete with its plastic library box. Taken as a whole, this is a most attractive set. Boehm has a somewhat unsmiling countenance here and there (at least by the side of Beecham in Nos. 3 and 5), but the playing of the Berlin Philharmonic is generally distinguished. Certainly the Berlin wind are a joy to listen to in most of these symphonies, and in Nos. 6, 8 and 9 Boehm is among the very best of Schubertians. It is only in the early symphonies that he sometimes fails to capture the youthful sparkle of these delightful scores. The *Rosamunde* excerpts are beautifully played: the opening of the *Overture* offers a splendidly dramatic flourish, and Boehm phrases the music which follows with the utmost grace. The recording is first-class and the tape transfers very sophisticated. The quality in the first two symphonies seems slightly drier than the rest, but it suits their character. Elsewhere the warmth and bloom over

the orchestra give much pleasure, yet there is the most refined detail. There are two tiny blemishes. There is a hint of roughness in the finale of No. 4 when the music expands into the movement's climax and a curious drop of pitch in the most famous *Ballet music* from *Rosamunde*. As this is not mirrored on the reverse of the cassette it must have come from the master tape and will presumably be common to all copies.

Karajan's cycle represents him at his freshest and most direct. Anyone who knows the DG version of the *Great C major symphony* will be astonished at the transformation here from self-consciousness to open lyricism. Tempi tend to be fast, both in outer movements and in slow movements, but with characteristically polished playing from the Berlin Philharmonic, there is rarely if ever any sense of unwanted haste. Though one misses the loving touches of personal magic that characterized Beecham's interpretations, the stylishness of the Berlin woodwind is pointed just as aptly towards a more rustic manner than usual, as for example in the second subject of the first movement in Symphony No. 3. The largeness of scale even in the early symphonies is more open to criticism, but the high spirits of the young Schubert are consistently conveyed. Karajan's far from characteristic simplicity is at its most effective in the *Unfinished symphony*, which is the more moving and intense for the degree of understatement. Warm, atmospheric recording. The set is rather handsomely packaged by EMI's usual standards, and with a large box the booklet uses a readable size of print. But the transfers lack the refinement of the DG set. In tuttis throughout the series there is a hint of roughness, and the focus of the upper strings is not always absolutely clean. It is easy to exaggerate this defect, but undoubtedly the sound DG provide for Boehm is sweeter.

Symphonies Nos. 3 in D major, D.200; 5 in B flat major, D.485.

⊛ (M) *** HMV TC-EXE 184. RPO, Beecham.

**(*)Decca KSXC 6799 [Lon. 5-7020]. Israel PO, Mehta.

Beecham's are magical performances in which every phrase breathes. There is no substitute for imaginative phrasing, and here each line is shaped with affection and spirit. Sunny, smiling performances with beautifully alive rhythms and luminous textures. The recording is faithful in timbre, well balanced and spacious. This is an indispensable recording for all collections. The cassette transfer is of good quality, warm yet clear and well balanced.

Because of the total memorability of Beecham's coupling it would be easy to underestimate the qualities of Mehta's tape. Except in the minuet of No. 5, his rhythmic manner is notably less persuasive than that of Beecham, although in the minuet of No. 3 the *Ländler*-like trio is particularly characterful. Sensitive as Mehta unfailingly is, the results are heavy by comparison. Yet the robust feeling of the account of the *D major Symphony* is exhilarating, and these performances are by no means to be dismissed. The Decca transfer, with its characteristic freshness and bloom (the delicacy of string texture at the opening of the *Fifth* is notable too), gives much pleasure.

Symphonies Nos. 3 in D major, D.200; 8 in B minor (Unfinished), D.759.
　**(*) DG 3300 475. Berlin PO, Boehm.

The coupling of Boehm's *Third* and *Eighth* is available on tape only: they are differently paired on disc. The *Third* is finely played, with splendid, disciplined ensemble from the Berlin Philharmonic. Perhaps there is a lack of youthful freshness, but this is certainly a well-made account. The *Unfinished* is a masterly performance, combining deep sensitivity with great refinement, and the points of detail as well as the overall warmth put this version among the very finest. The opening of the development – always a key point – is magically done, and the superb recording quality throughout gives unusual clarity, while allowing the Berlin Philharmonic ensemble its natural opulence. The transfer is of generally good quality. The focus in the middle and lower strings in No. 3 is not quite as clean here as in the complete set (which one assumes was a later retransfer and offers very sophisticated quality), and this is noticeable at the closing climax of the first movement. But the *Unfinished* has a fine impact and good detail, and both works have no lack of bloom.

Symphonies Nos. 4 in C minor (Tragic), D.417; 5 in B flat major, D.485.
　*(*) Decca KSXC 6483 [Lon. 5-6682]. Vienna PO, Kertesz.

Apart from a few extreme tempi – a fast minuet in No. 4, a fast first movement and a slow start to the second in No. 5 – this coupling offers attractive, stylish Schubert playing. Kertesz does not always find the smile in Schubert's writing, but the playing of the Vienna Philharmonic is beyond reproach and the recording exemplary. The cassette transfer, however, is disappointing, not up to Decca's usual high standard. The sound in the *Fourth Symphony* is muggy in the bass, and the overall texture is not clear. No. 5 is better but hardly brilliant.

Symphonies No. 4 in C minor (Tragic), D.417; 8 in B minor (Unfinished), D.759.
　** DG 3301 047 [id.]. Chicago SO, Giulini.
　*(*)Decca KSXC 6845. Israel PO, Mehta.

Giulini's account of the *Tragic* is controversial in its choice of tempi. He makes heavy weather of the first-movement allegro (at roughly minim 92), adopting a speed which offers insufficient contrast with the *Andante*, and which impedes a proper sense of flow. In the second movement he applies the brakes just before the return of the main theme (bar 110) and passes some less than perfect intonation in the ensuing section. The scherzo is not remotely *vivace*, and the finale is only a little less pedestrian. The recording is full-blooded and the transfer is at an unusually high level for DG (the first chord sends the level indicators up into the red area) so has good detail and range, although the bass needs cutting back somewhat. Mehta in the *Tragic* chooses sensible tempi and secures decent enough playing from the Israel orchestra; the performance has an almost rustic bounce and energy. The same goes for his account of the *Unfinished*, and the Decca sound throughout is characteristically bright and vivid. Giulini offers a deeply-felt reading of the latter, with much carefully considered detail. There are some magical things, such as the phrasing of the opening of the development of the first movement. By comparison Mehta seems markedly less refined and imaginative, but even so Giulini does not match here his earlier (1962) Philharmonia performance (see below).

Symphonies Nos. 5 in B flat major, D.485; 8 in B minor (Unfinished), D.759.

> * Philips 7300 512 [id.]. Concertgebouw Orch., Haitink.

Disappointingly dull performances from Haitink, with slow tempi the rule. It is a bad sign when one does not welcome the exposition repeat in the first movement of the *Unfinished*.

Symphony No. 8 in B minor (Unfinished), D.759.

> ⊛ (M) *** World Records TC-SH 290. Philharmonia Orch., Can-

telli – MENDELSSOHN: *Symphony No. 4.****

> (M) *** HMV TC-SXLP 30278. Philharmonia Orch., Giulini – BRAHMS: *Variations.***(*)

> *** Decca KSXC 6090. Vienna PO, Kertesz – *Overtures.***(*)

> **(*) DG 923057 [id.]. Berlin PO, Karajan – BEETHOVEN: *Overtures.***(*)

> **(*) Decca KSXC 6539. ECO, Britten – MOZART: *Symphony No. 38.***(*)

> (M) ** DG Privilege 3335 103. Berlin PO, Maazel – BEETHOVEN: *Symphony No. 5; BRAHMS: Tragic overture.***

> ** HMV TC-ASD 3203. Berlin PO, Karajan – HAYDN: *Symphony No. 104.**

Cantelli's moving account of the *Unfinished* was recorded a year before his premature death. It was made in genuine stereo and few allowances have to be made for its age. As always with Cantelli, the playing is remarkably fresh and alive. There are no 'interpretative touches' of the kind favoured by 'great' conductors, and yet for all that (or perhaps because of it) it is deeply personal and committed. The orchestral blend is an object lesson for its kind, and every phrase is carefully thought out yet at the same time spontaneous. There have been memorable accounts of the *Unfinished* since 1955, notably from Walter and Karajan, but this takes its place among the recorded classics. The transfer is beautifully managed, well balanced and clear.

Giulini's 1962 Philharmonia performance is refreshingly straightforward, yet full of imaginative detail. It is superlatively well played by the Philharmonia, and the result is more spontaneous than Giulini's much more recent Chicago version for DG (coupled with the *Tragic*; see above). The recording does not in the least sound its age, and the transfer is very successful, clean and well balanced and mellower than its Brahms coupling (which is also splendidly played).

Kertesz's reading is one of the finest of his Schubert cycle, spacious and unaffected and supported by fine orchestral playing. The recording is of the highest quality, with a wide dynamic range so that the woodwind solos in the second movement tend to sound a little distant. The *pianissimo* at the opening, however, immediately creates a degree of tension that is to be sustained throughout the performance. The cassette transfer is notably clear and vivid in Decca's best manner (although the couplings are slightly less well managed).

Karajan on DG characteristically gives extraordinary polish to the *Unfinished*, lighting up much that is often obscured. The first movement is extremely compelling, and the slow movement too brings tingling precise attack and a wonderful sense of drama. Particularly with a coupling of Beethoven overtures, this may not be the best general recommendation, but it is certainly a remarkably individual one. On tape the recording is well balanced and lacks only the last degree of brilliance. For best results a cut-back in the bass will be useful. The transfer handles the resonant acoustic quite well and although the *pianissimo* detail is not very clear there is a compensating atmosphere and warmth.

Britten also takes an individual view of the *Unfinished*, setting off at a fastish tempo for the first movement, refusing to inflate the cello theme, but underlining the symphonic tensions with crisp rhythms in the development. The second movement too is strongly rhythmic – an individual and refreshing interpretation, beautifully recorded. Apart from one or two moments when the sound congeals slightly in the middle frequencies at tuttis, the quality is dramatically vivid, with plenty of detail and wide dynamic contrasts.

A fresh approach is always acceptable with the *Unfinished*, but Maazel's first

movement is relatively uneventful and the second is without the sustained sense of lyricism and tension that a Beecham can bring. Nevertheless, the playing is for the most part excellent; the recording is good, and the transfer well balanced and clear. This is an acceptable coupling for a brilliant reading of Beethoven's *Fifth*.

Karajan's newer version of the *Unfinished* on HMV does not match his DG account in its drama and directness of utterance, but its simplicity of approach is disarmingly effective. The recording is full and the transfer quite well managed.

Symphony No. 9 in C major (Great), D.944.

*** Philips 7300 510 [id.]. Concertgebouw Orch., Haitink.

(M) *** DG Privilege 3318 050. Bavarian Radio Orch., Jochum – WEBER: *Der Freischütz overture.***

**(*)DG 3300 882 [id.]. Chicago SO, Giulini.

(M) **(*) HMV TC-SXLP 30267. Hallé Orch., Barbirolli.

**(*)Decca KSXC 6729. Israel PO, Mehta.

(M) **(*) Philips 7317 191 [7310 054]. Dresden State Orch., Sawallisch.

(M)*(**)Decca KCSP 467. LSO, Krips.

(M) * DG Privilege 3335 290 [3300 013]. Berlin PO, Karajan.

Haitink's is a fresh and beautiful performance, marked by superb playing from the Concertgebouw. The interpretative approach is generally direct, so that the end of the first movement brings fewer and less marked rallentandos than usual, with the result sounding natural and easy. The slow movement, more measured than usual, is lightened by superb rhythmic pointing, and the recording is both full and refined. The tape transfer is generally very successful –

certainly the best buy on cassette, though just occasionally one notices a lack of refinement in the textural detail; but the richness and warmth of the orchestra more than compensate, and the wind and strings alike have a fine overall bloom.

Jochum's performance is not available on disc. The recording dates from 1958, but no one would ever guess it from this splendidly vivid tape, which, though bright and detailed and with strong impact, has no lack of depth. Moreover this is the only version to include a fill-up and a very considerable one, an exciting account of Weber's *Der Freischütz overture*. The performance of the symphony is at the opposite pole from those of Haitink and Giulini. The reading is immensely dramatic, with great vitality and unleisurely tempi that are varied flexibly with the ebb and flow of the music. The slow movement has less repose than usual (although there is no suggestion of hurry) and it has a climax of great power. The compelling thrust of the reading extends through the exhilarating scherzo to a finale which has an irresistible onward impulse. Jochum's use of light and shade is never more effective than here, and the slightly higher transfer level on side two of the tape gives an exciting presence and projection to the performance. (Unfortunately this tape has been withdrawn just as we go to press.)

Giulini's is a distinctive reading, generally relaxed but with a dramatic finale. He seeks to establish a modular tempo through different sections, so that the slow introduction leads into the *Allegro* without any change of pulse. He draws the most beautiful playing from the Chicago orchestra, and the result, if somewhat self-conscious, is often persuasive. The recording has transferred splendidly to tape, the quality warm and refined, with excellent detail yet plenty of bloom. Side two is transferred at a marginally higher level than side one, and this seems to bring extra bite to the finale, which is most vividly projected.

Barbirolli gives a warm, lyrical reading, with the speeds perfectly chosen to solve all the notorious interpretative traps with the minimum of fuss. The Hallé playing may not be quite so polished as that of, say, the Concertgebouw on the Haitink version; but it is far more important that the Barbirolli magic is conveyed at its most intense. Barbirolli is completely consistent, and although, characteristically, he may always indulge in affectionate phrasing in detail, he is usually steady in maintaining tempi broadly throughout each movement. The second subject of the first movement, for example, brings no 'gear-change', but equally no sense of the music being forced; and again with the tempo changes at the end of the movement, Barbirolli's solution is very satisfying. The recording is basically full and ample, but the high-level transfer, while clear and well detailed, is a little lacking in richness and warmth (although the bass response is adequate), and there seems an absence of bloom on the upper range of the string tone.

Mehta's is a sunny performance, well-paced and well-sprung, with the Israel orchestra in amiable form. The very start brings a full *mezzo forte* in the opening horn melody, but that sign of insensitivity is an exception, and generally Mehta solves all the many interpretative problems of the work naturally and convincingly, observing the exposition repeat in the first movement, but then in the scherzo omitting the second repeat, as is common. The recording is beefy, with a boosted bass to balance a brilliant treble, not quite so refined in sound as some other versions; but the cassette transfer is highly successful, rich and full.

Sawallisch's reading, like his other recordings of the Schubert symphonies, is refreshingly direct. In this symphony some will find the result undercharacterized, but with refined playing from the Dresden orchestra and recording refined for its age it can be recommended at medium price. The transfer is smooth yet well detailed.

485

It is a great pity that the transfer of the vintage performance by Josef Krips with the LSO has been made at fractionally too high a level, producing marginal congestion at the peaks of the outer movements and the climax of the slow movement. The performance itself has a direct, unforced spontaneity which shows Krips's natural feeling for Schubertian lyricism at its most engaging. The playing is polished yet flexible, strong without ever sounding aggressive. In the two final movements Krips finds an airy exhilaration which makes one wonder how ever other conductors can keep the music earthbound as they do. The pointing of the trio in the scherzo is delectable, and the feathery lightness of the triplets in the finale makes one positively welcome every single one of its many repetitions. As a whole this reading represents the Viennese tradition at its very finest.

Karajan's 1971 DG recording, reissued on Privilege, is an intense disappointment, with the ruggedness of the writing smoothed over to a degree surprising even from this conductor. The tempi are fast; but, as other conductors have shown, that does not necessarily mean that the work need be weakened. But Karajan skates over the endless beauties. There is no impression of glowing expansiveness: this is a tour of a chromium heaven. The transfer produces lively but rather brash orchestral quality.

CHAMBER MUSIC

(i; ii) *Fantasia in C major* (for violin and piano), *D.934;* (i–iii) *Piano trio No. 2 in E flat major, D.929;* (iv) *String quartets Nos. 8 in B flat major, D.112; 14 in D minor* (*Death and the Maiden*), *D.810; 15 in G major, D.887.*

⊛ (M) *** World Records TC-SHB 53. (i) Adolf Busch (violin); (ii)

Rudolf Serkin (piano); (iii) Hermann Busch (cello); (iv) Busch Qt.

This set represents a miraculous achievement. All these recordings come from the 1930s, but in no way are they of purely historic interest or addressed primarily to the nostalgia market. Thanks to the ministrations of Anthony Griffith they sound miraculously fresh – the string tone is unbelievably natural, and the presence of the artists is at times uncanny. Try the opening of the *Piano trio* as a sampler: its detail is remarkable, and the electricity of the playing communicates from the very first bar. Throughout the set we are offered searching and moving performances that possess a songful spontaneity and humanity that are as consistent as they are inspiriting. The Busch Quartet play with the complete authority of masters in total communion, and their serenity and sensibility shine across the four decades that have elapsed since the recordings were made. The transfers are superbly done. Older recordings often sound especially well on tape, and there is no better example than this; the balance and detail are admirable, and the range of the sound is no less striking. It is difficult at times to believe that these are 'historic' recordings at all (the style of the actual string phrasing dates the performances more than the sound itself) and no one need hesitate on technical grounds here.

Octet in F major (for clarinet, horn, bassoon and strings), *D.803.*

**(*) Philips 7300 613. Academy of St Martin-in-the-Fields Chamber Ens.

(M) *** Decca Ace of Diamonds KSDC 508. New Vienna Octet.

(M) ** Turnabout KTVC 34152. Munich Octet.

The performance by the Academy of St Martin-in-the-Fields Chamber Ensemble is both warmly affectionate and impetuous. The playing is sometimes slightly indulgent in its control of tempi (notably in the first movement). The slow movement is most beautifully played, almost narcissistic in its tonal beauty, but very persuasive just the same. The fourth-movement variations are leisurely but imaginatively done, and the finale, after a striking opening, has plenty of impetus. The recording is rich and spacious, very warm and natural and with a fine balance between tonal blend and detail. The high-level transfer is generally of very good quality, although when the horn is playing loudly and, notably, at the passionate opening of the finale, there are hints that the level is fractionally too high.

Mellifluous would be the word to describe the playing of the New Vienna Octet. This is a charming performance, superbly recorded. On tape the sound quality is smoothly and nicely blended, if not especially sharp in inner detail.

On Turnabout a friendly and very agreeable performance, and the warm recording suits it admirably. It may seem leisured at times, but there is no lack of spontaneity and the players communicate their enjoyment readily. The recording is homogeneous in blend yet quite clear. Although not the most sophisticated version this is attractive, and a good bargain.

Piano quintet in A major (*Trout*), *D.667.*

> ***Philips 7300 648 [id.]. Alfred Brendel (piano), members of the Cleveland Qt.
> (M) **(*) Philips Festivo 7300 115. Ingrid Haebler (piano), Arthur Grumiaux (violin), Georges Janzer (viola), Eva Czako (cello), Jacques Cazauran (double bass).
> (B) **(*) Classics for Pleasure TC-CFP 40085. Moura Lympany (piano), principals of the LSO.
> (M) **(*) Decca Ace of Diamonds

KSDC 185. Clifford Curzon, members of the Vienna Octet.
> (M) *(*) Turnabout KTVC 34140. Louis Kentner, Hungarian Qt (augmented).
> (B) * RCA Camden C4-5046. Festival Qt (augmented).

Piano quintet in A major (*Trout*); *Notturno in E flat major* (for piano trio), *D.897.*

> **(*) CRD CRDC 4052. Clifford Benson, Nash Ens.
> (M) ** DG Privilege 3335 332. Christoph Eschenbach, members of the Koeckert Qt.

Piano quintet in A major (*Trout*); *String quartet No. 12 in C minor* (*Quartettsatz*), *D.703.*

> ** DG 3300 646 [id.]. Emil Gilels, Amadeus Qt (augmented).

(i) *Piano quintet in A major* (*Trout*); (ii) *Violin sonatina No. 2 in A minor*, *D.385.*

> (B) *(*) DG Heliodor 3348 122. (i) Joerg Demus, Schubert Qt; (ii) Wolfgang Schneiderhan (violin), Walter Klien (piano).

The *Trout* is remarkably well represented on cassette, and bearing in mind the excellence of the various budget-priced versions, the first choice is perhaps not absolutely clear-cut. Undoubtedly the new Brendel/Cleveland performance heads the list. If it lacks something in traditional Viennese charm, it has a compensating vigour and impetus, and the work's many changes of mood are encompassed with freshness and subtlety. The second movement *Andante* is radiantly played, and the immensely spirited scherzo has a most engagingly relaxed trio, with Brendel at his most persuasive. His special feeling for Schubert is apparent throughout: the deft pictorial imagery at the opening of the variations is delightful. The recording is well balanced and wide in range, and the transfer, made

487

at quite a high level, is of superior quality, full and clear. There is a hint of edginess on the violin timbre but not enough to withhold the strongest recommendation.

From Haebler a small-scale performance which is nonetheless very enjoyable. There is some admirably unassertive and deeply musical playing from Miss Haebler and from the incomparable Grumiaux, and it is this freshness and pleasure in music-making that render this account memorable. These artists do not try to make 'interpretative points' but are content to let the music speak for itself. The balance is not altogether perfect, but the quality of the recorded sound is good and the transfer natural in timbre and detail. The smoothness in the upper range is pleasing and the separation and spread more than adequate.

Moura Lympany's performance sets off with a brisk manner, the playing lively and fresh. In the second movement the interpretation relaxes, and the variations are attractively done. The matter-of-fact approach is balanced by the overall spontaneity of the music-making. The balance favours the piano, and the first violin seems backwards. But in most respects this is a lively and enjoyable account, not wanting in perception, and the Classics for Pleasure transfer has a vivid life about it and plenty of dramatic contrast. The variations, in particular, have a fine presence. The level is high but the quality is good, often excellent, though perhaps a trifle light in the bass.

The Decca Ace of Diamonds recording offers a classic performance, with a distinguished account of the piano part from Clifford Curzon and splendidly stylish support from the Vienna players. Schubert's warm lyricism is caught with remarkable freshness, and the stereo is of first-class quality. Some might find the brilliant scherzo a little too fierce to match the rest of the performance, but such vigorous playing introduces an element of contrast at the centre of the interpretation. The cassette transfer, however, seems to show up the age of the original

recording, with a somewhat unnatural quality to the string tone and a plummy quality to the bass. Careful use of the controls can help to smooth the sound, but the overall effect is not completely convincing.

The fresh vigour of the Nash Ensemble's playing has the spontaneity of a live concert performance. Tempi throughout are buoyant, which does not mean that the players cannot relax when necessary, but that the music-making has a spirited quality which is persuasive throughout. The account of the *Notturno* (a more intense piece than the title might suggest) is no less sympathetic, and with bold, clear recording and a good balance this is a most attractive coupling on both disc and tape. The transfer lacks the very last degree of range in the treble and the forward balance seems to reduce the dynamic range slightly. But the sound is more refined than nearly all the other cassette versions and it has plenty of body and detail.

Among the other full-price Trouts that have strong claims for consideration is the DG issue including an excellent account of the *Quartettsatz*. In the main work there is a masterly contribution from Gilels, and the Amadeus play with considerable freshness. The recording is of good quality, but the cassette transfer lacks range in the strings. The timbre given to the first violin is not too natural, nor is it very clean in focus. Moreover the overall sound picture is not ideally transparent.

An enjoyably alert performance from Christoph Eschenbach and members of the Koeckert Quartet. There is a good deal of sparkle and character – the variations are given plenty of individual interest, the outer movements striking momentum – and Eschenbach himself plays with genuine elegance. The recording acoustic is clear and rather dry; some may find it a trifle unexpansive. However, it has been given a first-class tape transfer and the sound is pleasingly natural, lacking only the last degree of range.

The balance is forward but not oppressively so. The *Notturno* has the advantage of a warmer acoustic and is most sympathetically played, although the more resonant recording is marginally less well focused. If this issue still yields to the Haebler/Grumiaux version, now also on a mid-priced label, it remains an attractive alternative, particularly in view of the fill-up.

An excellent performance on Heliodor, with Demus dominating, partly because the piano recording and balance are bold and forward and the string tone is thinner. There is – as befits the name of the string group – a real feeling for Schubert, and the performance has spontaneity and style. The first movement is especially arresting, and the *Theme and variations* are well shaped. The tape transfer, however, seems to emphasize the thinness of the strings (the recording dates from 1961), although the piano image is lifelike. The *Violin sonatina*, a most acceptable bonus, is well played and recorded.

Although on Turnabout Louis Kentner plays with distinction, this *Trout* is also let down by indifferent recording, thin and lacking in body. The string playing too has an unsmiling approach, and all in all this issue is not very competitive.

The performance by the so-called Festival Quartet (with Stuart Sankey, double-bass, but the pianist remaining anonymous) is an attractive one, with plenty of impulse and spontaneity throughout and no lack of imagination in the variations. Unfortunately this is another Camden issue where the Dolby treatment has been ineffective and the music-making is sadly muffled.

String quartets Nos. 8 in B flat major, D.112; 10 in E flat major, D.87.
> **(*)DG 3300 899. Melos Qt of Stuttgart.

These performances come from a complete Schubert cycle issued (on disc only) in 1975. The Melos are an impressive body whose performances here are unmannered and on the whole sympathetic. These early quartets date from 1813–14 (when Schubert was in his mid-teens), and their invention are an altogether disarming grace and innocence. Perhaps their atmosphere is not entirely captured here, but the playing does not lack dedication (or polish). For some reason the *B flat major Quartet*, which is on the second side, is transferred at a slightly higher level than No. 10 and is that much more vivid. Neither transfer level is really adventurous (which means that the background is not absolutely silent), but the string quality is most natural and the balance very good; indeed at times the projection in No. 8 is first-class.

String quartet No. 12 in C minor (Quartettsatz), D.703.
> ***CRD CRDC 4034. Alberni Qt
> – BRAHMS: *String sextet No. 1.****

A fresh and agreeably warm account of this fine single-movement work, originally intended as part of a full string quartet but finally left by Schubert to stand on its own. The coupling with the Brahms *Sextet* is appropriate, for it was Brahms who in 1870 arranged for the first publication of the *Quartettsatz*. The transfer is of excellent quality, and this tape is highly recommended.

String quartets Nos. 12 in C minor (Quartettsatz), D.703; 15 in G major, D.887.
> ***Decca Ace of Diamonds KSDC 512. Gabrieli Qt.

The *G major Quartet* is one of Schubert's most profound and searching utterances, and it is a pleasure to record that the Gabrieli Quartet have its measure. Their performance is compelling from beginning to end and has genuine sensitivity and depth of feeling. Moreover, the Decca engineers have achieved a marvellously blended sound which is beautifully natural and unforced, just like the Gabrielis' playing. The performance of the splendid C minor *Quartettsatz* is comparably eloquent. The cassette compares very favourably indeed with the LP. Just a little treble reduction may be useful on some machines, but then the quality is well-nigh perfect, with absolutely no background noise.

String quartets Nos. 14 in D minor (Death and the Maiden), D.810; 12 in C minor (Quartettsatz), D.703.
   (M)**(*)DG Privilege 3335 314. Amadeus Qt.

These Amadeus performances give a wonderful impression of unity as regards the finer points of phrasing, for example at the very beginning of the variations in D.810. The transfer is successful; the level is modest (although it seems to rise and bring rather more bite in the finale of D.810 and in the *Quartettsatz*) but the quality is generally smooth and pleasing, and tends to disguise the comparatively early date of the recording. This is a worthwhile issue, even if the account of the *Death and the Maiden quartet* has not the depth of the Busch version (see above).

String quintet in C major, D.956.
   ***CRD CRDC 4018. Alberni Qt, Thomas Igloi (cello).
   **(*) DG 3300 980. Melos Qt, Mstislav Rostropovich (cello).

The Alberni Quartet with the late Thomas Igloi give a richly enjoyable performance, one which naturally conveys the give and take of ensemble playing. The record (rightly) won glowing opinions when imported into the United States, where till then this British group was unknown, and that may point a contrast with higher-powered but less intensely communicative readings. The concentration here justifies the exposition repeat in the long first movement,

and though the Albernis do not match the hushed simplicity of the Aeolians in the sublime *Adagio*, theirs too conveys deep dedication. The last two movements receive spirited, unexaggerated performances. The recording is excellent, with a fine atmospheric bloom on it. On tape the quality is rich, even ripe in texture, and the overall balance and layout are most natural. Some ears may crave a more obviously extended range, but the sound spectrum is very well balanced, so that even if the last degree of sparkle is missing in the treble response, there is clear detail, while the homogeneity of the timbre overall is undoubtedly both satisfying and realistic.

Rostropovich plays as second cello in the DG performance, and no doubt his influence from the centre of the string texture contributes to the eloquence of the famous *Adagio*, which like the performance as a whole is strongly, even dramatically characterized. The emphasis of the rhythmic articulation of the outer movements leaves no doubt as to the power of Schubert's writing, and while there is no lack of atmosphere in the opening and closing sections of the slow movement, the performance is in the last analysis less persuasive than the Alberni version with its greater emotional resilience and flexibility. The DG transfer is live and immediate. The upper strings are sometimes a little husky in focus, but there is a good balance and excellent presence.

The famous performance by the Aeolian Quartet on Saga (CA 5266) is, alas, not Dolbyized.

Violoncello sonata in A minor (originally for arpeggione; revised Fournier), *D.821.*
   (M)(**)HMV TC-HQS 1398. Paul Tortelier (cello), Robert Weisz (piano) – GRIEG: *Cello sonata.*(**)

A clear, direct account of Schubert's amiable sonata is played here in a version 'arranged and transcribed by Pierre Fournier'. The playing has plenty of life, and the recording (which dates from 1962) still sounds well. However the transfer of this coupling is not a success and the opening of the Schubert brings discoloration of the cello tone.

Piano music

Allegretto in C minor, D.915; Moments musicaux Nos. 1–6, D.780; 2 Scherzi, D.593; 12 Valses nobles, D.969.

** DG 3300 996. Daniel Barenboim.

Some of the finest playing here comes in the *Two Scherzi*. In the first Barenboim's pointing is a delight, and he is equally persuasive in the trio of the second. The *Allegretto in C minor* is given an effective improvisatory quality, but the *Twelve Valses nobles* are played too forcefully for their full charm to be revealed. In the *Moments musicaux* there is much to admire: Barenboim's mood is often thoughtful and intimate; at other times there are bursts of impetuosity. On the whole Curzon (see below) catches the simplicity and innocent poetic feeling of this music more memorably. The piano tone on DG has impressive presence and weight but does not often display the richness of timbre Schubert's music ideally calls for. The transfer is of high quality, clear and clean.

Fantasia in C major (The Wanderer), D.760.

** Decca Phase 4 KPFC 4433 [Lon. 5-21183]. Ilana Vered – BEET" HOVEN: *Piano sonata No. 21.***

Ilana Vered's approach to the opening section is almost uncompromisingly bold. A little more resilience always pays dividends in Schubert, and as soon as Miss Vered reaches the *Adagio* she meltingly shows us the affinity this work

has with the *Impromptus*. Her directness of manner returns in the finale, and again one feels that her approach is too positive, not yielding to the special qualities of Schubert's inspiration. The clear, forward piano balance, slightly larger than life, obviously adds to this strong projection. The transfer is clean and well balanced.

Fantasia in C major (The Wanderer), D.760; Moments musicaux Nos. 1–6, D.780.

(M) **(*) DG Privilege 3335 271. Wilhelm Kempff.

A charming coupling of one of the most original of Schubert's solo piano pieces with the six trifles which under the title *Moments musicaux* range so much farther than one expects from their scale. Kempff characteristically gives intimate performances. His allegros are never very fast, and the results sing in the most relaxed way. In the *Wanderer fantasia* the high drama is not emphasized but the result is no less compelling, with a moulding of the structure which gives the illusion of spontaneity. Although the last degree of range is missing the transfers are of quite good quality. The piano tone is pleasingly warm in the *Moments musicaux*, but there is some hardness to edge the tone in the *Wanderer fantasia* and a hint of roughness on one or two of the loudest chords.

Fantasia in C major (The Wanderer), D.760; Piano sonata No. 16 in A minor, D.845.

**(*) DG 3300 504 [id.]. Maurizio Pollini.

This is piano-playing of an altogether exceptional order. Pollini's account of the *A minor Sonata* is searching and profound. He is almost without rival in terms of sheer keyboard control, and his musical insight is of the same order. The piano sound is musically balanced, but the cassette transfer offers a rather hard edge to the piano image in the louder moments; in the quieter ones the image has less presence and refinement of detail.

Impromptus Nos. 1–4, D.899; Nos. 5–8, D.935.
　⊛ *** Philips 7300 587. Alfred Brendel.
　(M) *** Philips 7317 147. Ingrid Haebler.
　**(*) DG 3300 986. Daniel Barenboim.
　(M) ** Turnabout KTVC 34141 [CT 2130]. Alfred Brendel.

Brendel's complete set of *Impromptus* on Philips has previously been split into two separate groups (each coupled with other music of Schubert). Now they are joined and the result is truly magical. The recording is quite superb, rich with a glowing middle range, fine sonority in the bass, and a gentle focus in this admirable transfer. It is difficult to imagine finer Schubert playing than this; to find more eloquence, more profound musical insights one has to go back to Edwin Fischer, and even here comparison is not always to Brendel's disadvantage. A superb issue in every way.

Ingrid Haebler, at medium price, is only marginally less beautifully recorded than Brendel and although her approach is rather more romantic, her *rubato* is so natural and musical that, irrespective of price, hers has strong claims to be numbered the finest single-tape recording after Brendel's. At times her playing has the most disarming innocence, at others great maturity and poise, and she often surprises the listener, for instance by her direct way with the famous *A flat impromptu*, D.935/2. The natural Philips recording is beautifully transferred to tape, sounding warm and full.

Barenboim's performances too are full of interest, with a wide range of mood, predominantly extrovert, yet relaxing beautifully to produce the greatest delicacy of touch. The playing is full of

character (witness the gentle, precise articulation of the opening of the *C minor Impromptu* or the flowing lyricism of the famous piece in G flat major, both from D.899). The piano timbre is bold and clear (the recording is extremely lifelike, the image on tape given excellent presence), but the instrument's singing quality is less readily revealed here than in the more melting performances from both Brendel and Haebler.

On Brendel's earlier Turnabout tape his approach is more matter-of-fact, often classical in manner rather than romantic. But the unaffected eloquence of the playing carries its own rewards, and the recording is surprisingly good, on cassette as on disc. However, in this price range Ingrid Haebler is a clear first choice.

Impromptus Nos. 1–4, D.899; Moments musicaux Nos. 1–6, D.780.
　(B) *** DG Heliodor 3348 246. Joerg Demus.

A first-class coupling. Demus's performances are direct and unforced, expressive and stylish. Their undoubted sensibility finds an admirable balance between the romantic and classical feeling of the music's inspiration. The *Impromptus* are especially well characterized, and although the recording is a little dry it is truthful. The cassette transfer is of high quality, clear and well balanced. This is an excellent bargain.

Moments musicaux Nos. 1–6, D.780.
　*** Decca KSXC 6523. Clifford Curzon – BEETHOVEN: *Eroica variations.****
Moments musicaux Nos. 1–6, D.780; Impromptus (Klavierstücke), D.946, Nos. 1–3.
　(M) *** Turnabout KTVC 34142 [(d) CT 2151]. Alfred Brendel.

Curzon gives superb performances of the *Moments musicaux*. These readings are among the most poetic now in the catalogue. The Turnabout recording is no less highly recommendable in its price-range. The performances have a simple, direct eloquence that is quite disarming, and the sound is astonishingly good. The three *Klavierstücke* are an acceptable bonus. The cassette transfers are both very well managed. Decca's piano timbre for Curzon is agreeably mellow, lacking the last degree of brilliance but with a quality that fits the music-making admirably. The Turnabout image is full and bold, with plenty of body.

Piano sonatas Nos. 2 in C major, D.279; 21 in B flat major, D.960.
(M) *** DG Privilege 3335 240. Wilhelm Kempff.

It is a tribute to Kempff's artistry that with most relaxed tempi he conveys such consistent, compelling intensity in the *B flat major Sonata*. Hearing the opening one might feel that this is going to be a lightweight account of Schubert's greatest sonata, but in fact the long-breathed expansiveness is hypnotic, so that here quite as much as in the *Great C major Symphony* one is bound by the spell of heavenly length. Rightly Kempff repeats the first-movement exposition with the important nine bars of lead-back, and though the overall manner is less obviously dramatic than is common, the range of tone colour is magical, with sharp terracing of dynamics to plot the geography of each movement. Though very much a personal utterance, this interpretation is no less great for that. It belongs to a tradition of pianism that has almost disappeared, and we must be eternally grateful that its expression has been so glowingly captured. Certainly the tape quality is agreeably warm, although the level of transfer might have been higher. The coupling, an unfinished early work in C major, is given an appropriately direct performance. Here the recording is somewhat lacking in lustre, and there is a touch of hardness.

Piano sonatas Nos. 5 in A flat major, D.557; 20 in A major, D.959.
*** Decca KSXC 6771. Radu Lupu.

The particular beauty of Radu Lupu's fine performance of the *A major Sonata* lies in the outer movements, which are wholly unmannered and free from expressive or agogic distortion. Lupu strikes the perfect balance between Schubert's classicism and the spontaneity of his musical thought, and at the same time he leaves one with the impression that this achievement is perfectly effortless. The scherzo has great sparkle and delicacy, and the slow movement has an inner repose and poetic feeling that remain memorable long after the cassette deck has stopped. Yet the strength of the interpretation lies in its sensitivity to detail and appreciation of the structure as a whole. The companion sonata is no less persuasively presented, and the recording is as natural and fresh as the performances themselves. The cassette transfer is very impressive.

Piano sonatas Nos. 15 in C major (Reliquie), D.840; 21 in B flat major, D.960.
**(*)DG 3300 995. Daniel Barenboim.

To say that Barenboim gives a Kempff-like reading of Schubert's greatest sonata (D.960) is not to deny his characteristic individuality but to point out that his is a reflective, lyrical view of the work, marked by exquisitely clean semiquaver passagework and strong, sharp dynamic contrasts. The second movement is slow and concentrated, the third light and sparkling, and the finale sharpened with its clean-cut contrasts. This issue is the more attractive for its imaginative coupling with the unfinished *C major Sonata*, a formidable large-scale argument presented in its full stature by Barenboim. The transfer is bold and clear, the focus equally clean at all dynamic levels, and not lacking range and depth, although there is a hint of hardness on fortissimos.

Piano sonata No. 17 in D major, D.850; 4 German dances from D.366.
*** Decca KSXC 6739. Vladimir Ashkenazy.

The fresh simplicity of Ashkenazy's reading of the sonata is wonderfully compelling, intense without being over-weighted. In each movement he holds the structure together naturally and unaffectedly, and though he is rarely seduced by incidental beauties the result is sunny and warm, never severe. Excellent recording and a first-class cassette transfer.

Piano sonata No. 17 in D major, D.850; Impromptus in G flat major, D.899/3; in A flat major, D.899/4.
*** Decca KSXC 6135. Clifford Curzon.

The passage to try first in the sonata is the beginning of the last movement, an example of the Curzon magic at its most intense, for with a comparatively slow speed he gives the rhythm a gentle 'lift' which is most captivating. Some who know more forceful interpretations – Richter (on disc) did a marvellous one – may find this too wayward, but Schubert surely thrives on some degree of coaxing. Curzon could hardly be more convincing – the spontaneous feeling of a live performance better captured than in many earlier recordings – and the *Impromptus* make an attractive fill-up. On tape the sound is generally excellent, and the transfer sophisticated in matters of balance and security. Just occasionally the upper treble notes of the piano harden under pressure and lose their bloom. But this will be more noticeable on some reproducers than others, and there is no reason to withhold a full recommendation.

Piano sonata No. 21 in B flat major, D.960; Impromptu in A flat major, D.935/2.
*** Decca KSXC 6580. Clifford Curzon.

This is one of the finest accounts of the *B flat Sonata* available on either tape or disc. Tempi are beautifully judged, and everything is in fastidious taste. Detail is finely drawn but never emphasized at the expense of the architecture as a whole. It is beautifully recorded, and the piano sounds marvellously truthful in timbre. On tape the balance is perhaps just a little lacking in sparkle, though undoubtedly the warmth of timbre suits the music, and the *Impromptus* on side two are marginally lighter in texture.

VOCAL AND CHORAL MUSIC

'Favourite songs': (i) *Abschied;* (ii) *An die Musik;* (iii) *An Sylvia;* (iv) *Du bist die Ruh;* (iii) *Erlkönig;* (v) *Die Forelle; Gretchen am Spinnrade;* (iv) *Heidenröslein;* (iii) *Im Abendrot;* (ii) *Der Musensohn;* (i) *Ständchen* (*Leise flehen*); (vi) *Ständchen* (*Zögernd leise*).
(M) ** Decca KCSP 524. (i) Tom Krause (bar.), Irwin Gage (piano); (ii) Kathleen Ferrier (contralto), Phyllis Spurr (piano); (iii) Hermann Prey (bar.), Karl Engel (piano); (iv) Stuart Burrows (tenor), John Constable (piano); (v) Margaret Price (soprano), James Lockhart (piano); (vi) Helen Watts (contralto), Elizabethan Singers, Halsey; Viola Tunnard (piano).

Certainly these are favourite songs, and the recital is enjoyable with its vividly projected sound (although the high-level transfer hovers a little close to the danger area). One assumes that such a concert is aimed at the inexperienced listener, so it would have been more helpful to provide the texts; or at the very least a synopsis of what each song is about should have been included. The performances are mixed in appeal. The opening items (*Die Forelle* and *Gretchen am Spinnrade*), sung by Margaret Price, are full of character, and Hermann Prey's group has plenty of atmosphere (especially *Im Abendrot*, with its beautiful pianissimo ending). Stuart Burrows's contributions are direct but not very subtle; on the other hand Tom Krause is on top form, and his *Abschied*, which ends side two, is most attractively sung. A good but not really outstanding anthology.

Lieder: *An die Laute; An die Musik; An Silvia; Auflösung; Bei dir allein; Dass sie hier gewesen; Der Einsame; Fischerweise; Die Forelle; Ganymed; Liebesbotschaft; Der Schiffer; Ständchen; Die Sterne; Über Wildemann; Der Wanderer an den Mond.*
 **(*)Enigma κ 453531. Ian Partridge (tenor), Jennifer Partridge (piano).

The fresh, lyrical flow of the singing here gives much pleasure. Ian Partridge is an imaginative Schubertian; his range of tone colour is matched by his feeling for the Schubertian phrase, shown immediately in the lovely *Liebesbotschaft*, which opens the recital. There are many favourite songs here, and the intelligence of the interpretations matches the tonal beauty of the voice. If there is a criticism it is that there is not enough variety of mood; warmth and flexibility are paramount, sometimes at the expense of dramatic emphasis. Jennifer Partridge accompanies sensitively and matches her brother's lyrical smoothness. The recording is good and the transfer offers natural quality and a good balance. No translations are provided and the notes are in abysmally small print.

'Favourite Lieder': (i; x) *An die Musik;* (ii; x) *Auf dem Wasser zu singen;* (iii; x) *Erlkönig;* (iv; xi) *Die Forelle;* (v; xii) *Frühlingsglaube;* (ii; x) *Heidenröslein;* (iv; xi) *Im Abendrot;* (vi; x) *Lachen und weinen;* (i; x) *Litanei auf das Fest aller Seelen;* (vii; xiii) *Der Musensohn;* (i; xiv) *Nacht und Träume;* (ii; x) *Nähe des Geliebten;* (viii; xv) *Die schöne Müllerin: Das Wandern; Ungeduld;* (vi; x) *Seligkeit;* (vii; xiii) *Wanderers Nachtlied;* (ii; x) *Wiegenlied;* (ix; x) *Die Winterreise: Der Lindenbaum.*
 (B) *** DG Heliodor 3348 268. (i) Grace Bumbry (mezzo-soprano); (ii) Rita Streich (soprano); (iii) Kim Borg (bass); (iv) Fritz Wunderlich (tenor); (v) Walther Ludwig (tenor); (vi) Irmgard Seefried (soprano); (vii) Dietrich Fischer-Dieskau (bar.); (viii) Ernst Haefliger (tenor); (ix) Hans Hotter (bar.); pianists: (x) Erik Werba; (xi) Hubert Giesen; (xii) Walter Bohle; (xiii) Joerg Demus; (xiv) Sebastian Peschko; (xv) Jacqueline Bonneau.

A fascinating recital, generous in offering eighteen songs and a most distinguished roster of artists. Rita Streich makes a particularly charming contribution, and her sweetness of timbre (which over the span of a whole tape might become too soft-centred) here effectively contrasts with other, more robust voices. Kim Borg is memorably dramatic in *Erlkönig;* Fischer-Dieskau inspirational in *Wanderers Nachtlied* (a most moving performance); and Irmgard Seefried shows an impressive control of colour in *Seligkeit.* Ernst Haefliger is a little stiff in *Das Wandern,* but unwinds for the famous *Ungeduld,* and if Grace Bumbry is a little heavyweight in *An die Musik,* Miss Streich is at her most delightful in the

Wiegenlied (D.468), which touchingly ends side one. Hans Hotter's *Der Lindenbaum* too is nobly sung. The recording is generally kind to the voices, with just a hint of peaking once or twice (the level of transfer is quite high). The piano timbre is natural, although the balance tends to vary from item to item. A most rewarding issue and excellent value.

Mass No. 5 in A flat major, D.678.
 **(*) Argo KZRC 869. Wendy Eathorne, Bernadette Greevy, Wynford Evans, Christopher Keyte, St John's College Choir, Academy of St Martin-in-the-Fields, Guest; John Scott (organ).

This is not quite so successful a performance as George Guest's earlier version of the *E flat Mass*, which has not been issued on cassette. The present work dates from 1822, though it was probably begun a few years earlier and was certainly revised later. It has many beauties and in a fervently inspired reading can sound most impressive. This performance is faithful but just lacks the distinction that marked Guest's disc recordings of the Haydn Masses on this label; neither the singing nor the playing is in the least routine, but it lacks the personality that these musicians brought to the Haydn and the later Schubert. The recording is very fine, though not every strand of texture comes through. However, this beautiful piece is not otherwise available at present on cassette, and as the transfer is of good quality, this issue can be recommended without serious reservations.

Rosamunde: Overture (*Die Zauberharfe, D.644*); incidental music (complete), *D.797.*
 *** Decca KSXC 6748 [Lon. 5-26444]. Rohangiz Yachmi (contralto), Vienna State Opera Chorus, Vienna PO, Münchinger.
(M) *** Philips Festivo 7310 053 [id.]. Aafje Heynis (contralto), Netherlands Radio Chorus, Concertgebouw Orch., Haitink.
**(*) HMV TC-ASD 3498. Ileana Cotrubas (soprano), Leipzig Radio Chorus, Dresden State Orch., Boskovsky.

Münchinger's recent Decca recording now seems marginally the first choice here. It is beautifully recorded and offers admirable freshness, first-class orchestral playing and a good contribution from the soloist and chorus. Münchinger can sometimes seem unsmiling in Schubert, but here he is at his best, and the tape transfer offers a pleasing bloom on the sound that is most persuasive.

Haitink shows the simple eloquence and musical sensitivity that he found also for his companion Festivo cassette of the incidental music for Mendelssohn's *A Midsummer Night's Dream*. The recording is a trifle resonant for scoring that was expressly (and skilfully) designed for the theatre-pit, but the tape transfer is well managed and the reverberation overhang is only really noticeable in the overture. Haitink does the third *Entr'acte* and the second *Ballet* quite beautifully, and Aafje Heynis is in fine voice as soloist in the lovely *Romance* (*The full moon shines on mountain peaks*). The chorus is excellent in the music for Spirits, Shepherds and Weberian Huntsmen, although the focus lacks something in crispness here. For the most part the sound is clear and vivid.

In seeking authenticity Boskovsky puts his selection to a slight disadvantage. He chooses to open with the overture *Alfonso and Estrella*, which Schubert used in the original production, even though it was written for an earlier opera. It is not one of the composer's more memorable orchestral pieces and thus gets this tape off to a rather dull start. Boskovsky keeps back the familiar *Zauberharfe* overture to form an encore item at the end. The music is sympathetically phrased and beautifully played throughout and there is no lack of drama. Ileana Cotrubas's contribution is distinguished, and the chorus is excellent. Yet in the last analysis there is a pervading seriousness about the music-making here, and although there is no lack of drama, there is a shortage of charm. The recording is well balanced, atmospheric and spacious, but the tape transfer is somewhat lacking in sparkle.

Song cycles: *Die schöne Müllerin, D.795; Schwanengesang, D.957; Die Winterreise, D.911.*

⊛ (M) *** DG 3371 029. Dietrich Fischer-Dieskau (bar.), Gerald Moore (piano).

Fischer-Dieskau and Moore had both recorded these great cycles of Schubert several times already before they embarked on this set as part of DG's Schubert song series. It was no mere repeat of earlier triumphs. If anything these performances – notably that of the greatest and darkest of the cycles, *Winterreise* – are even more searching than before, with Moore matching the hushed concentration of the singer in some of the most remarkable playing that even he has ever recorded. This splendid box was the first major Lieder recording to be issued on tape and it sets the highest standards of naturalness. Fischer-Dieskau's voice is caught with all its timbre fully conveyed, and the balance with the piano is admirable.

Die schöne Müllerin (song cycle), *D.795.*).

*(*) Telefunken CX4.41892. Nigel Rogers (tenor), Richard Burnett (Graf Hammerflügel fortepiano).

The interest in Nigel Rogers's version of *Die schöne Müllerin* lies in the use of a contemporary instrument for the accompaniment; but quite apart from the lowering of pitch involved and the twangy timbre, the demands of scholarship seem to have detracted from the energy of the performers. Rogers has an individual voice, but there are far better disc recordings representing his artistry. The recording could be more sharply focused, but the transfer is of good quality.

Schwanengesang (song cycle), *D.957.*

*** Enigma K 453459. John Shirley-Quirk (bar.), Steuart Bedford (piano).

Schwanengesang, containing some of Schubert's last and most memorable songs, presents the interpreter with an insuperable problem in that no single voice is suited to every one of them. John Shirley-Quirk's special success is in creating a feeling of unity over the whole group. He does this partly by strong characterization of each song, with the contrasts calculated so that each song seems to prepare the way for the one that follows. The flowing lyricism of *Liebesbotschaft* is thus dramatically halted by the declamation of *Kriegers Ahnung*, and at the close of the collection the graduation of mood from *Am Meer*, through the powerful account of *Der Doppelgänger* (one of Schubert's most original and forward-looking inspirations), to the welcome relaxation of tension for *Die Taubenpost* is masterly. Steuart Bedford provides equally imaginative accompaniments, and the recording gives the artists good presence and an excellent balance, which has been faithfully transferred on to this excellent cassette. There are no translations, however, and only sparse, poorly printed notes.

COLLECTIONS

'*Favourite composer*': (i; ii) *Rosamunde: Overture* (*Die Zauberharfe, D.644*); incidental music: *Entr'acte*

497

in B flat major; Ballet music Nos. 1 and 2, D.797; (i; iii) Symphony No. 8 in B minor (Unfinished), D.759; (iv) Piano quintet in A major (Trout), D.667; (v) Impromptu in B flat major, D.935/3; Moment musical in F minor, D.780/3; (vi) An Sylvia; (vii) Die Forelle; Heidenröslein; (viii) Ständchen.

(B) ** Decca KDPC 545/6. (i) Vienna PO; (ii) Monteux; (iii) Schuricht; (iv) Clifford Curzon (piano), members of the Vienna Octet; (v) Wilhelm Backhaus (piano); (vi) Hermann Prey (bar.), Karl Engel (piano); (vii) Margaret Price (soprano), James Lockhart (piano); (viii) Tom Krause (bar.), Irwin Gage (piano).

This makes a fairly satisfactory anthology, with a good if not very dramatic performance of the Unfinished and an outstanding one of the Trout quintet. The songs are well chosen and delightfully sung, and if Backhaus, as recorded, sounds somewhat brittle, this is still playing of character. The tape (unlike the disc) has the recording of the Trout complete on one side, giving the advantage of continuity, but the cassette sound seems to emphasize the touch of edginess to the string quality, and is similarly rather dry in the Rosamunde excerpts.

'The world of Schubert': (i) Rosamunde: Ballet music No. 2, D.797; (ii) Symphony No. 8 in B minor (Unfinished), D.759: 1st movt; (iii) Octet in F major, D.803: 3rd movt; (iii; iv) Piano quintet in A major (Trout), D.667: 4th movt; (iv) Impromptu in A flat major, D.899/4; Moment musical in F major, D.780/3; (v) Piano sonata No.18 in G major, D. 894: 3rd movt; (vi) An Sylvia; vii) Ave Maria; (viii)

Heidenröslein; (ix) Die schöne Müllerin: Wohin; (x) Ständchen.

(M) *** Decca KCSP 426. (i) Suisse Romande Orch., Ansermet; (ii) LPO, Stokowski; (iii) Vienna Octet; (iv) Clifford Curzon (piano); (v) Vladimir Ashkenazy (piano); (vi) Hermann Prey (bar.), Karl Engel (piano); (vii) Joan Sutherland (soprano), Ambrosian Singers, New Philharmonia Orch., Bonynge; (viii) Stuart Burrows (tenor), John Constable (piano); (ix) Peter Pears (tenor), Benjamin Britten (piano); (x) Tom Krause (bar.), Irwin Gage (piano).

The world of Schubert is another of those happy Decca compilations that has been assembled with loving skill to produce a first-class miniature concert. The Lieder are particularly successful, and if Joan Sutherland's Ave Maria with chorus is on the lush side, this is not likely to prove a drawback for someone wanting to explore the Schubertian world, of which it is certainly a part. Excellent sound throughout, and a first-class cassette transfer.

Schumann, Robert (1810–56)

Piano concerto in A minor, Op. 54.
(*) Philips 7300 113 [id.]. Stephen Bishop-Kovacevich, BBC SO, Colin Davis – GRIEG: Concerto.(*)

(B) **(*) Pye ZCCOB 656. Shura Cherkassky, LPO, Boult – GRIEG: Concerto.**(*)

(*) Decca KSXC 6624. Radu Lupu, LSO, Previn – GRIEG: Concerto.(*)

**(*) Enigma K 453564. Judit

Jaimes, LSO, Mata – GRIEG: *Concerto*.***

** DG 3301 042 [id.]. Martha Argerich, National SO of Washington, Rostropovich – CHOPIN: *Piano concerto No. 2*.**

** HMV TC-ASD 3521. Horacio Gutiérrez, LPO, Tennstedt – GRIEG: *Concerto*.**

** DG 923016 [id.]. Géza Anda, Berlin PO, Kubelik – GRIEG: *Concerto*.**

*(*) HMV TC-ASD 3133 [Angel 4xs 36899]. Sviatoslav Richter, Monte Carlo National Opera Orch., Matačić – GRIEG: *Concerto*.*(*)

As in Grieg so in Schumann, Bishop-Kovacevich and Davis give an interpretation which is both fresh and poetic, unexaggerated but powerful in its directness and clarity. Bishop-Kovacevich more than most shows the link between the central introspective slow movement and the comparable movement of Beethoven's *Fourth Concerto*, and the spring-like element of the outer movements is finely presented by orchestra and soloist alike. Unfortunately the cassette transfer, though smooth, is disappointingly lacking in sparkle and detail. The orchestra tends to sound mushy, and the low level means that hiss is a problem.

The partnership between Cherkassky and Boult provides one of the most satisfying accounts of this elusive concerto available on any label at any price. The recording was originally issued by World Record Club and later appeared first on Music for Pleasure and then on that same company's Fanfare label, but it is at present not available on disc in any form. Unfortunately the Pye transfer has been made at a very ambitious level and – as can be heard in the opening flourish – it is fractionally too high; the quality of the tuttis lacks freshness. But this concerto is lightly scored and for nearly all the time the sound is very pleasing, and the piano

image is clear and truthful. The balance remains good. The reading strikes a near-perfect balance between romantic boldness – the masculine element – and feminine waywardness and charm. The pastel shades of the opening pages are realized with delicacy, while the first-movement dialogues between the solo piano and the orchestral woodwind are most sensitively managed. Later the interplay with the strings in the *Andante* has an appealing simplicity. Boult's warmth can be felt here in the gracious string-playing, and he shows his control of the overall structure in the finale, which moves forward with a splendid impetus. Cherkassky's contribution is not without the occasional idiosyncrasy, but the spontaneity of the performance means that the listener's attention is always held.

The Decca cassette is strikingly bright and clear; the vivid recording projects the music-making with admirable life and presence. However, Lupu's performance with Previn is not so successful as the Grieg coupling. The clean boldness of approach is enjoyable enough, but the elusive poetry of this most romantic of concertos is not always fully revealed. The end of the slow movement is not as magical as it might be, and the finale, although brilliantly played, lacks the forward surge of the very finest accounts.

A fine performance of the Schumann concerto from Judit Jaimes and Eduardo Mata – sensitive and strong to match the brilliant Grieg coupling. There is nothing wilting about the piano-playing here, yet the romantic qualities of the music emerge alongside the vigour, and the freshness of the outer movements is balanced by the agreeable lightness of touch in the *Intermezzo*. The interplay between the orchestral wind soloists and the solo piano is persuasive, although it has not quite the degree of poetic feeling of the Bishop and Cherkassky versions; tempo changes are managed with flexibility and spontaneity. The recording is admirably vivid and clear, with a bold, natural piano image. Some might feel the acoustic a little lacking in warmth (and the violins in tutti a shade too brightly lit) but there is admirable detail, and the transfer to cassette is first-class in every way.

The partnership of Rostropovich and Argerich produces a performance which is full of contrast – helped by a recording of wide dynamic range – and strong in temperament. There is an appealing delicacy in the *Andantino*, and the outer movements have plenty of vivacity and colour. Yet in the last analysis the work's special romantic feeling does not fully blossom here, although the playing is not without poetry. The recording is admirably lifelike and well balanced and the transfer has excellent life and detail, even though both piano and orchestral images tend to recede somewhat in pianissimos.

The performance by Horacio Gutiérrez is well played and recorded, and the transfer is of first-class quality, the bold piano image matched by the clarity, depth and brilliance of the orchestra. But the reading fails to satisfy, and this cannot compete with the most imaginative and poetic alternative versions.

Anda's performance is thoroughly musical and Schumannesque in feeling, and while it does not probe any depths this account, with good orchestral support, is attractive. However, the DG transfer is somewhat thickly textured (this was a comparatively early tape issue), and the treble lacks some of the sparkle of the Grieg coupling, although it is not muffled.

Richter's reading of the Schumann, like that of the Grieg on the reverse, is extraordinarily wayward. Though with this composer Richter can hardly help bringing occasional illumination, this remains on the whole a disappointing version. The tape transfer is of good quality, not as striking as the Decca, but with bold piano tone and plenty of body to the orchestra, yet no lack of clarity.

(i) *Piano concerto in A minor, Op. 54;*
(ii) *Violoncello concerto in A minor, Op. 129.*

(M) ** DG Privilege 3318 009. (i) Sviatoslav Richter, Warsaw PO, Rowicki; (ii) Mstislav Rostropovich, Leningrad PO, Rozhdestvensky.

(M) *(*) Philips 7328 610. (i) Byron Janis, Minneapolis SO, Skrowaczewski; (ii) Maurice Gendron, Vienna SO, Dohnányi.

Richter's DG version of the *Piano concerto* is not so interesting as one would expect. Its opening speed is fast and the interpretation is in the main without idiosyncrasy, but only in the finale does one feel that vibrant quality in his playing which marks Richter out among even the greatest virtuosos. One suspects that the orchestra was partly to blame, and that its comparative sluggishness affected Richter's concentration. Not that the performance lacks style, but the intensity could be greater. Rostropovich's account of the *Cello concerto* is another matter. This is a superbly made performance, introspective yet at the same time outgoing, with a peerless technique at the command of a rare artistic imagination. The transfers are of good rather than outstanding quality. The *Piano concerto* sounds rather dry; the *Cello concerto* has more warmth and resonance, but is a little bottom-heavy.

Gendron's account of the *Cello concerto* is every bit as fine as Rostropovich's. It is youthful and passionate, full of verve and temperament. Gendron's style is less introspective than Rostropovich's, but the music is no less deeply felt. The balance places the cello well forward, but the orchestra comes into the picture. Unfortunately the orchestral sound itself is not too well focused – the fault of the original recording, not the tape transfer, which is certainly vivid. But for some reason the *Piano concerto* (on side one) is transferred at a much lower level, and here the orchestral sound has very little substance and even less impact. It is not all the fault of the recording balance, either, and although Byron Janis's playing is not insensitive the performance as a whole fails to hold the listener's attention.

(i) *Piano concerto in A minor, Op. 54;* (ii) *Symphony No. 1 in B flat major* (*Spring*), *Op. 38.*
> (M)**Decca KCSP 493. (i) Friedrich Gulda, Vienna PO, Andreae; (ii) LSO, Krips.

Gulda's account of the *Piano concerto* is refreshingly direct, with a brisk basic tempo in the first movement (the tempo in the coda is really nippy), yet with light, crisp playing the movement never sounds rushed. Similarly the *Intermezzo* is moved along, but remains delicate in feeling, with nicely pointed pianism. The finale is just right, with an enjoyable rhythmic lilt. The recording is full and pleasing, with excellent piano tone, but when one turns over for the symphony the quality is obviously less rich, with rather dated upper string timbre. This emphasizes the lightweight nature of the performance, though it comes over freshly enough, for the transfer itself is well made.

(i) *Violin concerto in D minor;* (ii) *Violoncello concerto in A minor, Op. 129.*
> (M)*Turnabout KTVC 34631. (i) Susanne Lautenbacher, Radio Luxembourg Orch., Cao; (ii) Laszlo Varga, Westphalian SO, Landau.

As far as the *Violin concerto* is concerned Susanne Lautenbacher has the cassette field to herself. Here is a good but unremarkable performance. In the *Cello concerto* Laszlo Varga is outclassed by Gendron (see above). In both works the

forward placing of the soloist and the impoverished orchestral sound prevent any serious consideration of this issue. Collectors especially interested in the *Violin concerto* might be advised to wait until a more distinguished recording comes on the market.

Violoncello concerto in A minor, Op. 129.
> *(*) HMV TC-ASD 3334 [Angel 4xs 37256]. Mstislav Rostropovich, Orchestre National de France, Bernstein – BLOCH: *Schelomo.*(***)

Except in the finale, where energy triumphs, the collaboration of Rostropovich and Bernstein in Schumann sounds disappointingly self-conscious, quite unlike the Bloch performance on the reverse. Rostropovich is at his most self-indulgent, not least in the lovely slow section, which is pulled about wilfully at a very slow basic tempo. The ripe recording, favouring the soloist, is not too securely transferred (our copy had a hint of 'pulsing'), and generally the sound is not very clearly focused, although it is acceptable. Rostropovich's earlier version and Gendron's (see above under the *Piano concerto*) are far preferable.

Konzertstück for 4 horns and orchestra in F major, Op. 86.
> ***DG 3300 939. Dale Clevenger, Richard Oldberg, Thomas Howell, Norman Schweikert (horns), Chicago SO, Barenboim – *Symphony No. 2.****

The Chicago orchestra has long had a reputation for its unique horn section, and here in the *Kanzertstück* is ample proof of breathtaking virtuosity and compelling artistry from the latest quartet of principals. Their playing not only conveys brilliance of an order rarely achieved before in recordings of this music; the joyfulness of Schumann's inspiration comes over superbly. This makes a generous and vividly enjoyable coupling to an outstanding version of the *Second Symphony*. The tape transfer balances the four horns rather too forwardly, so that their combined tone is almost overwhelming. Otherwise the recording is very good, with plenty of body and firmly focused, and the orchestra does not lack impact, even if it makes about the same volume as the soloists.

Symphony No. 1 in B flat major (Spring), Op. 38; Overture, Scherzo and Finale, Op. 52.
　　**(*)Decca KSXC 6486. Vienna PO, Solti.

Solti's performance of Schumann's *Spring symphony* does not quite match the glowing inspiration of his companion performances, but it provides a very welcome completion to the cycle, particularly with the unjustly neglected *Overture, Scherzo and Finale* provided as an ideal coupling. Solti's fine springing of rhythm is always a delight, and he shows conclusively how many imaginative points of orchestration Schumann devised for this work, whatever may have been said over the years. Excellent recording, and a lively tape transfer of generally good quality.

Symphonies Nos. 1 in B flat major (Spring), Op. 38; 4 in D minor, Op. 120.
　　*** Decca KSXC 6819 [Lon. 5-7039]. Vienna PO, Mehta.
　　** DG 3300 660 [id.]. Chicago SO, Barenboim.

Mehta draws a sharp contrast of mood and manner between these two symphonies. His view of the *Spring symphony* is resilient and light-hearted – with the Vienna Philharmonic at its most affectionate and spontaneous-sounding – while in No. 4 he brings out the darkly

dramatic qualities of this cyclic work, giving in relatively little to its charm. But the freshness of the music-making here is in no doubt, and with glorious Decca recording this is a very attractive issue; the performance of the *B flat major Symphony* is one of the finest available. The cassette transfer is of Decca's highest quality: there is a splendid body of sound, with a fine bloom on wind and strings alike, excellent detail and spaciousness. A first-class cassette in every way.

The *Fourth Symphony* brings the one serious disappointment in Barenboim's cycle of the Schumann symphonies. Here he seems at times too conscious of the example of Furtwängler before him, for he echoes some of the idiosyncrasies of that maestro on his classic mono disc recording, but without conveying the same spontaneous urgency. In the first movement, the playing of the Chicago orchestra is notably less well drilled than in the other symphonies, and the recording balance exposes some unexpectedly thin violin tone. The *First Symphony* is far more successful as a performance, matching the freshness and high spirits of Barenboim's reading of the *Second*. The tape offers clear, incisive sound, fresh and attractive if a little dry in the bass.

Symphony No. 2 in C major, Op. 61.
　　*** DG 3300 939. Chicago SO, Barenboim – *Konzertstück for 4 horns.****

Barenboim's exhilarating account of the *Second Symphony* stands out in his complete cycle with the Chicago orchestra, not only for the brilliance of the playing but for the sense of purpose conveyed from beginning to end, in a work which more than its companions can seem diffuse. The only possible reservation concerns the slow movement, where Barenboim adopts a more heavily expressive style in the radiant opening melody than some will approve; but his approach in that movement is quite consistent with the ripe healthy romanticism which pervades the whole performance. Ripe recording to match, and the tape transfer, though it loses something in brightness, is well detailed, with a strong clear bass line.

Symphony No. 2 in C major, Op. 61; Overture Hermann und Dorothea, Op. 136.
> **(*)HMV TC-ASD 3648. Philharmonia Orch., Muti.

A sensitive performance of the *Second Symphony* which offers orchestral playing of the highest quality. In no sense does the playing here compare unfavourably with that of the Vienna Philharmonic for Solti, and Muti is less concerned to push things along. Yet there is no want of vitality or momentum. The engineers are not always entirely successful in clarifying the admittedly dense textures Schumann favours, although the balance has a convincing enough perspective. The *Hermann und Dorothea overture* is not one of Schumann's stronger works, but it includes an engagingly lightweight quotation from the *Marseillaise*. The transfer is well managed, the quality bright and full; sometimes the focus is not absolutely clean, notably in the first movement of the symphony, but this is a marginal criticism. The overture sounds particularly fresh.

Symphony No. 2 in C major, Op. 61; Julius Caesar overture.
> ***Decca KSXC 6487. Vienna PO, Solti.

Anyone who has ever doubted whether Solti could convey genuine *Innigkeit*, with unwanted tensions removed and a feeling of spontaneous lyricism paramount, should hear the slow movement in this magnificent performance of Schumann's least popular symphony. Both there and in the other movements Solti's performance glows with Viennese warmth, a masterly culmination of his excellent cycle of Schumann symphonies.

The *Julius Caesar overture* is no masterpiece, but it makes an enjoyable fill-up. Excellent recording, and a good cassette transfer, although the sound seems marginally less well focused in the overture than in the symphony (where the string sound in the slow movement is particularly rich).

Symphony No. 3 in E flat major (Rhenish), Op. 97; Manfred overture, Op. 115.
> **(*)DG 3300 940. Chicago SO, Barenboim.

Barenboim's performance of the *Rhenish* strongly brings out the long-established German sympathies of the Chicago orchestra. Richly impressive, with superb horn-playing (so vital in this symphony), the performance is above all weighty, with the first movement less lightly sprung than usual in its compound time, but the more powerful for that, and with the Cologne Cathedral movement taken very slowly and heavily. Some will find this an ideal reading for those very points, and the forward and opulent recording quality matches the interpretation. The playing in the overture is marginally less polished than in the symphony, but that too has a strong and enjoyable reading. The transfer to tape offers clean, fresh sound, with plenty of body.

Symphonies Nos. 3 in E flat major (Rhenish), Op. 97; 4 in D minor, Op. 120.
> ***Decca KSXC 6356. Vienna PO, Solti.

This is a generous coupling of two symphonies which in Solti's hands glow with exuberance. Maybe it takes a great conductor to present this music with the intensity it deserves, making light of the problems of balance in the orchestration. Solti's sense of rhythm in Schumann is strikingly alert, so that the first movement of the *Rhenish* hoists one aloft on its soaring melodies, and the drama of the *Fourth Symphony* is given full force without ever falling into excessive tautness: there is still room to breathe. Karajan's Berlin Philharmonic performance of No. 3 is even finer, but it is not at present available on tape, and in any case Solti's generous coupling provides an admirable alternative at what in effect is a very reasonable price. Good recording quality; the cassette transfer is satisfactory but not as clean as the disc.

Symphony No. 4 in D minor, Op. 120.
    (***) HMV TC-ASD 3365. New Philharmonia Orch., Muti – MENDELSSOHN: *Symphony No. 4.*(***)

Muti gives a strong, attractive performance, which more than usual brings out the Mendelssohnian charm as well as the characteristic toughness of Schumann in D minor mood. Inevitably, when this is compared with Klemperer and the vintage Philharmonia Orchestra (available on disc only) one notes that the NPO in 1977 was not quite so polished a body, at least in the violin section, but with good, warm recording, not quite as defined as it might be, this makes a good coupling for the excellent version of Mendelssohn's *Italian* on the reverse. Unfortunately, although the transfer is smoother than in the Mendelssohn coupling, the outer movements are not free from roughness at peaks, and there is a degree of congestion at one or two climaxes in the finale.

Andante and variations in B flat major for 2 pianos, 2 violoncellos and horn.
    (M) **(*) Turnabout KTVC 34204. Toni and Rosi Grünschlag (pianos), Walther Tomböck (horn), Richard Harand, Gunther Weiss (cellos) – DUSSEK: *Double concerto.**(*)

This broadly romantic and not ineffective work is something of a musical curiosity. Presumably it was written for the composer's circle of intimate friends, for the subsidiary instrumental parts are not very demanding, except for the main horn variation, which demands a repeated leap, a cello acting in the place of 'second horn'. Before the music was published Schumann deleted these mainly instrumental (as distinct from pianistic) sections and the work has become known for two pianos alone. However, the original scheme can be very effective and the spontaneous playing on this Turnabout issue catches the style and brings the music's lyricism fully and enjoyably to life. The cassette transfer is acceptable but not outstanding, lacking the last degree of bite and presence.

Piano quartet in E flat major, Op. 47; Piano quintet in E flat major, Op. 44.
    *** CRD CRDC 4024. Thomas Rajna, members of the Alberni Qt.

Although the playing here may not be quite flawlessly polished, these performances are in their way as urgent and enjoyable as any available on disc. The recording is bright and crisp, which gives an extra (and not unlikeable) edge to the performances, and the transfer to tape is very successful. The sound has a natural balance and splendid body and detail; the piano tone is first-class, and altogether this is an excellent issue in every way.

String quartet No. 1 in A minor, Op. 41/1.
    (M) *** Decca Ace of Diamonds KSDC 510. Musikverein (Küchl) Qt – BRAHMS: *String quartet No. 3.****

The Musikverein Quartet (formerly known as the Küchl after the first violin) made a great impression with their recording of two late Mozart quartets, and this fine performance of the Schumann maintains their reputation for fine ensemble and natural musicality. There is a total absence of affectation here; the dynamic shading arises as a natural part of the music and never seems painted on. This is in some ways fresher than the fine Italian Quartet recording (not available on cassette), and the engineering is beyond reproach. A rewarding issue, and one of the best chamber-music cassettes available, notable for the freshness of the string textures as well as the warmth.

Arabeske in C major, Op. 18; Faschingsschwank aus Wien, Op. 26; Kinderscenen (Scenes from Childhood), Op. 15; Papillons, Op. 2.
> (M) *(*) Turnabout KTVC 34438. Walter Klien (piano).

Klien, always a thoughtful artist, is at his best in the *Arabeske* and, especially, in the *Kinderscenen*, which he plays very beautifully. But the impulsive manner in the *Faschingsschwank aus Wien* is not helped by a very hard and uncongenial recorded quality, and the same is true for *Papillons*, where the recording is only marginally better.

5 Études, Op. posth; Études symphoniques, Op. 13; Papillons, Op. 2.
> **(*) CBS 40-76635 [Col. MT 34539]. Murray Perahia (piano).

Beautifully poetic accounts that can be strongly recommended. Perahia has a special feeling for the *Symphonic studies* which is in evidence both on the concert platform and here, and makes every expressive point in the most natural and unfussy way. He plays the additional five studies that Schumann omitted from the published score as an addendum rather than inserting them into its course. The *Papillons* are unrivalled at present on disc or tape and are unlikely to be surpassed. The engineers give Perahia too close a balance to be ideal and the transfer does not offer especially distinguished sound:

the quality on side one (the *Études symphoniques*) is rather thick-textured, without sparkle in the treble; side two is brighter but harder in outline, although the delicate piano timbre in *Papillons* is effectively coloured.

Fantasia in C major, Op. 17.
> ** Decca KSXC 6756. Alicia de Larrocha (piano) – LISZT: *Piano sonata.***

Alicia de Larrocha is an artist of temperament and personality. Her Schumann *Fantasy* is perhaps too personal for a strong recommendation, but there are many good things in its favour, not least its excellent recording. However, on disc there are recordings available by Pollini, Richter, Arrau and Ashkenazy, and collectors would not be well advised to acquire this in preference to them unless a cassette version is essential. This is not to say that Larrocha's playing is not eminently worth hearing.

Fantasiestücke, Op. 12.
> ⊛ *** RCA RK 12397 [ARK 12397]. Artur Rubinstein (piano) – BEETHOVEN: *Piano sonata No. 18.****

In his ninetieth year, at the time of his last recital in London and with his sight already impaired, Rubinstein made what was to prove one of his most electrifying recordings, coupling Schumann and Beethoven. The personality of the pianist and his positive view of Schumann leap out from the very first bar, and though this may not be so deeply poetic and introspective a reading as Murray Perahia's (which is in any case not available on tape), it consistently has fuller, brighter colour, presented with a vitality that is irresistible. There is rhythmic latitude but none that is excessive, and with its range of tone colour and clarity of articulation it stands as a glowing monument to a master pianist whose eight decades of concert life led consistently upwards. The transfer offers one of the most realistic piano recordings available on tape, and certainly the finest sound Rubinstein has received in any of his recordings of the romantic piano literature. The tone is most agreeably full and warm, yet is clear in outline and wide in range. A highly satisfying production.

Frauenliebe und Leben (song cycle), *Op. 42.*

> (M) *(**) Saga CA 5277. Janet Baker (contralto), Martin Isepp (piano) – *Lieder recital.*(**)

Janet Baker's range of expression here runs the whole gamut from a joyful golden tone-colour in the exhilaration of *Ich kann's nicht fassen*, through an ecstatic half-tone in *Süsser Freund* (the fulfilment of the line *Du geliebter Mann* wonderfully conveyed) to the dead, vibratoless tone of agony in the final song. The Saga recording is far from perfect in the matter of balance and excess separation between piano and voice, and the transfer produces some distortion of both voice and piano at climaxes.

'Favourite composer': (i; ii) *Piano concerto in A minor, Op. 54;* (i) *Carnaval, Op. 9;* (iii) *Kinderscenen, Op. 15: Träumerei;* (iv) *Romance in F sharp major, Op. 28/2;* (v) *Symphony No. 1 in B flat major (Spring), Op. 38;* (vi) *Frauenliebe und Leben, Op. 42.*

> (B) * Decca KDPC 623/4. (i) Julius Katchen; (ii) Israel PO, Kertesz; (iii) Ilana Vered; (iv) Joseph Cooper; (v) LSO, Krips; (vi) Kathleen Ferrier, John Newmark.

A disappointing issue. Katchen's virtuoso reading of the *Concerto*, always brightly recorded, sounds shallow here, and the piano timbre of the monosourced recording of *Carnaval* also gives a hard, brittle image without bloom. When one samples the performances by

Ilana Vered and Joseph Cooper on the second tape the quality is altogether more congenial, but Kathleen Ferrier's account of *Frauenliebe und Leben* again suffers from too bright a sound, which mercilessly exposes the age of the recording. The *Symphony* comes off best, but that is available otherwise coupled.

Schütz, Heinrich (1585–1672)

Musikalische Exequien. Motets: *Die Himmel erzählen die Ehre Gottes; Ich bin ein rechter Weinstock; Selig sind die Toten.*

> * Advent D 1030 (see p. xxiii) [id.]. Cantata Singers, Harbison.

Schütz is otherwise unrepresented on cassette, though he is generally well served on disc. This account of the *Musikalische Exequien* is well prepared and conscientiously performed, but it is let down by the recording, which is made in a smaller acoustic than desirable and which in louder choral passages ccomes close to discoloration. This lack of smoothness, unusual from this source, diminishes the desirability of this issue. The motets are placed at the end of the *Musikalische Exequien*, leaving side two free for domestic use.

Scriabin, Alexander (1872–1915)

Piano concerto in F sharp minor, Op. 20; Prometheus –The poem of fire, Op. 60.

> *** Decca KSXC 6527. Vladimir Ashkenazy (piano), LPO, Maazel.

This is an admirable introduction to Scriabin's art and a very distinguished issue in every respect. Ashkenazy plays the *Piano concerto* with great feeling and authority, and the Decca recording has both clarity and luminosity. Moreover Maazel accompanies most sympathetically throughout. *Prometheus* too is given a thoroughly poetic and committed reading by Maazel and the LPO, Ashkenazy coping with the virtuoso obbligato part with predictable distinction. Powerfully atmospheric and curiously hypnotic, the score reeks of Madame Blavatsky and Scriabin's wild mysticism, while abounding in the fanciful lines of *art nouveau*. Given such outstanding recording and performance, this makes a splendid starting point for any Scriabin collection. It was issued on 6 January 1972, the centenary of the composer's birth. The cassette transfer is of generally good quality.

Poème de l'extase (*Poem of ecstasy*), *Op. 54.*
*** Decca Phase 4 KPFC 4333 [Lon. 5-21117]. Czech PO, Stokowski – RIMSKY-KORSA-KOV: *Capriccio espagnol***(*); DVOŘÁK: *Slavonic dance No. 10.***

Stokowski's version of the *Poème de l'extase* was recorded live, when the nonagenarian conductor visited Prague. The result, tactfully edited from more than one performance, has all the passionate commitment of a concert-hall performance, with the ebb and flow of tension and the flexibility of phrasing the more compellingly captured. The Phase Four recording highlights individual instruments, but not so aggressively as in the studio recording of the Rimsky-Korsakov on the reverse. The excellent cassette transfer provides sound which is robust and clear, with plenty of weight at climaxes.

Piano sonatas Nos. 2 (*Sonata-fantasy*) *in G sharp minor, Op. 19; 7 in F sharp major* (*White Mass*), *Op. 64; 10 in C major, Op. 70; Deux Danses, Op. 73; Deux Poèmes, Op. 32; Quatre Morceaux, Op. 56.*
*** Decca KSXC 6868 [Lon. 5-7087]. Vladimir Ashkenazy (piano).

This issue fulfils the high expectations engendered by Ashkenazy's earlier Scriabin recital (see below). Ponti, Ogdon and Roberto Szidon have all given us complete Scriabin sonata cycles on disc, but none has matched Ashkenazy's commanding authority and sense of vision in this repertoire. Whether one likes this music or not, there is no questioning the demonic, possessed quality of the playing. The cassette faithfully reproduces the sound one finds on the disc; indeed there is remarkably little to choose between the two formats.

Piano sonatas Nos. 3 in F sharp minor, Op. 23; 4 in F sharp major, Op. 30; 5 in F sharp major, Op. 53; 9 in F major (*Black Mass*), *Op. 68.*
*** Decca KSXC 6705 [Lon. 5-6920]. Vladimir Ashkenazy (piano).

Performances of the highest quality, superbly recorded. Of these four sonatas, three (Nos. 3, 5 and 9) were recorded by Horowitz (only No. 5 now remains in the catalogue, and is not available on tape). But Ashkenazy is hardly less magnificent, and readers interested in Scriabin's development could scarcely find a more indispensable issue. The cassette transfer is admirably faithful, offering remarkably pure, clean and secure piano tone.

Shostakovich, Dmitri (1906–75)

Piano concertos Nos. (i; ii) *1, Op. 35;* (i) *2, Op. 101. 3 Fantastic dances, Op. 5.*

 ***HMV TC-ASD 3081. Cristina Ortiz (piano), with (i) Bournemouth SO, Berglund; (ii) Rodney Senior (trumpet).

Cristina Ortiz gives fresh and attractive performances of both concertos, a degree under-characterized, but beautifully recorded and with a fine accompaniment from the Bournemouth orchestra. This HMV coupling also offers the *3 Fantastic dances*, which are played with splendid character. They sound especially well on the cassette, which offers excellent piano tone; and though the orchestral image on tape lacks the last degree of crispness, the overall sound has a pleasing bloom and undoubtedly makes enjoyable listening.

Violoncello concerto No. 2, Op. 126.
 DG 3300 653 [id.]. Mstislav Rostropovich, Boston SO, Ozawa – GLAZOUNOV: *Chant du ménestrel.*

Shostakovich's *Second Cello concerto* first appeared in the mid-1960s, but whereas Rostropovich recorded the *First* almost immediately, this concerto languished for a decade unrepresented in the catalogue. The *Second* is completely different from its predecessor; its first movement is closer to the ruminative *Nocturne* of the *First Violin concerto* than to the taut, concentrated *Allegro* of the *Cello concerto No. 1.* At first it appears to lack density of musical incident and seems deceptively rhapsodic, but closer acquaintance reveals its strength. Indeed it is an evocative and haunting work, and the rhapsodic opening *Largo* seems curiously

dreamlike until one realizes how purposeful is the soloist's course through its shadowy landscape. There is a short, succinct scherzo (in some ways the least musically substantial of the three movements) and a haunting, lyrical finale, gently discursive, sadly whimsical at times, and tinged with a smiling melancholy that suggests deeper sorrows. At first this finale too seems insubstantial, but it possesses concentration of mood rather than of musical matter and lingers in the listener's mind long after the performance is over. Rostropovich plays with beautifully controlled feeling and without the excessive vehemence which at times affects his art, while Seiji Ozawa brings sympathy and fine discipline to the accompaniment, and secures admirably expressive playing from the Boston orchestra. The recording is absolutely first-class, though Rostropovich is a trifle too forward. This apart, however, the balance is impeccably judged and the most is made of the spacious and warm acoustic. The cassette transfer is well managed too: the recording is pleasingly warm and natural, with a convincing perspective, but there is a slight lack of sparkle in the upper range. Even so the overall balance of sound is very musical.

Symphony No. 4 in C minor, Op. 43.
 **HMV TC-ASD 3440. Chicago SO, Previn.

An eminently straightforward, superlatively played and vividly recorded account of the problematic *Fourth Symphony*, whose publication Shostakovich withheld from 1936 to the early 1960s. So far Ormandy and Kondrashin have recorded this anguished score on disc, but neither version can be said to match the present issue in terms of the sheer quality of the orchestral response (the Chicago orchestra is untroubled here by the problems of woodwind intonation that have occasionally beset them elsewhere) or the body and presence of the recording. This conscientious and well-prepared performance is unlikely to be superseded for a very long time. The quality on tape has plenty of amplitude and warmth and certainly does not lack an edge of brilliance, although occasionally under pressure the clarity slips a little. The resonant sound does not offer transfer problems, but the inner detail of the recording lacks the last degree of transparency.

Symphony No. 5 in D minor, Op. 47.
(M) (***) RCA Gold Seal GK 42690. LSO, Previn.
(M) ** HMV Greensleeve TC-ESD 7029. Bournemouth SO, Berglund.
*(*) HMV TC-ASD 3443 [Angel 4xs 37285]. Chicago SO, Previn.
* RCA RK 11712. Philadelphia Orch., Ormandy.

Previn's RCA version with the LSO, which dates from the mid-sixties, is an altogether superlative account. The recording too was outstanding in all departments of the orchestra. Unfortunately the cassette transfer – although it generally sounds well – has a compressed dynamic range (the climax of the first movement is very much less telling here than on the equivalent disc). The freshness and vitality of the reading and the first-class playing of the LSO combine to produce a performance that is literal without lacking spontaneity. The kind of radiance that the strings achieve at the opening of the great slow movement is totally memorable; and throughout there is great intensity and eloquence. The buoyancy of the scherzo and the élan of the finale are highly exhilarating. Clearly this is the finest performance available on tape, and it is a great pity that the RCA engineers were intimidated by the wide dynamic range.

Berglund and the Bournemouth orchestra are superbly recorded, and the cassette transfer has captured the spectacular quality for which the disc has been rightly admired. The performance, however, is measured, even sober, although it has both atmosphere and eloquence. It is not the most exciting version available on disc, but on tape it will have to suffice until a completely recommendable alternative comes along. (Our review copy had some unattractive 'pulsing' unsteadiness at the opening of the slow movement, but this is unlikely to be found on tapes currently available.)

Previn's second recording of the *Fifth*, made in Chicago, does not match his earlier RCA version in intensity. His view of the work does not appear to have changed greatly in the intervening years, and although the playing of the Chicago orchestra is of the highest quality, there is little sense of freshness and urgency. The first movement is a good deal slower than usual, so much so that one feels the want of momentum. The scherzo is impressively played, but the slow movement is without a sense of forward movement and the climax, so impressive in the earlier version, lacks real urgency. The recorded sound is extremely impressive and the transfer is vividly detailed, with plenty of range and impact.

The Philadelphia Orchestra made the very first recording of the *Fifth Symphony*, and Ormandy has always shown a special feeling for Shostakovich. However, on the RCA tape one does not sense the commitment that marked Ormandy's early LP of the *First Symphony* and his more recent disc of the *Thirteenth*: there is too little sense of atmosphere, and the orchestral playing is surprisingly routine at times. It is all eminently well shaped but wanting in freshness. Matters are not helped by the RCA engineers, who favour a close balance, and on tape this results in coarsened climaxes and an absence of pianissimos.

Symphony No. 6 in B minor, Op. 54.
(*) HMV TC-ASD 3029. LSO, Previn – PROKOFIEV: *Lieutenant Kijé.*(*)

509

The opening slow movement of the *Sixth Symphony* is parallel to those of the *Fifth* and the *Eighth*, each among the composer's finest inspirations. Here Previn shows his deep understanding of Shostakovich in a powerfully drawn, unrelenting account of that massive structure, his slow tempo adding to the overall impact. After that the offhand wit of the central scherzo comes over the more delicately at a slower tempo than usual, leaving the hectic finale to hammer home the deceptively joyful conclusion to the argument. Even at the end Previn effectively avoids bombast in the exuberance of joy. Excellent recording, and the cassette transfer is generally of good quality, lacking only the last degree of refinement of detail.

Symphony No. 10 in E minor, Op. 93.
> **(*) Decca KSXC 6838 [Lon. 5-7061]. LPO, Haitink.
> (M)**HMV Greensleeve TC-ESD 7049. Bournemouth SO, Berglund.
> *RCA RK 25049. National PO, Tjeknavorian.

As a recording Bernard Haitink's Decca version is in the demonstration class. It has impressive body, range and definition: the balance is very natural, yet every detail of Shostakovich's score registers, and the climaxes are astonishingly lifelike. Haitink really has the measure of the first movement, whose climaxes he paces with an admirable sense of architecture, and he secures sensitive and enthusiastic playing from the LPO both here and in the scherzo. In the third movement he adopts a slower tempo than usual, which would be acceptable if there were greater tension or concentration of mood. But here and in the slow introduction to the finale the sense of concentration falters, though this must not be allowed to detract from the overall integrity and eloquence that Haitink largely

achieves. The sound quality from the cassette is hardly less impressive than that of the disc. It is admirably clear in detail, with a strikingly clean, natural bass response and a very good overall balance.

Berglund has a strong grip on the architecture of the work and is refreshingly straight: there is no attempt to interpose his personality between the music and the listener. He draws playing of high quality from the Bournemouth orchestra and is given sound quality of stunning realism. Berglund has a genuine sense of the music's scale but ultimately he is let down by a want of inner tension. Nevertheless this performance is not without strength or atmosphere, although there is an element of literalness and sobriety. There is more to this symphony than Berglund reveals. However, technically this is a most impressive issue; the transfer to tape is one of EMI's best; the strings have warmth and attack and the wind and brass have plenty of bloom. The recording is atmospheric, and the resonance does not obscure detail. Although the last degree of range is missing, the overall balance is very good.

Tjeknavorian's version is a non-starter. He unwisely chooses so leisurely a tempo that it is impossible to maintain tension. There is, consequently, no real gain in breadth, and although there is atmosphere, the lack of a compelling forward thrust is constantly apparent. The recording is as good as any on the market, and the tape is technically satisfactory. Although there is a touch of harshness and a minor deterioration of focus at the loudest fortissimos, caused by the reverberation, the transfer is generally well managed, and the sound is certainly vivid, with attractively warm string textures.

Symphony No. 15 in A major, Op. 141.
> ⊛ *** Decca KSXC 6906. LPO, Haitink.

The second issue in Haitink's Shostakovich series brings a performance which is a revelation. Early readings of the composer's last symphony seemed to underline the quirky unpredictability of the work, with the collage of strange quotations – above all the *William Tell* galop, which keeps recurring in the first movement – seeming joky rather than profound. Haitink by contrast makes the first movement sound genuinely symphonic, bitingly urgent. He underlines the purity of the bare lines of the second movement, and after the Wagner quotations which open the finale his slow tempo for the main lyrical theme gives it heartaching tenderness, not the usual easy triviality. The playing of the LPO is excellent, with refined tone and superb attack, and the recording is both analytical and atmospheric, as impressive on cassette as on disc. Although the textures are generally spare the few heavy tuttis are difficult for the engineers, and Decca sound copes with them splendidly. Indeed the witty opening movement offers demonstration quality of just how clean and sparkling a cassette transfer can be.

Violin sonata, Op. 134.
  *** Advent E 1069 (see p. xxiii) [id.]. Emanuel Borok (violin), Tatiana Yampolsky (piano) – PROKOFIEV: *Violin sonata No. 1.****

Emanuel Borok shows beyond doubt on this his debut recording that he is an artist of formidable technique and musicianship. The Shostakovich sonata is available on disc played by its dedicatee, David Oistrakh (it was composed to mark his sixtieth birthday), and also by Gidon Kremer, but it is unrepresented on a commercial cassette. Borok's account is scarcely less masterly than Oistrakh's (though the latter has slightly greater lyrical intensity) and is excellently recorded. The sonata makes use of a twelve-note row and is one of Shostakovich's least approachable pieces. Yet given

playing of this quality and such excellent recorded sound, the effort is well rewarded.

Preludes, Op. 34, Nos. 1, 4, 10, 12, 14–16, 19, 22, 24.
  *** DG 3301 096 [id.]. Lazar Berman (piano) – MUSSORGSKY: *Pictures.****

A thoroughly worthwhile coupling for Mussorgsky's *Pictures at an Exhibition*. Berman obviously finds great sympathy for these diverse miniatures, and his characterization is highly imaginative. The playing has more warmth than on some of Berman's other recordings; indeed it is very distinguished. The consistent element of spontaneity brings the music fully to life. The recording is splendid and the transfer admirably balanced, full, sonorous and clear.

Sibelius, Jean
(1865–1957)

Violin concerto in D minor, Op. 47.
  *** Decca KSXC 6493. Kyung-Wha Chung, LSO, Previn – TCHAIKOVSKY: *Concerto.****
  (M) **(*) Decca KCSP 398. Ruggiero Ricci, LSO, Fjeldstad – DVOŘÁK: *Concerto.***
  (*) Pye ZCPNH 14. Yuval Yaron, LPO, Soudant – TCHAIKOVSKY: *Concerto.(*)*
  ** DG 3300 496 [id.]. Pinchas Zukerman, LPO, Barenboim – BEETHOVEN: *Romances.***
  (B) *(*) DG Heliodor 3348 264. Miriam Fried, Belgian Radio and TV SO, Defossez – CHAUSSON: *Poème.**

Violin concerto; Humoresque No. 5, Op. 89/3; Serenades Nos. 1 in D major; 2 in G major, Op. 61/1–2.
> ****(*)** HMV TC-ASD 3199. Ida Haendel, Bournemouth SO, Berglund.

Violin concerto; Finlandia, Op. 26; Kuolema (incidental music): *Valse triste, Op. 44.*
> ****(*)** DG 923077. Christian Ferras, Berlin PO, Karajan.

Kyung-Wha Chung gives a most beautiful account of the work, poetic, brilliant and thoroughly idiomatic. She has impeccable style and an astonishing technique, and her feeling for the Sibelius *Concerto* is second-to-none. André Previn's accompanying cannot be too highly praised: it is poetic when required, restrained, full of controlled vitality and well-defined detail. The recording is superbly balanced and the cassette transfer is natural in quality, providing a smooth solo image and a warm orchestral backcloth; it is not as vividly detailed as some Decca issues but pleasingly atmospheric.

Ida Haendel brings virtuosity and attack to this score, and there is a refreshing want of egocentricity to her interpretation. She plays with dash and authority, even though there are certain passages where Kyung-Wha Chung brings greater poetic refinement. Berglund accompanies sympathetically, though the finale could go with greater panache. The two *Serenades* are marvellously atmospheric and Miss Haendel does them proud in this première recording. The recording is most impressive in detail and body. Had Berglund greater atmosphere in the *Concerto* this would compete more strongly with the first recommendation, Kyung-Wha Chung. Even so the performance is richly enjoyable, for Miss Haendel's tone and phrasing have memorable warmth and eloquence. The cassette transfer is of good quality. Although it has a slightly restricted dynamic range, the spacious richness of the sound and the intensity of the performance tend to minimize this defect.

Ricci has the clean, clear-cut, and effortless kind of technique that is a prime necessity for the Sibelius *Concerto*, and he makes light of its many difficulties. The reading is straightforward, with no lack of dash and intensity. A great contribution to the success of the performance is made by Fjeldstad and the orchestra. Fortunately the recording is very good indeed: the soloist, although well forward, is sufficiently detached from the orchestra to give an impression of depth. The cassette transfer is clear and bold in its projection of detail, and lacks only the very last degree of refinement; it can be made to sound very well.

Yuval Yaron plays the opening very gently, and the rocking accompaniment on the strings is not very distinctly focused. But the recording soon fills out in detail and at the first *tutti* the wide dynamic range reveals the weight of the orchestra within a fairly resonant acoustic. Yaron has a splendid technique, but the close microphone balance sometimes prevents the utmost smoothness of timbre when he is playing full-out. And this is undoubtedly a passionate performance, with the *Adagio* played with great eloquence (and splendidly shaped by Soudant). At times in the outer movements the impetuosity of the soloist makes one feel a lack of compensating poise, but the urgency of the music-making is in no doubt. The recording has transferred well to tape and has plenty of life and impact.

Ferras's performance is also a very good one. It has the advantage of being very well recorded, but, although Ferras begins the work with a winningly golden tone, when he is under stress at the end of the first movement and in the finale, his intonation and general security are no match for the superbly accurate Kyung-Wha Chung performance. But there is still much to enjoy and Ferras develops a rich, romantic tone for the main tune of the slow movement. The principal coupling is an extremely expansive reading of *Finlandia*, in which Karajan broadens the grand tune almost as far as it will go to accentuate its patriotic dignity. Only Karajan could bring this off, and he does, with superb Berlin Philharmonic brass playing to support him. The transfer of the *Concerto* is finely balanced, with a pleasing image for the violin soloist. The recording of *Finlandia* is well managed, but the strings are a little fierce in the climax of *Valse triste*. The performance of the *Violin concerto* is also available in a DG box together with the Ferras/Karajan versions of the Beethoven, Brahms and Tchaikovsky concertos (3371 021).

Zukerman has a sweet tone and a formidable technique that is much in evidence, particularly in the finale. There is no want of genuine feeling in the slow movement, though for those who prefer understatement here, he might be thought to pitch too high an emotional temperament; he does not match the aristocratic feeling that Kyung-Wha Chung gives us. His opening is beautiful and so is that of the first movement, though suddenly at bars 18–19 there are some upward swoops that are not in good style and elsewhere some *espressivo* throbs which are too much of a good thing. All this is a matter of taste, no doubt, and there are some beautiful passages where both Zukerman and Barenboim show great poetic feeling. There is a warm acoustic and a good recording, albeit a forward balance for the soloist. The transfer is of good quality, well balanced and detailed. The tape turns over before the finale, which is on side two with the Beethoven *Romances*.

Miriam Fried is a young Israeli violinist who won first prizes at the Genoa Paganini Competition in 1968 and the Concours Reine Elisabeth in Brussels in 1971. The Sibelius was recorded on the latter occasion. The reading is a highly romantic, self-indulgent affair and will appeal to those who like their Sibelius played with the last ounce of emotion. The Chausson coupling would be more acceptable if it were not recorded with piano accompaniment. Not a distinguished issue. The transfer is well managed, although the solo timbre sounds rather thin.

Finlandia, Op. 26; Karelia suite, Op. 11; Legends: The Swan of Tuonela, Op. 22/2; En Saga, Op. 9.
  (B) ** Classics for Pleasure TC-CFP 40247. Vienna PO, Sargent.

Sargent's collection is highly successful. Without being especially idiomatic, each performance has conviction and character, and the four works complement each other to make a thoroughly enjoyable programme. The Vienna Philharmonic Orchestra bring a distinct freshness to their playing of music which must have been fairly unfamiliar to them, and Sir Malcolm imparts his usual confidence. The brass is especially full-blooded in *En Saga*, and even *Finlandia* sounds unhackneyed. Perhaps Sir Malcolm's tempi for *Karelia* are on the brisk side, but the music projects vividly and the orchestral playing is excellent. The cassette transfers have plenty of life and colour, but a limited dynamic range reduces the impact and excitement of *En Saga* and *Finlandia*, and to a lesser extent the outer movements of *Karelia*.

Finlandia, Op. 26; Karelia suite, Op. 11; Kuolema (incidental music): *Valse triste, Op. 44; Legends: The Swan of Tuonela, Op. 22/2.*
  *(*) Decca Phase 4 KPFC 4378. New Philharmonia Orch., Kord.

This collection of popular Sibelius offers somewhat short measure. The recordings are bright and vivid in the Phase Four manner (with a fairly successful cassette transfer) but are not unmusically balanced. The performances, however, do not rise much above the routine.

Finlandia, Op. 26. King Christian II suite, Op. 27: Élégie; Musette. Kuolema: Valse triste, Op. 44. Pelléas et Mélisande, Op. 46: No. 8, Entr'acte.
(M) *** Decca KCSP 91. London Proms Orch., Mackerras –
  GRIEG: *Elegiac melodies* etc.***

The performance of *Finlandia* is brashly exciting, but other versions make a greater impact with a more sonorous sound balance. In the rest of the pieces the sound is first-rate and the programme is sheer joy. The *Musette* from the *King Christian II suite* is enchanting, and the *Entr'acte* from *Pelléas* is almost equally delightful: both have the kind of vivid colouring which has made the *Karelia suite* so famous. The *Elegy* too is beautiful, and this attractive collection is well worth its modest cost in this admirably clear transfer.

Finlandia, Op. 26; Kuolema (incidental music): complete (*Valse romantique, Op. 62b; Canzonetta, Op. 62a; Kurkikohtaus* (*Scene with cranes*), *Op. 44/2; Valse triste, Op. 44*); *Scènes historiques, Opp. 25, 66.*
(M) ** Decca Ace of Diamonds KSDC 489. Hungarian State SO, Jalas.

As Sibelius's son-in-law, Jussi Jalas brings a special authority to this repertoire, but his Hungarian orchestra is not of the first rank. The strings are a little wanting in lustre and richness of tone, and the wind playing is not distinguished. Jalas takes some of the *Scènes historiques* rather faster than did Barbirolli or Beecham; it must be assumed that this reflects the composer's wishes, but Gibson's account (see below) is much better, and is well recorded. The *Canzonetta* and *Valse romantique, Op. 62*, are

the two additional pieces Sibelius wrote for a later production of *Kuolema*. The *Scene with cranes* from the same play (Sibelius had an almost mystical feeling for swans, geese, cranes etc.) lacks the last degree of poetic intensity here, but *Finlandia* fares better and is given with some vigour. The recording is not really distinguished, though it is by no means unacceptable. The acoustic could be more open and the string tone have more blossom. The brass sound is impressive at the beginning of *Finlandia*, though, and there is virtually no difference between disc and cassette here.

Finlandia, Op. 26. Kuolema: Valse triste, Op. 44. Legends: The Swan of Tuonela, Op. 22/2. Tapiola (symphonic poem), *Op. 112.*
*** DG 923069 [id.]. Berlin PO, Karajan.

This is a first-rate cassette in every way. *Finlandia* is one of the finest performances available (tremendous orchestral tone from the Berliners), and the transfer provides a spectacularly vivid balance, with superb brass. *Tapiola* is also impressive, a performance of great intensity, offering superlative playing. The climax on the strings is given splendid projection on cassette, and the detail throughout is excellent. *Valse triste* is played slowly but is not without atmosphere, and *The Swan of Tuonela* is highly successful given such a rich sheen of sound.

Finlandia, Op. 26. Legends: The Swan of Tuonela, Op. 22/2. En Saga, Op. 9. Tapiola (symphonic poem), *Op. 112.*
*** HMV TC-ASD 3374 [Angel 4XS 37408]. Berlin PO, Karajan.

This almost duplicates Karajan's DG Sibelius anthology (see above), except that *En Saga* replaces *Valse triste*. This is Karajan's third recording of *Tapiola* but his first of *En Saga*, where he is a brisk story-teller, more concerned with narrative than atmosphere at the beginning; but the *lento assai* section and the coda are quite magical. *Finlandia* is superbly played and most realistically recorded. The new *Tapiola* is broader and more expansive than the DG version, and at the storm section beginning at bar 513 Karajan's more spacious tempo is vindicated; the effect is altogether more electrifying. The HMV recording is more forward and possesses great body and presence, so much so that some listeners may prefer the slightly more recessed yet atmospheric sound in the DG version. In any event both are great performances and totally committed. There is an ugly blemish in bar 598, where some of the cellos play D sharp and the others D natural. This should have been corrected. The cassette produces impressive results and has ample body and firmness. Only *The Swan* sounds a little too overnourished by comparison with the earlier version, but there is no lack of atmosphere.

4 Legends, Op. 22 (*Lemminkäinen and the Maidens of Saari; The Swan of Tuonela; Lemminkäinen in Tuonela; Lemminkäinen's Return*).
*** HMV TC-ASD 3644. Philadelphia Orch., Ormandy.
**(*) RCA RK 25172. Scottish National Orch., Gibson.
(**) HMV TC-ASD 3092. Royal Liverpool PO, Groves.
4 Legends, Op. 22; In Memoriam (funeral march), *Op. 59.*
(M) *(*) Decca Ace of Diamonds KSDC 488. Hungarian State SO, Jalas.
4 Legends, Op. 22; Karelia suite, Op. 11.
(***) DG 3300 656. Helsinki Radio Orch., Kamu.

Ormandy's version must be the first recommendation here. It offers an extremely fine recording that comes near to doing justice to the Philadelphia sound (though it is not so spectacularly successful as their *Pictures at an Exhibition* with Muti). In the first of the *Legends*, the wind are more closely observed than is ideal, and the sound would benefit from greater depth. Ormandy's account of the first *Legend* is not as spacious as Jensen's pioneering disc, but it is marvellously passionate. (These Maidens of Saari must have given Lemminkäinen quite a wild time!) Ormandy's *Swan of Tuonela* is among the very finest, full of atmosphere and poetry, and the third *Legend* is brooding and menacing. In *Lemminkäinen's Return*, he comes close to the famous hell-for-leather excitement generated in Beecham's old 78 set. Among cassette versions, Ormandy's is by far the fleetest horse. The tape transfer is slightly sharper in detail than the LP and rather less rich in the middle range; but the difference is not great.

In comparison with the Philadelphia version it would be easy to underestimate the excellence of the RCA recording under Sir Alexander Gibson. The Scottish National Orchestra does not produce quite the rich body of tone of the American orchestra but they play freshly and with much commitment. This is by far the finest Sibelius recording Gibson has given us to date. The *Swan of Tuonela* has a darkly brooding primeval quality, and there is an electric degree of tension in the third *Legend, Lemminkäinen in Tuonela*. The two outer pieces have ardent rhythmic feeling, and altogether this is highly successful. The RCA recording is spacious and the transfer is generally well managed, although the climaxes do not have quite the expansive fullness of the HMV tape. The musical notes are printed in almost unreadably small print.

Okko Kamu's account of *Lemminkäinen and the Maidens of Saari* is a trifle brisk, but his is a very fine performance of the *Legends*. He handles pictorial detail most imaginatively and at the same time

515

conveys the strongest feeling for shape. In *Lemminkäinen's Return* he is very good indeed. The Helsinki orchestra responds with enthusiasm and good ensemble to his direction, and the engineers provide a well-balanced and truthful sound picture. Unfortunately the DG cassette transfer offers very subfusc orchestral quality.

Sir Charles Groves is an admirable Sibelian, but he does not succeed in generating the powerful atmosphere necessary if these pieces are to work their magic. The cassette transfer, moreover, is very disappointing, curiously opaque and with a muddy bass that fails to tell. The lack of an open acoustic robs the music-making of atmosphere and deadens the orchestral impact.

In the performances conducted by Jussi Jalas, the composer's son-in-law, the Hungarian State Symphony Orchestra are not really inside the Sibelius idiom. Although there are good things in this reading, undistinguished orchestral playing and very ordinary recording quality diminish the appeal of this issue, even though it includes a welcome rarity, *In Memoriam*. The cassette transfer is clear, with good detail, but this only serves to emphasize the lack of body in the orchestral sound.

The Oceanides (tone poem), *Op. 73; Pelléas et Mélisande* (incidental music), *Op. 46: suite; Tapiola* (symphonic poem), *Op. 112.*
  (M) *** HMV TC-EXE 180. RPO, Beecham.

The *Pelléas et Mélisande* performance is one of the classics of recording history. Never have Sibelius's textures sounded more luminous and magical. Beecham lavished enormous attention on details of phrasing, and the results have a special eloquence. Sibelius himself asked Beecham to record *The Oceanides*, the only one of his tone poems not directly related to Nordic mythology. This is his most poetic evocation of the sea, and this mar-

vellous performance captures every nuance of the score. *Tapiola* has all the requisite brooding power and must be numbered among the very finest accounts ever recorded (alongside Kajanus, Koussevitzky and Karajan) and the quality of these transfers (the performances date from the 1950s) completely belies their age. The cassette has a fine bloom and atmosphere: there is a noticeable hiss, transferred from the elderly mastertape, but the climax of *Tapiola* is managed impressively.

Rakastava (suite), *Op. 14; Scènes historiques, Opp. 25, 66; Valse lyrique, Op. 96/1.*
  **(*) RCA RK 25051. Scottish National Orch., Gibson.

Written for a patriotic pageant, the *Scènes historiques* are vintage Sibelius; some of them (the *Scena*, Op. 25, No. 2, and the *Love song*, Op. 66, No. 2) plumb real depths of feeling, while others, like *The Chase*, Op. 66, No. 1, have a sense of the sweep and grandeur of nature. In the *Love song* Gibson strikes the right blend of depth and reticence, while elsewhere he conveys a fine sense of controlled power. Convincing and eloquent performances that have a natural feeling for the music. Gibson's *Rakastava* is beautifully unforced and natural, save for the last movement, which is a shade too slow. The *Valse lyrique* is not good Sibelius, but everything else on this tape is, and Gibson plays this repertoire with real commitment. The recorded sound is basically excellent, with the relationships between the various sections of the orchestra very well judged. The tape transfer, however, tends to harshen the treble response, and takes much of the bloom and freshness from the string tone. A treble cut improves matters considerably, and the woodwind detail remains vivid, but the sound overall is not as sweet and refined as on LP.

Symphonies Nos. 1–7.
> **(*)** Decca κ 3 ε 9. Vienna PO, Maazel.

Symphonies Nos. 1–7; The Bard, Op. 64; En Saga, Op. 9; Scènes historiques, Op. 25; (i) *Kullervo, Op. 7.*
> ** HMV TC-SLS 5129. Bournemouth SO, Berglund, (i) with Raili Kostia (soprano), Usko Viitanen (bass-bar.), Helsinki University Choir.

Maazel's cycle with the Vienna Philharmonic is still the best all-round version of the complete Sibelius symphonies, even though there are individual weaknesses: No. 6 is not particularly successful or idiomatic, and the slow movement of No. 3 also misses the point. In the first two and in Nos. 4 and 7 Maazel remains superb; it is strange that the mystery and breadth of No. 5 should elude him, since he has done it admirably in the concert hall. The Decca engineers have succeeded in improving the already excellent sound in these transfers, but with the individual symphonies now available on Jubilee, the attractions of this box are less obvious than when it was first issued.

Berglund's set is the only way in which tape collectors can purchase a recording of Sibelius's very first symphonic venture, *Kullervo,* and it has been magnificently transferred to tape, with fine body and impact, the chorus even clearer and more incisive than on disc. The work itself is an impressive five-movement piece on a Mahlerian scale; it predates *En Saga* and contains some vividly imaginative choral writing. The box also includes other shorter orchestral works. As for the symphonies themselves, they have their merits but in each instance one can do rather better from other sources (Maazel in Nos. 1 and 2; Davis in 3; Davis, Maazel or Karajan in 4; Karajan or Bernstein in 5; Davis in 6; Maazel or Davis in 7). As recordings it would be difficult to improve on this set, and the tape transfers are consistently successful, if not always quite as clean or as rich as the LPs. The orchestral playing is of high quality too. But judged by the highest standards these conscientious and well-prepared versions remain just a shade too literal and earthbound to be recommended without qualification. The layout, with Nos. 1 and 2, 3 (plus *The Bard*) and 4, 5 and 6 all back to back, and the *Seventh* coupled to *En Saga,* is admirable, and the notes are clearly printed. There is, however, no indication of the contents on the labels of the cassettes, an irritating economy which EMI occasionally favour.

Symphony No. 1 in E minor, Op. 39; Finlandia, Op. 26.
> **Philips 7300 517 [id.]. Boston SO, Colin Davis.

Symphony No. 1; Karelia suite, Op. 11.
> (M) **(*)** Decca Jubilee κjbc 42. Vienna PO, Maazel.

Symphony No. 1; Kuolema: Valse triste, Op. 44.
> (M) **(*)** CBS Classics 40-61804. New York PO, Bernstein.

Maazel's version of the *First Symphony* leads the field. It has freshness of vision to commend it, along with careful attention both to the letter and to the spirit of the score. The Vienna Philharmonic responds with enthusiasm and brilliance and the Decca engineers produce splendid detail. The performance of the *Karelia suite* is first-rate. The transfer is fairly sophisticated, but it seems not to have been remastered for its Jubilee reissue, and although the quality is full-blooded it lacks the crispness of detail of the others in this series. In the first movement the bass seems flabby, but when one turns over for the finale the level rises slightly and brings more bite. But *Karelia,* although rich-textured, lacks the last degree of sparkle.

Colin Davis secures idiomatic playing from the Boston Symphony Orchestra.

Tempi are well judged and there is a genuine sense of commitment. The recording, however, is less than distinguished. The perspective has little depth, and the string tone could be fresher at the top. The tape transfer is well managed, but the overall sound picture lacks something in range and brilliance. The quality is slightly more vivid in *Finlandia*.

Bernstein's account is impassioned and strong, as well as reasonably free from mannerisms. The power and eloquence of the string playing (especially in the finale) are most satisfying, and this is worth considering as an alternative to the Maazel. The tape transfer, although one of CBS's best, is rather less sophisticated than the Decca. Nevertheless the weight of string tone (very striking in the great tune of the finale) is well conveyed, even if the bright treble needs tempering, and (as in the rest of Bernstein's series) the bass is rather dry.

Symphony No. 2 in D major, Op. 43.
   (M) *** Decca Jubilee KJBC 43. Vienna PO, Maazel.
   (M) *** Philips Festivo 7310 084 [id.]. Concertgebouw Orch., Szell.
   *** Philips 7300 518 [id.]. Boston SO, Colin Davis.
   (M) **(*) Decca KECC 789. LSO, Monteux.
   (M) *(**) RCA Gold Seal GK 25011. RPO, Barbirolli.
   (M) ** CBS Classics 40-61805 [Col. MT 31827]. New York PO, Bernstein.
   ** HMV TC-ASD 3497. Bournemouth SO, Berglund.
   *(*) HMV TC-ASD 3414 [Angel 4XS 37444]. Pittsburg SO, Previn.
   (B) (**) RCA Camden C4-5029. Stockholm PO, Dorati.
   (B) * Pye ZCCCB 15003. LPO, Pritchard.

The *Second Symphony* is exceptionally well served on cassette. Szell's performance with the Concertgebouw Orchestra, on Philips's mid-price label, is classically conceived, tautly held together and superbly played. This may well be first choice for some readers, since the transfer is clear and vivid, a little lacking in opulence but otherwise very truthful: it suits Szell's conception very well. However, the reissue of Maazel's performance on Decca's Jubilee label makes it very competitive indeed, for the Decca sound is splendid, the transfer very sophisticated. Maazel's account is more traditionally lush: it is sumptuously recorded and beautifully played by the Vienna Philharmonic, but his reading leans more to the romantic view of the work favoured by some virtuoso conductors. The Tchaikovskian inheritance is stressed, rather than the classical forebears. The sound on the cassette is splendidly rich and brilliant, and the finale expands into a magnificent climax. A first-class issue which, technically, easily leads the field.

Colin Davis gives a dignified and well-proportioned account that is free from any excesses or mannerisms. Although it does not displace Maazel's or Szell's accounts (and is not as well recorded), it has sensitivity and freshness in its favour. The sound is not as open at the top as is desirable and there is a certain tubbiness in the middle-to-bottom range. However, this is an impressive performance, even in a field where competition is strong. The cassette transfer is of good quality and well balanced. The sound here is rather more impressive than in the Davis cassette of the *First Symphony*: it has body and spaciousness, and the violins have brightness and impact. This is quite satisfying, but the versions by Maazel and Szell are more vivid.

At medium price, Monteux and the LSO give a thoroughly acceptable and agreeably unmannered account of the work, and Decca accord them excellent sound. Again the cassette is excellent, the brightly lit recording transferring well to tape.

Barbirolli's version is marvellously alive. It has a spontaneity and vitality that capture the enthusiasm of the listener right from the outset, while the quality of the recorded sound has immediacy and presence. This has all the qualities of a live concert performance, and though it does not displace Maazel and Szell at the top of the list, it deserves to be recommended alongside them. Though less classical in outlook, it will be preferred by many readers. However, the RCA transfer does not match the best of those listed above in body and richness, and although it is otherwise quite well balanced there is an absence of bloom on the string tone.

There is no lack of spirit or warmth in Bernstein's version, which offers some thrilling orchestral playing from the New York Philharmonic. There are some mannered touches in the slow movement and the finale, but on the whole this performance has a spontaneity and virtuosity that are impressive. The recorded sound, however, is not comparable with the Maazel, Szell and Davis versions, though it is fully acceptable.

Berglund's is essentially a broad view. The lack of urgency is immediately felt at the opening of the first movement, and while the scherzo has plenty of impetus and the finale provides a satisfyingly broad culmination, the tension is slackly held in the slow movement. Overall the lack of dynamism must be counted a drawback in a symphony which is justly famous for engendering a high level of excitement. The recording is rich and spacious and the transfer is of first-class quality, virtually indistinguishable from the disc.

Previn's version is very well recorded and the transfer has plenty of body, though the middle string detail sounds rather husky. Unfortunately the quality of the orchestral playing is not comparable with that of the finest international orchestras, and while Previn eschews any

egocentric interpretative gestures, his performance is not wholly free from the charge of undercharacterization. Put bluntly, this has less personality and conviction than its rivals.

Dorati's is a well-shaped performance that is amazing value. It dates from the late 1960s and is admirably recorded. However, neither in the quality of the orchestral playing nor in definition and presence does it match the best available, and even at bargain price the cassette is put out of court by the poor management of the Dolby process, which damps down the treble response.

Pritchard's version with the LPO on Pye is a worthy if unremarkable reading, well enough recorded but in no way outstanding.

Symphony No. 3 in C major, Op. 52; (i) *Violin concerto in D minor, Op. 47.*

> (M) ** CBS Classics 40-61809. New York PO, Bernstein, (i) with Zino Francescatti (violin).

Bernstein's account of the *Third Symphony* is eminently well-shaped, but he does not penetrate the secrets of the slow movement as imaginatively as Colin Davis does (see below). However, at its modest price, and with a strong account of the *Violin concerto* from Zino Francescatti, there is much to commend in this issue, not least the spirited playing of the New York Philharmonic Orchestra. The recording does not quite match that of the rival Decca or Philips versions of the *Third*, and in the transfer of the *Violin concerto* the very bright treble needs considerable cutting back.

Symphony No. 3 in C major, Op. 52; Pelléas et Mélisande (incidental music): *suite, Op. 46.*

> ** HMV TC-ASD 3629. Bournemouth SO, Berglund.

Eminently well recorded performances of the *Third Symphony* and the complete

519

suite from *Pelléas et Mélisande* (Beecham – see above – omits the short atmospheric movement *By the seashore*). The symphony receives a sturdy, sober performance, well proportioned but ultimately uninspired. Nor do the *Pelléas* movements emerge with the magic of Beecham. However, the orchestral playing is altogether excellent and the sound exemplary.

Symphonies Nos. 3 in C major, Op. 52; 6 in D minor, Op. 104.
**(*) Philips 7300 519 [id.]. Boston SO, Colin Davis.
(M) *(**) Decca Jubilee KJBC 44. Vienna PO, Maazel.

Colin Davis's account of the *Third Symphony* undoubtedly leads the field. He judges the tempi in all three movements to perfection; no conductor has more effectively captured the elusive spirit of the slow movement or the power of the finale. In this respect he surpasses even the authoritative Kajanus set of pre-war days. He is well recorded too. The *Sixth* is impressive, though not as poetic in feeling as Karajan's (whose tape is not Dolbyized). However, the tape transfer has been made at a very low level. In consequence the sound has lost some of its vividness of detail and although, provided the volume is turned well up, it is perfectly acceptable, hiss problems do occur.

In the *Third Symphony* Maazel keeps a firm grip on the proceedings. He moulds phrases naturally and without affectation, and his build-up in the finale is most impressive. The slow movement is not quite poetic or reflective enough; he has little success in achieving the tranquillity and rapture (at fig. 6) that made Kajanus's set such a memorable experience. The *Sixth* is much less successful than the *Third*; Maazel does not penetrate beneath the surface and seems to have little sympathy for this most elusive and refined of Sibelius's scores. It is a pity that this issue is only partly success-

ful; the recording is first-class, and apart from a short passage where the timpani cause a little muddle in the climax of the first movement of No. 3 the transfer is sophisticated, with plenty of body and detail throughout.

Symphony No. 4 in A minor, Op. 63; The Bard (symphonic poem), *Op. 64.*
(**)HMV TC-ASD 3340. Bournemouth SO, Berglund.
Symphony No. 4; Tapiola (symphonic poem), *Op. 112.*
***Philips 7300 520 [id.]. Boston SO, Colin Davis.
(M) *** Decca Jubilee KJBC 45. Vienna PO, Maazel.
*** HMV TC-ASD 3485. Berlin PO, Karajan.

The coupling of the *Fourth Symphony* with *Tapiola* has been extraordinarily successful in the recording studio, and any of the three available cassettes may be purchased with confidence, though Colin Davis's is marginally the least vivid as sound because of the unadventurous level of the Philips transfer. Even so, the overall quality remains natural and well balanced, and hiss is not too troublesome. Undoubtedly this is a totally idiomatic and thoroughly concentrated account of the *Fourth Symphony*, arguably the finest of Davis's Sibelius cycle; there is a powerful sense of mystery, and the slow movement in particular conveys the feeling of communion with nature that lies at the heart of its inspiration. Tempi relate beautifully and Davis has the courage to take the slow movement really slowly. This is one of the finest recordings of the *Fourth* ever made and is coupled with an outstanding *Tapiola*, atmospheric and superbly played.

The *Fourth* is also the most impressive of Maazel's Sibelius cycle. The orchestral tone is less richly upholstered than that of the Berlin Philharmonic in Karajan's account, and Maazel brings to the music great concentration and power: the first movement is as cold and unremitting as one could wish, and throughout the work Maazel comes closer to the atmosphere and mystery of this music than almost anyone since Beecham. Apart from the slow movement, which could be a little more poetic, and one or two small points, there are no real reservations to be made. The recording here is superbly opulent and vivid. Maazel also gives a most impressive account of *Tapiola*. It is not so atmospheric as Karajan's at the outset, but it grows in power and impact as it proceeds. Maazel takes the famous storm section very slowly, and it gains immeasurably from this. Colin Davis's Boston account is superior to Maazel's in terms of sheer mystery and power, although the storm section is not as effectively done, and on tape the Philips sound is less vivid, for the transfer of Maazel's performances is of Decca's highest quality, with the most refined detail, the orchestral sound given splendid weight and atmosphere. At the climax of *Tapiola* there is just a hint of shrillness in the upper strings; otherwise this is a demonstration tape. Moreover the symphony is complete on side one without a turnover break before the finale. At medium price this issue is a real bargain.

In some ways Karajan's re-recording of the *Fourth Symphony* for HMV must be counted controversial. He gives broadly spacious – and highly atmospheric – accounts of the first and third movements, a good deal slower than in his earlier DG version (not available on cassette). He conveys eloquently the other-worldly quality of the landscape in the third movement, even if in atmosphere the Colin Davis account is more natural and intense. The first movement undoubtedly has great mystery and power. The recording is superb and the tape transfer is highly successful (one of HMV's very best cassettes), admirably rich and full, yet with no lack of detail and bite. The resonant warmth in the

bass is very striking, yet the upper range too is very good. Karajan's *Tapiola*, which is discussed above under its alternative coupling with *Finlandia* (TC-ASD 3374), is hardly less impressive, despite the error in bar 598.

Berglund's recording is not wanting in atmosphere; the brooding opening of the symphony is imaginatively caught. The contrasts of the slow movement are emphasized by the creation of a background of desolation from which the surges of emotional feeling well up with impressive force. But the comparative restraint of the interpretation as a whole, with its elegiac conclusion, lacks the power and concentration of the competing versions. The HMV sound is rich and spacious, but the tape transfer has poor definition, notably in the middle strings. Berglund's performance of *The Bard* is outstandingly fine, and the orchestral playing here (as in the symphony) is first-class. But this tape cannot really compete with the three outstanding versions listed above.

Symphony No. 4 in A minor, Op. 63; (i) *Luonnotar* (for soprano and orchestra), *Op. 70.*

> (M) *(*) CBS Classics 40-61807 [(d) Col. MT 32843]. New York PO, Bernstein, (i) with Phyllis Curtin (soprano).

Bernstein takes a dramatic view of the *Fourth*; indeed some will find it over-dramatized. The slow movement will prove too glamorized for some tastes and the finale too measured. Yet Bernstein is no mean Sibelian and his thoughts on this score are by no means to be discounted. What cannot be recommended, alas, is the *Luonnotar*, which is insensitive and wanting in mystery. Phyllis Curtin's contribution is not helped by the transfer, which tends to edge the voice somewhat uncomfortably. Otherwise the sound on tape is acceptable, if not outstanding.

Symphonies Nos. 4 in A minor, Op. 63; 5 in E flat major, Op. 82.

521

*RCA RK 11747. RPO, Tjekna-
vorian.

Tjeknavorian and the RPO are well
recorded. Tempi are brisk in the *Fourth
Symphony*, except in the finale, and Tjeknavorian plays the *Fifth* with almost no
pause between movements. His tempo is
well-judged for the first movement but a
good deal faster than is desirable in the
middle movement. These are unegotistic
and unmannered readings but basically
rather ordinary. The transfers are only a
mixed success. Although No. 5 generally
has more body than No. 4, where the
massed upper strings are fierce, the upper
range of the recording tends to lack focus
at times and tuttis are often brash and ill-
defined.

*Symphony No. 5 in E flat major, Op.
82; En Saga, Op. 9.*
*** HMV TC-ASD 3409 [Angel
4XS 37490]. Berlin PO,
Karajan.
(B) *(*) Classics for Pleasure TC-
CFP 40218. Scottish National
Orch., Gibson.
Symphony No. 5; Finlandia, Op. 26.
*** DG 923039 [id.]. Berlin PO,
Karajan.
*Symphony No. 5; Pohjola's Daugh-
ter* (symphonic poem), *Op. 49.*
(M) **(*) CBS Classics 40-61808.
New York PO, Bernstein.

The newest HMV issue is Karajan's
fourth recording of Sibelius's *Fifth Symphony*, and in many respects it must be
counted the finest, although even so it by
no means displaces the 1965 DG version.
The first movement is broader and more
spacious on HMV and Karajan achieves
a remarkable sense of its power and
majesty. His transition from the work's
first section to the 'scherzo' is slightly
more abrupt than in the 1965 recording,
and the tempi generally in the work's
first half are rather more extreme. The
variety of tone colour and above all the

weight of sonority that the Berlin Philharmonic have at their command are
astonishing, and the bassoon lament in
the development section finds the Berlin
strings reduced to the merest whisper.
Both the slow movement and finale are
glorious and have real vision, and the recording is excellent (as indeed it is in the
1965 DG version too). Some Sibelians
are worried by the richness and sensuousness that Karajan brings to this score, but
the sheer power and depth of this reading
should convince. The performance of *En
Saga*, which is discussed above under its
alternative coupling with *Finlandia* (TC-
ASD 3374), is no less compelling. The
transfer to tape offers satisfyingly rich
orchestral sound; although the detail of
climaxes lacks the last degree of definition, the refinement does not slip. The
sheer weight of sound in *En Saga* is
undoubtedly thrilling.

Turning to Karajan's earlier reading
for DG, one finds that the newly Dolbyized transfer offers astonishingly vivid
sound, with more range and detail than in
the HMV version. There is perhaps
slightly less body, but this was always a
full-blooded recording and there is certainly no lack of weight. The bite and
detail of the recording are impressive
throughout and reveal a sense of power
and atmosphere in the orchestral playing
that all but matches the newer version.
The finale is riveting; the Berlin Philharmonic brass create some superb sonorities here. Those preferring *Finlandia* to
En Saga as a filler will find that this too is
splendidly played, and brilliantly and
sonorously transferred. This is a very
good tape indeed.

Bernstein's *Fifth* is splendidly played
and totally unmannered. It is in fact a
reading of genuine stature, among the
finest currently available. Its price tells in
its favour as well, and though the recording is not as rich as in both of Karajan's
versions, the quality of this performance
earns it the strongest recommendation.
The fill-up is a finely proportioned reading of *Pohjola's Daughter*. On tape the

sound has undoubted weight and impact, although the bass is rather dry and the treble needs cutting back. But a good balance can be achieved, and this is certainly a thrilling performance.

Gibson's Scottish version is straightforward and refreshingly unmannered, and has the advantage of spacious and well-balanced recording. An eminently serviceable but far from outstanding tape: both the interpretation and the orchestral playing are sound rather than inspired. The transfer is vivid, though it has a somewhat limited dynamic range. However, the performance of the symphony is not entirely robbed of its dynamic contrasts, and *En Saga* is effective too.

Symphonies Nos. 5 in E flat major, Op. 82; 7 in C major, Op. 105.
  (M) **(*) Decca Jubilee KJBC 46. Vienna PO, Maazel.
  **(*) Philips 7300 415 [id.]. Boston SO, Colin Davis.

Maazel's *Fifth Symphony* is terribly fast, though it sets out at the same tempo as Karajan's. His second movement is twice as fast as Karajan's versions; hence there is little sense of space or breadth – or for that matter mystery – in this performance. The *Seventh*, on the other hand, is marvellous: this is the greatest account of the work since Koussevitzky's 78 r.p.m. recording, and has a rugged, epic power that is truly thrilling. Indeed the closing pages are as fine as Koussevitzky's, and no praise could be higher. The recording is superlative, with an excellent cassette transfer of striking range and definition – well up to the high standard of this excellent Jubilee series.

Good unfussy performances from Colin Davis and the Boston orchestra, though in the *Seventh* he is no match for Maazel or Koussevitzky. The *Fifth* is a little lacking in atmosphere, though it is more idiomatic than Maazel's. The recording is not the equal of the Decca version (it is curiously two-dimensional and a little lacking in transparency), and we could do without Colin Davis's vocalizations. The cassette transfer is faithful, although made at rather a low level.

Symphonies Nos. 6 in D minor, Op. 104; 7 in C major, Op. 105.
  (M) ** CBS Classics 40-61806. New York PO, Bernstein.

Bernstein's account of the *Sixth* is an eminently recommendable one, but he is by no means as sensitive in his handling of detail as Davis (see above under the *Third Symphony*). Yet the basic shape and atmosphere are right, and the recording is eminently acceptable, even if the dynamic range could be wider. The *Seventh* is finer still and has something of the spirit of Koussevitzky about it, even if the recording is not in the first flight. The transfer is generally acceptable, although some rebalancing will be necessary – the bass is light and the treble bright – but there is no lack of underlying weight even if the strings at the opening and close of No. 6 are a little wanting in body.

Karajan's tape of this coupling is not Dolbyized.

Tapiola (symphonic poem), *Op. 112:* see under *Finlandia, The Oceanides,* and *Symphony No. 4.*

The Tempest (incidental music), *Op. 109: Suites Nos. 1 and 2; In Memoriam* (funeral march), *Op. 59.*
  ** HMV TC-ASD 2961. Royal Liverpool PO, Groves.

The EMI recording for *The Tempest* music is naturally balanced and well detailed. In the *Oak-tree* and *The Chorus of the Winds* Groves does not distil the magic that distinguished Beecham's famous mono set, but the playing is eminently satisfactory. The tape transfer is not brilliant but quite acceptable: the sound has plenty of body. A little more sparkle would have been welcome, but the treble is not muffled.

Songs: *Arioso; Diamenten på Marss-non; Den Första Kyssen; Flickan kom ifrån sin älsklings möte; Höst-kväll; Kom nu hit; Men min Fågel märks dock icke; Om Kvällen; På Verandan vid Havet; Säf, säf, susa; Se'n har jag ej frågat mera; Svarta Rosor; Var det en dröm; Våren fly-ktar hastigt.*

(M) *** Decca Eclipse KECC 794. Kirsten Flagstad (soprano), LSO, Fjeldstad.

The songs of Sibelius command a much smaller audience than his symph-onies, but they are not less reflective of his genius for melody. Some of the songs were orchestrated by the composer, but seven of them remained in their original form (voice and piano) until trans-formed, usually with great skill, by such arrangers as Jalas, Pingoud, Fougsted, and Hellman. This recording, made in the early days of stereo, still sounds astonish-ingly good, and Sibelius-singing doesn't come like this any more! These classic performances give a magnificent impres-sion of Sibelius's not inconsiderable range as a song composer. Songs such as *Höstkväll (Autumn evening)* are among his greatest works apart from the symph-onies, and never have they been more radiantly performed. The tape transfer is admirably clear and well balanced, but it produces a touch of edge on the voice. This can be smoothed satisfactor-ily with the controls without further im-pairing the orchestral detail (which is atmospheric rather than crystal-clear). Recommended.

'*Favourite composer*': (i; ii) *Violin concerto in D minor, Op. 47; (iii) Fin-landia, Op. 26; (ii; iv) Karelia suite, Op. 11; (iii) Kuolema: Valse triste, Op. 44; Legend: The Swan of Tuo-nela, Op. 22/2; (ii; v) Symphony No. 2 in D major, Op. 43.*

(B) **(*)Decca KDPC 531/2. (i)

Ruggiero Ricci (violin), cond. Fjeldstad; (ii) LSO; (iii) Hunga-rian State SO, Jalas; (iv) Gibson; (v) Monteux.

There is nothing seriously to fault here, though it is a pity that Maazel's version of *Karelia* was not chosen instead of the relatively flabby account under Gibson. The main works are given distinguished performances, and *The Swan of Tuonela* even seems to sound more atmospheric here than on the parent LP. The cassettes are brilliantly transferred, the sound rather brighter than on the LPs. The symphony (on the second tape) sounds freshly incisive without being aggressive in its string timbre.

Smetana, Bedřich (1824–84)

Má Vlast (Vyšehrad; Vltava (Moldau); Sárka; From Bohemia's Woods and Fields; Tábor; Blaník).
   HMV TC-SLS 5151. Dresden State Orch., Berglund (with DVOŘÁK: *Scherzo capriccioso; Slavonic rhapsody No. 3*).
   (M) **(*) Supraphon 0450521. Czech PO, Ančerl.
   **(*)DG 3300 895. Boston SO, Kubelik.
   (M)(*)Decca KDPC 2 7044. Vienna PO, Kubelik.

Paavo Berglund's new complete *Má Vlast* with the Dresden Staatskapelle is undoubtedly the finest recording of this elusive cycle of symphonic poems to have appeared in stereo, on tape or disc. Whereas so many recorded performances have done well by *Vltava* and *From Bohemia's Woods and Fields* and then fallen short on the other four pieces, it is in these lesser-known works that

Berglund is most impressive. Indeed if there is a criticism of this set it is that *Vltava*, although splendidly played, seems slightly under-characterized alongside the other sections of the score. The opening *Vyšerad* is most beautifully played, full of lyrical evocation and atmosphere, while *Sárka* is arrestingly dramatic. *Tábor* and *Blaník* are played together and so often in previous accounts they have become engulfed in rhetoric: but not here. Berglund never lets the forceful rhythms hammer the listener into the ground, and the national feeling that is the basis of their inspiration here sounds surgingly jubilant. The closing pages of *Tábor* are beautifully managed, and the pastoral interlude in *Blaník* is engagingly lightweight, so that when the closing chorale appears it has a lilting step and conjures up memories of *The Bartered Bride* rather than bombastic militarism. The end of the work has a joyous release. Berglund does not shirk the melodrama, but he never lets it get the better of him. The Dresden orchestra plays magnificently and the recording is rich and full-blooded, the sound on tape virtually indistinguishable from the LPs. The two Dvořák bonuses are no less engagingly played (the *Slavonic rhapsody* is delightfully fresh), and the recording is equally successful here.

The Supraphon issue of *Má Vlast*, complete on one medium-priced tape, is not only a fine bargain but is a clear case where the sound on tape is preferable to the equivalent LPs, which sound edgy and artificially bright. On tape the quality is clear and sparkling, but there is little edge and a good overall balance producing plenty of weight. The performances have fine character, and the playing of the Czech Philharmonic adds a special degree of colour and rhythmic feeling to Ančerl's performances. The patriotism in the two final works is not overdone and while the recording does not match those from the finest Western sources it is fully acceptable.

Kubelik's DG performance is much more perceptive and penetrating than his earlier Decca set. He is careful to temper the bombast which too readily comes to the surface in this music (in *Tábor* and *Blaník* especially), and his skill with the inner balance of the orchestration brings much felicitous detail. The performances of the two unquestioned masterpieces of the cycle, *Vltava* and *From Bohemia's Woods and Fields*, are very well made, and throughout the orchestral playing is first-class. Just occasionally a touch more flair would have brought the orchestral colours out more vividly, but this lack of colour is partly caused by the DG sound, which, although admirably brilliant and clear, rather lacks sumptuousness and warmth of texture. However, this has the advantage that the louder, brassy passages are not allowed to degenerate into noise. The tape issue is fairly economically priced, since it offers the content of two LPs on one full-priced cassette, and the quality is good, full-bodied (in some ways more so than in the equivalent discs) but slightly below DG's highest standards. There is a slight lack of range in the treble, and every now and then our review copy had some fluttering discoloration in the wind (first noticed in the clarinet solo in *Vyšehrad*). However, this may have been cured in later copies.

The Decca set must be discounted on grounds of recording. The strings are thin and papery, the high treble peaky, and there is a feeling of congestion at climaxes. The Vienna Philharmonic are on good form, but Kubelik's readings here are somewhat lacking in purpose and colour. The tape is more satisfactory than the discs.

Má Vlast: Vyšehrad; Vltava.
  (*) DG 923049 [id.]. Berlin PO, Karajan – LISZT: *Hungarian rhapsody No. 2; Les Préludes.*(*)
Má Vlast: Vltava.
  *(**)HMV TC-ASD 3407 [Angel 4xs 37437]. Berlin PO, Karajan

– DVOŘÁK: *Symphony No. 9.**(**)

Vltava is such a well-made piece that it cannot but suit the virtuoso conductor, who has only to conjure first-rate playing, following the score, and the music makes its own points. On DG Karajan brings the music fully alive, and he is also most persuasive in the beautiful opening and closing pages of *Vyšehrad*, dominated by the bard-like harp. The central section is less convincing, but perhaps this is partly the composer's fault. Brilliant recording, generally well transferred, if not quite as clean in focus as the equivalent LP. The more recent recording of *Vltava* on HMV is also very well played; the recording, although rich, is not ideally refined in detail.

Má Vlast: Vltava; From Bohemia's Woods and Fields.
(M) **(*) DG Privilege 3318 047. Boston SO, Kubelik – DVOŘÁK: *String serenade.****

It was a happy idea to couple the two favourites from *Má Vlast* with Dvořák's *String serenade*. Hearing them out of context, however, one is more conscious that the recordings, while admirably clear and well-balanced, are slightly dry and lacking in atmosphere, and this is reflected in the otherwise admirable cassette transfer.

Má Vlast: Vltava. The Bartered Bride: Overture; Polka; Furiant; Dance of the Comedians.
(M) *(**) HMV TC-EXE 182. LPO, Boult – TCHAIKOVSKY: *Romeo and Juliet.***(*)

There is splendid life and colour in these performances, which are well played and recorded. Boult's account of *Romeo and Juliet* has an element of reserve, but in all other respects this coupling can be strongly recommended. The cassette is very highly modulated and there is some roughness in places, although the quality is otherwise vivid.

String quartets Nos. 1 in E minor (From my life); 2 in D minor.
(M) *** Decca Ace of Diamonds KSDC 529. Gabrieli Qt.

The only other issue that couples these two works together is the Supraphon version by the Smetana Quartet, and that is not available on cassette. Even if the competition were stiff, however, the Gabrielis would have strong claims: artistically both performances are first-class; technically they offer vivid and well-balanced recorded sound which has transferred to cassette with exemplary smoothness and range; and moreover they are at medium price. The *Second Quartet* is not the equal of the more popular autobiographical E minor work, but it is attractive nonetheless. This issue will give great satisfaction whether on disc or cassette. Strongly recommended.

10 Czech dances: Furiant; Slepička; Oves; Medved; Cibulička; Dupak; Hulán; Obkrocák; Sousedská; Skočná.
(M) ** Turnabout KTVC 34673. Rudolf Firkusny (piano).

These ten dances comprise Smetana's second set, written in 1879, some five years after the onset of his deafness, and they include some remarkably fine music. The piano recording is not of the first class: the balance is close and it tends to be slightly bottom-heavy. Yet with suitable adjustment of the controls it can be made to yield pleasing results, and there is little to choose between the disc and the cassette as far as quality is concerned.

Smyth, Ethel
(1858–1944)

The Wreckers: overture.
> (***) HMV TC-ASD 2400. Scottish National Orch., Gibson – HARTY: *With the Wild Geese;* MACCUNN: *Land of Mountain and Flood;* GERMAN: *Welsh rhapsody.*(***)

Ethel Smyth, one of the first emancipated English feminists, almost unbelievably managed to get all six of her operas produced during the time when the suffragette movement was gathering momentum. The best-known is *The Wreckers* (first performed in England in 1909), and we must hope that one day the piece will be revived. Meanwhile the *Overture* is a strong meaty piece, which shows the calibre of this remarkable woman's personality, for while the material itself is not memorable it is put together most compellingly and orchestrated with real flair. The story concerns the wrecking of ships by false signal lights on the Cornish coast. The recording is full-blooded, but the tape transfer has a narrowed dynamic range; the orchestral textures are thick and lacking in transparency of detail.

Soler, Antonio
(1729–83)

Keyboard sonatas: in A minor; C minor; D major (2); D minor; D flat major; F major; F sharp major; G major; G minor.
> *(*) Advent E 1050 (see p. xxiii) [id.]. Fernando Valenti (harpsichord).

Vital performances of ten sonatas by Soler, who, although not the equal of Domenico Scarlatti, is still a rewarding enough composer to warrant attention. The harpsichord is vividly (if somewhat closely) recorded, but satisfactory results may be obtained by reducing the level at which the sound is reproduced. Heard one after the other, the effect of these sonatas is a trifle monotonous, but taken in small doses, the rewards are greater. The transfer is immaculate.

Sor, Fernando
(1778–1839)

Sonata in C major (Deuxième grande sonate), Op. 25.
> (***) RCA RK 10711 [ARK 1 0711]. Julian Bream (guitar) – GIULIANI: *Le Rossiniane.*(***)

Sor's *Sonata* is an extremely inconsequential work, here beautifully played and immaculately recorded. Like the coupling this is instantly forgettable music. The transfer is admirably clean and clear.

Sousa, John Philip
(1854–1932)

Marches: El Capitan; Hands across the Sea; High School Cadets; The Invincible Eagle; King Cotton; Liberty Bell; Manhattan Beach; The Picadore; Semper fidelis; Stars and Stripes Forever; The Thunderer; Washington Post.
> (***) Decca Phase 4 KPFC 4134. Grenadier Guards Band, Bashford.

527

The buoyant breeziness of the presentation here is admirable and the piccolo solo in *Stars and Stripes* floats out beautifully. This tape includes a highly enjoyable programme of some of Sousa's best and most famous pieces. Unfortunately the current transfer of this collection has not been well-managed. The opening *Stars and Stripes* is badly clouded with bass-drum reverberation and elsewhere the high-level transfer produces congestion.

Marches: *El Capitan; High School Cadets; The Invincible Eagle; King Cotton; Liberty Bell; Manhattan Beach; The Picadore; Semper fidelis; Stars and Stripes Forever; Washington Post.*
(M)**Decca KCSP 404. Grenadier Guards Band, Harris.

These are fresh 'marching' performances in the English manner, well played and alive, if without the unbuttoned American exuberance one would expect from the other side of the Atlantic. The sound is excellent, crisp and clear, and the cassette transfer is good, with only a marginal loss of crispness in the transients.

Stainer, John
(1840–1901)

The Crucifixion.
(M) ** Enigma K 423523. James Griffett (tenor), Michael George (bass), Peterborough Cathedral Choir, Vann; Andrew Newberry (organ).

This performance is sincere and eloquent in a modestly restrained way. In his efforts not to overdramatize the narrative, Stanley Vann falls into the opposite trap of understatement, and there is a lack of vitality at times. The two soloists

make a stronger contribution, and the tenor, James Griffett, is pleasingly lyrical. However, the style of presentation does not wholly avoid hints of the sentimentality that hovers dangerously near all performances of this work. The recording is atmospheric, the choral sounds warm rather than incisive; but the tape transfer is of excellent quality. The soloists are projected well, and Andrew Newberry's fine organ accompaniment is well balanced.

Strauss, Franz
(1822–1905)

Horn concerto in C minor, Op. 8.
(M) *(*) Decca Jubilee KJBC 17. Barry Tuckwell, LSO, Kertesz
— R. STRAUSS: *Horn concertos.***

This concerto by Franz Strauss, Richard's father, has its moments, but it shows a distressing tendency to fall into the style of the cornet air with variations. There are some bright ideas in the work too, of course, but nothing to stop the score being put back in the attic where it rightly belongs. The transfer is clear and detailed in spite of a fair degree of resonance. The recording seems slightly richer than in the coupling.

Strauss, Johann, Snr
(1804–49)

Strauss, Johann, Jnr
(1825–99)

Strauss, Josef
(see also below)
(1827–70)

Strauss, Eduard
(1835–1916)

(All music listed is by Johann Strauss Jnr unless otherwise stated)

Bal de Vienne (ballet suite for *Die Fledermaus*, Act 2, arr. from Johann Snr and Jnr and Josef Strauss by Douglas Gamley); *Le Beau Danube* (ballet suite, arr. Désormière); *Die Fledermaus: overture.*
> *** Decca KSXC 6701 [Lon. 5-6896]. National PO, Bonynge.

Bonynge gives a straight-faced account of the *Die Fledermaus overture* but comes into his own in the vivacious ballet music, which is presented with effervescent sparkle. Much of the music here is unfamiliar Strauss, but it is all tuneful and gay in spirit. The Decca recording is superb, and the tape transfer is extremely brilliant.

Le Beau Danube (ballet suite, arr. Désormière).
> (B) *** DG Heliodor 3348 248. Berlin Radio Orch., Paul Strauss – OFFENBACH: *Gaîté Parisienne.****

Le Beau Danube as a score is not so adroitly chosen as *Graduation Ball*, but it is entertaining, if lightweight, and it is played here with vivacity and style,

though without the superb élan of the coupling. The recording sparkles and does not sound its age. The cassette transfer is splendid, every bit as good as the disc.

Graduation Ball (ballet, arr. Dorati).
> **(*) Decca KSXC 6867. Vienna PO, Dorati.

(i) *Graduation Ball;* (ii) *Die Fledermaus: overture and ballet music.*
> (M) ** Decca KCSP 406. Vienna PO, (i) Boskovsky; (ii) Karajan, with Vienna State Opera Chorus – WEBER: *Invitation to the Dance.***

Since Dorati arranged the music for *Graduation Ball* it was understandable that Decca should choose him to direct their third recording of this attractive score (the first, and best, was conducted by Fistoulari in the mono era). In his liner-notes Dorati tells us that he regards the work (written in partnership with the choreographer David Lichine for the Ballets Russes de Monte Carlo) as a 'youthful prank' or 'escapade', and his musical direction follows this mood. It is immensely spirited, even exhilarating, but barely hints at the charming romanticism with which the ballet itself is imbued. Both the opening of the work and the nostalgic closing section lack a sense of atmosphere, not helped by Decca's brilliantly lit recording. However, many of the flamboyant solo dances come off vividly, and the waltzes are not without lilt, so that in its zestful exuberance this is enjoyable enough, and Dorati welds the seams between the individual items skilfully. The transfer is extremely vivid and full-blooded, but it needs some treble cut if the upper strings are not to sound slightly fierce.

Boskovsky does not always treat *Graduation Ball* as a continuous ballet score; he obviously thinks of each item individually in terms of a concert performance. In consequence he inevitably loses some of the continuity of Dorati's clever patchwork quilt, which can form a surprisingly well integrated whole. Having said this, one can add that the playing is first-class and the recording lively. Its brightness is particularly attractive in the *Perpetuum mobile*, which Boskovsky does with great style. For this reissue Decca have added a bonus item, music from *Die Fledermaus* taken from Karajan's Decca complete set. All in all, this is well worth considering, and it is fairly priced; the cassette transfer is suitably brilliant, if a little sharp-edged.

COLLECTIONS OF WALTZES, POLKAS, etc.

(Listed in alphabetical order under the name of the conductor and then in numerical order using the manufacturers' catalogue numbers, which often produces a date-of-issue sequence)

Annen polka, Op. 117; An der schönen blauen Donau (Blue Danube) waltz, Op. 314; Geschichten aus dem Wiener Wald (Tales from the Vienna Woods) waltz, Op. 325; Overtures: *Die Fledermaus; Der Zigeunerbaron; Pizzicato polka* (written with Josef Strauss). STRAUSS, Johann, Snr: *Radetzky march, Op. 228.*

   (B)**(*)Pye ZCCCB 15024. Hallé Orch., Barbirolli.

Those who remember Sir John Barbirolli's Manchester Viennese concerts will find that he managed to capture much of the spontaneity of those occasions in this well-planned programme. Each side begins with an overture, presented with great panache and vivacity, and after the march or polkas comes one of the two greatest waltzes. The performance of the *Blue Danube* is especially successful, while the intimacy of atmosphere at the opening of *Tales from the Vienna Woods*

is no less beguiling. The recording has been vividly transferred to tape (the sound having more presence than on the equivalent disc), but the reverberation has brought some slipping of refinement in fortissimos. This is most noticeable in the *Radetzky march*, which is given an element of coarseness. But this remains a most enjoyable collection.

Perpetuum mobile, Op. 257; Polkas: *Annen, Op. 117; Unter Donner und Blitz (Thunder and Lightning), Op. 324; Tritsch-Tratsch, Op. 214; Pizzicato* (with Josef); Waltzes: *An der schönen blauen Donau, Op. 314; Kaiser (Emperor), Op. 437; Rosen aus dem Süden (Roses from the South), Op. 388.*

   *** DG 3300 299. Vienna PO. Boehm.

Boehm's affection is obvious throughout this concert, and he is especially warm in shaping the lovely preludes and postludes to the waltzes. His relaxed manner and unashamed rhythmic freedom are overtly personal, but there is undoubted spontaneity throughout and the lilt of the waltzes is persuasive. *Roses from the South* is outstanding; this is one of the finest versions in the catalogue. Perhaps the *Emperor* demands a shade more fervour, but Boehm's leisurely manner both here and in the *Blue Danube* is certainly beguiling. The polkas too are taken much slower than usual, but the VPO string playing in both the *Annen* and *Pizzicato* is memorable. The recording is first-class, with an atmospheric richness to suit the music-making. The tape we sampled was very sophisticated indeed, with fine detail and bloom.

'The world of Strauss', Vol. 2: Der Zigeunerbaron overture; Polkas: *Annen, Op. 117; Leichtes Blut, Op. 319; Neue Pizzicato, Op. 449; Tritsch-Tratsch, Op. 214;* Waltzes: *Accelerationen, Op. 234; Kaiser, Op.*

437; Künstlerleben (Artist's Life), Op. 316. STRAUSS, Johann, Snr: Radetzky march, Op. 228.

(M) ** Decca KCSP 73. Vienna PO, Boskovsky or Knappertsbusch.

Volume 1 is the best of the three collections Decca have issued in the *World of Strauss* series. Within a most attractively made programme it includes both *The Blue Danube* and *Tales from the Vienna Woods*, but the cassette (KCSP 10) is still non-Dolbyized and cannot be recommended until Decca decide to withdraw their pre-Dolby tapes and reissue them.

In Volume 2 Boskovsky shares the musical direction with Hans Knappertsbusch, who has earned a gramophone reputation for rather slow and sometimes lethargic tempi. But these performances (he conducts the *March*, all the polkas except the *New pizzicato*, and the *Accelerations waltz*) are lively and committed. Boskovsky conducts the rest of the programme, and the recording for his items adds an extra richness. The playing throughout has the authentic Viennese lilt and this is an enjoyable concert, though not as fine as the first volume of the series. The transfer is vivid, lacking only the last degree of refinement.

'The world of Strauss', Vol. 3: Persian march, Op. 289; Die Fledermaus overture; Polkas: Eljen a Magyar, Op. 332; Explosionen, Op. 43; Unter Donner und Blitz, Op. 324; Waltzes: Du und du (Fledermaus waltz), Op. 367; Liebeslieder; Morgenblätter (Morning Papers), Op. 279; Wein, Weib und Gesang (Wine, Woman and Song), Op. 333; Wiener Bonbons, Op. 307.

(M) *(*) Decca KCSP 312. Vienna PO, Boskovsky.

Most of these recordings date from the end of the fifties, but the resonance of the recording provides a pleasing bloom, characteristic of this series, and only the string tone hints at the age of the originals. The *Fledermaus waltz* with its massed upper strings sounds a little spiky but yields to the controls. Boskovsky and his orchestra are on top form throughout, playing the waltzes with affection but without slackness. The overture opens the concert, and the march and polkas are interspersed to make a most attractive selection. However, this is not one of Decca's best transfers: the bass line is not clear and there are patches of reverberation trouble with the bass drum. Side two is less clearly focused than side one.

'Favourite waltzes': An der schönen blauen Donau, Op. 314; Du und du, Op. 367; Frühlingsstimmen (Voices of Spring), Op. 410; Geschichten aus dem Wiener Wald, Op. 325; Kaiser, Op. 437; Künstlerleben, Op. 316; Rosen aus dem Süden, Op. 388; Tausend und eine Nacht (1001 Nights), Op. 346; Wein, Weib und Gesang, Op. 333; Wiener Blut (Vienna Blood), Op. 354; Wiener Bonbons, Op. 307.

(B) **(*) Decca KDPC 513/4. Vienna PO, Boskovsky.

One might think that a succession of Strauss waltzes spread over two cassettes would produce a degree of listening monotony, but that is never the case here, such is the composer's resource in the matter of melody and orchestration. There are some splendid performances, and the transfer is admirably smooth and vivid enough, though there is just a marginal lack of sparkle on the second of the two cassettes.

'Favourite composer': Overture: Die Fledermaus; Der Zigeunerbaron. Egyptian march, Op. 335. Perpetuum mobile, Op. 257. Polkas: Auf der Jagd, Op. 373; Explosionen, Op. 43; Neue Pizzicato, Op. 449; Pizzicato (with Josef); Unter Donner und Blitz,

531

Op. 324. Waltzes: *An der schönen blauen Donau, Op. 314; Du und du, Op. 367; Frühlingsstimmen, Op. 410; Geschichten aus dem Wiener Wald, Op. 325; Kaiser, Op. 437; Künstlerleben, Op. 316; Rosen aus dem Süden, Op. 388; Tausend und eine Nacht, Op. 346; Wein, Weib und Gesang, Op. 333; Wiener Blut, Op. 354.*

(B) **(*) Decca KDPC 549/50. Vienna PO, Boskovsky.

Following a tradition begun in the days of mono LPs with Clemens Krauss, Decca have over the years issued a series of incomparable stereo issues of the music of the Strauss family conducted with almost unfailing sparkle by Willi Boskovsky. The VPO have a tradition of New Year Strauss concerts, and it has become a happy idea at Decca to link the new issues with the year's turn. This two-cassette compilation, like the more expensive three-cassette set below, uses material from the recordings made during the early sixties, and with many favourites included it is a safe investment for those not objecting to a somewhat variable recorded quality. The cassette sound is markedly different between the two tapes. On the first it is agreeably smooth; on tape two the level is higher, which brings a more vivid effect but less refinement and rather too explosive sound effects in the *Explosionen polka*.

Waltzes: *An der schönen blauen Donau, Op. 314; Geschichten aus dem Wiener Wald, Op. 325; Kaiser, Op. 437; Rosen aus dem Süden, Op. 388; Wein Weib und Gesang, Op. 333; Wiener Blut, Op. 354.*

(M)**HMV Greensleeve TC-ESD 7025 [Angel 4xs 37070]. Johann Strauss Orch. of Vienna, Boskovsky.

Boskovsky's HMV recordings were made in the early seventies, and the qual-

ity is smoother than on the earliest of his Decca collections. However, the warm resonance of the sound does not provide a great deal of detail or sparkle, and although the playing is affectionate and idiomatic there is not the flair and spontaneity here that make Boskovsky's Decca series so distinctive. The cassette compares very favourably with the LP: there is very little difference, in fact.

'Music of the Strauss family': Polkas: *Champagne, Op. 211; Eljen a Magyar, Op. 332; Im Krapfenwald'l, Op. 336; Neue Pizzicato, Op. 449;* Waltzes: *Immer heiterer, Op. 235; Künstlerleben, Op. 316; Neu-Wien, Op. 342; Wo die Zitronen blühen (Where the Lemon Trees Bloom), Op. 364.* STRAUSS, Eduard: *Bahn frei polka galop, Op. 45.* STRAUSS, Johann, Snr: *Radetzky march, Op. 228; Seufzer-Galop, Op. 9.* STRAUSS, Josef: *Künstlergruss, Op. 274.*

(M)**HMV Greensleeve TC-ESD 7052. Johann Strauss Orch. of Vienna, Boskovsky.

This selection is imaginative and generous, and it is well played. But the polkas come off more successfully than the waltzes, where, though there is no absence of lilt, the rather suave style of the playing lacks the freshness of Boskovsky's Decca series. The recording is excellent, rich and with plenty of brilliance, and it has transferred to tape very successfully.

'Family concert': Spanish march, *Op. 433.* Polkas: *Demolirer, Op. 269; Pizzicato* (with Josef). *Du und du (Fledermaus waltz), Op. 367.* STRAUSS, Johann, Jnr, Josef, and Eduard: *Schützenquadrille.* STRAUSS, Eduard: *Bahn frei polka galop, Op. 45.* STRAUSS, Johann, Snr: *Radetzky march, Op. 228.* STRAUSS, Josef:

Brennende Liebe polka, Op. 129;
Transaktionen waltz, Op. 184.

(M) ** Decca Jubilee KJBC 28.
Vienna PO, Boskovsky.

In this further reshuffling of earlier
Boskovsky/VPO material for Decca's
Jubilee label there seems to be too great a
proportion of music in duple or quadruple time; there is only one waltz (from
Fledermaus). The programme opens with
the *Radetzky march*, and on tape this is
highly modulated, producing a rather
fierce sound, and a similar impression is
given in the *Bahn frei polka*, which
opens side two. Indeed although the
sound is lively and colourful throughout,
it is not as refined as on the best Decca
tapes, and the reverberation seems to give
too much emphasis at the bass end (although this can be corrected). The collection is valuable for the inclusion of the
Schützenquadrille, to which all three
brothers contributed (it was written for a
Viennese shooting contest in 1868).

'Invitation to a Strauss festival':
Marches: *Napoleon, Op. 156; Per-*
sian, Op. 289. Perpetuum mobile, Op.
257. Polkas: *Auf der Jagd, Op. 373;*
Banditen, Op. 378; Champagne, Op.
211; Eljen a Magyar, Op. 332; Ex-
plosionen, Op. 43; Neue Pizzicato,
Op. 449; Pizzicato (with Josef);
Unter Donner und Blitz, Op. 324.
Waltzes: *An der schönen blauen*
Donau, Op. 314; Frühlingsstimmen,
Op. 410; Geschichten aus dem Wiener
Wald, Op. 325; Kaiser, Op. 437;
Künstlerleben, Op. 316; Morgen-
blätter. Op. 279; Rosen aus dem
Süden, Op. 388; Wiener Blut, Op.
354; Wiener Bonbons, Op. 307;
Wo die Zitronen blühen, Op. 364.
STRAUSS, Eduard: *Bahn frei polka*
galop, Op. 45. STRAUSS, Josef:
Polkas: *Eingesendet, Op. 240; Feuer-*
fest, Op. 269; Jockey, Op. 278; Pla-
permäulchen, Op. 245. Waltzes:

Mein Lebenslauf ist Lieb' und Lust,
Op. 263; Sphärenklänge (*Music of*
the Spheres), *Op. 235.* STRAUSS,
Johann, Snr: *Radetzky march, Op.*
228.

(M) **(*) Decca KSDCC 7016/8.
Vienna PO, Boskovsky.

This anthology has been skilfully compiled from earlier recordings in the Boskovsky Decca series. They are perhaps
not so uniformly natural and rich as current ones, but from the beginning Decca
set a high technical standard, and if the
sound of the strings sometimes dates the
source of individual items the overall
ambient glow is consistent throughout.
The playing is reliably idiomatic and
usually has fine spontaneity and life, but
one or two of the more famous waltzes,
the *Blue Danube* and the *Emperor*, for
instance, have been recorded elsewhere
with greater distinction. But reservations
about a few individual items are forgotten in the excellence of the set as a whole.
The cassette transfer is generally of
Decca's top quality, more consistent
than the other Boskovsky sets mentioned
above (although for some reason side one
of the third cassette seems slightly less
bright than the rest of the programme).

'Champagne from Vienna': Banditen
polka, Op. 378; Egyptian march, Op.
335; Champagne polka (arr. Schönherr), *Op. 211;* Waltzes: *Künstlerle-*
ben, Op. 316; Wiener Bonbons, Op.
307. STRAUSS, Josef: Polkas: *Heite-*
rer Mut, Op. 281; Ohne Sorgen, Op.
271; Plappermäulchen, Op. 245;
Waltzes: *Delirien, Op. 212; Mein*
Lebenslauf ist Lieb' und Lust, Op.
263.

(M) *** Decca Ace of Diamonds
KSDC 474. Vienna PO, Bos-
kovsky.

This is a particularly satisfying anthology. Side one makes a splendid miniature concert, with two fine polkas to open

and close, *Artist's Life* and *Vienna Bonbons* in lilting performances in between, and the piquant *Egyptian march* as a centrepiece. The cassette transfer, made at a high level, has plenty of presence and body and only marginally less bloom than the disc. Often the quality reaches demonstration standard.

'Vienna imperial': Franz Josef I, Jubel march, Op. 126; Lagunen waltz, Op. 411; Orpheus quadrille, Op. 236 (formal and concert versions); *Schneeglöckchen waltz, Op. 143; S'Gibt nur a Kaiserstadt polka, Op. 291; So ängstlich sind wir nicht polka, Op. 413; Waldmeister overture.*
**(*) Decca KSXC 6419. Vienna PO, Boskovsky.

This collection is interesting in including two versions of the *Orpheus quadrille*, a gay Offenbach pot-pourri. We hear it through first comparatively slowly, in Viennese strict tempo! But the Viennese equivalent of *Come Dancing* has a good deal more grace and colour than the British product, to add to its formal elegance. Then on side two we are offered the concert version, and the music's irresistible high spirits come bubbling to the surface. There are other good things here too; the *Waldmeister overture* is full of striking tunes, and the two waltzes (especially *Lagunen*) are most fetching. On tape the sound has a striking overall bloom but the reverberation has brought some lack of clarity of focus, and the liveliness of the strings is accompanied by a certain amount of edge on the sheen of the violins.

'Happy New Year': Die Fledermaus: Czárdás; Bei uns z'Haus waltz, Op. 361; Indigo und die vierzig Räuber: Overture. STRAUSS, Johann, Jnr, Josef, and Eduard: *Schützenquadrille.* STRAUSS, Josef: *Die Schwätzerin, Op. 144; Im Fluge, Op. 230; Die Emancipierte, Op. 282; Extemporere, Op. 240; Auf Ferienreisen, Op. 133.* STRAUSS, Eduard: *Fesche Geister; Mit Extrapost.*
**(*) Decca KSXC 6495. Vienna PO, Boskovsky.

It would be difficult to find a tape with a gayer atmosphere. The programme is full of the most delicious Straussian confectionery, played with the lightest possible touch and beautifully recorded. The very Austrian *Bei uns z'Haus* waltz has one of Johann's most beguiling openings: it is a little-known piece that deserves to be more familiar. This and the *Indigo* overture offer a touch of extra substance among the sweetmeats, but the infectious quality of the playing ensures there is no danger that the ear is sated. There is not a dull moment here. On cassette the recording is admirably vivid and detailed, but somewhat over-bright, at times slightly fierce. The upper partials are not always entirely clean, which affects the focus of the side-drum.

'Welcome the New Year': Accelerationen waltz, Op. 234; Annen polka, Op. 117; Bitte schön polka, Op. 373; Freikugeln polka, Op. 326; Freut euch des Lebens waltz, Op. 340; Mephistos Höllenrufe waltz, Op. 101; Nordseebilder waltz, Op. 390; Russian march, Op. 426; Stürmisch in Lieb' polka, Op. 393. STRAUSS, Josef: *Frauenherz polka, Op. 166.*
*** Decca KSXC 6526. Vienna PO, Boskovsky.

Welcome the New Year is one of Boskovsky's happiest collections. Apart from the first two items listed, most of the music is completely unfamiliar and Boskovsky is a persuasive advocate. The music is played in a relaxed, completely assured manner, and the rich, spacious recording adds to the conductor's natural warmth. Side one closes with the *Rus-*

sian march, a characterful little piece that ends in the manner of a patrol, with the orchestration being gently reduced so that the music fades into the distance. This is done with simplicity and great charm and it alone is a strong enough recommendation for adding this tape to any collection. The sound is clear and clean, the reverberation adding a pleasing resonance and bloom. The strings have slightly more edge here than on the equivalent LP, but there is no lack of overall warmth. This is generally very sophisticated sound, although a slight treble cut is advisable.

'New Year concert 1973/4': *An der schönen blauen Donau waltz, Op. 314; Auf's Korn march, Op. 478; Carnaval in Rom: overture; Erinnerung an Covent-Garden waltz, Op. 329; Musikalischer Scherz, Op. 257; Perpetuum mobile, Op. 257; Sängerslust polka, Op. 328; Tik-Tak polka, Op. 365.* STRAUSS, Johann, Snr: *Wettrennen-Galopp, Op. 29.* STRAUSS, Josef: *Rudolfsheimer polka, Op. 153; Sphärenklänge waltz, Op. 235.*

*** Decca KSXC 6692. Vienna State Opera Chorus, Vienna PO, Boskovsky.

The novelty here is the inclusion of the Vienna State Opera Chorus in the original choral version of the *Blue Danube*. These are not the original words (which caused a political storm at the time). The use of the male chorus gives the piece an unexpectedly robust quality, attractive in its way but without the grace of the version for orchestra alone. The chorus also contributes with entirely fruitful effect to the *Sängerslust polka* and the *Auf's Korn march*; but perhaps the highlights of this collection are a beguiling performance of Josef's *Music of the Spheres waltz* and the attractive pot-pourri of English music-hall airs, *Erinnerung an Covent-Garden, Walzer nach englischen Volks-*

melodien (Strauss conducted a series of promenade concerts at Covent Garden during the summer and autumn of 1867). The piece is dominated by the tune *Champagne Charlie*, which sounds exotic in the context of a Strauss waltz. Excellent playing and recording throughout, and Boskovsky's final comment (in English) at the end of *Perpetuum mobile* is most apt. The cassette transfer is clear and vivid.

Ritter Pásmán: Csárdás, Op. 441. Perpetuum mobile, Op. 257. Polkas: *Annen, Op. 117; Auf der Jagd, Op. 373; Explosionen, Op. 43; Leichtes Blut, Op. 319; Stadt und Land, Op. 322; Vergnügungszug, Op. 281.* Overture: *Waldmeister.* Waltzes: *Bei uns z'Haus, Op. 361; Liebeslieder, Op. 114.* STRAUSS, Johann, Snr: *Radetzky march, Op. 228.*

**(*) Decca KSXC 6740. Vienna PO, Boskovsky.

Recorded 'live' in Vienna on New Year's Day 1975 this concert is not one of Boskovsky's more memorable Strauss anthologies. The applause between items is intrusive, and the extraneous 'train-whistle' used for the *Excursion-train polka* is clumsily balanced. The audience claps in disciplined fashion in the *Radetzky march*. The playing has plenty of life, but the sound has not the refinement of Boskovsky's best studio recordings. On tape the quality is both vivid and ripe in resonance, with plenty of body to the strings and only a hint of edge to their outline.

'New Year's Day concert in Vienna' (1979): Polkas: *Auf der Jagd, Op. 373; Bitte schön, Op. 372; Leichtes Blut, Op. 319; Pizzicato* (with Josef); *Tik-Tak, Op. 365.* Waltzes: *An der schönen blauen Donau, Op. 314; Bei uns z'Haus, Op. 361; Wein, Weib und Gesang, Op. 333.* STRAUSS, Johann, Snr: *Radetzky march, Op.*

228; Loreley-Rhein-Klänge waltz, Op. 154. STRAUSS, Eduard: *Ohne Bremse* (polka), *Op. 238.* STRAUSS, Josef: Polkas: *Die Emancipierte, Op. 282; Moulinet, Op. 57; Rudolfsheimer, Op. 153;* Waltz: *Sphärenklänge, Op. 235.*

*** Decca KSXC 2 7062 [Lon. LDR 5-10001/2]. Vienna PO, Boskovsky (with SUPPÉ: *Beautiful Galathea overture;* ZIEHRER: *Hereinspaziert waltz*).

Decca's 1979 New Year concert issue is a digital recording, which means, broadly speaking, that after the sound has reached the microphones it feeds directly into a computer, where all the information is transformed into a complicated numerical code. However, the signal is precise and there is no added or induced distortion in the recording system. The clarity, natural presence, and separation of detail are very striking, although in this instance the upper strings of the Vienna Philharmonic at times seem to have their upper partials slightly exaggerated, so that there is some lack of bloom at the top. In all other respects the recording is first-class and the excellence applies to the cassette as well as the discs. One notices the naturalness of the sound immediately in the very well focused audience applause at the opening, and the crispness of the side-drum (rarely caught well on cassette) is another striking feature, to say nothing of the freshness of the woodwind. The music-making itself gains much from the spontaneity of the occasion: its relaxed style is persuasive throughout, but one can feel the tension rising as the concert proceeds, and in the second half (and especially the encores) the electricity is very apparent. The performances are generally first-class and this is highly recommended, provided one can accept the applause and audience participation. The sound on disc and tape is almost identical, which bodes well for the future of digital cassettes.

Polkas: *Annen, Op. 117; Sturmisch in Lieb', Op. 393; Unter Donner und Blitz, Op. 324.* Waltzes: *An der schönen blauen Donau, Op. 314; Du und du, Op. 367; Geschichten aus dem Wiener Wald, Op. 325.* STRAUSS, Josef: *Dorfschwalben aus Österreich (Village Swallows).*

** Decca KSXCM 15014. Vienna PO, Boskovsky.

This is a tape-only compilation cunningly subtitled 'Strauss family favourites for the motorway' and obviously designed to get the best of both commercial worlds. However, the selection is neither particularly adventurous nor notably generous, and although the tape was originally offered at a special price, the full KSXC price makes it distinctly less enticing now. It includes both the *Blue Danube* and *Tales from the Vienna Woods*, which record collectors can get (on SPA 10) at budget price but tape collectors cannot, as the equivalent KCSP issue is not Dolbyized. The sound is generally good but not always absolutely clean in focus. Our review copy had hints of flutter too, but this is unlikely to be present on current tapes now in the shops.

Waltzes: *An der schönen blauen Donau,* Op. 314; *Frühlingsstimmen, Op. 410; Geschichten aus dem Wiener Wald, Op. 325; Künstlerleben, Op. 316; Rosen aus dem Süden, Op. 388.*

** Decca Phase 4 KPFC 4353 [Lon. 5-21144]. Boston Pops Orch., Fiedler.

These are characteristically lively performances, vividly recorded. There is no lack of flexibility, but no special magic either; yet this collection is enjoyable in its direct way. The cassette, like the disc, has plenty of sparkle.

Overture: *Die Fledermaus.* Polkas: *Annen, Op. 117; Eljen a Magyar, Op. 332; Tritsch-Tratsch, Op. 214.*

Waltzes: *An der schönen blauen Donau; Geschichten aus dem Wiener Wald, Op. 325; Kaiser, Op. 437.* STRAUSS, Johann, Snr: *Radetzky march, Op. 228.*

(M) **(*) DG Privilege 3318 062. Berlin Radio SO, Fricsay.

A highly attractive programme, including the three favourite waltzes. Fricsay's performances are undoubtedly rhythmically mannered, but they are full of character and personality. He can let the music relax in the most affectionate phrasing, yet he never loses the underlying tension. The *Tritsch-Tratsch* and *Eljen a Magyar* polkas are fast and racy, and the centrepiece of the *Radetzky march* has a splendid lilt. At the end of the *Annen polka* comes a charmingly individual combination of diminuendo and ritenuto. The recording is bright and well projected, with plenty of detail and warmth, and the transfer is vivid, the reverberation generally well managed.

Waltzes: *An der schönen blauen Donau, Op. 314; Kaiser, Op. 437; Künstlerleben, Op. 316; Wein, Weib und Gesang, Op. 333.*

(B) *(*) Classics for Pleasure TC-CFP 165. LPO, Guschlbauer.

Theodor Guschlbauer readily conveys his affection in these Viennese-style performances, and he makes the London Philharmonic play almost as if they were Vienna-born. The shaping of the opening of each waltz is very nicely done, and the orchestra are obviously enjoying themselves, even though the tension is held on comparatively slack reins. The recording, made in a reverberant acoustic, has warmth and bloom, but the resonance has presented problems in the cassette transfer. The side-drum, so crisp on LP, is less sharply focused here, and the upper strings lack the sweetness and refinement of the disc. Generally the quality is more than acceptable, but there is a degree of coarseness at times in *Wine, Woman and Song.*

Polkas: *Annen, Op. 117; Champagne, Op. 211; Eljen a Magyar, Op. 332; Leichtes Blut, Op. 319; Tritsch-Tratsch, Op. 214; Unter Donner und Blitz, Op. 324. Perpetuum mobile, Op. 257. Persian march, Op. 289.* Overtures: *Die Fledermaus; Der Zigeunerbaron.*

(B) *** Classics for Pleasure TC-CFP 40048. LPO, Guschlbauer.

Guschlbauer's collection of overtures and polkas sparkles from beginning to end. The playing is remarkably idiomatic and stylish, and the music-making is a constant joy. With the acoustic even better judged than on the first issue in terms of atmosphere, warmth and brilliance, the reproduction here is often of demonstration quality. The resonant sound has been expertly contained in the transfer. The balance is forward, but the dynamics are allowed to expand convincingly. *Perpetuum mobile,* which ends side two, is especially vivid.

Waltzes: *An der schönen blauen Donau, Op. 314; Geschichten aus dem Wiener Wald, Op. 325; Kaiser, Op. 437; Wein, Weib und Gesang, Op. 333; Wiener Blut, Op. 354.*

(M) *(**) RCA Gold Seal GK 25019. Vienna State Opera Orch., Horenstein.

Horenstein's performances are distinctive: they have a classical feeling in the Bruno Walter tradition. The rhythmic manner is comparatively straightforward, yet never inflexible, and the playing throughout has plenty of lift and sparkle. The shaping of the opening of the *Blue Danube* is evocative and the zither solo in *Tales from the Vienna Woods* has a disarming delicacy. In the *Emperor* the sweep of the upward curving

537

string tune is partly lost by the strong forward pulse of the playing, but it is this spirited momentum that is so generally effective. The transfer level is very high, and though the sound is comparably vivid it lacks refinement and the upper strings and brass tend to coarsen in tuttis.

Overtures: *Die Fledermaus; Der Zigeunerbaron.* Polkas: *Annen, Op. 117; Tritsch-Tratsch, Op. 214.* Waltzes: *An der schönen blauen Donau, Op. 314; Kaiser, Op. 437.*
   (*) HMV TC-ASD 3132 [Angel 4XS 37144]. Berlin PO, Karajan.

After the sumptuous *Die Fledermaus* overture, given rich, spacious recording, this collection is most disappointing. The *Annen polka* is stodgily phrased, and a similar heavy, mannered *rubato* takes most of the lilt out of the waltzes. The ample, resonant sound picture does not help to provide resilience to the actual orchestra sound. The cassette transfer is faithful enough, but not exactly sparkling.

Overtures: *Die Fledermaus; Der Zigeunerbaron.* Perpetuum mobile, *Op. 257.* Polkas: *Annen, Op. 117; Tritsch-Tratsch, Op. 214.* Waltzes: *An der schönen blauen Donau, Op. 314; Kaiser, Op. 437.* STRAUSS, Johann, Snr: *Radetzky march, Op. 228.* STRAUSS, Josef: *Delirien waltz, Op. 212.*
   ** DG 923025 [id.]. Berlin PO, Karajan.

This is much more successfully transferred than Karajan's later DG collection (see below) and the quality is fresh and bright. The playing is warmly idiomatic but has a touch of blandness too in the waltzes, although the polkas are lively enough.

Egyptian march, *Op. 335; Persian march, Op. 289.* Polkas: *Auf der Jagd, Op. 373; Pizzicato* (with Josef); *Unter Donner und Blitz, Op. 324.* Waltzes: *Geschichten aus dem Wiener Wald, Op. 325; Morgenblätter, Op. 279; Wiener Blut, Op. 354.*
   *(*) DG 3300 183 [id.]. Berlin PO, Karajan.

Karajan can be a persuasive conductor of Strauss waltzes, but he is not helped here by a transfer of indifferent quality which has little sparkle and muffled transients. The sound is well balanced, but it is markedly less brilliant than on the disc and has little projection. The polkas are lively enough (the *Pizzicato polka* is played gently as a foil to the others), but here the lack of crispness and bite is particularly serious. In the *Egyptian march* it is a curiosity indeed to hear the Berlin orchestral players making a robust vocal contribution to the middle section, which is made to sound like Ketèlbey.

Polkas: *Neue Pizzicato, Op. 449; Tik-Tak, Op. 365; Tritsch-Tratsch, Op. 214.* Waltzes: *Accelerationen, Op. 234; An der schönen blauen Donau, Op. 314; Rosen aus dem Süden, Op. 388; Wein, Weib und Gesang, Op. 333; Wiener Bonbons, Op. 307.*
   (B) ** Philips Fontana 7327 010. Vienna SO, Sawallisch.

This bargain-priced selection is quite generous and well compiled, and it makes an attractive concert: the *New Pizzicato polka* is a highlight. The transfer to cassette is notably successful, with crisp, lively sound, often preferable to that of the LP.

Waltzes transcribed by Schoenberg, Webern and Berg: *Kaiser, Op. 437; Rosen aus dem Süden, Op. 388* (both trans. Schoenberg); *Schatz waltz* (from *Der Zigeunerbaron*), *Op. 418*

(trans. Webern); *Wein, Weib und Gesang, Op. 333* (trans. Berg).
**(*)DG 3300 977 [id.]. Boston Symphony Chamber Players.

A fascinating curiosity. Schoenberg, Berg and Webern made these transcriptions for informal private performances. Schoenberg's arrangements of the *Emperor* and *Roses from the South* are the most striking, though Berg's *Wine, Women and Song* is sweetly appealing with its scoring for harmonium. As might be expected, Webern's *Schatz waltz* is aptly refined. Above all the spirit of Johann Strauss shines through, and his glorious melodies are unscathed. The playing here is affectionately rhythmic and very sophisticated. The image of a glorified Palm Court orchestra persists, but no café-band would have produced this degree of polish. The recording is sympathetically balanced, the transfer pleasing, if lacking the final degree of range. On two copies sampled there were momentary pitch slips, but that will probably have been cured by the time this book is in print.

OPERETTA

Die Fledermaus: complete.
(M) ***HMV TC-RLS 728. Elisabeth Schwarzkopf, Rita Streich, Nicolai Gedda, Helmut Krebs, Erich Kunz, Rudolf Christ, Philharmonia Chorus and Orch., Karajan.
**(*) Decca K 58 K 22. Hilde Gueden, Erika Köth, Waldemar Kmentt, Eberhard Waechter, Walter Berry, Giuseppe Zampieri, Regina Resnik, Vienna State Opera Chorus, Vienna PO, Karajan.
*(**) DG 3370 009 [id.]. Julia Varady, Lucia Popp, René Kollo, Bernd Weikl, Hermann Prey, Ivan Rebroff, Bavarian State Opera Chorus and Orch., Carlos Kleiber.

If the catalogue has never been infested with Fledermice, that is a recognition of the quality of earlier sets, notably Karajan's 1955 version (originally issued on Columbia), produced by Walter Legge and now reissued on HMV. This version has great freshness and clarity along with the polish which for many will make it a first favourite. Tempi at times are unconventional, both slow and fast, but the precision and point of the playing are magical and the singing is endlessly delightful. Schwarzkopf makes an enchanting Rosalinde, not just in the imagination and sparkle of her singing but also in the snatches of spoken dialogue (never too long) which leaven the entertainment. Needless to say she makes a gloriously commanding entry in the party scene, which is in every sense a highspot of Walter Legge's production. As Adèle, Rita Streich (like Schwarzkopf a pupil of Maria Ivogün) produces her most dazzling coloratura; Gedda and Krebs are beautifully contrasted in their tenor tone, and Erich Kunz gives a vintage performance as Falke. The original mono, crisply focused, has been given a brighter edge but otherwise left unmolested. However, the tape transfer softens this considerably, yet loses none of the vocal presence and detail. Indeed the atmosphere and naturalness of the recording balance are splendidly caught, and only the rather thin violin tone occasionally betrays the age of the recording. The last act (at the prison) is particularly evocative.

Karajan's 1960 Decca set was originally issued – with much blazing of publicity trumpets – as a so-called 'Gala performance', with various artists from the Decca roster appearing to do their turn at the 'cabaret' included in the Orlofsky ball sequence. This was a famous tradition of performances of *Die Fledermaus* at the New York Met. in the early years of this century. In due course Decca issued the set without the gala, and the gala album has been withdrawn. The performance itself has all the sparkle one could ask for. If anything, Karajan is even more brilliant than in the 1955 version, and the Decca recording is scintillating in its clarity. Where it does fall short, alas, is in the singing. Hilde Gueden is deliciously vivacious as Rosalinde, a beautifully projected interpretation, but vocally she is not perfect, and even her confidence has a drawback in showing how tentative Erika Köth is as Adèle, with her wavering *vibrato*. Indeed *Mein Herr Marquis* is well below the standard of the best recorded performances. Waldemar Kmentt has a tight, German-sounding tenor, and Giuseppe Zampieri as Alfred (a bright idea to have a genuine Italian for the part) is no more than adequate. The rest of the cast are very good, but even these few vocal shortcomings are enough to take some of the gilt off the gingerbread. It all depends on what you ask from *Fledermaus*; if it is gaiety and sparkle above everything, then with Karajan in control this is an excellent recommendation, and it certainly cannot be faulted on grounds of recording, which leaves nothing to be desired. The Decca transfer has characteristic brilliance and sparkle, yet plenty of weight in the orchestra. The agreeable resonance does not cloud detail, and the dialogue has good presence and atmosphere. Some slight smoothing of the treble might be useful on some players, but this is very sophisticated quality.

The glory of the DG set is the singing of the two principal women – Julia Varády and Lucia Popp magnificently characterful and stylish as mistress and servant – but much of the rest is controversial, to say the least. Many will be delighted by the incisive style of Carlos Kleiber, deliberately rejecting many older conventions. Though he allows plenty of rhythmic flexibility, he is never easy-going, for in every *rubato* a first concern is for precision of ensemble; and that does not always allow the fun and sparkle

of the score to emerge. But in its way the result is certainly refreshing, even electrically compelling, and the recording quality, both clear and atmospheric, is admirable. Hermann Prey makes a forthright Eisenstein, but René Kollo sounds lumberingly heavy as Alfred, and as for the falsetto Orlofsky of Ivan Rebroff, it has to be heard to be believed, unhealthily grotesque. For some ears this is so intrusive (as is the hearty German dialogue at times) as to make this set quite unacceptable for repeated listening. Although the transfer is made at rather a low level (notably on the first tape), the voices have plenty of presence and the dialogue is especially lively. The final act, in particular, is demonstration-worthy for its sense of presence. The libretto is clear but rather faintly printed.

Die Fledermaus: highlights.

*** HMV TC-ASD 2891. Anneliese Rothenberger, Renate Holm, Nicolai Gedda, Dietrich Fischer-Dieskau, Walter Berry, Brigitte Fassbaender, Vienna State Opera Chorus, Vienna SO, Boskovsky.

**(*) Decca KCET 600. Gundula Janowitz, Renate Holm, Waldemar Kmentt, Eberhard Waechter, Heinz Holecek, Erich Kunz, Wolfgang Windgassen, Vienna State Opera Chorus, Vienna PO, Boehm.

*(**) DG 3337 040 (from above set cond. Kleiber).

(M) Saga CA 5363. Rosette Anday, Georg Oggl, Hugo Meyer-Welfing, Ruthilde Bosch, Emmy Funk, Vienna Light Opera Chorus and Orch., Schönherr.

The HMV selection seems to find all that is most sparkling in the splendid Boskovsky performance. The famous *Trinke Liebchen* is matched by the ball scene where all sing in praise of champagne, and Orlofsky's *Chacun à son goût* is superb. The transfer is generally very successful, with a natural bloom on the voices and plenty of atmosphere. The singers, whether solo or in ensemble, are vividly projected. (The complete set from which this is taken is available on tape in the USA: Angel 4x2s 3790.)

Boehm conducts with great warmth and affection, if without the sparkle of Karajan. The complete recording (not available on tape) was made without dialogue and this is reflected in the highlights. The stars of the performance are undoubtedly Gundula Janowitz in rich voice as Rosalinde, and Renate Holm as Adèle, which of course she also sings on the HMV highlights tape. The male principals are less impressive. The use of a male Orlofsky has less dramatic point in a recording than on stage, and here Windgassen is vocally much inferior to Brigitte Fassbaender, who is so good in the HMV selection. However, to some ears he is vastly preferable to the blood-curdling sounds that Rebroff makes on DG. The transfer is successful in Decca's best manner, and with such sparkling sound the singers are projected with splendid life and presence.

With Kleiber as the principal – if at times controversial – attraction of the DG set, it was understandable that the overture would be included in this selection, but that means having less than usual of the finale of Act 2. The falsetto of Rebroff is the distinct drawback to an otherwise refreshingly different reading. The recording is full, and it has transferred brilliantly.

The Saga tape cannot be given any kind of recommendation at all, even at medium price. The sound in the overture resembles a transatlantic broadcast in the way it comes and goes in waves. When the voices enter it is slightly more stable, but the quality is grotesque. If this were a great historic performance one might make allowances, but the singing is merely fairly efficient and has no charm,

while the explosive sound from the orchestra is not improved by occasionally faulty intonation.

A Night in Venice (Eine Nacht in Venedig): complete.
  (M) *** HMV TC2-SXDWS 3043. Elisabeth Schwarzkopf, Nicolai Gedda, Erich Kunz, Peter Klein, Emmy Loose, Karl Dönch, Philharmonia Chorus and Orch., Ackermann.

A Night in Venice was drastically revised by Erich Korngold many years after Strauss's death, and it is that version, further amended, which appears in this charming 'complete' recording, a superb example of Walter Legge's Philharmonia productions, honeyed and atmospheric. As a sampler try the jaunty little waltz duet in Act 1 between Schwarzkopf as the heroine, Annina, and the baritone Erich Kunz as Caramello, normally a tenor role. Nicolai Gedda as the Duke then appropriates the most famous waltz song of all, the *Gondola song*, but with such a frothy production purism would be out of place. The excellent stereo transcription preserves the balance of the mono original admirably. The transfer is made at a rather lower level than either *Zigeunerbaron* or *Wiener Blut*, and the voices have rather less edge and presence. But the smoothness is not unattractive, and the chorus does not sound muddy. The music is happily spaced out on a single tape with Act 1 on side one and Acts 2 and 3 on side two. There is no libretto. The price of this issue reflects the fact that on disc the set is issued on three LP sides only. Highly recommended.

Wiener Blut (Vienna Blood): complete.
  ✸ (M) *** HMV TC2-SXDWS 3042. Elisabeth Schwarzkopf, Nicolai Gedda, Erika Köth, Erich Kunz, Emmy Loose, Karl

Dönch, Philharmonia Chorus and Orch., Ackermann.

To have Schwarzkopf at her most ravishing singing a waltz song based on the tune of *Morning Papers* is enough enticement for this superbly stylish performance of a piece which – with the composer a bored collaborator – was cobbled together from some of his finest ideas. The result may not be a great operetta, but in a recording it makes enchanting listening, with the waltz of the title made into the centrepiece. This Philharmonia version of the mid-fifties shows Walter Legge's flair as a producer at its most compelling, with Schwarzkopf matched by the regular team of Gedda and Kunz and with Emmy Loose and Erika Köth in the secondary soprano roles. The original mono recording was beautifully balanced, and the facelift given here is most tactfully achieved in this extremely successful stereo transcription. The transfer to tape is no less well managed, giving bright vivacious sound with plenty of atmosphere. Indeed this is technically the finest of the three HMV Johann Strauss operetta reissues. There is no libretto, but the single-tape format, with Act 1 on side one and Acts 2 and 3 on side two, is admirable, and the relatively small amount of spoken dialogue has fine presence.

Der Zigeunerbaron (*The Gipsy Baron*): complete.
> (M) *** HMV TC2-SXDW 3046.
> Elisabeth Schwarzkopf, Nicolai Gedda, Hermann Prey, Erich Kunz, Erika Köth, Monica Sinclair, Philharmonia Chorus and Orch., Ackermann.

The Gipsy Baron has had a poor showing in the recording studio, which is particularly surprising because there are relatively so few Strauss operettas, and by any standards this is outstanding. The plot (much praised in some quarters) is strangely offbeat, but the musical inspiration shows Strauss at his most effervescent, and this superb Philharmonia version from the mid-fifties has never been matched in its rich stylishness and polish. Schwarzkopf as the gipsy princess sings radiantly, not least in the heavenly Bullfinch duet (to the melody made famous by MGM as *One day when we were young*). Gedda, still youthful, sings with heady tone, and Erich Kunz as the rough pig-breeder gives a vintage echt-Viennese performance of the irresistible *Ja, das schreiben und das lesen*. The stereo transcription from excellent mono originals gives fresh and truthful sound, particularly in the voices. The transfer is admirably managed and, if the lively treble is cut back just a little, the fine atmosphere of the original recording (the chorus clear and the solo voices given plenty of sparkle) makes one almost think at times that this is real stereo. This set is presented on two cassettes in a box, but there is only a leaflet and no libretto; for some there may seem too much spoken dialogue without a translation.

COLLECTION

'*Your kind of Johann Strauss*': (i) *Perpetuum mobile, Op. 257*. Polkas: *Champagne, Op. 211;* (ii) *Tritsch-Tratsch, Op. 214;* (i) *Unter Donner und Blitz, Op. 324*. Waltzes: *An der schönen blauen Donau, Op. 314;* (ii) *Kaiser, Op. 437*. (iii) *Casanova: Nuns' chorus*. (iv) *Die Fledermaus: overture; Brüderlein und Schwesterlein; Chacun à son goût; Laughing song*. (i) STRAUSS, Johann, Snr: *Radetzky march, Op. 228*.
> (M) *** HMV TC-EXES 5014. (i) Hallé Orch., Barbirolli; (ii) Philharmonia Promenade Orch., Henry Krips; (iii) Elisabeth Schwarzkopf, Philharmonia Chorus and Orch., Ackermann; (iv) soloists, Vienna State

Opera Chorus, Vienna SO, Boskovsky.

Your kind of Johann Strauss features both father and son in an admirably made anthology, including as its highlights four excerpts from the outstanding Boskovsky set of *Die Fledermaus*. Brigitte Fassbaender's *Chacun à son goût* can rank with the finest performances of this sparkling song ever recorded. The programme opens with Barbirolli's *Blue Danube*, not as fine a performance as his Pye version but better recorded. Henry Krips's slightly indulgent version of the *Emperor waltz* is very enjoyable, and Barbirolli is heard at his very best in the polkas and in a most infectious account of *Perpetuum mobile*. With an extra bonus in Elisabeth Schwarzkopf's winning account of the *Nuns' chorus* (with the Philharmonia chorus sounding suitably opulent) this tape is brimming over with good things, and the sound is good throughout – lively in the polkas and warmly glowing in the *Fledermaus* excerpts.

Strauss, Josef
(1827–70)

'Prosit!': Polkas: *Feuerfest, Op. 269; Heiterer Mut, Op. 281; Im Fluge, Op. 230; Jockey, Op. 278; Ohne Sorgen, Op. 271; Plappermäulchen!, Op. 245.* Waltzes: *Delirien, Op. 212; Dorfschwalben aus Österreich, Op. 164; Mein Lebenslauf ist Lieb' und Lust, Op. 263; Transaktionen, Op. 184.*

⊛ ***Decca KSXC 6817. Vienna PO, Boskovsky.

Boskovsky here more than maintains the standards of his Strauss series (see above). The playing has marvellous life and warmth, and an essentially Viennese geniality. The silky phrasing of the strings is irresistible in *Transaktionen*, as is the delicious lilt of *Village Swallows*, one of the most delectable of the lighter waltzes. The polkas too have splendid vigour and sparkle. The recording is of superlative standard, and the cassette is marvellously done too. Our rosette is awarded not just to this issue but as a token of the overall achievement of Boskovsky's Strauss series – notably, on tape, KSXC 6526 and KSXC 6692 (see above).

Strauss, Richard
(1864–1949)

An Alpine symphony, Op. 64.
  **(*) HMV TC-ASD 3173. Dresden State Orch., Kempe.
  **(*) Decca KSXC 6752 [Lon. 5-6981]. Los Angeles PO, Mehta.
  (M)** RCA Gold Seal GK 42697. RPO, Kempe.

The *Alpine symphony* has all the rhetoric, confidence and opulence of the great Strauss tone poems, but, judged by the finest of them, its melodic invention is less fresh and its gestures sometimes ring a hollow note. But there is much to relish and enjoy when the performances are as good as these. Mehta's account with the Los Angeles Philharmonic is among the best Strauss he has yet given us, and he is supported by recording quality that is wide in range and rich in detail. It is not overlit as has sometimes been the case in their recordings, but the Decca engineers provide excellent internal focus without ever losing sight of the overall perspective. Mehta gives a virtuoso performance.

Kempe, however, brings a glowing warmth and humanity to this score, and there is no doubt that in his hands it sounds the greater work. He moulds each phrase with more sensitivity and life, and though, as with Mehta, there is a strong sense of forward movement, there is also a greater expressive freedom and flexibility of phrase. And, compared with the Los Angeles Philharmonic, the Dresden orchestra on Kempe's later HMV recording is the finer too; it produces richer, more cultured and essentially more vital tone quality. Kempe was a very great Strauss conductor and this tells. The EMI recording is impressively rich and full. It has on the whole transferred well to tape, although the recording has not quite the spectacular quality of the Decca cassette, which also has clearer inner detail. However, if the EMI tape is less adventurous in range it is satisfying nonetheless.

At medium price, Kempe's RCA reissue makes a fair recommendation, no less warm and committed than his later Dresden recording on HMV and on balance a shade more spontaneous-sounding. The recording quality is very good for its mid-sixties vintage, but on cassette there is a lack of range at both ends of the spectrum. The quality is respectable, but the treble lacks real sparkle and the transients are not ideally crisp, while the relative lack of bass detracts from the fullness.

Also sprach Zarathustra (symphonic poem), *Op. 30.*

> ***DG 3300 375 [id.]. Berlin PO, Karajan.
>
> (M) *** DG Privilege 3335 209 [3300 185]. Boston SO, Steinberg.
>
> **(*)Philips 7300 280 [id.]. Concertgebouw Orch., Haitink.

Sumptuous tone and virtuosity of the highest order make Karajan's DG version an electrifying *Zarathustra*, arguably the best on the market. The engineers produce recorded sound of the greatest realism and warmth, wholly natural in its aural perspective and free from gimmickry. Karajan's earlier account with the Vienna Philharmonic Orchestra (see below) is also a fine one, but the DG version eclipses it in almost every way. The DG engineers have transferred it at a high level, which means that at the opening and one or two points elsewhere there are hints of congestion. But these are not serious, and much of the richness and detail of this marvellous recording has been captured on the cassette, which is easily the most thrilling version of this work available on tape.

Steinberg's is another distinguished account. His tempi are fast, but there is a strong contrast in the lyrical sections of the score, which are highly evocative. Here the DG recording makes a contribution. Vivid in the moments of spectacle, it is more recessed and atmospheric in the music's reflective moments. The cassette transfer is very successful. The level of transfer is rather lower than with Karajan and there is no congestion; indeed the orchestral textures are richly spacious, while there is no lack of substance in the *pianissimo* sections of the score. A fine tape, not quite so overwhelming as Karajan's version, perhaps, but very rewarding, and it is excellent value, even though there are no fill-ups.

Haitink's account with the Concertgebouw Orchestra is hardly less impressive than Karajan's on DG, though the strings of the Berlin Philharmonic have greater rapture and lyrical intensity. When this recording was issued, very much in the shadow of the Karajan, its merits did not perhaps receive full recognition, and although Karajan remains first choice, Haitink's performance is a good second. The cassette transfer, however, has not been made at a very high level, and the sound has less impact than the DG tape. The recording is fully acceptable, but it is neither very rich (like the DG) nor especially brilliant or clear.

Symphonic poems: *Also sprach Zarathustra, Op. 30; Don Juan, Op. 20;*

*Till Eulenspiegels lustige Streiche,
Op. 28.*
> *** Decca KSXC 6749 [Lon. 5-
> 6978]. Chicago SO, Solti.
> (M)**(*) Decca Jubilee KJBC 27.
> Vienna PO, Karajan.

'Favourite composer': (i) *Also sprach
Zarathustra;* (ii) *Don Juan;* (i) *Till
Eulenspiegels lustige Streiche;* (ii)
*Der Rosenkavalier: 1st Waltz se-
quence;* (i) *Salome: Dance of the
Seven Veils.*
> (B) **(*) Decca KDPC 543/4.
> Vienna PO, (i) Karajan, (ii)
> Maazel.

With glorious performances, brilliantly recorded, of Strauss's three most
popular showpieces, Solti's generous
coupling can be warmly recommended.
The recording serves Strauss's ripe
orchestration superbly. Nor does Solti
give hasty performances, for in his
way he is more ripely expansive in *Also
sprach Zarathustra,* the longest of the
three, than his two-sided rivals. This is
Solti at his strongest, with the most
Germanic of American orchestras responding to the manner born. The
cassette transfer is well managed, although the two shorter works are rather
more sparklingly brilliant than *Also
sprach Zarathustra.*

Karajan's Vienna account of *Also
sprach Zarathustra,* famous for its spectacular recording with the widest dynamic range, dates from the early days of
stereo, and so do his *Till Eulenspiegel* and
Salome's *Dance,* but listening to them
one would scarcely imagine that they
were so old. Maazel's *Don Juan* is fine,
though not perhaps the equal of Karajan's, which is available either on the
Jubilee tape listed here or on KCSP 119
(see below) coupled to Tchaikovsky's
Romeo and Juliet. The transfers throughout the two-tape *Favourite composer* set
are brilliantly managed. The wide dynamic range of *Also sprach Zarathustra*
is successfully accomplished, with a re-

markably free sound at the complex
opening section. The *pianissimo* detail is
not sharply defined, but the climaxes
have fine presence. The surging string
sheen at the opening of Maazel's *Der
Rosenkavalier* waltz sequence is thrillingly vivid. However, the Jubilee tape has
the advantage of offering *Also sprach*
complete on one side, and it is certainly
good value. The Decca tape transfer gives
the impression that the almost too wide
dynamic range of the original recordings
has been slightly modified: the result is to
increase the impact of the quieter music
without spoiling the contrast. *Don Juan*
and *Till* are especially successful, but
there are problems at the very opening of
Also sprach Zarathustra, where the massive orchestral sound loses its security
momentarily.

*Also sprach Zarathustra, Op. 30; Till
Eulenspiegels lustige Streiche, Op.
28; Salome: Dance of the Seven
Veils.*
> (M) *** HMV Greensleeve TC-
> ESD 7026. Dresden State Orch.,
> Kempe.

Kempe's stature as a Strauss conductor has been challenged only by Karajan.
His *Also sprach Zarathustra* is completely
free of the sensationalism that marks so
many newer performances, though in
sheer opulence and virtuosity it must
yield to the Karajan DG version, which
offers more vivid sound but has no fill-
ups. Kempe's *Till Eulenspiegel* is excellent, though it does not obliterate memories of his marvellous (deleted) Berlin
Philharmonic account from the early
1960s (used as a fill-up to *Don Quixote*).
However, this is an eminently recommendable tape, securely transferred, with
fine body of tone, no distortion in *Also
sprach Zarathustra* and plenty of brilliance in the companion works.

*Also sprach Zarathustra, Op. 30;
Salome: Dance of the Seven Veils.*

(b) **(*) Classics for Pleasure TC-CFP 40289. LPO, Del Mar.

Norman Del Mar's account of *Also sprach Zarathustra* is very strongly characterized. It has a powerful, brooding opening (the timpani strokes dramatically clear), and the closing section of the score is given a memorably elegiac quality. The LP plays with great fervour and intensity, and the only slight snag on the tape is that the sound of the upper strings tends to lack body, although there is plenty of brilliance. A cut-back of treble improves the balance considerably, and there is no absence of vividness. This cassette makes the fullest impact, and the recording of *Salome's dance* has a sinuous translucence of texture that is highly effective. In its price range this is certainly competitive. The turnover break is quite well placed, but because side two is much longer than side one, there is an irritating hiatus while one spools back.

(i) *Burleske in D minor for piano and orchestra;* (ii) *Horn concertos Nos. 1 in E flat major, Op. 11; 2 in E flat major;* (iii) *Oboe concerto in D major;* (iv) *Violin concerto in D minor, Op. 8;* (v) *Duet-Concertino for clarinet and bassoon, strings and harp;* (vi) *Panathenäenzug for piano, left hand, and orchestra; Parergon to Sinfonia domestica for piano, left hand, and orchestra.*

  ***HMV TC-SLS 5067. Dresden State Orch., Kempe, with (i) Malcolm Frager (piano); (ii) Peter Damm (horn); (iii) Manfred Clement (oboe); (iv) Ulf Hoelscher (violin); (v) Manfred Weise (clarinet), Wolfgang Liebscher (bassoon); (vi) Peter Rösel (piano).

This Kempe compilation has much to recommend it, not least the superb playing of the Dresden orchestra and the splendidly vivid recordings. There are no alternative versions on disc or tape of the *Parergon* to the *Sinfonia domestica* or the *Panathenäenzug*, both written for the one-armed pianist Paul Wittgenstein, and impressively played here. Another recording of the *Violin concerto* was once briefly available, but it incorporated cuts, so Ulf Hoelscher's eloquent account of this attractive early piece is more than welcome. Manfred Clement's *Oboe concerto* is a sensitive reading, though his tone (these matters are personal) may not appeal to those brought up on Goossens; and for the *Horn concertos* serious collectors will not overlook Dennis Brain's recording (although this is available only on disc). But this is a set that will give undoubted pleasure, and in many ways the excellent cassette box is more attractive than the discs, for this is ideal music to dip into at will. On tape the recording is generally of first-class quality, admirably fresh, with a fine bloom, detail and body. The balance of the solo instruments is close but not oppressively so, and their subtleties of timbre are nicely caught (the *Oboe concerto* sounds especially beautiful). Only in the *Parergon* is there any lack of internal clarity, but this is caused mainly by the resonance and balance of the recording. The heavy Wagnerian orchestration of the *Panathenäenzug* is managed without strain.

(i) *Burleske in D minor for piano and orchestra;* (ii) *Violin concerto in D minor, Op. 8.*
  (***) HMV TC-ASD 3399 (as above).

This separate issue, for all the attractions of the coupling, has been virtually spoilt by the clumsiness of the transfer. The *Violin concerto* with its delightfully lyrical first movement and gay dance-like finale comes off best, although there is a general lack of refinement (noticeable in the upper partials of the violin tone at times). But in the *Burleske* the reverberation creates a muddiness that is often too coarse to give pleasure. The original transfers in the boxed set were far superior, fresh and clean in detail.

Horn concertos Nos. 1 in E flat major, Op. 11; 2 in E flat major.
(M) ** Decca Jubilee KJBC 17. Barry Tuckwell, LSO, Kertesz
– FRANZ STRAUSS: Horn concerto.*(*)

Tuckwell does not usually disappoint, but here he does not get the style right. One can play the *First Concerto* as a successor to Mozart and it can be effective that way; but better to bring out the *Don Juan* boldness that is also inherent in the music, as Dennis Brain readily demonstrated on his HMV disc. Tuckwell falls between the two, and his manner and line are unconvincing. He is at his best in the finale of the otherwise less memorable *Second Concerto*. The transfer to tape focuses the soloist cleanly, but the string textures are on the dry side and slightly lacking in warmth. With care the overall balance can be more than satisfactory and provide a fair degree of overall bloom.

Death and Transfiguration (Tod und Verklärung; symphonic poem), Op. 24.
** Advent D 1043 (see p. xxiii) [id.]. LSO, Horenstein – HINDEMITH: Mathis der Maler.**(*)

Horenstein's account of *Death and Transfiguration* is spacious, and the recorded sound is vivid and has presence, even though it is not ideally sumptuous. It is faithfully transferred: the Advent chrome tape matches the Unicorn LP fairly closely. However, Horenstein does not displace Karajan (see below) as the first recommendation.

Death and Transfiguration (Tod und Verklärung; symphonic poem), Op. 24; (i) Vier letzte Lieder (Four Last songs).

**(*) DG 3300 421. Berlin PO, Karajan, (i) with Gundula Janowitz (soprano).

In the *Four Last songs* Janowitz simply produces a beautiful flow of creamy soprano tone while leaving the music's deeper and subtler emotions underexposed. But with a superlative version of *Death and Transfiguration*, which can be regarded as a showpiece even among Karajan's Berlin recordings, this is an attractive coupling. The symphonic poem has transferred to cassette with impressive body and weight of orchestral tone. The quality is a little dry, but the bass line is not lacking in resonance and remains clean, and the strings and brass are given plenty of bite and attack. In the songs there is a touch of hardness to the voice, but careful use of the controls can minimize this, and the sound generally is atmospheric and sophisticated in detail and balance.

Don Juan, Op. 20.
(M) **(*) Decca KCSP 119. Vienna PO, Karajan – TCHAIKOVSKY: Romeo and Juliet.**(*)
(*) Philips 7300 344. Concertgebouw Orch., Haitink – ELGAR: Enigma variations.(*)

This early Decca recording of *Don Juan* is superbly played, and Karajan is as beguiling in the love music as he is exhilarating in the chase. The excellent recording has a wide dynamic range, and this has meant a transfer level that, for Decca, is relatively low, so that, though the climaxes are admirably vivid, some of the quieter passages, even for full strings, sound a little distant.

Haitink's version is given a very low-level transfer indeed, and the sound, although it has weight, is seriously lacking in sparkle. The fine performance – an unexpected coupling for a somewhat cautious account of *Enigma* – makes less impact than it should.

Don Quixote (fantastic variations), *Op. 35.*

> *** HMV TC-ASD 3118 [Angel 4xs 37057]. Mstislav Rostropovich (cello), Berlin PO, Karajan.
>
> (M) *** DG Privilege 3335 195. Pierre Fournier (cello), Berlin PO, Karajan.

The Karajan/Rostropovich account of *Don Quixote* is predictably fine, and many will feel that its artistic claims are stronger than Karajan's earlier DG version with Fournier. The only failing is a tendency for Rostropovich to dominate the aural picture. He dominates artistically too. His Don is superbly characterized, and the expressiveness and richness of tone he commands are a joy in themselves. There are moments when one wonders whether the intensity of his response does not lead to over-emphatic tone, but in general both the cello and the viola soloists and the Berlin orchestra under Karajan silence criticism. The HMV transfer is exceptionally successful, the sound rich and full-blooded yet not lacking detail.

The Fournier/Karajan partnership offers a less high-voltage reading, but Fournier's Don has no less nobility than Rostropovich's, and he brings great subtlety and (when required) repose to the part. The finale and Don Quixote's death are more moving in Fournier's hands (even more so in the earlier account he made with Krauss, which is available on cassette – see below – and is not to be forgotten). Amazingly there is great consistency in Karajan's handling of orchestral detail here and in his later recording, and though Fournier is forwardly balanced, the DG recording has such excellence that there is no need (given its price) to qualify a three-star recommendation. The transfer is well managed, and the sound has plenty of detail and impact.

(i) *Don Quixote, Op. 35. Don Juan, Op. 20.*

> **(*) Philips 7300 647 [id.]. Concertgebouw Orch., Haitink, (i) with Tibor de Machula (cello).

There are splendid things in Haitink's performance of *Don Quixote*, and his noble soloist is by no means lacking in personality or eloquence. Although it does not quite match the heady, intoxicating flamboyance of either of the Karajan versions, the orchestral playing is still superb: the Concertgebouw ranks with the very greatest orchestras in the world. Machula does not quite touch the depths of Fournier in the Don's dying peroration but he has great dignity and beauty of tone. The recording is excellent, and the *Don Juan* is one of the best in the catalogue. The transfer is made at a reasonably high level, but although the sound is basically full and natural the treble does not open up in *Don Quixote*, and the ear notices the lack of upper range, especially at climaxes. At the opening of *Don Juan* the level rises dramatically and the sound is strikingly more brilliant and vivid: indeed the climax of the piece, with its thrusting horns and soaring strings, is thrilling.

(i) *Don Quixote, Op. 35. Ein Heldenleben* (symphonic poem), *Op. 40.*

> (M)(***) Decca Historic KMON 2 7051. Vienna PO, Krauss, (i) with Pierre Fournier (cello).

No conductor came closer to the spirit of Strauss's epic scores than did Clemens Krauss. These richly idiomatic performances are in a class of their own, and the eloquent response of the Vienna Philharmonic Orchestra is testimony of Krauss's magic. His *Ein Heldenleben* has an impressive sweep and finely characterized detail; the *Don Quixote* has a warmth and humanity to which it is impossible not to respond. Fournier is at his noblest and most inspired. Needless to say, the recordings, made in the early 1950s, betray their years: climaxes need to open out, the upper strings are edgy and perspectives are not consistent. (The wind are suddenly very close in the 'critics' section of *Heldenleben* and so is Willi Boskovsky later in the work.) Technically the transfer of *Don Quixote* seems more successful than that of *Ein Heldenleben*, where the violin timbre lacks body and the acoustic and the orchestral balance within it seem variable. Textures seem less than perfectly secure in places. In *Don Quixote* the overall sound has more warmth and body, and Fournier's tone is well focused. The restricted range means that the detail of the more complex passages is only hinted at, but one can adjust to the overall sound picture and enjoy the nobility of the performance. Both works offer the advantage of unbroken continuity and are unique in this respect.

Ein Heldenleben, Op. 40.
   (M) *** DG Privilege 3335 194. Berlin PO, Karajan.
   **(*) Decca KCET 601. Vienna PO, Solti.
   **DG 3300 781 [id.]. Vienna PO, Boehm.

Karajan's 1959 *Heldenleben* sounds amazingly fresh in the Privilege transfer with its clarity of detail. It is a superb performance and at medium price can be confidently recommended. Playing of great power and distinction from the Berlin Philharmonic and in the closing section an altogether becoming sensuousness and warmth. The tape offers very good general quality, though the string sound is slightly dry – there is plenty of brilliance and attack, but less richness of sheen. The transfer is not made at the highest level, but thus accommodates the wide dynamic range without distortion.

Solti characteristically gives a fast-moving performance, tense to the point of fierceness in the opening tutti and elsewhere. It underlines the urgency rather than the opulence of the writing, and though many Straussians will prefer a warmer, more relaxed view, Solti finds his justification in a superb account of the final coda after the fulfilment theme, where in touching simplicity he finds complete relaxation at last, helped by the exquisite playing of the Vienna Philharmonic's concertmaster, Rainer Küchl. The Decca recording is formidably wide-ranging to match this high-powered performance. The transfer is made at the highest level and has an obvious feeling of spectacle. But when one turns over for the 'battle' sequence there is a hint of congestion, and although for the most part the sound is brilliant and vivid there is a suggestion that a few less decibels would have brought a degree more refinement. Nevertheless the impact of this tape is considerable.

Boehm's version is superbly played by the Vienna Philharmonic, but his reading lacks the dash and fire of the others. He is a shade dour and a little too conscious of his dignity by comparison with the swaggering hero of Karajan. DG provide splendidly detailed recording, with no lack of impact and presence, but the performance is ultimately uncompelling. The cassette transfer is clear.

Piano quartet in C minor, Op. 13.
   ** Advent E 1049 (see p. xxiii) [id.]. Irma Vallecillo (piano), Los Angeles String Trio.

Although Strauss's early *Piano quartet* (1884) is represented on disc, this Los Angeles version has the cassette field to itself. It is a derivative piece, though there are already signs of Strauss's rich lyrical generosity. The performance is tautly conceived and finely played, and though the studio is evidently on the small side and the recording balance closer than ideal, it is nonetheless most vividly recorded. The whole work is accommodated on one side, lasting more than forty minutes, the second side being left blank.

Elektra (opera): complete.

**(*) Decca K 124 K 22. Birgit Nilsson, Marie Collier, Regina Resnik, Gerhard Stolze, Tom Krause, Vienna State Opera Chorus, Vienna PO, Solti.

This Decca set of *Elektra* was a *tour de force* of John Culshaw and his engineering team. Not everyone will approve of the superimposed sound-effects, but as in Wagner every one of them has justification in the score, and the end result is a magnificently vivid operatic experience created without the help of vision. Nilsson is undoubtedly incomparable in the part, with the hard side of Elektra's character brutally dominant. Only when – as in the recognition scene with Oreste – she tries to soften the naturally bright tone does she let out a suspect flat note or two. As a rule she is searingly accurate in approaching even the most formidable exposed top notes. One might draw a parallel with Solti's direction – sharply focused and brilliant in the savage music which predominates, but lacking the languorous warmth one really needs in the recognition scene, if only for contrast. The tape transfer emphasizes the recording's brilliance. It is clinically clear, but lacks a balancing sumptuous quality. One needs a treble cut if the effect is not to become aggressive. The libretto is excellently done.

Der Rosenkavalier (opera): complete.

(M)***HMV TC-SLS 810. Elisabeth Schwarzkopf, Christa Ludwig, Otto Edelmann, Eberhard Waechter, Teresa Stich-Randall, Philharmonia Chorus and Orch., Karajan.

***Decca K 3 N 23 [Lon. 5–1435]. Régine Crespin, Yvonne Minton, Otto Wiener, Manfred Jungwirth, Helen Donath, Vienna State Opera Chorus, Vienna PO, Solti.

**(*) Philips 7699 045 [id.]. Evelyn Lear, Frederica von Stade, Jules Bastin, Ruth Welting, Derek Hammond-Stroud, Netherlands Opera Chorus, Rotterdam PO, de Waart.

From Karajan one of the greatest opera sets that Walter Legge ever produced, a classic performance. Schwarzkopf points her phrases, underlining the meaning of the words after the manner of a Lieder-singer, bringing out a character at once human and emotional yet at the same time restrained and an object for admiration. She makes of the Marschallin more of a lover figure than a mother figure, and that is something which adds to the reality of the situation. Instead of the buxom prima donna we have a mature woman, still attractive, whom it would be quite understandable and sympathetic for the young Octavian to love. The moment in Act 1 when she tells Octavian how sometimes in the middle of the night she comes downstairs and stops all the clocks, so disturbed is she about the passage of time and the approach of old age, is particularly moving. With Schwarzkopf one feels that the singer is still young and attractive enough to feel this emotion as a pressing thing. She is matched by an Octavian in Christa Ludwig who has a rich mezzo but one which is neither fruity nor womanly, but steady and youthful-sounding. Teresa Stich-Randall too is wonderfully steady but her light soprano is exquisitely sweet, so that when in the presentation of the silver rose she sings the soaring phrase *Wie himmlische* one wants to use this same phrase ('How heavenly!') to describe her singing. In the final trio three such beautifully contrasted yet steady voices make a perfect match. Karajan here, as in the other emotional climaxes, chooses a speed rather slower than is customary. Some have objected, but when the result is vocally so secure and the playing of the Philharmonia Orchestra is so full-blooded the music can certainly take this treatment, and the emotional peak seems even higher than usual. These emotional climaxes are places where – as in Puccini – Strauss seems to intend his audience to weep, and Karajan plays up to this. Otto Edelmann's Ochs is rather coarser than the characterizations of some previous singers in the part, and he exaggerates the Viennese accent on such words as *Polizei, gut* and *herzel*; but vocally it is most commendable, for Edelmann really does sing on the notes and does not merely give the impression in sing-speech. The recording was splendidly refurbished for its LP reissue to produce sound of very high quality, and this has been well transferred to tape, though without so wide a dynamic range as on the discs. The vocal balance tends to be fairly forward, yet the glorious backcloth provided by the Philharmonia Orchestra is glowingly caught. The levelling of the dynamics, however, seems to have brought up the background hiss transferred from the early master tape. Nevertheless this set makes very satisfying listening.

On two counts Solti scores over any other rival in this much-recorded opera. First, he opens out all the tiny cuts which over the years have been sanctioned in opera-house performances (often with the composer's blessing). In the second place the recording is sumptuously fine. The smoothly vivid richness has been well transferred to tape, and if the quality is marginally less open and sharply defined than on disc, the special effects and general detail are superior to the EMI production (although considering its age the latter measures up remarkably well). The big question for most lovers of this opera will be the contrasting merits of the two Marschallins. Crespin is here at her finest, with tone well-focused; the slightly maternal maturity of her approach will for many appear ideal, but the range of expression, verbal and musical, in Schwarzkopf's interpretation stands un-

rivalled, one of the great recorded performances. Manfred Jungwirth makes a firm, virile if not always imaginative Ochs, Yvonne Minton a finely projected Octavian and Helen Donath a sweet-toned Sophie. Solti's direction is fittingly honeyed, with tempi even slower than Karajan's in the climactic moments. The one serious disappointment is that the great concluding *Trio* does not quite lift one to the tear-laden height one ideally wants.

The glory of the set conducted by Edo de Waart is the singing of Frederica von Stade as Octavian, a fresh youthful performance, full of imagination. Next to her the others are generally pleasing but rarely a match for the finest performers on other sets, though it is good to have the vignette of Derek Hammond-Stroud's Faninal. Evelyn Lear produces her creamiest, most beautiful tone but spreads uncomfortably in the Act 3 *Trio*. Jules Bastin gives a virile performance as Ochs; the disappointment is the Sophie of Ruth Welting, often shallow of tone. The Rotterdam orchestra plays well for its principal conductor and is beautifully recorded. The transfer, although not at the highest level, is refined in detail and gives a fresh presence to the voices. The focus clouds just a little once or twice in complex ensembles but for the most part is pleasingly clean. The recording (especially of the orchestra) is rather dry, but not without bloom and atmosphere. The set is quite well laid out, although Act 3 starts part-way through side four (of three cassettes). The libretto is clear, even though the type size is small.

Der Rosenkavalier: highlights.
**(*) Decca KCET 487 (from above set cond. Solti).

This is a good, generous selection from a superb set. It was an early tape (the highlights were issued before the complete work), and the quality is not as vivid as in the opera itself; but it is still very good.

Salome (opera): complete.

   *** Decca κ 111 κ 22. Birgit Nils-
son, Grace Hoffman, Gerhard
Stolze, Waldemar Kmentt,
Eberhard Waechter, Vienna
PO, Solti.

   *(**) HMV TC-SLS 5139. Hil-
degard Behrens, Agnes Baltsa,
Karl-Walter Böhm, Wieslaw
Ochman, José van Dam,
Vienna PO, Karajan.

The Solti recording was the first Decca
'Sonicstage' production (strange jar-
gon), with its remarkable combination of
clarity and opulence: so often with
Strauss recordings we have had to choose
between brilliance, with details so clear
they sound fussy, and rich, fruity sound
that swallows up most of the inner parts.
Here the orchestral balance brings out
details never heard in the opera-house,
yet never getting the proportions wrong
so that, say, a flute swamps the violins.
The balance between voices and orchestra is just as precisely calculated. Some
may complain that in the big climaxes the
orchestra is too dominant, but what is
remarkable is that even then the voice is
clearly separated, an ideal solution. The
technical trickery is on the whole discreet,
and when it is not – as in the close-up
effect at the end when Salome in delighted horror whispers 'I have kissed thy
mouth, Jokanaan!' – it is very much in the
interests of the drama, the sort of effect
that any stage producer would include
were it possible in the theatre.

Nilsson is splendid. She is hard-edged
as usual but on that account more convincingly wicked: the determination and
depravity are latent in the girl's character
from the start. In the final scene she rises
to new heights, compelling one to accept
and even enjoy the horror of it, while the
uncleanness is conveyed more vividly
than I can ever remember. One's spine
tingles even as one squirms.

Of this score Solti is a master. He has
rarely sounded so abandoned in a re-

corded performance. The emotion swells
up naturally even while the calculation of
impact is most precise. Waechter makes a
clear, young-sounding Jokanaan. Gerhard Stolze portrays the unbalance of
Herod with frightening conviction, and
Grace Hoffman does all she can in the
comparatively ungrateful part of Hero-
dias. The tape transfer is outstandingly
successful, capturing the clarity and opulence of the recording with the widest
dynamic range and an amazing feeling of
spaciousness. The power of the opera's
climax is given tremendous presence and
projection. The libretto is admirably
clear, although, curiously, the side breaks
are not indicated.

Recorded for EMI by Decca engineers
in the Sofiensaal in Vienna, Karajan's
sumptuously beautiful version faithfully
recaptures the flair and splendour of the
Salzburg production, which Karajan
produced as well as conducted. It was
daring of him when preparing both recording and stage production to choose
for the role of heroine a singer then relatively unknown, but Hildegard Behrens
is triumphantly successful, a singer who
in the early scenes has one actively
sympathizing with the girlish princess,
and who keeps that sympathy and
understanding to a stage where most sopranos have been transformed into raging
harpies. The sensuous beauty of tone is
ravishingly conveyed, but the recording –
less analytical than the Decca set under
Solti, also recorded in the Sofiensaal – is
not always fair to her fine projection of
sound, occasionally masking the voice.
All the same the feeling of a live performance has been well captured, and the rest
of the cast is of the finest Salzburg standard. In particular José van Dam
makes a gloriously noble Jokanaan, and
in the early scenes his offstage voice from
the cistern at once commands attention,
underlining the direct diatonic strength
of his music in contrast to the exoticry
representing Salome and the court. Karajan – as so often in Strauss – is at his
most commanding and sympathetic, with

the orchestra, more forward than some will like, playing rapturously. This is a performance which, so far from making one recoil from perverted horrors, has one revelling in sensuousness. Unfortunately the tape transfer has an over-resonant bass which muddies the climaxes, notably at the end of the *Dance of the seven veils* and in the opera's closing pages. But the ear notices it at once, very near the opening, and while the sound generally is rich and atmospheric the element of distortion of the lower frequencies returns sporadically, and the sound lacks the freedom and range of the Decca set. The libretto is partly printed in white type on a coffee-coloured background, and is not nearly so easy to follow as the Decca booklet.

Salome (opera): *Dance of the seven veils; Closing scene.* Lieder: *Cäcilie; Ich liebe dich; Morgen!; Wiegenlied; Zueignung.*
> **(*) DG 3300 963 [id.]. Montserrat Caballé (soprano), French National Orch., Bernstein.

One of Caballé's earliest and most refreshingly imaginative opera sets was Strauss's *Salome* with Leinsdorf conducting. This version of the final scene, recorded over a decade later with a very different conductor, has much of the same imagination, the sweet innocent girl still observable next to the bloodthirsty fiend. The other side of the tape is less recommendable, partly because Caballé underlines the expressiveness of works that remain Lieder even with the orchestral accompaniment. Bernstein too directs an overweighted account of the *Dance of the seven veils.* The recording is basically warm and full but the transfer to tape is top-heavy: the strings have an over-accented upper range and are fierce. A strong treble cut smooths the sound considerably but leaves the violin sheen lacking ripeness, although Caballé is given plenty of presence.

Stravinsky, Igor
(1882–1971)

Violin concerto in D major.
> *** Decca KSXC 6601. Kyung-Wha Chung, LSO, Previn – WALTON: *Concerto.*⊛***

Kyung-Wha Chung is at her most incisive for the spikily swaggering outer movements, which with Previn's help are presented here in all their distinctiveness, tough and humorous at the same time. In the two movements labelled *Aria* Chung brings fantasy as well as lyricism; she is less overtly expressive than her rivals on disc, but conveys instead an inner brooding quality. Excellent recording, and an outstandingly fine cassette transfer. The vivid orchestral colours in the Stravinsky (the tuba especially well caught) are of demonstration quality.

Complete ballets: (i) *The Firebird (L'Oiseau de feu); Petrushka* (original 1911 score); (ii) *The Rite of Spring (Le Sacre du printemps).*
> **(*) Philips 7699 060. LPO, Haitink.
> *(**) CBS 40-79318. (i) New York PO; (ii) Cleveland Orch.; both cond. Boulez.

The Firebird (ballet): *suite* (1919 score). Complete ballets: *Petrushka* (1911 score); *The Rite of Spring.*
> (B) **(*) Decca KDPC 2 7052. Paris Conservatoire Orch., Monteux.

If Haitink's readings of these three great ballets of Stravinsky's early career seem rather understated, their focus and rhythmic point certainly make them satisfying on repetition. Haitink leaves the music to speak for itself; he is unhurried yet never sluggish, and there is a marvellous freshness about all three readings. The result is always musical, never brilliant for its own sake – as in the evocative music at the start of *Firebird*. In *Le Sacre* he makes no gestures to the groundlings; indeed some may find him too cautious in the *Danse sacrale* and not atmospheric enough at the opening of the second part. In general, however, the performances must be counted among the very best in the catalogue. The transfers to tape have been made at a comparatively modest level, and this has led to a feeling of restricted range in the treble. There is a lack of sparkling transients, which reduces the glitter in *Petrushka* and smooths over the gauze-like delicacy of texture in *The Firebird*. Indeed the separate cassette of this work (an earlier issue), or at least our review copy of it, seems to show greater range. The bloom of the resonance is retained, and there are some glowing orchestral colours throughout, but there is occasionally some harshness in *tutti*, noticeable in the opening and closing tableaux of *Petrushka* and in *The Rite of Spring*, where the tam-tam, for instance, loses focus. These two ballets are back to back on the first cassette, with *The Firebird* complete on the second.

Pierre Monteux, the conductor on the 'Double-Decca' tape, was closely associated with Stravinsky at the time when he was composing his major ballet scores, and Monteux conducted the first performance of *The Rite of Spring*. In spite of the lack of polish of the French orchestral playing (most noticeable in the *Firebird suite* – although there is also some lack of absolute assurance in the *Rite*), this is vivid music-making throughout and Julius Katchen, no less, was recruited for the solo piano part in *Petrushka*. This is the finest of the three performances and is helped by a recording with plenty of atmosphere and detail. The transfers are of good quality, though some care is necessary in setting the controls or a touch of harshness creeps in. But with any reservations these are still fine recordings, projected here with life and detail.

Boulez recorded the third of the three early ballets with the Cleveland Orchestra some years before the other two, and one would deduce that that is the key work for him. Having the three performances together underlines the consistency of Boulez's approach, with *Firebird* and *Petrushka* leading logically to the *Rite*. So it is that *Firebird*, for all the beauty of the New York orchestra's playing (where Boulez habitually was a more expressive conductor than before), is remarkable for strength and power rather than for sensuously evocative atmosphere. *Petrushka* similarly may lack some of the wit and sparkle which other conductors give it; but the score's strength leads even more obviously towards the *Rite*. As for the *Rite* itself, Boulez's spaciously paced, superbly forceful reading remains among the most satisfying ever recorded. The transfers have been made at a comparatively high level which brings good projection and vivid detail but some attendant drawbacks. In *Firebird* the bass drum muddies the texture occasionally (although otherwise the sound is often impressive); in *Petrushka* the upper strings are fierce (the woodwind has no lack of bloom), and in the *Rite* there is both harshness and, on side two, more congestion from the drums and a fair amount of coarseness in the work's closing pages.

The Firebird (*L'Oiseau de feu;* ballet): complete.
- *** Philips 7300 353 [id.]. LPO, Haitink.
- *** DG 3300 483 [id.]. LSO, Dorati.

No more refined performance of the complete *Firebird* has ever been recorded than Haitink's, and it is warmly recommended. The sheer savagery of *Kaschei's dance* may be a little muted, but the sharpness of attack and the clarity of detail make for a thrilling result, while the magic and poetry of the whole score are given a hypnotic beauty, with the LPO at its very finest. Recording of demonstration quality, and a beautiful cassette transfer which loses little in detail and atmosphere. It is perhaps a pity the level of transfer was not set marginally higher, but the fortissimos blaze to life vividly.

Dorati's newest recording of *The Firebird* with the RPO, using slightly faster tempi than those chosen by Haitink, is certainly dramatic and extremely vivid as a recording. However, the balance is rather close and relatively unatmospheric. The sound itself has superb bite and impact, and this may well appeal to those who like the Phase Four type of recording. It is exciting if lacking something in refinement.

The Firebird: suite (1919 score).
⊛ ***HMV TC-ASD 3645. Philadelphia Orch., Muti – MUSSORGSKY: *Pictures*.***

Muti secures superb playing from the Philadelphia Orchestra here. There have been many excellent accounts of this score in recent years, from Abbado, Giulini and others, but in terms of magic and poetry this surpasses them all. The *pianissimo* tone Muti draws from thhe Philadelphia strings is ravishing. This is a wonderful coupling, and the transfer to tape is first-class; the difference in soound between disc and cassette is minimal.

The Firebird: suite (1919 score); *Jeu de cartes* (ballet): complete.
*** DG 3300 483 [id.]. LSO, Abbado.

Stunning performances of great vitality and sensitivity. The LSO plays with superb virtuosity and spirit, and Abbado's feeling for atmosphere and colour is everywhere in evidence. Moreover the DG recording has plenty of detail, presence and impact, as well as an excellently judged musical perspective. The tape transfer is extremely vivid, the sound often approaching demonstration

standard in the *Firebird suite*. It is equally vibrant in *Jeu de cartes*, but here the transients are marginally less clean, although the detail and impact remain impressive.

(i) *The Firebird: suite* (1919 score); (ii) *Petrushka*: complete (1911 score).
(B)(**) RCA Camden C4-5034. (i) Paris Conservatoire Orch.; (ii) Boston SO; both cond. Monteux.

Monteux's Camden reissue includes the performance of the *Firebird suite* that is also available on Decca (see above) but uses a different version of *Petrushka*, made in Boston. This is an extremely lively performance and offers finer orchestral playing than the Paris version. There is a particularly exciting account of the final scene, all the bustle of the Shrovetide carnival brilliantly conveyed. The snag is the Boston acoustic, which adds a touch of harshness to the sound; and the Camden transfer is muffled and lacking in brilliance and sparkle, which makes matters even worse.

The Firebird: suite (1919 score); *The Song of the Nightingale* (symphonic poem).
(B) *** DG Heliodor 3348 145. Berlin PO, Maazel.

Le Rossignol is an underrated Stravinsky opera; its derivative opening, with overtones of *Nuages*, and its Rimskian flavour have led to its virtues being undervalued. Among them is its extraordinarily rich fantasy and vividness of colouring; and the symphonic poem that Stravinsky made from the material of this work deserves a more established place in the concert repertoire. The exotic effects and glittering colours are superbly caught here; the Berlin Philharmonic offers the utmost refinement. Maazel's reading of the *Firebird suite* too has an enjoyable *éclat*, and he has the advantage of the most beautiful woodwind playing, notably the oboe in the *Princesses' dance* and the bassoon in the *Berceuse*. The recording of both works was notable for its splendid atmosphere, and only the massed upper strings hint at its early date. The tape transfer is of sophisticated quality. The level seems a little low for *The Song of the Nightingale*, and the recording lacks the last degree of edge and range in the treble. But it remains very impressive, and there is no lack of brilliance in the *Firebird suite*.

The Firebird: suite (1945 revised version).

(M)*(*) RCA Gold Seal GK 42700 [AGK 1 1528]. Boston SO, Leinsdorf – RIMSKY-KORSAKOV: *Le Coq d'or*.*(*)

Leinsdorf uses the revised 1945 score with the extra movements (and the *Dance with the golden apples* is one of the most effective numbers here). The over-resonant sound clouds the vivid detail of Stravinsky's orchestration, although in some ways the cassette has rather more impact than the disc. There is fine playing and atmosphere, but this cannot compare with the finest versions of the 1919 suite.

Petrushka (ballet): complete (1911 score).

*** DG 3300 711 [id.]. LPO, Dutoit.
**(*) Philips 7300 354 [id.]. LPO, Haitink.

Petrushka is not a work one associates with DG, but it is brilliantly conducted by Charles Dutoit, and this issue is a splendid achievement. In many ways this is the freshest, most vivid account to be recorded since Ansermet's famous LP mono version. Interestingly it was made almost impromptu: a planned opera recording fell through and sessions were hastily reallotted with little advance planning. The result is triumphantly spontaneous in its own right, with rhythms that are incisive yet beautifully buoyant, and a degree of expressiveness in the orchestral playing that subtly underlines the dramatic atmosphere, and is especially magical in the Third Tableau. The final section too is strongly coloured, so that the gentle closing pages make a touching contrast to the gaiety of the early part of the scene. The recording is rich and sparkling, the only fault of balance being the prominence of the concertante piano soloist, Tamás Vásáry, who (ably as he plays) is given a ridiculously out-of-proportion star billing. The tape transfer, although not made at the highest level, offers DG's most sophisticated quality.

Haitink's *Petrushka* is faithful, well-delineated and musically rewarding, though some may feel that it errs occasionally on the side of understatement. Excellent recording: the firm definition and the perfectly proportioned and truthful aural perspective make it a joy to listen to. However, the Philips transfer, although good, is not quite as vividly detailed as Dutoit's DG issue.

Petrushka: complete (1947 score).

**(*) Philips 7300 653 [id.]. Concertgebouw Orch., Colin Davis.
*(*) Decca KSXC 6883 [Lon. 5-7106]. Vienna PO, Dohnányi.

Colin Davis's Philips version of the 1947 score combines brilliant and rich recording with a performance which to an exceptional degree makes a positive case for the 1947 score over the original. The recording has some curious and not always perfectly balanced spotlighting of instruments (most unexpected from Philips), but it reveals details of the rich texture that are normally obscured. From first to last Davis makes it clear that he regards this as fun music, drawing brilliantly precise playing from the Concertgebouw and rarely if ever forcing the pace, though always maintaining necessary excitement. The piano solo starts a little cautiously in the Russian dance, but that is an exception in an unusually positive reading. The transfer is slightly soft-grained in the treble, and the tone of the upper strings is somewhat lacking in body compared with the rest of the orchestra; otherwise the quality is vivid.

Christoph von Dohnányi's measured approach has a certain warmth, matched by the playing of the VPO, for whom the score is an obvious novelty. The sound is rich but not very sharply detailed, and this effect is emphasized on tape by the mellow quality of the transfer. The lack of drama and bite (the trumpet flourishes at the close are curiously laboured) is a serious drawback, and there is no compensating imaginative feel for the work's atmosphere. The solo pianist (Horst Gobel) provides a very mundane contribution. This cannot compare with Dutoit's splendid DG version (see above) or Colin Davis's Philips issue. Moreover the Decca turnover is clumsily placed (on disc as well as tape), in the middle of the Third Tableau.

(i) *Pulcinella* (ballet after Pergolesi): complete. *Suites Nos. 1 and 2.*
   ***HMV TC-ASD 3604. Northern Sinfonia Orch., Rattle, (i) with Jennifer Smith (soprano), John Fryatt (tenor), Malcolm King (bass).

Simon Rattle, helped rather than hindered by a somewhat dry recording acoustic which gives the flavour of a small theatre, conveys far more than usual the links between this score and the much later neo-classical opera *The Rake's Progress*. As one hears this genial theatrical entertainment, Rattle might be directing it as an adjunct to *The Rake's Progress* at Glyndebourne. With lively colourful playing from the Northern Sinfonia (the solos strong and positive) and with first-rate contributions from the three soloists, all of them artists who deserve to record much more, the high spir-

its of this score come over superbly. The high-level transfer has a wide range and gives orchestra and voices alike the most vivid presence and detail. A little smoothing of the treble improves the naturalness of the sound, but the overall projection is dramatic in its colour and impact.

Pulcinella: suite.
   *(**) Pye ZCPCNHX 3. Orch. of St John's, Smith Square, Lubbock – BARTÓK: *Rumanian dances***; RAVEL: *Ma Mère l'Oye suite.**(**)

Lubbock directs a fine bouncing performance of the *Pulcinella suite*, warmly recommended to anyone who fancies the coupling. The cassette transfer is lively, but there is a hint of coarseness in the acoustic, noticeable immediately at the opening.

The Rite of Spring (Le Sacre du printemps; ballet): complete.
   ***DG 3300 884 [id.]. Berlin PO, Karajan.
   *** Decca KSXC 6691 [Lon. 5-6885]. Chicago SO, Solti.
   ***DG 3300 635. LSO, Abbado.
   **(*)Philips 7300 585 [id.]. Concertgebouw Orch., Colin Davis.
   **(*)Philips 7300 278 [id.]. LPO, Haitink.
   (M) **(*) Enigma K 423520. National Youth Orch. of Great Britain, Rattle.
   (M) **(*) Philips 7317 119. LSO, Colin Davis.
   **(*)CBS 40-76676 [Col. XMT 34557]. New York PO, Mehta.
   *(**) CBS 40-72807. Cleveland Orch., Boulez.
   *(*)RCA RK 25130. LPO, Tjeknavorian.

Karajan's earlier LP recording of Stravinsky's masterpiece came in for much snide criticism from the composer, who described one passage as being a 'tempo di hoochie-koochie', and doubted whether Berlin Philharmonic traditions could compass music from so different a discipline. In this more recent recording, tougher, more urgent, less mannered and certainly exhilarating, Karajan goes a long way towards rebutting Stravinsky's complaints, and the result is superb. Karajan and his great orchestra are at their very finest, persuasive still (the opening of Part 2 is wonderfully atmospheric) but never obtrusively so, and above all powerfully and incisively dramatic. The transfer to tape is stunningly successful, with an extremely wide dynamic range yet admirable subtlety of detail in the *piano* and *pianissimo* passages. The tuttis is given a superb bite, and the cutting edge of the strings is splendidly managed without any feeling of unnatural abrasiveness. The spectacle on side two (marvellous drums) is riveting.

Solti's is a powerful, unrelenting account of Stravinsky's revolutionary score, with virtuoso playing from the Chicago orchestra and recording that demonstrates with breathtaking clarity the precision of inner detail. Some of the gentler half-tones of the score are presented rather glaringly, but this view of the work is magnificently consistent, showing Solti at his most tautly dramatic. The cassette is of demonstration quality. It is transferred at a high level and is splendidly vivid, with crisp transients and a fine sense of spectacle. The recording expands without strain for the climaxes, and there is both warmth and atmosphere in the lyrical moments.

There is a degree of detachment in Abbado's version with the LSO, which is arguably apt. In every way this is an outstanding reading, certain to excite the keenest admiration if not the warmest affection. Abbado even more than most rivals seems to have answered every problem on even the slightest point of detail. His observance of markings is meticulous, and an orchestra whose members have sometimes claimed they could play this score without a conductor (it has long been a favourite with the LSO) revels in the security given by Abbado's direction. The recording is breathtakingly brilliant, with a range of dynamic exceptionally wide even by latterday standards. The cassette transfer is splendid too, offering fresh, clear sound in spite of the wide range of dynamics. The edge and presence of the brass are especially impressive, and the overall effect is highly spectacular.

Colin Davis has his idiosyncrasies in this score (one of them his strange hold-up on the last chord), but in the new Concertgebouw recording he shows that his basic view of the work has not changed since his earlier LSO version of the mid-sixties. But here, with superb orchestral playing, this unusually direct view brings results that are strong, forthright and powerful. Some will prefer a more obviously involving reading, but the opulent sound of the Concertgebouw Orchestra, richly recorded, and the physical impact of this performance are still irresistible. The broadly resonant recording has been quite well transferred; there are some striking large-scale effects on side two: the horns are superbly caught, and the bass drum too. But the upper range of the recording lacks glitter and bite and the strings are given insufficient edge of attack, even in a performance as broadly conceived as this.

The natural and unforced qualities of Haitink's reading of Stravinsky have real compulsion. In a work which challenges the conductor to the utmost, Haitink is rather like one of those effortless golf wizards who hardly seem to strain a muscle but who drive farther than anyone. Other versions hammer the listener more powerfully, thrust him along more forcefully, but the sheer beauty of sound here, as well as the bite and precision of the playing, is most impressive.

For those who want to see beyond the brutality of the work, this performance could be a good first choice. Those wanting a stronger and more incisive reading could well turn to Solti or Karajan.

The performance of the National Youth Orchestra in this once-feared showpiece is not just 'good considering', but 'good' absolute; the youngsters under their young conductor produce warm, spontaneous and often very vivid playing. The conviction of the performance is the more evident because it was recorded in long takes, and the penalty of having a few imprecisions and errors is minimal. At medium price this is well worth considering, and the sound on tape is first-class. A slight treble cut may be useful on some players, but the recording has fine depth and atmosphere (the timpani, superbly played, make a spectacular effect) and the resonance does not cloud detail. An exciting issue.

Colin Davis's earlier LSO version is characteristically straightforward and thrusting. Sometimes he misses out on detail, but his full-bloodedness is certainly effective. This is good value at medium price, and the Philips recording, if not super-brilliant, is still very good.

Mehta's first recording with the New York Philharmonic after being appointed principal conductor duplicated a work he had already recorded with the Los Angeles orchestra (see below). As before, the reading is strong and dramatic, but the recording quality for CBS is less sharply defined than in the incisive Decca tape. It is pleasant, atmospheric sound, with plenty of weight, very different from the usual spotlit CBS style, but hardly as revealing as the best rivals. The transfer is faithful and particularly impressive in the latter half of the work, where the recording has striking depth and amplitude.

Boulez developed his reading of Le Sacre over the years so that finally he came to this recorded view that tempi should be generally measured, approaching those of Stravinsky himself in his final

recorded disc version. Boulez is less lyrical than the composer, but compensates with a relentless rhythmic urgency. Unfortunately the recording – thrilling on LP – has lost its transient bite in the tape transfer. Thus while its massiveness (matching the monolithic quality of the interpretation) remains, the cutting edge is all but blunted. This lessens the impact of such moments as the brass contrasts in *Jeux des cités rivales*.

Tjeknavorian's RCA version is undistinguished, its rhythms ponderous rather than powerful. The LPO produces some fine playing, notably at the atmospheric opening of Part 2, but the forward balance of the wind soloists reduces the dynamic contrast. The resonant acoustic produces a lack of inner clarity and coupled to the lack of any thrusting quality this tape cannot be recommended.

The Rite of Spring: complete; *8 Instrumental miniatures for 15 players.*
**(*)Decca KSXC 6444. Los Angeles PO or Chamber Ens., Mehta.

Mehta, in contrast with Boulez – whose Cleveland version (see above) appeared in the same month as this – favours very fast tempi in such passages as the *Spring augurs* and the final *Danse sacrale*. By contrast some of the contemplative passages, such as the *Rondes printanières*, are unusually expansive. It is an individual and interesting reading, and the playing, while not achieving Cleveland polish, is extremely brilliant. The *Eight Miniatures* are a comparatively late orchestration of some of the easy piano pieces Stravinsky labelled *Cinq doigts, Five-finger exercises*: an attractive fill-up but not so important as to affect the list of preferences in the *Rite*. On cassette the *Miniatures* are played first, making a very attractive prelude to Stravinsky's ballet score. The transfer is of first-class Decca quality, extremely brilliant and with an appropriate incisive edge.

559

The Rite of Spring: complete; (i) *The King of the Stars (Le Roi des Étoiles;* cantata).

> (M)**(*)DG Privilege 3335 222 [3300 269]. Boston SO, Tilson Thomas, (i) with New England Male Conservatory Chorus.

Michael Tilson Thomas's version of *The Rite of Spring* has an important if brief makeweight in the rare cantata of the same period – unperformed for several decades but here shown as an intensely imaginative, evocative choral work. The major offering is presented in a warmly expressive reading that misses some of the music's bite. The amply reverberant recording matches the approach, and although it has, on the whole, transferred successfully to tape some of the detail is less sharply defined than in other versions. *Le Roi des Étoiles* is used to open the cassette and proves an effective curtain-raiser.

The Soldier's Tale (L'Histoire du soldat): complete.

> *** Argo KZNC 15. Rudolph Nureyev, Michael MacLiammoir, Glenda Jackson, Instrumental Ens., Zalkowitsch.

Gennady Zalkowitsch directs an urgently vigorous performance of Stravinsky's score which conveys the element of earthiness. It is more Russian than neoclassic, with Erich Gruenberg an excellent violin soloist. In this version the narrator – the tough Glenda Jackson – has more to do than usual, while Nureyev as the Soldier and Michael MacLiammoir as the Devil are sharply contrasted. Good, clear recording which rather favours the voices, and the transfer is admirably clear and natural. Because the voices are well forward one is immediately involved in the narrative, and the balance between the actors and the illustrative commentary of the music is well maintained.

Three movements from Petrushka.

> **(*) Decca Phase 4 KPFC 4362 [Lon. 5–21148]. Ilana Vered (piano) – TCHAIKOVSKY: *Piano concerto No. 1.***(*)

Ilana Vered's performance is predictably brilliant, and shows a splendid feeling for the score's colour and atmosphere. The Decca piano tone is very brightly lit, the image close; on tape the quality is clean and natural.

(i) *Mass for voices and woodwinds;* (ii) *Les Noces* (ballet): complete.

> *** DG 3300 880 [id.]. English Bach Festival Chorus, Bernstein, with (i) Trinity Boys', Choir, members of the English Bach Festival Orch.; (ii) Anny Mory (soprano), Patricia Parker (mezzo-soprano), John Mitchinson (tenor), Paul Hudson (bass), Martha Argerich, Krystian Zimerman, Cyprien Katsaris, Homero Francesch (pianos), English Bach Festival Percussion Ens.

Bernstein directs characterful performances of these works, unexpectedly but imaginatively coupled. He reinforces the point that both the *Mass* and the much earlier ballet illustrating a folk wedding ceremony are intensely Russian in their inspiration. In the *Mass* the style is overtly expressive, with the boys of Trinity Choir responding freshly, but it is in *Les Noces* that Bernstein conveys an electricity, a dramatic urgency which at last give the work its rightful stature as one of the composer's supreme masterpieces, totally original and still today unexpected, not least in its black-and-white instrumentation for four pianos and percussion. The star pianists here make a superb team. Good atmospheric recording, and the transfer is first-class, the choral textures clean and incisive, the percussive transients in *Les Noces* admirably crisp. A demonstration tape.

Oedipus Rex (opera-oratorio): complete.

> *** Decca KCET 616. Alec Mc-Cowen (narrator), Peter Pears, Kerstin Meyer, Donald McIntyre, Stafford Dean, Ryland Davies, Benjamin Luxon, John Alldis Choir, LPO, Solti.

Solti's view of this highly stylized work is less sharp-edged than one would expect, and the dominant factor in the performance is not so much the conductor's direction as the heartfelt singing of Sir Peter Pears in the title role. It was he who sang the part in the composer's first LP recording twenty years earlier, and here the crispness and clarity of his delivery go with an ability to point the key moments of deep emotion with extraordinary intensity. The rest of the vocal team is good, if not outstanding, and the narrations (in English) of Alec McCowen are apt and undistracting. The outstandingly full and brilliant recording has transferred to tape with superb vividness. The chorus is given a splendidly incisive projection, and the balance of the soloists is wholly natural, with the most vivid orchestral detail throughout. A demonstration tape of the highest quality.

Sullivan, Arthur
(1842–1900)

Henry VIII: incidental music; *Macbeth: Overtures*: see under *Trial by Jury*.

Imperial march: see under *Utopia Ltd*.

In Memoriam overture; The Merchant of Venice: suite; The Tempest: incidental music.

> (M) *** HMV Greensleeve TC-ESD 7057. City of Birmingham SO, Dunn.

The longest work here, the suite of incidental music for *The Tempest*, dates from 1861, when the student composer was only nineteen. Not surprisingly it made him an overnight reputation, for it displays an astonishing flair and orchestral confidence. The *Introduction* may be melodramatic but it is memorably atmospheric too, and although some of the other items are conventional, the *Banquet dance* is charmingly scored and the *Dance of the Nymphs and Shepherds* is already anticipating *Iolanthe*. The *In Memoriam overture* opens with a hymn tune (*andante religioso*) which at the close is blown up, complete with organ, into an irresistibly self-confident 'transfiguration'. This work was written for the 1866 Norwich Festival, and although officially dedicated to the memory of Sullivan's recently deceased father, the composer obviously had his eye on a popular success, for there can be few less elegiac tributes to a departed relative. The shorter *Merchant of Venice* suite was composed five years later, and almost immediately the writing begins to anticipate the lively style which was so soon to find a happy marriage with Gilbert's words. The performance here is highly infectious. Sir Vivian Dunn also proves himself (understandably as an ex-director of the Band of HM Royal Marines) a master of musical grandiloquence in his account of *In Memoriam*. The recording is excellent throughout, and it is vividly transferred. It sounds best with the treble cut back a bit, but the big climax at the end of the overture is spectacularly handled, without congestion.

Marmion overture: see under *The Gondoliers*.

Overtures: (i; ii) *Di Ballo*; (i; iii) *The*

561

Gondoliers; (iv; v) *HMS Pinafore;* (i; iii) *Iolanthe; The Mikado;* (iv; iii) *The Pirates of Penzance;* (iv; vi) *The Yeomen of the Guard.*

> (M) *** Decca KCSP 259. (i) New SO of London; (ii) Collins; (iii) Godfrey; (iv) RPO; (v) Walker; (vi) Sargent.

The performances of the opera overtures are taken from the Decca complete sets. They readily reflect the unfailing sparkle and spontaneity that Isidore Godfrey brought to his performances and the remarkably consistent quality of the Decca recording. The acoustic is slightly dry but gives an authentic flavour of the theatre. *HMS Pinafore* is directed by James Walker and represents the best part of an otherwise disappointing set (no longer available on tape), while *The Yeomen of the Guard* reflects the extra spaciousness Sir Malcolm Sargent brought to this score. As a bonus Decca have discovered a vivacious recording of the *Di Ballo overture* conducted by Anthony Collins which must date from the mid-fifties yet still provides stereo of excellent quality. This is much the best available collection of Sullivan overtures and makes a splendid bargain. The cassette transfer is of good quality, crisp and clean.

Overtures: *The Gondoliers; HMS Pinafore; Iolanthe; The Mikado; The Pirates of Penzance; The Yeomen of the Guard.*

> (M) *(*) HMV TC-EXE 35. Pro Arte Orch., Sargent.

In spite of the warm, vivid recording one cannot praise Sir Malcolm's collection of overtures. The playing and tempi are comparatively limp, and there is an absence of vivacity and sparkle. The transfers are generally fresh and clear and enjoyably bright. There is just a hint of coarsening once or twice in loud moments, but generally this is well managed.

Pineapple Poll (ballet music, arr. Mackerras).

> (M) *** HMV Greensleeve TC-ESD 7028. RPO, Mackerras.

If ever there was a definitive recording, here is one from Mackerras of his own brilliantly witty score. The orchestral playing is immaculate; among the fine wind-playing the solo oboe is especially delightful. HMV have provided a quite outstanding recording, colourful, wide in range, with a splendid bloom and ambience, which will surely be hard to beat. Generally the tape sound is excellent, and the resonance of the recording seems to offer no problems. There is plenty of brilliance here, and the overall balance is very similar to the disc, which has only a touch more refinement.

OPERAS

The Savoy operas are well represented on tape. Decca have usually chosen to make available the newer series of D'Oyly Carte recordings under Royston Nash, rather than the earlier Godfrey recordings. They are presented in box form with two cassettes matching the discs in layout. HMV have generally chosen a single-tape format for their series conducted by Sir Malcolm Sargent, with the double advantages of continuity and economy.

(i) *Cox and Box*; (ii) *The Zoo.*

> **(*) Decca KTXC 128 [Lon. 5-1171]. D'Oyly Carte Opera Chorus, RPO, Royston Nash, with (i) Gareth Jones, Geoffrey Shovelton, Michael Rayner; (ii) Meston Reid, Kenneth Sandforth, John Ayldon, Julia Goss, Jane Metcalfe.

The Zoo (with a libretto by Bolton Rowe, a pseudonym for B. C. Stevenson) dates from June 1875, only three months after the success of *Trial by Jury*, which it obviously seeks to emulate, as the music more than once reminds us. With some initial success the piece was restaged in 1879, but after eighteen performances was withdrawn. Unpublished, the score lay neglected for nearly a century in the vaults of a London bank. This recorded performance is the first to be associated with the D'Oyly Carte Company. Although the libretto lacks the finesse and whimsicality of Gilbert, it is not without humour, and many of the situations presented by the plot (and indeed the actual combinations of words and music) are typical of the later Savoy operas. Thomas Brown (the disguised Duke of Islington) has a charmingly pompous number, *Ladies and gentlemen*, in which he addresses the crowd and requires their good-humoured prompting in the presentation of his speech, and Eliza's song *I'm a simple little child* catches the metre and style of the Victorian music-hall. The musical invention itself is often delightful and shows Sullivan's characteristic craftsmanship. The two couples are given a fetching double-duet, with a romantic melody and a patter song ingeniously combined. The plot contains reminders of Offenbach's *La Périchole*, which at the time of the first production of *The Zoo* was playing at another theatre in London, in harness with *Trial by Jury*. As the piece has no spoken dialogue it is provided here with a stylized narration, well enough presented by Geoffrey Shovelton. A recording of the animals at London Zoo sets the scene fairly effectively, but the return of the animal noises at the end is an unnecessary intrusion. The performance, however, is first-class, splendidly sung, fresh as paint, and admirably recorded, with a natural and lively tape transfer. The coupling is a new recording of *Cox and Box*, rather fuller than the earlier D'Oyly Carte version (coupled to *The Gondoliers* and not yet available on tape), and complete with its charming miniature overture. The per-

formance is sprightly but not as memorable as that splendid earlier performance, which featured Alan Styler, Joseph Riordan and Donald Adams. The captivating *Bacon 'Lullaby'* is not as beguilingly sung here as it was by Joseph Riordan. Moreover the recording (as in the Nash remake of *Trial by Jury*) pushes all the soloists forward and thus loses much of the feeling of a stage perspective. The tape transfer is made at a very high level and gives the solo voices a degree of edginess, but is otherwise vivid.

The Gondoliers: complete, with dialogue; *Marmion overture*.
** Decca K 73 K 22 [Lon. 5-12110]. John Reed, Kenneth Sandford, Meston Reid, Michael Rayner, Barbara Lilley, Jane Metcalfe, Julia Goss, Geoffrey Shovelton, Lyndsie Holland, D'Oyly Carte Opera Company, RPO, Nash.

There are two stereo D'Oyly Carte versions of *The Gondoliers* in the current Decca catalogue. The earlier classic set, under Godfrey (one of the finest recordings he ever made), is unfortunately not available on cassette; instead Decca have chosen the later 1977 recording under Royston Nash for their tape issue. Both on disc and cassette it is fitted on to four sides (the tapes are in a box) even though it includes the dialogue. And it is the dialogue that will be the stumbling block for most listeners: the stylized speech of Casilda – her assumed impediment provides the consonant 'w' in place of every 'r', thus altering 'Barataria' to 'Bawatawia' – becomes irritating before the opera is over. The performance is generally fresh and lively, although in the overture Nash's rather heavy pointing of the gavotte immediately shows less rhythmic resilience than in Godfrey's classic account. The singing is generally good, and

John Reed is on top form. The recording is clear, and especially lively in the tape version, but not as richly expansive as on the earlier Decca set. The *Marmion overture*, inspired by Walter Scott's poem, makes an interesting if not indispensable bonus.

The Gondoliers: complete, without dialogue.
  (M) ** HMV TC2-SXDW 3027. Alexander Young, Richard Lewis, Edna Graham, Elsie Morison, Geraint Evans, John Cameron, Marjorie Thomas, Owen Brannigan, Glyndebourne Festival Chorus, Pro Arte Orch., Sargent.

One would have thought that, after *Yeomen*, *The Gondoliers* would be the most readily responsive of the popular operas to the full operatic treatment. However, Sargent's set, for all its virtues, is not a complete success, and strangely enough it is in the long opening scene, where one would have expected Sir Malcolm's forces to be completely captivating, that there is some lack of spontaneity. At the entrance of the Duke of Plaza-Toro things warm up considerably (although the side-drum without snares feels curiously out of key), and Owen Brannigan, as a perfectly cast Don Alhambra, sings a masterly *No possible doubt whatever*. From then onwards and throughout the rest of the opera there is much to delight the ear. Edna Graham's Casilda is charmingly small-voiced (by the same token Elsie Morison is a little heavy in her song at the beginning of side two). Sir Malcolm adopts some unaccountably slow tempi in places, especially for the *Cachucha*, but the small ensembles and unaccompanied singing are lovely. There is a great deal of musical pleasure to be had from this set, and, having the advantage of a single-tape format, it is certainly competitive on grounds of price. The sound is of high quality, with a natural bloom on the voices and plenty of warmth, yet no lack of vividness.

The Grand Duke: complete.
  **(*) Decca K 17 K 22 [Lon. 5-12106]. John Reed, Kenneth Sandford, John Ayldon, Julia Goss, Jane Metcalfe, Lyndsie Holland, Meston Reid, Michael Rayner, D'Oyly Carte Opera Company, RPO, Nash.

The Grand Duke was the fourteenth and last of the Savoy operas. In spite of a spectacular production and a brilliant first night on 7 March 1896, the work only played for 123 performances and then lapsed into relative oblivion, although it has been revived by amateur societies. The present recording came after a successful concert presentation in 1975, and the recorded performance, which has both polish and vigour, represents perhaps the ideal way to sample Sullivan's least-known major score. Less than first-rate Sullivan can still make rewarding listening, even though, compared with the sparkle and melodic inspiration of *HMS Pinafore*, the music shows a sad decline. Gilbert's libretto is impossibly complicated, but there are many felicities in the lyrics to reward the dedicated enthusiast. The tape transfer is extremely vivid, with excellent presence and detail. There is sometimes just a touch of hardness to the female voices, but the sound has no lack of body and atmosphere.

HMS Pinafore: complete, with dialogue.
  *** Decca K 123 K 22 [Lon. 5-1277]. John Reed, Jeffrey Skitch, Thomas Round, Donald Adams, Jean Hindmarsh, Joyce Wright, Gillian Knight, D'Oyly Carte Opera Chorus, New SO of London, Godfrey.

Everyone has their own G. and S. favourite and *HMS Pinafore* is mine (I.M. writing). There is a marvellous spontaneity about the invention, and somehow the music has a genuine briney quality. *Pinafore* also contains Dick Deadeye, the strangest character in all the Savoy operas, who seems to have popped suddenly to the surface – in Freudian fashion – from Gilbert's subconscious, a more powerful figure than any of the matronly ladies at whom Gilbert liked to poke fun. It would be difficult to imagine a better recorded performance of *Pinafore* than this one. It is complete with dialogue, and while there is controversy about this (I personally find that I never tire of the best lines), here the dialogue is vital in establishing the character of Deadeye, since much of his part is spoken rather than sung. The dialogue is spoken extremely well here. Donald Adams is a totally memorable Deadeye and his larger-than-life personality underpins the whole piece. Among the others Jeffrey Skitch is a first-class Captain; Jean Hindmarsh is absolutely convincing as Josephine (it was a pity she stayed with the company for so short a time), and she sings with great charm. Thomas Round is equally good as Ralph Rackstraw. Little Buttercup could be slightly more colourful, but this is a small blemish, and among the minor parts George Cook is a most personable Bill Bobstay. The choral singing is excellent, the orchestral playing good, and Isidore Godfrey conducts with marvellous spirit and lilt. The recording has splendid atmosphere. It was, however, one of the earliest of Decca's series of D'Oyly Carte recordings in stereo. The transfer is made at the highest level, and at times there are hints that the transfer engineers have been marginally too ambitious. There is some lack of refinement at fortissimos, and the orchestral strings sound fierce. One or two choral climaxes bring a hint of congestion. For the most part the sound is extremely vivid, with voices (both in songs and dialogue) well projected, and one would not want to withhold a strong recommendation. The quality improves greatly when the treble is cut back. However, the sound from the discs is undoubtedly smoother, although for some reason sides two and four sound slightly mellower on cassette than sides one and three.

HMS Pinafore: complete, without dialogue.

(M) *** HMV TC2-SXDW 3034. George Baker, John Cameron, Richard Lewis, Owen Brannigan, Elsie Morison, Monica Sinclair, Glyndebourne Festival Chorus, Pro Arte Orch., Sargent – *Trial by Jury*.***

For their issue of *HMS Pinafore* and *Trial by Jury* EMI abandoned the single-tape format used for the rest of the series and here provided two tapes in a box, with a leaflet giving the plot synopses etc. The performance of *Pinafore* is undoubtedly very successful, and the transfer is of good quality, bright and lively, yet with plenty of warmth and atmosphere. The last degree of refinement is missing, perhaps, but overall there is little to grumble at in the general balance and clarity. It is to Owen Brannigan's great credit that, little as he had to do here, without the dialogue, he conveyed the force of Deadeye's personality so strongly. For those who find the dialogue tedious in repetition this is a very happy set, offering some good solo singing and consistently lovely ensemble singing and chorus work. The whole of the final scene is musically quite ravishing, and throughout if Sir Malcolm fails to find quite all the wit in the music he is never less than lively. George Baker is of course splendid as Sir Joseph, and John Cameron, Richard Lewis and (especially) Monica Sinclair, as Buttercup, make much of their songs. Elsie Morison I found disappointing; she spoils the end of her lovely song in Act 1 by singing sharp.

However, she brings plenty of drama to her *Scena* in Act 2. The male trio near the end of Act 1 is quite outstandingly well sung – full of brio and personality. The coupling with *Trial by Jury* makes this a fine bargain.

Iolanthe: complete, with dialogue.
**(*) Decca K 2 C 35 [Lon. 5-12104]. John Reed, Pamela Field, Judi Merri, Lyndsie Holland, Malcolm Williams, Kenneth Sandford, Michael Rayner, John Ayldon, D'Oyly Carte Opera Chorus, RPO, Nash.

As with *The Gondoliers*, Decca have chosen to issue on tape the more recent set of *Iolanthe* conducted by Royston Nash rather than the very successful early version under Godfrey. But the relative merits of the two recordings are here much closer. John Reed played the Lord Chancellor in both, and his portrayal has understandably matured: in the newer set the character has a real vintage quality. The vocal inflections, squeaks and other speech mannerisms are a delight. Only in the *Nightmare song* does one feel that familiarity has bred too easy a manner, and with hardly any sense of bravura (so fluently do the words trip out) some of the electricity is lost. But as a whole this version has undoubted charm and sparkle, and Nash's refined manner is immediately apparent in the overture. The latest Queen of the Fairies has a splendidly ripe speaking voice, yet when she sings the tone is less resonant. Pamela Field makes a suitably pert Phyllis and her spoken exchanges with the two Earls in Act 2 are superbly managed, helped by the vivid recording quality on tape, which projects the spoken dialogue with almost uncanny presence. John Ayldon's singing voice is rather throaty, and Michael Rayner as Strephon is very dark-toned. Kenneth Sandford too is not quite his usual impressive self; his *Sentry song*

lacks something in authority. However, there is much to enjoy; the two Earls are excellent and the choral singing is first-rate throughout. The tape transfer is extremely successful, and gives splendid detail and realism, although for best results a treble cut is needed to remove a touch of edge to the strings and voices.

Iolanthe: complete, without dialogue.
(M) **(*) HMV TC2-SXDW 3047. George Baker, Ian Wallace, John Cameron, Alexander Young, Owen Brannigan, Monica Sinclair, Elsie Morison, Glyndebourne Festival Chorus, Pro Arte Orch., Sargent.

There is much to praise in this HMV set, and EMI have refurbished the recording very successfully; it suits the studio-based performance and projects the music brightly without loss of inner warmth. The climax of Act 1, the scene of the Queen of the Fairies' curse on members of both Houses of Parliament, shows most excitingly what can be achieved with the 'full operatic treatment': this is a dramatic moment indeed. George Baker too is very good as the Lord Chancellor; his voice is fuller and more baritonal than the dry monotone we are used to from John Reed, yet he provides an equally individual characterization. For some listeners John Cameron's dark timbre may not readily evoke an Arcadian Shepherd, although he sings stylishly. The Peers' chorus is not a highlight. It is treated lyrically, and the tenors are not very incisive: some might wish for a more robust effect here. Nevertheless there is much to enjoy. The two Earls and Private Willis are excellent, the famous *Nightmare song* is very well and clearly sung, and all of the second act (except perhaps Iolanthe's recitative and ballad near the end) goes very well. The famous *Trio* with the Lord Chancellor and the two Earls is a joy. The opening scene of Act 1 is effectively atmospheric, with Monica Sinclair a splendid Fairy Queen. The orchestral playing is refined, and it is a pity that in the beautifully played overture the clarinet solo is very slightly discoloured in its upper partials in the tape transfer (at least on our copy). Otherwise the sound on cassette is first-class, warm and spacious yet with the refinement of detail fairly consistent. The voices are clearly projected.

The Mikado: complete, without dialogue.
*** Decca K 22 K 22 [Lon. 5-12103]. John Ayldon, Colin Wright, John Reed, Kenneth Sandford, Valerie Masterson, Lyndsie Holland, D'Oyly Carte Opera Chorus, RPO, Nash.
(M) ** HMV TC2-EXE 1021. Richard Lewis, Geraint Evans, Ian Wallace, Owen Brannigan, Elsie Morison, Monica Sinclair, Glyndebourne Festival Chorus, Pro Arte Orch., Sargent.

The most recent D'Oyly Carte *Mikado* is a complete success in every way and (apart from individual performances like Donald Adams's famous portrayal of the Mikado himself) it eclipses the earlier Decca set (which is not available on tape) in almost every respect. The effect is like a coat of bright new paint, and the G. and S. masterpiece emerges with a new sparkle. Musically this is by far the finest version the D'Oyly Carte Company have ever recorded. The choral singing is first-rate, with much refinement of detail. The glees, *Brightly dawns* and *See how the fates*, are robust in the D'Oyly Carte manner but more polished than usual. The words throughout are exceptionally clear without sizzling sibilants. This applies to an important early song in Act 1, *Our great Mikado*, which contains the seeds of the plot and is sometimes delivered in a throaty indistinct way. Not so

here: every word is crystal-clear. Of the principals, John Reed is a delicious Ko-Ko, a refined and individual characterization, and his famous *Little list* song has an enjoyable lightness of touch. Kenneth Sandford gives his customary vintage projection of Pooh Bah – a pity none of his dialogue has been included. Valerie Masterson is a charming Yum-Yum; *The sun whose rays* has rarely been sung with more feeling and charm, and it is followed by a virtuoso account of *Here's a how-de-do* which one wants to encore (and with a cassette one can, of course, if one wishes). Colin Wright's vocal production has a slightly nasal quality, but one soon adjusts to it and his voice has the proper bright freshness of timbre for Nanki-Poo. John Ayldon's Mikado has not quite the satanic glitter of Donald Adams in the earlier version, but he provides a laugh of terrifying bravura. Katisha (Lyndsie Holland) is commanding, and her attempts to interrupt the chorus in the finale of Act 1 are superbly believable and dramatic. With excellent sound throughout and an expert tape transfer, this set offers fine presence and realism.

The reissue of EMI's first stereo *Mikado*, under Sir Malcolm Sargent, makes a fascinating comparison with the D'Oyly Carte versions. Certainly in this HMV set we have much sheer musicality – the grand operatic style to the finales of both acts, the trio about the 'death' of Nanki-Poo and the glee which follows: these are beautifully sung and played. But taken as a whole this is not as enjoyable as the D'Oyly Carte set. There is less sheer style, and the basic humour of the piece is only sporadically caught. Geraint Evans cannot hold a candle to John Reed in the patter songs (nor in *Tit Willow*). Owen Brannigan makes a brave show of the Mikado, and the other star performance on HMV is Richard Lewis, who sings delightfully throughout. Monica Sinclair, however, has not the courage of her convictions when she exclaims *These arms shall thus enfold you*; but Elsie Morison sings nicely as Yum Yum. Generally the sound on tape is bright and clear; there is a hint that the last degree of refinement is missing in the big ensembles, but it is marginal, and the balance is good. The advantage of having the work complete on two sides is somewhat counteracted by the ill-judged side-turn; it comes in the finale of Act 1, only a few minutes before the end of the act. It would have taken only a little more tape to give each act complete on a single side.

The Mikado: abridged, without dialogue.
*** Pye ZCP 13. Donald Adams, Thomas Round, John Cartier, Lawrence Richard, Michael Wakeham, Valerie Masterson, Helen Landis, Gilbert and Sullivan Festival Chorus and Orch., Murray.

This first-class tape can be strongly recommended. The selection is generous (John Cartier even provides a miniature encore in his *Little list* song, which is wittily done), and there is not a weak member of the cast. Thomas Round's *Wand'ring minstrel* is matched by Valerie Masterson's charming *Sun whose rays*, and all the glees go especially well, from *I am so proud* to *Here's a how-de-do*. The three little maids are very petite and the famous trio describing the 'execution scene' is delightful. To round it all off Donald Adams produces a positively maniacal laugh in his superbly done *Mikado's song*, which has to be heard to be believed. The tape transfer is vivid; the small string section sounds rather sharp-edged, but the sound is admirably crisp, and the voices are naturally caught and convincingly projected. This is generally preferable to the equivalent disc.

Patience: complete, with dialogue.
**(*) Decca K 76 K 22. Mary Sansom, Donald Adams, John Cartier, Philip Potter, John Reed, Kenneth Sandford, Jennifer Toye, Gillian Knight, D'Oyly Carte Company, Godfrey.

In the cassette version of the D'Oyly Carte *Patience* the difference in level between music and dialogue one noticed on the original LPs has been put right. In the dialogue itself the reverberation is perhaps somewhat overdone, but the overall sound is convincingly managed, and the recording has fine body and warmth. The voices are natural and without edge. Indeed the whole presentation is such as to make one reappraise the score, and forget its uneven patches. There is much charming music here, even if it is Sullivan's primary colours that come off best, rather than the pastel shades. Certainly *When I first put this uniform on* and *The soldiers of the Queen* are among the very best of all Sullivan's military numbers. Donald Adams is a worthy successor to Darrell Fancourt in these. Patience herself is well characterized by Mary Sansom, but her singing is less impressive. She is thoroughly professional, and excellent in the dialogue, but her songs lack style, although they are not without moments of charm. All the dialogue is here, and very important it is to the action. Unfortunately the poems are spoken with rather too much intensity, whereas they need throwing off if the barbs of the satire are to be lightly pointed as Gilbert intended. In all other respects both Bunthorne and Grosvenor are well played. Both chorus and orchestra have never sounded better, and Isidore Godfrey displays his usual skill with the accompaniments, which have a splendid bounce. The wide dynamic range of the recording (which is resplendent in the loud music) is well captured here.

Patience: complete, without dialogue.
(M) **(*) HMV TC2-SXDW 3031. Elsie Morison, Alexander

Young, George Baker, John Cameron, Marjorie Thomas, Monica Sinclair, Heather Harper, Elizabeth Harwood, Glyndebourne Festival Chorus, Pro Arte Orch., Sargent.

The HMV set of *Patience* was another of the great successes of the Sargent series, and it is in almost every way preferable to the Decca D'Oyly Carte version. Although there is no dialogue there is more business than is usual from HMV and a convincing theatrical atmosphere. The recording is vivid, with no lack of warmth, and the singing is consistently good. The opening scene is far more effective than with Decca and so is the Act 1 finale. The chorus is a strong feature throughout, and where the men and women sing different melodic lines the clarity of each is admirable. Elsie Morison's Patience, George Baker's Bunthorne and John Cameron's Grosvenor are all admirably characterized, while the military men are excellent too. The many concerted items continually beguile the ear and Sir Malcolm's accompaniments tell splendidly. All in all, this is the sort of production we anticipated when HMV first began their 'Glyndebourne' series, and it can be heartily recommended. The tape transfer (again conveniently on one double-length cassette) needs a strong treble reduction or the vocal consonants are given an unnatural sibilance and the strings sound thin. However, it can be made to sound well.

The Pirates of Penzance: complete, with dialogue.
*** Decca к 61 к 22. John Reed, Donald Adams, Philip Potter, Valerie Masterson, Christine Palmer, Owen Brannigan, D'Oyly Carte Opera Chorus, RPO, Godfrey.

Isidore Godfrey is helped by a more uniformly excellent cast than was present on the earlier Decca stereo recording, and now for the first time we are given all the dialogue too. The theatrical spontaneity is well maintained, and the spoken scenes with the Pirate King are particularly effective. Donald Adams has a great gift for Gilbertian inflection and some of his lines give as much pleasure as his splendidly characterized singing. Christine Palmer's Ruth is not quite so poised, but her singing is first-rate – her opening aria has never been better done. John Reed does not show the Martyn Green poise in the patter songs (Green always seems to take a fiendish delight in the profusion of tongue-twisting consonants, where others just manage to negotiate them), but this is a real characterization of the part and it grows on one. Valerie Masterson is an excellent Mabel, and if her voice is not creamy throughout its range, she controls it with great skill to delight us often. Her duet with Frederick, *Leave me not to pine alone*, is enchanting, sung very gently. Godfrey has prepared us for it in the overture, and it is one of the highlights of the set. Godfrey's conducting is as affectionate as ever, more lyrical here, without losing the rhythmic buoyancy, and one can hear him revelling in the many touches of colour in the orchestration, which the Royal Philharmonic Orchestra present with much sophistication. But perhaps the greatest joy of the set is Owen Brannigan's Sergeant of Police, a part this artist was surely born to play. It is a marvellously humorous performance, yet the humour is never clumsy, and the famous *Policeman's song* is so fresh that it is almost like hearing it for the first time. The recording is superbly spacious and clear throughout, with a fine sense of atmosphere. The transfer level is remarkably high, and the sound has superb presence, bloom and detail, while the loudest climaxes are accommodated with ease. Only at the very end of Act 2 does the work's climax offer the slightest suspicion that the level is too high, but that is carping; this is demonstration-worthy in every sense.

The Pirates of Penzance: complete, without dialogue.

(M) *** HMV TC2-SXDW 3041. George Baker, James Milligan, John Cameron, Richard Lewis, Owen Brannigan, Elsie Morison, Glyndebourne Festival Chorus, Pro Arte Orch., Sargent.

This was one of the finest of Sir Malcolm Sargent's Gilbert and Sullivan sets. Besides a performance which is stylish as well as lively, conveying both the fun of the words and the charm of the music, the HMV recording has more atmosphere than usual in this series. Undoubtedly the star of the piece is George Baker; he is a splendid Major-General. Here is an excellent example of a fresh approach yielding real dividends, and Sargent's slower than usual tempo for his famous patter song means that the singer can relax and add both wit and polish to the words. Owen Brannigan, as in the Decca set, gives a rich portrayal of the Sergeant of the Police. The performance takes a little while to warm up: Sargent's accompaniment to the Pirate King's song is altogether too flaccid. Elsie Morison is a less than ideal Mabel: her opening cadenza of *Poor wandering one* is angular and over-dramatic, and she is not relaxed enough throughout. However, elsewhere she is much more convincing, especially in the famous duet, *Leave me not to pine alone*. The choral contributions (the opening of Act 2, for instance) are pleasingly refined, yet have no lack of vigour. *Hail poetry* is resplendent, while the choral finale is managed with poise and a balance which allows the inner parts to emerge pleasingly. The whole performance is in fact more than the sum of its parts.

The recording has transferred smoothly and vividly to tape, and the reverberation has been successfully contained, so the focus is nearly always clean. A little treble cut may be useful, for the voices and chorus have plenty of presence. The single-tape format is doubly attractive here, as the two acts are given a complete side each.

Princess Ida: complete, without dialogue.

*** Decca K 66 K 22. Elizabeth Harwood, Kenneth Sandford, Donald Adams, Jeffrey Skitch, John Reed, D'Oyly Carte Opera Chorus, RPO, Sargent.

When first issued, Sir Malcolm Sargent's stereo recording of *Princess Ida* suffered from comparison with Isidore Godfrey's earlier mono set, which was altogether more sprightly. But returning to the recording again in this outstanding tape transfer one finds that Sir Malcolm's broadly lyrical approach has much to offer in this 'grandest' of the Savoy operas. Elizabeth Harwood in the name part sings splendidly, and John Reed's irritably gruff portrayal of the irascible King Gama is memorable. He certainly is a properly 'disagreeable man'. The rest of the cast is no less strong, and with excellent teamwork from the company as a whole and a splendid recording, spacious and immediate, this has much to offer, even if Sullivan's invention is somewhat variable. The quality of the sound really is first-class, with splendid bloom and colour throughout and everything admirably clear.

Ruddigore: complete, without dialogue.

(M) *** HMV TC2-SXDW 3029. George Baker, Richard Lewis, Owen Brannigan, Harold Blackburn, Elsie Morison, Pamela Bowden, Monica Sinclair, Glyndebourne Festival Chorus, Pro Arte Orch., Sargent.

**(*) Decca K 75 K 22. John Reed, Thomas Round, Kenneth

Sandford, Donald Adams, Jean Hindmarsh, Gillian Knight, Jean Allister, D'Oyly Carte Opera Chorus, Orch. of the Royal Opera House, Covent Garden, Godfrey.

Sargent's approach is essentially lyrical and emphasizes the associations this lovely score so often finds with the music of Schubert. The performance is beautifully sung and the excellence is uniform. Perhaps George Baker sounds a little old in voice for Robin Oakapple, but he does the *Poor little man ... poor little maid* duet in Act 1 with great charm and manages his 'character transformation' later in the opera splendidly. Pamela Bowden is a first-class Mad Margaret, and her short Donizettian scena is superbly done. Equally Richard Lewis is an admirably bumptious Richard. Perhaps, surprisingly, Owen Brannigan does not make quite as much of the *Ghosts' high noon* song as Donald Adams on the D'Oyly Carte set, but his delicious Act 2 duet with Mad Margaret has an irresistible gentility (and one can visualize their traditional little dance movements, so evocatively is this section managed). The drama of the score is well managed too: Sir Despard's Act 1 entry has real bravado (the words of the chorus here are wonderfully crisp), and later the scene in the picture gallery (given a touch of added resonance by the recording) is effectively sombre. Even the slightly prissy crowd effects in Act 1 seem to fall into place, giving an attractive feeling of stylization. A superb reissue, transferred with admirable life and presence and making very enjoyable listening. It has the great advantage of being complete on two sides.

Ruddigore is one of Godfrey's less successful D'Oyly Carte recordings. There are several instances of tempi that are fractionally too brisk, and altogether a degree of charm is missing throughout. Savoyards will not be disappointed; here, very well recorded, is the production they

are used to, but in the Act 2 duet for Mad Margaret and Sir Despard the point is missed and this becomes another standard song. The omission of the dialogue was a mistake: the scene mentioned above is incomplete without the delightful spoken interchange about Basingstoke. Instead of the dialogue we are given the original overture complete with the music for the original finale to whet our appetites. The performance also includes the attractive duet *The battle's roar is over*, which is now (for whatever reason) traditionally omitted. There is much to enjoy here. The principals are good, especially Gillian Knight and Donald Adams (whose *Ghosts' high noon* is a marvellous highlight), and the chorus and orchestra are excellent. The transfer is smooth, offering warmly agreeable sound and a somewhat intimate effect at times to suit this very Schubertian score. There is not so much edge on the voices as on some of the D'Oyly Carte tape sets, but the colour and naturalness of the sound compensate for any slight lack of range, and the words are admirably clear.

Trial by Jury: complete.

(M) *** HMV TC2-SXDW 3034. George Baker, John Cameron, Richard Lewis, Owen Brannigan, Elsie Morison, Monica Sinclair, Glyndebourne Festival Chorus, Pro Arte Orch., Sargent – *HMS Pinafore*.***

An outstanding, thoroughly musical account, with a shade more 'production' than usual in the HMV series. The casting is excellent, and George Baker makes a fine judge. The recording is one of the best HMV have given us so far for G. and S.: it is clear, spacious and bright, and has some good but unexaggerated stereo effects. In many ways this is the finest available recording of *Trial by Jury*, and it is well transferred to tape. It is a great

571

pity, however, that it could not have been given side four of this boxed tape set to itself. Not a great deal of tape has been saved by setting the beginning of the work clumsily just before the end of side three.

(i) *Trial by Jury*: complete. *Overture Macbeth; Henry VIII* (incidental music): *March; Graceful dance*.
**(*) Decca KTXC 113 [Lon. 5-1167]. RPO, Nash, (i) with John Reed, Michael Rayner, Colin Wright, Julia Goss, Kenneth Sandford, John Ayldon, D'Oyly Carte Opera Chorus.

The fillers here are inconsequential; the *Macbeth overture* is brightly coloured, but not really inspired, and the orchestration is without the felicity Sullivan showed in the opera pit: it sometimes sounds curiously thin. The performance of *Trial by Jury* is thoroughly professional and alive, with first-class individual contributions from the small cast, notably John Reed. But the forward balance, all the voices projected out, does not help to create atmosphere, and one has the impression of everyone trying too hard. Every bit of choral 'business' is put over emphatically, and while the impact is never in doubt the whole effect is unsubtle. The HMV version (see above) is the one to go for if the coupling is right. The cassette transfer is vivid; the chorus is a little coarse-grained, but the solo voices sound admirably natural.

Utopia Ltd: complete. *Imperial march*.
**(*) Decca K 2 C 17 [Lon. 5-12105]. Pamela Field, Lyndsie Holland, John Ayldon, John Reed, Kenneth Sandford, Jon Ellison, Michael Buchan, James Conroy-Ward, D'Oyly Carte Opera Company, RPO, Nash.

Utopia Ltd was first performed in 1893, ran for 245 performances and then remained unheard (except for amateur productions) until revived for the D'Oyly Carte centenary London season in 1974, which led to this recording. Its complete neglect is unaccountable; the piece stages well, and if the music is not as consistently fine as the best of the Savoy operas, it contains much that is memorable. Moreover Gilbert's libretto shows him at his most wittily ingenious, and the idea of a Utopian society *inevitably* modelled on British constitutional practice suggests Victorian self-confidence at its most engaging. Also the score offers a certain nostalgic quality in recalling earlier successes. Apart from a direct quote from *Pinafore* in the Act 1 Finale, the military number of the First Light Guards has a strong flavour of *Patience*, and elsewhere *Iolanthe* is evoked.

Make way for the Wise Men, near the opening, immediately wins the listener's attention, and the whole opera is well worth having in such a lively and vigorous account. Royston Nash shows plenty of skill in the matter of musical characterization, and the solo singing is consistently assured. When Meston Reid as Captain Fitz-Battleaxe sings 'You see I can't do myself justice' in *Oh, Zara*, he is far from speaking the truth – this is a performance of considerable bravura. The ensembles are not always as immaculately disciplined as one is used to from the D'Oyly Carte, and *Eagle high* is disappointingly focused: the intonation here is not completely secure. However, the sparkle and spontaneity of the performance as a whole are irresistible, with vivid recording and a first-class tape transfer which has striking presence and clarity. As there is no overture as such, the recording uses Sullivan's *Imperial march*, written for the opening – by the Queen – of the Imperial Institute, five months before the première of the opera. It is an effective enough piece, but not a patch on the *March of the Peers* from *Iolanthe*.

The Yeomen of the Guard: complete, without dialogue.

   *** Decca ᴋ 60 ᴋ 22. Anne Hood, Elizabeth Harwood, John Reed, Philip Potter, Kenneth Sandford, Donald Adams, Gillian Knight, D'Oyly Carte Opera Chorus, RPO, Sargent.

   (ᴍ) **(*) HMV ᴛᴄ2-sxᴅw 3033. Marjorie Thomas, Elsie Morison, Geraint Evans, Richard Lewis, Owen Brannigan, John Carol Case, Monica Sinclair, Glyndebourne Festival Chorus, Pro Arte Orch., Sargent.

Here are two first-class performances of *The Yeomen of the Guard* both conducted by Sir Malcolm Sargent. The Decca set has the advantage of superior and more modern recording, but the HMV issue, with the music complete on two sides of a single tape, offers considerable economy and hardly less musical pleasure. In the Decca version Sir Malcolm's breadth of approach is at once apparent in the overture. The spinning number which follows also begins deliberately; it has a striking lyricism, with much play with echo effects, but has not quite the lightness of touch that Godfrey would have managed. This is not to imply that Sargent's result is less effective, only that it is not quite what one expects from a traditional D'Oyly Carte reading on Decca. As soon as the chorus enter (*Tower warders*), the degree of Sargent's 'grand operatic' approach makes a remarkable impact; indeed one has seldom heard the choruses in *Yeomen* expand with such power, nor indeed has the orchestra (especially the brass) produced such a regal sound. As the work proceeds the essential lyricism of Sargent's reading begins to emerge more and more, and the ensemble singing is especially lovely. There is no lack of drama either, and indeed the only aspect of the work to be played down somewhat is the humorous side. The interjections of Jack and Wil-

fred in the Act 1 finale are obviously seen as part of the whole rather than a suggestion of the humour that somehow seems to intrude into the most serious of human situations. The pathos of the famous Jester's song in the second act is played up, and the only moment to raise a real smile is the duet which follows, *Tell a tale of cock and bull*. But with consistently fine singing throughout from all the principals (and especially Elizabeth Harwood as Elsie), supported by perfectly balanced recording, this *Yeomen* is unreservedly a success. Apart from the brilliant and atmospheric Decca recording, the style of this performance is not so very different from Sargent's earlier one. The cassette transfer has splendid presence and immediacy, of Decca's best quality.

The singing on the HMV recording (which dates from 1960) is also very persuasive. As on Decca the trios and quartets with which this score abounds are most beautifully performed and skilfully balanced, and the ear is continually beguiled. Owen Brannigan's portrayal of Wilfred is splendidly larger than life and Monica Sinclair is a memorable Dame Carruthers. The finales to both acts have striking breadth, and the delightfully sung trio of Elsie, Phoebe and the Dame in the finale of Act 2 is a good example of the many individual felicities of this set. *Strange adventure*, too, is most beautifully done. As in the Decca recording there is very little feeling of humour, but the music triumphs. The sound on the tape is generally good. There is a reduction of absolute refinement at the highest levels, but this is only marginal; generally the voices have warmth and presence, and the music-making sounds vivid. Once or twice there is a hint of peaking on the female solo contributions, but for the most part the effect is congenial.

COLLECTIONS

'Favourites': highlights from *The Gondoliers; HMS Pinafore; Iolan-*

the; The Mikado; The Pirates of Penzance; Ruddigore; Trial by Jury; The Yeomen of the Guard.

** Pye ZCP 16. John Cartier, Donald Adams, Thomas Round, Valerie Masterson, Michael Wakeham, Lawrence Richard, Helen Landis, Ann Hood, Gilbert and Sullivan Festival Chorus and Orch., Murray.

This highlights tape is generously full, with nine numbers to each side. It is a pity it opens with the *Cachucha* from *The Gondoliers*, and closes with the *Policeman's song* from *Pirates*, which has to be quickly faded at the end; but with some of the most famous numbers from the eight operas featured it is very entertaining. Helen Landis, Donald Adams, John Cartier, Thomas Round and Valerie Masterson are all heard to good effect, and the recording has generally good projection.

'Festival of Gilbert and Sullivan': excerpts from *The Gondoliers; HMS Pinafore; Iolanthe; The Mikado; Patience; The Pirates of Penzance; Princess Ida; Ruddigore; The Sorcerer; Trial by Jury; The Yeomen of the Guard.*

(M)**(*) Decca K 3 G 13. D'Oyly Carte Opera Company, Godfrey, Nash, or Sargent.

There is much attractive music here, and the standard of performance is consistently high. But the term *Festival* implies something special, perhaps a collection of really outstanding versions of key numbers. In fact the selection (on three cassettes) is clumsily balanced, with curious omissions (*Prithee, pretty maiden* is not here, and *Patience* is represented by two numbers only). Both *Iolanthe* and *The Mikado* are given more than their share of space, and to end a selection of

eight numbers from *Iolanthe* with *My lord, a suppliant* instead of the famous trio tends to leave the listener unsatisfied, both dramatically and musically. However, on the credit side there are three first-class excerpts each from *Princess Ida* and *The Sorcerer*, and the order of the programme generally provides an agreeable listening sequence. The recording is excellent and the tape transfer of high quality; the sound is full and atmospheric as well as having plenty of life and presence.

'Highlights' from *The Gondoliers; HMS Pinafore; Iolanthe; The Mikado; The Pirates of Penzance; The Yeomen of the Guard.*

(B) *** Classics for Pleasure TC-CFP 40238. Richard Lewis, Monica Sinclair, Geraint Evans, John Cameron, George Baker, Elsie Morison, Marjorie Thomas, Owen Brannigan, Glyndebourne Festival Chorus, Pro Arte Orch., Sargent.

An attractive selection of highlights, generously offering samples of six of Sir Malcolm Sargent's HMV recordings. There is some distinguished solo singing, and if the atmosphere is sometimes a little cosy (the *Cachucha* from *The Gondoliers* sounds slower than ever, heard out of the context of the complete performance), there is a very great deal to enjoy. The recording has transferred well, and the quality is first-class.

'Highlights', Vol. 2, from *The Gondoliers; Iolanthe; The Mikado; Patience; The Pirates of Penzance; Trial by Jury.*

(B)**(*) Classics for Pleasure TC-CFP 40260. Artists as on above tape cond. Sargent.

This is generally a less attractive compilation than the earlier one (above). Of course there are some good things here, notably Owen Brannigan's *Sentry song* from *Iolanthe* and the items from *The Pirates of Penzance*. But generally these excerpts show Sargent's broad manner and occasional lack of sparkle, and this is reflected especially in the numbers from *The Mikado* and *The Gondoliers*. The recording is good, and the high-level transfer is generally admirable, with plenty of presence and atmosphere, and only the very occasional slip of absolute refinement of focus.

'Gilbert and Sullivan spectacular': excerpts from *HMS Pinafore; The Mikado; The Pirates of Penzance; Ruddigore.*

   ** Decca Phase 4 KPFC 4097. John Reed, Donald Adams, Kenneth Sandford, Valerie Masterson, soloists, D'Oyly Carte Opera Chorus, RPO, Sargent.

Basically the recording here is certainly spectacular, with a rich overall ambience and the soloists spotlighted well forward. The choral sound, however, is somewhat grainy, and the very loudest moments have a touch of discoloration. The conducting is musical and solid, without the wit of Godfrey but genial in its way. The memorable items are *A wandering minstrel*, very nicely turned by Philip Potter, and Donald Adams's superb versions of the Mikado's famous song (that laugh sounds even more horrifying than usual in Phase Four) and the *Policeman's song* from *Pirates* (which he does not usually sing). John Reed's contributions are very closely microphoned indeed and reveal a break in the voice occasionally.

'If patriotic sentiment is wanted': excerpts from: *The Gondoliers; HMS Pinafore; Iolanthe; Patience; The Yeomen of the Guard; Utopia Ltd.*

   (M) *(*) Decca KCSP 515. John Reed, Alan Styler, Kenneth Sandford, John Ayldon, Gillian Knight, D'Oyle Carte Opera Company, RPO or New SO, Godfrey, Nash or Walker.

A selection of patriotic items would seem a good idea for an anthology just after a royal jubilee, but in the event this selection is disappointing. It opens dramatically enough with a side-drum roll heralding the Peers from *Iolanthe*, but the sound seems artificially brilliant and the tape transfer offers edgy consonants and rather fierce strings. A degree of control is possible, but the balance remains top-heavy. The selection itself is generous but does not gell into a really memorable concert.

'The very best of Gilbert and Sullivan': medleys from: *The Gondoliers; HMS Pinafore; Iolanthe; The Mikado; The Pirates of Penzance.*

   ** Columbia Studio 2 TC-TWOX 1066. Morriston Orpheus Choir, HM Royal Marines Band, Neville.

Strictly not for purists, these are bandstand style pot-pourris (arranged by Ray Woodfield) which embellish the harmony as well as the instrumentation and often alter the rhythms too. However, the manner – even if it has a somewhat camp 'pop' flavour at times – is affectionate and the fervour of the singing is disarming, often when the presentation is furthest from the original style. As is usual with a good Welsh choir the lyrical music comes off best, and the character of some of the more vigorous writing is intense rather than sparkling. The chorus has some problems with dancing the *Cachucha* in stereo, and the ensemble here is hardly polished. The Marines Band provides a splendidly professional accompaniment throughout and although it is disconcerting to hear so many solo numbers in choral dress, the selection is so generous (nearly forty items are included) and the presentation so warm-hearted that the entertainment must give pleasure to all but the most zealous and particular Savoyards. The recording is rich and splendidly spacious and considering the resonance the tape transfer is remarkably well focused.

'Time for Gilbert and Sullivan': excerpts from: The Gondoliers; The Grand Duke; HMS Pinafore; Iolanthe; The Mikado; Patience; The Pirates of Penzance; Princess Ida; Ruddigore; Utopia Ltd; The Yeomen of the Guard.

> (M) *** Decca KMOR 2 8086. Various soloists from the D'Oyly Carte Opera Company, D'Oyly Carte Opera Chorus, RPO, New SO, or Royal Opera House, Covent Garden, Orch., Godfrey, Nash or Sargent.

This double-length cassette is one of a series of 'middle-of-the-road' tapes specifically intended for in-car use. But the recording is of first-class quality, indeed often of demonstration standard, and the very generous selection is arranged with great skill. This is now the most attractive single anthology of this repertoire available in tape form (there is no disc equivalent). Side two is particularly felicitous in its arrangement of items, and reminds one of the kind of skill that Charles Mackerras showed in the opening sections of Pineapple Poll. But here, of course, they are not snippets. Opening with three of the most attractive numbers from Patience, the concert continues with selections from Yeomen and Iolanthe and concludes with two little-known items, one each from Utopia Ltd and The Grand Duke, which show both composer and librettist on top form. Highly recommended.

'The world of Gilbert and Sullivan': excerpts from The Gondoliers; HMS Pinafore; The Mikado; Patience; Princess Ida.

> (M) *** Decca KCSP 28. D'Oyly Carte Opera Company, Godfrey or Sargent.

This is a brilliant anthology which is successful in picking some of the outstanding highlights not only from these operas but also from the recordings of them. With perhaps the single exception of the Princess Ida item, For a month to dwell (not showing Sir Malcolm Sargent in top form), everything is infectious and highly enjoyable. The other Princess Ida excerpt, If you give me your attention, is a favourite patter song, and John Reed does it well. The perfomances here are all from the Decca G. and S. complete sets, which are excellent technically, and indeed the tape opens with a stunning piece of atmospheric business before I am the monarch of the seas begins a trio of songs from Pinafore. The Mikado songs too (and this was not one of the best of Godfrey's series) are cleverly chosen to show the cast at their most sparkling. A wandering minstrel (Thomas Round), Three little maids and Tit willow (Peter Pratt) are all excellent. The Gondoliers was perhaps the best thing Godfrey did, and all five excerpts are winners. Perhaps most striking of all are the Patience songs, with Donald Adams in splendid form in his Catalogue song and When I first put this uniform on. This issue is especially valuable to tape collectors, as not all of Godfrey's complete recordings are available on cassette. The transfer is of good quality, and after the double-length Time for Gilbert and Sullivan cassette (see above), this is now the best G. and S. anthology available at any price.

'The world of Gilbert and Sullivan', Vol. 2: excerpts from Iolanthe; The Pirates of Penzance; Ruddigore; The Yeomen of the Guard.

> (M) **(*) Decca KCSP 29. D'Oyly

Carte Opera Company, Godfrey or Sargent.

This second tape is worth having for Donald Adams's classic performance of *When the night wind howls* from *Ruddigore*, which is superbly done. The selection also includes *I know a youth*, with its Schubertian charm, and the patter trio *My eyes are fully open*, which is very successful. There is a nice selection from *Iolanthe*, ending with the vivacious final trio, and the *Pirates* excerpts are most enjoyable too. In the *Yeomen* section the chorus *Tower warders* comes before *When maiden loves*, but that seems sensible enough in this context. Good sound throughout, both on disc and on tape, though the transfer is not always as vividly clear as in the complete sets from which these items are extracted. The quality in the solo songs is often first-rate, but the choral items sometimes sound slightly over-resonant and lack bite.

*'The world of Gilbert and Sullivan',
Vol. 3*: excerpts from *The Gondoliers; Iolanthe; The Mikado; Patience; Ruddigore; The Sorcerer; Trial by Jury.*
　(M) ** Decca KCSP 147. D'Oyly Carte Opera Company, Godfrey.

The third selection in this series is notable for a marvellous performance by John Reed in *My name is John Wellington Wells*, from *The Sorcerer*. This is one of Gilbert's very finest inspirations and the music points the words to perfection, but it comes from an otherwise comparatively unmemorable performance, as the companion duet, *Oh, I have wrought much evil with my spells*, readily shows. There are some good excerpts from *The Gondoliers* and *Patience*, and the selection is generous enough to merit recommendation even though one or two items have to be very quickly faded out at the end. In a selection of this kind, and with the whole range of operas to choose from, it ought to be possible to exclude pieces that do not extract easily from the master tape. The transfers are well managed.

Suppé, Franz von (1819–95)

Overtures: *Beautiful Galathea; Boccaccio; Light Cavalry; Morning, Noon and Night in Vienna; Pique Dame; Poet and Peasant.*
　(B) ** DG Heliodor 3348 030. Polish Radio SO, Rachon.
　*(*) Philips 7300 612 [id.]. LPO, Marriner.
　(B) (**)Philips Fontana 7328 008. Detroit SO, Paray.

Of these three issues the one by the Polish Radio orchestra under Stefan Rachon is much to be preferred. The transfer offers virtually no problems, even though the recording is quite resonant. The performances are extremely lively, and the two least-known overtures, *Boccaccio* and *Beautiful Galathea*, are especially good. There is not the kind of sophistication that one finds with Karajan (see below), but the alert, direct approach has plenty of sparkle. The recording is brilliant. On tape a degree of top cut is needed to remove an occasional touch of shrillness, but very satisfactory results can be obtained when the bass is brought up a little.

Marriner's collection is certainly well played (although the LPO violins do not show the virtuosity of the Berlin Philharmonic – the ensemble in *Light Cavalry*, for instance, is not as clean as it might be). Marriner is at his best in the overtures where elegance can add an attractive outer veneer to the music-making. Other versions of *Light Cavalry* are rhythmically more exhilarating, and the reprise of the fanfare theme in the coda is awkwardly managed. The opening of *Poet and Peasant* is so broad that it is almost sluggish. The warmly reverberant recording has not transferred satisfactorily to cassette; the transients are muddled, and the all-important side-drum is singularly ill-focused.

Paray's collection, dating from the early sixties, offers playing of great verve and élan. The playing has not the last degree of polish and there are some unashamedly scrambled fast string passages, but the flair and exhilaration of the music-making here are irresistible, and it is a great pity that the tape transfer is a failure, with the resonance causing patches of uncomfortable congestion at climaxes.

Overtures: *Beautiful Galathea; The Jolly Robbers; Light Cavalry; Morning, Noon and Night in Vienna; Pique Dame; Poet and Peasant.*
> *(**) DG 3300 222 [id.]. Berlin PO, Karajan.

Karajan's collection is superbly played, a swaggering display of orchestral virtuosity, but unfortunately the cassette transfer is not very successful. The basic resonance of the recording produces some lack of refinement in tuttis, and the side-drum snares are poorly focused. The opening of *The Jolly Robbers* overture readily shows this problem.

Overtures: *Light Cavalry; Morning, Noon and Night in Vienna; Pique Dame; Poet and Peasant.*
> (M)**(*)Decca KCSP 374 [Lon. 5-6779]. Vienna PO, Solti.

With only four overtures included (admittedly the most popular four) this cassette, even at medium price, would be difficult to recommend were not both performances and recordings so brilliant.

The recording has a wide dynamic range, perhaps too wide for the cello solos in *Morning, Noon and Night* and *Poet and Peasant*, where the instrument is backwardly balanced and sounds not unlike a viola. But if you like the old-fashioned, rather mellow type of Suppé performance, be warned, this is not the shop for that. The cassette transfer is extremely vivid and brilliant, frequently approaching demonstration quality.

There is also another Decca (Phase Four) cassette offering this same programme played by the London Festival Orchestra under Robert Sharples. But this is simply not competitive: the performances are much less distinguished, the transfer is less secure, and the price is much higher.

Surinach, Carlos
(born 1915)

Piano concerto.
> **(*) Decca KSXC 6757 [Lon. 5-6990]. Alicia de Larrocha, RPO, Frühbeck de Burgos – MONTSALVATGE: *Concerto breve.****

Carlos Surinach's *Piano concerto* was written for Alicia de Larrocha. The writing is not particularly individual though it is often far from ineffective. Ultimately, however, it is an obstinately unmemorable work, though it would be difficult to imagine a more persuasive advocate than Mme Larrocha, who enjoys excellent support from the RPO under Frühbeck de Burgos. The recording too has admirable clarity and warmth, and readers with a specialist interest in Spanish music might well want to investigate it. The coupling, a not-so-short *Concerto breve* by Xavier Montsalvatge, a composer of the same generation, is well worth hearing, even though it is not of compelling originality. The transfer is brilliantly done, though the resonance of the acoustic is not so cleanly controlled here as in the coupling, and the refinement slips just a little at times.

Szymanowski, Karol
(1882–1937)

King Roger (opera): complete.
(***) Rediffusion KAUR 5061/2. Andrzej Hiolski, Hanna Rumowska, Zdislaw Nikodem, Kazimierz Pustelak, Marek Dabrowski, Warsaw State Opera House Chorus and Orch., Mierzejewski.

Recorded in Poland in the mid-sixties with a near-ideal cast, this magnificent performance of Szymanowski's operatic masterpiece establishes very clearly its unique and compelling qualities. True the plot is baldly unoperatic, more the subject for a cantata than a true opera: the strange and handsome young shepherd who visits King Roger's court in medieval Sicily and tempts away Queen Roxana emerges as Dionysus. The characterization is simple and direct, but as in Beethoven's *Fidelio* symbolic figures genuinely live as believable characters. What is very striking if one follows the recording in the English translation (no Polish text is provided) is that not only the dramatic situations but the precise sentences are immediately identifiable, so sharply defined in the music is the tone of voice of the words.

The ritualistic element of the work is beautifully conveyed in the magnificent choruses, and the choir of the Warsaw State Opera House as well as the orchestra perform with passion from first to last. The inspired conductor is Mieczyslaw Mierzejewski; King Roger is nobly taken by Andrzej Hiolski, the Shepherd

by Kazimierz Pustelak, and the only character to give even a few moments of doubt is the soprano, Hanna Rumowska, as Roxana. The vividly atmospheric recording does not begin to show its age, but the tape transfer is made at a very high level, and while for the most part the sound is vivid and atmospheric (if not rich), the choral climaxes are over-modulated. There is a constricted feeling – the fortissimos blare – and the solo voices have an element of peaking too. Overall, listening is not very comfortable.

Tallis, Thomas
(*c*. 1505–1585)

The Lamentations of Jeremiah the Prophet.
*** HMV TC-CSD 3779. The King's Singers – BYRD: *Ave verum* etc.***

It makes a refreshing change to have this great church music sung by a consort of voices instead of a full choir and with a fairly secular-sounding acoustic instead of a reverberant cathedral. Though the absence of that atmosphere may reduce the appeal of this tape for some listeners, the refinement and precision of the King's Singers are, as ever, superb, even more here than in the motets on the reverse, and the magnificent *Lamentations* are given a new and intense slant. The recording is excellent and the tape transfer admirably clean.

Tartini, Giuseppe
(1692–1770)

Violoncello concerto in A major.
*** DG 3300 974 [id.]. Mstislav

579

Rostropovich, Zurich Collegium Musicum, Sacher – BOC-
CHERINI and VIVALDI: *Concertos.****

As with the other works in this collection, Rostropovich's view of Tartini's
concerto is larger than life, but the eloquence of the playing disarms criticism,
even when the cellist plays cadenzas of his
own that are not exactly in period. The
lively accompaniment is matched by
bright, vivid recording which has transferred to tape with plenty of presence.

Tausky, Vilem
(born 1910)

Concertino (for harmonica).
*** Argo KZRC 856. Tommy
Reilly (harmonica), Academy
of St Martin-in-the-Fields,
Marriner – JACOB: *5 Pieces;*
MOODY: *Little suite;* VAUGHAN
WILLIAMS: *Romance.****

Tausky's *Concertino* is an extremely
well made little work and it is beautifully
played and recorded here. In the last analysis it is not really memorable, except
for a theme in the first movement that
recalls *Land of Hope and Glory* (in contour rather than substance). The cassette
transfer is of excellent quality.

Tchaikovsky, Peter
(1840–93)

(i) *Between Birthdays* (*Children's
Album*), *Op. 39* (with verses by
Ogden Nash). *Nutcracker suite, Op.
71a.*
(M) * CBS Classics 40-61832.
Orch., Kostelanetz, (i) with
Peter Ustinov (narrator).

The *Between Birthdays* suite is an orchestration (presumably by Kostelanetz)
of Tchaikovsky's *Children's Album* for
the piano. The scoring is witty, and its
touch of vulgarity is rather effective.
Each little piece sparkles and would make
delightful listening without the overlay of
Nash's often clumsy verses. The *Nutcracker suite* is given a bright lively performance with very forward sound (the
dynamics are thus levelled – there is no
hint of a *piano* in the *Miniature overture*).
Once again the ever-present words will
surely daunt even the most receptive
listener on a second or third hearing. The
recording of the orchestra has transferred
vividly, but Peter Ustinov's narration is
rather less crisply focused. The transfer
level is high.

Capriccio italien, Op. 45. (i) *Piano
concerto No. 1 in B flat minor, Op. 23.*
(ii) *Violin concerto in D major, Op.
35. Marche slave, Op. 31; Nutcracker
suite, Op. 71a; Romeo and Juliet* (fantasy overture); *Serenade for strings in
C major, Op. 48; Symphonies Nos. 4–
6;* (iii) *Variations on a rococo theme,
Op. 33.*
(M) **(*) DG 3378 045. Berlin PO
(or (i) Vienna SO), Karajan,
with (i) Sviatoslav Richter
(piano); (ii) Christian Ferras
(violin); (iii) Mstislav Rostropovich (cello).

On the whole this is a distinguished
collection, and it has been uniformly well
transferred to cassette, with consistently
high levels and clear, slightly dry but
always vivid sound. A little treble cut restores most of the bloom to the upper
strings, leaving plenty of brilliance and

detail though sometimes a touch of glare. About the performances the only serious reservations concern the *Piano concerto*; this version is discussed below, as are the other shorter works. The symphonies are Karajan's earlier recordings and they are not lacking in flair and excitement; indeed the *Pathétique* is in many ways a more attractive performance than Karajan's later version. The layout on six cassettes is sensible, with one exception: the *String serenade* begins on cassette No. 3, the first movement following the close of the *Pathétique symphony*; the other three movements are on cassette No. 4 (coupled to the *Nutcracker suite*). This piece of clumsiness, which saves very little tape, makes the opening of the work for strings somewhat inaccessible. The notes are clearly printed.

(i) *Capriccio italien, Op. 45;* (i; iv) *Piano concerto No. 1 in B flat minor, Op. 23;* (i) *1812 overture, Op. 49; Symphonies Nos.* (ii) *4 in F minor, Op. 36;* (iii) *5 in E minor, Op. 64; 6 in B minor (Pathétique), Op. 74.*

  (B) **(*) Rediffusion Legend KLGDD 101. Czech PO, cond. (i) Ančerl; (ii) Slovak; (iii) Matačić; (iv) with Sviatoslav Richter (piano).

This four-cassette box is undoubtedly a bargain. Ančerl's performances of the *Capriccio* and *1812* are in no way exceptional, but they are certainly alive and are well played. Because of the absence of cannon in the overture, the closing climax is accommodated without the break-up of quality that mars almost all the other cassette versions. Richter's performance of the *Piano concerto* is a mono original (dating from 1960) and the sound is confined, but not unacceptably so. The performance is exciting enough, if without any special insights. The symphonies are a different matter. They are all refreshingly direct performances with plenty of excitement and excellent

orchestral playing. Ladislav Slovak's account of the *Fourth* is almost as strong as any available, fully characterized and vividly played. Matačić's *Fifth* has the drawback of a wobbly, very open-toned horn solo in the slow movement, and the finale lacks something in body of string tone at its opening; but otherwise the performance has splendid urgency and excitement. The *Pathétique* is even finer, the first-movement development really riveting, and the scherzo/march splendidly judged. The finale is eloquent in a richly romantic way without slipping over the edge. Throughout the symphonies the sound is vivid, and the high-level transfers offer a clear (if not especially rich) sound picture with only the occasional slipping of refinement, much preferable to the comparatively dim sound of the equivalent LPs.

Capriccio italien, Op. 45.
  (*)DG 923031 [id.]. Berlin PO, Karajan – *Violin concerto.*(*)

Karajan's account of the *Capriccio* is brilliant, the Berlin Philharmonic brass telling especially well. The combination of sophistication and panache (without any special affection conveyed) makes for a very professional kind of excitement, and the recording is bright and full-blooded. The tape transfer has both weight and brilliance, but the upper focus lacked the last degree of crispness in the copy we sampled.

Capriccio italien, Op. 45. (i) *1812 overture, Op. 49. Marche slave, Op. 31.*
  *(*) Decca KSXC 6895 [Lon. 5-7118]. Detroit SO, Dorati.
  (M) *(*) Decca KCSP 108. LSO, Alwyn, (i) with Band of Grenadier Guards.

Dorati's tape is generally better engineered than the Alwyn alternative, but the performances have less flair. There is no lack of direct excitement in *1812*, and the *Capriccio* has elegance, but none of the music-making is really memorable and *Marche slave* seems excessively sombre until the change of mood at the coda, which is taken briskly. The transfers are not wholly successful: the reverberation brings clouding of focus at times and although the levels are manipulated at the end of *1812* there is still a degree of coarseness.

Kenneth Alwyn shows a flair for Tchaikovsky rare in English conductors, and all three performances generate a real intensity and excitement while at the same time showing Alwyn's fine sense of style and care for detail. But this was an early cassette issue and the sound has a lack of refinement at climaxes that one would not expect in a current Decca tape. We have tried a new copy and the climaxes show a tendency to coarseness, although much of the sound is tolerable. What is not acceptable is the turnover break in the middle of the *Capriccio italien*. The *Marche slave* sounds best, and the guns at the end of *1812* are not too badly managed.

(i; ii) *Capriccio italien, Op. 45;* (i; iii) *1812 overture, Op. 49;* (i; ii) *Romeo and Juliet* (fantasy overture); (iv) *Sleeping Beauty, Op. 66: Rose adagio; Panorama.*
  (B) (*) Philips Fontana 7327 009.
    (i) Concertgebouw Orch.; (ii) Haitink; (iii) Markevitch; (iv) Vienna SO, Sawallisch.

Although the performances are good this bargain-priced cassette is only suitable for small players. Resonance clouds the *Capriccio italien*, and the boomy climaxes of *1812* are the opposite of spectacular. *Romeo and Juliet* has transferred more successfully, but this collection is not really recommendable.

Capriccio italien, Op. 45; Marche slave, Op. 31; Mazeppa: Gopak.
  *(**) HMV TC-ASD 3093 [Angel 4XS 37227]. LPO, Boult – RIMSKY-KORSAKOV: *Capriccio espagnol* etc.*(**)

Sir Adrian Boult made a famous recording of the *Capriccio italien* in the Colston Hall, Bristol, in the days of 78 r.p.m. discs. The present recording is certainly spectacular provided one can accept the resonance, which creates a very full-blooded, if larger-than-life effect. The performance, however, is very broad and in the last analysis lacks sheer vitality. The *Marche slave*, with its sombre opening, is well characterized if a little mannered, but the *Gopak* comes off well enough. The cassette transfer is not very successful, with a low frequency ceiling and the reverberation producing a muffled effect in the tuttis.

Capriccio italien, Op. 45; Marche slave, Op. 31; Nutcracker suite, Op. 71a.
  (B) **(*) DG Heliodor 3348 275. Berlin PO, Leitner.

Ferdinand Leitner's collection dates from the early sixties but the sound has been successfully refurbished, and apart from a hint of boominess in the deep bass (which is easily cut back) the quality is remarkably fresh. The *Capriccio italien* is not especially Italianate, but it is played with style and creates plenty of excitement without being frenzied. The *Marche slave* has dignity, and the *Nutcracker suite* is rather gently played, with considerable effect. An excellent bargain.

Capriccio italien, Op. 45; Romeo and Juliet (fantasy overture); *Eugene Onegin: Waltz.*
  * Decca Phase 4 KPFC 4388. RPO, Vonk.

These performances are marvellously recorded, and the cassette transfer is brilliantly managed, but Hans Vonk's directing hand produces little more than a routine account of *Romeo and Juliet*, and the *Capriccio* is similarly without flair.

Piano concerto No. 1 in B flat minor, Op. 23.
*** DG 3300 677 [id.]. Lazar Berman, Berlin PO, Karajan (with *Eugene Onegin Polonaise***).
(M) *** DG Privilege 3335 295. Martha Argerich, RPO, Dutoit (with *Nutcracker: Waltz of the Flowers***).
*** Decca KSXC 6840. Vladimir Ashkenazy, LSO, Maazel – MUSSORGSKY: *Pictures at an Exhibition.***(*)
(*) Decca Phase 4 KPFC 4362 [Lon. 5-21148]. Ilana Vered, LSO, Kord – STRAVINSKY: *Three movements from Petrushka.*(*)
(*) Decca Phase 4 KPFC 2 7004. Ivan Davis, RPO, Henry Lewis – RACHMANINOV: *Piano concerto No. 2.*(*)
(M) **(*) Decca Jubilee KJBC 29. Clifford Curzon, Vienna PO, Solti (with LITOLFF: *Scherzo***).
(M) **(*) RCA Gold Seal GK 25013. Earl Wild, RPO, Fistoulari.
(M) ** CBS Classics 40-61697. Nelson Freire, Munich PO, Kempe – GRIEG: *Piano concerto.***
HMV TC-ASD 3262 [Angel 4XS 37177]. Horacio Gutierrez, LSO, Previn – LISZT: *Piano concerto No. 1.*
(B) *(*) Classics for Pleasure TC-CFP 115. Peter Katin, LPO,

Pritchard – LITOLFF: *Scherzo.****
(B) *(*) DG Heliodor 3348 261. Valery Afanassiev, Orchestre National de Belgique, Defossez.
(B) * Pye ZCCOB 652. Shura Cherkassky, LPO, Boult – LITOLFF: *Scherzo.***
(**) DG 923021 [id.]. Sviatoslav Richter, Vienna SO, Karajan (with *Marche slave***(*)).

Even after the exaggerated fanfares of publicity which greeted the arrival of Lazar Berman in the West, this first of his concerto recordings outside the Soviet Union lived up to all expectations. It is interesting that credit for the incandescence of the performance must go almost as much to the conductor as to the pianist, and yet the conductor is Karajan, who has sometimes seemed too aloof as a concerto accompanist. Berman's character is firmly established in the massive chords of the introduction (though curiously he hustles the first group of all), and from there his revelling in dramatic contrast, whether of texture, tone colour, dynamic or tempo, makes this one of the most exciting readings ever put on record. It is not just a question of massive bravura but of extreme delicacy too, so that in the central *scherzando* of the slow movement, it almost sounds as though Berman is merely breathing on the keyboard, hardly depressing the notes at all. The ripe playing of the Berlin Philharmonic backs up the individuality of Berman's reading, and the recording is massively brilliant to match. The tape transfer is excellent, with brilliant weighty sound (the opening strings sound splendidly rich): in the very quietest moments the definition is marginally less refined in detail than on the disc but it is still very good. The *Polonaise* bonus, an older recording, has noticeably more edge; the performance has fine rhythmic vigour.

The sheer weight of the opening horn figure creates the mood of the big, broad performance from Martha Argerich and Charles Dutoit. The recording too is splendid, full-bodied, wide in dynamic range, and yet with a surprisingly natural balance. Martha Argerich's conception encompasses the widest range of tonal shading. In the finale she often produces a scherzando-like effect; then the orchestra thunders in with the Russian dance theme to create a real contrast. The quality of Charles Dutoit's contribution to the music-making is never in doubt. The tempo of the first movement is comparatively measured, seeking power rather than surface excitement, and again when the build-up begins for the final statement of the great lyrical tune of the finale, the conductor creates his climax in deliberate, measured fashion. The slow movement is strikingly atmospheric, yet delicate, its romanticism lighthearted. A most satisfying account in every way. The transfer is at a fairly high level and has plenty of body and good piano tone, though the treble range is less open than on the disc. The cassette offers a bonus, the *Waltz of the Flowers* elegantly played by the Berlin Philharmonic Orchestra under Leitner.

Originally issued spread uneconomically over two cassette sides, Ashkenazy's version now occupies only one, and is coupled to Mussorgsky. The new transfer is of the highest quality. A slight degree of bass cut is useful, but then the piano sounds splendidly bold, and clear, while the orchestral balance is most realistic. Ashkenazy's essentially lyrical performance offers a genuine alternative to those of Berman and Argerich. They remain more obvious first recommendations, but there are many who will enjoy Ashkenazy's thoughtfulness and his refusal to be stampeded by Tchaikovsky's passionate rhetoric. The biggest climaxes of the first movement are made to grow out of the music, instead of being part of a sweeping forward momentum, and the lyrical side of the writing associated with the beautiful second subject is distilled with obvious affection. In the *Andantino* too, Ashkenazy refuses to play flashily and thus uses the middle section as a contrasting episode to set in the boldest relief the return of the opening tune, which is played very beautifully. The finale is very fast and brilliant, yet the big tune is broadened at the end in a most convincing way.

The brilliantly recorded Phase Four tape by Ilana Vered also deserves an honourable place. The larger-than-life sound (the piano very forward and real, so that one almost feels able to touch it) is immensely dramatic, and if the overall balance is not quite natural, one forgives that when the immediacy is given to such exciting playing. Alongside the bravura, there are many imaginative touches from the soloist and a freshness in the orchestra which is similarly appealing. The refinement of piano tone at the opening and close of the slow movement, played with the utmost delicacy, gives much pleasure, and the finale has no lack of brilliance and power. The coupling is played with comparable command and undoubtedly increases the interest of this issue. The cassette transfer is extremely brilliant.

The partnership of Ivan Davis and Henry Lewis is successful in providing a fresh look at Tchaikovsky's masterpiece. In spite of the strong opening, with plenty of weight from the strings, the first movement is without a thrustful forward momentum, but is spacious, pianist and conductor both relaxing to take in the movement's lyrical detail. The *Andantino* is played simply, and as in the first movement the element of contrast is strong. The restatement of the main theme is played very slowly and gently, the performers' affection clearly shown. The finale is comparatively lightweight but has genuine sparkle, and the closing pages have plenty of impact. The Decca sound is brilliant, clear and immediate, without any special Phase Four exaggerations. The cassette sound is not quite as transparent as in the Rachmaninov coupling, and it is transferred at a lower level. But it has fine body and sonority and the piano tone is most convincing.

Sir Clifford Curzon's 1969 recording emerges here as fresh as new paint. The bold, full-blooded transfer covers up most of the sins of the fairly old recording, although some faults of balance remain and there are one or two obvious joins in the master tape. But Curzon matches thoughtfulness to unostentatious bravura, and the performance has fine zest and spontaneity. The coupling is not generous, but the performance is as scintillating as the recording, and the transfer is of demonstration quality.

Even in the shadow of Berman, the RCA Gold Seal issue by Earl Wild, with the RPO under Fistoulari, stands as one of the finest accounts of this much-recorded work. The recording was made originally for Reader's Digest and has lain in the RCA vaults for some years, but it needs no apology for its sound. From the fine sweep of the opening the reading is distinguished by its feeling of directness and power, yet the lyrical side of the music (the first movement's second subject, the outer sections of the *Andantino*) brings a comparable sensitivity. In the big cadenza one is reminded of Horowitz when Wild, by impetuous tempo changes in the imitative passages, makes himself sound almost like a piano duo. The finale too, taken with crackling bravura, again recalls the famous Horowitz/Toscanini record, and Fistoulari – splendidly assured throughout – makes a superb final climax. The transfer is generally successful but has not quite the sophistication of the Decca and DG tapes above. The piano tone is bold and clear, but the orchestral sound, although full-blooded, lacks the last degree of refinement.

Freire's is a strongly impetuous, youthful performance, which may be a little short of poise but is certainly exciting. The dash of the opening passage is exhilarating, and the conductor provides

strong support. The recording – brilliant and with a forwardly balanced piano in the transatlantic manner – has a touch of crudeness about it (the string sheen is too brightly lit for complete naturalness), but it rather suits the virility of the playing. Those looking for elegance in the central movement will be disappointed (the soloist's lead back to the main theme is rather clumsy), but there is no lack of adrenalin in the finale, and with a good coupling this cassette is distinctly competitive. The transfer has been made at a high level and the sound has plenty of range, while the piano timbre is substantial, bright but not too brittle.

Gutierrez was hailed by EMI (with publicized support from Previn) as a virtuoso of prodigious ability. His playing is certainly impressive here, but in fact it is in the work's lyrical passages rather than the moments of extreme bravura that this performance communicates more readily. It is certainly enjoyable, but it lacks the gripping compulsion of the best accounts. The rich sound seems ineffectively balanced at the opening, where the massed orchestral violins fail to tell in their famous sweeping romantic tune.

Katin's Classics for Pleasure version is given a brilliant, modern recording (paid for by Wills' cigarettes), and this is basically quite a strong, musical reading. But somehow there is a lack of drama, and the absence of extrovert bravura from the soloist (especially in the middle section of the slow movement) produces an impression of facelessness. But no one could fault this tape on grounds of taste, and it has an excellent filler. The transfer is of excellent quality, full-blooded and clear, with realistic piano tone.

Valery Afanassiev's performance was recorded at a public concert, but the audience is very well-behaved, although the vociferous applause begins before the last chords of the finale have ended. The enthusiasm is understandable, for Afanassiev plays extremely well and is especially impressive in the slow movement. However, the orchestral balance is poor, so that the strings are given little body and substance, and the piano, forwardly placed, easily dominates the sound balance. The transfer is acceptable if at rather a low level. The piano tone is good, but the orchestral focus is not ideally clear.

Cherkassky's version (originally issued by World Record Club) offers a genuine attempt to rethink the music, with generally slow tempi (even in the finale). Conductor and pianist work well together, but the result – although it has its moments – sounds rather unspontaneous. The first movement is too measured and there is no sense of any spirited 'battle' between soloist and orchestra. For all the attraction of having the lyrical orchestral theme in the finale really played lyrically, there is not enough sheer bravura here to carry a movement which is in essence a Russian dance. The recording is good (although the big opening string tune does not make as much impact as it might), and the transfer offers a natural sound balance. However, there is an incredibly clumsy turnover break in the slow movement, not even at the end of the *Andantino* section but in the middle of it. The soloist is playing so beautifully at the moment when it happens that one is exasperated to the point of fury at such witless engineering.

The element of struggle for which this work is famous is only too clear in the Richter/Karajan performance on DG. Richter and Karajan, not surprisingly, do not always agree. Each chooses a different tempo for the second subject of the finale and maintains it in spite of the other. However, in both the dramatic opening and the closing pages of the work they are agreed in a hugely mannered, bland stylization which is not easy to enjoy. Elsewhere in the first movement both conductor and pianist play havoc with any sense of forward tempo (although they both produce some real bursts of excitement here and there), and Richter's excessive *rubato* in the lyrical second-subject group is unspontaneous.

Clearly two major artists are at work, but it is difficult to praise the end product as a convincing reading. The recording is full-blooded, with a firm piano image. The tape offers the bonus of Karajan's fine performance of the *Marche slave*, which is well transferred.

(i) *Piano concerto No. 1 in B flat minor, Op. 23;* (ii) *Violin concerto in D major, Op. 35.*
> (M) *(*) Philips Festivo 7310 028. Rotterdam PO, Edo de Waart, with (i) Rafael Orozco; (ii) Mayumi Fujikawa.

Orozco's version of the *Piano concerto* is flamboyant enough, but in spite of the bravura, and although it is well recorded, this performance fails to be memorable. The *Prestissimo* central section of the slow movement is certainly intended by the composer as an opportunity for the soloist to show his mettle, but the lack of refinement here is unattractive. Mayumi Fujikawa's account of the *Violin concerto* has a great deal more finesse, and in the slow movement her warmly lyrical phrasing gives much pleasure, particularly as the supporting woodwind detail is nicely played. But the first movement lacks impetus, and in spite of the attraction of the coupling this cassette is not such a bargain as it looks. The transfers are made at a modest level, and the *Violin concerto* in particular lacks vividness unless the playback level is set very high.

(i) *Piano concerto No. 1 in B flat minor, Op. 23;* (ii) *Concert fantasia* (for piano and orchestra) *in G major, Op. 56.*
> (M) **(*) Decca KCSP 168. Peter Katin, with (i) LSO, Kundell; (ii) LPO, Boult.

The Decca recording of the *First Piano concerto* is bold and vivid, clear and immediate, and excellently balanced. The performance is equally alive and direct, the opening big tune taken fairly fast but with a fine sweep, the *Andantino* played very stylishly and the finale with plenty of bravura. Katin's Kempff-like clarity perfectly suits the *Concert fantasia*, with its *Nutcracker* overtones in the first movement. This two-movement piece is much less ambitious than the well-known concerto. Boult as well as Katin obviously relishes the delicacy of much of this music, and he induces his players to give a rhythmic spring which compensates completely for the occasional fault of ensemble. There is an overall freshness about the playing – in the full emotional passages as well as the rest – which should help to bring the piece the attention and popularity it deserves. The stereo is clear, the piano tone firm and bright. Altogether this is a most enjoyable and a very happily planned coupling. The cassette transfer is well managed: it is not quite so refined as the full-priced Ashkenazy version of the concerto (for instance) but still very good, the sound rather fuller on side one than side two (the *Fantasia*), where there is a compensating freshness.

Piano concerto No. 2 in G major, Op. 44 (original version).
> (M) *(*) Philips 7317 196. Werner Haas, Monte Carlo Opera Orch., Inbal.

Werner Haas is an intelligent and masterly player and he is on top form here. Unfortunately the orchestral accompaniment is less imaginative. The outer movements have plenty of vigour (although the finale lacks wit and sparkle), but the slow movement is undistinguished, and the solo playing of the principal violin and cello lacks flair and spontaneity. The performers are not helped by the Philips recording, which although full-blooded lacks brilliance and thus sounds overweighted in the bass. This is not the fault of the transfer, which is made at quite a high level and is well balanced.

Piano concerto No. 2 in G major, Op. 44 (arr. Siloti).
> (B) ** DG Heliodor 3348 298. Shura Cherkassky, Berlin PO, Richard Kraus.

This famous recording now reappears in excellent mono sound. Relatively few allowances have to be made for it, though it dates from 1955. DG are to be congratulated for not trying to transcribe it for stereo, since the overall effect is perfectly acceptable, though one could wish for a richer, fresher string sound. Cherkassky's playing is superb throughout, and although it is a drawback that he uses the truncated Siloti edition, his flair and poetry more than compensate. The cassette is slightly less smooth than the disc, but readers should not allow minor reservations to put them off this classic account, which is modestly priced.

Violin concerto in D major, Op. 35.
> *** Decca KSXC 6493. Kyung-Wha Chung, LSO, Previn – SIBELIUS: *Concerto.****
> *** Decca Phase 4 KPFC 4345 [Lon. 5-21116]. Ruggiero Ricci, Netherlands Radio Orch., Fournet – MENDELSSOHN: *Concerto.****
> **(*) Pye ZCPNH 14. Yuval Yaron, LPO, Soudant – SIBELIUS: *Concerto.**(*)
> **(*) DG 923031 [id.]. Christian Ferras, Berlin PO, Karajan – *Capriccio italien.**(*)
> *(*) Philips 7300 583. Henryk Szeryng, Concertgebouw Orch., Haitink – MENDELSSOHN: *Concerto* etc.*(*)

Violin concerto; Sérénade mélancolique, Op. 26; Valse-scherzo, Op. 34.
> **(*) Philips 7300 514 [id.]. Salvatore Accardo, BBC SO, Colin Davis.

(i) *Violin concerto;* (ii) *Souvenir d'un*

lieu cher: Meditation; Scherzo, Op. 41/1–2 (orch. Glazounov); *Valse-scherzo.*

(M) **(*) HMV TC-SXLP 30225. Nathan Milstein, with (i) Pittsburgh SO, Steinberg; (ii) orch., Irving.

Violin concerto; Souvenir d'un lieu cher: Meditation, Op. 42/1 (orch. Glazounov).

**(*) CBS 40-76725. Isaac Stern, National SO, Rostropovich.

Violin concerto; Valse-scherzo.

*** Decca KSXC 7854 [Lon. 5-7076]. Boris Belkin, New Philharmonia Orch., Ashkenazy.

Although the coupling is not generous, the newest Decca recording of Tchaikovsky's concerto by Boris Belkin with the LSO under Vladimir Ashkenazy lays a fair claim to head the list of available versions, particularly as the recording is of such outstanding, demonstration quality. This is a performance of genuine distinction and strong personality. Belkin brings temperament and flair to the solo part besides great sympathy, and everything he does rings true; one feels he is discovering the beauties of the score for the very first time. There is no trace of routine either in his playing or in the orchestral accompaniment under Ashkenazy, and the freshness and spontaneity that they communicate, as well as the Slavonic authenticity of feeling, make this a memorably winning account. The Decca recording is beautifully focused and well defined: there is splendid body and no want of smoothness and refinement. One or two extraneous noises are present on both cassette and disc, but these are of minor account. A most poetic and imaginative account, as fine as any now before the public. The charming *Valse-scherzo* makes an admirable fill-up. There is no appreciable difference between disc and cassette.

Like the Sibelius with which it is coupled, Kyung-Wha Chung's performance of the Tchaikovsky concerto is among the finest in the catalogue. Her technique is impeccable and her musicianship of the highest order, and Previn's accompanying is highly sympathetic and responsive. This has warmth, spontaneity and discipline; every detail is beautifully shaped and turned without a trace of sentimentality. The recording is well balanced and detail is clean, though the acoustic is warm. This is a very distinguished issue, and the transfer is admirably smooth and truthful, the sound well balanced, yet vivid, with expansive tuttis and a natural image for the soloist.

Ricci made an outstanding record of this concerto in the early days of mono LP. He then recorded it in stereo with rather less success, but his newer Phase Four recording with Fournet restores his reputation fully. The characteristic intense *vibrato* may not be to all tastes, but the ear readily submits to the compulsion and colour of the playing, which shows a rock-steady technique and a splendid lyrical feeling. Even though Ricci is very near the microphone, so secure is his left hand that the rich stream of tone is always securely based, and the larger-than-life image is attractive when the orchestral impact and detail are so vividly conveyed. The cassette transfer is outstandingly realistic.

A fine performance from Stern, lyrical in feeling yet with plenty of sparkle and bravura and a matching accompaniment under Rostropovich. The *Canzonetta* is most beautifully played, and the contrasts inherent in the finale are well brought out, yet with the Russian dance element dominating attractively. The balance, however, places the soloist well forward in the CBS manner, and the close microphone produces a degree of fierceness in the solo violin timbre under pressure, which the tape transfer seems to emphasize in the first movement. Otherwise the quality is vivid and detailed and the resonant acoustic is well caught. The *Meditation* makes an attractive filler; but in the last analysis this does not really compete with the more richly recorded Belkin and Chung versions on Decca. Moreover, as with many CBS issues on tape, no musical notes are provided.

The young Israeli virtuoso Yuval Yaron gives a most impressive performance. Like Belkin he takes the first movement at a comparatively spacious tempo, and revels in its lyrical detail. Soudant brings plenty of rhythmic resilience to the tuttis, and the partnership is undoubtedly successful. Yaron is balanced well forward by the truthful recording, but his technique stands up to the spotlight thus provided. He plays the *Canzonetta* most tenderly, giving it an elegiac atmosphere; then Soudant prepares the finale rather deliberately so that the start of the allegro makes a striking contrast. The woodwind interchanges in the finale are very relaxed, and the soloist too brings out the lyricism of these interludes between the bravura very pleasingly. The performance as a whole is an individual one, the interpretation well thought out. There is just a hint of over-deliberation at times, but this remains a very recommendable version, and the tape transfer is splendidly vivid, both sparkling and full-blooded.

Salvatore Accardo's account combines poise and freshness with flair. He has a keen lyricism and a fine sense of line, as one would expect, and he is sensitively accompanied by Colin Davis and the BBC Symphony Orchestra. Like Belkin he plays the *Concerto* complete, and an additional attraction is that he includes both the *Sérénade mélancolique* and the *Valse-scherzo*. Accardo's reading of the concerto has a refinement and restraint that mark it off from the traditional virtuoso approach, and no doubt for some collectors it will lack the passionate sweep they look for. Accardo has a marvellous purity, and if the recording was as good, it would carry a three-star grading. As it is, the soloist is a shade too close to the microphone to do his tone full justice, and the tape transfer (which is

otherwise a good one) tends to bring out the slight edginess of timbre which results.

Milstein's HMV recording of the concerto is no less competitive than Accardo's, particularly at medium price. Although in this transfer the recording needs a little smoothing at the top, it sounds amazingly fresh for its age. Milstein is both vital and sensitive, and there is no question of mere virtuosity and display dominating the proceedings. Moreover the couplings are substantial and presented very persuasively. The tape opens with the *Valse-scherzo*, placed as a prelude to the first movement of the concerto (which is less than ideal in this medium). Side two contains the other two concerto movements plus the *Souvenir d'un lieu cher*, which certainly makes an attractive encore.

Consideration of the Ferras/Karajan performance must be affected by personal reactions to Ferras's characteristic tone, with its rather close *vibrato* in lyrical passages and tendency to emphasize the schmalz on the G string. One finds too that Ferras's playing tends to lack charm, but some may react differently, and this is a well-conceived reading, with Karajan shaping the work as a whole very convincingly. The recording is excellent, the transfer kind to the soloist, who is given a sweet, rich timbre, especially in the upper range. There is some lack of absolute precision of focus in the recently made copy we tried, but the sound is full and well balanced. This performance is also available in a DG box with versions of the Beethoven, Brahms and Sibelius concertos played by the same artists (3371 021).

Szeryng is sweetly lyrical, but he is not helped by Haitink, who provides a rather slack accompaniment. The relaxed manner of the performance of the first movement is in some ways like the Belkin version on Decca, but that performance has strikingly more forward momentum and impulse. In the finale too Belkin shows a fire that Szeryng, although spirited, misses. The transfer, which is rather dim and at a very low level, lacks sparkle. The solo violin is very natural in timbre, if without any striking presence.

(i) *1812 overture, Op. 49. Francesca da Rimini* (fantasy), *Op. 32; Marche slave, Op. 31.*
    **(*) Philips 7300 253 [id.]. Concertgebouw Orch., Haitink, (i) with members of the Royal Netherlands Military Band.

As was noticed in reviewing the equivalent LP, the recordings here seem to have been balanced to give a brilliant edge to the sound. This means that, although the tape transfer has been made at a relatively low level, there is no lack of presence and detail, although in *Francesca de Rimini* the internal focus of the orchestra is not remarkably crisp. The recording has a wide dynamic range, and the tape needs a high-level playback (which brings up the hiss) if the opening of *1812* is not to lack substance. However, the climaxes open out impressively, the cymbals sound especially clear, and the final climax is accommodated with a genuine sense of spectacle yet very little congestion. The *Marche slave* also comes off splendidly, and Haitink conveys his affection readily. The performance itself is not unlike Kenneth Alwyn's on Decca (see above), with a fast coda. The richness and detail of the sound are impressive. Apart from the hiss this is certainly one of the more successful anthologies on cassette which include *1812*.

1812 overture, Op. 49; Marche slave, Op. 31; Romeo and Juliet (fantasy overture).
    **(*) DG 923045 [id.]. Berlin PO, Karajan.
    (***) HMV TC-ASD 2894 [Angel 4xs 36890]. LSO, Previn.

Karajan's performance of *1812* is another of the few versions that have trans-

ferred to cassette without losing the sense of spectacle in an orgy of coarseness or distortion. True the cannon at the end do offer some problems, tending to blot out the music itself, and one can sense the German engineers at their mixing panel adding and subtracting the bells strictly according to the conductor's demands. The choral opening comes off quite effectively, and with superb orchestral playing there is a good deal of excitement. Moreover the excellence of the transfer extends to the other items. *Marche slave* is presented with its full solemn character, and the richly vivid recording does it justice. It is a work that the Berlin orchestra do especially well. *Romeo and Juliet* is no less effective; Karajan's interpretation blends passion and a sombre dignity very judiciously, and the sound is first-class.

The HMV transfer of Previn's performances is much less successful. The quality is full-blooded, although the range is noticeably narrower than on the disc. The explosive noises which serve the climax of *1812* are uncomfortable rather than exciting. Previn takes a clearheaded, totally unsentimental view of the music, and as a result the three works emerge stronger in design (even *1812*) and no less exciting than usual. But the recording precludes a recommendation.

Francesca da Rimini (fantasy), *Op. 32; Romeo and Juliet* (fantasy overture).
    *** HMV TC-ASD 3567. LPO, Rostropovich.

Like Rostropovich's accounts of the symphonies these are intensely individual readings with loving concern for orchestral detail. The ebb and flow of tension have the spontaneity of live performances, and although Rostropovich's pacing is as free as his moulding of the melodic lines, the listener is carried along by the expressive vitality of the orchestral playing. At the opening of *Romeo and Juliet* there are bold accents in the lower strings; later there is a compulsive *accele-*

rando before the final romantic climax, yet the love theme is introduced with the greatest tenderness. It is an epic rather than a romantic approach, and *Francesca* has a similar sense of scale and high drama, with a breathtaking finale, yet touching delicacy in the work's central section, with radiant sounds from the LPO woodwind. The recording is resonant and spacious, with great body and impact; the transfers are mostly first-class, although in *Francesca* there is a slight slipping of internal focus at the *fortissimo* in the strings before the inferno music returns. But this is a thrilling tape that will give much satisfaction.

Hamlet (fantasy overture), *Op. 67a.*
 (M) ** Decca Jubilee KJBC 20. Vienna PO, Maazel – *Symphony No. 1.***(*)

Tchaikovsky's fantasy overture *Hamlet* did not repeat the success of *Romeo and Juliet*, but, as Stokowski has shown on disc (Everest SDBR 3011), it can be made to sound an inspired piece even if the secondary lyrical material is less memorable (and less felicitously scored) than the famous 'love theme' of the better-known work. *Hamlet* is, however, very strong on atmosphere, and the opening and closing pages have a sombre colouring which catches the essence of Shakespeare's tragedy remarkably well. It is here that Maazel's directness is simply not imaginative enough to bring out the full character of the writing, although the performance as a whole is not without drama and excitement. The recording is excellent and it has been vividly transferred. A more than generous coupling for a fine performance of the *Winter Day-dreams symphony*.

Manfred symphony, Op. 58.
 ***Decca KSXC 6853. New Philharmonia Orch., Ashkenazy.
 **(*) HMV TC-ASD 3018. LSO, Previn.

 (M) ** Decca Jubilee KJBC 26. Vienna PO, Maazel.
 *(*) DG 3300 878 [id.]. LSO, Ahronovich.

It is astonishing that this once totally neglected work should now be represented by four different cassette recordings. Each has its own merits, but the inspirational qualities of Vladimir Ashkenazy's reading, with its natural expressiveness and surging spontaneity, bring a uniquely rewarding performance that is as exciting as it is imaginative. The atmosphere and power of the opening movement are fully realized, and the scherzo has the most refined lyrical impulse, with wonderfully fresh string playing and sparkling articulation in the outer sections. The *Andante* is even finer; indeed in Ashkenazy's hands it is revealed as one of Tchaikovsky's most successful symphonic slow movements, full of lyrical fervour when the playing shows such strength of feeling yet is completely without exaggeration. The reading culminates in a stunning account of the finale, Ashkenazy opting for a fast tempo and providing a tremendous forward momentum. The *fugato* section is especially incisive, and the work's closing pages are given a satisfying feeling of apotheosis. The recording is immensely full-blooded and brilliant, yet natural in perspective; the tape transfer is highly sophisticated, both rich and detailed, with splendid weight and impact. A direct A/B comparison with the disc, however, shows that (as in Ashkenazy's version of the *Fifth Symphony*) the climaxes on cassette are marginally less richly expansive, although elsewhere the sound is almost identical in both media.

After Ashkenazy, Previn's account seems comparatively lacking in forward thrust but it remains a reading of considerable weight, with many imaginative touches. The scherzo is particularly fine, but the performance as a whole is helped by superb recording of great richness. Considering the amplitude, the HMV cassette is remarkably successful. The transfer has been made at the highest level and the climaxes expand impressively, with very little slipping in the overall refinement.

Maazel's is a fresh, straightforward performance and by no means to be dismissed. At Jubilee price it is excellent value, for the recording is first-class and the tape transfer vividly detailed, with brilliant, expansive climaxes. The music is quite strongly characterized and well played, though the reading lacks the distinctive qualities that make Ashkenazy's version so memorable.

Yuri Ahronovich's reading is very personal, with an extreme *ritenuto* style to exaggerate the Byronic melodrama. It is effective in its way, but the eccentricities seem likely to become less satisfactory on repetition. The recording is rich but the comparatively low transfer level means that the last degree of bite and sparkle are missing.

The Nutcracker (ballet), *Op. 71:* complete.

  (M) *** Philips 7505 076 [id.]. Concertgebouw Orch. (with chorus), Dorati.

  (B) *** Decca KDPC 2 7043. Suisse Romande Orch. (with chorus), Ansermet.

  (M) *** HMV TC2-SXDW 3028. Bolshoi Theatre Orch. (with chorus), Rozhdestvensky.

  **(*) HMV TC-SLS 834 [Angel 4x2s 3788]. LSO (with Ambrosian Singers), Previn.

  **(*) Decca KSXC 2 7059. National PO, Bonynge.

Tchaikovsky's enchanting score for the *Nutcracker* ballet has been exceptionally lucky in the recording studio since the earliest days of stereo, when Ansermet's magical set was among Decca's first releases. But, fine though that still is, the recording shows some signs of its age (mainly at the bass end of the audio spec-

trum, which now seems a little dead and lacking in natural resonance), and Dorati's set (issued here at medium price) must now take precedence. Although some might feel that the Concertgebouw acoustic is a little ample for a score designed for the theatre-pit, in all other respects the Philips sound is of the highest quality, both dramatically expansive and with a warmth and bloom given to wind and strings alike. The playing of the Concertgebouw Orchestra is immensely refined, and Dorati's attention to detail is loving rather than in any way clinical. The vitality of the playing is noticeable from the *Overture* onwards, with a delightful rhythmic spring and no forcing of accents, and the strings produce some lovely sounds. Dorati's conception is both vivid and strong; the *Transformation scene* has never before sounded quite so dramatic in a recording, and it is built to a tremendous climax. Then the *Waltz of the Snowflakes* produces the most delightfully soft-grained choral quality from the Boys' Choir of St Bavo Cathedral, Haarlem. In the dances which make up Act 2, Dorati's characterization is sure, although the *Waltz of the Flowers* could ideally have more lilt. Nevertheless this is a set that will give great satisfaction. The cassette transfer is of very high quality, though with marginally less brilliance in the upper frequencies than the equivalent LPs. It has the advantage of being complete on two sides of a single cassette.

Ansermet's Decca set has also been reissued in an excellent tape transfer on a single cassette. The performance is undoubtedly one of Ansermet's finest, and the Decca recording still sounds remarkably rich and vivid, with a freshness and sparkle to match the conductor's approach. Ansermet's feeling for orchestral colour and detail tells throughout, and the short dances of Act 2 have much piquancy of characterization.

Rozhdestvensky's recording has a very strong Russian colouring, nowhere more strikingly different from a Western approach than in the *Waltz of the Snow-flakes*, with the treble voices singing lustily. The timbres of woodwind and brass are strong-textured, the colouring bold with plenty of edge. The *March* is unexpectedly 'brassy', quite unlike the more piquant stylization one normally expects. The strings too have bite (and this is not just the nature of the recording balance), and there is never the slightest hint of sentimentalizing the music. The result is refreshingly spontaneous and full of character. Every point of the music tells, and if at times the extremely vivid sound lacks refinement, the sheer life of the playing disarms criticism. This too is an excellent single-tape issue; the quality has splendid edge and projection.

The alternative HMV set is affectionately and sumptuously played by Previn and the LSO. The playing is warm and pleasing in the opening scene, but immediately becomes more vivid and dramatic on side two when, after the end of the children's party, the magic begins to work. The *Transformation scene* is richly done, and the famous dances of Act 2 are played with much sophistication: indeed the orchestral playing throughout is of very high quality. This set can be recommended most warmly, even if the reading has not the individuality which both Dorati and Ansermet provide in their different ways. The cassette transfer is smooth, perhaps a little lacking in brilliance.

Bonynge's set is richly and brilliantly recorded. In its reissue format it is complete on a single cassette (like all the other tape versions except Previn's). Bonynge's approach is sympathetic and he secures fine playing from the National Philharmonic recording group. In the opening scene the music-making seems somewhat literal and lacking atmosphere, but with the beginning of the magic as the Christmas tree expands, the playing catches fire and the *Transformation scene* is finely done. Here one notices that on tape the climaxes do not expand expand as spectacularly as on disc, and in

the battle scene the sound sometimes lacks the last degree of crispness, an unusual fault for Decca. But in the latter part of the ballet Bonynge is at his best, with fine passion in the Act 2 *Pas de deux* and plenty of colour in the characteristic dances.

The Nutcracker, Op. 71: highlights.
　(M) **(*) Decca KCSP 357 (from above set cond. Ansermet).
　**(*) HMV TC-ASD 3051 (from above set cond. Previn).
　**(*) Decca KSXC 6821 (from above set cond. Bonynge).

These tapes reflect the qualities of the sets from which they come. Both Ansermet and Bonynge are rather more generous than Previn, and Ansermet's selection also has the advantage of being on Decca's cheapest label. The transfer is good but uneven; side two is outstandingly clear and vivid, side one rather less so. The sumptuous HMV recording has plenty of colour, but the textures are not always completely transparent and the choral focus in the *Waltz of the snow-flakes* is not absolutely clean. Elsewhere the refinement slips very slightly now and then, but generally the spectacular resonance is well managed. Bonynge's cassette represents high quality, technically speaking, and there is striking brilliance and detail. But, although the dynamic range is wide, the biggest climaxes do not seem to expand as dramatically as on the very finest Decca issues.

Nutcracker suite, Op. 71a.
　(M) *** Decca Jubilee KJBC 16 [Lon. 5-6420]. Vienna PO, Karajan – GRIEG: *Peer Gynt.****
　*** Decca Phase 4 KPFC 4352 [Lon. 5-21142]. Boston Pops Orch., Fiedler – GRIEG: *Peer Gynt.****

Anyone who wants the coupling with *Peer Gynt* should be well satisfied with

593

Karajan's tape. The readings are characteristically broad; the *Overture* is less miniature in effect than usual; the *Chinese dance* could be more piquant, and the Waltz could have a lighter touch, but these are mere carping criticisms. This is typical Karajan conducting, with its usual panache, and the fine orchestral playing is matched by vivid recording of Decca's best quality. The transfer is first-rate.

Fiedler's performance has marvellous spirit and vigour; the music is played with striking élan and colour. The vividly coloured recording helps to project the music-making, but the spontaneity and life of the playing itself are in no doubt. This is a demonstration of Phase Four at its very best. The cassette transfer is excellent.

(i) *Nutcracker suite, Op. 71a;* (ii) *Romeo and Juliet* (fantasy overture).
(M)**DG Privilege 3318 049. (i) Berlin PO, Leitner; (ii) Dresden (Saxon) State Orch., Sanderling.

Leitner's neat, pleasingly lightweight account of the *Nutcracker suite* is also available differently coupled (see under *Capriccio italien*). Here it is paired to Sanderling's *Romeo and Juliet*, a performance of genuine romantic flair and spontaneity. The recording is excellent in both works, and the tape transfer is vivid, though its brightness needs a little control (in the *Nutcracker* especially) if the upper strings are to retain their full body of sound.

(i) *Nutcracker suite, Op. 71a;* (ii) *Serenade for strings in C major, Op. 48.*
(M) *(*) Philips Festivo 7310 027. (i) LPO, (ii) LSO; both cond. Stokowski.

Both these recordings date from the mid-seventies, preceding Stokowski's Indian summer in the CBS recording studios just before he died. The *Nut-*

cracker suite, although it has its moments, is disfigured by a ridiculously fast tempo for the *March*, which is so swiftly paced that the flutes cannot properly articulate their semiquavers in the middle section. The *Dance of the Sugar Plum Fairy* has some added string tremolandos at the opening and is very mannered in its phrasing and *rubato*; there is a dramatic *fortissimo* towards the end of the *Waltz of the Flowers*. Altogether this does not have the magic of Stokowski's famous 78 r.p.m. set. The *Serenade* is straighter, bold and strong, with a passionate *Elegy*; but it is lacking in charm. The recording is excellent throughout, and the transfer, made at a high level for Philips, is admirably detailed and full-blooded.

Nutcracker suite, Op. 71a; The Sleeping Beauty, Op. 66: excerpts; *Swan Lake, Op. 20:* suite.
**(*) HMV TC-ASD 3584. LSO, Previn.

This HMV issue is generous in offering the complete *Nutcracker suite*, the usual concert suite from *Swan Lake* together with four items from *The Sleeping Beauty* (including the *Panorama*, which Previn floats magically). The performances show Previn's view of these works in the best light: the *Nutcracker suite* has glowing orchestral colours well caught in the warmly vivid sound. The 'plushy' effect characteristic of the other complete sets is not minimized here by the recording balance, which is rich and full rather than especially brilliant. But this tape makes very congenial listening. Original copies had minor pitch variations in the *Trepak* from *Nutcracker*, but current tapes are coming through without this fault.

Romeo and Juliet (fantasy overture).
***HMV TC-ASD 3488. Philharmonia Orch., Muti – *Symphony No. 2.*(**)
***DG 3300 284 [id.]. San Fran-

cisco SO, Ozawa – BERLIOZ: *Roméo et Juliette: Love scene;* PROKOFIEV: *Romeo and Juliet suite.****

(M)**(*)Decca KCSP 119. Vienna PO, Karajan–R. STRAUSS: *Don Juan.***(*)

(M) **(*) World Records TC-SH 287. Philharmonia Orch., Cantelli – WAGNER: *Siegfried idyll.***(*)

(M) **(*) HMV TC-EXE 182. LPO, Boult – SMETANA: *Vltava* etc.*(**)

(M) ** Decca Jubilee KJBC 21. Vienna PO, Maazel – *Symphony No. 2.**(*)

(M) *(*) Philips 7320 045. LSO, Dorati – BERLIOZ: *Roméo et Juliette: Love scene.**(*)

Muti's *Romeo and Juliet* is distinguished, one of the finest available, and full of imaginative touches. The opening has just the right degree of atmospheric restraint and immediately creates a sense of anticipation; the great romantic climax is noble in contour yet there is no lack of passion, while the main allegro is crisply and dramatically pointed. The repeated figure on the timpani at the coda is made to suggest a tolling bell and the expressive woodwind playing which follows gently underlines the feeling of tragedy. The full, rich recording suits the interpretation admirably, and the transfer has plenty of weight and generally good detail.

In the DG collection of musical evocations of *Romeo and Juliet* it was inevitable that the Tchaikovsky fantasy overture should be included. This is a thoroughly worthwhile anthology and Ozawa draws from the San Francisco orchestra warmly committed playing, very well recorded. The transfer is admirable, and this should not disappoint anyone who likes the idea of having three Romeos contrasted.

Karajan's *Romeo* is both dramatic and exciting. The tension relaxes in the quieter music, but if the reading is carefully drawn there is no lack of passion. The recording is splendid, except perhaps for a slight over-balance of percussion against the massed strings in the climaxes. The illusion of the concert hall is well conveyed. The cassette transfer is not one of Decca's best: although the climaxes are vivid (the bass drum and cymbals well accommodated), the quiet string passages tend to recede slightly and lose something in definition.

Guido Cantelli's recording, like his account of the *Siegfried idyll*, was made during the 1951 season, his first with the Philharmonia. There is no lack of concentration, yet nothing is overdriven. There is fine ensemble and marvellously articulated detail (a minor lapse of chording during the opening is hardly worth mentioning) and there is total commitment and a refreshing absence of any egocentricity. The sound quality is remarkably good; few allowances have to be made on this score. There have been distinguished performances of this work in the intervening years (from Karajan, Abbado, Sanderling and so on) but this version still belongs among their number. The cassette transfer is smooth and well balanced, but this is a work that needs stereo to make its fullest impact.

Boult's performance has a spacious romanticism that approaches nobility, but there are some curious tempi: the opening, after the first few bars, has a not quite convincing *accelerando*, and the closing chords of the work seem marginally to hang fire. These are small points in an otherwise rewarding performance, finely recorded. The cassette transfer is generally good, but in the Smetana coupling it is too highly modulated for comfort.

Maazel's *Romeo and Juliet* is characteristically brilliant, and this is emphasized by the tape transfer, which is clear but rather dry and unexpansive in quality, tending to exaggerate the surface excitement of the music-making.

A direct account from Dorati, not short on drama but lacking the full degree of romantic expansiveness. One needs a high volume setting for maximum impact, and that brings up the background. This is not really a very recommendable coupling.

Serenade for strings in C major, Op. 48.

*** Argo KZRC 848 [id.]. Academy of St Martin-in-the-Fields, Marriner – DVOŘÁK: *Serenade.****

*** Philips 7300 532 [id.]. ECO, Leppard – DVOŘÁK: *Serenade.****

(M) ** Decca KCSP 375. Israel PO, Solti - DVOŘÁK: *Serenade.***

(M) (***) HMV TC-SXLP 30239. LSO, Barbirolli – ARENSKY: *Variations.*(***)

(B) *(*) DG Heliodor 3348 121. Dresden State Orch., Suitner – DVOŘÁK: *Serenade.****

Both the Leppard and the Marriner performances use a less than full-sized string section, but Leppard is given some advantage in the richness and body of the Philips recording, slightly fuller than the Argo (recorded earlier). However, Marriner's performance compensates with expressive phrasing, and the relative opulence of the tone produced by the Academy group is balanced by the imagination and freshness of the performance. In each case the tape transfer is outstanding, matching the disc quality closely. Both issues are of excellent quality, and Leppard's more direct manner does not inhibit him in the *Waltz*, which is beautifully done.

Solti's is an early stereo recording but technically it is impressive. The brilliant sound balance tends to emphasize the glossiness of the playing of the Israel strings as well as their undoubted virtuosity. The performance is certainly gripping, yet Solti overplays the work; it wants more elegance and repose, and the *Waltz* has insufficient lustre. Solti brings considerable intensity to the *Elegy* and he catches the evocative atmosphere of the opening of the finale especially well. The tape reflects the disc quality, brightly lit, the string textures somewhat grainy.

Barbirolli uses the full LSO string section, recorded within a resonant acoustic, to give a rich, broad sonority. The recording dates from the mid-sixties and, if not quite as refined as the Philips sound for Leppard, is still remarkably good. The strength of the sweeping introductory theme establishes the ripeness of Barbirolli's approach, although later the *Allegro*'s secondary theme is nicely articulated. The *Waltz* is passionate rather than elegant, and the climax of the *Elegy* is characteristically full-blooded. The finale has vigour and bustle, and this version, with its unusual coupling, is very attractive. Unfortunately the tape transfer is overmodulated and is rather unrefined.

Suitner too has the advantage of a full orchestral string complement, and the strings of the Dresden State Orchestra have splendid warmth and bloom. However, the Heliodor transfer lacks clarity of focus and the resonant recording is not well caught, although the coupling is excellently managed.

Serenade for strings in C major, Op. 48; Nutcracker suite, Op. 71a.

**(*) DG 923046 [id.]. Berlin PO, Karajan.

Karajan takes the first movement of the *Serenade* very fast and the brilliance of the Berlin Philharmonic articulation is impressive. However, the music is robbed of some of its charm and the Mozartian element is minimized. The *Waltz* is richly done, and the slow movement is played expressively without underlining. The finale has splendid vigour. The recording is first-class and the transfer vivid and well detailed. The performance of the

Nutcracker suite is softer-grained than Karajan's Decca Jubilee version, helped by the recording balance, which although not lacking brilliance has a softer outline. The playing of the orchestra is again first-class, but some might feel that the homogeneity of timbre reduces the piquancy of the characteristic dances. Nevertheless this is an enjoyable coupling and the transfer is vivid and full, with plenty of detail.

Serenade for strings in C major, Op. 48; Souvenir de Florence (Sextet in D minor), Op. 70 (orchestral version).
*** Argo KZRC 584 [id.]. Academy of St Martin-in-the-Fields, Marriner.

Though Tchaikovsky asked for as big a body of strings as possible in his delectable *Serenade*, there is much to be said, in these days of increased string resonance and clever microphone placing, for having a modest band like the Academy of St Martin's. The insight of Marriner's performance, its glowing sense of joy combined with the finest pointing and precision of ensemble, put it in a class of its own. The unanimity of phrasing of the Academy's violins in the intense slow movement is breathtaking in its expressiveness, although here one does notice the lack of the sheer tonal weight that a bigger body of strings would afford. The coupling could hardly be more delightful, with the Academy tackling a work normally played by six solo strings and producing delectable results. The haunting second subject of the opening movement should certainly be sampled. The one snag is that to fit it on one LP record side, the work was subjected to some tactful cutting. Excellent, vividly atmospheric recording quality; the tape transfer was one of Argo's earliest cassette issues, but current copies show sophisticated quality. The sound is rich and clear in the *Serenade*, though there is a touch of shrillness which needs control in the *Souvenir de Florence*.

The Sleeping Beauty (ballet), *Op. 66*: complete.
**(*) Decca K 78 K 33 [Lon. 5-2316]. National PO, Bonynge.
(M) *(**) HMV TC-SLS 5001 [Angel 4x3s 3812]. LSO, Previn.

Of the three great Tchaikovsky ballets, *The Sleeping Beauty* is the most difficult to bring off away from the theatre. Bonynge secures brilliant and often elegent playing from the National Philharmonic Orchestra, and his rhythmic pointing is always characterful. As recorded the upper strings lack sumptuousness, and in this tape transfer the upper focus is sometimes rather feathery. Otherwise the wide-ranging recording has transferred with plenty of detail, although at times the bass line seems resonantly heavy (and the finale of Act 3 is made to seem rather stolid in consequence). There is much to give pleasure, however, and Bonynge is especially good at the close of Act 2 when, after the magical *Panorama*, the princess is awakened. There is a frisson of tension here, and the atmosphere is most evocative. In Act 3 Previn, helped by the richer HMV sound, finds more colour in the various characteristic dances, but generally the Decca sound has more sparkle, and the solo violinist (Mincho Minchev) and cellist (Francisco Gabarro) play their solos most appealingly.

Previn's set has somewhat plushy sound. It is rich and pleasing, but however one manipulates the controls it is difficult to achieve any sense of glitter or real brilliance. The orchestral playing is very polished, and Previn conveys his affection throughout, but too often there is a lack of vitality. In the *Entr'acte* (No. 18), with its violin solo by John Brown, the atmosphere is so cosy that the style hovers perilously near that of the salon. On the other hand the *Panorama* which comes immediately before shows Previn and his orchestra at their very best, the tune floating over its rocking bass in the most magical way. The cassette transfer has a comparatively restricted dynamic range but is otherwise acceptable.

The Sleeping Beauty, Op. 66: highlights.

> (M) **(*) Decca KCSP 358. Suisse Romande Orch., Ansermet.
>
> ** HMV TC-ASD 3370 (from above set cond. Previn).

Ansermet's selection faithfully reflects the character of the complete set from which it is taken (which has not yet been issued on tape). The excerpts from the Prologue and Act 1 are rather cool and literal, although there is no lack of dramatic effect. With the opening of side two and Act 2, the music is projected more vividly. The tape transfer – an early one – seems to have more range and sparkle on side one than side two, which is mellower; but the difference is not enough to mar enjoyment.

Previn's selection is well made and makes a very successful compilation. The tape transfer was originally too highly modulated, producing distortion in the final climax, but the level has now been reduced. The sound is sumptuous, but the reverberant acoustic minimizes the internal detail, and the upper range lacks edge and brilliance.

The Sleeping Beauty, Op. 66: suite; Swan Lake, Op. 20: suite.

> (M) **(*) Decca Jubilee KJBC 35. Vienna PO, Karajan.
>
> *(**) DG 3300 205 [id.]. Berlin PO, Karajan.
>
> (M)(***) HMV TC-EXE 183. Philharmonia Orch., Karajan (with MUSSORGSKY: *Khovantschina: Dance of the Persian slaves*(**)).
>
> (B)*Philips Fontana 7327 006. Vienna SO, Ančerl.

Karajan has recorded this coupling three times in stereo. The first was one of the outstanding issues in EMI's early stereo catalogue, with excitingly vivid playing and rich, atmospheric recording. Then it reappeared on HMV Concert Classics; originally the tape transfer was of good quality but accidentally missed off the Mussorgsky coupling. Now it has been remastered, but the level is marginally too high and the focus of the tuttis is rough. There are shrill strings in the *Sleeping Beauty suite*, and in the splendidly played Mussorgsky. *Dance* the gritty upper range is unacceptable.

The DG performances are the first choice on disc, with a superb contribution from the Berlin Philharmonic and plenty of charisma from Karajan, whose extrovert approach creates a high level of tension and electricity, and no lack of colour and warmth. Disappointingly DG have over-modulated the tape transfer and the spectacular climaxes are rough, with muddle from the bass drum in particular. At a slightly lower level this could have been an outstanding issue.

The Decca recording, now reissued on Jubilee, dates from 1965. The sound is brilliant, and the performances have panache and much of the extrovert excitement of the DG versions. The bright, vivid sound picture, not as ample as the DG, has transferred splendidly to tape, and this makes a clear first choice.

Ančerl's performances are routine ones and the recording is good rather than outstanding. The transfer lacks vividness and presence.

The Sleeping Beauty, Op. 66: suite; Swan Lake, Op. 20: suite; Eugene Onegin: Polonaise.

> (B) *(*) DG Heliodor 3348 125. Warsaw PO, Rowicki.

Rowicki is sometimes mannered and he chooses some curious tempi; the opening oboe theme of *Swan Lake*, for instance, is surprisingly slow. But this is mostly excellent playing with plenty of life in it, and the Polish woodwind soloists have strong individual personalities.

The recording is bright, with a tendency for the brass to blare a little, but at the price this is a reasonable coupling, in spite of dated string tone. The cassette transfer is fairly good: the quality is brilliant but also somewhat brash.

Suite No. 3 in G major, Op. 55.
    *** CBS 40-76733. Los Angeles PO, Tilson Thomas.
    *(**) HMV TC-ASD 3135. LPO, Boult.
    ** Decca KSXC 6857. Vienna PO, Maazel.

The performance of Tchaikovsky's *Third Suite* by Michael Tilson Thomas and the Los Angeles Philharmonic is in a class of its own; indeed it is one of the finest Tchaikovsky performances in the catalogue. So often the first three movements of this work are dwarfed by the finale, which undoubtedly contains the finest music, but here the conductor achieves a perfect balance. He opens and closes the first movement quite magically and takes its climax with just the right degree of romantic melodrama. The rhythmic character of the *Valse mélancolique* is deftly managed, and the crisp, gay scherzo is delightful, its middle section wittily and delicately pointed. At the opening of the fourth movement Tchaikovsky's great melody is splendidly shaped, and the variations unfold with gripping spontaneity, their sheer diversity a constant joy. The two variants featuring the cor anglais soloist and the concertante violin are beautifully played, and when the transformed melody swells out on the massed strings the effect is heartwarmingly eloquent. Tchaikovsky's closing *Polacca* is superbly prepared and Tilson Thomas ushers in the principal theme with a calculated *ritenuto* worthy of Sir Thomas Beecham. The trio has a swinging animation, and the piece closes with glorious vigour. The recording is vivid and well balanced, with fine detail. It lacks something in bloom and warmth in the middle area of the orches-

tra but does not want brilliance, and the transfer to tape is well judged, so that the final climax opens up splendidly.

Boult's warmly lyrical performance is much admired, and certainly the first three movements respond to such unforced eloquence, the scherzo daintily pointed. The *Variations* are also affectionately characterized, although there is some lack of drama and sheer gusto in the closing *Polacca*. However, the spectacularly ample recording has not been satisfactorily transferred; the sound is smooth but the climaxes fail to open up as they should.

The Decca recording for Maazel's version (not nearly so imaginative a performance) is infinitely more vivid; the reading is freshly conceived, and Maazel is supported by refined playing from the Vienna Philharmonic. The recording is beautifully clear and sparkling; woodwind detail has a pleasing individuality of colour. But the performance throughout is just that bit too literal, and any charm comes from the music itself rather than any melting quality in the music-making or any memorable shapeliness of phrasing. The transfer is first-class, with plenty of weight and brilliance and a strikingly clear internal focus achieved without any loss of bloom.

Swan Lake (ballet), *Op. 20*: complete.
    **(*) Decca K 37 K 33 [Lon. 5-2315]. National PO, Bonynge.
    *(**) HMV TC-SLS 5070 [Angel 4x3s 3834]. Ida Haendel (violin), LSO, Previn.

Bonynge's approach is essentially strong and vigorous, bringing out all the drama of the score if less of its charm. The forward impulse of the music-making is immediately striking, and Decca have matched the interpretation with a somewhat dry acoustic, producing leonine string tone and comparatively little feeling of sumptuousness. This is not to say that the richness of Tchaikovsky's scoring fails to tell, but the brightly lit sound picture provides robust detail in the place of glamour. The brass sounds too are open and vibrant, and the 'fairy castle' fanfares have here more of the atmosphere of a medieval tournament. The overall balance is well managed, although the violin solos sound rather larger than life. Perhaps they fail (like the performance as a whole) to distil all the romantic essence of this masterly score, but the commitment of the orchestral playing is never in doubt. There is consistent freshness here, and many of the spectacular moments are thrilling. The transfer to tape is eminently successful. The quality has rather more warmth, yet there is little if any loss of detail and inner refinement. The effect is to make the score sound richer, more romantic, and the wide dynamic range of the recording is captured without difficulty.

Previn's set, like his recordings of the other Tchaikovsky ballets, offers extremely polished orchestral playing, with beautiful wind solos, helped by a warm, resonant recording which gives plenty of bloom to the overall sound picture. Ida Haendel's contribution is first-class, and there is much refined detail and no lack of drama when the music calls for it. And yet something is missing. One hesitates to use the adjective 'cosy', but there is nevertheless a feeling here of over-sumptuousness, helped by the indulgent textures of the recording. Many may find this exactly to their taste, but there is an inherent vitality about the Bonynge set which is less apparent here. The HMV tape transfer is acceptable, but less refined in sound than the discs, and the solo violin tone is given something of an edge by the brightness of the overall sound balance.

Swan Lake, Op. 20: slightly abridged recording of the European score.
  (B) **(*) Decca KDPC 2 7058. Suisse Romande Orch., Ansermet.

Returning to Ansermet's 1959 recording of *Swan Lake* one is amazed by the vigour of the playing and the excellence of the recording. The Drigo version of the score which Ansermet uses dates from 1895. Drigo added orchestrations of his own, taken from Tchaikovsky's piano music (Op. 72), yet left out some sixteen hundred bars of the original score. Ansermet offers the Act 1 Introduction and Nos. 1–2, 4, 7 and 8; Act 2, Nos. 10–13; Act 3, Nos. 15, 17–18 and 20–23, with No. 5 (the *Pas de deux*) then interpolated before Nos. 28 and 29 from Act 4. In spite of the obvious gaps, most of the familar favourites are included here, and the music-making has such zest and colour that one cannot but revel in every bar. The solo wind-playing is not always as sweet-timbred as in some other versions, but the violin and cello solos are well done, and there is not a dull moment throughout this generously full double-length tape, which is in effect at bargain price. The transfer is very well managed, full-blooded and bright, although a little smoothing of the treble improves the timbre of the upper strings. Excellent value.

Swan Lake, Op. 20: highlights.
  *** HMV TC-ASD 3491 (from above set cond. Previn).
  (M) **(*) Philips 7317 103. LSO, Monteux.
  ** Decca Phase 4 KPFC 4375. Netherlands Radio Orch., Fistoulari.

Previn's selection is both generous and felicitous. It is superbly played and shows the very best qualities of the complete Previn set, with splendid solo wind playing and a rich-toned contribution from Ida Haendel. The recording is sumptuous and full-blooded, and considering its weight and amplitude the quality of the high-level transfer is admirable. The detail is good and the resonance well managed, the refinement of detail hardly slipping at all in the huge climaxes. The warmth and colour of the sound are highly congenial. Indeed this is more successfully balanced than the complete set from which it comes.

The Monteux cassette is one of Philips's very best medium-priced issues. The recording (on disc as well as tape) lacks the last degree of brilliance, but it is splendidly balanced and in the finale, which Monteux takes broadly and grandly, the richness and weight of the sound make a superb effect. Monteux's approach generally is affectionate rather than seeking a high level of tension. The LSO playing is beautifully turned. Excellent value.

Fistoulari's cassette is valuable in offering a generous selection from what is in many ways the finest complete recorded performance of *Swan Lake* and is not available on tape. Its drawback is the Phase Four recording, with a comparatively dry acoustic and unnatural balance. The tape transfer is very lively but not so smooth or refined as the equivalent LP, and the brilliance is slightly aggressive at times.

Symphonies Nos. 1–6.
    **(*) Decca κ 95 κ 63 [Lon. csp 5-10]. Los Angeles PO, Mehta.
Symphonies Nos. 1–6; Manfred symphony, Op. 58.
    **(*) HMV tc-sls 5099. LPO, Rostropovich.

Rostropovich recorded his Tchaikovsky cycle concurrently with live performances at the Royal Festival Hall, and though at certain points (as in some of the *fugato* development sections) the ensemble could be a shade crisper, the performances have not only passion and electricity but great charm and refinement too. The first three symphonies are superbly done in every way – Rostropovich manages to choose his tempi most persuasively, and his rhythmic pointing is consistently delectable – outshining here almost any opposition. Symphonies Nos.

4 to 6 are all characterized by relatively slow but well-pointed accounts of the first movements, and only in No. 5 is there a suspicion of the argument dragging. Otherwise these are sensitive, deeply felt readings which should be easy to live with. *Manfred* too is most persuasively done, with a scherzo of Berliozian refinement, though the recording in that work is not quite so rich and atmospheric as in the rest of the cycle. The *pianissimo* string tone is particularly beautiful. The transfer to tape offers acceptable rather than notable quality. The overall sound is less refined and transparent than in the outstanding equivalent LPs. One notices that the muted string tone lacks delicacy of texture and the middle strings are husky, making the *First Symphony* sound more robust in atmosphere, while the finale of the *Second* has poor transients and therefore the cymbals lack crispness. There is some coarseness of texture at the opening of *Manfred*, but on the whole the last three symphonies are reasonably well managed, although none of these cassettes offers the demonstration quality of the discs.

Mehta's set, superbly recorded by Decca in Los Angeles, has much to commend it. The performances are consistently strong and brilliant, and if the readings lack the distinctive individuality of the Rostropovich album (which also includes *Manfred*) this is not entirely a disadvantage for repeated listening. The directness of the music-making and its undoubted freshness, with orchestral playing vividly committed throughout, create a spontaneity that retains its hold on the listener. In the first three symphonies there is not the degree of charm that Rostropovich distils, but the music springs infectiously to life and the fine solo wind-playing never lacks character. The *Andante marziale* of No. 2, paced faster than usual, but deftly shaped, is a highlight; and the diversity of melodic style which distinguishes No. 3 gives much pleasure here. For the last three symphonies Mehta consciously changes his approach, with greater flexibility of tempo and much more use of *stringendo* (especially in the first movement of the *Fourth*). The *Fifth* is given a vibrant reading throughout, with the *Waltz* treated as an interlude and an incisively rhythmic presentation of the big tune in the coda of the finale. The first movement of the *Pathétique* has similar urgency and excitement – the development section is given a tremendous climax – and although some might find the 5/4 movement too fast and intense, the performance as a whole is highly eloquent. The recording is richly full-blooded and has the widest possible dynamic range; but the cassette transfer (although otherwise of first-class quality) is much less expansive and the louder fortissimos offer less weight than on the discs, making the contrasts less dramatic.

Symphony No. 1 in G minor (Winter Day-dreams), Op. 13.
(M) *** Philips Festivo 7310 160. LSO, Markevitch.
(M) **(*) Decca Jubilee KJBC 20. Vienna PO, Maazel – Hamlet.**
(***) HMV TC-ASD 3213. New Philharmonia Orch., Muti.

Tchaikovsky's marking *Allegro tranquillo* for the first movement presents problems of interpretation for any conductor. If the metronome marking is observed faithfully the result sounds rather tense and breathless, until sixty or so bars later the music comes to need that urgency. Markevitch choses a fast pace for the opening, yet skilfully retains the delicate Mendelssohnian atmosphere. The playing creates plenty of excitement but never loses the music's scale or charm. The opening of the slow movement is superbly evocative; the delightful scherzo has sylvan lightness, and the waltz at its centre is deftly pointed. The finale is no less successful, with an eloquent opening and a rousing close, before

which Markevitch creates a haunting sense of desolation at the reprise of the *Andante lugubre*. In all, this is a splendid version, as fine as any available. The recording (from the mid-sixties) has been freshly remastered and sounds full and clear. There is no appreciable difference in quality between cassette and disc, and at medium price this makes a clear first choice.

Muti, like Markevitch, has a fast tempo from the start, and needs no speed-change. It is the only questionable point of tension in a beautiful reading, which is helped by glowing recording quality and warmly sympathetic playing. There is no mistaking the way the performance takes wing, with a glorious climax to the horn melody in the slow movement, a light and lilting scherzo, and an urgent finale, with less feeling of *maestoso* than in Maazel's reading. Unfortunately, although the tape transfer is of good basic quality, the dynamic range has been severely cut back, and until this tape is remastered it is not acceptable.

On Decca the sound on cassette is in some ways more attractive than on the LP. There seems to be a slight reduction of dynamic range on these Maazel transfers, but the contrast remains wide and the effect seems more to increase the overall vividness than to give the impression of any lack of dynamic variety. The performance itself is much less mellow than Muti's. The opening movement is driven hard and the Mendelssohnian quality is played down, but there is also evidence of the care with which the conductor has studied the score. Much felicitous detail emerges afresh, and the scherzo comes to life splendidly, showing a real feeling for the line of the waltz. The finale too is very successful; even Tchaikovsky's somewhat academic *fugato* section comes off, with short stabbing emphases of each entry of the theme. The slow movement is not as dreamy as one might ideally ask, but the style of the playing, with strong, thrusting horn-playing for the final statement of the main tune, is convincing enough in the context of the other movements. This climax seems particularly effective on tape, the sound remarkably open and free.

Symphony No. 2 in C minor (Little Russian), Op. 17.
> (M) *** Philips Festivo 7310 161. LSO, Markevitch.
> *(**) HMV TC-ASD 3488. Philharmonia Orch., Muti – *Romeo and Juliet*.***
> (M) *(*) Decca Jubilee KJBC 21. Vienna PO, Maazel – *Romeo and Juliet*.**

Markevitch's Festivo reissue makes a clear first choice. The recording dates from 1967 but is well balanced, with plenty of body and detail. The performance is direct yet imaginative. After the finely played opening horn solo – which catches the folk quality of the melody admirably – some might feel that Markevitch's clean-cut rhythmic vigour is a little square. But the impetus of the first movement is strongly maintained, and the *Andantino marziale* is played with appealing delicacy. The scherzo is vivacious; the closing variations unfold with an attractive simplicity, and the secondary theme is nicely elegant. This is very much a performance to live with, especially when the sound is so natural. Apart from a moment of minor disturbance on the very opening chord, the cassette sound matches the disc almost exactly; it is in no way inferior.

Muti's account is characteristically fresh and imaginative. His warmth brings an agreeable geniality to the first movement, which does not lack excitement but is not too aggressively pointed. His *Andantino* takes Tchaikovsky's *marziale* rather literally, but its precise rhythmic beat has character without heaviness. Perhaps here, as in the finale, there is less than the full degree of charm, but the scherzo is vivacious and clean. In the finale Muti's degree of relaxed affection

produces much colour and the movement has strong character, even if the performance lacks a strong forward thrust of excitement. The recording is rich and full and generally well transferred until the finale, when the bass drum gives problems and the textures are muddied.

Maazel's hard-driving *brio* does not always suit this work. The reverberant recording apparent on the LP has obviously offered transfer problems, and the middle and lower frequencies seem to have been 'dried out' to some extent. The resulting sound balance is clear and brilliant but lacks warmth.

Symphony No. 3 in D major (Polish), Op. 29.
> (M) *** Philips Festivo 7310 162. LSO, Markevitch.
> (M) **(*) Decca Jubilee KJBC 22. Vienna PO, Maazel.
> **(*) HMV TC-ASD 3449. Philharmonia Orch., Muti.

Markevitch continues his highly successful series with a very enjoyable account of the *Polish symphony*. The Philips recording tends to emphasize the orchestra's middle frequencies and is slightly lacking in upper range (this is most noticeable in the scherzo). In that respect the cassette is marginally brighter than the disc, although otherwise the balance is virtually identical. The rhythmic vigour of the opening movement is striking, but the strong accents emphasize the weight of the allegro's main theme rather than its incandescence, and Tchaikovsky's somewhat academic development section is left to sound rather homespun. Markevitch chooses slow tempi for both the *Alla tedesca* and the *Andante*, and his warmth is readily conveyed. The scherzo is deftly lightweight and the finale strongly full-blooded, although the recording is a little thick in the final peroration. The whole performance has admirable consistency, and especially in such a good transfer it makes a clear first choice, with its wide dynamic contrasts and freedom from congestion.

With the alternative versions by Maazel and Muti, the order of preference would undoubtedly be reversed on disc. But on tape the infinitely more sophisticated Decca engineering means that of these two issues it is the Maazel Jubilee cassette that makes much the more vivid listening. A direct comparison with the equivalent LP reveals that Decca have slightly narrowed the dynamic range on the tape, but the main effect of this is to bring up the level of the pianissimos somewhat, while the climaxes are still able to expand impressively. The colour and detail of the sound are matched by its clarity and warmth, which suit Maazel's straightforward freshness of approach and provide the outer movements with plenty of thrust. In the central movements Maazel is undoubtedly sympathetic and he uncovers plenty of orchestral detail to delight the ear, but the woodwind playing (particularly that of the oboe) is more warmly sensitive in Muti's HMV version. Indeed in these three movements the Philharmonia playing is full of charm, bringing out the ballet associations of which Tchaikovsky was not in the least ashamed. Although Muti's performance has not the strong forward impulse of Maazel's in the outer movements, and he is not entirely successful in bringing off the rather grandiose peroration at the end of the finale (here Maazel's directness pays off admirably), his sensitivity and imagination uncover the full colour of the second and fourth movements and the lyrical expressiveness of the third. The opening movement too is not without vigour, and the wide dynamic range of the HMV recording permits an impressively weighty climax. On tape, however, the sound here is somewhat harsh (although elsewhere the climaxes expand quite well), and the recording, although warm and glowing, lacks the refined detail and transient crispness of the Decca cassette.

Symphony No. 4 in F minor, Op. 36.
- *** DG 3300 883 [id.]. Berlin PO, Karajan.
- *** DG 3300 651. Berlin PO, Abbado.
- (M) *** Decca Jubilee KJBC 23. Vienna PO, Maazel.
- (M) *** Philips Festivo 7310 153. LSO, Markevitch.
- (M) **(*) Decca KCSP 206. LSO, Szell.
- **(*) HMV TC-ASD 3647. LPO, Rostropovich.
- **(*) DG 3301 078. LSO, Boehm.
- ** Advent E 1020 (see p. xxiii) [id.]. LSO, Kosler.
- (B) * RCA Camden C4-5036. Boston SO, Munch.

(i) *Symphony No. 4;* (ii) *Marche slave, Op. 31.*
- (B) *(*) DG Heliodor 3348 176. Berlin PO, cond. (i) Maazel, (ii) Leitner.

Karajan's new performance of Tchaikovsky's *Fourth* is outstandingly fine. Its directness, coupled with remarkably fine orchestral playing and richly resonant recording, will make it first choice for many. Nevertheless Abbado's performance remains even more memorable. From the riveting opening fanfare, the drama and weight of the reading are apparent. The beginning of the *Allegro*, with its very Russian melancholy, brings an elegiac quality of string tone, yet this swiftly erupts into a spontaneously passionate *forte*. The second subject is beautifully prepared and delicately phrased, the counter-melody graceful in the strings. Then comes a superbly graduated climax from the fragile *pianissimo* of magically rocking strings to the strong culmination where the horns blaze out with their big tune, a 4. The second movement is as near perfection as one could hope for, with its gentle oboe solo, and the contrasting vigour of the dotted secondary section in the strings, which takes flight gloriously. At the end of the movement the reprise of the main theme is deliciously decorated. The scherzo is witty, the trio superbly articulated by wind and brass alike, and the finale too has sparkle as well as power. Other performances (Karajan's, for instance) have more weight, but not more of the spirit of the Russian peasant dance which was the source of Tchaikovsky's inspiration. The recording offers brilliant, extremely vivid sound. The copies now appearing in the shops, however, are slightly variable, and while the sound remains very good the comparatively low transfer level means that a high playback level is necessary for maximum impact, as the dynamic range is very wide.

Karajan's newest DG recording is a far more compelling performance than his previous versions (for DG and EMI). At the opening of the first movement, after the dramatic fanfare (even more robust than Abbado's), the theme of the *Allegro* steals in silkily on the strings and although its atmosphere has a tinge of melancholy, there is a hint of suaveness of tone also. But one's doubts are swept aside by the vitality and drive of the performance as a whole, and the beauty of the wind-playing at the opening and close of the slow movement can give nothing but pleasure. The dotted secondary theme on the strings, however, is played with its rhythm less incisively articulated than with Abbado; and because of the resonance of the recording the pizzicato strings of the scherzo have less presence and point, and the woodwind detail in the trio is more bland in effect. The finale has tremendous force and momentum and sweeps the listener along. The dynamic range of the sound is very wide indeed, which brings a familiar DG/Karajan recording characteristic, the recession of the orchestral image in pianissimos. Yet as the tuttis blaze into life the orchestra is given the most exciting presence. The fullness and weight of the sound are very impressive, and undoubtedly the orches-

tra is given more richness and substance here than in some more recent copies of the Abbado cassette; and there is very little slipping of refinement at climaxes.

The strength of Maazel's Decca recording is its basic simplicity and lack of personal mannerism. The dramatic and emotional power of the writing emerges in consequence with great effect; in the first movement the appearance of the relatively gentle second subject is not over-romanticized, and the contrast Tchaikovsky intended is underlined by this lack of emphasis. The slow movement is played most beautifully, and the scherzo is not too fast. The finale explodes just as it should. The tape transfer is admirably full-blooded; the central movements have fine bloom and vivid detail. However, compared to the Karajan and Abbado tapes the outer movements have a much less dramatic dynamic range. Of course this means that in the *piano* passages the orchestra is given more presence than on either of the DG tapes; but compared to the Decca LP, the biggest climaxes have marginally less amplitude and force.

Markevitch's version is as exciting as any available. It has a superbly thrusting first movement *Allegro*, and although Markevitch allows himself a lilting degree of *rubato* in the rocking crescendo passage it is the forward momentum of the performance that captures the listener. At the climax of the development Markevitch produces an exhilarating *stringendo* and then relaxes for the reprise of the second subject. The close of the movement, like the coda of the finale, brings the highest degree of tension and a real sense of triumph. The central movements are no less striking, with a vigorous dotted climax to the *Andantino* contrasting with the repose of the outer sections, and a fast scherzo where the duple rhythms of the woodwind trio are emphasized to bring out the peasant imagery. The recording is admirably full-blooded, and its spectacle and wide range have transferred to tape without any loss of impact and detail compared with the disc.

Szell's recording dates from a short but particularly successful period with Decca, when he also recorded Handel's *Fireworks* and *Water music suites*. Like that recording, this version of Tchaikovsky's *Fourth* is highly recommendable. The interpretation is satisfyingly direct; the first movement takes a little while to generate full tension, but the characterization of the central movements is strong, and the finale is superbly exciting. The Decca transfer was an early one but outstanding for its date, with plenty of brilliance and crisp detail (particularly in the scherzo) and yet no lack of weight in the finale. Some care with the controls is necessary to get the best balance but in Decca's lowest price-range this tape is undoubtedly recommendable, with one important reservation: the turnover break comes in the middle of the slow movement. It is quite well placed, but this kind of thoughtless production decision to save a few inches of tape is quite exasperating. To Decca's credit it is something that never happens now, and perhaps one day this issue will be remastered.

Rostropovich's reading of the outer movements is broadly spacious, and this gives the first movement a certain epic quality, particularly as the climaxes achieve the highest level of tension. Indeed the electricity of this performance is never in doubt. The slow movement is eloquent, with beautiful orchestral playing; the reprise of the main theme on the strings, deliciously decorated by the woodwind, is memorable. The scherzo is fast, with the balalaika effect well conveyed and a strongly characterized central section. The rich, full-blooded recording has created some problems in the high-level transfer: sometimes the refinement slips a little and there are moments of slight roughness in the finale.

Boehm's reading is intensely individual, and the frequent changes of tempo in the first movement are mercur-

ial to the point of eccentricity. Even on a second and third hearing the ear is taken by surprise by the conductor's unashamed impulsiveness. Yet underlying the waywardness is an undoubted feeling for the symphony's structural whole, and in the *Andantino* there is an inherent classicism. The basic tempo is measured, the oboe solo beautifully poised, and after a strong central climax the reprise is gently elegiac. The scherzo and finale maintain this controlled mood until the coda, which swiftly gathers momentum and ends the work in a blaze of virtuosity. Overall this is a distinctive, unconventional interpretation, undoubtedly imaginative, though not an obvious first choice as the only version of the symphony in a small collection. The wide-ranging recording is admirably clear and full-blooded and the tape transfer is first-class, well detailed and with truthful perspectives and plenty of brilliance and body.

Kosler's account on Advent is broadly conceived, and its spaciousness is supported by a first-class recording. However, there is at times a feeling of a lack of impetus, notably in the development section of the first movement, although the reading is not without its sense of power. The slow movement is sympathetically played but not distinctive, and in the third movement the section for the woodwind is rather square. The finale is very exciting, helped by the amplitude and brilliance of the tape transfer, which is one of Advent's best and demonstrates the wider frequency range possible with chrome tape. The symphony is complete on one side; the second is left blank for home recording.

Maazel's earlier Berlin Philharmonic recording was made in a very resonant acoustic, which tends to submerge detail to some extent. The performance is not dull but not very individual either, though with an exciting finale it might be considered at bargain price, particularly with Leitner's excellent version of *Marche slave* as a bonus. This is very successfully transferred, whereas in the symphony the orchestra seems too recessed.

The other bargain version, by Munch on Camden, suffers from an inefficient Dolby transfer, so that if one uses the Dolby circuitry for playback the treble loses its bite, although otherwise the sound is well balanced. The performance has considerable character, with a slow build-up of tension to an impressive climax in the first movement. The orchestral playing in the central movements is freshly characterized (the scherzo really vivacious), but the finale lacks the uninhibited excitement of the finest versions.

Symphonies Nos. (i) *5 in E minor, Op. 64;* (ii) *6 in B minor (Pathétique), Op. 74.*
> (M) **(*) World Records TC2-SHB 52. (i) Orch. of La Scala, Milan; (ii) Philharmonia Orch.; both cond. Cantelli.

With the exception of a couple of rather sudden tempo changes in the two outer movements, Cantelli's version of the *Fifth* is remarkably straight and unaffected. Its feeling is keen yet well controlled, so that the overall impression is of freshness and vigour. There is a splendid sense of line, rhythmic discipline and fine proportions. The Orchestra of La Scala responds with playing of classical finesse and aristocratic poise. Some allowance has to be made for the recording, which comes from the early 1950s, as there is a degree of shallowness in the tuttis. However, the transfer is well managed and with careful setting of the controls a very acceptable balance can be achieved. The quality in the *Pathétique* is first-class in every way and the transfer admirably vivid, so that – in spite of the absence of stereo – the ear adjusts immediately. The performance is memorable: there is no hint of overstatement or self-indulgence, yet the music is deeply felt and the reading has true nobility. The third movement is superb, the balance

between scherzo and march marvellously calculated, and here the crisp, clean sound balance is admirable.

Symphony No. 5 in E minor, Op. 64.
> *** Decca KSXC 6884. Philharmonia Orch., Ashkenazy.
> **(*) HMV TC-ASD 3641. LPO, Rostropovich.
> (M) ** Decca Jubilee KJBC 24. Vienna PO, Maazel.
> (M) ** RCA Gold Seal GK 25007. New Philharmonia Orch., Horenstein.
> ** DG 3300 888 [id.]. Boston SO, Ozawa.
> ** Decca KSXC 6754 [Lon. 5-6983]. Chicago SO, Solti.
> (M) *(*) Philips Festivo 7310 110. LSO, Markevitch.

Symphony No. 5; Marche slave, Op. 31.
> *** DG 3300 699 [id.]. Berlin PO, Karajan.
> *(**) Philips 7300 365 [id.]. Concertgebouw Orch., Haitink.
> (M) *(*) Philips 7321 003. LSO or Minneapolis SO, Dorati.

Karajan's and Haitink's recordings arrived within six months of each other, and on disc they posed a problem of choice. But on tape this is more easily resolved, for Karajan's DG transfer is of outstanding quality, the range and clarity of the recording in every way the equal of the disc, whereas the low-level transfer favoured by Philips reduces the impact and detail of a recording which on LP is of demonstration standard. Karajan's account is undoubtedly the more physically exciting, the climax of the slow movement grippingly intense, but Haitink's approach has more warmth and humanity. His refinement of detail is readily shown in the gently sensitive way the Concertgebouw strings phrase their secondary theme in the first movement, and in the elegiac quality of the opening bars of the *Andante*, preparing for the noble horn solo which follows. Karajan's reading is altogether more romantic here, taking Tchaikovsky at his word: *con alcuna licenza*. Some will undoubtedly feel that Haitink does not take enough licence, but with such naturally expressive playing the ear is easily convinced. Haitink's *Waltz* is presented rather precisely, at a moderate tempo; Karajan finds more character here. In the finale Karajan drives much harder, creating an electrifying forward thrust, whereas with Haitink one has more of a sense of the space and architecture of the movement. One can readily yield to the greater tension Karajan generates, but one can luxuriate with equal pleasure in the breadth and richness of the Concertgebouw playing. Certainly on DG the sound is sometimes too dry (the massed violins at the climax of the slow movement, for instance, which lack body), although the German recording has great projection and impact. The cassette is virtually indistinguishable from the disc, and as a bonus (not on the LP) adds Karajan's fine performance of *Marche slave*. Philips have the same coupling on their tape issue but it cannot compete with the DG issue in sonic terms.

Discounting the performance of the *Classical symphony* included in Ashkenazy's album of the Prokofiev *Piano concertos*, this recording of Tchaikovsky's *Fifth* is his recording debut on the rostrum in a major symphonic work. The result is something of a revelation: a performance of the *Fifth* as distinguished as any available, and one which (and this is surely a mark of greatness) throws new light on a familiar masterpiece. The quality of lyrical fervour and warmth that Ashkenazy brings to his reading is not achieved at the expense of excitement. Indeed his finale is as compelling as any available, yet it is full of affectionate detail. Tempi are admirably chosen throughout, and the forward flow of the music in all four movements is as natural as it is spontaneous. The second subject

of the first movement is allowed to blossom with a most appealing romanticism; the slow movement is very beautiful, the sense of repose in the opening and closing sections making an admirable framework for the passionate central climaxes. The *Waltz*, light and lilting, acts like an intermezzo between the second movement and the red-blooded finale with its gloriously rich string and brass tone. The recording is one of Decca's very best, rich and warm and with splendid detail and bloom; and on tape the sound is no less beautiful. But the sophistication of the transfer has been achieved by a very subtle reduction of the dynamic range, which means that the loudest climaxes do not expand quite so spectacularly as on the disc. The difference is marginal but it is apparent because of the closer than usual balance of the basic recording (so that on disc as well as tape the opening clarinet solo is not as hushed as in other versions). Readers must decide for themselves whether this tiny compromise (for the dynamic contrast which remains is still very impressive) is acceptable to achieve such splendour of sound.

Slow tempi predominate in Rostropovich's reading, and some may find his pacing too deliberate in the outer movements. Yet the playing is fully characterized, as the opening clarinet's *chalumeau* readily demonstrates, and even in the very broad statement of the finale's principal tune the eloquence of the music-making is in no doubt. The slow movement creates the highest degree of tension at its hushed opening; later the entries of the motto theme are suitably portentous, but lack the sheer drama of some other versions. The full-blooded richness of the recording and the fine playing of the LPO consistently sustain the conductor's approach, but on cassette the quality is less warm and refined than on disc (although a treble cut helps to smooth out the balance) and the total effect not so sumptous and compelling.

Maazel's Decca recording is excellent, but his is rather a cool reading. In the

Andante he brings in the motto theme pungently enough, but the movement as a whole has no broad emotional sweep, although the horn solo is beautifully phrased. The finale too begins and closes without a great deal of conviction, although the string-playing at the opening of the *Allegro vivace* is taut. The recording is full and vivid (the first movement especially so). The upper strings are a little lacking in bloom, but this tape can be made to give impressive results.

The RCA transfer of Horenstein's recording is acceptable but does not approach the Decca recording in fullness. Horenstein's reading has distinction, and if it lacks the compelling tension of the very finest versions, it remains enjoyable, with well-chosen tempi and lively, sensitive playing throughout. The only real idiosyncrasy is Horenstein's *ritenuto* in the coda of the first movement, which returns to the sombre mood of the opening rather than leading the listener expectantly on to the second movement.

Ozawa has the advantage of excellent DG sound. The transfer level is high, and the richness of the recording is matched by the freshness of the string sound. In the finale the brass is superb: this is undoubtedly the finest movement. The music-making springs vividly to life and the listener is swept along by the impact and projection of the orchestra. But the first three movements are disappointing, and until the finale the performance is a routine one.

Solti first recorded the *Fifth* in stereo in the mid-fifties with the Paris Conservatoire Orchestra (and that version is still available on disc: Decca SPA 223). In Paris Solti did not secure the most polished orchestral playing but in some ways that earlier record was more naturally exciting and spontaneous than his newer Chicago version, where the tension seems forced and the pulse too rigid. Of course there is some brilliant orchestral playing on this issue, and Tchaikovsky's score cannot fail to tell when the impact of the music-making is so strong. But the

brightly lit sound adds to the impression of inflexibility and brings also a hint of fierceness, on disc as on the tape, which lacks the last degree of refinement.

After a somewhat unevocative opening Markevitch applies to the first movement of the *Fifth* the forthright, highly charged approach which was so effective in the *Fourth*. He makes no concessions to the second subject group, which is presented with no let-up on the fast pace at which he takes the main allegro; Tchaikovsky's romanticism evaporates, as does the intended contrast. The slow movement is undoubtedly powerful, but the *Waltz* has no charm and the finale lacks warmth: the final statement of the big tune is slow and rather stolid. A disappointing issue after the success of Markevitch's versions of the first four symphonies. The sound is full and there is little difference between tape and disc.

Dorati's reading steers a midway course. The first movement, after a finely atmospheric opening, has a strong momentum; its changes of mood are perhaps a little under-characterized, but the overall shaping is impressive. The slow movement – beautifully played, and with a fine horn solo – is not as intense or flexible as in some performances, but the passion erupts at both climaxes. The *Waltz* is elegantly done, but the finale, with the main *Allegro* taken at a steady pace, makes only a moderate impact until the brass interjections arrive to add weight. The tape transfer is of only moderate quality. The level is low, and the upper strings are rather fizzy. Unless one uses a high volume setting the impact is poor. The bass is not very clean in the *Marche slave*.

Symphony No. 6 in B minor (Pathétique), Op. 74.
*** DG 3300 774 [id.]. Berlin PO, Karajan.
(*) DG 923122 [id.]. Berlin PO, Karajan (with BRAHMS: *Hungarian dances Nos. 1, 18–20*).

*** HMV TC-ASD 3515. LPO, Rostropovich.

(M)**(*)HMV TC-EXE 191. Philharmonia Orch., Giulini.

(M) **(*) Philips Festivo 7310 047. LSO, Markevitch.

**(*)Philips 7300 063 [id.]. Concertgebouw Orch., Haitink.

(M) ** Decca Jubilee KJBC 25. Vienna PO, Maazel.

** DG 3300 405 [id.]. Vienna PO, Abbado.

** Decca KDPC 2 7054. Vienna PO, Martinon – DVOŘÁK: Symphony No. 9.**(*)

*(*) Decca KSXC 6814 [Lon. 5-7034]. Chicago SO, Solti.

*(*)RCA RK 11744. LSO, Tjeknavorian.

(M) *(*) Philips 7321 024. LSO, Dorati (with Nutcracker: Waltz of the snowflakes*(*))

Within the last decade and a half Karajan has recorded the Pathétique three times, twice for DG and once for EMI (the least successful version: TC–ASD 2816). The interpretations are all very similar, and in many ways the newest issue (3300 774) is marginally the finest of the three. But, as in Karajan's latest recording of the Fifth, the sound is rather dry, and some may prefer the acoustic of the earlier version, dating from 1964. However, the early tape transfer (923122) is somewhat lacking in life and sparkle on side one, though on side two, with an increase of level, the quality is admirably brilliant and vivid. This issue offers a bonus of four Brahms Hungarian dances, and here the sound has almost too much brightness. The newer issue has a strikingly wide dynamic range, giving the climax of the first movement tremendous impact and the coda a contrasting sombre dignity. The famous secondary theme is perhaps more consciously moulded in this performance and is made to sound comparatively reticent by the lack of glow on the recorded strings; and again in the 5/4 movement the orchestra's expressive phrasing is not warmed by any noticeable acoustic bloom. The scherzo/march is brilliantly played, and if one senses that with a riper recording the lower brass could have added more resonance and weight, the movement's climax is given great edge and attack. In the finale the Berlin Philharmonic play with eloquence born of restraint, and the nobility of the performance is beyond question. The tape transfer of this issue is highly sophisticated, and on an A/B comparison one is often hard put to tell which is the disc and which the cassette.

Of the Rostropovich readings of the three last Tchaikovsky symphonies the Pathétique can be recommended virtually without reservation. Like the others it is a personal view, but its eloquence is direct and its specially Russian lyric fervour is highly compelling. The outer movements have strength and nobility and the finale balances passionate melancholy with restraint. The scherzo/march is perhaps less exhilarating than in some other versions, but it readily takes its place within the overall conception. The recording is splendidly full-blooded and the tape transfer is first-class, with plenty of body and detail.

Giulini's is a very direct reading; the opening is clear-cut and precise, and the whole exposition is laid before the listener in a rather matter-of-fact way. Yet there is an underlying strength, and Giulini attacks the development furiously, with matching tautness from the Philharmonia. The rest of the score unfolds in the same way, the conductor letting the music speak for itself. The finale is made the emotional peak of the work, as it undoubtedly is; but as a whole this reading, although splendidly played, is rather circumspect. The recording is clear and vivid, and the cassette transfer is first-class, having slightly more warmth and bloom than the disc, and no suggestion of restriction in the treble.

Markevitch brings great intensity to his account of the first movement. He takes the allegro at a fast pace and drives hard throughout, producing a *stringendo* that further tautens the climax at the reprise of the second subject. The effect is undoubtedly powerful, but with a touch of harshness to the recording some might feel that Markevitch is too aggressive, even though the performance is always under emotional control. The second movement has both warmth and elegance, and the march is treated broadly, providing suitable contrast before a deeply felt performance of the finale, where the second subject is introduced with great tenderness. The close of the symphony has an elegiac quality to complete a reading which has a wide emotional range and is gripping from first to last. The full, resonant recording is well transferred.

Haitink's performance has less obvious excitement than Karajan's, and it is less brilliantly recorded, but it is not less satisfying. Indeed it could be said that the comparative sobriety of Haitink's approach is ideal for this work, especially for repeated listening as a recording. The great second theme of the first movement is shaped with moving restraint: no other performance offers quite this quality of gentle dignity, and after the fiery development section, the slow, stately coda makes a fitting culmination. Equally in the second movement the pathos of the throbbing middle section is perfectly judged. Haitink's third movement has a true *scherzando* lightness, and the broadening for the final statement of the march is expertly managed. However, the cassette is a fairly early Philips transfer and lacks something in range and refinement. The sound is vivid enough but is apt to harshen somewhat at the loudest moments.

Maazel's is a good straightforward account, most impressive in the first and third movements, with a somewhat deadpan account of the second and a restrained finale, lacking in emotional depth. But this clean, unmannered playing offers its own rewards, and the recording is brilliant, with plenty of resonance, as in the rest of Maazel's series. The transfer is of outstanding quality, beautifully rich and detailed. However, this has been achieved by slightly reducing the dynamic range of the recording. Thus Tchaikovsky's *pianissimo* at the opening of the first movement is not fully achieved, and the big climax of the third movement does not expand as excitingly as it might.

Abbado's account, like his performance of the *Fifth*, is relatively lightweight. He provides a strong impulse throughout, and the second subject of the first movement sounds remarkably fresh, with radiant sounds from the strings. The climax, however, is slightly underpowered, and the finale too is restrained. The third movement is essentially a scherzo, the march-rhythms never becoming weighty and pontifical. This has many attractions for those who prefer a reading that is not too intense, and the slightly dry recording matches Abbado's conception, clean and clear in sound, rather than ripe.

Martinon's version has the advantage of being complete on one side of a Double Decca tape, coupled to Kertesz's brilliant early recording of the *New World symphony*. The performance is attractive enough to make the issue competitive, even if the reading as a whole has a certain Gallic impetuosity and tends to be somewhat lacking in depth of feeling. The first movement is well shaped and there is plenty of excitement; the second is slightly mannered but not lacking elegance, the scherzo straightforward, the finale somewhat underpowered, emotionally speaking. The recording is well balanced, with plenty of body and lacking the last degree of bloom, which betrays the age of the original recording.

With dangerously fast tempi throughout the first and third movements, the element of hysteria is never far away in

Solti's intense reading; and the element of nobility, so necessary to provide emotional balance, is missing. The scherzo/march loses all charm at this hectic pace; indeed the march element almost disappears altogether. The finale is more controlled in feeling but does not resolve the performance in any satisfactory way. Brilliantly clear recording to match the playing, but a treble cut is needed if the violins are not to sound excessively bright.

Tjeknavorian's first movement is curiously literal, everything laid out in front of the listener in a measured fashion, but the final spark of spontaneity missing. The 5/4 movement too lacks any kind of lilt in the rhythm. The last two movements are much more successful, especially the third, helped by fine recording; but the cassette transfer does not match the LP in its resplendent richness.

Dorati's recording is not ideally focused and the string tone lacks body. The reading has plenty of dynamism in the first movement, with a fast basic tempo and a strong climax. But the briskness extends to the 5/4 movement, where it is less welcome. There are some minor eccentricities of tempo in the scherzo/march, but the finale is finely done. However, the sound balance precludes a very strong recommendation in spite of the bonus, an excerpt from Dorati's early Minneapolis recording of *The Nutcracker*.

Variations on a rococo theme (for cello and orchestra), *Op. 33*.
  (*) DG 923098 [id.]. Mstislav Rostropovich, Berlin PO, Karajan – DVOŘÁK: *Cello concerto.*(*)

No grumbles about Rostropovich's performance here. He plays as if this were one of the greatest works for the cello, and he receives glowing support from Karajan and the Berlin Philharmonic. The *Rococo variations* is a delightful work, and it has never sounded

finer than it does here. However, the transfer to tape, while giving the orchestral tuttis plenty of life, offers a less well-defined solo image; the balance gives Rostropovich's cello less body and substance than it has in reality.

Piano trio in A minor, Op. 50.
  (B) *(**) Rediffusion Legend KLGD 026. Suk Trio.

An attractively bold and spontaneous account of Tchaikovsky's epic *Piano trio*, one of his most inspired works. All three instrumentalists play with strong personality, and it is a pity that the cellist is backwardly balanced in relation to the violin, for when the two instruments are playing together the cello tone tends to be somewhat submerged. Yet the cello solos emerge vividly, and one can feel the strength of the cellist's contribution, in spite of the balance. The first movement has splendid impetus, red-blooded and strong, with the kind of extrovert bravura the music demands. The variations too have both vigour and variety of mood, if rather less of a sense of elegance. Nevertheless this performance is enjoyable from the first note to the last, and it is a great pity that the tape transfer has been made at marginally too high a level, bringing a roughness to the upper focus of the sound which cannot be smoothed out with the controls.

Eugene Onegin (opera): complete.
  **(*) Decca K 57 K 32. Teresa Kubiak, Bernd Weikl, Stuart Burrows, Anna Reynolds, Nicolai Ghiaurov, Julia Hamari, Michel Sénéchal, John Alldis Choir, Orch. of the Royal Opera House, Covent Garden, Solti.

In terms of recorded sound, this set has remarkable transparency and detail; and in addition the orchestral playing is a delight. Solti, characteristically crisp in attack, has plainly warmed to the score, allowing his singers full rein in *rallentando* and *rubato* to a degree one might not have expected of him. The Tatiana of Teresa Kubiak is most moving – rather mature-sounding for the *ingénue* of Act 1, but with her golden, vibrant voice rising to the final confrontation of Act 3 most impressively. The Onegin of Bernd Weikl may have too little variety of tone, but again this is firm singing that yet has authentic slavonic tinges. Onegin becomes something like a first-person story-teller. The rest of the cast is excellent, with Stuart Burrows as Lensky giving one of his finest recorded performances yet. Here for the first time the full range of musical expression in this most atmospheric of operas is superbly caught, with the Decca recording capturing the off-stage effects with richness as well as brilliance. The transfer to tape is marginally short of Decca's highest standard. Perhaps the reverberation of the Kingsway Hall offered some problems, but the upper range is not quite so sweet and clean as on the very finest Decca opera issues. However, a careful smoothing of the treble removes the slight edginess yet leaves the vivid detail unimpaired. The recording has plenty of bloom, although the choral recording in the *Polonaise* scene at the opening of Act 3 lacks the last degree of refinement of focus. The set has a first-class and very clearly printed booklet, with libretto, and the layout on two cassettes is admirable. In spite of the reservations noted this set can be made to yield very good quality, and the splendid performance gives enormous pleasure.

Eugene Onegin: excerpts (Act 2: *Entr'acte and Waltz*; Act 3: *Polonaise*).
(*) Decca KCET 622 (from above set) – BIZET: *Carmen*: excerpts(*); BORODIN: *Prince Igor: Polovtsian dances*.***

An attractive collection of colourful and attractive opera excerpts taken from earlier Solti recordings, notably the complete sets of *Carmen* and *Eugene Onegin*. The transfers are well managed; the excerpts from *Onegin* tend to be smoother than the complete set, yet the sound remains vividly bright. However, the premium price of this tape will be questioned for such a reissue.

COLLECTIONS

'Favourite composer': (i–iii) *Piano concerto No. 1 in B flat minor, Op. 23;* (ii; iv) *1812 overture, Op. 49;* (v) *The Nutcracker, Op. 71; Trepak; Dance of the Sugar Plum Fairy; Waltz of the Flowers; Swan Lake, Op. 20: Waltz; Scene; Dance of the Little Swans; Czardas;* (vi) *Symphony No. 6 in B minor (Pathétique), Op. 74.*

(B) *(*) Decca KDPC 547/8. (i) Peter Katin (piano); (ii) LSO; (iii) Kundell; (iv) Alwyn, with Band of Grenadier Guards; (v) Suisse Romande Orch., Ansermet; (vi) RPO, Henry Lewis.

Katin's performance of the *Piano concerto* is a strong one, and the recording sounds as vivid here as ever. Unfortunately the set is let down by the performance of the *Pathétique*, by no means outstanding and marred by a very dry acoustic. The other works are well done, although it is a pity that room was not found for the full *Nutcracker suite*. The transfer of the *Piano concerto* is exceptionally clear and lively (with only a marginal hint of hardness), and *1812* is generally well accommodated, although the closing pages are not absolutely clean and free. The *Swan Lake* and *Nutcracker* excerpts sound well, if a little lacking in sparkle. In the symphony the string textures in the third movement are not as refined as on some Decca transfers, and there was also a fractional and momentary pitch slip in the first movement on our copy.

'The world of Tchaikovsky': (i) Piano concerto No. 1 in B flat minor, Op. 23: 2nd movt; (ii) 1812 overture, Op. 49: finale; (iii) Romeo and Juliet (fantasy overture); (iv) Swan Lake, Op. 20: Act 3: Pas de deux; (v) Symphony No. 6 in B minor (Pathétique), Op. 74: 4th movt; (vi) Eugene Onegin: Tatiana's letter scene.

(M) * Decca KCSP 142. Various orchestras, (i) cond. Henry Lewis, Ivan Davis (piano); (ii) Alwyn; (iii) Stokowski; (iv) Ansermet; (v) Henry Lewis; (vi) Valeria Heybalova (soprano).

This is designed to attract the filmgoer who saw The Music Lovers. The selection is arbitrary, and the only complete work is Romeo and Juliet, curiously given in Stokowski's truncated version with the ending cut off, so that the piece closes quietly. The excerpt from Tatiana's letter scene is not ideally secure vocally. The transfer is of only moderate quality, and the sound varies from item to item. The end of 1812 is coarse and distorted.

'Your kind of Tchaikovsky': (i–iii) Piano concerto No. 1 in B flat minor, Op. 23: opening section; (ii; iv) 1812 overture, Op. 49: finale; (v; vi) The Nutcracker, Op. 71: Chinese dance; Arab dance; Trepak; Dance of the Sugar Plum Fairy; (v; iii) Serenade for strings in C major, Op. 48: Waltz; (ii; viii) Swan Lake, Op. 20: Waltz; Scene; Dance of the Little Swans; (ii; ix) Symphony No. 6 in B minor (Pathétique), Op. 74: 3rd movt; (ii; x) String quartet No. 1 in D major, Op. 11: Andante cantabile (arr. Schmidt); (xi) None but the lonely heart.

(M) ** HMV TC-EXES 5004. (i) John Ogdon (piano); (ii) Philharmonia Orch.; (iii) Barbirolli; (iv) Royal Marines Band, Weldon; (v) LSO; (vi) Previn;

(vii) RPO, Boult; (viii) cond. Kurtz, Yehudi Menuhin (violin); (ix) Kletzki; (x) orchestral strings, Fistoulari; (xi) Boris Christoff (bass), Alexandre Labinsky (piano).

The only incomplete movement offered here is the opening of the First Piano concerto, an excerpt familiar from the days of 78 r.p.m. records. The rest of the programme is vividly presented and generally well recorded (although, as usual on tape, the end of 1812, which is also an excerpt, offers congestion rather than spectacle). It was a happy idea to include None but the lonely heart sung in the original Russian. Otherwise the selection offers the expected favourites and certainly demonstrates what a supreme melodic gift provided the underlying inspiration for all Tchaikovsky's music.

Telemann, Georg Philipp (1681–1767)

(i) Viola concerto in G major. Don Quichotte suite; Overture in D major for 2 oboes, 2 horns and strings.

*** Argo KZRC 836 [id.]. Academy of St Martin-in-the-Fields, Marriner, (i) with Stephen Shingles.

Anyone daunted by the sheer volume of Telemann's instrumental music could not do better than to investigate this splendid collection, which is superbly played and recorded. It presents a nicely varied group of works, not just the relatively well-known Viola concerto (with Stephen Shingles a stylish soloist) but the colourful and endearing Don Quichotte suite, a vivid example of early programme music, and the amazing Overture in D, written in 1765 when Telemann was well on in his eighties but still retained all his creative flair. Each movement is intensely individual, and the work ends with a graceful carillon for oboes and pizzicato strings and a final rumbustious *Tintamare*. The excellent cassette transfer is clear and clean, although the upper string tone has slightly less body than on the equivalent LP.

(i–iii) *Double concerto in G major for 2 violas and strings;* (i; iii) *Viola concerto in G major; Suite in D major for viola da gamba and strings;* (iv) *Triple violin concerto in F major.*

> (M) *(*) Turnabout κτνc 34288. (i) Ernst Wallfisch (viola or viola da gamba); (ii) Ulrich Koch (viola); (iii) Württemberg CO, Faerber; (iv) Georg Egger, Susanne Lautenbacher, Adelhaid Schaeffer (violins), Stuttgart Soloists.

The *Viola concerto* is well-known as one of Telemann's most striking works, and the *Concerto in F major for three violins* has a similar attractive affinity with Bach (and Handel too). The expressive slow movement is notable. The playing here is alive and musicianly, the slight snag being the recording, which has a rather fizzy upper register. However, the tape transfer tends to smooth this somewhat, though the sound is acceptable rather than outstanding. It is at its best in the *Triple violin concerto* (but that is also available in a cleaner recording on a Rediffusion cassette: see below).

Triple violin concerto in F major; Suite in E flat major for strings (La Lyra); Suite in D major for violoncello, strings and continuo.

> (M) ** Rediffusion Royale κRoy 2008. Soloists, Slovak CO, Warchal.

The *Triple Violin concerto*, which opens like Handel (the scalic passage anticipating the *Arrival of the Queen of Sheba*) and has a finale like the Bach of the *Brandenburg concertos*, is a busy, inventive work, and it is given an alert performance here. The *La Lyra suite* offers a set of strongly characterized dance movements and its genially extrovert qualities are well caught, although the hurdygurdy imitation in the third movement is less piquant here than it has sounded in some other (disc) recordings. The *Suite in D major* is a concertante work where the solo cello plays an important but not dominating role. The spirited style of the playing is attractive throughout the collection, and although the recording is a trifle dry (and light in the bass as transferred to tape) it has plenty of life and detail.

Overture in C major (Hamburger Ebb und Fluth); Overture des nations anciens et modernes; Overture in C major.

> *** Argo κzrc 837 [id.]. Academy of St Martin-in-the-Fields, Marriner.

Here is another outstanding Argo issue to match and supplement the companion tape including the *Viola concerto* and *Don Quichotte*. This triptych of diverse Telemann suites is irresistible. The *Hamburg Ebb and Flow* has programmatic implications in the manner of Vivaldi, but the musical descriptions are never too literal and the titular associations with the figures of classical mythology serve only to inspire the composer's imagination. Similarly the *Ancient and Modern Nations* provide paired dances given colour by their contrasts of manner. If the Hamburg suite evokes the spirit of Handel, there are Bachian overtones too, and these extend to the dances in both the other suites. Certainly the C major work which has no title is no less distinguished in invention. With a high-level transfer the sound has fine body and no lack of detail, but in comparison with some other Argo issues one senses a very marginal lack of refinement of texture. This is judging by the very highest standards and (on side two especially) the sound often approaches demonstration quality.

Overtures: in C major (Hamburger Ebb und Fluth); in F sharp minor; in G minor.
>   **(*)HMV TC-ASD 3631. Prague CO, Björlin.

These are good performances of some of Telemann's most appealing orchestral pieces. Ulf Björlin, a Swedish conductor best known here for a set of Berwald symphonies on EMI (not available on cassette), has some feeling for period style, though these perfomances are not quite as elegant as Marriner's on the Argo issue (see above), nor are they quite so well recorded. The transfers, however, are fresh, crisp and clean, with plenty of body, the treble brightly resonant.

Suite in A minor for flute and strings.
>   ** Enigma K 453538. Ingrid Dingfelder (flute), ECO, Leonard – HOFFMEISTER: *Concerto.***

Telemann's splendid *A minor Suite for flute and strings* has much in common with Bach's similar work in B minor. It is an inspired work, offering the soloist plenty of opportunity to show finesse as well as bravura. This account is uncommonly well played by the solo flautist, Ingrid Dingfelder. Lawrence Leonard favours brisk tempi and crisp rhythmic pointing, so that the music is almost overcharacterized at times. Certainly the second movement, *Les plaisirs*, marked *presto*, becomes *prestissimo* here, and the ensemble between strings and continuo suffers marginally. But otherwise the alert orchestral playing is attractive, and the harpsichord is nicely balanced to make a positive contribution. Indeed the recording (although forward) is of excellent quality and with a little trimming at the top becomes very realistic. The pro-

gramme notes are printed in type too small to read.

Suite in F major for 4 horns, 2 oboes and string orchestra.
>   (M) *(*) Turnabout KTVC 34078. Mainz CO, Kehr – ROSETTI: *Concerto* *(*); VIVALDI: *Double concerto.*(**)

The *Suite in F* is one of Telemann's most striking and original works. Interestingly enough it uses the key that was not to settle down as the natural 'home' key of the french horn until the end of the nineteenth century (D or E flat being favoured before then). It is a good key for the instrument, bright as well as flexible, and Telemann's writing, although it demands virtuosity, is very sympathetic as well as imaginative. The work's programme conjures up Greek mythology, but transferred to the Alster riverside in Hamburg, Telemann's home town. There are echoes, of course, and shepherds and nymphs, but the most striking and original item is a concert by frogs and crows. The music is not strictly speaking imitative, but the writing for the horns is surprisingly modern. The recording is atmospheric but unfortunately the transfer has been clumsily managed: there is coarseness in the orchestral sound, noticeable immediately in the overture, and the hint of overloading from the horns is even more striking here than on the equivalent LP.

Flute sonatas, Op. 2, Nos. 1 in G major; 2 in E minor; 3 in D major; 4 in B minor; 5 in A major; 6 in E major.
>   (M) *** HMV TC-HQS 1368. Michel Debost, James Galway (flutes).

This is charming music, the epitome of Telemann's *galant* style, showing a striking facility of invention and a thorough and ingenious exploration of the possibilities of the flute duet. Perhaps because of the pure sound characteristic of the flute, with its lack of overtones, the blend between the two instruments is absolute, with interweaving polyphony admirably balanced with a sure harmonic implication. Academic devices, especially imitative techniques, canon and fugue, are employed most imaginatively, and although one would not suggest this is a cassette to listen to all at once, the diversity of the music (and its melodic appeal) are remarkable. It is beautifully played and recorded with the utmost refinement and naturalness. The tape transfer is excellent too, with occasionally just a touch of 'fluff' in the treble which can be minimized with the controls.

Tippett, Michael
(born 1905)

Fantasia concertante on a theme of Corelli; Little music for strings.
   (M) *(*) Pye ZCTPL 13069. Orch. of St John's, Smith Square, Lubbock – ELGAR: *Introduction and allegro; Serenade.**

Although the account of the *Little music* is well managed, the *Fantasia* seems somewhat under-rehearsed. This is music which needs extreme precision in its playing if its expressive effect is to blossom freely. Here the players give more than a hint of the difficulty of the score's more complex moments. The cassette transfer has rather less bite and detail than in the Elgar coupling; there is some lack of range, but it does not seriously interfere with the music.

Turina, Joaquín
(1882–1949)

Danzas fantásticas, Op. 22.
   (B) ** DG Heliodor 3348 284. Monte Carlo Opera Orch., Frémaux – MILHAUD: *Le Carnaval d'Aix***(*) (with BRITTEN: *Young Person's Guide*).

Atmospheric and thoroughly sympathetic performances from Frémaux, although the evocation is as much French in flavour as Spanish. However, the music-making is undoubtedly very agreeable (the opening *Exaltación* comes off especially well) and the recording has been smoothly transferred. The Britten *Variations* are less successful, but the Milhaud *Carnaval* is a delightful piece and very well brought off.

Vaughan Williams, Ralph
(1872–1958)

Concerto grosso; Fantasia on a theme of Thomas Tallis; Partita for double string orchestra.
   *** HMV TC-ASD 3286. LPO, Boult.

Sir Adrian's noble reading of the *Tallis Fantasia*, never before so gravely intense as here in a recording of the ripest fidelity, is interestingly coupled with two much rarer string works. The *Partita for double string orchestra* (one without double-basses) is chiefly remembered for the *Intermezzo* headed 'Homage to Henry Hall', a unique tribute to the leader of a dance-band. The work is attractive but not as catchy as one always hopes. The *Concerto grosso*, written with young players in mind and calling for different degrees of accomplishment in each

617

section, is far more than a didactic piece, as this splendid performance brings out. The cassette transfer is rich and full, with a wide dynamic range.

English folksongs suite; Toccata marziale.
*** Enigma κ 453565. London Wind Orch., Wick – HOLST: *Military band suites; Hammersmith.****

As in the Holst suites the pace of these performances is attractively zestful, and if the slow movement of the *English folksongs suite* could have been played more reflectively, the bounce of *Seventeen come Sunday* is irresistible. The *Toccata marziale*, written in 1924 for the British Empire Exhibition at Wembley, has plenty of flourish. The sound is first-rate and most vividly transferred to tape.

(i) Fantasia on Greensleeves; Fantasia on a theme of Thomas Tallis; Five Variants of Dives and Lazarus; (i; ii) The Lark ascending. (iii) Songs: Linden Lea; Orpheus with his Lute; The Water Mill.
*** Argo KZRC 15696. (i) Academy of St Martin-in-the-Fields, Marriner; (ii) Iona Brown (violin); (iii) Robert Tear (tenor), Philip Ledger (piano).

Superbly balanced and refined performances of four favourite Vaughan Williams orchestral works, which with the help of sumptuous recorded sound have great power and intensity. The transfer to tape is admirable, offering the most beautiful string timbre. The climaxes of the *Tallis fantasia* are wonderfully rich and totally without unnatural edge, and the solo violin in *The Lark ascending* is naturally focused. As a bonus the cassette offers Robert Tear's comparatively robust, yet not inexpressive perform-

ances of three favourite songs (these are not on the equivalent LP). In all a richly rewarding collection.

Fantasia on a theme of Thomas Tallis.
**(*) Advent E 1047 (see p. xxiii) [id.]. RPO, Stokowski – DVOŘÁK: *String serenade* **(*); PURCELL: *Dido's lament.*(*)

(M) (**) HMV TC-EXE 39. Philharmonia Orch., Sargent – ELGAR: *Enigma variations.*(**)

Stokowski's care with tonal balance brings radiant antiphonal effects as the different string groups are contrasted. Surprisingly the performance is unusually straightforward; there is less speed variation than is common, and there is little *stringendo* at the approach of the main climax. Stokowski is more serene than Silvestri (see below), yet his restraint does not in any way interfere with the music's forward momentum. He conjures the ripest string playing from the RPO, who are very well recorded on this chrome tape. The sound has fine body and a wide range, although the extreme top loses the last degree of sweetness of focus at times. But this can be effectively tidied with the controls; there is no edginess.

One could hardly fail to be moved by the richness and body of string tone that HMV provide, but Sir Malcolm's performance is disappointing. He is content simply to play the notes and there is little spiritual quality. The tape transfer sounds somewhat fresher than the coupling, but our copy was spoilt by the curious 'pulsing' effect which affected some early transfers. This may have been cured on later copies.

Fantasia on a theme of Thomas Tallis; The Wasps: overture.
(M) **(*) HMV Greensleeve TC-ESD 7013. Bournemouth SO,

Silvestri – ELGAR: *In the South.****

Those wanting Silvestri's exhilaratingly memorable account of Elgar's *In the South* need not be deterred if they already have Marriner's account of the *Tallis fantasia*. This reading is quite different, more brilliant, less expansive, with remarkable tension in the opening and closing pages, and a touch of restraint in the handling of the second orchestra. But the central climax of the work is tremendously passionate, in a tighter, more direct way. The playing is excellent, the recording only marginally less good. Silvestri's account of the *Wasps overture* makes the most of the *brio*, with crisp, fast tempi and the expansiveness of the great tune in the middle not allowed to interfere with the forward momentum. The vivacity of the playing and the vivid recording (only a trifle less good than *In the South*) make this very enjoyable indeed. The cassette transfer is marginally less secure in texture here than in the Elgar coupling, but the climaxes have plenty of clarity and projection and this remains an impressive coupling.

Romance in D flat major for harmonica, string orchestra and piano.
*** Argo KZRC 856. Tommy Reilly, Academy of St Martin-in-the-Fields, Marriner – JACOB: *5 Pieces;* MOODY: *Little suite;* TAUSKY: *Concertino.* ***

Vaughan Williams's atmospheric *Romance*, if not one of his most inspired works, is still worth having, but it is the Jacob and Moody works that make this anthology worth exploring. The recording on the cassette is of very good quality.

A Sea symphony (No. 1).
(M) *** Decca KECC 583. Isobel Baillie (soprano), John Cameron (bar.), LPO Choir, LPO, Boult.

In the early days of LP this was a famous demonstration recording, and it was used by the late Gilbert Briggs in his large-scale Festival Hall concerts of recorded music to show just how clear and realistic recorded sound could be. Even today the famous opening has a presence and impact to startle the listener: the clarity of the chorus and rich bite of the brass are as stunning as ever. Only the upper string tone betrays the age of the original. The stereo transcription has been expertly transferred to tape and loses nothing of the sense of spectacle and range. As for the performance, Boult is at his most inspired. However diffuse the argument may seem on paper, the urgency of a live performance is unfailingly conveyed, and only the finale, nearly half an hour long, outstays its welcome at all. What comes out is how much the work forecasts the later Vaughan Williams, and what a striking achievement it was from a composer who far too readily has been dubbed a late developer. This performance has still not been outshone in the recording studio: it did after all have the benefit of the composer's presence at the sessions.

A London symphony (No. 2).
(B) **(*) Classics for Pleasure TC-CFP 40286. LPO, Handley.
**(*) RCA RK 6860. LSO, Previn.

Vernon Handley's performance with the LPO has not the subtlety and power of Previn's version, but it is direct and enjoyable. Tempi are well chosen, the climaxes of the slow movement and the finale (before the *Epilogue*) have undoubted eloquence, and the orchestral playing is sensitive throughout (notably in the closing pages of the *Lento*). The recording has plenty of weight, and the tape transfer accommodates the dynamic contrasts without difficulty. The upper range is very slightly restricted (the muted strings in the slow movement are not absolutely clean), but generally this sounds

619

far more impressive than the RCA Previn cassette, and at bargain price it must be a first choice on tape if not on disc.

Previn underlines the greatness of this work as a symphony, not just a sequence of programmatic impressions. Though the actual sonorities are even more subtly and beautifully realized here than in rival versions, the architecture is equally convincingly presented, with the great climaxes of the first and last movements powerful and incisive. Most remarkable of all are the pianissimos, which here have new intensity, a *frisson* as in a live performance. The LSO plays superbly. Unfortunately the RCA transfer suffers from the low level that apparently was necessary to accommodate the wide dynamic range. The sound is basically good (if not outstandingly refined in detail), but at the level of reproduction needed to make a real impact the background noise comes up, in spite of Dolby. Also, most irritatingly, a turnover break is made in the slow movement, so very near the end that one is exasperated by such wanton disregard for the listener's concentration just to save a very few inches of tape. To make matters worse, having made a positive and well-placed break, the sound is faded back up again on side two. But with all the faults the warm recording is undoubtedly well enough transferred to be enjoyable.

(i) *A Pastoral symphony (No. 3). Symphony No. 5 in D major.*
    (M) *** Decca KECC 607. LPO, Boult, (i) with Margaret Ritchie (soprano).

These are both fine, indeed historic performances (with the composer in attendance in the recording studio), and their preservation on tape is most welcome. The account of No. 5 is really outstanding, with a breadth and richness which Boult uniquely brings to the music of Vaughan Williams. The transfers have been skilfully managed and No. 5, which

depends a great deal on big washes of string tone, is surprisingly warm and full. The *Pastoral symphony* is an earlier recording (both, of course, are stereo transcriptions of mono originals), and here the string tone is less rich, but the overall warmth of the recording remains pleasing. The ethereal opening pages have great delicacy of texture. The only tiny fault is a hint of textural insecurity in one or two very quiet wind solos, but otherwise the sound is clear and vivid and the intensity of the music-making in No. 5 is fully conveyed.

Sinfonia Antartica (No. 7).
    *** HMV TC-ASD 2631. Norma Burrowes (soprano), LPO Choir, LPO, Boult.
    (M)**(*) Decca Eclipse KECC 577. Margaret Ritchie (soprano), LPO Choir, LPO, Boult; superscriptions spoken by John Gielgud.

The *Antartica* may be episodic but it is still a vital and dramatic symphony, deriving as it does from the score to the film *Scott of the Antarctic*. Sir Adrian gives a stirring account in his newest HMV recording and is splendidly served by the HMV engineers. The high-level transfer is admirably rich and full-blooded and provides a fine moment of spectacle at the entry of the organ on side two (which contains the last three movements).

The earlier Decca recording was also outstanding in its day, and the stereo transcription has been faithfully transferred to tape, with the famous organ solo no less dramatic sonically. Generally the recording has sparer textures than the stereo remake, but that is not always a drawback in an evocative piece of this nature, and there is no lack of vividness. The performance itself has plenty of electricity and atmosphere. John Gielgud's superscriptions before each section are effectively intimate and certainly not intrusive, recorded at a slightly lower volume level than the orchestra. It is a pity, however, that a turnover break had to be made in the slow movement.

VOCAL AND CHORAL MUSIC

(i) *2 Preludes on Welsh folk songs; Romanza (The White Rock); Toccata (St David's Day); 3 Preludes on Welsh hymn tunes (Bryn Calfaria; Rhosymedre; Hyfrydol).* (ii) *A Choral flourish; 100th Psalm; O vos omnes; A Vision of Aeroplanes; A Voice out of the Whirlwind.*

> (M) *(*) RCA Gold Seal GK 25016. (i) Timothy Farrell (organ); (ii) Exultate Singers, Garrett.

A Vision of Aeroplanes, says the front of this medium-price RCA issue, adopting the most eye-catching title from the works listed. It makes a misleading introduction for an unassuming collection of some of Vaughan Williams's smaller choral and organ works (the piece in question has words from the Old Testament), but this tape has its gentle delights, not least in the motet *A Voice out of the Whirlwind*, to more Biblical words, from Job. As a culmination the composer quotes the most colourful theme from his ballet *Job*, the *Galliard for the Sons of the Morning*, and the music leaps to life. The organ pieces have attractive themes too. Committed rather than refined performances; fair recording, and a fair cassette transfer, not always absolutely clear and less successful in the organ music, where there are patches of minor roughness of focus.

(i) *Fantasia on Christmas carols.* Arrangements: *And all in the morning; Wassail song.* (Also includes: trad., arr. WARLOCK: *Bethlehem down; Adam lay y-bounden.*)

> (M) ** HMV Greensleeve TC-ESD 7021. Guildford Cathedral Choir, Pro Arte Orch., Barry Rose, (i) with John Barrow (bar.) – HELY-HUTCHINSON: *Carol symphony.*(**)

Vaughan Williams's joyful *Fantasia* is comparatively short. It was written for performance in 1912 in Hereford Cathedral, so the acoustic at Guildford Cathedral is well chosen. The performance is suitably exuberant, and John Barrow is an eloquent if not outstanding soloist. The rest of the side is made with an attractive selection of traditional carols in arrangements by Vaughan Williams and Warlock. The recording is of good quality, and the transfer of the Vaughan Williams side is much more successful than the Hely-Hutchinson coupling, having altogether more substance.

Folk-song arrangements: *A I walked out; Ballade de Jésus Christ; The brewer; Bushes and briars; The captain's apprentice; Chanson de Quête; The cuckoo; Geordie; How cold the wind doth blow; Joseph and Mary; The lawyer; The maiden's lament; The morning dew; On board a 98; The ploughman; Réveillez-vous Piccarz; Rolling in the dew; The Saviour's love; Searching for lambs; She's like the swallow; The truth sent from above.*

> (M) *** HMV TC-HQS 1412. Robert Tear (tenor), Philip Ledger (piano), Hugh Bean (violin).

Robert Tear, who earlier made a delightful record (not yet available on tape) of Benjamin Britten's folk-song settings, here turns to the very different, more innocent settings of Vaughan Williams, and conveys comparable intensity, not least in those songs where the singer has a stanza or so unaccompanied. The selection could hardly be more attractive or varied in mood and expression. Stylish accompaniments. Excellent recording and a smoothly natural tape transfer which is also kind to Hugh Bean's sensitive violin obbligati in the three closing songs of the recital (*The lawyer*, *Searching for lambs* and *How cold the wind doth blow*).

Verdi, Giuseppe
(1813–1901)

Ballet music from: *Don Carlos; Otello; I Vespri siciliani*.
*** Decca KSXC 6726 [Lon. 5-6945]. Cleveland Orch., Maazel.

Maazel secures really first-class playing from the Cleveland Orchestra (listen, for instance, to the oboe at the beginning of the third of the *Four Seasons* from *I Vespri siciliani*), and he is given a recording that, though bright, is not clinical, and offers plenty of detail without any loss of atmosphere. The transfer is first-class, of top Decca ballet quality, with warmth, brilliance and plenty of sparkle in the percussion.

Ballet music from: (i) *Otello*; (ii) *Il Trovatore; I Vespri siciliani*.
(M) ** Philips 7317 197. (i) LSO; (ii) Monte Carlo Opera Orch.; both cond. Almeida.

Strong, colourful performances of undemanding music that for practical reasons no longer gets performed in the opera-house. Two-steps, waltzes fast and slow, galops and lyrical adagios, all have a place here, all unmistakably the work of a master, and well worth hearing if not with any solemnity. The *Otello* items, in which the LSO appears, are markedly more spirited in performance. Good recording, but the rather low-level transfer means that although the sound is well balanced, the upper range has less brilliance and glitter than on disc. This is good value at medium price but by no means as distinguished as Maazel's anthology (see above).

Overtures and Preludes (complete): *Aïda* (Prelude); *Alzira; Aroldo* (Overtures); *Attila; Un Ballo in maschera* (Preludes); *La Battaglia di Legnano; Il Corsaro* (Sinfonias); *Ernani* (Prelude); *La Forza del destino; Un Giorno di regno; Giovanna d'Arco* (Sinfonias); *Luisa Miller* (Overture); *Macbeth; I Masnadieri* (Preludes); *Nabucco* (Overture); *Oberto, Conte di San Bonifacio* (Sinfonia); *Rigoletto; La Traviata* (Preludes); *I Vespri siciliani* (Sinfonia).
*** DG 3370 010 [id.]. Berlin PO, Karajan.

Make no mistake, this playing is in a class of its own and has an electricity, refinement and authority that sweep all before it. Some of the overtures are little known (*Aroldo*, *Alzira* and *La Battaglia di Legnano*), and all are given with tremendous panache and virtuosity. These are performances of real spirit, and the recording is extremely vivid and spectacular in its range of dynamic contrast and colour. The climaxes are accommodated with aplomb in spite of the high transfer level, and only in the coda of *Giovanna d'Arco* (at the end of side two) does the bass drum temporarily disturb the security of texture. Elsewhere the weight and amplitude of the tuttis are impressive, although the upper strings are rather dryly recorded, with a touch of fierceness at times.

A single-tape selection is also available (3301 145), including the items from *Aïda, Un Ballo in maschera, Il Corsaro, La Forza del destino, Luisa Miller, Macbeth, Nabucco, Rigoletto, La Traviata* and *I Vespri siciliani*.

Overtures: *Aïda* (reconstructed and arr. Spada); *Aroldo; La Forza del destino; Luisa Miller; Nabucco; I Vespri siciliani.*
*** RCA RK 31378. LSO, Abbado.

Of the three collections of Verdi overtures available on cassette, Abbado's is a clear first choice for those not insisting on a complete set. The RCA tape has been transferred with great flair. The orchestral brass is superbly rich, and the resonant acoustic has been caught with the upper focus clear and sparkling. The strings have a striking lustre (the atmospheric opening of the *Aïda* overture is ravishingly beautiful). Abbado directs strong and brilliant performances and his selection includes Verdi's most substantial works in this form. The novelty is the introduction which Verdi originally wrote for the first Italian performance of *Aïda* and subsequently rejected. It is a considerably extended piece; in Spada's reconstruction one can see why the composer did not want in instrumental terms to anticipate effects far more telling in the full operatic setting, but heard independently it is most entertaining and deftly scored. Highly recommended.

Overtures and Preludes: *La Battaglia di Legnano; La Forza del destino; Giovanna d'Arco; Luisa Miller; Nabucco; I Vespri siciliani.*
*** HMV TC-ASD 3366. New Philharmonia Orch., Muti.

Along with his recent recordings of Tchaikovsky's second and third sym-

phonies, this must be numbered among Riccardo Muti's most successful ventures into the recording studio. The playing has great spirit and character, and the New Philharmonia responds to his direction with evident warmth. Naturally balanced orchestral sound (richer than on Karajan's DG set) makes this a highly desirable issue. On cassette the recording is immensely vivid and full-blooded; on the whole the reverberant acoustic has transferred well, although there is at times just a hint that the quality lacks the last degree of refinement. But the brass is rich and the woodwind warmly coloured, and the occasional touch of coarseness (as at the very end of *Forza del destino*) is acceptable when the overall impact is undoubtedly very exciting.

Requiem Mass.
**(*) Decca K 85 K 22 [Lon. 5-1275]. Joan Sutherland, Marilyn Horne, Luciano Pavarotti, Martti Talvela, Vienna SO Chorus, Vienna PO, Solti.
*(**) HMV TC-SLS 909. Elisabeth Schwarzkopf, Christa Ludwig, Nicolai Gedda, Nicolai Ghiaurov, Philharmonia Chorus and Orch., Giulini.
(*) DG 3370 002 [id.]. Mirella Freni, Christa Ludwig, Carlo Cossutta, Nicolai Ghiaurov, Vienna Singverein, Berlin PO, Karajan.

Of the available cassettes of Verdi's *Requiem* the Decca Solti version is (so far) easily the most satisfactory from the technical point of view. The famous *Dies Irae*, with its spectacular use of the bass drum, is not absolutely free from distortion, either at its first appearance or when it dramatically interrupts the *Libera me*, and elsewhere the choral peaks are not always as open in sound as on disc. But the soloists, whether singing alone or in ensemble, are naturally caught and the overall sound has good detail and no lack of bloom. The *Sanctus* is infinitely clearer here than in the Giulini set. Solti's performance is not really a direct rival to any other, for with the wholehearted co-operation of the Decca engineers he has played up the dramatic side of the work at the expense of the spiritual. There is little or nothing reflective about this account, and those who criticize the work for being too operatic will find plenty of ammunition here. The team of soloists is a very strong one, though the matching of voices is not always ideal. The choral singing is not so incisive as on the HMV set, even though the clearer Decca transfer is an obvious advantage. The HMV performance undoubtedly conveys more of the work's profundity than this, but Solti's extrovert approach is given plenty of projection by the engineering.

It is the refinement quite as much as the elemental strength which comes across under Giulini. Such passages as the *Dies Irae* are overwhelmingly exciting (though never merely frenetic), and the hushed tension of the chorus's whispers in the same movement and the warm lyricism of the solo singing are equally impressive. What Giulini proves is that refinement added to power can provide an even more intense experience than the traditional Italian approach. In this concept a fine English chorus and orchestra prove exactly right: better-disciplined than their Italian counterparts, less severe than the Germans. The array of soloists could hardly be bettered. Schwarzkopf caresses each phrase, and the exactness of her voice matches the firm mezzo of Christa Ludwig in their difficult octave passages. Again with Ludwig you have to throw aside conventional Italian ideas of performance, but the result is undeniably more musical. Gedda is at his most reliable, and Ghiaurov with his really dark bass actually manages to sing the almost impossible *Mors stupebit* in tune without a suspicion of wobble. The solo voices are well caught in the tape version and the

overall balance is good. But the wrath of the Day of Judgement falls on the transfer engineers for underestimating the amplitude of the great *Dies Irae* chorus: each time this appears the recording breaks up into unpleasant distortion. The *Sanctus* too lacks refinement of detail.

Karajan smoothes over the lines of Verdi's masterpiece with the help of a mellow Berlin acoustic. The result is undeniably beautiful, but it loses most of its dramatic bite. The tape transfer is of disappointingly poor quality, with recessed pianissimos and generally poor focus.

Four Sacred pieces (Ave Maria; Stabat Mater; Laudi alla Vergine; Te Deum).
    *** Decca KCET 602. Chicago Symphony Chorus and Orch., Solti.
    (M) **(*) Philips 7317 192. Leipzig Radio Chorus and SO, Kegel.

Solti's brand of dedication is one of brightness and tension. The Chicago Symphony Chorus cannot quite match the finest in Europe, but Solti draws finely shaded performances from his forces, and the electricity is never in doubt. Moreover he never runs the risk of seeming mannered in his moulding. The climaxes of the *Stabat Mater* and *Te Deum* are thrilling, and their effect is enormously enhanced by bold, brilliant recording which has been transferred with riveting clarity and weight to this splendid tape. Because of this the music makes far more impact on the listener than the superbly sung version under Herbert Kegel, which perhaps lacks something in its smaller, less spacious scale.

However, Kegel's magnificent choir presents these very late fragments of Verdian inspiration with a directness that is intensely refreshing. There is a case for the deeply introspective view of Giulini in this music (his version is not available on cassette), but the sharp focus of Kegel and the cleanly balanced recording make for an electric immediacy. This is music great enough to be effective even in maximum simplicity. The transfer offers a warmly atmospheric sound picture. The wide dynamic range has meant a moderate transfer level and the pianissimos are smooth rather than clearly defined. However, the climaxes expand impressively. Side two, which contains the *Laudi* and *Te Deum*, seems slightly fresher, with a little more range than side one, but the difference is marginal.

OPERA

Aïda: complete.

*** Decca K 64 K 32 [Lon. 5-1393]. Leontyne Price, Jon Vickers, Rita Gorr, Robert Merrill, Giorgio Tozzi, Rome Opera Chorus and Orch., Solti.

**(*) Decca K 2 A 20 [Lon. 5-1313]. Renata Tebaldi, Carlo Bergonzi, Giulietta Simionato, Cornell MacNeil, Arnold van Mill, Fernando Corena, Vienna Singverein, Vienna PO, Karajan.

**(*) HMV TC-SLS 977 [Angel 4x3s 3815]. Montserrat Caballé, Placido Domingo, Fiorenza Cossotto, Piero Cappuccilli, Nicolai Ghiaurov, Chorus of the Royal Opera House, Covent Garden, New Philharmonia Orch., Muti.

(M) *(**) HMV TC-SLS 5108. Maria Callas, Richard Tucker, Fedora Barbieri, Tito Gobbi, Chorus and Orch. of La Scala, Milan, Serafin.

(M) *(**) RCA RK 40005 [ARK 3 2544]. Leontyne Price, Placido Domingo, Grace Bumbry, Sherrill Milnes, Ruggero Rai-

mondi, John Alldis Choir, LSO, Leinsdorf.

Of the five recordings of *Aïda* available on tape, the earlier of the two Leontyne Price versions (with Solti), recorded by Decca in Rome in 1962, is undoubtedly the most successful. It easily outshines the later Price version, recorded by RCA at Walthamstow ten years later, in sound as in performance. Price is an outstandingly assured Aïda, rich, accurate and imaginative, while Solti's direction is superbly dramatic, notably in the Nile Scene. Anyone wanting a more expansive, contemplative view still has the option of Karajan, but this Decca set is more clearly red-blooded in its Verdian commitment. Merrill is a richly secure Amonasro, Rita Gorr a characterful Amneris, and Jon Vickers is splendidly heroic as Radames. The transfer to tape is most successful. The vibrant solo singing is vividly projected, and the spectacle of the Triumphal Scene in Act 2 (the ballet music too most colourful) is given sumptuous sound, with the trumpets ringing out in gloriously brazen tones. Equally the quality in the Nile Scene is robustly dramatic, and the opening of Act 4 (the confrontation of Radames and Amneris) has great power. Occasionally the quieter choral detail lacks sharpness of focus (the Priests in Act 4), but generally this is of demonstration quality. As in all the other sets, the opera is accommodated on two tapes, one act on each of the four sides. This set is accompanied by an exceptionally clear libretto, in large, readable type.

The spectacular Decca set with Karajan and the Vienna Philharmonic is one of those almost ideal recorded performances: the more you hear it the more satisfying it becomes, largely because it lays stress all the time on the musical values, if necessary at the expense of the dramatic ones. In this Karajan is of course helped by having a Viennese orchestra rather than an Italian one determined to do things in the 'traditional' manner. The chorus too is a very different thing from a normal Italian opera-house chorus, and the inner beauty of Verdi's choral writing at last manages to come out. But most important of all is the musicianship and musical teamwork of the soloists. Bergonzi in particular emerges here as a model among tenors, with a rare feeling for the shaping of phrases and attention to detail. Cornell MacNeil too is splendid. Tebaldi's interpretation of the part of Aïda is well-known and much loved. Her creamy tone colour rides beautifully over the phrase (what a wonderful vehicle for sheer singing this opera is), and she too acquires a new depth of imagination. Too dominant a characterization would not have fitted Karajan's total conception, but at times Tebaldi is too selfless. Vocally there are flaws too: notably at the end of *O patria mia*, where Tebaldi finds the cruelly exposed top notes too taxing. Among the other soloists Arnold van Mill and Fernando Corena are both superb, and Simionato provides one of the very finest portrayals of Amneris we have had in a complete *Aïda*. The recording has long been famous for its technical bravura and flair. But – and it is an important but – the dynamic range between loud and soft is almost too great, and for the quiet passages not to sound too distant, giving a 'back of the gallery' effect, the big climaxes must be played at a very high level, perhaps too high a level for small rooms. The cassette transfer has problems with the wide dynamic range of the recording, but the quality is good, if not as vividly clear as on the discs.

Caballé's portrait of the heroine is superb, full of detailed insight into the character and with countless examples of superlative singing. The set is worth having for her alone, and Cossotto makes a fine Amneris. Domingo produces glorious sound, but this is not one of his most imaginative recordings, while the Amonasro of Piero Cappuccilli is prosaic. So is much of Muti's direction – no swagger in the Triumphal Scene, unfeeling met-

rical rhythms in the Death Scene – and the recording, not quite boldly expansive enough, is a shade disappointing, not so vivid as the Decca sets of a decade and more earlier. The transfer to tape is well managed, the quality rich and atmospheric (Caballé's voice sounding especially beautiful). The spectacular choral scenes are weighty rather than brilliantly clear. The transfer level rises strikingly on side four, bringing a dramatic edge to Amneris's *scena* and the duet with Radames at the opening of the last act. The libretto is clear.

The Nile Scene – focus of the central emotional conflict in a masterpiece which is only incidentally a pageant – has never been so full of power and character in the recording studio as in the reissued Callas set of the mid-fifties. Though Callas is hardly as sweet-toned as some will insist on for an Aïda, her detailed imagination is irresistible, and she is matched by Tito Gobbi at the very height of his powers; Tucker gives one of his very finest recorded performances, and Barbieri is a commanding Amneris. The tape transfer is generally well managed, but from the sound point of view the set must be clearly regarded as 'historic'. The solo voices are vivid, full and immediate (although there is occasionally some peaking at climaxes), but the moments of spectacle have to be listened to with a tolerant ear. The biggest ensembles are congested, with a tendency to harshness. The libretto is clearly and pleasantly printed.

There is much to commend in Leontyne Price's 1971 recording of *Aïda*, and with a fine cast at less than full price it is worth considering. But it comes inevitably into direct comparison with Price's earlier set and by that standard it is a little disappointing. Price's voice is not so glowing as it was, and though there are moments where she shows added insight, it is the earlier performance which generates more electricity, has more dramatic urgency. Domingo makes a warm and stylish Radames, Milnes a strong if hardly electrifying Amonasro and Bumbry a superb imaginative Amneris. It is a pity that the recording, by the latest standards, does not capture the glamour of the score. Most of the earlier sets are more impressive in sound. The tape transfer offers a basically warm acoustic, with plenty of bloom on the voices, but the spectacular climaxes are congested. There was some flutter on our copy of the second tape, especially noticeable at the beginning of side three. The libretto, although miniature in size to fit the small RCA box, is quite readable.

Aïda: highlights.
> **(*) Decca KSXC 2242 [Lon. 5-25206] (from above set cond. Karajan).
> ** HMV TC-ASD 3292 (from above set cond. Muti).

For anyone choosing one of the other complete versions of *Aïda* the Decca tape will be a splendid reminder of the musical and technical excellence of Karajan's set, although not all its magnetisim can be fully revealed in a collection of excerpts, however generous and well managed. The cassette transfer is good: its slightly reduced dynamic range is an advantage, and the big Triumphal Scene is handled spectacularly. There is a touch of hardness on Tebaldi's upper notes; otherwise the quality is excellent.

Muti's set of highlights is transferred at a slightly higher level than the complete set from which it comes. This makes the sound brighter but gives the voices more edge: Caballé's voice is dramatically projected but is given less bloom. The Triumphal Scene has more brilliance but less richness and weight. However, as a sampler of this performance the tape serves well enough.

Attila: highlights.
> (M) *** Philips Festivo 7310 064. Ruggero Raimondi, Cristina Deutekom, Carlo Bergonzi, Sherrill Milnes, Ambrosian Singers, Finchley Children's Music Group, RPO, Gardelli.

This is the first of an excellent series of medium-priced Festivo issues of highlights from Philips' distinguished recordings of lesser-known Verdi operas, splendidly conducted by Lamberto Gardelli. A youthfully urgent work like *Attila* makes one marvel at the way Verdi consistently entertains, and in a well-chosen set of excerpts like this the musical unevenness is much less apparent. The dramatic anticipations of *Macbeth* (Attila himself is far more than a simple villain), the musical anticipations of *Rigoletto*, helped by fine singing, make this a most enjoyable selection. Deutekom, not the most sweet-toned of sopranos, has never sung better in the recording studio, and the rest of the cast is outstandingly good. As in other issues in this series, the layout is somewhat controversial. Here two excerpts from Act 1 are placed at the end of side two to 'round off' the selection. This is less of a good idea on tape than on disc, yet it is undoubtedly effective musically (the finale from Act 1 is a vintage Verdi ensemble), especially as the level of the transfer – slightly higher on the second side – brings richly vivid sound and striking weight and amplitude.

Un Ballo in maschera: complete.
> **(*) HMV TC-SLS 984. Martina Arroyo, Reri Grist, Fiorenza Cossotto, Placido Domingo, Piero Cappuccilli, Chorus of the Royal Opera House, Covent Garden, New Philharmonia Orch., Muti.

The quintet of principals here is unusually strong, but it is the conductor who takes first honours in a warmly dramatic reading. His rhythmic resilience and consideration for the singers go with keen concentration, holding each act together in a way he did not quite achieve in his earlier recording for HMV of *Aïda*.

Arroyo, rich of voice, is not always imaginative in her big solos, and Domingo rarely produces a half-tone, though the recording balance may be partly to blame. The sound is opulent, and the tape transfer is of good quality, but it has a rather narrow dynamic range. There is plenty of vocal projection but not enough light and shade.

Il Corsaro: highlights.
(M) *** Philips Festivo 7310 068. Jessye Norman, Montserrat Caballé, José Carreras, Gian-Piero Mastromei, John Noble, Ambrosian Singers, New Philharmonia Orch., Gardelli.

The first performance of *Il Corsaro* was given in Trieste in 1848. Though the characterization of the opera is rudimentary, the contrast of the two heroines is effective, with Gulnara, the Pasha's slave, carrying conviction in the *coup de foudre* which has her promptly worshipping the Corsair, an early example of the Rudolph Valentino figure. The rival heroines are splendidly taken here, with Jessye Norman as the faithful wife, Medora, actually upstaging Caballé as Gulnara. Many will feel that a collection of highlights is an attractive way of approaching this opera, particularly as likenesses in the key numbers to some of the greatest passages in *Rigoletto*, *Trovatore* and *Traviata* give the opera vintage Verdi flavour, and the orchestration is often masterly. Gardelli directs vividly; there is fine singing from José Carreras, and Gian-Piero Mastromei rises to the challenge of the Pasha's Act 3 *scena*. The other items are divided between Acts 1 and 3 plus Gulnara's Act 2 aria, *Nè sulla terra ... Ah conforto*. The transfer is vividly natural, and the sound opens up splendidly in the big Act 3 finale.

Don Carlo: complete.
*** Decca K 128 K 43. Renata Tebaldi, Grace Bumbry, Carlo Bergonzi, Dietrich Fischer-Dieskau, Nicolai Ghiaurov, Chorus and Orch. of the Royal Opera House, Covent Garden, Solti.

Unlike earlier 'complete' recordings of *Don Carlo*, which used the four-act revision, this Decca version includes the important passages excised, notably the Fontainebleau scene, and that may underline the one major deficiency of the set, that the dramatic temperature fails to rise as it should until the duet between Philip and Rodrigo at the end of Act 2 (Act 1 in the four-act version). Till then Solti tends to be somewhat rigid, but once the right mood is established he does marvellously with his Covent Garden forces, and the result in the *Auto da fe* scene is very fine. Tebaldi too in this most exciting Verdian role warms up well, and gives a magnificent account of *Tu che la vanità*. Bumbry and Bergonzi both sing splendidly, and after some rather gritty singing early on, Fischer-Dieskau rises fittingly to Rodrigo's great death scene, sounding almost (but not quite) as moving as Gobbi in the old HMV set (mono, and not yet reissued on tape). Ghiaurov as Philip is obviously not so dramatic as Christoff was in both HMV and DG sets, but the straighter approach brings a nobility, a sense of stoic pride, that is most compelling. The recording is of Decca's usual high standard and it has been given a vibrant transfer, splendidly detailed (as the opening scene shows immediately) and strongly projected. The cassette layout is satisfactory and the libretto admirably bold and clear.

I due Foscari: complete.
*** Philips 7699 057 [id.]. Katia Ricciarelli, José Carreras, Piero Cappuccilli, Samuel Ramey, Austrian Radio Chorus and SO, Gardelli.

As in so many of Verdi's most telling dramatic situations, it is the father–

daughter relationship in *I due Foscari* which prompts some of the finest music, including superb duets. It had better be explained that the precise relationship between the Doge of Venice, Francesco Foscari, and the heroine, Lucrezia, is father and daughter-in-law, but the wonder is that with a very limiting plot – based loosely on one of Byron's undramatic dramas – Verdi overcomes the shortcoming that nothing changes much in the relationships from beginning to end, and that in any case the wicked are left unpunished with the good brought low. Even so there are Verdian high spirits in plenty, which erupt in swinging cabalettas and much writing that anticipates operas as late as *Simon Boccanegra* (obvious enough in the Doge's music) and *La Forza del destino* (particularly in the orchestral motifs which act as labels for the principal characters).

The cast is first-rate, with Katia Ricciarelli giving her finest performance in the recording studio to date and with José Carreras singing tastefully as well as powerfully, not least in the prison aria, which even suggests that Verdi knew his *Fidelio*. Piero Cappuccilli as the Doge brings out the likenesses with *Boccanegra*. The crispness of discipline among the Austrian Radio forces is admirable, but there is less sense of atmosphere than in the earlier London-made recordings in the series; otherwise good clean Philips recording. The transfer too is admirably clean, and the sense of perspective is excellent: where there are distanced effects the clarity of focus is retained. Miss Ricciarelli's voice (and to a lesser extent that of José Carreras) tends to harden slightly when the recording is under pressure by strongly projected top notes. However, the sound has plenty of depth and is often impressively detailed. The presentation allows only very small print for the libretto, and there is no attempt to make the ends of the acts coincide with cassette sides.

Falstaff: complete.
(M) **(*) Decca K 110 K 32. Geraint Evans, Robert Merrill, Ilva Ligabue, Mirella Freni, Rosalind Elias, Giulietta Simionato, Alfredo Kraus, RCA Italiana Opera Chorus and Orch., Solti.
(M) **(*) HMV TC-SLS 5037. Tito Gobbi, Rolando Panerai, Elisabeth Schwarzkopf, Anna Moffo, Nan Merriman, Fedora Barbieri, Nicola Zaccaria, Luigi Alva, Philharmonia Chorus and Orch., Karajan.

The combination of Solti and Geraint Evans is irresistible. Their set comes up as sparkling as ever in this modestly priced Decca tape issue. There is an energy, a sense of fun, a sparkle that outshine rival versions, outstanding as they may be. Evans has never sounded better in the recording studio, and the rest of the cast admirably lives up to his example. Solti drives hard, and almost any comparison with the ancient Toscanini set will show his shortcomings, but it is still an exciting and well-pointed performance, the rest of the cast well contrasted. The transfer to tape is clean and lively. The orchestral brass sounds a little brash, and a touch of hardness on the voices in ensemble brings a hint of fierceness at climaxes. But the sound generally is more atmospheric and expansive than in the alternative Karajan set. The layout has Act 1 on the first cassette (with one scene on each side) and Acts 2 and 3 each complete on the remaining two sides. The libretto is beautifully clear, printed in an ideal typeface.

Karajan's version of *Falstaff* presents not only the most pointed account orchestrally of Verdi's comic masterpiece (the Philharmonia Orchestra at its very peak) but the most sharply characterful cast ever gathered for a recording. If you relish the idea of Tito Gobbi as Falstaff (his many-coloured voice, not quite fat-sounding in humour, presents a sharper character than usual), then this is clearly the best choice, for the rest of the cast is a delight, with Schwarzkopf a tinglingly masterful Mistress Ford, Anna Moffo sweet as Nannetta and Rolando Panerai a formidable Ford. The sound, of excellent late-fifties vintage, has been revamped, and at medium price no one will complain. One reason why the whole performance hangs together so stylishly is the production of Walter Legge: this is a vintage example of his work. The cassette transfer is brilliantly clear and vivid but dry in the bass. For best results one needs a treble cut (which also removes a good deal of the background noise inherent in the early master tape) and a bass boost. But the recording is otherwise vivid and well detailed, and in spite of the high level of the transfer there is only the very occasional hint of vocal 'peaking'. The work is divided on to the two tapes with Act 1 complete on side one; Act 2, Scene 1, on side two; Act 2, Scene 2, and Act 3, Scene 1, on side three; and the opera is concluded on side four.

La Forza del destino: slightly abridged recording.

    (M) **(*) HMV TC-SLS 5120. Maria Callas, Richard Tucker, Nicola Rossi-Lemeni, Elena Nicolai, Carlo Tagliabue, Renato Capecchi, Plinio Clabassi, Chorus and Orch. of La Scala, Milan, Serafin.

Callas was at her very peak when she took the role of Leonora in the Scala recording. Hers is an electrifying performance, providing a focus for an opera normally regarded as diffuse. Though there are classic examples of Callas's raw tone on top notes, they are insignificant next to the wealth of phrasing which sets a totally new and individual stamp on even the most familiar passages. The pity is that the stereo transcription process has (on tape as well as LP) taken away some of the brightness and edge of the recording as originally issued in mono;

but in compensation one of the major cuts (at the opening of the final scene) has now been opened out. Apart from his tendency to disturb his phrasing with sobs, Richard Tucker sings superbly; but not even he and certainly none of the others – including the baritone Carlo Tagliabue, well past his prime – begin to rival the dominance of Callas. Serafin's direction is crisp, dramatic and well-paced, again drawing the threads together; and the recording has plenty of atmosphere, which is retained in the tape transfer. The detail is remarkably good, and the solo voices are smoothly natural without any peaking. The libretto, however, is in very small type.

La Forza del destino, Act 3: *Solenne in quest'ora.*

    (M) **(*) Decca KCSP 496. Giuseppe di Stefano (tenor), Leonard Warren (bar.), Orch. of St Cecilia Academy, Rome, Previtali – PUCCINI: *Collection of duets.***(*)

This single Verdi item is included within a collection of operatic duets by Puccini. It is a fine, dramatic performance and the voices are well projected by the recording, which only betrays its age by the quality of the string tone.

Un Giorno di regno (*King for a Day*): highlights.

    (M) *** Philips Festivo 7310 066. Fiorenza Cossotto, Jessye Norman, José Carreras, Ingvar Wixell, Wladimiro Ganzarolli, Ambrosian Singers, RPO, Gardelli.

Un Giorno di regno was Verdi's second work for the stage. It may not be the greatest comic opera of the period, but it clearly reveals the young Verdi as a potent rival even in this field to his immediate predecessors, Rossini and Donizetti. The Rossinian echoes are particularly infectious, though every number of this generous set of highlights (six excerpts from Act 1 and five, including the finale, from Act 2) reveals that Verdi is more than an imitator, and there are striking passages which clearly give a foretaste of successes to come. But it is essentially a lightweight work and this collection of highlights provides an entertainment as sparkling and frothy as anyone could want. Excellent singing from a fine team, with Jessye Norman and José Carreras outstanding. The recording is superbly full-blooded and the transfer is well balanced and vivid, lacking only the last bit of range at the top.

I Lombardi: highlights.
> (M) *** Philips Festivo 7310 065. Cristina Deutekom, Placido Domingo, Ruggero Raimondi, Ambrosian Singers, RPO, Gardelli.

I Lombardi, first produced in 1843, followed *Nabucco*, which had appeared the year before. If you are looking for sophisticated perfection this is not the opera to sample, but the directness of Verdi's inspiration is in no doubt. The selection here does not attempt to follow the intricacies of the plot but presents some of the most stirring music. It opens with the pilgrims' chorus from Act 3 (*Gerusalem . . . Gerusalem!*) and then returns to Act 2 for Oronte's cavatina. Another splendid chorus is at the centre of side two (*O Signore*), and the tape provides a memorable climax with the famous *Trio* (and finale) of Act 4, well-known from the days of 78 recordings. By those standards Cristina Deutekom is not an ideal Verdi singer. Her tone is sometimes hard and the voice is not always perfectly in control, yet there are some glorious moments too and the phrasing is often impressive. Domingo as Oronte is in superb voice, and the villain, Pagano, is well characterized by Raimondi. The selection might have been more generous (there is an unnecessary

fade after Oronte's Act 2 cavatina), but the recording is extremely vivid and the transfer – made at a higher level than usual for Philips – has plenty of presence and projection. There is a hint of fierceness at climaxes, but it is not unacceptable.

Luisa Miller: complete.
> **(*) Decca K 2 L 25 [Lon. 5-13114]. Montserrat Caballé, Anna Reynolds, Luciano Pavarotti, Sherrill Milnes, Bonaldo Giaiotti, Richard van Allan, London Opera Chorus, National PO, Maag.

The Met. in New York had one of its most striking successes with this improbable opera (Montserrat Caballé in the name part), and though Verdi jogs along for much of the time, the big emotional moments prod him to characteristic heights of inspiration. Caballé, not as flawless vocally as one would expect (where is her trill?), yet gives a splendidly dramatic portrait of the heroine. Maag's conducting too underlines the light and shade, the atmospheric qualities of a score which, for all its imagination, can start sagging. Pavarotti's performance is comparable to Caballé's, full of detailed, seemingly spontaneous imagination, a creative interpreter, not just a beautiful singer of notes. Though Anna Reynolds cannot match Shirley Verrett on the RCA set (not yet issued on cassette), the Decca version, brilliantly played and vividly recorded, has the balance of advantage, and the tape transfer is first-class: it offers vibrant orchestral sound and yet has plenty of atmosphere, with the voices naturally projected. The layout is well managed, with Act 1 given a cassette to itself and the second and third acts a side each. The booklet is clearly printed.

Macbeth: complete.
> *** DG 3371 022 [id.]. Piero

Cappuccilli, Shirley Verrett, Niçolai Ghiaurov, Placido Domingo, Chorus and Orch. of La Scala, Milan, Abbado.

*** HMV TC-SLS 992 [Angel 4x3s 3833]. Sherrill Milnes, Fiorenza Cossotto, Ruggero Raimondi, José Carreras, Ambrosian Opera Chorus, New Philharmonia Orch., Muti.

In Abbado's scintillating performance the diamond precision of ensemble has one thinking of Toscanini. The conventional rum-ti-tum of witches and murderers' choruses is transformed, becomes tense and electrifying, helped by the immediacy of sound. At times Abbado's tempi are unconventional, but with slow speeds he springs the rhythm so infectiously that the results are the more compelling. Based on the Giorgio Strehler production at La Scala, the whole performance gains from superb teamwork, for each of the principals is far more meticulous than is common about observing Verdi's detailed markings, above all those for *pianissimo* and *sotto voce*. Verrett, hardly powerful above the stave, yet makes a virtue out of necessity in floating glorious half-tones, and with so firm and characterful a voice she makes a highly individual, not at all conventional Lady Macbeth. As for Cappuccilli he has never sung with such fine range of tone and imagination in a recording as here, and José Carreras makes a real, sensitive character out of the small role of Macduff. The tape transfer is exceptionally sophisticated, the orchestra very real at spectacular moments and lower levels too (the bass drum is impressively caught). There is plenty of atmosphere (the Act 2 finale is a splendid example), and the voices sound extremely natural. There is relatively little vocal edge, and this slightly reduces the sense of presence as compared with the discs, but that is a marginal criticism. Overall the acoustic and production are most convincing. As usual with

DG, the three tapes follow the layout of the records.

Muti's version appeared within weeks of Abbado's, confirming that new standards were being set in this opera on record. Though Muti and his team do not quite match the supreme distinction of Abbado and his Scala forces, they provide a distinct and valid alternative that some will prefer. Quite apart from preference for individual singers – on which each collector will have his own views – there is the contrast of sound between the extremely sharp focus of the DG set and the more comfortable warmth of this EMI one, which conceals any slight shortcomings of ensemble compared with the superlative Scala standards. Both Milnes and Cossotto sing richly, and are richly convincing in their relatively conventional views of their roles. As an appendix the set includes some valuable extra material from Verdi's first version of the opera; the death arioso for Macbeth is also included in the DG version (in its place in the last scene, not as an appendix). The recording is generally very good. The opera is spread over two tapes, with no attempt to match one act to each side. On the second tape there are some thrilling sounds in the spectacular scenes of Acts 3 and 4, the chorus projecting splendidly and supported by excitingly rich brass sonorities. On the first cassette some of the *pianissimo* detail is less than sharp in image, and Lady Macbeth's voice offers the occasional peak, but overall this makes very enjoyable listening. The libretto is clear.

Macbeth: highlights.
  *** DG 3306 045 (from above set cond. Abbado).

Though inevitably with so rich a score favourite passages have to be left out, *Macbeth* is a good opera to sample in highlights. This well-balanced selection from an outstanding set can be thoroughly recommended, and is well transferred to tape. The level is not especially ambitious, but the quality has rather more presence and edge than in the complete recording.

I Masnadieri: complete.

*** Philips 7699 010. Montserrat Caballé, Carlo Bergonzi, Ruggero Raimondi, Piero Cappuccilli, Ambrosian Singers, New Philharmonia Orch., Gardelli.

'We take this to be the worst opera which has been given in our time at Her Majesty's Theatre', wrote the critic Henry Chorley after the first performance of this, the one opera which Verdi wrote for London. 'Verdi is finally rejected', he said firmly. With Queen Victoria present at the première and the role of the heroine taken by the young Jenny Lind, the piece was an instant success, but not for long. As this excellent recording makes plain, its long neglect is totally undeserved, despite a libretto which is a bungled adaptation of a Schiller play. Few will seriously identify with the hero-turned-brigand who stabs his beloved rather than lead her into a life of shame, but in a recording flaws of motivation are of far less moment than on the stage. The melodies may only fitfully be out of Verdi's top drawer, but the musical structure and argument often look forward to a much later period in hints of Forza, Don Carlo and even Otello. With Gardelli as ever an urgently sympathetic Verdian and a team of four excellent principals, this can be warmly recommended. The recording is splendid, and the cassette transfer is admirable, one of the most vivid of all the Philips operas available on tape.

I Masnadieri: highlights.

(M) *** Philips Festivo 7310 067 (from above set cond. Gardelli).

The selection here is rather arbitrary; nothing is included from Act 1 and the Act 3 finale is moved forward to

'round off' side one. The listener then returns to the Amalia/Carlo duet (Dio, ti ringrazio!) before moving on to the fairly extended excerpts from Act 4 including the trio and finale (Qui son essi!). The music is all gripping, and the recording – transferred at a high level – is as vivid here as in the complete set from which it comes.

Nabucco: complete.

*** Decca K 126 K 32. Tito Gobbi, Elena Suliotis, Carlo Cava, Bruno Prevedi, Dora Carral, Vienna State Opera Chorus and Orch., Gardelli.

**(*) HMV TC-SLS 5132. Matteo Manuguerra, Renata Scotto, Nicolai Ghiaurov, Veriano Luchetti, Elena Obraztsova, Ambrosian Opera Chorus, Philharmonia Orch., Muti.

In 1966 Decca set impressive standards in this first opera of Verdi's to show him at full stretch. True, the choral contribution was less committed than one would ideally like in a work which contains a chorus unique in Verdi's output, Va, pensiero, but in every other way this is a masterly performance, with dramatically intense and deeply imaginative contributions from Tito Gobbi as Nabucco and Elena Suliotis as the evil Abigaille. Gobbi was already nearing the end of his full career, but even he rarely recorded a performance so full of sharply dramatic detail, while Suliotis made this the one totally satisfying performance of an all-too-brief recording career, wild in places but no more than is dramatically necessary. Though Carlo Cava as Zaccaria is not ideally rich of tone, it is a strong performance, and Gardelli, as in his later Verdi recordings for both Decca and Philips, showed what a master he is at pointing Verdian inspiration, whether in the individual phrase or over a whole scene, simply and naturally without ever forcing. The mid-sixties recording is brilliant and atmospheric, although the tape transfer (otherwise vividly detailed) needs a fair degree of control in the treble if the upper range is to sound completely natural. The rather fierce treble focus is noticeable immediately in the overture, but the quality seems to mellow on the second of the two tapes. The opera is admirably laid out, with each of the four acts given a cassette side to itself. The libretto is bold and clear.

When a decade later HMV attempted to rival the Decca set, the choice of Muti as conductor was promising, but in the event he failed to match Gardelli, either in detail or overall. The cast, as impressive as could be gathered at the time – with Manuguerra (an outstanding Scarpia in the Rostropovich *Tosca*) an imaginative choice as Nabucco – failed nevertheless to equal the three-dimensional characterizations of the earlier team. Renata Scotto sang well but was far less inside the role than Suliotis; Manuguerra was strong and reliable but lacked the flair of Gobbi; and although Elena Obraztsova proved stronger vocally than Dora Carral as Fenena, the casting was inappropriate. The recording quality, firm and warm, the resonance bringing added richness but less choral clarity, offered more problems in transfer to tape; the focus in spectacular moments is less refined than on Decca, although there is no lack of bloom and immediacy for the soloists. The layout, on two tapes, matches the Decca set.

Otello: complete.
    *** Decca K 102 K 32 [Lon. 5-13130]. Carlo Cossutta, Margaret Price, Gabriel Bacquier, Vienna Boys' Choir, Vienna State Opera Chorus, Vienna PO, Solti.
    (M) **(*) Decca K 55 K 32 [Lon. 5-1324]. Mario del Monaco, Renata Tebaldi, Aldo Protti, Vienna Grisstadtkinderchor, Vienna State Opera Chorus, Vienna PO, Karajan.
    (**) RCA RK 40001. Jon Vickers, Leonie Rysanek, Tito Gobbi, Rome Opera Chorus and Orch., Serafin.

Although Solti recorded outstanding versions of *Aïda* and *Falstaff* in the sixties, latterly he has neglected Verdi in his recording programme, so that the warmth and tenderness of his reading of *Otello* as well as its incisive sense of drama take one freshly by surprise. The recording is bright and atmospheric to match, which leaves the vocal contributions as a third and more debatable deciding point. Of the very finest quality is the singing of Margaret Price as Desdemona, a ravishing performance with the most beautiful and varied tonal quality allied to deep imagination. Carlo Cossutta as Otello is not so characterful a singer, but more than most rivals he sings with clear, incisive tone and obvious concern for musical qualities. Gabriel Bacquier gives a thoughtful, highly intelligent performance as Iago, but his relative weakness in the upper register brings obvious disappointment. A choice between this and the Karajan set is not easy to make on performance grounds, although the newest Decca tape transfer is undoubtedly very sophisticated. The spectacle of the opening scene is managed with characteristic Decca flair, and the sense of perspective is admirably conveyed. The recording itself has splendid warmth and bloom. Some may like to temper the very brilliant treble, but the sparkle and detail of the sound are matched by plenty of body and weight. Technically this set is in a class of its own. Each act is complete on one of the four cassette sides and the libretto booklet is printed in large, clear type.

If only the two casts on the Decca Karajan and the RCA set could have been combined. If Vickers and Gobbi had been in the Decca recording it could have stood unchallenged for ever, or even if just Gobbi replaced the inadequate

Protti. As it is, both sets are flawed. Karajan is much more dramatic in his conducting than Serafin; often he even rivals Toscanini. This is a different Karajan from the one who directed the Decca *Aïda*. Restraint is no longer the keynote: drama rather. Once again, clarity of texture, helped by the recording and the precision of players and singers, will tell the discerning listener that this is not an Italian group, but it is still completely idiomatic. Tebaldi and Monaco give one of their finest recorded performances, but Vickers, potentially at least one of the finest Otellos in the world today, is excellent too and on many points of style he shows up Monaco. Protti is admittedly not nearly so inadequate as Iago as one expected. His performance is always reliable, if never imaginative and never sinister – and that is a drawback in an opera whose plot hinges on Iago's machinations. Gobbi on RCA is far superior, as dramatically imaginative as one would expect. But what undoubtedly gives the older Decca set the advantage over the RCA is the quality of the recording. The transfer handles the spectacular crowd scenes with characteristic Decca aplomb and the overall ambience has striking warmth and colour, with good inner detail. The RCA transfer is much less sophisticated, conveying little of the sense of spectacle, while the break between sides three and four is very badly chosen.

Rigoletto: complete.

*** Decca K 2 A 3 [Lon. 5-13015]. Joan Sutherland, Sherrill Milnes, Luciano Pavarotti, Martti Talvela, Huguette Tourangeau, Ambrosian Opera Chorus, LSO, Bonynge.

(M) *(**) HMV TC-SLS 5018. Maria Callas, Tito Gobbi, Giuseppe di Stefano, Nicola Zaccaria, Chorus and Orch. of La Scala, Milan, Serafin (with recital by Callas: arias from ROSSINI: *Il Barbiere di Siviglia;* MEYERBEER: *Dinorah;* DELIBES: *Lakmé;* VERDI: *I Vespri siciliani***(*)).

Just over ten years after her first recording of this opera Sutherland appeared in it again, and the set was far more than a dutiful remake. Richard Bonynge from the very start shows his feeling for the resilient rhythms, and the result is fresh and dramatic, underlining the revolutionary qualities in the score which nowadays we tend to ignore. Pavarotti too is an intensely characterful Duke: an unmistakable rogue but an unmistakable charmer too. Thanks to him and to Bonynge above all, the *Quartet* for once on a complete set becomes a genuine musical climax. Sutherland's voice has acquired a hint of a beat, but there is little of the mooning manner which disfigured her earlier assumption, and the result is glowingly beautiful as well as supremely assured technically. Milnes is a strong Rigoletto, vocally masterful and with good if hardly searching presentation of character. Urgently enjoyable, with good atmospheric recording, both on disc and on tape, where the transfer is up to Decca's usual high standard.

There has never been a more compelling performance of the title role in *Rigoletto* than that of Gobbi on his classic Scala set of the fifties, originally mono, here given a generally effective stereo transcription. At every point, in almost every single phrase, Gobbi finds extra meaning in Verdi's vocal lines, with the widest range of tone colour employed for expressive effect. Callas, though not naturally suited to the role of the wilting Gilda, is compellingly imaginative throughout and di Stefano gives one of his finer performances. The inclusion of some of Callas's finest aria recordings of the late fifties is most welcome. The tape transfer has more presence for the solo voices and chorus than in some other

635

EMI transfers in this vintage series, but it is not without a degree of roughness at peaks. Gobbi's voice is very well caught, however. The recording of the Callas recital, which is on side four (of two cassettes), is also not free from peaking on loud high notes and offers far from perfect focus at times. The layout of the opera gives Acts 1 and 2 on the first cassette (the side break is in the middle of Act 1) and Act 3 complete on side three.

Rigoletto: highlights.
*** Decca KCET 580 (from above set cond. Bonynge).

This is a well-made and generous selection, reflecting the fine singing of the complete set and the warmly resonant recording, so kind to the voices, which is generally managed without problems here. It is a pity that *Questa o quella* had to be faded at the end, especially as this is the first item; but after this the selection is well edited.

Simon Boccanegra: complete.
*** DG 3371 032 [id.]. Piero Cappuccilli, Mirella Freni, Nicolai Ghiaurov, José van Dam, José Carreras, Chorus and Orch. of La Scala, Milan, Abbado.
(M)(***) HMV TC-SLS 5090. Tito Gobbi, Victoria de los Angeles, Boris Christoff, Walter Monachesi, Paolo Dari, Chorus and Orch. of Rome Opera, Santini (with recital by Christoff: arias from VERDI: *La Forza del destino; Nabucco;* BELLINI: *Norma* (***)).

Abbado's recording of *Simon Boccanegra*, directly reflecting the superb production which the Scala company brought to London, is one of the most beautiful Verdi sets ever made. From this one can appreciate not just the vigour of the composer's imagination but the finesse of the colouring, instrumental and vocal. Under Abbado the playing of the orchestra is brilliantly incisive as well as refined, so that the drama is underlined by extra sharpness of focus. The cursing of Paolo after the great Council Chamber Scene makes the scalp prickle, with the chorus muttering in horror and the bass clarinet adding a sinister comment, here beautifully moulded. Cappuccilli, always intelligent, gives a far more intense and illuminating performance than the one he recorded for RCA earlier in his career. He may not match Gobbi in range of colour and detail, but he too gives focus to the performance, and Ghiaurov as Fiesco sings beautifully too, though again not so characterfully as Christoff on the HMV set. Freni as Amelia sings with freshness and clarity, while José van Dam is an impressive Paolo. With electrically intense choral singing too, this is a set to put alongside Abbado's superb *Macbeth* with the same company. Although the level of transfer is comparatively modest, the sound quality and detail are good, with the distant choral perspectives generally convincing. The solo voices are natural and have presence, while the overall balance is well managed. There is some background hiss, but it is not too intrusive. The libretto, however, is in appallingly small type and often faintly printed.

The role of Boccanegra inspired Tito Gobbi to one of the most magnificent and intense performances he ever recorded, and his incomparable contribution is matched by the equally vivid and distinctive singing of Boris Christoff in the role of his enemy, Fiesco. That alone would give the HMV mono set of the mid-fifties a special status, but Victoria de los Angeles too sings most affectingly, and although the conducting of Santini cannot match that of Abbado on the DG set in precision and purposefulness, the great recognition scene between Boccanegra and his daughter is even more richly compelling, an emotional culmination. The others in the cast are never less than acceptable, and the stereo transcription, though limited in range, catches the voices vividly. Unfortunately the tape transfer has been clumsily managed. The first of the three cassettes, containing the Prologue and the first part of Act 1, offers a pleasingly warm projection of the solo voices, although the choral sound is muddy. But from the second cassette onwards the level rises and roughness appears, giving an unattractive degree of edge to the voices for the rest of the opera and producing patches of distortion on the valuable Christoff recital which is used to fill up the sixth side. The libretto is clearly printed, but the typeface is very small.

Simon Boccanegra: highlights.
    *** DG 3306 046 (from above set cond. Abbado).

Those who for any reason resist the complete set of *Simon Boccanegra* should certainly consider this well-chosen collection of highlights, an excellent sampler of a superb issue. The cassette transfer is extremely vivid and the level seems higher than in the complete set, with correspondingly more presence and detail.

La Traviata: complete.
    **(*) Decca K 19 K 32 [Lon. 5-1366]. Joan Sutherland, Carlo Bergonzi, Robert Merrill, Chorus and Orch. of Maggio Musicale Fiorentino, Pritchard.
    **(*) DG 3370 024 [id.]. Ileana Cotrubas, Placido Domingo, Sherrill Milnes, Bavarian State Opera Chorus and Orch., Carlos Kleiber.
    (M) **(*) HMV TC-SLS 5097. Victoria de los Angeles, Carlo del Monte, Mario Sereni, Chorus and Orch. of Rome Opera, Serafin.

Opinions on Sutherland's Violetta are sharply divided, and this characteristic performance from her will not win over her determined critics. It is true that her diction is poor, but it is also true that she has rarely sung with such deep feeling in the recording studio as in the final scene here. The *Addio del passato* (both stanzas included and sung with an unexpected lilt) merely provides a beginning, for the duet with Bergonzi is most winning and the final death scene, *Se una pudica vergine*, is overwhelmingly beautiful. This is not a sparkling Violetta, true, but it is more perfect vocally than almost any other in a complete set. Bergonzi is an attractive Alfredo and Merrill an efficient Germont. Pritchard sometimes tends to hustle things along, with too little regard for shaping Verdian phrases, but the recording quality is outstandingly good. The transfer to tape is one of Decca's very best. The sparkle and atmosphere of the opening scene are well caught, and the distant effects nicely brought off; moreover the individual voices are given naturalness and bloom. The balance with the orchestra, warmly and vividly recorded, is excellent and the reverberation nicely calculated.

The DG recording too has been transferred to tape with great sophistication, no doubt helped by the multi-microphone techniques employed in the recording. But what is disappointing in this set is that the microphone placing exaggerates technical flaws in Cotrubas's contribution. Not only is her breathing too often audible, but her habit of separating coloratura with intrusive aitches is underlined, and the *vibrato* becomes too obvious at times. However, such is her magic that many will forgive such faults, for her characterization combines both strength and vulnerability. The contributions of Domingo and Milnes also add to the considerable appeal of the performance, but Carlos Kleiber's direction is controversial, with more than a hint of Toscanini-like rigidity in the party music and occasionally too much insistence on

637

discipline. But the sound on tape is a compensating factor. It is clear, freshly detailed and offers natural vocal and choral timbres, excellent presence and a convincing balance with the orchestra. In many ways this is demonstration quality, even if it has been artificially contrived. The libretto, however, is another of DG's failures, with unacceptably small print.

Even when Victoria de los Angeles made this HMV recording in the late fifties, the role of Violetta lay rather high for her voice. Nonetheless it drew from her much beautiful singing, not least in the coloratura display at the end of Act 1, which, though it may lack easily ringing top notes, has delightful sparkle and flexibility. As to the characterization, Los Angeles was a far more sympathetically tender heroine than is common, and though neither the tenor nor the baritone begins to match her in artistry, their performances are both sympathetic and feeling, thanks in part to the masterly conducting of Serafin. All the traditional cuts are made, not just the second stanzas. The sound on tape is vivid and clear and seldom betrays the age of the recording. Los Angeles's voice is given both bloom and brilliance; only very occasionally is there a slipping of overall refinement in the choruses and a hint that the level is approaching its point of upper tolerance.

La Traviata: highlights.
**(*) DG 3306 047 (from above set cond. Kleiber).
**(*) Decca KCET 483. Pilar Lorengar, Giacomo Aragall, Dietrich Fischer-Dieskau, Chorus and Orch. of German Opera, Berlin, Maazel.

Though Cotrubas as Violetta is unflatteringly recorded, hers is certainly a performance, touching and intense, to which the listener must respond, and the DG collection of highlights makes a convenient substitute for the complete

set, valuable too for Carlos Kleiber's distinctive reading and the firm, musicianly contributions of Domingo and Milnes. The transfer to tape is clear and clean, but the level is disappointingly low, which brings an attendant degree of hiss.

Instead of offering a selection from the Sutherland version Decca have chosen to issue highlights from their later recording conducted by Lorin Maazel. (This is available in complete form on tape in the USA: Lon. 5-1279.) Listeners' response to this performance will depend on their reactions to Lorengar's voice. Her interpretation is most affecting, deeply felt and expressively presented, but the *vibrato* is often intrusive to the point where the tone colour is seriously marred. That will not worry all ears and in any case, with Fischer-Dieskau a searchingly intense Germont (if hardly an elderly one) and Aragall making impressive trumpet-sounds as Alfredo, this is a strong cast. Maazel's conducting is characteristically forceful. The selection is generous and includes most of the favourite excerpts; the transfer to tape is excellent, clear and well balanced, with particularly natural vocal production.

Il Trovatore: complete.
**(*) HMV TC-SLS 5111. Leontyne Price, Franco Bonisolli, Elena Obraztsova, Piero Cappuccilli, Ruggero Raimondi, Chorus of German Opera, Berlin, Berlin PO, Karajan.
** Decca K 82 K 32 [Lon. 5-13124]. Joan Sutherland, Marilyn Horne, Luciano Pavarotti, Ingvar Wixell, Nicolai Ghiaurov, London Opera Chorus, National PO, Bonynge.
(M) *(**) HMV TC-SLS 869. Maria Callas, Giuseppe di Stefano, Fedora Barbieri, Rolando Panerai, Chorus and Orch. of La Scala, Milan, Karajan (with recital by Callas: arias from

BOITO: *Mefistofele;* CATALANI: *La Wally;* CILEA: *Adriana Lecouvreur;* GIORDANO: *Andrea Chénier* *(**)).

(***) RCA RK 40002. Leontyne Price, Placido Domingo, Fiorenza Cossotto, Sherrill Milnes, Ambrosian Opera Chorus, New Philharmonia Orch., Mehta.

In spite of the apparent profusion of available recordings, *Il Trovatore* has not been very lucky in its tape transfers. The famous RCA recording, which comes nearest to Caruso's summation of the opera's needs – 'the four greatest singers in the world' (on top form) – has been coarsely transferred: the level is too high and the sound is generally uncongenial and congested at peaks. Until RCA remaster this set it must be reluctantly placed at the bottom of the list. The newer Karajan HMV set also casts Leontyne Price as Leonora: she often sings beautifully, and though the performance does not match the RCA version it easily leads the available cassette versions. The soloists are generally distinguished and Karajan coaxes a splendid response from orchestra and chorus (the *Soldiers' chorus* is particularly good, with fast, lilting rhythms). There is certainly no lack of dramatic effect and although the tension is very unevenly held, this is partly the fault of the curiously variable recording balance, the product of multi-channel technique exploited overenthusiastically. The images come forward and recede in the strangest way: the opening scene is a good example, the focus less than exact, then an explosive climax at the end. Yet it is imaginatively sung. There are many similar instances. Manrico's off-stage solo in Act 1 is far too distanced, as is the chorus in the Convent Scene. The introduction to *Di quella pira* provides full-blooded orchestral sound, but then the orchestra fades down for the entry of the tenor. There is a touch of coarseness to his singing, but it is unde-

niably exciting. Generally the sound on tape is rich and atmospheric and the dynamic range is undoubtedly wide even if at times one gets a 'back-of-the-circle' effect. The opera is well laid out and the libretto is first-class.

Bonynge in most of his opera sets has been unfailingly urgent and rhythmic, but this new Decca account of *Il Trovatore* is at an altogether lower level of intensity, with elegance rather than dramatic power the dominant quality. Nor does the role of Leonora prove very apt for the latter-day Sutherland. The coloratura passages are splendid, but a hint of unsteadiness is present too in much of the rest. Pavarotti for the most part sings superbly but falls short, for example, in the semiquaver groups of *Di quella pira*, and, like Sutherland, Marilyn Horne as Azucena does not produce consistently firm tone. Wixell as the Count sings intelligently, but a richer tone is needed. Most recommendable in the set is the complete ballet music, more brilliantly recorded as well as better played than the rest. The transfer to tape brings characteristic Decca presence and atmosphere, with plenty of weight in the orchestra and a fine overall perspective.

The combination of Karajan and Callas is formidably impressive. There is a toughness and dramatic determination in Callas's singing – whether in the coloratura or in the dramatic passages. It gives the heroine an unsuspected depth of character which culminates in Callas's fine singing of an aria which used often to be cut entirely – *Tu vedrai che amore in terra*, here with its first stanza alone included. Barbieri is a magnificent Azucena, Panerai a strong, incisive Count and di Stefano at his finest as Manrico. Though the stereo transcription is limited in range, it is well balanced. But unfortunately the transfer to tape has been made at marginally too high a level and the sound is not always comfortable. The chorus varies from a lively if rather fierce sound (in the *Soldiers' chorus*) to mushiness when the vocal image recedes, and there is often blurring at tuttis. Callas's voice offers moments of peakiness, and the other voices also suffer from a general huskiness of focus. The arias which are used to fill up the last part of side four also lack refinement of sound at peaks, which is a pity, for they are beautifully sung. With careful setting of the controls these faults can be minimized, but the hint of distortion remains under the surface of the music. The opera is well laid out and the libretto is clearly printed.

Il Trovatore: highlights (in English).
> (M) **(*) HMV Greensleeve TC-ESD 7027. Elizabeth Fretwell, Patricia Johnson, Charles Craig, Peter Glossop, Donald McIntyre, Rita Hunter, Sadler's Wells Opera Chorus and Orch., Moores.

Anyone seeking a potted version of *Il Trovatore* in English should be well satisfied with this vividly recorded HMV Greensleeve cassette. The words are admirably clear and there is plenty of drama in the presentation. Away from the stage some of the singing does not stand up too well, but Elizabeth Fretwell is undoubtedly both strong and stylish, even if *Tacea la notte* is rather shaky. Charles Craig is as ringing and well-controlled a tenor as you will find anywhere. Patricia Johnson and Peter Glossop are not quite up to their stage form, but their singing has plenty of conviction, and the presence and depth of the recording are very persuasive, with excellent clarity when the chorus is in distant perspective. Indeed the ensembles, the *Miserere* and the finale to the Convent Scene, have splendid attack, while the famous *Home to our mountains* duet is beautifully sung.

Il Trovatore: 'Great arias and choruses'.
> (M)*(*) Decca KCSP 513. Renata Tebaldi, Mario del Monaco, Ugo Savarese, Giulietta Simio-nato, Giorgio Tozzi, Maggio Musicale Fiorentino Chorus, Théâtre de Genève Orch., Erede.

Renata Tebaldi's vocal personality – the voice at its freshest – dominates this selection from Decca's 1956 recording of *Il Trovatore*. Del Monaco has the right tone colour for Manrico, and it is the greatest of pities that he fails so lamentably to do much more than sing consistently at the top of his voice. Even in excerpts it becomes wearing after a time. Simionato's contribution was one of the strongest elements in the complete set, but here she emerges less strongly, although her singing is always reliable. The conducting too does not have quite the lift and dramatic tension this opera above all calls for. The recording sounds astonishingly fresh for its age and is often strikingly vivid. There is some woolliness in the bass, which the tape transfer tends to exaggerate (notably in the *Soldiers' chorus*); generally the sound is excellent.

COLLECTIONS

Choruses: *Aïda: Gloria all'Egitto. Don Carlo: Spuntato ecco il dì. Ernani: Sì, redesti il leon di Castiglia. I Lombardi: Gerusalem. Macbeth: Patria oppressa. Nabucco; Gli arredi festivi; Va, pensiero (Chorus of Hebrew slaves). Otello: Fuoco di gioia. Il Trovatore: Vedi, le fosche (Anvil chorus).*
> ⊛ *** DG 3300 495 [id.]. Chorus and Orch. of La Scala, Milan, Abbado.

This is a superb tape, quite the finest collection of operatic choruses available. The combination of precision and tension in these La Scala performances is riveting, and the recording is of superlative standard, offering a wide dynamic range, fine detail in the pianissimos and marvellous weight in the moments of spectacle. The diminuendo at the end of the *Anvil chorus* is most subtly managed, while the rhythmic bounce of *Sì, redesti* (from *Ernani*) is matched by the expansive brilliance of the excerpts from *Aïda* (lovely fruity trumpets) and *Don Carlo*, and by the atmospheric power of *Patria oppressa* from *Macbeth*. The cassette transfer is of demonstration quality throughout.

Arias: *Aïda: Se quel guerrier . . . Celeste Aïda. Un Ballo in maschera: Di' tu se fedele; Non possono* (chorus). *Ernani: Mercè, diletti. La Forza del destino: La vita è inferno . . . Della natal! . . . Fu vana impresa! . . . O tu che in seno agli angeli. Luisa Miller: Oh! fede negar potessi . . . Quando le sere. Macbeth: O figli . . . Ah, la paterna mano. Otello: Dio! mi potevi scagliar tutti i mali; Niun mi tema. Rigoletto: Questa o quella . . . La costanza tiranna del core; La donna è mobile. La Traviata: Lungo da lei . . . De' miei bollenti spiriti. Il Trovatore: Il presagio . . . Ah sì, ben mio; Di quella pira.*

(M) *** Philips 7317 160. Carlo Bergonzi (tenor), Ambrosian Singers, New Philharmonia Orch., Santi.

This collection is taken from a three-disc anthology offering arias spanning the whole of Verdi's career. The single-tape selection is both generous and apt, and though Bergonzi almost inevitably fails to contrast the characters very distinctly, few tenors of his generation could have undertaken this exacting project with such consistently satisfying musicianship. Good clear recording and generally stylish accompaniments. The level of transfer is characteristically modest, but the sound quality is excellent, the orchestral detail good, the voice warmly natural and with no lack of presence. The vocal fortissimos are clear and free.

Arias: *Ernani: Surta è la notte; Ernani, involami. I Vespri siciliani: Mercè, dilette.*

(M) **(*) Decca Ace of Diamonds KSDC 146. Joan Sutherland (soprano), Paris Conservatoire Orch., Santi – DONIZETTI: *Linda di Chamounix; Lucia: arias.***(*)

It is primarily for the Donizetti items that this magnificent recital is famous, but these Verdi arias show a comparable level of memorability, with superb singing throughout. The transfer, however, was an early Decca tape issue and the sound loses the last degree of refinement at peaks. Basically the quality is good, with a bloom on the voice and the orchestral backing well detailed, but the moments of minor peakiness – untypical of Decca – must be mentioned. No doubt in due course this issue will be remastered.

'Favourite composer': arias, duets and choruses: *Aïda:* (i) *Se quel guerrier . . . Celeste Aïda; Su! del Nilo . . .* (ii) *Ritorna vincitor;* (iii) *Triumphal march and ballet music;* (i; iv) *Già i sacerdoti . . . Ah! tu dei. Un Ballo in maschera:* (v) *Morrò, ma prima in grazia. Don Carlo:* (vi) *O don fatale. Falstaff:* (vii) *Ehi! Paggio! La Forza del destino:* (viii) *Overture; Morir! tremenda cosa! . . . Urna fatale. Luisa Miller:* (ii) *Oh! fede negar potessi . . . Quando le sere. Macbeth:* (ix) Apparition Scene. *Nabucco:* (x) *Va, pensiero (Chorus of Hebrew slaves). Otello:* (v) *Willow song; Ave Maria. Rigoletto:* (xi) *Gualtier Maldè . . . Caro nome;* (xii) *La donna è mobile. La Traviata:* Prelude to Act 1; (xi; i) *Brindisi; Un dì felice. Il Trovatore:*

VERDI

(xiii) *Vedi, le fosche (Anvil chorus);*
(xiv) *Di quella pira;* (xiv; ii) *Miserere.*

(B) *** Decca KDPC 555/6. (i)
Carlo Bergonzi; (ii) Renata
Tebaldi; (iii) Vienna Singverein,
Vienna PO, Karajan; (iv) Giulietta Simionato; (v) Régine
Crespin; (vi) Grace Bumbry;
(vii) Geraint Evans; (viii) Leonard Warren, Santa Cecilia
Orch., Previtali; (ix) Dietrich
Fischer-Dieskau, Ambrosian
Chorus, LPO, Gardelli; (x)
Chorus and Orch. of St Cecilia
Academy, Rome, Franci; (xi)
Joan Sutherland; (xii) Luciano
Pavarotti; (xiii) Chorus and
Orch. of Maggio Musicale Fiorentino, Erede; (xiv) Mario del
Monaco.

An outstanding set in every way and
much more cleverly selected than the
World of Verdi (see below). The first tape
opens with an impressively vibrant account of the *Chorus of Hebrew slaves* (a
different recording from the one on KCSP
447), and there are many memorable
items, from the electrifying *Macbeth* excerpt to Sutherland's beautiful *Caro
nome* and Crespin's *Willow song* and *Ave
Maria* from *Otello.* Geraint Evans's
scene from *Falstaff* and of course the excerpts from the spectacular Karajan *Aïda.*
As should always happen with an anthology of this kind, each item balances
with what has gone before and what is to
follow. The recording (except perhaps in
the *Forza* overture) is of uniformly good
quality and the cassette transfers are
admirably vivid.

'Gala night at La Scala': *Un Ballo in
maschera:* (i) *Teco io sto. Don Carlo:*
(ii) *Ella giammai m'amò;* (iii) *Nel
giardin del bello saracin ostello. Rigoletto:* (iv; v) Act 3: finale. *La Traviata:* (vi) *Ah, fors'è lui. Il Trovatore: Gipsy chorus; Soldiers' chorus;*
(vi) *Tutto è deserto; Il balen.*

(B) *(*) DG Heliodor 3348 280.
Chorus and Orch. of La Scala,
Milan, various conductors,
with (i) Antonietta Stella,
Gianni Poggi; (ii) Boris Christoff; (iii) Fiorenza Cossotto;
(iv) Renata Scotto; (v) Carlo
Bergonzi, Dietrich Fischer-
Dieskau, Ivo Vinco; (vi) Ettore
Bastianini, Ivo Vinco.

The title *Gala night at La Scala* suggests something of an occasion, but
a good deal of the content of this tape
is rather routine in presentation. The
choruses, for instance, somewhat dryly
recorded, are not especially exciting.
The most distinguished items here are
from *Don Carlo*, though Amelia and
Richard's duet from *Un Ballo in maschera* is attractively spirited. The tape
closes with the finale to *Rigoletto*, and
that is movingly done. The transfer is
generally successful, vivid with just an
occasional peak (on a female-voiced
climax).

'The world of Verdi': *Aïda:* (i) *Se quel
guerrier . . . Celeste Aïda. Don Carlo:*
(i; ii) *Ascolta! le porte . . . Dio che nell'
alma infondere. La Forza del destino:* (iii) *Overture. Luisa Miller:* (i)
*Oh! fede negar potessi . . . Quando le
sere. Nabucco:* (iv) *Va, pensiero.
Otello:* (v) *Willow song. Rigoletto:*
(vi) *La donna è mobile;* (v; vii) *Quartet: Bella figlia. La Traviata:* (viii)
Prelude to Act 1; (ii) *Di Provenza il
mar. Il Trovatore:* (ix) *Vedi, le fosche;*
(x) *Stride la vampa. I Vespri siciliani:*
(xi) *Mercè, dilette.*

(M) ** Decca KCSP 447. (i) Carlo
Bergonzi; (ii) Dietrich Fischer-
Dieskau; (iii) Santa Cecilia
Orch., Previtali; (iv) Vienna

642

State Opera Chorus and Orch., Gardelli; (v) Joan Sutherland; (vi) Luciano Pavarotti; (vii) Stefania Malagù, Renato Cioni, Cornell MacNeil; (viii) German Opera Orch., Berlin, Maazel; (ix) Chorus and Orch. of Santa Cecilia Academy, Rome, Franci; (x) Marilyn Horne; (xi) Maria Chiara.

Although this selection is generous, it is less attractive than the two-tape *Favourite composer* set (see above), which is better value. The *Forza overture*, which opens this tape, lacks richness and lustre, and the following *Chorus of Hebrew slaves* is not very clearly focused. After this the recording settles down, although the transfer seems to project everything vividly forward, and there is some lack of light and shade. There are some very good things later, including Sutherland's *Willow song*, Bergonzi's *Celeste Aïda*, and (especially) Maria Chiara's beautiful and sparkling *Mercè, dilette*. The Bergonzi/Fischer-Dieskau duet from *Don Carlo* rounds off the recital dramatically, and many may feel that this tape is worth exploring for side two alone.

'Your kind of Verdi': Requiem Mass: (i) *Sanctus. Aïda:* (ii) *Gloria all'Egitto;* (iii) *Celeste Aïda. Don Carlo:* (iv) *O don fatale. La Forza del destino:* (v) *Rataplan. Nabucco:* (ii) *Va, pensiero. Otello: Fuoco di gioia;* (vi) *Ave Maria. Rigoletto:* (vii) *La donna è mobile. La Traviata:* (viii; ix) *Brindisi; Sempre libera. Il Trovatore:* (x) *Vedi, le fosche;* (xi) *Di quella pira;* (xi; xii) *Miserere.*
- (M) **(*)HMV TC-EXES 5015. (i) Philharmonia Chorus and Orch., Giulini; (ii) Chorus and Orch. of the Royal Opera House, Covent Garden, Gardelli; (iii) Placido Domingo; (iv) Shirley Verrett; (v) Bianca-

Maria Casoni, Ambrosian Opera Chorus, RPO, Giulini; (vi) Montserrat Caballé; (vii) Nicolai Gedda; (viii) Carlo del Monte; (ix) Victoria de los Angeles; (x) Rome Opera Chorus and Orch., Schippers; (xi) Franco Corelli; (xii) Gabriella Tucci.

The compiler of this anthology managed to avoid producing just a series of purple patches, yet has found room for many favourite items. There is plenty of contrast, and the distinguished cast list ensures a sprinkling of outstanding performances (notably those by Caballé, Los Angeles and Shirley Verrett). The recording is remarkably consistent. The *Aïda* march lacks something in brilliance, but the *Sanctus* from the *Requiem* sounds well.

Vieuxtemps, Henri (1820–81)

Violin concertos Nos. 4 in D minor, Op. 31; 5 in A minor, Op. 37.
- **(*) HMV TC-ASD 3555. Itzhak Perlman, Orchestre de Paris, Barenboim.

Vieuxtemps wrote six violin concertos, and it is surprising that so few violinists have attempted to resurrect more than the odd one. This coupling of two of the best-known is apt, and it presents superbly stylish readings, with Perlman both aristocratically pure of tone and intonation and passionate of expression. In his accompaniments Daniel Barenboim draws warmly romantic playing from the Paris Orchestra. However, the basically full recording has lost some of its refinement in the transfer to tape. The forward placing of the soloist brings a degree of fierceness to the solo violin timbre (the level is high), and some of the orchestral tuttis are not very smooth.

Violin concerto No. 5 in A minor, Op. 37.

*** Decca KSXC 6759 [Lon. 5-6992]. Kyung-Wha Chung, LSO, Foster – SAINT-SAËNS: *Violin concerto No. 3.****

Even more than the Saint-Saëns on the reverse, the Vieuxtemps concerto needs persuasive advocacy, and that is certainly what Kyung-Wha Chung provides, not just in her passionate commitment in the bravura sections but in the tender expressiveness of the slow movement, so much more compelling than the usual more extrovert manner. Excellent recording, and the transfer is generally first-class, although the sound here is marginally less precisely focused than in the Saint-Saëns coupling. But the soloist is given a warm, natural tone.

Villa-Lobos, Heitor
(1887–1959)

Bachianas Brasileiras No. 3; Mômoprecóce (fantasy for piano and orchestra).

**(*) HMV TC-ASD 3429. Cristina Ortiz (piano), New Philharmonia Orch., Ashkenazy.

No. 3 of the *Bachianas Brasileiras*, which dates from 1938, is the only one of the series to involve the piano. The *Mômoprecóce* began life in 1920 (while the composer was living in Paris) as the set of piano pieces called *Carnaval das Crianças* and was reworked in this form later. The score is rowdy and colourful, like so much of Villa-Lobos's music, and

its sheer zest for life and unrelieved cheerfulness may be too much for some people. It is not music of great substance and is best taken in small doses. Cristina Ortiz plays with appropriate vigour and colour and Ashkenazy gives splendid support. The recording is first-class, and the sound on tape is clean and clear – a little lacking in bloom in the treble, but less so on side two (the *Mômoprecóce*). At the end of this piece there are slight problems with an over-resonant bass drum, but otherwise the exotic percussive detail and piano timbre have plenty of sparkle.

Bachianas Brasileiras No. 5.

(M) (**) RCA RK 42006. Anna Moffo (soprano), American SO, Stokowski – CANTELOUBE: *Chants d'Auvergne;* RACHMANINOV: *Vocalise.*(**)

Anna Moffo gives a seductive performance of the most famous of the *Bachianas Brasileiras*, adopting a highly romantic style (matching the conductor) and warm tone colour. Warm recording to match, but unfortunately the cassette transfer is rather shrill.

Guitar concerto.

CBS 40-76369 [Col. MT 33208]. John Williams, ECO, Barenboim – RODRIGO: *Concierto de Aranjuez.(*)

(*) DG 3300 718 [id.]. Narciso Yepes, LSO, Navarro – CASTELNUOVO-TEDESCO: *Concerto.*(*)

John Williams's compelling performance makes the very most of Villa-Lobos's slight but curiously memorable little concerto. The rhapsodic quality of the *Andantino* is well brought out. The CBS recording balances the soloist well forward, but the orchestral detail comes through, and the tape transfer, while lacking the last degree of upper range, offers greater freshness than in the Rodrigo coupling.

Yepes's performance too is a good one, if without quite the individuality of John Williams's. The accompaniment is vividly managed and the recording well transferred. The DG recording, both here and in the Castelnuovo-Tedesco coupling, has rather more range and naturalness than the CBS one, but is smooth rather than brilliant.

12 Études for guitar; Suite populaire brésilienne.
   ***RCA RK 12499. Julian Bream (guitar).

Bream engages the listener's attention from the opening of the first study and holds it to the last. The vigour and energy of the playing are matched by its spontaneity, and there is considerable subtlety of colour. The recording is immaculate and it has transferred cleanly and realistically. The *Suite* is no less strongly characterized, although the music is lighter in mood and less concentrated in structure. The recording here is slightly more resonant, and effectively so. The only real criticism of this cassette concerns the liner notes, which are reproduced in almost unreadable small type.

Études Nos. 1, 3, 5–8, 11, 12; Gavota-Chôro; Mazurka-Chôro; 5 Preludes; Schottisch-Chôro; Suite populaire brésilienne; Valsa-Chôro.
   (M) **(*) Saga CA 5453. Eric Hill (guitar).

An ambitious recital. Eric Hill is especially good in the *Five Preludes*: these performances are first-class. He makes less of a case for the short lightweight pieces, but brings out the full character and contrasts inherent in the *Études*. The guitar is balanced very forwardly, and its closeness to the microphone reduces the range of dynamic in writing which sometimes demands strongly marked crescendos and diminuendos as part of its structure.

But this is fine playing, and when the music creates atmosphere and requires a kind of musing ebb and flow, Eric Hill is at his best. The transfer is made at a very high level (one needs the volume low for a realistic image), and undoubtedly the recording is full and naturally balanced, if the image be larger than life-size. Only in the last two studies, at the end of the recital, do the expansive textures (played with considerable bravura) cause the focus of the sound to blur, suggesting that (on side two at least) a slightly lower level would have been more prudent.

5 Preludes.
   *** CBS 40-73545 [Col. MT 34198]. John Williams (guitar) – SCARLATTI: *Sonatas.****

CBS provides excellent recording for John Williams's performance of the *Preludes*. Although he is closely balanced, his playing is of the highest order of mastery. A lower level-setting compensates for the close balance, and enables this artist's playing to register effectively. These are as perfect and as finely turned as any performances in the catalogue, on tape or disc, and the cassette transfer is well managed, clear and clean.

(i)   *Carnaval das Crianças (Children's Carnival): suite. A Fiandeira (The Spinning Girl); A Lenda do Caboclo (The Legend of Caboclo); Rudepoêma; Saudades des Sélvas Brasileiras; New York Skyline (2nd version); Suite floral (Três peças), Op. 97.*
   ***DG 3300 634. Roberto Szidon (piano), (i) with Richard Metzler.

Bright, attractive music that is unfailingly inventive and enjoyable and excellently played by Robert Szidon. *Rudepoêma*, written in the first half of the 1920s, is one of Villa-Lobos's best pieces in this medium. Szidon is a brilliant player, and in the *Carnaval das Crianças* for piano, four hands (though some of the pieces are for only one pianist), he is well supported by Richard Metzler. The recording is a shade close but eminently realistic; the tape transfer is slightly drier in sound than the LP.

Vivaldi, Antonio
(1675–1741)

L'Estro armonico (12 concertos), *Op. 3*: complete.
  *** Argo K 119 K 22. Christopher Hogwood, Colin Tilney (harpsichords and organ), Robert Spencer (chitarrone), Academy of St Martin-in-the-Fields, Marriner.

As so often, Marriner directs the Academy in radiant and imaginative performances of baroque music and yet observes scholarly good manners. The delightful use of continuo – lute and organ as well as harpsichord – the sharing of solo honours, and the consistently resilient string-playing of the ensemble make for compelling listening. The recording is immaculate, and it is a positive advantage that the twelve concertos are fitted on to four sides, since Vivaldi in effect grouped them in four sets of three. The transfer is made at a very high level, and although it has striking presence and sophisticated detail, the upper range in *tutti* is marginally less sweet and refined than on disc, though the loss is not serious enough to prevent a firm recommendation.

L'Estro armonico, Op. 3: Violin concerto No. 6 in A minor; Double violin concerto No. 8 in A minor; Violin concerto No. 9 in D major; Quadruple violin concerto No. 10 in B minor.

** Philips 7300 526. Henryk Szeryng, Maurice Hasson, Gerard Poulet, Claire Bernard (violins), ECO, Szeryng.

Immaculate playing, polished, attentive accompaniments, first-class recording; but there is something faceless about the style of the music-making here. The clean lines and the sophistication lack baroque exuberance of spirit, though at times the music springs more fully to life. A disappointing collection, nevertheless, although the tape transfer has splendid immediacy and warmth and is for the most part of demonstration quality, the balance admirably realistic.

L'Estro armonico, Op. 3: Violin concerto No. 6 in A minor; Double violin concerto No. 8 in A minor. Double violin concerto in C minor, P. 436; Violoncello concerto in D minor, P. 287.

  (M)*(*) Rediffusion Royale KROY 2006. Bohdan Warchal, Viliam Dobrucky, Anna Holblingova, Quido Hobling (violins), Juraj Alexander (cello), Slovak CO, Warchal.

L'Estro armonico, Op. 3: Quadruple violin concerto No. 10 in B minor; Concerto No. 11 in D minor for strings. Triple violin concerto in F major, P. 278; Double concerto for violin and violoncello, P. 308.

  (M)*(*) Rediffusion Royale KROY 2010. Soloists, Slovak CO, Warchal.

Bohdan Warchal has already given us a fairly successful tape of *The Four Seasons*, and this pair of cassettes offers groups of string concertos, each including two from *L'Estro armonico* plus two other miscellaneous works. The playing is characteristically alert, the soloists assured, and there is plenty of dynamic contrast. That said, one must add that rhythmically the music-making seems rather metronomic and somewhat lacking in flexibility and resilience. The best performance is Bohdan Warchal's own of the *Violin concerto*, Op. 3/6, where the expressive solo contribution in the slow movement is memorable. But elsewhere the music tends to jog along (spiritedly, to be sure) in a somewhat unimaginative fashion. The recording is very bright and forward, with somewhat grainy string textures, emphasized by the tape transfer, which needs a strong treble cut if it is to sound natural in timbre. Neither cassette liner provides sufficient documentation, and (as on other issues in this Royale series) there is no information about the music itself.

Trial between Harmony and Invention (12 violin concertos), *Op. 8:* complete.

    (*) Telefunken MH 435386. Alice Harnoncourt (violin), Jürg Schaeftlein (oboe), Vienna Concentus Musicus (using original instruments), Harnoncourt.

(i) *Trial between Harmony and Invention;* (ii) *Flute concerto in D major, RV. 429;* (iii) *Violoncello concerto in B minor, RV. 424.*

    (*) CRD CRD 4025 (Nos. 1–4; see also below); CRD 4048 (Nos. 5–10); CRD 4049 (Nos. 11–12; Flute and cello concertos). English Consort (using original instruments), Pinnock, with (i) Simon Standage (violin); (ii) Stephen Preston (flute); (iii) Anthony Pleeth (cello).

The first four concertos of Op. 8 are a set within a set, forming what is (deservedly) Vivaldi's most popular work, *The Four Seasons*. Their inspirational force and their eloquence and tunefulness tend to dwarf the remaining eight concertos, but there is some splendid music through-

out the complete work, well worth exploring. The Telefunken box includes one of the most imaginative accounts of *The Four Seasons* to be recorded since Marriner's famous 1970 version (see below). Alice Harnoncourt's timbre is leonine, and her tone production somewhat astringent, bringing out the pithiness of timbre inherent in her baroque instrument (although some of this emphasis is contributed by the brightly lit recording). But the dramatic style of the solo playing is at one with the vivid pictorialism of Vivaldi's imagery. The shepherd's dog in *Spring* barks vociferously, and the dance rhythms of the finale of the same concerto are extremely invigorating. The interpretative approach throughout emphasizes the element of contrast. The languorous opening of *Summer* makes a splendid foil for the storm and the buzzing insects, yet the zephyr breezes are wistfully gentle. The continuo uses a chamber organ, to great effect, and piquant touches of colour are added to the string textures, which are rather grainy, although the quality seems to mellow on the second tape. Concertos Nos. 9 and 12 are played on the tape by Jürg Schaeftlein, who makes a first-class contribution, and this choice of instrumentation further varies the colouring of Vivaldi's score. The transfer is made on chromium dioxide tape and the wide frequency range is very obvious: indeed there is too much brilliance in the treble, and even with the controls in use a degree of edge remains on the sound picture. Otherwise the recording is very sophisticated and secure, with a silent background. There is an excellent booklet of notes, clearly printed.

The CRD version of *The Four Seasons* is also a highly imaginative one and like the Telefunken set features a baroque violin. As this tape was issued separately, in advance of the other two, it is considered below with the other cassettes containing the first four concertos only. On disc the two remaining records of this set were issued in a double-sleeve, but the three cassettes are all individually packaged. Because six concertos are fitted on the second tape, the third is able to include two bonus concertos, of which the *Flute concerto* is particularly attractive. The performances throughout are alert and full of character, with eloquent slow movements. As on the Telefunken set, there is a quality of astringency to the sound (although the treble is bright rather than edgy) which emphasizes the neat, scaled-down imagery. The acoustic is comparatively dry, and although here too a chamber organ is used in the continuo to add extra touches of colour, there is little suggestion of fantasy or Mediterranean glow. Nevertheless these are undoubtedly distinguished performances even if they are perhaps over-serious in their presentation of music that was designed primarily to entertain. The transfers are immaculately clean and clear, if not especially rich.

The Four Seasons, Op. 8/1–4 (from *Trial between Harmony and Invention*).

> *** Argo KZRC 654 [id.]. Alan Loveday, Academy of St Martin-in-the-Fields, Marriner.
>
> (M) *** Decca Jubilee KJBC 63 [Lon. 5-6809]. Konstanty Kulka, Stuttgart CO, Münchinger.
>
> *** CRD CRD 4025. Simon Standage, English Consort, Pinnock (see also above).
>
> (B) *** Philips Fontana 7327 003. Astorre Ferrari, Stuttgart Soloists, Couraud.
>
> (M) *** DG Privilege 3318 042. Wolfgang Schneiderhan, Lucerne Festival Strings, Baumgartner.
>
> *** DG 3300 300 [id.]. Michel Schwalbé, Berlin PO, Karajan.
>
> **(*) HMV TC-ASD 3293 [Angel

4xs 37053]. Itzhak Perlman, LPO.

> (M) **(*) Turnabout KTVC 34040. Susanne Lautenbacher, Württemberg CO, Faerber.
>
> (B) **(*) DG Heliodor 3348 005. Monique Frasca-Colombier, Kuentz CO, Kuentz.
>
> (B) **(*) Classics for Pleasure TC-CFP 40016. Kenneth Sillito, Virtuosi of England, Davison.
>
> **(*) Philips 7300 527 [id.]. Felix Ayo, Berlin CO, Negri.
>
> (M) ** Rediffusion Royale KROY 2001. Bohdan Warchal, Slovak CO.
>
> ** Philips 7300 176. Felix Ayo, I Musici.
>
> *(*) CBS 40-73097 [Col. MT 31798]. Pinchas Zukerman, ECO.
>
> (M) *(*) Saga CA 5443. Giuliano Badini, Sinfonia di Siena – ALBINONI: *Adagio.* *
>
> (M) * RCA Gold Seal RK 25061. Ralph Holmes, Cantilena, Shepherd.
>
> * CBS 40-76717. John Holloway, La Grande Écurie et la Chambre du Roy, Malgoire.

With eighteen recordings already available on cassette (including James Galway's transcription for flute: see below) it seems incredible that Vivaldi's masterpiece remained almost unknown and unperformed after his death until Münchinger's pioneering early LP record, with Rudolf Barchet as soloist, once more brought it before the musical public in 1951. Even today it is a work much more frequently heard in recordings than in the concert hall. The Academy of St Martin's gives a magical performance, with an element of fantasy that makes the music sound utterly new. The continuo, for example (beautifully played by Simon Preston), uses a wide variety of tone colour, and for the slow movement of *Winter*, with its pizzicato accompaniment under a rich violin arioso, Preston switches to the organ and avoids confusion of texture. The opulence of string tone – helped by the acoustic of St John's, Smith Square, where the recording was made – will be too romantic for some, but there is no self-indulgence in this interpretation, no sentimentality, for the contrasts are made sharper and fresher, not smoothed over. The rustic dance which ends *Spring*, for example, has rarely if ever sounded so light and pointed. On disc the recording is of demonstration quality; the transfer to tape was an early one and opens with gleaming, bright strings. The sound is generally good throughout, although by the highest Argo standards the consistency of quality is not absolute, and side two is less clean and refined than side one. Nevertheless this remains a top recommendation.

Münchinger and the Stuttgart Chamber Orchestra, whose early LPs did so much to reawaken interest in Vivaldi, here show that their stylish and lively manner is as compelling as ever, helped by vivid recording. Though this is brighter than many versions, it stands as one of the most satisfying. The cassette, like the disc, offers first-class sound; the transfer is fresh and transparent, the continuo and inner detail coming through naturally. At Jubilee price this is a bargain.

The CRD performance is certainly an individual one. Simon Standage uses a baroque violin and the rest of the string group play 'authentic' instruments, while Trevor Pinnock directs from the harpsichord. As might be expected, the continuo comes through most successfully and yet not too insistently, providing extra colour as well as decoration. The slow movement of *Autumn*, where the harpsichord plays simple arpeggios against the sustained strings, is most beautiful. But essentially this is a dramatic performance strongly characterized. That is well illustrated by the *Adagio* of

Summer, where the soloist is songfully poised while the bustling strings threaten the approaching storm, which when it arrives has the fury of a tempest. This same vigour produces elsewhere tempi that verge on being too fast, but the vivacity is never in doubt and the dark colouring from the lower strings in *tutti* is another mark of the special character of this account. The transfer is admirably vivid and clear, although the treble needs just a little softening. When this is done the textures are clean and transparent.

The bargain-priced Fontana reissue has a great deal to offer. Neither soloist nor orchestra plays with the final degree of polish, but there is striking commitment to the music throughout. Witness the short slow movement of *Autumn*, where the intensity is beautifully controlled, or indeed the vigour of any of the allegros, where the players' enjoyment is obvious. The music-making is helped by the excellent recording, smooth and warm yet vivid, giving Ferrari a gleaming tonal line, and enough detail for the orchestra without spotlighting any lack of precision. With such good sound and genuine stylistic sympathy this is very competitive. The cassette transfer is demonstration-worthy in its crisp immediacy and detail, with no lack of body.

Schneiderhan's fine performance has transferred to tape with great success. The quality is highly sophisticated, with a really beautiful orchestral string sound and a realistic balance. The timbre of the soloist is beautifully caught, and the lack of bass noticeable on the equivalent LP seems less apparent here. However, the LP offers an extra item, a violin concerto from *L'Estro armonico* (Op. 3/11); but although the cassette contains only the main work, it remains competitive. Schneiderhan's tempi are lively, and the whole performance has fine spontaneity as well as excellent detail.

Michel Schwalbé is a truly memorable soloist. His playing is neat, precise and wonderfully musical, with a touch of Italian sunshine in the tone. His sparkling playing is set against radiant Berlin Philharmonic string textures, and the engineers appear to have damped down the bass end of the audio spectrum to prevent too cushioned a sound. The tonal beauty of Karajan's conception is not achieved at the expense of vitality, and although the harpsichord hardly comes through, the overall scale is acceptable. Not a conventional account, then, but very rewarding of its kind. The transfer – made at a moderately high level – is not quite as robust in focus and texture as the LP, but the quality is very good and there is no lack of refinement.

The finesse of Perlman as a great violinist is evident from first to last in his account of *The Four Seasons*. Though some will demand more reticence in baroque concertos, Perlman's imagination holds the sequence superbly together, and there are many passages of pure magic, as in the central *Adagio* of *Summer*. With an intimate acoustic, the sound is never inflated but in scale and sharply defined. The cassette transfer, however, is very bright, less refined than the disc.

Lautenbacher's performance is beautifully made. At times her languorous approach misses some of the work's Italianate fire, but the orchestra plays with fine freshness and makes a good foil for her polished if sometimes slightly too relaxed manner. The recording is really first-rate, with gleaming tone for the soloist and splendid richness and clarity combined. This is an outstanding cassette in every way and excellent value at the price asked.

The Heliodor issue is another bargain-price version which is excellent value for money. The soloist, Monique Frasca-Colombier, plays nimbly and is thoroughly musical. The timbre of the solo violin (small-toned but not thin) is bright and so are the orchestral strings, while the acoustic is warm but not too resonant for the continuo to come through. Throughout the playing has plenty of character, and the cassette transfer, like the disc, offers excellent quality, transparent yet with no lack of body.

An enjoyable performance from Arthur Davison and the Virtuosi of England, marked by assured solo playing from Sillito. He is balanced rather too far forward, which detracts from gentler expressiveness, but otherwise the sound is vivid and clear; this is excellent value at CFP price. The transfer is one of the best from this label, smooth and firm, with plenty of body and no lack of life and detail.

With a talented group from East Berlin Felix Ayo secures playing of microscopic precision, and the string tone is sweet and resonant. It remains a solid middle-of-the-road version, marred only by one or two miscalculations, as in the very fast opening of *Winter* and occasional squeezed tone in lyrical slow movements. Warm recording, and a faithful cassette transfer producing a sense of cosiness in its richness of texture.

Warchal's performance with the Slovak Chamber Orchestra has plenty of character. The soloist plays cleanly and produces fine tone; his avoidance of romanticism is in no way clinical, and there is some luminous playing from orchestra and continuo in the slow movements (that of *Autumn* most memorable). The rhythms of the allegros are crisp and buoyant, and the high-level transfer brings vividness but no lack of refinement. This is good value, though the effect of the recording is less sophisticated than the cheaper Ferrari Fontana issue.

Felix Ayo's performance with I Musici dates from the beginning of the sixties, but the warm, reverberant recording still sounds well. This will be enjoyed by those for whom richness of sound is paramount, even at the cost of vitality. Felix Ayo produces lovely tone throughout and he plays as stylishly as ever. The transfer has a fairly low level on side one (with an attendant degree of hiss); side two is slightly brighter and brings more detail and immediacy. This issue seems uncompetitive at full price.

Zukerman's recording comes from his complete set of Op. 8, of which only *The Four Seasons* has been issued on tape. The performance brings out all the music's drama, and the expressive qualities of the playing are in no doubt. On side one the transfer is agreeable but has a limited range, and the treble is subdued, lacking bite (although the continuo still comes through). The level on side two is slightly higher, giving the sound rather more impact but also less refinement.

Giuliano Badini on Saga proves an excellent soloist, and he is given a spirited accompaniment. The slow movement of *Winter* is a highlight, but *Autumn* and *Summer* too have plenty of character. The sound is resonant, the frequency range comparatively restricted. The side break comes after the slow movement of *Summer*; side two seems marginally fresher than side one, but generally the quality will be acceptable on a small player.

Ralph Holmes is also an excellent soloist; his lyrical style is very appealing, and he is supported by a good continuo player, who is especially impressive in the slow movement of *Autumn*. But the orchestral recording is rather resonant, and the allegros are somewhat clouded by the acoustic. Although this is an enjoyable version, it is not among the finest available. Moreover the transfer is not very sophisticated, with a glare on the treble and (on our copy) some curious peaky distortion on the upper partials of the solo violin.

At full price the version by John Holloway and La Grande Écurie et la Chambre du Roy is not competitive. It is another 'authentic performance' but the rather meagre textures are not given enough dramatic contrast by the recording. The soloist plays well, but this reading lacks the degree of imagination shown in the CRD version, or by Harnoncourt in the Telefunken complete set (see above). The transfer lacks range and immediacy, although the sound is pleasant enough.

The Four Seasons, Op. 8/1–4 (arr. for flute and strings).
> *(**) RCA RK 25034 [LRK 1 2284]. James Galway (flute), I Solisti di Zagreb.

James Galway's transcription is thoroughly musical and so convincing that at times one is tempted to believe that the work was conceived in this form. The playing itself is marvellous, full of detail and imagination, and the recording is good, even if the flute is given too forward a balance. The cassette transfer is acceptable but over-bright, without the supporting richness of middle and lower frequencies that gives warmth to the LP. However, with the treble cut back and the bass increased, an acceptable if not absolutely refined sound can be achieved.

La Cetra (12 violin concertos), *Op. 9*: complete.
> *** Argo K 99 K 33. Iona Brown (violin), Academy of St Martin-in-the-Fields.

Iona Brown, for some years now the leader of the St Martin's Academy, here acts as director in the place of Neville Marriner. From the resilience and imagination of the results one would hardly detect any difference from the immaculate and stylish Vivaldi playing in earlier Academy issues. The recording is outstandingly vivid even by Argo standards and the tape transfer is of demonstration quality. The treble is softer-grained than on some earlier Argo issues of Telemann and Vivaldi, and the full richness and amplitude of the sound are accommodated naturally. The continuo, whether harpsichord or chamber organ, comes through subtly. The concertos are spaced over two cassettes (three to a side) as against three discs.

Flute concertos, Op. 10, Nos 1 in F major (La Tempesta di mare), P.261; 2 in G minor (La Notte), P.342; 3 in D major (Il Cardellino), P.155; 4 in G major, P.104; 5 in F major, P.262; 6 in G major, P.105.

(M) *(*) Turnabout KTVC 34023. Jean-Pierre Rampal (flute), Robert Veyron-Lacroix (harpsichord continuo), Louis de Froment Chamber Ens.

Jean-Pierre Rampal plays with style and expertise, but his accompaniment lacks something in body, although it sounds less meagre here than on the equivalent disc. The continuo (an imaginative one, as it happens) is also recorded too close to the microphones. However, the transfer is secure and can be made to yield an acceptable balance.

Concertos for diverse instruments

Flute concertos: in D major, P.205/ RV.429; in G major, RV.435; Sopranino recorder concerto in C major, P.79/RV.443; Treble recorder concertos: in A minor, P.77/RV.108; in F major, RV.434.

*** HMV TC-ASD 3554. Hans-Martin Linde (flute or recorder), Prague CO.

Hans-Martin Linde, the West German flautist, has an attractively fresh tone both on the flute and on the two sizes of recorder he uses for three of the concertos here. Only two of the regular Op. 10 works are included – No. 4 was one expressly written for transverse flute, and No. 5 was expressly written for treble recorder as it is played here. Rhythmically lively, Linde is splendidly accompanied by the excellent strings of the Prague Chamber Orchestra, with the accompaniments slightly scaled down for the piquant sounds of the sopranino recorder. The whole effect is highly engaging, and although the recording on tape is not quite so warm and rounded as on disc, it is bright and full; with a slight

treble smoothing it can be made to yield a clean, realistic sound picture, admirably suited to the music.

Double horn concerto in F major, P.320.

(M) (**) Turnabout KTVC 34078. Alois Spach, Gottfried Roth, Mainz CO, Kehr – ROSETTI: *Concerto;* TELEMANN: *Suite.*(*)

The *Double horn concerto* is characteristic, with an imaginative and very striking finale. It receives here an excellent performance, but the recording has been very coarsely transferred to tape, and there is roughness throughout.

Lute concerto in D major, P.209.

** RCA RK 11673 [RK 1052]. Julian Bream, Julian Bream Consort – BRITTEN: *Courtly dances;* RODRIGO: *Concierto de Aranjuez.***(*)

This is not one of Vivaldi's most memorable concertos, but it is brilliantly played. The actual arrangement and the close placing of the small chamber group give the music-making a curiously modern sound. The transfer is faithful and clean.

Double mandolin concerto in G major, P.133; Mandolin concerto in C major, P.134; Lute concerto in D major, P.209; Trio in G minor for violin, lute and continuo.

(M) **Turnabout KTVC 34153 [CT 2128]. Paul Grund, Artur Rumentsch (mandolins), Anton Stingl (lute), Rudolf Breitschmid (violin), Württemberg CO, Faerber.

An attractively fresh and genial collection of music for lute and mandolin. Vivaldi's invention is not always at its most imaginative here, but the diverse effects of timbre, the lively playing and the warm recording make a good effect. The accompaniment is stylish and the recording has a sense of space, although the soloists are placed well forward. An enjoyable tape, but not to be taken all at once. The transfer is well managed; the balance is quite realistic and the solo instruments are natural in timbre and focus. The resonance brings just a hint of blurring in the orchestral tuttis, but the string sound is pleasingly full, and there is an agreeable overall bloom.

Concertos with organ: *Concerto in due cori for 4 flutes, 4 violins, strings and 2 organs in A major, P.226; Concerto for oboe, violin, organ and strings in C major, P.36; Concertos for violin, organ and strings: in F major, P.274; in D minor, P.311.*

　　*** DG 3300 652. André Isoir (organ), Paul Kuentz CO, Kuentz.

The playing here is spirited and accomplished, and the engineers have produced some excellent quality. The music itself has its share of stock Vivaldi responses, but on the whole the invention is vital enough to hold the listener. The tape transfer is of very good quality, though it seems to emphasize the forward balance of the solo instruments at the expense of the overall dynamic range. But the sound itself is first-class.

Concertos for strings: in D minor (Madrigalesco), P.86; in G major (Alla rustica), P.143; Violin concertos: in D major (L'Inquietudine), P.208; in E major (L'Amoroso), P.246; Double violin concerto in A major, P.28; Sinfonia in B minor (Al Santo Sepolcro), P.21.

　　**(*) DG 3300 207. Soloists, Berlin PO, Karajan.

Karajan relaxes with members of his Berlin orchestra far away from the city on an annual working holiday. The relaxation and enjoyment, coupled with extraordinary refinement of execution, make this a tape which stands out among most Vivaldi offerings, but there is an element of self-indulgence in Karajan's interpretations that may make the result seem too sweet for some tastes, quite apart from scholarly considerations of style. Refined recording to match the performances, which include four memorable nicknamed concertos. The *Sinfonia* is an amazing piece, considering the date of composition. Undoubtedly this is a rewarding and enjoyable collection, and the superb playing tends to sweep reservations aside. The transfer is well balanced but lacks the freedom at both ends of the audio spectrum of the best DG tapes. The bass is rather dry and confined, and the treble, although smooth, lacks range. There is no lack of bloom, however, and the solo instruments are well focused.

Violin concertos: in E minor (Il Favorito), P.106/RV.277; in G major, P.107/RV.308; in D major, P.147/RV.230; in E major (L'Amoroso), P.246/RV.271; in C minor (Il Sospetto), P.419/RV.199.

　　*** HMV TC-ASD 3690. Werner Grobholz (violin), Prague CO, Vajnar.

An outstanding collection. P.106 and P.107 are the more substantial works: their playing time almost equals that of the other three put together. But the C minor work (*Il Sospetto*) has a hauntingly original *Andante*, fascinatingly oblique in its harmonic implications, where the soloist joins the ripieno violins in a sinuous melody that sounds astonishingly modern. Werner Grobholz is especially good in the slow movements, playing the leisurely *arioso* of *Il Favorito* with memorable expressive feeling. He is no less eloquent in the *Largo cantabile* of P.107, where the simple bass continuo accompaniment is beautifully managed. The orchestra plays the outer movements with vigorous warmth, producing the full body of tone that is characteristic of string ensembles from Eastern Europe. The recording is bright, almost completely refined in the upper range, and has plenty of body in this successful transfer.

Violoncello concertos in C major, P.31; in G major, P.120.

*** DG 3300 974 [id.]. Mstislav Rostropovich, Zurich Collegium Musicum, Sacher – BOCCHERINI and TARTINI: *Concertos.****

Performances of great vigour and projection from Rostropovich. The playing is superbly brilliant and immensely strong in character; it may be somewhat large-scale for Vivaldi's two quite short concertos, but undoubtedly every bar of the music comes fully to life. Splendidly lively accompaniments and excellent recording, bright and clean, yet with no lack of depth. The tape transfer too is admirable.

Miscellaneous collections

Bassoon concerto in A minor, P.70; Flute concerto in C minor, P.440; Oboe concerto in F major, P.264; Concerto for 2 oboes, bassoon, 2 horns and violin, P.273.

*** Argo KZRC 839. Martin Gatt (bassoon), William Bennett (flute), Neil Black, Celia Nicklin (oboes), Timothy Brown, Robin Davis (horns), Academy of St Martin-in-the-Fields, Marriner.

This issue will give enormous pleasure. The playing is splendidly alive and characterful, with crisp, clean articulation and well-pointed phrasing, free from over-emphasis. The work for oboes and

horns is agreeably robust; the *A minor Bassoon concerto* has a delightful sense of humour, while the flute and the oboe concertos, if not showing Vivaldi at his most inventive, are still very compelling and worthwhile. The recording is a model of clarity and definition and has striking richness and atmosphere too. This is one of the very finest Vivaldi collections on tape.

Bassoon concerto in A minor, P.70; Concerto in C major for 2 oboes and 2 clarinets, P.73; Concerto in G major for oboe and bassoon, P.129; Oboe concerto in C major, P.41.

(M) ** Turnabout KTVC 34025. Soloists, Gli Accademici di Milano.

This is another Turnabout issue that tends to sound more attractive on tape than on disc. The transfer is smooth and clean, with realistic presence and detail. The balance places the solo instruments too far forward, but the intimacy of the comparatively dry acoustic means that the ear does not rebel at the relatively limited dynamic range. The *Concerto for two oboes and two clarinets* is charming, and even if Vivaldi would not have recognized the sound of the modern instruments, the colouristic effect more than justifies the anachronism. Both the *Oboe concerto* and the work for oboe and bassoon are highly engaging, and although in the *Bassoon concerto* the larger-than-life solo instrument produces a faintly lugubrious effect, the result is humorous rather than grotesque. On the whole the quick movements come off better than the slow ones, where there is a tendency to plod, with the continuo unimaginatively realized. But generally the freshness of Vivaldi's inspiration is readily communicated.

(i) *Flute concertos, Op. 10, Nos. 1 in F major (La Tempesta di mare), P.261; 2 in G minor (La Notte), P.342; 3 in D major (Il Cardellino), P.155. Con-*

certo for strings in D minor (*Madriga-lesco*), *P.86.* (ii) *Double violin concerto in A major* (*Echo*), *P.222. Sonata a quattro for strings in E flat major* (*Al Santo Sepolcro*).

(M) *** Philips Universo 7317 098.
I Musici, with (i) Severino Gazzelloni (flute); (ii) Franco Tamponi, Walter Gallozzi (violins).

This cassette successfully balances a trio of expertly played flute concertos with three generally more expressive works for strings. Gazzelloni's tempestuous scales in Op. 10/2 display bravura of the highest order, and these performances have splendid life and vivacity, though it might have been a better arrangement to alternate the works for flute with those for violins. Certainly the string-playing is of high quality (particularly fine in the *Sonata*), and the echo effects in P.222 are nicely managed. A first-class issue in every way, and splendidly recorded on cassette as on disc, the former being of demonstration standard, with fresh, transparent textures of complete naturalness.

Flute concerto in F major (*La Tempesta di mare*), *Op. 10/1; Double mandolin concerto in G major, P. 133; Oboe concerto in A minor, P.42; Double violin concerto in A minor, P. 28; Violin concerto in E major* (*L'Amoroso*), *P.246.*

*** Philips 7300 387. Gastone Tassinari (flute), G. Vescovo, T. Ruta (mandolins), Leo Driehuys (oboe), Felix Ayo, Roberto Michelucci (violins), I Musici.

As this is a tape-only compilation, it seems perverse that the short first movement of the *Flute concerto* is placed after the two violin concertos at the end of side one, instead of the more sensible course of having the whole work complete on side two. Nevertheless this is a very attractive collection, beautifully recorded. Felix Ayo's performance of *L'Amoroso* is appropriately warm, and a similar richly sensuous style brings the *Double violin concerto* glowingly to life. Yet there is no lack of vitality; the *Flute concerto* makes a refreshingly piquant contrast, and the jolly *Concerto for two mandolins* has an attractive spontaneity. The concert is rounded off with stylish playing from Leo Driehuys in the work for oboe. The transfer is demonstration-worthy throughout.

Double flute concerto in C major, RV.533; Concertos for strings in D minor (*Madrigalesco*), *P. 86/ RV.129; in G major* (*Alla rustica*), *P.143/RV.151; Double trumpet concerto in C major, P.75/RV.537; Double violoncello concerto in G minor, RV.531; Concerto for 2 violins and 2 cellos in D major, RV.564.*

(***) Oiseau-Lyre KDSLC 544.
Academy of Ancient Music, Hogwood.

Not everything in this issue is of equal substance. The invention in the *Double trumpet concerto* is not particularly strong, and on tape the sound is coarsened by too high a transfer level. This persists on side two, if with a less unpleasant effect. The best-known concertos here are the *Madrigalesco* and the *Alla rustica*, but some of the others are no less captivating. The *Concerto for two flutes* has great charm and is decorated with vigour and aplomb. Performances are first-rate throughout, and much of the music demonstrates the imaginative power of this often unexpectedly rewarding composer, whose unpredictability continues to astonish. But until this issue is remastered at a lower level, readers would do better with the equivalent disc.

Double horn concerto in F major, P.321; Double oboe concerto in D minor, P.302; Concerto in F major for 2 oboes, bassoon, 2 horns and violin, P.319; Piccolo concerto in C major, P.79.

*** Argo KZRC 840. Soloists, Academy of St Martin-in-the-Fields, Marriner.

The musical substance may not be very weighty, but Vivaldi was rarely more engaging than when, as here, he was writing for wind instruments, particularly when he has more than one in his team. This delectable collection makes a splendid supplement to the earlier one from the Academy (KZRC 839: see above). The transfer is of very good quality if perhaps slightly less consistently fresh and open than the companion tape. The delightful *Piccolo concerto* performance with its surprising element of fantasy comes off best (this offers demonstration quality); the sound in the opening *Double horn concerto* seems to have marginally less range. An enchanting collection all the same.

Piccolo concertos: in C major, P.78; in A minor, P.83; Concerto in D minor for viola d'amore and lute, P.266; Viola d'amore concerto in D minor.

(M) ** Turnabout KTVC 34009. Soloists, Württemberg CO, Faerber.

An enjoyable collection of Vivaldi concertos, featuring two bright little works for piccolo, in which Hans-Martin Linde proves an admirable soloist. The less robust sounds of lute and viola d'amore offer a complete contrast to the piccolo, and both these *D minor Concertos* are attractive. The chamber orchestra, like the soloists, is well recorded. The transfer is generally good: Linde's sopranino recorder is beautifully caught; but the viola d'amore is a little lacking in presence, and the orchestral string tone sometimes gives a slightly subfusc impression.

(i) *Piccolo concerto in C major, P.79;* (ii) *Concerto in D minor for viola d'amore and lute, P.266;* (iii; v) *Double violin concerto in A major (Echo), P.222;* (iv; v) *Violoncello concerto in E minor.*

(M) **(*)DG Privilege 3335 200.
(i) Hans-Martin Linde (sopranino recorder), Emil Seiler CO, Hofmann; (ii) Monique Frasca-Colombier (viola d'amore), Narciso Yepes (guitar), Paul Kuentz CO, Kuentz; (iii) Walter Prystawski, Herbert Höver (violins); (iv) Pierre Fournier (cello); (v) Lucerne Festival Strings, Baumgartner.

The *Cello concerto* is an arrangement by Vincent d'Indy and Paul Bazelaire of a sonata for solo cello, and a very good concerto it makes, played here by Fournier with élan and obvious enjoyment. The *Double concerto in D minor* also makes an alteration to Vivaldi's original, very effectively substituting a guitar for the lute. It is an excellent performance, as is that of the *Echo concerto*, which has rather more subtlety and delicacy of phrasing than in the I Musici version (on Philips Universo 7317 098: see above). However, on tape the Philips recording has more body and firmness of texture, without loss of transparency of detail. Hans-Martin Linde is in excellent form: his playing in P.79 is perkily vivacious. Generally the Privilege transfer is well managed and truthful, if not so strikingly fresh as the Philips I Musici cassette.

CHORAL MUSIC

Beatus vir; Gloria in D major.
*(*) CBS 40-76596. Mary Burgess, Jocelyn Chamonin (sopranos), Carolyn Watkinson (contralto), Raphael Passaquet Vocal Ens., La Grande Écurie

et la Chambre du Roy, Malgoire.

Gloria in D major.

(*) Argo KZRC 505. Elizabeth Vaughan (soprano), Janet Baker (contralto), King's College Choir, Academy of St Martin-in-the-Fields, Willcocks – PERGOLESI: *Magnificat.*(*)

(M)*(*) Turnabout KTVC 34029. Friederike Sailer (soprano), Margarethe Bence (contralto), Stuttgart Pro Musica Choir and Orch., Couraud – MOZART: *Benedictus sit Deus; Exsultate jubilate.**

Gloria in D major; Magnificat (ed. Malipiero).

(**) HMV TC-ASD 3418. Teresa Berganza (mezzo-soprano), Lucia Valentini-Terrani (contralto), New Philharmonia Chorus and Orch., Muti.

(i) *Gloria in D major;* (ii) *Nulla in mondo pax sincera.*

*** Oiseau-Lyre KDSLC 554. Christ Church Cathedral Choir, Oxford, Academy of Ancient Music, Preston, with (i) Judith Nelson (soprano), Carolyn Watkinson (contralto); (ii) Emma Kirkby (soprano).

Magnificat (short choral version).

** Argo KZRC 854. King's College Choir, Academy of St Martin-in-the-Fields, Ledger – BACH: *Magnificat.***

The freshness and point of the Christ Church performance of Vivaldi's *Gloria* are irresistible, and anyone who normally doubts the attractiveness of authentic string technique should sample this; here the absence of *vibrato* adds a tang exactly in keeping with the performance. The soloists too keep *vibrato* to the minimum, adding to the freshness, yet Carolyn Watkinson rivals even Dame Janet Baker in the dark intensity of the central Bach-like aria for contralto, *Domine Deus, Agnus Dei*. The choristers of Christ Church Cathedral excel themselves, and the recording is of excellent quality, though on cassette there is a degree of thickness of texture in the choral fortissimos. The solo motet provided as coupling has Emma Kirkby coping splendidly with the bravura writing for soprano and singing the expressive music with an eloquent line and memorable tonal beauty. The recording here, on tape and disc, is of demonstration quality.

Malgoire has the virtue of commitment and spirit, and if the singing were better and the orchestral playing a little more polished this would be recommendable. Period instruments are used, but surely the wind intonation need not be as awry as it is. Despite their vitality and robustness, these performances are not really satisfying enough to suffer repeated hearing, even though there are some stylish touches. As far as recording is concerned, the CBS acoustic is not quite expansive enough for comfort, and the cassette transfer, although quite well balanced, is limited in range. This is most striking on side one; the level rises on side two (the break comes between the *Domine Fili* and the *Domine Deus, Agnus Dei* of the *Gloria*), but although this makes the sound more vivid, it then loses refinement of focus.

The Argo version of the *Gloria* is much to be preferred. It uses comparatively small forces, and save for the occasional trace of preciosity it is very stylish indeed. It has an excellent team of soloists and is very well recorded. The transfer is of characteristically sophisticated Argo quality. There is a very slight blurring of the focus of the choir by the King's acoustic, but the solo voices have a natural presence and the overall balance is excellent. The orchestral introduction is arresting in its vividness, with splendid attack in the strings, beautifully caught. Some might feel that the exaggerated consonants are tiresome, but this is unquestionably a most vivid performance.

The Turnabout performance is altogether more homely, with adequate rather than outstanding soloists. However, the simple style of presentation is quite effective. There is no lack of freshness and the recording is good, if not sophisticated. The balance places the orchestra well forward, and although the chorus is further back the sound is clear. The high-level transfer is agreeably bright and lacks only the last degree of refinement, comparing favourably with the disc. This would be fair value at medium price, but unfortunately the Mozart coupling is less distinguished.

Although the HMV Muti cassette and the Argo King's coupling with Bach both list Vivaldi's *Magnificat*, these are two quite different versions of the same basic work. Muti offers the more expansive score, including extended solo arias. The Argo recording shares some material, such as the opening chorus, but here the music is on a much smaller scale. Ledger opts for boys' voices in the solos, such as the beautiful duet, *Esurientes*, and though the singers are taxed by ornamentation, the result has all the accustomed beauty of this choir's recordings, set warmly against the chapel's acoustic. This makes a fascinating and attractive coupling for the grander Bach setting of the *Magnificat*. The transfer to tape has been quite well managed but this is not one of Argo's finest cassette issues; the choral sounds are not always outstandingly clear in focus.

Muti's approach, both in the *Magnificat* and in the *Gloria*, is altogether blander than the Argo performances. His expansiveness suits the larger-scaled *Magnificat* (which has transferred quite well, if with no remarkably vivid qualities) better than the *Gloria*, which lacks the incisiveness and freshness of the Argo performance. Moreover on our copy the high-level recording produced

'crumbling' of texture at the opening, and the duet *Laudamus te* had an uncomfortable peakiness.

COLLECTIONS

'Favourite composer': (i) *The Four Seasons, Op. 8/1–4;* (ii) *L'Estro armonico: Concerto in B minor, Op. 3/10;* (iii) *Flute concerto in G minor (La Notte), Op. 10/2;* (iv; v) *Bassoon concerto in A minor, P.70/RV.498;* (vi) *Concerto for strings in G major (Alla rustica), P.143/RV.151;* (vii; v) *Double trumpet concerto in C major, P.75/RV.537;* (viii) *Gloria in D major.*

(B) *** Decca KDPC 609/10. (i) Stuttgart CO, Münchinger; (ii) Moscow CO, Barshai; (iii) Stephen Preston (flute), Academy of Ancient Music, Hogwood; (iv) Martin Gatt (bassoon); (v) Academy of St Martin-in-the-Fields, Marriner; (vi) Lucerne Festival Strings, Baumgartner; (vii) John Wilbraham, Philip Jones (trumpets); (viii) soloists, King's College Choir, Academy of St Martin-in-the-Fields, Willcocks.

An outstandingly generous set, which can be cordially recommended on all counts. The *Four Seasons* is Münchinger's latest recording (1974), with Konstanty Kulka as the stylish soloist, and the other performances are all first-rate, with the bassoon and flute concertos as highlights. The recording is of consistently excellent quality, and the transfer (although very bright and needing a little taming) is vivid and detailed, only slipping a little in refinement in the *Concerto for two trumpets*. The *Gloria*, however, is especially successful, the choral sound sounding fresher here than on the full-priced Argo tape from which it comes (see above). This set would make a splendid basis for any Vivaldi collection.

'The world of Vivaldi': (i) *The Four Seasons: Spring, Op. 8/1;* (ii) *Flute concerto in G minor (La Notte), Op. 10/2;* (iii) *Concerto in G major for strings (Alla rustica), P.143;* (iv; v) *Double trumpet concerto in C major, P.75;* (v; vi) *Quadruple violin concerto in B minor, Op. 3/10;* (vii) *Gloria in D major:* excerpts.

(M) *(*) Decca KCSP 526. (i) Werner Krotzinger (violin), Stuttgart CO, Münchinger; (ii) Stephen Preston (flute), Academy of Ancient Music, Hogwood; (iii) Lucerne Festival Strings, Baumgartner; (iv) John Wilbraham, Philip Jones (trumpets); (v) Academy of St Martin-in-the-Fields, Marriner; (vi) Alan Loveday, Carmel Kaine, soloists; (vii) King's College Choir, Academy of St Martin-in-the-Fields, Willcocks.

This is a less attractive collection than it looks. It opens with *Spring* from the rather staid, Germanic account of *The Four Seasons* recorded by Münchinger in the early days of stereo, which was less successful than his 1951 mono version, and which he later superseded. The recording in this tape transfer lacks freshness, and it is even less well focused in the excerpts from the *Gloria*. Side two generally sounds fresher than side one and contains the most memorable performance here, the splendidly regal account of the *Double trumpet concerto,* with very distinguished soloists and the St Martin's Academy on top form. The concerto from *L'Estro armonico,* Op. 3/10, is also successfully transferred, although the volume needs to come up a bit after the

trumpet work if the recording is not to sound a trifle bland. Stephen Preston's performance of *La Notte* uses an early instrument for authenticity. (Incidentally, as a sampler this issue fails in its purpose, as nearly all the records from which the performances are taken have not been transferred to tape.)

Wagner, Richard (1813–83)

Siegfried idyll.

*** DG 3370 023 [id.]. Berlin PO, Karajan – BRUCKNER: *Symphony No. 7.****

*** Decca KCET 2 7046 (original scoring). Vienna PO, Solti – BRUCKNER: *Symphony No. 7.***

(M) **(*) World Records TC-SH 287. Philharmonia Orch., Cantelli – TCHAIKOVSKY: *Romeo and Juliet.***(*)

Karajan uses a full body of strings and secures some splendidly rich and radiant playing from the Berlin Philharmonic Orchestra. There is no finer recorded performance currently available, and the tape transfer has fine body and detail. A most successful issue.

So rich is the sound Decca provide for Solti that one never has any sense of asceticism in the original scoring, and the playing is similarly warm and committed. Only in the central climax does one feel the need for a larger body of strings, but the reading as a whole is so compelling that criticism is confounded. The transfer is of first-class quality.

Cantelli's performance was recorded in the wake of his first London season with the Philharmonia Orchestra in 1951. *Siegfried idyll* was first issued on 78s in the following year and was highly acclaimed. Andrew Porter thought it sublime, and the late Eric Blom wrote that he could never hope on this earth to hear a more heavenly performance. They were right. It is beautifully shaped, tender and eloquent, and though there are other magnificent performances, from Furtwängler, Walter and Karajan, this eloquent reading holds its own with any of them. The recording is beautifully blended and betrays relatively few signs of its age. Of course it is not quite as expansive as recordings made a few years later, but the balance is impeccably judged. On tape the quality is full and clear, only marginally less fresh and secure than the LP.

Siegfried idyll; Lohengrin: Prelude to Act 1; Die Meistersinger: Prelude to Act 1; Tristan und Isolde: Prelude and Liebestod.

(M) *** DG Privilege 3335 212. Berlin PO, Kubelik.

This is an outstanding tape, beautifully balanced and totally free from distortion. Although the transfer level is not quite as high as it might be, the fresh liveliness of the treble response means that some degree of treble cut is possible without taking the bloom away from the pianissimos in the *Lohengrin Prelude* and the *Siegfried idyll*. The slightly dry bass means that the *Meistersinger Prelude* is clean in detail as well as having impressive weight. There is some marvellous playing from the Berlin Philharmonic. Kubelik's readings are expansive and relaxed rather than gripping, but the *Siegfried idyll*, if a little cool at the opening, is beautifully shaped and, like the *Tristan* and *Meistersinger Preludes*, is built to a satisfying climax.

Der fliegende Holländer: overture; Götterdämmerung: Siegfried's Rhine journey; Siegfried's funeral music; Lohengrin: Preludes to Acts 1

and 3; Die Meistersinger: Prelude to Act 1; Dance of the apprentices and Entry of the masters; Parsifal: Prelude to Act 1; Das Rheingold: Entry of the Gods into Valhalla; Rienzi: overture; Siegfried: Forest murmurs; Tannhäuser: overture; Prelude to Act 3; Tristan: Prelude and Liebestod; Die Walküre: Ride of the Valkyries.

(M) *(**) HMV TC-SLS 5075. Philharmonia Orch., Klemperer.

In the tape age bleeding chunks of Wagner would seem less appropriate, although the already large (and growing) collection of purely orchestral excerpts suggests an equally wide public for this kind of issue. Certainly Klemperer's readings, solidly concentrated, are characterful enough to stand presentation in a box like this. The six sides present a fascinating comment on the composer. Generally good, atmospheric recording. The tape transfers are of mixed quality. Often the sound is very good: the first tape, with *Rienzi*, *The Flying Dutchman*, *Tannhäuser* (very impressive) and the *Prelude to Act 1* of *Lohengrin*, is the best, although there is a hint of pulsing in the sustained string tone in the last piece. The *Prelude to Act 3* of *Lohengrin* and the *Meistersinger overture* also generally sound well, but elsewhere there are moments when the refinement slips; and on the third tape there is serious coarseness in the *Entry of the Gods into Valhalla* and *Siegfried's Rhine Journey*.

Der fliegende Holländer: overture; Lohengrin: Preludes to Acts 1 and 3; Die Meistersinger: Prelude to Act 1; Tristan und Isolde: Prelude and Liebestod.

**(*) Decca KSXC 6656. Vienna PO, Stein.

A brilliant attempt to get the full panoply of Wagnerian orchestration on to cassette. The transfer is full in body and wide in range, and the level is high. The sound is not entirely free from congestion, but usually there is only a hint, and many machines will produce spectacular results. The performances are marvellously vivid and rich, intense and spontaneous: the only miscalculation is the use of the operatic ending of the *Prelude to Act 3* of *Lohengrin*, which tapers off into *Here comes the bride* instead of the dash of the concert ending used by most conductors. But this is a small blemish when the *Tristan Prelude and Liebestod* is so finely moulded and the *Lohengrin Prelude to Act 1* (an elusive piece in the recording studio) played so radiantly, its great climax so well placed. The *Meistersinger Prelude* is a richly spacious reading, although the *Flying Dutchman overture*, given a similarly broad treatment, has some lack of electricity.

Der fliegende Holländer: overture; Die Meistersinger: Prelude to Act 1; Tannhäuser: overture; Tristan: Prelude to Act 1.
  (M) * Supraphon 045134. Czech PO, Konwitschny.

These are distinguished performances. They have consistent spontaneity and electricity, and the playing of the Czech Philharmonic shows splendid fervour in the *Tristan Prelude*; *Die Meistersinger* is spacious yet has plenty of momentum. The recording too is warmly atmospheric, and it is a pity that its resonance has meant a lack of clarity and brilliance in these transfers. Side one (including *Tannhäuser* and *Die Meistersinger*) seriously lacks range in the treble, and although the level rises on side two and brings greater vividness, the quality could not be described as sparkling or refined.

Der fliegende Holländer: overture; Die Meistersinger: Prelude to Act 1; Tannhäuser: overture (original version); *Tristan und Isolde: Prelude and Liebestod.*

*(**) Decca KSXC 6856 [Lon. 5-7078]. Chicago SO, Solti.

The recording of the *Flying Dutchman overture* comes from Solti's complete set and sounds rather fierce in the present tape transfer. *Die Meistersinger*, previously used as a (somewhat unlikely) coupling for the Decca cassette of Elgar's *Second Symphony*, sounds more substantial. The powerful reading of the Dresden version of *Tannhäuser* has its intensity sharpened by the very brilliant sound, and in general here the treble needs softening if it is not to seem overbright. In the *Tristan Prelude and Liebestod* Solti shows more tenderness than in his performance within the complete set (see below), but again the recording quality tends to overintensify the effect of the music-making; and on two copies we tried there was a hint of unsteady 'pulsing' in the sustained string textures.

(i; ii) *Der fliegende Holländer: overture;* (ii; iii) *Rienzi: overture;* (iv–vi) *Tannhäuser: overture and Venusberg music;* (v; vii) *Die Walküre: Ride of the Valkyries.*
  (M)*(*)Decca KCSP 468. (i) New Philharmonia Orch.; (ii) Paita; (iii) Netherlands Radio PO; (iv) LSO Chorus; (v) LSO; (vi) Leinsdorf; (vii) Stokowski.

This collection is notable for Leinsdorf's performance of the *Tannhäuser overture and Venusberg music* (a sumptuous version with chorus) and Carlos Paita's excellent account of the *Rienzi overture*. The other two items are less impressive, and the recording of the *Flying Dutchman overture* has one or two rough moments; but the transfer is otherwise quite well managed.

Götterdämmerung: Dawn and Siegfried's Rhine journey; Siegfried's funeral music; Siegfried: Forest murmurs; Tannhäuser: Prelude to Act 3;

661

Tristan und Isolde: Prelude to Act 3; Die Walküre: Ride of the Valkyries.
*(*) HMV TC-ASD 2934. LPO, Boult.

In the last analysis this is a disappointing collection. It is for the most part finely played, but too often the electricity is missing, and even *Forest murmurs* lacks atmosphere. The most striking performance is the beautiful original version of Wagner's *Prelude to Act 3, Tannhäuser*. This is a comparatively extended synthesis of the motifs associated with Elisabeth; the orchestration is gentle and evocative, and Boult presents it with a simple eloquence which is extremely effective. However, the characterization elsewhere is less sure and *Siegfried's funeral music* has not the breadth that some other conductors find. The recording is generally of good quality, although the first climax of the opening item (*Dawn*) is slightly muddled by the resonance. The tape transfer generally lacks sparkle in the treble, and the engineers have obvious trouble with the bass drum.

Götterdämmerung: Siegfried's Rhine journey; Siegfried's funeral music; Final scene; Das Rheingold; Entry of the gods into Valhalla; Siegfried: Forest murmurs; Die Walküre: Ride of the Valkyries; Wotan's farewell and magic fire music.
**(*) Decca KSXC 6743. National SO of Washington, Dorati.

Dorati's orchestral selection from *The Ring* is essentially dramatic. The *Ride of the Valkyries* comes off especially well, as do the three excerpts from *Götterdämmerung* (with a superbly played horn solo in *Siegfried's Rhine journey*). But in the final scene from *Die Walküre* the lack of the richness and body of string tone that this orchestra can produce limits the effect of Dorati's eloquence; and it is the brass and wind playing one remembers most in the *Das Rheingold* and *Siegfried*

excerpts. Nevertheless, with brilliant Decca sound there is much that is exciting in this collection, and the programme is well balanced. The cassette transfer is of high quality, although compared to the equivalent LP the sound is slightly drier, with marginally less bloom. The recording remains impressive; the big climaxes are caught with no feeling of discomfort.

Lohengrin: Preludes to Acts 1 and 3; Die Meistersinger: Prelude to Act 1; Parsifal: Prelude to Act 1; Tristan und Isolde: Prelude and Liebestod.
*** Philips 7300 391 [id.]. Concertgebouw Orch., Haitink.

Haitink's tape is outstandingly fine, the performances of the highest quality, less sensuous than Karajan's but no less telling. Compared to Karajan's Berlin version (see below), Haitink's climax in the *Lohengrin Prelude to Act 1* is not so finely graduated, but there is a superb sense of drama, and after the riveting brass chords the great cymbal clash is placed unerringly. Haitink's characteristic restraint brings great dignity and nobility to the *Parsifal* excerpts, and undoubtedly his performance of the *Meistersinger* overture is the finest in the current catalogue. At the very opening the recording shows a touch of overresonance, but that is momentary, and the sound generally is wonderfully rich and spacious. The cassette transfer is of excellent quality, offering first-rate Philips sound, and the level is not low considering the richness and body of the recordings. The collection is well planned and ends stirringly with the *Third act Lohengrin Prelude*, complete with concert ending.

(i) *Lohengrin: Preludes to Acts 1 and 3;* (ii) *Parsifal: Prelude and Good Friday music;* (i) *Tannhäuser: overture.*
(B) * DG Heliodor 3348 221. Lam-

oureux Orch., Markevitch; (ii)
Bavarian Radio SO, Jochum.

Markevitch's Lamoureux performances are very much Wagner with a French accent, and the recording lacks the full amplitude one needs in this music, notably in *Tannhäuser*, which sounds rather meagre. Jochum's account of the *Parsifal* excerpts is justly famous; unfortunately the tape transfer loses some of the amplitude of the disc and the brass tends to sound brash. Also at the opening of the *Lohengrin Prelude to Act 1* there is some slight discoloration of the upper partials, while the *Third act Prelude* lacks body and substance.

Lohengrin: Prelude to Act 1; Tannhäuser: overture and Venusberg music; Tristan und Isolde: Prelude and Liebestod.
*** HMV TC-ASD 3130 [Angel 4xs 37097]. Chorus of German Opera, Berlin, Berlin PO, Karajan.

These Karajan performances are in a class of their own. The body of tone produced by the Berlin Philharmonic gives a breathtaking richness to the climaxes. That of the *Lohengrin prelude* is superbly graduated, and in the *Tristan Liebestod* the orgasmic culmination is quite overwhelming. The same superb sense of timing and spaciousness is applied to the *Tannhäuser overture and Venusberg music*. If you want this selection there is no need to look elsewhere, for EMI's sound is first-class, though on the otherwise spectacular tape the massed strings show a hint of the 'pulsing' beat that seems to afflict some cassettes. However, this may have been cured on later copies.

VOCAL MUSIC

Das Liebesmahl der Apostel (cantata).
(*) Symphonica CSYM 11. Ambrosian Male-Voice Chorus, Symphonica of London, Morris – BRUCKNER: *Helgoland*.*

The disappointment of Wyn Morris's account of Wagner's strange Pentecostal cantata, written originally for massed choirs in Dresden at a time when he was composing *Tannhäuser*, is that the male chorus sounds comparatively small, whereas Wagner undoubtedly envisaged a more spectacular effect. With homophonic writing the rule, the squareness and plainness of Wagner's invention are underlined, where ideally one wants a more persuasive manner. But with a fascinating Bruckner coupling, this is still a recording to cherish. The unaccompanied opening sections are splendidly vivid and immediate, helped in this admirable transfer by a recording of remarkable presence and wide dynamic range. As the work expands the chorus recedes within the orchestral framework, and the balance remains attractively spacious if lacking the monumental qualities Wagner obviously intended.

OPERA

Der fliegende Holländer (The Flying Dutchman): complete.
**(*) Decca K 24 K 32 [Lon. 5-13119]. Norman Bailey, Janis Martin, Martti Talvela, René Kollo, Werner Krenn, Isola Jones, Chicago Symphony Chorus and Orch., Solti.
**(*) DG 3371 017 [id.]. Thomas Stewart, Gwyneth Jones, Karl Ridderbusch, Herman Esser, Harald Elk, Sieglinde Wagner, Bayreuth Festival (1971) Chorus and Orchestra, Boehm.

Solti's first Wagner opera recording in Chicago marks a distinct change from the long series made in Vienna. The playing is superb, the singing cast is generally impressive and the recording is vividly immediate. On tape the quality seems slightly dry in the overture, but when the opera itself begins there is no sense of being confined, in spite of the close balance. The presence of the voices is matched by the brilliance and weight of orchestral tone. What will disappoint some who admire Solti's earlier Wagner sets is that this most atmospheric of Wagner operas is presented with no Culshaw-style production whatever, merely as a concert performance. Characters halloo to one another when evidently standing elbow to elbow, and even the Dutchman's ghostly chorus sounds very close and earthbound. But with Norman Bailey a deeply impressive Dutchman, Janis Martin generally a sweet-toned Senta, Martti Talvela a splendid Daland, and René Kollo, for all his occasional coarseness, an illuminating Erik, it surpasses all current competition (on disc as well as tape). But the break between the two cassettes comes at an inconvenient point, and on at least one copy tried several bars are snipped out. This will probably have been corrected by the time we are in print.

Tape-collectors wanting a real feeling of atmosphere in *Der fliegende Holländer* must at present turn to the alternative set from Boehm, recorded at the 1971 Bayreuth Festival. This too has been vividly transferred to tape, with excellent presence for soloists and chorus alike and a fine bloom on the orchestra. The sense of perspective is much more successfully conveyed, but there are also the usual drawbacks inherent in recording a live performance. The chorus is poorly disciplined in its singing, and its members are distractingly noisy on the stage. Gwyneth Jones sings beautifully in *pianissimo* passages but develops a wobble which worsens as she puts pressure on the voice. Thomas Stewart is better focused in tone than he sometimes is. Boehm's searching interpretation is well worth hearing. The transfer has been made at

quite a high level and considering the warmly resonant acoustic, the detail is excellent, and the upper focus is very good, if not always absolutely clean. Undoubtedly the sense of spontaneity conveyed by this recording makes up to a considerable extent for its defects.

Der fliegende Holländer: highlights.
**(*) Decca KCET 626 (from above set cond. Solti).

The Flying Dutchman lends itself to excerpts more readily than some of Wagner's later operas; but even so *Senta's ballad* is terminated here without a satisfactory cadence and the *Norwegian sailors' chorus* also ends in mid-air. Here too the sound is not very refined, with a degree of blare in the orchestra. On side one the quality is warmer and well focused; but the opera's closing scene is less sweetly focused. Nevertheless the transfer does not lack vividness throughout, and the excerpts show the consistency of the performance and the vibrancy of Solti's direction.

Götterdämmerung: complete.
*** Decca K 4w 32 [Lon. 5-1604]. Birgit Nilsson, Wolfgang Windgassen, Dietrich Fischer-Dieskau, Gottlob Frick, Gustav Neidlinger, Claire Watson, Christa Ludwig, Vienna State Opera Chorus, Vienna PO, Solti.
(M) *** DG 3378 048 [id.], Helga Dernesch, Helge Brilioth, Thomas Stewart, Karl Ridderbusch, Zoltan Keleman, Gundula Janowitz, Christa Ludwig, German Opera Chorus, Berlin, Berlin PO, Karajan – *Das Rheingold.****

In Decca's formidable task of recording the whole *Ring cycle* under Solti, *Götterdämmerung* provided the most daunting challenge of all; but characteristically Solti, and with him the Vienna Philharmonic and the Decca recording team under John Culshaw, were inspired to heights even beyond earlier achievements. Even the trifling objections to earlier issues have been eliminated here. The balance between voices and orchestra has by some magic been made perfect, with voices clear but orchestra still rich and near-sounding. Above all Solti has undoubtedly matured into a warmer and wiser director. He drives hard still, but no longer is there any feeling of over-driving, and even the *Funeral music*, which in Solti's early Covent Garden performances was brutal in its power, is made into a natural not a forced climax. There is not a single weak link in the cast. Nilsson surpasses herself in the magnificence of her singing: even Flagstad in her prime would not have been more masterful as Brünnhilde. As in *Siegfried*, Windgassen is in superb voice; Frick is a vivid Hagen, and Fischer-Dieskau achieves the near-impossible in making Gunther an interesting and even sympathetic character. As for the recording quality, it surpasses even Decca's earlier achievement. No more magnificent set has appeared in the whole history of recording, and Decca have also surpassed themselves in the excellence of the tape transfer, which is wonderfully vivid and clear.

Karajan like Solti before him reserved for the concluding *Ring* opera his finest achievement. His singing cast is marginally even finer than Solti's, and his performance conveys the steady flow of recording sessions prepared in relation to live performances. But ultimately he falls short of Solti's achievement in the orgasmic quality of the music, the quality which finds an emotional peak in such moments as the end of Brünnhilde's and Siegfried's love scene, the climax of the *Funeral music* and the culmination of the *Immolation*. At each of these Karajan is a degree less committed, beautifully as the players respond, and warm as his overall approach is. Dernesch's Brünnhilde is

warmer than Nilsson's, with a glorious range of tone. Brilioth as Siegfried is fresh and young-sounding, while the Gutrune of Gundula Janowitz is far preferable to Claire Watson on Decca. The matching is otherwise very even. The balance of voices in the recording may for some dictate a choice: the DG brings the singers closer, gives less brilliance to the orchestral texture. On tape only. the Karajan *Götterdämmerung* is issued in a 'chunky' box together with *Das Rheingold* at what is virtually bargain price. The transfers are of good quality but made at a generally lower level than the Decca Solti recordings, which are fuller and more vivid in sound. The DG layout, with cassettes covering the two operas, is also less satisfactory than the Decca, which where possible allots a single cassette to each act. The narrow DG libretto booklet is not ideal either, especially in the size of the typeface chosen.

Twilight of the Gods (*Götterdämmerung*): complete (in English).

*** HMV TC-SLS 5118. Rita Hunter, Alberto Remedios, Norman Welsby, Aage Haugland, Derek Hammond Stroud, Margaret Curphey, Katherine Pring, English National Opera Chorus and Orch., Goodall.

Goodall's account of the culminating opera in Wagner's tetralogy may not be the most powerful ever recorded, and certainly it is not the most polished, but it is one which, paradoxically, by intensifying human as opposed to superhuman emotions enhances the epic scale. The very opening may sound a little tentative (like the rest of the Goodall English *Ring*, this was recorded live at the London Coliseum), but it takes no more than a few seconds to register the body and richness of the sound, on tape as well as disc. The occasional slight imprecision and the occasional rawness of wind tone actually seem to enhance the earthiness of Goodall's view with more of the primeval saga about it than the magnificent polished studio-made *Ring* cycles of Solti and Karajan.

In some ways both Rita Hunter and Alberto Remedios were more considerately recorded on the earlier Unicorn version of the final scenes (at one time available on a vivid Pye cassette, but temporarily out of the catalogue), with more bloom on their voices, but their performances here are magnificent in every way. In particular the golden beauty of Remedios's tenor is consistently superb, with no Heldentenor barking at all, while Aage Haugland's Hagen is giant-sounding to focus the evil, with Gunther and Gutrune mere pawns. The voices on stage are in a different, drier acoustic from that of the orchestra, but on tape that helps to give them clarity against the richness of the supporting orchestral tapestry. Considering the problems the balance is very impressive. As for Goodall, with his consistently expansive tempi he carries total concentration – except, curiously, in the scene with the Rhinemaidens, whose music (as in *Rheingold* too) lumbers along heavily here. The transfer, its level obviously carefully calculated to encompass the recording's wide dynamic range, is notable for the warmth and bloom it gives to voices and orchestra alike. The orchestral brass sounds superbly full-blooded and more than compensates for the lack of the vivid brilliance and range in the treble that Decca provide in Wagner. The focus is good and only slips a little in *Siegfried's funeral music* and the Immolation Scene, where the sheer amplitude of the recording brings a hint of congestion. But for the most part the ear is beguiled by the glorious richness and atmosphere of the music-making.

Götterdämmerung: highlights.
　**(*) Decca ksxc 6220 (from above set cond. Solti).

The recording of the Decca *Götterdämmerung* was celebrated by one of the classics of television film, Humphrey Burton's *The Golden Ring*. This selection from the complete recording was timed to appear for one of the film's presentations, and it makes an excellent reminder not only for nostalgic viewers but for anyone daunted by the size of the complete set. The items could hardly be better chosen, with the rallying chorus of Act 2 a welcome addition to the obvious, predictable items. This was an early Decca transfer, made some time before the complete *Ring* cycle was issued on tape. The quality is comparatively unrefined, with rough edges, an occasional hint of flutter and some coarseness at the climax of *Siegfried's funeral music*. Even so the sheer drama of the sound is well projected. The balance is clear but light in the bass.

Götterdämmerung: orchestral highlights: *Siegfried's Rhine journey; Siegfried's funeral music; Brünnhilde's immolation.*
　(*)RCA rk 11317 [ark 1 1317]. LSO, Stokowski.

This is a disappointing issue on all counts. The Stokowskian magic comes over only sporadically, and Brünnhilde's Immolation Scene loses most of its effect without the vocal part of the score. To make matters worse the recording is badly focused and badly balanced, and in any case the tape issue produces serious congestion in the louder climaxes (the Immolation Scene is very uncomfortable indeed); the general focus is very poor.

Lohengrin: complete.
　(m)(***)HMV tc-sls 5071. Jess Thomas, Elisabeth Grümmer, Dietrich Fischer-Dieskau, Christa Ludwig, Gottlob Frick, Vienna State Opera Chorus, Vienna PO, Kempe.

Kempe's is a rapt account of *Lohengrin* which has never been surpassed in the recording studio, one of his finest monuments in sound. After all, Kempe looked at Wagner very much from the spiritual side, giving *Lohengrin* perspectives deeper than is common. The link with early Wagner is less obvious than usual, and instead one sees the opera as the natural pair with *Parsifal*, linked no doubt in Wagner's mind too, since in mythology Parsifal was the father of Lohengrin. The intensity of Kempe's conducting lies even in its very restraint, and throughout this glowing performance one senses a gentle but sure control, with the strings of the Vienna Philharmonic singing radiantly. The singers too seem uplifted, Jess Thomas singing more clearly and richly than usual, Elisabeth Grümmer unrivalled as Elsa in her delicacy and sweetness, Gottlob Frick gloriously resonant as the king. But it is the partnership of Christa Ludwig and Fischer-Dieskau as Ortrud and Telramund that sets the seal on this superb performance, giving the darkest intensity to their machinations in Act 2, their evil heightening the beauty and serenity of so much in this opera. The transfer to tape is of disappointing quality. For the most part the solo voices sound well, but the opening *Prelude* is not quite secure, and there is coarseness in the treble at fortissimos, causing lack of focus to the choral passages. There is a general lack of refinement of detail, with occasional discoloration in the orchestral wind (in the *Third act Prelude* the clarinets suffer). At the opening of side six (Act 3, Scene 3) the brass fanfares and the orchestral section which follows are very rough.

Die Meistersinger von Nürnberg (*The Mastersingers*): complete.

**(*)DG 3378 068 [id.]. Dietrich Fischer-Dieskau, Caterina Ligendza, Peter Lagger, Roland Hermann, Placido Domingo, Horst Laubenthal, Christa Ludwig, Chorus and Orch. of German Opera, Berlin, Jochum.

**(*) Decca κ 13 κ 54 [Lon. 5-1512]. Norman Bailey, Hannelore Bode, Kurt Moll, Bernd Weikl, René Kollo, Adolf Dallapozza, Julia Hamari, Gumpoldskirchner Spatzen, Vienna State Opera Chorus, Vienna PO, Solti.

Jochum's is a performance which more than any captures the light and shade of Wagner's most warmly approachable score, its humour and tenderness as well as its strength. The recording was made at the same time as live opera-house performances in Berlin, and the sense of a comedy being enacted is irresistible. With Jochum the processions at the start of the final Festwiese have sparkling high spirits, not just German solemnity, while the poetry of the score is radiantly brought out, whether in the incandescence of the Act 3 prelude (positively Brucknerian in hushed concentration) or the youthful magic of the love music for Walther and Eva. Above all Jochum is unerring in building long Wagnerian climaxes and resolving them – more so than his recorded rivals. The cast is the most consistent yet assembled in the recording studio. Though Caterina Ligendza's big soprano is a little ungainly for Eva, it is an appealing performance, and the choice of Domingo for Walther is inspired. The key to the set is of course the searching and highly individual Sachs of Fischer-Dieskau, a performance long awaited. Obviously controversial (you can never imagine this sharp Sachs sucking on his boring old pipe), Fischer-Dieskau with detailed word-pointing and sharply focused tone gives new illumination in every scene. The Masters – with not one woolly-toned member – make a superb team, and Horst Laubenthal's finely tuned David matches this Sachs in applying Lieder style. The recording balance favours the voices, which is a pity, but is otherwise refined, with a comparatively low-level transfer to match. The sound is warmly musical but cannot begin to match the Solti Decca recording in immediacy or range at either end of the spectrum. The balance is good and there are no hiss problems; one can find great musical pleasure in this issue (the sound matching the warmth and humanity of Jochum's conception), but the moments of spectacle lack the kind of vividness that Decca have accustomed us to in Wagner's music. Moreover the layout on five cassettes produces an extra side-turn in Acts 1 and 3. The libretto is clear but the print is small.

The great glory of Solti's long-awaited set is not the searing brilliance of the conductor but rather the mature and involving portrayal of Sachs by Norman Bailey. For his superb singing the set is well worth investigating, and there is much else to enjoy, not least the bright and detailed sound which the Decca engineers have, as so often in the past, obtained with the Vienna Philharmonic, recording Wagner in the Sofiensaal. Kurt Moll as Pogner, Bernd Weikl as Beckmesser (really singing the part) and Julia Hamari as Magdalene (refreshingly young-sounding) are all excellent, but the shortcomings are comparably serious. Both Hannelore Bode and René Kollo fall short of their far-from-perfect contributions to earlier sets, and Solti for all his energy gives a surprisingly square reading of this most appealing of Wagner scores, exaggerating the four-square rhythms with even stressing, pointing his expressive lines too heavily and failing to convey real spontaneity. It remains an impressive achievement, and those who must at all costs hear Bailey's marvellous Sachs should not be deterred. The Decca transfer produces electrically vivid sound. The transfer is at the highest level and the range of the recording at both ends of the spectrum is very striking. There are moments when the brilliance verges on fierceness and the focus can

occasionally slip, but generally the sound has quite remarkable bloom, projection and detail, and much beauty of texture too. The opera is conveniently set out on four cassettes, with Acts 1 and 2 sensibly given a cassette each and Act 3 complete on the remaining four sides. The libretto booklet is beautifully clearly printed.

Die Meistersinger von Nürnberg: highlights.
> **(*)** Decca KCET 625 (from above set cond. Solti).

This generous selection from Solti's variably successful set effectively minimizes the principal flaws (the contributions of Hannelore Bode and René Kollo as Eva and Walther) and rightly highlights Norman Bailey's noble characterization of Sachs. Kurl Moll as Pogner is also well represented. The brilliantly vivid sound, with its hint of fierceness in the transfer, reflects the range and presence of the complete set.

Parsifal: complete.
> *** Decca K 113 K 54. René Kollo, Christa Ludwig, Dietrich Fischer-Dieskau, Hans Hotter, Zoltan Kelemen, Gottlob Frick, Vienna Boys' Choir, Vienna Opera Chorus, Vienna PO, Solti.

It was natural that after Solti's other magnificent Wagner recordings for Decca, he should want to go on to this last of the operas. In almost every way it is just as powerful an achievement as any of his previous Wagner recordings in Vienna, with the Decca engineers surpassing themselves in vividness of sound and the Vienna Philharmonic in radiant form. The singing cast could hardly be stronger, every one of them pointing words with fine, illuminating care for detail. The complex balances of sound, not least in the *Good Friday music*, are beautifully caught, and Solti throughout shows his sustained intensity in Wagner. There remains just one doubt, but that rather serious – the lack of the spiritual quality that can make live performances so involving. Maybe it is better after all not to record this opera in the studio. The transfer is basically of high quality, and the last two acts produce most beautiful sound, spacious, clear and full. However, the opening *Prelude* suggests a fractionally too high transfer level; there is some slight lack of refinement and even a hint of unsteadiness of texture. This returns in the choral music of Scene 2, and then disappears – the great choral climax at the end of the act is resplendently expansive. The layout on tape is superior to the LP format in offering Act 1 spread over the first four sides, and Acts 2 and 3 each complete on two. The libretto is clearly printed, but, irritatingly, shows the side breaks for the discs.

Das Rheingold: complete.
   *** Decca к 2 w 29 [Lon. 5-1309].
    George London, Kirsten Flagstad, Set Svanholm, Gustav Neidlinger, Vienna PO, Solti.
   (M) *** DG 3378 048 [id.]. Dietrich Fischer-Dieskau, Josephine Veasey, Gerhard Stolze, Zoltan Kelemen, Berlin PO, Karajan – *Götterdämmerung*.***

The Decca set was the first recording ever issued commercially of the opening drama in the *Ring* cycle. Solti gives a magnificent reading of the score, crisp, dramatic and direct. He somehow brings a freshness to the music without ever overdriving or losing an underlying sympathy. Vocally the set is held together by the unforgettable singing of Neidlinger as Alberich. Too often the part – admittedly ungrateful on the voice – is spoken rather than sung, but Neidlinger vocalizes with wonderful precision and makes the character of the dwarf develop from the comic creature of the opening scene to the de-mented monster of the last. Flagstad specially learnt the part of Fricka for this recording, and her singing makes one regret that she never took the role on stage. But regret is small when a singer of the greatness of Flagstad found the opportunity during so-called retirement to extend her reputation with performances such as this. Only the slightest trace of hardness in the upper register occasionally betrays her, and the golden power and richness of her singing are for the rest unimpaired – enhanced even, when the recorded quality is as true as this. As Wotan, George London is sometimes a little rough – a less brilliant recording might not betray him – but this is a dramatic portrayal of the young Wotan. Svanholm could be more characterful as Loge, but again it is a relief to hear the part really sung. Much has been written on the quality of the recording, and without any doubt it deserves the highest star rating. Decca went to special trouble to produce the recording as for a stage performance and to follow Wagner's intentions as closely as possible. They certainly succeeded. Even those who are sometimes troubled by the almost excessive sharpness of definition Decca provide in complex scores – the 'Festival Hall' effect – will find that here the clarity does not prevent Wagner's orchestral effects from coming over in their full bloom of richness. An outstanding achievement, and so is the cassette transfer, offering sound that equals and even at times outshines the disc versions. As in the other issues in this remarkable Decca cassette edition of *The Ring*, the richness and spread of the sound are matched by its range and clarity.

Karajan's account is more reflective than Solti's. The very measured pace of the *Prelude* indicates this at the start, and there is often an extra bloom on the Berlin Philharmonic playing. But Karajan's very reflectiveness has its less welcome side, for the tension rarely varies. One finds such incidents as Alberich's stealing of the gold or Donner's hammer-blow passing by without one's pulse quickening as it should. Unexpectedly, Karajan is not so subtle as Solti in shaping phrases and rhythms. There is also no doubt that the DG recording managers were not so painstaking as John Culshaw's Decca team, and that too makes the end-result less compellingly dramatic. But on the credit side the singing cast has hardly any flaw at all, and Fischer-Dieskau's Wotan is a brilliant, memorable creation, virile and expressive. Among the others Veasey is excellent, though obviously she cannot efface memories of Flagstad; Gerhard Stolze, with his flickering almost *Sprechstimme* as Loge, gives an intensely vivid if, for some, controversial interpretation. The recording is excellent but does not outshine the Decca, and neither does the tape transfer: the sound is warm and refined but lacks the vivid presence and projection of the Decca set.

The Rhinegold: complete (in English).

   ***HMV TC-SLS 5032. Norman Bailey, Derek Hammond Stroud, Katherine Pring, Emile Belcourt, Helen Attfield, Anne Collins, Lois McDonall, Robert Lloyd, Clifford Grant, English National Opera Orch., Goodall.

It is a practical comment on Goodall's slow tempi in Wagner that unlike other versions the *Rhinegold* from the English National Opera Company's production spreads on to four records or cassettes instead of three. For the first three sides the temperature is low, reflecting hardly at all the tensions of a live performance, even though this was taken from a series of London Coliseum presentations. The recording too, admirably clean and refined, is less atmospheric than that of *Siegfried*, the first of the series to be recorded. Nonetheless the momentum of Wagner gradually builds up, so that by the final scenes both the overall teamwork and the individual contributions of such singers as Norman Bailey, Derek Hammond Stroud and Clifford Grant come together impressively. Hammond Stroud's vivid representation of Alberich culminates in a superb account of the curse. The spectacular orchestral effects are vividly caught by the engineers, even if balances (inevitably) are sometimes less than ideal. The transfer to tape is outstanding, even among the generally high standard of these EMI English *Ring* issues. The voices have a natural presence and the detail is remarkably clear; yet there is plenty of warmth and bloom on voices and orchestra alike. The special stage effects produce a riveting sense of spectacle, and the big climaxes are admirably managed, except for the very closing bars, where there is a touch of congestion. The only drawback is that the tape issue follows the discs by placing the recording on eight sides; it would have fitted comfortably on four. The libretto is clearly printed.

Siegfried: complete.

   ***Decca K 3 W 31 [Lon. 5-1508]. Wolfgang Windgassen, Birgit Nilsson, Hans Hotter, Gerhard Stolze, Gustav Neidlinger, Kurt Böhme, Marga Höffgen, Joan Sutherland, Vienna PO, Solti.

   (M) ** DG 3378 049 [id.]. Jess Thomas, Helga Dernesch, Thomas Stewart, Gerhard Stolze, Zoltan Kelemen, Karl Ridderbusch, Oralia Dominguez, Berlin PO, Karajan – *Die Walküre*.**(*)

Siegfried has too long been thought of as the grimmest of the *Ring* cycle, with dark colours predominating. It is true that the predominance of male voices till the very end, and Wagner's deliberate matching of this in his orchestration, give a special colour to the opera, but a performance as buoyant as Solti's reveals that more than in most Wagner the message is one of optimism. Each of the three acts ends with a scene of triumphant optimism – the first act in Siegfried's forging song, the second with him hot in pursuit of the woodbird, and the third with the most opulent of love duets. Solti's array of singers could hardly be bettered. Windgassen is at the very peak of his form, lyrical as well as heroic. Hotter has never been more impressive in a recording, his Wotan at last captured adequately. Stolze, Neidlinger and Böhme are all exemplary, and predictably Joan Sutherland makes the most seductive of woodbirds. Only the conducting of Solti leaves a tiny margin of doubt. In the dramatic moments he could hardly be more impressive, but that same woodbird scene shows up the shortcomings. The bird's melismatic carolling is plainly intended to have a degree of freedom, whereas Solti allows little or no lilt in the music at all. But it is a minute flaw in a supreme achievement. With singing finer than any opera-house could normally provide, with masterly playing from the Vienna Philharmonic, and Decca's most opulent recording this is a set likely to stand comparison with anything the rest of the century may provide. The tape transfer is of outstanding quality, with spectacular range and clarity to match the others in Decca's tape edition of *The Ring*.

When Siegfried is outsung by Mime, it is time to complain, and though the DG set has many fine qualities – not least the Brünnhilde of Helga Dernesch – it hardly rivals the Solti version. Windgassen on Decca gave a classic performance, and any comparison highlights the serious shortcomings of Jess Thomas. It only makes matters worse that the DG balance favours the voices more than the Decca. Otherwise the vocal cast is strong, and Karajan provides the seamless playing which characterizes his cycle. Recommended only to those irrevocably committed to the Karajan cycle. The tapes are issued coupled to *Die Walküre* at a very reasonable price, but

the transfer has not the flair and immediacy of the Decca versions. The set is divided over six cassettes (covering both operas) and the side breaks are not always ideal; neither is the long narrow libretto booklet.

Siegfried: complete (in English).
(M) *** HMV TC-SLS 875. Alberto Remedios, Rita Hunter, Norman Bailey, Gregory Dempsey, Derek Hammond Stroud, Clifford Grant, Anne Collins, Sadler's Wells Orch., Goodall.

Compounded from three live performances at the London Coliseum, this magnificent set gives a superb sense of dramatic realism. More tellingly than in almost any other Wagner opera recording, Goodall's spacious direction here conveys the genuine dramatic crunch that gives the experience of hearing Wagner in the opera-house its unique power, its overwhelming force. In the *Prelude* there are intrusive audience noises, and towards the end the Sadler's Wells violins have one or two shaky moments, but this is unmistakably a great interpretation caught on the wing. Remedios, more than any recorded rival, conveys not only heroic strength but clear-ringing youthfulness, caressing the ear as well as exciting it. Norman Bailey makes a magnificently noble Wanderer, steady of tone, and Gregory Dempsey is a characterful Mime, even if his deliberate whining tone is not well caught in the recording. The sound is superbly realistic, even making no allowances for the conditions. Lovers of opera in English should grasp the opportunity of hearing this unique set. The tape transfer is admirably vivid and detailed, kind to the voices, with a natural presence so that the words are clear, yet there is no edge or exaggeration of consonants. The orchestral recording is drier than in the others of the series; the brass sound brassier, less rounded than in *The Twilight of the Gods*, for instance, but not less effective. The strings, however, have plenty of body and bloom. The overall clarity compensates for any lack of sumptuousness. The layout is admirable, with each of the three acts complete on one cassette. The libretto is clear and the type not too small.

Tannhäuser (Paris version): complete.
> **(*) Decca K 80 K 43. René Kollo, Helga Dernesch, Christa Ludwig, Hans Sotin, Victor Braun, Werner Hollweg, Vienna State Opera Chorus, Vienna PO, Solti.

Solti provides an electrifying experience, demonstrating beyond a shadow of doubt how much more effective the Paris revision of *Tannhäuser* is, compared with the usual Dresden version. The differences lie mainly – though not entirely – in Act 1 in the scene between Tannhäuser and Venus. Wagner rewrote most of the scene at a time when his style had developed enormously. The love music here is closer to *Walküre* and *Tristan* than to the rest of *Tannhäuser*. The hero's harp song enters each time in its straight diatonic style with a jolt, but this is only apt, and the richness of inspiration, the musical intensification – beautifully conveyed here – transform the opera. The Paris version has never been recorded before, and that alone should dictate choice. But quite apart from that Solti gives one of his very finest Wagner performances to date, helped by superb playing from the Vienna Philharmonic and an outstanding cast, superlatively recorded. Dernesch as Elisabeth and Ludwig as Venus outshine all rivalry, and Kollo, though not ideal, makes as fine a Heldentenor as we are currently likely to hear. The transfer is extremely brilliant, not quite so smooth and sweet on the top as in some Decca opera sets, but very vivid. The distant choral effects are gorgeously atmospheric; the moments of

spectacle come off well, though there is just a hint of roughness at times (in the *Grand March* scene, for instance). But that is judging by Decca's own very high standards: this is still a three-star set.

Tristan und Isolde: complete.
> (M) *** Decca K 41 K 53. Fritz Uhl, Birgit Nilsson, Regina Resnik, Arnold van Mill, Tom Krause, Vienna PO, Solti.
> **(*) DG 3378 069 [id.] (with rehearsal sequence). Wolfgang Windgassen, Birgit Nilsson, Christa Ludwig, Martti Talvela, Eberhard Waechter, Bayreuth Festival (1966) Orch., Boehm.

Solti's performance is less flexible and sensuous than Karajan's (not yet available on tape), but he shows himself ready to relax in Wagner's more expansive periods. On the other hand the end of Act 1 and the opening of the *Love duet* have a knife-edged dramatic tension. Birgit Nilsson responds superbly to Solti's direction. There are moments when the great intensity that Flagstad brought to the part is not equalled, but more often than not Nilsson is masterly in her conviction, and – it cannot be emphasized too strongly – she never attacks below the note as Flagstad did, so that miraculously at the opening of the *Love duet* the impossibly difficult top Cs come out and hit the listener crisply and cleanly, dead on the note; and the *Liebestod* is all the more moving for having no soupy swerves at the climax. Fritz Uhl is a really musical Heldentenor. Only during one passage of the *Love duet* (*O sink' hernieder*) does he sound tired, and for the most part this is a well focused voice. Dramatically he leaves the centre of the stage to Isolde, but his long solo passages in Act 3 are superb and make that sometimes tedious act into something genuinely gripping. The Kurwenal of Tom Krause and the King Mark of Arnold van Mill are both excellent, and it is only Regina Resnik as Brangaene who gives any disappointment. The production has the usual Decca/Culshaw imaginative touch, and like the *Ring* transfers this is a splendid demonstration of the high standards achieved by Decca in the tape medium. The clear projection of the voices against an often sumptuously glowing orchestral texture is matched by the sense of perspective and atmosphere of the recording. The work's climaxes (the end of Act 1 as well the *Love duet* and *Liebestod*) are impressively free and spectacular. Each of the three acts is complete on a single cassette, and there is a very clear libretto.

Boehm's account was taken from a live performance at Bayreuth, but apart from such passages as the *Prelude* and concluding *Liebestod*, where the experience is vivid, the performance too often acquires tension of the wrong sort, and Boehm's speeds are surprisingly fast. Nilsson is here more expressive but less bright-toned than in the Decca set, and Windgassen – in his time an incomparable Tristan – begins to show signs of wear in the voice. The other two male principals are first-rate, but Christa Ludwig's Brangaene is unexpectedly marred by a pronounced *vibrato* in the great warning solos that punctuate the *Love duet*. The recording favours the voices, suffering inevitably from live recording conditions. The transfer, made at quite a high level, is extremely vivid and clear; the solo voices have believable naturalness and presence. The orchestral sound at climaxes is somewhat dry – more resonance would have given greater beauty to the sound – but the *Liebestod* is captured without any fall-off in quality at its peak, and generally, considering the recording date, the sound is excellent. Side ten includes excerpts from Boehm's rehearsals; one is struck by the beauty of the violin timbre in the empty auditorium. The libretto is printed in very small type and is not really satisfactory.

Tristan und Isolde: highlights.
(M) **(*) DG Privilege 3335 243 [922029] (from above set cond. Boehm).

Boehm's reading of *Tristan* lacks – in the love music at least – the glowing expansive warmth one ideally needs. But a one-tape selection covering the obvious high points of the opera is welcome, and though the recording – made live in the Festspielhaus – has dated a little, this can be safely recommended. The transfer is of excellent quality; it is a little dry in the bass, but offers (perhaps in consequence) a high level and a general body and spaciousness in the strings as well as being kind to the voices.

Tristan und Isolde: scenes (Act 1: *Isolde's narrative and curse;* Act 2: *Love duet;* Act 3: *Liebestod*).
*(*) HMV TC-ASD 3354. Helga Dernesch, Jon Vickers, Christa Ludwig, Chorus of German Opera, Berlin, Berlin PO, Karajan.

This is a sensible selection from Karajan's fine complete set, but the drawback is that the recording is hastily faded in at the opening of the excerpt from Act 1, and no less clumsily faded out again at the 'end' of the Act 2 *Love duet*. The sound on side one tends to be muffled in detail in the orchestra; side two is clearer but lacks richness in the orchestral sound and the distant perspectives for the voices are exaggerated. Throughout one is conscious of a lack of range.

Die Walküre: complete.
***Decca K 3 w 30 [Lon. 5-1509]. Birgit Nilsson, Régine Crespin, Christa Ludwig, James King, Hans Hotter, Gottlob Frick, Vienna PO, Solti.
(M) **(*) DG 3378 049 [id.]. Régine Crespin, Gundula Janowitz, Josephine Veasey, Jon

Vickers, Thomas Stewart, Martti Talvela, Berlin PO, Karajan – *Siegfried*.**

Solti's conception of *Die Walküre* is more lyrical than one would have expected from his recordings of the three other *Ring* operas. He sees Act 2 as the kernel of the work, perhaps even of the whole cycle. Acts 1 and 3 have their supremely attractive set-pieces, which must inevitably make them more popular as entertainment, but here one appreciates that in Act 2 the conflict of wills between Wotan and Fricka makes for one of Wagner's most deeply searching scenes. That is the more apparent when the greatest of latterday Wotans, Hans Hotter, takes the role, and Christa Ludwig sings with searing dramatic sense as his wife. Before that Act 1 seems a little underplayed, not nearly so sharp-edged as in Decca's earlier version with Leinsdorf (not available on tape). This is partly because of Solti's deliberate lyricism – apt enough when love and spring greetings are in the air – but also (on the debit side) because James King fails to project the character of Siegmund, fails to delve into the word-meanings, as all the other members of the cast consistently do. Crespin has never sung more beautifully in the recording studio, but even that cannot cancel out the shortcoming. As for Nilsson's Brünnhilde it has grown mellower since she made the earlier Decca recording, the emotions are clearer, and under-the-note attack is almost eliminated. Some may hesitate in the face of Hotter's obvious vocal trials but the unsteadiness is if anything less marked than in his EMI disc recordings of items done many years ago. Superlative recording, and a first-class cassette transfer, matching the rest of this splendid Decca series in its vividness and breadth.

The great merits of Karajan's version in competition with Solti's are the refinement of the orchestral playing and the heroic strength of Jon Vickers as Siegmund. With that underlined, one cannot but note that the vocal shortcomings here are generally more marked, and the total result does not add up to quite so compelling a dramatic experience; one is less involved. Thomas Stewart may have a younger, firmer voice than Hotter, but the character of Wotan emerges only partially. It is not just that he misses some of the word-meaning, but that on occasion – as in the kissing away of Brünnhilde's godhead – he underlines too crudely. A fine performance nonetheless, and Josephine Veasey as Fricka matches her rival Ludwig in conveying the biting intensity of the part. Gundula Janowitz's Sieglinde has its beautiful moments, but the singing is ultimately a little static. Crespin's Brünnhilde is impressive, but nothing like so satisfying as her study of Sieglinde on the Decca set. The voice is at times strained into unsteadiness, which the microphone seems to exaggerate. The DG recording is good, but not quite in the same class as the Decca – though some machines may favour things the other way round. The cassette version too is less impressive than the Decca, transferred at a lower level. It is issued, competitively priced, coupled to *Siegfried* in a 'chunky' box, with the usual DG small print in the libretto.

The Valkyrie: complete (in English).
*** HMV TC-SLS 5063. Rita Hunter, Alberto Remedios, Margaret Curphey, Norman Bailey, Clifford Grant, Ann Howard, English National Opera Company and Orch., Goodall.

Like the others in this series, *The Valkyrie* under Reginald Goodall was recorded live at the London Coliseum, and with minor reservations it fills the bill splendidly for those who want to hear the *Ring* cycle in English. With the voices balanced a little closer than in *Siegfried*, the words of Andrew Porter's translation are a degree clearer, but the atmosphere is less vivid. The glory of the performance lies not just in Goodall's spacious direction but in the magnificent Wotan of Norman Bailey, noble in the broadest span but very human in his illumination of detail. Rita Hunter sings nobly too, and though she is not quite so commanding as Nilsson is in the Solti cycle, she is often more lyrically tender. Alberto Remedios as Siegmund is more taxed than he was as Siegfried in the later opera (lower tessituras are not quite so comfortable for him), but his sweetly ringing top register is superb. If others, such as Ann Howard as Fricka, are not always kindly treated by the microphone, the total dramatic compulsion is irresistible. On tape the sound is vivid within a dry acoustic. The voices are forwardly projected and the words clear, although in Act 2 Ann Howard's voice is given a rather hard edge. Later the moments of spectacle are well handled, although in the *Ride of the Valkyries* the internal focus of detail is less than crisp. But on the whole this is exciting sound, if lacking in sumptuousness.

COLLECTIONS

'The "Golden" Ring'; Das Rheingold: Entry of the gods into Valhalla; Die Walküre: Ride of the Valkyries; Siegfried: Forest murmurs; Götterdämmerung: Prelude; Siegfried's Rhine journey; Rhinemaidens' song; Siegfried's funeral music. Siegfried idyll.

> ***Decca KSXC 6421. Birgit Nilsson (soprano), Wolfgang Windgassen (tenor), Vienna PO, Solti.

This collection of 'pops' from *The Ring*, plus the *Siegfried idyll*, makes a generous tape, highly recommendable to anyone just setting out on the path of Wagner-worship. Fine performances from the complete cycle, and brilliant re-

cording. The transfer is admirably clear throughout; *Siegfried's funeral music* sounds much more assured here than on the *Götterdämmerung* highlights cassette, and the quality in the *Siegfried idyll* is most beautiful. An impressive collection.

The Ring: excerpts: *Das Rheingold*: Scene 4: *Zur Burg führt die Brücke; Die Walküre*: Act 1: *Ein Schwert verhiess mit der Vater*; Act 3: *Ride of the Valkyries; Loge, hör; Magic fire music; Siegfried*: Act 1: *Notung!; Götterdämmerung*: Act 3: *Siegfried's death and funeral music.*

> (M) **(*) DG Privilege 3335 239 (from above complete sets cond. Karajan).

The task of selecting highlights from the whole of the *Ring* cycle is an impossible one, but on this mid-priced sampler tape from Karajan's DG cycle no one would seriously object to any of the items, all of them among the Wagnerian peaks. Good, generally refined recording, and the tape transfer is mostly of excellent quality, clear and expansive. The excerpts are nicely tailored so that one is never left unsatisfied after a clumsy fade-out. This is a much more successful cassette than the Decca *World of Wagner* issue (see below).

'Favourite composer': (i) *Der fliegende Holländer: Overture;* (ii) *Senta's ballad;* (iii; iv) *Götterdämmerung: Siegfried's Rhine journey;* (v) *Lohengrin: Prelude to Act 1;* (vi) *Die Meistersinger: Prelude to Act 1;* (vii) *Prize song;* (iii; iv; viii) *Parsifal: Ich sah das Kind;* (vi) *Das Rheingold: Entry of the Gods into Valhalla;* (ix) *Tannhäuser: Pilgrims' chorus;* (x) *Todesahnung . . . O du mein holder Abendstern (O star of eve);* (iii; iv) *Tristan und Isolde: Prelude to Act 1;*

(iii; xi) *Die Walküre: Ride of the Valkyries; Magic fire music.*
(B) *(*) Decca KDPC 625/6. (i) Orch. of the Royal Opera House, Covent Garden, Dorati; (ii) Gwyneth Jones; (iii) Vienna PO; (iv) Knappertsbusch; (v) New Philharmonia Orch., Hurst; (vi) LSO, Stokowski; (vii) James King; (viii) Kirsten Flagstad; (ix) Kingsway Chorus and SO, Camarata; (x) Tom Krause; (xi) Otto Edelmann, various soloists, cond. Solti.

A well-made selection, but hardly an imaginative one, as is underlined by the inclusion of the Camarata/Kingsway version of the *Pilgrims' chorus*, which is sturdily unmemorable. Highlights include Gwyneth Jones's noble account of *Senta's ballad* (vividly transferred) and the brief contributions by Kirsten Flagstad, James King and Tom Krause. George Hurst's account of the *Lohengrin Prelude* has a very forward balance which prevents a real *pianissimo*, although the climax is impressively spacious. Elsewhere the slightly too ambitious transfer level brings fierceness and intermittent patches of congestion, noticeable in the opening overture, and especially in the fizzy *Meistersinger Prelude* and *Siegfried's Rhine journey*, which Knappertsbusch directs eloquently. The extended extracts from Solti's 1958 recording of Act 3 of *Die Walküre* sound quite well here.

'The world of Wagner': (i; ii) *Götterdämmerung: Siegfried's Rhine journey; Siegfried's funeral music; Tannhäuser: Overture;* (iii) *Elisabeth's greeting;* (iv) *O star of eve; Tristan und Isolde:* (i) *Liebestod; Die Walküre: Ride of the Valkyries;* (v) *Magic fire music.*
(M) (**) Decca KCSP 317. Vienna PO, Solti, with (i) Birgit Nilsson; (ii) Wolfgang Windgassen; (iii) Helga Dernesch; (iv) Victor Braun; (v) Hans Hotter.

These 'bleeding chunks' let blood sometimes at both ends, with fades-in as well as fades-out. Wagner is very difficult to summarize in this way (if the excerpts are taken from complete versions), for his music seldom produces a suitable cadence where it might be wanted. Of course, these performances are of the highest quality, but this is a most unsatisfying set of excerpts, and it would certainly have been better to have chosen Hotter's *Magic fire music* scene to end the tape (as it comes to a proper finish) than leaving us in mid-air at the end of *Siegfried's funeral music*. The transfers are almost too brilliant, with a hint of shrillness, and the heavy modulation at the climax of the *Liebestod* at the end of side one brings harshness too. However, the tape compares quite well with the disc.

'Your kind of Wagner': (i) *Siegfried idyll*: excerpt; (ii) *Der fliegende Holländer: Spinning chorus;* (iii) *Götterdämmerung: Siegfried's Rhine journey; Siegfried's funeral music;* (ii) *Lohengrin: Bridal chorus;* (iv) *Die Meistersinger: Prelude to Act 1;* (ii) *Tannhäuser: Pilgrims' chorus; Die Walküre:* (iii) *Ride of the Valkyries;* (v) *Wotan's farewell and Magic fire music.*
(M) ** EMI TC-EXES 5016. (i) ECO, Barenboim; (ii) Bavarian State Opera Chorus and Orch., Heger; (iii) LPO, Boult; (iv) LSO, Barbirolli; (v) Hans Hotter (bar.), Philharmonia Orch., Ludwig.

On the whole an agreeable collection, but room should have been found for the complete *Siegfried idyll* instead of only this (substantial) excerpt. The sound is warm and quite well balanced, if lacking brilliance, and the two famous choruses are reasonably well focused. Barbirolli's account of the *Mastersingers overture* (which opens the tape) is very spacious but a little lacking in vitality.

Waldteufel, Emil (1837–1915)

Polkas: *Bella Bocca, Op. 163; L'Esprit français, Op. 182; Minuit, Op. 168; Prestissimo-Galop, Op. 152.* Waltzes: *Acclamations, Op. 223; España, Op. 236; Estudiantina, Op. 191; Les Patineurs (The Skaters), Op. 183.*

> (M) ** HMV Greensleeve TC-ESD 7012. Monte Carlo National Opera Orch., Boskovsky.

Waltzes: *Dolores; España; Les Grenadiers; Mon Rêve; Les Patineurs; Pomone; Toujours ou jamais.*

> *** Decca KSXC 6704. National PO, Gamley.

Waltzes: *Les Grenadiers; Mon Rêve; Pomone; Pluie de diamants; Les Sirènes; Très jolie.*

> (M) **(*) HMV Greensleeve TC-ESD 7070. LPO, Boskovsky.

Waldteufel's waltzes have a direct, breezy vivacity. They lack the underlying poetic feeling that takes the works of Johann Strauss into the concert hall, but their spontaneity and wit more than compensate for any lack of distinction in the tunes. Undoubtedly *The Skaters* is Waldteufel's masterpiece, but *Pomone, Mon Rêve* and the less well-known *Toujours ou jamais* all show the composer at his best. *España* is, of course, a direct crib from Chabrier, but is enjoyable enough, even if it does not match the original score in exuberance. Rhythmic zest

and vitality are the keynote of Douglas Gamley's performances. He does not forget that Waldteufel was French. There is just the right degree of sophistication and affection in the phrasing, and the fine Decca recording, made in a well-chosen resonant acoustic, has both brilliance and bloom. The cassette transfer is very successful: the sparkling treble is matched by a feeling of weight, yet the bass line, although telling, is not over-emphasized and indeed is admirably clean. A demonstration tape.

Boskovsky's first tape is enjoyable too and has the advantage of including, besides *Estudiantina* (which is unaccountably omitted from the Decca collection), some attractive polkas. In his notes to this EMI issue Peter Gammond comments that 'the music of Waldteufel remains a mainly untapped fountain', and another novelty, *Acclamations* (which Boskovsky opens very persuasively), emphasizes the truth of this. Boskovsky's manner is understandably *echt* Viennese, and some might feel that his style is too cosy for such Gallic inspiration. *The Skaters* undoubtedly responds well to such warmth, but perhaps the closing polka, *L'Esprit français*, sounds too much like *l'esprit viennois*. The cassette transfer offers a much brasher sound than the disc, lively certainly, but somewhat unrefined. However, the character of the music-making is well projected.

Boskovsky's second collection is if anything more attractive than the first. The Viennese manner is again predominant: the opening of *Pomone* is deliciously pointed, and the main theme is phrased very affectionately. *Les Sirènes*, appropriately, also has a seductive principal melody, and Boskovsky's treatment shows subtlety as well as affection. *Les Grenadiers*, however, seems unnecessarily brisk at its opening fanfare, and the principal tune is given a rather mannered rhythmic emphasis. *Mon Rêve* combines vivacity with warmth in a most appealing way. The recording is agreeably full and resonant;

677

the tape transfer has not the upper range of the Decca issue, but is well balanced and pleasing.

Les Patineurs (The Skaters) waltz, Op. 183.

⊛ (M) ***HMV TC-SXLP 30224. Philharmonia Orch., Karajan – GOUNOD: *Faust ballet***(*); OFFENBACH: *Gaîté Parisienne.****

This is a classic performance, the finest available of any Waldteufel waltz, with the incomparable Dennis Brain creating a *frisson* of magic as he lovingly phrases the opening horn solo with a tone of the softest velvet. Excellent recording, and the tape is crisply and freshly transferred.

Walton, William (born 1902)

Violin concerto.

⊛***Decca KSXC 6601. Kyung-Wha Chung, LSO, Previn – STRAVINSKY: *Violin concerto.****

*** HMV TC-ASD 3483. Ida Haendel, Bournemouth SO, Berglund – BRITTEN: *Violin concerto.*⊛***

The *Violin concerto*, written for Heifetz in 1939, shows Walton at his most distinctively compelling. Even he has rarely written melodies so ravishingly beautiful, so hauntingly romantic, yet his equally personal brand of spikiness has rarely if ever been presented with more power. Kyung-Wha Chung recorded this rich work immediately after playing a long sequence of live performances, and the brooding intensity of the opening presents the first melody with a depth of ex-

pressiveness, tender and hushed, that has never been matched in a recording, not even by Heifetz himself. With Previn as guide, and with the composer himself a sympathetic observer at the recording sessions, Chung then builds up a performance which must remain a classic, showing this concerto as one of the greatest of the century. Outstandingly fine recording, and a first-class cassette transfer, rich-textured and with plenty of detail.

A sunny, glowing, Mediterranean-like view of the concerto from Ida Haendel, with brilliant playing from the soloist and eloquent orchestral support from the Bournemouth orchestra under Paavo Berglund. Kyung-Wha Chung's version is wirier and in some ways more in character, but many collectors will respond equally (or even more) positively to Miss Haendel's warmth. There is an unrelieved lyricism about her tone that may not be to all tastes, but given the quality of both playing and recording (as well as the interest of the no less successful performance of the Britten coupling) this is an eminently desirable issue. The transfer is rich and has good detail (although the percussion once or twice lacks the last degree of transient crispness) and overall provides a pleasingly natural balance.

Crown Imperial; Orb and Sceptre (coronation marches).

(*) HMV TC-ASD 3388 [Angel 4XS 37436]. LPO, Boult – ELGAR: *Pomp and Circumstance marches* etc.(*)

Walton's two coronation marches make the ideal coupling for Boult's collection of Elgar marches. It was Boult who first conducted them in Westminster Abbey (in 1937 and 1953 respectively) and he brings even more flamboyance to them than to the Elgar items. The recording is immensely rich and spectacular and its wide amplitude is, on the whole, satisfactorily caught in the tape transfer, although the focus in the bass is not very clean and there are minor hints that the level is just fractionally too high.

Façade: Suites Nos. 1 and 2. BACH (arr. Walton): *The Wise Virgins: ballet suite.*
   ** HMV TC-ASD 3317. City of Birmingham SO, Frémaux.

Watton's arrangements of movements from Bach cantatas give off electric sparks (except of course in *Sheep may safely graze*), and Frémaux's version is most welcome. In *Façade* his manner is not quite as light and sparkling as it might be, but his rhythmic control gives a fresh new look to the music. The reverberant recording produces a pleasing sound, but the lack of sparkle in the upper transients means that the *Façade* suites lack a degree of bite and crispness, an essential component of the music. One notices this at the opening fanfare; however, the ear quickly adjusts, and otherwise the quality is good throughout, though the fourth movement of *The Wise Virgins* is rather noisy.

Symphony No. 1 in B flat minor.
   **(*) RCA GK 42707. LSO, Previn.
   ** Enigma K 453557. Royal Liverpool PO, Handley.

Previn gives a marvellously biting account of this magnificent symphony. His fast tempi may initially make one feel that he is pressing too hard, but his ability to screw the dramatic tension tighter and tighter until the final resolution is most assured, and certainly reflects the tense mood of the mid-thirties, as well as the youthful Walton's own dynamism. (The composer has since told us that the tensions express a very personal period of stress in his own emotional life.) '*Presto con malizia*' says the score for the scherzo, and malice is exactly what Previn conveys, with the hints of vulgarity and humour securely placed. In the slow movement Previn finds real warmth,

giving some of the melodies an Elgarian richness, and the finale's electricity here helps to overcome any feeling that it is too facile, too easily happy a conclusion. The bright recording quality (late-sixties vintage) has on the whole transferred adequately to cassette, the scherzo sounding especially effective. The recording does not display the widest dynamic range, and the lack of expansive richness at the ends of the outer movements means that a high playback level is needed for maximum impact; but the orchestral sound has good detail and presence.

Vernon Handley's interpretation of this work matured when he conducted a number of performances with the Royal Liverpool Philharmonic Orchestra during Walton's seventy-fifth birthday celebrations. It is essentially a broad view and tends to play down the work's cutting edge: there is very little suggestion of *malizia* in the scherzo. Indeed it must be said that the reading tends to under-characterize the music. While the first-movement climax is impressively shaped to a considerable peak of excitement, it is the orchestral brass that make the most striking effect; the string playing lacks bite and incisiveness, both here and in the finale. The recording is resonant and spacious, and the balance does not give the violins any special emphasis, but the lack of body to the tone is not really the fault of the engineers. Overall the sound is impressive, and the closing spectacle of the finale is generally well managed in the tape transfer. But Previn has shown us that this symphony can produce far more impact than it does here.

(i) *Belshazzar's Feast* (oratorio); (ii) Coronation *Te Deum.*
   *** Decca KCET 618 [Lon. 5-26525]. London Philharmonic Chorus, LPO, Solti, with (i) Benjamin Luxon (bar.); (ii) Choirs of Salisbury, Winchester and Chichester Cathedrals.

679

Whether or not prompted by the composer's latterday dictum that *Belshazzar's Feast* is more a choral symphony than an oratorio, Sir Georg Solti directs a sharply incisive performance which brings out the symphonic basis rather than the atmospheric story-telling. Fresh, scintillating and spiky, it is a performance that gives off electric sparks, not always quite idiomatic but very invigorating. Solti observes Walton's syncopations very literally, with little or none of the flexibility that the jazz overtones suggest, and his slow tempo for the lovely chorus *By the waters of Babylon* remains very steady, with little of the customary *rubato*. But with brilliant recording to match the orchestra's contribution, with generally excellent singing from the chorus and with a sympathetic contribution from Luxon (marred only slightly by *vibrato*) this is a big-scale reading which overall is most convincing. Moreover from the very opening, with its dramatic trombone solo, one is aware that this is to be one of Decca's demonstration tapes, with superbly incisive and clear choral sound, slightly sparer of texture in *Belshazzar's Feast* than in the *Te Deum*, a splendid occasional piece which makes the ideal coupling. The orchestra and percussive effects too have striking detail and presence.

(i; ii) *Gloria.* (ii) Coronation *Te Deum. Crown Imperial; Orb and Sceptre* (coronation marches).
*(**) HMV TC-ASD 3348. City of Birmingham SO, Frémaux, with (i) Barbara Robotham (mezzo-soprano), Anthony Rolfe Johnson (tenor), Brian Rayner Cook (bar.); (ii) CBSO Chorus, Choristers of Worcester Cathedral.

'Shatteringly apt displays of pomp and circumstance' is the delightful description of Frank Howes for the three Walton works inspired by coronations,

and here they are splendidly coupled with the grand setting of the *Gloria* which Walton wrote in 1961 for a double celebration at Huddersfield, the 125th anniversary of the Choral Society and the thirtieth anniversary of its association with Sir Malcolm Sargent. That last work, the longest of the four, has not quite the same concentration as the others, for it represents Walton tending to repeat himself in his jagged Alleluia rhythms and jazzy fugatos. Frémaux directs a highly enjoyable performance nonetheless, but it rather pales before the Coronation *Te Deum*, which may use some of the same formulas but has Walton electrically inspired. It is a grand setting which yet has a superb formal balance (almost a sonata form) while exploiting every tonal and atmospheric effect imaginable between double choirs and semi-choruses. The two splendid marches are marvellously done too. Frémaux uses the original full version of *Crown Imperial* instead of observing the cuts suggested by Walton (which reduce it by about a third), and that is the right decision.

The tape transfer has been made at the most ambitious level, and while the sound is spectacular it could hardly be described as refined! The reverberation obviously offers problems, and the chorus focus is often poor, although the *Te Deum* (on side two) seems somewhat clearer than the *Gloria*. The marches are affected by the resonance too, and although the element of spectacle remains, the clouding of the transients is unattractive, and there is considerable coarseness at climaxes.

Warlock, Peter
(1894–1930)

Songs: *After two years; As ever I saw; The Bayly berith the bell away; The birds; The cricketers of Hambledon; The droll lover; Elore Lo; Fair and true; The fox; The frostbound wood; Ha'nacker Mill; Jillian of Berry; My own country; Passing by; Pretty ring time; Robin Good-fellow; Roister doister; Romance; Sigh no more, ladies; Sleep; There is a lady sweet and kind; To the memory of a great singer; Twelve oxen; When as the rye reach to the chin; Yarmouth Fair; Youth.*

**(*) Oiseau-Lyre KDSLC 19. Norman Bailey (bass-bar.), Geoffrey Parsons (piano).

Over two dozen of Warlock's songs, displaying the art of the miniaturist, whether in the brisk items which have crisp pay-offs (not always so lightly pointful here as they should be) or in such intense songs as *The frostbound wood*. Though Norman Bailey is consistently thoughtful in his singing, charm is not one of his great qualities, and the vocal tone is somewhat lacking in variety. But with superb, stylish accompaniments (and an effective five-voiced chorus joining in for the final number on each side) this is a valuable and attractive anthology, very well, if rather resonantly, recorded. The transfer is clean and clear.

Waxman, Franz (1906–67)

Film scores: *Bride of Frankenstein: Creation of the female monster. Old Acquaintance: Elegy for strings. Philadelphia Story: Fanfare; True love. A Place in the Sun: suite. Prince Valiant: suite. Rebecca: suite. Sunset Boulevard: suite. Taras Bulba: The ride to Dublo.*

⊛ ***** RCA RK 11711. National PO, Gerhardt.

Of the many European musicians who crossed the Atlantic to make careers in Hollywood, Franz Waxman was among the most distinguished. Born in Upper Silesia, he had his early musical training in Germany. He was immensely gifted, and much of his music can stand on its own without the screen images it originally served to accompany. His first important score was for James Whale's *Bride of Frankenstein*, a horror movie to which many film buffs give classic status. His marvellously evocative music (a haunting, almost Wagnerian crescendo built over a throbbing timpani beat) for *The creation of the female monster* (visually most compelling in the film sequence) was restored by the conductor, mainly from listening to the film soundtrack, as the orchestral parts are lost. It builds on a memorable three-chord motif which seems instantly familiar. Readers will soon discover its associations for themselves: sufficient to say that the more familar use of this melodic fragment comes from a score written by another composer some fourteen years later. The *Bride of Frankenstein* music dates from 1935. Waxman stayed on to write for 188 films over thirty-two years. The opening of the first item on this tape, the *Suite* from *Prince Valiant*, immediately shows the vigour of Waxman's invention and the brilliance of his Richard-Straussian orchestration, and this score includes one of those sweeping string tunes which are the very epitome of Hollywood film music. Perhaps the finest of these comes in *A Place in the Sun*, and in the *Suite* it is used to preface an imaginative rhapsodical movement for solo alto sax (brilliantly played here by Ronnie Chamberlain). The reprise of the main tune, also on the alto sax but decorated by a characteristic counter-theme in the upper strings, is a moment of the utmost magic. In this work, incidentally, there is another curious anticipation of music written by another composer: a fugal section of Waxman's score is remarkably like the end of the second movement of Shostakovich's *Eleventh Symphony* (written seven years after the film, which was not shown in the Soviet Union). To make the coincidence complete it was Waxman who conducted the West Coast première of the symphony in 1958.

All the music on this tape is of high quality, and for any movie buff this is desert-island material. It nostalgically includes the famous MGM introductory title fanfare, which Waxman wrote as a backcloth for Leo the Lion. The orchestral playing throughout is marvellously eloquent, and the conductor's dedication is obvious. The recording is rich and full, with no lack of brilliance in this very successful transfer to tape.

Weber, Carl Maria von (1786–1826)

Andante and Hungarian rondo in C minor (for bassoon and orchestra), *Op. 35; Bassoon concerto in F major, Op. 75.*

(M) ** Turnabout KTVC 134039. George Zukerman, Württemberg CO, Faerber – MOZART and BOISMORTIER: *Bassoon concertos.***

The *Bassoon concerto* is somewhat insubstantial, without much orchestral interest, but the *Andante and Hungarian rondo* (originally written for viola and rescored for bassoon by the composer) is more characteristic of Weber's usual instrumental and melodic facility. Both performances are excellent. The cassette transfer is clear, but unfortunately the clarity tends to emphasize the thinness of the orchestral strings. The solo bassoon, however, is caught most naturally.

(i; ii) *Clarinet concerto No. 1 in F minor, Op. 73;* (i; iii) *Clarinet concertino in C minor, Op. 26;* (iv) *Romanza siciliana in G minor for flute and small orchestra;* (i; v) *Clarinet quintet in B flat major, Op. 34.*

(M) *** Turnabout KTVC 134151. (i) David Glazer (clarinet); (ii) Württemberg CO, Faerber; (iii) Innsbruck SO, Robert Wagner; (iv) Peter Thalheimer (flute), Hamburg SO, Neidlinger; (v) Kohon Qt.

This is an outstanding tape anthology, offering first-class quality throughout. The performances are all good, and the little bonus, the *Romanza siciliana*, not on the equivalent LP, is charming. The sound is smoother and rather more natural than on disc.

Piano concertos Nos. 1 in C major, Op. 11; 2 in E flat major, Op. 32.

(M) ** Turnabout KTVC 34155. Friedrich Wuehrer, Vienna Pro Musica Orch., Swarowsky.

Weber's enjoyable piano concertos, written in 1810 and 1812, postdate all five of Beethoven's concertos, yet they seem to lie at the musical crossroads of the early nineteenth century: they have inherited little of Beethoven's grandeur, and although they are romantic in the operatic sense they anticipate neither the feminine gentility of Schumann's concerto, nor the sweep of Tchaikovsky's. Certainly the *E flat Concerto* – the more ambitious of the two – has a theatrical feeling very much the composer's own, with a horn solo to add to the operatic associations and a jolly, extrovert finale. But on the whole the *C major Concerto* seems the more successful with its characteristic principal subject, its short but expressive adagio with a serene melody on the cellos, and the spontaneous finale with its attractive flowing triplet figuration. Wuehrer shows a special feeling for the Weberian style and Swarowsky directs the characteristic dotted rhythms with equal sympathy. The orchestral playing is committed if not polished; it is better disciplined in the *First Concerto*. The recording, a stereo transcription of an old mono recording, is rather thin, and this is not disguised in the tape transfer, which shows some harshness at times (notably at the end of the first movement of the *Second Concerto*, which comes on side one); but the ear adjusts. The *First Concerto* seems to have marginally more bloom on the sound.

Invitation to the Dance, Op. 65 (arr. Berlioz).
>   (M) ** Decca KCSP 406. Vienna PO, Boskovsky – J. STRAUSS: *Graduation Ball* etc.**

This performance has no special felicities, but it is neatly played and brightly recorded. The sound on the cassette is slightly brighter than on the disc.

Overtures: *Abu Hassan; Beherrscher der Geister; Euryanthe; Der Freischütz; Oberon; Peter Schmoll.*
>   **(*) DG 3300 294 [id.]. Berlin PO, Karajan.

Karajan's collection of Weber overtures is performed with great style and refinement, but the transfer of the excellent recording to cassette loses the sparkle and finesse of the equivalent disc.

Der Freischütz: overture.
>   (M) *** DG 3318 050. Bavarian Radio Orch., Jochum – SCHUBERT: *Symphony No. 9.****

This excitingly dramatic performance acts as a superb bonus for Jochum's outstanding account of Schubert's *Great C major Symphony*. (Unfortunately this tape was withdrawn just as we went to press.)

Oberon: overture.
>   **(*) Decca KSXC 16829 [Lon. 5-7057]. Chicago SO, Solti – BEETHOVEN: *Symphony No. 3.*(***)
>   (M) ** CBS Classics 40-61019. Cleveland Orch., Szell – MENDELSSOHN: *Symphony No. 4* etc.**

Weber's *Oberon overture*, although brilliantly played in Solti's version, makes a curious match for Beethoven's *Eroica symphony*, to which it acts as encore (on tape only). Its fairy atmosphere is literally rather than affectionately delineated, but the allegro has splendid energy and fire.

Szell's performance is beautifully played but lacks somthing in romanticism. The recording is good and the transfer clean and well balanced.

Clarinet quintet in B flat major, Op. 34.
>   (M) (***) HMV TC-HQS 1395. Gervase de Peyer, Melos Ens. – MOZART: *Clarinet quintet.**(**)

In this medium-priced reissue the HMV recording of Weber's *Clarinet quintet* is coupled with a recommendable performance of the Mozart. The performance of the Weber, with its extrovert dotted rhythms in the first movement and almost bucolic scherzo, is very assured, and the bravura playing in the finale is memorable. On tape the sound is basically well balanced but on our review copy the upper focus was disfigured by harmonic distortion caused by a marginally too high transfer level. Later copies may well have improved in this respect.

Grand duo concertante in E flat major (for clarinet and piano).
>   **Enigma K 453533. Keith Puddy (clarinet), Ian Brown (piano) – BRAHMS: *Clarinet trio.***

683

Weber's youthfully ambitious *Grand duo concertante* makes an apt and attractive coupling for the beautiful Brahms *Trio*. Again the performance lacks something in bravura and flair, but with clean, rather close recording it is a fair recommendation. On tape the recorded outline is rather soft-grained. The sound is well balanced but the definition could be more vividly focused.

Der Freischütz (opera): complete.
> ***DG 3371 008 [id.]. Gundula Janowitz, Edith Mathis, Peter Schreier, Theo Adam, Siegfried Vogel, Franz Crass, Leipzig Radio Chorus, Dresden State Orch., Carlos Kleiber.

This marked Carlos Kleiber's first major recording venture. The young conductor, son of a famous father, had already won himself a reputation for inspiration and unpredictability, and this fine, incisive account of Weber's atmospheric and adventurous score fulfilled all expectations. With the help of an outstanding cast, excellent work by the recording producer, and electrically clear recording, this is a most compelling version of an opera which lends itself well to recording. Only occasionally does Kleiber betray a fractional lack ˙of warmth.

Although this was a very early transfer, one of the first operas DG issued on tape in Dolby form, the quality is surprisingly good, with a generally clear focus and natural projection of the soloists. The opera's closing scene is notably well managed, and here the full, vivid sound approaches demonstration standard. The layout on three cassettes follows the discs. The libretto is clear and readable, though in small print.

Weill, Kurt
(1900–1950)

Kleine Dreigroschenmusik (Suite from The Threepenny Opera).
> *** Advent F 1036 (see p. xxiii) [id.]. Contemporary Chamber Ens., Weisberg – BOLCOM: *Frescoes;* MILHAUD: *La Création du monde.****

This *Suite from The Threepenny Opera*, dating from January 1929, was compiled at Otto Klemperer's suggestion, and his classic Philharmonia performance is still available on disc, although the tape issue has been withdrawn. A direct comparison between Klemperer's reading and this version by Arthur Weisberg and his chamber group reveals the former as rather more tonally robust and obviously Germanic in feeling. But the two accounts are surprisingly similar, both rhythmically and in nuance and choice of tempi. The playing of the Contemporary Chamber Ensemble has both vigour and sensibility, and Weisberg shows himself naturally sympathetic to the sharply characteristic scoring and the slightly decadent atmosphere. The recording has the great advantage of chrome tape with its extended range, which gives a demonstration presence to the brass and an effective subtlety to the percussive effects.

Widor, Charles-Marie
(1844–1937)

Organ symphony No. 5 in F major, Op. 42/1.
> **(*) Advent D 1017 (see p. xxiii) [id.]. Richard Ellsasser (organ of the Hammond Museum, Gloucester, Mass.).

(M) *(**) HMV TC-HQS 1406. Jane Parker-Smith (organ of Salisbury Cathedral; with GRISON: *Toccata in F major;* JONGEN: *Sonata eroica, Op. 94*(**)).

Organ symphonies Nos. 5 (complete); *6 in G major, Op. 42/2:* 1st movt; *8 in B major:* 4th movt.

(M) *** Saga CA 5439. David Sanger (organ of St Peter's Italian Church, Clerkenwell, London).

Recordings of the complete *Organ symphony No. 5* are useful, if only to show that the extraction of the famous *Toccata* finale for separate performance is entirely justified; the writing in the rest of the work is comparatively conventional and in no way equal to this famous piece. David Sanger's account of the whole symphony is first-class in every respect and recorded with fine bloom and clarity. His restraint in registering the central movements prevents Widor's cosy melodic inspiration from sounding banal, and the finale is exciting without sounding over-blown. The other symphonic movements are well done, but serve to confirm the conclusion that the *Toccata* was Widor's one masterstroke. The tape transfer is astonishingly successful, the dynamic range wide, so that the *Toccata* bursts on the listener brilliantly. The quality here is much smoother than on the HMV tape, with little loss of refinement at climaxes. This is excellent value.

Richard Ellsasser is an eloquent and musical advocate, but his performance lacks the flamboyant flair of David Sanger's, and he seems reluctant to draw on the big guns, even in the *Toccata* itself, which here is comparatively restrained. The organ he uses is a large-scale one (10,000 pipes, four manuals and 144 stops), built by John Hays Hammond in a stone tower of his castle home, and Advent's transfer, on chrome tape, of the well-balanced Nonesuch recording is immaculate in every respect. It is placed complete on side one of the cassette, the second side being left blank.

Jane Parker-Smith also gives a first-class account of Widor's most famous *Organ symphony*, and she is well recorded, especially in the brilliantly played *Toccata*. Her encores are also very acceptable: Jules Grison's *Toccata* is suitably flamboyant, and the Jongen *Sonata eroica* is a well-made if not distinctive piece, also with a spectacular finale, which is played with fine flair. On tape the sound is good for the most part, but there are moments here and there when the quality crumbles a little under stress.

Williams, John
(20th century)

Close Encounters of the Third Kind: suite; *Star Wars:* suite (film incidental music).

**(*) RCA RK 12698. National PO, Gerhardt.

**(*) Decca KSXC 6885. Los Angeles PO, Mehta.

Star Wars: suite.

**(*) Decca KSXC 6880 (as above, cond. Mehta; with R. STRAUSS: *Also sprach Zarathustra, Op. 30:* opening (theme from film *2001*); HOLST: *The Planets, Op. 32: Jupiter; Mars* *(*)).

The great popularity of these two space-age films has created more than usual interest in the background music written by John Williams. However eclectic his inspiration, both scores are undeniably attractive, and each draws considerable appeal from the imaginative orchestration. The music from *Star Wars* forms a definite suite of six movements; the shorter piece from *Close Encounters* is continuous and essentially atmospheric.

Gerhardt has the full measure of both, and the National Philharmonic Orchestra plays marvellously for him; the sweeping strings have an eloquence in the best Hollywood tradition. He shows particular skill in the *Close Encounters* sequence, creating genuine tension and evocative feeling, whereas Mehta tends to over-dramatize the climax. In *Star Wars* the Hollywoodian theme picturing Princess Leia includes a horn solo which is played quite gorgeously, to create a frisson of pleasure, and the closing section has a swagger of *nobilmente*. Mehta is good here too, and the sheer gusto of his approach is undoubtedly exhilarating, as it is also in the opening section. But although the Los Angeles orchestra play splendidly they do not always show the flair that makes Gerhardt's coupling so memorable. They do, however, have the advantage of much richer recording, and the Decca transfer is more sophisticated than the RCA in its balance. At the opening fanfare of *Star Wars* there is some lack of focus on the RCA tape, and at climaxes the orchestra has less body, although the resonance is well controlled. But on sonic grounds the Decca tape easily wins.

There seems no reason to recommend the alternative Decca issue coupling *Star Wars* (alone) with music by Richard Strauss and Holst, especially as the level in these additional items is fractionally too high and the recording tends to coarsen a little at climaxes.

Wolf-Ferrari, Ermanno (1876–1948)

Il segreto di Susanna (Susanna's Secret; opera): complete.
*** Decca KCET 617 [Lon. 5-1169]. Maria Chiara (soprano), Bernd Weikl (bar.), Orch. of the Royal Opera House, Covent Garden, Gardelli.

Though *Susanna's Secret* never quite lives up to the effervescence of its delectable (and deservedly popular) overture, it is a charming piece that in a performance like this has an individual magic, not least in the equally popular *Intermezzo*. The plot about the anti-smoking husband and the wife who in secret (and against Edwardian convention) smokes has an obvious period flavour, but the humour is well pointed. Excellent singing and playing, brilliant recording, and a demonstration-worthy cassette with sparkling orchestral sound and splendid presence and immediacy for the voices. The overall balance is first-rate.

Collections

Concerts of Orchestral and Concertante Music

Academy of Ancient Music, Hogwood

'The world of the baroque orchestra': STAMITZ: *Symphony in D major, Op. 3/2.* PURCELL: *Abdelazar: suite.* GEMINIANI: *Concerto grosso in E minor, Op.3/3.* BACH, J. C.: *Overture No. 2 in D major.* VIVALDI: *Flute concerto in G minor (La Notte), Op. 10/2.* HANDEL: *Water music: Trumpet suite in D major.*

(M)**Decca KCSP 544.

A generously diverse sampler of baroque music played on 'original instruments' with a robust, invigorating style and a comparative lack of Italianate charm. The playing is vividly alert throughout, the recording rather forward which means some reduction of light and shade, if no lack of presence and detail. The key change between the end of the Stamitz and the beginning of Purcell's suite is uncomfortably sudden, but otherwise the arrangement of items is well chosen. The transfer, however, made at a high level, brings less than absolute refinement at times, noticeably at the opening of the Stamitz, J. C. Bach and Handel items.

Academy of St Martin-in-the-Fields, Marriner

ALBINONI: *Adagio in G minor* (arr. Giazotto) *for strings and organ.* MENDELSSOHN: *Octet in E flat major, Op. 20: Scherzo.* HANDEL: *Bere-*nice: Minuet. Messiah: Pastoral symphony. MOZART: *March in D major, K.335/1. German dance (Sleighride), K.605/3.* BACH: *Christmas oratorio, BWV 248: Sinfonia. Suite No. 3 in D major, BWV 1068: Air.* PACHELBEL: *Canon in D major.* BEETHOVEN: *12 Contretänze.*

*** HMV TC-ASD 3017 [Angel 4xs 37044].

This account of Albinoni's *Adagio* must be the most refined in the catalogue, although (as also in the gravely measured performance of the Pachelbel *Canon*) the beautiful playing is matched by a strongly characterized overall conception. One special delight here is the Beethoven *Contretänze,* with their sudden reminder of the finale of the *Eroica symphony,* but the whole programme gives the fullest pleasure and is beautifully recorded. The tape transfer is good too; it lacks the last degree of range on side one but is often excellent on side two.

'The Academy in concert': MOZART: *Serenade No. 13 in G major (Eine kleine Nachtmusik), K.525.* GLUCK: *Orfeo ed Euridice: Dance of the Blessed Spirits.* MOZART, Leopold: *Toy symphony* (attrib. Haydn). SCHUBERT: *Rosamunde, D.797: Entr'acte in B flat major.* HANDEL: *Xerxes: Ombra mai fù (Largo).* BACH: *Cantata No. 147: Jesu, joy of man's desiring.*

687

** HMV TC-ASD 3375 [Angel 4xs 37443].

The highlight here is an enchanting version of the *Toy symphony* with some delightfully piquant sounds. The programme is a frankly popular one; for all the delicacy of the scoring of Handel's *Largo*, one still craves the vocal line – an arrangement sits uneasily within this kind of programme. The most famous of Mozart's serenades is graciously played, if with a hint of blandness, and the flute solo in the Gluck piece is matched by the beautiful wind-playing in the *Rosamunde* melody – a little spoilt on our copy by the impure upper harmonics of the transfer. The sound is generally smooth, if lacking in range and the last degree of refinement.

'The world of the Academy': HANDEL: *Solomon: Arrival of the Queen of Sheba.* TELEMANN: *Trumpet concerto in D major.* MOZART: *Divertimento for strings No. 1 in D major, K.136.* HAYDN: *6 Allemandes.* ROSSINI: *String sonata No. 1.* MENDELSSOHN: *Octet in E flat major, Op. 20: Scherzo.* TCHAIKOVSKY: *Serenade for strings, Op. 48: Waltz.*

(M) *** Argo KCSP 101.

This sampler offers a very happy collection of lollipops. It opens stylishly and infectiously with the *Arrival of the Queen of Sheba*, and among its special delights are the spirited and buoyant finale of the Mozart *Divertimento*, the genial Rossini *Sonata*, the beautifully played Mendelssohn *Scherzo* and the elegant Tchaikovsky *Waltz*. The recording is smooth, rich and completely natural in timbre; the tape has been remastered since it was first issued and is of striking demonstration quality. The *Arrival of the Queen of Sheba* sounds wonderfully fresh; the trumpet in the Telemann is admirably crisp, and the Rossini *Sonata* sparkles as if newly minted. There are few better cassettes than this.

'The world of the Academy', Vol. 2: VIVALDI: *The Four Seasons: Winter, Op. 8/4.* BACH: *Suite No. 2 in B minor, BWV 1067: Minuet; Badinerie. Suite No. 3 in D major, BWV 1068: Air.* HANDEL: *Berenice: Minuet.* HUMMEL: *Trumpet concerto in E flat major: Finale.* GRIEG: *Holberg suite, Op. 40: Prelude.* ELGAR: *Serenade for strings in E minor, Op. 20.* BARTÓK: *Music for strings, percussion and celesta:* 2nd movt. STRAVINSKY: *Pulcinella: Vivo; Minuetto; Finale.*

(M) **(*) Argo KCSP 163.

Even more than the first *World of the Academy* collection, this tape offers an exceptionally fine selection of masterly performances of outstandingly memorable music. The Hummel finale is especially captivating, and it is good to have the Elgar *Serenade*, even if the performance here is not entirely idiomatic. The recording is basically of high quality, but the tape transfer, though brilliant and with a wide range, seems to exaggerate the upper partials of the string tone, and a fairly strong treble cut is needed to give the violins the body of tone the ear would normally expect. However, the tape responds to the controls, although the detail in the Hummel excerpt is not ideally clean.

'A baroque festival' (with various soloists): VIVALDI: *L'Estro armonico: Quadruple violin concerto in B minor, Op. 3/10; Double violin concerto in A minor, Op. 3/8. La Stravaganza: Violin concerto in B flat major, Op. 4/1. Double trumpet concerto in C major, P. 75.* CORELLI: *Concerto grosso in G minor (Christmas concerto), Op. 6/8.* BACH: *Double concerto in D minor for violin and oboe (from BWV 1060). Flute concerto in G minor (from BWV*

1056). TELEMANN: *Trumpet concerto in D major. Viola concerto in G major.* ARNE: *Harpsichord concerto No. 5 in G minor.* HANDEL: *Concerto grosso, Op. 3/1. Oboe concerto No. 3 in G minor. Organ concerto No. 16 in D minor, Op. 7/4.* FASCH: *Trumpet concerto in D major.*

(M) *** Argo K 69 K 33.

A superb set. The music, like the performances, is of the highest quality, and the recording offers some really gorgeous sound. The string textures here are wonderfully warm yet transparent, and the soloists, flute, oboe, or harpsichord, are natural in both balance and timbre. Only in the trumpet concertos is there a suggestion that the upper range of the recording is not quite so free as elsewhere, and that is marginal. The compilation is ideal for tape listening; one can join the music anywhere and wallow in the finely balanced combination of vitality and serenity that is present throughout. Highly recommended.

(i) **Academy of St Martin-in-the-Fields, Marriner;** (ii) **ECO, Leppard**

'*Famous baroque and rococo dances*': (i) BOCCHERINI: *Quintet in E major, Op. 13/5: Minuet.* MOZART: *Divertimento No. 17 in D major, K.334: Minuet. Symphony No. 40 in G minor, K.550: Minuet.* (ii) HANDEL: *Water music: Sarabande; Rigaudon.* BACH: *Suite No. 1 in C major, BWV 1066: Minuets 1 and 2. Suite No. 2 in B minor, BWV 1067: Polonaise. Suite No. 3 in D major, BWV 1068: Gavottes 1 and 2.* HAYDN: *Symphony No. 48 in C major (Maria Theresia): Minuet.* (i) *Symphony No. 53 in D major (L'Impériale): Minuet.* (ii) BACH, J. L.: *Suite in G major: Minuet; Gavotte.*

(M) ** Philips 7317 109.

A concert with such a profusion of minuets is bound to have some lack of variety, however imaginatively the dance form is treated by different composers. In the event this programme shows more diversity than one might expect. The transfer gives warm agreeable sound, though in some tracks the resonance of the recording produces some lack of refinement. Undoubtedly the spacious warmth of string tone offered here suits a programme like this.

Adler, Larry (harmonica)

Concert (with Orch., Gamley): GERSHWIN: *Porgy and Bess: Summertime.* JOPLIN: *The Entertainer.* RODRIGO: *Concierto de Aranjuez: 2nd movt.* ADLER: *Genevieve waltz. Screws blues.* KHACHATURIAN: *Gayaneh: Sabre dance.* DINICU: *Hora staccato.* DEBUSSY: *Suite bergamasque: Clair de lune.* ALFVÉN: *Swedish rhapsody No. 1.* MASSENET: *Thaïs: Meditation.* FALLA: *El amor brujo: Ritual fire dance.*

** (*) Decca Phase 4 KPFC 4429.

Larry Adler's admirers will welcome this well-chosen anthology. It was he above all who won for the humble mouth-organ universal acceptance as a genuine musical instrument, and here he displays his consummate technique and his musical sensitivity and imagination over an attractively varied selection. The opening *Summertime* shows just how hauntingly he can phrase a simple melody, and he is equally good in Debussy's *Clair de lune* and the *Meditation* from Massenet's *Thaïs*. Naturally enough the programme includes Adler's own incidental music for the famous film *Genevieve*. The recording spotlights the solo harmonica so that there is comparatively little dynamic range between this and the backing orchestra; however, the ear adjusts. The tape transfer is generally well managed at a high level, although there is a touch of roughness in the upper focus of the solo instrument at times on side one (notably in *The Entertainer*).

Works for harmonica and orchestra (with (i) Morton Gould Orch.; (ii) RPO; both cond. Gould): (i) GERSHWIN: *Three-quarter blues; Merry Andrew; Lullaby time.* (ii) BENJAMIN: *Harmonica concerto.* VAUGHAN WILLIAMS: *Romance.* ARNOLD: *Harmonica concerto, Op. 46.* MILHAUD: *Suite.*

(M) *(**) RCA GK 42747.

This is an indispensable collection. The four major works were all written for Larry Adler, and the Gershwin pieces make an irresistible miniature suite, as tuneful and inspired as any of the more formal concertos. Of these Malcolm Arnold's is particularly rewarding; the opening *Grazioso* is immediately appealing, and there is one of those swinging finales at which this composer is so adept. The Benjamin work is also felicitously conceived, with its haunting *Canzona* and amiable closing rondo; and Milhaud's *Suite* has a racy, extrovert inventive style which Adler captures with infectious spirit. Indeed the playing throughout is marvellous. The soloist tells us in his witty liner-note that he had problems learning the music (playing more readily by ear than from music), but none of that shows here. The recording is good but has offered transfer problems, especially in the Gershwin, where the harmonica's upper partials are fizzy and blurred. One needs a filter or strong treble cut. Side two (which includes the last three works listed) is somewhat cleaner, although there is an element of harshness in the orchestral sound.

André, Maurice (trumpet)

'Trumpet concertos' (with Berlin PO, Karajan): HUMMEL: *Concerto in E flat major.* MOZART, Leopold: *Concerto in D major.* TELEMANN: *Concerto in D major.* VIVALDI: *Concerto in A flat major.*

*(**) HMV TC-ASD 3044.

An attractive collection of trumpet concertos, brilliantly played by Maurice André. His manner is somewhat deadpan in the three baroque concertos, though his security in the upper register in the work by Leopold Mozart and the fine Telemann concerto is impressive. The jaunty quality of the Hummel is not missed, and the finale of this work, taken at breakneck pace, is certainly exhilarating. The recording has been transferred at fractionally too high a level and lacks the last degree of refinement on side one (the trumpet image tends to blur a little), but side two (the Hummel) is generally good, except for a lack of detail in the finale, where the orchestra sounds mushy.

'More trumpet concertos' (with ECO, Mackerras): HANDEL: *Concerto in D minor* (reconstituted and orch. Thilde). ALBINONI: *Concertos: in B flat major; in D major* (arr. Paumgartner). TELEMANN: *Concerto in D major* (ed. Töttcher-Grebe). HERTEL: *Concerto in E flat major.*

*(**) HMV TC-ASD 3394.

Arrangements of concertos originally written for flute or oboe obviously call for high bravura when played on the trumpet, and Maurice André is on top form here. The works by Albinoni sound perhaps excessively robust in these transcriptions, but the Telemann concerto is particularly agreeable. For trumpet fans this should prove a worthwhile anthology, although on tape the recording is acceptable only, with a lack of refinement of detail in the accompanying strings and a tendency for the trumpet's upper harmonics to lack the clean bright purity which was obviously present on the master recording.

Baroque music (with Franz Liszt CO, Frigyes): BACH: *Suite in B minor, BWV 1067.* HAYDN, Michael: *Trumpet concerto in D major.* TELEMANN: *Concerto in D major for trumpet, 2 oboes, bassoon and harpsichord.*
** HMV TC-ASD 3595.

The unlikely arrangement of Bach's B minor suite with the flute part played by a solo trumpet comes off well enough, partly by clever balancing and partly because Maurice André's virtuosity (even in the *Badinerie*) is almost self-effacing. It makes the music sound like a new work rather than an arrangement, even though the effect is instrumentally clumsier, more robust, less mercurial. Skilful balancing also makes the Telemann concerto delightful listening, with the trumpet felicitously combining with the woodwind. The sound is good and the transfers excellent, except in the Michael Haydn concerto, where there is some discoloration on the solo instrument (even though the level is only marginally higher). However, this may not be present on all copies.

'Animals in music'

(i) LSO; (ii) Julius Katchen, Gary Graffman (pianos); cond. Henderson; (iii) Varda Nishry (piano); (iv) Suisse Romande Orch., Ansermet; (v) George Malcolm (harpsichord); (vi) Orch. of Royal Opera House, Covent Garden, Boult; (vii) Clifford Curzon (piano), members of the Vienna Octet; (viii) Sargent: (i; ii) SAINT-SAËNS: *Carnival of the Animals.* (iii) IBERT: *Le Petit Âne blanc* (*The Little White Donkey*). (iv) TCHAIKOVSKY: *The Sleeping Beauty: Puss-in-Boots and the White Cat.* (v) RIMSKY-KORSAKOV: *Tsar Saltan: Flight of the bumble bee* (arr. Malcolm). (vi) BACH: *Cantata No.*

208: Sheep may safely graze. (vii) SCHUBERT: *Piano quintet in A major (Trout), D.667: Theme and variations.* (i; viii) PROKOFIEV: *Peter and the Wolf* (abridged and without narration).
(M) **(*) Decca KCSP 366.

This is not quite so successful as the companion anthology, *Birds in music*, but it is an attractive compilation provided one can accept the abridged version of *Peter and the Wolf* (with no narration). The *Carnival of the Animals* is given a strongly characterized performance and demonstration sound quality. (It was originally issued with the Ogden Nash verses but they are mercifully omitted here.) The *Flight of the bumble bee* played by George Malcolm on the harpsichord makes a delightful closing encore. The transfer is sophisticated, the quality warm and vivid, crystal-clear in the *Carnival of the Animals*.

Ashkenazy, Vladimir (piano)

'*Ashkenazy in concert*': TCHAIKOVSKY: *Piano concerto No. 1 in B flat minor, Op. 23* (with LSO, Maazel). RACHMANINOV: *Piano concerto No. 2 in C minor, Op. 18* (with Moscow PO, Kondrashin). MOZART: *Piano concerto No. 20 in D minor, K.466* (with LSO, Schmidt-Isserstedt). BEETHOVEN: *Piano concerto No. 5 in E flat major (Emperor), Op. 73* (with Chicago SO, Solti). BRAHMS: *Piano concerto No. 2 in B flat major, Op. 83* with LSO, (Mehta).
(M) *** Decca K 64 K 33.

On tape this makes a first-class compilation. Each work is complete on a single side except the Brahms, which splits conveniently in half. The quality is Decca's very best, and the richness and detail (with a bold, natural piano image) give immediate pleasure at the opening of the Tchaikovsky concerto. Only in the first movement of the *Emperor* is the orchestral focus slightly less clean. Ashkenazy has made a more recent recording of the Rachmaninov *Second Concerto* (with Previn), and one wonders why Decca did not choose that version; but this earlier performance is certainly a fine one, while the Brahms is given such a vivid sound picture that the performance seems to spring fully to life. The poetry of Ashkenazy's contribution is in no doubt here and in the Mozart D minor work, where the orchestral score is played with somewhat less flexibility.

Ballet

'Favourite ballets' (with (i) Orch. of Royal Opera House, Covent Garden; (ii) Lanchbery; (iii) Paris Conservatoire Orch.; (iv) Martinon; (v) Suisse Romande Orch., Ansermet; (vii) LSO, Monteux; (viii) Maag; (ix) Israel PO, Solti): excerpts from: (i; ii) HÉROLD: *La Fille mal gardée*, (iii; iv) ADAM: *Giselle*. (v) DELIBES: *Coppélia*. TCHAI-KOVSKY: (i; vi) *Swan Lake;* (vii) *The Sleeping Beauty;* (v) *Nutcracker*. (iii; viii) CHOPIN (orch. DOUGLAS): *Les Sylphides*. (ix) ROSSINI (arr. Respighi): *La Boutique fantasque*.

(B) **(*) Decca KDPC 515/6.

These sets of excerpts are quite cleverly edited so that they often amount to a miniature suite of highlights. The performances are generally distinguished, though it is a pity that the *Panorama* was chosen for inclusion within Monteux's *Sleeping Beauty* selection: he plays it rather too fast. The recording standard is high, only the Ansermet *Coppélia* slipping a little below the overall quality, which mixes brilliance and warmth very agreeably. Of course the choice of items from the Tchaikovsky ballets is arbitrary, but they sound well in context. The excerpts from *La Fille mal gardée* (including

the *Clog dance*) and *Giselle* are particularly enjoyable.

'Favourite ballet suites' (with (i) LPO; (ii) RPO; (iii) Netherlands Radio PO; (iv) LSO; all cond. Black): (i) DELIBES: *Coppélia; Sylvia*. (ii) TCHAIKOVSKY: *Nutcracker, Op. 71a*. (iii) MASSENET: *Le Cid*. MEYER-BEER (arr. Lambert): *Les Patineurs*. (iv) KHACHATURIAN: *Gayaneh*.

(B) ** Decca KDPC 605/6.

These two cassettes are inexpensive and offer a great deal of music. The orchestral playing under Stanley Black is generally first-class, and the music-making has plenty of life and colour. The Delibes suites seem marginally less bright in sound here than in their separate issue, but the balance is agreeably warm and full. Indeed the transfers throughout are sophisticated and *Gayaneh* is transferred with a keen edge of brilliance that many will find exciting. The Massenet and Meyerbeer suites are particularly successful in their transient sparkle, although on our copy there were one or two quiet passages where the orchestral texture was fractionally insecure. But the one real drawback to the set is the recording of the *Nutcracker suite*, where there is very little dynamic range and the orchestral wind solos are consistently larger than life. The *Miniature overture* starts after the last two numbers of *Sylvia*, and the increase in level is startling – there is absolutely no suggestion of the gentle opening that Tchaikovsky intended.

'The world of ballet', Vol. 2 – 'Ballet music from the opera' (cond. Gibson, Kertesz, Gardelli, Ansermet): GOUNOD: *Faust*, Act 5: ballet suite. SMETANA: *The Bartered Bride: Polka; Furiant*. PONCHIELLI: *La Gioconda: Dance of the hours*. BORODIN: *Prince Igor: Polovtsian dances* (with chorus).

(M) ** Decca KCSP 97.

Volume 1 of *The world of the ballet* (KCSP 55) was a very early tape and is still not available in Dolbyized form. Volume 2 was given the Dolby treatment, but the fairly high-level transfer does not always retain its crispness of focus in the climaxes of Gibson's admirably stylish account of the *Faust* ballet music. One would not wish to exaggerate this: the recording remains enjoyably lively, but it is not quite so smooth as on disc. The *Dance of the hours* comes from the complete opera recording, and the surprise entry of the chorus near the beginning also brings a touch of roughness; but the splendidly played *Bartered Bride* dances come over vividly, and Ansermet's set of the *Polovtsian dances* is well managed.

(i) **Bamberg SO;** (ii) **Berlin Radio Orch.**

'Opera intermezzi' (cond. (iii) Kulka; (iv) Leitner; (v) Strauss; (vi) Fricsay) from: (i; iii) MASCAGNI: *Cavalleria Rusticana.* (ii; v) *L'Amico Fritz.* (i; iv) LEONCAVALLO: *I Pagliacci,* Act 1. (ii; v) PUCCINI: *Manon Lescaut,* Act 3. *Suor Angelica.* (i; iii) SCHMIDT: *Notre Dame.* (ii; v) WOLF-FERRARI: *Il Campiello. I Quattro rusteghi.* GIORDANO: *Fedora,* Act 2. CILEA: *Adriana Lecouvreur,* Act 2. (ii; vi) PONCHIELLI: *La Gioconda: Dance of the hours.*

(B)**DG Heliodor 3348 279.

These recordings come from a number of sources, and yet the sound is remarkably consistent. There is some lack of sumptuousness but overall the balance is good and because the transfer is a lively one it is possible to produce a smooth body to the string timbre (which dominates many of these pieces), cut back the hiss, and yet not lose the life of the recordings. The most distinguished items are those originally issued on an outstanding early stereo ten-inch LP by the Berlin Radio Orchestra under Paul Strauss.

These include the two Wolf-Ferrari pieces, delectable morsels exquisitely played, a very good *Manon Lescaut* excerpt and equally characterful intermezzi from *Fedora, Adriana Lecouvreur* and (especially) *L'Amico Fritz.* This is well worth its modest cost.

Berlin PO, Karajan

'The wonder of Karajan': overtures: MENDELSSOHN: *The Hebrides (Fingal's Cave), Op. 26.* NICOLAI: *The Merry Wives of Windsor.* WEBER: *Der Freischütz.* WAGNER: *Der fliegende Holländer (The Flying Dutchman). Lohengrin: Prelude to Act 1.*

(M)**HMV TC-EXE 205.

The title *The wonder of Karajan* covers a collection originally recorded for the Columbia label in the early sixties and later reissued by World Record Club. The performances are all strongly characterized, and the reverberant acoustic and forward balance give them a robustness - one would not expect from Karajan's later DG recordings. *Fingal's Cave* and the *Lohengrin Prelude* are especially successful, although some might find the lack of a real *pianissimo* at the opening and close of the latter piece a drawback. The transfer is made at a high level, the reverberation reasonably well controlled, and although there is some lack of ultimate refinement, the quality is undoubtedly vivid.

'Opera intermezzi' from: VERDI: *La Traviata (Prelude to Act 3).* MASCAGNI: *L'Amico Fritz; Cavalleria Rusticana.* PUCCINI: *Suor Angelica; Manon Lescaut.* LEONCAVALLO: *I Pagliacci.* MUSSORGSKY: *Khovantschina (Prelude to Act 4).* SCHMIDT: *Notre Dame.* MASSENET: *Thaïs (Meditation).* GIORDANO: *Fedora.* CILEA: *Adriana Lecouvreur.* WOLF-FERRARI: *I Gioielli della*

Madonna (Jewels of the Madonna).
**(*)DG 923047.

Karajan shows his mastery of phrase and idiom immediately in the opening *La Traviata Prelude*, which is beautifully done, and the same poise gives distinction to the famous *Cavalleria Rusticana Intermezzo* and indeed the Puccini items. Where high drama is called for, as in the music of the verismo school, Karajan rises to the occasion and one can hear the resin sizzle as those Berlin string bows bite. The pervading atmosphere of melancholy and melodrama is lightened only in the Wolf-Ferrari piece, and because of this lack of variety of mood one's recommendation must be slightly tempered. However, those who fancy the programme will not be disappointed by the performances or the recording, which is extremely vivid. The very wide dynamic range of the climaxes of *L'Amico Fritz* and the *Pagliacci* intermezzi has meant a relatively low transfer level, but the sound remains well detailed, and the atmospheric acoustic is exactly right. The orchestral playing is marvellous.

'Ballet from the opera': BORODIN: *Prince Igor: Polovtsian dances.* TCHAIKOVSKY: *Eugene Onegin: Polonaise; Waltz.* VERDI: *Aïda: ballet music. Otello: ballet music.* PON-CHIELLI: *La Gioconda: Dance of the hours.*
**(*)DG 3300 206.

Although the recording here sounds just a trifle dated, without quite the body to the upper strings, or the overall sumptuousness of timbre, we would expect now, the transfer to cassette has been quite successful, offering a good balance and range. The orchestral playing is first-class, and Karajan's approach from first to last shows a care for detail and a freshness as if he were coming to these pieces for the first time. There is vivid excitement in the *Polovtsian* dances and an attractively light touch in the Tchaikovsky

waltz. The sinuous phrasing of the *Dance of the priests* from *Aïda* (which opens side two) is matched by the charm and colour of the opening section of the *Dance of the hours*. An enjoyable collection.

'Adagio': ALBINONI: *Adagio in G minor* (arr. Giazotto) *for strings and organ.* PACHELBEL: *Canon and Gigue in D major* (arr. Seiffert). BOCCHERINI: *Quintettino (La musica notturna di Madrid).* RESPIGHI: *Ancient airs and dances: Suite No. 3.* VIVALDI: *Concerto for strings in G major (Alla rustica), P.143.*
***DG 3300 317 [id.].

Karajan's performance of Albinoni's famous *Adagio* must be the plushiest ever, and in its way it is irresistible, like a particularly enticing meringue. The playing is very beautiful indeed, as it is also in Pachelbel's *Canon* (another curiously memorable trifle), where the orchestral tone is utterly sumptuous, the harpsichord emerging through the rich textures like a piquant condiment. The *Gigue* that follows, however, is too thick-textured to sound spritely, though it remains pleasingly elegant. The Boccherini *Quintettino* is unusually evocative and most engagingly presented, while the Vivaldi concerto (which is not included on the equivalent disc) and the Respighi suite have an appealing grace. The recording is first-class and the tape transfer of very high quality.

'Karajan festival': MOZART: *Serenade No. 13 in G major (Eine kleine Nachtmusik), K.525.* SMETANA: *Má Vlast: Vltava.* BRAHMS: *Hungarian dances Nos. 1 in G minor; 3 in F major; 5 in G minor; 6 in D major.* LISZT: *Les Préludes* (symphonic poem), *G.97.*
(M)***DG 3308 071.

With its bright yet full-blooded sound this is one of DG's most successful cassettes; *Les Préludes* is more effective as a recording here than on the several LPs on which this performance appears. *Eine kleine Nachtmusik* is given a singularly fresh performance, and *Vltava* is beautifully played. The Brahms *Dances* too are bright without being fierce. A most enjoyable medium-priced cassette: highly recommended.

'The waltz': waltzes from DELIBES: *Coppélia* (*Swanilda's scene*). CHOPIN: *Les Sylphides* (*Opp. 18, 64/2*). BERLIOZ: *Symphonie fantastique* (*Un bal*). TCHAIKOVSKY: *Nutcracker* (*Waltz of flowers*). *Serenade for strings, Op. 48.* SIBELIUS: *Kuolema: Valse triste, Op. 44.* STRAUSS, Johann: *An der schönen blauen Donau* (*Blue Danube*), *Op. 314.*

(M)**(*)DG Privilege 3318 010.

This is a more successful compilation on tape than on disc. The recording is pleasingly warm and smooth, yet clear too, and should make admirable late-evening listening. The performances are suave but beautifully made: the caressing way Karajan begins the waltz from Tchaikovsky's *String serenade* is characteristic, and the excerpts from *Coppélia* and *Les Sylphides* are very successful, as is the waltz from the *Symphonie fantastique*, which sounds surprisingly well in this context. Only the *Blue Danube* is slightly disappointing: it has an atmospheric opening, but Karajan is too mannered and loses much of the inherent vitality of the piece.

'Dreams': BACH: *Suite No. 2 in B minor, BWV 1067: Rondeau. Suite No. 3 in D major, BWV 1068: Air.* MOZART: *Serenade No. 13 in G major* (*Eine kleine Nachtmusik*), *K. 525: Romanze.* DELIBES: *Coppélia: Ballade.* MASSENET: *Thaïs: Meditation.* CHOPIN (orch. Douglas): *Les Sylphides: Prelude; Nocturne.* SIBEL-

IUS: *Legends: The Swan of Tuonela, Op. 22/2.* DEBUSSY: *Prélude à l'après-midi d'un faune.*

(M)**(*)DG Privilege 3308 019.

Karajan's perfumed Bach performances are best heard as a pleasing background for the late evening, when one can perhaps admire the superbly polished orchestral playing (the harpsichord tinking just audibly in the background). The rest of the programme is first-rate in every way, and this anthology is most successfully compiled. The recording is resonantly atmospheric in exactly the right way and the high-level transfer has brought demonstration sound quality, particularly in the latter part of the programme, where the performances are highly distinguished. The Debussy *Prélude* sounds quite ravishingly beautiful.

'Hi-fi Karajan': BIZET: *Carmen suite No. 1.* STRAUSS, Johann: *Wiener Blut* (*Vienna Blood*) *waltz, Op. 354.* MOZART: *Serenade No. 6 in D major* (*Serenata notturna*), *K.239.* ROSSINI: *La Gazza ladra* (*The Thieving Magpie*) *overture.* MENDELSSOHN: *The Hebrides* (*Fingal's Cave*) *overture, Op. 26.*

(M)*(*)DG Privilege 3335 253.

The opening of this cassette, the suite from *Carmen*, certainly fits its title, *Hi-fi Karajan*, for the sound is brilliant and sparkling to match the sophisticated orchestral playing. The *Serenata notturna*, which comes next, is duller in quality (as well as not showing the conductor at his most sparkling), and *Vienna Blood* is only moderately successful. The recording of *La Gazza ladra*, which opens side two, is reverberant and rather confused at the opening, but *Fingal's Cave* is successful, with generally good sound to match fine playing.

Overtures: BEETHOVEN: *Fidelio, Op. 72b.* MENDELSSOHN: *The Hebrides*

695

(*Fingal's Cave*), *Op. 26*. WEBER: *Oberon*. SUPPÉ: *Light Cavalry*. STRAUSS, Johann: *Die Fledermaus*. ROSSINI: *William Tell*.

(M)**DG Privilege 3335 310.

These are all first-class performances. The *Hebrides* and *Oberon*, besides being beautifully played, show considerable poetry and romantic feeling, while *Light Cavalry* and *Die Fledermaus* have plenty of zest and panache. The recordings are of basically high quality, but it is a pity that the tape opens with *Fidelio*, where the tuttis show an element of congestion. The focus is not always crisp in *Oberon*, but otherwise the sound is generally good if not outstanding.

'*Allegro non troppo*' (with (i) Berlin PO, Karajan; (ii) Munich CO, Stadlmair; (iii) Berlin Radio Orch., Maazel): (i) DEBUSSY: *Prélude à l'après-midi d'un faune*. DVOŘÁK: *Slavonic dance No. 7 in C minor, Op. 46/7*. RAVEL: *Boléro*. SIBELIUS: *Kuolema: Valse triste, Op. 44*. (ii) VIVALDI: *Concerto for 2 oboes, 2 clarinets and strings, P. 74*: 1st movt. (iii) STRAVINSKY: *Firebird suite*: excerpts.

(M)**DG Privilege 3335 400.

This selection was inspired by Bruno Bozzetto's cartoon film *Allegro non troppo*, which was not without wit or imaginative imagery, but was rather spoiled by the heavy humour of the photographed orchestral scenes. However, those who enjoyed the film and want a reminder of it will find that the performances here are all first-class. The recording tends to be bright, and on tape the upper string sound is rather thin at the climax of the Debussy *Prélude*; and it has a positive cutting edge in the Dvořák *Slavonic dance*. But the overall balance is good.

'*Karajan highlights*': GRIEG: *Peer Gynt suite No. 1, Op. 46: Morning*.

PONCHIELLI: *La Gioconda: Dance of the hours*. SUPPÉ: *Light Cavalry overture*. WEBER: *Invitation to the Dance, Op. 65* (arr. Berlioz). VIVALDI: *The Four Seasons: Spring, Op. 8/1*. SIBELIUS: *Finlandia, Op. 26*. TCHAIKOVSKY: *Eugene Onegin: Waltz; Polonaise*. STRAUSS, Johann, Jnr, and Josef: *Pizzicato polka*.

(M)*(*)DG 3345 034.

Immaculate playing and a varied if rather bitty programme. The *Dance of the hours* is a highlight, but all the music-making is strongly characterized. The recording is good, but the rather low transfer level detracts from the immediacy and sharpness of detail. However, the quality is fully acceptable, even if one knows that the parent tapes of some of these items produce fuller and more vivid results.

(i) Berlin PO; (ii) Philharmonia Orch.; Karajan

'*Karajan favourites*': (i) SMETANA: *Má Vlast: Vltava*. MENDELSSOHN: Overture: *The Hebrides* (*Fingal's Cave*), *Op. 26*. (ii) TCHAIKOVSKY: *1812 overture, Op. 49*. CHABRIER: *España*. ROSSINI: Overture: *Il Barbiere di Siviglia*. BIZET: *Carmen: Suite No. 1*. LISZT: *Hungarian rhapsody No. 2, G.359*. LEONCAVALLO: *I Pagliacci: Intermezzo*. BORODIN: *Prince Igor: Polovtsian dances*. WALDTEUFEL: *Les Patineurs* (*The Skaters*) *waltz, Op. 183*. STRAUSS, Johann, Snr: *Radetzky march*.

(M)**HMV TC-SXDW 3048.

Vintage Karajan performances offering superb orchestral playing and strongly characterized music-making throughout. Chabrier's *España* is not a work one associates with Karajan, but it certainly sparkles. The recording is full and vivid, and it is a pity that the first of the two cassettes is fractionally over-modulated, causing occasional patches of roughness, most noticeable in *1812* (and not only at the final climax) and *España.*

Berlin PO, Solti

'The world of Russia': MUS-SORGSKY: *Night on the Bare Mountain. Khovantschina: Prelude to Act 1; Persian dance.* BORODIN: *Prince Igor: Overture.* GLINKA: *Russlan and Ludmilla: Overture.*

(M)***Decca KCSP 257.

It is fascinating to compare this concert with the similar collection Solti made with the LSO (*Romantic Russia:* see below). The great Berlin orchestra obviously had a softening effect on Solti's vibrant musical nature, and the tightly strung nervous tension characteristic of the earlier collection has mellowed slightly here. *Night on the Bare Mountain* is splendidly exciting, yet the interpretation is a spacious one and the lyrical closing section must be one of the sweetest ever recorded. A similar radiance pervades the beautifully flowing *Khovantschina Prelude,* which is very successful, and there is sensuous orchestral playing in the *Persian dance. Russlan and Ludmilla* has a fraction less impetus here than in the London performance, and some may enjoy it for this slightly more relaxed air (in London the dash and virtuosity of the LSO's playing were paramount). The performance of the *Prince Igor overture* is extremely romantic, with an unexpected ritenuto for the second subject. This is disconcerting on first hearing, but one soon adjusts when the playing is so warmly committed and the recording so richly projected. On tape the resonance prevents crystal clarity in the *Russlan overture,* but the *Khovantschina* items are really demonstration-worthy, with a fine bloom on wind and strings alike. On side two *Night on the Bare Mountain* has plenty of weight and the overture to *Prince Igor* is richly-bodied. This is excellent value.

Berlin Radio SO, Fricsay

'Opera ballets': GOUNOD: *Faust: ballet suite.* VERDI: *Aïda: ballet music. Otello: ballet music.* PONCHIELLI: *La Gioconda: Dance of the hours.* TCHAIKOVSKY: *Eugene Onegin: Polonaise; Waltz.*

(B)**DG Heliodor 3348 133.

Fricsay is at his most vividly incisive in the *Otello* ballet music, which begins side two. His performance of the *Dance of the hours* is no less alert, and is notable for vivacity rather than warmth – Karajan (see above) is more beguiling. The two Tchaikovsky dances which close the concert are strongly rhythmic and full of personality (there is a characteristic broadening of tempo at the final reprise of the main waltz tune before the coda). Side one, which on tape is transferred at a lower level, offers much more mellow music-making in the *Faust* ballet music, with more recessed sound to match the almost sleepy tempi; and the sensuous elements of the *Aïda* score are emphasized. An enjoyable collection; the sound is not too dated.

'Birds in music'

(i) LSO; (ii) Kertesz; (iii) James Bowman, Peter Pears, John Shirley-Quirk, with Benjamin Britten; (iv) George Malcolm (harpsichord); (v) Joan Sutherland, LSO, Bonynge; (vi) Gamba; (vii) Wilhelm Backhaus (piano); (viii) Jascha Silberstein (cello), Marie Goossens (harp); (ix) Consuelo Rubio (soprano), National Orch. of Spain, Argenta; (x) Vienna PO, Boskovsky: (i; ii) RESPIGHI: *The Birds* (suite): excerpts. (iii) PURCELL: *When the cock begins to crow.* (iv) DAQUIN: *Le Coucou.* (v) BENEDICT: *The Gypsy and the Bird.* (i; vi) ROSSINI: Overture: *La Gazza ladra* (*The Thieving Magpie*). (vii) SCHUMANN: *Waldsce-*

697

nen: The prophet bird. (viii) SAINT-SAËNS: *Carnival of the Animals: The swan.* (ix) GRANADOS: *Goyescas: La maja y el ruisenor (The maiden and the nightingale).* (x) STRAUSS, Josef: *Dorfschwalben aus Österreich (Village Swallows) waltz, Op. 164.* Wildlife recordings: Dawn chorus; cockerels; cuckoos; linnet; magpies; green woodpecker; nightingale.

⊛ (M) *** Decca KCSP 367.

A quite delightful anthology, with bird songs very happily edited into the fabric as introductions to each piece. The playing and singing are throughout of the very highest quality, and the recording – wonderfully rich and warm and vivid – is matched by a transfer at the highest level. A most desirable issue and an ideal gift tape.

Bolshoi Theatre Orchestra Violins, Reyentovitch

'Presenting the Violins of the Bolshoi Theatre': music by GRANADOS; DEBUSSY; DINICU; SAINT-SAËNS; GRIEG; KHACHATURIAN; RUBINSTEIN; FAURÉ; SARASATE; RAVEL; SIBELIUS; HANDEL; LULLY; PARADIS; BACH–GOUNOD; SCHUBERT; MENDELSSOHN; SMETANA; DVOŘÁK; GRIEG; RIMSKY-KORSAKOV; VLASOV; PROKOFIEV.

(M)** HMV TC-ESDW 707.

This much more extended HMV collection is presumably played by the same group as that on the Heliodor tape below. The repertoire is similar, the acoustic resonant, although the recording is clear and for the most part cleanly transferred. Often the sound is excellent, with body and lustre as well as good detail. Just occasionally the transfer loses its refinement of focus, as in the *Navarra* of Sarasate, where the solo violins featured bring a peaky overmodulation. There are many favourite tunes here, and the concert includes minor contributions from three vocal soloists. Grieg's *Ich liebe dich* sounds well in Russian when sung so reasonantly (by Ivan Petrov). If you enjoy light classical music, veering towards the salon but always tuneful, this pair of tapes should give satisfaction. The notes quote Sir Thomas Beecham's remark that music 'should allure, enchant the ear, never mind the inner significance'. He would undoubtedly have enjoyed conducting many of the items here, and Yuri Reyentovitch presents most of them with undoubted flair. The closing *Waltz* from Prokofiev's *War and Peace* is very nicely done.

Bolshoi Violin Ens., Reyentovitch

'Russian melodies': RIMSKY-KORSAKOV: *Tsar Saltan: Flight of the bumble bee.* SHOSTAKOVICH: *The Gadfly: Romance.* FIBICH: *Poème.* DVOŘÁK: *Gipsy melody. Serenade for strings in E major, Op. 22.* SVETLANOV: *Aria.* PROKOFIEV: *War and Peace: Waltzes.* RACHMANINOV: *Vocalise, Op. 34/14.* RUBINSTEIN: *Melody in F major, Op. 3/1.*

(B)** DG Heliodor 3348 270.

A fascinating 'old-world' collection recalling the Palm Court days, although the sound this group of excellent string players makes is lusciously rich, souped up by the resonance. Do not be put off by the opening *Flight of the bumble bee,* which produces a curiously gritty sound. After this the recording settles down and is agreeably rich and lustrous. To make the sound even more nostalgic a 'piano continuo' is used; the pianist stays at the keyboard through 'the Dvořák *String serenade* (played complete) and even makes an effective concertante contribution to the *Larghetto.* But it is for melodies like the *Poème* of Fibich and the Rubinstein *Melody in F* that this collection is memorable, and they are splendidly done – which is not to say that the Dvořák work is not very effectively presented too.

Boston Pops Orch., Fiedler

'Fiedler encores': SIBELIUS: Finlandia, Op. 26. SMETANA: Má Vlast: Vltava. DVOŘÁK: Slavonic dance No. 1 in C major, Op. 46/1. VAUGHAN WILLIAMS: English folksongs suite. IVES: Variations on 'America' (orch. Schuman).
** Decca Phase 4 KPFC 4426 [Lon. 5–21178].

A characteristically lively concert. Arthur Fiedler always keeps the musical pot boiling, even if his balance of the various ingredients lacks subtlety. The robust items come off best, notably the outer movements of the Folksongs suite and the splendidly rumbustious performance of Ives's Variations on 'America'. Finlandia is quite exciting, although at the opening the recording seems over-resonant in the bass. The overall balance is forward, which precludes wide dynamic contrasts but ensures good projection and detail if not the last degree of refinement.

Bournemouth Sinfonietta, Wagenheim

Italian baroque concertos: BARSANTI: Concerto grosso in D major, Op. 3/10. GEMINIANI: Concerto grosso in E minor, Op. 3/3. ALBINONI: Sinfonia in G major. MANFREDINI: Double trumpet concerto in D major (with Keith Chalmers and Malcolm Weale, trumpets).
** HMV TC-ASD 3630.

These are strong, spirited performances, vividly played and richly and clearly recorded. Volker Wagenheim is at his very best in the delightful Op. 3/3 of Geminiani with its gracious opening Adagio e staccato. This is played with much character, and the work's slow movement is admirably expressive. But in some of the other movements here the playing seems too rhythmically forceful. These are Italian concertos, and one feels at times one has removed to Northern Europe, with its less sunny atmosphere. However, the playing is always alert and the balance allows the continuo to come through clearly. The transfer is full and clean, with excellent detail, although the sound has a slight edge, which increases the feeling that the allegros lack resilience.

Bournemouth SO, Berglund

'Entry of the Boyars': SCHALASTER: Dance Liana. BULL, Ole: The Herd Girl's Sunday. GLINKA: Waltz fantasy. RIMSKY-KORSAKOV: May Night: Overture. GLAZOUNOV: Concert waltz No. 1 in D major, Op. 47. HALVORSEN: Entry of the Boyars. SIBELIUS: Karelia suite, Op. 11: Intermezzo; Alla marcia. Spring song, Op. 16. Scènes historiques, Op. 25: Festivo.
** HMV TC-ASD 3514.

A generally attractive concert. The Herd Girl's Sunday by Ole Bull is especially fetching, reminding one of the Norwegian melodies of Grieg. The three Russian pieces go especially well: they are lively and colourful, and the Glazounov Concert waltz has never been recorded with such sparkle before. The Sibelius items are a little disappointing, especially Karelia, which is not given enough joie de vivre. The recording is rich, with plenty of bloom, and the tape transfer is good, although the sound in the title piece, which opens the concert, is not always completely refined.

Bournemouth SO, Silvestri

'Stereo showpieces': MUSSORGSKY: Night on the Bare Mountain. RAVEL: Pavane pour une infante défunte.

SAINT-SAËNS: *Danse macabre, Op. 40.* SIBELIUS: *Finlandia, Op. 26.* BORODIN: *In the Steppes of Central Asia.* DUKAS: *L'Apprenti sorcier.*

(M) *** HMV Greensleeve TC-ESD 7064.

The late Constantin Silvestri is heard at his very best here, especially in the pieces which call for brilliance. Moreover the Studio Two recording – originally slightly dry – has transferred splendidly to tape: the sound has both breadth and sparkle and is admirably clear in detail. *Night on the Bare Mountain* opens the concert vividly, and both the *Danse macabre* and *The Sorcerer's Apprentice* are exciting and colourful. *Finlandia* too is done with plenty of gusto. The slower pieces lack the last degree of expansiveness and poetry, but within the context of the programme they are undoubtedly enjoyable when the overall transfers are so successful.

Bournemouth SO, Susskind

'Invitation to the waltz': STRAUSS, Johann: *Frühlingsstimmen (Voices of Spring), Op. 410.* WEBER: *Invitation to the Dance.* WALDTEUFEL: *Les Patineurs (The Skaters), Op. 183.* STRAUSS, Josef: *Sphärenklänge (Music of the Spheres), Op. 235.* TCHAIKOVSKY: *Eugene Onegin: Waltz.* KHACHATURIAN: *Masquerade: Waltz.* LEHÁR: *The Merry Widow: Waltz.*

(M) *(**) HMV Greensleeve TC-ESD 7056.

The novelty here is Weber's *Invitation to the Dance*, not in the usual Berlioz arrangement but in a version by Weingartner. With a conductor's flair for 'what comes off' the orchestration has some attractive colourings, and at the end Weingartner brings the main tune back in the brass. The performances here are all polished, the *Waltz* from *Eugene*

Onegin being specially affectionate. The recording is warmly resonant and all the music is played with character. *Voices of Spring* and the *Skaters' waltz* (with a fine horn solo at the beginning) are strikingly vivacious. Unfortunately the high-level transfer is coarsened at times by the considerable reverberation, although no one could complain that the results are not vivid.

Brüggen, Frans (recorder)

'Recorder concertos' (with Vienna Concentus Musicus, Harnoncourt): VIVALDI: *Concerto in C minor, P.440.* SAMMARTINI: *Concerto in F major.* TELEMANN: *Concerto in C major.* NAUDOT: *Concerto in G major.*

**(*) Telefunken CX 4.41095.

Frans Brüggen is probably the greatest master of the recorder now before the public, and he gives these four assorted concertos keen advocacy. (In the Vivaldi he even takes part in the tutti.) In his hands, phrases are turned with the utmost sophistication, intonation is unbelievably accurate and matters of style exact. There is spontaneity too, and for its superb musicianship, excellent recording, and well-balanced orchestral contribution this collection can earn nothing but praise. The Telemann concerto is an especially fine one, and Brüggen and Harnoncourt bring out the music's grace with sure sensitivity. In the Vivaldi the roulades are thrown off with consummate ease, and even the less striking Naudot piece emerges as music of character. The transfer is very lively, but this was an early Telefunken issue and the chrome tape produces a degree of edginess towards the end of side two (the Naudot); and the orchestral textures at times have a lack of complete security – the timbre (not the pitch) is sometimes a little unsteady. But for the most part this can be made to sound very well.

Cantilena, Shepherd

'*English music 1600–1750*': HANDEL: *Concerto grosso in D major, Op. 6/5.* PURCELL: *Chacony in G minor.* FERRABOSCO: *Pavane.* BRADE: *Suite of 3 dances.* BOYCE: *Concerto grosso in B minor.*

(M) *(*) RCA Gold Seal GK 25135.

This *Concerto grosso* is one of the very finest of Handel's Op. 6 set. It has six movements of great variety and resource and is the very epitome of the baroque instrumental spirit. It is given a strong, almost aggressive performance here, and the same alert, vigorous playing extends throughout this attractively balanced programme. The recording is brightly lit and is cleanly transferred, with the continuo coming through well. However, the music never seems to relax and smile. It is partly the fault of the transfer, which lacks something in bloom, but it also stems from the playing, which, though it has plenty of life and impulse, less readily creates a feeling of repose.

'Capriccio espagnol'

(i) LSO, Martinon; (ii) Suisse Romande Orch., Ansermet; (iii) LSO, Argenta; (iv) Paris Conservatoire Orch., Morel: (i) RIMSKY-KORSAKOV: *Capriccio espagnol, Op. 34.* (ii) GLINKA: *Jota aragonesa.* (iii) MOSZKOWSKI: *Spanish dances, Book 1, Op. 12.* (iv) RAVEL: *Rapsodie espagnole.*

(M) *(**) Decca KCSP 182.

Martinon's *Capriccio espagnol* is among the most brilliant available, but Morel's account of Ravel's *Rapsodie*, although well played, is rather deadpan. Argenta, however, does the charming Moszkowski dances most vivaciously, and Ansermet is predictably colourful in the *Jota aragonesa*. With excellent recording quality throughout, this could be a

most attractive collection of Spanish music by non-Spanish composers, but unfortunately the early tape transfer produces a rather muddy bass. The opening of the *Capriccio* is confused and there are moments elsewhere when there seems marginally too much amplitude. Our copy (a new tape sampled at the time of going to press) also had moments of 'pulsing' at climaxes in the *Capriccio* and the *Rapsodie.* For much of the time the sound is excellent, with plenty of bloom and warmth, and the Moszkowski *Dances* make a delightful effect. However, this issue obviously needs remastering.

'Carnival'

(i) LSO; (ii) Kertesz; (iii) Paris Conservatoire Orch.; (iv) Morel; (v) Suisse Romande Orch., Ansermet; (vi) Martinon; (vii) Monteux; (viii) Katchen, Graffman (pianos); cond. Henderson: (i; ii) DVOŘÁK: *Carnaval overture, Op. 92.* (iii; iv) ALBÉNIZ: *Iberia: Fête-Dieu à Séville.* (v) SCHUMANN: *Carnaval* (ballet): excerpts. (iii; vi) BERLIOZ: *Le Carnaval romain overture, Op. 9.* (i; vii) DEBUSSY: *Nocturnes: Fêtes.* (i; viii) SAINT-SAËNS: *Carnival of the Animals:* excerpts.

(M) *(*) Decca KCSP 174.

'Carnival' is an ingenious basis for a selection, and this programme is imaginatively chosen. It opens well with a distinguished and exciting account of Dvořák's overture, but one immediately notices that this was an early Decca transfer and there is some clouding in the bass at climaxes. This happens in the Albéniz too, and the recording of the *Carnival of the Animals* does not sparkle here as it does in its other (complete) appearance in a Decca anthology, *Animals in music* (see above).

Casals, Pablo (cello and cond.)

'Song of the birds': TRAD. (arr. Casals): *Song of the birds; St Marti del Canigo* (with Prades Festival Orch.). BACH: *Organ pastorale in F major; Aria* (with Perpignan Festival Orch.). *Organ concerto No. 3* (trans. Rosanoff). HAYDN: *Piano sonata No. 9 in D major: Adagio.* FALLA: *7 Spanish popular songs: Nana* (with E. Istomin, piano). SCHUMANN: *5 Pieces in folk style* (with L. Mannes, piano).

(M) ** CBS 40–61579.

The main interest here is the title piece, which seems to have caught the public fancy. The rest of the programme is most notable for Casals's own vocal contribution – various grunts and expressions of ardour accompanying the playing. The recording is good but a trifle dry and the transfer is acceptable (not wide in range but quite convincingly balanced), even if the upper focus of the cello timbre is not always quite clean.

Chacksfield, Frank, and his Orch.

'The world of immortal classics': DEBUSSY: *Suite bergamasque: Clair de lune.* SAINT-SAËNS: *Carnival of the Animals: The swan.* ELGAR: *Salut d'amour.* TCHAIKOVSKY: *Nutcracker: Waltz of the flowers.* LISZT: *Liebestraum No. 3.* RUBINSTEIN: *Melody in F.* GRIEG: *Peer Gynt: Morning.* DVOŘÁK: *Humoresque.* BACH: *Suite No. 3: Air.* ALSTONE: *Valse d'été.*

(M) *** Decca KCSP 176.

The title *Immortal classics* suggests that this might be a glamorous selection, and that is certainly so. Purists are urged to keep well away, but those who like to wallow in gorgeously rich orchestral textures should sample this. The arrangements are unashamedly vulgar (yet in an essentially stylish way), with Saint-Saëns's *Swan* portrayed on divided strings floating serenely as on a Disneyland lake against a reflected Hollywood sunset. The sound really is luscious throughout and each piece is ripely characterized, with Alstone's charming *Valse d'été* fetchingly lightweight at the close. The cassette is very highly modulated but there is barely a ripple of interference at the climaxes, for the sound offers wide dynamic contrasts (inherent in the playing), with splendid detail and range.

'The world of immortal serenades' from: BIZET: *The Fair Maid of Perth.* ROMBERG: *The Student Prince.* MOZART: *Don Giovanni.* OFFENBACH: *The Tales of Hoffmann: Barcarolle.* DONIZETTI: *Don Pasquale.* BERLIOZ: *La Damnation de Faust: Mefistofeles' serenade.* MASCAGNI: *Cavalleria Rusticana: Siciliano.* TCHAIKOVSKY: *Romeo and Juliet:* Love theme. TOSELLI: *Serenade.* PIERNE: *Serenade.* DRIGO: *Serenade: Les Millions d'Arlequin.* SCHUBERT: *Ständchen.* BRAGA: *Angel's serenade.* YOUNG: *Serenade to a Mandarin.*

(M) *** Decca KCSP 298.

This is a most enjoyable collection, with vivacious, smiling orchestral playing which sounds as if players and conductor alike are hugely enjoying this feast of good tunes. The arrangements are romanticized but usually tasteful, and even the truncated version of Tchaikovsky's *Romeo and Juliet* is rather well managed. All the lighter pieces are given plenty of sparkle and colour, and the operatic melodies from *Don Pasquale* and *The Fair Maid of Perth* have the lilt of enjoyment that permeates this whole tape. As with KCSP 176 (above), if you are a purist, stay away; otherwise this is a first-class entertainment, and the excellence of the cassette transfer is striking, with vivid orchestral colours, detail and sparkle. The orchestral quality is less sumptuous than the equivalent disc, notably in the matter of the body of string tone, but this is a most enjoyable tape.

Chicago SO, Barenboim

LISZT: *Les Préludes* (symphonic poem), *G.97*. DVOŘÁK: *Slavonic dances in C major and G minor, Op. 46/1 and 8*. SMETANA: *Má Vlast: Vltava*. BRAHMS: *Hungarian dances Nos. 1 in G minor; 3 in F major; 10 in F major*.
**(*) DG 3301 054.

A highly imaginative performance of *Vltava* from Barenboim, beautifully played by the Chicago orchestra – the moonlight flickering in the water is memorably evocative – and a fine version of *Les Préludes* too, with dignity as well as excitement. The Brahms and Dvořák dances make attractive encores (especially the delightfully phrased *Hungarian dance No. 3 in F major*), but some may feel that Barenboim would have done better to include more substantial fare to fill the rest of each side. The recording is rich and atmospheric, notably full in amplitude, but the low-level transfer of our (German-manufactured) review copy, sophisticated though it is, means that the treble response is not as wide-ranging as it might be, although there is no muffling and the cymbals tell convincingly, provided one has the volume well up.

Chicago SO, Solti

'*Five favourite overtures*': WAGNER: *Die Meistersinger* (*Prelude to Act 1*). BERLIOZ: *Les Francs-Juges, Op. 3*. ROSSINI: *Il Barbiere di Siviglia*. BEETHOVEN: *Egmont, Op. 84. Leonora No. 3, Op. 72b*.
*(**) Decca KSXCP 6684 [(d) Lon. 5–6800].

This cassette is disappointingly transferred. The reverberant sound suits the Berlioz best; the Beethoven overtures and the Wagner tend to be rather muddy and lack impact from the upper strings. The performances, of course, are of high quality; the Beethoven items are especially successful.

City of Birmingham SO, Frémaux

'*Louis Frémaux conducts*': RAVEL: *Boléro*. DUKAS: *L'Apprenti sorcier* (*The Sorcerer's Apprentice*). CHABRIER: *España*. DEBUSSY: *Prélude à l'après-midi d'un faune*. SAINT-SAËNS: *Danse macabre, Op. 40*.
**(*) HMV TC-ASD 3008.

These are all enjoyable performances, and the resonant recording brings out their colour. The climax of *Boléro* is well graduated, and there is plenty of excitement at the end, including an effective bass drum. *The Sorcerer's Apprentice* has plenty of life and sparkle, and Chabrier's *España* is hardly less vivid. The Debussy *Prélude* creates an attractive contrast of mood and Frémaux shapes it poetically, while the *Danse macabre* is undoubtedly lively and exciting. Taken as a whole this collection is very satisfying and can be cordially recommended. The transfer to tape has been well managed – especially considering the resonance – and if the last degree of detail is missing, the ripeness of the orchestral texture is effectively handled. There is a momentary problem with the bass drum in *España*, but the end of *Boléro* is not distorted.

Clarinet

'*The world of the clarinet*' (with (i) Alfred Prinz, Stuttgart CO, Münchinger; (ii) Gervase de Peyer, with Cyril Preedy (piano); (iii) Alfred Boskovsky, with members of the Vienna Octet): (i) MOZART: *Clarinet concerto in A major, K.622*. (ii)

WEBER: *Grand duo concertante in E flat major, Op. 48.* DEBUSSY: *Petite Pièce.* HOROVITZ: *2 Majorcan pieces.* (iii) WAGNER: *Adagio for clarinet and strings.* BRAHMS: *Clarinet quintet in B minor, Op. 115:* 3rd movt.

(M) *** Decca KCSP 395.

Such a collection must inevitably include Mozart's *Clarinet concerto,* the most beautiful lyrical concertante work written for any wind instrument; but this (in a fine performance by Alfred Prinz) tends to put the rest of the programme in the shade. Nevertheless the music on side two is imaginatively chosen, and the individual items fit together very well. In particular the Debussy *Petite Pièce* and the two Majorcan miniatures by Horovitz make a witty closing section after the classical and romantic repertoire. The recording is first-rate throughout and the transfers of excellent quality.

'Classical favourites'

(i) ECO, Bonynge; (ii) LSO; (iii) Solti; (iv) Orch. of the Royal Opera House, Covent Garden, Boult; (v) Suisse Romande Orch., Ansermet; (vi) Stuttgart CO, Münchinger; (vii) Kertesz; (viii) Vienna Mozart Ens., Boskovsky; (ix) Vienna PO, Knappertsbusch: (i) HANDEL: *Solomon: Arrival of the Queen of Sheba.* (ii; iii) *Water music: Air. Xerxes: Largo.* (iv) BACH: *Cantata No. 208: Sheep may safely graze.* (v) *Suite No. 3 in D major, BWV 1068: Air. Cantata No. 12: Sinfonia.* (vi) BOCCHERINI: *Quintet in E major, Op. 13/5: Minuet and Trio.* HAYDN (attrib. Hofstetter): *String quartet No. 17 in F major, Op. 3/5: Serenade.* (ii; vii) MOZART: *Masonic funeral music, K.477.* (viii) *German dance, K.605/3: Sleighride. Divertimento No. 17 in D major,*

K.334: Minuet and Trio. (ix) SCHUBERT: *Marche militaire in D major, D.733/1.*

(M) ** Decca KCSP 510.

This agreeable collection of favourites, stylishly performed, is given a consistently high-level transfer, which has the effect of presenting all the music on much the same dynamic plane. Good for the car; and although the last degree of refinement is missing, this makes effective background listening for late evening.

'Classical favourites for the motorway'

(i) Vienna PO, Boskovsky; (ii) Suisse Romande Orch., Stein; (iii) LSO, Abbado; (iv) New Philharmonia Orch., Frühbeck de Burgos; (v) ECO, Britten; (vi) Vienna PO, Mehta; (vii) LSO, Kertesz; (viii) Los Angeles PO, Mehta: (i) REZNIČEK: *Donna Diana: overture.* (ii) SIBELIUS: *Finlandia, Op. 26.* (iii) PROKOFIEV: *Symphony No. 1 in D major (Classical), Op. 25.* (iv) MENDELSSOHN: *A Midsummer Night's Dream overture, Op. 21.* (v) GRAINGER: *Shepherd's Hey.* (vi) WAGNER: *Lohengrin: Prelude to Act 3.* (vii) RESPIGHI: *The Birds: Prelude.* (viii) HOLST: *The Planets, Op. 32: Jupiter.*

**(*) Decca KSXC 15011.

This diverse collection is unexpectedly successful: the element of contrast is effectively used to provide an entertaining concert for the car. The performances are all good ones (Abbado's mellow account of the Prokofiev *Classical symphony* comes up with striking freshness) and the recording consistently good. The transfer was a comparatively early one and the sound has not quite the brilliance of the newest Decca issues; but it is well balanced and sounds congenial at home as well as in the car. Some might feel, however, that the KSXC price-range is too high for an anthology of reissues.

Cleveland Orch., Maazel

Overtures: VERDI: *La Forza del destino.* BEETHOVEN: *The Creatures of Prometheus, Op. 43.* BERLIOZ: *Le Carnaval romain, Op. 9.* GLINKA: *Russlan and Ludmilla.* BRAHMS: *Academic Festival overture, Op. 80.* ROSSINI: *La Gazza ladra (The Thieving Magpie).*
*** Decca KSXC 6782 [Lon. 5–7006].

A most enjoyable tape; the sound balance is in many ways preferable to the disc equivalent. Maazel's charisma is especially well demonstrated by the opening *Forza del destino,* which is superbly played, the arching string cantilena persuasively shaped, and the brass vibrantly exciting. The full-blooded recording is no less impressive in *Le Carnaval romain,* another demonstration item. The only relative disappointment is *La Gazza ladra,* where the reverberation prevents the side-drum from being crystal-clear. But the sound is suitably rich in the *Academic Festival overture,* and the orchestral response throughout the programme is very lively.

Czech PO, Ančerl

'Russian music': TCHAIKOVSKY: *1812 overture, Op. 49. Capriccio italien, Op. 45.* GLINKA: *Russlan and Ludmilla overture.* BORODIN: *In the Steppes of Central Asia.*
(B) (*) Rediffusion Legend KLGD 008.

This collection is notable for including an outstanding performance of Borodin's masterly tone poem *In the Steppes of Central Asia,* as fine as any in the catalogue. The *Capriccio italien* is lively too, but the cassette cannot be recommended:

the sound is meagre, with papery strings in *1812* and curiously insubstantial cannon.

Dances

'The Phase Four world of spectacular dances' (with (i) RPO; (ii) Black; (iii) New Philharmonia Orch., Stokowski; (iv) LSO, Sharples; (v) Kingsway SO, Camarata; (vi) LPO; (vii) Herrmann): (i; ii) GLIÈRE: *The Red Poppy: Russian sailors' dance.* (iii) TCHAIKOVSKY: *Swan Lake: Dance of the Little Swans.* (iv) *Nutcracker: Trepak.* (v) RIMSKY-KORSAKOV: *The Snow Maiden: Dance of the Tumblers.* (vi; vii) RAVEL: *Five o'clock foxtrot.* (vi; ii) OFFENBACH: *Orpheus in the Underworld: Can-can.* WEBER (arr. Berlioz): *Invitation to the dance.* (i; ii) SAINT-SAËNS: *Danse macabre, Op. 40.*
(M) ** Decca KCSP 407.

The Glière *Russian sailors' dance* that opens this concert certainly justifies the title, both as a performance and as a recording; and elsewhere the playing is mostly lively enough, except perhaps in the *Danse macabre,* which is a trifle sober. The Ravel *Five o'clock foxtrot* does not really fit either, but its individual colouring and rhythmic style make for an excellent contrast. The recording is consistently bright, sometimes over-bright, for instance in the *Dance of the Tumblers,* which has thin, edgy upper strings. In the Weber and Saint Saëns the string tone is a little thin too; but the transfer is of high quality, extremely vivid in detail and colour, and many will enjoy this.

Early Music Consort of London, Munrow

'Greensleeves to a ground': ANON.: *Greensleeves to a ground.* DOWLAND: *5 Dances.* WILLIAMS: *Sonata*

in imitation of birds. PURCELL: *Chaconne.* PAISIBLE: *Sonata for 4 recorders.* VAUGHAN WILLIAMS: *Fantasia on Greensleeves. Suite for pipes.* WARLOCK: *Capriol suite: Bransles.* RUBBRA: *Meditazioni.* RICHARDSON: *Beachcomber.*

***HMV TC-CSD 3781.

There is some enchanting music here. One would expect the Elizabethan items to steal the honours, and certainly the Dowland *Dances* (and the famous title piece) are effective, while William Williams's *Trio sonata in imitation of birds* (1703) is charming. But most memorable of all are the Warlock *Bransles* (deliciously scored), the Vaughan Williams *Suite for pipes*, and Richardson's *Beachcomber*, with its enchanting ocarina effects. The only comparatively clumsy arrangement is of Vaughan Williams's *Greensleeves fantasia*, where the piano accompaniment is no substitute for strings. The playing throughout is flawless, and the modest instrumentation has transferred to tape immaculately.

'*Renaissance suite':* music composed and arranged by David MUNROW for the film *La Course en tête*, including excerpts from PRAETORIUS: *Terpsichore;* SUSATO: *The Danserye;* and music by HASSLER; MACQUE; PHALESE; CORELLI.

(M)**(*)HMV TC-HQS 1415.

This music was arranged by the late David Munrow for the film *La Course en tête*, which focused on the cycle races at Grenoble. The suite is divided into twelve movements, each with a title, and the writing seems to increase in imaginative and instrumental resource as it proceeds. The music on side one is infectious and varied enough, ending with a superbly atmospheric item from Praetorius's *Terpsichore* (subtitled *In the mountains*) with trumpet echo effects finally disappearing into the distance. Side two has many de-

lights, not least the exotically scored *Six days of Grenoble* (an original composition by Munrow himself); the beautiful *Tristan's lament* (a fourteenth-century Italian melody); *Why suffer?* (a regal solo of great character); and finally some excellent variations on Corelli's *La Folie d'Espagne* for the full group, with superb recorder flourishes. The sound has marvellous piquancy and is splendidly recorded. On tape the transfer is not quite so crisp and clean on side one as on side two, where the instrumental group has a presence of demonstration quality.

'*Festival of early music':* '*Ecco la primavera'* (Florentine music of the 14th century): including anonymous works and music by LANDINI; PIERO; TERANO; GIOVANNI DA FIRENZE; JACOPO DA BOLOGNA. '*Music of the Crusades':* including anonymous works and music by MARCABRU; Guiot de DIJON; VOGELWEIDE; Le Chatelain de COUCY; GAUCELEM FAIDIT; CONON DE BETHUNE; RICHARD COEUR-DE-LION; THIBAUT DE CHAMPAGNE. '*The triumphs of Maximilian I':* including anonymous works and music by SENFL; ISAAC; KOTTER; FINCK; KREUTZENHOFF.

(M)***Argo K 40 K 33.

This box happily combines three Argo anthologies originally issued separately. They are even more rewarding heard in juxtaposition, though it is not recommended to listen to all three at one session. Tape is the ideal medium for dipping into a collection of this kind – one can so easily take up where one left off. The recording throughout is first-class in every way and the transfers are of demonstration quality, wonderfully clear and vivid. There is an excellent booklet of notes detailing music and instrumentation and providing useful background information.

The fourteenth-century Florentine music on the first cassette should have a wide general appeal. Landini's works are immediately approachable, and so is much else on this fine tape. No one knows exactly how or on what instruments the accompaniment would originally have been performed; the Early Music Consort solve the problem with their usual combination of scholarship and imagination. The singers include artists of the distinction of James Bowman, and the players are quite first-rate. David Munrow's recorder-playing is virtuosic. Attractive music, expertly transcribed and played, and well recorded.

Despite the title of the second cassette, not all the music can be associated with the Crusades themselves, but Ian Bent in his scholarly and informative note does not make particular claims that it is. Again, most of the accompaniments are purely speculative (only the melodic line survives in some cases), so that listeners should be prepared to approach these lively performances for what they are, imaginative reconstructions rather than exact reproductions of what was heard in the thirteenth century. The performances, like the realizations, are brilliantly effective.

Maximilian I was inordinately vain. He was also shrewd enough to see that lavish patronage of the arts would ensure that posterity would remember him. His dedicated support meant that the decade between 1486 and 1496 became a watershed for the medieval development of the German Lied. Clearly the mid-century had been dominated by the music of Ludwig Senfl (who died about 1555), and Senfl's music is rightly given the lion's share of the excellent third tape of this collection. To sample the individuality of Senfl's musical personality try the fourth piece on side one, the piquant bell ringers' trio, *Das Gläut zu Speyer*. In variety of arrangement and sophistication of presentation this tape represents the zenith of the achievement of David Munrow and his Consort.

'*The art of the recorder*' (with Norma Burrowes, soprano; Martyn Hill, tenor; James Bowman, counter-tenor; Robert Lloyd, bass): ANON.: *English dance* (13th century); *Saltarello* (14th century). BARBIREAU: *Een Vrolic Wesen*. ATTAIGNANT (publisher): *4 Chansons*. BYRD: *The leaves be green* (Fantasy). HOLBORNE: *5 Dances*. SCHMELZER: *Sonata à 7 flauti*. PURCELL: *Fantasia: 3 Parts upon a ground*. VIVALDI: *Concerto in A minor*. BASTON: *Concerto in D major*. HANDEL: *Acis and Galatea: O ruddier than the cherry*. BACH: *Cantata No. 208: Sheep may safely graze. Cantata No. 106: Sonatina. Magnificat, BWV 243: Esurientes*. ARNE: *As You Like It: Under the greenwood tree*. COUPERIN: *2 Musettes*. BRITTEN: *Scherzo*. HINDEMITH: *Plöner Musiktag: Trio*. BUTTERLEY: *The white-throated warbler*. DICKINSON: *Recorder music*.

(M) **(*) HMV TC-SLS 5022.

This cleverly arranged anthology shows the recorder in all its roles, from the comparatively simple medieval instrumentation through the Renaissance to the baroque and classical periods; the delightful decorative effect on vocal music is well represented, and the collection ends with some formidable modern examples. The recording is admirably clear and forward, with a fine presence, but there seems to be very little dynamic range in the tape transfer and the ear is troubled after a while by the relative absence of light and shade. The modern scores seem most affected, with the textures and imagery giving a larger-than-life effect.

(i) **Early Music Consort;** (ii) **Morley Consort**

'Two Renaissance dance bands' (both dir. Munrow): (i) SUSATO: *12 Dances from 'The Danserye'.* (ii) *Dances for broken consort from Thomas Morley's First Booke of Consort Lessons.*

(M)**HMV TC-EXE 104.

Tielman Susato (who lived in the first half of the sixteenth century) left no orchestration for his *Danserye*, directing that the music should be played on musical instruments of all kinds ('as is pleasing and appropriate'). The Early Music Consort take him at his word and provide a galaxy of crumhorns, cornetts, sackbuts, recorders and string instruments, with a regal thrown in for good measure. The instrumentation is nicely varied, with the full forces employed for the set pieces like the *Pavane la bataille*. Perhaps the playing itself is more sophisticated than sixteenth-century listeners would have expected, but it is lively and direct, and the effect is to bring the music fully back to life. The dances from Morley's *First Booke* are given a softer, more delicate instrumentation, which matches well the melancholy grace of the Elizabethan court dance style. Again the playing is committed and there are some really lovely sounds here, which the atmospheric recording sets in excellent perspective. Altogether this is a valuable and enjoyable issue, as useful for schools as for the home, where it will provide some unusual and colourful incidental music. The transfer level is relatively modest to accommodate the wide amplitude of the opening *Mourisque* from the Susato dances, and this means that (especially on side one) the transients are not very crisp. But the recorders make some delightful sounds and in the Morley group on side two the quality seems cleaner.

'Encore'

(i) Berlin PO; (ii) Fricsay; (iii) Bamberg SO, Kraus; (iv) Berlin Radio SO; (v) Leitner: (i; ii) SMETANA: *Má Vlast: Vltava.* (iii) LISZT: *Hungarian rhapsody No. 1, G.359.* (ii; iv) STRAUSS, Johann: *Kaiser* (*Emperor*) *waltz, Op. 437.* (i; v) TCHAIKOVSKY: *Capriccio italien, Op. 45.*

(B)**DG Heliodor 3348 249.

Fricsay's volatile performance of *Vltava* is highly dramatic in its musical characterization and romantic in conception. Making full use of a wide range of dynamic contrasts it is undeniably exciting, and it is matched by Fricsay's equally individual approach to the *Emperor waltz* (rhythmically very flexible, with a mannered coda). Leitner's account of Tchaikovsky's *Italian caprice* is similarly individual (not very Italianate), while Richard Kraus indulges in unashamed *rubato* in the Liszt *Hungarian rhapsody* but brings it off by the vigour of his conception. With full-blooded sound these performances make a successful collection, and the slight lack of refinement in the transfer (due to the high level) can be forgiven when the overall presentation is so vivid.

England

'Music from England' (with (i) LSO, Jochum; (ii) RPO, Del Mar; (iii) Hart House Orch., Toronto, Neel; (iv) Boston SO, Steinberg; (v) ECO, Barenboim): ELGAR:(i) *Variations on an original theme* (*Enigma*), *Op. 36: Nimrod;* (ii) *Pomp and Circumstance march No. 1 in D major, Op. 39;* (iii) *Serenade for strings in E minor, Op. 20.* (iv) HOLST: *The Planets, Op. 32: Jupiter.* (v) DELIUS: *On Hearing the First Cuckoo in Spring; Summer Night on the River.* VAUGHAN WILLIAMS: *Fantasia on Greensleeves.*

(M)*(*)DG Privilege 3335 250.

The compiler of this programme (was it chosen in Hanover or London, one wonders?) seems determined to present the English as a rather sleepy, unenergetic lot. Jochum's version of *Nimrod* was not a good choice as opening. Poetic it certainly is, when heard in context; but on its own it tends to sound lethargic, particularly as the sound quality lacks sharpness of focus. An absence of transient glitter adversely affects *Jupiter*, and even the two Delius pieces lack the clarity of outline one finds in the original ECO collection from which they are taken (DG 3300 500: see below and under Delius). This tape springs to life at last with the Boyd Neel performance of Elgar's *Serenade*, which ends the concert in spirited fashion and which is given a cleaner and better-projected recording than most of the rest of the programme.

ECO, Asensio

'*Preludes and Intermezzos from Zarzuelas*': CHAPI: *El Tambor de Granaderos. La Revoltosa.* GIMENEZ: *El Baile de Luis Alonso. Los Borrachos. El Patinillo. La Boda de Luis Alonso.* BRETON: *La Verbena de la Paloma.* CHUECA: *El Bateo.*

(M) ** Rediffusion Royale KROY 2013.

With good tunes and brightly coloured scoring (primary colours and robust instrumentation), this collection of music from the world of Spanish operetta, which will be totally unknown to most readers, can be cordially recommended. The strong Spanish flavour is well caught by Asensio and his players; the recording is bright and lively, and it has transferred to tape with admirable crispness. On our copy the last few bars of the music on side one were cut off in the editing, but this is unlikely to be common to all copies. No notes about the music are included, but the writing is diverse and entertaining even without knowledge of its context.

ECO, Barenboim

'*Greensleeves*' (with (i) Pinchas Zukerman, violin): VAUGHAN WILLIAMS: *Fantasia on Greensleeves.* (i) *The Lark ascending.* WALTON: *Henry V: Passacaglia – Death of Falstaff; Touch her soft lips and part.* DELIUS: *2 Aquarelles. Fennimore and Gerda: Intermezzo. On Hearing the First Cuckoo in Spring. Summer Night on the River.*
*** DG 3300 500 [id.].

Barenboim creates richly spun orchestral textures, and some might feel that these performances almost have a touch of decadence; but such gorgeous sounds are hard to resist. Zukerman's account of *The Lark ascending* is ravishing and entirely convincing even if it is not perhaps totally idiomatic. The spacious recording suits the music-making perfectly; this is a fascinating and rewarding tape, beautifully transferred.

ECO, Garcia

'*English music*': BOYCE: *Symphony No. 4 in F major.* VAUGHAN WILLIAMS: *Fantasia on Greensleeves.* DELIUS: *Hassan: Serenade and Intermezzo.* PURCELL: *Chacony in G minor. Dido and Aeneas: suite.* HANDEL: *Solomon: Arrival of the Queen of Sheba.* ELGAR: *Chanson de matin; Chanson de nuit, Op. 15/1 and 2.* WARLOCK: *Capriol suite for strings.*
** CBS 40–76719.

This is a distinguished concert, the programme wide-ranging, its diversity causing the separate works to set off sparks from each other. The Purcell chaconne is splendidly done, with strong, expressive playing and an imaginative use of dynamic contrast. This closes side one; side two, with its rather lighter mood, offers warm and stylish music-making, from the

709

freshness of the *Queen of Sheba* to the neoclassicism of Warlock's *Capriol suite*. The recording is natural and admirably balanced, and it is a pity that the tape transfer has not more life in the treble. The quality is pleasing (the bass well focused), but there is not enough bite: the Boyce symphony loses much of its resilience when the top is so soft-edged. Nevertheless this is enjoyable listening for the late evening, though the LP offers a more realistic projection.

Ensemble d'Archets Eugène Ysaÿe, Bobesco

'Music of Venice': ALBINONI: *Adagio in G minor* (arr. Giazotto) *for strings and organ. Sonata a cinque in E minor, Op. 5/9.* GEMINIANI: *Concerto grosso* (from Corelli's *Violin sonata in D minor* (*La Follia*), *Op. 5/ 12*). PACHELBEL: *Canon in D major* (arr. Münchinger). ROSSINI: *String sonata No. 3 in C major.* YSAÿE: *Paganini variations.*

(B) *(*) DG Heliodor 3348 219.

The curiously solemn style of the playing here leaves this programme of essentially Italian music lacking in the Mediterranean warmth and sparkle it needs. The Rossini sonata which opens the concert is entirely without humour, and Pachelbel's famous canon is played very seriously indeed. There is a touch of Gallic elegance in the Albinoni, but the most interesting novelty, the Ysaÿe variations on the famous Paganini theme, is much too deadpan. The recording is warm and full, especially good on side two (the Geminiani and Pachelbel), where the transfer offers strikingly realistic quality.

Ewerhart, Rodolf (organ and cond.)

'Festive music from the 18th century for two and four organs, with brass' (with Franz Lehrndorfer, Hans Has-

elböck, Wolfgang Oehms (organs), brass ens., timpani): ALBERTIN: *Sonata in D major for 4 organs, 4 trumpets, 4 horns and timpani.* MULLER: *Sonatas for 4 organs: in A major; in C major: in B flat major.* ANON.: *Intrada pastorale; Intrada* (both for 2 organs, 2 trumpets, 2 horns and timpani).

(M) ** Turnabout KTVC 34216.

The *concertato* device of writing music for two or more organs originated in Venice but its novelty soon spread to other parts of Europe, and in a musical era which loved imitative devices and echo effects its appeal is understandable. Marian Muller (born in 1724) was a musician-priest (later abbot) of the Benedictine monastery at Einsiedeln who studied in Milan and no doubt took the *concertato* style home with him. His compositions for four organs are in single-movement form and were intended for performance on the principal holy days of the church calendar (the A major work was written for Christmas, the C major for Easter and the B flat for Whitsun). They are inventive pieces and cleverly conceived so that the part-writing integrates naturally and smoothly. The performances here are excellent and the recording is first-class, with an admirably smooth tape transfer. The works featuring brass instruments are much more conventional: the opening piece by Alfons Albertin seems to be all tonic and dominant, and the anonymous *Intradas* are rooted to the natural harmonic series of the brass instruments. The performances are straightforward, and the recording has transferred quite well to cassette.

'Favourite orchestral music'

Volume 1 (with (i) London Proms SO, Mackerras; (ii) LSO; (iii) Fjeldstad; (iv) Suisse Romande Orch., Ansermet; (v) Maag; (vi) Stuttgart CO, Münchinger; (vii)

Alwyn): (i) SIBELIUS: *Finlandia, Op. 26.* (ii; iii) GRIEG: *Peer Gynt suite No. 1, Op. 46.* (iv) RAVEL: *Boléro.* DEBUSSY: *Suite bergamasque: Clair de lune.* (ii; v) MENDELSSOHN: *The Hebrides (Fingal's Cave) overture, Op. 26.* (vi) MOZART: *Serenade No. 13 in G major (Eine kleine Nachtmusik), K.525.* (ii; vii) TCHAIKOVSKY: *Capriccio italien, Op. 45. Marche slave, Op. 31.*

   (B) ** Decca KDPC 511/2.

On the whole a very successful compilation, with generally excellent performances supporting a well-balanced programme. The sound is somewhat variable; the end of the *March slave* and the climaxes of the *Capriccio italien* are lacking in refinement, but this is good value for money.

Volume 2 (with (i) LSO; (ii) Stokowski; (iii) Black; (iv) LPO; (v) RPO; (vi) Herrmann): (i; ii) WAGNER: *Die Walküre: Ride of the Valkyries.* DEBUSSY: *Prélude à l'après-midi d'un faune.* MUSSORGSKY (arr. Stokowski): *Night on the Bare Mountain.* RAVEL: *Daphnis et Chloé: Suite No. 2* (with chorus). BERLIOZ: *La Damnation de Faust: Dance of the Sylphs.* (i; iii) DVOŘÁK: *Slavonic dance No. 1 in C major, Op. 46/1.* SMETANA: *Má Vlast: Vltava.* (iii; iv) CHABRIER: *España.* (iii; v) SAINT-SAËNS: *Danse macabre, Op. 40.* (iv; vi) FAURÉ: *Pavane, Op. 50.* DUKAS: *L'Apprenti sorcier (The Sorcerer's Apprentice).*

   (B) ** Decca KDPC 519/20.

The excellent is always the enemy of the good, and in this two-cassette concert the performances by Stokowski (which are mixed between the two tapes) stand out as having far more character and life than the rest. The Debussy and Ravel items are very successful, and the short Berlioz dance makes a delicious encore at the end. *Night on the Bare Mountain* is given in Stokowski's own version (although the notes do not make this clear) and is vividly dramatic. The rest of the music-making is acceptable: Stanley Black keeps the pot boiling very successfully, but Bernard Herrmann's account of *L'Apprenti sorcier* lacks spontaneity and sparkle. The recording is excellent throughout but the transfers occasionally show a hint of strain at climaxes, although this is not too serious.

'Favourite piano concertos'

(i) Peter Katin; (ii) LSO, Kundell; (iii) New SO (of London); (iv) Colin Davis; (v) LPO; (vi) Friedrich Gulda, Vienna PO, Andreae: (i; ii) TCHAIKOVSKY: *Concerto No. 1 in B flat minor, Op. 23.* (i; iii; iv) RACHMANINOV: *Concerto No. 2 in C minor, Op. 18.* (i; iv; v) GRIEG: *Concerto in A minor, Op. 16.* (vi) SCHUMANN: *Concerto in A minor, Op. 54.*

   (B) * Decca KDPC 503/4.

There seems little point in a compilation of this kind except a slight price saving; and the performances here are hardly among the most riveting available, though all are acceptable. The transfers are not especially brilliant, and the Rachmaninov sounds lacklustre, with a dull treble response and too much bass emphasis.

'Favourite symphonies'

Volume 1 (with Vienna PO, cond. (i) Monteux; (ii) Kubelik; (iii) Münchinger): (i) BEETHOVEN: *Symphony No. 6 in F major (Pastoral), Op. 68.* (ii) DVOŘÁK: *Symphony No. 9 in E minor (From the New World), Op. 95.* (iii) SCHUBERT: *Symphony No. 8 in B minor (Unfinished), D.759.*

   (B) (*) Decca KDPC 501/2.

Some advantage could have been gained from the tape format here by putting the *New World symphony* complete on a single cassette side. Instead it is not only split (after the *Largo*), but the last two movements come on the second cassette. It would be difficult to imagine a more clumsy arrangement! In any case the transfer of the Dvořák is very undistinguished, with a boomy, resonant bass that quite spoils a good performance. The other music fares better, but this set cannot be recommended.

Volume 2 (with (i) New Philharmonia Orch., Giulini; (ii) Suisse Romande Orch., Ansermet; (iii) LSO, Josef Krips): (i) MOZART: *Symphony No. 40 in G minor, K.550.* (ii) MENDELSSOHN: *Symphony No. 4 in A major (Italian), Op. 90.* BEETHOVEN: *Symphony No. 5 in C minor, Op. 67.* (iii) SCHUMANN: *Symphony No. 1 in B flat major (Spring), Op. 38.*

(B) * Decca KDPC 527/8.

There seems little reason to commend a popular anthology of this kind that includes at its centre the Ansermet performance of Beethoven's *Fifth*, a conscientious but uninspired piece of music-making which cannot be counted among the several recommended versions in the Decca catalogue. The other performances have varying degrees of merit, and the recording is good.

'Favourite violin concertos'

(i–iii) Ruggiero Ricci, LSO, cond. (i) Gamba; (ii) Sargent; (iii) Fjeldstad: (i) BRUCH: *Violin concerto No. 1 in G minor, Op. 26.* MENDELSSOHN: *Violin concerto in E minor, Op. 64.* (ii) TCHAIKOVSKY: *Violin concerto in D major, Op. 35.* (iii) SIBELIUS: *Violin concerto in D minor, Op. 47.*

(B) **(*) Decca KDPC 505/6.

No one should be disappointed in this collection; indeed the performances of the Bruch and Mendelssohn concertos are among the finest in the catalogue, and they are very well recorded and admirably transferred. The performance of the Tchaikovsky concerto is less distinctive but like the vivid reading of the Sibelius it is certainly enjoyable. The transfers are well managed.

Galway, James (flute)

'*The man with the golden flute*' (with (i) National PO, Gerhardt; (ii) Anthony Goldstone (piano); (iii) Lucerne Festival Strings, Baumgartner): (i) BACH: *Suite No. 2 in B minor, BWV 1067: Minuet; Badinerie.* PAGANINI: *Moto perpetuo, Op. 11.* VIVALDI: *Flute concerto in G minor (La Notte), Op. 10/2.* GLUCK: *Orfeo ed Euridice: Dance of the Blessed Spirits.* (ii) DEBUSSY: *Suite bergamasque: Clair de lune. The Little Shepherd. Syrinx for solo flute.* BERKELEY: *Flute sonatina, Op. 13.* (iii) MOZART: *Andante for flute and orchestra in C major, K.315.*

(M) **(*) RCA Gold Seal GK 25160 [LRK 1 5094].

James Galway's genial charisma, the beauty of his tone, and the spectacular brilliance of his technique command the widest possible audience, yet one is left in no doubt that besides his sense of fun he possesses the keenest musical sensibility. His phrasing is masterly and its inevitability contributes a good deal towards his special gift of making the listener forget that he is often listening to transcriptions of music written with a quite different tone colour in mind. This sampler of Galway's skill and musicianship over a fairly diverse repertoire is an obvious choice because of its price, and it includes several items from the finest of his four available anthologies, *Showpieces* (see below). One of these is Paganini's *Moto perpetuo,* which shows off Galway's bravura in its irrepressible stream of notes. The famous *Dance of the Blessed Spirits* draws an appealing beauty of line and phrase, while the spontaneous little Berkeley *Sonatina* is a welcome novelty. The balance here (as throughout the concert) places Galway well forward, but the pianist, Anthony Goldstone, manages to remain in the picture. The piano, however, is rather dryly recorded. Debussy's *Clair de lune* is also given a piano accompaniment and the arrangement is clumsy, beautifully as Galway plays the melodic line. The Vivaldi concerto too is hardly refined in its accompanying detail. The transfer is generally of good quality, the solo flute truthfully caught, while the resonant acoustic does not blur the orchestral focus.

'Showpieces' (with National PO, Gerhardt): DINICU: *Hora staccato.* DRIGO: *Les Millions d'Arlequin: Serenade.* PAGANINI: *Moto perpetuo, Op. 11.* BACH: *Suite No. 2 in B minor, BWV 1067: Minuet; Badinerie.* MIYAGI: *Haru no Umi.* GODARD: *Suite of 3 pieces, Op. 116: Waltz.* RIMSKY-KORSAKOV: *Tsar Saltan: Flight of the bumble bee.* SAINT-SAËNS: *Ascanio* (ballet): *Adagio and variation.* CHOPIN: *Waltz in D flat major (Minute), Op. 64/1.* GLUCK: *Orfeo ed Euridice: Dance of the Blessed Spirits.* DÖPPLER: *Fantaisie pastorale hongroise, Op. 26.* ***RCA RK 11719.

This collection of 'lollipops' shows the flair and sparkle of James Galway's playing at its most captivating, besides demonstrating a technical command to bring wonder: Paganini himself must have astonished his listeners in this way. The bravura pieces, including the Dinicu *Hora staccato,* Rimsky-Korsakov's *Flight of the bumble bee* and Godard's deliciously inconsequential little waltz, are nicely balanced by the expressive music, and there are several attractive novelties. Only Bach's famous *Badinerie* seems a shade too fast, and even this is infectious. Charles Gerhardt's accompaniments are characteristically adroit, and the transfer is of excellent quality.

'The magic flute of James Galway' (with National PO, Gerhardt): HANDEL: *Solomon: Arrival of the Queen of Sheba.* RACHMANINOV: *Vocalise, Op. 34/14.* BACH: *Sonata in C minor: Allegro.* MENDELSSOHN: *A Midsummer Night's Dream, Op. 61: Scherzo.* SCHUMANN: *Kinderscenen: Träumerei.* GOSSEC: *Tambourin.* CHOPIN: *Variations on a theme from Rossini's 'La Cenerentola'.* KREISLER: *Schön Rosmarin.* DVOŘÁK: *Humoresque in G flat major, Op. 101/7.* BRISCIALDI: *Carnival of Venice.* **(*) RCA RK 11745 [LRK 1 5131].

Galway's gift for making transcriptions sound as if the music had been originally conceived for the flute almost succeeds in the *Arrival of the Queen of Sheba,* and his exuberant roulades in the Chopin *Variations* and (especially) the *Carnival of Venice* are very fetching. The *Midsummer Night's Dream Scherzo* has an iridescent sparkle, and, among the lyrical items, Schumann's *Träumerei* is beautifully phrased. The flair and sparkle of Galway's bravura never fail to astonish, though the Bach *Allegro* is outrageously fast. The recording balances the flute well forward with an unashamed spotlight, and the transfer has plenty of life.

'Songs for Annie' (with (i) National PO, Gerhardt; (ii) Marisa Robles Harp Ens.; (iii) Kevin Conneff, Irish drum): (i) MARAIS: *Le Basque.* VILLA-LOBOS: *Bachianas Brasileiras No. 5: Aria.* FAURÉ: *Dolly suite: Berceuse.* MOZART: *Piano sonata No. 15 in C major, K.545: Allegro.* DENVER:

Annie's song. HASSE: *Tambourin.* DEBUSSY: *La plus que lente.* TRAD.: (ii) *Brian Boru's march.* (iii; played on a tin whistle) *Belfast hornpipe.* (i) BIZET-BORNE: *Carmen fantasy.* TRAD.: *Spanish love song.*

**(*)RCA RK 25163.

This collection, dedicated to Galway's wife, includes the John Denver song which took him into the charts (quite an achievement for a modest flute!); but in fact the one totally memorable item here is the opening *Le Basque* of Marais. Its simple *moto perpetuo* theme registers with indelible charm and remains in the memory long after the cassette has finished playing. The rest of the programme is a characteristically fetching array of clever arrangements by either Galway or Duthoit; but one would not give this collection a first place among Galway's anthologies. The recording and transfer are both well managed, although there is some lack of upper range. The flute is admirably caught, even though the balance is larger than life.

Grumiaux, Arthur (violin)
'Violin romances' (with New Philharmonia Orch., de Waart): BEETHOVEN: *Romances Nos. 1 in G major, Op. 40; 2 in F major, Op. 50.* BERLIOZ: *Rêverie et Caprice, Op. 8.* TCHAIKOVSKY: *Sérénade mélancolique, Op. 26.* WIENIAWSKI: *Violin concerto No. 2 in D minor, Op. 22: Romance* (2nd movt). *Légende, Op. 17.* SVENDSEN: *Romance in G major, Op. 26.*

(M)**(*)Philips 7317 104.

This is a splendid anthology, offering solo playing of superlative quality. There have been very few finer performances of the Beethoven *Romances*, and the account of the Berlioz *Rêverie et Caprice* is no less distinguished. Of the slighter pieces, the delightful Svendsen *Romance*

(which some readers may remember from 78 days) is presented with style and charm. The soloist's warmth for such a perfectly made miniature is understandable. The accompaniment is well in the picture throughout, although the balance treats the solo violin and the orchestral backing on equal terms, which rather reduces the effect of light and shade. The sound of the tape is very pleasant and agreeable, with the soloist well focused, but the orchestral quality is rather plushy, and in fully scored passages it lacks something in inner definition. The equivalent disc has more refinement of detail, but as a late-evening concert the cassette is acceptably smooth.

Hallé Orch., Barbirolli

'Music of Vienna': STRAUSS, Johann, Jnr: *An der schönen blauen Donau (Blue Danube), Op. 314.* Polkas: *Unter Donner und Blitz (Thunder and Lightning), Op. 324; Champagne, Op. 211. Zigeunerbaron overture. Perpetuum mobile, Op. 257.* STRAUSS, Johann, Snr: *Radetzky march, Op. 228.* LEHÁR: *Gold and Silver, Op. 75.* STRAUSS, Richard: *Der Rosenkavalier: Waltz suite.*

(M)**HMV Greensleeve TC-ESD 7067.

Although this is enjoyable (and a good tape for the car), only the *Perpetuum mobile* – given a deliciously pointed, sprightly, yet relaxed performance – is vintage Barbirolli. *The Blue Danube* sounds rather bland, and even *Gold and Silver* (a piece this conductor always did well) is somewhat over-indulged. The polkas are lively, and there are some characteristically sensuous moments in the *Rosenkavalier* excerpts; but for some reason Barbirolli used a modernized version of the *Radetzky march* (by Gordon Jacob). The sound still has the artificial brilliance of the Studio Two original and is sometimes fierce. The transfer is on the whole well managed, but it needs taming and is not always clean in focus (notably in *Radetzky*).

(Richard) Hickox Orch., Hickox

ALBINONI: *Adagio in G minor* (arr. Giazotto) *for organ and strings. Oboe concerto in D minor, Op. 9/2* (with Sara Barrington, oboe). PACHEL-BEL: *Canon in D major* (arr. Münch-inger). BONONCINI: *Sinfonia da chiesa a quattro, Op. 5/1.* PURCELL: *Chacony in G minor.*
　(***) Argo KZRC 866.

This performance of Albinoni's *Adagio* must be among the most tasteful available, yet the playing has no lack of warmth. Similarly the climax of Pachelbel's famous *Canon* is graduated with great skill; the Purcell *Chacony* is no less effective, and the delightful Albinoni *Oboe concerto* makes a splendid bonus. The recording too is absolutely first-class, and it is a pity that the tape transfer has been made at too high a level, so that there is distortion at the climaxes of the Albinoni and Pachelbel works.

Holliger, Heinz (oboe)

'Oboe concertos' (with Frankfurt Radio SO, Inbal, and (i) Aurèle Nicolet, flute): BELLINI: *Oboe concerto in E flat major.* MOLIQUE: *Concertino in G minor.* (i) MOSCHELES: *Concerto in F major for flute and oboe.* RIETZ: *Konzertstück in F minor, Op. 33.*
　** Philips 7300 515 [id.].

The playing here is of high quality throughout, but not all the music is inspired. The two-movement Bellini concerto is delightful, and the Moscheles *Double concerto* is attractively inventive too, the first movement especially fetching. But the other works are more conventional. The recording is full and natu-

ral, but its resonance has led to a comparatively low-level transfer without much sparkle. In the Bellini the orchestral tuttis are not always completely refined.

Hundred Best Tunes: see *Your Hundred Best Tunes.*

'Hush-a-bye-baby'

Combined uterus sounds; sounds through the placenta and navel cord (synthesized by Howard Blaikley); also classical music 'suitable for young babies' by PACHELBEL; MOZART: FAURÉ; POULENC; DE-BUSSY; R. STRAUSS; CANTELOUBE; DVOŘÁK; VIVALDI (with various artists).
　** RCA RK 42751.

This extraordinary compilation is designed to be played to a new-born baby, and provide emotional sustenance and relaxation by combining carefully chosen soporific music with synthesized memories of its prenatal residence in the womb. Most adults will no doubt fail to remember and identify with the throbbing womb vibrations, which sound a bit like *Dr Who*, but the music is delightful. It is slightly marred by the inclusion of two very artificial synthesized arrangements of Debussy by Tomita and a closing lullaby sung sincerely but rather gauchely by Dr Michèle Clements, who devised the recording. But the rest, with James Galway's flute featuring prominently, makes a highly agreeable concert, with a memorable *Pie Jesu* from Fauré's *Requiem* (Alain Clement) as a central highlight. The recording is first-class and the transfers offer consistently warm glowing sound quality.

'Immortal classics'

Various artists: music by CLARKE; HANDEL; BEETHOVEN; HOOK;

MOZART; MENDELSSOHN; GLINKA; LISZT; GOUNOD; RIMSKY-KORSAKOV; DEBUSSY; CHABRIER; WALDTEUFEL; LEHÁR; STRAUSS, Johann; OFFENBACH; WAGNER; PUCCINI; MASSENET; MASCAGNI; SINDING; ELGAR.

(B) ** Decca KDPC 615/6.

Not everyone will respond to the title, but this anthology of twenty-five favourites is well made and offers a diverse mixture of orchestral, vocal and piano pieces. Opening with Stokowski's ostentatiously romantic conception of the *Trumpet voluntary*, the programme mixes *The Lass from Richmond Hill* and *You Are My Heart's Delight* (Kenneth McKellar) and *Vilja* (Joan Sutherland) with Liszt's *Liebestraum* (Ilana Vered) and Sinding's *Rustle of Spring* (Joseph Cooper). The orchestral items include Chabrier's *España* (Argenta), the Offenbach *Barcarolle* (Solti), *Fingal's Cave* (Ansermet, not Maag), *The Ride of the Valkyries* (Stokowski) and Massenet's *Meditation* from *Thaïs* (with Josef Sakonov as the lushly romantic soloist). The recording is good throughout; the transfers are almost always well managed and sometimes excellent.

'Invitation to the Dance'

Various artists: WEBER: *Invitation to the Dance, Op. 65* (arr. Berlioz). TCHAIKOVSKY: *Swan Lake: Waltz. The Nutcracker: Waltz of the Flowers. Eugene Onegin: Waltz. The Sleeping Beauty: Waltz.* STRAUSS, Richard: *Der Rosenkavalier: Waltz sequence.* GOUNOD: *Faust, Act 1: Waltz.*

(B) ** DG Heliodor 3348 174.

A spirited collection, well recorded (although the recordings are rather dated) and brightly transferred. Fricsay conducts the *Invitation to the Dance* and waltzes from *Eugene Onegin* and *Faust* in

lively fashion but does not forgo elegance. Rowicki, who does the *Swan Lake* and *Sleeping Beauty* excerpts, is very brisk indeed, but Leitner's *Waltz of the Flowers* makes a suitably mellow interlude. Karl Boehm is obviously thoroughly at home in the *Rosenkavalier* sequence.

Israel PO, Mehta

'Showcase': ROSSINI: *La Scala di seta: overture.* VERDI: *La Traviata: Preludes to Acts 1 and 3. I Vespri siciliani: overture.* WEBER: *Oberon: overture.* MENDELSSOHN:*A Midsummer Night's Dream, Op. 61: Nocturne; Scherzo.*

** (*) Decca KSXC 6843 [Lon. 5–7065].

A first-class tape offering Decca's best quality. There is splendid detail; the characteristic brightness of the Israeli strings is well conveyed and there is an excellent bloom on wind and brass alike. With such vivid quality the performances must be well projected (especially the Rossini and the Mendelssohn *Scherzo*), and one can accept the lack of a really distinguished line in the *La Traviata Preludes*.

(Philip) Jones Brass Ens.

'Renaissance brass' (music of 1400–1600): FRANCHOS: *Trumpet intrada.* PASSEREAU: *Il est bel et bon* (arr. REEVES). AGRICOLA: *Oublier veul* (arr. HOWARTH). LASSUS: *Madrigal dell'eterna* (arr. JONES). VECCHI: *Saltarello.* SUSATO: *Suite of 6 dances.* BYRD: *Earl of Oxford's march.* FARNABY: *Suite of 6 dances.* GIBBONS: *Royal pavane. In nomine.*

** Argo KZRC 823.

An attractive collection, not all of which was originally intended for brass. In fact the madrigals and keyboard dances are among the more effective numbers but the comparatively limited range of colour possible with such a group tells if the music is taken in larger doses. The recording is basically very good and the transfer level high, but there is an element of harshness in the louder, fanfare-like pieces.

'*Easy winners*': music by JOPLIN; MOZART; HAZELL; MONTI; DE-BUSSY; PREMRU and TRAD.
**Argo KZRC 895.

The collector's item here is an arrangement of Monti's *Czardas*, offering a display of breathtaking bravura by Ivor James on the horn. The rest of the collection is pleasantly easy-going, though it is doubtful if Mozart's *Eine kleine Nachtmusik* on four tubas has more than novelty value, skilfully done as it is. This and Scott Joplin, plus a couple of rather attractive pieces by the recording's producer, Chris Hazell, are the most striking numbers. The playing is first-class, of course, and so is the sound.

Light classics

'*Festival of light classics*' (with (i) Czech PO; (ii) Stokowski; (iii) Netherlands Radio PO; (iv) Fistoulari; (v) LSO; (vi) Josef Sakonov (violin); (vii) London Festival Orch.; (viii) New Philharmonia Orch.; (ix) Black; (x) Kingsway SO, Camarata; (xi) Vonk; (xii) Sharples; (xiii) Civil; (xiv) Herrmann; (xv) Frank Chacksfield and his Orch.; (xvi) LPO; (xvii) John Wilbraham (trumpet), cond. Camarata; (xviii) David Parkhouse (piano)): (i; ii) RACHMANINOV: *Prelude in C sharp minor, Op. 3/2* (orch. Stokowski). (iii; iv) TCHAIKOVSKY: *Swan Lake: Waltz.* (v; ii) *Chant sans paroles, Op. 40/6.* (vi; vii) *None but the lonely heart.* (viii; ii) *The Sleeping Beauty: Waltz.* (iii; ix) MASSENET: *Le Cid: Aragonaise.* (x) STRAUSS,

Johann: *The Blue Danube waltz.* (v; ii) CLARKE: *Trumpet voluntary.* (v; xi) GLINKA: *Russlan and Ludmilla: overture.* (vii; ix) PROKOFIEV: *The Love of Three Oranges: March; Scherzo.* (i; ii) ELGAR: *Enigma variations, Op. 36: Nimrod.* (x) BACH–GOUNOD: *Ave Maria* (with chorus). STRAUSS, Johann: *Tritsch-Tratsch polka;* (with Josef) *Pizzicato polka.* (vii; xii) SUPPÉ: *Light Cavalry overture.* (vii; xiii). BIZET: *Carmen: Flower song* (arr. Civil). (i; ii) DVO-ŘÁK: *Slavonic dance in E minor, Op. 72/2.* (vii; xiv) WEILL: *Threepenny Opera: Mack the knife.* (xv) HUM-PERDINCK: *Hansel and Gretel: Prayer.* (vii; ix) KHACHATURIAN: *Gayaneh: Sabre dance.* (xvi; ix) LISZT: *Hungarian rhapsody No. 2.* (v; ix) SMETANA: *The Bartered Bride: Polka; Dance of the Comedians.* (v; ii) SCHUBERT: *Moment musical in F minor* (orch. Stokowski). (xvii; vii) ARBAN: *Carnival of Venice.* (xvi; xiv) DEBUSSY: *Suite bergamasque: Clair de lune.* (vi; vii) MASSENET: *Thaïs: Meditation.* (x) STRAUSS, Johann, Snr: *Radetzky march.* (v; ix) GRIEG: *Peer Gynt: Anitra's dance.* (vi; vii) PONCE: *Estrellita.* (vii; xiv; xviii) GERSHWIN: *Variations on 'I got rhythm'.*
(M) *(*) Decca K 2 C 6.

This kind of compilation is very suitable for tape issue in a box, particularly when the contents of three discs are tailored to fit a pair of cassettes. The programme is quite imaginatively chosen and well laid out for maximum contrast, and those whose musical taste lies in this area of lighter classical music will have no real cause to fault the performances. It is a pity that a little more care was not taken with the transfer level on the first cassette. The opening Rachmaninov *Prelude* in

Stokowski's somewhat exotic arrangement offers a degree of congestion in the bass at the first climax; in the Tchaikovsky *Waltz* that follows there is a similar feeling of constriction, which returns every now and then throughout the first two sides. On sides three and four the quality is crisper and brighter, although sometimes a trifle fierce (the *Meditation* from *Thaïs* is very forwardly balanced). This yields to the controls readily enough, but one cannot cure the boomy bass on sides one and two.

Light music

'*Festival of light music*' (with (i) LPO; (ii) Black; (iii) London Festival Orch.; (iv) New SO, Godfrey; (v) Rawicz and Landauer; (vi) Mantovani and his Orch.; (vii) Derek Collier (violin), Daphne Ibbott (piano); (viii) Sharples; (ix) Josef Sakonov (violin); (x) Kingsway SO, Camarata; (xi) RPO; (xii) Rogers): (i; ii) OFFENBACH: *Orpheus in the Underworld: overture.* (ii; iii) GROFÉ: *Grand Canyon suite: On the trail.* (iv) SULLIVAN: *Iolanthe overture.* (v; vi) ADDINSELL: *Warsaw concerto.* (vii) KREISLER: *Caprice viennoise.* (iii; viii) SUPPÉ: *Poet and Peasant overture.* (ix; iii) SARASATE: *Zigeunerweisen.* (vi) CHAMINADE: *Autumn.* (x) STRAUSS, Johann: *Die Fledermaus overture.* (vi) *Waltzes: Morning Papers; Roses of the South.* LEHÁR: *The Merry Widow: Waltz.* (xi; xii) KETÈLBEY: *In a Monastery Garden; In a Persian Market* (both with chorus). (vii) PAGANINI: *Valse.* arr. KREISLER: *Londonderry air.* (ix; iii) KORNGOLD: *Garden scene.* (xi; xii) BERNSTEIN: *Candide overture.* (i; ii) CHABRIER: *España.* (xi; ii) TCHAIKOVSKY: *Marche slave.*

(M)*(*) Decca K 45 K 33.

The *Festival of light music* charts a curious path within Decca's catalogue, mixing Mantovani with the LSO and choosing, for instance, Johann Strauss performances by the Kingsway Symphony Orchestra when there are readily available versions by Boskovsky and the VPO: this is as inexplicable as the inclusion of the Korngold and Leonard Bernstein items in a collection of this nature. Moreover for a three-tape compilation the content is not generous: most of the sides have only three items on them, and the playing time is undoubtedly short measure. However, anyone for whom this mixture has an appeal will find that most of the transfers are well managed. The opening Offenbach overture is not very clean, but generally the sound is brilliant, although the pieces for violin and piano are much too forward and one needs to turn the volume down to get a realistic image.

Light Music Society Orch., Dunn

'*Britain's choice*': LANGFORD: *March from the Colour suite.* FARNON: *À la claire fontaine.* TOMLINSON: *Suite of English folk dances.* DUNCAN: *March from A Little suite* (theme for *Dr Finlay's Casebook*). CURZON: *The Boulevardier.* BINGE: *The Watermill.* DOCKER: *Tabarinage.* POPE: *Ring of Kerry: suite.*

(M)**HMV Greensleeve TC-ESD 7063.

The programme opens attractively with the *March* from Langford's *Colour suite* (very reminiscent of Malcolm Arnold: without that composer's final touch of exuberance, but infectious nonetheless). The rest of the music here either has ingenuous atmosphere, like Robert Farnon's *À la claire fontaine* or Ronald Binge's engaging pastel portrait of *The Watermill*, or is lively in an English folksy way. Ernest Tomlinson's *English folk dances* have not quite the character of

Vaughan Williams's *Folksongs suite*, but they are cleverly scored. Dunn's advocacy is persuasive and the orchestral playing excellent, but the recording, although vivid, lacks something in bloom. The resonant acoustic has obviously offered slight problems in the transfer, and the upper range is bright rather than smoothly refined.

LPO, Lloyd-Jones

'Concert of Russian music': MUSSORGSKY: *Night on the Bare Mountain* (original version). BALAKIREV: *King Lear overture*. RIMSKY-KORSAKOV: *Sadko, Op. 5*. BORODIN: *Symphony No. 3 in A minor* (*Unfinished;* orch. Glazounov).

(M) *** Philips 7317 032.

David Lloyd-Jones, who is perhaps best-known for his work on television opera and with the English National Opera company (his conducting of Prokofiev's *War and Peace* was a formidable achievement), made a splendid recording début with this concert. The items are unexpected but make a satisfying and highly enjoyable group. Most fascinating is the original version of *Night on the Bare Mountain*, which in Mussorgsky's own score has many angular passages, eartickling to any listener today, not shocking at all. Rimsky-Korsakov's 'musical picture' *Sadko* – not to be confused with the opera of the same name written twenty-five years later – and the unfinished Borodin *Symphony* are both pointedly and atmospherically done, while it is good to have so brilliant a version of Balakirev's *King Lear* overture, whose quirky ideas remind one of Berlioz. The recording quality is excellent, and the transfers are generally of the best Philips quality. Only the opening *Sadko* is a little lacking in brilliance, but the Borodin *Symphony*, which follows, is admirably vivid; and when one turns over, the Mussorgsky and Balakirev pieces offer first-class sound.

LPO, Mackerras

TCHAIKOVSKY: *1812 overture, Op. 49* (with Welsh Guards Band). GLINKA: *Russlan and Ludmilla: Overture.* WAGNER: *Lohengrin: Prelude to Act 3.* MUSSORGSKY: *Night on the Bare Mountain.*

(B) ** Classics for Pleasure TC-CFP 101.

Bright, alert performances, well played and recorded. *1812* appears to use mortar-fire at the end; the effect is small-scale, and combined with a low-level transfer, this means that the climax of the work is transferred without the usual distortion. On side one the level is higher and the other works are consequently more vivid in detail. The sound is brightly lit throughout. This is good value, but none of the performances is memorable.

LSO, Argenta

Spanish music: RIMSKY-KORSAKOV: *Capriccio espagnol, Op. 34*. GRANADOS: *Spanish dance No. 5 in E minor, Op. 37* (*Andaluza*). CHABRIER: *España.* MOSZKOWSKI: *5 Spanish dances, Book 1, Op. 12*.

(M) *** Decca Eclipse KECC 797.

This is a glittering mixture of recorded Spanishry, mostly from the pens of non-Spaniards. The performances are all excellent, sometimes missing the final degree of urgency, but always with plenty of colour. The slight Moszkowski dances are beautifully played, and the last three are especially successful. *España* lacks the last degree of panache but has plenty of sparkle, for Ataulfo Argenta knows what he is about; there is no better recorded version. Both this and the Rimsky-Korsakov have already been mentioned in the composer index, but the collection as a whole is rather more than the sum of its parts. The tape transfer has vividly brilliant sound, and is especially good in the Moszkowski and Granados pieces. This is excellent value.

LSO, Previn

'André Previn's Music Night': WAL-TON: Orb and Sceptre (coronation march). DUKAS: L'Apprenti sorcier (The Sorcerer's Apprentice). ALBI-NONI: Adagio in G minor (arr. Giazotto) for strings and organ. HUMPERDINCK: Hansel and Gretel: Overture. RAVEL: La Valse. DVO-ŘÁK: Slavonic dance No. 9 in B major, Op. 72/1.
**(*)HMV TC-ASD 3131.

An admirably enjoyable collection of favourites, demonstrating Previn's charisma at the peak of his success with the LSO. Only Albinoni's Adagio lacks full conviction, and perhaps for that one cannot blame Previn: its inclusion was no doubt dictated by commercial rather than musical considerations. The sound is very good on side one of the tape, sparkling and bright, but on our copy side two had noticeably less range in the treble, although the balance remained good.

'André Previn's Music Night', Vol. 2: GLINKA: Russlan and Ludmilla: Overture. BARBER: Adagio for strings. FALLA: The Three-cornered Hat: 3 dances. DEBUSSY: Prélude à l'après-midi d'un faune. BUTTER-WORTH: The Banks of Green Willow. STRAUSS, Johann: Kaiser (Emperor) waltz, Op. 437.
**HMV TC-ASD 3338.

Especially fine performances here of Barber's Adagio and the Debussy Pré-lude (with some beautiful flute-playing from William Bennett). The Falla suite also has splendid life and colour, but like the Russlan overture it is discoloured by a degree of coarseness in the climaxes (in the Falla it is the finale that is affected). The Emperor waltz is disappointing, a straightforward account not showing any real feeling for the idiom.

'In concert': BEETHOVEN: The Creatures of Prometheus: Overture, Op. 43. ALBINONI: Adagio in G minor (arr. Giazotto) for strings and organ. TCHAIKOVSKY: Marche slave, Op. 31. HOLST: The Planets, Op. 32: Jupiter. VAUGHAN WILLIAMS: Fantasia on Greensleeves. ENESCO: Roumanian rhapsody No. 1. PROKOFIEV: Romeo and Juliet: Montagues and Capulets. WALTON: Portsmouth Point: Overture.
(M)**HMV TC-ESD 7011.

This is essentially a sampler and as such it serves well enough, although the curious juxtaposition of items (Beethoven, Albinoni–Giazotto and Tchaikovsky make odd bedfellows) is singularly inept. Highlights are the Enesco and Walton pieces, and the Tchaikovsky Marche slave is stirringly done. The transfer is generally well managed, the sound full-blooded if not always clean in the bass.

LSO, Solti

'Romantic Russia': BORODIN: Prince Igor: Overture; Polovtsian dances (with LSO Chorus). GLINKA: Russlan and Ludmilla: overture. MUS-SORGSKY: Night on the Bare Mountain. Khovantschina: Prelude.
***Decca KSXC 6263.

Stunning recording from Decca, vivid and rich, with marvellous detail and heart-warming cello tone. This version of the Polovtsian dances, probably the best in the catalogues, is also available on Decca's Georg Solti conducts collection (see below under Solti). The chorus in the opening dances is lyrical and polished in a characteristically English way, but when the music warms up the performance is as exciting as anyone could wish. A very fast *Russlan and Ludmilla overture* (with the LSO on the tips of their toes, but never sounding out of breath) is very diverting, and *Night on the Bare Mountain*, played without eccentricity, but with a tender closing section, cannot fail with this quality of recording. The marvellously evocative *Khovantschina Prelude* is not quite as successful here as in Solti's Berlin performance (see under Berlin Philharmonic above), but the *Prince Igor overture* has fine dash and spontaneity, yet is romanticized by the richly recorded textures. The transfer to tape is one of Decca's very best. Side two is especially good with exceptional bite and life in the *Russlan and Ludmilla overture* and amazing depth and weight in *Night on the Bare Mountain*. The *Polovtsian dances* sound extremely brilliant too, and the *Khovantschina Prelude* is beautifully pellucid and clear.

LSO, Stokowski

'60th anniversary concert': WAGNER: *Die Meistersinger: Prelude to Act 1*. DEBUSSY: *Prélude à l'après-midi d'un faune*. GLAZOUNOV: *Violin concerto in A minor, Op. 82* (with Silvia Marcovici, violin). BRAHMS: *Symphony No. 1 in C minor, Op. 68*. TCHAIKOVSKY: *Marche slave, Op. 31*.
**Decca Phase 4 KPFC 3/4.

This pair of tapes celebrates a historic occasion in June 1972 when, almost exactly sixty years after his first appearance with the London Symphony Orchestra – in 1912, just before he went to Philadelphia – Stokowski conducted the London orchestra in an identical programme. Decca recorded the whole concert at the Royal Festival Hall, as well as the repeat concert the following day at the Royal Albert Hall. The recordings represent an edited amalgam of the two occasions, so catching the extra vividness of live music-making but gaining a degree of polish and precision usually associated with recordings made in the studio. The Phase Four techniques achieve characteristically forward placing of the woodwind solos, and plenty of clarity. The acoustic, however, is rather dry, and neither the Wagner nor the Brahms has quite the expansive richness (or reverberation) one would expect from a normal Decca production. The miracle is that Stokowski, even at ninety-one, was as much a magician as ever in his orchestral control and the ability to draw from his players sounds utterly distinctive to himself. Yet the performances are surprisingly unindulgent; the rich panoply of Wagner's *Die Meistersinger* and the hazy summer atmosphere of the Debussy *Prélude* are presented straightforwardly, although with obvious affection. The Glazounov *Concerto* is a splendid performance; Silvia Marcovici is full of romantic fire and has just the right temperament for this quixotic work. The Brahms *Symphony* is a highly romantic interpretation, with considerable flexibility, but Stokowski was always convincing in everything he does and the forward impulse of the music is never allowed to flag. Tchaikovsky's *Marche slave* acts as a generous encore and is announced by the conductor in a curiously gentle voice. Needless to say there is plenty of electricity here, and the orchestral playing has a feeling of conscious bravura. Quite apart from their historic importance these two tapes make highly enjoyable listening, in spite of the close-up recording and the feeling of dryness in the orchestral middle frequencies. The transfers are on the whole well balanced. The cassettes are issued normally and are not packaged in a box.

Marches

'March' (with various artists): VERDI: *Aïda: Grand march* (St Cecilia

Chorus and Orch.). GOUNOD: *Funeral march of a marionette* (cond. Gibson). BERLIOZ: *La Damnation de Faust: Hungarian march* (cond. Martinon). CHABRIER: *Marche joyeuse* (cond. Morel). GRIEG: *Sigurd Jorsalfar: Homage march* (cond. Fjeldstad). ELGAR: *Pomp and Circumstance march No. 1* (cond. Bliss). PROKOFIEV: *Love of Three Oranges: March* (cond. Ansermet). RIMSKY-KORSAKOV: *Tsar Saltan march* (cond. Martinon). TCHAIKOVSKY: *The Nutcracker: Miniature march* (cond. Ansermet); *Marche slave* (LSO, Alwyn).

(M) *** Decca KCSP 173.

This collection has been chosen and programmed with real imagination and is very entertaining. The sound is often spectacular, but, because of the variety within the music chosen, the excitement is never oppressive. There is not an indifferent performance here; Ansermet's two items (by Prokofiev and Tchaikovsky) have splendid flair, and Gibson's account of the *Funeral march of a marionette* has delicacy and charm. The concert ends splendidly with Alwyn's *Marche slave*. Technically the cassette transfer is outstandingly successful, skilfully handling a wide dynamic range and offering plenty of brilliance as well as weight.

'Radetzky march' (with (i) Bavarian Radio Orch., Kubelik; (ii) Capella Coloniensis; (iii) Leitner; (iv) Nordmark SO, Heinrich Steiner; (v) Bamberg SO, Richard Kraus; (vi) Berlin Radio SO, Fricsay; (vii) Berlin PO; (viii) Monte Carlo Opera Orch., Frémaux): (i) MENDELSSOHN: *A Midsummer Night's Dream: Wedding march; Fairies' march.* (ii; iii) MOZART: *March, K.237.* (iv) GRIEG: *Sigurd Jorsalfar: Homage march;* (v) *Peer Gynt: In the Hall of the Mountain King.* (vi) BERLIOZ: *La Damnation de Faust: Hungarian march.* (vii; iii) TCHAIKOVSKY: *Marche slave.* (viii) PROKOFIEV: *March, Op. 99.* (vi) STRAUSS, Johann, Snr: *Radetzky march.*

(B) *(*) DG Heliodor 3348 148.

This Heliodor tape cannot match the Decca compilation above in sophistication, but it is inexpensive and quite enjoyable. On side one the recording is not always too clean in focus, but side two (from Berlioz onwards) is brilliant and full-blooded. Both Fricsay and Leitner produce first-rate music-making, and the items by Mozart and Prokofiev make attractive mid-side contrast.

Menuhin, Yehudi (violin)

Violin concertos (with (i) Bath Festival Orch., cond. Menuhin; (ii) Rudolf Barshai (viola); (iii) Vienna PO, Silvestri; (iv) Philharmonia Orch., (v) Kurtz; (vi) Susskind; (vii) Berlin PO, Kempe): (i) MOZART: *Violin concerto No. 3 in G major, K.216.* (i; ii) *Sinfonia concertante in E flat major, K.364.* (iii) BEETHOVEN: *Violin concerto in D major, Op. 61.* (iv; v) MENDELSSOHN: *Violin concerto in E minor, Op. 64.* (iv; vi) BRUCH: *Violin concerto No. 1 in G minor, Op. 26.* (vii) BRAHMS: *Violin concerto in D major, Op. 77.*

(M) **(*) HMV TC-SLS 5106.

Many will be glad to have Menuhin's recordings of the major concertos gathered so conveniently together. The performances are not always technically immaculate but they have a warmth and humanity that command attention. The Mendelssohn and Bruch are among the finest versions ever recorded; they are also available separately, but that cassette is in non-Dolby form. Generally these transfers are excellent. The Beethoven is smooth yet clear; the Mozart works have fresh tuttis and the soloists beautifully focused (just a hint once or twice of the refinement slipping, but nothing serious). The Bruch and Mendelssohn concertos have the level set very high and are brightly lit, the detail very clear (some top cut may be needed here); the Brahms is well balanced, with plenty of orchestral weight and good presence.

'Romances' (with Philharmonia Orch., Pritchard): BEETHOVEN: *Romances Nos. 1 in G major, Op. 40; 2 in F major, Op. 50.* WIENIAWSKI: *Légende, Op. 17.* CHAUSSON: *Poème, Op. 25.* BERLIOZ: *Romance, Rêverie et Caprice, Op. 8.*
(M)**HMV TC-SXLP 30249.

This is not among Menuhin's most rewarding issues. The performances are good rather than outstanding, and none has any special charisma. Menuhin's tone seems uncovered at times and his intonation is sometimes suspect. The Berlioz and Wieniawski pieces do not receive the special kind of advocacy they need if they are to make their full effect; and there is a finer version of the elusive Chausson *Poème* (by Milstein). Readers are referred to Grumiaux's similar anthology (see above); it is not as clearly recorded, but is generally preferable to this. However, the HMV transfer is of good quality, clearly detailed, well balanced and nearly always refined.

Monte Carlo Opera Orch., Frémaux

'French overtures' from: BIZET: *Carmen* (*Prelude*). THOMAS: *Mignon.* ADAM: *Si j'étais roi.* BOIELDIEU: *Le Calife de Bagdad. La Dame blanche.* AUBER: *Fra Diavolo.*
(B)**DG Heliodor 3348 260.

Louis Frémaux shows himself thoroughly at home in this repertoire, played with the proper French accent. The music is all attractively scored and felicitous in invention, and if the horn soloist at the beginning of *Mignon* is not especially gracious, that is the only contribution from the wind which is below par, and the string-playing is neat and stylish, notably so in *Si j'étais roi.* The two charming Boieldieu overtures are shaped with warmth and elegance, and *Fra Diavolo* has point and wit. The transfers are of good quality, with well-balanced sound, lacking the last degree of range (the level is rather low) but agreeably bright and full. On our review copy there was just a suspicion of discoloration occasionally in the upper wind partials.

'Italian overtures' from: VERDI: *La Forza del destino. I Vespri siciliani.* ROSSINI: *La Scala di seta. Il Barbiere di Siviglia. L'Italiana in Algeri.* BELLINI: *Norma* (*Prelude*).
(B)*(*)DG Heliodor 3348 265.

Frémaux directs lively performances of these Italian overtures, but, as might be expected, his orchestra is not so naturally at home in this repertoire as in the companion tape of French music. The playing is not without finesse, but it lacks the final degree of stylishness which would make this music sparkle. The recording is quite good; the strings are bright but somewhat lacking in body. There is a fair amount of hiss.

Musica Antiqua, Uridge

Renaissance music, Vol. 1: Early dance and instrumental music of the Trouvères; 13th-century French motets; French songs; 16th-century rustic dances.
(B) * Rediffusion Legend KLGD 024.
Renaissance music, Vol. 2: Elizabethan England; Italian Renaissance music; Spanish organ music; German song and dance; French songs.
(B) * Rediffusion Legend KLGD 025.

The above headings give an outline of a diverse collection ranging from early music for pipes, the cabinet organ and Minnelieder through to songs by Dowland and Josquin des Prés, organ music by Milan and Narvaéz, and dances by Hassler and Scheidt. The anthology has the merit of enthusiasm and it is far from unintelligently planned. There are certain drawbacks: the performances are a little wanting in polish, and the recording is just a trifle too forward at times (audible intakes of breath by singers). The cassette transfer does not produce distinguished sound: it is edgy and wanting in smoothness.

National PO, Gerhardt

'Classic film scores': Title fanfares: WAXMAN: MGM; NEWMAN: Selznick; 20th-Century Fox (with Cinemascope extension); STEINER: Warner Bros. Excerpts from film scores: KORNGOLD: Captain Blood; Elizabeth and Essex. STEINER: Now Voyager; Gone with the Wind; The Caine Mutiny. HERRMANN: Citizen Kane; King of the Khyber Rifles. ROZSA: Knights of the Round Table; Hawks in Flight; Julius Caesar. WAXMAN: Objective Burma; Peyton Place. TIOMKIN: Guns of Navarone; The Thing from Another World. AMFITHEATROF: Salome's Dance of the Seven Veils.

*(**)RCA RK 42005.

This fascinating collection will obviously catch the eye of film buffs, and while these are mostly snippets, the diversity of the programme has an obvious appeal. The opening fanfares are repetitive in style but have a documentary as well as a nostalgic interest. As for the incidental music itself, it is all highly professional, but its musical quality is very uneven. Hollywoodian invention was often extremely conventional and sus-

tained only by colourful orchestration and fine orchestral playing (to say nothing of the vigour of the action which it accompanied). There is, of course, no lack of high-flown rhetoric, and there are moments of individuality, notably from Bernard Herrmann, while Tiomkin's science fiction excerpt is imaginatively scored and well above average. Charles Gerhardt secures committed and idiomatic playing from this first-class orchestra and the recording has the right vivid qualities. Unfortunately the tape transfer is very variable from excerpt to excerpt. The opening fanfares lack sparkle (and there is too much bass), although later the sound is better balanced.

National PO, Herrmann

'Music from great Shakespearean films': SHOSTAKOVICH: Hamlet (incidental music): suite. WALTON: Richard III; Prelude. ROZSA: Julius Caesar (incidental music): suite.

**(*)Decca Phase 4 KPFC 4315 [Lon. 5–21132].

This is in some ways a less attractive collection than Bernard Herrmann's tapes of his own music. The Shostakovich score for Hamlet is impressively dramatic and atmospheric, very much in the Soviet tradition set by Prokofiev, and the Walton Prelude is a fine piece too. But Rozsa's suite is not in this class; its rhetoric seems empty in a typical Hollywood way. The recording, however, does much to commend the programme: it is spacious and resonant yet has plenty of bite and colour. The Shostakovich is given plenty of impact; only in the Rozsa do the textures tend to congeal a little, and that is at least partly the fault of the scoring. However, no one can complain of a lack of spectacle here, or any shortage of exotic orchestral effects.

'Great British film music': LAMBERT: Anna Karenina: suite. BAX: Oliver

Twist: 2 Lyrical pieces. BENJAMIN: *An Ideal Husband: Waltz; Galop.* WALTON: *Escape Me Never: Ballet.* VAUGHAN WILLIAMS: *49th Parallel: The invaders.* BLISS: *Things to Come: suite.*

**(*) Decca Phase 4 KPFC 4363.

A most attractive collection, very well recorded and splendidly transferred at a high level. The music by Constant Lambert, Bax and Benjamin is well worth having, tuneful and vividly scored: the *Ideal Husband Waltz* is particularly stylish and appealing. The performances are generally well played and sympathetic, but the conductor blots his copybook in the *Things to Come suite* which he treats Symphonically with a rather self-conscious capital S. The result is that the famous march is slow and turgid instead of urgent and exciting (Bliss's own recording on Ace of Diamonds – disc only – shows just how it should be done). But even with that drawback this is a very enticing issue.

Netherlands Radio Orch., Paita

'Great overtures': BEETHOVEN: *Leonora No. 3, Op. 72b.* BERLIOZ: *Le Carnaval romain, Op. 9.* BRAHMS: *Academic Festival overture, Op. 80.* WAGNER: *Rienzi.*

**(*) Decca Phase 4 KPFC 4297.

Brilliantly played performances, showing Carlos Paita and the Dutch orchestra on top form. There is plenty of drama and undoubted spontaneity; *Leonora No. 3* creates tension from the very opening bar, and *Rienzi* is played with warmth and spirit. The recording is full-blooded in Decca's best Phase Four manner, and the transfer misses only the very last degree of refinement at climaxes. But the wide dynamic range increases one's enjoyment of the performances.

New Philharmonia Orch., Gerhardt

'Elizabethan serenade': BINGE: *Elizabethan serenade.* ELGAR: *Chanson de matin, Op. 15/2. Variations on an original theme (Enigma), Op. 36: Nimrod.* WALTON: *Henry V: Touch her soft lips and part.* TOYE: *The Haunted Ballroom.* BRITTEN: *The Young Person's Guide to the Orchestra (Variations and fugue on a theme of Purcell), Op. 34.* ARNOLD: *4 Scottish dances.*

(M) (***) RCA Gold Seal GK 25006.

Charles Gerhardt is an immensely gifted and versatile musician; whatever he touches seems to spring to life, and that is shown throughout this diverse and attractively chosen programme. The opening title piece is given a persuasive freshness, and Toye's charming *Haunted Ballroom* has splendid atmosphere. Arnold's *Scottish dances* are as exuberant as anyone could wish; the lovely melody of the third dance (famous as a TV signature tune) is beautifully played. The account of the Britten *Variations* is attractively alive and direct. Altogether a first-rate anthology, and it is a pity that the tapes we tried have been of unreliable quality, with coarseness at fortissimos, flutter and pitch unsteadiness. The basic sound is vivid and it may be that by the time we are in print these faults which bedevilled all early copies of this issue will have been cured.

New Philharmonia Orch., Mackerras

'Favourite ballet music': ballet suites from: ROSSINI: *William Tell.* DELIBES: *Sylvia. Coppélia.* GOUNOD: *Faust.*

(B) **(*) Classics for Pleasure TC-CFP 40229.

This is an exceptionally vivid tape, with sound of demonstration quality.

The acoustic is ideal for the music and the glowing orchestral colouring is balanced by sparkling overall sound. The dynamic range is reduced to achieve a very high level of transfer, but this seems to be only occasionally noticeable, most markedly in *Coppélia*, where some of the composer's contrasts are minimized.

New SO (of London), Agoult

'*Clair de lune*': MASSENET: *Thaïs: Meditation. La Vierge: Dernier sommeil de la Vierge.* TCHAIKOVSKY: *Chant sans paroles, Op. 2/3. Andante cantabile for strings.* FAURÉ: *Pavane, Op. 50.* ELGAR: *Dream Children, Op. 43/1 and 2.* DEBUSSY: *Suite bergamasque: Clair de lune.* BACH: *Wachet auf:* choral variation. GLUCK: *Orfeo ed Euridice: Dance of the Blessed Spirits.*

(M)*** Decca KCSP 111.

This cassette offers particularly stylish performances of the *Dance of the Blessed Spirits*, Fauré's *Pavane*, and the *Dream Children* of Elgar, where the lovely woodwind playing catches the wistful charm of this music very well indeed. The Tchaikovsky *Andante cantabile* is conceived so gently and tastefully that the intimate nature of the composer's original string-quartet medium is preserved. Excellent recording, and a splendid transfer: the upper strings hint at the early recording date, but the overall ambient richness is nicely set off by the bright treble, and this is for the most part of very high quality indeed.

New York Trumpet Ens., Schwarz

'*A festival of trumpets*': BIBER, Heinrich: *Sonata a 7 in C major.* PEZEL: *Sonata a 7 in C major. Sonatinas Nos. 61–2, 65–6.* BIBER, Carl: *Sonata in C major. Sonata for two choirs.* GABRIELI, Giovanni: *Sonata.* SCHEIDT: *Canzona.* RATHGEBER: *Concerto in*

E flat major, Op. 6/15. MOLTER: *Symphony in C major.*

*** Advent D 1039 (see p. xxiii) [id.].

Outstanding quality, in no way inferior to a gramophone record. The first side contains almost three quarters of an hour of brilliantly played and vividly recorded brass music. As so often in recordings from this source, the balance is very forward and there is little ambience. The B side is left blank so that one can use it domestically.

Overtures

'*The Phase Four world of concert overtures*' (with various orchestras, cond. (i) Vonk; (ii) Sharples; (iii) Black; (iv) Stokowski; (v) Foster; (vi) Paita): overtures: (i) GLINKA: *Russlan and Ludmilla.* (ii) SUPPÉ: *Light Cavalry.* (iii) SMETANA: *The Bartered Bride.* (iv) BEETHOVEN: *Egmont.* (v) MOZART: *Le Nozze di Figaro.* (vi) WAGNER: *Der fliegende Holländer.*

(M)** Decca KCSP 409.

The performances here are lively (if not always especially polished) and the recording always vivid. The best items are Stokowski's fine *Egmont* and the exciting *Flying Dutchman* from Carlos Paita (although there is a hint of roughness in the tape sound here). Generally the transfers are strong in impact and detail.

(Orchestre de) Paris, Jacquillat

MESSAGER: *Les Deux Pigeons:* suite; *Isoline:* suite. LALO: *Scherzo for orchestra.* PIERNÉ: *Marche des petits soldats de plomb.* DE LISLE (arr. Berlioz): *La Marseillaise* (with soloists and chorus).

(M)*** HMV Greensleeve TC-ESD 7048.

An utterly delectable concert, splendidly played and recorded, and most successfully transferred to cassette. The Messager scores are full of charm and colour; the Lalo *Scherzo* is a first-rate piece, and Pierné's *March of the little lead soldiers* is deliciously piquant. Berlioz's arrangement of *La Marseillaise* (all verses included) for soloists, choirs and orchestra is irresistibly life-enhancing, and it is done with great flair and commitment here. Highly recommended.

(Orchestre de) Paris, Rostropovich

'*Russian orchestral music*': GLINKA: *Russlan and Ludmilla: Overture. Valse-fantaisie in B minor.* MUS-SORGSKY: *Night on the Bare Mountain.* BORODIN: *In the Steppes of Central Asia.* RIMSKY-KORSAKOV: *Capriccio espagnol, Op. 34.*

*(**)HMV TC-ASD 3421 [Angel 4xs 36889].

Rostropovich's music-making has plenty of colour and spirit. The Glinka *Valse-fantaisie* is given a particularly elegant performance, and *In the Steppes of Central Asia* is poetically shaped. However, both here and in the slow section of the *Capriccio* (where the strings have the tune) the phrasing is sometimes apt to sound too broad and the onward flow of the music loses some of its impetus. The recording is very reverberant, and this has reduced the sparkle in the upper register. The absence of glittering transients means that in the *Capriccio* the triangle solo is curiously blurred. *Night on the Bare Mountain* loses its bite too, and the overture similarly could do with more edge. It must be emphasized that there is no coarseness of tone, and the sound is agreeably warm.

(Orchestre de) Paris, Rozhdestvensky

'*A Russian festival gala*': BORODIN: *Prince Igor: Polovtsian dances.*

RIMSKY-KORSAKOV: *Capriccio espagnol, Op. 34. Russian Easter Festival overture, Op. 36.* MUSSORGSKY: *Night on the Bare Mountain.*

(M) (***) HMV Greensleeve TC-ESD 7006.

Exciting performances, brilliantly played. The tension is kept at a high level throughout the concert, and yet the characterization of each piece is very well done. The *Russian Easter Festival overture* is among the finest available performances of this piece, and the *Capriccio espagnol* is also outstanding. The *Polovtsian dances* and the *Capriccio* are both vividly transferred, with everything projected forward, but the dynamics have been condensed and eventually the consistently loud orchestral sound becomes tiresome. The *Festival overture* survives rather better, but the quiet music at the end of *Night on the Bare Mountain* offers too little contrast with what has gone before.

'Pas de deux'

(i) LSO, Bonynge; (ii) Suisse Romande Orch., Ansermet; (iii) Paris Conservatoire Orch., Martinon. (i) MINKUS: *Don Quixote: Pas de deux.* (ii) TCHAIKOVSKY: *The Sleeping Beauty: Blue Bird pas de deux. Swan Lake,* Act 3: *Pas de deux. The Nutcracker,* Act 2: *Pas de deux of the Sugar Plum Fairy.* (iii) ADAM: *Giselle,* Act 1: *Peasant pas de deux;* Act 2: *Grand pas de deux and Finale.*

(M)***Decca KCSP 487.

Robert Irving's similar collection on Classics for Pleasure (see under RPO below) is spoiled by a clumsy tape transfer, so this brilliant Decca issue is most welcome. Bonynge's account of the *Don Quixote pas de deux* is especially welcome; it is a sparkling performance, as are the *Giselle* excerpts from Martinon. The Ansermet recordings are good too and the transfers throughout are very vivid indeed, although the orchestral quality is sometimes a little dry.

Philadelphia Orch., Ormandy

'Sabre dance': TCHAIKOVSKY: *Swan Lake, Op. 20: suite.* MUSSORGSKY: *Night on the Bare Mountain.* BORODIN: *Prince Igor: Polovtsian dances. Nocturne for strings.* KHACHATURIAN: *Gayaneh: Sabre dance.*
  (M)*(*)CBS Embassy 40–30100.

Brilliant playing throughout, with the customary Philadelphia panache, though not the display of colour in the wind solos that one would expect in a European recording. The sound is very bright in the American manner and it has transferred quite well, especially in the *Polovtsian dances.* For some reason the *Swan Lake* suite is split up, with the famous oboe tune opening the concert (where the upper partials of the oboe timbre are less than perfectly clean) and the rest at the end of side two.

Philadelphia Orch. or LSO, Ormandy

'Commercial break': BACH: *Suite No. 3 in D major: Air* (Benson & Hedges). TCHAIKOVSKY: *Nutcracker suite: Dance of the Flutes* (Cadbury's). DVOŘÁK: *Symphony No. 9 (New World): Largo* (Hovis). ORFF: *Carmina Burana:* excerpt (Old Spice). HANDEL: *Royal Fireworks music: overture* (Loewenbrau). ELGAR: *Enigma variations: Nimrod* (St Bruno). GRIEG: *Peer Gynt suite No. 1: Dawn* (Nescafé). BEETHOVEN: *Symphony No. 6 in F major (Pastoral)* (Blue Band). STRAUSS, Richard: *Also sprach Zarathustra:* opening.
  (M)*CBS Classics 40–61836.

With so many TV commercials currently featuring themes drawn from the classical repertoire this was a good idea for a collection, and the performances here are nearly all distinguished, if sometimes rather leisurely. The Dvořák *Largo* certainly takes that tempo indication literally, but is sustained by beautiful playing. The opening of the *Royal Fireworks music,* however, is excessively slow. The recordings are all basically good, but the tape transfer is patchy: the refinement slips at the climaxes of the Dvořák, the *Carmina Burana* excerpt is fuzzy, and the Beethoven is not ideally clear either.

Philharmonia Orch. or RPO, Weldon

'British concert pops': COLERIDGE-TAYLOR: *Petite suite de concert.* ELGAR: *Chanson de matin, Op. 15/1.* DELIUS: *La Calinda* (arr. Fenby). VAUGHAN WILLIAMS: *Fantasia on Greensleeves. English folksongs suite: Folk songs from Somerset* (arr. Jacob). HARTY: *Irish symphony: The fair day* (scherzo). COATES: *London suite: Covent Garden (Tarantelle)* ARNOLD: *4 Scottish dances: No. 1.* TRAD.: *Suo-gan* (arr. Weldon). GRAINGER: *Londonderry air.*
  (M)**(*)HMV TC-SXLP 30243.

Coleridge-Taylor's *Petite suite de concert* seems to have no place in today's repertoire. It is light music at its best – a sophisticated extension of the Palm Court tradition, but imaginatively scored for the kind of orchestra (double or single woodwind, brass and strings) that used to play at spas and seaside resorts two generations ago. There is a vast library of music by composers like Haydn Wood, Percy Fletcher, Curzon, Quilter and countless others which is tuneful, put together with real craftsmanship, and shows a fine understanding of the orchestral palette, but is never heard live today. The *Petite suite* epitomizes this tradition, and listeners responding to its freshness in this splendid performance will join us in wishing that more was available in recordings of this calibre. Most of the rest of the programme is more familiar. Eric Coates, whose energetic *Tarantelle* from the *London suite* is a highlight, managed to bridge the gap into the mid-twentieth century by writing successful film music. The delicious scherzo from Harty's *Irish symphony* is especially welcome; but this collection is first-class in every way, and the bright recording has generally transferred well to cassette, with only the occasional slip of refinement (notably in the Vaughan Williams and Malcolm Arnold), caused by the resonant fortissimos.

'Pomp and Circumstance'

(i) LSO, Bliss; (ii) Simon Preston (organ); (iii) Grenadier Guards Band, Bashford; (iv) Philip Jones Brass Ens.; (v) Chorus, LSO, Britten: (i) ELGAR: *Pomp and Circumstance marches, Op. 39/1–5.* (ii) *Imperial march, Op. 32.* (iii) COATES: *Dambusters march.* (iv) BLISS: *Antiphonal fanfare for 3 brass choirs.* (ii) WALTON: *Crown Imperial.* (iv) BAX: *Fanfare for the wedding of Princess Elizabeth* (1948). BRITTEN: *Fanfare for St Edmundsbury.* (v) arr. BRITTEN: *National anthem.*

(M) *** Decca KCSP 419.

A transfer of Decca's top quality makes this a highly attractive issue. Bliss's account of the *Pomp and Circumstance marches* is extremely lively, never sentimentalizing, yet not missing the *nobilmente*. There is a slight edge in the sound of No. 1, betraying the early stereo recording. The brass fanfares by Bliss, Bax and Britten, contrasted in range and style, are very appealing when the stereo effect is so impressive. One might have preferred an orchestral version of *Crown*

Imperial, but the recording here is of demonstration quality, and Simon Preston is an eloquent advocate.

Prague SO, Dixon

'Romantic overtures': SCHUMANN: *Manfred, Op. 115.* BRAHMS: *Tragic overture, Op. 81.* WAGNER: *A Faust overture.* MENDELSSOHN: *Die schöne Melusine (Fair Melusina), Op. 32.*

(B) *(*) Rediffusion Legend KLGD 014.

These four overtures make a rather successful anthology, particularly as the performances are strong and well played. The recording, however, does not sound very modern, and although it is full-blooded the tape transfer provides little bloom on the upper strings. A treble cut can smooth this out to a considerable extent without muffling the overall texture, but the sound image remains rather dated.

Royal Liverpool PO, Groves

'Rule Britannia': ELGAR: *Pomp and Circumstance marches, Op. 39, Nos. 1 and 4.* HOLST: *Song without words No. 2: Marching song.* ARNE: *British Grenadiers* (arr. Robinson). *Rule Britannia* (arr. Sargent; with Anne Collins, Liverpool Philharmonic Choir). VAUGHAN WILLIAMS: *Coastal Command: Dawn patrol.* DAVIES: *RAF march past.* WALTON: *Henry V: Touch her soft lips and part; Agincourt song.* arr. WOOD: *Fantasia on British sea songs: Hornpipe.* COATES: *Dambusters march.* BLISS: *Processional.* ALFORD: *On the Quarter Deck.*

** HMV TC-ASD 3341.

A genial collection, nicely varied in content. Groves's way with the music is relaxed but often agreeably fresh. The best items are the *RAF march past* and the *Dambusters* (lightweight but breezy), and the two Elgar marches have a spacious *nobilmente*. Anne Collins seems to overemphasize her consonants in *Rule Britannia*, and here as in the famous *Hornpipe* one misses the ambience of the Proms. The transfer is generally full-blooded, but the resonance prevents crispness of transients and the quality is smooth rather than sharply focused.

Royal Opera House, Covent Garden, Orch., Solti

'Solti at the opera': VERDI: *La Traviata: Preludes to Acts 1 and 3.* ROSSINI: Overtures: *L'Italiana in Algeri; Semiramide.* OFFENBACH: *Les Contes d'Hoffmann: Barcarolle.* GOUNOD: *Faust: Ballet music.* PONCHIELLI: *La Gioconda: Dance of the hours.*
> (M) **(*) Decca KCSP 347 [Lon. 5-6753].

Solti's characteristically intense reading of the *Traviata* preludes is neatly offset by the crisp account of Rossini's *Italian Girl in Algiers* overture (with the oboe solo nicely done); and the warmth and rich colouring of the famous Offenbach *Barcarolle* are matched by the exhilarating elegance of the *Dance of the hours* with its glowing wind colours. On side one the recording is of demonstration quality, wide in range, resonant and clear in the bass; on side two the sound is less open in quality (the tuttis of the *Faust* ballet music are not cleanly transferred), but this remains an enjoyable collection.

RPO, Beecham

'Beecham conducts famous overtures': BEETHOVEN: *The Ruins of Athens, Op. 113.* ROSSINI: *La Gazza ladra.* MENDELSSOHN: *A Midsummer Night's Dream, Op. 21.* BERLIOZ: *Le Corsaire, Op. 21.* BRAHMS: *Academic Festival overture, Op. 80.* SUPPÉ: *Poet and Peasant.*
> (M) HMV TC-EXE 70.

A most attractive collection with Beecham on top form is spoilt here by inept engineering. The basic quality of the tape transfer is dull and muddy, with very little treble response, while the orchestral texture is curiously insecure. The writer drew EMI's attention to the fault when the tape was first issued, but a current copy shows no improvement.

RPO, Irving

'Pas de deux' from: TCHAIKOVSKY: *The Sleeping Beauty,* Act 3. *The Nutcracker.* DELIBES: *Sylvia,* Act 3. ADAM: *Giselle,* Act 1 (*Valse*). CHOPIN (arr. Douglas): *Les Sylphides.* MINKUS: *Don Quixote.* ROSSINI-RESPIGHI: *La Boutique fantasque: Can-can.* PROKOFIEV: *Romeo and Juliet.*
> (B) (**) Classics for Pleasure TC-CFP 40274.

An attractive selection of ballet snippets in strong, stylish performances. The recording is a little dated, with unnaturally bright upper strings, but it is basically excellent, with a lively stereo acoustic and good presence. Unfortunately side one, containing the two Tchaikovsky excerpts plus the *Pas de deux* from *Sylvia*, is transferred at a ridiculously high level and the fortissimos distort constantly. Side two is much better but still has patches of unrefinement at peaks.

Russian music

'Concert of Russian favourites' (with (i) Dresden State Orch., Sanderling; (ii) Monte Carlo Opera Orch., Frémaux; (iii) Leningrad PO, Rozhdestvensky; (iv) Berlin PO; (v) Maazel;

(vi) Leitner): (i) BORODIN: *In the Steppes of Central Asia.* (ii) *Prince Igor; Polovtsian dances.* (iii) KHACHATURIAN: *Gayaneh: Sabre dance.* (iv; v) MUSSORGSKY: *Night on the Bare Mountain.* RIMSKY-KORSAKOV: *Capriccio espagnol, Op. 34.* (iv; vi) TCHAIKOVSKY: *Marche slave, Op. 31.*

(B)**DG Heliodor 3348 269.

This is a fairly successful reissue of a cassette formerly on Privilege. The sound is drier in this presentation: *In the Steppes of Central Asia* lacks warmth, and the *Polovtsian dances* have more brilliance than colour. But the *Capriccio espagnol,* superbly played by the Berlin orchestra, comes off effectively (even if the upper range lacks the last degree of refinement), and the overall balance, both here and in Leitner's excellent *Marche slave,* is well managed. The opening *Sabre dance* makes a splendid impact, and taken as a whole this modestly priced cassette is quite good value.

'Sabre dance'

(i) Leningrad PO, Rozhdestvensky; (ii) Berlin PO; (iii) Karajan; (iv) Berlin Radio Orch., Maazel; (v) Monte Carlo Opera Orch., Frémaux; (vi) Boehm; (vii) Boston SO, Tilson Thomas: (i) KHACHATURIAN: *Gayaneh: Sabre dance.* (ii; iii) RAVEL: *Boléro.* (iv) FALLA: *The Three-cornered Hat: Jota.* (v) BORODIN: *Prince Igor: Polovtsian dances.* (ii; vi) STRAUSS, Richard: *Salome: Dance of the Seven Veils.* (vii) STRAVINSKY: *The Rite of Spring: Danse sacrale.*

(M)**DG Privilege 3335 254.

Including as it does Karajan's Berlin Philharmonic version of Ravel's *Boléro,* Boehm's sensuous performance of Salome's dance, and opening with an

exciting account of the title piece from Rozhdestvensky, this is an attractive enough compilation. The sound is variable but always acceptable, though sometimes lacking the last degree of range and edge. The *Danse sacrale* from *The Rite of Spring* is especially good and ends the programme spectacularly.

Scheit, Karl (guitar)

Guitar concertos (with Vienna Festival CO, Boettcher): GIULIANI: *Guitar concerto No. 1 in A major, Op. 30.* CARULLI: *Guitar concerto in A major.* PAGANINI: *Romanze for solo guitar in A minor.* TORELLI: *Double concerto for violin, guitar and strings in A major.*

(M)*(*)Turnabout KTVC 34123.

In the Giuliani concerto, which fills the first side, Boettcher shapes the orchestral ritornelli with character – his opening is particularly well managed – but Scheit is not a player of strong personality, and as recorded his image is often rather dim. This detracts from the listener's enjoyment, here and also in Carulli's equally personable one-movement concerto, which is the main piece on side two. The other two works are characteristic but short, and again in the Torelli the orchestral contribution tells where the soloist is more withdrawn. The transfer is more vivid on side two.

Scottish Baroque Ens., Friedman

'At Hopetown': TRAD. (ed. Elliott): *Airs and dances of Renaissance Scotland.* MCGIBBON: *Sonata No. 5 in G major.* PURCELL: *Chaconne in G major.* HANDEL: *Trio sonata in C minor, Op. 2/1.* HAYDN: *12 Little divertimenti.*

**CRD CRDC 4028.

This collection offers well-established masterpieces alongside little-known

731

Scottish music. The Purcell *Chaconne* and the Handel and Haydn pieces are given with good style and musicianship. The Renaissance dances from Scotland edited by Kenneth Elliott are a useful addition to the catalogue and are quite attractive; the sonata by William McGibbon (1690–1756), avowedly written in the style of Corelli, is not without charm. The recording is somewhat over-resonant and in the cassette form the treble needs to be tamed a little.

'Scandinavian serenade': GRIEG: *Holberg suite, Op. 40.* NIELSEN: *Little suite for string orchestra, Op. 1.* SIBELIUS: *Canzonetta, Op. 62a.* WIREN: *Serenade for strings, Op. 11.*
**CRD CRDC 4042.

Good accounts of all these pieces, let down by a rather forward balance which prevents the players making the most of *pianissimo* markings. The quality of the cassette transfer is not particularly distinguished but is perfectly acceptable. The Sibelius *Canzonetta*, which derives from the incidental music to *Kuolema*, is beguilingly played. The first movement of the Dag Wiren *Serenade* sounds a shade untidy at times and the quality above the stave is spiky.

Sea music

'The world of the sea' (with (i) New Philharmonia Orch., Paita; (ii) Suisse Romande Orch., Ansermet; (iii) Kenneth McKellar (tenor), David Woolford (piano); (iv) Orch. of the Royal Opera House, Covent Garden; (v) Britten; (vi) London Wind Quintet; (vii) Ambrosian Singers, ECO): (i) WAGNER: *Der fliegende Holländer* (*The Flying Dutchman*)*: overture.* (ii) RIMSKY-KORSAKOV: *Scheherazade, Op. 35: The sea and Sinbad's ship.* DEBUSSY:

La Mer: Dialogue du vent et de la mer. (iii) IRELAND: *Sea fever.* (iv; v) BRITTEN: *Peter Grimes: 4 Sea interludes: 1, Dawn; 2, Storm.* (vi) ARNOLD: *3 Shanties for wind quintet.* (vii; v) GRAINGER: *Scotch strathspey and reel.*
(M)** Decca KCSP 396.

An imaginative idea for an anthology, quite well realized. It is perhaps a pity that the *Scheherazade* excerpt was included, since surely many collectors will already possess a complete version. It is of course a reasonable choice in the context, but the transfer is one of the least successful excerpts, emphasizing the upper partials of the string tone. There is also a touch of roughness in Paita's vivid Wagner performance (caused by the highly modulated transfer). But this collection is made especially attractive by the inclusion of the witty Arnold *Shanties* and the two Britten *Interludes*, which offer very good sound. Taken as a whole this is a rewarding collection.

'Serenade'

(i) Vienna Mozart Ens., Boskovsky; (ii) Gabriel Bacquier (bar.), ECO, Bonynge; (iii) Janáček Qt; (iv) Melos Ens.; (v) Tom Krause (bar.), Irwin Gage (piano); (vi) LSO, Kertesz; (vii) Academy of St Martin-in-the-Fields, Marriner; (viii) Stuart Burrows (tenor), John Constable (piano); (ix) Stuttgart CO, Münchinger; (x) Stockholm Radio Orch., Westerberg: (i) MOZART: *Serenade No. 13 in G major* (*Eine kleine Nachtmusik*)*, K.525:* 1st movt. (ii) *Don Giovanni: Deh vieni alla finestra.* (iii) HAYDN (attrib. Hofstetter): *String quartet No. 17 in F major, Op. 3/5: Serenade.* (iv) BEETHOVEN: *Serenade in D major for flute, violin and viola, Op. 25.* (v) SCHUBERT: *Schwanenge-*

sang: Ständchen. (vi) BRAHMS: *Serenade No. 1 in D major, Op. 11:* 4th movt. (vii) TCHAIKOVSKY: *Serenade for strings in C major, Op. 48: Waltz.* DVOŘÁK: *Serenade for strings in E major, Op. 22:* 1st movt. (vi) *Serenade (for wind) in D minor, Op. 44:* 2nd movt. (vii) ELGAR: *Serenade for strings in E minor, Op. 20:* 2nd movt. (viii) TOSELLI: *Serenata.* (ix) SUK: *Serenade for strings, Op. 6:* 2nd movt. (x) WIREN: *Serenade for strings, Op. 11:* finale.

(M)***Decca KCSP 323.

Serenade is another of Decca's felicitous compilations where the items are chosen and set out so as to lead the ear on readily from each piece to the next. The collection opens conventionally, perhaps, but less well-known excerpts by Beethoven, Brahms and Suk are forthcoming to add freshness and novelty to what is in essence popular repertoire. All the performances are of very high quality and the transfers are splendidly managed so that there is a variety of dynamic level as well as the obvious contrasts of instrumental, orchestral and vocal forms. A highly recommendable tape from every point of view, equally useful for in-car or domestic listening.

Solti, Georg

'Georg Solti conducts' (with various orchestras): GLINKA: *Russlan and Ludmilla overture.* GLUCK: *Orfeo ed Euridice: Dance of the Blessed Spirits.* TCHAIKOVSKY: *Serenade for strings: Waltz.* BORODIN: *Prince Igor: Polovtsian dances* (with LSO Chorus). BIZET: *Carmen: Prelude.* MAHLER: *Symphony No. 5: Adagietto.* ROSSINI: *La Boutique fantasque: suite.*

(M)***Decca KCSP 127.

As a portrait of a great contemporary

conductor this is uncannily effective. Each side opens with an overture, one by Glinka, the other by Bizet, both of which show the zestful vitality and energy which inspire almost everything Solti does. Equally the Tchaikovsky *Waltz* is irresistible for its sheer energy, and of course the *Polovtsian dances* are marvellously alive. The Mahler *Adagietto* shows strikingly the special intensity Solti can bring to slow music for strings. It is perhaps surprising that Decca did not choose to include some Wagner. *La Boutique fantasque* completes the picture by showing the other side of the coin, brilliant, even infectious playing, but very little charm. Excellent sound, brightly etched to suit the music-making. A fine tribute and a well-made concert.

Stern, Isaac (violin)

'Great violin favourites' (with Columbia SO, Katims): TCHAIKOVSKY: *None but the lonely heart.* BRAHMS: *Hungarian dance No. 5.* GERSHWIN: *Porgy and Bess: Bess, you is my woman now.* RIMSKY-KORSAKOV: *Tsar Saltan: Flight of the bumble bee.* FOSTER: *Jeannie with the light brown hair.* KREISLER: *Liebeslied.* TRAD.: *Greensleeves.* DVOŘÁK: *Humoresque.* DEBUSSY: *Suite bergamasque: Clair de lune.* BENJAMIN: *Jamaican rumba.* SCHUBERT: *Ave Maria.* COPLAND: *Rodeo: Hoe-down.*

(M)(*)CBS Classics 40–61039.

Stern is balanced much too closely, but he plays with persuasive warmth and richness of tone. The arrangements, by Arthur Harris, are generally effective; the version of *Greensleeves* is nicely introduced, while Benjamin's *Jamaican rumba* and Copland's *Hoe-down* bring in an attractive element of contrast. Stern plays the lyrical melodies very beautifully and is warmly accompanied. It is a pity that the tape transfer is too poorly focused to afford much enjoyment.

Stokowski, Leopold

'Stokowski encores' (with (i) Czech PO, (ii) LSO): (i) RACHMANINOV: *Prelude in C sharp minor, Op. 3/2*. (ii) CHOPIN: *Mazurka in A minor, Op. 17/4*. SCHUBERT: *Moment musical in F minor, D. 780/3*. BYRD: *Earl of Salisbury pavan and galliard*. (i) DVOŘÁK: *Slavonic dance No. 10 in E minor, Op. 72/2*. (ii) TCHAIKOVSKY: *Chant sans paroles, Op. 40/6*. CLARKE: *Trumpet voluntary*. DUPARC: *Extase*. (i) ELGAR: *Variations on an original theme* (*Enigma*), *Op. 36: Nimrod* (only).

**(*) Decca KPFC 4351.

Many of these items are transcriptions showing Stokowski at his most imaginative, with no inhibitions about stylistic exactitude. If the famous Rachmaninov *Prelude* cannot really be transcribed for orchestra, the sounds here are certainly novel, while the Chopin *Mazurka* is delightful, made to sound almost like French music. The scoring is at its most individual in the Byrd and Clarke items but it is undoubtedly effective; and Elgar's *Nimrod* is played most tenderly, sounding for all the world like a completely separate piece. With very good orchestral playing and vivid sound, transferred with fine presence and colour, this is a first-class tape, although just once or twice on our copy there was a hint of the strings 'pulsing'.

'The Phase Four world of Leopold Stokowski' (with various orchestras): RAVEL: *Fanfare for 'L'Éventail de Jeanne'*. TCHAIKOVSKY: *Marche slave, Op. 31; The Sleeping Beauty: Waltz; Swan Lake: Dance of the Little Swans*. STRAVINSKY: *Pas-*

torale. WAGNER: *Die Walküre: Ride of the Valkyries*. MUSSORGSKY: *Pictures at an Exhibition: The hut on fowl's legs; The Great Gate of Kiev*. (M) * Decca KCSP 159.

This is certainly a characteristic collection, with Stokowski's feeling for orchestral colour producing exotic and fascinating sounds in the Ravel *Fanfare* and the attractive Stravinsky *Pastorale*. Stokowski the magician is shown in the two Tchaikovsky dances, the music glowing with life and warmth; and Stokowski the extrovert show-off is suitably brilliant in the *Ride of the Valkyries*, the sound aggressive in its brightness. But the Phase Four engineers really go to town in *Marche slave* and the Mussorgsky: these are both too highly modulated for comfort, and there is generally a tendency for the transfer to sound unrefined.

Stuttgart CO, Münchinger

CORELLI: *Concerto grosso, Op. 6, No. 8 in G minor* (*Christmas concerto*). PACHELBEL: *Canon in D major* (arr. Münchinger). RICCIOTTI: *Concertino No. 2 in G major*. GLUCK: *Chaconne*. BACH: *Christmas oratorio, BWV 248: Sinfonia*.

(M) **(*) Decca Ace of Diamonds KSDC 411 [Lon. 5–6206].

An enjoyable collection. Corelli's beautiful *Christmas concerto* is especially successful, and if occasionally there is a suggestion of the stiffness of manner that has marred some recordings from this source, it detracts little from the general appeal of the music-making. The transfer is very successful; there is striking detail, yet the strings have a fine bloom and naturalness, although they are brightly lit. The recording for Münchinger's newer version of the Pachelbel (see below) is even more richly sumptuous, but this transfer is first-class in every way.

'Baroque music': PACHELBEL: *Canon in D major* (arr. Münchinger). *Gigue in D major* (arr. Seiffert). ALBINONI: *Adagio in G minor* (arr. Giazotto) *for strings and organ*. BACH: *Cantata No. 147: Jesu, joy of man's desiring. Cantata No. 208: Sheep may safely graze*. HANDEL: *Solomon: Arrival of the Queen of Sheba. Organ concerto No. 4 in F major, Op. 4/4* (soloist Ulrich Bremsteller). *Overture: Berenice*.

*(*) Decca KSXC 6862.

Richly beautiful recorded quality distinguishes this concert: indeed the sound is gorgeously ripe and ample. The balance is close, which does not permit much dynamic contrast in the Pachelbel *Canon*, although the *Gigue* certainly sounds gracious. If the playing possessed a compensating alertness and vitality, the romantic overtones of such a sound balance would have been minimized; but as it is, the Handel pieces are lethargic (although the *Organ concerto*, with Ulrich Bremsteller, is nicely registered), and the Albinoni *Adagio* sounds unbelievably soupy.

Thames CO, Dobson

'The baroque concerto in England' (with Neil Black, oboe, William Bennett, flute): ANON. (probably HANDEL): *Concerto grosso in F major*. BOYCE: *Concerti grossi: in E minor for strings; in B minor for 2 solo violins, cello and strings*. WOODCOCK: *Oboe concerto in E flat major; Flute concerto in D major*.

***CRD CRD 4031.

A wholly desirable collection, beautifully played and recorded. Indeed the tape transfer has splendid life and presence and often offers demonstration quality – try the opening of the Woodcock *Flute concerto*, for instance. The music is all highly rewarding. The opening concerto was included in Walsh's first edition of Handel's Op. 3 (as No. 4) but was subsequently replaced by another work. Whether or not it is by Handel it is an uncommonly good piece, and it is given a superbly alert and sympathetic performance here. Neil Black and William Bennett are soloists of the highest calibre, and it is sufficient to say that they are on top form throughout this most enjoyable concert.

Tone poems

'Great tone poems' (with (i) New Philharmonia Orch., Kord; (ii) RPO; (iii) Henry Lewis; (iv) Kingsway SO, Camarata; (v) LPO, Herrmann; (vi) LSO; (vii) Black; (viii) Stokowski): (i) SIBELIUS: *Finlandia, Op. 26. Legends: The Swan of Tuonela, Op. 22/2*. (ii; iii) STRAUSS, Richard: *Till Eulenspiegels lustige Streiche, Op. 28*. (iv) BORODIN: *In the Steppes of Central Asia* (arr. Camarata). (v) DUKAS: *L'Apprenti sorcier (The Sorcerer's Apprentice)*. (vi; vii) SMETANA: *Mà Vlast: Vltava*. (ii; vii) SAINT-SAËNS: *Danse macabre, Op. 40*. (vi; viii) DEBUSSY: *Prélude à l'après-midi d'un faune*. MUSSORGSKY: *Night on the Bare Mountain* (arr. Stokowski).

(B)*(*)Decca KDPC 601/2.

An impressive anthology that is apparently good value for money; but there are a few drawbacks. Although the transfers are mostly strikingly full, clear and vivid (notably in the Sibelius pieces and *Till Eulenspiegel*), there are moments when the high level causes the refinement to slip – in *The Sorcerer's Apprentice* (which is disappointing as a performance too), *Vltava*, and the powerful Stokowski *Night on the Bare Mountain*. The performances, apart from the Stokowski, and to a lesser extent Henry Lewis's *Till*

Eulenspiegel, are good but not outstanding. *In the Steppes of Central Asia* is enjoyably eloquent, but is heard in a slightly abbreviated arrangement.

Vienna PO, Boskovsky

'Overtures of old Vienna': STRAUSS, Johann: *Die Fledermaus. Prinz Methusalem.* NICOLAI: *The Merry Wives of Windsor.* REZNIČEK: *Donna Diana.* HEUBERGER: *Der Opernball* (Opera Ball).

(M)*** Decca Jubilee KJBC 47.

Vivid performances given a spectacular recording. The balance is sometimes a little larger than life, but in music for sheer entertainment like this the extra projection is effective enough. The authentic Viennese lilt gives special charm to the *Opera Ball overture*; and Johann Strauss's *Prinz Methusalem*, with its well-managed off-stage band effect in the middle, is a vivacious novelty. The exhilarating forward impulse of *Donna Diana* is nicely judged. The tape transfer is splendidly managed, with fine sparkle and atmosphere. Highly recommended: this is a demonstration issue, as was the equivalent disc before it.

'New Year in Vienna': SUPPÉ: *Beautiful Galathea: overture.* STRAUSS, Johann, Jnr: *Explosionen* (*Explosions*) *polka, Op. 43. Lob der Frauen polka, Op. 315. Morgenblätter* (*Morning Papers*) *waltz, Op. 279. Persian march, Op. 289. Unter Donner und Blitz* (*Thunder and Lightning*) *polka, Op. 324.* STRAUSS, Johann, Snr: *Sperl galop. Piefke und Pufke polka.* STRAUSS, Josef: *Eingesendet polka, Op. 240.* LEHÁR: *Gold and Silver waltz, Op. 79.* ZIEHRER: *Hereinspaziert! waltz, Op. 518.*

*(**) Decca KSXC 6572.

The Decca New Year concerts by Boskovsky and the VPO have traditionally included only music of the Strauss family, but this one (dating from 1972) broke with precedent. It opens with a vivacious account of Suppé's *Beautiful Galathea overture* and includes as a highlight a gorgeous performance of Lehár's *Gold and Silver waltz.* Another attractive novelty is the *Hereinspaziert! waltz* of Carl Ziehrer. Translated literally the title is an invitation to enter, and it represents the call of the barker outside a fairground booth. The piece is characteristically robust, as is the *Sperl galop* of Johann Senior, which many will recognize without knowing the title. The playing throughout is of the finest Boskovsky/VPO vintage, and it is a pity that the basically excellent but reverberant recording has brought transfer problems. There are muddled transients (noticeable immediately in the overture) and other moments of roughness. The effects in the *Explosions polka* and the percussion in *Thunder and Lightning* are uncomfortably congested.

Violin

'The world of the violin' (with violinists (i) John Georgiadis, (iv) Willi Boskovsky, (vi) Ruggiero Ricci, (vii) Itzhak Perlman, (x) Alfredo Campoli; (ii) LSO; (iii) Bonynge; (v) Vienna Mozart Ens.; (viii) Vladimir Ashkenazy (piano); (ix) Gamba; (xi) E. Gritton (piano); (xii) Sargent): (i–iii) MASSENET: *Thaïs: Meditation.* (ii; v) BEETHOVEN: *Romance No. 2 in F major, Op. 50.* (vi) PAGANINI: *Caprice No. 13 in B flat major, Op. 1.* (vii; viii) FRANCK: *Violin sonata in A major:* 4th movt. (vi; ii; ix) MENDELSSOHN: *Violin concerto in E minor, Op. 64:* finale. BRUCH: *Violin concerto No. 1 in G minor, Op. 26: Adagio.* SARASATE: *Zigeunerweisen.* (x; xi) KREISLER: *Liebeslied.* (vi; ii;

xii) TCHAIKOVSKY: *Violin concerto in D major, Op. 35:* finale.

(M)*(*)Decca KCSP 350.

A well-laid-out anthology that somehow fails to gell and seems unsatisfying and bitty. It is partly that the recordings tend to vary in level and balance; the excerpt from the Franck *Violin sonata*, for instance, lacks presence compared with the piece immediately before it. The transfers are generally well managed; but apart from the excerpts from the Mendelssohn and Bruch concertos, this programme is only intermittently beguiling. (For Volume 2 of this series, see under Collier in the Instrumental Recitals section.)

Warsaw National PO, Semkow

'España': CHABRIER: *España*. RIMSKY-KORSAKOV: *Capriccio espagnol, Op. 34*. RAVEL: *Rapsodie espagnole*. FALLA: *El amor brujo: Pantomime; Dance and Ritual fire dance*.

(B)***DG Heliodor 3348 029.

An extraordinarily successful bargain collection which amounts to more than the sum of its parts. Chabrier's *España* is as zestful as anyone could wish, a little brash but undoubtedly exhilarating; Rimsky's *Capriccio* offers rather measured basic tempi but the orchestral playing is alert and sympathetic (the horns are gorgeously rich) and there is excellent detail. The Ravel *Rapsodie* is memorably sensuous, with richly spun melodic lines, and the three excerpts from *El amor brujo* only serve to whet the appetite for more. The recording is splendid, full, atmospheric, with flashing percussion and plenty of warmth and depth. It is quite admirably transferred to tape, the treble fractionally too bright, perhaps, but with clean transients, full body and a natural atmospheric resonance. Highly recommended.

Williams, John (oboe), Bournemouth Sinfonietta, Wagenheim

Oboe concertos: VIVALDI: *Oboe concerto in D minor, F.7/1*. ALBINONI: *Oboe concerto in B flat major, Op. 7/3*. TELEMANN: *Oboe concerto in F minor*. HUMMEL: *Introduction, theme and variations for oboe and orchestra, Op. 102*. HANDEL (attrib.): *Oboe concerto in E flat major*.

***HMV TC-ASD 3609.

John Williams is a delightful soloist here. He plays sensitively and with exactly the right degree of elegance in the attractive Hummel work, and the slow movement of the Telemann concerto demonstrates his expressive phrasing at its most engaging. In this work as in the Hummel he dominates the music-making; elsewhere Volker Wagenheim's strong and vigorous tuttis sometimes seem to overstate the case, although such a bold orchestral backing makes a good foil for the pertly delicate oboe image. The recording is vivid and clear and the transfer admirably crisp and clean, though it has a certain edge, which adds even more emphasis to the fortissimos. Nevertheless this is a first-class collection.

World of the Academy, World of ballet, etc.: see under *Academy, Ballet*, etc.

Your Hundred Best Tunes

'The world of Your Hundred Best Tunes' (from BBC radio programme; played and sung by various artists).

(M)(**)Decca KCSP 112 (*Vol. 1*).
(M)*(*)Decca KCSP 155 (*Vol. 2*).
(M)*(*)Decca KCSP 205 (*Vol. 3*).
(M)*(*)Decca KCSP 264 (*Vol. 4*).
(M)**Decca KCSP 299 (*Vol. 5*).
(M)*(*)Decca KCSP 316 (*Vol. 6*).
(M)**Decca KCSP 355 (*Vol. 7*).

(M)*(*) Decca KCSP 356 (*Vol. 8*).
(M)*(*) Decca KCSP 373 (*Vol. 9*).
(M)*(*) Decca KCSP 400 (*Vol. 10*).
(M)*** Decca KHBC 1/1; KHBC 1/2 (*'The top 25'*).

This was a brilliantly commercial idea for a series of anthologies, and it has had great success on disc and cassette alike. Unfortunately most of the tape transfers date from Decca's earliest period, and the varying degrees of level and amplitude between items obviously gave problems until techniques became more sophisticated. In the reissue of the 'top twenty-five' of the hundred 'tunes' in a remastered form the sound is very much more sophisticated than in the individual issues. This collection includes *Finlandia*, the *Nuns' chorus* from *Casanova* (with Joan Sutherland), the *Adagio* from Bruch's *Violin concerto* (Ricci), *Jesu, joy of man's desiring*, the finale from Beethoven's *Pastoral symphony*, the *Intermezzo* from *Cavalleria Rusticana, The Hebrides overture* (Maag), Allegri's *Miserere* (abridged), Handel's *Largo*, the *Meditation* from *Thaïs*, the *Toccata* from Widor's *Organ symphony No. 5* (Simon Preston), the *Largo* from the *New World symphony* (cleverly abridged) and Pavarotti's *Nessun dorma* from *Turandot*. For one or two of the excerpts a different recording is used in the newer issue. In the case of Pavarotti (replacing Kenneth McKellar) this is an obvious advantage, but elsewhere the reverse applies: for instance, *Tales from the Vienna Woods* is now played by Mantovani instead of the LPO under Dorati. However, the sound on the reissue is so much more satisfactory than on the KCSPs that the choice is clear.

Of the remaining issues, Volumes 4, 6, 8, 9, and 10 all suffer to some extent from variable sound. Volume 5 has slight problems with the *Trumpet voluntary*, but is generally successful and includes Tchaikovsky's *Capriccio italien* (Alwyn), *Jerusalem, The Lost Chord* (Stuart Burrows)

and eloquent versions of *I know that my Redeemer liveth* (Joan Sutherland) and Dvořák's *Invocation to the moon* from *Rusalka* (Pilar Lorengar). Volume 7 is notable for Solti's brilliant account of the *Dance of the hours*, the *Hallelujah chorus* (under Boult), Kathleen Ferrier's *Che farò*, and the finale of the *Emperor concerto* (Katchen).

The whole set has now also been issued in two boxes (K 4 M 18 and 19), which again offer more modern transfers, and should be considered by those for whom this repertoire has great interest. It is certainly a good way for inexperienced listeners to discover the source of much music to which they cannot put a name.

'Your Hundred Best Tunes: new chart' (from BBC radio programme; played and sung by various artists).

(M)**(*) Decca KCSP 491 (*Vol. 1*).
(M)**(*) Decca KCSP 488 (*Vol. 2*).

The two issues from the 'new chart' are comparatively recent transfers and the sound quality is mostly of a high standard. At the opening of Volume 1 the string tone is somewhat shrill in the *Prelude to Act 1* of *La Traviata* (Solti), but this responds to the controls, and the sound thereafter is clear and full-bodied, with plenty of range and detail. The vocal items in this collection are especially good; they include *Che gelida manina* (Pavarotti), the *Serenade* from *The Fair Maid of Perth* (McKellar), Tchaikovsky's *None but the lonely heart* (Ghiaurov), Sherill Milnes's splendid *Largo al factotum* (from *The Barber of Seville*), and a lovely performance of Brahms's *Lullaby* from Tebaldi to end the concert.

The famous duet *Au fond du temple saint* (from *The Pearl Fishers*) was especially recorded for Volume 2 by Pavarotti and Ghiaurov, and they give it a fine lyrical lift. Once again vocal excerpts dominate, including Joan Sutherland in excellent form dreaming about marble halls (from *The Bohemian Girl*), and Pavarotti in *La donna è mobile* from *Rigoletto*. Non-vocal items include the second movement from Rodrigo's *Concierto de Aranjuez* and the *Orpheus in the Underworld overture*, which, with an over-resonant bass, is the only technical blot in a most attractive collection, otherwise well transferred.

Brass and Military Band Concerts

Berlin Philharmonic Wind Ens., Karajan

'Prussian and Austrian marches'.
  *DG 3308 196/7.

Karajan presents here a collection of thirty marches from composers as diverse as Beethoven and Suppé, Fučik and Johann Strauss. The Prussian marches are played with the proper rhythmic stiffness; the Austrian marches, appropriately, are more flexible. The recording is admirably full-blooded but unfortunately the cassette transfers are unacceptably lacking in bite in the treble. The transients are very poor indeed. The level of transfer is low, and the effect is too bass-heavy, even for this repertoire. The two tapes are available separately. On 3308 196 there is a march called *Entry into Paris* which is anonymous: no wonder!

Black Dyke Mills Band, Brand or Newsome

'The best of the Black Dyke Mills Band': CHABRIER: *Marche joyeuse.* arr. LANGFORD: *Drink to me only; Fantasy on British sea songs; British Grenadiers; All through the Night; Blaydon Races; Greensleeves; The Girl I Left Behind Me.* ROSSINI: *La Danza.* TOMLINSON: *Best Foot Forward.* ORD HUME: *Brilliant march.* NEWSOME: *Concorde.* ALFORD: *Colonel Bogey.* SOUSA (arr. Langford): *Marching with Sousa.*
  **(*)RCA PK 25025.

The Black Dyke Mills and the Grimethorpe Colliery Bands (see below) are currently creating astonishing new standards in their field. The playing here is of the utmost sophistication. Any thought of amateurism is banished; the ensemble, execution and the sheer style of the music-making suggest professionalism of an international standard. This is a lightweight programme, but the panache of the presentation is irresistible. The recording has generally transferred satisfactorily to tape, and much of it sounds very well. At the opening of the Chabrier *Marche joyeuse* the reverberation prevents the transients from being ideally crisp in the percussion, but the overall focus is good.

Black Dyke Mills Band, Newsome or Parkes

'British music for brass bands': ELGAR: *Severn suite, Op. 87.* RUBBRA: *Variations on 'The Shining River', Op. 101.* FLETCHER: *An Epic Symphony.* BALL: *Sinfonietta.*
  ***RCA RK 25078.

This is certainly one of the finest brass-band collections ever recorded. The performance of the *Severn suite* is definitive and is discussed, along with the rest of the programme, in its entry for Elgar above. The RCA sound is bright rather than richly sonorous, but this remains an indispensable issue for admirers of the British brass-band movement. Roy Newsome conducts the *Severn suite* and Rubbra *Variations;* the lighter works are the province of Major Peter Parkes.

'Triple champions': GREGSON: *Connotations for brass band.* BAILEY: *Diadem of Gold: overture.* MATHIAS:

Vivat Regina suite, Op. 75. LANG-FORD: *Harmonious variations on a theme of Handel.*
***RCA PK 25143.

A splendid tape, more richly recorded than the earlier Black Dyke Mills collection of British brass-band music. Once again the playing has memorable zest and sophistication. The issue celebrates the band's 'hat trick' in winning the national championships for the third year running, and the two 1977 test pieces (for the Great Britain and British Open Championships) are included here. Gregson's *Connotations* has a genuine nobility in its sustained passages, and vigorous invention elsewhere; *Diadem* is a perfect vehicle for the bravura this band so readily displays. William Mathias's *Vivat Regina* is an attractively spontaneous suite, with a spirited air of pageantry, while the Langford *Variations* show every conceivable diversity in their brilliant scoring. The invention too certainly does not lack imagination. When played like this all the music sounds better than it is. Peter Parkes conducts the test pieces; the remaining two items are directed by Roy Newsome. There are, shamefully, no notes about the music.

'Sound of brass': March: *Viva Birkinshaw. Spanish caprice. Hat trick* (horn trio). *Mexico Grandstand.* FARNON: *Une Vie de matelot. Overture: The Mill on the Cliff. From the Shores of the Mighty Pacific.* Hymn: *Sandon.* DVOŘÁK: *Symphony No. 9 (New World):* finale.
(M)*******Decca KSBC 324.

As is perhaps indicated by the absence of composers' names (on liner note and labels), the programme here is essentially basic repertoire, known better to brass-band enthusiasts than in the general musical world. But it serves to demonstrate the homogeneity and superb tonal blending (to say nothing of the bravura of individual soloists) characteristic of the Black

Dyke band in 1976 when this recording was made. Robert Farnon's *Une Vie de matelot* was the test piece which won the band their 1975 championship. Here the instrumental detail has an orchestral finesse; the arrangement of the finale from the *New World symphony,* however, does not attempt to imitate the orchestra, and it is very effective in brass-band terms. The recording is first-class, rich and full-blooded yet clear, and the transfer has splendid sonority and refinement.

BMC, Fairey and Foden's Bands, Mortimer

'The world of brass bands': ROSSINI: *William Tell overture:* Finale. HEYLER: *Three of a kind.* MEYERBEER: *Le Prophète:* Coronation march. FRIML: *Donkey serenade.* SIBELIUS: *Finlandia.* CLARKE: *Trumpet voluntary.* HEYKENS: *Serenade.* SCULL: *Trombones to the Fore.* HAYSOME: *Whispering Brass. Spanish Harlequin.* GERMAN: *Merrie England:* selection.
(M)*(*)Decca KCSP 20.

The first of a series, this collection dates from a period when Harry Mortimer was exerting an important dual influence – helping (partly via the BBC) to place the brass band before a wider musical public and providing the musical inspiration to ensure that spontaneity went hand in hand with higher standards of performance. There is a characteristic exuberance about the playing here, and the contrast between the massive sounds of *Trombones to the Fore* and the ingenuous novelty, *Whispering Brass,* which follows immediately after, is brilliantly underlined. An enjoyable programme throughout, with extremely full-blooded sound. The high-level transfer was an early issue, however; on our copy the upper transients were not always too clean, and the quality breaks up somewhat in *Finlandia*. The exuberant selection from *Merrie England* which ends the tape tends to lack definition, although there is no distortion.

'The world of brass bands', Vol. 2 (with Sale and District Choir): SEYMOUR: *Marching Trumpets*. BALL: *2nd Rhapsody on Negro Spirituals*. GOULD: *Brass Band blues*. WAGNER: *Tannhäuser: Grand march*. SCHUBERT: *Lilac Time:* selection. OFFENBACH: *Orpheus in the Underworld: overture*. arr. GEEHL: *Watching the Wheat*. STANTON: *Flanagan's Mare*. STRAUSS, Johann: *Chit chat polka*. GOUNOD: *Faust: Soldiers' chorus*. ADAMS: *The Holy City*.

(M)*(*)Decca KCSP 68.

These breezy performances again demonstrate the vigour and expertise of Harry Mortimer and his group of bandsmen. The music-making smiles genially throughout, and the playing is first-class. The programme is neatly devised to provide contrast, and the inclusion of the Sale and District Choir perpetuates a long-established partnership between massed brass and voices. The recording is full and bright, although again the rather fuzzy transients show the early date of the transfer. The choral sound is slightly pithy, but otherwise not badly focused, although the level in the *Tannhäuser* excerpt is miscalculated: there is some congestion here.

'The world of brass bands', Vol. 3: SULLIVAN: *The Pirates of Penzance: overture*. ALFVÉN: *Swedish rhapsody*. MARTYN: *Napoleon galop*. SCULL: *A Trumpet piece for a ceremonial occasion*. HANDEL: *Queen of Sheba: Grand march*. TCHAIKOVSKY: *Marche slave*. arr. MORTIMER: *John Peel*. SEYMOUR:

Zamora. CHOPIN: *Military polonaise*. GREEN: *Sunset*.

(M)**(*)Decca KCSP 306.

This is the last of the three concerts assembled from recordings Harry Mortimer made with this group at the end of the 1950s. In some ways this is vintage material, but it is splendidly recorded (except perhaps for the Chopin, which is a mono transcription). Nowhere are the vigour and style of the playing heard to better effect than in Tchaikovsky's *Marche slave;* although judiciously cut, this has the flair and panache of a first-rate orchestral version. It is this same spirited quality that makes all the first three *World of brass bands* issues so enjoyable. The witty *Napoleon galop* too demonstrates just how professional is the expertise of these players. The transfers here are crisper than in the first two tapes and are often very good indeed, although the programme itself has rather less musical interest than the earlier ones.

Brass bands

'The world of brass bands', Vol. 4 (with Black Dyke Mills Band, Newsome or Brand; Brighouse and Rastrick Band, Scott; City of Coventry Band, Chappell; Fairey Band, Dennison; Manchester CWS Band, Gartside; Yorkshire Imperial Metals Band, Worsley): BROADBENT: *Centaur march*. ARNOLD: *Little suite, Op. 80*. PUCCINI: *La Bohème: Musetta's waltz song*. BINGE: *Cornet carillon*. GEEHL: *Romanza*. GREGSON: *Prelude for an occasion*. VERDI: *Aïda: Grand march*. BOEME: *Trumpet concerto:* 1st movt. STRAUSS, Johann: *Tritsch-Tratsch polka, Op. 214*. HAYDN: *String quartet, Op. 3/5: Serenade*. HUMPERDINCK: *Hansel and Gretel: Prelude*.

(M)**(*)Decca KCSP 413.

743

Decca's fourth *World of brass bands* anthology moves away from the early Mortimer BMC/Foden's/Fairey combination (see above) and includes excerpts from recordings made more than a decade later. The expertise of the playing here is matched by the very high quality of the recording and by the immaculate transfers, rich in sonority and wide in range, crisp in detail. The sound is often of demonstration standard, though the acoustic is rather more confined and 'studioish' than on the early cassettes. The players show great confidence and skill but the music-making, although lively, only occasionally displays the sheer infectious high spirits of the Mortimer recordings (compare the *Tritsch-Tratsch polka*, for instance). On the other hand the lovely *Hansel and Gretel Prelude* (not the overture) and Arnold's attractive *Little suite* show just how polished is the finest brass-band playing of the seventies.

'*Festival of championship brass*' (with Black Dyke Mills, Brighouse and Rastrick, City of Coventry, Cory, Fairey, Grimethorpe Colliery, GUS, Hampshire Youth, Manchester CWS, Ransome, Hoffman and Pollard, Rochdale, Stanshawe, Bristol, Tredegar Junior, Yorkshire Imperial Metals Bands, under their own conductors): *The National Anthem*. WALTERS: *Flourish for brass*. GERMAN: *The President: march*. MENDELSSOHN: *Symphony No. 4* (*Italian*): *Saltarello*. ELGAR: *Severn suite: Fugue*. VERDI: *La Forza del destino: overture*. STRAUSS, Johann, Snr: *Radetzky march*. BERLIOZ: *Le Corsaire overture*. JOHNSON: *Ceramic City festival*. DAMARE: *Cleopatra polka*. SHOSTAKOVICH: *Festival overture*. POWELL: *The Tops; Duo for euphoniums*. WRIGHT: *Concerto for cornet: Rondo*. CHABRIER: *Marche joyeuse*. WATTERS: *A*

Cotswold lullaby. WINDSOR: *Alpine echoes*. YORKE: *The Shipbuilders suite*. GOLD: *Exodus theme*. HOLST: *Moorside suite*. GUNGL: *Casino dances*. KAYE: *Queensbury*. BOEKEL: *Scherzo*. MUSSORGSKY (arr. Hurst): *Night on the Bare Mountain*. SMETANA: *The Bartered Bride: Polka*.
(M) **(*) Decca K 28 K 32.

Most of the famous names are in the roster of bands here, and *aficionados* will find this an inexpensive way of representing each within a modest collection. The concert opens splendidly with Walters's aptly-named *Flourish for brass*, and it is a pity that the National Anthem, which follows on, produces some minor distortion, for generally the sound here is so-phisticated, bright and full, with excellent detail. The programme ranges wide but is well balanced. One or two items come from live concerts and include audience reaction, but as these performances provide some of the most exciting playing, few will grumble. Among the highlights are an ebullient *Le Corsaire overture*, Chabrier's *Marche joyeuse* and the Holst *Moorside suite* (which sounds as superb as on its parent tape), but Mendelssohn's *Italian symphony* and Mussorgsky's *Night on the Bare Mountain* transcribe rather clumsily: the string detail cannot readily be copied by brass instruments, however sophisticated the playing. The transfer level varies a little, but not enough to be a nuisance. The contents of three LPs are here sensibly spaced out on to two tapes, and in general this box can be cordially welcomed.

Brighouse and Rastrick Band (conductor unnamed)

'*The floral dance*' (collection of popular and traditional melodies).
***Logo KLOGO 1001.
'*Love you a little bit more*' (pop songs).
**Logo KLOGO 1006.

744

The Brighouse and Rastrick Band achieved the top of the hit parade with their catchy version of *The floral dance*. None of the other items on their first tape quite matches this, but the arrangements are cleverly made and tunes like *Scarborough Fair, Try to remember, Solitaire* (and even, surprisingly, the famous *Lara's theme* from *Dr Zhivago*) are highly effective. Both playing and recording are first-class and the transfer is of excellent quality. The second collection offers background-music-styled versions of tunes like *When I fall in love, I'm in the mood for love, Twelfth of never*, and *How deep is the ocean*. The brass timbres are skilfully and soporifically blended; one hardly expects a brass band to provide a romantic atmosphere, but Derek Broadbent's scoring gets very near to the late-evening effect achieved more readily by string-based orchestrations. Again the sound is good and the transfer is immaculate.

Coldstream Guards Band, Pope

'The voice of the guns': ALFORD: *The Voice of the Guns.* STARKE: *With Sword and Lance.* GANNE: *Le Père de la victoire.* LATANNE: *Light of Foot.* PLANQUETTE: *Sambre et Meuse.* BLON: *Under the Banner of Victory.* LOTTMAN: *Anchors Aweigh.* FUČIK: *Entry of the Gladiators.* FREDERIKSEN: *Copenhagen march.* STRAUSS, Johann, Snr: *Radetzky march.* COSTA: *A Frengesa.* JAVALOYES: *El Abanico.* BAGLEY: *National Emblem.* THOMAS: *The Consort.*

(M) ** Decca Eclipse KECC 2172.

A first-class collection of British and continental marches, played with vigour and spirit, fairly fast, well recorded, with plenty of weight as well as life in the sound balance. The side-drum and cymbal transients lack crispness, but in all other respects the transfer is well managed, although a slight bass cut improves the balance.

Fairey Band, Dennison

'A concert entertainment': GLINKA: *Russlan and Ludmilla: overture.* WEBBER: *Jesus Christ Superstar: I don't know how to love him.* CLARKE: *Carnival of Venice.* OFFENBACH: *Orpheus in the Underworld: overture.* BERLIOZ: *Hungarian march.* TRAD.: *Scarborough Fair.* PHILLIPS: *Escapada.* MASCAGNI: *Cavalleria Rusticana: Intermezzo.* COATES: *The Three Bears.*

(M) *(*) Decca KSBC 323.

A disappointing concert. The sound is vividly close and the transfer admirably faithful, but there is no atmosphere and Kenneth Dennison does not achieve the sparkle and spontaneity of live music-making. The Berlioz *Hungarian march* falls flat, and *Orpheus in the Underworld* has no flair. In the opening Glinka overture the sharp detail of the recording reveals that some of the running passages are slightly fumbled, while at the centre of *The Three Bears* fantasy the syncopated rhythms go awry for a bar or two. *Scarborough Fair* is given an over-elaborate arrangement, and *Escapada* (subtitled *A Mexican Elopement*) is a singularly dull and repetitive piece.

Grenadier Guards Band, Bashford or Parkes

'The world of the Grenadier Guards': PARKES: *The White Plume.* HANDEL: *Scipio.* ZEHLE: *Wellington.* arr. BASHFORD: *Old London medley. When Johnny comes marching home.* SOUSA: *The Thunderer. Stars and Stripes Forever.* PLANQUETTE: *Sambre et Meuse.* NEWMAN: *Captain from Castile: Conquest.* RODGERS: *Victory at Sea: Guadalcanal march.*

TRAD. (arr. Rogers): *She Wore a Yellow Ribbon.* TEIKE: *Steadfast and True.*

(M) *** Decca KCSP 248.

A very well compiled collection, vividly and brilliantly transferred. The level is very high, but any slight lack of refinement is more than compensated for by the presence and clarity of the recording. The *Old London medley* (wittily arranged) offers demonstration quality, and the closing *Stars and Stripes Forever* has irresistible élan, with a splendid effect from the piccolos in the Trio. This is the least expensive and the best of the Grenadier Guards cassettes.

'Great continental marches' (cond. Parkes): LINCKE: *Father Rhine.* RADECK: *Fridericus Rex.* BERLIOZ: *Hungarian march.* FUČIK: *Fearless and True.* DUNKLER: *Dutch Grenadiers' march.* MARQUINA: *Espani cani.* GANNE: *Marche Lorraine.* TRAD.: *Le Baroudeur.* LEEMANS: *March of the Belgian parachutists.* FREDERIKSEN: *Copenhagen march.* DONIZETTI (arr. Horabin): *Daughter of the Regiment.* KRAL: *Hoch Hapsburg.*

(M) ** Decca KBSC 713.

These are clean, vigorous 'marching' performances, crisply played and admirably recorded (although the band is rather close). But there is some lack of flair and exuberance (the Berlioz march is not built to a climax as it can be). The transfer is vivid, and cleanly detailed.

'The sound of pageantry – Music for a royal occasion' (cond. Bashford): BASHFORD: *Fanfare for a Jubilee. A Windsor flourish.* Arrangements: *The Agincourt song. A Purcell suite: Rondo.* SULLIVAN: *Henry VIII: Graceful dance.* arr. DART: *Royal music of King James I: 3 Almandes.*

FLETCHER: *The Spirit of Pageantry.* ELGAR: *Imperial march, Op. 32.* KETÈLBEY: *With Honour Crowned.* WALTON: *Coronation march: Crown Imperial.* COATES: *The Three Elizabeths. Youth of Britain.*

(M) ** Decca KBSC 715.

Again Decca's close recording balance is a drawback here. It minimizes the light and shade in the Dart arrangements (although the playing here is hardly subtle), and in the marches there is a lack of atmosphere. However, Percy Fletcher's *Spirit of Pageantry* is brightly done, as is the Eric Coates. The Walton suffers most from the comparative lack of resonance. The recording is undoubtedly bright and vivid and the transfer crisp, sonorous and clean.

Grimethorpe Colliery Band, Howarth

'Band of the year': LEAR: *Red Sky at Night. Hogarth's Hoe Down. Barney's tune. Chinese Take Away. Parade. Paris le soir.* FOSTER: *I Dream of Jeannie with the Light Brown Hair.* HOWARTH: *Cornet concerto. Mosaic.* SOUSA: *Stars and Stripes Forever.*

(M) *** Decca KSBC 325.

The astonishing bravura of the execution here is apparent in every moment of every piece. The arrangements are ingenious and make the fullest use of the sophistication of the playing. The running passages, taken at a fantastic speed, are heard immediately in the opening *Red Sky at Night*, and even more entertainingly in *Chinese Take Away,* which has an element of wit. The impeccable intonation, the blend of the chording, and the exactness of the articulation remind the listener of the sort of brass ensemble he would expect from an international symphony orchestra. *Hogarth's Hoe Down* shows gripping rhythmic energy, and *Paris le soir* has remarkable atmosphere.

The music itself is harmonically conventional, but the playing almost redeems it. Strangely the only disappointment is *Stars and Stripes*, well enough played but lacking sheer high spirits. The recording is first-class, and for once Decca's close balance is an advantage rather than a drawback in displaying the remarkable detail and the richness of sonorities with great presence. The transfer is immaculate: this is a real demonstration tape.

'*Classics for brass*': HOLST: *A Moorside suite*. IRELAND: *A Comedy overture*. ELGAR: *Severn suite, Op. 87*. BLISS: *Kenilworth*.
*** Decca KSXC 6820.

The Grimethorpe Colliery Band provides here a splendid programme made entirely from music originally written for brass band. It is superbly recorded and the tape transfer offers richer, more glowing sound than the RCA cassette by the Black Dyke Mills Band which also includes the *Severn suite*. The performances are discussed under each composer above.

Grimethorpe Colliery Band, Thomson

'*Band of the Year*': THOMSON: *The Nybbs*. arr. LANGFORD: *Lark in the Clear Air. Sarie Marais*. TCHAIKOVSKY: *The Sleeping Beauty: Waltz*. DAMARE: *Cleopatra*. HOLST: *Suite No. 1: March*. TOMLINSON: *Overture on famous English airs*. MASCAGNI: *Cavalleria Rusticana: Intermezzo*. CLARKE: *Trumpet voluntary*. DAVIE: *Variations*.
*** RCA PK 25048.

Sparkling playing and demonstration recording make this a particularly attractive issue. Indeed it is technically one of the very best tapes available of brass-band music; the sound is at once sonorous and yet clear, with splendid bite

and projection. The programme is lightweight but it is all played with great spontaneity and the transcriptions are notably successful.

Military bands

'*The world of military bands*', *Vol. 2* (with (i) Bands and Drums of Parachute Regiment; (ii) Life Guards and Royal Horse Guards; (iii) Grenadier Guards; (iv) Scots and Welsh Guards): (i) BROWN: *Moonshot. In Martial Mood*. DAVIES: *RAF march past*. WAGNER: *Die Walküre: Ride of the Valkyries*. (ii) SCULL: *Trombones to the Fore*. ELGAR: *Pomp and circumstance March No. 1: Land of Hope and Glory*. (iii) WARD: *Sussex by the Sea*. WILLSON: *Music Man. Seventy-six trombones*. arr. WINDRAM: *On Ilkley Moor* (medley). PHILLIPS: *US Marine Corps hymn*. SOUSA: *King Cotton*. ANKA: *The Longest Day*. (iv) WALTERS: *Trumpets Wild*.
(M) * Decca KCSP 66.

The first volume in this Decca series (KCSP 18) is not available in Dolby form. This second collection is a very early transfer; the sound is thick, with fuzzy side-drums and, in the *US Marine Corps hymn*, an exaggerated bass drum. The performances are vigorous, as the opening *Seventy-six Trombones* demonstrates, but much of the music is loud, and with unrefined sound the tape is in need of remastering.

'*The very best of military bands*' (with (i) HM Royal Marines Band, Dunn or Neville; (ii) Royal Artillery Band, Hays; (iii) Band of Royal Engineers, Patch; (iv) Royal Artillery Mounted Band, Kenney; (v) Scots Guards Band, Beat; (vi) RAF Central Band, Wallace or Davies; (vii)

Regimental Bands of Scottish Division, Briggs): (i) SOUSA: *King Cotton*. KNIPPER: *Cavalry of the Steppes*. ALFORD: *On the Quarter Deck*. FARNON: *Colditz march*. TIOMKIN: *The Guns of Navarone* (theme). BARRATT: *March of the Cobblers*. (ii) KOENIG: *Post Horn galop*. ALFORD: *Standard of St George*. (iii) TRAD.: *Hoedown in the Highlands*. (iv) MANTOVANI: *Brass Buttons*. (v) GAYFER: *Royal Visit*. (vi) BATH: *Out of the Blue*. GOODWIN: *633 Squadron theme*. ANDERSON: *Trumpeter's lullaby*. TRAD.: *Portsmouth*. WAGNER: *Nibelungen march*. VINTER: *The Dover Coach*. (vii) *Pride of Princes Street*.

**(*) EMI Studio Two TC-TWOX 1070.

By grouping out the pieces the bands are allowed to establish their individual identities, notably those of the RAF and the Marines. The programme is effectively varied; highlights include the *Colditz march* and *Guns of Navarone*, both sounding suitably resplendent, plus, of course, the Alford march, from the Royal Marines; an excellent *Post Horn galop* from the Royal Artillery; Leroy Anderson's *Trumpeter's lullaby* and Gilbert Vinter's imaginatively scored *Dover Coach* from the RAF. Gayfer's *Royal Visit* (Scots Guards) is conventional Elgar-derived pageantry but is crisply presented. The transfers are generally first-rate, although there is a shade too much bass drum in the (attractive) arrangement of *Portsmouth*, and the focus in the *Pride of Princes Street*, which closes the concert, is rather fizzy. But this is an invigorating compilation.

Mortimer, Harry, and All-Star Brass

'*A lifetime of music*': DOUGLAS: *Mephistopheles*. MONCKTON: *Arca-dians overture*. PURCELL, E.: *Passing By*. DOUGHTY: *Air and variations on Grandfather's Clock*. arr. NEWSOME: *Sandon* (hymn). HALL: *Death or Glory*. SCHUBERT: *Marche militaire*. POWELL: *The Tops*. FLETCHER: *March of the Manikins*. YOUMANS: *No, no, Nanette: Tea for Two*. FRASER SIMSON: *Love Will Find a Way*. NORTON: *She Will Say her Say*. *Robbers' chorus*. BIZET: *L'Arlésienne: Farandole*.

(M)*(**) EMI TC-NTS 145.

This aptly celebrates Harry Mortimer's long service to the world of brass, for the selection is characteristic of the kind of lightweight programme he can bring off so effectively. Unfortunately the transfer is not altogether successful. The transient crispness so necessary in this music is sadly lacking, and the climax of the *Arcadians overture* becomes congested. The wide reverberation brings problems of clarity of detail, which is a pity; Harry Mortimer's direction is as buoyant as ever and the playing is excellent.

Royal Air Force Central Band, Davies or Wallace

'*The best of the Central Band of the Royal Air Force*': DAVIES: *RAF march past*. THEODORAKIS: *Zorba the Greek*. BIDGOOD: *Sons of the Brave*. GOODWIN: *The Battle of Britain march*. ALFORD: *Old Panama*. *The Thin Red Line*. *Colonel Bogey on Parade* (medley). BARRATT: *Tango Taquin*. ROSSINI–RESPIGHI: *La Boutique fantasque*: excerpts. COATES: *Dambusters march*. arr. ROPER: *Clochemerle*. LOCKYER: *The Pathfinders*. SOUSA (arr. Langford): *Marching with Sousa* (medley).

(M)**(*) EMI TC-EXE 151.

An excellent collection, with spirited playing and a well-balanced programme. *Zorba the Greek* and the Rossini–Respighi selection are especially vivid, and the Sousa medley makes a lively conclusion. The transfers are well managed and are bright and full, although the refinement slips just a little in *The Pathfinders*. Otherwise this is most enjoyable.

'*Marching with the RAF*': ALFORD: *Old Panama. The Thin Red Line.* BRIDGER: *Airborne Division.* STANLEY: *The Contemptibles.* HALL: *Officer of the Day.* BREPSANT: *Belphegor.* SOUSA (arr. Langford): *Marching with Sousa.* LANGFORD: *Prince of Wales march.* PANELLA: *On the Square.* LOEFFLER: *Ad astra.* SIEBERT: *The Rover's Return.* SCHRAMMEL: *Wien bleibt Wien.* DAVIES: *Anniversary march.*

(M)**EMI TC-OU 2188.

These marches are rather a mixed bag, and the playing, though vigorous, lacks the panache that the Marines Band can find for such a programme. The recording is good and the transfer well balanced if not brilliant.

(HM) Royal Marines Band, Dunn or Neville

'*Marching with the Marines*': RUSSELL: *A Life on the Ocean Wave.* ZIMMERMAN: *Anchors Aweigh.* ALFORD: *Army of the Nile. HM Jollies.* HOLST: *Suite No. 2: March.* ARNOLD: *Little suite, Op. 53: March.* DUNN: *Under the White Ensign. Cockleshell Heroes.* SOUSA: *Manhattan Beach. Semper fidelis. The Pride of the Wolverines.* GRAHAM: *The Champion.* WILLIAMS: *Blue Devils.*

(M)**(*)HMV TC-EXE 59.

The Royal Marines Band (that is, the Band of the Royal Marines School of Music) has established an enviable reputation, not just for the excellent standards of the playing itself, but also for its continued identification with the pageantry of Britain's past imperial role. There is something about the way the Marines play a march. Without choosing an especially fast tempo, they achieve an irresistible forward momentum and convey an unexaggerated sense of confidence. Here is a lively selection played with the celebrated swagger. The sound is good on side one and often very good on side two, which contains much of the most rewarding music, including the marches by Holst and Malcolm Arnold (a particularly fetching piece). The programme – made up of early recordings – is conducted by Sir Vivian Dunn.

'*Crown Imperial*': BAX: *Royal Wedding fanfare No. 1.* NEVILLE: *Sword of Honour.* ELGAR (all abridged): *Young Winston: Medley. Caractacus: Triumphal march. Enigma variations: Nimrod. Pomp and Circumstance march No. 4. Land of Hope and Glory. Cockaigne.* ARNOLD: *Homage to the Queen.* arr. WOOD: *Fantasia on British sea songs* (excerpts). ARNE: *Rule Britannia.* BOYCE: *Heart of oak.* GRANT: *Crimond. Evening hymn* (arr. Dunn). GREEN: *Sunset.* DUNN: *Salute to the Colours.* HOLST (arr. Dunn): *I vow to thee my country.* WALTON: *Orb and Sceptre. Crown Imperial.*

*(**)EMI TC-NTS 123.

This was the finest of the various band collections of *nobilmente* music issued in Jubilee year, and it has a splendid feeling of pageantry throughout. Paul Neville's own march, *Sword of Honour*, written in the Elgar/Walton tradition, is an attractively spontaneous piece, and the performance of *Crown Imperial* which ends the concert has a proper regal splendour. Among the other items one must mention

Nimrod, cleverly transcribed, with a finely played horn solo to make it memorable. This is a most entertaining tape for in-car use, and it is a pity that the spectacularly reverberant recording has offered considerable transfer problems, with patches of congestion, notably in the Arnold *Homage to the Queen* and the bugles' fanfare; these spoil the reproduction domestically. Both conductors participate.

'*The very best of the Band of the Royal Marines*': ALFORD: *Colonel Bogey. Standard of St George. Great Little Army.* JAVOLOYES: *El Abanico.* BAGLEY: *National Emblem.* ZIMMERMAN: *Anchors Aweigh.* SOUSA: *Semper fidelis.* DUNN: *Cockleshell Heroes.* CHABRIER: *España.* RUSSELL: *A Life on the Ocean Wave.* ISAAC: *Warship theme.* PANELLA: *On the Square.* BACHARACH: *This Guy's in Love with You. What the World Needs Now Is Love.* MCCUNN: *Sutherland's Law theme.* MANDEL: *Shadow of Your Smile.* PROKOFIEV: *Lieutenant Kijé: Troika.* TROMBEY: *Eye Level.* SIMPSON: *On the track.* TRAD.: *When the Saints Come Marching In.*
**(*)EMI Studio Two TC-TWOX 1063.

The very best of the Band of the Royal Marines is aptly named, for the selection is generous and represents the band and its distinguished conductors on top form. The Alford marches are superbly done, with the relaxed swagger that this band have made their own, and on side two Panella's *On the Square* is equally invigorating. The heavy brass in Bagley's *National Emblem* is rousing indeed. After the marches comes a selection of lighter fare. The Bacharach numbers are most

successful (the reeds beautifully mellifluous and the intonation impeccable) and the *Sutherland's Law theme* is also delightfully scored. In the *Troika* from *Lieutenant Kijé* there is a real sense of style. Dunn conducts the marches on side one, Neville the varied items on side two. The recording is always very good, sometimes excellent, and the transfers are well managed. The cymbal transients on side one are not absolutely sharp in focus, but in all other respects the sound is vividly detailed.

'*A concert programme*': ADDISON: *A Bridge Too Far* (theme). TARREGA: *Recuerdos de la Alhambra.* BARRATT-SIEBER: *Piper in the Meadow.* WHITCOMB: *Evening Breeze.* ANDERSON: *Penny Whistle song.* JACOB: *Concerto for band.* WILSON: *The Adventurer.* LOEWE: *My Fair Lady: symphonic scenario* (arr. Cacavas). WILLIAMS: *Star Wars suite.*
** EMI Studio Two TC-TWOX 1075.

Basically a lightweight concert programme. The arrangement of Tarrega's guitar piece *Recuerdos de la Alhambra* does not come off, but elsewhere there is sophisticated use of wind-band scorings, especially in Ken Whitcomb's *Evening Breeze*, the Leroy Anderson flute trio and the elaborate *My Fair Lady* selection. This is let down by some lack of vitality in the music-making, and though Gordon Jacob's *Concerto* is beautifully played and well worth recording, the performance lacks something in communicated zest. However, the band is on top form in the *Star Wars suite*. Paul Neville is the musical director throughout. The sound is good and the transfer smooth and full-bodied, lacking something in glitter and edge at the top.

Instrumental Recitals

Adeney, Richard (flute), **Ian Brown** (piano)

'Classical flute': MOZART: Flute sonata in F major, K.13. SCHUBERT: Introduction and variations on an original theme, Op. 160. BEETHOVEN: Flute sonata in B flat major; National themes and variations, Op. 107, Nos. 3 and 7.

**(*) Enigma K 453540.

An attractive programme, immaculately played. There is undoubtedly spontaneity here, but the players do not always exploit the full possibilities of light and shade, and they are not helped by the close balance, which minimizes the dynamics as well as giving a larger-than-life effect. However, the recording quality itself is admirably truthful, and the transfer has a demonstration faithfulness of body and presence. There is much to enjoy here, but it is not a recital to be taken all at once. The programme notes are printed in unbelievably small type.

Andre, Maurice (trumpet), **Jane Parker-Smith** (organ)

'Music for trumpet and organ': BACH: (Unaccompanied) Violin partita No. 3 in E major, BWV 1006: Gavotte; Rondeau. Cantata No. 68: My heart ever faithful. Suite No. 3 in D major, BWV 1068: Air. (Unaccompanied) Violoncello suite No. 4 in E flat major, BWV 1010: Bourrée. BACH–GOUNOD: Ave Maria. CHARPENTIER, Marc-Antoine: Te Deum: Opening fanfare. ALBINONI: Adagio (arr. Giazotto). HANDEL: Xerxes: Largo. Gloria in excelsis Deo. SCHUBERT: Ave Maria. CLARKE: Trumpet voluntary. SENAILLE: Sonata No. 3: Allegro spiritoso. STANLEY: Trumpet tune. MOZART: Exsultate jubilate, K.165: Alleluia (arrangements by Jean-Michel Defaye).

**(*) HMV TC-ASD 3453.

Really splendid playing from Maurice André. His phrasing is impeccable: even the Ave Maria settings of Gounod and Schubert are successful, so sure is his feeling for the music's line. Elsewhere he shows an attractive 'baroque' exuberance, notably in Albinoni's Adagio, which he plays in a recitative style, providing a florid climax that is undoubtedly thrilling. The combination of trumpet and organ may not be to all tastes, but the advocacy here is persuasive and the reverberant recording is remarkably well captured in the tape transfer, although the focus on side two is rather less clean than on side one.

Barrueco, Manuel (guitar)

VILLA-LOBOS: Études Nos. 1–3, 5, 7, 8, 11, 12. Suite populaire brésilienne. GUARNIERI: Estudo No. 1. CHAVEZ: 3 Pieces.

(M)**(*) Turnabout KTVC 34676.

Manuel Barrueco is a strong player and shows himself completely at home in the Villa-Lobos Études, which he plays with impressive technical command and considerable intensity. His performance of the Suite populaire brésilienne is not as beguiling as Julian Bream's (see under Villa-Lobos in the Composer index), but the other works are well done. The recording is full and natural, a little larger than life, perhaps, but not enough to mar enjoyment. The transfer is immaculate, bold and clean.

Berman, Lazar (piano)

RACHMANINOV: *Preludes Nos. 1 in C sharp minor, Op. 3/2; 6 in G minor, Op. 23/5; 16 in G major, Op. 32/5.* SCRIABIN: *Études in B Flat minor; in D sharp minor, Op. 8/11 and 12.* KHACHATURIAN: *Toccata.* PROKOFIEV: *Love of Three Oranges: March.* BEETHOVEN: *Sonata No. 20 in G major, Op. 49/2: Minuet. The Ruins of Athens, Op. 113: Turkish march.* CHOPIN: *Étude in C sharp minor, Op. 25/7.* LISZT: Concert paraphrases (Schubert Lieder): *Gretchen am Spinnrade, G.558/8; Erlkönig, G.558/4.* FALLA: *El amor brujo: Ritual fire dance.*

> *(**) CBS 40–76612 [Col. MT 34545].

Berman shows here the wide range of his sympathies. This is an attractive collection of miniatures played with the flair of a virtuoso in love with the keyboard. The Liszt paraphrases of Schubert songs are particularly valuable, and so are the Soviet items. The recording is good, but the transfer is limited in range; there is a lack of open quality at climaxes which inhibits the sound, although the force of the playing comes through.

Bilson, Malcolm (fortepiano)

'The Viennese fortepiano', Vol. 1: MOZART: *Rondos: in A minor, K.511; in D major, K.485.* BEETHOVEN: *Piano sonatas Nos. 13 in E flat major, Op. 27/1; 14 in C sharp minor (Moonlight), Op. 27/2.*

> ** Advent E 1056 (see p. xxiii) [id.].

'The Viennese fortepiano', Vol. 2:

HAYDN: *Piano sonatas Nos. 54 (H.40) in G major; 62 (H.52) in E flat major.* MOZART: *Piano sonata No. 9 in D major, K.311.*

> ** Advent E 1059 (see p. xxiii) [id.].

The instruments used here are copies made by Philip Belt of Indiana of a fortepiano by Jean-Louis Dulcken (c. 1795) and one by Gabriel Anton Walter of Vienna (c. 1790), who built the fortepiano owned by himself. Malcolm Bilson is a professor of piano at Cornell University who has specialized in the fortepiano, and his playing is both scholarly and musical. The recording balance is rather close, in fact too close for some tastes; but in all other respects, the recording is clean and truthful, with the wide range and crispness of outline characteristic of Advent tapes. Apart from the balance, this is a worthwhile project, interestingly realized.

Bolcom, William (piano)

'Pastimes and piano rags': JOPLIN: *Efficiency rag; Modesty rag; New Era rag; Troubadour rag; Great Scott rag.* MATTHEWS: *Pastimes rags Nos. 1–5.*

> **(*) Advent D 1041 (see p. xxiii) [id.].

Splendidly robust and spirited playing, and excellent quality from the engineering point of view. The only snag here is the close balance, which in time tends to tire the ear somewhat. But there are no complaints about the lively playing or the entertaining music, or about the technical excellence of the transfer.

Bonell, Carlos (guitar)

'Guitar music of Spain': RODRIGO: *Pequenas Sevillanas. Ya se van los pastores. Fandango.* TORROBA: *Burgalesa.* SANZ: *Espanoleta. Canarios.* SOR: *Fantasiá elegiaca.* PUJOL: *Gua-*

jira (Evocación Cubana). Tango.
TARREGA: *Sueno* (mazurka). *Maria*
(gavotte). *Capricho Arabe. Gran
Jota.* TRAD. (arr. BONELL): *4 Spanish
folksongs.*

**Enigma K 453527.

'Baroque guitar works': PURCELL
(arr. BONELL): *The Fairy Queen:
Rondeau; Dance of the fairies. Chaconne.* WEISS: *Tombeau sur la mort de
Monsieur Comte de Logy.* VISÉE:
Suite in G major. BACH: *Suite in A
minor, BWV 997.*

**Enigma K 453555.

Carlos Bonell is a bold player and he
characterizes the music strongly. This is
emphasized by the close microphone placing of the Enigma recording, which tends
to reduce the light and shade; but, the
sound is clean and natural. Much of the
Spanish music is imaginatively played
(and one can hear that Bonell is seeking
dynamic contrast in spite of the close
microphone). The baroque programme is
also attractive in its way, although the
presentation is direct rather than displaying expressive subtleties. In both cases the
tape transfers are of immaculate clarity
and provide good presence, but the overall effect is positive rather than beguiling.

Bream, Julian (lute)

'The woods so wild': BYRD: *The
woods so wild.* MILANO: *Fantasias
Nos. 1–8.* CUTTING: *Packington's
round.* DOWLAND: *Walsingham. Go
from my window. Bonnie sweet
Robin. Loth to depart.* HOLBORNE:
*Fairy round. Heigh ho holiday.
Heart's ease.* ANON: *Greensleeves.*

***RCA RK 11708.

This is an exceptionally vivid recital of
lute music. The title piece, in Byrd's
setting with variations, is immediately
striking, and all the items have strong

individuality; the Milano *Fantasias* are
particularly distinctive, both in quality of
invention and in the opportunity they
afford for bravura. Try *La Compagna*
(No. 4), which ends side one – most fetching and exciting. The mood of gentle
melancholy which is a special feature of
Elizabethan music makes effective contrasts to the virtuosity; and nowhere
more touching than in the delightful closing piece, *Loth to depart*, appropriate for
such a memorable concert. The recording
projects the instrument with fine realism,
and the transfer to tape is excellent. There
is a slightly metallic quality to the sound,
but this responds to the treble control.

Bream, Julian (guitar)

'Julian Bream and friends' (with (i)
George Malcolm (harpsichord); (ii)
members of the Cremona Qt; (iii)
Julian Bream Consort): BOCCHER-
INI: (i) *Introduction and Fandango.*
(ii) *Guitar quintet in E minor.* (iii)
BRITTEN: *Gloriana: Courtly dances.*
(ii) HAYDN: *Guitar quartet in E
major, Op. 2/2.*

(M) **(*) RCA Gold Seal GK
42753.

This rearrangement of Bream
repertoire makes a most agreeable
medium-priced recital. The Boccherini
Quintet is an attractive work with an appealing slow movement; the colourful
Introduction and Fandango comes from
the *Quintet, Op. 50/2.* The Haydn work is
the usual arrangement from an early
string quartet. What adds piquancy to
the collection is the inclusion of the
Courtly dances from *Gloriana* (also available coupled to Rodrigo – see the Composer index). The recording is good, if a
little dated (it has not the presence and
body of a modern recording, except in the
Britten). The transfer is smooth and has a
natural ambience.

'The art of Julian Bream': FRES-
COBALDI: *Aria detta La Frescobalda
with variations.* ALBÉNIZ, Mateo:
Sonata. SCARLATTI, Domenico:
(Keyboard) *Sonatas, L.33, L.352.*
CIMAROSA: *Sonatas in C sharp
minor and A major.* BERKELEY:
Sonatina, Op. 51. RODRIGO: *En los
trigales.* RAVEL: *Pavane pour une infante défunte.* ROUSSEL: *Segovia, Op.
29.*

**(*) RCA RK 11735.

This recital opens eloquently with the
adaptation (by Segovia) of Frescobaldi,
and the predominantly classical items on
the first side are played stylishly. However, more variety would have been welcome: all the music here is engaging, but
its atmosphere remains very similar. Side
two brings a refreshing move into the
twentieth century and a much greater
diversity of harmonic colour. Lennox
Berkeley's *Sonatina* is imaginatively conceived, but it is the beautiful arrangement (by Bream himself) of Ravel's
Pavane that stays in the listener's
memory at the conclusion of the tape.
Excellent playing and truthful recording;
the transfer is of demonstration quality,
the guitar timbre clean and crisp yet with
a natural resonance.

Bream, Julian, and John Williams
(guitars)

'Live': JOHNSON: *Pavane and Gal-
liard.* TELEMANN: *Partie polonaise.*
SOR: *Fantaisie, Op. 54.* BRAHMS:
Theme and variations, Op. 18 (trans.
Williams). FAURÉ: *Dolly suite, Op.
56.* DEBUSSY: *Rêverie. Children's
Corner: Golliwog's cakewalk. Suite
bergamasque: Clair de lune.* ALBÉ-
NIZ: *Castilla.* GRANADOS: *Spanish
dance No. 2 (Oriental).*

**(*)RCA RK 03090.

This recital was recorded live in
Boston and New York during a North
American tour. The sound is first-class,
every bit as good as anything these artists
have done in the studio. The drawback is
the applause, which, though shortened in
the editing, is still very intrusive on repeated hearings. The playing is of the
highest quality although perhaps at times
slightly self-conscious (the Granados
encore has an almost narcissistic tonal
beauty). As a whole there is not quite the
electricity of this team's other recitals.
Fauré's *Dolly suite* sounds a little cosy
and the transcription of the *Variations*
from Brahms's *B flat major Sextet* is not
entirely effective. But the *Golliwog's
cakewalk* and the Albéniz *Castilla* are
highly enjoyable. The transfer is immaculate, offering superb quality, clear and
naturally balanced, but the 'double-
length' tape is not generously filled, and
it is expensive. Moreover, apart from the
titles it gives no information whatsoever
about the music or the source of the recital.

'Together': LAWES: *Suite for 2 guitars.* CARULLI: *Duo in G major, Op.
34.* SOR: *L'encouragement, Op. 34.*
ALBÉNIZ: *Cordoba.* GRANADOS:
Goyescas: Intermezzo. FALLA: *La
vida breve: Spanish dance No. 1.*
RAVEL: *Pavane pour une infante
défunte.*

***RCA RK 11626.

'Together again': CARULLI: *Serenade, Op. 96.* GRANADOS: *Danzas
españolas Nos. 6 and 11.* ALBÉNIZ:
*Bajo la Palmera, Op. 232. Iberia:
Evocación.* GIULIANI: *Variazioni
concertanti, Op. 130.*

***RCA ARK 1 0456.

In this case two guitars are better than
one; these two fine artists clearly strike
sparks off each other. On the first tape,
Albéniz's *Cordoba* is hauntingly memor-

able and the concert closes with a slow stately version of Ravel's *Pavane* which is unforgettable. On the second tape it is again music of Albéniz that one remembers for the haunting atmosphere the two artists create together, but it is irritating that the *Evocación* from *Iberia* is broken for the side turn. The recording has good presence, although on the second tape one notices a tendency to a metallic colouring of the timbre when the instruments are playing loudly together; some treble cut is useful here. Much of the music, however, sounds very realistic against the virtually silent background possible with tape.

Brendel, Alfred (piano)

'Alfred Brendel plays': BEETHOVEN: *Sonata No. 8 in C minor (Pathétique), Op. 13. Bagatelle No. 1 in G minor, Op. 119. 6 Variations on the Turkish march from 'The Ruins of Athens' Op. 76. Für Elise.* SCHUBERT: *Impromptus Nos. 2 in E flat major; 3 in G flat major, D.899. Moment musical No. 3 in F minor, D.780.* BALAKIREV: *Islamey.* LISZT: *Hungarian rhapsody No. 11 in A minor, G.244. Études d'exécution transcendante d'après Paganini, G.140: No. 3, La Campanella.*
(M) ** Decca KCSP 249.

A sampler to show the scope and diversity of Alfred Brendel's musicianship. The performance of the *Pathétique sonata* was not one of the finest of his Turnabout cycle, but the other Beethoven miniatures are very enjoyable, and the Schubert performances are outstanding. The quality of the recording in these Schubert items is strikingly clear and full-bodied, although elsewhere the sound is shallower, notably in the Liszt rhapsody and *Islamey*. The tape transfer is faithful and this makes an enjoyable recital.

Brüggen, Frans (recorder)

'Music for recorder' (with Nikolaus Harnoncourt, viola da gamba, Gustav Leonhardt, harpsichord): PARCHAM: *Solo for recorder and continuo.* VAN EYCK: *Pavane lachrymae.* LOEILLET: *Sonata for recorder and continuo in C minor.* DIEUPART: *Suite in G major for recorder and continuo.* TELEMANN: *Fantasies in C major; in A minor.*
**(*) Telefunken CX 4.41203.

This is a delightful recital, showing Brüggen on top form, especially in the unaccompanied *Pavane* by Jacob van Eyck. The recording is made at a comparatively low level and because of this the harpsichord does not tell as strongly as it might; but the sound is good, and for those whose tastes lie in this repertoire the cassette can be recommended strongly. It is on chrome tape, but because of the low level its possibilities are not fully realized.

Byzantine, Julian (guitar)

VILLA-LOBOS: *Preludes Nos. 1–5. Chôro typico.* PONCE: *Campo.* MAZA: *Homenaje a la guiterra.* LAURO: *Danza negra. Suite venezolana: Valse. Valse No. 3.*
(B) **(*) Classics for Pleasure TC-CFP 40209.

A pleasing recital, offering thoughtful and thoroughly musical playing, although there is not perhaps the distinction and individuality of Julian Bream or John Williams in the attractive Villa-Lobos *Preludes*. The recording is attractively live and immediate; the transfer level is high, and one needs to set the volume back or the guitar sounds larger than life.

755

Collier, Derek (violin), Daphne Ibbott (piano)

'The world of the violin', Vol. 2: PAGANINI: *Valse.* MENDELSSOHN: *Song without words: May breezes.* KREISLER: *Caprice Viennois. Schön Rosmarin.* FAURÉ: *Nocturne, Op. 57.* DVOŘÁK: *Slavonic dance No. 2, Op. 46/2.* SCHUBERT: *Cradle song, Op. 105. Valse sentimentale in A minor.* RIMSKY-KORSAKOV: *Sadko: Chant hindou.* ALBÉNIZ: *Sevilla, Op. 47.* RAMEAU: *Tambourin.* TRAD.: *Londonderry air.* BRANDL: *The Old Refrain.* KORNGOLD: *Much Ado About Nothing* (incidental music): *Garden scene.* BRAHMS: *Hungarian dance No. 17* (arr. Kreisler). BACH: *Arioso* (from *Clavier concerto, BWV 1056*).

(M)**Decca KCSP 405.

Polished playing of an attractive lightweight programme, beautifully recorded and immaculately transferred. The balance is realistic, and both violin and piano sound eminently natural. The music-making, however, is just a little lacking in personality. (Volume 1 of this series includes concertante orchestral works and is reviewed in the Concerts section.)

Cooper, Joseph (piano)

'Face the music': CHOPIN: *Étude in E major, Op. 10/3.* LISZT: *Liebesträume, G.541.* GRIEG: *Lyric pieces: Nocturne in C major, Op. 54/4.* BRAHMS: *Waltz in A flat major, Op. 39/15.* SCARLATTI: *Sonata in C major, L.104.* SCHUBERT: *Impromptu in A flat major, D935.* SCHUMANN: *Kinderscenen, Op. 15: Träumerei.* COOPER: *Hidden melodies* in the styles of Bach, Liszt, Brahms, Scarlatti, Tchaikovsky, Schumann, Grieg, Mozart, Schubert and Chopin.

**(*)CRD CRDC 4006.

Following the huge success of Joseph Cooper's television show, it was CRD who first had the bright idea of recording a selection of his *Hidden melodies.* There are ten of them here, and the allusions to the melodic and harmonic quirks of the concealed composers are as ingenious as ever. The pieces simulating Schubert and Scarlatti are charming, and there is real wit in the version of *Jingle bells* in the manner of . . .? The other discovery that CRD made was that J.C.'s friendly musical advocacy is not dampened in the recording studio. Thus the popular piano pieces which make up the rest of the recital are no less persuasively played than his own pastiches. The Grieg, Liszt and Schumann works are particularly beautiful, and are well recorded too. The cassette transfer is an early one, however, good in its day (1974) but not as secure or as brightly focused as the Decca recitals below.

'The world of Joseph Cooper': ALBÉNIZ: *Seguidillas, Op. 232/5.* BRAHMS: *Intermezzo in B flat minor, Op. 117/2.* BEETHOVEN: *Für Elise, G.173.* GRIEG: *Wedding Day at Troldhaugen, Op. 65/6.* FAURÉ: *Impromptu in F minor, Op. 31/2.* CHOPIN: *Prelude No. 15 in D flat major (Raindrop), Op. 28.* MENDELSSOHN: *Song without words: Bees' Wedding, Op. 67/4.* GRANADOS: *Goyescas: The Maiden and the Nightingale.* SCHUMANN: *Romance in F sharp major, Op. 28/2.* LISZT: *Valse oubliée No. 1, G.21.* DVOŘÁK: *Humoresque in G flat major, Op. 101/7.* TCHAIKOVSKY: *Humoresque in G major, Op. 10/2.* SCHUBERT: *Impromptu in E flat major, D.899/2.* DEBUSSY: *Suite bergamasque: Clair de lune.*

(M)***Decca KCSP 372.

'The world of Joseph Cooper'. Vol. 2:
SINDING: *Rustle of Spring*. BEET-
HOVEN: *Piano sonata No. 8 in C
minor (Pathétique), Op. 13:* 2nd
movt. RACHMANINOV: *Prelude in C
sharp minor, Op.3/2*.BADARZEWSKA:
The Maiden's Prayer. LISZT: *Paraphrase on Chant polonais No. 5 of
Chopin, G.480*. DOHNÁNYI: *Rhapsody No. 3 in C major, Op. 11/3*. DE-
BUSSY: *Préludes, Book 1: La Fille
aux cheveux de lin*. COOPER: *Hidden
melodies* in the styles of Mendelssohn, Bach, Debussy, Scarlatti,
Schumann, Schubert, Chopin,
Rachmaninov and Brahms.

(M) *** Decca KCSP 473.

'The world of Joseph Cooper', Vol. 3:
MOZART: *Sonata No. 11 in A major,
K.331: Rondo alla turca*. GRIEG: *But-
terfly, Op. 43/1*. RACHMANINOV:
Polichinelle, Op. 3/4. MACDOWELL:
*Woodland sketches: To a wild rose;
To a water lily, Op. 51/1 and 6*. RAFF:
La Fileuse, Op. 157/2. CHOPIN: *Noc-
turne in E flat major, Op. 9/2; Polo-
naise in A flat major, Op. 53*.
BRAHMS: *Ballade in G minor, Op.
118/3*. GRAINGER: *Country Gardens*.
MAYERL: *Marigold, Op. 78*. COOPER:
Hidden melodies in the styles of
Mozart, Delius, Brahms, Grieg and
Chopin.

(M) **(*) Decca KCSP 519.

Since Decca took over Joseph
Cooper's recording contract in 1975 they
have issued an annual recital of popular
repertoire on their cheapest label. The
first collection is particularly enticing, the
programme nicely balanced and played
with consistent freshness and spontaneity. Highly recommended, even
though there are no *Hidden melodies*.
Volume 2 includes nine, with *Three Blind
Mice* heard first as the 'joy of man's desiring' and later in a clever Debussian pas-

tiche; perhaps most imaginative of all is
the *Lambeth Walk* in the style of Rachmaninov. The recital is first-class in every
way, strongly characterized playing projected with great zest and feeling. Volume
3 offers five more *Hidden melodies* (with
an entertaining 'crib' at the end); the
Delius and Grieg arrangements are delightful and the Brahms is wittily gruff.
The recital is a shade less spontaneous
than the first two issues; the Chopin
items, for instance, show J.C. on slightly
less than top form, but Rachmaninov's
Polichinelle is beautifully played, and the
miniatures by MacDowell and Billy
Mayerl are refreshingly alert. Throughout all three issues the piano tone is warm
and full yet clear, and the tape transfers
are admirably faithful.

'An evening with Joseph Cooper':
SCHUMANN: *Widmung*. SCHUBERT:
7 Waltzes. An die Musik. BEET-
HOVEN: *Piano sonata No. 14 in C
sharp minor (Moonlight), Op. 27/2*.
RACHMANINOV: *Humoresque, Op.
10/5*. PADEREWSKI: *Minuet in G
major, Op. 14/1*. CHOPIN: *Con-
tredanse*. MACDOWELL: *AD
MDCXX, Op. 53/3*. DEBUSSY: *Children's Corner: Golliwog's cakewalk*.
MAYERL: *Parade of the Sandwich-
board Men*. COOPER: *Hidden melody*
in the style of Chopin.

(M) ** Decca KCSP 542.

The inclusion of a complete performance of the *Moonlight sonata* in this 1978
issue was unwise, even though the recording is linked to the live lecture-recitals
which are a current feature of Joseph
Cooper's musical advocacy. The performance is perfectly acceptable but not distinguished: the middle section of the
minuet is too heavily played, and the articulation in the finale lacks the proper
degree of bravura and sparkle. On the
other hand the opening *Widmung* is
undoubtedly stylish, and the Rachmani-

nov, Paderewski and (especially) Mayerl encores are most enjoyable. Only one *Hidden melody*, but a rather fetching example. The piano timbre is broad and full. The transfer is made at the highest level and just once or twice gives a hint that the upper tolerance is dangerously near; the louder passages are not quite as fresh as on the earlier recitals.

Curley, Carlo (Allen electronic organ)

'Organ spectacular': SCHUBERT: *Marche militaire, D.733. Moment musical No. 3, D.780.* SAINT-SAËNS: *Suite algérienne: Marche militaire française.* BACH: *Suite No. 3 in D major, BWV 1068: Air. Cantata No. 29: Sinfonia.* MENDELSSOHN: *Athalie: War march of the Priests.* SOUSA: *Liberty Bell.* MASSENET: *Thaïs: Meditation.* HAYDN: *St Anthony chorale.* DUSSEK: *Andante in F major.* WAGNER: *Tannhäuser: Grand march.*

> (M)**Rediffusion Royale KROY 2015.

For this recording Carlo Curley transported his Allen concert touring organ (a 5500-watt electronic instrument, operated by digital computers, which has 164 stops and can produce about 600 different sound timbres through 380 speakers) into the organ hall at Alexandra Palace. The result was to provide a cocoon of reverberation to match this old-fashioned programme of transcriptions, which Curley plays brightly and spectacularly. He over-romanticizes everything, and even creates a swell in the middle of the *St Anthony chorale*. There is no clarity (but neither was there on the disc), but the sounds are certainly sumptuous. The success of the tape transfer is little short of astonishing: the spectacle is accommodated with virtually no signs of strain.

'Dreaming'

Romantic piano music (with (i) Wilhelm Kempff; (ii) Tamás Vásáry; (iii) Stefan Askenase; (iv) Christoph Eschenbach; (v) Joerg Demus; (vi) Dino Ciani; (vii) Sviatoslav Richter; (viii) Rudolf Firkusny): (i) SCHUMANN: *Kinderscenen, Op. 15:* excerpts. (vi) *Novelette in F major, Op. 21/2.* (ii) CHOPIN: *Fantaisie-impromptu in C sharp minor, Op. 66. Étude in A flat major, Op. 25/1.* (iii) *Waltz in A flat major, Op. 69/1.* (i) BEETHOVEN: *Piano sonata No. 8 in C minor (Pathétique), Op. 13:* 2nd movt. (iii) MENDELSSOHN: *Song without words in E major, Op. 19/1.* (iv) MOZART: *Piano sonata No. 15 in C major, K.545:* 1st movt. (v) SCHUBERT: *Impromptu in A flat major, D.899/4.* (i) BRAHMS: *Intermezzo in E flat major, Op. 117/1.* (vii) DEBUSSY: *Estampes: Jardins sous la pluie.* (viii) MUSSORGSKY: *Pictures at an Exhibition: The Great Gate of Kiev.* (vii) RACHMANINOV: *Prelude No. 5 in D major, Op. 23/4.*

> (M)**(*)DG 3308 236.

A most attractively planned recital. The roster of artists is impressive and they nearly all give of their best. Kempff opens poetically with Schumann, Stefan Askenase makes two memorable contributions and Christoph Eschenbach's Mozart is crisp and clean. The recording of the excerpt from *Estampes* sounds slightly insubstantial, but the other Richter performance (Rachmaninov) is first-class. It follows most successfully after Firkusny's bold portrait of *The Great Gate of Kiev*. The piano recording is nearly always first-rate and the transfer of consistent excellence, clear and natural in balance.

Eden, Bracha, and Alexander Tamir
(piano duet)

'*The world of two pianos*': BRAHMS: *Hungarian dances Nos. 5 and 6.* DVOŘÁK: *Slavonic dances, Op. 46/1 and 6.* DEBUSSY: *Petite suite.* RACHMANINOV: *Prelude No. 1 in C sharp minor, Op. 3. Barcarolle, Op. 5.* WEINBERGER: *Schwanda the Bagpiper: Polka and fugue.* MILHAUD: *Scaramouche suite.*

(M) *** Decca KCSP 349.

A most attractive and brilliantly played recital which suits the cassette medium especially well. The anthology has been put together with the characteristic Decca flair and as a collection is as enjoyable as the best of the full-priced LP recitals by these two artists. Debussy's *Petite suite* and the Weinberger and Milhaud items are highlights. The recording varies in clarity and body between items, but is nearly always of demonstration quality.

Empire Brass Quintet

'*Renaissance and Baroque brass music*': HANDEL: *Aria.* ANON. (attrib. PALESTRINA): *Ricercare del primo tuono.* ALBINONI: *Suite in G major.* PEUERL: *Canzon no. 1.* PEZEL: *Intrade, Sarabande and Bal.* PURCELL: *King Arthur: Allegro and Air.* JOSQUIN DES PRÉS: *Heth sold ein Meisken.* BACH: *The Art of fugue: Contrapunctus No. 9. Fantasia in C major.* GABRIELI, Giovanni: *Canzona per Sonare No. 2.* HOLBORNE: *5 Pieces.* PRIULI: *Canzone seconda a 6.* SCHEIN: *Paduana and Galliard. Canzona bergamasca.* BYRD: *Alleluia.*

*** Advent E 1067 (see p. xxiii) [id.].

A superb cassette in every way. The recording, made in St George's Russian Church, Brookline, Massachusetts, is excellently balanced. The ensemble blends admirably and there is sufficient ambience to give depth to the recording. The Empire Brass Quintet won the 1976 Walter Naumberg Award for excellence in chamber music and is a first-rate ensemble. Three of the members hail from the Boston Symphony, and the group is Quintet-in-Residence at Boston University. There is some very distinguished playing here and the recording is of demonstration standard.

Georgiadis, John (violin), Susan Georgiadis (piano)

'*Moto perpetuo*': MORTENSEN: *The Laughing Violin.* MASSENET: *Thaïs: Meditation.* KREISLER: *Liebesfreud. Liebeslied. Schön Rosmarin. Praeludium and allegro.* TOSELLI: *Serenata, Op. 6.* PAGANINI: *Moto perpetuo, Op. 11.* POLIAKIN: *Le Canari* (polka). SARASATE: *Romanza andaluza, Op. 22/1.* BAZZINI: *La Ronde des lutins, Op. 25.* TCHAIKOVSKY: *Melody, Op. 42/3.*

**(*) CBS 40-73690.

The Laughing Violin, which opens this somewhat old-fashioned programme, has a music-hall vulgarity about it but should certainly raise a smile. The playing throughout is stylishly romantic (the Kreisler pieces and the Massenet *Meditation* very nicely done) or shows striking bravura. The Paganini *Moto perpetuo* which ends side one has some superbly articulated *spiccato* playing, and Bazzini's *La Ronde des lutins* is a breathtaking example of fiddlistic fireworks, with cascades of pizzicatos mixed into the melodic line. The recording balance is lifelike, with the piano (reasonably enough in this repertoire) placed backwardly, and the transfer to tape is smooth and natural, with rather more presence on side two.

Hasson, Maurice (violin), Ian Brown (piano)

'Brilliant showpieces for the violin': WIENIAWSKI: Polonaise in D major. Scherzo tarantelle. PAGANINI: Cantabile in D major. Introduction and variations on one string on a theme by Rossini. Caprices, Op. 1, Nos. 5 and 13. PARADIS: Sicilienne. RIMSKY-KORSAKOV: Tsar Saltan: Flight of the bumble bee. RAVEL (arr. CATHERIN): Rapsodie espagnole: Habañera. BLOCH: Nigun. GLUCK (arr. KREISLER): Orfeo ed Euridice: Dance of the Blessed Spirits. BRAHMS: Scherzo in C minor (F.A.E). STRAVINSKY (arr. DUSHKIN): Russian maiden's song.
***Enigma K 453537.

A splendid tape. The reproduction is admirably realistic, the balance favouring the violin but not excluding the piano. The recital is certainly not misnamed; the sparkling bravura in the out-and-out showpieces is matched by rich tone and seductive phrasing in the lyrical music. The Paganini Cantabile immediately shows Hasson's control of colour; Ravel's Habañera and the Gluck confirm his artistry. The Brahms Scherzo adds substance to the close of the programme. The transfer is immaculate, clear, full and clean. Highly recommended.

Katchen, Julius (piano)

'Encores': BACH (arr. HESS): Cantata No. 147: Jesu, joy of man's desiring. BRAHMS: Rhapsody No. 2 in G minor, Op. 79. BEETHOVEN: Sonata No. 8 in C minor (Pathétique), Op. 13: 2nd movt. LISZT: Hungarian rhapsody No. 12, G.244. MENDELSSOHN: On Wings of Song. Rondo capriccioso, Op. 14. MOZART: Sonata No. 15 in C major, K.545: 1st movt. CHOPIN: Fantaisie-impromptu in C sharp minor, Op. 66. Polonaise No. 6 in A flat major, Op. 53. DEBUSSY: Suite bergamasque: Clair de lune. FALLA: El amor brujo: Ritual fire dance.
(M)**(*) Decca KCSP 110.

As a popular piano recital this is wholly successful. The programme is admirably planned so that each piece makes a good contrast with its predecessor; the mood and style of the music range widely, and Katchen shows the breadth of his sympathies too. Best are the rhapsodies by Brahms (splendidly impulsive) and Liszt (the ear revels in such glittering cascades) and a delightfully brittle and poised Rondo capriccioso. Then comes a lovely performance of On Wings of Song to melt the ear afterwards. But everything is good: the Bach is poised, the Polonaise strong-fingered and passionate, and the Fantaisie-impromptu ripples off the fingers with consummate ease. Clair de lune is evocative and the Ritual fire dance suitably powerful, with a characteristic mannerism just before the end. By comparison with the equivalent LP the piano tone here is curiously soft-edged – bold enough, but without the sharpness of outline characteristic of many of Katchen's Decca recordings. The result is undoubtedly pleasing and suits many items in the programme very well. The transfer level is high.

Kempff, Wilhelm (piano)

Piano transcriptions (arr. Kempff): BACH: Chorale preludes: Nun komm der Heiden Heiland, BWV 659; Befiehl du deine Wege, BWV 727; In dulci jubilo, BWV 751; Wachet auf, BWV 140; Ich ruf' zu dir, BWV 639; Jesus bleibet meine Freude, BWV 147/6. Flute sonata in E flat major, BWV 1031: Siciliano. Cantata No.

29: *Sinfonia. Harpsichord concerto No. 5 in F minor BWV 1056: Largo.* HANDEL: *Minuet in G minor.* GLUCK: *Orfeo ed Euridice: Ballet music.*

**(*)DG 3300 647.

The Kempff magic is never entirely absent from any of this great pianist's recordings, but some may feel that it makes its presence felt rather unevenly in this recital. Several of the chorale preludes are played in a very studied way. The presentation of *Wachet auf* is very firm and clear, the background embroidery precisely articulated, and *Jesu, joy of man's desiring* is played with less delicacy, more extrovert projection than usual. The *Siciliano* from BWV 1031, however, is given an appealing lyrical flow, and the *Orfeo* excerpts, which close the recital, are very beautiful. Kempff is splendidly recorded; the piano tone is full and clear, and the tape transfer is immaculate.

'*Für Elise*': BEETHOVEN: *Für Elise, G.13. Rondo à capriccio in G major (Rage over a lost penny), Op. 129.* MOZART: *Fantasy in D minor, K397.* SCHUBERT: *Moments musicaux, D.780, Nos. 1, 3 and 5.* BRAHMS: *3 Intermezzi, Op. 117.* SCHUMANN: *Papillons, Op. 2.*

(B)**(*)DG Heliodor 3348 137.

This is a well-planned tape, and although the piano tone is variable (the acoustic changes strikingly on side two) it does give a fair idea of Kempff's range. *Für Elise* is simple and totally unromantic, and the Brahms *Intermezzi* are most beautifully done; but the highlight of the collection is unquestionably the really wonderful performance of the Mozart *Fantasia*, played simply but with great art lying beneath the music's surface. The transfer is of excellent quality throughout, clean and clear, with pleasingly warm timbre in the Brahms.

'The king of instruments'

Organ music played by (i) Fernando Germani, Selby Abbey; (ii) Simon Preston, Westminster Abbey; (iii) Lionel Rogg, Royal Festival Hall, London; (iv) David Willcocks, King's College Chapel, Cambridge; (v) Nicholas Kynaston, Westminster Cathedral; (vi) Noel Rawsthorne, Liverpool Cathedral; (vii) George Thalben Ball, Temple Church; (viii) Nicholas Danby, Blenheim Palace; (ix) Francis Jackson, York Minster; (x) Alan Wicks, Canterbury Cathedral: (i) WIDOR: *Symphony No. 5 in F minor, Op. 42/1: Toccata.* (ii) MURRILL: *Carillon.* (iii) BUXTEHUDE: *Prelude and fugue in G minor.* (iv) BACH: *Chorale prelude: Wachet auf, BWV 645.* (v) VIERNE: *Carillon de Westminster.* (vi) KARG-ELERT: *Chorale improvisation: Nun danket alle Gott.* (vii) PURCELL: *Voluntary on the Old Hundredth.* (viii) BOËLL-MANN: *Suite gothique: Toccata.* (ix) COCKER: *Tuba tune.* (x) BACH: *Toccata and fugue in D minor, BWV 565.*

(M)**EMI TC-MCS 12.

This collection was originally issued on disc as a sampler to tempt collectors to explore the series of HMV organ records from which the excerpts were taken. Many of these are deleted now and none has been issued on tape, but the compilation is valuable in its representation of many fine British organs and their players. The only disappointment is the Widor *Toccata*, which offers crumbling bass sound, but that was poorly focused on disc too. The other items have all transferred surprisingly well and are nearly all free from congestion. Alan Wick's performance of the famous Bach *Toccata and fugue* is strangely slow; but Cocker's *Tuba tune*, recorded at York, and (especially) the delightful Westminster *Carillon* are splendidly played. The sound is well balanced if sometimes rather thick in texture.

Klien, Walter (piano)

'*Romantic piano music*': BEET-HOVEN: *Sonata No. 14 in C sharp minor (Moonlight), Op. 27/2.* LISZT: *Liebestraum No. 3, G.541.* CHOPIN: *Étude in E major, Op. 10/3. Waltz in D flat major, Op. 70/3.* MENDELS-SOHN: *Song without words: Spring song.* DEBUSSY: *Suite bergamasque: Clair de lune.* TCHAIKOVSKY: *Chant sans paroles, Op. 2/3.* SCHUMANN: *Kinderscenen: Träumerei.* BRAHMS: *Waltz in A flat major, Op. 39/15.*

(M)**Turnabout KTVC 37033.

The performance of the *Moonlight sonata* is rather deliberate, but the rest of this programme offers playing of the highest order. Klien's taste is sure and he plays each piece with well-judged characterization and style. Highlights are a quite deliciously delicate *Spring song*, a passionate and controlled *Liebestraum*, a very sensitive *Clair de lune*, and a poised and beautifully shaped *Träumerei*. The recording as transferred is basically warm and pleasing, offering covered piano timbre in the romantic genre pieces, but in the occasional *fortissimo* the tone hardens and in the finale of the *Moonlight sonata* it becomes clattery.

Klien, Walter and Beatriz (piano duet)

'*Music for piano, four hands*': BRAHMS: *Waltzes, Op. 39.* DVOŘÁK: *Legends, Op. 59.* SCHUBERT: *3 Marches militaires, D.733.* GRIEG: *4 Norwegian dances, Op. 35.*

(M)**(*)Turnabout KTVC 34041.

A fine collection in every way. If the art of the piano duet has lost its place in the television-bound home, the exhilaration of playing in duet (one of the most intense musical experiences for even a second-rate amateur pianist) is here conveyed in full force. The Schubert should be tried first; the three marches are positively intoxicating. The other items are all played with enormous brio and sympathy, and, needless to say, rather more accurately than is customary on the drawing-room upright. The piano focus is not always quite perfect in the Schubert, but elsewhere the recording is excellent, bold and clear.

Larrocha, Alicia de (piano)

'*Favourite Spanish encores*': ALBÉ-NIZ, Mateo: *Sonata in D major.* ALBÉNIZ, Isaac: *Recuerdos de Viaje Nos. 5 and 6. Pavana–Capricho, Op. 12. Tango, Op. 165/2. Malaguena, Op. 165/3. Suite espagnole: No. 3, Sevillanas.* SOLER: *Sonatas in G minor; in D major.* GRANADOS: *Danzas españolas Nos. 5 and 7.* TUR-INA: *5 Danzas gitanas, 1st series: No. 5, Sacro-monte, Op. 55. 3 Danzas Andaluzas: No. 3, Zapateado, Op. 8.*

**(*)Decca KSXC 6734 [Lon. 5–6953].

An entirely delightful collection of lightweight Spanish keyboard music, played with such skill and simplicity that even the slightest music never becomes chocolate-boxy. The eighteenth-century classicism of the sonatas by Soler and Mateo Albéniz makes a splendid foil for the warmer romanticism of Isaac Albéniz and the vivid colours of Granados and Turina. The transfer offers very lifelike piano tone, warm and natural, although side one (where the level seems fractionally lower) has a marginal lack of crispness in the treble.

Ledger, Philip (organ of King's College Chapel, Cambridge)

'Organ music from King's': BACH: *Toccata and fugue in D minor, BWV 565.* BRAHMS: *Chorale prelude: Es ist ein' Ros' entsprungen, Op. 122/8.* LISZT: *Prelude and fugue on the name BACH, G.260.* VAUGHAN WILLIAMS: *Rhosymedre.* FRANCK: *Choral No. 3 in A minor.* VIERNE: *Pièces en style libre: No. 19, Berceuse.* WIDOR: *Symphony No. 5 in F minor, Op. 42/1: Toccata.*
(M)(**)HMV TC-HQS 1356.

Fine playing, but the transfer lacks refinement during the Franck and Widor pieces, in spite of the limited dynamic range, which spoils the ubiquitous Bach *Toccata and fugue in D minor* and certainly damps down Liszt's flamboyant *Prelude and fugue on BACH.*

Lloyd Webber, Julian (cello), Yitkin Seow (piano)

'The romantic cello': POPPER: *Elfentanz, Op. 39.* SAINT-SAËNS: *Carnival of the Animals: The swan. Allegro appassionato, Op. 43.* FAURÉ: *Après un rêve.* MENDELSSOHN: *Song without words, Op. 109.* RACHMANINOV: *Sonata, Op. 19: Slow movement.* DELIUS: *Romance.* CHOPIN: *Introduction and polonaise brillante, Op. 3.* ELGAR: *Salut d'amour, Op. 12.*
**(*)Enigma K 423524.

The clean, clear recording balance, admirably natural but not especially resonant, produces a cello image where the upper tonal range predominates. There is some lack of ripeness in the bass, but this accords well with Julian Lloyd Webber's approach to this repertoire, sympathetically stylish, never romantically indulgent. The bravura is accomplished with enviable ease, and the balance permits Yitkin Seow, who plays splendidly, to form an equal partnership in the slow

movement of Rachmaninov's *Cello sonata.* In the last analysis perhaps the sound is a fraction too dry, but the transfer is immaculately realistic, with splendid presence and focus.

Menuhin, Yehudi, and Stéphane Grappelli (violins)

'Jealousy' (*Hits of the thirties*): GADE: *Jealousy.* RODGERS: *Blue room. The Lady is a Tramp.* KERN: *A Fine Romance. Pick Yourself Up.* GRAPPELLI: *Billy. Aurore. Errol. Jermyn Street.* GERSHWIN: *Love Is Here To Stay. Lady Be Good.* PORTER: *Night and Day.* MCHUGH: *I Can't Believe That You're In Love With Me.* STRACHEY: *These Foolish Things.* BERLIN: *Cheek to Cheek.*
***EMI TC-EMD 5504.

The partnership of Menuhin and Grappelli started in the television studio; their brief duets (tagged on to interviews) were so successful that the idea developed of recording a whole recital. This was the first selection, and found each maestro striking sparks off the other in style but matching the other remarkably closely in matters of tone and balance. The result is delightful, particularly in numbers such as *Pick Yourself Up* where the arrangement directly tips a wink towards Bachian figuration. Excellently focused recording, and the transfer is nearly always crisp and clean.

'Fascinatin' Rhythm': GERSHWIN: *Soon. Summertime. Nice Work If You Can Get It. Embraceable You. Fascinatin' Rhythm. Liza. 'S Wonderful. I Got Rhythm.* KERN: *Why Do I Love You. All the Things You Are.* PORTER: *Just One of Those Things. Looking at You. I Get a Kick Out of You.* GRAPPELLI: *Johanny aime. Minuet pour Menuhin.*
***EMI TC-EMD 5523.

One of the secrets of the success of this partnership lies in the choice of material. All these items started out as first-rate songs with striking melodies which live in whatever guise, and here with ingenious arrangements they spark off the individual genius of each violinist both as a challenge and towards the players' obvious enjoyment. The high spirits of the collaboration are caught beautifully, and like the other recordings in the series this can be recommended unreservedly to anyone fancying the offbeat mixture. Good vivid sound and the high-level transfer has plenty of life (although the balance is very forward).

'Tea for Two': MEYER and KAHN: *Crazy Rhythm*. GERSHWIN: *The Man I Love. A Foggy Day*. YOUMANS: *Tea for Two*. RODGERS: *My Funny Valentine. Thou Swell*. KERN: *Yesterdays*. ARLEN: *Between the Devil and the Deep Blue Sea*. BRAHAM: *Limehouse Blues*. HARRIS: *Air on a Shoe String. Viva Vivaldi*. GRAPPELLI: *Highgate village. Adelaide Eve* (played by Menuhin on violin with Grappelli on piano).

***EMI TC-EMD 5530.

This third issue shows Menuhin and Grappelli even more confident in their harmoniously clashing partnership. Inevitably, with swung rhythms the essential element of the exercise, Grappelli is generally the dominant partner, but most successful of all are the items by Max Harris, *Air on a Shoe String* and *Viva Vivaldi*, which, with harpsichord (played by Laurie Holloway) an important element, pay more than lip-service to classical tradition. Vivid immediate recording and a splendidly clean transfer. Taking quality of sound into account as well as the vibrant playing, this is the most attractive of the Menuhin/Grappelli tapes.

Moore, Edward (piano)

'The world's best-loved piano music': SÉVERAC: *An old musical box*. DVOŘÁK: *Humoresque in G flat major, Op. 101/7*. PADEREWSKI: *Minuet in G major, Op. 14/1*. MACDOWELL: *To a wild rose, Op. 51/1*. SINDING: *Rustle of Spring, Op. 32/3*. GRANADOS: *Andaluza (Spanish dance No. 5)*. BEETHOVEN: *Minuet in G major*. CHOPIN: *Mazurka in B flat major, Op. 7/1. Preludes, Op. 28: Nos. 7 in A major; 20 in C minor*. BACH: *Cantata No. 147: Jesu, joy of man's desiring* (arr. Hess). arr. GRAINGER: *Londonderry air*. DEBUSSY: *Suite bergamasque: Clair de lune. Préludes, Book 1: La fille aux cheveux de lin*. MENDELSSOHN: *Spring song, Op. 62/6*. BRIDGE: *Rosemary*. GRIEG: *Butterfly, Op. 43/1*. ALBÉNIZ: *Tango in D major, Op. 165/2*. LIADOV: *A musical snuff-box, Op. 32*.

(M)*(*)Saga CA 5400.

An unassuming recital, offering nineteen miniatures of which a great many are certainly favourites. The playing is freshly direct, with no interpretative subtleties but responding to the atmosphere of each piece and avoiding clumsy over-emphasis or exaggerated *rubato*. The recording is bright, slightly shallow, but suitably mellow in the gentle pieces. It is not very expansive, but it is secure. The upper focus is smooth if sometimes not perfectly clean. Taken overall the issue is not really distinguished, but it is inexpensive and will undoubtedly give pleasure.

'Musical instruments at the Victoria and Albert Museum'

Virginals; ivory lute; baroque oboe; baroque violin; writing-case virginals; baroque guitar; baroque flute; baryton; hurdy-gurdy; Taskin harpsichord; giraffe piano; French hand-horn (played by various artists). Narration and illustrated booklet by Carole Patey (with 53 colour slides).

Available from HM Stationery Office.

At the centre of this presentation is an eighty-minute cassette on which each instrument is introduced by Carole Patey with interspersed anecdotes using additional voices (after the manner of a BBC radio programme) to increase the dramatic effect. The illustrated talk is in two halves; at the end of each there is a further short recital using the instruments discussed. This is the least effective part of the tape: the playing still sounds illustrative rather than creating the ambience of proper performances. However, the production generally is admirable, entertaining and informative. The cassette is of very good quality and the recording truthful. Each instrument is naturally balanced, and the narrating voice is given a friendly forward projection. The instrumental sound lacks the very fullest frequency range (the upper partials of the baroque instruments are smoothed off somewhat), but this is not a really serious criticism: the recording remains very effective for its purpose. A simple cue sheet, for amateur or professional use, is provided so that the colour slides can be fitted to the narrative. This is a first-class idea, efficiently realized.

Ogdon, John (piano)

'Popular piano favourites': BACH: Cantata No. 147: Jesu, joy of man's desiring. BEETHOVEN: Für Elise. IRELAND: The Holy Boy. April. POULENC: Mouvement perpétuel No. 1. IBERT: Histoires: 2, Le petit âne blanc. CHAMINADE: Automne, Op. 35. MOSZKOWSKI: Valse in E major, Op. 34/1. RACHMANINOV: Prelude in C sharp minor, Op. 3/2. GRANADOS: Goyescas: 4, The Maiden and the Nightingale. ALBÉNIZ: Tango in D major, Op. 165/2. SINDING: Rustle of Spring, Op. 32/3. SCOTT, Cyril: Lotus Land, Op. 47/1. Danse nègre, Op. 58/5. GRIEG: Lyric pieces: Wedding Day at Troldhaugen, Op. 65/6.

(M)*(*)HMV TC-EXE 178.

A highly musical but rather sturdy recital, somewhat lacking incandescence in the Granados but with Ogdon at his very best in the French and English music. The opening Bach chorale immediately sets the atmosphere of rather studied care in the matter of articulation and phrasing. The piano recording is basically excellent: on our copy the quality was clear but rather dry on side one; on side two a higher transfer level brought a fuller and brighter sound but also, every now and then, a hint of congestion.

Organ music

'Favourite organ music' (with (i) Karl Richter, organ of Victoria Hall, Geneva; (ii) Simon Preston, Westminster Abbey or King's College Chapel, Cambridge; (iii) Karl Richter, cond. and organ of St Mark's, Munich, with CO; (iv) Michael Nicholas, Norwich Cathedral): (i) BACH: Toccata and fugue in D minor, BWV 565. Fantasia and fugue in G minor, BWV 542. (ii) Chorale prelude: Wachet auf, BWV 645. (iii) HANDEL: Organ concertos: in B flat major, Op. 4/2; in D minor, Op. 7/4. (iv) Water music: Air. Xerxes: Largo. CLARKE: Trumpet voluntary. DAVIES: Solemn melody. BOËLLMANN: Suite gothique: Toccata. KARG-ELERT: Chorale improvisation: Nun danket alle Gott. (ii) PURCELL: Trumpet tune. FRANCK: Pièce héroïque. WAGNER: Tannhäuser:

765

Pilgrims' chorus. WIDOR: *Symphony No. 5 in F minor, Op. 42/1: Toccata.* (B)**Decca KDPC 523/4.

Economically priced, this pair of tapes would have been a 'best buy' among organ recitals on cassette had the engineering been more consistent. The first tape is first-class in every way; the music here is played either by Simon Preston at Westminster and King's or by Michael Nicholas at Norwich. The standard of performance is very high indeed and the music is splendidly projected, highlights being the Widor *Toccata* (reproduced with admirable realism and smoothness) and the Boëllmann, which offers a real sense of spectacle. The transfer level is admirably judged. On the second tape the level rises, and immediately at the opening of Karl Richter's Bach (BWV 565) there is congestion in the bass. A feeling of slight discomfort prevails throughout the two Bach pieces, although the Handel *Organ concertos* are smooth (almost too much so). These are well played, if with little suggestion of imaginative flair; Op. 7/4 is more successful than Op. 4/2.

'The world of the organ' (with (i) Jeanne Demessieux, Liverpool Met. Cathedral; (ii) Edward Higginbottom, Corpus Christi College, Cambridge; (iii) Simon Preston, Westminster Abbey; (iv) D. J. Rees, Alltwen Chapel, Pontardawe; (v) Douglas Haas, with Württemberg CO, Faerber; (vi) Karl Richter, Victoria Hall, Geneva; (vii) Jiři Ropek, St Giles, Cripplegate): (i) WIDOR: *Symphony No. 5 in F minor, Op. 42/1: Toccata.* (ii) FRANCK: *Pièce héroïque.* (iii) PURCELL: *Trumpet tune.* CLARKE: *Trumpet voluntary.* (iv) DAVIES: *Solemn melody.* (v) ALBINONI: *Adagio in G minor* (arr. Giazotto) *for strings and organ.* (vi) BACH: *Toccata and fugue in D minor, BWV 565.* (vii) *Chorale prelude:*

Wachet auf, BWV 542. Fantasia and fugue in G minor, BWV 542. (M)**(*)Decca KCSP 262.

An admirably planned recital, offering first-rate playing throughout and a fairly wide range of organ sound within different ambiences. The recording is excellent but the tape transfer has been made at fractionally too high a level on side one; there is some roughness in the upper partials in the Widor *Toccata* and the Purcell *Trumpet tune*, but it is marginal and can be smoothed out by cutting the treble back. The other pieces on side one are relatively unblemished, and side two, where the level is lower, sounds fine. This contains the three Bach items; the two played by Ropek are particularly successful.

Perlman, Itzhak, and Pinchas Zukerman (violins)

Duets for two violins: LECLAIR: *Sonata No. 5 in E minor.* WIENIAWSKI: *Études-Caprices Nos. 1 and 2.* HANDEL: *Passacaglia in G minor* (arr. HALVORSEN). SPOHR: *Duo concertante in D major, Op. 67/2.* **HMV TC-ASD 3430.

Predictably brilliant playing from Perlman and Zukerman, though a whole tape of this medium may prove too daunting for some tastes. The Spohr is an interesting piece, and collectors with a taste for violinistic wizardry will want to investigate this recital. Good, realistic recording quality and a smooth, clean transfer.

Piano music

'Favourite piano music' (with (i) Julius Katchen; (ii) Friedrich Gulda; (iii) Wilhelm Kempff; (iv) Peter Katin): (i) BACH: *Cantata No. 147: Jesu, joy of man's desiring* (arr. Hess). MOZART: *Piano sonata No. 15 in C major, K.545:* 1st movt.

BEETHOVEN: *Piano sonata No. 8 in C minor (Pathétique), Op. 13:* 2nd movt. (ii) *Piano sonata No. 14 in C sharp minor (Moonlight), Op. 27/2* (iii) *Für Elise.* (i) MENDELSSOHN: *On wings of song* (arr. Liszt). BRAHMS: *Hungarian dance No. 5 in F sharp minor. Intermezzo in E flat major, Op. 117/1.* (iv) *Rhapsody in G minor, Op. 79/2.* (i) CHOPIN: *Polonaise in A flat major.* (iii) *Impromptu No. 1 in A flat major, Op. 29. Ballade No. 3 in A flat major, Op. 47. Piano sonata No. 2 in B flat minor (Funeral march), Op. 35:* 3rd movt. *Fantaisie-impromptu in C sharp minor, Op. 66.* (iv) *Waltzes: in D flat major, Op. 64/1; in C sharp minor, Op. 64/2.* (ii) DEBUSSY: *Suite bergamasque: Clair de lune.* (iv) LISZT: *Liebestraum No. 3, G.541. Consolation No. 3, G.172.* SCHUMANN: *Romance, Op. 28/2.*

(B)**Decca KDPC 509/10.

This collection would have been more useful issued on one double-length tape for late-evening use. The selection has been intelligently made but it does not really gell into a recital. However, the performances show consistent musical sensitivity and (especially from Katchen) moments of distinction. The recording is of good quality and the transfer is also well done.

Polanska, Elena (harps and tambourin), **Roger Cotte** (recorder), **Guy Durand** (vièle and recorder)

'*Medieval and Renaissance music for the Irish and Medieval harps with vièle, recorders and tambourin*'.

(M)**Turnabout KTVC 34019.

The performance of medieval music is inevitably conjectural, but Roger Cotte, in the excellent notes which accompany this tape, suggests that a performing musician's sensibility and good taste should govern the choice of instrumentation. Certainly the slender and piquant sounds here recorded have a convincing atmosphere. The delicacy of texture extends to the vièle, the ancestor of the violin, which Guy Durand plays stylishly. The attractive programme, which ranges from the thirteenth century to the sixteenth, certainly does not lack melodic appeal; and the balance, although forward, creates a proper sense of scale and allows dynamic contrast. The transfer is of immaculate quality, clean and clear throughout.

Preston, Simon (organ of Westminster Abbey)

'*Crown Imperial*': WALTON: *Crown Imperial march.* CLARKE: *Prince of Denmark's march.* HANDEL: *Saul: Dead March.* PURCELL: *Trumpet tune.* ELGAR: *Imperial march.* VIERNE: (Organ) *Symphony No. 1:* Finale. WAGNER: *Tannhäuser: Pilgrims' chorus.* GUILMANT: *March on a theme of Handel.* SCHUMANN: *Study No. 5.* KARG-ELERT: *Marche triomphale ('Now thank we all our God').*

(M)***Argo KCSP 507.

A spectacular tape which is in every way successful. Simon Preston uses wide dynamic contrasts to increase the impact of his programme, and Walton's *Crown Imperial* has a panoply of sound which compares very favourably with an orchestral recording. The Vierne and the Karg-Elert items both lend themselves admirably to such flamboyance and tonal opulence. The transfer to tape is of high quality, clean, and with the wide dynamic range accommodated without stress, even when the high-level transfer takes the indicator needles into the red area.

Ragossnig, Konrad, and Walter Feybli (guitars)

'Music for two guitars': BARRIOS: *Danza Paraguaya.* CRESPO: *Nortena.* LAURO: *Vals Venezelano.* PONCE: *Valse. 3 Mexican popular songs.* VILLA-LOBOS: *Chôros No. 1. Cirandinhas Nos. 1. and 10.* TRAD.: *Boleras sevillanas. Salamanca. Villancico. De blanca tierra. Buenos reyes. Linda amiga. El puerto. El pano moruno. Cantar montanes. Tutu maramba. Cubana.*

(M)**(*)Saga CA 5412.

This attractive recital of Spanish and South American music features a guitar duo of some personality; they make a good team and bring their diverse programme fully alive. The recording is good and the transfer near excellent. A genuine bargain.

Richter, Sviatoslav (piano)

BACH: *The Well-tempered Clavier, Book 1, Nos. 1, 4, 5, 6 and 8.* SCHUBERT: *Allegretto in C minor, D. 915. Ländler in A major, D.336/1.* SCHUMANN: *Abegg variations, Op. 1.* RACHMANINOV: *Prelude in G sharp minor, Op. 32/12.* PROKOFIEV: *Visions fugitives, Op. 22, Nos. 3, 6, 9.*

(B)***DG Heliodor 3348 286.

This live recital dates from 1962, and although the audience betrays its presence with the usual coughs and rustles, it is not too distracting. The quality of sound is good, a little dry but completely acceptable. The transfer is made at a high level, and successfully encompasses the wide dynamic range of Richter's Bach playing. His style is coolly expressive, thoughtful, and makes no concessions to the harpsichord: this is Bach on the piano and no mistake about it. The effect is undoubtedly refreshing. The rest of the programme is repertoire in which Richter is thoroughly at home, and the playing is

masterly: here the piano timbre seems marginally less rich. An excellent bargain nonetheless.

Robles, Maria (harp)

'The world of the harp': FALLA: *The Three-cornered Hat: Danza del Corregidor.* ALBÉNIZ: *Romores de la Caleta. La torre bermeja.* GURIDI: *Viejo Zortzico.* MOZART: *Theme, Variations and Rondo pastorale.* BEETHOVEN: *Variations on a Swiss air.* BRITTEN: *A Ceremony of Carols: Interlude.* FAURÉ: *Impromptu, Op. 86.* PIERNÉ: *Impromptu-caprice, Op. 9.* SALZEDO: *Chanson de la nuit.*

(M)(***)Decca KCSP 348.

Potentially an attractive anthology, this tape is spoiled by too high a level of transfer, which produces uncomfortable sound and a frequent hint of underlying harmonic distortion. Some pieces come off better than others, but this is not a tape to recommend except for a very small player.

Romero, Angel (guitar)

'Spanish virtuoso': TORROBA: *Madroños.* ALBÉNIZ: *Córdoba, Op. 232/4. Tango, Op. 163/2.* GRANADOS: *La maja de Goya.* RODRIGO: *Fandango.* TARREGA: *Preludes Nos. 2 and 5. Estudio brillante. Mazurka. Maria. Marieta. Adelita.* TURINA: *Fandanguillo. Garrotín. Soleares. Ráfaga.*

(M)*(*)HMV TC-HQS 1401.

Angel Romero, as we know from his recording of the Rodrigo guitar concerto with Previn, is an excellent artist, but away from the stimulus of orchestra and conductor his manner of playing sometimes seems self-effacing. The opening *Madroños* of Torroba is striking enough, and the *Córdoba* of Albéniz which follows is certainly evocative, but later, particularly on the second side, which features the music of Turina and Tarrega, the introvert manner fails to grip the listener. The recording is smooth to match, and this is pleasant enough for late-evening background music.

Romero, Pepe (guitar)

'Famous guitar music': TARREGA: *Recuerdos de la Alhambra. Capricho Arabe.* VILLA-LOBOS: *Prelude No. 1 in E minor. Étude No. 1 in E minor.* LAURO: *El Marabino.* ALBÉNIZ: *Asturias.* SAGRERAS: *El Colibri.* SOR: *Variations on a theme by Mozart, Op. 9. Sonata in C major, Op. 15.*
  * Philips 7300 566 [id.].

This collection is aptly named: it includes many of the most famous short pieces guitarists love to play to show what miracles of technique are possible on this instrument, or how strongly the guitar can project a simple, well-made tune. *Recuerdos de la Alhambra* is an example of the first genre with its fluttering sustained effects, and Pepe Romero's performance of it immediately shows his approach to the whole collection. The technique is there, but there is no electricity, and Romero's advocacy of the music throughout is singularly unpersuasive. 'Here are all the pieces you insist on my playing,' he seems to imply; 'take them or leave them, as you wish.' The recording is excellent and well transferred, but this makes dull listening.

Rubinstein, Artur (piano)

'L'Amour de la vie' (music from his film biography): CHOPIN: *Polonaise in A flat major, Op. 53. Nocturne in D flat major, Op. 27/2.* VILLA-LOBOS: *Polichinelle.* SCHUMANN: *Fantasiestücke, Op. 12: Des Abends.* PROKO-FIEV: *The Love of Three Oranges: March.* BEETHOVEN: *Sonata No. 23 in F minor (Appassionata), Op. 57:* 1st movt. LISZT: *Liebestraum No. 3,*

G.541. MENDELSSOHN: *Spinning song.* FALLA: *Ritual fire dance.*
  (M) *** RCA Gold Seal GK 42708.

The issue of a Rubinstein recital on a mid-price label was prompted by the pianist's film biography. Some of the playing is marvellous, the melting Chopin *Nocturne*, the richly romantic yet never sentimental *Liebestraum*, and the perky Prokofiev *March*; and the collection ends with Rubinstein's favourite encore, the Falla *Ritual fire dance*, sounding for all the world as if it were originally written for the piano. The tautly tuned instrument usually favoured by Rubinstein for recording produces some shallowness of tone in fortissimos, but the great pianist coaxes a warm, singing timbre from it for the lyrical music. The transfer is crisply focused and has excellent range.

Sanger, David (harpsichord)

'Harmonious blacksmith': PARA-DISI: *Sonata No. 6 in A major.* HAN-DEL: *Suite No. 5: The harmonious blacksmith.* COUPERIN: *Pièces: Les barricades mysterieuses; Les moissonneurs; Le moucheron.* SCARLATTI, D.: *Sonata in E major, L.23.* LOEIL-LET: *Sonata in G minor.*
  (M) ** Saga CA 5384.

David Sanger's repertoire is more adventurous than his playing, which is sometimes rather circumspect in this admirably balanced programme, with Handel's famous *Harmonious blacksmith* variations as its centrepiece. The recording is vivid but a trifle over-resonant; the transfer level is high, the focus acceptable. This is fair value.

Schäffer, Michael (lute)

'French lute music': ATTAIGNANT: *Chanson: Tant que vivray. 5 Dances.* MOUTON: *Allemande: La dialogue des graces sur Iris. Sarabande: La*

769

Mallassis. Canarie: L'amant content. LE SAGE DE RICHEE: *Ouverture.* VISÉE: *Suite in D minor.* BITTNER: *Praeludium. Allemande. Courante. Sarabande: Passacaglia.*

(M)***Turnabout KTVC 34137.

This is an exceptionally rewarding tape. Michael Schäffer is obviously a player of some distinction and his feeling for style is highly developed. The repertoire he includes here will be unfamiliar to all except specialists, but it can be confidently recommended to the general music-lover. The Attaignant dances are charming, and so are the Mouton works. The Visée suite is perhaps the best-known piece (Bream has recorded it) and Schäffer plays it with great taste and accomplishment. The recording produces a slightly fuller quality than one expects from a lute, but there is no harm in that and generally speaking the sound is beautifully engineered. The transfer, at a high level, is of immaculate quality: this cassette loses nothing on the disc it mirrors. It makes ideal late-night listening.

Segovia, Andrés (guitar)

'Reveries': GLUCK: *Orfeo ed Euridice: Dance of the Blessed Spirits.* SCHUMANN: *Album for the Young, Op. 68, Nos. 1–2, 5–6, 9–10, 16 and 26. Scenes from Childhood, Op. 15: Träumerei. Romanza.* ASENCIO: *Mystic suite.* CASTELNUOVO-TEDESCO: *Ronsard.* MORENO-TORROBA: *Castellana.*

***RCA RK 12602 [ARK 1 2602].

At once intimate and gently evocative, this 1977 recital was carefully programmed so as not to strain the eighty-four-year-old maestro's resources. Indeed he shows admirable technical assurance. The music is slight, but undoubtedly charming, and is presented with great affection. The playing throughout has a degree of spontaneity rare in guitar recordings, especially where the element of repose is inherent in the atmosphere. The recording is completely real and the transfer immaculate.

Stringer, Alan (trumpet), Noel Rawsthorne (organ of Liverpool Cathedral)

'Trumpet and organ': CHARPENTIER, Marc-Antoine: *Te Deum: Prelude.* STANLEY: *Voluntary No. 5 in D major.* PURCELL: *Sonata in C major. Two Trumpet tunes and Air.* BOYCE: *Voluntary in D major.* CLARKE: *Trumpet voluntary.* BALDASSARE: *Sonata No. 1 in F major.* ROMAN: *Keyboard suite in D major: Non troppo allegro; Presto (Gigue).* FIOCCO: *Harpsichord suite No. 1: Andante.* BACH: *Cantata No. 147: Jesu, joy of man's desiring.* attrib. GREENE: *Introduction and trumpet tune.* VIVIANI: *Sonata No. 1 in C major.*

**(*)CRD CRDC 4008.

This collection is extremely well recorded and immaculately transferred. The reverberation of Liverpool Cathedral is under full control and both trumpet and organ are cleanly focused, while the trumpet has natural timbre and bloom. Alan Stringer is at his best in the classical pieces, the *Voluntary* of Boyce, the *Trumpet tunes* and *Sonata* of Purcell and the stylishly played *Sonata* of Viviani, a most attractive little work. He also gives a suitably robust performance of the famous *Trumpet voluntary*. Elsewhere he is sometimes a little square: the Bach chorale is rather too stiff and direct. But admirers of this repertoire will find much to enjoy, and the *Andante* of Fiocco has something in common with the more famous *Adagio* attributed to Albinoni in Giazotto's famous arrangement.

Tarr, Edward (trumpet and baroque trumpet), George Kent (organ)

'Baroque masterpieces for trumpet and organ': BOYCE–GREENE: *Suite of trumpet voluntaries in D major.* PRENTZL: *Sonata in C major.* KREBS: *Wachet auf* (2 settings). *Gott der Vater wohn' uns bei. In allen meinen Taten.* PEZEL: *Sonata in C major. Sonatinas Nos. 1–3 and 6 in C major* (for 2 trumpets and continuo). PURCELL: *Voluntary for organ in D minor.* STANLEY: *Suite of trumpet voluntaries in D major.* VIVIANI: *Sonatas Nos. 1–2 for trumpet and organ.* FANTINI: *Sonatas Nos. 3 and 8 in C major for trumpet and organ.* FRESCOBALDI: *Toccata per l'Elevazione.* TELEMANN: *Air de trompette in C major.*

***Advent F 1038 (see p. xxiii) [id.].

Each side or 'volume' (as the presentation enclosed with the cassette has it) lasts some three quarters of an hour. It is not recommended for continuous listening, but that is no criticism of the distinction of these performances but rather of the aural limitations of the medium itself: these pieces are undoubtedly baroque, but whether they are all 'masterpieces' is another matter. What is not in doubt is the quality of the playing and the excellence of the recording, which has outstanding presence without lacking any depth. A demonstration tape.

Tortelier, Paul (cello)

'Encores' (with Shuki Iwasaki, piano): SAINT-SAËNS: *Carnival of the Animals: The swan.* RAVEL: *Pièce en forme de habanera.* FAURÉ: *Papillon, Op. 77. Après un rêve.* MASSENET: *Elégie, Op. 10.* TORTELIER: *Pisanetto.* GRANADOS: *Goyescas: Intermezzo.* SARASATE: *Zapateado.* VALENTINI: *Violoncello sonata No. 10 in E major.* PAGANINI: *Moto perpetuo.*

Variations on a theme of Rossini. DVOŘÁK: *Rondo in G minor, Op. 94.* CHOPIN: *Prelude in E minor, Op. 28/4.*

(M)**HMV TC-EXE 179.

Tortelier is on top form here: Saint-Saëns's noble portrayal of *The swan,* which opens the recital, is beautifully played, and later the upper-register histrionics demanded by the display pieces of Sarasate and Paganini evoke an equally impressive bravura. Eloquent phrasing is matched by good taste, and if this kind of programme appeals it could hardly be better done. The recording spotlights the cello at the expense of the piano accompaniments, but the ultimate lack of range in the transfer also detracts somewhat from the presence of the artists.

'Träumerei'

Romantic piano music (with (i) Christoph Eschenbach; (ii) Joerg Demus; (iii) Wilhelm Kempff; (iv) Tamás Vásáry; (v) Géza Anda; (vi) Sviatoslav Richter; (vii) Stefan Askenase): (i) SCHUMANN: *Kinderscenen, Op. 15: Träumerei. Waldscenen, Op. 82: Einsame Blumen.* (ii) SCHUBERT: *Impromptu in A flat major, D.899/4.* (iii) BEETHOVEN: *Für Elise.* BRAHMS: *Rhapsody in G minor, Op. 79/2.* (iv) LISZT: *Polonaise No. 2 in E major.* (v) CHOPIN: *Prelude in D flat major, Op. 28/15.* (vi) *Ballade No. 4 in F minor, Op. 52.* (vii) *Waltz No. 7 in C minor, Op. 64/2.*

(M)**DG Privilege 3318 004.

If the compiler of this programme was thinking of a moonlit romantic atmosphere, then it opens well with Christoph Eschenbach's restrained yet admirably sensitive performances of Schumann's title piece and the picture of *Einsame Blumen* (*Lonely flowers*). Anda's account of the well-known Chopin *Prelude* maintains the mood, and Richter's *Bal-*

771

lade shows a remarkable concentration and atmosphere (it was recorded at a live recital). On side two Demus's neat, small-scale Schubert is matched by Kempff's Brahms *Rhapsody*, which is comparatively reticent in mood. Liszt's *Polonaise* closes the recital robustly. The tape transfer is well managed, with clear, full piano tone and surprisingly little difference of timbre between the items, which all have different sources.

Tyler, James (lute, baroque guitar, mandora)

'*Music of the Renaissance virtuosi*' (with Nigel North, lute, theorbo, cittern; Douglas Wootton, lute, bandora; Jane Ryan, bass viol): ANON.: *Zouch, his march.* VALLET: *Suite.* BORRONO: *3 Pieces from the Castelione Book.* CORBETTA: *Suite.* DE RORE/TERZI: *Contrapunto sopra 'Non mi toglia il ben mio'.* ALLISON: *Sharp pavin.* BERNIA: *Toccata chromatica.* KAPSPERGER: *Toccata.* PICCININI: *Toccata.* FERRABOSCO: *Spanish pavan.* CASTELLO: *Sonata.* DOWLAND: *Fantasia.*

(M)***Saga CA 5438.

A civilized and rewarding anthology, far more varied in sonority than the list of contents would lead one to expect. The playing of James Tyler is splendidly musical and effortlessly virtuosic. The mandora (or mandola) is an obsolete instrument related to the mandolin; the bandora (or pandora) is a metal-strung instrument like the cittern. There is some highly interesting repertoire here, and the performances are really distinguished. Unfortunately the cassette gives no liner presentation. The recording reproduces these subdued instruments truthfully and with no attempt to make them larger than life. Strongly recommended.

Walker, Luise (guitar)

'*Guitar music in Vienna*' (with Gottfried Hechtle, flute; Paul Roczek, violin; Jürgen Geise, viola; Wilfried Tachezi, cello): SCHUBERT: *Quartet for guitar, flute, viola and violoncello, D.96.* WEBER: *Minuet and trio for guitar, flute and viola.* HAYDN: *Cassation in C major* (for guitar, violin, cello).

(M)**Turnabout KTVC 34171.

These works are all arrangements. The 'Schubert' piece is not by Schubert at all, although he had a hand in its final form; it is an arrangement of a trio by a Bohemian contemporary called Matiegka. Schubert added the cello part and a trio to the minuet. The first movement indeed sounds very Schubertian; its spontaneity comes as much from its delightful texture as from its thematic content. Weber's *Minuet and trio* is very personable but short. The Haydn work is an arrangement (probably by the composer) of a string quartet (Op. 1/6). It has a particularly fine adagio in which the guitar merely accompanies a long solo violin cantilena, superbly played here by Paul Roczek. This is perhaps the highlight of a pleasant, very well recorded tape that might be useful for late-evening background listening. The transfer is refined and clear, and is quite the match of the equivalent disc.

Williams, John (guitar)

Guitar recital 1: ALBÉNIZ: *La torre bermeja.* PONCE: *3 Mexican popular songs.* VILLA-LOBOS: *Étude No. 1 in E minor.* CRESPO: *Nortena.* DUARTE: *Variations on a Catalan folk song, Op. 25.* SOR: *Variations on a theme of Mozart, Op. 9.* SEGOVIA: *Oración study in E major. Estudio. Humorada.* TANSMAN: *Barcarolle.* GRANADOS: *La maja de Goya.* LAURO: *Valse criollo.*

Guitar recital 2: BACH: (Unaccompanied) *Violoncello suites Nos. 1 in G major, BWV 1007; 3 in C major, BWV 1009.* SCARLATTI, D.: *Sonata in E minor, L.352.* SCARLATTI, A.: *Gavotte.*

(B)**(*) Decca KDPC 579/80.

This collection dates from 1959 and was originally issued (in disc form) on the Delysé label. When Decca took over the catalogue the material was remastered and rearranged into this double-recital format, with the classical items (Bach and Scarlatti) in one group and the other devoted to the mainly Latin material. John Williams's playing shows complete technical assurance and his keenly intelligent mind provides concentration even in the trifles (he is nowhere more beguiling than in the little Tansman *Barcarolle*). There is undoubtedly a lack of temperament in the Spanish repertoire, but the playing is never dull; the control of colour and dynamic keeps the music alive. The Bach suites, arranged by John Duarte, are transcribed into keys suitable to the guitar: No. 1 is transposed up a fifth to D and No. 3 down a third to A minor. They are played soberly and conscientiously, and some may seek more flair: yet the thoughtfulness of the music-making, with its conscious use of light and shade, is certainly impressive. The recording is of high quality; it does not sound in the least dated, and with the volume carefully set these tapes give a remarkable illusion of the presence of the soloist, with the guitar recorded in the right scale.

'The best of John Williams': BACH: *Lute suite No. 4: Gavotte.* GRANADOS: *Spanish dance No. 5.* FALLA: *The Three-cornered Hat: Miller's dance.* ALBÉNIZ: *Asturias.* TARREGA: *Recuerdos de la Alhambra.* VILLA-LOBOS: *Prelude No. 2.* PRAETORIUS: *La Volta.* TELEMANN: *Bourrée alla polacca* (with instrumental group). SCARLATTI, D.: *Sonata in E major, L.23.* SAGRERAS: *El Colibri.* TRAD.: *El Testamen de Amelia.* LAURO: *Valse criollo.* PONCE: *Scherzino Mexicano.* VIVALDI: *Guitar concerto in D major* (with ECO).

(M)**(*) CBS 40–61843 [(d) Col. MT 31407].

The best of John Williams spans just over a decade of recording with CBS. Much of the material here has previously been available on a now deleted compilation called *Greatest hits.* The anthology is an essentially popular one and although it concentrates on Latin repertoire there is a leavening of baroque (including a short concerto by Vivaldi), and even a contribution from Praetorius. For those who are not guitar specialists it represents excellent value, although not better than the more extensive and better-balanced anthology in the Decca set above. The recording is excellent and the transfer is acceptable, though not as crisp as some of John Williams's full-priced tapes; the orchestral detail in the Vivaldi is unrefined.

'More virtuoso music': MUDARRA: *Fantasia. Diferencias sobre el Conde Claros.* REUSNER: *Suite No. 4 in C minor: Paduana.* PRAETORIUS: *Terpsichore: Ballet. La Volta.* BACH: *Prelude, fugue and allegro, BWV 998.* GIULIANI: *Guitar sonata, Op. 15:* 1st movt. VILLA-LOBOS: *Preludes Nos. 2 in E major; 4 in E minor.* TORROBA: *Aires de la Mancha.*

**(*) CBS 40–72526.

The recital which preceded this, called *Virtuoso music for guitar* (40-72348), is not available in Dolby form; but this successor will do very nicely. It offers superior playing, as might be expected, although self-conscious bravura is seldom part of John Williams's musical personality. Indeed his reserve is such as to produce rather literal accounts of the Mudarra and Giuliani works. But in the Praetorius pieces he is superb. Here the cool style is exactly right, and the music has great classical poise and character. The Villa-Lobos *Preludes* are subtle and show a fine sense of atmosphere. Williams returns, effectively, to his neo-classical manner for the Torroba suite of *Aires de la Mancha*. Clear, forward CBS sound and a faithful transfer.

'Virtuoso variations': BACH: *Violin partita in D minor: Chaconne.* DOWLAND: *Queen Elizabeth, her galliard. Earl of Essex, his galliard.* BATCHELOR: *Mounsiers almaine.* PAGANINI: *Caprice No. 24, Op. 1.* GIULIANI: *Variations on a theme by Handel, Op. 107.* SOR: *Variations on a theme by Mozart, Op. 9.*
  ***CBS 40–72728.

This is one of John Williams's most attractive recitals, offering plenty of opportunity for virtuosity. In the Bach *Chaconne* – superbly played – it is virtuosity by restraint, but in *Mounsiers almaine* (which is given a touch of humour) there are some glittering roulades towards the end. The two Dowland pieces are done with a most fetching, dignified reserve. Both the Paganini and the Giuliani are technically sparkling, and if the *rubato* in the ear-tickling Sor *Variations on a theme by Mozart* seems not entirely spontaneous, this is still a brilliant performance. The recording is immaculate and the transfer is smooth and clear; there is a great deal to enjoy here.

'More Spanish music': TARREGA: *Recuerdos de la Alhambra.* GRANADOS: *Spanish dance No. 5.* TORROBA: *Aires de la Mancha.* VILLA-LOBOS: *Preludes Nos. 2 in E major. 4 in E minor.* ALBÉNIZ: *Sevilla.* SOR: *Variations on a theme by Mozart, Op. 9.* FALLA: *Homenaje.* MUDARRA: *Fan-*

tasia. TURINA: *Fandanguillo, Op. 36.*
  ***CBS 40–72950.

John Williams plays Spanish music not in a direct, intense manner (like Yepes, for instance) but thoughtfully, and evocatively, with instinctive control of atmosphere and dynamics. His approach can be heard at its most magical in Turina's *Fandanguillo.* The sophisticated use of *rubato* and colour in the Granados *Spanish dance* is almost orchestral and very effective. Above all the playing sounds spontaneous, and (as the restrained virtuosity of the famous fluttering *Recuerdos de la Alhambra* readily shows) Williams's technique is phenomenal and always at the service of the music. There is some superb *pianissimo* evocation in the Villa-Lobos *Prelude,* while the control of *rubato* is at its most subtle in the middle section of the Albéniz *Sevilla,* which ends side one. The recording is clear and immediate and admirably transferred to tape.

'Music from Japan, England and Latin America': YOCOH: *Theme and variations on 'Sakura'.* DODGSON: *Fantasy-Divisions.* PONCE: *Sonatina Meridional.* VILLA-LOBOS: *Chôros No. 1.* LAURO: *Valse criollo.* CRESPO: *Nortena.* SOJO: *5 Venezuelan pieces.* BARRIOS: *Danza Paraguaya.*
  ***CBS 40–73205.

An exotic and lively programme and not an insubstantial one. The Dodgson piece is by no means lightweight, and it makes a good foil for the Villa-Lobos *Chôros* which it follows. In his programme note John Williams draws the parallel between the guitar and the Japanese koto and certainly the *Sakura* variations transcribe effectively to the Western instrument. The Venezuelan pieces are inventive and colourful too. Williams is a superbly assured and stylish advocate, and the recording here has fine presence in an excellent transfer.

'John Williams and friends' (with Carlos Bonell, guitar; Brian Gascoign, Morris Pert, marimbas and vibraphone; Keith Marjoram, bass): VIVALDI: *Double guitar concerto in G major* (originally for 2 mandolins). DAQUIN: *Le Coucou.* BACH: *Violoncello suite No. 3: Bourrée. Cantata No. 147: Jesu, joy of man's desiring. Trio sonata in C major, BWV 1037: Gigue.* TELEMANN: *Bourrée alla polacca.* PURCELL: *Trio sonata No. 11 in F minor.* MOZART: *Adagio (for glass harmonica), K.356. Piano sonata No. 11 in A major, K. 331: Rondo alla turca.*

*CBS 40–73487.

There is nothing inherently wrong in using an offbeat instrumental and percussive combination for a concert of mainly baroque music, so long as the chosen timbres do not rob the music of vitality. But this collection is too soft-centred by half. Bach and Vivaldi are vitiated by marimbas – at least as presented here – and only Daquin's *Le Coucou* (although it sounds chocolate-boxy) begins to justify the experiment. For the rest the flabby sounds created will appeal only to the listener more oriented to 'pop' than the concert hall. The recording is good, but the transfer is not very crisp.

'The John Williams collection': VILLA-LOBOS: *Prelude No. 1 in E minor.* DOWLAND: *Fantasie No. 7.* BARRIOS: *Madrigal Gavota.* RODRIGO: *Concierto de Aranjuez: Adagio* (with ECO, Barenboim). BACH: *Cantata No. 147: Jesu, joy of man's desiring.* ALBÉNIZ, Mateo: *Sonata in D major.* ALBÉNIZ, Isaac: *Asturias.* PAGANINI: *Caprice No. 24, Op. 1.* GRANADOS: *La maja de Goya.* MOZART: *Piano sonata No. 11 in A major, K.331: Rondo alla turca.*

**(*)CBS 40–73784.

This is a further shrewd compilation made from John Williams's earlier recordings and it deserves to be a bestseller. Opening atmospherically with Villa-Lobos the programme shows this artist's wide talents at their best. Whether in the charmingly ingenuous sonata by Mateo Albéniz or the lyrical intensity of the Rodrigo *Adagio* (marvellously played) or the sheer electricity of Isaac Albéniz's *Asturias*, Williams is totally compelling. The drawback for some will be the Bach and Mozart pieces with marimbas and vibraphone ad lib, taken from *John Williams and friends* (see above). The recording has been strikingly well transferred to tape; the sound is admirably crisp and clean, and in the concerto the orchestra has good presence.

Yepes, Narciso (guitar)

'The world of the Spanish guitar': VILLA-LOBOS: *Chôros No. 1. Prelude No. 1.* TARREGA: *Recuerdos de la Alhambra. Capricho Arabe.* TURINA: *Garrotín. Soleares. Ráfaga.* TORROBA: *Madronos.* SOR: *Variations on a theme by Mozart, Op. 9.* ALBÉNIZ: *La torre bermeja. Granada. Asturias. Romores de la Caleta.* FALLA: *The Three-cornered Hat: Miller's dance.*

(M)***Decca KCSP 179.

Narciso Yepes's characteristic fluency and the natural freedom of his style are immediately noticeable in the opening Villa-Lobos pieces. This playing has striking temperament and the improvisatory flair which can give the solo guitar its special magnetism. The recording is not new and the solo image has less body than in Yepes's more modern DG recitals, but the quality is perfectly acceptable and always true in timbre and clear in focus. The items by Albéniz are particularly colourful (notably the *Asturias*), and the flexibility of Sor's *Mozart Variations* is most appealing. An excellent bargain at the price; the tape compares well with the disc.

'The world of the Spanish guitar',
Vol. 2: NARVAEZ: *4 Variations on*
Guardame las vacas. SANZ: *Suite*
española. SOR: *Minuet in D major.*
Study in E minor. TARREGA: *Prelude*
in G major. Gran Jota. MALATS: *Impresiones de España: Serenata*
española. PUJOL: *El Abejorro.* MAZA:
Habanera. PIPO: *Cancion y danza.*
VILLA-LOBOS: *Prelude No. 3. Étude*
No. 1. SAVIO: *Escenas Brasilenas.*
YEPES: *Danza Inca.*
　(M)***Decca KCSP 278.

If you have been pleased with Volume 1 of Yepes's *World of the guitar* you should be well satisfied with the second. The recording is always good, with no lack of body. Sometimes, as in the *Gran Jota* of Tarrega, one might ask for more sparkle, but Yepes's conception is intimate, so the sound fits quite well. There is some delightful music in this piece, comparatively extended by guitar standards. Side two of the recital makes a particularly attractive selection including a favourite among the Villa-Lobos *Preludes:* No. 3, a haunting melody, which Yepes plays with great freedom. The fluttering flight of Pujol's bumble bee (*El Abejorro*) might have taken wing with more conscious bravura, but this is not Yepes's manner. He is especially good at creating colour and atmosphere; witness the cool, serious melancholy of the opening of Sanz's *Suite española* or the character of Sor's *E minor Study*. Above all Yepes sustains the tension in his playing, and his own *Inca dance* makes an attractively piquant ending to the programme, which is given plenty of presence in this transfer.

'Guitarra romantica': GIULIANI:
Sonata in C major, Op. 15: Sonatina

in D major, Op. 71/3. SOR: *Variations*
on 'Marlborough', Op. 28. TARREGA: *Preludes: in D minor; in E*
major. 'Marieta' Mazurka. Capricho
Arabe. Serenata.
　**DG 3300 871.

Whether or not the title has anything to do with it, Yepes's performances here are very relaxed and wayward. In the two sonatas by Giuliani which form the main part of the recital a more positive approach would have benefited the music, which is not always very substantial. As it is, Yepes's use of dynamics as well as his *rubato* seem wilful and not always convincingly spontaneous. The other items are successful enough but hardly arresting. The recording is excellent and the transfer immaculate.

'Baroque works for guitar': BACH:
Prelude in C minor, BWV 99. Bourrée in E minor. Sarabande in E minor.
WEISS: *Suite in E major.* SCARLATTI,
Domenico: *Sonata in E minor.* SANZ:
Suite española.
　(M)**DG Privilege 3318 038.

The Bach pieces are played rather soberly, and it must be said that baroque or classical music does not always bring out the flair in Yepes's playing. Nevertheless this programme is musical and without romantic distortions. The recording is warmly atmospheric, though not as sparkling as Yepes's DG tape of Spanish music (see below); but the transfer is particularly vivid and has plenty of presence as well as warmth of tone.

'Spanish guitar music': ALBÉNIZ:
Asturias. Rómores de la Caleta. La
torre bermeja. GRANADOS: *Spanish*
dance No. 4: Villanesca. TARREGA:
Recuerdos de la Alhambra. Tango.
LLOBET: *La filla del marxant. La*
canço del Lladre. RUIZ-PIPÓ: *Danza*

No. 1. VILLA-LOBOS: *Preludes Nos. 1 and 3.* FALLA: *El amor brujo: El círculo mágico. The Three-cornered Hat: Farruca.*

(M)***DG Privilege 3335 182.

Narciso Yepes's performance of the Falla ballet excerpts reminds one of Beethoven's assertion that a guitar is an orchestra all by itself. This music-making has remarkable projection and atmosphere; the whole recital shows Yepes's striking ability to create tension in a recording studio – something too few guitarists can do. The programme is generally on a high level of interest; the *Spanish dance* of Granados is particularly gay and colourful. The transfer is excellently managed and sounds convincingly realistic. Highly recommended.

Zaradin, John (guitar)

WEISS: *Ballette.* FRESCOBALDI: *Air and variations* (arr. SEGOVIA). LAURO: *Valse criollo.* ALBÉNIZ: *Granada* (arr. TARREGA). MALATS: *Spanish serenade.* RODRIGO: *Concierto de Aranjuez.*

(B)**Classics for Pleasure TC-CFP 40012.

Classics for Pleasure had the excellent idea of coupling their recording of the Rodrigo *Concierto de Aranjuez* (reviewed above) with a recital by the soloist. His playing has plenty of character, and there are some attractive miniatures here. The recording is good and the transfer well managed, faithful and with bloom as well as clarity.

Vocal Recitals and Choral Collections

Anderson, Moira (soprano)

'The world of Moira Anderson', Vol. 1: LANE: *Finian's Rainbow: On a clear day you can see forever.* BOCK: *Fiddler on the Roof: Matchmaker.* ADAMS: *The holy city.* TRAD.: *Eriskay love lilt; John Anderson; Willie's gone to Melville Castle; The lea rig; Waltzing in the clouds; Once upon a time; My cup runneth over; Perfect day.* SULLIVAN: *The Pirates of Penzance: Poor wandering one.*

(M) *** Decca KCSP 345.

Moira Anderson's freshness of style and unaffected eloquence are matched by the beauty of her voice. She sings Scottish songs with an artless simplicity that is very appealing, and she judges the degree of sentiment in the sacred music so that it is never cloying. This well-planned recital is one of five with a similar mixture of operetta, ballads, folk and religious material (*Vol. 2*, KCSP 346; *Vol. 3*, KCSP 352; *Vol. 4*, KCSP 353; *Vol. 5*, KCSP 354). She is brightly accompanied (but sometimes, for instance in the excerpt from *The Pirates of Penzance*, the arrangements are tarted up) and well recorded; the transfers too are generally of good quality.

There are also two EMI collections, but these specialize in specific repertoire: musicals (*Someone wonderful*, TC-EMC 3040) and *The auld Scots sangs* (TC-EMC 3071). This is a particularly delightful collection, although some of the songs are over-arranged to include a discreet but rather soupy choral accompaniment. But Miss Anderson is in ravishing voice throughout.

Bach Choir

'Great choral classics' (with Thames CO, Willcocks): HANDEL: *Coronation anthems: Zadok the Priest; The King shall Rejoice. Israel in Egypt: Hailstones chorus.* BACH: *Cantata No. 147: Jesu, joy of man's desiring. Cantata No. 22: Awake us Lord and hasten. Cantata No. 140: Zion hears the watchmen's voices; Glory now to God we render (Sleepers, awake).* MOZART: *Ave verum corpus, K.618.* HAYDN: *The Creation: Introduction (Representation of chaos); In the beginning ... And the Spirit of God; The heavens are telling* (with Sally Burgess, soprano, Stuart Horner, tenor, Michael Leighton Jones, bar.).

(M) **(*) Decca KCSP 527.

A singularly vivid collection, splendidly sung and recorded. Although most of the choruses are spectacular ones there is enough lyrical music to make the concert reasonably varied. The contrasts of *The Creation* excerpts are most dramatically made. The transfer is made at a very high level and is not without a hint of roughness at one or two peaks, but for the most part it offers fine presence and detail.

Bailey, Norman (bass-bar.)

'Ballads and sacred songs' (with Geoffrey Parsons, piano): SPEAKS: *On the road to Mandalay.* KEEL: *Trade winds.* IRELAND: *Sea fever.* STANFORD: *Songs of the Sea: Drake's drum.* VAUGHAN WIL-

LIAMS: *The Vagabond. Linden Lea*. HAYDN WOOD: *A brown bird singing*. MOSS: *The floral dance*. HANDEL: *Silent worship*. MURRAY: *I'll walk beside you*. BRAHE: *Bless this house*. ADAMS: *The holy city*. RASBACH: *Trees*. SULLIVAN: *The lost chord*. SIBELIUS: *Be still, my soul*. WOLCOTT: *Blessed is the spot. O Thou, by whose name*. MALOTTE: *The Lord's Prayer*.

**Oiseau-Lyre KDSLC 20.

Fine operatic artist as he is, Norman Bailey is not the most responsive recitalist. Nor is the voice – noble-toned on stage in Wagner – one which takes smoothly to being recorded. For those reasons this is not the most successful of ballad recitals, but it will certainly please Bailey's admirers with its excellent choice of items and superb accompaniments from Geoffrey Parsons. The high-level transfer is of good quality, the voice resonantly caught and the balance good.

Baker, Janet (mezzo-soprano)

'*Favourites*' (with Gerald Moore, piano): R. STRAUSS: *Ständchen*. MENDELSSOHN: *Auf Flügeln des Gesanges*. SCHUBERT: *Heidenroslein*. SCHUMANN: *Der Nussbaum*. GOUNOD: *Sérénade*. MASSENET: *Crépuscule*. CHABRIER: *Villanelle des petites canards*. HAHN: *L'heure exquise*. BAX: *Me suis mis en dance*. SULLIVAN: *Orpheus with his lute*. PARRY: *O Mistress mine*. QUILTER: *It was a lover and his lass*. FINZI: *It was a lover and his lass*. IRELAND: *The Sally Gardens*. HOWELLS: *Gavotte*. TRAD.: (arr. Vaughan Williams): *Bushes and briars*. ANON.: (arr. Anderson) *Drink to me only;* (arr. Hughes) *I know where I'm going*.

*(**)HMV TC-ASD 2929.

A wholly enchanting recital that shows the sheer diversity of Janet Baker's art with captivating charm. Gerald Moore's accompaniments are a model, participating in the mood and colour of every song. The recording is basically excellent and well transferred on side one, but several copies sampled showed a degree of congestion on side two caused by the higher level of transfer.

'*Lieder*' (with Martin Isepp, piano): SCHUMANN: *Frauenliebe und Leben* (song cycle), *Op. 42*. BRAHMS: *Das Mädchen spricht; Die Mainacht; Nachtigall; Von ewiger Liebe*. SCHUBERT: *Die abgeblühte Linde; Heimliches Lieben; Minnelied; Der Musensohn*.

(M)*(**)Saga CA 5277.

Janet Baker's inspirational early Saga recording of *Frauenliebe und Leben* is discussed in our Composer index. The Schubert songs are not quite on this level (*Der Musensohn* is a little jerky), but the Brahms are beyond praise. The singing is of a quality that you find only once or twice in a generation; this is undoubtedly a collector's piece, whether on tape or disc. The transfer produces some distortion on the voice at loud climaxes, but then so did the LP, and it is mostly good, although the piano tone shows a minor degree of harmonic distortion at times.

'*Arie amorose*' (with Academy of St Martin-in-the-Fields, Marriner): arias by GIORDANI; CACCINI; STRADELLA; SARRI; CESTI; LOTTI; ALESSANDRO SCARLATTI; CALDARA; BONONCINI; DURANTE; PERGOLESI; MARTINI; PICCINI; PAISIELLO.

**(*)Philips 7300 691.

A delightful recital of classical arias, marred only by the absence of libretti or any kind of documentation about the music beyond the titles; the extensive liner-notes concentrate on Janet Baker's career. The programme is cleverly arranged to contrast expressive with sprightly music, and the wide range of Janet Baker's tonal graduation and her beautiful phrasing are matched by an artless lightness of touch in the slighter numbers. The accompaniments are intimate and tasteful: there is no more fetching example than Pergolesi's *Ogni pena più spietata*, with its deft bassoon obbligato, or the short closing song with harpsichord, Paisiello's *Nel cor più non mi sento*. The recording has a warm acoustic, and the resonance does not always provide the last degree of crispness of orchestral detail, but the transfer is kind to the voice.

Berganza, Teresa (mezzo-soprano)

'The art of zarzuela', Vol. 1: CHUECA: *Agua azucarillos y aguardiente: Prelude. La Granvia: Tango de la Menegilda. Schotis del Eliseo.* LUNA: *El Niño Judio: Canción española.* CHAPI: *El Barquillero: Romanza. La Chavala: Canción de la Gitana. Las Higas del Zebedeo: Carceleras.* GIMENEZ: *Soleares: Intermezzo. La Tempranica: Romanza de Tempranica; Zapateado.*

(M)**(*) Rediffusion KROY 2011.

The complete lack of documentation here is a disgrace. There is nothing whatsoever about the source of the music: not even the composers are named. But Teresa Berganza was at her absolute prime when the recordings were made. The voice is rich and creamy on top, darkly resonant in the middle and lower registers. The singing is at once vibrant, capriciously enchanting and, of course, very Spanish. The scintillating bravura in the *Zapateado* from *La Tempranica* is unforgettable, but undoubtedly the highlight of the recital is the richly seductive performance of the *Romanza* from *El Barquillero* with its gently syncopated melody that is a kind of Spanish *Im cham-*

bre séparée. Berganza sings it as enchantingly as Schwarzkopf does that famous number in her operetta recital (see below). The recording here is attractively resonant and the high-level transfer catches the voice vividly (and the suitably brash orchestral backing). There is a hint of peaking once or twice, and the sound lacks the last degree of refinement, but this cassette is a very rewarding one and readily demonstrates that the world of Spanish zarzuela is a still unexplored treasure-chest.

'Spanish songs from the Middle ages and Renaissance' (with Narciso Yepes, guitar): songs by TORRE; VALDERRABANO; MILAN; TRIANA; ENCINA; VASQUES; NARVAÉZ; MUDARRA; FUENLLANA; ALFONSO X; and anonymous composers.

***DG 3300 477.

This delectable collection is sung with disarming eloquence by Teresa Berganza, who is on top form and is obviously in love with her repertoire. Narciso Yepes accompanies with great sympathy and makes a major contribution to the success of the recital. The two artists are most naturally balanced and the transfer is very sophisticated, the voice caught with remarkable realism and presence. This is not a specialist recital: the music communicates readily in the most direct way, and excellent notes are provided.

Bergonzi, Carlo (tenor)

'Famous tenor arias' from: VERDI: *Aïda; Luisa Miller; La Forza del destino; Il Trovatore; Un Ballo in maschera; La Traviata.* PONCHIELLI: *La Gioconda.* PUCCINI: *La Bohème; Tosca; Manon Lescaut.*

(M)**(*) Decca KCSP 535.

Mostly dating from the late fifties, these recordings of favourite Verdi and Puccini arias (with one Ponchielli thrown in) show Bergonzi in his finest form. He does not attempt the rare *pianissimo* at the end of *Celeste Aïda*, but here among Italian tenors is a thinking musical artist who never resorts to vulgarity. The recording, of whatever vintage, is clear and gives the right bloom to the voice. The transfer is full-blooded (in the opening *Aïda* excerpt there is a hint of over-modulation in the brass) and it is reliable, though sometimes (notably in the Puccini arias) it does not produce a very convincing focus for the upper strings.

Best, Martin (tenor, lute and psaltery)

'*The dawn of romance*': Songs and music of the early troubadours of Provence including VENTADORN; BORNELH; BLAYE; FAIDIT; MARCABRU; VAQUEIRAS; VIDAL; RIQUIER; and traditional and anonymous music.

***HMV TC-CSD 3785.

A splendid recital. Martin Best's robust vocal style readily brings this music to life and there are some infectious sounds from the accompanying group of instrumentalists, who have plenty of opportunities for display. That these instrumental sounds are largely conjectural is obvious enough, but one is easily convinced when the effect is so exhilarating. There is a contribution also from members of the Geoffrey Mitchell Choir. The transfer to tape is of demonstration quality, with fine presence and life for both voice and instruments. The overall ambience is slightly resonant and is admirably judged; it is beautifully caught here.

Boston Camerata, Cohen

'*Courts and chapels of Renaissance France*': Music for voices and early instruments from Paris, Dijon, Geneva and Avignon, c. 1450–1600 by: DUFAY; BINCHOIS; MORTON; CERTON; SERMISY; JANNEQUIN; GERVAISE; PASSEREAU; JACOTIN;

DU TERTRE; GOUDIMEL; LASSUS; LE JEUNE; and anonymous composers.

** Advent D 1008 (see p. xxiii) [id.].

The Burgundian part of this collection comprises vocal pieces by Dufay and Binchois interspersed with instrumental works by Robert Morton and a transcription of Dufay'§ *J'ay grant douleur*. It is followed by a compilation of pieces from about 1530 by composers such as Sermisy, Jannequin and Gervaise. The expert performers of the Boston Camerata under Joel Cohen are rather forwardly balanced, though not unacceptably so, but a greater dynamic range would have registered were they slightly more distant. There is far too little space between the various pieces. The B side brings psalm settings by Goudimel in sober performances, and a variety of other pieces from Lassus, Le Jeune and others. The performances are a little wanting in flair and imagination if one compares with Munrow, and played at one sitting the uniform sound level proves tiring. The actual quality of the recording is first-class, and if the performances were just a little more spirited and poetic, this would deserve three stars.

'*Musica Teutonica*': German music of the Middle Ages and Renaissance by: RÜGEN; REVENTAL; REGENBOGEN; WOLKENSTEIN; ISAAC; BRUCK; GREITER; REGNART; HASSLER; SENFL; LASSUS; and anonymous composers.

*(**)Advent E 1031 (see p. xxiii) [id.].

The brief of this anthology is to illustrate the growth of the Minnesinger tradition. It includes intelligent performances of such pieces as the beautiful narrative of Abraham's sacrifice, *Gott Vater sprach*, by Regenbogen and Oswald von Wolkenstein's *Wach auf, mein hort*, and takes us up to Hassler, Senfl and Lassus. The performances are spirited and often sensitive, and the quality of the sound itself is quite outstanding. Made at the Museum of Fine Arts, Boston, the recording was transferred to cassette bypassing many of the usual procedures involved in cassette manufacture. Unfortunately the balance is much too forward at times, and the instrumental pieces are aggressive in their presence.

'A Renaissance Christmas': MOU-TON: *Noe, noe.* ANON. (Gregorian): *Veni redemptor gentium.* RASELIUS; RESINARIUS; ECCARD: *Nun komm der Heiden Heiland* (four settings). JOSQUIN DES PRÉS: *In principio erat verbum.* ANON.: *Nova nova; Salve, lux fidelium; Joseph est bien marié; Marvel not, Joseph; Riu riu chiu.* OBRECHT: *Magnificat.* WAL-THER: *Joseph, lieber Joseph mein.* VICTORIA: *O magnum mysterium.* PRAETORIUS: *Quem pastores laudavere; Wie schön leuchtet der Morgenstern.* GUERRERO: *Virgen santa; Los Reyes siguen la estrella.* CLEMENS NON PAPA: *Vox in Rama.* ATTEY: *Sweet was the song the Virgin sung.* BYRD: *Lullaby.*
** Advent E 1032 (see p. xxiii) [id.].

Recorded in the Museum of Fine Arts, Boston, this celebration of Christmas collects various pieces from Jean Mouton to Praetorius and Byrd in performances of uneven quality. There is a certain stiffness and rectitude about these readings (the Byrd is a good instance in point) that diminishes pleasure. The performers are not greatly helped by the very forward balance; the transfer, however, is of the high quality one associates with this label.

'The roots of American music': Renaissance melodies in traditional music of the New World (Provence, c.

1200; New Mexico, 1953; Music in Renaissance Mexico (from Spain); Old and new France; Wandering songs and ballads; Folk polyphony in the United States).
*** Advent E 1062 (see p. xxiii) [id.].

A presented recital recorded before an audience and designed to show the European roots of indigenous American music. It begins with an interesting parallel between *Kalenda Maya* from twelfth-century Provence and a Mexican processional from a medieval-style mystery play collected in New Mexico in the 1950s. There are other parallels, between folksongs collected in Quebec and French songbooks of the early Renaissance, between songs from the southern Appalachians and Elizabethan music, and the anthems of Billings and Elizabethan madrigals. The programme also includes some of the repertoire composed for the cathedrals and churches of Mexico and New Spain during the Renaissance by Francesco Franco. The performances are spirited and sympathetic, and they are more naturally balanced than some of the studio recordings in the Advent catalogue. The transfer is of excellent quality throughout. There is audience applause and a useful (albeit somewhat off-mike) commentary. An unusual and interesting anthology.

Brannigan, Owen (bass), Elizabeth Harwood (soprano)

'Sing the songs of Britain' (with Hendon Grammar School Choir, Pro Arte Orch., Mackerras): *Bay of Biscay. Cherry ripe. It was a lover. There was a jolly miller. The oak and the ash. Sigh no more, ladies. Early one morning. The bailiff's daughter of Islington. Charlie is my darling. A hunting we will go. The ash grove. Heart of oak. Ye banks and braes.*

The keel row. John Peel. Where the bee sucks. The vicar of Bray.
(M)**HMV Greensleeve TC-ESD 7002.

The partnership of Owen Brannigan, with his jaunty humour, and Elizabeth Harwood in freshest voice prevents this collection from becoming too soft-centred, although the arrangements do not avoid a degree of over-sweetness from the children's choir. It is all agreeably spontaneous and well recorded, though the transfer to tape lacks something in crispness of focus at times.

Browne, Sandra (mezzo-soprano)

'Spanish collection' (with Michael Isador, piano): RODRIGO: *Cançó del Teuladí; Trovadoresca; Cuatro madrigales amatorios.* GRANADOS: *Tonadillas: La maja dolorosa Nos. 1–3; Amor y odio; El mirar de la maja; El majo timido; Callejo; El majo discreto; El tra la la y el punteado.* FALLA: *Siete cançiones populares españolas.* MONTSALVATGE: *3 songs from Cinco cançiones negras.*
**(*)Enigma K 453563.

Sandra Browne's is a characterful, full-bodied voice, not always perfectly under control in the lighter songs, but excitingly vibrant in some of the more robust items. She is well supported by Michael Isador's vivid accompaniments and the performances here convey the point and sparkle of a delightful selection of Spanish songs, including many favourites. The recording – forwardly balanced – has great presence and has been admirably transferred to tape, giving plenty of projection. The liner-notes, although still in small print, are an improvement of some of Enigma's ealier issues.

Burrows, Stuart (tenor)

'Songs for you' (with (i) John Constable or Eurfryn John, piano;

(ii) Ambrosian Singers, Morris; Martin Neary, organ): (i) TOSELLI: *Serenata.* GLOVER: *Rose of Tralee.* WILLIAMS: *My little Welsh home.* SANDERSON: *Until.* BOUGHTON: *The Immortal Hour: Faery song.* CLAY: *I'll sing thee songs of Araby.* JACOBS-BOND: *A perfect day.* WOODFORDE-FINDEN: *Kashmiri song.* LESLIE: *Annabelle Lee.* D'HARDELOT: *Because.* RASBACH: *Trees.* MARSHALL: *I hear you calling me.* PURCELL, E.: *Passing by.* HAYDN WOOD: *Roses of Picardy.* MURRAY: *I'll walk beside you.* BRAHE: *Bless this house.* (ii) SULLIVAN: *The lost chord.* GOUNOD: *O divine Redeemer.* PARRY: *Jesu, lover of my soul.* NEGRO SPIRITUALS: *Steal away; Jericho.* DVOŘÁK (arr. Ditson): *Goin' home.* MALOTTE: *The Lord's Prayer.* ADAMS: *The holy city.* TCHAIKOVSKY: *The crown of roses.* LIDDLE: *How lovely are Thy dwellings.* SCHUBERT: *Ave Maria.* MONK: *Abide with me.*
(B)**(*)Decca KDPC 607/8.
'The world of sacred songs' (as section ii above).
(M)***Decca KCSP 219.

Stuart Burrows's headily beautiful tenor and fresh open manner could hardly be more apt for this collection of popular songs and ballads. His is a voice which takes naturally to being recorded, and the results can be warmly recommended to anyone tempted by the selection. Some may wish that the singing was more strongly characterized, but much of this repertoire responds to a lyrical presentation. The *Songs for you* collection consists of three recitals from different sources. The second tape, which is also available separately, concentrates on sacred music, with a backing by the Ambrosian Singers; it is very well recorded and excellently transferred throughout. The two recitals on the first tape have different accompanists. The recording on side one (John Constable accompanying) comes from the Oiseau-Lyre catalogue and is beautifully transferred. Side two (with Eurfryn John), like the sacred music, originated on the Delysé label and is a stereo transcription of mono, with a degree of edginess on the voice at times.

'Great Welsh songs' (with John Constable, piano): songs by HUGHES; LEWIS; NICHOLAS; WILLIAMS; HENRY; DAVIES; Joseph PARRY; Bradwen JONES; and traditional.

**Enigma K 453559.

Six of the songs presented here are Victorian in origin, ballads strong in drama and much favoured at concerts and Eisteddfods along with the traditional material. It was against this background that Joseph Parry, R. S. Hughes, John Henry, and William Davies composed their rather more sophisticated music. This recital admirably spans the whole range, and Stuart Burrows is suitably robust or gently lyrical by turns. He is well recorded, although the sound has not the bloom of the best of the Decca set above; the transfer is clear and clean. John Constable accompanies attentively.

Caballé, Montserrat (soprano)

Arias (with Barcelona SO, Gatto or Guadagno) from: VERDI: *Macbeth; Il Trovatore.* MASCAGNI: *Cavalleria Rusticana.* PUCCINI: *Turandot.* CATALANI: *La Wally.* PONCHIELLI: *La Gioconda.* GIORDANO: *Andrea Chénier.*

**(*)Decca KSXC 6825 [Lon. 5-26497].

Caballé produces much beautiful singing, but with slack accompaniments the overall results are variable. Challenged by the weighty roles of Lady Macbeth and Turandot, Caballé rises superbly,

both in vocal terms and in projecting the words; Leonora in *Trovatore* provides ideal material for her, and though in the other items the voice is at times under obvious stress, this is an impressive recital. The tape transfer is admirably clear and offers natural vocal timbre and good presence. Although the level is high, there is seldom any hint of peakiness, and there are good transients and truthful colour.

Callas, Maria (soprano)

'The unreleased recordings': VERDI: *Il Corsaro: Egli non riede ancor . . . Non so le tetre immagini; Ne sulla terra . . . Vola talor dal carcere. Il Trovatore: Tacea la notte placida . . . Di tale amor. Un Ballo in maschera: Morrò, ma prima in grazia.* BELLINI: *La Sonnambula: Compagne, teneri amici . . . Come per me serena; Ah, se una . . . Ah, non credea mirarti.*

***HMV TC-ASD 3535.

The fear was that a collection of Maria Callas's unreleased recordings would include items that never appeared because of all-too-obvious vocal shortcomings (it is common knowledge that right at the end of her career Callas made duet recordings which have never been released). In fact every one of these items is richly enjoyable. The solos from *Sonnambula* were recorded as early as 1955 with Callas in her prime, if anything more relaxed than in her performances on the complete set of 1957; but comparing this (and the *Ballo* aria) with Callas's singing in complete sets, the remarkable thing is the total consistency: most details are identical. Best of all – because most revealing – are the two arias from *Il Corsaro*, recorded as late as 1969, showing the vocal technique at its most assured (particularly in legato phrasing) and the artistry at its most commanding. The recordings vividly capture the unique voice, and the tape transfer is admirably smooth, catching the vocal timbre glowingly.

'Operatic recital': arias from: ROS-SINI: *Il Barbiere di Siviglia.* VERDI: *Macbeth; Don Carlo.* PUCCINI: *Tosca.* GLUCK: *Alceste.* BIZET: *Carmen* (with Nicolai Gedda, tenor). SAINT-SAËNS: *Samson et Dalila.* MASSENET: *Manon.*

(M)**HMV TC-EXE 74.

This medium-priced collection ranges wide over Callas's EMI recordings, from a gloriously fiery account of Rosina's aria from *Barbiere di Siviglia* (the force of her enunciation of the word *ma* ('but') has to be heard to be believed) to some of her relatively late performances of French items, with the *Carmen* excerpts taken from the complete set. All of this is vintage Callas and well worth collecting. The transfer (an early EMI issue) is made at a rather low level, and although the voice is treated kindly the orchestral detail lacks sparkle.

'La Divina' (*The art of Maria Callas*): arias from: MASCAGNI: *Cavalleria Rusticana.* CILEA: *Adriana Lecouvreur.* PUCCINI: *Manon Lescaut; La Bohème; Turandot; Madama Butterfly.* PON-CHIELLI: *La Gioconda.* CHERUBINI: *Medea.* SPONTINI: *La Vestale.* MAS-SENET: *Le Cid; Werther.* ROSSINI: *Il Barbiere di Siviglia.* BELLINI: *La Sonnambula; I Puritani; Norma; Il Pirata.* MEYERBEER: *Dinorah.* L-LIBES: *Lakmé.* THOMAS: *Hamlet.* DONIZETTI: *Lucia di Lammermoor.* VERDI: *Rigoletto; I Vespri siciliani; Ernani; Don Carlo; Nabucco; Un Ballo in maschera; Attila; Macbeth; Il Trovatore.*

*(**)HMV TC-SLS 5057.

So generous a selection from the recordings of Maria Callas must inevitably bring up much exciting material, and no admirer of the singer should be without this set; but a serious shortcoming is the absence of information on the times and places of the recordings, particularly when the dates of copyright given are downright misleading. And the order of the items is by genre, which makes it still more difficult for the non-specialist to fathom which vintage of Callas recording he is listening to. But the wonders of vocal imagination here far exceed any frustrations: each side, indeed every item, brings memorable moments totally unique to Callas. The tape transfer is well managed throughout the first two tapes, the sound clear and vivid. But on side five (the Mad scene from *Il Pirata*) the level rises and the sound becomes fierce, with bad peaking and roughness at climaxes; and throughout the last two sides the vocal quality is shrill.

'Maria Callas album': arias from: BELLINI: *Norma; I Puritani; La Sonnambula.* ROSSINI: *Il Barbiere di Siviglia; Il Turco in Italia.* PUCCINI: *Manon Lescaut; Turandot; Gianni Schicchi; Madama Butterfly; La Bohème* (with Giuseppe di Stefano, tenor); *Tosca.* MASSENET: *Manon.* VERDI: *La Forza del destino; Rigoletto; Aïda; Macbeth; Il Trovatore; Un Ballo in maschera.* LEON-CAVALLO: *I Pagliacci.* DONIZETTI: *Lucia di Lammermoor.* GLUCK: *Alceste.* BIZET: *Carmen.* MASCAGNI: *Cavalleria Rusticana.* SAINT-SAËNS: *Samson et Dalila.*

**(*)HMV TC-SLS 5104.

Most of the twenty-four items in this superb collection date from the mid-fifties, when Maria Callas was at the very peak of her formidable powers. The majority come from the complete sets she recorded with such conductors as Serafin and Karajan, in London or at La Scala, but the shrewdness of the choice is illustrated by the selection of Rosina's *Una voce poco fa* in the more sharply characterful and sparkling version from

Callas's 1954 recital and not from her complete set of *Barbiere*. Dates and recording venues are meticulously given, with full texts and an essay on Callas, and the booklet is beautifully printed in clear, readable type. The stereo transcriptions (many of these recordings come from mono originals) catch the voice well and the transfers are bright and clear, but (especially on the second tape) there is a degree of edginess. However, the level has been well calculated to avoid blasting, with only a hint of peaking at times. Do not judge the sound by the opening *Casta diva* with its fuzzy chorus.

Cambridge Consort, Cohen

'Songs of a traveling apprentice' (*A musical entertainment from Germany, Flanders and Italy, c. 1500*): music by: HOFHAYMER; ISAAC; JOSQUIN DES PRÉS; AGRICOLA; CARA; FRANCESCO DA MILANO; FORSTER; LEONHARD VON LANGENAU; SENFL; LEMLIN; and anonymous composers.

*(*) Advent D 1023 (see p. xxiii) [id.].

This recital sets out to re-create the kind of entertainment an adventurous traveller might have heard while wandering through Europe at the turn of the sixteenth century. It ranges from Hofhaymer to Josquin, from simple to relatively sophisticated secular music. The performances by the Cambridge Consort under Joel Cohen are scholarly enough but somewhat joyless, though this overall impression may well be enhanced by the unrelieved uniformity of the level of the recorded sound. The balance is somewhat forward, so that there is relatively little sense of depth and ambience. The quality itself is clean and clear.

Carreras, José (tenor)

'Be my love' (with ECO, Benzi): LARA: *Granada*. TOSTI: *Malia*. BIXIO: *Parlami d'amore*. DE CURTIS: *Non ti scorda; Ti voglio tanto bene*. CARDILLO: *Core 'ngrato*. BRODSZKY: *Be my love*. BUZZI-PECCIA: *Lolita*. CASTALDON: *Musica proibita*. LEHÁR: *The Land of Smiles: Dein is mein ganzes Herz* (*You are my heart's delight*).

**(*)Philips 7300 707.

José Carreras here joins the cohort of celebrated tenors who have attempted to storm the profitable middle-of-the-road market, and he is no better and no worse than most. The presentation is attractive, with sumptuous accompaniments recorded in an agreeable, reverberant acoustic. The arrangements are generally better than usual, and although, predictably, there are moments of sentimentality, the opening *Granada* and the famous *You are my heart's delight* come off well. The recording has a wide dynamic range and it is well encompassed by the transfer, which is made at quite a high level. The treble is marginally less open than on the LP, but otherwise the sound is rich and well balanced.

Caruso, Enrico (tenor)

'Legendary performer' (recordings processed by digital computer): arias from: LEONCAVALLO: *I Pagliacci*. PUCCINI: *Tosca*. VERDI: *Rigoletto; Aïda; Il Trovatore*. MEYERBEER: *L'Africana*. HALÉVY: *La Juive*. PONCHIELLI: *La Gioconda*. BIZET: *Carmen*. GOUNOD: *Faust*. DONIZETTI: *L'Elisir d'amore*. FLOTOW: *Martha*. HANDEL: *Xerxes*.

**(*)RCA RK 11749.

These transfers of pre-electric recordings made by the legendary Caruso were produced through an exceedingly laborious computer process that sought to eliminate the unnatural resonances of the acoustic recording horn, and though in some ways they still have not the freshness of the original 78 discs when reproduced in ideal conditions, there is no doubt of their superiority to previous transfers. The illusion of presence is striking; one can imagine far more easily than usual what it was actually like to hear the great tenor, and the selection of items is excellent. Unfortunately on cassette the sound has not quite the open quality which makes the LP so impressive, but the voice is smoothly caught.

Chiara, Maria (soprano)

'*Presenting Maria Chiara*' (with Vienna Volksoper Orch., Santi): arias from: DONIZETTI: *Anna Bolena*. BELLINI: *I Puritani*. VERDI: *Aïda*. BOITO: *Mefistofele*. PUCCINI: *La Bohème; Suor Angelica; Manon Lescaut; Turandot*. MASCAGNI: *Lodoletta*.

**(*) Decca KSXC 6548.

Few if any début recitals can equal this satisfying anthology in vocal beauty and freshness. One remembers in particular Tebaldi's early mono collection on LP (LXT 2507) from the early fifties: Maria Chiara certainly recalls the rich sweetness of the youthful Tebaldi, but here the artistic personality is already fuller, the sense of line and control of phrase pointing the way to early maturity. The limpid flexibility and bloom of the voice are readily apparent in the opening Donizetti and Bellini arias, and so are the floating quality of the line and the exquisitely free *pianissimo;* but these features are matched by the *legato* phrasing in *O patria mia* and the frisson created by the sudden darkening of tone at the cadence of the excerpt from *Mefistofele*. Mimi is portrayed with poignancy, but the highlight of side two is the ravishing account of the little-known aria from *Lodoletta*. The recording throughout is Decca's best and it is a great pity that the transfer level is marginally too high; while the sound is vivid, there is some peaking of the voice at climaxes.

Choral music

'*Great choral classics*' (with (i) South German Madrigal Choir, Gönnenwein; (ii) New Philharmonia Chorus, Frühbeck de Burgos; (iii) Ambrosian Singers, Mackerras; (iv; v) Chœurs René Duclos, cond. (iv) Cluytens, (v) Hartemann; (vi) Philharmonia Chorus, Giulini; (vii) King's College Choir, Willcocks; (viii) Hallé and Sheffield Choirs, Barbirolli; (ix) French Radio Chorus, Prêtre): (i) BACH: *St Matthew Passion: O Haupt voll Blut und Wunden*. (ii) MOZART: *Requiem, K.626: Dies irae*. (iii) HANDEL: *Messiah: For unto us a child is born*. (ii) MENDELSSOHN: *Elijah: And then shall your light break forth*. (iv) BERLIOZ: *L'Enfance du Christ: Shepherds' chorus*. (v) GOUNOD: *Messe solennelle Sainte Cécile: Domine salvum*. (vi) VERDI: *Requiem: Sanctus*. (vii) FAURÉ: *Requiem: Sanctus*. (viii) ELGAR: *Dream of Gerontius: Praise to the holiest*. (vii) VAUGHAN WILLIAMS: *Mass in G minor: Kyrie*. (ix) POULENC: *Gloria in G: Gloria in excelsis*.

(M)**HMV TC-MCS 14.

Considering the variety of sources, the sound on side one of our copy of this cassette (Bach, Handel, Poulenc, Mendelssohn, Berlioz, Saint-Saëns) was good, the level high. But on side two there was some lack of refinement, notably in the Fauré and Elgar excerpts. But the *Sanctus* from Verdi's *Requiem* seems rather clearer here than on the transfer of the complete set from which it comes, although the sound is not entirely free. Such a collection may well tempt purchasers to explore further, but, perversely, not all the performances from which these excerpts are taken are available on tape.

Christoff, Boris (bass)

'*Music from the Slavonic Orthodox Liturgy*' (with Alexander Nevsky Cathedral Choir, Sofia, Konstantinov) by CHESNOKOV; ZINOVIEV; KOCHETOV; HRISTOV; DINEV; STROUMSKI; LYUBIMOV; BORTNYANSKI.

***HMV TC-ASD 3513.

Boris Christoff's glorious voice is superbly caught in these items stemming directly from the traditions of the Russian Orthodox Church. The vividly atmospheric recording matches the evocative music, and the warmly reverberant sound is richly caught in the transfer, which rarely slips from its general refinement.

'*The 1949–52 recordings*'; excerpts from: MUSSORGSKY: *Boris Godunov; Khovantschina.* GLINKA: *A Life for the Tsar.* TCHAIKOVSKY: *Eugene Onegin.* RIMSKY-KORSAKOV: *Sadko; The Invisible City of Kitezh.* GLUCK: *Iphigenia in Aulis.* MOZART: *Don Giovanni.* VERDI: *Ernani; I Vespri siciliani; Don Carlo.* BOITO: *Mefistofele.* BORODIN: *Prince Igor. Russian songs; songs by* MUSSORGSKY *and* BORODIN.

(M)***HMV TC-RLS 735.

The magnetic quality of Christoff's singing is instantly established in the opening item, a magnificent recording of the big solo from *A Life for the Tsar*, previously unpublished; and from then on the compulsion of the singer's artistry as well as the vivid individuality of his bass timbres make this a total portrait, not just a collection of items. There are eleven other previously unpublished recordings, all of them valuable, and most of the rest has been out of the catalogue for years. The transcriptions from the original 78s have been well managed, and the cassette transfer has plenty of life and

presence, although in some of the earliest recordings there is a degree of edge on the voice.

'*Russian romances and folk songs*' (with Russian Balalaika Orch., Liakoff): *Alas fate . . . O bitter fate. Grief, affliction, all hope gone. O pain, pass away. The nightingale. Natasha. Masha may not go down to the river. I am grieved. Two guitars. Do not touch me. How the wind howls. Where the eternal snow. Come, my guitar.*

**DG 3336 115 [id.].

Admirers of Christoff will find here that the voice turns readily from drama to characteristic Russian melancholy. The accompaniments are varied, using not only balalaikas but also a small instrumental group (featuring flute and cor anglais) and the piano (Gesine Tiefuhr). The recording balance is forward, so the voice projects well and the accompanying detail is clear.

Domingo, Placido (tenor)

'*Be my love*' (with LSO, Loges; Marcel Peters, piano): LEHÁR: *The Land of Smiles: Dein ist mein ganzes Herz.* Popular and Neapolitan songs.

*(*)DG 3300 700.

This collection does not show Domingo at his best. The performances are lusty and the recording is not very refined, the voice projected forward and the whole presentation without subtlety. The transfer is vivid but coarse.

Early Music Consort of London, Munrow (see also under Concerts)

'*Monteverdi's contemporaries*': vocal and instrumental music by MAINERIO; GUAMI; LAPPI; PRIOLI;

PORTA; BUSATTI; DONATI; D'INDIA; GRANDI.
**HMV TC-ASD 3393.

Contemporaries of Monteverdi but not associates, and these two sides – one of instrumental music, one of church music – give a fair idea of the range of expression of the composers of the time. The extraordinary motet *O vos omnes* by Grandi, for example, has amazing chromaticisms. David Munrow's direction is characteristically spirited, particularly in the instrumental items. It is a pity that on tape the opening instrumental piece by Mainerio on side one offers unrefined sound, as for the most part the quality is good in the instrumental section and often very good in the vocal music on side two, where the resonant acoustic is well managed. The lack of upper range is more noticeable on side one.

'Late 14th-century avant-garde': ballades, virelai, motets, canons, rondeaux and dances by VAILLANT; PYKINI; CASERTA; PERUSIO; HASPROIS; GRIMACE; FRANCISCUS; BORLET; SOLAGE; MERUCO; and anonymous composers.
**(*)HMV TC-ASD 3621.

This collection, taken from a three-disc album called *The art of courtly love* (not available on cassette), leavens the fourteenth-century ballades and virelai with instrumental rondeaux and dance music. The programme is primarily vocal, however, and as its melodic structure is rather bare and austere, it will not be to all tastes. But the music is presented with characteristic vitality and there are some piquant sounds, including crumhorns, shawms, citole, korthold, bass rebec, and other instrumental exotica. The closing item, the anonymous virelai *Restoés, restoés*, has irresistible sparkle, and the adventurous will find that much of the programme will reward perseverance. The recording is very good indeed and the transfer immaculate.

Evans, Wynford (tenor)

'To entertain the stealth of love' (with Carl Shavitz, lute; Peter Vel, viola da gamba): *Songs and ayres* by DOWLAND; FERRABOSCO; CAMPION; JONES; ROSSETER; BARTLETT.
**Enigma K 453535.

With one side devoted to a selection of Dowland's finest songs, the other to the younger Ferrabosco's Ben Jonson settings as well as other items, this makes an attractive recital, not always as lively in performance as it might be, but always tasteful and sensitive. The close recording is not entirely kind to the voice, but the balance with the lute is realistic. However, the amount of available light and shade is reduced by the microphone placing. The quality of the transfer is excellent.

'Mirror of love' (with Carl Shavitz, lute; Peter Vel, viola da gamba): songs by DOWLAND; DANYEL; CORKINE; ATTLEY; JONES; CAMPION.
*(*)Enigma K 453562.

As in his other Enigma collection of Elizabethan music, Wynford Evans proves a tasteful and sweet-toned tenor but his interpretations are disappointingly colourless, cautious even. The music requires more positive characterization if its springing vitality is to come over to the modern listener. The somewhat undifferentiated recording tends to exaggerate this shortcoming, although the transfer is well managed.

Ferrier, Kathleen (contralto)

'Folksongs and songs by Roger Quilter': Folksongs: *Ma bonny lad. The keel row. Blow the wind southerly. I have a bonnet trimmed with blue. My boy Willie. I know where I'm going. The fidgety bairn. I will walk with my love. Ca' the yowes. O waly waly. Willow willow. Stuttering lovers.*

Have you seen but a whyte lillie grow? Ye banks and braes. Drink to me only. Down by the Sally Gardens. The lover's curse. QUILTER: *Now sleeps the crimson petal; The fair house of joy; To daisies; Over the mountains.*

(M)***Decca KACC 309.

Kathleen Ferrier's freshness and warmth in this repertoire, which she obviously loved, make this an indispensable recital, and the transfers are of excellent quality, the voice open with a natural bloom on it. This compares well with the disc, and considering the source of the orignals there is miraculously little background noise.

'The world of Kathleen Ferrier': TRAD.: *Blow the wind southerly; The keel row; Ma bonny lad; Kitty my love.* BRIDGE: *Go not happy day.* arr. BRITTEN: *Come you not from Newcastle.* SCHUBERT: *An die Musik; Der Musensohn.* BRAHMS: *Sapphische Ode.* JENSEN: *Altar.* MAHLER: *Rückert Lieder: Um Mitternacht.* HANDEL: *Rodelinda: Art thou troubled? Messiah: He was despised.* GLUCK: *Orfeo: Che puro ciel; Che farò.* BACH: *St Matthew Passion: Have mercy, Lord.* GRÜBER: *Silent night.*

(M)**(*)Decca KCSP 172.

This selection admirably shows Kathleen Ferrier's range, and most of her famous recordings are here (though not, surprisingly, *O rest in the Lord*). It will be treasured especially for her spoken introduction to the Jensen song (taken from a BBC broadcast), which she then sings exquisitely. The transfers are vivid and made at a high level; they seem almost to accentuate the faults of the originals from which they are taken (mostly 78 r.p.m discs), with clicks and background noises and occasional blasting. But some items,

including the Bach, Handel and Mahler, are unblemished.

Ghiaurov, Nicolai (bass)

Russian songs (with Zlatina Ghiaurov, piano): TCHAIKOVSKY: *None but the lonely heart; Not a word, O my love; Don Juan's serenade; It was in the early spring; Mid the noisy stir of the ball; I bless you, woods.* BORODIN: *From the shores of your far-off native land.* GLINKA: *Midnight review.* RUBINSTEIN: *Melody.* DARGOMIZHSKY: *The worm; Nocturnal breeze; The old corporal.*

**Decca KSXC 6530.

This is a fascinating recital of Russian songs, many of them not otherwise available in recordings; but Ghiaurov is not at his most imaginative, nor is the voice well projected, except in some of the Tchaikovsky songs. Such music needs more of an illusion of live performance. The recording is excellent.

'Popular Russian songs' (with Kaval Chorus and Orch., Margaritov): *The cliff. Volga boatmen. Dubinushka. Bandura. Styen'ka Razin. Along Petersburg Street. In the dark forest. Dark eyes. Dear little knight. Twelve brigands. Farewell joy.*

***Decca KSXC 6659.

These are all items originally made famous outside Russia by the greatest of all Russian basses, Chaliapin, but Nicolai Ghiaurov with his gloriously dark tone and fine projection is almost as persuasive. A fascinating, individual collection very well recorded. The transfer to tape has been admirably managed, with excellent detail and atmosphere. The dynamic range is well demonstrated by the slow choral crescendo in the famous *Volga boatmen* song.

791

Gigli, Beniamino (tenor)

'The best of Gigli': BIZET: *Agnus Dei.* Arias from LEONCAVALLO: *I Pagliacci.* VERDI: *Rigoletto; Aïda.* PUCCINI: *Tosca; La Bohème.* DONIZETTI: *L'Elisir d'amore.* MASSENET: *Manon.* BIZET: *Carmen; Les Pêcheurs de perles.* HANDEL: *Xerxes.* GOUNOD: *Faust.*

***HMV TC-ALP 1681.

For most collectors this single-tape anthology will make an ideal representation of Gigli's art. The recordings all date from the thirties and are of excellent quality. In every item his individuality is clear, buoyant and charming, using his unique golden tone (never more telling than in the Donizetti and Puccini items) with cavalier freedom. There are stylistic points to query, but the natural magnetism is consistently compelling. The recording shows a somewhat limited top, but this affects the orchestral accompaniments rather than impairing the freshness of the vocal quality. The transfers are well managed, at a generally high level: the *Aïda* aria (*Ritorna vincitor*), for instance, has striking presence. There are excellent notes giving the recording dates and relating the music to Gigli's career.

'Sacred songs and favourite ballads': HANDEL: *Xerxes: Ombra mai fù* (*Largo*). *Ave Maria* settings by SCHUBERT; BACH–GOUNOD; GIBILARO. SCHUBERT: *Serenade.* BIZET: *Agnus Dei.* FRANCK: *Panis angelicus.* SULLIVAN: *The lost chord.* YRADIER: *La Paloma.* LEONCAVALLO: *Mattinata.* DENZA: *Occhi di fata.* ROSSINI: *La Danza.* MARTINI: *Plaisir d'amour.* MURRAY: *I'll walk beside you.* TOSTI: *Goodbye.*

(M)**(*)HMV TC-HLM 7019.

Good taste was never Gigli's strong suit, but his way with these trifles is nothing if not winsome, with the pouting manner outrageously but compellingly used. Even at his least defensible – and the intrusive aitches in Schubert's *Ave Maria* hardly improve the music's line – Gigli emerges as a major, totally unmistakable artist. His passionate advocacy of Bizet's *Agnus Dei* (which uses a tune from *L'Arlésienne*) completely triumphs over the rather woolly recording of the accompanying chorus, while Rossini's *La Danza* has a memorable sparkle. The two closing ballads are sung in English: *I'll walk beside you* has a gloriously honeyed closing cadence. The recordings date from the thirties, except Schubert's *Ave Maria*, which comes from 1947. The tape transfer has excellent clarity and presence and there is excellent documentation.

'The art of Gigli' (1918–46): religious arias; songs; arias and duets from: PONCHIELLI: *La Gioconda.* GIORDANO: Fedora. MASCAGNI: *Cavalleria Rusticana; Lodoletta; L'Amico Fritz; Isabeau.* LEONCAVALLO: *I Pagliacci.* MASSENET: *Manon; Werther.* DONIZETTI: *L'Elisir d'amore; La Favorita.* PUCCINI: *Tosca; La Bohème; Manon Lescaut.* BIZET: *Carmen.* VERDI: *Aïda; Il Trovatore.* MOZART: *Don Giovanni.* CILEA: *L'Arlesiana.* HALÉVY: *La Juive.* LALO: *Le Roi d'Ys.* BOITO: *Mefistofele.* GOUNOD: *Faust.*

(M)***HMV TC-RLS 729.

In the rich generation of Italian tenors following Caruso, Gigli stood out as the most honey-toned and positive of character. He was a natural star, and though his musical taste was not impeccable this wide-ranging selection from his recordings for HMV – missing out an important period in the late twenties – consistently reveals that star quality. It is fascinating to compare early and late recordings, but the marvel is the voice's consistency. The recording is smooth, but in general these transfers have too little top, robbing the voice of some of its brightness. However, the tape transfers are of admirably consistent quality (some of the recordings made in the forties sound delectably creamy), and the sound balance is if anything more convincing on tape than on disc. The three cassettes are well filled and there is a clearly printed booklet.

'The art of Gigli', Vol. 2 (1947–55): songs; ballads; arias from operettas and from CESTI: *Orontea.* MONTE-VERDI: *Arianna.* ALFANO: *Don Juan de Mantua.* MASCAGNI: *L'Amico Fritz.* HANDEL: *Atalanta.* GIORDA-NO: *Marcella.* DONIZETTI: *L'Elisir d'amore.* PUCCINI: *Turandot.* Duets (with Rina Gigli) from: VERDI: *Otello.* MASCAGNI: *L'Amico Fritz.* BOITO: *Mefistofele.*

(M)**(*)HMV TC-RLS 732.

It would be only too easy to under-estimate the worth of this additional box of Gigli recordings. The second and third tapes contain a great deal of lightweight material – Neapolitan songs, and items like *Mother Machree* and *The Rosary* which are of very limited musical interest. But Gigli sang this material with inimit-able style: his *Funiculi, funicula,* for in-stance, has irresistible zest, and although the voice had darkened by the mid-fifties, surprisingly often the bloom comes back to give a frisson of pleasure. The set opens with a series of operatic recordings made in 1947–9 (Gigli already in his late fifties) and the voice shows an astonish-ing freshness: the late account of *Nessun dorma* (1949) has undoubted interest alongside the 1951 recordings of duets with his daughter. Among the treasures here is Gigli's very last session, recorded in March 1955 at the Kingsway Hall in experimental stereo, a touching close to a great career. Perhaps this is a box more for Gigli devotees than the general collec-tor, but lovers of Italian popular song will find much to enjoy, particularly as

the sound is so consistently good, open and clear at the top, and often with con-vincing orchestral quality too. The trans-fers to tape are first-class, vivid and kind to the voice.

Gobbi, Tito (bar.)

'The art of Tito Gobbi': including Italian songs; songs; ballads; arias from: CILEA: *L'Arlesiana.* PUCCINI: *La Fanciulla del West.* VERDI: *Don Carlos; Otello; La Forza del destino; Macbeth; Un Ballo in maschera; Nabucco.* MOZART: *Le Nozze di Figaro.* DONIZETTI: *L'Elisir d'am-ore.* BERLIOZ: *La Damnation de Faust.* ROSSINI: *William Tell.*

(M)***HMV TC-RLS 738.

This magnificent collection includes Gobbi recordings from three decades – the early (1942) recordings made in Italy, English-made recordings from the late forties and mid-fifties, and a 1965 collec-tion of Italian songs. All are fascinating. Jack Rance's *arioso* from *Fanciulla del West* is included both in the youthful 1942 version and in a 1955 version, never previously issued, which shows how the voice had grown darker and richer and the artistry enormously intensified. Of the early recordings the most valuable is of the Death of Rodrigo from *Don Carlos,* a performance as compelling in its way as the classic one in the later complete re-cording. And although there is some roughness of tone and expression in places, Gobbi consistently claims atten-tion as the most characterful and mag-netic of dramatic baritones of his period. The transcriptions from 78s are well managed; some of the earliest recordings display a degree of shallowness, and the voice is not always given the fullest bloom, but the transfers to tape have plenty of life and presence.

Gomez, Jill (soprano)

'Spanish songs' (with John Const-able, piano): GRANADOS: *Tonadillas*

al estilo antiguo, Nos. 1–6. TURINA: *Poema en forma de canciones, Op. 19.* FALLA: *Trois mélodies; Siete cançiones populares españolas.*

(M)**(*)Saga CA 5409.

Jill Gomez's delectable recital of Spanish songs, including Falla's *Seven Spanish popular songs*, is one of the highlights of the Saga catalogue. The transfer is more than acceptable: although there is not the fullest range, the sound is reasonably clear, the voice well caught, while the plumminess in the piano timbre responds to a bass cut. LP pressings of this issue were seldom silent-surfaced and many will find the cassette preferable by far.

Gueden, Hilde (soprano)

'The world of operetta' (with Vienna State Opera Chorus and Orch., Schönherr): excerpts from: STRAUSS, Johann, Jnr: *Wiener Blut; Die Fledermaus; Die Tänzerin Fanny Elssler.* KREISLER: *Sissy.* KÁLMÁN: *Gräfin Mariza.* STRAUS: *The Chocolate Soldier; Rund um die Liebe; Ein Walzertraume.* FALL: *Madame Pompadour; The Dollar Princess.* ASCHER: *Hoheit tanzt Walzer.* ZIEHRER: *Der Schätzmeister.* LEHÁR: *Der Zarewitsch; Schön ist die Welt; The Merry Widow; Zigeunerliebe.*

(M)** Decca KCSP 52.

Hilde Gueden was in vivacious form when these recordings were made, and the programme includes, alongside favourites, many little-known excerpts from operettas long forgotten in this country. The recording is basically an early mono one, and although the engineers have smoothed out the treble the orchestral sound is obviously dated at the opening. But the vocal quality is unimpaired and has plenty of life, especially on side two. In many ways the cassette sound is more successful than the disc in

disguising the fact that the stereo is simulated and has less body than one expects in a modern recording.

Hammond, Joan (soprano), Charles Craig (tenor)

'Love duets' (sung in English; with RPO, Tausky): PUCCINI: *La Bohème: Your tiny hand is frozen; They call me Mimi; Lovely maid in the moonlight. Tosca: Mario, Mario. Madama Butterfly: Ah, love me a little.* GOUNOD: *Faust: The hour is late.* VERDI: *Aïda. Nile scene.*

(M) **(*) HMV Greensleeve TC-ESD 7033.

Joan Hammond and Charles Craig, both in their vocal prime when they recorded these duets, were artists seriously neglected by the record companies. Another area of neglect was the performance of opera in English, and both those points make this a valuable collection. Moreover the artists are well caught by the microphone, and their brimming sincerity, coupled with warm expressiveness, makes for consistently enjoyable performances of these well-chosen items. The transfers are made at a comparatively high level, and the voices have fine presence. There is a touch of edginess too, but most of this can be smoothed. In the excerpt from *Madam Butterfly* the climaxes lose the last degree of refinement, but this is not serious.

Harvey, Frederick (bar.)

'Songs of land and sea' (with (i) Royal Marines Band, Dunn; (ii) Irish Guards Band, Jaeger; (iii) Philharmonia Orch., Weldon; (iv) Gerald Moore, piano): (i) PHILLIPS: *The fishermen of England.* STANFORD: *3 Songs of the Sea.* SANDERSON: *Up from Somerset;* (ii) *Drake goes west;* (iii) *Devonshire cream and cider.* (i) GERMAN: *Glorious Devon;*

(ii) *Merrie England: The yeomen of England.* KEEL: *Trade winds.* LONGSTAFFE: *When the sergeant-major's on parade.* (iii) PEEL: *In summertime on Bredon.* (iv) ELGAR: *Shepherd's song.* VAUGHAN WILLIAMS: *Silent noon.* BUTTERWORTH: *A Shropshire Lad: Loveliest of trees.* GURNEY: *I will go with my father a-ploughing.* (iii) TRAD.: *David of the White Rock; Blow the wind southerly;* (arr. Kennedy-Fraser) *Eriskay love lilt.*
(M)***HMV Greensleeve TC-ESD 7054.

One of the finest recitals of its kind ever issued, this entertaining collection is not only generous but is given added interest by the variety of the accompaniments. No one has ever recorded Stanford's vigorous *Sea Songs* with more panache or natural sympathy, and the folksy Devon ballads are no less stimulating. *When the sergeant-major's on parade* has a splendid twinkling swagger, and the lyrical settings which form the closing part of the recital are beautifully sung. The acoustic has just the right degree of resonance to give the voice warmth and bloom, and the band accompaniments have plenty of sonority. Just occasionally in the items with piano (near the end) the resonance clouds the focus marginally, but for the most part the transfer here is very good indeed. Highly recommended.

Hill, Martyn (tenor)

'*French romantic songs*' (with John Constable, piano): MASSENET: *Chant provençal; Sérénade d'automne; Nuit d'Espagne; Stances; Un adieu; Vous aimerez demain; Élégie.* HAHN: *D'une prison; Mai; L'Heure exquise; Si mes vers avaient des ailes; Le rossignol des lilas; Offrande; Paysage.* FAURÉ: *Chanson d'amour; Au*
bord de l'eau; Nell; Sylvie; Clair de lune; Lydia; Après un rêve.*
(M)***Saga CA 5419.

Martyn Hill is best-known for his singing of early music but has latterly extended his repertory, and his pleasing, heady tenor tone admirably suits these favourite French songs. The style is not always completely idiomatic, but with sensitive accompaniment by John Constable this makes a valuable medium priced issue. The transfer is not made at a very ambitious level, but the voice is naturally caught and the balance with the piano is realistic. This is one of Saga's very best tapes.

Holm, Renate (soprano), Werner Krenn (tenor)

'*Wine, women and song*' (with Vienna Volksoper Orch., Paulik): arias from: STRAUSS, Johann, Jnr: *Der Zigeunerbaron; Eine Nacht in Venedig.* MILLÖCKER: *Der Bettelstudent.* SUPPÉ: *Boccaccio.* LEHÁR: *The Merry Widow; The Land of Smiles; Schön ist die Welt; Paganini; Der Zarewitsch; Der Graf von Luxemburg; The Circus Princess.* DOSTAL: *Clivia; Die ungarische Hochzeit.* KÜNNEKE: *Cousin from Nowhere.* KATTNIGG: *Bel Ami; Maidens from the Rhine.* ZERNIK: *Chi sa?* (song).
(B)***Decca KDPC 595/6.

Renate Holm and Werner Krenn make an excellent partnership in this repertoire; their voices have plenty of individual character yet blend well together. Much of the singing is warmly beautiful, and it is sometimes vivacious; but the programme was chosen to include rather too much lyrical music of a similar style. This was originally issued on Decca's top-priced LP label, and it is a pity that the recording budget was not extended to include a chorus and feature more contrasting lively numbers. Even so, this is a valuable and comprehensive selection, and on a pair of cassettes it can easily be dipped into rather than taken all at once. The transfer is of demonstration quality, giving a lovely bloom to the voices and sparkle and warmth to the orchestra. The effect is highly beguiling.

'Italian opera festival'

With Joan Sutherland, Renata Tebaldi, Zinka Milanov, Teresa Berganza, Giulietta Simionato, Carlo Bergonzi, Luciano Pavarotti, Mario del Monaco, Giuseppe di Stefano, Ettore Bastianini, Fernando Corena, Geraint Evans, George London, Cesare Siepi: excerpts from: ROSSINI: *La Gazza ladra* (*overture*); *Il Barbiere di Siviglia; L'Italiana in Algeri.* BELLINI: *Norma.* DONIZETTI: *L'Elisir d'amore; Lucia di Lammermoor.* VERDI: *Nabucco; Rigoletto; Il Trovatore; La Traviata; La Forza del destino; Aïda; Otello.* BOITO: *Mefistofele.* PONCHIELLI: *La Gioconda.* LEONCAVALLO: *I Pagliacci.* MASCAGNI: *Cavalleria Rusticana.* CILEA: *L'Arlesiana.* GIORDANO: *Andrea Chénier.* PUCCINI: *La Bohème; Madama Butterfly; Turandot; Tosca.*

(M) ** Decca Ace of Diamonds KGOCA 7013/5.

As a potted history of nineteenth-century Italian opera this three-tape anthology is well documented – the items in broad (though not exact) historical sequence, and with synopses of plots and translations of the excerpts. But the performances are rather a mixed bag, and the recordings too, besides varying greatly in level, also vary in quality, from the excellence of *Aïda* to the distinctly dated, plummy quality of the *Anvil chorus* from the early complete *Il Trovatore*. In fact the excerpts have obviously been chosen (sensibly enough) as characteristic favourites from each opera

rather than because they are jewels as performances. Thus the opening Rossini items tend to lack sparkle (although, apart from *Largo al factotum*, they are well recorded), and choices like the *Quartet* from *Rigoletto* and the *Cav.* and *Pag.* excerpts are hardly collector's items. However, there are some fine things here, notably the excerpts from *Lucia* (the *Sextet*, a tour de force), *Mefistofele* (an imaginative choice), the sumptuous Karajan *Aïda*, and *Madama Butterfly*, with Tebaldi and Bergonzi. The reverberation of the opening overture means the sound is not too clean, and the *Tosca* excerpt too is ill-focused; but generally the transfers are successful, especially on the second and third cassettes.

King's College Choir, Cambridge, Ledger

'Music for Holy Week' by LOTTI; HORSLEY; KING JOHN IV OF PORTUGAL; GIBBONS; WEBBE-MILLER; LEIGHTON; SHEPHERD; and traditional music. VICTORIA: *O vos omnes; Videte omnes populi.* LASSUS: *Tristis est anima mea.* TAVERNER: *Dum transisset sabbatum.*

***HMV TC-ASD 3450.

An admirable compilation, ranging widely from the music of Victoria, Lassus and Morley to more modern contributions. The recording has transferred well to tape, with sophistication of detail and no lack of overall refinement. The King's acoustic is not easy to capture with the smoothness that is achieved here.

'Carols for Christmas Eve' by WOODWARD; HOWELLS; WISHART; KIRKPATRICK; LEDGER; LEIGHTON; HADLEY; MENDELSSOHN; arrangements by VAUGHAN WILLIAMS; STAINER; PEARSALL; RUTTER; WILLCOCKS. TRAD.: *I saw three ships; O come all ye faithful.*

(***)HMV TC-CSD 3774.

The joyful opening of Woodward's *Up! Good Christian folk, and listen* is typical of this attractive concert, which gives a new freshness to many favourites by the refinement and expressive vigour of the singing. With seventeen items included this is excellent value, and one can only report sadly that the tape transfer has been too highly modulated and there is intermittent coarseness, although some of the quieter music is unaffected.

King's College Choir, Cambridge, Willcocks

'*The Psalms of David*': Nos. 122, 42, 43, 104, 61, 24, 121, 23, 46, 84, 15, 137, 147–50.
**(*)HMV TC-CSD 3656.

In pioneer days the early Christians took over the Psalter along with the Old Testament teachings from the Hebrew Temple, and the Psalms have always been an integral part of Anglican liturgy. Although they are called 'The Psalms of David' it has long been recognized that the original Hebrew collection (some 150 strong) was gathered together over a period of several hundred years, and the writings are from many different anonymous hands. The Anglican settings used on these recordings have offered their composers a fairly wide range of expressive potential, yet the music itself, perhaps because of the stylized metre and the ritual nature of its use, seldom approaches the depth and resonance which is found in the music of the great composers of the Roman Catholic faith, Palestrina, Victoria and so on. The King's College Choir, conducted by Sir David Willcocks from the organ, give an eloquent account of a cross-section of the Psalter on this tape; they are beautifully recorded, and the transfer is impeccably smooth.

'*Anthems from King's*': English cathedral anthems 1890–1940 (with James Lancelot, organ) by PARRY; BULLOCK; BAIRSTOW; LEY; NAYLOR; GARDINER; HARWOOD; STANFORD; BAINTON; WOOD; DARKE; HADLEY; HARRIS.
**HMV TC-CSD 3752.

An attractive and representative collection of English cathedral music from just before the turn of the century until about halfway through our own. A good deal of the writing is not very adventurous, harmonically speaking, but it is all effective and some of it is memorable. Highlights include Edward Bairstow's eloquent *Let all mortal flesh keep silence*, the fine Balfour Gardiner *Evening hymn* and Stanford's *Beati quorum via*. The last four items, by Charles Wood, Harold Darke, Patrick Hadley and William Harris, are here especially effective for being heard together, four diverse yet complementary settings that sum up the twentieth-century Anglican tradition rather well. The tape transfer is generally made at a low level but is otherwise of pleasing quality; only in the comparatively ambitious *I was glad* by Parry do the clarity and refinement of the recording slip.

'*The world of Christmas*': The first nowell. While shepherds watched. I saw three ships. Ding dong merrily on high. King Jesus hath a garden. In dulci jubilo. Unto us is born a son. O come all ye faithful. Away in a manger. O little town of Bethlehem. The holly and the ivy. God rest ye merry, gentlemen. See amid the winter's snow. Past three o'clock. MENDELSSOHN: *Hark the herald angels.*
(M)***Argo KCSPA 104.

The items in this cheap sampler of carols are taken from some of Argo's many fine recordings of King's College Choir, made over a dozen or so years. The annual carol service has after all become such a national institution that the choir's choice of carol directly influences fashion and popularity. The mixture here naturally concentrates on established favourites, all performed with the poise, point and refinement for which King's is famous, but one or two items, like *Past three o'clock*, are designed to get the listener inquiring further. No other carol collection can match it at the price. The tape transfer was an early Decca issue, and at first it suffered from roughness caused by the high level. However, current copies have cured this fault: the level remains high but the sound is now smoothly detailed, with plenty of atmosphere.

'The world of King's' (with soloists): VIVALDI: *Gloria:* excerpt. TALLIS: *Sancte Deus*. GIBBONS: *This is the record of John*. HANDEL: *Coronation anthem: Zadok the Priest*. BYRD: *Ave verum corpus*. SCHOLEFIELD: *The day Thou gavest*. BACH: *O Jesu so meek*. ALLEGRI: *Miserere (Psalm 51)*.

(M)**(*) Argo KCSPA 245.

This anthology is designed as a sampler of the King's style, but in its own right it makes an outstanding concert of Renaissance and baroque choral music. The resplendent opening of Vivaldi's *Gloria* is followed by the wonderful *Sancte Deus* of Tallis. The Gibbons verse anthem, however, is recorded with a curiously forward effect, so that the singing is too much on top of the listener. Side two opens with the familiar performance of *Zadok the Priest*; the beautiful flowing lines of Byrd's *Ave verum* make a perfectly calculated contrast, and after the short Bach part-song, the concert ends with the famous King's recording of Allegri's *Miserere*, with its soaring treble line marvellously sung by Master Roy Goodman. This superbly confident piece of singing, of almost unbelievable perfection, is alone worth the modest

price of the tape. The transfers are made at a high level and some machines may show a hint of strain at the opening of the Vivaldi, and in *Zadok the Priest* and the Gibbons, but for the most part the live immediacy of the sound is impressive.

'The world of Christmas music' (with (i) Andrew Davis or Simon Preston, organ; (ii) Hervey Alan, bass-bar., LSO): (i) *Once in Royal David's city*. DAVIES: *O little town of Bethlehem*. TRAD.: *Blessed be that maid Mary; Infant Holy; Gabriel's message; Sussex carol; Coventry carol; Shepherds in the field abiding*. ORDE: *Adam lay y-bounden*. arr. HOLST: *Lullay my liking*. DARKE: *In the bleak midwinter*. JOUBERT: *Torches*. (ii) VAUGHAN WILLIAMS: *Fantasia on Christmas carols*.

(M)** Decca KCSP 501.

The newest Argo reissue of Christmas music from King's is generously full and includes for a highlight on side two a superbly joyful performance of Vaughan Williams's *Fantasia on Christmas carols*. The sound is fresh and full here, but on side one, which contains the first eight items, the quality is less cleanly focused by the high-level transfer. The collection opens with the famous processional version of *Once in Royal David's city*. The choir is on top form throughout the programme.

'A festival of lessons and carols as sung on Christmas Eve, 1964' (with Andrew Davis, organ).

(M)*** Argo KCSP 528.

The well-tried formula never fails. This was the last of the series of carol-service recordings made with this choir by Argo, and with its mixture of the well-known and the unusual it remains perhaps the loveliest of all, with fine atmospheric recording. The name of Andrew

Davis, the organ scholar of the time, has since become famous throughout the world of music, and no doubt his musicianship powerfully reinforced that of David Willcocks. As in the actual service at Christmas the opening *Once in Royal David's city* is sung as a processional, and the recording reproduces vividly the slow approach of the choir. Modern carols by Peter Wishart and Peter Racine Fricker are included among the traditional ones. Two of the loveliest are *There is no rose* and *Lullay my liking*, both of the fifteenth century, the latter in Holst's inspired arrangement. The transfer to tape is immaculate. Only very occasionally is the choral focus less well defined than on the disc, and the click-free background of the cassette is an obvious advantage during the opening processional.

'Christmas music from King's' (with Andrew Davis, organ, and Douglas Whittaker, flute, Christopher van Kempen, cello): VICTORIA: *O magnum mysterium; Senex puerum portabat.* BYRD: *Senex puerum portabat; Hodie beata virgo.* GIBBONS: *Hosanna to the Son of David.* WEELKES: *Hosanna to the Son of David; Gloria in excelsis.* SWEELINCK: *Hodie Christus natus est.* WATTS: *Watts's cradle song.* Arrangements by: MACONCHY: *Nowell!;* BRITTEN: *The holly and the ivy;* HUGHES: *Angelus ad Virginum;* POSTON: *Angelus ad Virginum; My dancing day;* BERKELEY: *I sing of a maiden;* HOLST, Imogen: *The Lord that lay;* WARLOCK: *Where riches is everlasting.*

(M) **(*) HMV Greensleeve TC-ESD 7050.

A happily chosen survey of music inspired by the Nativity from the fifteenth century up to the present. As might be expected, the King's Choir confidently

encompasses the wide variety of styles, from the spiritual serenity of the music of Victoria to the attractive arrangements of traditional carols by modern composers, where an instrumental accompaniment is added. These items are quite delightful and they are beautifully recorded. Generally the transfer to tape offers refined sound; the focus never slips more than fractionally.

'The sound of King's': choral music by SWEELINCK; HANDEL; POSTON; CHARPENTIER, Marc-Antoine; BYRD; FAURÉ; PARRY; VAUGHAN WILLIAMS; HAYDN etc.

(M) HMV TC-MCS 13.

Like the Argo collection *The world of King's,* this anthology ranges wide in its choice of items, and their attractions are obvious, except that the original purpose of the equivalent LP issue, to act as a sampler of the King's repertoire, is lost on tape, since little of the material is available in cassette form. But in any case the transfers are so inept – the sound is unrefined from the very opening piece – that this cannot be recommended.

(The) King's Singers

'German and Spanish part-songs' by HASSLER; SENFL; LASSUS; VON BRUCK; SCHEIN; ENCIŇA; ESCOBAR; VASQUEZ; ROMAN; PONCE and anonymous composers.

**(*)HMV TC-ASD 3557.

'A French collection' (with Early Music Consort, Munrow): Renaissance chansons by JANNEQUIN; JACOTIN; PASSEREAU; WILLAERT; CERTON; MORNABLE; ARBEAU; LE JEUNE. POULENC: *Songs.*

***HMV TC-CSD 3740.

'Madrigal collection': madrigals by MORLEY; WEELKES; WILBYE; BENNETT: FARMER; FESTA; HOSTIA; DE

WERT; CAIMO; DA NOLA; BANCH-
IERI; GASTOLDI; LASSUS.

**(*)HMV TC-CSD 3756.

'Concert collection': madrigals by
HENRY VIII; DAGGERE; FARMER;
TOMKINS; MORLEY. Sacred music
by: GIACOBBI; HANDL; VITTORIA.
Chansons and songs by: RIDOUT;
JOSQUIN DES PRÉS; JANNEQUIN;
LEGRAND; GRIEG. Traditional
pieces.

**(*)HMV TC-CSD 3766.

'Out of the blue' (popular and folk
songs).

*(**)EMI TC-EMC 3023.

'Lollipops' (includes: I'm a train;
Ding a dong; Marry a woman uglier
than you; Ob-la-di; There are bad
times just around the corner; Les trois
cloches).

*(**)EMI TC-EMC 3093.

'Swing' (includes music by Duke
Ellington, Irving Berlin and others).

**EMI TC-EMC 3157.

'Flanders and Swann and Noël
Coward'.

***EMI TC-EMC 3196.

'Tempus fugit' (popular music by
Dylan, Lennon and McCartney,
etc.).

**EMI TC-EMC 3268.

'The King's Singers' (sampler:
mostly popular songs).

(M)*(*)EMI TC-EXE 200.

'Tenth Anniversary Concert' (recorded live at the Royal Festival
Hall):

Vol. 1: music by JANNEQUIN; BYRD;
WEELKES; FARMER; BANCHIERI; DE
WERT; POULENC; GLASSER.

***EMI TC-KS 1001.

Vol. 2: popular music, including Ten
years on; In the mood; The mermaid;
Greens; I'm a train; Ob-la-di; Rag;
Widdicombe fair.

***EMI TC-KS 1002.

With the Tenth Anniversary Concert,
recorded live, there are a round dozen
cassettes available to show the remarkably diverse talents of the King's
Singers. The group have successfully
bridged the gap between classical and
popular traditions, and if occasionally
one feels that the smooth homogeneity of
their style is in danger of devitalizing
some of their repertoire, there is such
consistent imagination and life in the
presentation that criticism is often
disarmed.

The sheer professionalism of the group
is irresistible in the collection of German
and Spanish part-songs, material which
would normally seem somewhat esoteric.
This anthology may well not appeal to
everyone, but the very opening part-song
on the German side, Tanzen und springen,
fizzingly sets the pattern for the whole.
The Spanish side is more varied, with
some material from before 1500, the rest
from the sixteenth century. The recording
is good and the transfer full and clear. It
is a pity that, unlike the equivalent LP,
the cassette format does not include the
full translations.

The French collection makes a successful juxtaposition of Renaissance chansons and all the male-voiced choral songs
of Poulenc. The guiding hand of David
Munrow ensures stylish and spirited
music-making here; the recording is of
high quality and the transfer fresh and
immediate. The Madrigal collection too
has both charm and character; the robust
qualities of Banchieri's Contrappunto
bestiale, with its lively animal imitations,
is well brought out. Here the recording
balance is very forward. The transfer is
smooth but lacks something in presence
and bite. The programme of the Concert
collection ranges from Elizabethan music
to the songs of Grieg and even includes
an arrangement of Puppet on a string.
The transfer is of good quality and this is
an enjoyable concert.

Out of the blue offers some extremely
effective modern arrangements, notably
those of Richard Rodney Bennett. Wish

you were here has a nimble horn obbligato (it sounds like Alan Civil), and there is an equally vivacious Gershwin number, *It's a great little world.* This is a most entertaining mix and it is a pity that the quality of the transfer is unrefined at times, with poor transients, variable focus, and limited range. *Lollipops* is strong in presence, but the full, bright sound sometimes overloads and the quality coarsens. The exhilarating *I'm a train*, ingenious settings of *Phil the fluter's ball* and Noël Coward's *There are bad times just around the corner*, plus *Ding a dong* and *Les trois cloches* are all memorable. The *Swing* anthology is mainly lyrical, less extrovert than one might expect. Highlights here include the arrangements by Richard Rodney Bennett of *Blue skies* and *Bye-bye blues*; and a superbly imaginative band imitation (complete with a simulated 78 r.p.m. background swish) is featured in *I only have eyes for you.* This is essentially a nostalgic rather than a vigorous look at a past era. The transfers are mostly smooth.

As we go to press, the most recent issue, *Tempus fugit*, takes the group nearer to the disco scene than they have been before. The style of the Ray Conniff Singers springs to mind in numbers like *Don't let the sun go down on me* and the richly vocalized *Mr Tambourin Man*, although the vocal lines here are more complex. *Space oddity* includes rather contrived sound effects; it does not really take off, but reminds one of the Beatles' *Yellow submarine* in its presentation. There are two lyrical Beatles numbers as highlights: *Things we said today* and *Strawberry fields forever.* The backing varies, often orchestral with strong rhythms: the opening *Monday* inhabits the world of not-so-heavy rock. This will not be to all tastes, but it is a diverting tape for the car and is well recorded, the sound full and clear in the generally good transfer.

If one had to pick a single cassette showing the group at their freshest and most imaginative it would surely be the splendid compilation of the songs of Noël Coward and Flanders and Swann. The opening *Transport of delight* lives up to its name, and *The slow train, The Wompon, Rockall* and *The sloth* are all unforgettable. *Mad dogs and Englishmen* has snippets of *Rule Britannia* spliced in, and throughout the Coward numbers there is ample wit, with *There are bad times just around the corner* a *tour de force* at the end. The recording is excellent and the transfer smooth, lacking only the last degree of life and presence. After this the medium-priced sampler seems pleasant rather than outstanding, although it includes a haunting George Martin piece called *The game* and the delightful *My colouring book* (arranged by Christopher Broadbent). The high-level transfer brings good projection, but also patches where the aural refinement slips.

The *Tenth Anniversary Concert* can be recommended with the greatest enthusiasm. The presence of the audience means that there are spoken introductions (generally witty) and the kind of spontaneity that can only come from a live recording. The atmosphere of the occasion is splendidly caught and the transfer quality is excellent throughout. The first half is serious, the second a fun collection, opening irresistibly with *Ten years on* and including, near the end, the audience's own sung birthday tribute to the group. There are many favourites here, and two most welcome encores.

Lloyd, Robert (bass)

'Sea fever' (with Nina Walker, piano): songs by IRELAND; KEEL; GERMAN; PURCELL; WARLOCK; HARTY; ARMSTRONG GIBBS; STANFORD; HEAD; and traditional shanties.

**(*)HMV TC-ASD 3545.

Robert Lloyd opens with a beautiful performance of Ireland's setting of the title piece; he is especially good in two of Stanford's *Songs of the Sea* (*The old Superb* and *Drake's drum*), and his characterization of the closing item, *What shall we do with the drunken sailor?*, is equally enjoyable. Not all the singing is quite so imaginative as this, but the anthology is cleverly selected and is entertaining, provided it is not taken all at once. Nina Walker accompanies strongly. Both artists are well recorded and realistically balanced; the transfer is full and clear, with only the slightest suggestion of edge on the voice at times.

London Festival Brass Ens., Trinity School Choir, Pearson

'*The magic of Christmas*': *O come all ye faithful; Ding dong merrily on high; Jingle bells; The first nowell; The holly and the ivy; O come Emmanuel; Christmas is coming; Away in a manger; Good King Wenceslas.* BERLIN: *White Christmas.* GRÜBER: *Silent night.* MENDELSSOHN: *Hark the herald angels.*

*** Decca Phase 4 KPFC 4316.

An attractive offbeat Christmas collection. Leslie Pearson's imaginative arrangements are highly infectious, though not for purists. The opening *Jingle bells* is typical, with the chorus heard against a background of syncopated brass chords. *Ding dong merrily on high* features harpsichord, glockenspiel and trumpets, while *O come Emmanuel* even has a moment of Latin American rhythm. Undoubtedly the most fetching item of all is the closing *Good King Wenceslas*, wittily syncopated. The choral singing is excellent, and the recording has a proper touch of spectacle. The tape transfer is excellent, with crisp detail and no congestion.

Luxon, Benjamin (bar.)

'*Break the news to mother*' (*Victorian and Edwardian ballads;* with David Willison, piano): SANDERSON: *Up from Somerset.* CAREY: *Nearer my God to Thee.* MCCALL: *Boots.* HARRIS: *Break the news to mother.* HATTON: *The wreck of the Hesperus.* CAPEL: *Love, could I only tell thee.* BLANEY: *Mr Bear.* JACOBS-BOND: *Just a' wearying for you.* SULLIVAN: *The lost chord.* WOODFORDE-FINDEN: *Kashmiri song.* HARPER: *A bandit's life.* PENN: *Smilin' through.* PETRIE: *Asleep in the deep.*

(M) *** Argo KZKC 42.

Benjamin Luxon has made something of a speciality of singing Edwardian ballads, whether in company with Robert Tear or on his own. The bluff hints of characterization here never step into the area of outright send-up, which on a recording is just as well, and this warmly characterful collection is guaranteed to delight any who have enjoyed this singer's recitals on television or in the concert hall. Good atmospheric recording and a splendid transfer, giving the voice fine bloom and resonance and placing the piano realistically.

McCormack, John (tenor)

'*Legendary performer*' (recordings processed by digital computer): arias from HANDEL: *Semele;* MOZART: *Don Giovanni;* BIZET: *Les Pêcheurs de perles;* DONIZETTI: *La Fille du régiment.* BIMBONI: *Sospiri miei andante.* PARKINS: *Le Portrait.* SCHUMANN: *The singer's consolation.* RACHMANINOV: *When night descends.* TOSTI: *Venetian song.* BARTLETT: *A dream.* BALFE: *Come into the garden, Maude.* LEHMANN: *Ah, moon of my delight; Bonny wee thing.* arr. HUGHES: *The next market day; A Ballynure ballad; The bard of Armagh.*

**(*) RCA RK 12472.

Like the Caruso collection on the same label, these transfers have been made from 78s with the help of a digital computer to eliminate unwanted resonances. The result – if anything even more vitally than with Caruso – has a living quality which makes one relish the light, bright tones of McCormack in his prime. There is some superb singing here – this account of *Il mio tesoro* from *Don Giovanni* is a classic of vocal recording – to have one appreciating the special status of the Irish tenor in his earlier career. Recommended even to those who do not usually respond to McCormack's highly individual timbre. The tape is well balanced and clean if not quite as revealing as the disc.

McKellar, Kenneth (tenor)

'The world of Kenneth McKellar': Roamin' in the gloamin'. Annie Laurie. Song of the Clyde. My love is like a red, red rose. Skye boat song. The end of the road. Wi' a hundred pipers. Ye banks and braes. The tartan. My ain folk. Scotland the brave. Will ye no come back again.

(M) *** Decca KCSP 11.

This enchanting tape is aptly named, for Kenneth McKellar has made these songs his own. *My ain folk* and, especially, *Will ye no come back again* show his matchless feeling for phrasing and sentiment without sentimentality. Lively songs too are given a rhythmic bounce that is irresistible: *Scotland the brave* is wonderfully exhilarating. Sometimes the songs are over-produced: the fanfare that heralds *Wi' a hundred pipers* is quite unnecessary; on the other hand the harpsichord for *Ye banks and braes* (most beautifully sung) was a happy choice. The programme itself is well chosen – there is not a second-rate piece of singing here and side two gets better and better. The transfer is of demonstration quality; the voice is fresh and natural and admirably projected (although the balance is more forward in some songs than others), and the accompaniment has plenty of life and sparkle.

'The world of Kenneth McKellar', Vol. 2: Trottin' to the fair. Danny boy. The star of the County Down. My Lagan love. The old turf fire. Macushla. Hame o' mine. The hiking song. O sing to me the auld Scots sangs. We're no awa to bide awa'. The wee cooper o' Fife. Auld lang syne.

(M) *** Decca KCSP 67.

Some of the items here are romantic ballads where the music has a touch of sentimentality, like *Macushla* or *O sing to me*, but McKellar presents them with admirable restraint, and in items like *Trottin' to the fair* or *The wee cooper o' Fife* he is incomparable. Another irresistible collection to show what a great artist McKellar is in the field of Celtic folk music. The transfer is particularly pleasing, the voice agreeably natural and warm, the accompaniments, including the supporting chorus, smooth yet realistic and with no lack of detail. The third issue in this series, *The evergreen world of K.M.* (KCSP 149), includes pop songs, which are definitely not Kenneth McKellar's métier, making an uneasy mixture of different styles.

'Kenneth McKellar sings Robert Burns': 25 folk songs.

(B) **(*) Decca KDPC 2 8087.

The songs of Robert Burns have been cleverly collected on this double-length tape from a number of discs recorded over the last decade. This is the material in which McKellar has no peer and many of these songs are sung very beautifully indeed. *Ae fond kiss, Ye banks and braes, Afton Water* (ravishingly done), *Bonnie wee thing, Ca' the ewes, My love is like a red, red rose* and many others are included here, to give constant delight. The voice is clearly recorded and the transfers are on the whole very well managed. The one exception is *Scots wha ha'e*, which before each verse has horridly intrusive brass fanfares that should have been edited out; they are not even very well played, and the high modulation causes coarseness and blasting. However, this is the last item on side one and one can always stop and spool on, even though McKellar's singing is first-class.

'Songs of the British Isles': Ye banks and braes. David of the White Rock. Cockles and mussels. Villikens and his Dinah. Island moon. Sweet lass of Richmond Hill. Ellan Vannin. Dance to your daddy. O, waly, waly. Bonnie labouring boy. Twa corbies. Greensleeves. Rising of the lark. Ball of Kirriemuir. The last rose of summer.

(M) *** Decca Eclipse KECC 2155.

Songs of the British Isles is thoroughly recommendable. Bob Sharples has excelled himself in the arrangements, which are neat and imaginative; McKellar is in excellent voice and can delight by his humour (as in *Villikens and his Dinah*) and ravish with his phrasing (as in the very beautiful song from the Isle of Lewis, *Island moon*). There is pathos too in *Twa corbies* (very nicely judged) and, to round off a splendid recital, an unaffectedly lovely account of *The last rose of summer*. The recording is first-rate in every way – perhaps the best McKellar has received – and the tape transfer, made at a high level, has fine presence and detail.

'Focus on Kenneth McKellar': songs; Celtic folk songs; arias from: PUCCINI: *La Bohème;* HANDEL: *Ptolemy.*

(B) ** Decca KFOC 2 8053.

This bargain-priced double-length tape mixes Scottish folk music with other repertoire in which Kenneth McKellar is less stylistically secure. There are some attractive things here, notably the ravishing performance of *Land of heart's desire* and sparkling versions of the *Uist tramping song* and *Road to the isles*; but as a collection this does not match the earlier issues listed above. The recording has been transferred at the highest possible level, and just occasionally the refinement of focus slips a little.

'Roamin' in the gloamin' ': Road to the isles. Star o' Robbie Burns. The cockle gatherer. Bonnie Mary of Argyle. Afton Water. Roamin' in the gloamin'. Scotland the brave. Song of the Clyde. Bonnie wee thing. Westering home. Keep right on to the end of the road. arr. KENNEDY-FRASER: Eriskay love lilt.

✸ *** Decca KSKC 4034.

This was Kenneth McKellar's first stereo recital, recorded very early in his career, when the voice was at its peak, with a marvellous freshness and bloom. The simple style, natural warmth, and sure sense of line, the lyrical music tonally ravishing, and the jaunty tunes sung with a nicely humorous touch, all combine to provide a recital of the utmost distinction. Even *Keep right on to the end of the road,* presented with robust sincerity, sounds better than it is; and for the most part the programme is compiled from songs of great beauty and character. The orchestral arrangements are nicely judged, and show none of the excesses that mar some of McKellar's later recordings. The transfer is first-class, clear, clean and naturally balanced. Highly recommended.

There are two other McKellar Scottish collections available. *I belong to Scotland* (KMORC 508), a medium-priced tape, is mainly notable for a rumbustious, music-hall-style account of *I belong to Glasgow* and some lively Scottish dance numbers, but it also contains an outrageously sentimental performance of *Auld Scotch mither mine;* several other modern songs are included which show an element of vulgarity. *The romantic Scotland* (KSKC 5177) returns to the traditional material that Kenneth McKellar can make sound magical, but here he is not at his best and displays a tendency almost to croon the lyrical songs.

(Geoffrey) Mitchell Choir, ECO, Heath

'The joy of Christmas': TRAD.: *The twelve days of Christmas. Ding dong merrily on high. In dulci jubilo. The birds. When the crimson sun had set. I saw three ships. Sussex carol. Good King Wenceslas. The holly and the ivy. Unto us a Son is born. We wish you a merry Christmas.* arr. RUBBRA: *Infant Holy.* MENDELSSOHN: *Hark the herald angels.* TCHAIKOVSKY: *The crown of roses.* arr. VAUGHAN WILLIAMS: *Gloucestershire wassail.* arr. RUTTER: *Christmas bells.*

*** HMV TC-CSD 3784.

None of Edward Heath's recordings demonstrates more readily than this his balanced musicianship and real gifts as a conductor. The freshness of the singing is apparent from the very opening of this invigorating collection, and the sparkle of both singing and playing carries spontaneity throughout. The care in preparation is shown in many touches of detail, and the vigour of the direction is especially striking in Rubbra's imaginative arrangement of the traditional Polish carol *Infant Holy*, where the lyrical fervour of the singing blossoms as at a live performance. *I saw three ships* is delightful with its skipping rhythmic flow, and Mendelssohn's angels are gloriously eloquent. A most enjoyable concert, very well recorded and given one of EMI's best transfers, full-blooded, nearly always clearly focused, and sometimes approaching demonstration standard.

Mormon Tabernacle Choir

'We wish you a merry Christmas' (with the Philadelphia Brass Ens., percussion, Condie; Alexander Schreiner, organ): favourite carols.

(M)(***)CBS Classics 40–61771.

The sheer joy of the singing makes this collection of carols unique. *O come, O come, Emmanuel* is built to a breathtaking climax on a wave of jubilation, and *We wish you a merry Christmas* really communicates its greeting. *The carol of the bells* is delightfully done; *O Tannenbaum* has a racy vivaciousness of spirit that is totally disarming, and *Silent night* is presented solemnly but with great warmth. Unfortunately, although the basic recording is excellent the technical quality of the transfer is shameful, with generally ill-focused sound and rough climaxes.

'The white cliffs of Dover' (with Robert Merrill, bar., Columbia SO, Ottley): popular American and English songs.

(M)(**) CBS Classics 40–61791.

The Mormons bring a show-biz sparkle to numbers like *Over there* and *This is the army, Mr Jones*, and a warm sentimentality to *Keep the home fires burning. Tipperary* is appropriately spirited, but the title piece is made to sound rather soupy. The recording is full-blooded and the transfer slightly (only slightly) better-focused than the others in this series.

'Beloved choruses' (with Philadelphia Orch., Ormandy): BACH: *Sheep may safely graze; Jesu, joy of man's desiring;* and choruses from: *St Matthew Passion;* HAYDN: *The Creation;* HANDEL: *Messiah;* and by SCHUBERT; RIMSKY-KORSAKOV; SIBELIUS.

(M)(**)CBS Classics 40–61829.

Although the Mormons sing with characteristic intensity throughout, there is a good deal of slow, sustained music here, and the tape transfer provides rather mushy sound. The upper frequencies are limited and the sound focus is never sharp. It is at its best in the choral version of *Finlandia*, sung with thrilling fervour, although at the end the orchestral percussion is muddled. The closing *Hallelujah* from *Messiah* is similarly thrilling in its intensity.

Morriston Orpheus Choir

'*Corau Mawr Cymru*' (cond. Sims): *Land of my fathers*. CANDISH: *Song of the Jolly Roger*. HUGHES: *Tydi a roddaist*. FALFAN: *Roll, Jordan, roll*. TRAD.: *Rock of Cader Idris; All through the night*. JONES: *We'll keep a welcome*. RICHARDS: *God bless the Prince of Wales*. arr. PARRY: *Aberystwyth*. BRAHMS: *Lullaby*. VERDI: *Nabucco: Chorus of Hebrew slaves*. JONES: *Deus salutis* (*Llef*). SULLIVAN: *The long day closes*. JAMES: *Hen wlad fy Nhadau*.

(M) **(*) Decca Daffodil KDAFC 208.

This strikingly successful tape is a reissue of a collection that Decca first issued on LP in the earliest days of stereo. The slightly dry acoustic has produced a transfer of demonstration standard, the sound rich and clear, yet not lacking ambience. The choir shows plenty of character but no special sense of discipline; the opening and closing *Land of my fathers* is rather slow, and among the other items it is the gentle pieces that come off best. In particular Brahms' *Lullaby* and *All through the night* are both beautifully sung. Elsewhere, and particularly in the Verdi chorus, the presentation is robust and forthright rather than subtle in shading. The singing is often unaccompanied, and the organist's contribution is discreet but effective.

(i) **Morriston Orpheus Male Choir;** (ii) **Pendyrus Male Choir;** (iii) **Treorchy Male Choir**

'*The world of Wales in song*' (with (iv) Thomas L. Thomas. (v) David Lloyd): (i) *God bless the Prince of Wales; Tydi a roddaist; We'll keep a welcome; Hen wlad fy*. (ii) *Hyfrydol; Llef; Cwm Rhondda; Cysga di*. (iii) *Y deryn pur; Sospan fach; All thro' the night; Myfanwy; Hob y deri dando*. (iv) *Dafydd y garreg wen*. (v) *My little Welsh home*.

(M) ** Decca KCSP 42.

A well-made collection, using three choirs and with two attractive solo interludes. The transfers are well done, and the choirs have plenty of resonance and atmosphere. The snag is that the items from the Treorchy Choir have a mono source, and the sound, although always acceptable, is less well focused. But there are plenty of favourites here, and the tape is generously full.

Opera

'*Favourite opera*': solos, duets and choruses from: MOZART: *Le Nozze di Figaro* (inc. *Overture*); *Don Giovanni*. GLUCK: *Orfeo*. ROSSINI: *Il Barbiere di Siviglia*. DONIZETTI: *L'Elisir d'amore; Lucia di Lammermoor* (including *Sextet*). VERDI: *Nabucco; Rigoletto* (including *Quartet*); *Aïda*. BIZET: *Carmen*. SAINT-SAËNS: *Samson et Dalila*. MASCAGNI: *Cavalleria Rusticana* (including *Intermezzo*). LEONCAVALLO: *I Pagliacci*. PUCCINI: *La Bohème; Gianni Schicchi; Madama Butterfly; Turandot*.

(B) ** Decca KDPC 507/8.

This is a sound collection; the order has been sensibly arranged so that items follow on naturally, and the transfers are good (the *Barber* and *Carmen* excerpts lack sparkle in the orchestra, but these are isolated instances). After an attractive Mozartian start, the Donizetti, Verdi and Puccini selections are excellently chosen. Artists include Lisa della Casa and Cesare Siepi (Mozart), Teresa Berganza (Gluck), di Stefano, Sutherland (Donizetti and Verdi), Resnik (Saint-Saëns), Tebaldi and Bergonzi (Puccini).

'Grand opera festival' (with Janet Baker, Joan Sutherland, Teresa Berganza, Cesare Siepi, Cristina Deutekom, Luciano Pavarotti, Renata Tebaldi, Mario del Monaco, Sherrill Milnes, Leontyne Price, Jussi Bjoerling, Felicia Weathers, Fiorenza Cossotto, Pilar Lorengar, Marilyn Horne, Giuseppe di Stefano, Regina Resnik, Hilde Gueden, Elisabeth Söderström, Otto Edelmann and other artists): excerpts from: MONTEVERDI: *Orfeo.* PURCELL: *Dido and Aeneas.* HANDEL: *Alcina.* GLUCK: *Orfeo.* MOZART: *Don Giovanni; Così fan tutte; Le Nozze di Figaro; Die Zauberflöte.* ROSSINI: *Il Barbiere di Siviglia.* DONIZETTI: *La Fille du régiment.* VERDI: *Luisa Miller; Rigoletto; Il Trovatore; Un Ballo in maschera; Aïda.* PONCHIELLI: *La Gioconda.* PUCCINI: *La Bohème; Gianni Schicchi; Madama Butterfly; Tosca.* DVOŘÁK: *Rusalka.* MUSSORGSKY: *Boris Godunov.* DELIBES: *Lakmé.* GOUNOD: *Faust.* BIZET: *Carmen.* MASSENET: *Manon.* SAINT-SAËNS: *Samson et Dalila.* BEETHOVEN: *Fidelio.* R. STRAUSS: *Der Rosenkavalier.* WAGNER: *Die Walküre.*

(M) **(*) Decca K 2 C 7.

This *Grand opera festival* with its star-studded cast is the finest of the three principal Decca opera compilations. It is supported by excellent notes by Stelios Galatopoulos which place the excerpts in historical sequence, even though they are not all performed in strict order of composition. In this respect it is a pity that in putting the contents of three discs on two cassettes the excerpts from Verdi's *Un Ballo* (Sherrill Milnes) and Leontyne Price's *Ritorna vincitor* (from *Aïda*) have been interpolated between the Mozart and the naturally following sequence of Rossini's *La calunnia* (Nicolai Ghiaurov) and the singing lesson from *La Fille du régiment* (Joan Sutherland). However, there is so much to enjoy here, from Janet Baker in Dido's lament and Teresa Berganza in Gluck and Mozart, on through the fine Verdi and Puccini and the French opera to Richard Strauss and Wagner. The recordings have transferred very successfully (although the level is somewhat variable – side four shows a marked increase over side three).

'Opera gala': Arias from: LEONCAVALLO: *I Pagliacci.* VERDI: *La Traviata; Rigoletto; Aïda; Il Trovatore.* ROSSINI: *Il Barbiere di Siviglia.* GOUNOD: *Faust.* PUCCINI: *Turandot.* BIZET: *Carmen.*

(B) **DG Heliodor 3347 272.

An acceptable collection at bargain price but hardly a 'gala'! It opens well with a distinguished account of the *Prologue* from *Pagliacci* by Giuseppe Taddei, and there is a vibrant *Celeste Aïda* from Carlo Bergonzi, followed by a strong but slightly stiff *Stride la vampa* from Fiorenza Cossotto. Teresa Berganza's *Una voce poco fa* is reliable, but a little too positive: heard away from the complete set it lacks a feeling of capriciousness. Then comes the other highlight, Montserrat Caballé's sparkling version of the *King of Thule* and *Jewel song* from *Faust*. After this Antonietta Stella sounds rather shrill during *In questa reggia*, and Grace Bumbry's closing *Habanera* iss rather deadpan. The transfers are well managed.

'The world of opera':

Vol. 1: excerpts from: ROSSINI: *Il Barbiere di Siviglia* (*Overture*). MOZART: *Le Nozze di Figaro.* DONIZETTI: *L'Elisir d'amore.* VERDI: *Il Trovatore; Don Carlos; Rigoletto* (*Quartet*). GOUNOD: *Faust.* BEETHOVEN: *Fidelio.* DVOŘÁK: *Rusalka.* PUCCINI: *La Bohème; Gianni Schicchi; Tosca.*

(M)**Decca KCSP 449.

Vol. 2: excerpts from: HANDEL: *Rodelinda.* MOZART: *Le Nozze di Figaro.* ROSSINI: *Il Barbiere di Siviglia.* VERDI: *Aïda; Nabucco; La Traviata* (*Prelude, Act I*); *Rigoletto.* WAGNER: *Tannhäuser.* BIZET: *Carmen.* PUCCINI: *Tosca; Madama Butterfly.*

(M)**Decca KCSP 450.

Vol. 3: excerpts from: ROSSINI: *La Scala di seta* (*Overture*). GLUCK: *Orfeo.* MOZART: *Don Giovanni.* VERDI: *La Traviata; Aïda; La Forza del destino.* SAINT-SAËNS: *Samson et Dalila.* WAGNER: *Die Meistersinger.* PUCCINI: *Madama Butterfly; Tosca; La Bohème.*

(M)**(*)Decca KCSP 489.

Vol. 4: excerpts from: GLUCK: *Orfeo.* MOZART: *Don Giovanni.* BELLINI: *Norma.* VERDI: *Il Trovatore.* PUCCINI: *La Bohème; Turandot.* PONCHIELLI: *La Gioconda.* BIZET: *Carmen.* LEONCAVALLO: *I Pagliacci.* MASCAGNI: *Cavalleria Rusticana.*

(M)**(*)Decca KCSP 490.

These are all agreeable collections but the series has improved as it has proceeded. Moreover the quality of the transfers is smoother in Volumes 3 and 4 than in 1 and 2. After a not very sparkling account of the Rossini overture, the highlights on the first tape include Teresa Berganza's fresh *Voi che sapete* and Joan Sutherland's *Jewel song*. There seems to be slight unsteadiness of texture in the recording of the Moon invocation from *Rusalka*, but the sound is brilliant for the closing *Te Deum* from *Tosca*. The highlight of the second volume is Joan Sutherland's ravishing performance of *Caro nome* (from her first complete set). Placido Domingo's *Celeste Aïda* is matched by Tom Krause's excellent *Tannhäuser* aria. The recording is lively throughout, but there is some peaking in Teresa Berganza's stylish *Una voce poco fa*, and the orchestra strings sound shrill in the Tebaldi/ Bergonzi love duet from *Madama Butterfly*.

Volume 3 opens well with the neatly played overture, followed by Teresa Berganza's cool but distinguished *Che puro ciel* from *Orfeo* (she provides *Che farò* in an equally fine version in Volume 4). Then comes a melting *Ritorna vincitor* from Maria Chiara, and James King eloquent in the *Prize song* from *Die Meistersinger*. Unexpectedly the moving performance of *One fine day* is by Felicia Weathers, and the collection ends with a nicely tailored *Musetta's waltz scene* from *La Bohème* (the Serafin set). The sound is generally excellent. Volume 4 offers Sutherland's *Casta diva*, Maria Chiara as Mimi, an enterprising excerpt from *La Gioconda* (with Milanov) and lively items from *Cav.* and *Pag.*, with the famous *Intermezzo* from the former opera placed before the final excerpt, Placido Domingo's *Nessun dorma*. The sound is mostly very good.

Opera choruses

'Famous opera choruses' from: WEBER: *Der Freischütz.* WAGNER: *Der fliegende Holländer; Tannhäuser; Lohengrin.* VERDI: *Il Trovatore; La Traviata.* BERLIOZ: *La Damnation de Faust.* BEETHOVEN: *Fidelio.*

(B)*(*)DG Heliodor 3348 212.

There are some excellent performances here, notably the vivacious Weber *Huntsmen's chorus* (conducted by Jochum) and the *Prisoners' chorus* from *Fidelio* (directed by Fricsay). The Verdi choruses come from La Scala complete sets. The transfer is generally well managed, with well-focused choral tone and plenty of body and life. Side two is marginally brighter than side one and contains the one miscalculation: the *Soldiers' chorus* from Markevitch's set of *La Damnation de Faust* is recorded at a higher level than the other items, and brings coarseness into the sound picture.

'*Favourite opera choruses*' from: VERDI: *Il Trovatore; I Lombardi; Nabucco; Aïda; Otello; Macbeth.* LEONCAVALLO: *I Pagliacci.* PUCCINI: *Madama Butterfly.* WAGNER: *Der fliegende Holländer; Tannhäuser.* GOUNOD: *Faust.* BIZET: *Carmen.* TCHAIKOVSKY: *Eugene Onegin.* BORODIN: *Prince Igor.* MUSSORGSKY: *Boris Godunov.*

(B)*Decca KDPC 525/6.

A pair of cassettes filled with opera choruses seems too much of a good thing, even when (as with *Otello, The Flying Dutchman* and *Boris Godunov*) quite long excerpts are sometimes chosen. Moreover the transfers have obviously offered almost insuperable problems, with the balance and amplitude of the sound varying from piece to piece. Quite a lot of the excerpts come from complete sets; including the early *Il Trovatore* (where the *Anvil chorus* is muddy in the bass); *The Flying Dutchman* (under Dorati), where there is congestion at climaxes; and the spectacular Act 1 choral scene from *Otello* (Erede), which is not very refined either. There is much here that sounds satisfactory: the *Humming chorus* from *Butterfly* (from the Serafin set), the *Polovtsian dances* (Ansermet) and, notably, the *Coronation scene* from *Boris Godunov* (the Covent Garden chorus under

Edward Downes and Joseph Rouleau as Boris); but this set cannot receive an enthusiastic recommendation. Incidentally, although the cassette labels are correct, the liner notes are wrongly printed, each describing the contents of the other tape.

'*Great opera choruses*' from: VERDI: *Nabucco; Il Trovatore; Aïda.* BELLINI: *Norma.* LEONCAVALLO: *I Pagliacci.* WAGNER: *Tannhäuser.* BEETHOVEN: *Fidelio.* GOUNOD: *Faust.* BIZET: *Carmen.* MUSSORGSKY: *Boris Godunov.*

(M)**(*) Decca KCSP 296.

This imaginatively chosen collection is preferable in every way to Decca's double-tape *Favourite choruses* (see above). Most of the excerpts come from distinguished complete sets, notably the *Pilgrims' chorus* scene from Solti's *Tannhäuser*, which has a memorable sense of perspective. Bonynge conducts the *War chorus* from *Norma* and the *Soldiers' chorus* from *Faust*, and Karajan directs the *Coronation scene* from *Boris Godunov*. The transfers are generally good and often excellent. There is a slight lack of refinement in the spectacular march scene from *Aïda*, but the one real misjudgement is the *Prisoners' chorus* from *Fidelio*, which follows the Wagner on side one: the level suddenly rises and the sound becomes fierce, so for this item one needs to cut back both the volume and the treble response. But taken as a whole this is excellent value: the *Toreador chorus* is especially vivid.

Opera marches

Marches from: MOZART: *Die Entführung aus dem Serail.* BEETHOVEN: *Fidelio.* ROSSINI: *William Tell.* BIZET: *Carmen.* VERDI: *Aïda; Il Trovatore; Don Carlos.* WAGNER: *Tannhäuser; Lohengrin.*

(B) * DG Heliodor 3348 277.

These are, of course, not just orchestral marches: many of them feature the chorus, and some, like the *Soldiers' chorus* from *Il Trovatore* (one of the best items here), are not really marches at all. The performances are vivid, often distinguished, but the collection is spoilt by the great variance in quality of sound between the different transfers. The opening *Chorus of Janissaries* from *Die Entführung* sounds muddled, with no crispness of focus at all, and the *Don Carlos* excerpt on side two is similarly poorly focused. On the other hand the spectacular march from *Aïda* comes over well. The quality in the Wagner excerpts, very well sung, is again disappointingly lacking in crispness at climaxes.

Operatic duets

'*Favourite operatic duets*' from ROSSINI: *Semiramide*. VERDI: *Il Trovatore; La Traviata; Don Carlos; La Forza del destino*. PUCCINI: *Tosca; Madama Butterfly; La Bohème*. BIZET: *Les Pêcheurs de perles; Carmen*. BERLIOZ: *Béatrice et Bénédict*.

(B) ** Decca KDPC 517/8.

The Sutherland/Horne Act 1 duet from *Semiramide* is a classic by any standards, and there are other interesting inclusions here too: the Bergonzi/Fischer-Dieskau duet from Act 2 of *Don Carlos* (superbly exciting) and by contrast the lovely *Nocturne* from *Béatrice et Bénédict* (April Cantelo and Helen Watts). Perhaps most interesting of all, however, is the successful transfer of an early Decca mono recording of *Au fond du temple saint* stirringly sung by Libero de Luca and Jean Borthayre. The rest of the programme includes oft-used Decca items by familiar artists such as Tebaldi and Bergonzi. The closing scene of *Carmen* (Resnik and del Monaco) is vibrant enough, although here and in the excerpts on side four from *La Bohème* and *Madama Butterfly* the recording lacks the usual Decca sparkle

in the orchestra. For the most part the transfers are of good quality and there is no congestion.

Operetta

'*The world of operetta favourites*': excerpts from: STRAUSS, Johann, Jnr: *Die Fledermaus; Der Zigeunerbaron; Casanova*. ZELLER: *Der Obersteiger*. STRAUS: *The Chocolate Soldier*. OFFENBACH: *Orpheus in the Underworld; La Périchole*. LECOCQ: *Le Cœur et la main*. LEHÁR: *The Merry Widow; The Land of Smiles*.

(M) **(*) Decca KCSP 466.

An attractive programme with a major contribution from Hilde Gueden, in very good form indeed. Other highlights include Régine Crespin's Letter song from *La Périchole* and Joan Sutherland's *Boléro* from a little-known piece by Lecocq. The collection opens spiritedly with the ubiquitous *Die Fledermaus overture* and the transfers are well managed until the beginning of side two, when the other overture, *Orpheus in the Underworld*, produces congestion at the opening; but after this the quality settles down again.

Palmer, Felicity (soprano)

'*Love's old sweet song*' (Victorian and Edwardian ballads; with John Constable, piano): SULLIVAN: *My dearest heart*. HAYDN WOOD: *A brown bird singing; Bird of love divine*. EDEN: *What's in the air today*. TRAVERS: *A mood*. MOIR: *Down the vale*. SQUIRE: *If I might come to you*. BRAHE: *Two little words*. D'HARDELOT: *Three green bonnets*. EVERARD: *It's all right in the summertime*. BINGHAM: *Love's old sweet song*. SPEAKS: *Morning*. MURRAY: *I'll walk beside you*. SANDERSON: *The valley of laughter.* SILESU: *Love, here is my heart.* LEHR: *Whatever is – is best.* BEHREND: *Daddy.*

(M)**(*)Argo KZRC 45.

The ear-catching item here is Everard's *It's all right in the summertime,* which Felicity Palmer delivers in true music-hall style with a cor-blimey Cockney accent. Even if the off-key piano postlude is also off-key in the wrong sense (not matching the humour of the rest at all), the result is a glorious tour de force, and sets the tone for one of the most warmly characterful recitals of this kind. These were all drawing-room songs which for decades were despised; now their overtly sentimental charm can be enjoyed afresh as a delightful period offering in performances like these, superbly accompanied by John Constable. The acoustic is reverberant, not like a drawing-room at all, but the sound is full and vivid, and generally well caught by the transfer.

Partridge, Ian (tenor)

'An album of English songs' (with Jennifer Partridge, piano): BRITTEN: *Winter Words* (song cycle to poems by Thomas Hardy). HOLST: *A little music; The thought; A floral bandit.* QUILTER: *Go lovely rose; O mistress mine.* ARMSTRONG GIBBS: *A song of shadows; The fields are full.* GURNEY: *Under the greenwood tree; The ploughman singing; Nine of the clock.* WARLOCK: *To the memory of a great singer; As ever I saw.* BUSH: *Echo's lament for Narcissus; The wonder of wonders.*

***Enigma K 453539.

The Britten song cycle is the best-known item here, but it is not that alone which makes this one of the most warmly attractive recorded collections of English song; Ian Partridge, with his headily beautiful voice, an ideal instrument for

recording, gives each of the separate songs on side two a touching, expressive individuality, responding not just to the gentle melodies but to the tender moods and sensitive setting of English lyrics. This is an area of song still seriously neglected, and Ian Partridge points the way, helped by fresh and imaginative accompaniment from his sister Jennifer. Partridge's approach to the Britten cycle is refreshingly different from that of Peter Pears, not nearly so heavily pointed but full of detailed insights, and, with beauty the keynote, it is just as revealing of Britten and Hardy.

Pavarotti, Luciano (tenor)

'The world's favourite arias' from: LEONCAVALLO: *I Pagliacci.* FLOTOW: *Martha.* BIZET: *Carmen.* PUCCINI: *La Bohème; Tosca; Turandot.* VERDI: *Rigoletto; Aïda; Il Trovatore.* GOUNOD: *Faust.*

**(*)Decca KSXC 6649.

As one would expect from Pavarotti, there is much to enjoy in his ripe and resonant singing of these favourite arias, but it is noticeable that the finest performances are those which come from complete sets, conducted by Karajan (*Bohème*), Mehta (*Turandot*) and Bonynge (*Rigoletto*), where with character in mind Pavarotti's singing is the more intense and imaginative. The rest remains very impressive, though at under forty minutes the measure is short. The transfer is generally brilliant, the level high; the Verdi items are especially vivid and only the *Turandot* excerpt (*Nessun dorma*), with its none too clear choral contribution, falls slightly below the general high standard.

'King of the high Cs': arias from: DONIZETTI: *La Fille du régiment; La Favorita.* VERDI: *Il Trovatore.* R. STRAUSS: *Der Rosenkavalier.*

ROSSINI: *Guglielmo Tell*. BELLINI: *I Puritani*. PUCCINI: *La Bohème*.

*** Decca KSXC 6658 [Lon. 5–26373].

The punning title may not be to everyone's taste, but in recent years there have been few finer or more attractively varied collections of tenor arias than this, a superb display of Pavarotti's vocal command as well as his projection of personality. The selections come from various sources and the recording quality is remarkably consistent, the voice stirringly vibrant and clear, even though the transfers are all made at maximum level. The accompanying detail and contributions of the chorus are well managed too.

'*O holy night*' (with Wandsworth Boys' Choir, National PO, Adler): sacred music by ADAM; STRADELLA; MERCADANTE; SCHUBERT; BIZET; BERLIOZ. FRANCK: *Panis angelicus*. BACH–GOUNOD: *Ave Maria* (2).

**(*)Decca KSXC 6781.

It is a long-established tradition for great Italian tenors to indulge in such songs as these, most of them overtly sugary in their expression of (no doubt) sincere religious fervour. Pavarotti is hardly a model of taste, but more than most of his rivals (even a tenor as intelligent as Placido Domingo) he avoids the worst pitfalls; and if this sort of recital is what you are looking for, then Pavarotti is a good choice, with his beautiful vocalizing helped by full, bright recording. Note too that one or two of these items are less hackneyed than the rest, for instance the title setting by Adam, Mercadante's *Parola quinta* and the *Sanctus* from Berlioz's *Requiem mass*. The transfer is admirably clear and clean; the chorus too is naturally caught.

'*The art of Pavarotti*': arias from: DONIZETTI: *L'Elisir d'amore; Maria Stuarda; La Fille du régiment;*

Lucia di Lammermoor. VERDI: *Un Ballo in maschera; Rigoletto; Macbeth; Requiem (Ingemisco)*. ROSSINI: *Stabat Mater (Cujus animam)*. PUCCINI: *Turandot*.

***Decca KSXC 6839.

A generous and well-varied collection of Italian arias which superbly displays the magnificent qualities of Luciano Pavarotti. It is remarkable that an Italian tenor with a voice that has specific lyrical echoes of Gigli as well as heroic echoes of the greatest of his predecessors should also be a thinking and imaginative musician. Those qualities are repeatedly demonstrated here, even if at times Pavarotti's positive character takes him near danger. There is nothing weak or undercharacterized about this singing, yet it is never vulgar, and the ease with which he sings up to his top Cs and (in *Cujus animam*) up to D flat is phenomenal. Culled from different complete sets, the recordings – all with excellent Decca characteristics – are admirably consistent. The transfers too are well managed, although there is sometimes a slight lack of bloom on the choral fortissimos.

'*Pavarotti sings duets*' (with (i) Nicolai Ghiaurov; (ii) Joan Sutherland; (iii) Renata Tebaldi; (iv) Montserrat Caballé; (v) Mirella Freni; (vi) Rolando Panerai): excerpts from: (i) BIZET: *Les Pêcheurs de perles*. (ii) DONIZETTI: *La Fille du régiment*. BELLINI: *I Puritani*. (iii) VERDI: *Un Ballo in maschera;* (iv) *Luisa Miller*. (v; vi) PUCCINI: *La Bohème;* (v) *Madama Butterfly*.

***Decca KSXC 6858.

The great Bizet duet – an enormously popular item, but one far too rarely recorded – was done separately (for the *Your Hundred Best Tunes* series – see above), but otherwise this collection is cunningly assembled from Pavarotti's most successful complete opera sets, including the sparkling *Fille du régiment* and the superb *Madama Butterfly* conducted by Karajan. It makes an irresistible anthology. Not many tenors today could begin to match this range of expression, technical mastery and sheer beauty of tone, and Pavarotti is splendidly partnered here. The layout of the duets, too, is particularly felicitous, each following on naturally, with the rapturously joyous duet from Act 2 of *Un Ballo in maschera* (*Teco io sto*) to end side one and the great love duet from Act 1 of *Madama Butterfly* to close side two. For some reason, in both these items the treble becomes slightly over-bright and needs control; otherwise the transfers are of very high quality throughout. There are few more thoroughly enjoyable vocal recitals available than this.

Price, Leontyne (soprano)

'*Christmas with Leontyne Price*' (with Vienna Singverein, Vienna PO, Karajan): GRÜBER: *Silent night.* MENDELSSOHN: *Hark the herald angels.* HOPKINS: *We three kings.* TRAD.: *Angels we have heard on high; O Tannenbaum; God rest ye merry; Sweet li'l Jesus.* WILLIS: *It came upon the midnight clear.* BACH: *Vom Himmel hoch.* BACH–GOUNOD: *Ave Maria.* SCHUBERT: *Ave Maria.* ADAM: *O holy night.* MOZART: *Alleluja, K.165.*

(M)**(*) Decca Jubilee KJBC 38.

There is much beautiful singing here, but the style is essential operatic. The rich, ample voice, when scaled down (as for instance in *We three kings*), can be very beautiful, but at full thrust it does not always catch the simplicity of melodic line which is characteristic of many of these carols. Yet the vibrant quality of the presentation is undoubtedly thrilling, and it can charm too, as in *God rest ye merry*, with its neat harpsichord accompaniment. The transfer is admirably rich and vivid.

Purcell Consort, Grayston Burgess

'*Music of the High Renaissance in England*' (with Jaye Consort of Viols, Simon Preston, organ and harpsichord): GIBBONS: *O God the King of Glory; Great Lord of Lords; Lord Salisbury's pavan.* FERRABOSCO: *Pavan for viols.* BYRD: *O Lord, how vain; Elegy on the death of Tallis; Lord Salisbury's pavan; In Nomine a 5 for viols.* WEELKES: *As Vesta was from Latmos hill descending.* MORLEY: *Hard by a crystal fountain.* BULL: *Prelude; In Nomine.* TOMKINS: *The Lady Folliott's galliard.*

(M)***Turnabout KTVC 34017.

A beautifully planned and executed concert which blends vocal music, harpsichord pieces, splendidly played by Simon Preston, and music for viols. All the music-making is stylish, spontaneous and highly enjoyable, and this makes a fine sequel to the Purcell Consort's collection of early Renaissance music (see below). The level of the tape transfer is high: the rather forward balance of the recording tends to minimize the dynamic range somewhat, but in every other respect the sound is fresh and clear, with excellent projection and a fine bloom on the voices.

'*John Dunstable and his contemporaries: Music of the early Renaissance*' (with Musica Reservata): DUNSTABLE: *Ave maris stella* (hymn); *O rosa bella* (song); *Quam pulchra es; Veni sancte spiritus; Veni creator* (motets). DUFAY: *Ave regina coelorum* (motet); *Franc cueur gentil* (song). ANON.: *Sing we to this merry company* (carol); *Filles à marier* (song); *Deo gratias Anglia* (The Agincourt carol); *Basse dance: La Spagna.* PLAINSONG: *Salve regina, mater misericordiae; Reges*

Tharis (Offertorium); *Alma redemptoris mater*. LANTINS: *In tua memoria* (motet). FRYE: *Ave regina coelorum* (motet).

(M)***Turnabout KTVC 34058.

In his day Dunstable was the most famous musician in Europe, and the legacy of music he left us reveals him an unquestioned master; his beautiful isorhythmic motet *Veni sancte spiritus* shows this readily. From this fine collection Dunstable's originality stands out (in spite of the fact that doubt is cast on whether he was in fact the composer of *O rosa bella*, one of the highlights). The Lantins *In tua memoria* is a lovely piece, and Dufay and Frye both emerge as strong personalities. The performances throughout are wonderfully fresh and alive. The sweet tone of the soprano, Barbara Elsy, and the flexible melisma of the tenor, Ian Partridge, stand out from a vocal group which displays a skill and security usually associated with instrumental music. The recording too is excellent, clear yet with a perfectly judged acoustic, and the transfer is smooth and clean. This is very highly recommended.

'*English madrigals from the courts of Elizabeth I and James I*' by BENNET; BYRD; WEELKES; MORLEY; FARNABY; KIRBYE; FARMER; GREAVES; VAUTOR; BATESON; GIBBONS; ALISON; TOMKINS; WILBYE; WARD.

(M)***Turnabout KTVC 34202.

A first-rate collection, superbly sung by a group of six singers who individually are fine artists and collectively make a splendid team. The first two items, John Bennet's *All creatures now are merry-minded* and Byrd's *This sweet and merry month*, are full of the joy of spring, and the spontaneity and freshness of the performances match the composers' inspiration. And whether in the lively interplay of parts of *Wither away so fast?* or the sustained intensity of *Construe my mean-*

ing the singers show both their versatility and sense of contrast. Byrd's *Lullaby* is most gently sung, and the melancholy *Retire, my troubled soul*, which closes the recital, is quite ravishing. The concert is admirably planned, not only in the choice and order of items but also in the happy idea of having the Elizabethan madrigals grouped on side one and those from the Succession on side two. The cassette transfer is full and natural; on our tape there seemed rather more immediacy for the voices on side two, and rather less projection on side one, but current copies may have evened up this difference.

'*To entertain a king*' (*Music for Henry VIII*; with Musica Reservata, Morrow): music by CORNISH; BARBIREAU; HENRY VIII; RICHEFORT; ISAAC; BUSNOIS; DAGGERE; and anonymous dance music.

(M)***Argo KZKC 24.

The Musica Reservata group, which joins the Purcell Consort here, has a reputation for robust and vital readings of neglected repertoire. They sometimes resist the delicacy of nuance and preciosity of much madrigal singing, drawing their analogy with the kind of vocal production one encounters in folk singing, not always to the music's advantage. Here, however, they form a harmonious partnership with the Purcell Consort to present a varied and entertaining programme that might have been heard at the court of Henry VIII. The singing is both refined and robust. Cornish's delightful *Ah Robin* is matched by the gentle melancholy of the anonymous *Where be ye my love*, while the boisterous *I am a jolly foster* reminds one of the glee sung by the crew in Sullivan's *HMS Pinafore*. The instrumental pieces are piquantly scored, and, like the interludes for harpsichord, are played with much character. The whole programme is beautifully recorded and admirably transferred to cassette: the atmosphere is at once intimate and lively.

'The triumphs of Oriana' (*Music to entertain Elizabeth I*; with London Cornet and Sackbut Ens., Elizabethan Consort of Viols): music by PEEL; BENNET; MORLEY; HUNT; WEELKES; WILBYE; HOLMES; MUNDY; FARMER; MARSON; TOMKINS; EAST; and anonymous dances.
(M)**Argo KZKC 25.

This cassette attempts to re-create the atmosphere of Windsor in 1593, when a tournament was given in honour of Queen Elizabeth I and this grand collection of madrigals by the country's most famous composers was presented for the first time. With debatable success each side opens with crowd noises to provide atmosphere, and the madrigals themselves are performed by a choir big enough for open-air performances, not by the regular small consort. Some of the bigger madrigals are backed with brass, and the viol music provides attractive dance interludes. There is certainly an element of spectacle here, although the basically excellent recording has sometimes been transferred at fractionally too high a level and the refinement slips just a little with the wide amplitude of the choral climaxes.

Rothenberger, Anneliese (soprano)

'Anneliese Rothenberger sings operetta': excerpts from: KATTNIGG: *Balkanliebe*. STRAUSS, Johann, Jnr: *Casanova; Die Fledermaus*. DOSTAL: *Clivia; Die ungarische Hochzeit*. LINCKE: *Frau Luna*. LEHÁR: *The Merry Widow; Giuditta*. KÜNNEKE: *Die lockende Flamme*. BENATZKY/STOLZ: *White Horse Inn*. KÁLMÁN: *Gräfin Maritza*. ZELLER: *Der Vogelhändler*.
(M) *(*) HMV Greensleeve TC-ESD 7043.

The very forward balance of the voice here tends to detract from the presenta-

tion, although the excerpts mix familiar with unfamiliar in an imaginative programme. Miss Rothenberger's even delivery and reliably firm vocal line are impressive, although *Vilja* (for instance) has more lyrical ardour than charm. *Ich bin verliebt* (from *Clivia*), with its decorative vocal flourishes, brings genuine bravura, and the lively numbers are often infectiously vivacious (*Lind ist die Bacht* from *Die lockende Flamme* is a good example). There is much to praise and enjoy, but the tape transfer is overmodulated and rough in places and is noticeably unkind in its focus of the chorus used in some of the items. The accompaniments, which come from a variety of sources, are generally well managed (the conductors include Willy Mattes, Carl Michalski, Willi Boskovsky and Robert Stolz).

Rothenberger, Anneliese, and Nicolai Gedda (tenor)

'Favourite operetta duets' (with Graunke SO, Mattes or Stolz): from: KÁLMÁN: *Czardasfürstin; Gräfin Maritza*. LEHÁR: *The Land of Smiles; Giuditta; The Merry Widow*. STOLZ: *Frühling im Prater; Zwei Herzen im Dreivierteltakt*. MILLÖCK ER: *Die Dubarry*. STRAUSS, Johann, Jnr: *Casanova; Wiener Blut*.
**HMV TC-CSD 3748.

Good, stylish performances of a number of favourites, interspersed with less familiar but not less attractive excerpts. The transfer is restricted in dynamic range, but the sound is undoubtedly vivid. There is much to charm here, notably *Bei einem Tea en deux* from *The Land of Smiles* and the famous *Merry Widow waltz*. Elsewhere the singing is sometimes more routine in presentation, but always stylish.

815

Royal Choral Society

'*Crown imperial*' (with Norma Procter, contralto, LPO, Andrew Davis; Nicholas Kynaston, organ): arr. BLISS: *God save the Queen.* HANDEL: *Zadok the Priest.* ELGAR: *Pomp and circumstance march No. 1, Op. 39.* arr. VAUGHAN WILLIAMS: *Old Hundredth.* ARNE: *Rule Britannia.* WALTON: *Crown imperial.* PARRY: *Jerusalem.*

(B)(**)Classics for Pleasure TC-CFP 198.

Strong vigorous performances, well balanced and recorded if lacking something in spectacle; *Rule Britannia* and *Jerusalem* do not manage to conjure up the 'Proms' atmosphere. The Walton lacks the rich, resplendent quality of Boult's performance (for instance). The tape transfer has, alas, been made at marginally too high a level and there are recurring patches where the sound coarsens.

Royal Liverpool Philharmonic Choir and Orch., Walters

'*A song for Christmas*' (with Woodfall Junior School Choir; Robert Tear, tenor): TRAD.: *Born in Bethlehem; Over the snow; Babe of Bethlehem; The Bells; The little camel boy; Chester carol; Jingle bells; Deck the hall; The Virgin Mary had a baby boy; A Czech rocking carol; Cuckoo carol.* ANDERSON: *Sleigh-ride.* ARTHUR: *Tua Bethlem dref.* WALTERS: *Iona; Ding-dong doh.* VAUGHAN WILLIAMS: *Wither's rocking carol.* GRÜBER: *Silent night.*

(M)***HMV Greensleeve TC-ESD 7024.

This must be the happiest of all carol collections. The annual carol concert of the Royal Liverpool Philharmonic Society goes back more than forty years, and its essential participants are children (in the audience as well as the choir). For this recording a special evening session was convened to record *Jingle bells*, in which the audience joins for the chorus. The sheer exhilaration of this joyous singing is such as to place this number alongside the famous Manchester schoolchildren's recordings made for Columbia in the late twenties. But the whole programme is delightful. Its freshness is mirrored in the orchestral arrangements, and Robert Tear's solo contribution is memorable too, especially in the moving performance of *Tua Bethlem dref*, sung in Welsh. But it is the children one remembers, and they sing enchantingly, especially in *The little camel boy* and *Ding-dong doh.* The orchestral arrangements are scored with loving expertise, and the whole concert has the spontaneity of a live occasion. The recording is warmly glowing and the tape transfer has captured the resonance beautifully. Only just occasionally the clarity of the transients slips; for the most part the sound is first-class, and no more so than in the closing *Silent night*, which radiates a wonderful stillness.

Sacred music

'*The world of sacred music*', Vol. 2: *Famous airs and choruses from:* BACH: *Mass in B minor.* HANDEL: *Messiah; Judas Maccabaeus; Samson.* VERDI: *Requiem.* BRAHMS: *A German Requiem.* MENDELSSOHN: *Elijah.* BERLIOZ: *L'Enfance du Christ.*

(M)*(**)Decca KCSP 297.

This is an attractive selection, and the solo items, which include Kathleen Ferrier, Joan Sutherland and Kenneth McKellar singing Handel, and Geraint Evans in Mendelssohn, are beautifully sung and well transferred. The snag is that the choruses have offered transfer problems. The opening Bach *Sanctus* has a degree of roughness, and although the *Sanctus* from Verdi's *Requiem*, which closes side two, has a more convincing sound quality the choral contribution to the *Elijah* excerpts hints at congestion. On the other hand Joan Sutherland's splendid performance of *Let the bright seraphim* is demonstration-worthy.

St John's College Choir, Cambridge, Guest

'The world of Christmas', Vol. 2 (with Brian Runnett, organ): BRITTEN: *A Ceremony of Carols.* JOUBERT: *Torches; There is no rose.* WARLOCK: *Adam lay y-bounden; Balulalow.* arr. SHAW: *My dancing day; The seven joys of Mary; Cherry tree carol.* WILLIAMSON: *Ding dong merrily.* TRAD.: *Adeste fideles; Up! good Christian folk; Rocking.*
(M)***Argo KCSPA 164.

The outstanding performance of the *Ceremony of Carols* (discussed in the Britten section above) would alone make this tape worth having, but the other carols are imaginatively chosen and beautifully sung too. The transfer is admirably natural, clean and secure. Treble voices are not always the easiest sound to focus cleanly in a cassette transfer, but the Argo engineers have managed exceptionally well here, and the Britten often approaches demonstration quality.

'The world of St John's': music by WEELKES; PURCELL; DAVY; S. S. WESLEY; HOWELLS; VAUGHAN WILLIAMS; MONTEVERDI; BANCHIERI; HAYDN; MENDELSSOHN; MESSIAEN.
(M)**(*)Argo KCSP 300.

As can be heard from these recordings, St John's College Choir, trained and directed by George Guest, have run the more celebrated King's College Choir at Cambridge very close. The style, while remaining refined, is often more robust than that at King's: no suspicion here of

being over-mannered. The variety of the music represented here is encompassed with confidence. The Davy and Vaughan Williams works are settings of similar words (taken from Psalm 47) and they are sung with fine vigour (the Vaughan Williams has the advantage of a jubilant brass accompaniment). The Purcell *Jehova, quam multi sunt hostes mei* is also a splendid piece, while the collection closes with an eloquent *O for the wings of a dove* (from Master Alastair Roberts) and – following after with surprising success – Messiaen's *O sacrum convivium.* They are both beautifully recorded and well transferred, as in most of the programme, although the focus slips a little in the opening Weelkes *Alleluia* and the *Kyrie* from Haydn's *Paukenmesse.*

'Christmas at St John's': GRÜBER: *Silent night.* RUTTER: *Shepherd's pipe carol.* MENDELSSOHN: *Hark the herald angels. O little town of Bethlehem; Born on earth; The twelve days of Christmas; Up! good Christian folk; Good King Wenceslas; While shepherds watched; God rest you merry, gentlemen; The holly and the ivy; Away in a manger; The first nowell; I saw three ships; Suo Gan.*
***Argo KZRC 782.

This is first-rate in every way, a wholly successful concert of mostly traditional carols, in sensitive arrangements without frills. The singing is straightforwardly eloquent, its fervour a little restrained in the Anglican tradition, yet with considerable underlying depth of feeling. The full character of every carol, is well brought out: the expressive simplicity of *I saw three ships* and Rutter's *Shepherd's pipe carol* is most engaging. The recording is excellent and the tape transfer one of Argo's very best, full, yet clear, with the natural resonance well caught.

Sass, Sylvia (soprano)

'Presenting Sylvia Sass' (with LSO, Gardelli): arias from: PUCCINI: *Turandot; Tosca; Manon Lescaut; Madama Butterfly.* VERDI: *Aïda; Macbeth; I Lombardi.*

*** Decca KSXC 6841 [Lon. 5-26524].

Glamorous and vibrant in personality and appearance as well as of voice, Sylvia Sass immediately establishes her star status at the very start of Turandot's big aria, *In questa reggia.* The Puccini excerpts stand any kind of competition in their range and expression, searching as well as beautiful, and though the Verdi items occasionally betray tiny chinks in the technical armour, there have been few more exciting soprano recital recordings in recent years. The transfer to tape has brought a touch of hardness to edge the vibrancy of the voice, and the orchestral strings too sound somewhat thin. But the recording is otherwise vivid and clear, and the refinement of detail creates the most beautiful orchestral textures in the introductions to the scenes from *Macbeth* and *I Lombardi.*

'Dramatic arias' (with National PO, Gardelli): BELLINI: *Norma: Sediziose voci . . . Casta diva.* VERDI: *La Traviata: E strano . . .Ah, fors'è lui. Il Trovatore: Vanne, lasciami . . . D'amor sull'ali rosee. Macbeth: Nel dì della vittoria . . . Vieni! t'affretta! La luce langue.* PONCHIELLI: *La Gioconda: Suicidio!*

**(*) Decca KSXC 6921.

Sylvia Sass's account of *Casta diva*, which opens this recital, reveals both her magnetism and her technical finesse at their most impressive. This is singing which keeps producing echoes of Callas on the one hand, Sutherland on the other, while remaining totally individual, and the beat in the voice is kept well in check.

The other performances are more controversial, sometimes exaggerated in their expression, but Sass is nothing if not a compelling singer, and her vibrancy is never for a moment in doubt. Not many sopranos today could sound so commanding in so formidable a collection of arias. The transfers are made at a very high level and the sound is clear rather than rich (the orchestra lacking warmth), with the voice tending to harden at *fortissimo* and a marginal hint of peaking in the *La Traviata* scene.

(The) Scholars

'When the winds breathe soft – Glees from Georgian England': LINLEY: *Let me, careless.* WEBBE: *When the winds breathe soft; You gave me your heart.* BATTISHILL: *Amidst the myrtles.* COOKE: *Deh! Dove?; In paper case.* CALLCOTT: *O snatch me swift.* DANBY: *The nightingale.* WALMISLEY: *Music, all powerful.* BEALE: *The humble tenant.* ATTWOOD: *To all that breathe.*

***Oiseau-Lyre KDSLC 33.

The Georgian glee had its heyday during the last half of the eighteenth century and the first two decades of the nineteenth. Derived from the madrigal, the form is sometimes simple, sometimes complex, with as many as eight parts. This admirably chosen selection shows the freshness and diversity of some of the best examples: the atmospheric title piece (which comes second) is enchanting. The singing here is of the highest quality, the voices well integrated yet never bland. Words are clear, consonants unexaggerated. The whole effect – whether the music is expressive or lively – is consistently spontaneous. The recording is superb and the transfer of demonstration quality: the voices have presence and a lovely warmth and bloom. Highly recommended.

Schwarzkopf, Elisabeth (soprano)

'Elisabeth Schwarzkopf sings operetta' (with Philharmonia Chorus and Orch., Ackermann): HEUBERGER: Der Opernball: Im chambre séparée. ZELLER: Der Vogelhändler: Ich bin die Christel; Schenkt man sich Rosen. Der Obersteiger; Sie nich bös. LEHÁR: Der Zarewitsch: Einer wird kommen. Der Graf von Luxemburg: Hoch Evoë; Heut noch werd ich Ehefrau. Giuditta: Meine Lippen. STRAUSS, Johann, Jnr: Casanova: Nuns' chorus; Laura's song. MILLÖCKER: Die Dubarry: Ich schenk mein Herz; Was ich im Leben beginne. SUPPÉ: Boccaccio: Hab ich nur deine Liebe. SIECZYNSKY: Wien du Stadt meiner Träume (Vienna, city of my dreams; song).

✲***HMV TC-ASD 2807.

This is one of the most delectable recordings of operetta arias ever made, and it is here presented with excellent sound. Schwarzkopf's 'whoopsing' manner (as Philip Hope-Wallace called it) is irresistible, authentically catching the Viennese manner, languor and sparkle combined. Try for sample the exquisite Im chambre séparée or Sei nicht bös; but the whole programme is performed with supreme artistic command and ravishing tonal beauty. This outstanding example of the art of Elisabeth Schwarzkopf at its most enchanting is a tape which ought to be in every collection. The transfer is beautifully managed and provides presence yet retains the full vocal bloom.

Scottish National Chorus

'Great songs of Scotland' (with Moira Anderson, soprano, BBC Scottish Orch., Currie): The bonnie Earl o' Moray; O whistle; Afton Water; Durisdeer; Scots wha hae; Annie Laurie; Gae bring to me a pint of wine; The wee cooper o' Fife; Ye banks and braes; The Birks o' Aberfeldy; Ca the yowes; Sleeps the noon; I'll aye ca in by yon toun; This is no my plaid; Loch Lomond; Auld lang syne.

**Enigma K 423522.

This is well produced and the orchestrations are tastefully arranged. The opening of The bonnie Earl o' Moray, with its dramatic fanfares, sets the seal on the presentation, which sometimes detracts from the simplicity of these beautiful songs. On the other hand the orchestral preludes and postludes are very pleasing. These are songs intended for the solo voice, as Moira Anderson demonstrates whenever she sings alone, and very engagingly too. In Loch Lomond the chorus takes over from her, not really to the music's advantage. But those who like choral singing will find the Scottish National group sings with vigour and polish: they are splendid in Auld lang syne. The recording is richly atmospheric and has trasferred very well to tape.

Scotto, Renata (soprano), **Placido Domingo** (tenor)

Duets: MASSENET: Manon: Toi! Vous! GOUNOD: Roméo et Juliette: Va, je t'ai pardonné. GIORDANO: Fedora: E lui! E lui! Andate. MASCAGNI: I Rantzau: Giorgio si batte.

**(*)CBS40-76732.

Fine, rich, mellifluous singing from both soprano and tenor in an interesting group of duets. Mascagni's I Rantzau may not be a masterpiece, but in its warmly lyrical way the Act 4 duet is highly effective, and it is a great pity that the cassette is even less generous than the disc in providing any sort of background information about it (there are no musical notes other than the titles). Scotto is at her most compelling characterizing Manon, less aptly cast as Juliette. In all four duets it is the warmth of the singing rather than dramatic pointing which stands out. The transfers are adequate, clear but lacking range on top and with hints of peaking on the soprano voice in the strongest climaxes.

Soviet Army Ens., Alexandrov

Song of youth; A birch tree in a field; Far away; Volga boat song; You are always beautiful; Along Peter's Street; Tipperary; Kalinka, Babdura; Oh no! John; Snow flakes; Ukrainian poem. SHAPORIN: *The Decembrists: Soldiers' chorus.*

(M)**EMI TC-EXE 155.

There is plenty of character and exuberance here. The recording wants a little taming, to take off a touch of stridency, but the vitality of the singing and playing comes through. The familiar items like *Kalinka* and the *Volga boat song* are well done, but our favourite was a surprisingly idiomatic *O no! John*, sung in English and with a twinkle of humour, missing the dead-pan 'art-song' treatment which often spoils the home product. On the whole the transfer is clear and well-focused. However, the sound in the last item on side two, the *Ukrainian poem*, is coarse, with the voices tending to blast.

Stade, Frederica von (mezzo-soprano)

'French arias' (with LPO, Pritchard) from: MEYERBEER: *Les Huguenots.* GOUNOD: *Roméo et Juliette.* BERLIOZ: *Béatrice et Bénédict; La Damnation de Faust.* MASSENET: *Werther; Cendrillon.* OFFENBACH: *La Grande-Duchesse de Gérolstein.* THOMAS: *Mignon.*

***CBS 40–76522.

'The problem is simply how to convey her excellence in temperate language',

said one reviewer of this splendid recital of varied and attractive French arias. Von Stade's is an outstandingly rich and even mezzo-soprano, and she uses it with a rare technical finesse, so that trills and ornaments have a clarity and precision not often encountered. The range of expression is comparably wide: here she commandingly compasses formidably contrasted roles, from page in the Meyerbeer and Gounod to *grande dame* in the two delectable Offenbach arias, the comedy delectably pointed but never guyed. The transfer is of good quality, kind to the voice and naturally balanced. Side two has a higher level than side one.

'Mozart and Rossini arias' (with Rotterdam PO, de Waart) from: MOZART: *Le Nozze di Figaro; La Clemenza di Tito; Don Giovanni.* ROSSINI: *Il Barbiere di Siviglia; Otello; La Cenerentola.*

***Philips 7300 511 [id.].

It was as Cherubino in *Figaro* at Glyndebourne that Frederika von Stade first made her mark in Britain, at once demonstrating electrifying qualities of projection and voice. Much of that electricity is caught here, not just in Mozart but if anything more impressively still in her finely characterized and superbly sung Rossini portraits, the minx-like Rosina, the sparkling Cinderella and the agonized Desdemona, at once poised and deeply involved. Excellent, refined recording with the voice well balanced; the transfer is rather more vivid in the Rossini than in the Mozart, and at climaxes there is sometimes a feeling that the amplitude of the vocal texture does not expand quite naturally.

Recital (with Martin Katz, piano): DOWLAND: *Come again, sweet love; Sorrow stay.* PURCELL: *The Blessed Virgin's expostulation.* LISZT: *Die drei Zigeuner; Einst; Oh! quand je dors.* DEBUSSY: *Chansons de Bilitis*

Nos. 1–3. arr. CANTELOUBE: *Auprès de ma blonde; Où irai-je me plaindre; Au pré de la Rose; D'où venez-vous fillette.* HALL: *Jenny Rebecca.*
**(*)CBS 40–76728.

The delectable Frederica von Stade is as always magically compelling here, both in vocal personality and in the vocal production itself. If in some of these songs Schwarzkopf, Janet Baker and others have sometimes been more positive, this memorable recital becomes more than the sum of its parts, closing with an engagingly gentle encore piece by Carol Hall. The accompaniments by Martin Katz are poised and sensitive. The transfers are clean and faithful, although the treble is not as soft-grained as on LP and there is a touch of hardness on the upper range of the voice. Our copy has 'print-through' on both sides, so that in the silences between the songs the sound on the reverse tracks can be faintly heard.

Stefano, Giuseppe di (tenor)

'The world of Neapolitan song' (with New SO, Pattacini, or Orch., Olivieri): songs by DE CURTIS; CESARINI; LAZZARO; BIXIO; CARDILLO; BARBERIS; TAGLIAFERRI; CALIFANO; COSTA; NICOLAVENTE; and traditional songs.
(M)***Decca KCSP 313.

Di Stefano was still in magnificent voice in the mid-sixties when he recorded these popular Neapolitan songs – including many comparative rarities as well as obvious choices like *Torna a Surriento, Catari, catari,* and *Addio, mia bella Napoli.* The selection on tape has been generously extended, with about half a dozen extra items added to the content of Decca's original full-priced LP recital (SXL 6176). Despite the inevitable touches of vulgarity the singing is both rich-toned and charming. The transfer is clear and vivid.

Sutherland, Joan (soprano)

'Romantic French arias' (with Geneva Grand Theatre Chorus, Suisse Romande Orch., Bonynge) from: OFFENBACH: *Robinson Crusoé; Les Contes d'Hoffmann (Doll song); La Grande-Duchesse de Gérolstein.* MEYERBEER: *Dinorah.* CHARPENTIER: *Louise.* AUBER: *Manon Lescaut; Fra Diavolo.* BIZET: *Les Pêcheurs de perles.* MASSENET: *Cendrillon.* GOUNOD: *Mireille.*
***Decca KCET 454.

This is a special tape-only issue selecting much of the cream from a two-disc album (SET 454/5). It will come as a delightful surprise to many that Offenbach's *Robinson Crusoé* includes an irresistible waltz song for the heroine as she steps ashore on Crusoe's island and is met by cannibals (*Take me to the man I adore*). Sutherland sings that and all the other brilliant numbers with great flair and abandon, relishing her virtuosity, while the romantic side is represented by such enchanting items as Massenet's sad little Cinderella aria, Dinorah's sweet lullaby for her pet goat, and a ravishing account of *Depuis le jour* from *Louise* to make most modern rivals sound thin and pale. Even among Sutherland's recitals this shines out for its fidelity in capturing the voice in its range of tone and dynamic. Except in the aria from *The Pearl Fishers* she is in delightfully fresh voice. The transfer is of excellent quality, although different on each side. Side one is very brilliant, the upper orchestral strings a little sharp-edged; side two is mellower, with slightly less presence to the voice but a rather more natural focus for the upper range of the orchestra. There is no lack of sparkle throughout.

'The world of Joan Sutherland': arias from: GOUNOD: *Faust.* DONIZETTI: *La Fille du régiment.* VERDI: *Rigo-*

letto; La Traviata. BELLINI: *Norma.*
DELIBES: *Lakmé.* CHARPENTIER:
Louise. HANDEL: *Messiah.* STRAUSS,
Johann, Jnr: *Casanova (Nuns'
chorus).* COWARD: *Conversation
Piece (I'll follow my secret heart).*
LEONCAVALLO: *La Mattinata.*
TRAD. (arr. Gamley): *The twelve
days of Christmas.*

(M) *(**) Decca KCSP 100.

Few if any vocal bargains match this –
a full hour of Sutherland at her finest,
ranging over the widest possible list of
items. This is of course intended as a sampler, a bait for the collector to purchase
much more, and in that it should be very
successful. The only pity is that nothing is
included from Sutherland's most famous
role, *Lucia di Lammermoor*, but the two
big solos from that are presented with
unrivalled freshness in the reissue of
Sutherland's first recital after her great
1959 triumph (KSDC 146 – see within the
composer index under Donizetti and
Verdi). However, KCSP 100 was an early
transfer and is now in need of remastering. The quality on side one is generally
good, but the voice tends to peak slightly
on high notes; on side two the focus of
the recording is less secure and there
are moments of fuzziness of outline
that we would not expect in a modern
transfer.

'Joy to the world' (Christmas carols,
all arr. GAMLEY; with Ambrosian
Singers, New Philharmonia Orch.,
Bonynge): HANDEL: *Joy to the world.*
WILLIS: *It came upon the midnight
clear.* ADAM: *O holy night.* GOUNOD:
O Divine Redeemer. TRAD.: *What
child is this?; Adeste fideles; The
twelve days of Christmas; Good King
Wenceslas; The holly and the ivy;
Angels we have heard on high; Deck
the hall.* REGER: *The Virgin's slum-
ber song.* MENDELSSOHN: *Hark the*

herald angels. SCHUBERT: *Ave
Maria.*

**(*) Decca KSXC 6193.

These are sugar-coated versions of
carols arranged by Douglas Gamley, but
who is going to complain when the result
cocoons the listener in a web of opulent
sound? A popular carol tape like this
may be hard to take at a single sitting, but
of its kind this is very good indeed, with
an unforgettably resilient performance of
The twelve days of Christmas. The transfer is of excellent quality, bold and clear.

Sutherland, Joan, and Luciano Pava-rotti (tenor)

Operatic duets (with National PO,
Bonynge) from: VERDI: *La Traviata;
Otello; Aïda* (with chorus). BELLINI:
La Sonnambula. DONIZETTI: *Linda
di Chamounix.*

*** Decca KSXC 6828.

This collection offers a rare sample of
Sutherland as Aïda (*La fatale pietra . . . O
terra, addio* from Act 4), a role she sang
only once on stage, well before her international career began; and with this and
her sensitive impersonations of Desdemona, Violetta and the Bellini and
Donizetti heroines, Sutherland might
have been expected to steal first honours
here. In fact these are mainly duets to
show off the tenor, and it is Pavarotti
who runs away with the main glory,
though both artists were plainly challenged to their finest and the result, with excellent accompaniment, is among the
most attractive and characterful duet recitals. The recording is admirably clear
and well focused, and the sophistication
of orchestral detail is striking in the
Otello and *Aïda* scenes which close the
recital.

Swingle II

'English and French part-songs':
VAUGHAN WILLIAMS: *Full fathom*

five; The cloud-capp'd towers; Over hill, over dale. STANFORD: *The blue bird.* BRITTEN: *Hymn to St Cecilia.* ELGAR: *The shower.* DEBUSSY: *Trois chansons de Charles d'Orléans.* SAINT-SAËNS: *Les fleurs et les arbres; Calme des nuits.* RAVEL: *Trois chansons.* POULENC: *Un soir de neige.*

**(*)RCA RK 25112.

The vocal precision, clever use of colour, and perfect blending of voices here remind one of an instrumental group, each instrument perfectly in tune, the textures completely homogeneous. Swingle II, of course, have much in common with the King's Singers, and they are on top form in this enterprising programme of part-songs, although more often they are heard in arrangements. This is superb singing, and the music is fully characterized. The tape transfer projects the singers well forward and seems to compress the dynamic range slightly. The quality on side two is slightly crisper in outline than side one, articulating the French accents clearly.

Tear, Robert (tenor)

'I dream of Jeanie' (with Philip Ledger, piano): MARSHALL: *I hear you calling me.* PURCELL, E.: *Passing by.* FRASER SIMSON: *Christopher Robin.* GODARD: *Angels guard thee.* RIEGO: *Homing.* WARLOCK: *The first mercy.* VAUGHAN WILLIAMS: *Silent noon.* RUSSELL: *Vale.* ROSS: *The cherry hung with snow.* ANDROZZO: *If I can help somebody.* LEHMANN: *The cuckoo.* COLERIDGE-TAYLOR: *Big Lady Moon.* PICCOLOMINI: *Ora pro nobis.* HEAD: *The little road to Bethlehem.* FOSTER: *I dream of Jeanie.* TOSELLI: *Serenata.* SANS-SOUCI: *When song is sweet.*

**(*)Argo KZKC 76.

Robert Tear chooses an attractive selection of songs and ballads which skirt the very cliff-edge of sentimentality. He points them well, with only the occasional hint of parody; the fine songs by Vaughan Williams, Head and Warlock cap the rest nicely. The recording is well balanced in a slightly resonant acoustic, and the transfer level is high; the sound is for the most part clear and clean, although at climaxes there is the slightest hint of peaking, more noticeable on side one.

Tebaldi, Renata (soprano)

'Great soprano arias' from: PUCCINI: *La Bohème; Tosca; Manon Lescaut; Madama Butterfly; Gianni Schicchi.* VERDI: *La Forza del destino; Il Trovatore; Otello.*

(M) *** Decca Ace of Diamonds KSDC 481.

A highly attractive collection, for the most part showing Tebaldi on peak form, the voice at its creamiest and with no lack of drama. The opening *scena* from *Forza del destino* is particularly fine, and other highlights include the excerpts from *Bohème, Manon Lescaut* and, of course, the outstanding *Un bel dì* from Butterfly. It was a good idea to rescue the *Tacea la notte*, which comes from a generally undistinguished complete set of *Trovatore.* The recording is excellent throughout, and considering the variety of sources the transfers are remarkably even in quality.

Tenors

'Great tenors of today' (with (i) Carlo Bergonzi; (ii) Franco Corelli; (iii) Placido Domingo; (iv) Nicolai Gedda; (v) James McCracken; (vi) Luciano Pavarotti; (vii) Jon Vickers): (ii) VERDI: *Aïda: Se quel guerrier . . . Celeste Aïda.* (v) *Otello: Niun mi tema.* (i) *La Forza del des-*

tino: O tu che in seno. (iv) BIZET: *Les Pêcheurs de perles: Je crois entendre.* (vii) *Carmen: Flower song.* (i) PUCCINI: *Tosca: E lucevan le stelle.* (ii) *Turandot: Nessun dorma.* (iii) *Manon Lescaut: Donna non vidi mai.* (ii) GIORDANO: *Andrea Chénier: Come un bel dì.* (vi) MASCAGNI: *L'Amico Fritz: Ed anche . . . oh amore.* (iv) GOUNOD: *Faust: Salut! Demeure.* (viii) SAINT-SAËNS: *Samson et Dalila: Arrêtez, ô mes frères.*

**(*) HMV TC-ASD 3302.

HMV compiled this anthology ingeniously from many sources. For example Luciano Pavarotti, an exclusive Decca artist from early in his international career, had earlier still taken part in EMI's complete set of *L'Amico Fritz*, so providing the excerpt which completes this constellation of great tenors. Not that each is necessarily represented in the most appropriate items, and the compilation does have one wishing (for example) that Vickers rather than McCracken was singing *Otello*, though that excerpt is valuable for preserving a sample of Barbirolli's complete set of that opera, short-lived in its regular issue. And although Vickers does not make an ideal Don José, it is useful to have his *Flower song*, since the set from which it comes is one of the less recommendable versions. The transfers are good, and though the recording quality is not consistent the voices are well reproduced, with warm orchestral accompaniments.

'*Great tenors of the world*' (with (i) Enrico Caruso; (ii) Tito Schipa; (iii) Beniamino Gigli; (iv) Richard Tauber; (v) Helge Roswaenge; (vi) Marcel Wittrisch; (vii) John McCormack; (viii) Heddle Nash; (ix) Lauritz Melchior; (x) Jussi Bjoerling; (xi) Georgess Thill): arias from: (i) LEONCAVALLO: *I Pagliacci.* (ii) DONIZETTI: *L'Elisir d'amore.* (iii) VERDI:

Rigoletto. GIORDANO: *Andrea Chénier.* (iv) FLOTOW: *Martha.* (v) ADAM: *Le Postillion de Longjumeau.* MOZART: *Die Entführung aus dem Serail.* (vi) MEYERBEER: *Les Huguenots* (duets with Margarete Teschemacher). (vii) HANDEL: *Atalanta.* (viii) MASSENET: *Manon.* (ix) WAGNER: *Tannhäuser (Rome narration).* (x) PUCCINI: *Turandot.* MEYERBEER: *L'Africaine.* (xi) BERLIOZ: *Les Troyens.*

(M) **(*) HMV TC-HLM 7004.

This makes a fascinating comparison with HMV's other tenor anthology (see above). No more distinguished list of tenors of the inter-war years could be assembled than this, and the items have been skilfully chosen, some entirely predictable, like Caruso's *Vesti la giubba*, Schipa's *Una furtiva lagrima*, or Gigli's *La donna è mobile*, but including such rare treasures as Helge Roswaenge's magnificent account of the bravura aria (*Freunde, vernehmet die Geschichte*) from *Le Postillion de Longjumeau*. While in the more modern recordings (like Jussi Bjoerling's 1944 version of *Nessun dorma*) the voices are not damped down, in the transcriptions from 78 the top is generally restricted to cut back the background noise of the originals. This is immediately noticeable in Caruso's opening item, and discerning collectors may feel that at times it has been overdone, although the tape transfers are full and clear.

Treorchy Male Choir, Jones

'*Climb every mountain*': excerpts from: VERDI: *I Masnadieri; La Forza del destino.* RODGERS: *The Sound of Music.* Music by SCHUBERT; CARTER; MCCARTNEY; DYLAN; and others.

**(*) Columbia TC-SCX 6593.

The ingenuous vigour of the tenor soloist, Wyn Davies, in the introduction to the *Robbers' chorus* from *I Masnadieri*, which opens this concert, is very much in the Welsh tradition. There is much eloquent feeling in the singing throughout, and if sometimes its intensity is slightly misplaced, one cannot but respond when the recording is so impressively rich and resonant. Indeed this is one of the very best available cassettes of Welsh choral singing; the quality of the transfer only falls below the highest EMI standards in the last item, the finale to Act 2 of Verdi's *Forza del destino*, where there is (on our copy) some curious distortion in the voice of the soprano, Mary Davies. She is not the most stylish of singers, and the other solo contributions are not always up to the standard of the choir. However, the programme mixes traditional Welsh concert material with pieces like *Yesterday* (which sounds rather inflated) and *Blowin' in the wind* quite effectively.

Valente, Benina (soprano)

Lieder (with Richard Goode, piano): MOZART: *Un moto di gioia; Als Luise; Das Veilchen; Der Zauberer.* WOLF: *Auch kleine Dinge; Mir ward gesagt; Wer rief dich denn? Du denkst mit einem Fädchen; Wie lange schon; Ihr jungen Leute; Mein Liebster singt; Schweig' einmal still; Ich hab' in Penna.* SCHUBERT: *Heidenröslein; An die Nachtigall; Nacht und Träume; Rastlöse Liebe.* BRAHMS: *Therese; Der Tod; Meine Liebe ist grün; Nachtigall; Auf dem Kirchhofe; Vergebliches Ständchen.*
**(*)Advent E 1048 (see p. xxiii) [id.].

An accomplished singer, Benina Valente seems equally at home in Mozart and in Wolf. The first side of the recital, which takes some twenty minutes, is mostly given over to Wolf, while the second is divided between Schubert and Brahms. Richard Goode is a sympathetic

accompanist, and the balance between voice and piano is excellent. There is some print-through on the copy submitted for review, and there could be longer pauses between the songs, but the quality is otherwise excellent.

Vienna State Opera Chorus

'Grand opera choruses' (with Vienna PO, (i) Karajan, (ii) Gardelli, (iii) Solti, (iv) Maazel) from: (i) MUSSORGSKY: *Boris Godunov.* (ii) VERDI: *Nabucco;* (i) *Otello.* PUCCINI: *Madama Butterfly.* (iii) WAGNER: *Die Meistersinger; Tannhäuser; Parsifal.* (iv) BEETHOVEN: *Fidelio.*
**Decca KSXC 6826.

This tape is over-priced. Although the performances are generally distinguished they come from complete sets, and there are several unsatisfactory closing fadeouts, notably in the Wagner excerpts. The Verdi transfers have brilliant sound (there is a touch of roughness in the chorus from Act 1 of *Otello*); and the *Humming chorus* from *Butterfly* and the scene from Act 1 of *Parsifal* both offer beautifully atmospheric quality. The liner note provides a eulogy of the Chorus itself but no details of what they are singing about.

Welsh choirs

'The very best of Welsh choirs', Vol. *1* (with Morriston Orpheus Choir, Harry or John; Monmouthshire Male Choir, Jenkins; Treorchy Choir (with Cory Band), V. Jones).
(**)EMI TC-EMC 3099.
Vol. 2 (with Dowlais Male Choir, W. Jones; Morriston Orpheus Choir (with GUS Band), Harry or John; Monmouthshire Male Choir, Jenkins).
*(*)EMI TC-EMC 3154.

These are both excellent compilations from the fine EMI back catalogue of

Welsh choral recordings. Volume 1, however, suffers from technical problems. The transfer (on our copy, at least) offered consistent 'pulsing' throughout and the focus of the choir was rather furry. The programme contains many favourites, including *Men of Harlech*, *Llef*, Parry's *Myfanwy*, *All through the night*, *Cartref* and *Cwm Rhondda*, and the recording is basically excellent; but this issue needs remastering. Volume 2 is tonally secure, and the choral groups are richly and resonantly recorded. The lack of bite in the treble is a drawback in the more incisive pieces, but *Comrades in arms* comes over quite well; and the *Chorus of Hebrew slaves* from *Nabucco* is eloquently atmospheric. When one turns to side two the lack of crisp transients in the *Soldiers' chorus* from *Faust* rather spoils the effect. However, the sustained music is successful.

White, Robert (tenor)

'*When you and I were young, Maggie*' (with Samuel Sanders, piano): BUTTERFIELD: *When you and I were young, Maggie.* FOSTER: *Beautiful dreamer.* FOOTE: *An Irish folk song.* TOURS: *Mother o' mine.* arr. TAYLOR: *May day carol.* SPEAKS: *Sylvia.* NEVIN: *Little Boy Blue; The Rosary.* PENN: *Smilin' through.* ROOT: *The vacant chair.* BOND: *I love you truly.* MCGILL: *Duna.* EDWARDS: *By the bend of the river.* DANKS: *Silver threads among the gold.* WESTENDORF: *I'll take you home again, Kathleen.* BOND: *A perfect day.*
**(*) RCA RK 11698.

Robert White is a tenor with a very individual timbre which may not appeal to every ear but certainly has a special fascination for those who – broadly generalizing – like an Irish tenor sound. White is in fact American, though clearly enough (his father was a close friend of John McCormack) he deliberately cultivates his Irish sound in such repertory as this. His manner is totally unsentimental, the style pleasingly direct and fresh, full of unforced charm. Fresh, clear recording to match, and the transfer too is clean, with an excellent balance and natural piano tone. There is a touch of edge on the voice, but this can be smoothed with a slight treble cut.

'*I hear you calling me*' (with Samuel Sanders, piano): CROUCH: *Kathleen Mavourneen.* MARTIN: *Come to the fair.* LEHMANN: *In a Persian garden; Ah moon of my delight.* arr. HUGHES: *A Ballynure ballad.* TRAD.: *Danny boy; The last rose of summer.* ADAMS: *The bells of St Mary's.* HAYDN WOOD: *Roses of Picardy.* ALLITSEN: *The Lord is my light.* MARGETSON: *Tommy, lad!* arr. STANFORD: *Molly Brannigan.* arr. SANDERS: *Molly Malone.* CRAXTON: *Mavis.* MARSHALL: *I hear you calling me.*
**(*) RCA RK 12450 [ARK 1 2450].

After the success of Robert White's first recording of ballads, it was to be expected that RCA would offer a second instalment. The result has all the disarming qualities of the first and can be recommended with equal enthusiasm to anyone charmed by this very individual voice. The recital again evokes the spirit of John McCormack by opening with a tenderly stylish account of *Danny boy*. The transfer is rather smoother and warmer than for the first recital and is generally very good indeed.

Winchester Cathedral Choir, Neary

'*Christmas carols*': *Once in Royal David's city; Alma redemptoris mater; When Christ was born; We three kings; Coventry carol; Angels from the realms of glory; Whence is that goodly fragrance; Unto us a son; See amid the winter snow.* GRÜBER: *Silent night.* BERLIOZ: *L'Enfance du Christ: L'adieu des bergers.* MENDELSSOHN: *Hark the herald angels.* BYRD: *Lullaby.* PRAETORIUS: *Es ist ein' Ros' entsprungen.*

(M)** Philips 7317 134.

A pleasingly intimate collection. The mood is set at the opening when *Once in Royal David's city* begins with a treble solo (beautifully sung by an unnamed member of the choir), and then the carol is taken up gently by the rest of the group. The recording throughout is atmospheric and truthful (though not sharply focused), and the selection, while including plenty of favourites, is not unadventurous. The *Coventry carol* is one of the highlights, its gentle melancholy beautifully caught. A good background tape for Christmas Eve.

Cassettes for the Car and Background Listening

The possibilities of tape for specific in-car use, as background music for a dinner party, or simply to create a pleasantly romantic late-evening atmosphere remain comparatively unexplored. Sophisticated orchestral arrangements of the best of the twentieth century's popular music can be very entertaining and a pleasant accompaniment to a long drive, or used as a backcloth for conversation and cocktails. Of course there are plenty of individual 'middle-of-the-road' cassettes of this kind, but most are of indifferent technical quality, many (including virtually all the early James Last repertoire) are only available in non-Dolby form, and almost all are too short to be really useful. Decca's seven *Easy listening* anthologies (KCSP 289–94 and 435) are generally well chosen and offer a reasonable standard of sound, but if they had been issued on double-length tapes they would have been far more useful. EMI's *The very best of Manuel* (a pseudonym for the brilliant arranger Geoff Love) meets this criticism halfway by providing some twenty items in a longer than usual standard tape (TC–EMC 1051). The Manuel brand of Latin kitsch is certainly colourful and there are many good tunes in this collection; it is an

excellent in-car tape, but the technical quality of the transfer is less satisfactory for domestic reproduction. Similarly *The very best of Ron Goodwin* (TC–TWOX 1064) is an entertaining mixture of film and show music, plus some memorable standards (eighteen items in all), but the reproduction is disappointing when listened to on high-grade equipment, although in the car it produces vivid results. One other EMI tape can be mentioned here, and this at least is double-length. Those who like the smoky-timbred, close-microphoned clarinet-playing of Acker Bilk will find plenty of favourite melodies in *The golden treasury of Acker Bilk* (TC2 EXE 1008), and the recording is adequate.

If one is prepared to accept single-length cassettes Decca have a generally well-engineered *Sounds* series. These are attractively compiled, although, curiously, the same track sometimes appears on two different cassettes. *Sounds romantic* (KMORC 2), *Sounds relaxed* (KMORC 3), *Sounds from the shows* (KMORC 8), *Sounds wide screen* (KMORC 9) and *Sounds of the seasons* (KMORC 13) are among the best of this series.

However, there are two double-length cassettes, *Soft and easy, Volumes 1* (KDPC 2 8039) and *2* (KDPC 2

8064), which are even more attractive. Each contains about two dozen standards; the selection on the first tape is particularly engaging. One would think it an easy matter to string together an anthology of really catchy arrangements of favourites, but compilers seem all too willing to pad out a collection with less than first-rate material. Another Decca double-length cassette series is spoiled in this way: *Focus on Frank Chacksfield* (KFOC 2 8057) includes a proportion of old mono recordings which sound distinctly thin; while *Focus on Ronnie Aldrich* (KFOC 2 8047) has patches of rough sound, although the programme includes a fair share of good tunes and the arrangements, featuring a double (stereo) piano image with orchestral backing, are effective.

For more than a decade Klaus Wunderlich has held the undisputed crown among the Hammond organists of the popular musical world. His superb technique, zippy rhythmic style, and wide stylistic sympathies, coupled to crisp Telefunken recording, have established an immediately recognizable image. Until recently most of his cassettes have been in non-Dolby versions, but now Decca have started reissuing the earlier recordings on their own label. *The unique Klaus Wunderlich sound* (KDPC2–R 8094) is one such compilation, featuring a series of medleys which are characteristically wide in range, from *Moonlight serenade* and *Tico tico* to *Summertime* and *Raindrops keep falling on*

my head. The transfer is first-class throughout, rich and smooth, yet with no lack of bite. Klaus Wunderlich is not only a brilliant organist but an electronics expert, and he balances the master tapes himself in his own studio. His latest foray is a cleverly engineered anthology featuring three new Hohner instruments, an electra-piano (which sounds like a celesta, but has also the possibilities of the vibraphone), a clavinet (which evokes harpsichord and guitar) and an electronic imitation of orchestral strings (which is uncannily accurate at times). On *Dream concerto* (KDKC 2 8072) he plays all three, and the different master recordings are cleverly mixed. The result (ranging from *Liebestraum* and the *Meditation* from *Thaïs* to *Clair* and *Wandering star*) is highly effective, and the tape transfer is immaculate.

Finally we turn to a new Decca series of double-length cassettes which provide the kind of background listening that has an all-purpose suitability. From this *Time for . . .* series four issues stand out. They are generally vividly engineered, though there is just the occasional patch of roughness, which is not noticeable in the car. *Time for piano* (KMOR 2 8081) offers twenty-eight tunes and a wide-ranging artists' roster. *Time for romance* (KMOR 2 8091) offers some very stylish piano-playing from Stanley Black, but is mostly orchestral and has plenty of atmosphere. *Time for strings* (KMOR 2 8083) is rather more mixed in appeal but agreeable enough, although the sound is somewhat variable. *Time for brass* (KMOR 2 8084) offers twenty-four brass and military band items, skilfully selected to provide an extremely buoyant and vivid programme. Band enthusiasts will find this a most invigorating cassette for the car, although domestically the high level brings some roughness of focus at times.

Talking Books and Plays

The growing number of spoken word recordings on tape (an obviously superior medium to disc for this repertoire) has been spearheaded by the Listen for Pleasure series, each consisting of two cassettes, with an average total playing time of about two hours, issued in a neatly devised package at just over £4 (and about to be launched in North America as we go to press). They are all obvious bargains, with many famous readers (notably David Niven with his autobiography) and with three full-length plays (including Dame Edith Evans's unforgettable portrayal of Lady Bracknell) among the initial releases. Aimed at the widest market and with the family car journey particularly in mind, they deserve success.

The Argo series is adventurous and distinguished, but costs much more. Argo cassettes are at the top end of the medium price-range, and if (as is often the case) a book or play extends to four tapes it becomes expensive, perhaps over-priced. But this is compensated by the sophistication of the production. We have space to mention only a few here, but the issues featuring Roy Dotrice and Glenda Jackson are certainly outstanding. *Watership Down* is totally compelling: it stretches to four tapes but is not a moment too long, and the vocal characterization (especially of Big Ears) is brilliantly perceptive. *Peter Pan* too is dramatized in the most vivid way (the novel, not the play, is used). The opening is rather wordy, but once under way it has a strong narrative flow, with a vocal portrayal of Captain Hook that cunningly recalls a famous film actor. Glenda Jackson, with her clean delivery and complete participation, is a natural choice for stories like *The Secret Garden* and *Little Women*, and her groups of fairy tales are very stylish. In Rudyard Kipling's *Jungle Book* Ian Richardson is superb; again the vocal colouring for the different characters is highly imaginative. Laurie Lee's readings from *Cider with Rosie* are another much-acclaimed item from the same catalogue, and we shall always be grateful that Bing Crosby, not long before he died, was persuaded to record *The Adventures of Tom Sawyer*. The characterization is no great shakes, but the easy manner and the golden voice earn their own welcome.

On their cheapest label (KABC) Argo have reissued at a price not too far above the Listen for Pleasure range some of their earlier dramatized recordings, notably *Alice in*

833

Wonderland with Jane Asher (and Margaretta Scott as a delightful narrator) and the magical *Wind in the Willows*, immortalizing Richard Goolden as Mole.

These comments only scratch the surface of the repertoire, and the list below selects the cream of the available recordings; but many readers will simply want to know that it exists. There are few better ways of passing a car journey than with a really good tale – even if the family have heard it before.

ADAMS, Richard
> *Watership Down.* Argo K 30 K 44. Roy Dotrice (with music by Butterworth).
> Argo KZDAC 176. Scenes from above recording.

ALCOTT, Louisa May
> *Little Women.* Argo K 98 K 33. Glenda Jackson.

ALDISS, Brian
> *Frankenstein Unbound.* Listen for Pleasure (L.f.P.) TC–LFP 7027. The author.

AUSTEN, Jane
> *Emma.* L.f.P. TC–LFP 7033. Dame Peggy Ashcroft.
> *Pride and Prejudice.* L.f.P. TC–LFP 7042. Celia Johnson.

AWDRY, Rev. W.
> *Railway Stories.* Decca KCSP 270 (*Volume 1*); KCSP 271 (*Volume 2*). Johnny Morris.

BARRIE, James
> *Peter Pan.* Argo K 90 K 33. Roy Dotrice and family (with music by Mendelssohn).

BETJEMAN, John
> *Banana Blush* (poems with music by Jim Parker). Charisma 7208 570. The author.

BRONTË, Charlotte
> *Jane Eyre.* L.f.P. TC–LFP 7029. Dame Wendy Hiller.

BRONTË, Emily
> *Wuthering Heights.* L.f.P. TC–LFP 7017. Daniel Massey.

BURNETT, Frances Hodgson
> *The Secret Garden.* Argo K 4 J 15. Glenda Jackson (with music by Kenny Clayton).

CARROLL, Lewis
> *Alice in Wonderland.* Argo KABC 1/2. Dramatized by Douglas Cleverdon, with Jane Asher, Vivienne Chatterton, Tony Church, Frank Duncan, Deryck Guyler, Carleton Hobbs, Norman Shelley, Ian Wallace, Marjorie Westbury; narrator: Margaretta Scott.
> *Alice through the Looking Glass.* Argo KABC 3/4. Dramatized and with cast similar to above.

CARTLAND, Barbara
> *I Search for Rainbows.* L.f.P. TC–LFP 7025. The author.
> '*Children's stories with strings*': *Jabberwocky; Jack and the Beanstalk; Tweedle Dum and Tweedle Dee; Father William; Rapunzel.* Argo KZDSW 706. Richard Baker (with music by Alan Ridout).

COLLODI, Carlo
> *Pinocchio.* Argo K 107 K 22. Bernard Cribbens.

CONAN DOYLE, Arthur
> *The Hound of the Baskervilles.*

L.f.P. TC–LFP 7005. Hugh
Burden.

COOLIDGE, Susan M.
What Katy Did. L.f.P. TC–LFP
7008. Gwen Watford.

DICKENS, Charles
A Christmas Carol. Argo KZSW
584/5. Roy Dotrice.
David Copperfield. Argo K 116 K
22. Roy Dotrice.
Doctor Marigold. Argo KZDSC
713. Roy Dotrice.
Oliver Twist. L.f.P. TC–LFP 7016.
Ron Moody.
Oliver Twist: Sikes and Nancy.
Argo KZDSC 711. Roy Dotrice.
*The Pickwick Papers: Bardell and
Pickwick*. Argo KZDSC 709.
Roy Dotrice.
*The Pickwick Papers: Mr Bob
Sawyer's party. The Signalman*
(ghost story). Argo KZDSC 710.
Roy Dotrice.
*A Tale of Two Cities: The Bastille
prisoner*. Argo KZDSC 712. Roy
Dotrice.

DURRELL, Gerald
My Family and Other Animals.
L.f.P. TC–LFP 7011. Gerald
Harper.

EDWARDS, Dorothy
*All About My Naughty Little
Sister*. L.f.P. TC–LFP 7013.
Felicity Kendal.

ELIOT, T. S.
*Four Quartets; The Waste Land;
Poems*. Argo K 2 P 24. Alec
Guinness.
Murder in the Cathedral. L.f.P.
TC–LFP 7045. Robert Donat
and the Old Vic Company.
*Old Possum's Book of Practical
Cats*. Argo KABC 22. The
author.

Fairy stories
'My favourite fairy stories'. L.f.P.
TC–LFP 7003. Nanette
Newman, Richard Norman,
Judi Dench, Pete Murray.

FORSYTH, Frederick
The Odessa File. L.f.P. TC–LFP
7030. Patrick Allen.

FRANCIS, Dick
High Stakes. L.f.P. TC–LFP 7005.
James Bolam.

GALLICO, Paul
The Snow Goose. RCA PK 11765.
Narrated by Spike Milligan with
Ludmilla Nova (with music).
*The Snow Goose; The Small Mir-
acle*. L.f.P. TC–LFP 7023. Sir
John Mills.

GRAHAME, Kenneth
The Reluctant Dragon. Argo
KZSWC 567. Michael Hordern
(with music).
The Wind in the Willows. Argo
KABC 5/6. Dramatized by Tony
Robertson, with Richard Gool-
den, Norman Shelley, Frank
Duncan, Tony Church and Pat-
rick Wymark.

HARDY, Thomas
Tess of the d'Urbervilles. Argo K
146 K 33. Moira Shearer.

HAWKESWORTH, John
*Upstairs, Downstairs: Book 1
(1903–1908)*. L.f.P. TC–LFP
7002. Hannah Gordon.

HERRIOT, James
*If Only They Could Talk; It
Shouldn't Happen to a Vet*.
L.f.P. TC–LFP 7024. The
author.

HYDE, H. Montgomery
Crime Has its Heroes. L.f.P. TC–LFP 7015. Frank Windsor.

Jackson, Glenda
'The Glenda Jackson Story Book'. Argo KZSWC 559 (*Volume 1: Goldilocks; Little Red Riding Hood; Snow White and the Seven Dwarfs*); KZSWC 560 (*Volume 2: The Frog Prince; The Story of Joseph; The Emperor's New Clothes*). Glenda Jackson (with music by Kenny Clayton).

Jesus
The Story of Jesus (abridged version taken from the four Gospels). L.f.P. TC–LFP 7009. Robert Dougal.

KENT, Alexander
Richard Bolitho, Midshipman. L.f.P. TC–LFP 7004. Anthony Valentine.

KIPLING, Rudyard
The Jungle Book. Argo KZSWC 525/7. Ian Richardson.
Just So Stories. Argo KABC 18/19 18/19 (*Vol. 1*); KABC 20/21 (*Vol. 2*). Richard Johnson, Barbara Jefford, Michael Hordern.

LEE, Laurie
Cider with Rosie. Argo K 91 K 33. The author (music by the Yetties).

MacLEAN, Alistair
The Guns of Navarone. L.f.P. TC–LFP 7014. Patrick Allen.

MILNE, A. A.
The House at Pooh Corner. Argo K 36 K 43. Norman Shelley, who also sings the *Hums* to music by H. Fraser Simson.

Now We Are Six. Argo KZSWC 569. Norman Shelley.
Now We Are Six; When We Were Very Young. Lf.P. TC–LFP 7038. Sir John Mills and Hayley Mills.
When We Were Very Young. Argo KZSWC 568. Norman Shelley.
Winnie the Pooh. Argo K 3 K 16. Norman Shelley (with *Hums* as above).

MONSARRAT, Nicholas
The Cruel Sea. L.f.P. TC–LFP 7036. Robert Powell.

NESBIT, E.
The Railway Children. L.f.P. TC–LFP 7006. Dinah Sheridan.

NIVEN, David
The Moon's a Balloon. L.f.P. TC–LFP 7010. The author.

PEMBERTON, Victor
Dr Who and the Pescatons. Argo KZSWC 564. Tom Baker, Elisabeth Sladen, Bill Mitchell.

PLOMER, William
The Butterfly Ball and The Grasshoppers' Feast. Argo KZSWC 2 8043. Judi Dench and Michael Hordern (with music).

SAGAN, Françoise
A Certain Smile. L.f.P. TC–LFP 7019. Anna Massey.

SAINT-EXUPÉRY, Antoine de
The Little Prince. Argo KABC 16/17. Peter Ustinov.

SCHAEFER, Jack
Shane. L.f.P. TC–LFP 7032. Peter Marinker.

SEWELL, Anna
Black Beauty. L.f.P. TC–LFP 7026. Hayley Mills.
Argo K 106 K 22. Angela Rippon.

SHAKESPEARE, William
Recordings by Marlowe Society of Cambridge, dir. George Rylands:
Antony and Cleopatra. Argo K 72 K 43.
As You Like It. K 46 K 32.
Hamlet. K 33 K 53.
Henry IV, Part 1. K 54 K 42.
Julius Caesar. K 32 K 32.
King Lear. K 53 K 43.
King Richard II. K 35 K 32.
Macbeth. K 14 K 32.
The Merchant of Venice. K 143 K 42.
A Midsummer Night's Dream. K 52 K 32.
Much Ado About Nothing. K 70 K 32.
Othello. K 49 K 43.
Richard III. K 142 K 43.
Romeo and Juliet. K 15 K 42.
Twelfth Night. K 16 K 32.

1957 Old Vic production:
Hamlet. L.f.P. TC–LFP 7021. John Gielgud, Leon Quartermaine, Yvonne Mitchell, Coral Browne, etc., dir. John Gielgud and John Richmond.

SHERIDAN, Richard
The School for Scandal. L.f.P. TC–LFP 7028. Dame Edith Evans, Claire Bloom, Harry Andrews, Alec Clunes, Michael Gough, Athene Seyler, Cecil Parker.

SPYRI, Johanna
Heidi. Argo K 122 K 22. Judi Dench.

STEVENSON, Robert Louis
Dr Jekyll and Mr Hyde. Argo K 149 K 22. Tom Baker.

Treasure Island. L.f.P. TC–LFP 7018. Anthony Bate.

THOMAS, Dylan
Under Milk Wood. Argo K 84 K 22. Original BBC production with Richard Burton, Hugh Griffith etc.
'*The world of Dylan Thomas*': *Under Milk Wood* (excerpts); *Poems.* Argo KCPA 166. Richard Burton, Emlyn Williams, Richard Bebb.

TOLKIEN, J. R.
The Hobbit. Argo K 4 D 27. Nicol Williamson.

TRUEMAN, Fred
Ball of Fire. L.f.P. TC–LFP 7022. The author.

TWAIN, Mark
The Adventures of Tom Sawyer. Argo K 3 K 34. Bing Crosby (with music by Tommy Reilly, harmonica).

Ustinov, Peter
Cautionary verse by Browning and Carroll; Belloc: *Cautionary tales.* Argo KABC 11. Peter Ustinov.

UTTLEY, Alison
Little Grey Rabbit stories. L.f.P. TC–LFP 7031. Beryl Reid.

VERNE, Jules
Journey to the Centre of the Earth. Argo KZSWC 565/6. Tom Baker.

WILDE, Oscar
Children's stories: The Happy Prince; The Star Child; The Nightingale and the Rose; The Selfish Giant; The Young King. Argo KZSWC 547/8 (available separately). Robert Morley.

The Importance of Being Earnest.
L.f.P. TC–LFP 7001. John Gielgud, Dame Edith Evans, Celia
Johnson, Pamela Brown,
Roland Culver etc.

WILLIAMSON, Henry
Tarka the Otter. L.f.P. TC-LFP
7034. David Attenborough.

WILSON, Harold
'*A Prime Minister on Prime Ministers': Winston Churchill and
Harold Macmillan.* L.f.P. TC–
LFP 7035. The author.